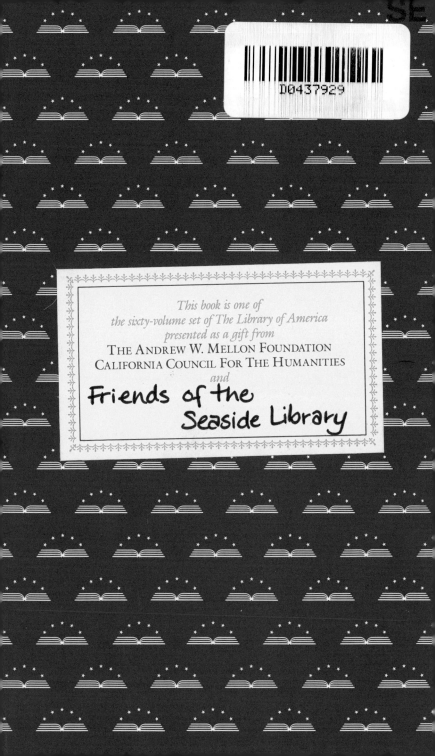

THE DEBATE ON
THE CONSTITUTION

PART TWO

THE DEBATE ON THE CONSTITUTION

Federalist and Antifederalist Speeches, Articles,
and Letters During the Struggle over Ratification

PART TWO

DEBATES IN THE PRESS AND IN PRIVATE CORRESPONDENCE

January 14–August 9, 1788

DEBATES IN THE STATE RATIFYING CONVENTIONS

South Carolina, May 12–24, 1788
Virginia, June 2–27, 1788
New York, June 17–July 26, 1788
North Carolina, July 21–August 4, 1788

THE LIBRARY OF AMERICA

Distributed to the trade in the United States
and Canada by the Viking Press.

Library of Congress Catalog Number: 92–25449
For cataloging information, see end of Index.
ISBN 0–940450–64–X

First Printing
The Library of America—63

Manufactured in the United States of America

BERNARD BAILYN
SELECTED THE CONTENTS AND WROTE
THE HEADINGS AND NOTES FOR THIS VOLUME

The publishers wish to thank
The Lynde and Harry Bradley Foundation
for funding the publication of The Debate on the Constitution.

The publishers also express their appreciation to
John P. Kaminski and Gaspare J. Saladino, editors of
The Documentary History of the Ratification of the Constitution,
and the State Historical Society of Wisconsin, the publisher,
for editorial assistance, the use of archival materials, and
permission to reprint extensive excerpts.

Grateful acknowledgment is made to the National Endowment for
the Humanities, the Ford Foundation, and the Andrew W. Mellon
Foundation for their generous support of this series.

Contents

DEBATES IN THE STATE
RATIFYING CONVENTIONS

South Carolina Ratifying Convention, May 12–24, 1788

Virginia Ratifying Convention, June 2–27, 1788

APPENDIX

DEBATES IN THE PRESS
AND IN PRIVATE
CORRESPONDENCE

January 14–August 9, 1788

ON THE LIKELY FAILURE OF LIBERTY:
THE DISSENT OF TWO NEW YORK DELEGATES
TO THE PHILADELPHIA CONVENTION

Robert Yates and John Lansing, Jr., to
Governor George Clinton

Daily Advertiser (New York), January 14, 1788

Albany, Dec. 21, 1787.

SIR, We do ourselves the honor to advise your Excellency, that, in pursuance of concurrent resolutions of the Honorable Senate and Assembly, we have, together with Mr. Hamilton, attended the Convention appointed for revising the articles of Confederation, and reporting amendments to the same.

It is with the sincerest concern we observe, that in the prosecution of the important objects of our mission, we have been reduced to the disagreeable alternative of either exceeding the powers delegated to us, and giving our assent to measures which we conceived destructive of the political happiness of the citizens of the United States; or opposing our opinion to that of a body of respectable men, to whom those citizens had given the most unequivocal proofs of confidence. Thus circumstanced, under these impressions, to have hesitated would have been to be culpable. We therefore gave the principles of the Constitution, which has received the sanction of a majority of the Convention, our decided and unreserved dissent; but we must candidly confess, that we should have been equally opposed to any system, however modified, which had in object the consolidation of the United States into one Government.

We beg leave briefly to state some cogent reasons which, among others, influenced us to decide against a consolidation of the States. These are reducible into two heads.

First. The limited and well defined powers under which we acted, and which could not, on any possible construction,

3

embrace an idea of such magnitude as to assent to a general Constitution in subversion of that of the State.

Secondly. A conviction of the impracticability of establishing a general Government, pervading every part of the United States, and extending essential benefits to all.

Our powers were explicit, and confined to the *sole and express purpose of revising the articles of Confederation*, and reporting such alterations and provisions therein, as should render the Federal Constitution adequate to the exigencies of Government, and the preservation of the Union.

From these expressions, we were led to believe that a system of consolidated Government, could not, in the remotest degree, have been in contemplation of the Legislature of this State, for that so important a trust, as the adopting measures which tended to deprive the State Government of its most essential rights of Sovereignty, and to place it in a dependent situation, could not have been confided, by implication, and the circumstance, that the acts of the Convention were to receive a State approbation, in the last resort, forcibly corroborated the opinion, that our powers could not involve the subversion of a Constitution, which being immediately derived from the people, could only be abolished by their express consent, and not by a Legislature, possessing authority vested in them for its preservation. Nor could we suppose, that if it had been the intention of the Legislature to abrogate the existing Confederation, they would, in such pointed terms, have directed the attention of their delegates to the revision and amendment of it, in total exclusion of every other idea.

Reasoning in this manner, we were of opinion, that the leading feature of every amendment ought to be the preservation of the individual States, in their uncontroled constitutional rights; and that, in reserving these, a mode might have been devised, of granting to the Confederacy, the monies arising from a general system of revenue, the power of regulating commerce, and enforcing the observance of Foreign treaties, and other necessary matters of less moment.

Exclusive of our objections, originating from the want of power, we entertained an opinion that a general Government, however guarded by declarations of rights or cautionary provisions, must unavoidably, in a short time, be productive of the destruction of the civil liberty of such citizens who could be effectually coerced by it; by reason of the extensive territory of the United States; the dispersed situation of its inhabitants, and the insuperable difficulty of controling or counteracting the views of a set of men (however unconstitutional and oppressive their acts might be) possessed of all the powers of Government, and who, from their remoteness from their constituents, and necessary permanency of office, could not be supposed to be uniformly actuated by an attention to their welfare and happiness; that however wise and energetic the principles of the general Government might be, the extremities of the United States could not be kept in due submission and obedience to its laws at the distance of many hundred miles from the seat of Government; that if the general Legislature was composed of so numerous a body of men as to represent the interest of all the inhabitants of the United States in the usual and true ideas of representation, the expence of supporting it would become intolerably burthensome, and that if a few only were invested with a power of legislation, the interests of a great majority of the inhabitants of the United States must necessarily be unknown, or if known even in the first stages of the operations of the new Government, unattended to.

These reasons were in our opinion conclusive against any system of consolidated Government: to that recommended by the Convention we suppose most of them forcibly apply.

It is not our intention to pursue this subject further than merely to explain our conduct in the discharge of the trust which the Honorable the Legislature reposed in us—interested however, as we are in common with our fellow citizens in the result, we cannot forbear to declare that we have the strongest apprehensions that a Government so organized as that recommended by the Convention, cannot afford that security to equal and permanent liberty, which we wished to make an invariable object of our pursuit.

We were not present at the completion of the New Constitution; but before we left the Convention, its principles were so well established as to convince us that no alteration was to be expected, to conform it to our ideas of expediency and safety. A persuasion that our further attendance would be fruitless and unavailing, rendered us less solicitious to return.

We have thus explained our motives for opposing the adoption of the National Constitution, which we conceived it our duty to communicate to your Excellency, to be submitted to the consideration of the Hon. Legislature.

We have the Honor to be, with the greatest Respect, your Excellency's most obedient and very humble Servants,

Hugh Ledlie to John Lamb

Hartford, Connecticut, January 15, 1788

The length of time, since our acquaintance first commenced in N York about the years 1765 & 1766 makes me almost diffident whether you continue the same Patriot & friend to your Country; I then found you together with Sears, Robinson, Wiley, Mott, Light Scott Hazard &c &c and many others whose Names I have forgot a Committee for opposeing the diabolical and oppressive Stamp Act, when Pintard Williams &c were brought to the Stool or rather Stage of repentance for Acts of high crimes and misdemeanors committed against the then sons of liberty throughout the Continent—But to return, I say, I sho'd not have dared to Venture a line to you on the subject I am about to say a few words upon, if I had not accidentally seen your Name with others (good men) in some of our publick newspapers handled in a very rough, ungentlemanlike manner—but even then I remain'd Ignorant who those scurrilous, defamatory, backbiting writers meant, untill a few days since being in company with Genl. James Wadsworth who first told me it was you, & aded an Anecdote—the other day or some time since a gentleman one Mr. Hamilton meeting you in the street Asked you how you could be so much against the New Constitution, for it was pretty certain your old good friend Genl. Washington would in all probability be the first President under it; to which you reply'd that in that case all might be well, but perhaps after him Genl Slushington might be the next or second President. This Sir, was the very first hint I had of your opposing it and was confirmed in the same by the Approbrous indecent & I believe false speeches made use of at our late C——n in this place by some sly mischevious insinuations viz that out of the impost £8000 was paid by this State Annually to the State of

7

N York out of which you recd. upwards of £900 which enabled you & others to write the foederal farmer & other false Libels and send them into this & the Neighbouring States to poison the minds of the good people against the good C——n.—They say a Lamb, a Willet, a Smith, a Clinton, & a Yates's Salleries are paid by this State through your State impost, the late C——n which Met in this town the 3d. Inst.—and Voted the New C—stn the 9th. in the evening & finished the 10th. was carried on by what I can learn with a high hand against those that disapproved thereof, for if I am not misinform'd when the Latter were speaking which by the by were far from being the best Orators (a few excepted) they were brow beaten by many of those Cicero'es as they think themselves & others of Superiour rank as they call themselves, as also by the unthinking deluded Multitude who were previously convened as it is thought by many for that purpose, which together with Shuffleing & Stamping of feet, caughing talking spitting & Whispering, as well by some of the Members as Spectators with other interruptions &c &c: too many to be here inumerated which I am told is true for I was not there myself being at that time confined by a Slight touch of the Gout, all these Menaces & Stratagems were used by a Junto who tries to carry all before them in this State, as well by writing as every other diabolical & evil pretence   And as the Press's in this State are open to them, but evidently shut against all those that would dare & presume to write on the other side against the N Cs——n they have greatly the Advantage & by these means Stigmatise every one they think Acts or thinks to the contrary of what they say or do. Witness our late landholder & some others of the same class against Richard Henry Lee Esqr. Mr. Mason, Mr. Geary &c &c yet notwithstanding all their long laboured scurilous, Vindictive, bitter, Malicious, & false insinuations there was found in our C n n forty one righteous men, that did not bow the knee to Baal but in the midts of all the storms of reproaches &c &c stood their ground firm tho' 127. of those (called by some of the first rank by their soft smooth speaches just at the close Voted for the New Con——n a C—n n that in the end will work the ruin of the freedom & liberty of these thirteen disunited States—I am not alone in this opinion for there are

many of the first abilities in this & the Neighbouring States
with whom I correspond as well by letters as otherways besides the above 41., that think this n C——n a guilded Pill,
but some of them notwithstanding the guilding is so artfully
laid on can discern the Arsanac & Poison through the outside
colouring—and our good Printers (after the Nag was stolen I
think after they had spent all their Venom which came from
the Quills of the Junto in favour of the N C——n & just
before the sitting of our C——n) then & not till then they
published a pompious libel, that then & at all times they
would publish on both sides—but the D——l trust them
says many that from principle are against the N. C——n and
so none that I know of was ever sent them, well knowing it
must run the gauntlet through all these infernal grubstreet,
hireling scurrilous scriblers, that watch & guard the posts of
the Printers doors in this town, & who are daily attending for
the selfsame purpose of disjointing, Mangleing & torturing
every piece that don't please their pallet—This Sir, is some of
the reasons why so few or none are sent—another reason is
they have got almost all the best Writers (as well as speakers)
on their side tho' we vie with & I believe over ballance them
in point of honesty and integrity—the piece aluded to as
above teems with trying to sow discord & contention between the United States, by insinuating that Richard H. Lee
Esqr. has and is a great enemy to Genl. Washington & that he
endeavored to get his cousin Genl. Lee to be commander of
our late Army &c &c in short they leave as the old saying is
no stone unturn'd but they compass Sea and land, they rake
H—l and scim the D—l to make one proselite, and when
they have found him, they make him two fold more the child
of h. l. than he was before, this proverb is of late verified by
their turning from light to darkness Copper, Wimble & some
others whom at present I'll forbear to name—We that are
against the N— C——n are stigmatis'd by those mighty men
of Moab by the approbious Name of Wrongheads, if they are
nam'd right I believe there is a Majority in this State against
the N. C——n for it is thought by the best judges that if the
Freemen &c of this State could be convened together in one
body the greatest Number would Vote against the new propos'd C——n notwithstanding all that is held out to the

people at large in the publick Newspapers in this State—We
wish here we had some of your good Writers and a free Press
we would souse some of our upstart sons of Apollo that pretend to great things—

One worthless man that gains what he pretends
disgusts a thousand unpretending friends
trials light as Air—are to the jealous confirmation strong
as proofs of holy Writ—the Wise too Jealous are
fools too secure—Beware beware beware
    for I apprehend a dreadful snare
is laid for Virtuous innocence
under a friends false pretence—

Now Sir on the whole let me tell you, that those gentlemen
at least, those that I can unite with, have no greater hope
(besides that of an over ruling providence) than in the Virtue
& wisdom of your State together with that of Virginia &
Massachusetts not adopting the N. C——n and I have heard
some of the first Characters that composed our late C——n
say that if nine States did adopt the C——n and N York rejected it, they would remove into your State where they could
injoy freedom & liberty, for which they had fought & Bled
heretofore, and if your State is not by that means one of the
most populous flourishing states on the Continent I am much
Mistaken not by emigrants only that are or will be disatisfied
with the N. C——n from the different states, but also from
Europe, I myself if I am able to buy a small farm in your State
somewhere about the South Bay Fairhaven Crownpoint, up
the Mohawk river German flatts, fort Stanwix, Wood Creek,
the Onoida Lake, Trouviers on the Annodanga River, Sho-
haryskill, Bradstreets island in Lake Ontario in the Mouth of
the River St Lawrence Oswego only excepted Niagara &
above all some where on the South banks of Lake Erie—
most or all of those places I am acquainted with, & if the
proposed C——n takes place & Providence permitts I will
with others remove into your State, provided you do not
adopt it for many of the Convention that attended it (for as I
said before I did not attend myself in person) told me that the
Conv—n was one of the most overbearing Assemblys that
ever sat in this State and as the N. Cs——n gives all the power

both of the Sword & purse into the hands of the C—n—ss our people reckon it leads to and opens a door for despotism Tyranny, Anarchy & confusition and every evil Work. I am afraid Sir for want of knowing whom to put confidence in you (if you sent any) sent your books into the wrong hands as they never appeared or could be seen except a few sent to Genl. J. W. tho I never could see one untill a few days before our C—v—n set the rest besides those sent as above were all secreted, burnt and distributed amongst those for the N. C t. n in order to torture ridicule & make shrewd remarks & may game of, both of the pamphlet and them that wrote and sent them, all which they did not spare to do in our public Newspapers by Extracts and detach'd sentences just such as served their Vile Malignant purpose long before I or any against the C—t. n ever saw (I mean) the foederal farmer—on the whole sho'd be glad to know who those Gentlemen are whom our heads of Wit takes in hand to Villifie in our public papers besides yourself, pray Sr. who is Mr. Willet, Mr. Smith Mr. Clinton & Mr Yates—is Mr. Willet he that defended so nobly at fort Stanwix in the late War—also who is Mr Smith, and is Mr. Clinton your Worthy Govr.—and pray who is Mr Yates—two of those Names viz Judge Yates & Melankton Smith Esqr. lodged at my house upwards of 20 days in Decemr. 1787. together with Mr. Duane, your Mayor Chancellor Livingston Judge Herring, Mr. Benson your Attorney Genl. & Mr. DeWitt your Surveyor Genl. shod be glad to know which or whether all or any of the above gentlemen, are against or for the New proposed Constitution—our 41 Members of Convention that opposed the Constitution went home very heavy hearted and discouraged to think that by one stroke they had lost all their liberty & priviledges both Civil & Sacred as well as all their property money &c &c by a set of men who's aim is entirely popularity as they think will please the bulk of the people & procure them places, Sallery, & Pensions under the New Constitution, as I am inform'd that many who are now in office & who it is said were dicidedly against it untill they came to this town to Conven—n then they were told plainly, that if they did not turn & Vote for it they must not expect any places either of trust or profitt under the New Constitution, thus this capital stroke was reserved for the finishing blow, as those concerned well knew the pulse's of these sort of men—for as one of your City said att the beginning of the late War he then being on Long Island & settleing some affairs from this State that he could buy any Counseller in this state for a half Joe. or a Pd. of Irish linnen—there is nothing that works so effectually as interest so it is well verified as to some of our great men in the present case some of whom I believe I could call by name but at present I'll forbear only that I will add one sentiment more & have done untill I hear from N York viz That I verily believe we have some of the most selfish, Avericious, narrow contracted set of Mortals that now exist in these thirteen disunited States you'll please to excuse some low scurrilous Vulgar language the want of diction & grammer as I am not a man of a liberal Education and only follow the plough having no other employ to get my bread but by the sweat of my brow for I injoy neither place nor pension, as they that are for the N Constitution in this state & I am sure I shall never have any except I turn to their side, which at present I have no thoughts of—Sr. you'll please to forgive this lengthy unconnected scrawl as it hastily flew from one of the pens of the family of the wrongheads so called by the tory roundheads—We this way fear this N Constitution will work much mischief before it is adopted, & the destruction & ruin of the thirteen States if it takes place. Please to give my Compliments to all the before named gentlemen and Hugh Hughes Esqr. being one of the old committee more especially to those that are decidedly against the N Constitution

P.S. Sir, General James Wadsworth is one of the many studs that has behaved in character against the N Constitution and stood firm & intriped, notwithstanding all the scoffs flirts brow beatings, flings, coughs shuffles, threats, & maneces of the opisite faction in Convention, the sophistry, colouring, and smoth speeches of those great men which spoke last gave a turning cast to the whole, & thereby gave the weaker brethren a different turn of mind from what they had when they came from home & or the instructions they receiv'd from the towns to which they belonged—but further these forty one good men in the Minority say in the Name of

common sense why was the people in the different States so
blind to their own interest, as, at first to choose & send to the
general Convention at Philadela. men then belonging to Congress, but more especially afterwards to send those very men
to the State Convention to confirm their own dear Acts &
doings at Philadelphia—it is beyond all conceptions that
Wise men should act in this form, as to send the very men
whose interest it is to Vote themselves places of honour &
trust, profitt, & Money into their own pockets just so things
were managed at our late Convention in this town the very
men that fram'd the new Constitution at Philadelphia, together with our present Govr. Lieut. Govr. Judges of our
Supr. & Inferior Courts, present delegates to Congress,
Judges of probates Lawyers tagrag & bobtail with some Revd
Divines & placemen Sallerymen sinecures & expectants of every denomenation whatsoever, were the men chosen in this
State to attend our Convention, and who Voted to a man for
the New Constn. only the honest forty one who enjoyed none
of the above Lucrative places, posts or pensions &c &c &c
and that stood free & unbiased in their minds & were the
only honest disinterested men that Voted in the negative—We this way hope that if a Convention is form'd in
your State (which we hope will not be) that none of this sort
of self Interested gentry may be chosen which was evidently
the case here, which in the opinion of many honest good &
disinterested men disaffected the honest true & simple desire
of not only framing a good constitution at Philadelphia but
adopting the Constitution in our late Convention in this
town—Now Sr. I don't mean to be understood, that there
was not a number of worthy characters (provided they had
been disinterested) that Voted for the N Constitution, but in
the name of common sense how can these men who it is said
has their Chests & trunks, &c filled with publick securities
bought up by their emissaries heretofore from 1/3 to 6/8 on
the pound and the Moment the N Constitution takes place
they are all to be made good (as they imagine with Interest
from their date) and equal to gold and silver—so that the
poor first proprietor will be obliged to Work perhaps at hard
labour to pay 20/. and the interest thereon for what he sold for
2/6.—in short these and many other iniquituous practices

that has been & now is carrying on by many of those great
and mighty men that has heretofore made their Jack out of
flour, & beef, Long Island Plunder, &c &c—you'll be so
good as not to let any one from this quarter see this letter &
indeed no one (excepted) some select friends & please not to
give or let any body have or see any copy extracts or detached
sentances as you may well learn the Malavelent Vindictive
tempers of some of these harpies at least I have found it so
against any one that dare either write Speak or Act or even
think against their New Dagon Constitution—Now Sr. as I
told you before that you must not look for either diction
Grammer or even connection from a Ploughman but this
much I can say that what ever is accuracies or incoherence or
sentiments thrown together that they come from a staunch
republican Whig who can trace his pedigree in that line much
farther back than Charles the 2d. even in Shorpshire near
Ludlow Castle, down to Henry the 2d. & before 14 Miles
above the City of Banwick on the banks of the Tweed—
Adieu my dear old friend & acquaintance, Please to write
how and by whom you receive this and how the land lies in
your state touching the new Constitutn. &c And what help
we may depend on from the known Virtue, Wisdom, and
good policy of your State in opposeing the new Constitution
you may depend on it you have many good & honest friends
this way Notwithstanding the many Surrilous inflamitory
Pieces published of late in our partial publick papers for it is
evident every thing was published that was in favour of the
New Constitution but on the contrary every thing hugger-
mugger'd & suppress'd that was truly alarming against it—I
believe by this time I have tired your patience therefore to
make any further apology would be to add to the length of
this long epistle therefore shall conclude—

NB. There is five gentlemen of the first characters on the
Continent that I formerly occasionally and now with some of
them that are now living correspond with (viz) Dr. Franklin,
Govr Franklin—Govr. Livingston now of the Jerseys, The
Honble. William Smith, and Sr. Henry Moore formerly of
your City, Dr. Johnson of this State and the Honble. Saml.
Adams of Boston all of whom the latter excepted I fear are

decidedly against me as to the New Constitution, what
Govr. Livingston's opinion is I can never learn, as it is somewhat above two years since I received a letter from him on
acct. of the Commutation and Cincinati affairs, I wish I
could know what part he takes as touching the New Constitution, if I did I would write him as well as my old friend
Saml. Adams (who by the by) is on the Right side of the
question & whose opinion in all Cases of Goverment &c especially when it coinsides with my weak Opinion I Value
much—I wish you would write which side of the Question
Govr. Livingston takes—Sr. Henry Moore William Smith
Esq. Phillip Livingston & William Livingston Esqrs. were
formerly some of the greatest & best friends I ever had in
America but my old friend William Smith Esqr. taking the
wrong side of the question from whom I had a letter some
time since, I from these connections & correspondants heretofore receiv'd great satisfaction in both Church & State
more especially from Govr. Livingston when he occasionally
corresponded with me when Writing against the Bishop of
Landaff &c—Dr. Johnson who is at present one of the best
friends I have in this State last May before he went to the
Convention at Philadelpa. was so kind as to spend part of
two afternoons with me & now an evening the 5th. Inst—in
May we talk'd much of the intended Convention at Philadel-
pha. the other evening more particularly of the N Constitution but altho we differ'd widely in sentiments about &
concerning the N Constitution & the doings of our then
present Convention so far as they had then transpired, yet all
these (as the old saying is) broke no squares in all our other
politicks or friendship—I have not seen or corresponded
with my old friend Dr. Franklin since Octr. 1775 then at
Cambridge at General Washingtons house & at Rox-
bury—on turtle I had the pleasure of dining with him the
Genl. &c &c two days this Journey I made particularly by
the Dr.s desire when the Colo. Harison & Mr. Lynche went
a Committee through this town from Congress to Genl
Washington &c at Cambridge except that I wrote the Dr.
last May by Dr Johnson

Nathaniel Barrell to George Thatcher

Boston, January 15, 1788

I can assure my friend Thatcher, his letter of 22d. ultimo was peculiarly flattering, and should have been answerd before, but for a variety of reasons any of which I persuade myself you will be satisfied with, when you come to be informd of them, but which I have not time now to mention—I am pleasd with the open freedom with which you touch political matters, and however we may differ on that point I hope we shall always view each other as friends to good Government—at present I confess to you we are not altogether agreed in sentiment respecting the federal frame which brings me to this town—the pamphlet you were pleasd to enclose on that subject I think is wrote in that easy familiar stile which is ever pleasing to me. but tho it has a tendency to elucidate if not remove some objections to the federal constitution, yet I dare not say 'tis a full answer to the many objections against it, however I think with you a great part of those objections are founded on remote possibilities—do realy what you so humourously define, spring from that doctrine I have heard you reprobate, as originating in the heart which we are told by him who made it, is as you say— but tho I give more credit to this declaration than you do, yet I would by no means treat congress, or such men as my friend Thatcher, as *"tho they were rogues"*—nay I have such an opinion of you Sir, that I would cheerfully consent to your being a leading man in the first congress, after we adopt the federal Government.—I hope you will not think me to familiar if I should say the manner in which you treat this subject is rather laughfable than serious—and that it is much easier to tell the objectors to turn their representatives out, than to do it—I cant but think you know how dificult it is to turn out a representative who behaves ill, even tho chosen but for one

year—think you not 'twould be more dificult to remove one
chosen for two years?—I could wish to lay my objections
before you in the same familiar manner you have been pleasd
to set me the example, but for want of your talents, I will do
it in my own way, which are such as if not removd will prevent my acceeding to it—because after all the Willsonian oro-
tary—after all the learned arguments I have seen written—
after all the labord speeches I have heard in its defence—and
after the best investigation I have been able to give it—I see
it pregnant with the fate of our libertys and if I should not
live to feel its baneful effects, I see it intails wretchedness on
my posterity—slavery on my children—for as it now stands
congress will be vested with much more extensive powers
than ever great Brittain exercisd over us—too great to intrust
with any set of men, let their talents & vertues be ever so
conspicuous—even tho composd of such exalted amiable
characters as the great Washington—for while we consider
them as men of like passion the same spontaneous inherent
thirst for power with ourselvs—great & good as they may be
when they enter upon this important charge, what dependance can we have on their continuing so?—but were we
sure they would continue the faithful guardians of our libertys, & prevent any infringments on the priviledges of the people—what assurance can we have that such men will always
hold the reins of Government?—that their successors will be
such—history tells us Rome was happy under Augustus, tho
wretched under Nero, who could have no greater power than
Augustus—and that the same Nero when young in power
could weep at signing a death warrant, tho afterwards became
so callous to the tender feelings of humanity as to behold
with pleasure Rome in flames.—but Sir I am convincd such
that six years is too long a term for any set of men to be at the
helm of Government for in that time they will get so firmly
rooted their influence will be so great as to continue them for
life—because Sir I am persuaded we are not able to support
the additional charge of such a Government and that when
our State Government is annihilated this will not suit our local concerns so well as what we now have—because I think
'twill not be so much for our advantage to have our taxes
imposd & levied at the pleasure of Congress as the method

now pursued—and because Sir I think a Continental collector at the head of a standing army will not be so likely to do
us justice in collecting the taxes, as the mode of colecting now
practicd—and to crown all sir, because I think such a Government impracticable among men with such high notions of
liberty as we americans. these are the general objections as
they occur to my mind, the perticulars I cant bring within the
bounds of a letter, all which convince me the federal constitution as it now stands, needs much amendment before 'twill be
safe for us to adopt it—therefore as wise men—as the faithful guardians of the peoples libertys—and as we wish well to
posterity it becomes to reject it unless such amendments take
place as will secure to us & ours that liberty without which
life is a burthen.—

Rawlins Lowndes and Edward Rutledge Debate in the South Carolina Legislature

January 16, 1788

Mr. Lowndes desired gentlemen to consider that his antagonists were mostly gentlemen of the law, who were capable of giving ingenious explanations to such points as they wished to have adopted. He explained his opinion relative to treaties to be, that no treaty concluded contrary to the express laws of the land could be valid. The king of England, when he concluded one, did not think himself warranted to go further than to promise that he would endeavor to induce his parliament to sanction it. The security of a republic is jealousy; for its ruin may be expected from unsuspecting security; let us not therefore receive this proferred system with implicit confidence, as carrying with it the stamp of superior perfection; rather let us compare it with what we already possess with what we are offered for it. We are now under government of a most excellent constitution—one that had stood the test of time, and carried us through difficulties generally supposed to be insurmountable—one that had raised us high in the eyes of all nations, and given to us the enviable blessings of liberty and independence—a constitution sent like a blessing from heaven, yet we were impatient to change it for another, that vested power in a few men to pull down that fabric which we had raised at the expence of our blood. Charters ought to be considered as sacred things; in England an attempt was made to alter the charter of the East India company, but they invoked heaven and earth in their cause—moved lords, nay even the king in their behalf, and thus averted the ruin with which they were threatened. It had been said, that this new government was to be considered as an experiment; he really was afraid it would prove a fatal one to our peace and happi-

ness—an experiment! what risque the loss of political existence on experiment? No, Sir, if we are to make experiments,
rather let them be such as may do good, but which cannot
possibly do any injury to us or our posterity. So far from
having any expectation of success from such experiments, he
sincerely believed that when this new constitution should be
adopted, the sun of the southern states would set never to
rise again. To prove this, he observed, that six of the eastern
states formed a majority in the house of representatives (in
the enumeration he passed Rhode Island, and included Pennsylvania.) Now was it consonant with reason—with wisdom—with policy, to suppose that in a legislature where a
majority of persons sat whose interests were greatly different
from ours, that we had the smallest chance of receiving adequate advantages? certainly not. He believed the gentlemen
that went from this state to represent us in the convention,
possessed as much integrity, and stood as high in point of
character as any gentlemen that could have been selected; and
he also believed, that they had done every thing in their
power to procure for us a proportionate share in this new
government; but the very little they had gained proved what
we might expect in future; and that the interest of the Northern states would so predominate, as to divest us of any pretensions to the title of a republic. In the first place, what cause
was there for jealousy of our importing negroes? Why confine
us to 20 years, or rather why limit us at all? For his part he
thought this trade could be justified on the principles of religion, humanity and justice; for certainly to translate a set of
human beings from a bad country to a better, was fulfilling
every part of these principles. But they don't like our slaves,
because they have none themselves, and therefore want to exclude us from this great advantage; why should the southern
states allow of this without the consent of nine states? (Judge
Pendleton observed, that only three states, Georgia, South
Carolina, and North Carolina, allowed the importation of
negroes, Virginia had a clause in her constitution for this
purpose, and Maryland, he believed, even before the war,
prohibited them.) Mr. Lowndes observed, that we had a law
prohibiting the importation of negroes for three years, a law
he greatly approved of, but there was no reason offered why

the southern states might not find it necessary to alter their conduct, and open their ports.—Without negroes this state would degenerate into one of the most contemptible in the union, and cited an expression that fell from general Pinckney, on a former debate, that whilst there remained one acre of swamp land in South Carolina, he should raise his voice against restricting the importation of negroes. Even in granting the importation for 20 years, care had been taken to make us pay for this indulgence, each negro being liable on importation to pay a duty not exceeding ten dollars, and in addition to this were liable to a capitation tax. Negroes were our wealth, our only natural resource, yet behold how our kind friends in the North were determined soon to tie up our hands, and drain us of what we had.—The Eastern states drew their means of subsistence in a great measure from their shipping, and on that head they had been particularly careful not to allow of any burthens—they were not to pay tonnage or duties, no not even the form of clearing out—all ports were free and open to them! Why then call this a reciprocal bargain, which took all from one party to bestow it on the other? (Major Butler observed, that they were to pay five per cent. impost) This Mr. Lowndes proved must fall upon the consumer. They are to be the carriers, and we being the consumers, therefore all expences would fall upon us. A great number of gentlemen were captivated with this new constitution, because those who were in debt would be compelled to pay; others pleased themselves with the reflection that no more confiscation laws could be passed; but those were small advantages in proportion to evils that might be apprehended from the laws that might be passed by Congress, whenever there was a majority of representatives from the Eastern states, who were governed by prejudices and ideas extremely different from ours. He was afraid in the present instance that so much partiality prevailed for this new constitution, that opposition from him would be fruitless; however he felt so much the importance of the subject, that he hoped the house would indulge him in a few words to take a view comparatively of the old constitution and the new one, in point of modesty.—Congress, labouring under many difficulties, asked to regulate commerce for 21 years, when the power reverted into the hands of those who originally gave it; but this infallible new constitution eased us of any more trouble, for it was to regulate commerce *ad infinitum*; and thus called upon us to pledge ourselves and posterity forever in support of their measures; so that when our local legislature had dwindled down to the confined powers of a corporation, we should be liable to taxes and excise; not perhaps payable in paper, but in specie. However they need not be uneasy, since every thing would be managed in future by great men, and great men every body knew were incapable of acting under influence of mistake or prejudice—they always were infallible—so that if at any future period we should smart under laws which bore hard upon us, and think proper to remonstrate, the answer would probably be—Go, you are totally incapable of managing for yourselves—go mind your private affairs—trouble not yourselves with public concerns—*mind your business*—the latter expression was already the motto of some coppers in circulation, and he thought it would soon be the style of language held out towards the southern states. The honorable member apologized for going into the merits of this new constitution, when it was ultimately to be decided on by another tribunal, but understanding that he differed in opinion with his constituents, who were opposed to electing any person as a member of the convention that did not approve of the proposed plan of government; he should not therefore have an opportunity of expressing those sentiments which occurred to him on considering the plan for a new federal government. But if it was sanctioned by the people it would have his hearty concurrence and support. He was very much originally against a declaration of independency—he also opposed the instalment law, but when they received the approbation of the people, it became his duty as a good citizen to promote their due observance.

Mr. E. Rutledge was astonished to hear the honorable gentleman pass such eulogium on the old confederation, and prefer it as he had done, to the one before the house. For his part he thought that confederation so very weak, so very inadequate to the purposes of the union, that unless it was materially altered, the Sun of American Independence would indeed soon set—never to rise again! What could be effected for

America under that highly extolled constitution? Could it obtain security for our commerce in any part of the world? Could it enforce obedience to any one law of the union? — Could it obtain one shilling of money for the discharge of the most honorable obligations? The honorable gentleman knew it could not. Was there a single power in Europe that would lend us a guinea on the faith of that confederation, or could we borrow one on the public faith of our own citizens? The people of America had seen these things—they had felt the consequences of this feeble government, if that deserved the name of government which had no power to enforce laws founded on solemn compact; and was it under the influence of those feelings that, with almost one voice, they had called for a different government. But the honorable gentleman had said, that this government had carried us gloriously through the last war; Mr. Rutledge denied the assertion—it was true that we had passed gloriously through the war while the confederation was in existence, but that success was not to be attributed to the confederation; it was to be attributed to the firm and unconquerable spirit of the people, who were determined, at the hazard of every consequence, to oppose a submission to British government; it was to be attributed to the armaments of an ally, and the pecuniary assistance of our friends: These were the wings on which we were carried so triumphantly through the war; and not this wretched confederation which is unable, by universal acknowledgment, to obtain a discharge of any part of our debts in the hour of the most perfect domestic tranquility.—What benefits then are to be expected from such a constitution in the day of danger?—without a ship—without a soldier—without a shilling in the federal treasury, and without a nervous government to obtain one, we hold the property that we now enjoy at the courtesy of other powers. Was this such a tenure as was suitable to the inclinations of our constituents? It certainly was not—they had called upon us to change their situation, and we should betray their interest, and our own honor, if we neglected it. But the gentleman had said, that there were points in this new confederation which would endanger the rights of the people—that the president and ten senators may make treaties, and that the balance between the states was not

sufficiently preserved—that he is for limiting the powers of
Congress, so that they shall not be able to do any harm; for if
they have the power to do any harm they may. To this Mr.
Rutledge observed, that the greatest part of the hon. gentleman's objection was founded in an opinion, that the choice of
the people would fall on the most worthless and the most
negligent part of the community; but if it was to be admitted,
it would go to the withholding of all power from all public
bodies. The gentleman would have done well to have defined
the kind of power that could do no harm; the very idea of
power included a possibility of doing harm; and if the gentleman would show the power that could do no harm, he would
at once discover it to be a power that could do no good. To
argue against the use of a thing from the abuse of it, had long
since been exploded by all sensible people. It was true, that
the president, with the concurrence of two thirds of the senate might make treaties and it was possible that the senators
might constitute the two thirds, but it was just within the
reach of possibility, and a possibility from whence no danger
could be apprehended; if the president or the senators abused
their trust, they were answerable for their conduct—they
were liable to impeachment and punishment, and the fewer
that were concerned in the abuse of the trust, the more certain would be the punishment. In the formation of this article, the delegates had done their duty fully—they had
provided that two thirds of the senate should concur in the
making of the treaties; if the states should be negligent in
sending their senators, it would be their own faults, and the
injury would be theirs, not the framers of the constitution;
but if they were not negligent, they would have more than
their share. Is it not astonishing that the gentleman who is so
strenuous an advocate for the powers of the people, should
distrust the people the moment that power is given to them,
and should found his objections to this article in the corruption of the representatives of the people, and in the negli-
gence of the people themselves. If such objections as these
have any weight, they tend to the destruction of all confidence—the withholding of all power—the annihilation of all
government. Mr. Rutledge insisted that we had our full share
in the house of representatives, and that the gentleman's fears

of the northern interest prevailing at all times were ill founded. The constitution had provided for a census of the people, and the number of representatives was to be directed by the number of the people in the several states; this clause was highly favorable to the southern interest. Several of the northern states were already full of people; it was otherwise with us, the migrations to the south were immense, and we should in the course of a few years, rise high in our representation, whilst other states would keep their present position. Gentlemen should carry their views into futurity, and not confine themselves to the narrow limits of a day when contemplating a subject of such vast importance. The gentleman had complained of the inequality of the taxes between the northern and southern states—that ten dollars a head was imposed on the importation of negroes, and that those negroes were afterwards taxed. To this it was answered, that the ten dollars per head, was an equivalent to the 5 per cent. on imported articles; and as to their being afterwards taxed, the advantage is on our side; or, at least not against us. In the northern states the labor is performed by white people, in the southern by black. All the free people, (and there are few others) in the northern states, are to be taxed by the new constitution; whereas only the free people and two-fifths of the slaves in the southern states are to be rated in the apportioning of taxes. But the principal objection is, that no duties are laid on shipping—that in fact the carrying trade was to be vested in a great measure in the Americans, and that the ship-building business was principally carried on in the northern states. When this subject is duly considered the southern states should be among the last to object to it. Mr. Rutledge then went into a consideration of the subject, after which the house adjourned.

"Publius," The Federalist XXXIX
[James Madison]

Independent Journal (New York), January 16, 1788

To the People of the State of New-York.

The last paper having concluded the observations which were meant to introduce a candid survey of the plan of government reported by the Convention, we now proceed to the execution of that part of our undertaking. The first question that offers itself is, whether the general form and aspect of the government be strictly republican? It is evident that no other form would be reconcileable with the genius of the people of America; with the fundamental principles of the revolution; or with that honorable determination, which animates every votary of freedom, to rest all our political experiments on the capacity of mankind for self-government. If the plan of the Convention therefore be found to depart from the republican character, its advocates must abandon it as no longer defensible.

What then are the distinctive characters of the republican form? Were an answer to this question to be sought, not by recurring to principles, but in the application of the term by political writers, to the constitutions of different States, no satisfactory one would ever be found. Holland, in which no particle of the supreme authority is derived from the people, has passed almost universally under the denomination of a republic. The same title has been bestowed on Venice, where absolute power over the great body of the people, is exercised in the most absolute manner, by a small body of hereditary nobles. Poland, which is a mixture of aristocracy and of monarchy in their worst forms, has been dignified with the same appellation. The government of England, which has one republican branch only, combined with a hereditery aristocracy and monarchy, has with equal impropriety been frequently placed on the list of republics. These examples, which are nearly as dissimilar to each other as to a genuine republic, shew the extreme inaccuracy with which the term has been used in political disquisitions.

If we resort for a criterion, to the different principles on which different forms of government are established, we may define a republic to be, or at least may bestow that name on, a government which derives all its powers directly or indirectly from the great body of the people; and is administered by persons holding their offices during pleasure, for a limited period, or during good behaviour. It is *essential* to such a government, that it be derived from the great body of the society, not from an inconsiderable proportion, or a favored class of it; otherwise a handful of tyrannical nobles, exercising their oppressions by a delegation of their powers, might aspire to the rank of republicans, and claim for their government the honorable title of republic. It is *sufficient* for such a government, that the persons administering it be appointed, either directly or indirectly, by the people; and that they hold their appointments by either of the tenures just specified; otherwise every government in the United States, as well as every other popular government that has been or can be well organized or well executed, would be degraded from the republican character. According to the Constitution of every State in the Union, some or other of the officers of government are appointed indirectly only by the people. According to most of them the chief magistrate himself is so appointed. And according to one, this mode of appointment is extended to one of the co-ordinate branches of the legislature. According to all the Constitutions also, the tenure of the highest offices is extended to a definite period, and in many instances, both within the legislative and executive departments, to a period of years. According to the provisions of most of the constitutions, again, as well as according to the most respectable and received opinions on the subject, the members of the judiciary department are to retain their offices by the firm tenure of good behaviour.

On comparing the Constitution planned by the Convention, with the standard here fixed, we perceive at once that it is in the most rigid sense conformable to it. The House of Representatives, like that of one branch at least of all the State Legislatures, is elected immediately by the great body of the people. The Senate, like the present Congress, and the Senate of Maryland, derives its appointment indirectly from the people. The President is indirectly derived from the choice of the people, according to the example in most of the States. Even the judges, with all other officers of the Union, will, as in the several States, be the choice, though a remote choice, of the people themselves. The duration of the appointments is equally conformable to the republican standard, and to the model of the State Constitutions. The House of Representatives is periodically elective as in all the States: and for the period of two years as in the State of South-Carolina. The Senate is elective for the period of six years; which is but one year more than the period of the Senate of Maryland; and but two more than of the Senates of New-York and Virginia. The President is to continue in office for the period of four years; as in New-York and Delaware, the chief magistrate is elected for three years, and in South-Carolina for two years. In the other States the election is annual. In several of the States however, no constitutional provision is made for the impeachment of the Chief Magistrate. And in Delaware and Virginia, he is not impeachable till out of office. The President of the United States is impeachable at any time during his continuance in office. The tenure by which the Judges are to hold their places, is, as it unquestionably ought to be, that of good behaviour. The tenure of the ministerial offices generally will be a subject of legal regulation, conformably to the reason of the case, and the example of the State Constitutions.

Could any further proof be required of the republican complextion of this system, the most decisive one might be found in its absolute prohibition of titles of nobility, both under the Federal and the State Governments; and in its express guarantee of the republican form to each of the latter.

But it was not sufficient, say the adversaries of the proposed Constitution, for the Convention to adhere to the republican form. They ought, with equal care, to have preserved the *federal* form, which regards the union as a *confederacy* of sovereign States; instead of which, they have framed a *national* government, which regards the union as a *consolidation* of the States. And it is asked by what authority this bold and radical innovation was undertaken. The handle which has been made of this objection requires, that it should be examined with some precision.

Without enquiring into the accuracy of the distinction on which the objection is founded, it will be necessary to a just estimate of its force, first to ascertain the real character of the government in question; secondly, to enquire how far the Convention were authorised to propose such a government; and thirdly, how far the duty they owed to their country, could supply any defect of regular authority.

First. In order to ascertain the real character of the government it may be considered in relation to the foundation on which it is to be established; to the sources from which its ordinary powers are to be drawn; to the operation of those powers; to the extent of them; and to the authority by which future changes in the government are to be introduced.

On examining the first relation, it appears on one hand that the Constitution is to be founded on the assent and ratification of the people of America, given by deputies elected for the special purpose; but on the other that this assent and ratification is to be given by the people, not as individuals composing one entire nation; but as composing the distinct and independent States to which they respectively belong. It is to be the assent and ratification of the several States, derived from the supreme authority in each State, the authority of the people themselves. The act therefore establishing the Constitution, will not be a *national* but a *federal* act.

That it will be a federal and not a national act, as these terms are understood by the objectors, the act of the people as forming so many independent States, not as forming one aggregate nation, is obvious from this single consideration that it is to result neither from the decision of a *majority* of the people of the Union, nor from that of a *majority* of the States. It must result from the *unanimous* assent of the several States that are parties to it, differing no other wise from their ordinary assent than in its being expressed, not by the legislative authority, but by that of the people themselves. Were the people regarded in this transaction as forming one nation, the will of the majority of the whole people of the United States, would bind the minority; in the same manner as the majority in each State must bind the minority; and the will of the majority must be determined either by a comparison of the individual votes; or by considering the will of a majority of the States, as evidence of the will of a majority of the people of the United States. Neither of these rules has been adopted. Each State in ratifying the Constitution, is considered as a sovereign body independent of all others, and only to be bound by its own voluntary act. In this relation then the new Constitution will, if established, be a *federal* and not a *national* Constitution.

The next relation is to the sources from which the ordinary powers of government are to be derived. The house of representatives will derive its powers from the people of America, and the people will be represented in the same proportion, and on the same principle, as they are in the Legislature of a particular State. So far the Government is *national* not *federal*. The Senate on the other hand will derive its powers from the States, as political and co-equal societies; and these will be represented on the principle of equality in the Senate, as they now are in the existing Congress. So far the government is *federal*, not *national*. The executive power will be derived from a very compound source. The immediate election of the President is to be made by the States in their political characters. The votes allotted to them, are in a compound ratio, which considers them partly as distinct and co-equal societies; partly as unequal members of the same society. The eventual election, again is to be made by that branch of the Legislature which consists of the national representatives; but in this particular act, they are to be thrown into the form of individual delegations from so many distinct and co-equal bodies politic. From this aspect of the Government, it appears to be of a mixed character presenting at least as many *federal* as *national* features.

The difference between a federal and national Government as it relates to the *operation of the Government* is supposed to consist in this, that in the former, the powers operate on the political bodies composing the confederacy, in their political capacities: In the latter, on the individual citizens, composing the nation, in their individual capacities. On trying the Constitution by this criterion, it falls under the *national*, not the *federal* character; though perhaps not so compleatly, as has been understood. In several cases and particularly in the trial of controversies to which States may be parties, they must be viewed and proceeded against in their collective and political capacities only. So far the national countenance of the Government on this side seems to to be disfigured by a few federal features. But this blemish is perhaps unavoidable in any plan; and the operation of the Government on the people in their individual capacities, in its ordinary and most essential proceedings, may on the whole designate it in this relation a *national* Government.

But if the Government be national with regard to the *operation* of its powers, it changes its aspect again when we contemplate it in relation to the *extent* of its powers. The idea of a national Government involves in it, not only an authority over the individual citizens; but an indefinite supremacy over all persons and things, so far as they are objects of lawful Government. Among a people consolidated into one nation, this supremacy is compleatly vested in the national Legislature. Among communities united for particular purposes, it is vested partly in the general, and partly in the municipal Legislatures. In the former case, all local authorities are subordinate to the supreme; and may be controuled, directed or abolished by it at pleasure. In the latter the local or municipal authorities form distinct and independent portions of the supremacy, no more subject within their respective spheres to the general authority, than the general authority is subject to them, within its own sphere. In this relation then the proposed Government cannot be deemed a *national* one; since its jurisdiction extends to certain enumerated objects only, and leaves to the several States a residuary and inviolable sovereignty over all other objects. It is true that in controversies relating to the boundary between the two jurisdictions, the tribunal which is ultimately to decide, is to be established under the general Government. But this does not change the principle of the case. The decision is to be impartially made, according to the rules of the Constitution; and all the usual and most effectual precautions are taken to secure this impartiality. Some such tribunal is clearly essential to prevent an appeal to the sword, and a dissolution of the compact; and that it ought to be established under the general, rather than under the local Governments; or to speak more properly, that it could be safely established under the first alone, is a position not likely to be combated.

If we try the Constitution by its last relation, to the authority by which amendments are to be made, we find it neither wholly *national*, nor wholly *federal*. Were it wholly national, the supreme and ultimate authority would reside in the *majority* of the people of the Union; and this authority would be competent at all times, like that of a majority of every national society, to alter or abolish its established Government. Were it wholly federal on the other head, the concurrence of each State in the Union would be essential to every alteration that would be binding on all. The mode provided by the plan of the Convention is not founded on either of these principles. In requiring more than a majority, and particularly, in computing the proportion by *States*, not by *citizens*, it departs from the *national*, and advances towards the *federal* character: In rendering the concurrence of less than the whole number of States sufficient, it loses again the *federal*, and partakes of the *national* character.

The proposed Constitution therefore is in strictness neither a national nor a federal constitution; but a composition of both. In its foundation, it is federal, not national; in the sources from which the ordinary powers of the Government are drawn, it is partly federal, and partly national: in the operation of these powers, it is national, not federal: In the extent of them again, it is federal, not national: And finally, in the authoritative mode of introducing amendments, it is neither wholly federal, nor wholly national.

"An Old State Soldier" I

Virginia Independent Chronicle (Richmond), January 16, 1788

An ADDRESS *to the* GOOD PEOPLE *of* VIRGINIA, *on the* NEW FŒDERAL CONSTITUTION, *by an old State Soldier, in answer to an Officer in the late American army.*

A fellow-citizen whose life has once been devoted to your service, and knows no other interest now than what is common to you all, solicits your attention for a new few moments on the new plan of government submitted to your consideration.

Well aware of the feebleness of a Soldier's voice after his service shall be no longer requisite, and sensible of the superiority of those who have already appeared on this subject, he does not flatter himself that what he has now to say will have much weight—Yet it may serve to contradict some general opinions which may have grown out of circumstances too dangerous to our reputations, to remain unanswered.

Conscious of the rectitude of his own intentions however, and trusting that "in searching after error truth will appear," he flatters himself he should be excused, were he to leave the merits of this cause to that more able ADVOCATE, the CONSTITUTION itself, and confine himself wholly to those general, plain, and honest truths which flow from the feelings of the warmest heart.

FREEDOM has its charms, and authority its use—but there are certain points beyond which neither can be stretched without falling into licentiousness, or sinking under oppression.

Here then let us pause!—and before we approach these dreadful extremes, view well the ground on which we now stand, as well as that to which we are about to step. Let it be remembered that after a long and bloody conflict, we have been left in possession of that great blessing for which we so long contended—and which was only obtained, and could not be perfectly founded at a time when there was only a chance for succeeding in the claim. The one being separate and distinct from the other at all times, a happy REVOLUTION therefore, has necessarily left incomplete the labors of the war for the more judicious and permanent establishment of the calms of peace. It was not expected, or even wished, that a SYSTEM, which was the mere OFFSPRING of NECESSITY, should govern and controul us when our object was changed, and another time than confusion should offer itself to our service for making choice of a better. But on the contrary the same mutual agreement which promised us success in our undertaking during the war, led us to hope for a happy settlement of those rights at the approach of peace—which alone can be done now by that policy which holds out at equal balance, strength and energy in the one hand, and justice, peace, and lenity in the other. Too much 'tis true may be surrendered up—but 'tis as certain too much may be retained, since there is no way more likely to lose ones liberty in the end than being too niggardly of it in the beginning. For he who grasps at more than he can possibly hold, will retain less than he could have handled with ease had he been moderate at first. *Omnes deteriores sumus licentia.* But how much is necessary to be given up is the difficulty to be ascertained. We all know however the more desperate any disease has become, so much more violent must be the remedy—that if there be now a danger in making the attempt, it is owing more to the putting off to this late period that which at some time or another is unavoidable, than to any thing in the design itself. Having neglected this business until necessity pressed us forward to it, we see an anxiety and hurry now in some which is extremely alarming to others—when in fact had it been attempted at the close of the war, it might have seemed nothing more perhaps than a necessary guard to that tender infant, INDEPENDENCE, to whom we had just given birth.

Long had the friends to the late REVOLUTION observed how incomplete the business was when we contented ourselves under that form of government, after the return of peace, which was only designed to bind us together the more effectually to carry on the war—and which could not be expected to operate effectually in many cases, the exspence of which no one at that time could foresee. At this late period then an attempt has been made to complete the designs of a war that ended many years before. And the first object which presented itself to our view in the business was the necessity of strengthening the UNION—the only probable way to do which, was the creating an authority whereby our credit could be supported—and in doing this (although it seems a single alteration in our old plan) the introduction of several other things was unavoidable. The credit of the UNION, like that of an individual, was only to be kept up by a prospect of being at some time or another able to pay the debts it had necessarily contracted—and that prospect could no way begin but by the establishment of some fund whereon the CONTINENT could draw with certainty. But the right of taxation (the only certain way of creating that fund) was too great a surrender to be made without being accompanied with some other alterations in the old plan. Among these the Senate, and the mode of proportioning the taxes with the representatives, seem to be the most material—the one acting as a curb, the other as a guide in the business. Though in fact the credit of the UNION depended on several other things besides the payment of its debts—Its internal defence, its compliance with its treaties, and the litigation of its own disputes, must be considered as inseparable from its national dignity. Therefore the additional authorities of the President, and the institution of the supreme court, were nothing more than necessary appendages to that AUTHORITY which every one seems to grant was necessary to be given up to strengthen our UNION and support our credit and dignity as a people—and when rightly considered can amount to nothing more than one alteration, so generally wished for, divided into several parts. One thing however appears to be entirely forgot: No one seems to remember that we had any fœderal constitution before this. Or if they do they have entirely forgotten what it was—it must be remembered however, that there was no other complaint made about that, but a want of energy and power. The removing this grand objection then, which seems to be the only material alteration made by this new Constitution, has not, as was expected, perfected the

UNION; but it has served only to make way for the discovery of smaller imperfections which were not before seen. The want of a bill of rights, a charter for the press, and a thousand other things which are now discovered, have been heretofore unnoticed although they existed then in as great a degree as they now do. Whenever any alterations have been made in any of these lesser faults, they have universally been for the better. For instance the appropriation of monies under pretence of providing for our national defence, which then was without hesitation, is now restricted to two years: For although Congress could not absolutely keep a large standing force in time of profound peace, yet they had it in their power to provide for an army when there was not an absolute war: For the declaration being at their sole will, and they not accountable for the necessity, left the appropriation which was given them for supporting the one, entirely at their discretion in time of the other. That when this article shall be viewed independent of the grand object, and considered as one of the smaller faults, separate and distinct from the right of taxation, it must be confessed that part of our SYSTEM has been altered for the better. And thus too respecting a bill of rights, and the liberty of the press, it may also be said, the objection has been diminished by the new plan: For what security had we on this head before but that which was in our state constitutions? And of what is the republican form of government which Congress is now to guarantee to each state to consist? Certainly of any thing each state shall think proper that does not take from Congress what this constitution absolutely claims. Even the very one we now have, or such parts of it as do not extend that far, may be that form of government which this new plan obliges Congress to guarantee. That so far from these objections being increased, they are diminished by the new plan; as there will not only be the same state security for these rights then, but also a continental conformation of them—there being nothing in the new system that excludes that part of the old. That it is not, because those smaller faults have not been before seen, they necessarily originate in, or are magnified by the new constitution: but the truth is, they have always been overlooked in beholding that grand blemish which marked the features of the old plan. The

representation which was much more unequal and far more
objectionable, then went unnoticed—as no one would observe the disproportion of the fingers while the whole carcase
was disjointing for the want of sinews. The general cry and
only wish then was, for more authority in our government. It
was not expected the amendments would extend much further—yet they have: Many inferior objections which existed
in the old plan, are in the new altered for the better. That
when we came to enquire into the merits of this matter fairly,
and set apart in the first place those things which are absolutely necessary to compose that alteration in our fœderal plan
which we all so ardently wished for, and then in the next
place give the proper credits to this new constitution for the
amendments made in the more inferior faults of the old, we
shall find there are but few things left worthy of grounding an
opposition on. 'Tis much to be lamented however that we
cannot avoid extremes on either side: For as all extremes are
subject to a union in the end, it will be well if our violent
opposition at this time, does not return to the most opposite
submission at another. Indeed the comparrison of this opposition among ourselves to that of the late one towards our
original situation, serves only to prove the likeness there is
between the beginning and ending of our liberty—for there
are no two things more strikingly alike than the first respira-
tions of life and the last melancholy gasps of existence. But
when confined to the likeness of situation itself, the same
comparison is entirely unjust: For formerly we were governed
by those who had no interest in our prosperity: But now it
is our FRIENDS, our COUNTRYMEN, and our BRETH-
REN, on whom we are called to rely, whose very existence is
so inseparable from our welfare as to render it impossible for
them to injure us without giving a fatal stab to themselves
and the happiness of their posterity. But to those who cannot
distinguish between a cause and a people, a sentiment and an
individual, the analogy may appear just, in its intended meaning—yet self-evident as the contrary is, it would illy become
those whose reputations are immediately concerned to stifle
an honest resentment on this occasion. When we behold the
character of individuals held up to view as an argument in
favor of any cause, we are sufficiently disgusted with the igno-

rance of the author; but when we see the credit of that ignorance (accompanied by illiberality) given to us who would
willingly merit a better appellation than the secret movers of
personal jealousy and detraction among citizens, we are doubly mortified—considering an endeavor to keep alive those*
distinctions now which owed their existence to the heat of
war, as illiberal as a suspicion over our best friends would be
unjust. The one serving only to keep up a perpetual war
among ourselves; and the other to make distrust a justification
for dishonesty—neither of which is a trait in the character of
a real soldier it is presumed: For besides the dishonor, he who
really knows what war is, would scarcely wish to keep it up
when he could have peace. But it is a trite remark that he who
is most violent in time of the one, has generally been the most
mild during the other. It is not at all surprising however that
you should be brought to believe your liberties are now in
danger, when you are thus shewn how that bravery you have
once felt in your favor, is likely to take residence in the breasts
of those thus capable of any thing. By thus assuming our
names and holding to view their own genuine characters, designing men do us more real injury, and their own cause more
essential service, than those who insinuate that we shall be
preferred from our former services to share the spoils when
our country shall fall a prey to aristocratical invasion. These
last only add insult to misfortune: For there is but little in our
influence to rouse your jealousy, and much less in our situations to excite your envy, unless the nobleness of your gratitude should make you wish to share in our poverty and
fears.—These being all we have obtained, there is but little
prospect of our becoming your tyrants, since misery and
wretchedness are seldom called in to share the dignities of
oppression. In short, as there is nothing in this constitution
itself that particularly bargains for a surrender of your liberties, it must be your own faults if you become enslaved. Men
in power may usurp authorities under any constitution—and
those they govern may oppose their tyranny: For although it
be wrong to refuse the legal currency of one's country, yet
there can be no harm in rejecting base coin, since there is no

*Whig and Torie. See *"An Officer in the late Am. Ar."* on Con.

state in the world which compels a man to take that which is under its own standard.

It cannot be denied however but this constitution has its faults—yet when the whole of those objections shall be collected together and compared to the excellence of the main object, we cannot but conclude that the opposition will be like quarrelling about the division of straws, and neglecting the management of the grain. The period is not far distant however when it must be determined whether it be best to adopt it as it now stands, or run the risk of losing it by attempting amendments. This last consideration, deeply impressed on the minds of those who are interested in the welfare of America, cannot fail to call forth your attention, when a fitter season shall demand it, and another paper give it circulation.

"Brutus" IX

New York Journal, January 17, 1788

The design of civil government is to protect the rights and promote the happiness of the people.

For this end, rulers are invested with powers. But we cannot from hence justly infer that these powers should be unlimited. There are certain rights which mankind possess, over which government ought not to have any controul, because it is not necessary they should, in order to attain the end of its institution. There are certain things which rulers should be absolutely prohibited from doing, because, if they should do them, they would work an injury, not a benefit to the people. Upon the same principles of reasoning, if the exercise of a power, is found generally or in most cases to operate to the injury of the community, the legislature should be restricted in the exercise of that power, so as to guard, as much as possible, against the danger. These principles seem to be the evident dictates of common sense, and what ought to give sanction to them in the minds of every American, they are the great principles of the late revolution, and those which governed the framers of all our state constitutions. Hence we find, that all the state constitutions, contain either formal bills of rights, which set bounds to the powers of the legislature, or have restrictions for the same purpose in the body of the constitutions. Some of our new political Doctors, indeed, reject the idea of the necessity, or propriety of such restrictions in any elective government, but especially in the general one.

But it is evident, that the framers of this new system were of a contrary opinion, because they have prohibited the general government, the exercise of some powers, and restricted them in that of others.

I shall adduce two instances, which will serve to illustrate my meaning, as well as to confirm the truth of the preceding remark.

In the 9th section, it is declared, "no bill of attainder shall be passed." This clause takes from the legislature all power to declare a particular person guilty of a crime by law. It is proper the legislature should be deprived of the exercise of this power, because it seldom is exercised to the benefit of the community, but generally to its injury.

In the same section it is provided, that "the privilege of the writ of habeas corpus shall not be suspended, unless when in cases of rebellion and invasion, the public safety may require it." This clause limits the power of the legislature to deprive a citizen of the right of habeas corpus, to particular cases viz. those of rebellion and invasion; the reason is plain, because in no other cases can this power be exercised for the general good.

Let us apply these remarks to the case of standing armies in times of peace. If they generally prove the destruction of the happiness and liberty of the people, the legislature ought not to have power to keep them up, or if they had, this power should be so restricted, as to secure the people against the danger arising from the exercise of it.

That standing armies are dangerous to the liberties of a people was proved in my last number—If it was necessary, the truth of the position might be confirmed by the history of almost every nation in the world. A cloud of the most illustrious patriots of every age and country, where freedom has been enjoyed, might be adduced as witnesses in support of the sentiment. But I presume it would be useless, to enter into a laboured argument, to prove to the people of America, a position, which has so long and so generally been received by them as a kind of axiom.

Some of the advocates for this new system controvert this sentiment, as they do almost every other that has been maintained by the best writers on free government.—Others, though they will not expressly deny, that standing armies in times of peace are dangerous, yet join with these in maintaining, that it is proper the general government should be vested with the power to do it. I shall now proceed to examine the arguments they adduce in support of their opinions.

A writer, in favor of this system, treats this objection as a ridiculous one. He supposes it would be as proper to provide against the introduction of Turkish janizaries, or against making the Alcoran a rule of faith.

From the positive, and dogmatic manner, in which this author delivers his opinions, and answers objections made to his sentiments—one would conclude, that he was some pedantic pedagogue who had been accustomed to deliver his dogmas to pupils, who always placed implicit faith in what he delivered.

But, why is this provision so ridiculous? because, says this author, it is unnecessary. But, why is it unnecessary? "because, the principles and habits, as well as the power of the Americans are directly opposed to standing armies; and there is as little necessity to guard against them by positive constitutions, as to prohibit the establishment of the Mahometan religion." It is admitted then, that a standing army in time of peace, is an evil. I ask then, why should this government be authorised to do evil? If the principles and habits of the people of this country are opposed to standing armies in time of peace, if they do not contribute to the public good, but would endanger the public liberty and happiness, why should the government be vested with the power? No reason can be given, why rulers should be authorised to do, what, if done, would oppose the principles and habits of the people, and endanger the public safety, but there is every reason in the world, that they should be prohibited from the exercise of such a power. But this author supposes, that no danger is to be apprehended from the exercise of this power, because, if armies are kept up, it will be by the people themselves, and therefore, to provide against it, would be as absurd as for a man to "pass a law in his family, that no troops should be quartered in his family by his consent." This reasoning supposes, that the general government is to be exercised by the people of America themselves—But such an idea is groundless and absurd. There is surely a distinction between the people and their rulers, even when the latter are representatives of the former.—They certainly are not identically the same, and it cannot be disputed, but it may and often does happen, that they do not possess the same sentiments or pursue the same interests. I think I have shewn, that as this government is constituted, there is little reason to expect, that the interest of the people and their rulers will be the same.

Besides, if the habits and sentiments of the people of America are to be relied upon, as the sole security against the encroachment of their rulers, all restrictions in constitutions are unnecessary; nothing more is requisite, than to declare who shall be authorized to exercise the powers of government, and about this we need not be very careful—for the habits and principles of the people will oppose every abuse of power. This I suppose to be the sentiments of this author, as it seems to be of many of the advocates of this new system. An opinion like this, is as directly opposed to the principles and habits of the people of America, as it is to the sentiments of every writer of reputation on the science of government, and repugnant to the principles of reason and common sense.

The idea that there is no danger of the establishment of a standing army, under the new constitution, is without foundation.

It is a well known fact, that a number of those who had an agency in producing this system, and many of those who it is probable will have a principal share in the administration of the government under it, if it is adopted, are avowedly in favour of standing armies. It is a language common among them, "That no people can be kept in order, unless the government have an army to awe them into obedience; it is necessary to support the dignity of government, to have a military establishment." And there will not be wanting a variety of plausible reason to justify the raising one, drawn from the danger we are in from the Indians on our frontiers, or from the European provinces in our neighbourhood. If to this we add, that an army will afford a decent support, and agreeable employment to the young men of many families, who are too indolent to follow occupations that will require care and industry, and too poor to live without doing any business we can have little reason to doubt, but that we shall have a large standing army, as soon as this government can find money to pay them, and perhaps sooner.

A writer, who is the boast of the advocates of this new constitution, has taken great pains to shew, that this power was proper and necessary to be vested in the general government.

He sets out with calling in question the candour and integrity of those who advance the objection, and with insinuating, that it is their intention to mislead the people, by alarming their passions, rather than to convince them by arguments addressed to their understandings.

The man who reproves another for a fault, should be careful that he himself be not guilty of it. How far this writer has manifested a spirit of candour, and has pursued fair reasoning on this subject, the impartial public will judge, when his arguments pass before them in review.

He first attempts to shew, that this objection is futile and disingenuous, because the power to keep up standing armies, in time of peace, is vested, under the present government, in the legislature of every state in the union, except two. Now this is so far from being true, that it is expressly declared, by the present articles of confederation, that no body of forces "shall be kept up by any state, in time of peace, except such number only, as in the judgment of the United States in Congress assembled, shall be deemed requisite to garrison the forts necessary for the defence of such state." Now, was it candid and ingenuous to endeavour to persuade the public, that the general government had no other power than your own legislature have on this head; when the truth is, your legislature have no authority to raise and keep up any forces?

He next tells us, that the power given by this constitution, on this head, is similar to that which Congress possess under the present confederation. As little ingenuity is manifested in this representation as in that of the former.

I shall not undertake to enquire whether or not Congress are vested with a power to keep up a standing army in time of peace; it has been a subject warmly debated in Congress, more than once, since the peace; and one of the most respectable states in the union, were so fully convinced that they had no such power, that they expressly instructed their delegates to enter a solemn protest against it on the journals of Congress, should they attempt to exercise it.

But should it be admitted that they have the power, there is such a striking dissimilarity between the restrictions under

which the present Congress can exercise it, and that of the
proposed government, that the comparison will serve rather
to shew the impropriety of vesting the proposed government
with the power, than of justifying it.

It is acknowledged by this writer, that the powers of Congress, under the present confederation, amount to little more
than that of recommending. If they determine to raise troops,
they are obliged to effect it through the authority of the state
legislatures. This will, in the first instance, be a most powerful
restraint upon them, against ordering troops to be raised. But
if they should vote an army, contrary to the opinion and
wishes of the people, the legislatures of the respective states
would not raise them. Besides, the present Congress hold
their places at the will and pleasure of the legislatures of the
states who send them, and no troops can be raised, but by the
assent of nine states out of the thirteen. Compare the power
proposed to be lodged in the legislature on this head, under
this constitution, with that vested in the present Congress,
and every person of the least discernment, whose understanding is not totally blinded by prejudice, will perceive, that they
bear no analogy to each other. Under the present confederation, the representatives of nine states, out of thirteen, must
assent to the raising of troops, or they cannot be levied: under
the proposed constitution, a less number than the representatives of two states, in the house of representatives, and the
representatives of three states and an half in the senate, with
the assent of the president, may raise any number of troops
they please. The present Congress are restrained from an
undue exercise of this power, from this consideration, they
know the state legislatures, through whose authority it must
be carried into effect, would not comply with the requisition
for the purpose, if it was evidently opposed to the public
good: the proposed constitution authorizes the legislature to
carry their determinations into execution, without the intervention of any other body between them and the people. The
Congress under the present form are amenable to, and removable by, the legislatures of the respective states, and are
chosen for one year only; the proposed constitution does not
make the members of the legislature accountable to, or removeable by the state legislatures at all; and they are chosen,

the one house for six, and the other for two years; and cannot be removed until their time of service is expired, let them conduct ever so badly.—The public will judge, from the above comparison, how just a claim this writer has to that candour he affects to possess. In the mean time, to convince him, and the advocates for this system, that I possess some share of candor, I pledge myself to give up all opposition to it, on the head of standing armies, if the power to raise them be restricted as it is in the present confederation; and I believe I may safely answer, not only for myself, but for all who make the objection, that they will be satisfied with less.

ON THE POWERS OF THE NATIONAL
GOVERNMENT: AN ANALYSIS OF ARMIES,
TAXATION, AND THE GENERAL WELFARE CLAUSE

"Publius," The Federalist XLI
[James Madison]

Independent Journal (New York), January 19, 1788

To the People of the State of New-York.

The Constitution proposed by the Convention may be considered under two general points of view. The FIRST relates to the sum or quantity of power which it vests in the Government, including the restraints imposed on the States. The SECOND, to the particular structure of the Government, and the distribution of this power, among its several branches.

Under the first view of the subject two important questions arise,—1. Whether any part of the powers transferred to the general Government be unnecessary or improper? —2. Whether the entire mass of them be dangerous to the portion of jurisdiction left in the several States?

Is the aggregate power of the general Government greater than ought to have been vested in it? This is the first question.

It cannot have escaped those who have attended with candour to the arguments employed against the extensive powers of the Government, that the authors of them have very little considered how far these powers were necessary means of attaining a necessary end. They have chosen rather to dwell on the inconveniences which must be unavoidably blended with all political advantages; and on the possible abuses which must be incident to every power or trust of which a beneficial use can be made. This method of handling the subject cannot impose on the good sense of the people of America. It may display the subtlety of the writer; it may open a boundless field for rhetoric and declamation; it may inflame the passions of the unthinking, and may confirm the prejudices of the misthinking. But cool and candid people will at once reflect, that the purest of human blessings must have a portion of alloy in them; that the choice must always be made, if not of the lesser evil, at least of the GREATER, not the PERFECT good; and that in every political institution, a power to advance the public happiness, involves a discretion which may be misapplied and abused. They will see therefore that in all cases, where power is to be conferred, the point first to be decided is whether such a power be necessary to the public good; as the next will be, in case of an affirmative decision, to guard as effectually as possible against a perversion of the power to the public detriment.

That we may form a correct judgment on this subject, it will be proper to review the several powers conferred on the Government of the Union; and that this may be the more conveniently done, they may be reduced into different classes as they relate to the following different objects;—1. security against foreign danger—2. regulation of the intercourse with foreign nations—3. maintenance of harmony and proper intercourse among the States—4. certain miscellaneous objects of general utility—5. restraint of the States from certain injurious acts—6. provisions for giving due efficacy to all these powers.

The powers falling within the first class, are those of declaring war, and granting letters of marque; of providing armies and fleets; of regulating and calling forth the militia; of levying and borrowing money.

Security against foreign danger is one of the primitive objects of civil society. It is an avowed and essential object of the American Union. The powers requisite for attaining it, must be effectually confided to the fœderal councils.

Is the power of declaring war necessary? No man will answer this question in the negative. It would be superfluous therefore to enter into a proof of the affirmative. The existing confederation establishes this power in the most ample form.

Is the power of raising armies, and equipping fleets necessary? This is involved in the foregoing power. It is involved in the power of self-defence.

But was it necessary to give an INDEFINITE POWER of raising TROOPS, as well as providing fleets; and of maintaining both in PEACE, as well as in WAR?

The answer to these questions has been too far anticipated, in another place, to admit an extensive discussion of them in this place. The answer indeed seems to be obvious and conclusive as scarcely to justify such a discussion in any place. With what colour of propriety could the force necessary for defence, be limited by those who cannot limit the force of offence. If a Federal Constitution could chain the ambition, or set bounds to the exertions of all other nations: then indeed might it prudently chain the discretion of its own Government, and set bounds to the exertions for its own safety.

How could a readiness for war in time of peace be safely prohibited, unless we could prohibit in like manner the preparations and establishments of every hostile nation? The means of security can only be regulated by the means and the danger of attack. They will in fact be ever determined by these rules, and by no others. It is in vain to oppose constitutional barriers to the impulse of self-preservation. It is worse than in vain; because it plants in the Constitution itself necessary usurpations of power, every precedent of which is a germ of unnecessary and multiplied repetitions. If one nation maintains constantly a disciplined army ready for the service of ambition or revenge, it obliges the most pacific nations, who may be within the reach of its enterprizes, to take corresponding precautions. The fifteenth century was the unhappy epoch of military establishments in time of peace. They were introduced by Charles VII. of France. All Europe has followed, or been forced into the example. Had the example not been followed by other nations, all Europe must long ago have worne the chains of a universal monarch. Were every nation except France now to disband its peace establishment, the same event might follow. The veteran legions of Rome were an overmatch for the undisciplined valour of all other nations, and rendered her mistress of the world.

Not less true is it, that the liberties of Rome proved the final victim to her military triumphs, and that the liberties of Europe, as far as they ever existed, have with few exceptions been the price of her military establishments. A standing force therefore is a dangerous, at the same time that it may be a necessary provision. On the smallest scale it has its inconveniences. On an extensive scale, its consequences may be fatal.

On any scale, it is an object of laudable circumspection and precaution. A wise nation will combine all these considerations; and whilst it does not rashly preclude itself from any resource which may become essential to its safety, will exert all its prudence in diminishing both the necessity and the danger of resorting to one which may be inauspicious to its liberties.

The clearest marks of this prudence are stamped on the proposed Constitution. The Union itself which it cements and secures, destroys every pretext for a military establishment which could be dangerous. America, united with a handful of troops, or without a single soldier, exhibits a more forbidding posture to foreign ambition, than America disunited, with an hundred thousand veterans ready for combat. It was remarked on a former occasion, that the want of this pretext had saved the liberties of one nation in Europe. Being rendered by her insular situation and her maritime resources, impregnable to the armies of her neighbours, the rulers of Great-Britain have never been able, by real or artificial dangers, to cheat the public into an extensive peace establishment. The distance of the United States from the powerful nations of the world, gives them the same happy security. A dangerous establishment can never be necessary or plausible, so long as they continue a united people. But let it never for a moment be forgotten, that they are indebted for this advantage to their Union alone. The moment of its dissolution will be the date of a new order of things. The fears of the weaker or the ambition of the stronger States or Confederacies, will set the same example in the new, as Charles VII. did in the old world. The example will be followed here from the same motives which produced universal imitation there. Instead of deriving from our situation the precious advantage which Great-Britain has derived from hers, the face of America will be but a copy of that of the Continent of Europe. It will present liberty every where crushed between standing armies and perpetual taxes. The fortunes of disunited America will be even more disastrous than those of Europe. The sources of evil in the latter are confined to her own limits. No superior powers of another quarter of the globe intrigue among her rival nations, inflame their mutual animosities, and render them the instruments of foreign ambition, jealousy and revenge. In America, the miseries springing from her internal jealousies, contentions and wars, would form a part only of her lot. A plentiful addition of evils would have their source in that relation in which Europe stands to this quarter of the earth, and which no other quarter of the earth bears to Europe. This picture of the consequences of disunion cannot be too highly coloured, or too often exhibited. Every man who loves peace, every man who loves his country, every man who loves liberty, ought to have it ever before his eyes, that he may cherish in his heart a due attachment to the Union of America, and be able to set a due value on the means of preserving it.

Next to the effectual establishment of the Union, the best possible precaution against danger from standing armies, is a limitation of the term for which revenue may be appropriated to their support. This precaution the Constitution has prudently added. I will not repeat here the observations, which I flatter myself have placed this subject in a just and satisfactory light. But it may not be improper to take notice of an argument against this part of the Constitution, which has been drawn from the policy and practice of Great-Britain. It is said that the continuance of an army in that kingdom, requires an annual vote of the Legislature; whereas the American Constitution has lengthened this critical period to two years. This is the form in which the comparison is usually stated to the public: But is it a just form? Is it a fair comparison? Does the British Constitution restrain the Parliamentary discretion to one year? Does the American impose on the Congress appropriations for two years? On the contrary, it cannot be unknown to the authors of the fallacy themselves, that the British Constitution fixes no limit whatever to the discretion of the Legislature, and that the American ties down the Legislature to two years, as the longest admissible term.

Had the argument from the British example been truly stated, it would have stood thus: The term for which supplies may be appropriated to the army-establishment, though unlimited by the British Constitution, has nevertheless in practice been limited by parliamentary discretion, to a single year. Now if in Great-Britain, where the House of Commons is elected for seven years; where so great a proportion of the members are elected by so small a proportion of the people; where the electors are so corrupted by the Representatives, and the Representatives so corrupted by the Crown, the Representative body can possess a power to make appropriations to the army for an indefinite term, without desiring, or without daring, to extend the term beyond a single year; ought not suspicion herself to blush in pretending that the Representatives of the United States, elected FREELY, by the WHOLE BODY of the people, every SECOND YEAR, cannot be safely entrusted with a discretion over such appropriations, expressly limited to the short period of TWO YEARS.

A bad cause seldom fails to betray itself. Of this truth, the management of the opposition to the Federal Government is an unvaried exemplification. But among all the blunders which have been committed, none is more striking than the attempt to enlist on that side, the prudent jealousy entertained by the people, of standing armies. The attempt has awakened fully the public attention to that important subject; and has led to investigations which must terminate in a thorough and universal conviction, not only that the Constitution has provided the most effectual guards against danger from that quarter, but that nothing short of a Constitution fully adequate to the national defence, and the preservation of the Union, can save America from as many standing armies as it may be split into States or Confederacies; and from such a progressive augmentation of these establishments in each, as will render them as burdensome to the properties and ominous to the liberties of the people; as any establishment that can become necessary, under a united and efficient Government, must be tolerable to the former, and safe to the latter.

The palpable necessity of the power to provide and maintain a navy has protected that part of the Constitution against a spirit of censure, which has spared few other parts. It must indeed be numbered among the greatest blessings of America, that as her Union will be the only source of her maritime strength, so this will be a principal source of her security against danger from abroad. In this respect our situation bears another likeness to the insular advantage of Great-Britain. The batteries most capable of repelling foreign enterprizers on our safety, are happily such as can never be turned by a perfidious government against our liberties.

The inhabitants of the Atlantic frontier are all of them deeply interested in this provision for naval protection, and they have hitherto been suffered to sleep quietly in their beds; if their property has remained safe against the predatory spirit of licencious adventurers; if their maritime towns have not yet been compelled to ransome themselves from the terrors of a conflagration, by yielding to the exactions of daring and sudden invaders, these instances of good fortune are not to be ascribed to the capacity of the existing government for the protection of those from whom it claims allegiance, but to causes that are fugitive and fallacious. If we except perhaps Virginia and Maryland, which are peculiarly vulnerable on their Eastern frontiers, no part of the Union ought to feel more anxiety on this subject than New-York. Her sea coast is extensive. The very important district of the state is an island. The state itself is penetrated by a large navigable river for more than fifty leagues. The great emporium of its commerce, the great recervoir of its wealth, lies every moment at the mercy of events, and may almost be regarded as a hostage, for ignominious compliances with the dictates of a foreign enemy, or even with the rapacious demands of pirates and barbarians. Should a war be the result of the precarious situation of European affairs, and all the unruly passions attending it, be let loose on the ocean, our escape from insults and depredations, not only on that element but every part of the other bordering on it, will be truly miraculous. In the present condition of America, the states more immediately exposed to these calamities, have nothing to hope from the phantom of a general government which now exists; and if their single resources were equal to the task of fortifying themselves against the danger, the object to be protected would be almost consumed by the means of protecting them.

The power of regulating and calling forth the militia has been already sufficiently vindicated and explained.

The power of levying and borrowing money, being the sinew of that which is to be exerted in the national defence, is properly thrown into the same class with it. This power also has been examined already with much attention, and has I trust been clearly shewn to be necessary both in the extent and form given to it by the constitution. I will address one additional reflection only to those who contend that the power ought to have been restrained to external taxation, by which they mean taxes on articles imported from other countries. It can not be doubted that this will always be a valuable source of revenue, that for a considerable time, it must be a principle source, that at this moment it is an essential one. But we may form very mistaken ideas on this subject, if we do not call to mind in our calculations, that the extent of revenue drawn from foreign commerce, must vary with the variations both in the extent and the kind of imports, and that these variations do not correspond with the progress of population, which must be the general measure of the publick wants. As long as agriculture continues the sole field of labour, the importation of manufactures must increase as the consumers multiply. As soon as domestic manufactures are begun by the hands not called for by agriculture, the imported manufactures will decrease as the numbers of people increase. In a more remote stage, the imports may consist in considerable part of raw materials which will be wrought into articles for exportation, and will therefore require rather the encouragement of bounties, than to be loaded with discouraging duties. A system of Government, meant for duration, ought to contemplate these revolutions, and be able to accommodate itself to them.

Some who have not denied the necessity of the power of taxation, have grounded a very fierce attack against the Constitution on the language in which it is defined. It has been urged and echoed, that the power "to lay and collect taxes, duties, imposts and excises, to pay the debts: and provide for the common defence and general welfare of the United States," amounts to an unlimited commission to exercise every power which may be alledged to be necessary for the common defence or general welfare. No stronger proof could be given of the distress under which these writers labour for objections, than their stooping to such a misconstruction.

Had no other enumeration or definition of the powers of the Congress been found in the Constitution, than the general expressions just cited, the authors of the objection might have had some colour for it; though it would have been difficult to find a reason for so aukward a form of describing an authority to legislate in all possible cases. A power to destroy the freedom of the press, the trial by jury or even to regulate the course of descents, or the forms of conveyances, must be very singularly expressed by the terms "to raise money for the general welfare."

But what colour can the objection have, when a specification of the objects alluded to by these general terms, immediately follows; and is not even separated by a longer pause than a semicolon. If the different parts of the same instrument ought to be so expounded as to give meaning to every part which will bear it; shall one part of the same sentence be excluded altogether from a share in the meaning; and shall the more doubtful and indefinite terms be retained in their full extent and the clear and precise expressions, be denied any signification whatsoever? For what purpose could the enumeration of particular powers be inserted, if these and all others were meant to be included in the preceding general power? Nothing is more natural or common than first to use a general phrase, and then to explain and qualify it by a recital of particulars. But the idea of an enumeration of particulars, which neither explain nor qualify the general meaning, and can have no other effect than to confound and mislead, is an absurdity which as we are reduced to the dilemma of charging either on the authors of the objection, or on the authors of the Constitution, we must take the liberty of supposing, had not its origin with the latter.

The objection here is the more extraordinary, as it appears, that the language used by the Convention is a copy from the articles of confederation. The objects of the Union among the States as described in article 3d. are, "their common defence, security of their liberties, and mutual and general welfare." The terms of article 8th. are still more identical. "All charges of war, and all other expences, that shall be incurred for the common defence or general welfare, and allowed by the United States in Congress, shall be defrayed out of a common treasury &c." A similar language again occurs in art. 9. Construe either of these articles by the rules which would justify, the construction put on the new Constitution, and they vest in the existing Congress a power to legislate in all cases whatsoever. But what would have been thought of that assembly, if attaching themselves to these general expressions, and disregarding the specifications, which ascertain and limit their import, they had exercised an unlimited power of providing "for the common defence and general welfare."? I appeal to the objectors themselves, whether they would in that case have employed the same reasoning in justification of Congress, as they now make use of against the Convention. How difficult it is for error to escape its own condemnation!

Henry Knox to John Sullivan

New York, January 19, 1788

(private)

The new Minister of France, the Count de Moutiers who arrived yesterday brought the enclosed letter from our common friend the Marquis de la Fayette. It is addressed to you on the supposition of your being in this city and President of Congress. But alass there is no Congress although two months have elapsed since one ought to have been assembled agreably to the confederation

The new constitution! the new Constitution! is the general cry this way. Much paper is spoiled on the subject, and many essays are written which perhaps are not read by either side. It is a stubborn fact however, that the present system called the confederation has run down—That the springs if ever it had others, than the late Army have utterly lost their tone, and the machine cannot be wound up again.

But something must be done speedily or we shall be involved in all the horrors of anarchy and seperate interests— This indeed appears to have been the serious judgement of all the states which have formally considered the new constitution, and therefore they have adopted it, not as a perfect system, but as the best that could be obtained under existing circumstances

If to those states which have already adopted it, Massachusetts and New Hampshire should be added, a doubt cannot be entertained, but that it will be received generally in the course of the present year—If Massachusetts and New Hampshire reject it we shall have to encounter a boisterous and uncertain ocean of events

Should you have leisure, I shall be much obliged by a confidential information of the disposition of New Hampshire on the subject, and you may rest assured that your confidence will not be misplaced

"Americanus" [*John Stevens, Jr.*] *VII*

Daily Advertiser (New York), January 21, 1788

Governor Randolph's letter to the Speaker of the House of Delegates of Virginia, on the Federal Constitution, has certainly great merit. A vein of candor, manliness, and at the same time delicacy, pervades every part, and prepossesses us strongly in favor of the author. But if the imagination is delighted by the purity and elegance of the diction, if the justness and propriety of sentiment display'd in this letter, brings full conviction to the mind, it only serves the more to encrease our mortification, when we reflect on the main scope and tendency of it. That a mind so fully convinced of the necessity of Union, and which views with horror the idea of a dissolution, should, notwithstanding, be made to hesitate and boggle, by objections so trivial and insignificant, is one of those melancholy instances of weakness, from which, even the best and most cultivated understandings are not exempt. My knowledge of his Excellency's character and sentiments, is wholly limited to what may be collected from this performance. But this alone is sufficient evidence of the integrity of the heart which dictated it. A sort of instinct, impels me to this conclusion, and convinces me I am right. This conviction, however, of the rectitude of his intentions, serves only to render his Excellency's conduct the more inexplicable. After surmounting all those great obstacles that have been thrown in the way, against the adoption of the new Constitution; After admitting the necessity of a standing army; the unlimited power of taxation, nay, that "the new powers must be deposited in a new body, growing out of a consolidation of the Union;" After surmounting, I say, these difficulties, he has suffered himself to be checked in his career, by objects of the smallest magnitude.

1. *All ambiguities of expression to be precisely explained.* But if

the late Convention could not avoid ambiguities, after four months application to this business, what reason have we to expect that a subsequent Convention will succeed any better. We all know that comments frequently obscure the text they were meant to elucidate, and render that ambiguous, which before was sufficiently plain and obvious. If there are really any ambiguous expressions contained in this Constitution, I am persuaded, the good sense of my fellow countrymen, will dictate to them the necessity of expunging them, the moment they shall feel the least inconvenience arising from them. The full discovery of these inaccuracies must necessarily be left to time.

2. *The President to be rendered ineligible, after a given number of years.* This is a political refinement, the necessity of which, is very problematical. It is difficult for us to divest ourselves entirely of the ideas we have imbibed from our English ancestors. The extensive prerogatives and regal state, which the Supreme Executive in England have always possessed, have ever been, and with reason too, the object of terror to the friends of liberty. All their efforts have been directed to the attainment of this important point, viz. to circumscribe and limit these dangerous powers within proper bounds. But on this side the Atlantic, all apprehensions arising from this source, are visionary. Why then should we tie up our own hands, and deprive ourselves of the services of a man, with whose conduct we are perfectly satisfied? For my part I confess, I can see no reason whatever, to induce us to adopt this amendment, and I firmly believe this to be the sentiment of the majority of the people of these States.

3. *In taking from him, either the power of nominating to the judiciary offices, or of filling up vacancies, which therein may happen during the recess of the Senate, by granting commissions, which shall expire at the end of their next sessions.* The design here, I suppose, is to prevent the President possessing too great an influence with respect to these appointments. But I am so unfortunate, that my sentiments, such as they are, with respect to this amendment, happen to be in direct opposition to those of Mr. Randolph's. Instead of controling the President still farther with regard to appointments, I am for leaving the appointment of all the principal officers under the

Federal Government *solely* to the President, and the subordinate ones to the heads of departments.

4. *To take from him the power of pardoning for treason.* This is a power that must necessarily be lodged some where, and where, I would ask, would we place it with greater safety and propriety?

5. *To draw the line between the powers of Congress and individual States; and to define the former; so as to leave no clashing of jurisdictions or dangerous disputes; and to prevent the one from being swallowed up by the other, under the cover of general words and implication.*

The objects of congressional Legislation are already enumerated and clearly defined in the Constitution. But it may be objected that by the last clause of the eighth section of the first article, an *indefinite* power of Legislation is given to the General Government. But no inference can be more unfair and disingenuous. It surely cannot be denied that the Federal head *must* possess the powers of *Legislation.* They *must* pass laws for laying and collecting taxes—for borrowing of money—for regulating commerce, &c. &c. And what is the purport and effect of this clause but *merely* a declaration of *this* power? Nothing can be clearer than that by this clause no *new* powers are granted. The fact is that though the *objects* of Legislation may be ascertained and defined in the body of a constitutional compact, yet from the very nature of this power the *manner* of exercising it must *necessarily* be *discretionary.* In this respect it must *unavoidably* remain *unlimited* and *indefinite.* The Constitution may say about *what*, but cannot say *how* this power shall be exercised. But it may be asked in what manner is this *discretionary* power to be kept within due bounds? I answer, that the Constitution itself is a *supreme law of the land*, unrepealable by any *subsequent law*: every law that is not made in conformity to *that*, is in itself nugatory, and the Judges, who by their oath, are bound to support the Constitution as the *supreme law of the land* must determine accordingly. But should those restraints, which is hardly supposable, prove insufficient, it then rests with the PEOPLE to restore to the Constitution its wonted vigor.

6. *To abridge the powers of the Senate to make treaties the supreme laws of the land.*

So far as an article of a treaty may be opposed to, or in any way contravene an existing law of the land, so far perhaps the concurrence of the whole Legislature might be proper to give it validity. It will not, however, be denied, that treaties ought to have the force of "laws of the land." And for a variety of reasons, I should presume, the Senate to be the only proper depositum of this power. Negociations of this nature require a management and secrecy ill suited to the turbulence and party violence of a numerous House of Representatives. They are, besides, too numerous and transitory a body to make the members thereof subjected to any great degree of responsibility. From local circumstances, treaties with foreign powers must necessarily contain some articles, which will be more advantageous or disadvantageous to one State than to another. And as there subsists so great a disparity between the States with respect to extent of territory and number of inhabitants, it would come within the power of three or four States to dictate the law to all the rest; and the interest of the smaller States would inevitably be sacrificed to the local interests or ambitious views of the larger.

7. *To provide a tribunal instead of the Senate, for the impeachment of Senators.*

Agreeably to the amendment I have proposed above, viz. that appointments should be in the President *only*, this tribunal would be unnecessary, as the business of the Senate (except that they constitute a Court for Trials on Impeachments) would thereby be confined *solely* to the business of Legislation, for which it is obvious they could not be made impeachable. And here candor obliges me to acknowledge, that the concurrence of the Senate, with regard to appointments, appears to me to be the greatest defect in this intended plan of Government. There is certainly a glaring impropriety in the Senators trying on impeachments those very officers, in whose appointments they have had a voice.

8. *To incapacitate the Congress to determine their own salaries.*

I have but one observation to make on this head. It does not appear to me to be an object of sufficient magnitude, to make it necessary to call together another convention.

9. *To limit and define the Judicial power.*

But is not the Judicial power limited and defined by the

second section of the third article, as precisely as the nature of the case will admit of. Without restraining Congress from the exercise of the powers of Legislation, how could the Judicial power be more precisely limited and defined.

Thus have I considered, in a summary manner, all the objections and proposed amendments, which Mr. Randolph has thought necessary to make to this new plan of Government. And I must here repeat again the observation I have already made—That these objections appear, to me at least, trivial and insignificant.

Mr. Randolph's scheme of appointing another Federal Convention, for the discussion of amendments, cannot now be carried into execution, as the Constitution, has already been adopted and ratified by four States, and probably will shortly be adopted by more.

Mr. Randolph has candidly confessed it as his opinion, that those two points, viz. "the equality of suffrage in the Senate, and the submission of commerce to a mere majority," which proved so very offensive to himself and Mr. Mason, "cannot be corrected." And of the nine other objections, which he has brought against the Constitution, some are disputable, the greater part insignificant, and none of sufficient consequence to render it necessary to call together another Convention. But what would be the probable issue of such a measure? Could the deliberations of such a Convention be confined solely to Mr. Randolph's objections, there might then, perhaps, be some chance of their rising in harmony and good humor, but so multifarious and contradictory are the objections which have been urged from different quarters, that human wisdom and human prudence must utterly despair of ever forming a consistent and uniform plan out of such incongruous and heterogeneous materials. Would not such a *Convention* be in the very predicament mankind were in at the building of BABEL? They set themselves about to build a CITY and a TOWER whose top might reach unto Heaven. But their *language* was CONFOUNDED, so that they did *not understand one another's speech. Therefore the name of it was called* BABEL.

"Publius," The Federalist XLII
[James Madison]

New-York Packet, January 22, 1788

To the People of the State of New-York.

The *second* class of powers lodged in the General Government, consists of those which regulate the intercourse with foreign nations, to wit, to make treaties; to send and receive Ambassadors, other public Ministers and Consuls; to define and punish piracies and felonies committed on the high seas, and offences against the law of nations; to regulate foreign commerce, including a power to prohibit after the year 1808, the importation of slaves, and to lay an intermediate duty of ten dollars per head, as a discouragement to such importations.

This class of powers forms an obvious and essential branch of the fœderal administration. If we are to be one nation in any respect, it clearly ought to be in respect to other nations.

The powers to make treaties and to send and receive Ambassadors, speak their own propriety. Both of them are comprized in the articles of confederation; with this difference only, that the former is disembarrassed by the plan of the Convention of an exception, under which treaties might be substantially frustrated by regulations of the States; and that a power of appointing and receiving "other public Ministers and Consuls," is expressly and very properly added to the former provision concerning Ambassadors. The term Ambassador, if taken strictly, as seems to be required by the second of the articles of confederation, comprehends the highest grade only of public Ministers; and excludes the grades which the United States will be most likely to prefer where foreign embassies may be necessary. And under no latitude of construction will the term comprehend Consuls. Yet it has been found expedient, and has been the practice of Congress to employ the inferior grades of public Ministers; and to send and receive Consuls. It is true that where treaties of commerce stipulate for the mutual appointment of Consuls, whose functions are connected with commerce, the admission of foreign Consuls may fall within the power of making commercial treaties; and that where no such treaties exist, the mission of American Consuls into foreign countries, may *perhaps* be covered under the authority given by the 9th article of the Confederation, to appoint all such civil officers as may be necessary for managing the general affairs of the United States. But the admission of Consuls into the United States, where no previous treaty has stipulated it, seems to have been no where provided for. A supply of the omission is one of the lesser instances in which the Convention have improved on the model before them. But the most minute provisions become important when they tend to obviate the necessity or the pretext for gradual and unobserved usurpations of power, a list of the cases in which Congress have been betrayed, or forced by the defects of the confederation into violations of their chartered authorities, would not a little surprize those who have paid no attention to the subject; and would be no inconsiderable argument in favor of the new Constitution, which seems to have provided no less studiously for the lesser, than the more obvious and striking defects of the old.

The power to define and punish piracies and felonies committed on the high seas, and offences against the law of nations, belongs with equal propriety to the general government; and is a still greater improvement on the articles of confederation. These articles contain no provision for the case of offences against the law of nations; and consequently leave it in the power of any indiscreet member to embroil the confederacy with foreign nations. The provision of the fœderal articles on the subject of piracies and felonies, extends no farther than to the establishment of courts for the trial of these offences. The definition of piracies might perhaps without inconveniency, be left to the law of nations; though a legislative definition of them, is found in most municipal codes. A definition of felonies on the high seas is evidently requisite.

Felony is a term of loose signification even in the common law of England; and of various import in the statute law of that kingdom. But neither the common, nor the statute law of that or of any other nation ought to be a standard for the proceedings of this, unless previously made its own by legislative adoption. The meaning of the term as defined in the codes of the several States, would be as impracticable as the former would be a dishonorable and illegitimate guide. It is not precisely the same in any two of the States; and varies in each with every revision of its criminal laws. For the sake of certainty and uniformity therefore, the power of defining felonies in this case, was in every respect necessary and proper.

The regulation of foreign commerce, having fallen within several views which have been taken of this subject, has been too fully discussed to need additional proofs here of its being properly submitted to the fœderal administration.

It were doubtless to be wished that the power of prohibiting the importation of slaves, had not been postponed until the year 1808, or rather that it had been suffered to have immediate operation. But it is not difficult to account either for this restriction on the general government, or for the manner in which the whole clause is expressed. It ought to be considered as a great point gained in favor of humanity, that a period of twenty years may terminate for ever within these States, a traffic which has so long and so loudly upbraided the barbarism of modern policy; that within that period it will receive a considerable discouragement from the fœderal Government, and may be totally abolished by a concurrence of the few States which continue the unnatural traffic, in the prohibitory example which has been given by so great a majority of the Union. Happy would it be for the unfortunate Africans, if an equal prospect lay before them, of being redeemed from the oppressions of their European brethren!

Attempts have been made to pervert this clause into an objection against the Constitution, by representing it on one side as a criminal toleration of an illicit practice, and on another, as calculated to prevent voluntary and beneficial emigrations from Europe to America. I mention these misconstructions, not with a view to give them an answer, for they deserve none; but as specimens of the manner and spirit in which some have thought fit to conduct their opposition to the proposed government.

The powers included in the *third* class, are those which provide for the harmony and proper intercourse among the States.

Under this head might be included the particular restraints imposed on the authority of the States, and certain powers of the judicial department; but the former are reserved for a distinct class, and the latter will be particularly examined when we arrive at the structure and organization of the government. I shall confine myself to a cursory review of the remaining powers comprehended under this third description, to wit, to regulate commerce among the several States and the Indian tribes; to coin money, regulate the value thereof and of foreign coin; to provide for the punishment of counterfeiting the current coin, and securities of the United States; to fix the standard of weights and measures; to establish an uniform rule of naturalization, and uniform laws of bankruptcy; to prescribe the manner in which the public acts, records and judicial proceedings of each State shall be proved, and the effect they shall have in other States; and to establish post-offices, and post-roads.

The defect of power in the existing confederacy, to regulate the commerce between its several members, is in the number of those which have been clearly pointed out by experience. To the proofs and remarks which former papers have brought into view on this subject, it may be added, that without this supplemental provision, the great and essential power of regulating foreign commerce, would have been incompleat, and ineffectual. A very material object of this power was the relief of the States which import and export through other States, from the improper contributions levied on them by the latter. Were these at liberty to regulate the trade between State and State, it must be foreseen that ways would be found out, to load the articles of import and export, during the passage through their jurisdiction, with duties which would fall on the makers of the latter, and the consumers of the former: We may be assured by past experience, that such a practice would be introduced by future contrivances; and both by that and a common knowledge of human affairs, that it would nourish unceasing animosities, and not improbably terminate in serious interruptions of the public tranquility. To those who do not view the question through the medium of passion or of interest, the desire of the commercial States to collect in any form, an indirect revenue from their uncommercial neighbours, must appear not less impolitic than it is unfair; since it would stimulate the injured party, by resentment as well as interest, to resort to less convenient channels for their foreign trade. But the mild voice of reason, pleading the cause of an enlarged and permanent interest, is but too often drowned before public bodies as well as individuals, by the clamours of an impatient avidity for immediate and immoderate gain.

The necessity of a superintending authority over the reciprocal trade of confederated States has been illustrated by other examples as well as our own. In Switzerland, where the Union is so very slight, each Canton is obliged to allow to merchandizes, a passage through its jurisdiction into other Cantons, without an augmentation of the tolls. In Germany, it is a law of the empire, that the Princes and States shall not lay tolls or customs on bridges, rivers, or passages, without the consent of the Emperor and Diet; though it appears from a quotation in an antecedent paper, that the practice in this as in many other instances in that confederacy, has not followed the law, and has produced there the mischiefs which have been foreseen here. Among the restraints imposed by the Union of the Netherlands, on its members, one is, that they shall not establish imposts disadvantageous to their neighbors, without the general permission.

The regulation of commerce with the Indian tribes is very properly unfettered from two limitations in the articles of confederation, which render the provision obscure and contradictory. The power is there restrained to Indians, not members of any of the States, and is not to violate or infringe the legislative right of any State within its own limits. What description of Indians are to be deemed members of a State, is not yet settled; and has been a question of frequent perplexity and contention in the Fœderal Councils. And how the trade with Indians, though not members of a State, yet residing within its legislative jurisdiction, can be regulated by an external authority, without so far intruding on the internal rights of legislation, is absolutely incomprehensible. This is not the only case in which the articles of confederation have inconsiderately endeavored to accomplish impossibilities; to reconcile a partial sovereignty in the Union, with compleat sovereignty in the States; to subvert a mathematical axiom, by taking away a part, and letting the whole remain.

All that need be remarked on the power to coin money, regulate the value thereof, and of foreign coin, is that by providing for this last case, the Constitution has supplied a material omission in the articles of confederation. The authority of the existing Congress is restrained to the regulation of coin *struck* by their own authority, or that of the respective States. It must be seen at once, that the proposed uniformity in the *value* of the current coin might be destroyed by subjecting that of foreign coin to the different regulations of the different States.

The punishment of counterfeiting the public securities as well as of the current coin, is submitted of course to that authority, which is to secure the value of both.

The regulation of weights and measures is transferred from the articles of confederation, and is founded on like considerations with the preceding power of regulating coin.

The dissimilarity in the rules of naturalization, has long been remarked as a fault in our system, and as laying a foundation for intricate and delicate questions. In the 4th article of the confederation, it is declared "that the *free inhabitants* of each of these States, paupers, vagabonds, and fugitives from justice excepted, shall be entitled to all privileges and immunities of *free citizens*, in the several States, and *the people* of each State, shall in every other, enjoy all the privileges of trade and commerce, &c." There is a confusion of language here, which is remarkable. Why the terms *free inhabitants*, are used in one part of the article; *free citizens* in another, and *people* in another, or what was meant by superadding "to all privileges and immunities of free citizens,"—"all the privileges of trade and commerce," cannot easily be determined. It seems to be a construction scarcely avoidable, however, that those who come under the denomination of *free inhabitants* of a State, although not citizens of such State, are entitled in every other

State to all the privileges of *free citizens* of the latter; that is, to
greater privileges than they may be entitled to in their own
State; so that it may be in the power of a particular State, or
rather every State is laid under a necessity, not only to confer
the rights of citizenship in other States upon any whom it
may admit to such rights within itself; but upon any whom it
may allow to become inhabitants within its jurisdiction. But
were an exposition of the term "inhabitants" to be admitted,
which would confine the stipulated privileges to citizens
alone, the difficulty is diminished only, not removed. The
very improper power would still be retained by each State, of
naturalizing aliens in every other State. In one State residence
for a short term confers all the rights of citizenship. In another qualifications of greater importance are required. An
alien therefore legally incapacitated for certain rights in the
latter, may by previous residence only in the former, elude his
incapacity; and thus the law of one State, be preposterously
rendered paramount to the law of another, within the jurisdiction of the other. We owe it to mere casualty, that very
serious embarrassments on this subject, have been hitherto escaped. By the laws of several States, certain descriptions of
aliens who had rendered themselves obnoxious, were laid under interdicts inconsistent, not only with the rights of citizenship, but with the privilege of residence. What would have
been the consequence, if such persons, by residence or otherwise, had acquired the character of citizens under the laws of
another State, and then asserted their rights as such, both to
residence and citizenship within the State proscribing them?
Whatever the legal consequences might have been, other consequences would probably have resulted of too serious a nature, not to be provided against. The new Constitution has
accordingly with great propriety made provision against
them, and all others proceeding from the defect of the confederation, on this head, by authorising the general government
to establish an uniform rule of naturalization throughout the
United States.

The power of establishing uniform laws of bankruptcy, is
so intimately connected with the regulation of commerce,
and will prevent so many frauds where the parties or their

property may lie or be removed into different States, that the expediency of it seems not likely to be drawn into question.

The power of prescribing by general laws the manner in which the public acts, records and judicial proceedings of each State shall be proved, and the effect they shall have in other States, is an evident and valuable improvement on the clause relating to this subject in the articles of confederation. The meaning of the latter is extremely indeterminate; and can be of little importance under any interpretation which it will bear. The power here established, may be rendered a very convenient instrument of justice, and be particularly beneficial on the borders of contiguous States, where the effects liable to justice, may be suddenly and secretly translated in any stage of the process, within a foreign jurisdiction.

The power of establishing post-roads, must in every view be a harmless power; and may perhaps, by judicious management, become productive of great public conveniency. Nothing which tends to facilitate the intercourse between the States, can be deemed unworthy of the public care.

"Publius," The Federalist XLIII
[*James Madison*]

Independent Journal (New York), January 23, 1788

To the People of the State of New-York.

The *fourth* class comprises the following miscellaneous powers.

1. A power "to promote the progress of science and useful arts, by securing for a limited time, to authors and inventors, the exclusive right, to their respective writings and discoveries."

The utility of this power will scarcely be questioned. The copy right of authors has been solemnly adjudged in Great Britain to be a right at common law. The right to useful inventions, seems with equal reason to belong to the inventors. The public good fully coincides in both cases, with the claims of individuals. The States cannot separately make effectual provision for either of the cases, and most of them have anticipated the decision of this point, by laws passed at the instance of Congress.

2. "To exercise exclusive legislation in all cases whatsoever, over such district (not exceeding ten miles square) as may, by cession of particular States and the acceptance of Congress, become the seat of the Government of the United States; and to exercise like authority over all places purchased by the consent of the Legislature of the States, in which the same shall be, for the erection of forts, magazines, arsenals, dockyards and other needful buildings."

The indispensible necessity of compleat authority at the seat of Government carries its own evidence with it. It is a power exercised by every Legislature of the Union, I might say of the world, by virtue of its general supremacy. Without it, not only the public authority might be insulted and its proceedings be interrupted, with impunity; but a dependence of the members of the general Government, on the State comprehending the seat of the Government for protection in the exercise of their duty, might bring on the national councils an imputation of awe or influence, equally dishonorable to the Government, and dissatisfactory to the other members of the confederacy. This consideration has the more weight as the gradual accumulation of public improvements at the stationary residence of the Government, would be both too great a public pledge to be left in the hands of a single State; and would create so many obstacles to a removal of the Government, as still further to abridge its necessary independence. The extent of this federal district is sufficiently circumscribed to satisfy every jealousy of an opposite nature. And as it is to be appropriated to this use with the consent of the State ceding it; as the State will no doubt provide in the compact for the rights, and the consent of the citizens inhabiting it; as the inhabitants will find sufficient inducements of interest to become willing parties to the cession; as they will have had their voice in the election of the Government which is to exercise authority over them; as a municipal Legislature for local purposes, derived from their own suffrages, will of course be allowed them; and as the authority of the Legislature of the State, and of the inhabitants of the ceded part of it, to concur in the cession, will be derived from the whole people of the State, in their adoption of the Constitution, every imaginable objection seems to be obviated.

The necessity of a like authority over forts, magazines &c. established by the general Government is not less evident. The public money expended on such places, and the public property deposited in them, require that they should be exempt from the authority of the particular State. Nor would it be proper for the places on which the security of the entire Union may depend, to be in any degree dependent on a particular member of it. All objections and scruples are here also obviated by requiring the concurrence of the States concerned, in every such establishment.

3. "To declare the punishment of treason, but no attainder of treason shall work corruption of blood, or forfeiture, except during the life of the person attainted."

As treason may be committed against the United States, the

authority of the United States ought to be enabled to punish it. But as new-fangled and artificial treasons, have been the great engines, by which violent factions, the natural offspring of free Governments, have usually wrecked their alternate malignity on each other, the Convention have with great judgment opposed a barrier to this peculiar danger, by inserting a constitutional definition of the crime, fixing the proof necessary for conviction of it, and restraining the Congress, even in punishing it, from extending the consequences of guilt beyond the person of its author.

4. "To admit new States into the Union; but no new State, shall be formed or erected within the jurisdiction of any other State; nor any State be formed by the junction of two or more States, or parts of States, without the consent of the Legislatures of the States concerned, as well as of the Congress."

In the articles of confederation no provision is found on this important subject. Canada was to be admitted of right on her joining in the measures of the United States; and the other *colonies*, by which were evidently meant, the other British colonies, at the discretion of nine States. The eventual establishment of *new States*, seems to have been overlooked by the compilers of that instrument. We have seen the inconvenience of this omission, and the assumption of power into which Congress have been led by it. With great propriety therefore has the new system supplied the defect. The general precaution that no new States shall be formed without the concurrence of the federal authority and that of the States concerned, is consonant to the principles which ought to govern such transactions. The particular precaution against the erection of new States, by the partition of a State without its consent, quiets the jealousy of the larger States; as that of the smaller is quieted by a like precaution against a junction of States without their consent.

5. "To dispose of and make all needful rules and regulations respecting the territory or other property belonging to the United States, with a proviso that nothing in the Constitution shall be so construed as to prejudice any claims of the United States, or of any particular State."

This is a power of very great importance, and required by

considerations similar to those which shew the propriety of the former. The proviso annexed is proper in itself, and was probably rendered absolutely necessary, by jealousies and questions concerning the Western territory, sufficiently known to the public.

6. "To guarantee to every state in the Union a Republican form of Government; to protect each of them against invasion; and on application of the Legislature, or of the Executive (when the Legislature cannot be convened) against domestic violence."

In a confederacy founded on republican principles, and composed of republican members, the superintending government ought clearly to possess authority to defend the system against aristocratic or monarchical innovations. The more intimate the nature of such a Union may be, the greater interest have the members in the political institutions of each other; and the greater right to insist that the forms of government under which the compact was entered into, should be *substantially* maintained. But a right implies a remedy; and where else could the remedy be deposited, than where it is deposited by the Constitution. Governments of dissimilar principles and forms have been found less adapted to a federal coalition of any sort, than those of a kindred nature. "As the confederate republic of Germany," says Montesquieu, "consists of free cities and petty states subject to different Princes, experience shews us that it is more imperfect than that of Holland and Switzerland." "Greece was undone" he adds, "as soon as the King of Macedon obtained a seat among the Amphyctions." In the latter case, no doubt, the disproportionate force, as well as the monarchical form of the new confederate, had its share of influence on the events. It may possibly be asked what need there could be of such a precaution, and whether it may not become a pretext for alterations in the state governments, without the concurrence of the states themselves. These questions admit of ready answers. If the interposition of the general government should not be needed, the provision for such an event will be a harmless superfluity only in the Constitution. But who can say what experiments may be produced by the caprice of particular states, by the ambition of enterprizing leaders, or by the intrigues and influence of foreign powers. To the second question it may be answered, that if the general government should interpose by virtue of this constitutional authority, it will be of course bound to pursue the authority. But the authority extends no farther than to a *guaranty* of a republican form of government, which supposes a pre-existing government of the form which is to be guaranteed. As long therefore as the existing republican forms are continued by the States, they are guaranteed by the Federal Constitution. Whenever the states may chuse to substitute other republican forms, they have a right to do so, and to claim the federal guaranty for the latter. The only restriction imposed on them is, that they shall not exchange republican for anti-republican Constitutions; a restriction which it is presumed will hardly be considered as a grievance.

A protection against invasion is due from every society to the parts composing it. The latitude of the expression here used, seems to secure each state not only against foreign hostility, but against ambitious or vindictive enterprizes of its more powerful neighbours. The history both of antient and modern confederacies, proves that the weaker members of the Union ought not to be insensible to the policy of this article.

Protection against domestic violence is added with equal propriety. It has been remarked that even among the Swiss Cantons, which properly speaking are not under one government, provision is made for this object; and the history of that league informs us, that mutual aid is frequently claimed and afforded; and as well by the most democratic, as the other Cantons. A recent and well known event among ourselves, has warned us to be prepared for emergencies of a like nature.

At first view it might seem not to square with the republican theory, to suppose either that a majority have not the right, or that a minority will have the force to subvert a government; and consequently that the fœderal interposition can never be required but when it would be improper. But theoretic reasoning in this, as in most other cases, must be qualified by the lessons of practice. Why may not illicit combinations for purposes of violence be formed as well by a majority of a State, especially a small State, as by a majority of a county or a district of the same State; and if the authority of the State ought in the latter case to protect the local magistracy, ought not the fœderal authority in the former to support the State authority? Besides, there are certain parts of the State Constitutions which are so interwoven with the Fœderal Constitution, that a violent blow cannot be given to the one without communicating the wound to the other. Insurrections in a State will rarely induce a fœderal interposition, unless the number concerned in them, bear some proportion to the friends of government. It will be much better that the violence in such cases should be repressed by the superintending power, than that the majority should be left to maintain their cause by a bloody and obstinate contest. The existence of a right to interpose will generally prevent the necessity of exerting it.

Is it true that force and right are necessarily on the same side in republican governments? May not the minor party possess such a superiority of pecuniary resources, of military talents and experience, or of secret succours from foreign powers, as will render it superior also in an appeal to the sword? May not a more compact and advantageous position turn the scale on the same side against a superior number so situated as to be less capable of a prompt and collected exertion of its strength? Nothing can be more chimerical than to imagine that in a trial of actual force, victory may be calculated by the rules which prevail in a census of the inhabitants, or which determine the event of an election! May it not happen in fine that the minority of CITIZENS may become a majority of PERSONS, by the accession of alien residents, of a casual concourse of adventurers, or of those whom the Constitution of the State has not admitted to the rights of suffrage? I take no notice of an unhappy species of population abounding in some of the States, who during the calm of regular government are sunk below the level of men; but who in the tempestuous scenes of civil violence may emerge into the human character, and give a superiority of strength to any party with which they may associate themselves.

In cases where it may be doubtful on which side justice lies, what better umpires could be desired by two violent factions, flying to arms and tearing a State to pieces, than the representatives of confederate States not heated by the local flame? To the impartiality of Judges they would unite the affection of friends. Happy would it be if such a remedy for its infirmities, could be enjoyed by all free governments; if a project equally effectual could be established for the universal peace of mankind.

Should it be asked what is to be the redress for an insurrection pervading all the States, and comprizing a superiority of the entire force, though not a constitutional right; the answer must be, that such a case, as it would be without the compass of human remedies, so it is fortunately not within the compass of human probability; and that it is a sufficient recommendation of the Fœderal Constitution, that it diminishes the risk of a calamity, for which no possible constitution can provide a cure.

Among the advantages of a confederate republic enumerated by Montesquieu, an important one is, "that should a popular insurrection happen in one of the States, the others are able to quell it. Should abuses creep into one part, they are reformed by those that remain sound."

7. "To consider all debts contracted and engagements entered into, before the adoption of this Constitution, as being no less valid against the United States under this Constitution, than under the Confederation."

This can only be considered as a declaratory proposition; and may have been inserted, among other reasons, for the satisfaction of the foreign creditors of the United States, who cannot be strangers to the pretended doctrine that a change in the political form of civil society, has the magical effect of dissolving its moral obligations.

Among the lesser criticisms which have been exercised on the Constitution, it has been remarked that the validity of engagements ought to have been asserted in favour of the United States, as well as against them; and in the spirit which usually characterizes little critics, the omission has been transformed and magnified into a plot against the national rights. The authors of this discovery may be told, what few others need be informed of, that as engagements are in their nature reciprocal, an assertion of their validity on one side necessarily involves a validity on the other side; and that as the article is merely declaratory, the establishment of the principle in one case is sufficient for every case. They may be further told that every Constitution must limit its precautions to dangers that are not altogether imaginary; and that no real danger can exist that the government would DARE, with or even without this Constitutional declaration before it, to remit the debts justly due to the public, on the pretext here condemned.

8. "To provide for amendments to be ratified by three-fourths of the States, under two exceptions only."

That useful alterations will be suggested by experience, could not but be foreseen. It was requisite therefore that a mode for introducing them should be provided. The mode preferred by the Convention seems to be stamped with every mark of propriety. It guards equally against that extreme facility which would render the Constitution too mutable; and that extreme difficulty which might perpetuate its discovered faults. It moreover equally enables the general and the state governments to originate the amendment of errors as they may be pointed out by the experience on one side or on the other. The exception in favour of the equality of suffrage in the Senate was probably meant as a palladium to the residuary sovereignty of the States, implied and secured by that principle of representation in one branch of the Legislature; and was probably insisted on by the States particularly attached to that equality. The other exception must have been admitted on the same considerations which produced the privilege defended by it.

9. "The ratification of the conventions of nine States shall be sufficient for the establishment of this Constitution between the States ratifying the same."

This article speaks for itself. The express authority of the people alone could give due validity to the Constitution. To have required the unanimous ratification of the thirteen States, would have subjected the essential interests of the whole to the caprice or corruption of a single member. It would have marked a want of foresight in the Convention, which our own experience would have rendered inexcusable.

Two questions of a very delicate nature present themselves on this occasion. 1. On what principle the confederation, which stands in the solemn form of a compact among the States, can be superceded without the unanimous consent of the parties to it? 2. What relation is to subsist between the nine or more States ratifying the Constitution, and the remaining few who do not become parties to it.

The first question is answered at once by recurring to the absolute necessity of the case; to the great principle of self-preservation; to the transcendent law of nature and of nature's God, which declares that the safety and happiness of society are the objects at which all political institutions aim, and to which all such institutions must be sacrificed. PERHAPS also an answer may be found without searching beyond the principles of the compact itself. It has been heretofore noted among the defects of the Confederation, that in many of the States, it had received no higher sanction than a mere legislative ratification. The principle of reciprocality seems to require, that its obligation on the other States should be reduced to the same standard. A compact between independent sovereigns, founded on ordinary acts of legislative authority, can pretend to no higher validity than a league or treaty between the parties. It is an established doctrine on the subject of treaties, that all the articles are mutually conditions of each other; that a breach of any one article is a breach of the whole treaty; and that a breach committed by either of the parties absolves the others; and authorises them, if they please, to pronounce the treaty violated and void. Should it unhappily be necessary to appeal to these delicate truths for a justification for dispensing with the consent of particular States to a dissolution of the federal pact, will not the complaining parties find it a difficult task to answer the MULTIPLIED and IMPORTANT infractions with which they may be confronted? The time has been when it was incumbent on us all to veil the ideas which this paragraph exhibits. The scene is now changed, and with it, the part which the same motives dictates.

The second question is not less delicate; and the flattering prospect of its being merely hypothetical, forbids an over-curious discussion of it. It is one of those cases which must be left to provide for itself. In general it may be observed, that although no political relation can subsist between the assenting and dissenting States, yet the moral relations will remain uncancelled. The claims of justice, both on one side and on the other, will be in force, and must be fulfilled; the rights of humanity must in all cases be duly and mutually respected; whilst considerations of a common interest, and above all the remembrance of the endearing scenes which are past, and the anticipation of a speedy triumph over the obstacles to re-union, will, it is hoped, not urge in vain MODERATION on one side, and PRUDENCE on the other.

THE FEDERALISTS' CONSPIRACY DETECTED:
"THE MOST ODIOUS SYSTEM OF TYRANNY THAT
WAS EVER PROJECTED . . . A CRIME OF
THE BLACKEST DYE"

"Centinel" [*Samuel Bryan*] *XII*

Independent Gazetteer (Philadelphia), January 23, 1788

To the People of Pennsylvania.

Fellow-Citizens, Conscious guilt has taken the alarm, thrown out the signal of distress, and even appealed to the generosity of patriotism. The authors and abettors of the new constitution shudder at the term *conspirators* being applied to them, as it designates their true character, and seems prophetic of the catastrophe: they read their fate in the epithet.

In dispair they are weakly endeavouring to screen their criminality by interposing the shield of the virtues of a Washington, in representing his concurrence in the proposed system of government, as evidence of the purity of their intentions; but this impotent attempt to degrade the brightest ornament of his country to a base level with themselves, will be considered as an aggravation of their treason, and an insult on the good sense of the people, who have too much discernment not to make a just discrimination between the honest mistaken zeal of the patriot, and the flagitious machinations of an ambitious junto, and will resent the imposition that Machiavelian arts and consummate cunning have practised upon our *illustrious chief.*

The term *conspirators* was not, as has been alledged, rashly or inconsiderately adopted; it is the language of dispassionate and deliberate reason, influenced by the purest patriotism: the consideration of the nature and construction of the new constitution naturally suggests the epithet; its justness is strikingly illustrated by the conduct of the patrons of this plan of government, but if any doubt had remained whether this epithet is merited, it is now removed by the very uneasiness it occasions; this is a confirmation of its propriety. Innocence would have nothing to dread from such a stigma, but would triumph over the shafts of malice.

The conduct of men is the best clue to their principles. The system of deception that has been practised; the constant solicitude shewn to prevent information diffusing its salutary light, are evidence of a conspiracy beyond the arts of sophistry to palliate, or the ingenuity of falsehood to invalidate: the means practised to establish the new constitution are demonstrative of the principles and designs of its authors and abettors.

At the time, says Mr. Martin (deputy from the state of Maryland in the general convention) when the public prints were announcing our perfect unanimity, discord prevailed to such a degree, that the minority were upon the point of appealing to the public against the machinations of ambition. By such a base imposition, repeated in every newspaper and reverberated from one end of the union to the other, was the people lulled into a false confidence, into an implicit reliance upon the wisdom and patriotism of the convention; and when ambition, by her deceptive wiles, had succeeded to usher forth the new system of government with apparent unanimity of sentiment, the public delusion was compleat. The most extravagant fictions were palmed upon the people, the seal of divinity was even ascribed to the new constitution; a felicity more than human was to ensue from its establishment;—overlooking the real cause of our difficulties and burthens, which have their proper remedy, the people were taught that the new constitution would prove a mine of wealth and prosperity equal to every want, or the most sanguine desire; that it would effect what can only be produced by the exertion of industry and the practice of œconomy.

The conspirators, aware of the danger of delay, that allowing time for a rational investigation would prove fatal to their designs, precipitated the establishment of the new constitution with all possible celerity; in Massachusetts the deputies of that convention, who are to give the final fiat in behalf of that great state to a measure upon which their dearest concerns depend, were elected by express in the first moments of blind enthusiasm; similar conduct has prevailed in the other states as far as circumstances permitted.

If the foregoing circumstances did not prove a conspiracy, there are others that must strike conviction in the most unsuspicious. Attempts to prevent discussion by shackling the press ought ever to be a signal of alarm to freemen, and considered as an annunciation of meditated tyranny; this is a truth that the uniform experience of mankind has established beyond the possibility of doubt. Bring the conduct of the authors and abettors of the new constitution to this test, let this be the criterion of their criminality, and every patriotic mind must unite in branding them with the stigma of conspirators against the public liberties.—No stage of this business but what has been marked with every exertion of influence and device of ambition to suppress information and intimidate public discussion; the virtue and firmness of some of the printers, rose superior to the menaces of violence, and the lucre of private interest; when every means failed to shackle the press, the free and independent papers were attempted to be demolished by withdrawing all the subscriptions to them within the sphere of the influence of the conspirators; fortunately for the cause of liberty and truth, these daring high handed attempts have failed except in one instance, where from a peculiarity of circumstances, ambition has triumphed. Under the flimsey pretence of vindicating the character of a contemptible drudge of party rendered ridiculous by his superlative folly in the late convention, of which the statement given in the Pennsylvania Herald, was confessedly a faithful representation, this newspaper has been silenced* by some hundreds of its subscribers (who it seems are generally among the devoted tools of party, or those who are obliged from their thraldom to yield implicit assent to the mandates of the junto) withdrawing their support from it; by this stroke the conspirators have suppressed the publication of the most valuable debates of the late convention, which would have

*The Herald it is said is to be discontinued the 23d instant, (the Editor is already dismissed.)

been given in course by the Editor of that paper, whose stipend now ceasing, he cannot afford without compensation the time and attention necessary to this business.

Every patriotic person who had an opportunity of hearing that illustrious advocate of liberty and his country, Mr. Findley, must sensibly regret that his powerful arguments are not to extend beyond the confined walls of the State-House, where they could have so limitted an effect; that the United States could not have been his auditory through the medium of the press. I anticipate the answer of the conspirators; they will tell you that this could not be their motive for silencing this paper, as the whole of the debates were taken down in short hand by another person and published, but the public are not to be so easily duped, they will not receive a spurious as an equivalent for a genuine production; equal solicitude was expressed for the publication of the former as for the suppression of the latter—the public will judge of the motives.

That investigation into the nature and construction of the new constitution, which the conspirators have so long and zealously struggled against, has, notwithstanding their partial success, so far taken place as to ascertain the enormity of their criminality. That system which was pompously displayed as the perfection of government, proves upon examination to be the most odious system of tyranny that was ever projected, a many headed hydra of despotism, whose complicated and various evils would be infinitely more oppressive and afflictive than the scourge of any single tyrant: the objects of dominion would be tortured to gratify the calls of ambition and cravings of power, of rival despots contending for the sceptre of superiority; the devoted people would experience a distraction of misery.

No wonder then that such a discovery should excite uneasy apprehensions in the minds of the conspirators, for such an attempt against the public liberties is unprecedented in history, it is a crime of the blackest dye, as it strikes at the happiness of millions and the dignity of human nature, as it was intended to deprive the inhabitants of so large a portion of the globe of the choicest blessing of life and the oppressed of all nations of an asylum.

The explicit language of the Centinel during the empire of delusion was not congenial to the feelings of the people, but truth when it has free scope is all powerful, it enforces conviction in the most prejudiced mind; he foresaw the consequence of an exertion of the good sense and understanding of the people, and predicted the defeat of the measure he ventured to attack, when it was deemed sacred by most men and the certain ruin of any who should dare to lisp a word against it: he has persevered through every discouraging appearance, and has now the satisfaction to find his countrymen are aware of their danger and are taking measures for their security.

Since writing the foregoing, I am informed that the Printer of the Pennsylvania Herald is not quite decided whether he will drop his paper; he wishes, and perhaps will be enabled, to persevere; however, the conspirators have effected their purpose; the editor is dismissed and the debates of the convention thereby suppressed.

"Brutus" X

New York Journal, January 24, 1788

To the PEOPLE *of the* STATE *of* NEW-YORK.

The liberties of a people are in danger from a large standing army, not only because the rulers may employ them for the purposes of supporting themselves in any usurpations of power, which they may see proper to exercise, but there is great hazard, that an army will subvert the forms of the government, under whose authority, they are raised, and establish one, according to the pleasure of their leaders.

We are informed, in the faithful pages of history, of such events frequently happening.—Two instances have been mentioned in a former paper. They are so remarkable, that they are worthy of the most careful attention of every lover of freedom.—They are taken from the history of the two most powerful nations that have ever existed in the world; and who are the most renowned, for the freedom they enjoyed, and the excellency of their constitutions:—I mean Rome and Britain.

In the first, the liberties of the commonwealth was destroyed, and the constitution overturned, by an army, lead by Julius Cesar, who was appointed to the command, by the constitutional authority of that commonwealth. He changed it from a free republic, whose fame had sounded, and is still celebrated by all the world, into that of the most absolute despotism. A standing army effected this change, and a standing army supported it through a succession of ages, which are marked in the annals of history, with the most horrid cruelties, bloodshed, and carnage;—The most devilish, beastly, and unnatural vices, that ever punished or disgraced human nature.

The same army, that in Britain, vindicated the liberties of that people from the encroachments and despotism of a tyrant king, assisted Cromwell, their General, in wresting from the people, that liberty they had so dearly earned.

You may be told, these instances will not apply to our case:—But those who would persuade you to believe this, either mean to deceive you, or have not themselves considered the subject.

I firmly believe, no country in the world had ever a more patriotic army, than the one which so ably served this country, in the late war.

But had the General who commanded them, been possessed of the spirit of a Julius Cesar or a Cromwell, the liberties of this country, had in all probability, terminated with the war; or had they been maintained, might have cost more blood and treasure, than was expended in the conflict with Great-Britain. When an anonimous writer addressed the officers of the army at the close of the war, advising them not to part with their arms, until justice was done them—the effect it had is well known. It affected them like an electric shock. He wrote like Cesar; and had the commander in chief, and a few more officers of rank, countenanced the measure, the desperate resolution had been taken, to refuse to disband. What the consequences of such a determination would have been, heaven only knows.—The army were in the full vigor of health and spirits, in the habit of discipline, and possessed of all our military stores and apparatus. They would have acquired great accessions of strength from the country.—Those who were disgusted at our republican forms of government (for such there then were, of high rank among us) would have lent them all their aid.—We should in all probability have seen a constitution and laws, dictated to us, at the head of an army, and at the point of a bayonet, and the liberties for which we had so severely struggled, snatched from us in a moment. It remains a secret, yet to be revealed, whether this measure was not suggested, or at least countenanced, by some, who have had great influence in producing the present system.—Fortunately indeed for this country, it had at the head of the army, a patriot as well as a general; and many of our principal officers, had not abandoned the characters of citizens, by assuming that of soldiers, and therefore, the scheme proved abortive. But are we to expect, that this will always be the case? Are we so much better than the people of other ages and of other countries, that the same allurements of power and greatness, which led them aside from their duty, will have no influence upon men in our country? Such an idea, is wild and extravagant.—Had we indulged such a delusion, enough has appeared in a little time past, to convince the most credulous, that the passion for pomp, power and greatness, works as powerfully in the hearts of many of our better sort, as it ever did in any country under heaven.—Were the same opportunity again to offer, we should very probably be grossly disappointed, if we made dependence, that all who then rejected the overture, would do it again.

From these remarks, it appears, that the evils to be feared from a large standing army in time of peace, does not arise solely from the apprehension, that the rulers may employ them for the purpose of promoting their own ambitious views, but that equal, and perhaps greater danger, is to be apprehended from their overturning the constitutional powers of the government, and assuming the power to dictate any form they please.

The advocates for power, in support of this right in the proposed government, urge that a restraint upon the discretion of the legislatures, in respect to military establishments in time of peace, would be improper to be imposed, because they say, it will be necessary to maintain small garrisons on the frontiers, to guard against the depredations of the Indians, and to be prepared to repel any encroachments or invasions that may be made by Spain or Britain.

The amount of this argument striped of the abundant verbages with which the author has dressed it, is this:

It will probably be necessary to keep up a small body of troops to garrison a few posts, which it will be necessary to maintain, in order to guard against the sudden encroachments of the Indians, or of the Spaniards and British; and therefore, the general government ought to be invested with power to raise and keep up a standing army in time of peace, without restraint; at their discretion.

I confess, I cannot perceive that the conclusion follows from the premises. Logicians say, it is not good reasoning to infer a general conclusion from particular premises: though I

am not much of a Logician, it seems to me, this argument is
very like that species of reasoning.

When the patriots in the parliament in Great-Britain, contended with such force of argument, and all the powers of
eloquence, against keeping up standing armies in time of
peace, it is obvious, they never entertained an idea, that small
garrisons on their frontiers, or in the neighbourhood of
powers, from whom they were in danger of encroachments,
or guards, to take care of public arsenals would thereby be
prohibited.

The advocates for this power farther urge that it is necessary, because it may, and probably will happen, that circumstances will render it requisite to raise an army to be prepared
to repel attacks of an enemy, before a formal declaration of
war, which in modern times has fallen into disuse. If the constitution prohibited the raising an army, until a war actually
commenced, it would deprive the government of the power
of providing for the defence of the country, until the enemy
were within our territory. If the restriction is not to extend to
the raising armies in cases of emergency, but only to the keeping them up, this would leave the matter to the discretion of
the legislature; and they might, under the pretence that there
was danger of an invasion, keep up the army as long as they
judged proper—and hence it is inferred, that the legislature
should have authority to raise and keep up an army without
any restriction. But from these premises nothing more will
follow than this, that the legislature should not be so restrained, as to put it out of their power to raise an army,
when such exigencies as are instanced shall arise. But it does
not thence follow, that the government should be empowered
to raise and maintain standing armies at their discretion as
well in peace as in war. If indeed, it is impossible to vest the
general government with the power of raising troops to garrison the frontier posts, to guard arsenals, or to be prepared
to repel an attack, when we saw a power preparing to make
one, without giving them a general and indefinite authority,
to raise and keep up armies, without any restriction or qualification, then this reasoning might have weight; but this has
not been proved nor can it be.

It is admitted that to prohibit the general government,

from keeping up standing armies, while yet they were authorised to raise them in case of exigency, would be an insufficient guard against the danger. A discretion of such latitude would give room to elude the force of the provision.

It is also admitted that an absolute prohibition against raising troops, except in cases of actual war, would be improper; because it will be requisite to raise and support a small number of troops to garrison the important frontier posts, and to guard arsenals; and it may happen, that the danger of an attack from a foreign power may be so imminent, as to render it highly proper we should raise an army, in order to be prepared to resist them. But to raise and keep up forces for such purposes and on such occasions, is not included in the idea, of keeping up standing armies in times of peace.

It is a thing very practicable to give the government sufficient authority to provide for these cases, and at the same time to provide a reasonable and competent security against the evil of a standing army—a clause to the following purpose would answer the end:

As standing armies in time of peace are dangerous to liberty, and have often been the means of overturning the best constitutions of government, no standing army, or troops of any description whatsoever, shall be raised or kept up by the legislature, except so many as shall be necessary for guards to the arsenals of the United States, or for garrisons to such posts on the frontiers, as it shall be deemed absolutely necessary to hold, to secure the inhabitants, and facilitate the trade with the Indians: unless when the United States are threatened with an attack or invasion from some foreign power, in which case the legislature shall be authorised to raise an army to be prepared to repel the attack; provided that no troops whatsoever shall be raised in time of peace, without the assent of two thirds of the members, composing both houses of the legislature.

A clause similar to this would afford sufficient latitude to the legislature to raise troops in all cases that were really necessary, and at the same time competent security against the establishment of that dangerous engine of despotism a standing army.

The same writer who advances the arguments I have noticed, makes a number of other observations with a view to prove that the power to raise and keep up armies, ought to be discretionary in the general legislature; some of them are curious; he instances the raising of troops in Massachusetts and Pennsylvania, to shew the necessity of keeping a standing army in time of peace; the least reflection must convince every candid mind that both these cases are totally foreign to his purpose—Massachusetts raised a body of troops for six months, at the expiration of which they were to disband of course; this looks very little like a standing army. But beside, was that commonwealth in a state of peace at that time? So far from it that they were in the most violent commotions and contests, and their legislature had formally declared that an unnatural rebellion existed within the state. The situation of Pennsylvania was similar; a number of armed men had levied war against the authority of the state, and openly avowed their intention of withdrawing their allegiance from it. To what purpose examples are brought, of states raising troops for short periods in times of war or insurrections, on a question concerning the propriety of keeping up standing armies in times of peace, the public must judge.

It is farther said, that no danger can arise from this power being lodged in the hands of the general government, because the legislatures will be a check upon them, to prevent their abusing it.

This is offered, as what force there is in it will hereafter receive a more particular examination. At present, I shall only remark, that it is difficult to conceive how the state legislatures can, in any case, hold a check over the general legislature, in a constitutional way. The latter has, in every instance to which their powers extend, complete controul over the former. The state legislatures can, in no case, by law, resolution, or otherwise, of right, prevent or impede the general government, from enacting any law, or executing it, which this constitution authorizes them to enact or execute. If then the state legislatures check the general legislatures, it must be by exciting the people to resist constitutional laws. In this way every individual, or every body of men, may check any government, in proportion to the influence they may have over the body of the people. But such kinds of checks as these, though they sometimes correct the abuses of government, oftner destroy all government.

It is further said, that no danger is to be apprehended from the exercise of this power, because it is lodged in the hands of representatives of the people; if they abuse it, it is in the power of the people to remove them, and chuse others who will pursue their interests. Not to repeat what has been said before, That it is unwise in any people, to authorize their rulers to do, what, if done, would prove injurious—I have, in some former numbers, shewn, that the representation in the proposed government will be a mere shadow without the substance. I am so confident that I am well founded in this opinion, that I am persuaded, if it was to be adopted or rejected, upon a fair discussion of its merits, without taking into contemplation circumstances extraneous to it, as reasons for its adoption, nineteen-twentieths of the sensible men in the union would reject it on this account alone; unless its powers were confined to much fewer objects than it embraces.

"Publius," The Federalist XLIV
[James Madison]

New-York Packet, January 25, 1788

To the People of the State of New-York.

A *Fifth* class of provisions in favor of the fœderal authority, consists of the following restrictions on the authority of the several States:

1. "No State shall enter into any treaty, alliance or confederation, grant letters of marque and reprisal, coin money, emit bills of credit, make any thing but gold and silver a legal tender in payment of debts; pass any bill of attainder, ex post facto law, or law impairing the obligation of contracts, or grant any title of nobility."

The prohibition against treaties, alliances and confederations, makes a part of the existing articles of Union; and for reasons which need no explanation, is copied into the new Constitution. The prohibition of letters of marque is another part of the old system, but is somewhat extended in the new. According to the former, letters of marque could be granted by the States after a declaration of war. According to the latter, these licenses must be obtained as well during war as previous to its declaration, from the government of the United States. This alteration is fully justified by the advantage of uniformity in all points which relate to foreign powers; and of immediate responsibility to the nation in all those, for whose conduct the nation itself is to be responsible.

The right of coining money, which is here taken from the States, was left in their hands by the confederation as a concurrent right with that of Congress, under an exception in favor of the exclusive right of Congress to regulate the alloy and value. In this instance also the new provision is an improvement on the old. Whilst the alloy and value depended on the general authority, a right of coinage in the particular States could have no other effect than to multiply expensive mints, and diversify the forms and weights of the circulating pieces. The latter inconveniency defeats one purpose for which the power was originally submitted to the fœderal head. And as far as the former might prevent an inconvenient remittance of gold and silver to the central mint for recoinage, the end can be as well attained, by local mints established under the general authority.

The extension of the prohibition to bills of credit must give pleasure to every citizen in proportion to his love of justice, and his knowledge of the true springs of public prosperity. The loss which America has sustained since the peace, from the pestilent effects of paper money, on the necessary confidence between man and man; on the necessary confidence in the public councils; on the industry and morals of the people, and on the character of Republican Government, constitutes an enormous debt against the States chargeable with this un-advised measure, which must long remain unsatisfied; or rather an accumulation of guilt, which can be expiated no otherwise than by a voluntary sacrifice on the altar of justice, of the power which has been the instrument of it. In addition to these persuasive considerations, it may be observed that the same reasons which shew the necessity of denying to the States the power of regulating coin, prove with equal force that they ought not to be at liberty to substitute a paper me-dium in the place of coin. Had every State a right to regulate the value of its coin, there might be as many different curren-cies as States; and thus the intercourse among them would be impeded; retrospective alterations in its value might be made, and thus the citizens of other States be injured, and animosi-ties be kindled among the States themselves. The subjects of foreign powers might suffer from the same cause, and hence the Union be discredited and embroiled by the indiscretion of a single member. No one of these mischiefs is less incident to a power in the States to emit paper money than to coin gold or silver. The power to make any thing but gold and silver a tender in payment of debts, is withdrawn from the States, on the same principle with that of striking of paper currency.

Bills of attainder, ex post facto laws, and laws impairing the obligation of contracts, are contrary to the first principles of the social compact, and to every principle of sound legislation. The two former are expressly prohibited by the declarations prefixed to some of the State Constitutions, and all of them are prohibited by the spirit and scope of these fundamental charters. Our own experience has taught us nevertheless, that additional fences against these dangers ought not to be omitted. Very properly therefore have the Convention added this constitutional bulwark in favor of personal security and private rights; and I am much deceived if they have not in so doing as faithfully consulted the genuine sentiments, as the undoubted interests of their constituents. The sober people of America are weary of the fluctuating policy which has directed the public councils. They have seen with regret and with indignation, that sudden changes and legislative interferences in cases affecting personal rights, become jobs in the hands of enterprizing and influential speculators; and snares to the more industrious and less informed part of the community. They have seen too, that legislative interference, is but the first link of a long chain of repetitions; every subsequent interference being naturally produced by the effects of the preceding. They very rightly infer, therefore, that some thorough reform is wanting which will banish speculations on public measures, inspire a general prudence and industry, and give a regular course to the business of society. The prohibition with respect to titles of nobility, is copied from the articles of confederation, and needs no comment.

2. "No State shall, without the consent of the Congress, lay any imposts or duties on imports or exports, except what may be absolutely necessary for executing its inspection laws, and the neat produce of all duties and imposts laid by any State on imports or exports, shall be for the use of the Treasury of the United States; and all such laws shall be subject to the revision and controul of the Congress. No State shall, without the consent of Congress, lay any duty on tonnage, keep troops or ships of war in time of peace; enter into any agreement or compact with another State, or with a foreign power, or engage in war unless actually invaded, or in such imminent danger as will not admit of delay."

The restraint on the power of the States over imports and exports is enforced by all the arguments which prove the necessity of submitting the regulation of trade to the fœderal councils. It is needless therefore to remark further on this head, than that the manner in which the restraint is qualified, seems well calculated at once to secure to the States a reasonable discretion in providing for the conveniency of their imports and exports; and to the United States a reasonable check against the abuse of this discretion. The remaining particulars of this clause, fall within reasonings which are either so obvious, or have been so fully developed, that they may be passed over without remark.

The sixth and last class consists of the several powers and provisions by which efficacy is given to all the rest.

1. "Of these the first is the power to make all laws which shall be necessary and proper for carrying into execution the foregoing powers, and all other powers vested by this Constitution in the government of the United States."

Few parts of the Constitution have been assailed with more intemperance than this; yet on a fair investigation of it, no part can appear more compleatly invulnerable. Without the *substance* of this power, the whole Constitution would be a dead letter. Those who object to the article therefore as a part of the Constitution, can only mean that the *form* of the provision is improper. But have they considered whether a better form could have been substituted?

There are four other possible methods which the Convention might have taken on this subject. They might have copied the second article of the existing confederation which would have prohibited the exercise of any power not *expressly* delegated; they might have attempted a positive enumeration of the powers comprehended under the general terms "necessary and proper;" they might have attempted a negative enumeration of them, by specifying the powers excepted from the general definition: They might have been altogether silent on the subject; leaving these necessary and proper powers, to construction and inference.

Had the Convention taken the first method of adopting the second article of confederation; it is evident that the new

Congress would be continually exposed as their predecessors have been, to the alternative of construing the term *"expressly"* with so much rigour as to disarm the government of all real authority whatever, or with so much latitude as to destroy altogether the force of the restriction. It would be easy to shew if it were necessary, that no important power, delegated by the articles of confederation, has been or can be executed by Congress, without recurring more or less to the doctrine of *construction* or *implication*. As the powers delegated under the new system are more extensive, the government which is to administer it would find itself still more distressed with the alternative of betraying the public interest by doing nothing; or of violating the Constitution by exercising powers, indispensably necessary and proper; but at the same time, not *expressly* granted.

Had the Convention attempted a positive enumeration of the powers necessary and proper for carrying their other powers into effect; the attempt would have involved a complete digest of laws on every subject to which the Constitution relates; accommodated too not only to the existing state of things, but to all the possible changes which futurity may produce: For in every new application of a general power, the *particular powers*, which are the means of attaining the *object* of the general power, must always necessarily vary with that object; and be often properly varied whilst the object remains the same.

Had they attempted to enumerate the particular powers or means, not necessary or proper for carrying the general powers into execution, the task would have been no less chimerical; and would have been liable to this further objection; that every defect in the enumeration, would have been equivalent to a positive grant of authority. If to avoid this consequence they had attempted a partial enumeration of the exceptions, and described the residue by the general terms, *not necessary or proper*: It must have happened that the enumeration would comprehend a few of the excepted powers only; that these would be such as would be least likely to be assumed or tolerated, because the enumeration would of course select such as would be least necessary or proper, and that the unnecessary and improper powers included in the residuum, would be less forceably excepted, than if no partial enumeration had been made.

Had the Constitution been silent on this head, there can be no doubt that all the particular powers, requisite as means of executing the general powers, would have resulted to the government, by unavoidable implication. No axiom is more clearly established in law, or in reason, than that wherever the end is required, the means are authorised; wherever a general power to do a thing is given, every particular power necessary for doing it, is included. Had this last method therefore been pursued by the Convention, every objection now urged against their plan, would remain in all its plausibility; and the real inconveniency would be incurred, of not removing a pretext which may be seized on critical occasions for drawing into question the essential powers of the Union.

If it be asked, what is to be the consequence, in case the Congress shall misconstrue this part of the Constitution, and exercise powers not warranted by its true meaning? I answer the same as if they should misconstrue or enlarge any other power vested in them, as if the general power had been reduced to particulars, and any one of these were to be violated; the same in short, as if the State Legislatures should violate their respective constitutional authorities. In the first instance, the success of the usurpation will depend on the executive and judiciary departments, which are to expound and give effect to the legislative acts; and in the last resort, a remedy must be obtained from the people, who can by the election of more faithful representatives, annul the acts of the usurpers. The truth is, that this ultimate redress may be more confided on against unconstitutional acts of the fœderal than of the State Legislatures, for this plain reason, that as every such act of the former, will be an invasion of the rights of the latter, these will be ever ready to mark the innovation, to sound the alarm to the people, and to exert their local influence in effecting a change of fœderal representatives. There being no such intermediate body between the State Legislatures and the people, interested in watching the conduct of the former, violations of the State Constitutions are more likely to remain unnoticed and unredressed.

2. "This Constitution and the laws of the United States which shall be made in pursuance thereof, and all treaties made, or which shall be made, under the authority of the United States, shall be the supreme law of the land, and the Judges in every State shall be bound thereby, any thing in the Constitution or laws of any State to the contrary notwithstanding."

The indiscreet zeal of the adversaries to the Constitution, has betrayed them into an attack on this part of it also, without which it would have been evidently and radically defective. To be fully sensible of this we need only suppose for a moment, that the supremacy of the State Constitutions had been left compleat by a saving clause in their favor.

In the first place, as these Constitutions invest the State Legislatures with absolute sovereignty, in all cases not excepted by the existing articles of confederation, all the authorities contained in the proposed Constitution, so far as they exceed those enumerated in the confederation, would have been annulled, and the new Congress would have been reduced to the same impotent condition with their predecessors.

In the next place, as the Constitutions of some of the States do not even expressly and fully recognize the existing powers of the confederacy, an express saving of the supremacy of the former, would in such States have brought into question, every power contained in the proposed Constitution.

In the third place, as the Constitutions of the States differ much from each other, it might happen that a treaty or national law of great and equal importance to the States, would interfere with some and not with other Constitutions, and would consequently be valid in some of the States at the same time that it would have no effect in others.

In fine, the world would have seen for the first time, a system of government founded on an inversion of the fundamental principles of all government; it would have seen the authority of the whole society every where subordinate to the authority of the parts; it would have seen a monster in which the head was under the direction of the members.

3. "The Senators and Representatives, and the members of the several State Legislatures; and all executive and judicial

officers, both of the United States, and the several States shall be bound by oath or affirmation, to support this Constitution."

It has been asked, why it was thought necessary, that the State magistracy should be bound to support the Fœderal Constitution, and unnecessary, that a like oath should be imposed on the officers of the United States in favor of the State Constitutions?

Several reasons might be assigned for the distinction. I content myself with one which is obvious & conclusive. The members of the Fœderal Government will have no agency in carrying the State Constitutions into effect. The members and officers of the State Governments, on the contrary, will have an essential agency in giving effect to the Fœderal Constitution. The election of the President and Senate, will depend in all cases, on the Legislatures of the several States. And the election of the House of Representatives, will equally depend on the same authority in the first instance; and will probably, for ever be conducted by the officers and according to the laws of the States.

4. Among the provisions for giving efficacy to the fœderal powers, might be added, those which belong to the executive and judiciary departments: But as these are reserved for particular examination in another place, I pass them over in this.

We have now reviewed in detail all the articles composing the sum or quantity of power delegated by the proposed Constitution to the Fœderal Government; and are brought to this undeniable conclusion, that no part of the power is unnecessary or improper for accomplishing the necessary objects of the Union. The question therefore, whether this amount of power shall be granted or not, resolves itself into another question, whether or not a government commensurate to the exigencies of the Union, shall be established; or in other words, whether the Union itself shall be preserved.

"*Publius*," *The Federalist XLV*
[*James Madison*]

Independent Journal (New York), January 26, 1788

To the People of the State of New-York.

Having shewn that no one of the powers transferred to the federal Government is unnecessary or improper, the next question to be considered is whether the whole mass of them will be dangerous to the portion of authority left in the several States.

The adversaries to the plan of the Convention instead of considering in the first place what degree of power was absolutely necessary for the purposes of the federal Government, have exhausted themselves in a secondary enquiry into the possible consequences of the proposed degree of power, to the Governments of the particular States. But if the Union, as has been shewn, be essential, to the security of the people of America against foreign danger; if it be essential to their security against contentions and wars among the different States; if it be essential to guard them against those violent and oppressive factions which embitter the blessings of liberty, and against those military establishments which must gradually poison its very fountain; if, in a word the Union be essential to the happiness of the people of America, is it not preposterous, to urge as an objection to a government without which the objects of the Union cannot be attained, that such a Government may derogate from the importance of the Governments of the individual States? Was then the American revolution effected, was the American confederacy formed, was the precious blood of thousands spilt, and the hard earned substance of millions lavished, not that the people of America should enjoy peace, liberty and safety; but that the Governments of the individual States, that particular municipal establishments, might enjoy a certain extent of power, and be arrayed with certain dignities and attributes of sovereignty? We have heard of the impious doctrine in the old world that the people were made for kings, not kings for the people. Is the same doctrine to be revived in the new, in another shape, that the solid happiness of the people is to be sacrificed to the views of political institutions of a different form? It is too early for politicians to presume on our forgetting that the public good, the real welfare of the great body of the people is the supreme object to be pursued; and that no form of Government whatever, has any other value, than as it may be fitted for the attainment of this object. Were the plan of the Convention adverse to the public happiness, my voice would be, reject the plan. Were the Union itself inconsistent with the public happiness, it would be, abolish the Union. In like manner as far as the sovereignty of the States cannot be reconciled to the happiness of the people. The voice of every good citizen must be, let the former be sacrificed to the latter. How far the sacrifice is necessary, has been shewn. How far the unsacrificed residue will be endangered, is the question before us.

Several important considerations have been touched in the course of these papers, which discountenance the supposition that the operation of the federal Government will by degrees prove fatal to the State Governments. The more I revolve the subject the more fully I am persuaded that the balance is much more likely to be disturbed by the preponderancy of the last than of the first scale.

We have seen in all the examples of antient and modern confederacies, the strongest tendency continually betraying itself in the members to despoil the general Government of its authorities, with a very ineffectual capacity in the latter to defend itself against the encroachments. Although in most of these examples, the system has been so dissimilar from that under consideration, as greatly to weaken any inference concerning the latter from the fate of the former; yet as the States will retain under the proposed Constitution a very extensive portion of active sovereignty, the inference ought not to be wholly disregarded. In the Achæan league, it is probable that the federal head had a degree and species of power, which gave it a considerable likeness to the government framed by the Convention. The Lycian confederacy, as far as its principles and form are transmitted, must have borne a still greater analogy to it. Yet history does not inform us that either of them ever degenerated or tended to degenerate into one consolidated government. On the contrary, we know that the ruin of one of them proceeded from the incapacity of the federal authority to prevent the dissentions, and finally the disunion of the subordinate authorities. These cases are the more worthy of our attention, as the external causes by which the component parts were pressed together, were much more numerous and powerful than in our case; and consequently, less powerful ligaments within, would be sufficient to bind the members to the head, and to each other.

In the feudal system we have seen a similar propensity exemplified. Notwithstanding the want of proper sympathy in every instance between the local sovereigns and the people, and the sympathy in some instances between the general sovereign and the latter; it usually happened that the local sovereigns prevailed in the rivalship for encroachments. Had no external dangers, enforced internal harmony and subordination; and particularly had the local sovereigns possessed the affections of the people, the great kingdoms in Europe, would at this time consist of as many independent princes as there were formerly feudatory barons.

The State Governments will have the advantage of the federal Government, whether we compare them in respect to the immediate dependence of the one or the other; to the weight of personal influence which each side will possess; to the powers respectively vested in them; to the predilection and probable support of the people; to the disposition and faculty of resisting and frustrating the measures of each other.

The State Governments may be regarded as constituent and essential parts of the federal Government; whilst the latter is nowise essential to the operation or organisation of the former. Without the intervention of the State Legislatures, the President of the United States cannot be elected at all. They must in all cases have a great share in his appointment, and will perhaps in most cases of themselves determine it. The Senate will be elected absolutely and exclusively by the State Legislatures. Even the House of Representatives, though drawn immediately from the people, will be chosen very much under the influence of that class of men, whose influence over the people obtains for themselves an election into the State Legislatures. Thus each of the principal branches of the federal Government will owe its existence more or less to the favor of the State Governments, and must consequently feel a dependence, which is much more likely to beget a disposition too obsequious, than too overbearing towards them. On the other side, the component parts of the State Governments will in no instance be indebted for their appointment to the direct agency of the federal government, and very little if at all, to the local influence of its members.

The number of individuals employed under the Constitution of the United States, will be much smaller, than the number employed under the particular States. There will consequently be less of personal influence on the side of the former, than of the latter. The members of the legislative, executive and judiciary departments of thirteen and more States; the justices of peace, officers of militia, ministerial officers of justice, with all the county corporation and town-officers, for three millions and more of people, intermixed and having particular acquaintance with every class and circle of people, must exceed beyond all proportion, both in number and influence, those of every description who will be employed in the administration of the federal system. Compare the members of the three great departments, of the thirteen States, excluding from the judiciary department the justices of peace, with the members of the corresponding departments of the single Government of the Union; compare the militia officers of three millions of people, with the military and marine officers of any establishment which is within the compass of probability, or I may add, of possibility, and in this view alone, we may pronounce the advantage of the States to be decisive. If the federal Government is to have collectors of revenue, the State Governments will have theirs also. And as those of the former will be principally on the sea-coast, and not very numerous; whilst those of the latter will be spread over the face of the country, and will be very numerous, the advantage in this view also lies on the same side. It is true that the confederacy is to possess, and may exercise, the power of collecting internal as well as external taxes throughout the

States: But it is probable that this power will not be resorted to, except for supplemental purposes of revenue; that an option will then be given to the States to supply their quotas by previous collections of their own; and that the eventual collection under the immediate authority of the Union, will generally be made by the officers, and according to the rules, appointed by the several States. Indeed it is extremely probable that in other instances, particularly in the organisation of the judicial power, the officers of the States will be cloathed with the correspondent authority of the Union. Should it happen however that separate collectors of internal revenue should be appointed under the federal Government, the influence of the whole number would not be a comparison with that of the multitude of State officers in the opposite scale. Within every district, to which a federal collector would be allotted, there would not be less than thirty or forty or even more officers of different descriptions and many of them persons of character and weight, whose influence would lie on the side of the State.

The powers delegated by the proposed Constitution to the Federal Government, are few and defined. Those which are to remain in the State Governments are numerous and indefinite. The former will be exercised principally on external objects, as war, peace, negociation, and foreign commerce; with which last the power of taxation will for the most part be connected. The powers reserved to the several States will extend to all the objects, which, in the ordinary course of affairs, concern the lives, liberties and properties of the people; and the internal order, improvement, and prosperity of the State.

The operations of the Federal Government will be most extensive and important in times of war and danger; those of the State Governments, in times of peace and security. As the former periods will probably bear a small proportion to the latter, the State Governments will here enjoy another advantage over the Federal Government. The more adequate indeed the federal powers may be rendered to the national defence, the less frequent will be those scenes of danger which might favour their ascendency over the governments of the particular States.

If the new Constitution be examined with accuracy and

candour, it will be found that the change which it proposes, consists much less in the addition of NEW POWERS to the Union, than in the invigoration of its ORIGINAL POWERS. The regulation of commerce, it is true, is a new power; but that seems to be an addition which few oppose, and from which no apprehensions are entertained. The powers relating to war and peace, armies and fleets, treaties and finance, with the other more considerable powers, are all vested in the existing Congress by the articles of Confederation. The proposed change does not enlarge these powers; it only substitutes a more effectual mode of administering them. The change relating to taxation, may be regarded as the most important: And yet the present Congress have as compleat authority to REQUIRE of the States indefinite supplies of money for the common defence and general welfare, as the future Congress will have to require them of individual citizens; and the latter will be no more bound than the States themselves have been, to pay the quotas respectively taxed on them. Had the States complied punctually with the articles of confederation, or could their compliance have been enforced by as peaceable means as may be used with success towards single persons, our past experience is very far from countenancing an opinion that the State Governments would have lost their constitutional powers, and have gradually undergone an entire consolidation. To maintain that such an event would have ensued, would be to say at once, that the existence of the State Governments is incompatible with any system whatever that accomplishes the essential purposes of the Union.

On the New Constitution

State Gazette of South Carolina (Charleston), January 28, 1788

In evil hour his pen 'squire Adams drew
Claiming dominion to his well born few:
In the gay circle of St. James's plac'd
He wrote, and, writing, has his work disgrac'd.
Smit with the splendor of a British King
The crown prevail'd, so once despis'd a thing!
Shelburne and Pitt approv'd of all he wrote,
While Rush and Wilson echo back his note.

Tho' British armies could not here prevail
Yet British politics shall turn the scale; —
In five short years of Freedom weary grown
We quit our plain republics for a throne;
Congress and *President* full proof shall bring,
A mere disguise for Parliament and King.

A standing army! — curse the plan so base;
A despot's safety — Liberty's disgrace. —
Who sav'd these realms from Britain's bloody hand,
Who, but the generous rustics of the land;
That free-born race, inur'd to every toil,
Who tame the ocean and subdue the soil,
Who tyrants banish'd from this injur'd shore
Domestic traitors may expel once more.

Ye, who have bled in Freedom's sacred cause,
Ah, why desert her maxims and her laws?
When *thirteen* states are moulded into *one*
Your rights are vanish'd and your honors gone;
The form of Freedom shall alone remain,
As Rome had Senators when she hugg'd the chain.

Sent to revise your systems—not to change—
Sages have done what Reason deems most strange:
Some alterations in our fabric we
Calmly propos'd, and hoped at length to see—
Ah, how deceived!—these heroes in renown
Scheme for themselves—and pull the fabric down—
Bid in its place Columbia's tomb-stone rise
Inscrib'd with these sad words—*Here Freedom lies!*

"Publius," The Federalist XLVI
[James Madison]

New-York Packet, January 29, 1788

To the People of the State of New-York.

Resuming the subject of the last paper, I proceed to enquire whether the Fœderal Government or the State Governments will have the advantage with regard to the predilection
and support of the people. Notwithstanding the different
modes in which they are appointed, we must consider both of
them, as substantially dependent on the great body of the citizens of the United States. I assume this position here as it
respects the first, reserving the proofs for another place. The
Fœderal and State Governments are in fact but different
agents and trustees of the people, constituted with different
powers, and designated for different purposes. The adversaries of the Constitution seem to have lost sight of the people altogether in their reasonings on this subject; and to have
viewed these different establishments, not only as mutual rivals and enemies, but as uncontrouled by any common superior in their efforts to usurp the authorities of each other.
These gentlemen must here be reminded of their error. They
must be told that the ultimate authority, wherever the derivative may be found, resides in the people alone; and that it will
not depend merely on the comparative ambition or address of
the different governments, whether either, or which of them,
will be able to enlarge its sphere of jurisdiction at the expence
of the other. Truth no less than decency requires, that the
event in every case, should be supposed to depend on the
sentiments and sanction of their common constituents.

Many considerations, besides those suggested on a former
occasion, seem to place it beyond doubt, that the first and

most natural attachment of the people will be to the governments of their respective States. Into the administration of these, a greater number of individuals will expect to rise. From the gift of these, a greater number of offices and emoluments will flow. By the superintending care of these, all the more domestic, and personal interests of the people will be regulated and provided for. With the affairs of these, the people will be more familiarly and minutely conversant. And with the members of these, will a greater proportion of the people have the ties of personal acquaintance and friendship, and of family and party attachments; on the side of these therefore the popular bias, may well be expected most strongly to incline.

Experience speaks the same language in this case. The fœderal administration, though hitherto very defective, in comparison with what may be hoped under a better system, had during the war, and particularly, whilst the independent fund of paper emissions was in credit, an activity and importance as great as it can well have, in any future circumstances whatever. It was engaged too in a course of measures, which had for their object, the protection of every thing that was dear, and the acquisition of every thing that could be desireable to the people at large. It was nevertheless, invariably found, after the transient enthusiasm for the early Congresses was over, that the attention and attachment of the people were turned anew to their own particular governments; that the Fœderal Council, was at no time the idol of popular favor; and that opposition to proposed enlargements of its powers and importance, was the side usually taken by the men who wished to build their political consequence on the prepossessions of their fellow citizens.

If therefore, as has been elsewhere remarked, the people should in future become more partial to the fœderal than to the State governments, the change can only result, from such manifest and irresistible proofs of a better administration, as will overcome all their antecedent propensities. And in that case, the people ought not surely to be precluded from giving most of their confidence where they may discover it to be most due: But even in that case, the State governments could have little to apprehend, because it is only within a certain sphere, that the fœderal power can, in the nature of things, be advantageously administered.

The remaining points on which I propose to compare the fœderal and State governments, are the disposition, and the faculty they may respectively possess, to resist and frustrate the measures of each other.

It has been already proved, that the members of the fœderal will be more dependent on the members of the State governments, than the latter will be on the former. It has appeared also, that the prepossessions of the people on whom both will depend, will be more on the side of the State governments, than of the Fœderal Government. So far as the disposition of each, towards the other, may be influenced by these causes, the State governments must clearly have the advantage. But in a distinct and very important point of view, the advantage will lie on the same side. The prepossessions which the members themselves will carry into the Fœderal Government, will generally be favorable to the States; whilst it will rarely happen, that the members of the State governments will carry into the public councils, a bias in favor of the general government. A local spirit will infallibly prevail much more in the members of the Congress, than a national spirit will prevail in the Legislatures of the particular States. Every one knows that a great proportion of the errors committed by the State Legislatures proceeds from the disposition of the members to sacrifice the comprehensive and permanent interest of the State, to the particular and separate views of the counties or districts in which they reside. And if they do not sufficiently enlarge their policy to embrace the collective welfare of their particular State, how can it be imagined, that they will make the aggregate prosperity of the Union, and the dignity and respectability of its government, the objects of their affections and consultations? For the same reason, that the members of the State Legislatures, will be unlikely to attach themselves sufficiently to national objects, the members of the Fœderal Legislature will be likely to attach themselves too much to local objects. The States will be to the latter, what counties and towns are to the former. Measures will too often be decided according to their probable effect, not on the national prosperity and happiness, but on the prejudices, interests and pursuits of the governments and people of the individual States. What is the spirit that has in general characterized the proceedings of Congress? A perusal of their journals as well as the candid acknowledgments of such as have had a seat in that assembly, will inform us, that the members have but too frequently displayed the character, rather of partizans of their respective States, than of impartial guardians of a common interest; that whereon one occasion improper sacrifices have been made of local considerations to the aggrandizement of the Fœderal Government; the great interests of the nation have suffered on an hundred, from an undue attention to the local prejudices, interests and views of the particular States. I mean not by these reflections to insinuate, that the new Fœderal Government will not embrace a more enlarged plan of policy than the existing government may have pursued, much less that its views will be as confined as those of the State Legislatures; but only that it will partake sufficiently of the spirit of both, to be disinclined to invade the rights of the individual States, or the prerogatives of their governments. The motives on the part of the State governments, to augment their prerogatives by defalcations from the Fœderal Government, will be overruled by no reciprocal predispositions in the members.

Were it admitted however that the Fœderal Government may feel an equal disposition with the State governments to extend its power beyond the due limits, the latter would still have the advantage in the means of defeating such encroachments. If an act of a particular State, though unfriendly to the national government, be generally popular in that State, and should not too grossly violate the oaths of the State officers, it is executed immediately and of course, by means on the spot, and depending on the State alone. The opposition of the Fœderal Government, or the interposition of Fœderal officers, would but inflame the zeal of all parties on the side of the State, and the evil could not be prevented or repaired, if at all, without the employment of means which must always be resorted to with reluctance and difficulty. On the other hand, should an unwarrantable measure of the Fœderal Government be unpopular in particular States, which would seldom fail to be the case, or even a warrantable measure be so, which may sometimes be the case, the means of opposition to it are powerful and at hand. The disquietude of the people, their repugnance and perhaps refusal to co-operate with the officers of the Union, the frowns of the executive magistracy of the State, the embarrassments created by legislative devices, which would often be added on such occasions, would oppose in any State difficulties not to be despised; would form in a large State very serious impediments, and where the sentiments of several adjoining States happened to be in unison, would present obstructions which the Fœderal Government would hardly be willing to encounter.

But ambitious encroachments of the Fœderal Government, on the authority of the State governments, would not excite the opposition of a single State or of a few States only. They would be signals of general alarm. Every Government would espouse the common cause. A correspondence would be opened. Plans of resistance would be concerted. One spirit would animate and conduct the whole. The same combination in short would result from an apprehension of the fœderal, as was produced by the dread of a foreign yoke; and unless the projected innovations should be voluntarily renounced, the same appeal to a trial of force would be made in the one case, as was made in the other. But what degree of madness could ever drive the Fœderal Government to such an extremity? In the contest with Great Britain, one part of the empire was employed against the other. The more numerous part invaded the rights of the less numerous part. The attempt was unjust and unwise; but it was not in speculation absolutely chimerical. But what would be the contest in the case we are supposing? Who would be the parties? A few representatives of the people, would be opposed to the people themselves; or rather one set of representatives would be contending against thirteen sets of representatives, with the whole body of their common constituents on the side of the latter.

The only refuge left for those who prophecy the downfal of

the State Governments, is the visionary supposition that the Fœderal Government may previously accumulate a military force for the projects of ambition. The reasonings contained in these papers must have been employed to little purpose indeed, if it could be necessary now to disprove the reality of this danger. That the people and the States should for a sufficient period of time elect an uninterrupted succession of men ready to betray both; that the traitors should throughout this period, uniformly and systematically pursue some fixed plan for the extension of the military establishment; that the governments and the people of the States should silently and patiently behold the gathering storm, and continue to supply the materials, until it should be prepared to burst on their own heads, must appear to every one more like the incoherent dreams of a delirious jealousy, or the misjudged exaggerations of a counterfeit zeal, than like the sober apprehensions of genuine patriotism. Extravagant as the supposition is, let it however be made. Let a regular army, fully equal to the resources of the country be formed; and let it be entirely at the devotion of the Fœderal Government; still it would not be going too far to say, that the State Governments with the people on their side would be able to repeal the danger. The highest number to which, according to the best computation, a standing army can be carried in any country, does not exceed one hundredth part of the whole number of souls; or one twenty-fifth part of the number able to bear arms. This proportion would not yield in the United States an army of more than twenty-five or thirty thousand men. To these would be opposed a militia amounting to near half a million of citizens with arms in their hands, officered by men chosen from among themselves, fighting for their common liberties, and united and conducted by governments possessing their affections and confidence. It may well be doubted whether a militia thus circumstanced could ever be conquered by such a proportion of regular troops. Those who are best acquainted with the late successful resistance of this country against the British arms will be most inclined to deny the possibility of it. Besides the advantage of being armed, which the Americans possess over the people of almost every other nation, the existence of subordinate governments to which the people are attached, and by which the militia officers are appointed, forms a barrier against the enterprizes of ambition, more insurmountable than any which a simple government of any form can admit of. Notwithstanding the military establishments in the several kingdoms of Europe, which are carried as far as the public resources will bear, the governments are afraid to trust the people with arms. And it is not certain that with this aid alone, they would not be able to shake off their yokes. But were the people to possess the additional advantages of local governments chosen by themselves, who could collect the national will, and direct the national force; and of officers appointed out of the militia, by these governments and attached both to them and to the militia, it may be affirmed with the greatest assurance, that the throne of every tyranny in Europe would be speedily overturned, in spite of the legions which surround it. Let us not insult the free and gallant citizens of America with the suspicion that they would be less able to defend the rights of which they would be in actual possession, than the debased subjects of arbitrary power would be to rescue theirs from the hands of their oppressors. Let us rather no longer insult them with the supposition, that they can ever reduce themselves to the necessity of making the experiment, by a blind and tame submission to the long train of insidious measures, which must precede and produce it.

The argument under the present head may be put into a very concise form, which appears altogether conclusive. Either the mode in which the Fœderal Government is to be constructed will render it sufficiently dependant on the people, or it will not. On the first supposition, it will be restrained by that dependence from forming schemes obnoxious to their constituents. On the other supposition it will not possess the confidence of the people, and its schemes of usurpation will be easily defeated by the State Governments; who will be supported by the people.

On summing up the considerations stated in this and the last paper, they seem to amount to the most convincing evidence, that the powers proposed to be lodged in the Fœderal Government, are as little formidable to those reserved to the individual States, as they are indispensibly necessary to accomplish the purposes of the Union; and that all those alarms which have been sounded, of a meditated or consequential annihilation of the State Governments, must, on the most favorable interpretation, be ascribed to the chimerical fears of the authors of them.

David Ramsay to Benjamin Lincoln

Charleston, South Carolina, January 29, 1788

I had the pleasure of receiving your letter by mr. Crocker. I shall be happy in rendering that young gentle man every civility in my power.

Our Assembly is now sitting & have unanimously agreed to hold a convention. By common consent the merits of the fœderal constitution were freely discussed on that occasion for the sake of enlightening our citizens. Mr Lownds was the only man who made direct formal opposition to it. His objections were local & proceeded from an illiberal jealousy of New: England men. He urged that you would raise freights on us & in short that you were too cunning for our honest people. That your end of the continent would rule the other. That the sun of our glory would set when the new constitution operated. He has not one fœderal idea in his head nor one that looks beyond Pedee. He is said to be honest & free of debt but he was an enemy to Independence & though our President in 1778 he was a British subject in 1780. His taking protection was rather the passive act of an old man than otherwise. He never aided nor abetted the British government directly but his example was mischievous. His opposition has poisoned the minds of some. I fear the numerous class of debtors more than any other. On the whole I have no doubt that it will be accepted by a very great majority of this State. The sentiments of our leading men are of late much more fœderal than formerly. This honest sentiment was avowed by the first characters. "New England has lost & we have gained by the war her suffering citizens ought to be our carriers though a dearer freight should be the consequence." Your delegates never did a more political thing than in standing by those of South Carolina about negroes. Virginia deserted them & was for an immediate stoppage of further importation. The dominion has lost much popularity by the conduct of her delegates on this head. The language now is "the Eastern states can soonest help us in case of invasion & it is more our interest to encourage them & their shipping than to join with or look up to Virginia". In short sir a revolution highly favorable to union has taken place. Fœderalism & liberality of sentiment has gained great ground. Mr Lownds still thinks you are a set of sharpers—does not wonder that you are for the new constitution as in his opinion you will have all the advantage. You begrudge us our negroes in his opinion. But he is almost alone. I have now nearly completed a general history of the late revolution & mean to publish it soon. I also have it in idea to visit Boston previously to its publication that I may trace the rise of the opposition. I wish to converse with some of your leading characters about 1767. I shall thank every body who will furnish me with any documents that may be of service.

John Williams to His Constituents

Albany Federal Herald, February 25, 1788

An Extract of a Letter from John Williams, Esq; at Pough-keepsie, to his Friends in Washington County, dated 29th January, 1788.

"The new constitution is not yet taken up, various are the opinions upon this subject; if I can have my opinion carried it will be this, let it come to the people without either recommending or disapprobation; let the people judge for themselves—if the majority is for it, let it be adopted—if they are against it, let it be rejected, as all powers are, or ought to be, in the people; they, and they only, have the right to say whether the form of government shall be altered. For my own part, I must confess, under the present situation of affairs, something must be done, but whether the present system is the best will be the question. The powers given to the president are very great. The elections may be so altered as to destroy the liberty of the people. The direct taxation, and to be collected by officers of Congress, are powers which cannot be granted agreeable to our present constitution, nor will it be very convenient for Congress officers, and our state collectors, to be collecting both at one time, and as Congress may lay a poll tax, how will that agree with us. I need not tell you the injustices of it. If the new constitution is adopted, Congress hath all the impost and excise; this latter may be laid heavy on taverns and spirits, so that the emoluments from taverns, which are now converted to the use of the poor, must go to Congress; and what is yet worse, all the duties arising from any duties or excise, are to be appropriated to the use of Congress.

"You will also observe that senators are for six years, and that small states have an equal number with large states, so that the advantage of having property in a maritime state, will be reduced to an equal value with the property where there is no navigation. If this is not taking our liberty, it is certainly diminishing our property, which is equal to it. What hath kept the taxes so low in this state—the reason is obvious, our impost duties. This is a privilege Providence hath endowed us with; our landed property will ever sell according to the conveniency of it; the lighter the tax, the higher the land; the nigher to market, the greater profits arising from our produce. Let our imposts and advantages be taken from us, shall we not be obliged to lay as heavy taxes as Connecticut, Boston, &c. What hath kept us from those burthens but the privileges, which we must lose if the present proposed constitution is adopted."

"Publius," The Federalist XLVII
[James Madison]

Independent Journal (New York), January 30, 1788

To the People of the State of New-York.

Having reviewed the general form of the proposed government, and the general mass of power allotted to it: I proceed to examine the particular structure of this government, and the distribution of this mass of power among its constituent parts.

One of the principal objections inculcated by the more respectable adversaries to the constitution, is its supposed violation of the political maxim, that the legislative, executive and judiciary departments ought to be separate and distinct. In the structure of the federal government, no regard, it is said, seems to have been paid to this essential precaution in favor of liberty. The several departments of power are distributed and blended in such a manner, as at once to destroy all symmetry and beauty of form; and to expose some of the essential parts of the edifice to the danger of being crushed by the disproportionate weight of other parts.

No political truth is certainly of greater intrinsic value or is stamped with the authority of more enlightened patrons of liberty, than that on which the objection is founded. The accumulation of all powers legislative, executive and judiciary in the same hands, whether of one, a few or many, and whether hereditary, self appointed, or elective, may justly be pronounced the very definition of tyranny. Were the federal constitution therefore really chargeable with this accumulation of power or with a mixture of powers having a dangerous tendency to such an accumulation, no further arguments would be necessary to inspire a universal reprobation of the system. I persuade myself however, that it will be made apparent to every one, that the charge cannot be supported, and that the maxim on which it relies, has been totally misconceived and misapplied. In order to form correct ideas on this important subject, it will be proper to investigate the sense, in which the preservation of liberty requires, that the three great departments of power should be separate and distinct.

The oracle who is always consulted and cited on this subject, is the celebrated Montesquieu. If he be not the author of this invaluable precept in the science of politics, he has the merit at least of displaying, and recommending it most effectually to the attention of mankind. Let us endeavour in the first place to ascertain his meaning on this point.

The British constitution was to Montesquieu, what Homer has been to the didactic writers on epic poetry. As the latter have considered the work of the immortal Bard, as the perfect model from which the principles and rules of the epic art were to be drawn, and by which all similar works were to be judged; so this great political critic appears to have viewed the constitution of England, as the standard, or to use his own expression, as the mirrour of political liberty; and to have delivered in the form of elementary truths, the several characteristic principles of that particular system. That we may be sure then not to mistake his meaning in this case, let us recur to the source from which the maxim was drawn.

On the slightest view of the British constitution we must perceive, that the legislative, executive and judiciary departments are by no means totally separate and distinct from each other. The executive magistrate forms an integral part of the legislative authority. He alone has the prerogative of making treaties with foreign sovereigns, which when made have, under certain limitations, the force of legislative acts. All the members of the judiciary department are appointed by him; can be removed by him on the address of the two Houses of Parliament, and form, when he pleases to consult them, one of his constitutional councils. One branch of the legislative department forms also, a great constitutional council to the executive chief; as on another hand, it is the sole depositary of judicial power in cases of impeachment, and is invested with the supreme appellate jurisdiction, in all other cases. The judges again are so far connected with the legislative department, as often to attend and participate in its deliberations, though not admitted to a legislative vote.

From these facts by which Montesquieu was guided it may clearly be inferred, that in saying "there can be no liberty where the legislative and executive powers are united in the same person, or body of magistrates," or, "or if the power of judging be not separated from the legislative and executive powers," he did not mean that these departments ought to have no *partial agency* in, or no *controul* over the acts of each other. His meaning, as his own words import, and still more conclusively as illustrated by the example in his eye, can amount to no more than this, that where the *whole* power of one department is exercised by the same hands which possess the *whole* power of another department, the fundamental principles of a free constitution, are subverted. This would have been the case in the constitution examined by him, if the King who is the sole executive magistrate, had possessed also the compleat legislative power, or the supreme administration of justice; or if the entire legislative body, had possessed the supreme judiciary, or the supreme executive authority. This however is not among the vices of that constitution. The magistrate in whom the whole executive power resides cannot of himself make a law, though he can put a negative on every law, nor administer justice in person, though he has the appointment of those who do administer it. The judges can exercise no executive prerogative, though they are shoots from the executive stock, nor any legislative function, though they may be advised with by the legislative councils. The entire legislature, can perform no judiciary act, though by the joint act of two of its branches. The judges may be removed from their offices; and though one of its branches is possessed of the judicial power in the last resort. The entire legislature again can exercise no executive prerogative, though one of its branches constitutes the supreme executive magistracy; and another, on the empeachment of a third, can try and condemn all the subordinate officers in the executive department.

The reasons on which Montesquieu grounds his maxim are a further demonstration of his meaning. "When the legislative and executive powers are united in the same person or body" says he "there can be no liberty, because apprehensions may arise lest *the same* monarch or senate should *enact* tyrannical laws, to *execute* them in a tyrannical manner." Again "Were the power of judging joined with the legislative, the life and liberty of the subject would be exposed to arbitrary controul, for *the judge* would then be *the legislator*. Were it joined to the executive power, *the judge* might behave with all the violence of *an oppressor*." Some of these reasons are more fully explained in other passages; but briefly stated as they are here, they sufficiently establish the meaning which we have put on this celebrated maxim of this celebrated author.

If we look into the constitutions of the several states we find that notwithstanding the emphatical, and in some instances, the unqualified terms in which this axiom has been laid down, there is not a single instance in which the several departments of power have been kept absolutely separate and distinct. New-Hampshire, whose constitution was the last formed, seems to have been fully aware of the impossibility and inexpediency of avoiding any mixture whatever of these departments; and has qualified the doctrine by declaring "that the legislative, executive and judiciary powers ought to be kept as separate from, and independent of each other *as the nature of a free government will admit; or as is consistent with that chain of connection, that binds the whole fabric of the constitution in one indissoluble bond of unity and amity*." Her constitution accordingly mixes these departments in several respects. The senate which is a branch of the legislative department is also a judicial tribunal for the trial of empeachments. The president who is the head of the executive department, is the presiding member also of the senate; and besides an equal vote in all cases, has a casting vote in case of a tie. The executive head is himself eventually elective every year by the legislative department; and his council is every year chosen by and from the members of the same department. Several of the officers of state are also appointed by the legislature. And the members of the judiciary department are appointed by the executive department.

The constitution of Massachusetts has observed a sufficient though less pointed caution in expressing this fundamental article of liberty. It declares "that the legislative department shall never exercise the executive and judicial powers, or either

of them: The executive shall never exercise the legislative and
judicial powers, or either of them: The judicial shall never
exercise the legislative and executive powers, or either of
them." This declaration corresponds precisely with the doctrine of Montesquieu as it has been explained, and is not in a
single point violated by the plan of the Convention. It goes
no farther than to prohibit any one of the entire departments
from exercising the powers of another department. In the
very constitution to which it is prefixed, a partial mixture of
powers has been admitted. The Executive Magistrate has a
qualified negative on the Legislative body; and the Senate,
which is a part of the Legislature, is a court of impeachment
for members both of the executive and judiciary departments.
The members of the judiciary department again are appointable by the executive department, and removeable by the
same authority, on the address of the two legislative branches.
Lastly, a number of the officers of government are annually
appointed by the legislative department. As the appointment
to offices, particularly executive offices, is in its nature an executive function, the compilers of the Constitution have in
this last point at least, violated the rule established by themselves.

I pass over the constitutions of Rhode-Island and Connecticut, because they were formed prior to the revolution; and
even before the principle under examination had become an
object of political attention.

The constitution of New-York contains no declaration on
this subject; but appears very clearly to have been framed with
an eye to the danger of improperly blending the different departments. It gives nevertheless to the executive magistrate a
partial controul to the legislative department; and what is
more, gives a like controul to the judiciary department, and
even blends the executive and judiciary departments in the
exercise of this controul. In its council of appointment, members of the legislative are associated with the executive authority in the appointment of officers both executive and
judiciary. And its court for the trial of impeachments and correction of errors, is to consist of one branch of the legislature
and the principal members of the judiciary department.

The constitution of New-Jersey has blended the different

powers of government more than any of the preceding. The governor, who is the executive magistrate, is appointed by the legislature; is chancellor and ordinary or surrogate of the state; is a member of the supreme court of appeals, and president with a casting vote, of one of the legislative branches. The same legislative branch acts again as executive council to the governor, and with him constitutes the court of appeals. The members of the judiciary department are appointed by the legislative department, and removeable by one branch of it, on the impeachment of the other.

According to the constitution of Pennsylvania, the president, who is head of the executive department, is annually elected by a vote in which the legislative department predominates. In conjunction with an executive council, he appoints the members of the judiciary department, and forms a court of impeachments for trial of all officers, judiciary as well as executive. The judges of the supreme court, and justices of the peace, seem also to be removeable by the legislature; and the executive power of pardoning in certain cases to be referred to the same department. The members of the executive council are made EX OFFICIO justices of peace throughout the state.

In Delaware, the chief executive magistrate is annually elected by the legislative department. The speakers of the two legislative branches are vice-presidents in the executive department. The executive chief, with six others, appointed three by each of the legislative branches, constitute the supreme court of appeals: He is joined with the legislative department in the appointment of the other judges. Throughout the states it appears that the members of the legislature may at the same time be justices of the peace. In this state, the members of one branch of it are EX OFFICIO justices of peace; as are also the members of the executive council. The principal officers of the executive department are appointed by the legislative; and one branch of the latter forms a court of impeachments. All officers may be removed on address of the legislature.

Maryland has adopted the maxim in the most unqualified terms; declaring that the legislative, executive and judicial powers of government, ought to be forever separate and distinct from each other. Her constitution, notwithstanding makes the executive magistrate appointable by the legislative department; and the members of the judiciary, by the executive department.

The language of Virginia is still more pointed on this subject. Her constitution declares, "that the legislative, executive and judiciary departments, shall be separate and distinct; so that neither exercise the powers properly belonging to the other; nor shall any person exercise the powers of more than one of them at the same time; except that the justices of the county courts shall be eligible to either house of assembly." Yet we find not only this express exception, with respect to the members of the inferior courts; but that the chief magistrate with his executive council are appointable by the legislature; that two members of the latter are triennially displaced at the pleasure of the legislature; and that all the principal offices, both executive and judiciary, are filled by the same department. The executive prerogative of pardon, also is in one case vested in the legislative department.

The constitution of North-Carolina, which declares, "that the legislative, executive and supreme judicial powers of government, ought to be forever separate and distinct from each other," refers at the same time to the legislative department, the appointment not only of the executive chief, but all the principal officers within both that and the judiciary department.

In South-Carolina, the constitution makes the executive magistracy eligible by the legislative department. It gives to the latter also the appointment of the members of the judiciary department, including even justices of the peace and sheriffs; and the appointment of officers in the executive department, down to captains in the army and navy of the state.

In the constitution of Georgia, where it is declared, "that the legislative, executive and judiciary departments shall be separate and distinct, so that neither exercise the powers properly belonging to the other." We find that the executive department is to be filled by appointments of the legislature; and the executive prerogative of pardon, to be finally exercised by the same authority. Even justices of the peace are to be appointed by the legislature.

In citing these cases in which the legislative, executive and judiciary departments, have not been kept totally separate and distinct, I wish not to be regarded as an advocate for the particular organizations of the several state governments. I am fully aware that among the many excellent principles which they exemplify, they carry strong marks of the haste, and still stronger of the inexperience, under which they were framed. It is but too obvious that in some instances, the fundamental principle under consideration has been violated by too great a mixture, and even an actual consolidation of the different powers; and that in no instance has a competent provision been made for maintaining in practice the separation delineated on paper. What I have wished to evince is, that the charge brought against the proposed constitution, of violating a sacred maxim of free government, is warranted neither by the real meaning annexed to that maxim by its author; nor by the sense in which it has hitherto been understood in America. This interesting subject will be resumed in the ensuing paper.

"Brutus" XI

New York Journal, January 31, 1788

The nature and extent of the judicial power of the United States, proposed to be granted by this constitution, claims our particular attention.

Much has been said and written upon the subject of this new system on both sides, but I have not met with any writer, who has discussed the judicial powers with any degree of accuracy. And yet it is obvious, that we can form but very imperfect ideas of the manner in which this government will work, or the effect it will have in changing the internal police and mode of distributing justice at present subsisting in the respective states, without a thorough investigation of the powers of the judiciary and of the manner in which they will operate. This government is a complete system, not only for making, but for executing laws. And the courts of law, which will be constituted by it, are not only to decide upon the constitution and the laws made in pursuance of it, but by officers subordinate to them to execute all their decisions. The real effect of this system of government, will therefore be brought home to the feelings of the people, through the medium of the judicial power. It is, moreover, of great importance, to examine with care the nature and extent of the judicial power, because those who are to be vested with it, are to be placed in a situation altogether unprecedented in a free country. They are to be rendered totally independent, both of the people and the legislature, both with respect to their offices and salaries. No errors they may commit can be corrected by any power above them, if any such power there be, nor can they be removed from office for making ever so many erroneous adjudications.

The only causes for which they can be displaced, is, conviction of treason, bribery, and high crimes and misdemeanors.

This part of the plan is so modelled, as to authorise the courts, not only to carry into execution the powers expressly given, but where these are wanting or ambiguously expressed, to supply what is wanting by their own decisions.

That we may be enabled to form a just opinion on this subject, I shall, in considering it,

1st. Examine the nature and extent of the judicial powers—and

2d. Enquire, whether the courts who are to exercise them, are so constituted as to afford reasonable ground of confidence, that they will exercise them for the general good.

With a regard to the nature and extent of the judicial powers, I have to regret my want of capacity to give that full and minute explanation of them that the subject merits. To be able to do this, a man should be possessed of a degree of law knowledge far beyond what I pretend to. A number of hard words and technical phrases are used in this part of the system, about the meaning of which gentlemen learned in the law differ.

Its advocates know how to avail themselves of these phrases. In a number of instances, where objections are made to the powers given to the judicial, they give such an explanation to the technical terms as to avoid them.

Though I am not competent to give a perfect explanation of the powers granted to this department of the government, I shall yet attempt to trace some of the leading features of it, from which I presume it will appear, that they will operate to a total subversion of the state judiciaries, if not, to the legislative authority of the states.

In article 3d, sect. 2d, it is said, "The judicial power shall extend to all cases in law and equity arising under this constitution, the laws of the United States, and treaties made, or which shall be made, under their authority, &c."

The first article to which this power extends, is, all cases in law and equity arising under this constitution.

What latitude of construction this clause should receive, it is not easy to say. At first view, one would suppose, that it meant no more than this, that the courts under the general government should exercise, not only the powers of courts of law, but also that of courts of equity, in the manner in which those powers are usually exercised in the different states. But this cannot be the meaning, because the next clause authorises the courts to take cognizance of all cases in law and equity arising under the laws of the United States; this last article, I conceive, conveys as much power to the general judicial as any of the state courts possess.

The cases arising under the constitution must be different from those arising under the laws, or else the two clauses mean exactly the same thing.

The cases arising under the constitution must include such, as bring into question its meaning, and will require an explanation of the nature and extent of the powers of the different departments under it.

This article, therefore, vests the judicial with a power to resolve all questions that may arise on any case on the construction of the constitution, either in law or in equity.

1st. They are authorised to determine all questions that may arise upon the meaning of the constitution in law. This article vests the courts with authority to give the constitution a legal construction, or to explain it according to the rules laid down for construing a law.—These rules give a certain degree of latitude of explanation. According to this mode of construction, the courts are to give such meaning to the constitution as comports best with the common, and generally received acceptation of the words in which it is expressed, regarding their ordinary and popular use, rather than their grammatical propriety. Where words are dubious, they will be explained by the context. The end of the clause will be attended to, and the words will be understood, as having a view to it; and the words will not be so understood as to bear no meaning or a very absurd one.

2d. The judicial are not only to decide questions arising upon the meaning of the constitution in law, but also in equity.

By this they are empowered, to explain the constitution according to the reasoning spirit of it, without being confined to the words or letter.

"From this method of interpreting laws (says Blackstone)

by the reason of them, arises what we call equity;" which is thus defined by Grotius, "the correction of that, wherein the law, by reason of its universality, is deficient; for since in laws all cases cannot be foreseen, or expressed, it is necessary, that when the decrees of the law cannot be applied to particular cases, there should some where be a power vested of defining those circumstances, which had they been foreseen the legislator would have expressed; and these are the cases, which according to Grotius, lex non exacte definit, sed arbitrio boni viri permittet."

The same learned author observes, "That equity, thus depending essentially upon each individual case, there can be no established rules and fixed principles of equity laid down, without destroying its very essence, and reducing it to a positive law."

From these remarks, the authority and business of the courts of law, under this clause, may be understood.

They will give the sense of every article of the constitution, that may from time to time come before them. And in their decisions they will not confine themselves to any fixed or established rules, but will determine, according to what appears to them, the reason and spirit of the constitution. The opinions of the supreme court, whatever they may be, will have the force of law; because there is no power provided in the constitution, that can correct their errors, or controul their adjudications. From this court there is no appeal. And I conceive the legislature themselves, cannot set aside a judgment of this court, because they are authorised by the constitution to decide in the last resort. The legislature must be controuled by the constitution, and not the constitution by them. They have therefore no more right to set aside any judgment pronounced upon the construction of the constitution, than they have to take from the president, the chief command of the army and navy, and commit it to some other person. The reason is plain; the judicial and executive derive their authority from the same source, that the legislature do theirs; and therefore in all cases, where the constitution does not make the one responsible to, or controulable by the other, they are altogether independent of each other.

The judicial power will operate to effect, in the most certain, but yet silent and imperceptible manner, what is evidently the tendency of the constitution:—I mean, an entire subversion of the legislative, executive and judicial powers of the individual states. Every adjudication of the supreme court, on any question that may arise upon the nature and extent of the general government, will affect the limits of the state jurisdiction. In proportion as the former enlarge the exercise of their powers, will that of the latter be restricted.

That the judicial power of the United States, will lean strongly in favour of the general government, and will give such an explanation to the constitution, as will favour an extension of its jurisdiction, is very evident from a variety of considerations.

1st. The constitution itself strongly countenances such a mode of construction. Most of the articles in this system, which convey powers of any considerable importance, are conceived in general and indefinite terms, which are either equivocal, ambiguous, or which require long definitions to unfold the extent of their meaning. The two most important powers committed to any government, those of raising money, and of raising and keeping up troops, have already been considered, and shewn to be unlimitted by any thing but the discretion of the legislature. The clause which vests the power to pass all laws which are proper and necessary, to carry the powers given into execution, it has been shewn, leaves the legislature at liberty, to do every thing, which in their judgment is best. It is said, I know, that this clause confers no power on the legislature, which they would not have had without it—though I believe this is not the fact, yet, admitting it to be, it implies that the constitution is not to receive an explanation strictly, according to its letter; but more power is implied than is expressed. And this clause, if it is to be considered, as explanatory of the extent of the powers given, rather than giving a new power, is to be understood as declaring, that in construing any of the articles conveying power, the spirit, intent and design of the clause, should be attended to, as well as the words in their common acceptation.

This constitution gives sufficient colour for adopting an equitable construction, if we consider the great end and design it professedly has in view—there appears from its preamble to be, "to form a more perfect union, establish justice, insure domestic tranquillity, provide for the common defence, promote the general welfare, and secure the blessings of liberty to ourselves and posterity." The design of this system is here expressed, and it is proper to give such a meaning to the various parts, as will best promote the accomplishment of the end; this idea suggests itself naturally upon reading the preamble, and will countenance the court in giving the several articles such a sense, as will the most effectually promote the ends the constitution had in view—how this manner of explaining the constitution will operate in practice, shall be the subject of future enquiry.

2d. Not only will the constitution justify the courts in inclining to this mode of explaining it, but they will be interested in using this latitude of interpretation. Every body of men invested with office are tenacious of power; they feel interested, and hence it has become a kind of maxim, to hand down their offices, with all its rights and privileges, unimpared to their successors; the same principle will influence them to extend their power, and increase their rights; this of itself will operate strongly upon the courts to give such a meaning to the constitution in all cases where it can possibly be done, as will enlarge the sphere of their own authority. Every extension of the power of the general legislature, as well as of the judicial powers, will increase the powers of the courts; and the dignity and importance of the judges, will be in proportion to the extent and magnitude of the powers they exercise. I add, it is highly probable the emolument of the judges will be increased, with the increase of the business they will have to transact and its importance. From these considerations the judges will be interested to extend the powers of the courts, and to construe the constitution as much as possi-. ble, in such a way as to favour it; and that they will do it, appears probable.

3d. Because they will have precedent to plead, to justify them in it. It is well known, that the courts in England, have by their own authority, extended their jurisdiction far beyond the limits set them in their original institution, and by the laws of the land.

The court of exchequer is a remarkable instance of this. It was originally intended principally to recover the king's debts, and to order the revenues of the crown. It had a common law jurisdiction, which was established merely for the benefit of the king's accomptants. We learn from Blackstone, that the proceedings in this court are grounded on a writ called quo minus, in which the plaintiff suggests, that he is the king's farmer or debtor, and that the defendant hath done him the damage complained of, by which he is less able to pay the king. These suits, by the statute of Rutland, are expressly directed to be confined to such matters as specially concern the king, or his ministers in the exchequer. And by the articuli super cartas, it is enacted, that no common pleas be thenceforth held in the exchequer contrary to the form of the great charter: but now any person may sue in the exchequer. The surmise of being debtor to the king being matter of form, and mere words of course; and the court is open to all the nation.

When the courts will have a precedent before them of a court which extended its jurisdiction in opposition to an act of the legislature, is it not to be expected that they will extend theirs, especially when there is nothing in the constitution expressly against it? and they are authorised to construe its meaning, and are not under any controul?

This power in the judicial, will enable them to mould the government, into almost any shape they please.—The manner in which this may be effected we will hereafter examine.

"Publius," The Federalist XLVIII
[James Madison]

New-York Packet, February 1, 1788

To the People of the State of New-York.

It was shewn in the last paper, that the political apothegm there examined, does not require that the legislative, executive and judiciary departments should be wholly unconnected with each other. I shall undertake in the next place, to shew that unless these departments be so far connected and blended, as to give to each a constitutional controul over the others, the degree of separation which the maxim requires as essential to a free government, can never in practice, be duly maintained.

It is agreed on all sides, that the powers properly belonging to one of the departments, ought not to be directly and compleatly administered by either of the other departments. It is equally evident, that neither of them ought to possess directly or indirectly, an overruling influence over the others in the administration of their respective powers. It will not be denied, that power is of an encroaching nature, and that it ought to be effectually restrained from passing the limits assigned to it. After discriminating therefore in theory, the several classes of power, as they may in their nature be legislative, executive, or judiciary; the next and most difficult task, is to provide some practical security for each against the invasion of the others. What this security ought to be, is the great problem to be solved.

Will it be sufficient to mark with precision the boundaries of these departments in the Constitution of the government, and to trust to these parchment barriers against the encroaching spirit of power? This is the security which appears to have been principally relied on by the compilers of most of the

American Constitutions. But experience assures us, that the efficacy of the provision has been greatly over-rated; and that some more adequate defence is indispensibly necessary for the more feeble, against the more powerful members of the government. The legislative department is every where extending the sphere of its activity, and drawing all power into its impetuous vortex.

The founders of our republics have so much merit for the wisdom which they have displayed, that no task can be less pleasing than that of pointing out the errors into which they have fallen. A respect for truth however obliges us to remark, that they seem never for a moment to have turned their eyes from the danger to liberty from the overgrown and all-grasping prerogative of an hereditary magistrate, supported and fortified by an hereditary branch of the legislative authority. They seem never to have recollected the danger from legislative usurpations; which by assembling all power in the same hands, must lead to the same tyranny as is threatened by executive usurpations.

In a government, where numerous and extensive prerogatives are placed in the hands of a hereditary monarch, the executive department is very justly regarded as the source of danger, and watched with all the jealousy which a zeal for liberty ought to inspire. In a democracy, where a multitude of people exercise in person the legislative functions, and are continually exposed by their incapacity for regular deliberation and concerted measures, to the ambitious intrigues of their executive magistrates, tyranny may well be apprehended on some favorable emergency, to start up in the same quarter. But in a representative republic, where the executive magistracy is carefully limited both in the extent and the duration of its power; and where the legislative power is exercised by an assembly, which is inspired by a supposed influence over the people with an intripid confidence in its own strength; which is sufficiently numerous to feel all the passions which actuate a multitude; yet not so numerous as to be incapable of pursuing the objects of its passions, by means which reason prescribes; it is against the enterprising ambition of this department, that the people ought to indulge all their jealousy and exhaust all their precautions.

The legislative department derives a superiority in our governments from other circumstances. Its constitutional powers being at once more extensive and less susceptible of precise limits, it can with the greater facility, mask under complicated and indirect measures, the encroachments which it makes on the co-ordinate departments. It is not unfrequently a question of real nicety in legislative bodies, whether the operation of a particular measure, will, or will not extend beyond the legislative sphere. On the other side, the executive power being restrained within a narrower compass, and being more simple in its nature; and the judiciary being described by land marks, still less uncertain, projects of usurpation by either of these departments, would immediately betray and defeat themselves. Nor is this all: As the legislative department alone has access to the pockets of the people, and has in some Constitutions full discretion, and in all, a prevailing influence over the pecuniary rewards of those who fill the other departments, a dependence is thus created in the latter, which gives still greater facility to encroachments of the former.

I have appealed to our own experience for the truth of what I advance on this subject. Were it necessary to verify this experience by particular proofs, they might be multiplied without end. I might find a witness in every citizen who has shared in, or been attentive to, the course of public administrations. I might collect vouchers in abundance from the records and archieves of every State in the Union. But as a more concise and at the same time, equally satisfactory evidence, I will refer to the example of two States, attested by two unexceptionable authorities.

The first example is that of Virginia, a State which, as we have seen, has expressly declared in its Constitution, that the three great departments ought not to be intermixed. The authority in support of it is Mr. Jefferson, who, besides his other advantages for remarking the operation of the government, was himself the chief magistrate of it. In order to convey fully the ideas with which his experience had impressed him on this subject, it will be necessary to quote a passage of some length from his very interesting "Notes on the State of Virginia." (P. 195.) "All the powers of government, legislative, executive and judiciary, result to the legislative body. The

concentrating these in the same hands is precisely the definition of despotic government. It will be no alleviation that
these powers will be exercised by a plurality of hands, and not
by a single one, 173 despots would surely be as oppressive as
one. Let those who doubt it turn their eyes on the republic of
Venice. As little will it avail us that they are chosen by ourselves. An *elective despotism*, was not the government we
fought for; but one which should not only be founded on
free principles, but in which the powers of government
should be so divided and balanced among several bodies of
magistracy, as that no one could transcend their legal limits,
without being effectually checked and restrained by the others. For this reason that Convention which passed the ordinance of government, laid its foundation on this basis, that
the legislative, executive and judiciary departments should be
separate and distinct, so that no person should exercise the
powers of more than one of them at the same time. *But no
barrier was provided between these several powers.* The judiciary
and executive members were left dependent on the legislative
for their subsistence in office, and some of them for their continuance in it. If therefore the Legislature assumes executive
and judiciary powers, no opposition is likely to be made; nor
if made can it be effectual; because in that case, they may put
their proceeding into the form of an act of Assembly, which
will render them obligatory on the other branches. They have
accordingly *in many* instances *decided rights* which should have
been left to *judiciary controversy*; and *the direction of the executive, during the whole time of their session, is becoming habitual
and familiar.*"

The other State which I shall take for an example, is Pennsylvania; and the other authority the council of censors which
assembled in the years 1783 and 1784. A part of the duty of this
body, as marked out by the Constitution was, "to enquire
whether the Constitution had been preserved inviolate in
every part; and whether the legislative and executive branches
of government had performed their duty as guardians of
the people, or assumed to themselves, or exercised other or
greater powers than they are entitled to by the Constitution."
In the execution of this trust, the council were necessarily
led to a comparison, of both the legislative and executive

proceedings, with the constitutional powers of these departments; and from the facts enumerated, and to the truth of
most of which, both sides in the council subscribed, it appears
that the Constitution had been flagrantly violated by the Legislature in a variety of important instances.

A great number of laws had been passed violating without
any apparent necessity, the rule requiring that all bills of a
public nature, shall be previously printed for the consideration of the people; altho' this is one of the precautions
chiefly relied on by the Constitution, against improper acts of
the Legislature.

The constitutional trial by jury had been violated; and
powers assumed, which had not been delegated by the Constitution.

Executive powers had been usurped.

The salaries of the Judges, which the Constitution expressly
requires to be fixed, had been occasionally varied; and cases
belonging to the judiciary department, frequently drawn
within legislative cognizance and determination.

Those who wish to see the several particulars falling under
each of these heads, may consult the Journals of the council
which are in print. Some of them, it will be found may be
imputable to peculiar circumstances connected with the war:
But the greater part of them may be considered as the spon-
tanious shoots of an ill constituted government.

It appears also, that the executive department had not been
innocent of frequent breaches of the Constitution. There are
three observations however, which ought to be made on this
head. *First*. A great proportion of the instances, were either
immediately produced by the necessities of the war, or recommended by Congress or the Commander in Chief. *Secondly*. in
most of the other instances, they conformed either to the declared or the known sentiments of the legislative department.
Thirdly. The executive department of Pennsylvania is distinguished from that of the other States, by the number of members composing it. In this respect it has as much affinity to a
legislative assembly, as to an executive council. And being at
once exempt from the restraint of an individual responsibility
for the acts of the body, and deriving confidence from mutual
example and joint influence; unauthorized measures would of

course be more freely hazarded, than where the executive department is administered by a single hand or by a few hands.

The conclusion which I am warranted in drawing from these observations is, that a mere demarkation on parchment of the constitutional limits of the several departments, is not a sufficient guard against those encroachments which lead to a tyrannical concentration of all the powers of government in the same hands.

"Publius," The Federalist XLIX
[James Madison]

Independent Journal (New York), February 2, 1788

To the People of the State of New-York.

The author of the "Notes on the state of Virginia," quoted in the last paper, has subjoined to that valuable work, the draught of a constitution which had been prepared in order to be laid before a convention expected to be called in 1783 by the legislature, for the establishment of a constitution for that commonwealth. The plan, like every thing from the same pen, marks a turn of thinking original, comprehensive and accurate; and is the more worthy of attention, as it equally displays a fervent attachment to republican government, and an enlightened view of the dangerous propensities against which it ought to be guarded. One of the precautions which he proposes, and on which he appears ultimately to rely as a palladium to the weaker departments of power, against the invasions of the stronger, is perhaps altogether his own, and as it immediately relates to the subject of our present enquiry, ought not to be overlooked.

His proposition is, "that whenever any two of the three branches of government shall concur in opinion, each by the voices of two thirds of their whole number, that a convention is necessary for altering the constitution or *correcting breaches of it,* a convention shall be called for the purpose."

As the people are the only legitimate fountain of power, and it is from them that the constitutional charter, under which the several branches of government hold their power, is derived; it seems strictly consonant to the republican theory, to recur to the same original authority, not only whenever it may be necessary to enlarge, diminish, or new-model the powers of government; but also whenever any one of the departments may commit encroachments on the chartered authorities of the others. The several departments being perfectly co-ordinate by the terms of their common commission, neither of them, it is evident, can pretend to an exclusive or superior right of settling the boundaries between their respective powers; and how are the encroachments of the stronger to be prevented, or the wrongs of the weaker to be redressed, without an appeal to the people themselves; who, as the grantors of the commission, can alone declare its true meaning and enforce its observance?

There is certainly great force in this reasoning, and it must be allowed to prove, that a constitutional road to the decision of the people, ought to be marked out, and kept open, for certain great and extraordinary occasions. But there appear to be insuperable objections against the proposed recurrence to the people, as a provision in all cases for keeping the several departments of power within their constitutional limits.

In the first place, the provision does not reach the case of a combination of two of the departments against a third. If the legislative authority, which possesses so many means of operating on the motives of the other departments, should be able to gain to its interest either of the others, or even one third of its members, the remaining department could derive no advantage from this remedial provision. I do not dwell however on this objection, because it may be thought to lie rather against the modification of the principle, than against the principle itself.

In the next place, it may be considered as an objection inherent in the principle, that as every appeal to the people would carry an implication of some defect in the government, frequent appeals would in great measure deprive the government of that veneration, which time bestows on every thing, and without which perhaps the wisest and freest governments would not possess the requisite stability. If it be true that all governments rest on opinion, it is no less true that the strength of opinion in each individual, and its practical influence on his conduct, depend much on the number which he supposes to have entertained the same opinion. The reason of man, like man himself is timid and cautious, when left alone;

and acquires firmness and confidence, in proportion to the number with which it is associated. When the examples, which fortify opinion, are *antient* as well as *numerous*, they are known to have a double effect. In a nation of philosophers, this consideration ought to be disregarded. A reverence for the laws, would be sufficiently inculcated by the voice of an enlightened reason. But a nation of philosophers is as little to be expected as the philosophical race of kings wished for by Plato. And in every other nation, the most rational government will not find it a superfluous advantage, to have the prejudices of the community on its side.

The danger of disturbing the public tranquility by interesting too strongly the public passions, is a still more serious objection against a frequent reference of constitutional questions, to the decision of the whole society. Notwithstanding the success which has attended the revisions of our established forms of government, and which does so much honour to the virtue and intelligence of the people of America, it must be confessed, that the experiments are of too ticklish a nature to be unnecessarily multiplied. We are to recollect that all the existing constitutions were formed in the midst of a danger which repressed the passions most unfriendly to order and concord; of an enthusiastic confidence of the people in their patriotic leaders, which stifled the ordinary diversity of opinions on great national questions; of a universal ardor for new and opposite forms, produced by a universal resentment and indignation against the antient government; and whilst no spirit of party, connected with the changes to be made, or the abuses to be reformed, could mingle its leven in the operation. The future situations in which we must expect to be usually placed, do not present any equivalent security against the danger which is apprehended.

But the greatest objection of all is, that the decisions which would probably result from such appeals, would not answer the purpose of maintaining the constitutional equilibrium of the government. We have seen that the tendency of republican governments is to an aggrandizement of the legislative, at the expence of the other departments. The appeals to the people therefore would usually be made by the executive and judiciary departments. But whether made by one side or the other, would each side enjoy equal advantages on the trial? Let us view their different situations. The members of the executive and judiciary departments, are few in number, and can be personally known to a small part only of the people. The latter by the mode of their appointment, as well as, by the nature and permanency of it, are too far removed from the people to share much in their prepossessions. The former are generally the objects of jealousy: And their administration is always liable to be discoloured and rendered unpopular. The members of the legislative department, on the other hand, are numerous. They are distributed and dwell among the people at large. Their connections of blood, of friendship and of acquaintance, embrace a great proportion of the most influencial part of the society. The nature of their public trust implies a personal influence among the people, and that they are more immediately the confidential guardians of the rights and liberties of the people. With these advantages, it can hardly be supposed that the adverse party would have an equal chance for a favorable issue.

But the legislative party would not only be able to plead their cause most successfully with the people. They would probably be constituted themselves the judges. The same influence which had gained them an election into the legislature, would gain them a seat in the convention. If this should not be the case with all, it would probably be the case with many, and pretty certainly with those leading characters, on whom every thing depends in such bodies. The convention in short would be composed chiefly of men, who had been, who actually were, or who expected to be, members of the department whose conduct was arraigned. They would consequently be parties to the very question to be decided by them.

It might however sometimes happen, that appeals would be made under circumstances less adverse to the executive and judiciary departments. The usurpations of the legislature might be so flagrant and so sudden, as to admit of no specious colouring. A strong party among themselves might take side with the other branches. The executive power might be in the hands of a peculiar favorite of the people. In such a posture of things, the public decision might be less swayed by prepossessions in favor of the legislative party. But still it could never be expected to turn on the true merits of the question. It would inevitably be connected with the spirit of pre-existing parties, or of parties springing out of the question itself. It would be connected with persons of distinguished character and extensive influence in the community. It would be pronounced by the very men who had been agents in, or opponents of the measures, to which the decision would relate. The *passions* therefore not *the reason*, of the public, would sit in judgment. But it is the reason of the public alone that ought to controul and regulate the government. The passions ought to be controuled and regulated by the government.

We found in the last paper that mere declarations in the written constitution, are not sufficient to restrain the several departments within their legal limits. It appears in this, that occasional appeals to the people would be neither a proper nor an effectual provision, for that purpose. How far the provisions of a different nature contained in the plan above quoted, might be adequate, I do not examine. Some of them are unquestionably founded on sound political principles, and all of them are framed with singular ingenuity and precision.

"Civis" [David Ramsay] to the Citizens of South Carolina

Columbian Herald (Charleston, S.C.), February 4, 1788

Friends, Countrymen, and Fellow Citizens, You have at this time a new federal constitution proposed for your consideration. The great importance of the subject demands your most serious attention. To assist you in forming a right judgment on this matter, it will be proper to consider,

1st. It is the manifest interest of these states to be united. External wars among ourselves would most probably be the consequence of disunion. Our local weakness particularly proves it to be for the advantage of South-Carolina to strengthen the federal government; for we are inadequate to secure ourselves from more powerful neighbours.

2d. If the thirteen states are to be united in reality, as well as in name, the obvious principle of the union should be, that the Congress or general government, should have power to regulate all general concerns. In a state of nature, each man is free and may do what he pleases; but in society, every individual must sacrifice a part of his natural rights; the minority must yield to the majority, and the collective interest must controul particular interests. When thirteen persons constitute a family, each should forego every thing that is injurious to the other twelve. When several families constitute a parish, or county, each may adopt any regulations it pleases with regard to its domestic affairs, but must be abridged of that liberty in other cases, where the good of the whole is concerned.

When several parishes, counties or districts form a state, the separate interests of each must yield to the collective interest of the whole. When thirteen states combine in one government, the same principles must be observed. These relinquishments of natural rights, are not real sacrifices: each person, county or state, gains more than it loses, for it only gives up a right of injuring others, and obtains in return aid and strength to secure itself in the peaceable enjoyment of all remaining rights. If then we are to be an united people, and the obvious ground of union must be, that all continental concerns should be managed by Congress—let us by these principles examine the new constitution. Look over the 8th section, which enumerates the powers of Congress, and point out one that is not essential on the before recited principles of union. The first is a power to lay and collect taxes, duties, imposts and excises, to pay the debts, and provide for the common defence and general welfare of the United States.

When you authorised Congress to borrow money, and to contract debts for carrying on the late war, you could not intend to abridge them of the means of paying their engagements, made on your account. You may observe, that their future power is confined to provide for the *common defence* and *general welfare* of the United States. If they apply money to any other purposes, they exceed their powers. The people of the United States who pay, are to be judges how far their money is properly applied. It would be tedious to go over all the powers of Congress, but it would be easy to shew that they all may be referred to this single principle, "that the general concerns of the union ought to be managed by the general government." The opposers of the constitution, cannot shew a single power delegated to Congress, that could be spared consistently with the welfare of the whole, nor a single one taken from the states, but such as can be more advantageously lodged in the general government, than in that of the separate states.

For instance—the states cannot emit money; this is not intended to prevent the emission of paper money, but only of state paper money. Is not this an advantage? To have thirteen paper currencies in thirteen states is embarrassing to commerce, and eminently so to travellers. It is obviously our interest, either to have no paper, or such as will circulate from Georgia to New-Hampshire. Take another instance—the Congress are authorised to provide and maintain a navy—Our sea coast in its whole extent needs the protection thereof; but if this was to be done by the states, they who build ships, would be more secure than they who do not. Again, if the local legislatures might build ships of war at pleasure, the Eastern would have a manifest superiority over the Southern states. Observe how much better this business is referred to the regulations of Congress. A common navy, paid out of the common treasury, and to be disposed of by the united voice of a majority for the common defence of the weaker as well as of the stronger states, is promised, and will result from the federal constitution. Suffer not yourselves to be imposed on by declamation. Ask the man who objects to the powers of Congress two questions. Is it not necessary that the supposed dangerous power be lodged somewhere? and secondly, where can it be lodged consistently with the general good, so well as in the general government? Decide for yourselves on these obvious principles of union.

It has been objected, that the eastern states have an advantage in their representation in Congress. Let us examine this objection—the four eastern states send seventeen members to the house of representatives, but Georgia, South-Carolina, North-Carolina and Virginia, send twenty-three. The six northern states send twenty-seven, the six southern thirty. In both cases we have a superiority;—but, say the objectors, add Pennsylvania to the northern states, and there is a majority against us. It is obvious to reply, add Pennsylvania to the Southern states, and they have a majority. The objection amounts to no more than that seven are more than six. It must be known to many of you, that the Southern states, from their vast extent of uncultivated country, are daily receiving new settlers; but in New-England their country is so small, and their land so poor, that their inhabitants are constantly emigrating. As the rule of representation in Congress is to vary with the number of inhabitants, our influence in the general government will be constantly increasing. In fifty years, it is probable that the Southern states will have a great ascendency over the Eastern. It has been said that thirty-five men, not elected by yourselves, may make laws to bind you. This objection, if it has any force, tends to the destruction of your state government. By our constitution, sixty-nine make a quorum, of course, thirty-five members may make a law to bind all the people of South-Carolina.—Charleston, and any one of the neighbouring parishes send collectively thirty-six members; it is therefore possible, in the absence of all others, that three of the lower parishes might legislate for the whole country. Would this be a valid objection against your own constitution? It certainly would not—neither is it against the proposed federal plan. Learn from it this useful lesson—insist on the constant attendance of your members, both in the state assembly, and Continental Congress: your representation in the latter, is as numerous in a relative proportion with the other states as it ought to be. You have a thirteenth part in both houses; and you are not, on principles of equality, entitled to more.

It has been objected, that the president, and two-thirds of the senate, though not of your election, may make treaties binding on this state. Ask these objectors—do you wish to have any treaties? They will say yes.—Ask then who can be more properly trusted with the power of making them, than they to whom the convention have referred it? Can the state legislatures? They would consult their local interests—Can the Continental House of Representatives? When sixty-five men can keep a secret, they may. Observe the cautious guards which are placed around your interests. Neither the senate nor president can make treaties by their separate authority.— They must both concur.—This is more in your favor than the footing on which you now stand. The delegates in Congress of nine states, without your consent can not bind you;—by the new constitution there must be two thirds of the members present, and also the president, in whose election you have a vote. Two thirds are to the whole nearly as nine to thirteen. If you are not wanting to yourselves by neglecting to keep up the states compliment of senators, your situation with regard to preventing the controul of your local interests by the Northern states, will be better under the proposed constitution than now it is under the existing confederation.

It has been said, we will have a navigation act, and be restricted to American bottoms, and that high freight will be the consequence. We certainly ought to have a navigation act, and we assuredly ought to give a preference, though not a monopoly, to our own shipping.

If this state is invaded by a maritime force, to whom can we apply for immediate aid?—To Virginia and North-Carolina?

Before they can march by land to our assistance, the country may be over run. The Eastern states, abounding in men and in ships, can sooner relieve us, than our next door neighbours. It is therefore not only our duty, but our interest, to encourage their shipping. They have sufficient resources on a few months notice, to furnish tonnage enough to carry off all your exports; and they can afford, and doubtless will undertake to be your carriers on as easy terms as you now pay for freight in foreign bottoms.

On this subject, let us consider what we have gained, & also what they have lost by the revolution. We have gained a free trade with all the world, and consequently a higher price for our commodities, it may be said, and so have they; but they who reply in this manner, ought to know, that there is an amazing difference in our favor: their country affords no valuable exports, and of course the privilege of a free trade is to them of little value, while our staple commodity commands a higher price than was usual before the war. We have also gained an exemption from quit rents, to which the eastern states were not subjected. Connecticut and Rhode-Island were nearly as free before the revolution as since. They had no royal governor or councils to control them, or to legislate for them. Massachusetts and New-Hampshire were much nearer independence in their late constitutions than we were. The eastern states, by the revolution, have been deprived of a market for their fish, of their carrying-trade, their ship building, and almost of every thing but their liberties.

As the war has turned out so much in our favor, and so much against them, ought we to begrudge them the carrying of our produce, especially when it is considered, that by encouraging their shipping, we increase the means of our own defence. Let us examine also the federal constitution, by the principle of reciprocal concession. We have laid a foundation for a navigation act.—This will be a general good; but particularly so to our northern brethren. On the other hand, they have agreed to change the federal rule of paying the continental debt, according to the value of land as laid down in the confederation, for a new principle of apportionment, to be founded on the numbers of inhabitants in the several states respectively. This is an immense concession in our favor.

Their land is poor; our's rich; their numbers great; our's small; labour with them is done by white men, for whom they pay an equal share; while five of our negroes only count as equal to three of their whites. This will make a difference of many thousands of pounds in settling our continental accounts. It is farther objected, that they have stipulated for a right to prohibit the importation of negroes after 21 years. On this subject observe, as they are bound to protect us from domestic violence, they think we ought not to increase our exposure to that evil, by an unlimited importation of slaves. Though Congress may forbid the importation of negroes after 21 years, it does not follow that they will. On the other hand, it is probable that they will not. The more rice we make, the more business will be for their shipping: their interest will therefore coincide with our's. Besides, we have other sources of supply—the importations of the ensuing 20 years, added to the natural increase of those we already have, and the influx from our northern neighbours, who are desirous of getting rid of their slaves, will afford a sufficient number for cultivating all the lands in this state.

Let us suppose the union to be dissolved by the rejection of the new constitution, what would be our case? The United States owe several millions of dollars to France, Spain, and Holland. If an efficient government is not adopted, which will provide for the payment of our debt, especially of that which is due to foreigners—who will be the losers? Most certainly the southern states. Our exports, as being the most valuable, would be the first objects of capture on the high seas; or descents would be made on our defenceless coasts, till the creditors of the United States had paid themselves at the expence of this weaker part of the union. Let us also compare the present confederation, with the proposed constitution. The former can neither protect us at home, nor gain us respect abroad: it cannot secure the payment of our debts, nor command the resources of our country, in case of danger. Without money, without a navy, or the means of even supporting an army of our own citizens in the field, we lie at the mercy of every invader; our sea port towns may be laid under contribution, and our country ravaged.

By the new constitution, you will be protected with the

force of the union, against domestic violence and foreign invasion. You will have a navy to defend your coasts.—The respectable figure you will make among the nations, will so far command the attention of foreign powers, that it is probable you will soon obtain such commercial treaties, as will open to your vessels the West-Indian islands, and give life to your expiring commerce.

In a country like our's, abounding with free men all of one rank, where property is equally diffused, where estates are held in fee simple, the press free, and the means of information common; tyranny cannot readily find admission under any form of government; but its admission is next to impossible, under one where the people are the source of all power, and elect either mediately by their representatives, or immediately by themselves the whole of their rulers.

Examine the new constitution with candor and liberality. Indulge no narrow prejudices to the disadvantage of your brethren of the other states; consider the people of all the thirteen states, as a band of brethren, speaking the same language, professing the same religion, inhabiting one undivided country, and designed by heaven to be one people. Consent that what regards all the states should be managed by that body which represents all of them; be on your guard against the misrepresentations of men who are involved in debt; such may wish to see the constitution rejected, because of the following clause "no state shall emit bills of credit, make any thing but gold and silver coin, a tender in payment of debts, pass any *expost facto* law, or law impairing the obligation of contracts." This will doubtless bear hard on debtors who wish to defraud their creditors, but it will be of real service to the honest part of the community. Examine well the characters & circumstances of men who are averse to the new constitution. Perhaps you will find that the above recited clause is the real ground of the opposition of some of them, though they may artfully cover it with a splendid profession of zeal for state privileges and general liberty.

On the whole, if the proposed constitution is not calculated to better your country, and to secure to you the blessings for which you have so successfully contended, reject it: but if it is an improvement on the present confederation, and contains within itself the principles of farther improvement suited to future circumstances, join the mighty current of federalism, and give it your hearty support. You were among the first states that formed an independent constitution; be not among the last in accepting and ratifying the proposed plan of federal government; it is your sheet anchor; and without it, independence may prove a curse.

"Agrippa" [*James Winthrop*] *XVIII*

Massachusetts Gazette (Boston), February 5, 1788

To the MASSACHUSETTS CONVENTION.
GENTLEMEN,
In my last address I ascertained, from historical records, the following principles, that, in the original state of government, the whole power resides in the whole body of the nation; that when a people appoint certain persons to govern them, they delegate their whole power; that a constitution is not itself a bill of rights; and that, whatever is the form of government, a bill of rights is essential to the security of the persons and property of the people. It is an idea favourable to the interest of mankind at large, that government is founded in compact. Several instances may be produced of it; but none is more remarkable than our own. In general I have chosen to apply to such facts as are in the reach of my readers. For this purpose I have chiefly confined myself to examples drawn from the history of our own country, and to the old testament. It is in the power of every reader to verify examples thus substantiated. Even in the remarkable argument on the fourth section, relative to the power over election, I was far from stating the worst of it, as it respects the adverse party. A gentleman, respectable in many points, but more especially for his systematick and perspicuous reasoning in his profession, has repeatedly stated to the Convention among his reasons in favour of that section, that *the Rhode-Island assembly have for a considerable time past had a bill lying on their table for altering the manner of elections for representatives in that state.* He has stated it with all the zeal of a person, who believed his argument to be a good one. But surely a *bill lying on a table* can never be considered as any more than an *intention* to pass it,

and nobody pretends that it ever actually did pass. It is in strictness only the intention of a part of the assembly, for nobody can aver that it ever will pass.* I write not with an intention to deceive, but that the whole argument may be stated fairly. Much eloquence and ingenuity have been employed in shewing that side of the argument in favour of the proposed constitution; but it ought to be considered, that if we accept it upon mere verbal explanations, we shall find ourselves deceived. I appeal to the knowledge of every one, if it does not frequently happen, that a law is interpreted in practice very differently from the intention of the legislature. Hence arises the necessity of acts to amend and explain former acts. This is not an inconvenience in the common and ordinary business of legislation; but is a great one in a constitution. A constitution is a legislative act of the whole people. It is an excellence that it should be permanent, otherwise we are exposed to perpetual insecurity from the fluctuation of government. We should be in the same situation as under absolute government, sometimes exposed to the pressure of greater, and sometimes unprotected by the weaker power in the sovereign.

It is now generally understood, that it is for the security of the people, that the powers of the government should be lodged in different branches. By this means publick business will go on, when they all agree, and stop when they disagree. The advantage of checks in government is thus manifested, where the concurrence of different branches is necessary to the same act; but the advantage of a division of business is advantageous in other respects. As in every extensive empire, local laws are necessary to suit the different interests, no single legislature is adequate to the business. All human capacities are limitted to a narrow space; and as no individual is capable of practising a great variety of trades no single legislature is capable of managing all the variety of national and state concerns. Even if a legislature was capable of it, the business of the judicial department must, from the same cause, be

---

*A writer in the Gazette of 29th Jan. under the signature of captain M'Daniel having with civility and apparent candour, called for an explanation of what was said in one of my former papers, I have chosen to mention him with respect, as the only one of my reviewers who deserves an answer.

slovenly done. Hence arises the necessity of a division of the business into national and local. Each department ought to have all the powers necessary for executing its own business, under such limitations as tend to secure us from any inequality in the operations of government. I know it is often asked against whom in a government by representation is a bill of rights to secure us? I answer, that such a government is indeed a government by ourselves; but as a just government protects all alike, it is necessary that the sober and industrious part of the community should be defended from the rapacity and violence of the vicious and idle. A bill of rights therefore ought to set forth the purposes for which the compact is made, and serves to secure the minority against the usurpation and tyranny of the majority. It is a just observation of his excellency doctor Adams in his learned defence of the American constitutions, that unbridled passions produce the same effect whether in a king, nobility, or a mob. The experience of all mankind has proved the prevalence of a disposition to use power wantonly. It is therefore as necessary to defend an individual against the majority in a republick, as against the king in a monarchy. Our state constitution has wisely guarded this point. The present confederation has also done it.

I confess that I have yet seen no sufficient reason for not amending the confederation, though I have weighed the argument with candour. I think it would be much easier to amend it than the new constitution. But this is a point on which men of very respectable character differ. There is another point in which nearly all agree, and that is, that the new constitution would be better in many respects if it had been differently framed. Here the question is not so much what the amendments ought to be, as in what manner they shall be made; whether they shall be made as conditions of our accepting the constitution, or whether we shall first accept it, and then try to amend it. I can hardly conceive that it should seriously be made a question. If the first question, whether we will receive it as it stands, be negatived, as it undoubtedly ought to be, while the conviction remains that amendments are necessary; the next question will be, what amendments shall be made? Here permit an individual, who glories in being a citizen of Massachusetts, and who is anxious that the character may remain undiminished, to propose such articles as appear to him necessary for preserving the rights of the state. He means not to retract any thing with regard to the expediency of amending the old confederation, and rejecting the new one totally; but only to make a proposition which he thinks comprehends the general idea of all parties. If the new constitution means no more than the friends of it acknowledge, they certainly can have no objection to affixing a declaration in favour of the rights of states and of citizens, especially as a majority of the states have not yet voted upon it.

"Resolved, that the constitution lately proposed for the United States be received only upon the following conditions:

"1. Congress shall have no power to alter the time, place or manner of elections, nor any authority over elections, otherwise than by fining such state as shall neglect to send its representatives or senators, a sum not exceeding the expense of supporting its representatives or senators one year.

"2. Congress shall not have the power of regulating the intercourse between the states, nor to levy any direct tax on polls or estates, nor any excise.

"3. Congress shall not have power to try causes between a state and citizens of another state, nor between citizens of different states; nor to make any laws relative to the transfer of property between those parties, nor any other matter which shall originate in the body of any state.

"4. It shall be left to every state to make and execute its own laws, except laws impairing contracts, which shall not be made at all.

"5. Congress shall not incorporate any trading companies, nor alienate the territory of any state. And no treaty, ordinance or law of the United States shall be valid for these purposes.

"6. Each state shall have the command of its own militia.

"7. No continental army shall come within the limits of any state, other than garrison to guard the publick stores, without the consent of such states in time of peace.

"8. The president shall be chosen annually and shall serve but one year, and shall be chosen successively from the different states, changing every year.

"9. The judicial department shall be confined to cases in which ambassadours are concerned, to cases depending upon treaties, to offences committed upon the high seas, to the capture of prizes, and to cases in which a foreigner residing in some foreign country shall be a party, and an American state or citizen shall be the other party; provided no suit shall be brought upon a state note.

"10. Every state may emit bills of credit without making them a tender, and may coin money, of silver, gold or copper, according to the continental standard.

"11. No powers shall be exercised by Congress or the president but such as are expressly given by this constitution and not excepted against by this declaration. And any offices of the United States offending against an individual state shall be held accountable to such state as any other citizen would be.

"12. No officer of Congress shall be free from arrest for debt by authority of the state in which the debt shall be due.

"13. Nothing in this constitution shall deprive a citizen of any state of the benefit of the bill of rights established by the constitution of the state in which he shall reside, and such bills of rights shall be considered as valid in any court of the United States where they shall be pleaded.

"14. In all those causes which are triable before the continental courts, the trial by jury shall be held sacred."

These at present appear to me the most important points to be guarded. I have mentioned a reservation of excise to the separate states, because it is necessary, that they should have some way to discharge their own debts, and because it is placing them in an humiliating & disgraceful situation to depute them to transact the business of internal government without the means to carry it on. It is necessary also, as a check on the national government, for it has hardly been known that any government having the powers of war, peace, and revenue, has failed to engage in needless and wanton expense. A reservation of this kind is therefore necessary to preserve the importance of the state governments; without this the extremes of the empire will in a very short time sink into the same degradation and contempt with respect to the middle state as Ireland, Scotland, & Wales, are in with regard to England. All the men of genius and wealth will resort to the seat of government, that will be center of revenue, and of business, which the extremes will be drained to supply.

This is not mere vision, it is justified by the whole course of things. We shall therefore, if we neglect the present opportunity to secure ourselves, only encrease the number of proofs, already too many, that mankind are incapable of enjoying their liberty. I have been the more particular in stating the amendments to be made, because many gentlemen think it would be preferrable to receive the new system with corrections. I have by this means brought the corrections into one view, and shewn several of the principal points in which it is unguarded. As it is agreed, at least professedly, on all sides, that those rights should be guarded, it is among the inferiour questions in what manner it is done, provided it is absolutely and effectually done. For my own part, I am fully of opinion, that it would be best to reject this plan, and pass an explicit resolve, defining the powers of Congress to regulate the intercourse between us and foreign nations, under such restrictions as shall render their regulations equal in all parts of the empire. The impost, if well collected, would be fully equal to the interest of the foreign debt, and the current charges of the national government. It is evidently for our interest that the charges should be as small as possible. It is also for our interest that the western lands should, as fast as possible, be applied to the purpose of paying the home debt. Internal taxation and that fund have already paid two thirds of the whole debt, notwithstanding the embarrassments usual at the end of a war.

We are now rising fast above our difficulties, every thing at home has the appearance of improvement, government is well established, manufactures increasing rapidly, and trade expanding. Till since the peace we never sent a ship to India, and the present year, it is said, sends above a dozen vessels from this state only, to the countries round the Indian ocean. Vast quantities of our produce are exported to those countries. It has been so much the practice of European nations to farm out this branch of trade, that we ought to be exceedingly jealous of our right. The manufactures of the state probably exceed in value one million pounds, for the last year. Most of the useful and some ornamental fabricks are established.

There is great danger of these improvements being injured unless we practice extreme caution at setting out. It will always be for the interest of the southern states to raise a revenue from the more commercial ones. It is said that the consumer pays it; But does not a commercial state consume more foreign goods than a landed one? The people are more crouded, and of consequence the lands is less able to support them. We know it is to be a favourite system to raise the money where it is. But the money is to be expended at another place, and is therefore so much withdrawn annually from our stock. This is a single instance of the difference of interest; it would be very easy to produce others. Innumerable as the differences of manners, and these produce differences in the laws. Uniformity in legislation is of no more importance than in religion; Yet the framers of this new constitution did not even think it necessary that the president should believe, that there is a God, although they require an oath of him. It would be easy to shew the propriety of a general declaration upon that subject. But this paper is already extended too far.

Another reason which I had in stating the amendments to be made, was to shew how nearly those who are for admitting the system with the necessary alterations, agree with those who are for rejecting this system and amending the confederation. In point of convenience, the confederation amended would be infinitely preferable to the proposed constitution. In amending the former, we know the powers granted, and are subject to no perplexity; but in reforming the latter, the business is excessively intricate, and great part of the checks on Congress are lost. It is to be remembered too, that if you are so far charmed with eloquence, and misled by fair representations and charitable constructions, as to adopt an undefined system, there will be no saying afterwards that you were mistaken, and wish to correct it. *It will then be the constitution of our country, and entitled to defence.* If Congress should chuse to avail themselves of a popular commotion to continue in being, as the fourth section justifies, and as the British parliament has repeatedly done, the only answer will be, that it is the constitution of our country, and the people chose it. It is therefore necessary to be exceedingly critical. Whatsoever way shall be chosen to secure our rights, the same resolve ought to contain the whole system of amendment. If it is rejected, the resolve should contain the amendations of the old system; and if accepted, it should contain the corrections of the new one.

"Publius," The Federalist LI [*James Madison*]

Independent Journal (New York), February 6, 1788

To the People of the State of New-York.

To what expedient then shall we finally resort for maintaining in practice the necessary partition of power among the several departments, as laid down in the constitution? The only answer that can be given is, that as all these exterior provisions are found to be inadequate, the defect must be supplied, by so contriving the interior structure of the government, as that its several constituent parts may, by their mutual relations, be the means of keeping each other in their proper places. Without presuming to undertake a full developement of this important idea, I will hazard a few general observations, which may perhaps place it in a clearer light, and enable us to form a more correct judgment of the principles and structure of the government planned by the convention.

In order to lay a due foundation for that separate and distinct exercise of the different powers of government, which to a certain extent, is admitted on all hands to be essential to the preservation of liberty, it is evident that each department should have a will of its own; and consequently should be so constituted, that the members of each should have as little agency as possible in the appointment of the members of the others. Were this principle rigorously adhered to, it would require that all the appointments for the supreme executive, legislative, and judiciary magistracies, should be drawn from the same fountain of authority, the people, through channels, having no communication whatever with one another. Perhaps such a plan of constructing the several departments would be less difficult in practice than it may in contemplation appear. Some difficulties however, and some additional expence, would attend the execution of it. Some deviations therefore from the principle must be admitted. In the constitution of the judiciary department in particular, it might be inexpedient to insist rigorously on the principle; first, because peculiar qualifications being essential in the members, the primary consideration ought to be to select that mode of choice, which best secures these qualifications; secondly, because the permanent tenure by which the appointments are held in that department, must soon destroy all sense of dependence on the authority conferring them.

It is equally evident that the members of each department should be as little dependent as possible on those of the others, for the emoluments annexed to their offices. Were the executive magistrate, or the judges, not independent of the legislature in this particular, their independence in every other would be merely nominal.

But the great security against a gradual concentration of the several powers in the same department, consists in giving to those who administer each department, the necessary constitutional means, and personal motives, to resist encroachments of the others. The provision for defence must in this, as in all other cases, be made commensurate to the danger of attack. Ambition must be made to counteract ambition. The interest of the man must be connected with the constitutional rights of the place. It may be a reflection on human nature, that such devices should be necessary to controul the abuses of government. But what is government itself but the greatest of all reflections on human nature? If men were angels, no government would be necessary. If angels were to govern men, neither external nor internal controuls on government would be necessary. In framing a government which is to be administered by men over men, the great difficulty lies in this: You must first enable the government to controul the governed; and in the next place, oblige it to controul itself. A dependence on the people is no doubt the primary controul on the government; but experience has taught mankind the necessity of auxiliary precautions.

This policy of supplying by opposite and rival interests, the defect of better motives, might be traced through the whole system of human affairs, private as well as public. We see it particularly displayed in all the subordinate distributions of power; where the constant aim is to divide and arrange the several offices in such a manner as that each may be a check on the other; that the private interest of every individual, may be a centinel over the public rights. These inventions of prudence cannot be less requisite in the distribution of the supreme powers of the state.

But it is not possible to give to each department an equal power of self defence. In republican government the legislative authority, necessarily, predominates. The remedy for this inconveniency is, to divide the legislature into different branches; and to render them by different modes of election, and different principles of action, as little connected with each other, as the nature of their common functions, and their common dependence on the society, will admit. It may even be necessary to guard against dangerous encroachments by still further precautions. As the weight of the legislative authority requires that it should be thus divided, the weakness of the executive may require, on the other hand, that it should be fortified. An absolute negative, on the legislature, appears at first view to be the natural defence with which the executive magistrate should be armed. But perhaps it would be neither altogether safe, nor alone sufficient. On ordinary occasions, it might not be exerted with the requisite firmness; and on extraordinary occasions, it might be perfidiously abused. May not this defect of an absolute negative be supplied, by some qualified connection between this weaker department, and the weaker branch of the stronger department, by which the latter may be led to support the constitutional rights of the former, without being too much detached from the rights of its own department?

If the principles on which these observations are founded be just, as I persuade myself they are, and they be applied as a criterion, to the several state constitutions, and to the federal constitution, it will be found, that if the latter does not perfectly correspond with them, the former are infinitely less able to bear such a test.

There are moreover two considerations particularly applicable to the federal system of America, which place that system in a very interesting point of view.

First. In a single republic, all the power surrendered by the people, is submitted to the administration of a single government; and usurpations are guarded against by a division of the government into distinct and separate departments. In the compound republic of America, the power surrendered by the people, is first divided between two distinct governments, and then the portion allotted to each, subdivided among distinct and separate departments. Hence a double security arises to the rights of the people. The different governments will controul each other; at the same time that each will be controuled by itself.

Second. It is of great importance in a republic, not only to guard the society against the oppression of its rulers; but to guard one part of the society against the injustice of the other part. Different interests necessarily exist in different classes of citizens. If a majority be united by a common interest, the rights of the minority will be insecure. There are but two methods of providing against this evil: The one by creating a will in the community independent of the majority, that is, of the society itself; the other by comprehending in the society so many separate descriptions of citizens, as will render an unjust combination of a majority of the whole, very improbable, if not impracticable. The first method prevails in all governments possessing an hereditary or self appointed authority. This at best is but a precarious security; because a power independent of the society may as well espouse the unjust views of the major, as the rightful interests, of the minor party, and may possibly be turned against both parties. The second method will be exemplified in the federal republic of the United States. Whilst all authority in it will be derived from and dependent on the society, the society itself will be broken into so many parts, interests and classes of citizens, that the rights of individuals or of the minority, will be in little danger from interested combinations of the majority. In a free government, the security for civil rights must be the same as that for religious rights. It consists in the one case in the multiplicity of interests, and in the other, in the multiplicity of sects. The degree of security in both cases will depend on the number of interests and sects; and this may be presumed to depend on the extent of country and number of people comprehended under the same government. This view of the subject must particularly recommend a proper federal system to all the sincere and considerate friends of republican government: Since it shews that in exact proportion as the territory of the union may be formed into more circumscribed confederacies or states, oppressive combinations of a majority will be facilitated, the best security under the republican form, for the rights of every class of citizens, will be diminished; and consequently, the stability and independence of some member of the government, the only other security, must be proportionally increased. Justice is the end of government. It is the end of civil society. It ever has been, and ever will be pursued, untill it be obtained, or untill liberty be lost in the pursuit. In a society under the forms of which the stronger faction can readily unite and oppress the weaker, anarchy may as truly be said to reign, as in a state of nature where the weaker individual is not secured against the violence of the stronger: And as in the latter state even the stronger individuals are prompted by the uncertainty of their condition, to submit to a government which may protect the weak as well as themselves: So in the former state, will the more powerful factions or parties be gradually induced by a like motive, to wish for a government which will protect all parties, the weaker as well as the more powerful. It can be little doubted, that if the state of Rhode Island was separated from the confederacy, and left to itself, the insecurity of rights under the popular form of government within such narrow limits, would be displayed by such reiterated oppressions of factious majorities, that some power altogether independent of the people would soon be called for by the voice of the very factions whose misrule had proved the necessity of it. In the extended republic of the United States, and among the great variety of interests, parties and sects which it embraces, a coalition of a majority of the whole society could seldom take place on any other principles than those of justice and the general good; and there being thus less danger to a minor from the will of the major party, there must be less pretext also, to provide for the security of the former, by introducing into the government a will not dependent on the latter; or in other words, a will independent of the society itself. It is no less certain than it is important,

notwithstanding the contrary opinions which have been entertained, that the larger the society, provided it lie within a
practicable sphere, the more duly capable it will be of self
government. And happily for the *republican cause*, the practicable sphere may be carried to a very great extent, by a judicious modification and mixture of the *federal principle*.

"A. B." [*Francis Hopkinson*], *The Raising: A New Song for Federal Mechanics*

Pennsylvania Gazette (Philadelphia), February 6, 1788

I.

Come muster, my Lads, your mechanical Tools,
Your Saws and your Axes, your Hammers and Rules;
Bring your Mallets and Planes, your Level and Line,
And Plenty of Pins of American Pine;
   For our Roof we will raise, and our Song still shall be—
   A Government firm, and our Citizens free.

II.

Come, up with *the Plates*, lay them firm on the Wall,
Like the People at large, they're the Ground-work of all;
Examine them well, and see that they're sound,
Let no rotten Parts in our Building be found;
   For our Roof we will raise, and our Song still shall be—
   Our Government firm, and our Citizens free.

III.

Now hand up *the Girders*, lay each in his Place,
Between them *the Joists* must divide all the Space;
Like Assembly-men, *these* should lye level along,
Like *Girders*, our Senate prove loyal and strong;
   For our Roof we will raise, and our Song still shall be—
   A Government firm, over Citizens free.

IV.

The Rafters now frame—your *King-Posts* and *Braces*,
And drive your Pins home, to keep all in their Places;
Let Wisdom and Strength in the Fabric combine,
And your Pins be all made of American Pine;
   For our Roof we will raise, and our Song still shall be—
   A Government firm, over Citizens free.

V.

Our *King-Posts* are Judges—how upright they stand,
Supporting the *Braces*, the Laws of the Land—
The Laws of the Land, which divide Right from Wrong,
And strengthen the Weak, by weak'ning the Strong;
   For our Roof we will raise, and our Song still shall be—
   Laws equal and just, for a People that's free.

VI.

Up! Up with the Rafters—each Frame is a State!
How nobly they rise! their Span, too, how great!
From the North to the South, o'er the Whole they extend,
And rest on the Walls, while the Walls they defend!
   For our Roof we will raise, and our Song still shall be—
   Combined in Strength, yet as Citizens free.

VII.

Now enter the *Purlins*, and drive your Pins through,
And see that your Joints are drawn home, and all true;
The *Purlins* will bind all the Rafters together,
The Strength of the Whole shall defy Wind and Weather;
   For our Roof we will raise, and our Song still shall be—
   United as States, but as Citizens free.

VIII.

Come, raise up the Turret—our Glory and Pride—
In the Centre it stands, o'er the Whole to preside;
The Sons of *Columbia* shall view with Delight
It's Pillars, and Arches, and Towering Height;
   Our Roof is now rais'd, and our Song still shall be—
   A Fœderal Head, o'er a People still free.

IX.

Huzza! my brave Boys, our Work is complete,
The World shall admire *Columbia*'s fair Seat;
It's Strength against Tempest and Time shall be Proof,
And Thousands shall come to dwell under our ROOF.
   Whilst we drain the deep Bowl, our Toast still shall be—
   Our Government firm, and our Citizens free.

"Brutus" XII

New York Journal, February 7 and 14, 1788

In my last, I shewed, that the judicial power of the United States under the first clause of the second section of article eight, would be authorized to explain the constitution, not only according to its letter, but according to its spirit and intention; and having this power, they would strongly incline to give it such a construction as to extend the powers of the general government, as much as possible, to the diminution, and finally to the destruction, of that of the respective states.

I shall now proceed to shew how this power will operate in its exercise to effect these purposes. In order to perceive the extent of its influence, I shall consider,

First. How it will tend to extend the legislative authority.

Second. In what manner it will increase the jurisdiction of the courts, and

Third. The way in which it will diminish, and destroy, both the legislative and judicial authority of the United States.

First. Let us enquire how the judicial power will effect an extension of the legislative authority.

Perhaps the judicial power will not be able, by direct and positive decrees, ever to direct the legislature, because it is not easy to conceive how a question can be brought before them in a course of legal discussion, in which they can give a decision, declaring, that the legislature have certain powers which they have not exercised, and which, in consequence of the determination of the judges, they will be bound to exercise. But it is easy to see, that in their adjudications they may establish certain principles, which being received by the legislature, will enlarge the sphere of their power beyond all bounds.

It is to be observed, that the supreme court has the power, in the last resort, to determine all questions that may arise in the course of legal discussion, on the meaning and construction of the constitution. This power they will hold under the constitution, and independent of the legislature. The latter can no more deprive the former of this right, than either of them, or both of them together, can take from the president, with the advice of the senate, the power of making treaties, or appointing ambassadors.

In determining these questions, the court must and will assume certain principles, from which they will reason, in forming their decisions. These principles, whatever they may be, when they become fixed, by a course of decisions, will be adopted by the legislature, and will be the rule by which they will explain their own powers. This appears evident from this consideration, that if the legislature pass laws, which, in the judgment of the court, they are not authorised to do by the constitution, the court will not take notice of them; for it will not be denied, that the constitution is the highest or supreme law. And the courts are vested with the supreme and uncontroulable power, to determine, in all cases that come before them, what the constitution means; they cannot, therefore, execute a law, which, in their judgment, opposes the constitution, unless we can suppose they can make a superior law give way to an inferior. The legislature, therefore, will not go over the limits by which the courts may adjudge they are confined. And there is little room to doubt but that they will come up to those bounds, as often as occasion and opportunity may offer, and they may judge it proper to do it. For as on the one hand, they will not readily pass laws which they know the courts will not execute, so on the other, we may be sure they will not scruple to pass such as they know they will give effect, as often as they may judge it proper.

From these observations it appears, that the judgment of the judicial, on the constitution, will become the rule to guide the legislature in their construction of their powers.

What the principles are, which the courts will adopt, it is impossible for us to say; but taking up the powers as I have explained them in my last number, which they will possess under this clause, it is not difficult to see, that they may, and probably will, be very liberal ones.

We have seen, that they will be authorized to give the constitution a construction according to its spirit and reason, and not to confine themselves to its letter.

To discover the spirit of the constitution, it is of the first importance to attend to the principal ends and designs it has in view. These are expressed in the preamble, in the following words, viz. "We, the people of the United States, in order to form a more perfect union, establish justice, insure domestic tranquility, provide for the common defence, promote the general welfare, and secure the blessings of liberty to ourselves and our posterity, do ordain and establish this constitution," &c. If the end of the government is to be learned from these words, which are clearly designed to declare it, it is obvious it has in view every object which is embraced by any government. The preservation of internal peace—the due administration of justice—and to provide for the defence of the community, seems to include all the objects of government; but if they do not, they are certainly comprehended in the words, "to provide for the general welfare." If it be further considered, that this constitution, if it is ratified, will not be a compact entered into by states, in their corporate capacities, but an agreement of the people of the United States, as one great body politic, no doubt can remain, but that the great end of the constitution, if it is to be collected from the preamble, in which its end is declared, is to constitute a government which is to extend to every case for which any government is instituted, whether external or internal. The courts, therefore, will establish this as a principle in expounding the constitution, and will give every part of it such an explanation, as will give latitude to every department under it, to take cognizance of every matter, not only that affects the general and national concerns of the union, but also of such as relate to the administration of private justice, and to regulating the internal and local affairs of the different parts.

Such a rule of exposition is not only consistent with the general spirit of the preamble, but it will stand confirmed by considering more minutely the different clauses of it.

The first object declared to be in view is, "To form a perfect union." It is to be observed, it is not an union of states or bodies corporate; had this been the case the existence of the state governments, might have been secured. But it is a union of the people of the United States considered as one body, who are to ratify this constitution, if it is adopted. Now to make a union of this kind perfect, it is necessary to abolish all inferior governments, and to give the general one compleat legislative, executive and judicial powers to every purpose. The courts therefore will establish it as a rule in explaining the constitution. To give it such a construction as will best tend to perfect the union or take from the state governments every power of either making or executing laws. The second object is "to establish justice." This must include not only the idea of instituting the rule of justice, or of making laws which shall be the measure or rule of right, but also of providing for the application of this rule or of administering justice under it. And under this the courts will in their decisions extend the power of the government to all cases they possibly can, or otherwise they will be restricted in doing what appears to be the intent of the constitution they should do, to wit, pass laws and provide for the execution of them, for the general distribution of justice between man and man. Another end declared is "to insure domestic tranquility." This comprehends a provision against all private breaches of the peace, as well as against all public commotions or general insurrections; and to attain the object of this clause fully, the government must exercise the power of passing laws on these subjects, as well as of appointing magistrates with authority to execute them. And the courts will adopt these ideas in their expositions. I might proceed to the other clause, in the preamble, and it would appear by a consideration of all of them separately, as it does by taking them together, that if the spirit of this system is to be known from its declared end and design in the preamble, its spirit is to subvert and abolish all the powers of the state government, and to embrace every object to which any government extends.

As it sets out in the preamble with this declared intention, so it proceeds in the different parts with the same idea. Any person, who will peruse the 8th section with attention, in which most of the powers are enumerated, will perceive that they either expressly or by implication extend to almost every thing about which any legislative power can be employed. But if this equitable mode of construction is applied to this part of the constitution; nothing can stand before it.

This will certainly give the first clause in that article a construction which I confess I think the most natural and grammatical one, to authorise the Congress to do any thing which in their judgment will tend to provide for the general welfare, and this amounts to the same thing as general and unlimited powers of legislation in all cases.

(To be continued.)

(Continued from last Thursday's paper.)

This same manner of explaining the constitution, will fix a meaning, and a very important one too, to the 12th clause of the same section, which authorises the Congress to make all laws which shall be proper and necessary for carrying into effect the foregoing powers, &c. A voluminous writer in favor of this system, has taken great pains to convince the public, that this clause means nothing: for that the same powers expressed in this, are implied in other parts of the constitution. Perhaps it is so, but still this will undoubtedly be an excellent auxilliary to assist the courts to discover the spirit and reason of the constitution, and when applied to any and every of the other clauses granting power, will operate powerfully in extracting the spirit from them.

I might instance a number of clauses in the constitution, which, if explained in an *equitable* manner, would extend the powers of the government to every case, and reduce the state legislatures to nothing; but, I should draw out my remarks to an undue length, and I presume enough has been said to shew, that the courts have sufficient ground in the exercise of this power, to determine, that the legislature have no bounds set to them by this constitution, by any supposed right the legislatures of the respective states may have, to regulate any of their local concerns.

I proceed, 2d, To inquire, in what manner this power will increase the jurisdiction of the courts.

I would here observe, that the judicial power extends, ex-

pressly, to all civil cases that may arise save such as arise between citizens of the same state, with this exception to those
of that description, that the judicial of the United States have
cognizance of cases between citizens of the same state, claiming lands under grants of different states. Nothing more,
therefore, is necessary to give the courts of law, under this
constitution, complete jurisdiction of all civil causes, but to
comprehend cases between citizens of the same state not included in the foregoing exception.

I presume there will be no difficulty in accomplishing this.
Nothing more is necessary than to set forth, in the process,
that the party who brings the suit is a citizen of a different
state from the one against whom the suit is brought, & there
can be little doubt but that the court will take cognizance of
the matter, & if they do, who is to restrain them? Indeed, I
will freely confess, that it is my decided opinion, that the
courts ought to take cognizance of such causes, under the
powers of the constitution. For one of the great ends of the
constitution is, "to establish justice." This supposes that this
cannot be done under the existing governments of the states;
and there is certainly as good reason why individuals, living in
the same state, should have justice, as those who live in different states. Moreover, the constitution expressly declares, that
"the citizens of each state shall be entitled to all the privileges
and immunities of citizens in the several states." It will therefore be no fiction, for a citizen of one state to set forth, in a
suit, that he is a citizen of another; for he that is entitled to all
the privileges and immunities of a country, is a citizen of that
country. And in truth, the citizen of one state will, under this
constitution, be a citizen of every state.

But supposing that the party, who alledges that he is a citizen of another state, has recourse to fiction in bringing in his
suit, it is well known, that the courts have high authority to
plead, to justify them in suffering actions to be brought before them by such fictions. In my last number I stated, that
the court of exchequer tried all causes in virtue of such a fiction. The court of king's bench, in England, extended their
jurisdiction in the same way. Originally, this court held pleas,
in civil cases, only of trespasses and other injuries alledged to
be committed *vi et armis*. They might likewise, says Black-

stone, upon the division of the *aula regia*, have originally held pleas of any other civil action whatsoever (except in real actions which are now very seldom in use) provided the defendant was an officer of the court, or in the custody of the marshall or prison-keeper of this court, for breach of the peace, &c. In process of time, by a fiction, this court began to hold pleas of any personal action whatsoever; it being surmised, that the defendant has been arrested for a supposed trespass that "he has never committed, and being thus in the custody of the marshall of the court, the plaintiff is at liberty to proceed against him, for any other personal injury: which surmise of being in the marshall's custody, the defendant is not at liberty to dispute." By a much less fiction, may the pleas of the courts of the United States extend to cases between citizens of the same state. I shall add no more on this head, but proceed briefly to remark, in what way this power will diminish and destroy both the legislative and judicial authority of the states.

It is obvious that these courts will have authority to decide upon the validity of the laws of any of the states, in all cases where they come in question before them. Where the constitution gives the general government exclusive jurisdiction, they will adjudge all laws made by the states, in such cases, void *ab initio*. Where the constitution gives them concurrent jurisdiction, the laws of the United States must prevail, because they are the supreme law. In such cases, therefore, the laws of the state legislatures must be repealed, restricted, or so construed, as to give full effect to the laws of the union on the same subject. From these remarks it is easy to see, that in proportion as the general government acquires power and jurisdiction, by the liberal construction which the judges may give the constitution, will those of the states lose its rights, until they become so trifling and unimportant, as not to be worth having. I am much mistaken, if this system will not operate to effect this with as much celerity, as those who have the administration of it will think prudent to suffer it. The remaining objections to the judicial power shall be considered in a future paper.

George Washington to
the Marquis de Lafayette

Mount Vernon, Virginia, February 7, 1788

You know it always gives me the sincerest pleasure to hear from you, my dear Marquis, and therefore I need only say that your two kind letters of the 9th & 15th. of Octo. so replete with personal affection and confidential intelligence, afforded me inexpressible satisfaction. I shall myself be happy in forming an acquaintance and cultivating a friendship with the new Minister Plenipotentiary of France, whom you have commended as "a sensible & honest man"—these are qualities too rare & too precious not to merit one's particular esteem—You may be persuaded he will be well received by the Congress of the United States, because they will not only be influenced in their conduct by his individual merits, but also by their affection for the nation of whose Sovereign he is the Representative.—For it is an undoubted fact, that the People of America entertain a greateful remembrance of past services as well as a favourable disposition for commercial and friendly connections with your Nation.—

You appear to be, as might be expected from a real friend to this Country, anxiously concerned about its present political situation. So far as I am able I shall be happy in gratifying that friendly solicitude. As to my sentiments with respect to the merits of the new Constitution, I will disclose them without reserve (although by passing through the Post offices they should become known to all the world) for, in truth, I have nothing to conceal on that subject. It appears to me, then, little short of a miracle, that the Delegates from so many different States (which States you know are also different from each other in their manners, circumstances and prejudices) should unite in forming a system of national Government, so little liable to well founded objections. Nor am I yet such an enthusiastic, partial or undiscriminating admirer of it, as not to perceive it is tinctured with some real (though not radical) defects. The limits of a letter would not suffer me to go fully into an examination of them; nor would the discussion be entertaining or profitable, I therefore forbear to touch upon it. With regard to the two great points (the pivots on which the whole machine must move) my Creed is simply:—

1st.—That the general Government is not invested with more Powers than are indispensably necessary to perform the functions of a good Government; and, consequently, that no objection ought to be made against the quantity of Power delegated to it:

2ly.—That these Powers (as the appointment of all Rulers will forever arise from, and, at short stated intervals, recur to the free suffrage of the People) are so distributed among the Legislative, Executive, and Judicial Branches, into which the general Government is arranged, that it can never be in danger of degenerating into a monarchy, an Oligarchy, an Aristocracy, or any other despotic or oppressive form; so long as there shall remain any virtue in the body of the People.—

I would not be understood my dear Marquis to speak of consequences which may be produced, in the revolution of ages, by corruption of morals, profligacy of manners, and listlessness for the preservation of the natural and unalienable rights of mankind; nor of the successful usurpations that may be established at such an unpropitious juncture, upon the ruins of liberty, however providently guarded and secured, as these are contingencies against which no human prudence can effectually provide. It will at least be a recommendation to the proposed Constitution that it is provided with more checks and barriers against the introduction of Tyranny, & those of a nature less liable to be surmounted, than any Government hitherto instituted among mortals, hath possessed. we are not to expect perfection in this world: but mankind, in modern times, have apparently made some progress in the science of Government.—Should that which is now offered to the People of America, be found on experiment less perfect than it can be made—a Constitutional door is left open for its amelioration. Some respectable characters have wished that the

States, after having pointed out whatever alterations and amendments may be judged necessary, would appoint another federal Convention to modify it upon those documents. For myself I have wondered that sensible men should not see the impracticability of the scheme. The members would go fortified with such Instructions that nothing but discordant ideas could prevail. Had I but slightly suspected (at the time when the late Convention was in session) that another Convention would not be likely to agree upon a better form of Government, I should now be confirmed in the fixed belief that they would not be able to agree upon any System whatever: — So many, I may add, such contradictory, and, in my opinion, unfounded objections have been urged against the System in contemplation; many of which would operate equally against every efficient Government that might be proposed. I will only add, as a farther opinion founded on the maturest deliberation, that there is no alternative—no hope of alteration—no intermediate resting place—between the adoption of this and a recurrence to an unqualified state of Anarchy, with all its deplorable consequences.—

Since I had the pleasure of writing to you last, no material alteration in the political State of affairs has taken place to change the prospect of the Constitution's being adopted by nine States or more. Pennsylvania, Delaware, Jersey and Connecticut have already done it. It is also said Georgia has acceded.—Massachusetts, which is perhaps thought to be rather more doubtful than when I last addressed you, is now in Convention.

A spirit of emigration to the western Country is very predominant. Congress have sold, in the year past, a pretty large quantity of lands on the Ohio, for public Securities, and thereby diminished the domestic debt considerably. Many of your Military acquaintances such as the Generals Parsons, Varnum and Putnam, the Colos. Tupper Sprout and Sherman, with many more, propose settling there. From such beginnings much may be expected.

The storm of war between England and your Nation, it seems, is dissipated. I hope and trust the political affairs in France are taking a favorable turn. If the Ottomans wod. suffer themselves to be precipitated into a war, they must abide the consequences. Some Politicians speculate on a triple Alliance between the two Imperial Courts & Versailles.

I think it was rather fortunate, than otherwise, that the incaution of an Ambassador and the rascality of a Rhinegrave prevented you from attempting to prop a falling fabric. —

It gives me great pleasure to learn the present ministry of France are friendly to America; and that Mr Jefferson & yourself have a prospect of accomplishing measures which will mutually benefit and improve the commercial intercourse between the two Nations.

"Publius," The Federalist LII
[James Madison]

New-York Packet, February 8, 1788

To the People of the State of New-York.

From the more general enquiries pursued in the four last papers, I pass on to a more particular examination of the several parts of the government. I shall begin with the House of Representatives.

The first view to be taken of this part of the government, relates to the qualifications of the electors and the elected. Those of the former are to be the same with those of the electors of the most numerous branch of the State Legislatures. The definition of the right of suffrage is very justly regarded as a fundamental article of republican government. It was incumbent on the Convention therefore to define and establish this right, in the Constitution. To have left it open for the occasional regulation of the Congress, would have been improper for the reason just mentioned. To have submitted it to the legislative discretion of the States, would have been improper for the same reason; and for the additional reason, that it would have rendered too dependent on the State Governments, that branch of the Fœderal Government, which ought to be dependent on the people alone. To have reduced the different qualifications in the different States, to one uniform rule, would probably have been as dissatisfactory to some of the States, as it would have been difficult to the Convention. The provision made by the Convention appears therefore, to be the best that lay within their option. It must be satisfactory to every State; because it is conformable to the standard already established, or which may be established by the State itself. It will be safe to the United States; because,

being fixed by the State Constitutions, it is not alterable by
the State Governments, and it cannot be feared that the people of the States will alter this part of their Constitutions, in
such a manner as to abridge the rights secured to them by the
Fœderal Constitution.

The qualifications of the elected being less carefully and
properly defined by the State Constitutions, and being at the
same time more susceptible of uniformity, have been very
properly considered and regulated by the Convention. A representative of the United States must be of the age of twenty-
five years; must have been seven years a citizen of the United
States, must at the time of his election, be an inhabitant of the
State he is to represent, and during the time of his service
must be in no office under the United States. Under these
reasonable limitations, the door of this part of the Fœderal
Government, is open to merit of every description, whether
native or adoptive, whether young or old, and without regard
to poverty or wealth, or to any particular profession of religious faith.

The term for which the Representatives are to be elected,
falls under a second view which may be taken of this branch.
In order to decide on the propriety of this article, two questions must be considered; first, whether biennial elections
will, in this case, be safe; secondly, whether they be necessary
or useful.

First. As it is essential to liberty that the government in
general, should have a common interest with the people; so it
is particularly essential that the branch of it under consideration, should have an immediate dependence on, & an intimate sympathy with the people. Frequent elections are
unquestionably the only policy by which this dependence
and sympathy can be effectually secured. But what particular
degree of frequency may be absolutely necessary for the
purpose, does not appear to be susceptible of any precise calculation; and must depend on a variety of circumstances with
which it may be connected. Let us consult experience, the
guide that ought always to be followed, whenever it can be
found.

The scheme of representation, as a substitute for a meeting
of the citizens in person, being at most but very imperfectly

known to ancient polity; it is in more modern times only, that we are to expect instructive examples. And even here, in order to avoid a research too vague and diffusive, it will be proper to confine ourselves to the few examples which are best known, and which bear the greatest analogy to our particular case. The first to which this character ought to be applied, is the House of Commons in Great Britain. The history of this branch of the English Constitution, anterior to the date of Magna Charta, is too obscure to yield instruction. The very existence of it has been made a question among political antiquaries. The earliest records of subsequent date prove, that Parliaments were to *sit* only, every year; not that they were to be *elected* every year. And even these annual sessions were left so much at the discretion of the monarch, that under various pretexts, very long and dangerous intermissions, were often contrived by royal ambition. To remedy this grievance, it was provided by a statute in the reign of Charles the second, that the intermissions should not be protracted beyond a period of three years. On the accession of Wil. III. when a revolution took place in the government, the subject was still more seriously resumed, and it was declared to be among the fundamental rights of the people, that Parliaments ought to be held *frequently*. By another statute which passed a few years later in the same reign, the term "frequently" which had alluded to the triennial period settled in the time of Charles II. is reduced to a precise meaning, it being expressly enacted that a new parliament shall be called within three years after the determination of the former. The last change from three to seven years is well known to have been introduced pretty early in the present century, under an alarm for the Hanoverian succession. From these facts it appears, that the greatest frequency of elections which has been deemed necessary in that kingdom, for binding the representatives to their constituents, does not exceed a triennial return of them. And if we may argue from the degree of liberty retained even under septennial elections, and all the other vicious ingredients in the parliamentary constitution, we cannot doubt that a reduction of the period from seven to three years, with the other necessary reforms, would so far extend the influence of the people over their representatives, as to satisfy us, that biennial elections under the fœderal system, cannot possibly be dangerous to the requisite dependence of the house of representatives on their constituents.

Elections in Ireland till of late were regulated entirely by the discretion of the crown, and were seldom repeated except on the accession of a new Prince, or some other contingent event. The parliament which commenced with George II. was continued throughout his whole reign, a period of about thirty-five years. The only dependence of the representatives on the people consisted, in the right of the latter to supply occasional vacancies, by the election of new members, and in the chance of some event which might produce a general new election. The ability also of the Irish parliament, to maintain the rights of their constituents, so far as the disposition might exist, was extremely shackled by the controul of the crown over the subjects of their deliberation. Of late these shackles, if I mistake not, have been broken; and octennial parliaments have besides been established. What effect may be produced by this partial reform, must be left to further experience. The example of Ireland, from this view of it, can throw but little light on the subject. As far as we can draw any conclusion from it, it must be, that if the people of that country have been able, under all these disadvantages, to retain any liberty whatever, the advantage of biennial elections would secure to them every degree of liberty which might depend on a due connection between their representatives and themselves.

Let us bring our enquiries nearer home. The example of these States when British colonies claims particular attention; at the same time that it is so well known, as to require little to be said on it. The principle of representation, in one branch of the Legislature at least, was established in all of them. But the periods of election were different. They varied from one to seven years. Have we any reason to infer from the spirit and conduct of the representatives of the people, prior to the revolution, that biennial elections would have been dangerous to the public liberties? The spirit which every where displayed itself at the commencement of the struggle; and which vanquished the obstacles to independence, is the best of proofs that a sufficient portion of liberty had been every where enjoyed to inspire both a sense of its worth, and a zeal for its

proper enlargement. This remark holds good as well with regard to the then colonies, whose elections were least frequent,
as to those whose elections were most frequent. Virginia was
the colony which stood first in resisting the parliamentary
usurpations of Great-Britain: it was the first also in espousing
by public act, the resolution of independence. In Virginia
nevertheless, if I have not been misinformed, elections under
the former government were septennial. This particular example is brought into view, not as a proof of any peculiar merit,
for the priority in those instances, was probably accidental;
and still less of any advantage in *septennial* elections, for when
compared with a greater frequency they are inadmissible: but
merely as a proof, and I conceive it to be a very substantial
proof, that the liberties of the people can be in no danger
from *biennial* elections.

The conclusion resulting from these examples will be not a
little strengthened by recollecting three circumstances. The
first is that the Fœderal Legislature will possess a part only of
that supreme legislative authority which is vested completely
in the British parliament, and which with a few exceptions
was exercised by the colonial Assemblies and the Irish Legislature. It is a received and well founded maxim, that, where
no other circumstances affect the case, the greater the power
is, the shorter ought to be its duration; and, conversely, the
smaller the power, the more safely may its duration be protracted. In the second place, it has, on another occasion, been
shewn that the Fœderal Legislature will not only be restrained by its dependence on the people as other legislative
bodies are; but that it will be moreover watched and controuled by the several collateral Legislatures, which other legislative bodies are not. And in the third place, no comparison
can be made between the means that will be possessed by the
more permanent branches of the Fœderal Government for seducing, if they should be disposed to seduce, the House of
Representatives from their duty to the people; and the means
of influence over the popular branch, possessed by the other
branches of the governments above cited. With less power
therefore to abuse, the Fœderal Representatives, can be less
tempted on one side, and will be doubly watched on the
other.

"Publius," The Federalist LIII
[James Madison]

Independent Journal (New York), February 9, 1788

To the People of the State of New-York.

I shall here perhaps be reminded of a current observation, "that where annual elections end, tyranny begins." If it be true as has often been remarked, that sayings which become proverbial, are generally founded in reason, it is not less true that when once established, they are often applied to cases to which the reason of them does not extend. I need not look for a proof beyond the case before us. What is the reason on which this proverbial observation is founded? No man will subject himself to the ridicule of pretending that any natural connection subsists between the sun or the seasons, and the period within which human virtue can bear the temptations of power. Happily for mankind, liberty is not in this respect confined to any single point of time; but lies within extremes, which afford sufficient latitude for all the variations which may be required by the various situations and circumstances of civil society. The election of magistrates might be, if it were found expedient, as in some instances it actually has been, daily, weekly, or monthly, as well as annual; and if circumstances may require a deviation from the rule on one side, why not also on the other side. Turning our attention to the periods established among ourselves, for the election of the most numerous branches of the state legislatures, we find them by no means coinciding any more in this instance, than in the elections of other civil magistrates. In Connecticut and Rhode-Island, the periods are half-yearly. In the other states, South-Carolina excepted, they are annual. In South-Carolina, they are biennial; as is proposed in the federal government. Here is a difference, as four to one, between the longest and shortest periods; and yet it would be not easy to shew that

Connecticut or Rhode-Island is better governed, or enjoys a greater share of rational liberty than South-Carolina; or that either the one or the other of these states are distinguished in these respects, and by these causes, from the states whose elections are different from both.

In searching for the grounds of this doctrine, I can discover but one, and that is wholly inapplicable to our case. The important distinction so well understood in America between a constitution established by the people, and unalterable by the government; and a law established by the government, and alterable by the government, seems to have been little understood and less observed in any other country. Wherever the supreme power of legislation has resided, has been supposed to reside also, a full power to change the form of the government. Even in Great-Britain, where the principles of political and civil liberty have been most discussed; and where we hear most of the rights of the constitution, it is maintained that the authority of the parliament is transcendent and uncontroulable, as well with regard to the constitution, as the ordinary objects of legislative provision. They have accordingly, in several instances, actually changed, by legislative acts, some of the most fundamental articles of the government. They have in particular, on several occasions, changed the periods of election; and on the last occasion, not only introduced septennial, in place of triennial, elections; but by the same act continued themselves in place four years beyond the term for which they were elected by the people. An attention to these dangerous practices has produced a very natural alarm in the votaries of free government, of which frequency of elections is the corner stone; and has led them to seek for some security to liberty against the danger to which it is exposed. Where no constitution paramount to the government, either existed or could be obtained, no constitutional security similar to that established in the United States, was to be attempted. Some other security therefore was to be sought for; and what better security would the case admit, than that of selecting and appealing to some simple and familiar portion of time, as a standard for measuring the danger of innovations, for fixing the national sentiment, and for uniting the patriotic exertions. The most simple and familiar portion of time, applicable to the subject, was that of a year; and hence the doctrine has been inculcated by a laudable zeal to erect some barrier against the gradual innovations of an unlimited government, that the advance towards tyranny was to be calculated by the distance of departure from the fixed point of annual elections. But what necessity can there be of applying this expedient to a government, limited as the federal government will be, by the authority of a paramount constitution? Or who will pretend that the liberties of the people of America will not be more secure under biennial elections, unalterably fixed by such a constitution, than those of any other nation would be, where elections were annual or even more frequent, but subject to alterations by the ordinary power of the government?

The second question stated is, whether biennial elections be necessary or useful? The propriety of answering this question in the affirmative will appear from several very obvious considerations.

No man can be a competent legislator who does not add to an upright intention and a sound judgment, a certain degree of knowledge of the subjects on which he is to legislate. A part of this knowledge may be acquired by means of information which lie within the compass of men in private as well as public stations. Another part can only be attained, or at least thoroughly attained, by actual experience in the station which requires the use of it. The period of service ought therefore in all such cases to bear some proportion to the extent of practical knowledge, requisite to the due performance of the service. The period of legislative service established in most of the states for the more numerous branch is, as we have seen, one year. The question then may be put into this simple form; does the period of two years bear no greater proportion to the knowledge requisite for state legislation, than one year does to the knowledge requisite for state legislation? The very statement of the question in this form, suggests the answer that ought to be given to it.

In a single state the requisite knowledge, relates to the existing laws which are uniform throughout the state, and with which all the citizens are more or less conversant; and to the general affairs of the state, which lie within a small compass, are not very diversified, and occupy much of the attention and

conversation of every class of people. The great theatre of the
United States presents a very different scene. The laws are so
far from being uniform, that they vary in every state; whilst
the public affairs of the union are spread throughout a very
extensive region, and are extremely diversified by the local affairs connected with them, and can with difficulty be correctly
learnt in any other place, than in the central councils, to
which a knowledge of them will be brought by the representatives of every part of the empire. Yet some knowledge of the
affairs, and even of the laws of all the states, ought to be
possessed by the members from each of the states. How can
foreign trade be properly regulated by uniform laws, without
some acquaintance with the commerce: the ports, the usages,
and the regulations, of the different states. How can the trade
between the different states be duly regulated without some
knowledge of their relative situations in these and other
points? How can taxes be judiciously imposed, and effectually
collected, if they be not accommodated to the different laws
and local circumstances relating to these objects in the different states? How can uniform regulations for the militia be
duly provided without a similar knowledge of many internal
circumstances by which the states are distinguished from each
other? These are the principal objects of federal legislation,
and suggest most forceably, the extensive information which
the representatives ought to acquire. The other inferior objects will require a proportional degree of information with
regard to them.

It is true that all these difficulties will by degrees be very
much diminished. The most laborious task will be the proper
inauguration of the government, and the primeval formation
of a federal code. Improvements on the first draught will
every year become both easier and fewer. Past transactions of
the government will be a ready and accurate source of information to new members. The affairs of the union will become
more and more objects of curiosity and conversation among
the citizens at large. And the increased intercourse among
those of different states will contribute not a little to diffuse a
mutual knowledge of their affairs, as this again will contribute
to a general assimilation of their manners and laws. But with
all these abatements the business of federal legislation must

continue so far to exceed both in novelty and difficulty, the legislative business of a single state as to justify the longer period of service assigned to those who are to transact it.

A branch of knowledge which belongs to the acquirements of a federal representative, and which has not been mentioned, is that of foreign affairs. In regulating our own commerce he ought to be not only acquainted with the treaties between the United States and other nations, but also with the commercial policy and laws of other nations. He ought not be altogether ignorant of the law of nations, for that as far as it is a proper object of municipal legislation is submitted to the federal government. And although the house of representatives is not immediately to participate in foreign negotiations and arrangements, yet from the necessary connection between the several branches of public affairs, those particular branches will frequently deserve attention in the ordinary course of legislation, and will sometimes demand particular legislative sanction and co-operation. Some portion of this knowledge may no doubt be acquired in a man's closet; but some of it also can only be derived from the public sources of information; and all of it will be acquired to best effect by a practical attention to the subject during the period of actual service in the legislature.

There are other considerations of less importance perhaps, but which are not unworthy of notice. The distance which many of the representatives will be obliged to travel, and the arrangements renderd necessary by that circumstance, might be much more serious objections with fit men to this service if limited to a single year than if extended to two years. No argument can be drawn on this subject from the case of the delegates to the existing Congress. They are elected annually it is true; but their re-election is considered by the legislative assemblies almost as a matter of course. The election of the representatives by the people would not be governed by the same principle.

A few of the members, as happens in all such assemblies, will possess superior talents, will by frequent re-elections, become members of long standing; will be thoroughly masters of the public business, and perhaps not unwilling to avail themselves of those advantages. The greater the proportion of new members, and the less the information of the bulk of the members, the more apt will they be to fall into the snares that may be laid for them. This remark is no less applicable to the relation which will subsist between the house of representatives and the senate.

It is an inconveniency mingled with the advantages of our frequent elections, even in single states where they are large and hold but one legislative session in the year, that spurious elections cannot be investigated and annulled in time for the decision to have its due effect. If a return can be obtained, no matter by what unlawful means, the irregular member, who takes his seat of course, is sure of holding it a sufficient time, to answer his purposes. Hence a very pernicious encouragement is given to the use of unlawful means for obtaining irregular returns. Were elections for the federal legislature to be annual, this practice might become a very serious abuse, particularly in the more distant states. Each house is, as it necessarily must be, the judge of the elections, qualifications and returns of its members, and whatever improvements may be suggested by experience for simplifying and accelerating the process in disputed cases. So great a portion of a year would unavoidably elapse, before an illegitimate member could be dispossessed of his seat, that the prospect of such an event, would be little check to unfair and illicit means of obtaining a seat.

All these considerations taken together warrant us in affirming that biennial elections will be as useful to the affairs of the public, as we have seen that they will be safe to the liberties of the people.

William Williams to the Printer

American Mercury (Hartford, Conn.), February 11, 1788

Mr. BABCOCK,

Since the Federal Constitution has had so calm, dispassionate and rational a discussion, and so happy an issue, in the late worthy Convention of this State; I did not expect any members of that hon. body to be challenged in a News-paper, and especially by name, and by anonymous writers, on account of their opinion, or decently expressing their sentiments relative to the great subject then under consideration or any part of it. Nor do I yet see the propriety, or happy issue of such a proceeding. However as a gentleman in your Paper, feels uneasy, that every sentiment contained in his publications, (tho' in general they are well written) is not received with perfect acquiescence and submission.

I will endeavour to satisfy him, or the candid reader, by the same channel that I am not so reprehensible as he supposes, in the matter refer'd to. When the clause in the 6th article, which provides that "no religious test should ever be required as a qualification to any office or trust, &c" came under consideration. I observed I should have chose that sentence and any thing relating to a religious test, had been totally omitted rather than stand as it did, but still more wished something of the kind should have been inserted, but with a reverse sense, so far as to require an explicit acknowledgment of the being of a God, his perfections and his providence, and to have been prefixed to, and stand as, the first introductory words of the Constitution, in the following or similar terms, viz. *We the people of the United States, in a firm belief of the being and perfections of the one living and true God, the creator and supreme Governour of the world, in his universal providence and the authority of his laws: that he will require of all moral agents an account of their conduct, that all rightful powers among men are ordained of, and mediately derived from God, therefore in a depen-dence on his blessing and acknowledgment of his efficient protection in establishing our Independence, whereby it is become necessary to agree upon and settle a Constitution of federal government for ourselves*, and in order to form a more perfect union &c. as it is expressed in the present introduction, do ordain &c. and instead of none, that no other religious test, should ever be required &c. and that supposing, but not granting, this would *be no security at all*, that it would make hypocrites &c. yet this would not be a sufficient reason against it; as it would be a public declaration against, and disapprobation of men, who did not, even with sincerity, make such a profession, and they must be left, to the searcher of hearts: that it would how-ever, be the voice of the great body of the people, and an acknowledgment proper and highly becoming them to ex-press on this great and only occasion, and according to the course of Providence, one mean of obtaining blessings from the most high. But that since it was not, and so difficult and dubious to get it inserted, I would not wish to make it a capital objection: that I had no more idea of a religious test, which should restrain offices to any particular, sect, class, or denomination of men or christians, in the long list of diver-sity, than to regulate their bestowments, by the stature or dress of the candidate; nor did I believe one sensible catholic man in the state wished for such a limitation; and that there-fore the News-Paper observations, and reasonings (I named no author) against a test, in favour of any one denomination of christians, and the sacriligious injunctions of the test laws of England &c. combatted objections which did not exist, and *was building up a man of straw and knocking him down again*. These are the same and only ideas and sentiments, I endeavoured to communicate on that subject, tho' perhaps not precisely in the same terms; as I had not written, nor preconceived them, except the proposed test, and whether there is any reason in them or not, I submit to the public.

I freely confess such a test and acknowledgment, would have given me great additional satisfaction: and I conceive the arguments against it, on the score of hypocricy, would apply with equal force against requiring an oath, from any officer of the united or individual states; and with little abatement, to

any oath in any case whatever: but divine and human wisdom, with universal experience, have approved and established them as useful, and a security to mankind.

I thought it was my duty to make the observations, in this
behalf, which I did, and to bear my testimony for God: and
that it was also my duty to say *the Constitution*, with this, and
some other faults of another kind, was yet too wise and too
necessary to be rejected.

P.S. I could not have suspected, the Landholder (if I know
him) to be the author of the piece refer'd to; but if he or any
other, is pleased to reply, without the signature of his proper
name, he will receive no further answer or notice from me.

Feb. 2d, 1788.

"Publius," The Federalist LIV
[James Madison]

New-York Packet, February 12, 1788

To the People of the State of New-York.

The next view which I shall take of the House of Representatives, relates to the apportionment of its members to the several States, which is to be determined by the same rule with that of direct taxes.

It is not contended that the number of people in each State ought not to be the standard for regulating the proportion of those who are to represent the people of each State. The establishment of the same rule for the apportionment of taxes, will probably be as little contested; though the rule itself in this case, is by no means founded on the same principle. In the former case, the rule is understood to refer to the personal rights of the people, with which it has a natural and universal connection. In the latter, it has reference to the proportion of wealth, of which it is in no case a precise measure, and in ordinary cases a very unfit one. But notwithstanding the imperfection of the rule as applied to the relative wealth and contributions of the States, it is evidently the least exceptionable among the practicable rules; and had too recently obtained the general sanction of America, not to have found a ready preference with the Convention.

All this is admitted, it will perhaps be said: But does it follow from an admission of numbers for the measure of representation, or of slaves combined with free citizens, as a ratio of taxation, that slaves ought to be included in the numerical rule of representation? Slaves are considered as property, not as persons. They ought therefore to be comprehended in estimates of taxation which are founded on property, and to be excluded from representation which is regulated by a census of persons. This is the objection, as I understand it, stated in its full force. I shall be equally candid in stating the reasoning which may be offered on the opposite side.

We subscribe to the doctrine, might one of our southern brethren observe, that representation relates more immediately to persons, and taxation more immediately to property, and we join in the application of this distinction to the case of our slaves. But we must deny the fact that slaves are considered merely as property, and in no respect whatever as persons. The true state of the case is, that they partake of both these qualities; being considered by our laws, in some respects, as persons, and in other respects, as property. In being compelled to labor not for himself, but for a master; in being vendible by one master to another master; and in being subject at all times to be restrained in his liberty, and chastised in his body, by the capricious will of another, the slave may appear to be degraded from the human rank, and classed with those irrational animals, which fall under the legal denomination of property. In being protected on the other hand in his life & in his limbs, against the violence of all others, even the master of his labor and his liberty; and in being punishable himself for all violence committed against others; the slave is no less evidently regarded by the law as a member of the society; not as a part of the irrational creation; as a moral person, not as a mere article of property. The Fœderal Constitution therefore, decides with great propriety on the case of our slaves, when it views them in the mixt character of persons and of property. This is in fact their true character. It is the character bestowed on them by the laws under which they live; and it will not be denied that these are the proper criterion; because it is only under the pretext that the laws have transformed the negroes into subjects of property, that a place is disputed them in the computation of numbers; and it is admitted that if the laws were to restore the rights which have been taken away, the negroes could no longer be refused an equal share of representation with the other inhabitants.

This question may be placed in another light. It is agreed on all sides, that numbers are the best scale of wealth and taxation, as they are the only proper scale of representation. Would the Convention have been impartial or consistent, if they had rejected the slaves from the list of inhabitants when the shares of representation were to be calculated; and inserted them on the lists when the tariff of contributions was to be adjusted? Could it be reasonably expected that the southern States would concur in a system which considered their slaves in some degree as men, when burdens were to be imposed, but refused to consider them in the same light when advantages were to be conferred? Might not some surprize also be expressed that those who reproach the southern States with the barbarous policy of considering as property a part of their human brethren, should themselves contend that the government to which all the States are to be parties, ought to consider this unfortunate race more compleatly in the unnatural light of property, than the very laws of which they complain!

It may be replied perhaps that slaves are not included in the estimate of representatives in any of the States possessing them. They neither vote themselves, nor increase the votes of their masters. Upon what principle then ought they to be taken into the fœderal estimate of representation? In rejecting them altogether, the Constitution would in this respect have followed the very laws which have been appealed to, as the proper guide.

This objection is repelled by a single observation. It is a fundamental principle of the proposed Constitution, that as the aggregate number of representatives allotted to the several States, is to be determined by a fœderal rule founded on the aggregate number of inhabitants, so the right of choosing this allotted number in each State is to be exercised by such part of the inhabitants, as the State itself may designate. The qualifications on which the right of suffrage depend, are not perhaps the same in any two States. In some of the States the difference is very material. In every State, a certain proportion of inhabitants are deprived of this right by the Constitution of the State, who will be included in the census by which the Fœderal Constitution apportions the representatives. In this point of view, the southern States might retort the complaint, by insisting, that the principle laid down by the Convention required that no regard should be had to the policy of particular States towards their own inhabitants; and consequently, that the slaves as inhabitants should have been admitted into the census according to their full number, in like manner with other inhabitants, who by the policy of other States, are not admitted to all the rights of citizens. A rigorous adherence however to this principle is waved by those who would be gainers by it. All that they ask is, that equal moderation be shewn on the other side. Let the case of the slaves be considered as it is in truth a peculiar one. Let the compromising expedient of the Constitution be mutually adopted, which regards them as inhabitants, but as debased by servitude below the equal level of free inhabitants, which regards the *slave* as divested of two fifths of the *man*.

After all may not another ground be taken on which this article of the Constitution, will admit of a still more ready defence. We have hitherto proceeded on the idea that representation related to persons only, and not at all to property. But is it a just idea? Government is instituted no less for protection of the property, than of the persons of individuals. The one as well as the other, therefore may be considered as represented by those who are charged with the government. Upon this principle it is, that in several of the States, and particularly in the State of New-York, one branch of the government is intended more especially to be the guardian of property, and is accordingly elected by that part of the society which is most interested in this object of government. In the Fœderal Constitution, this policy does not prevail. The rights of property are committed into the same hands with the personal rights. Some attention ought therefore to be paid to property in the choice of those hands.

For another reason the votes allowed in the Fœderal Legislature to the people of each State, ought to bear some proportion to the comparative wealth of the States. States have not like individuals, an influence over each other arising from superior advantages of fortune. If the law allows an opulent citizen but a single vote in the choice of his representative, the respect and consequence which he derives from his fortunate situation, very frequently guide the votes of others to the objects of his choice; and through this imperceptible channel the rights of property are conveyed into the public representation. A State possesses no such influence over other States. It is not probable that the richest State in the confederacy will ever influence the choice of a single representative in any other State. Nor will the representatives of the larger and richer States, possess any other advantage in the Fœderal Legislature over the representatives of other States, than what may result from their superior number alone; as far therefore as their superior wealth and weight may justly entitle them to any advantage, it ought to be secured to them by a superior share of representation. The new Constitution is in this respect materially different from the existing confederation, as well as from that of the United Netherlands, and other similar confederacies. In each of the latter the efficacy of the fœderal resolutions depends on the subsequent and voluntary resolutions of the States composing the Union. Hence the States, though possessing an equal vote in the public councils, have an unequal influence, corresponding with the unequal importance of these subsequent and voluntary resolutions. Under the proposed Constitution, the fœderal acts will take effect without the necessary intervention of the individual States. They will depend merely on the majority of votes in the Fœderal Legislature, and consequently each vote whether proceeding from a larger or a smaller State, or a State more or less wealthy or powerful, will have an equal weight and efficacy; in the same manner as the votes individually given in a State Legislature, by the representatives of unequal counties or other districts, have each a precise equality of value and effect; or if there be any difference in the case, it proceeds from the difference in the personal character of the individual representative, rather than from any regard to the extent of the district from which he comes.

Such is the reasoning which an advocate for the southern interests might employ on this subject: And although it may appear to be a little strained in some points, yet on the whole, I must confess, that it fully reconciles me to the scale of representation, which the Convention have established.

In one respect the establishment of a common measure for representation and taxation will have a very salutary effect. As the accuracy of the census to be obtained by the Congress, will necessarily depend in a considerable degree on the disposition, if not the co-operation of the States, it is of great importance that the States should feel as little bias as possible to swell or to reduce the amount of their numbers. Were their share of representation alone to be governed by this rule they would have an interest in exaggerating their inhabitants. Were the rule to decide their share of taxation alone, a contrary temptation would prevail. By extending the rule to both objects, the States will have opposite interests, which will controul and ballance each other; and produce the requisite impartiality.

"Publius," The Federalist LV [James Madison]

Independent Journal (New York), February 13, 1788

To the People of the State of New-York.

The number of which the House of Representatives is to consist, forms another, and a very interesting point of view under which this branch of the federal legislature may be contemplated. Scarce any article indeed in the whole constitution seems to be rendered more worthy of attention, by the weight of character and the apparent force of argument, with which it has been assailed. The charges exhibited against it are, first, that so small a number of representatives will be an unsafe depositary of the public interests; secondly, that they will not possess a proper knowledge of the local circumstances of their numerous constituents; thirdly, that they will be taken from that class of citizens which will sympathize least with the feelings of the mass of the people, and be most likely to aim at a permanent elevation of the few on the depression of the many; fourthly, that defective as the number will be in the first instance, it will be more and more disproportionate, by the increase of the people, and the obstacles which will prevent a correspondent increase of the representatives.

In general it may be remarked on this subject, that no political problem is less susceptible of a precise solution, than that which relates to the number most convenient for a representative legislature: Nor is there any point on which the policy of the several states is more at variance; whether we compare their legislative assemblies directly with each other, or consider the proportions which they respectively bear to the number of their constituents. Passing over the difference between the smallest and largest states, as Delaware, whose most numerous branch consists of twenty-one representatives, and Massachusetts, where it amounts to between three and four hundred; a very considerable difference is observable among states nearly equal in population. The number of representatives in Pennsylvania is not more than one-fifth of that in the state last mentioned. New-York, whose population is to that of South-Carolina as six to five, has little more than one third of the number of representatives. As great a disparity prevails between the states of Georgia and Delaware, or Rhode-Island. In Pennsylvania the representatives do not bear a greater proportion to their constituents than of one for every four or five thousand. In Rhode-Island, they bear a proportion of at least one for every thousand. And according to the constitution of Georgia, the proportion may be carried to one for every ten electors; and must unavoidably far exceed the proportion in any of the other States.

Another general remark to be made is, that the ratio between the representatives and the people, ought not to be the same where the latter are very numerous, as where they are very few. Were the representatives in Virginia to be regulated by the standard in Rhode-Island, they would at this time amount to between four and five hundred; and twenty or thirty years hence, to a thousand. On the other hand, the ratio of Pennsylvania, if applied to the state of Delaware, would reduce the Representative assembly of the latter to seven or eight members. Nothing can be more fallacious than to found our political calculations on arithmetical principles. Sixty or seventy men, may be more properly trusted with a given degree of power than six or seven. But it does not follow, that six or seven hundred would be proportionally a better depository. And if we carry on the supposition to six or seven thousand, the whole reasoning ought to be reversed. The truth is, that in all cases a certain number at least seems to be necessary to secure the benefits of free consultation and discussion, and to guard against too easy a combination for improper purposes: As on the other hand, the number ought at most to be kept within a certain limit, in order to avoid the confusion and intemperance of a multitude. In all very numerous assemblies, of whatever characters composed, passion never fails to wrest the sceptre from reason. Had every Athenian citizen been a Socrates; every Athenian assembly would still have been a mob.

It is necessary also to recollect here the observations which were applied to the case of biennial elections. For the same reason that the limited powers of the Congress and the controul of the state legislatures, justify less frequent elections than the public safety might otherwise require; the members of the Congress need be less numerous than if they possessed the whole power of legislation, and were under no other than the ordinary restraints of other legislative bodies.

With these general ideas in our minds, let us weigh the objections which have been stated against the number of members proposed for the House of Representatives. It is said in the first place, that so small a number cannot be safely trusted with so much power.

The number of which this branch of the legislature is to consist at the outset of the government, will be sixty five. Within three years a census is to be taken, when the number may be augmented to one for every thirty thousand inhabitants; and within every successive period of ten years, the census is to be renewed, and augmentations may continue to be made under the above limitation. It will not be thought an extravagant conjecture, that the first census, will, at the rate of one for every thirty thousand raise the number of representatives to at least one hundred. Estimating the negroes in the proportion of three fifths, it can scarcely be doubted that the population of the United States will by that time, if it does not already, amount to three millions. At the expiration of twenty five years, according to the computed rate of increase, the number of representatives will amount to two hundred; and of fifty years, to four hundred. This is a number which I presume will put an end to all fears arising from the smallness of the body. I take for granted here what I shall in answering the fourth objection hereafter shew, that the number of representatives will be augmented from time to time in the manner provided by the constitution. On a contrary supposition, I should admit the objection to have very great weight indeed.

The true question to be decided then is whether the small-

ness of the number, as a temporary regulation, be dangerous
to the public liberty: Whether sixty five members for a few
years, and a hundred or two hundred for a few more, be a
safe depositary for a limited and well guarded power of legislating for the United States? I must own that I could not give
a negative answer to this question, without first obliterating
every impression which I have received with regard to the
present genius of the people of America, the spirit, which
actuates the state legislatures, and the principles which are
incorporated with the political character of every class of citizens. I am unable to conceive that the people of America in
their present temper, or under any circumstances which can
speedily happen, will chuse, and every second year repeat the
choice of sixty five or an hundred men, who would be disposed to form and pursue a scheme of tyranny or treachery. I
am unable to conceive that the state legislatures which must
feel so many motives to watch, and which possess so many
means of counteracting the federal legislature, would fail either to detect or to defeat a conspiracy of the latter against the
liberties of their common constituents. I am equally unable to
conceive that there are at this time, or can be in any short
time, in the United States any sixty five or an hundred men
capable of recommending themselves to the choice of the
people at large, who would either desire or dare within the
short space of two years, to betray the solemn trust committed to them. What change of circumstances time and a fuller
population of our country may produce, requires a prophetic
spirit to declare, which makes no part of my pretensions. But
judging from the circumstances now before us, and from the
probable state of them within a moderate period of time, I
must pronounce that the liberties of America can not be
unsafe in the number of hands proposed by the federal constitution.

From what quarter can the danger proceed? Are we afraid
of foreign gold? If foreign gold could so easily corrupt our
federal rulers, and enable them to ensnare and betray their
constituents, how has it happened that we are at this time a
free and independent nation? The Congress which conducted
us through the revolution were a less numerous body than
their successors will be; they were not chosen by nor respon-

sible to their fellow citizens at large; though appointed from year to year, and recallable at pleasure, they were generally continued for three years; and prior to the ratification of the federal articles, for a still longer term; they held their consultations always under the veil of secrecy; they had the sole transaction of our affairs with foreign nations; through the whole course of the war, they had the fate of their country more in their hands, than it is to be hoped will ever be the case with our future representatives; and from the greatness of the prize at stake and the eagerness of the party which lost it, it may well be supposed, that the use of other means than force would not have been scrupled: yet we know by happy experience that the public trust was not betrayed; nor has the purity of our public councils in this particular ever suffered even from the whispers of calumny.

Is the danger apprehended from the other branches of the federal government? But where are the means to be found by the President or the Senate, or both? Their emoluments of office it is to be presumed will not, and without a previous corruption of the house of representatives cannot, more than suffice for very different purposes: Their private fortunes, as they must all be American citizens, cannot possibly be sources of danger. The only means then which they can possess, will be in the dispensation of appointments. Is it here that suspicion rests her charge? Sometimes we are told that this fund of corruption is to be exhausted by the President in subduing the virtue of the Senate. Now the fidelity of the other house is to be the victim. The improbability of such a mercenary and perfidious combination of the several members of government standing on as different foundations as republican principles will well admit, and at the same time accountable to the society over which they are placed, ought alone to quiet this apprehension. But fortunately the constitution has provided a still further safeguard. The members of the Congress are rendered ineligible to any civil offices that may be created or of which the emoluments may be increased, during the term of their election. No offices therefore can be dealt out to the existing members, but such as may become vacant by ordinary casualties; and to suppose that these would be sufficient to purchase the guardians of the people, selected by the people themselves, is to renounce every rule by which events ought to be calculated, and to substitute an indiscriminate and unbounded jealousy, with which all reasoning must be vain. The sincere friends of liberty who give themselves up to the extravagancies of this passion are not aware of the injury they do their own cause. As there is a degree of depravity in mankind which requires a certain degree of circumspection and distrust: So there are other qualities in human nature, which justify a certain portion of esteem and confidence. Republican government presupposes the existence of these qualities in a higher degree than any other form. Were the pictures which have been drawn by the political jealousy of some among us, faithful likenesses of the human character, the inference would be that there is not sufficient virtue among men for self government; and that nothing less than the chains of despotism can restrain them from destroying and devouring one another.

"Publius," The Federalist LVI
[James Madison]

Independent Journal (New York), February 16, 1788

To the People of the State of New-York.

The *second* charge against the House of Representatives is, that it will be too small to possess a due knowledge of the interests of its constituents.

As this objection evidently proceeds from a comparison of the proposed number of representatives, with the great extent of the United States, the number of their inhabitants, and the diversity of their interests, without taking into view at the same time the circumstances which will distinguish the Congress from other legislative bodies, the best answer that can be given to it, will be a brief explanation of these peculiarities.

It is a sound and important principle that the representative ought to be acquainted with the interests and circumstances of his constituents. But this principle can extend no farther than to those circumstances and interests, to which the authority and care of the representative relate. An ignorance of a variety of minute and particular objects, which do not lie within the compass of legislation, is consistent with every attribute necessary to a due performance of the legislative trust. In determining the extent of information required in the exercise of a particular authority, recourse then must be had to the objects within the purview of that authority.

What are to be the objects of federal legislation? Those which are of most importance, and which seem most to require local knowledge, are commerce, taxation, and the militia.

A proper regulation of commerce requires much information, as has been elsewhere remarked; but as far as this information relates to the laws and local situation of each individual state, a very few representatives would be very sufficient vehicles of it to the federal councils.

Taxation will consist, in great measure, of duties which will be involved in the regulation of commerce. So far the preceeding remark is applicable to this object. As far as it may consist of internal collections, a more diffusive knowledge of the circumstances of the state may be necessary. But will not this also be possessed in sufficient degree by a very few intelligent men diffusively elected within the state. Divide the largest state into ten or twelve districts, and it will be found that there will be no peculiar local interest in either, which will not be within the knowledge of the representative of the district. Besides this source of information, the laws of the state framed by representatives from every part of it, will be almost of themselves a sufficient guide. In every state there have been made, and must continue to be made, regulations on this subject, which will in many cases leave little more to be done by the federal legislature, than to review the different laws, and reduce them into one general act. A skilful individual in his closet, with all the local codes before him, might compile a law on some subjects of taxation for the whole union, without any aid from oral information; and it may be expected, that whenever internal taxes may be necessary, and particularly in cases requiring uniformity throughout the states, the more simple objects will be preferred. To be fully sensible of the facility which will be given to this branch of federal legislation, by the assistance of the state codes, we need only suppose for a moment, that this or any other state were divided into a number of parts, each having and exercising within itself a power of local legislation. Is it not evident that a degree of local information and preparatory labour would be found in the several volumes of their proceedings, which would very much shorten the labours of the general legislature, and render a much smaller number of members sufficient for it? The federal councils will derive great advantage from another circumstance. The representatives of each state will not only bring with them a considerable knowledge of its laws, and a local knowledge of their respective districts; but will probably in all cases have been members, and may even at the very time be members of the state legislature, where all the local information and interests of the state are assembled, and from whence they may easily be conveyed by a very few hands into the legislature of the United States.

The observations made on the subject of taxation apply with greater force to the case of the militia. For however different the rules of discipline may be in different states; They are the same throughout each particular state; and depend on circumstances which can differ but little in different parts of the same state.

The attentive reader will discern that the reasoning here used to prove the sufficiency of a moderate number of representatives, does not in any respect contradict what was urged on another occasion with regard to the extensive information which the representatives ought to possess, and the time that might be necessary for acquiring it. This information, so far as it may relate to local objects, is rendered necessary and difficult, not by a difference of laws and local circumstances within a single state; but of those among different states. Taking each state by itself, its laws are the same, and its interests but little diversified. A few men therefore will possess all the knowledge requisite for a proper representation of them. Were the interests and affairs of each individual state, perfectly simple and uniform, a knowledge of them in one part would involve a knowledge of them in every other, and the whole state might be competently represented, by a single member taken from any part of it. On a comparison of the different states together, we find a great dissimilarity in their laws, and in many other circumstances connected with the objects of federal legislation, with all of which the federal representatives ought to have some acquaintance. Whilst a few representatives therefore from each state may bring with them a due knowledge of their own state, every representative will have much information to acquire concerning all the other states. The changes of time, as was formerly remarked, on the comparative situation of the different states, will have an assimilating effect. The effect of time on the internal affairs of the states taken singly, will be just the contrary. At present some of the states are little more than a society of husbandmen. Few of them have made much progress in those branches of industry, which give a variety and complexity to the affairs of a nation. These however will in all of them be the fruits of a more advanced population; and will require on the part of each state a fuller representation. The foresight of the Convention has accordingly taken care that the progress of population may be accompanied with a proper increase of the representative branch of the government.

The experience of Great Britain which presents to mankind so many political lessons, both of the monitory and exemplary kind, and which has been frequently consulted in the course of these enquiries, corroborates the result of the reflections which we have just made. The number of inhabitants in the two kingdoms of England and Scotland, cannot be stated at less than eight millions. The representatives of these eight millions in the House of Commons, amount to five hundred fifty eight. Of this number one ninth are elected by three hundred and sixty four persons, and one half by five thousand seven hundred and twenty three persons.* It cannot be supposed that the half thus elected, and who do not even reside among the people at large, can add any thing either to the security of the people against the government; or to the knowledge of their circumstances and interests, in the legislative councils. On the contrary it is notorious that they are more frequently the representatives and instruments of the executive magistrate, than the guardians and advocates of the popular rights. They might therefore with great propriety be considered as something more than a mere deduction from the real representatives of the nation. We will however consider them, in this light alone, and will not extend the deduction, to a considerable number of others, who do not reside among their constituents, are very faintly connected with them, and have very little particular knowledge of their affairs. With all these concessions two hundred and seventy nine persons only will be the depository of the safety, interest and happiness of eight millions; that is to say: There will be one representative only to maintain the rights and explain the situation *of twenty eight thousand six hundred and seventy* constituents, in an assembly exposed to the whole force of executive influence, and extending its authority to every object of

*Burgh's polit. disquis.

legislation within a nation whose affairs are in the highest degree diversified and complicated. Yet it is very certain not only that a valuable portion of freedom has been preserved under all these circumstances, but that the defects in the British code are ·chargeable in a very small proportion, on the ignorance of the legislature concerning the circumstances of the people. Allowing to this case the weight which is due to it: And comparing it with that of the House of Representatives as above explained, it seems to give the fullest assurance that a representative for every *thirty thousand inhabitants* will render the latter both a safe and competent guardian of the interests which will be confided to it.

"Publius," The Federalist LVII
[James Madison]

New-York Packet, February 19, 1788

To the People of the State of New-York.

The *third* charge against the House of Representatives is, that it will be taken from that class of citizens which will have least sympathy with the mass of the people, and be most likely to aim at an ambitious sacrifice of the many to the aggrandizement of the few.

Of all the objections which have been framed against the Fœderal Constitution, this is perhaps the most extraordinary. Whilst the objection itself is levelled against a pretended oligarchy, the principle of it strikes at the very root of republican government.

The aim of every political Constitution is or ought to be first to obtain for rulers, men who possess most wisdom to discern, and most virtue to pursue the common good of the society; and in the next place, to take the most effectual precautions for keeping them virtuous, whilst they continue to hold their public trust. The elective mode of obtaining rulers is the characteristic policy of republican government. The means relied on in this form of government for preventing their degeneracy are numerous and various. The most effectual one is such a limitation of the term of appointments, as will maintain a proper responsibility to the people.

Let me now ask what circumstance there is in the Constitution of the House of Representatives, that violates the principles of republican government; or favors the elevation of the few on the ruins of the many? Let me ask whether every circumstance is not, on the contrary, strictly conformable to these principles; and scrupulously impartial to the rights and pretensions of every class and description of citizens?

Who are to be the electors of the Fœderal Representatives?

Not the rich more than the poor; not the learned more than the ignorant; not the haughty heirs of distinguished names, more than the humble sons of obscure and unpropitious fortune. The electors are to be the great body of the people of the United States. They are to be the same who exercise the right in every State of electing the correspondent branch of the Legislature of the State.

Who are to be the objects of popular choice? Every citizen whose merit may recommend him to the esteem and confidence of his country. No qualification of wealth, of birth, of religious faith, or of civil profession, is permitted to fetter the judgment or disappoint the inclination of the people.

If we consider the situation of the men on whom the free suffrages of their fellow citizens may confer the representative trust, we shall find it involving every security which can be devised or desired for their fidelity to their constituents.

In the first place, as they will have been distinguished by the preference of their fellow citizens, we are to presume, that in general, they will be somewhat distinguished also, by those qualities which entitle them to it, and which promise a sincere and scrupulous regard to the nature of their engagements.

In the second place, they will enter into the public service under circumstances which cannot fail to produce a temporary affection at least to their constituents. There is in every breast a sensibility to marks of honor, of favor, of esteem, and of confidence, which, apart from all considerations of interest, is some pledge for grateful and benevolent returns. Ingratitude is a common topic of declamation against human nature; and it must be confessed, that instances of it are but too frequent and flagrant both in public and in private life. But the universal and extreme indignation which it inspires, is itself a proof of the energy and prevalence of the contrary sentiment.

In the third place, these ties which bind the representative to his constituents are strengthened by motives of a more selfish nature. His pride and vanity attach him to a form of government which favors his pretensions, and gives him a share in its honors and distinctions. Whatever hopes or projects might be entertained by a few aspiring characters, it must generally happen that a great proportion of the men deriving their advancement from their influence with the people, would have more to hope from a preservation of the favor, than from innovations in the government subversive of the authority of the people.

All these securities however would be found very insufficient without the restraint of frequent elections. Hence, in the fourth place, the House of Representatives is so constituted as to support in the members an habitual recollection of their dependence on the people. Before the sentiments impressed on their minds by the mode of their elevation, can be effaced by the exercise of power, they will be compelled to anticipate the moment when their power is to cease, when their exercise of it is to be reviewed, and when they must descend to the level from which they were raised; there for ever to remain, unless a faithful discharge of their trust shall have established their title to a renewal of it.

I will add as a fifth circumstance in the situation of the House of Representatives, restraining them from oppressive measures, that they can make no law which will not have its full operation on themselves and their friends, as well as on the great mass of the society. This has always been deemed one of the strongest bonds by which human policy can connect the rulers and the people together. It creates between them that communion of interests and sympathy of sentiments of which few governments have furnished examples; but without which every government degenerates into tyranny. If it be asked what is to restrain the House of Representatives from making legal discriminations in favor of themselves and a particular class of the society? I answer, the genius of the whole system, the nature of just and constitutional laws, and above all the vigilent and manly spirit which actuates the people of America, a spirit which nourishes freedom, and in return is nourished by it.

If this spirit shall ever be so far debased as to tolerate a law not obligatory on the Legislature as well as on the people, the people will be prepared to tolerate any thing but liberty.

Such will be the relation between the House of Representatives and their constituents. Duty, gratitude, interest, ambition itself, are the chords by which they will be bound to fidelity and sympathy with the great mass of the people. It is possible that these may all be insufficient to controul the

caprice and wickedness of man. But are they not all that government will admit, and that human prudence can devise? Are
they not the genuine and the characteristic means by which
Republican Government provides for the liberty and happiness of the people? Are they not the identical means on which
every State Government in the Union, relies for the attainment of these important ends? What then are we to understand by the objection which this paper has combated? What
are we to say to the men who profess the most flaming zeal
for Republican Government, yet boldly impeach the fundamental principle of it; who pretend to be champions for the
right and the capacity of the people to chuse their own rulers,
yet maintain that they will prefer those only who will immediately and infallibly betray the trust committed to them?

Were the objection to be read by one who had not seen the
mode prescribed by the Constitution for the choice of representatives, he could suppose nothing less than that some unreasonable qualification of property was annexed to the right
of suffrage; or that the right of eligibility was limited to persons of particular families or fortunes; or at least that the
mode prescribed by the State Constitutions was in some respect or other very grossly departed from. We have seen how
far such a supposition would err as to the two first points.
Nor would it in fact be less erroneous as to the last. The only
difference discoverable between the two cases, is, that each
representative of the United States will be elected by five or
six thousand citizens; whilst in the individual States the election of a representative is left to about as many hundred. Will
it be pretended that this difference is sufficient to justify an
attachment to the State Governments and an abhorrence to
the Fœderal Government? If this be the point on which the
objection turns, it deserves to be examined.

Is it supported by *reason*? This cannot be said, without
maintaining that five or six thousand citizens are less capable
of chusing a fit representative, or more liable to be corrupted
by an unfit one, than five or six hundred. Reason, on the
contrary assures us, that as in so great a number, a fit representative would be most likely to be found, so the choice
would be less likely to be diverted from him, by the intrigues
of the ambitious, or the bribes of the rich.

Is the *consequence* from this doctrine admissible? If we say that five or six hundred citizens are as many as can jointly exercise their right of suffrage, must we not deprive the people of the immediate choice of their public servants in every instance where the administration of the government does not require as many of them as will amount to one for that number of citizens?

Is the doctrine warranted by *facts*? It was shewn in the last paper, that the real representation in the British House of Commons very little exceeds the proportion of one for every thirty thousand inhabitants. Besides a variety of powerful causes, not existing here, and which favor in that country, the pretensions of rank and wealth, no person is eligible as a representative of a county, unless he possess real estate of the clear value of six hundred pounds sterling per year; nor of a city or borough, unless he possess a like estate of half that annual value. To this qualification on the part of the county representatives, is added another on the part of the county electors, which restrains the right of suffrage to persons having a freehold estate of the annual value of more than twenty pounds sterling according to the present rate of money. Notwithstanding these unfavorable circumstances, and notwithstanding some very unequal laws in the British code, it cannot be said that the representatives of the nation have elevated the few on the ruins of the many.

But we need not resort to foreign experience on this subject. Our own is explicit and decisive. The districts in New-Hampshire in which the Senators are chosen immediately by the people are nearly as large as will be necessary for her representatives in the Congress. Those of Massachusetts are larger, than will be necessary for that purpose. And those of New-York still more so. In the last State the members of Assembly, for the cities and counties of New-York and Albany, are elected by very nearly as many voters, as will be entitled to a representative in the Congress, calculating on the number of sixty-five representatives only. It makes no difference that in these senatorial districts and counties, a number of representatives are voted for by each elector at the same time. If the same electors, at the same time are capable of choosing four or five representatives, they cannot be incapable of choosing one. Pennsylvania is an additional example. Some of her counties which elect her State representatives, are almost as large as her districts will be by which her Fœderal Representatives will be elected. The city of Philadelphia is supposed to contain between fifty and sixty thousand souls. It will therefore form nearly two districts for the choice of Fœderal Representatives. It forms however but one county, in which every elector votes for each of its representatives in the State Legislature. And what may appear to be still more directly to our purpose, the whole city actually elects a *single member* for the executive council. This is the case in all the other counties of the State.

Are not these facts the most satisfactory proofs of the fallacy which has been employed against the branch of the Fœderal Government under consideration? Has it appeared on trial that the Senators of New-Hampshire, Massachusetts, and New-York; or the Executive Council of Pennsylvania; or the members of the Assembly in the two last States, have betrayed any peculiar disposition to sacrifice the many to the few; or are in any respect less worthy of their places than the representatives and magistrates appointed in other States, by very small divisions of the people?

But there are cases of a stronger complexion than any which I have yet quoted. One branch of the Legislature of Connecticut is so constituted that each member of it is elected by the whole State. So is the Governor of that State, of Massachusetts, and of this State, and the President of New-Hampshire. I leave every man to decide whether the result of any one of these experiments can be said to countenance a suspicion that a diffusive mode of chusing representatives of the people tends to elevate traitors, and to undermine the public liberty.

Harry Innes to John Brown

Danville, Kentucky, February 20, 1788

I returned late last evening from Fayette & found Mr. La-casagne here on his way to Philadelphia. I have snatched up my pen to let you know that I am not altogether thoughtless of you; this letter should be more full but the bearer sets out early this morning & I am obliged to curtail it. I wrote you via Richmond very fully on the subject of your business & what I thought the Court would probably do at the March Term. I have nothing to add on that head but to assure you that everything in my power shall be done for the benefit of yours and your clients interest.

The subject of the Federal Constitution begins to engross the attention of the people & I am endeavoring to bring about a convention on that important subject big with the fate of Kentucky & the Western Country. The objections which have been generally made to the eastward are of a general nature and appear to affect the general interest of United America; they are of too much importance to be looked over. I need not repeat them here as they have often appeared in the Public Print, but my Dr. Sir. the adoption of that Constitution would be the destruction of our young & flourishing country which I shall endeavor to point out concisely to you, viz: All commercial regulations "are to be vested in the General Congress". Our interests and the interests of the Eastern states are so diametrically opposite to each other that there cannot be a ray of hope left to the Western Country to suppose that when once that interest clashes we shall have justice done us. There is no such idea as justice in a Political society when the interests of 59/60 are to be injured thereby and that this will be the case as soon as we have the liberty of exportation, is self evident. Is there an article that the Eastern States can export except Fish oil & rice that we shall not abound in. I say not one. So long therefore as Congress hath this sole power & a majority have the right of deciding on those grand questions we cannot expect to enjoy the navigation of the Mississippi, but another evil equally great will arise from the same point. If ever we are a great and happy people, it must arise from our industry and attention to manufactories. This desirable end can never be brought about so long as the state Legislatures have the power of prohibiting imports, can we suppose that Congress will indulge us with a partial import when we must otherwise procure all our resources from the Eastward, the consequence of which is that we will be impoverished and the Eastern States will draw all our wealth and emigration will totally cease.

The most particular objection is the power of the Judiciary if our separation takes place, there will probably arise disputes between the Citizens of New Jersey, Pennsylvania, Delaware, Maryland, Virginia, & North Carolina and the Citizens of Kentucky; it is hardly to be supposed that each of the Citizens of these States as may have disputes with the Citizens of Kentucky will sue in Kentucky we shall be drawn away to the Federal Court and the Citizens from Kentucky away from their local habitations will nine times out of ten fall a sacrifice to their contests.

there are with me three insurmountable objections to the New Constitution. I wish to see a convention of the people on the subject & to remonstrate against it through the convention of Virginia & if that cannot be done, at least to address. Our local situation must justify any measures which may be adopted upon this occasion, certain that if the Constitution is adopted by us that we shall be the mere vassals of the Congress and the consequences to me are horrible and dreadful.

I would write more, but am obliged to conclude but before I lay down my pen must observe that the Indians continue hostile. 25 horses were taken in the latter end of January when the earth was covered 5 inches of snow. Will Congress do anything for us. Let us hear from you as soon as possible. Mr. Lacasagne will stay some time in Philadelphia & hath promised me to inform you of his lodgings, & to undertake to forward any letter you may send to his care. Mr. Al Parker of Lexington will leave Philadelphia the beginning of April. We have had a most severe winter, which is not ended. I know of no changes among your acquaintances here. We are all well.

"Brutus" XIII

New York Journal, February 21, 1788

Having in the two preceding numbers, examined the nature and tendency of the judicial power, as it respects the explanation of the constitution, I now proceed to the consideration of the other matters, of which it has cognizance.—The next paragraph extends its authority, to all cases, in law and equity, arising under the laws of the United States. This power, as I understand it, is a proper one. The proper province of the judicial power, in any government, is, as I conceive, to declare what is the law of the land. To explain and enforce those laws, which the supreme power or legislature may pass; but not to declare what the powers of the legislature are. I suppose the cases in equity, under the laws, must be so construed, as to give the supreme court not only a legal, but equitable jurisdiction of cases which may be brought before them, or in other words, so, as to give them, not only the powers which are now exercised by our courts of law, but those also, which are now exercised by our court of chancery. If this be the meaning, I have no other objection to the power, than what arises from the undue extension of the legislative power. For, I conceive that the judicial power should be commensurate with the legislative. Or, in other words, the supreme court should have authority to determine questions arising under the laws of the union.

The next paragraph which gives a power to decide in law and equity, on all cases arising under treaties, is unintelligible to me. I can readily comprehend what is meant by deciding a case under a treaty. For as treaties will be the law of the land, every person who have rights or privileges secured by treaty, will have aid of the courts of law, in recovering them. But I do not understand, what is meant by equity arising under a treaty. I presume every right which can be claimed under a treaty, must be claimed by virtue of some article or clause contained in it, which gives the right in plain and obvious words; or at least, I conceive, that the rules for explaining treaties, are so well ascertained, that there is no need of having recourse to an equitable construction. If under this power, the courts are to explain treaties, according to what they conceive are their spirit, which is nothing less than a power to give them whatever extension they may judge proper, it is a dangerous and improper power. The cases affecting ambassadors, public ministers, and consuls — of admiralty and maritime jurisdiction; controversies to which the United States are a party, and controversies between states, it is proper should be under the cognizance of the courts of the union, because none but the general government, can, or ought to pass laws on their subjects. But, I conceive the clause which extends the power of the judicial to controversies arising between a state and citizens of another state, improper in itself, and will, in its exercise, prove most pernicious and destructive.

It is improper, because it subjects a state to answer in a court of law, to the suit of an individual. This is humiliating and degrading to a government, and, what I believe, the supreme authority of no state ever submitted to.

The states are now subject to no such actions. All contracts entered into by individuals with states, were made upon the faith and credit of the states, and the individuals never had in contemplation any compulsory mode of obliging the government to fulfil its engagements.

The evil consequences that will flow from the exercise of this power, will best appear by tracing it in its operation. The constitution does not direct the mode in which an individual shall commence a suit against a state or the manner in which the judgement of the court shall be carried into execution, but it gives the legislature full power to pass all laws which shall be proper and necessary for the purpose. And they certainly must make provision for these purposes, or otherwise the power of the judicial will be nugatory. For, to what purpose will the power of a judicial be, if they have no mode, in which they can call the parties before them? Or of what use will it be, to call the parties to answer, if after they have given judgment, there is no authority to execute the judgment? We must, therefore, conclude, that the legislature will pass laws which will be effectual in this head. An individual of one state will then have a legal remedy against a state for any demand he may have against a state to which he does not belong. Every state in the union is largely indebted to individuals. For the payment of these debts they have given notes payable to the bearer. At least this is the case in this state. Whenever a citizen of another state becomes possessed of one of these notes, he may commence an action in the supreme court of the general government; and I cannot see any way in which he can be prevented from recovering. It is easy to see, that when this once happens, the notes of the state will pass rapidly from the hands of citizens of the state to those of other states.

And when the citizens of other states possess them, they may bring suits against the state for them, and by this means, judgments and executions may be obtained against the state for the whole amount of the state debt. It is certain the state, with the utmost exertions it can make, will not be able to discharge the debt she owes, under a considerable number of years, perhaps with the best management, it will require twenty or thirty years to discharge it. This new system will protract the time in which the ability of the state will enable them to pay off their debt, because all the funds of the state will be transferred to the general government, except those which arise from internal taxes.

The situation of the states will be deplorable. By this system, they will surrender to the general government, all the means of raising money, and at the same time, will subject themselves to suits at law, for the recovery of the debts they have contracted in effecting the revolution.

The debts of the individual states will amount to a sum, exceeding the domestic debt of the United States; these will be left upon them, with power in the judicial of the general government, to enforce their payment, while the general government will possess an exclusive command of the most productive funds, from which the states can derive money, and a command of every other source of revenue paramount to the authority of any state.

It may be said that the apprehension that the judicial power will operate in this manner is merely visionary, for that the legislature will never pass laws that will work these effects. Or if they were disposed to do it, they cannot provide for levying an execution on a state, for where will the officer find property whereon to levy?

To this I would reply, if this is a power which will not or cannot be executed, it was useless and unwise to grant it to the judicial. For what purpose is a power given which it is imprudent or impossible to exercise? If it be improper for a government to exercise a power, it is improper they should be vested with it. And it is unwise to authorise a government to do what they cannot effect.

As to the idea that the legislature cannot provide for levying an execution on a state, I believe it is not well founded. I presume the last paragraph of the 8th section of article 1, gives the Congress express power to pass any laws they may judge proper and necessary for carrying into execution the power vested in the judicial department. And they must exercise this power, or otherwise the courts of justice will not be able to carry into effect the authorities with which they are invested. For the constitution does not direct the mode in which the courts are to proceed, to bring parties before them, to try causes, or to carry the judgment of the courts into execution. Unless they are pointed out by law, how are they to proceed, in any of the cases of which they have cognizance? They have the same authority to establish regulations in respect to these matters, where a state is a party, as where an individual is a party. The only difficulty is, on whom shall process be served, when a state is a party, and how shall execution be levied. With regard to the first, the way is easy, either the executive or legislative of the state may be notified, and upon proof being made of the service of the notice, the court may proceed to a hearing of the cause. Execution may be levied on any property of the state, either real or personal. The treasury may be seized by the officers of the general government, or any lands the property of the state, may be made subject to seizure and sale to satisfy any judgment against it. Whether the estate of any individual citizen may not be made answerable for the discharge of judgments against the state, may be worth consideration. In some corporations this is the case.

If the power of the judicial under this clause will extend to the cases above stated, it will, if executed, produce the utmost confusion, and in its progress, will crush the states beneath its weight. And if it does not extend to these cases, I confess myself utterly at a loss to give it any meaning. For if the citizen of one state, possessed of a written obligation, given in pursuance of a solemn act of the legislature, acknowledging a debt due to the bearer, and promising to pay it, cannot recover in the supreme court, I can conceive of no case in which they can recover. And it appears to me ridiculous to provide for obtaining judgment against a state, without giving the means of levying execution.

Hugh Williamson's Speech
at Edenton, North Carolina

delivered November 8, 1787, printed in the
Daily Advertiser (New York), February 25, 26, 27, 1788

The following Remarks on the New Plan of Government are handed us as the substance of Doctor WILLIAMSON's *Address to the Freemen of Edenton and the County of Chowan, in North-Carolina, when assembled to instruct their Representatives.*

Though I am conscious that a subject of the greatest magnitude must suffer in the hands of such an advocate, I cannot refuse, at the request of my fellow-citizens, to make some observations on the new Plan of Government.

It seems to be generally admitted, that the system of Government which has been proposed by the late Convention, is well calculated to relieve us from many of the grievances under which we have been laboring. If I might express my particular sentiments on this subject, I should describe it as more free and more perfect than any form of government that ever has been adopted by any nation; but I would not say it has no faults. Imperfection is inseparable from every human device. Several objections were made to this system by two or three very respectable characters in the Convention, which have been the subject of much conversation; and other objections, by citizens of this State, have lately reached our ears. It is proper that you should consider of these objections. They are of two kinds; they respect the things that are in the system, and the things that are not in it. We are told that there should have been a section for securing the Trial by Jury in Civil cases, and the Liberty of the Press: that there should also have been a Declaration of Rights. In the new system it is provided, that "*The Trial of all crimes*, except in cases of Impeach-

227

ment," *shall be by Jury*, but this provision could not possibly be extended to all *Civil* cases. For it is well known that the Trial by Jury is not general and uniform throughout the United States, either in cases of Admiralty or of Chancery; hence it became necessary to submit the question to the General Legislature, who might accommodate their laws on this occasion to the desires and habits of the nation. Surely there is no prohibition in a case that is untouched.

We have been told that the Liberty of the Press is not secured by the New Constitution. Be pleased to examine the plan, and you will find that the Liberty of the Press and the laws of Mahomet are equally affected by it. The New Government is to have the power of protecting literary property; the very power which you have by a special act delegated to the present Congress. There was a time in England, when neither book, pamphlet, nor paper could be published without a licence from Government. That restraint was finally removed in the year 1694 and by such removal, their press became perfectly free, for it is not under the restraint of any licence. Certainly the new Government can have no power to impose restraints. The citizens of the United States have no more occasion for a second Declaration of Rights, than they have for a section in favor of the press. Their rights, in the several States, have long since been explained and secured by particular declarations, which make a part of their several Constitutions. It is granted, and perfectly understood, that under the Government of the Assemblies of the States, and under the Government of the Congress, every right is reserved to the individual, which he has not expressly delegated to this, or that Legislature. The other objections that have been made to the new plan of Government, are: That it absorbs the powers of the several States: That the national Judiciary is too extensive: That a standing army is permitted: That Congress is allowed to regulate trade: That the several States are prevented from taxing exports, for their own benefit.

When Gentlemen are pleased to complain, that little power is left in the hands of the separate States; they should be advised to cast an eye upon the large code of laws, which have passed in this State since the peace. Let them consider how few of those laws have been framed, for the general benefit of the Nation. Nine out of ten of them, are domestic; calculated for the sole use of this State, or of particular citizens. There must still be use for such laws, though you should enable the Congress to collect a revenue for National purposes, and the collection of that revenue includes the chief of the new powers, which are now to be committed to the Congress.

Hitherto you have delegated certain powers to the Congress, and other powers to the Assemblies of the States. The portion that you have delegated to Congress is found to have been useless, because it is too small, and the powers that are committed to the assemblies of the several States, are also found to be absolutely ineffectual for national purposes, because they can never be so managed as to operate in concert. Of what use is that small portion of reserved power? It neither makes you respectable nor powerful. The consequence of such reservation is national contempt abroad, and a state of dangerous weakness at home. what avails the claim of power, which appears to be nothing better than the empty whistling of a name? The Congress will be chosen by yourselves, as your Members of Assembly are. They will be creatures of your hands, and subject to your advice. Protected and cherished by the small addition of power which you shall put into their hands, you may become a great and respectable nation.

It is complained that the powers of the national Judiciary are too extensive. This objection appears to have the greatest weight in the eyes of gentlemen who have not carefully compared the powers which are to be delegated with those that had been formerly delegated to Congress. The powers that are now to be committed to the national Legislature, as they are detailed in the 8th section of the first article, have already been chiefly delegated to the Congress under one form or another, except those which are contained in the first paragraph of that section. And the objects that are now to be submitted to the Supreme Judiciary, or to the Inferior Courts, are those which naturally arise from the constitutional laws of Congress. If there is a single new case that can be exceptionable, it is that between a foreigner and a citizen, or that between the citizens of different States. These cases may come up by appeal. It is provided in this system that there shall be no fraudulent tender in the payments of debts. Foreigners, with whom we have treaties, will trust our citizens on the faith of this engagement. And the citizens of different States will do the same. If the Congress had a negative on the laws of the several States, they would certainly prevent all such laws as might endanger the honor or peace of the nation, by making a tender of base money; but they have no such power, and it is at least possible that some State may be found in this Union, disposed to break the Constitution, and abolish private debts by such tenders. In these cases the Courts of the offending States would probably decide according to its own laws. The foreigner would complain; and the nation might be involved in war for the support of such dishonest measures. Is it not better to have a Court of Appeals in which the Judges can only be determined by the laws of the nation? This Court is equally to be desired by the citizens of different States. But we are told that justice will be delayed, and the poor will be drawn away by the rich to a distant Court. The authors of this remark have not fully considered the question, else they must have recollected that the poor of this country have little to do with foreigners, or with the citizens of distant States. They do not consider that there may be an Inferior Court in every State; nor have they recollected that the appeals being *with such exceptions*, and *under such regulations* as Congress shall make, will never be permitted for trifling sums, or under trivial pretences, unless we can suppose that the national Legislature shall be composed of knaves and fools. The line that separates the powers of the national Legislature from those of the several States is clearly drawn. The several States reserve every power that can be exercised for the particular use and comfort of the State. They do not yield a single power which is not purely of a national concern; nor do they yield a single power which is not absolutely necessary to the safety and prosperity of the nation, nor one that could be employed to any effect in the hands of particular States. The powers of Judiciary naturally arise from those of the Legislature. Questions that are of a national concern, and those cases which are determinable by the general laws of the nation, are to be referred to the national Judiciary, but they have not any thing to do with a single case either civil or criminal, which respects the private and particular concerns of a State or its citizens.

The possibility of keeping regular troops in the public service has been urged as another objection against the new Constitution. It is very remarkable that the same objection has not been made against the original Confederation, in which the same grievance obtained without the same guards. It is now provided, that no appropriation of money for the use of the army shall be for a longer time than two years. Provision is also made for having a powerful militia, in which case there never can be occasion for many regular troops. It has been objected in some of the Southern States, that the Congress, by a majority of votes, is to have the power to regulate trade. It is universally admitted that Congress ought to have this power, else our commerce, which is nearly ruined, can never be restored; but some gentlemen think that the concurrence of two thirds of the votes in Congress should have been required. By the sundry regulations of commerce, it will be in the power of Government not only to collect a vast revenue for the general benefit of the nation, but to secure the carrying trade in the hands of citizens in preference to strangers. It has been alledged that there are few ships belonging to the Southern States, and that the price of freight must rise in consequence of our excluding many foreign vessels: but when we have not vessels of our own, it is certainly proper that we should hire those of citizens in preference to strangers; for our revenue is promoted and the nation is strengthened by the profits that remain in the hands of citizens; we are injured by throwing it into the hands of strangers; and though the price of freight should rise for two or three years, this advantage is fully due to our brethren in the Eastern and middle States, who, with great and exemplary candor, have given us equal advantages in return. A small encrease in the price of freight would operate greatly in favor of the Southern States: it would promote the spirit of ship building; it would promote a nursery for native seamen, and would afford support to the poor who live near the sea coast; it would encrease the value of their lands, and at the same time it would reduce their taxes. It has finally been objected that the several States are not permitted to tax their exports for the benefit of their particular Treasuries. This strange objection has been occasionally repeated by citizens of this State.

They must have transplanted it from another State, for it could not have been the growth of North-Carolina. Such have been the objections against the new Constitution.

Whilst the honest patriot, who guards with a jealous eye the liberties of his country, and apprehends danger under every form: the placeman in every State, who fears lest his office should pass into other hands; the idle, the factious, and the dishonest, who live by plunder or speculation on the miseries of their country; while these, assisted by a numerous body of secret enemies, who never have been reconciled to our Independence, are seeking for objections to this Constitution; it is a remarkable circumstance, and a very high encomium on the plan, that nothing more plausible has been offered against it; for it is an easy matter to find faults.

Let us turn our eyes to a more fruitful subject; let us consider the present condition of the United States, and the particular benefits that North Carolina must reap by the proposed form of Government. Without money, no Government can be supported; and Congress can raise no money under the present Constitution: They have not the power to make commercial treaties, because they cannot preserve them when made. Hence it is, that we are the prey of every nation: We are indulged in such foreign commerce, as must be hurtful to us: We are prohibited from that which might be profitable, and we are accordingly told, that on the last two years, the Thirteen States have hardly paid into the Treasury, as much as should have been paid by a single State. Intestine commotions in some of the States: Paper Money in others, a want of inclination in some, and a general suspicion throughout the Union, that the burthen is unequally laid; added to the general loss of trade have produced a general bankruptcy, and loss of honor. We have borrowed money of Spain—she demands the principal, but we cannot pay the interest. It is a circumstance perfectly humiliating, that we should remain under obligations to that nation: We are Considerably indebted to France but she is too generous to insist upon what she knows we cannot pay, either the principal or interest. In the hour of our distress, we borrowed money in Holland; not from the Government, but from private citizens. Those who are called the Patriots were our friends, and they are oppressed in their turn by hosts of enemies: They will soon have need of money: At this hour we are not able to pay the interests of their loan. What is to be done? Will you borrow money again from other citizens of that oppressed Republic, to pay the interest of what you borrowed from their brethren? This would be a painful expedient, but our want of Government may render it necessary. You have two or three Ministers abroad; they must soon return home, for they cannot be supported. You have four or five hundred troops scattered along the Ohio to protect the frontier inhabitants, and give some value to your lands; those troops are ill paid, and in a fair way for being disbanded. There is hardly a circumstance remaining; hardly one external mark by which you can deserve to be called a nation. You are not in a condition to resist the most contemptible enemy. What is there to prevent an Algerine Pirate from landing on your coast, and carrying your citizens into slavery? You have not a single sloop of war. Does one of the States attempt to raise a little money by imposts or other commercial regulations.—A neighboring State immediately alters her laws and defeats the revenue, by throwing the trade into a different channel. Instead of supporting or assisting, we are uniformly taking the advantage of one another. Such an assemblage of people are not a nation. Like a dark cloud, without cohesion or firmness, we are ready to be torn asunder and scattered abroad by every breeze of external violence, or internal commotion.

Is there a man in this State who believes it possible for us to continue under such a Government?—Let us suppose but for a minute, that such a measure should be attempted.—Let us suppose that the several States shall be required and obliged to pay their several quotas according to the original plan. You know that North-Carolina, on the last four years, has not paid one dollar into the Treasury for eight dollars that she ought to have paid. We must encrease our taxes exceedingly, and those taxes must be of the most grievous kind; they must be taxes on lands and heads; taxes that cannot fail to grind the face of the poor; for it is clear that we can raise little by imports and exports. Some foreign goods are imported by water from the Northern States, such goods pay a duty for the benefit of those States, which is seldom drawn back; this operates as a tax upon our citizens. On this side, Virginia promotes her revenue to the amount of 25,000 dollars every year, by a tax on our tobacco that she exports: South-Carolina on the other side, may avail herself of similar opportunities. Two thirds of the foreign goods that are consumed in this State are imported by land from Virginia or South-Carolina; such goods pay a certain impost for the benefit of the importing States, but our Treasury is not profited by this commerce. By such means our citizens are taxed more than one hundred thousand dollars every year, but the State does not receive credit for a shilling of that money. Like a patient that is bleeding at both arms, North-Carolina must soon expire under such wasteful operations. Unless I am greatly mistaken, we have seen enough of the State of the Union, and of North-Carolina in particular, to be assured that another form of Government is become necessary. Is the form now proposed well calculated to give relief? To this, we must answer in the affirmative. All foreign goods that shall be imported into these States, are to pay a duty for the use of the nation. All the States will be on a footing, whether they have bad ports or good ones. No duties will be laid on exports; hence the planter will receive the true value of his produce, wherever it may be shipped. If excises are laid on wine, spirits, or other luxuries, they must be uniform throughout the States. By a careful management of imposts and excises, the national expences may be discharged without any other species of tax; but if a poll-tax, or land-tax shall ever become necessary, the weight must press equally on every part of the Union. For in all cases, such taxes must be according to the number of inhabitants. Is it not a pleasing consideration that North-Carolina, under all her natural disadvantages, must have the same facility of paying her share of the public debt as the most favored, or the most fortunate State? She gains no advantage by this plan, but she recovers from her misfortunes. She stands on the same footing with her sister States, and they are too generous to desire that she should stand on lower ground. When you consider those parts of the new System which are of the greatest import—those which respect the general question of liberty and safety, you will recollect that the States in Convention were unanimous; and you must re-

member that some of the members of that body have risqued
their lives in defence of liberty; but the system does not require the help of such arguments; it will bear the most scrupulous examination.

When you refer the proposed system to the particular circumstances of North-Carolina, and consider how she is to be
affected by this plan; you must find the utmost reason to rejoice in the prospect of better times—this is a sentiment that
I have ventured with the greater confidence, because it is the
general opinion of my late Honorable Colleagues, and I have
the utmost reliance in their superior abilities. But if our constituents shall discover faults where we could not see any, or if
they shall suppose that a plan is formed for abridging their
liberties when we imagined that we had been securing both
liberty and property on a more stable foundation; if they perceive that they are to suffer a loss where we thought they
must rise from a misfortune; they will at least do us the justice
to charge those errors to the head, and not to the heart.

The proposed system is now in your hands, and with it the
fate of your country. We have a common interest, for we are
embarked in the same vessel. At present she is in a sea of
troubles, without sails, oars, or pilot; ready to be dashed into
pieces by every flaw of wind. You may secure a port, unless
you think it better to remain at sea. If there is any man among
you that wishes for troubled times and fluctuating measures,
that he may live by speculations, and thrive by the calamities
of the State; this Government is not for him.

If there is any man who envies the prosperity of a native
citizen, who wishes that we should remain without native
merchants or seamen, without shipping, without manufactures, without commerce; poor and contemptible, the tributaries of a foreign country; this Government is not for him.

And if there is any man who has never been reconciled to
our Independence, who wishes to see us degraded and insulted abroad, oppressed by anarchy at home, and torn into
pieces by factions; incapable of resistance and ready to become a prey to the first invader; this Government is not for
him.

But it is a Government, unless I am greatly mistaken, that
gives the fairest promise of being firm and honorable; safe

from Foreign Invasion or Domestic Sedition. A Government by which our commerce must be protected and enlarged; the value of our produce and of our lands must be encreased; the labourer and the mechanic must be encouraged and supported. It is a form of Government that is perfectly fitted for protecting Liberty and Property, and for cherishing the good Citizen and the Honest Man.

"Centinel" [*Samuel Bryan*] *XVI*

Independent Gazetteer (Philadelphia), February 26, 1788

To the People of Pennsylvania.

Fellow-Citizens, The new constitution instead of being the panecea or cure of every grievance so delusively represented by its advocates will be found upon examination like Pandora's box, replete with every evil. The most specious clauses of this system of ambition and iniquity contain latent mischief, and premedated villainy. By section 9th of the 1st article, "No *ex post facto* law shall be passed." This sounds very well upon a superficial consideration, and I dare say has been read by most people with approbation. Government undoubtedly ought to avoid retrospective laws as far as may be, as they are generally injurious and fraudulent: Yet there are occasions when such laws are not only just but highly requisite. An ex post facto law is a law made after the fact, so that the Congress under the new constitution are precluded from all controul over transactions prior to its establishment. This prohibition would skreen the numerous public defaulters, as no measure could be constitutionally taken to compel them to render an account and restore the public money; the unaccounted millions lying in their hands would become their private property. Hitherto these characters from their great weight and numbers have had the influence to prevent an investigation of their accounts, but if this constitution be established, they may set the public at defiance, as they would be completely exonerated of all demands of the United States against them. This is not a strained construction of this section, but the proper evident meaning of the words, which not even the ingenuity, or sophistry of the *Caledonian*, can disguise from the meanest capacity. However if this matter admitted of any doubt, it would be removed by the following consideration, viz. that the new constitution is founded upon a dissolution of the present articles of confederation and is an original compact between those states, or rather those individuals who accede to it; consequently all contracts, debts and engagements in favor or against the United States, under the *old* government, are cancelled unless they are provided for in the *new* constitution. The framers of this constitution appear to have been aware of such consequence by stipulating in article 6th, that all debts contracted, and engagements entered into before the adoption of this constitution shall be valid *against* the United States under the new constitution, but there is no provision that the debts, &c. due *to* the United States, shall be valid or recoverable. This is a striking omission, and must have been designed, as debts of the latter description would naturally occur and claim equal attention with the former. This article implied, cancels all debts due to the United States prior to the establishment of the new constitution. If equal provision had been made for the debts due *to* the United States, as *against* the United States, the ex post facto clause would not have so pernicious an operation.

The immaculate convention, that is said to have possessed the fullness of patriotism, wisdom and virtue, contained a number of the principal public defaulters; and these were the most influential members, and chiefly instrumental in the framing of the new constitution: There were several of this description in the deputation from the state of Pennsylvania, who have long standing and immense accounts to settle, and MILLIONS perhaps to refund. The late Financier alone, in the capacity of chairman of the commercial committee of Congress, early in the late war, was entrusted with millions of public money, which to this day remain unaccounted for, nor has he settled his accounts as Financier. The others may also find it a convenient method to balance accounts with the public; they are sufficiently known and therefore need not be designated—This will account for the zealous attachment of such characters to the new constitution and their dread of investigation and discussion. It may be said that the new Congress would rather break through the constitution than suffer the public to be defrauded of so much treasure, when the burthens and distresses of the people are so very great;

but this is not to be expected from the characters of which that Congress would in all probability be composed, if we may judge from the predominant influence and interest these defaulters now possess in many of the states. Besides, should Congress be disposed to violate the fundamental articles of the constitution for the sake of public justice, they would be prevented in so doing by their oaths,* but even if this should not prove an obstacle, if it can be supposed that any set of men would perjure themselves for the public good, and combat an host of enemies on such terms, still it would be of no avail, as there is a further barrier interposed between the public and these defaulters, namely, the supreme court of the union, whose province it would be to determine the constitutionality of any law that may be controverted; and supposing no bribery or corrupt influence practised on the bench of judges, it would be their sworn duty to refuse their sanction to laws made in the face and contrary to the letter and spirit of the constitution, as any law to compel the settlement of accounts and payment of monies depending and due under the old confederation would be. The 1st section of 3d article gives the supreme court cognizance of not only the laws, but of all cases arising under the constitution, which empowers this tribunal to decide upon the construction of the constitution itself in the last resort. This is so extraordinary, so unprecedented an authority, that the intention in vesting of it must have been to put it out of the power of Congress, even by breaking through the constitution, to compel these defaulters to restore the public treasure.

    In the present circumstances these sections of the new constitution would be also productive of great injustice between the respective states; the delinquent states would be exonerated from all existing demands against them on account of the

---

*Article VI. "The senators and representatives beforementioned and the members of the several state legislatures, and all executive and judicial officers, both of the United States and of the several states, shall be bound by oath to support this constitution." Were ever public defaulters so effectually skreened! Not only the administrators of the general government, but also of the state governments, are prevented by oath from doing justice to the public; and the legislature of Pennsylvania could not without perjury insist upon the delinquent states discharging their arrears.

great arrearages of former requisitions, as they could not be constitutionally compelled to discharge them. And as the majority of the states are in this predicament, and have an equal voice in the senate, it would be their interest, and in their power by not only the constitution, but by a superiority of votes to prevent the levying of such arrearages; besides, the constitution, moreover, declares, that all taxes, &c. shall be uniform throughout the United States; which is an additional obstacle against noticing them.

The state of Pennsylvania in such case, would have no credit for her extraordinary exertions and punctuality heretofore; but would be taxed equally with those states which, for years past, have not contributed any thing to the common expences of the union; indeed, some of the states have paid nothing since the revolution.

Philadelphia, 23d February, 1788.

Jeremiah Hill to George Thatcher

Biddleford, Maine, c. February 26, 1788

I can with a good deal of Pleasure anticipate the glory, of this young Empire, dedicated to the fair Godess of Liberty. a friend to his Country when he sees a fair prospect of its increase in Honor & happiness anticipates the future Grandeur naturally resulting to its inhabitants from a well ordered Government. the same as we fond parents do the fair healthy promising boy rising to maturity—I am daily making Calculations for the United States to be adorned with her new *wedding Suit*. I will give you a short account of my Calculations. by the first of April next the present Congress will receive official Intelligence of nine States having adopted the new Constitution, they will then make the proper Arrangements for sending official orders to the several States who have adopted it, to make the resiquite Elections for organizing the new Congress. tho' they wont send out those orders untill every State in the Union has had the Constitution under debate and has either adopted or rejected it if they mean to do either, having made those necessary preresiquites Congress will adjourn leaving a Committee in the interregnum to manage such matters & things as may be necessary during that time, as the present Confederation authorises. then I shall expect to see my old friend again: I have made these Calculations to Mrss. Thatcher I assure you they were not disagreeable to her. . . . To return the several States will receive these official orders by the first of August and by the first of October will have compleated the different Elections, then the present Congress will all return to induct the new Congress agreeable to the Constitution, then I hope we shall all see and enjoy those Halcyon days which has been so long prognosticated, when the *Lincolnians* and *Shaysites* shall lie down together, beat their swords into plowshares and their spears into pruning hooks & learn *Insurgency* no more. then peace &

good order shall invade this Asylum of Liberty where every one shall set in his own Orchard in the Summer, & by his own fire in the winter, and there shall be nothing to make us afraid, only the rod of Correction which shall slay the wicked and ungodly, who shall presume to trample on its laws or violate its Council—I made these Calculations previous to seeing your Letter to brother Lee of the 10th. inst. which he has favored me with the perusal of—by that Letter I fear nine States won't have acted upon the new Constitution according to my Calculations. However, a month or so in the great Scale will be but in comparison of the great whole as a mote in the great Luminary of Heaven . . . the post has not come this way week on Account of the heavy Snow. the man is waiting to carry this to Kennebunk therefore you must excuse my not filing up the third page—

"A Deep Laid Scheme to Enslave Us . . . Invented in the Society of the Cincinnati"

Independent Gazetteer (Philadelphia), February 27, 1788

A correspondent says, that the cause of despotism has met with no very brilliant success in the state of Massachusetts Bay. From among near four hundred members in convention, after all the unfair play that had been used, only a majority of nineteen could be found, for the ratification of the new constitution with amendments. There were 168 who would not adopt the constitution with the proposed amendments, which seems the strongest protest which can be made against it. If the other states therefore should proceed to the ratification of the new constitution we shall be troubled with eternal dissentions. Time and investigation (says our correspondent) will prove that there has been a deep laid scheme to enslave us. This scheme was probably invented in the society of the Cincinnati, who were to start up in every state in favor of the new constitution, and to give their voice as the voice of the people. We have been very neglectful of our interests in suffering this society to exist among us. That the honor is not hereditary does not make the society in any manner less mischievous for the present. Mr. *Rufus King*, in the convention of Massachusetts, had the audacity to confess that there was a secret design in the continental convention, which they wished to conceal till it was ripe for execution. He said to have divulged it would have been as foolish as if General Washington had divulged his scheme to attack the British in Boston, when he planted his cannon upon Dorchester hills.

"Publius," The Federalist LXII
[*James Madison*]

Independent Journal (New York), February 27, 1788

To the People of the State of New-York.

Having examined the constitution of the house of representatives, and answered such of the objections against it as seemed to merit notice, I enter next on the examination of the senate. The heads into which this member of the government may be considered, are—I. the qualifications of senators—II. the appointment of them by the state legislatures—III. the equality of representation in the senate—IV. the number of senators, and the term for which they are to be elected—V. the powers vested in the senate.

I. The qualifications proposed for senators, as distinguished from those of representatives, consist in a more advanced age, and a longer period of citizenship. A senator must be thirty years of age at least; as a representative, must be twenty-five. And the former must have been a citizen nine years; as seven years are required for the latter. The propriety of these distinctions is explained by the nature of the senatorial trust; which requiring greater extent of information and stability of character, requires at the same time that the senator should have reached a period of life most likely to supply these advantages; and which participating immediately in transactions with foreign nations, ought to be exercised by none who are not thoroughly weaned from the prepossessions and habits incident to foreign birth and education. The term of nine years appears to be a prudent mediocrity between a total exclusion of adopted citizens, whose merit and talents may claim a share in the public confidence; and an indiscriminate and hasty admission of them, which might create a channel for foreign influence on the national councils.

II. It is equally unnecessary to dilate on the appointment of senators by the state legislatures. Among the various modes which might have been devised for constituting this branch of the government, that which has been proposed by the convention is probably the most congenial with the public opinion. It is recommended by the double advantage of favouring a select appointment, and of giving to the state governments such an agency in the formation of the federal government, as must secure the authority of the former; and may form a convenient link between the two systems.

III. The equality of representation in the senate is another point, which, being evidently the result of compromise between the opposite pretensions of the large and the small states, does not call for much discussion. If indeed it be right that among a people thoroughly incorporated into one nation, every district ought to have a *proportional* share in the government; and that among independent and sovereign states bound together by simple league, the parties however unequal in size, ought to have an *equal* share in the common councils, it does not appear to be without some reason, that in a compound republic partaking both of the national and federal character, the government ought to be founded on a mixture of the principles of proportional and equal representation. But it is superfluous to try by the standard of theory, a part of the constitution which is allowed on all hands to be the result not of theory, but "of a spirit of amity, and that mutual deference and concession which the peculiarity of our political situation rendered indispensable." A common government with powers equal to its objects, is called for by the voice, and still more loudly by the political situation of America. A government founded on principles more consonant to the wishes of the larger states, is not likely to be obtained from the smaller states. The only option then for the former lies between the proposed government and a government still more objectionable. Under this alternative the advice of prudence must be, to embrace the lesser evil; and instead of indulging a fruitless anticipation of the possible mischiefs which may ensue, to contemplate rather the advantageous consequences which may qualify the sacrifice.

In this spirit it may be remarked, that the equal vote allowed to each state, is at once a constitutional recognition of the portion of sovereignty remaining in the individual states, and an instrument for preserving that residuary sovereignty. So far the equality ought to be no less acceptable to the large than to the small states; since they are not less solicitous to guard by every possible expedient against an improper consolidation of the states into one simple republic.

Another advantage accruing from this ingredient in the constitution of the senate, is the additional impediment it must prove against improper acts of legislation. No law or resolution can now be passed without the concurrence first of a majority of the people, and then of a majority of the states. It must be acknowledged that this complicated check on legislation may in some instances be injurious as well as beneficial; and that the peculiar defence which it involves in favour of the smaller states would be more rational, if any interests common to them, and distinct from those of the other states, would otherwise be exposed to peculiar danger. But as the larger states will always be able by their power over the supplies to defeat unreasonable exertions of this prerogative of the lesser states; and as the facility and excess of law-making seem to be the diseases to which our governments are most liable, it is not impossible that this part of the constitution may be more convenient in practice than it appears to many in contemplation.

IV. The number of senators and the duration of their appointment come next to be considered. In order to form an accurate judgment on both these points, it will be proper to enquire into the purposes which are to be answered by a senate; and in order to ascertain these it will be necessary to review the inconveniencies which a republic must suffer from the want of such an institution.

First. It is a misfortune incident to republican government, though in a less degree than to other governments, that those who administer it, may forget their obligations to their constituents, and prove unfaithful to their important trust. In this point of view, a senate, as a second branch of the legislative assembly, distinct from, and dividing the power with, a first, must be in all cases a salutary check on the government. It doubles the security to the people, by requiring the concurrence of two distinct bodies in schemes of usurpation or perfidy, where the ambition or corruption of one, would otherwise be sufficient. This is a precaution founded on such clear principles, and now so well understood in the United States, that it would be more than superfluous to enlarge on it. I will barely remark that as the improbability of sinister combinations will be in proportion to the dissimilarity in the genius of the two bodies; it must be politic to distinguish them from each other by every circumstance which will consist with a due harmony in all proper measures, and with the genuine principles of republican government.

Secondly. The necessity of a senate is not less indicated by the propensity of all single and numerous assemblies, to yield to the impulse of sudden and violent passions, and to be seduced by factious leaders, into intemperate and pernicious resolutions. Examples on this subject might be cited without number; and from proceedings within the United States, as well as from the history of other nations. But a position that will not be contradicted need not be proved. All that need be remarked is that a body which is to correct this infirmity ought itself be free from it, and consequently ought to be less numerous. It ought moreover to possess great firmness, and consequently ought to hold its authority by a tenure of considerable duration.

Thirdly. Another defect to be supplied by a senate lies in a want of due acquaintance with the objects and principles of legislation. It is not possible that an assembly of men called for the most part from pursuits of a private nature, continued in appointment for a short time, and led by no permanent motive to devote the intervals of public occupation to a study of the laws, the affairs and the comprehensive interests of their country, should, if left wholly to themselves, escape a variety of important errors in the exercise of their legislative trust. It may be affirmed, on the best grounds, that no small share of the present embarrassments of America is to be charged on the blunders of our governments; and that these have proceeded from the heads rather than the hearts of most of the authors of them. What indeed are all the repealing, explaining and amending laws, which fill and disgrace our voluminous codes, but so many monuments of deficient wisdom; so many impeachments exhibited by each succeeding, against each preceding session; so many admonitions to the people of the value of those aids which may be expected from a well constituted senate?

A good government implies two things; first, fidelity to the object of government, which is the happiness of the people; secondly, a knowledge of the means by which that object can be best attained. Some governments are deficient in both these qualities: Most governments are deficient in the first. I scruple not to assert that in the American governments, too little attention has been paid to the last. The federal constitution avoids this error; and what merits particular notice, it provides for the last in a mode which increases the security for the first.

Fourthly. The mutability in the public councils, arising from a rapid succession of new members, however qualified they may be, points out in the strongest manner, the necessity of some stable institution in the government. Every new election in the states, is found to change one half of the representatives. From this change of men must proceed a change of opinions; and from a change of opinions, a change of measures. But a continual change even of good measures is inconsistent with every rule of prudence, and every prospect of success. The remark is verified in private life, and becomes more just as well as more important, in national transactions.

To trace the mischievous effects of a mutable government would fill a volume. I will hint a few only, each of which will be perceived to be a source of innumerable others.

In the first place it forfeits the respect and confidence of other nations, and all the advantages connected with national character. An individual who is observed to be inconstant to his plans, or perhaps to carry on his affairs without any plan at all, is marked at once by all prudent people as a speedy victim to his own unsteadiness and folly. His more friendly neighbours may pity him; but all will decline to connect their fortunes with his; and not a few will seize the opportunity of making their fortunes out of his. One nation is to another what one individual is to another; with this melancholy distinction perhaps, that the former with fewer of the benevolent emotions than the latter, are under fewer restraints also from taking undue advantage of the indiscretions of each other.

Every nation consequently whose affairs betray a want of wisdom and stability, may calculate on every loss which can be sustained from the more systematic policy of its wiser neighbours. But the best instruction on this subject is unhappily conveyed to America by the example of her own situation. She finds that she is held in no respect by her friends; that she is the derision of her enemies; and that she is a prey to every nation which has an interest in speculating on her fluctuating councils and embarrassed affairs.

The internal effects of a mutable policy are still more calamitous. It poisons the blessings of liberty itself. It will be of little avail to the people that the laws are made by men of their own choice, if the laws be so voluminous that they cannot be read, or so incoherent that they cannot be understood; if they be repealed or revised before they are promulged, or undergo such incessant changes that no man who knows what the law is to day can guess what it will be to morrow. Law is defined to be a rule of action; but how can that be a rule, which is little known and less fixed?

Another effect of public instability is the unreasonable advantage it gives to the sagacious, the enterprising and the moneyed few, over the industrious and uninformed mass of the people. Every new regulation concerning commerce or revenue; or in any manner affecting the value of the different species of property, presents a new harvest to those who watch the change, and can trace its consequences; a harvest reared not by themselves but by the toils and cares of the great body of their fellow citizens. This is a state of things in which it may be said with some truth that laws are made for the *few* not for the *many*.

In another point of view great injury results from an unstable government. The want of confidence in the public councils damps every useful undertaking; the success and profit of which may depend on a continuance of existing arrangements. What prudent merchant will hazard his fortunes in any new branch of commerce, when he knows not but that his plans may be rendered unlawful before they can be executed? What farmer or manufacturer will lay himself out for the encouragement given to any particular cultivation or establishment, when he can have no assurance that his preparatory labors and advances will not render him a victim to an inconstant government? In a word no great improvement or laudable enterprise, can go forward, which requires the auspices of a steady system of national policy.

But the most deplorable effect of all is that diminution of attachment and reverence which steals into the hearts of the people, towards a political system which betrays so many marks of infirmity, and disappoints so many of their flattering hopes. No government any more than an individual will long be respected, without being truly respectable, nor be truly respectable without possessing a certain portion of order and stability.

"The Impartial Examiner" I, part 2

Virginia Independent Chronicle (Richmond), February 27, 1788

(*Continued from our last.*)

Section 8th of the first article gives the Congress a power "to lay and collect, taxes, duties, imposts and excises." If it be a true maxim that those, who are entrusted with the exercise of the higher powers of government, ought to observe two essential rules; first in having no other view than the general good of all without any regard to private interest; and secondly, to take equal care of the whole body of the community, so as not to favor one part more than another: it is apparent that under the proposed constitution, this general confederated society, made up of thirteen different states, will have very little security for obtaining an observance, either of the one, or of the other, rule. For being different societies, though blended together in legislation, and having as different interests; to uniform rule for the whole seems to be practicable: and hence, it is to be feared, that the general good may be lost in a mutual attention to private views. From the same causes we may lament the probability of losing the advantage of the second rule; for it may be expected, in like manner, that the general care of the whole will be lost by the separate endeavors of different legislators to favor their own states. So long as mankind continues to be influenced by interest, the surest means of effecting an union of counsels in any assembly is by an union of interests. Now, if it be considered that it is this concert, that it is this union in promoting the *general good*, which alone can preserve concord in this great republic, and secure it success and glory,—unhappy will be the situation of America, if she once precludes the beneficial effects of such a good understanding. Yet, I apprehend that these evils may result in a great measure from an exercise of that branch of legislative authority, which respects internal direct taxation. For in this, it is scarcely probable that the interest, ease or convenience of the several states can be so well consulted in the fœderal assembly, as in their own respective legislatures. So different are many species of property, so various the productions, so unequal the profits arising, even from the same species of property, in different states, that no general mode of contribution can well be adopted in such a manner as at once to affect all in an equitable degree. Hence may arise disagreeable objects of contention. A diversity of interests will produce a diversity of schemes. Thus each state, as it is natural will endeavor to raise a revenue by such means, as may appear least injurious to its own interest: a source of dissention manifestly detrimental to that harmony, which is necessary to support the confederation. I cannot conceive it impracticable to reform the fœderal system in such a manner as to ensure a compliance with the necessary requisitions of Congress from the different state legislatures. Then all the several states being left to raise their own share of the revenue, and being the only proper judges of the mode most convenient to themselves, it is highly probable that this important branch of government would be carried on more generally to the satisfaction of each state; and would tend to promote a spirit of concord between all the parts of this great community. Because *each* being thus accommodated, and participating in the advantages of the union,—*none* subjected to any inconvenience thereby,—*all* would consequently concur in nourishing an affection for the government, which so cemented them.

I believe, it is acknowledged that the establishment of excises has been one of the greatest grievances, under which the English nation has labored for almost a century and an half. Although this may seem an œconomical tax, as arising out of manufactures, from which the *industrious* may derive advantages; and whereof the *wealthy* by consuming the greatest share, will of course contribute the largest proportion of the tax: yet the nature of it being such, as requires severe laws for its execution, it has justly become an object of general detestation. This has induced Judge Blackstone to declare that "the rigour and arbitrary proceedings of excise laws seem hardly compatible with the temper of a free nation." While, therefore, you are freemen—while you are unused to feel any other power, but such as can be exercised within the bounds of moderation and decency, it, doubtless, behoves you to consider whether it is an eligible step to subject yourselves to a new species of authority, which may warrant the most flagrant violations of the sacred rights of habitation. If this branch of revenue takes place, all the consequent rigour of excise laws will necessarily be introduced in order to enforce a due collection. On any charges of offence in this instance you will see yourselves deprived of your boasted trial by jury. The much admired common law process will give way to some quick and summary mode, by which the unhappy defendant will find himself reduced, perhaps to ruin, in less time than a charge could be exhibited against him in the usual course.

It has ever been held that standing armies in times of peace are dangerous to a free country; and no observation seems to contain more reason in it. Besides being useless, as having no object of employment, they are inconvenient and expensive. The soldiery, who are generally composed of the dregs of the people, when disbanded, or unfit for military service, being equally unfit for any other employment, become extremely burthensome. As they are a body of men exempt from the common occupations of social life, having an interest different from the rest of the community, they are wanton in the lap of ease and indolence, without feeling the duties, which arise from the political connection, though drawing their subsistence from the bosom of the state. The severity of discipline necessary to be observed reduces them to a degree of slavery; the unconditional submission to the commands of their superiors, to which they are bound, renders them the fit instruments of tyranny and oppression.—Hence they have in all ages afforded striking examples of contributing, more or less, to enslave mankind;—and whoever will take the trouble to examine, will find that by far the greater part of the different nations, who have fallen from the glorious state of liberty, owe their ruin to standing armies. It has been urged that they are necessary to provide against sudden attacks. Would not a well regulated militia, duly trained to discipline, afford ample security? Such, I conceive, to be the best, the surest means of protection, which a free people can have when not actually engaged in war. This kind of defence is attended with two advantages superior to any others; first, when it is necessary to embody an army, they at once form a band of soldiers, whose interests are uniformly the same with those of the whole community, and in whose safety they see involved every thing that is dear to themselves: secondly, if one army is cut off, another may be immediately raised already trained for military service. By a policy, somewhat similar to this, the Roman empire rose to the highest pitch of grandeur and magnificence.

The supreme court is another branch of fœderal authority, which wears the aspect of imperial jurisdiction, clad in dread array, and spreading its wide domain into all parts of the continent. This is to be co-extensive with the legislature, and, like that, is to swallow up all other courts of judicature.—For what is that judicial power which "shall extend to all cases in law and equity" in some having "original," in all others "appellate jurisdiction," but an establishment universal in its operation? And what is that "appellate jurisdiction both as to law and fact," but an establishment, which may in effect operate as original jurisdiction?—Or what is an appeal to enquire into facts after a solemn adjudication in any court below, but a trial *de novo*? And do not such trials clearly imply an incompetency in the inferior courts to exercise any kind of judicial authority with rectitude? Hence, will not this eventually annihilate their whole jurisdiction? Here is a system of jurisprudence to be erected, no less surprising than it is new and unusual. Here is an innovation, which bears no kind of analogy to any thing, that Englishmen, or Americans, the descendants of Englishmen, have ever yet experienced. Add to all, that this high prerogative court establishes no fundamental rule of proceeding, except that the trial by jury is allowed in some criminal cases. All other cases are left open—and subject "to such regulations as the Congress shall make."— Under these circumstances I beseech you all, as citizens of Virginia, to consider seriously whether you will not endanger the solemn trial by jury, which you have long revered, as a sacred barrier against injustice—which has been established by your ancestors many centuries ago, and transmitted to you, as one of the greatest bulwarks of civil liberty—which you have to this day maintained inviolate:—I beseech you, I say, as members of this commonwealth, to consider whether you will not be in danger of losing this inestimable mode of trial in all those cases, wherein the constitution does not provide for its security. Nay, does not that very provision, which is made, by being confined to a few particular cases, almost imply a total exclusion of the rest? Let it, then, be a reflection deeply impressed on your minds—that if this noble privilege, which by long experience has been found the most exquisite method of determining controversies according to the scale of equal liberty, should once be taken away, it is unknown what new species of trial may be substituted in its room. Perhaps you may be surprised with some strange piece of judicial polity,—some arbitrary method, perhaps confining all trials to the entire decision of the magistracy, and totally excluding the great body of the people from any share in the administration of public justice.

(*To be continued*)

Benjamin Rush to Jeremy Belknap

Philadelphia, February 28, 1788

In answer to your question respecting the conduct & opinions of the quakers in Pennsylvania, I am very happy in being able to inform you that they are all (with an exception of three or four persons only) highly fœderal.—There was a respectable representation of that Society in our Convention, all of whom voted in favor of the New Constitution. They consider very wisely that the Abolition of slavery in our country must be gradual in order to be effectual, and that the Section of the Constitution which will put it in the power of Congress twenty years hence to restrain it altogether, was a great point obtained from the Southern States. The appeals therefore that have been made to the humane & laudable prejudices of our quakers by our Antifœderal writers, upon the Subject of Negro Slavery, have been treated by that prudent Society with Silence and Contempt.—

Some of the same reasons have operated upon me, that have influenced you to admire & prefer the new government. If it held forth no other advantages that a future exemption from paper money & tender laws, it would be eno' to recommend it to honest men. To look up to a government that encourages Virtue—establishes justice ensures order, secures property—and protects from every Species of Violence, affords a pleasure that can only be exceeded by looking up in all circumstances to a *general providence*. Such a pleasure I hope is before us & our posterity under the influence of the new Government.—

The arguments, or to express myself more properly—the Objections of your minority, were in many respects the same as those which were urged by the Speakers in behalf of the minority of Pennsylvania. They both suppose that the men who are to be entrusted with the supreme power of our Country will become at once the receptacles of all the depravity of human nature.—They forget that they are to be part of ourselves, and if we may judge of their future conduct by what we have too Often Observed in the State governments, the Members of the fœderal legislature, will much Oftener injure their constituents by voting agreeably to their inclinations, than *against* them.

But in cherishing jealousies of our rulers, we are too apt to overlook the weaknesses & vices of the people. Is not history as full of examples of both in them, as it is of the crimes of kings? What is the present moral character of the inhabitants of the united States? I need not describe it. It proves too plainly that the *people*, are as much disposed to Vice, as their rulers, and that nothing but a vigorous & efficient government can prevent their degenerating into Savages, or devouring each other like beasts of prey.—

I pant for the time when the establishment of the new government, and the Safety to individuals which shall arise from it, shall excuse men who like myself wish only to be passengers, from performing the duty of Sailors on board the political Ship in which our all is embarked.—I have yeilded to a deep Sense of the extreme danger of my Country, in quitting the cabin for a Station at the pump. As soon as the storm is over, and our bark safely moored, the first wish of my heart will be to devote the whole of my time to the peaceable pursuits of Science, and to the pleasures of social and domestic life.—

"Brutus" XIV

New York Journal, February 28 and March 6, 1788

The second paragraph of sect. 2d. art. 3, is in these words: "In all cases affecting ambassadors, other public ministers and consuls, and those in which a state shall be a party, the supreme court shall have original jurisdiction. In all the other cases before mentioned, the supreme court shall have appellate jurisdiction, both as to law and fact, with such exceptions, and under such regulations as the Congress shall make."

Although it is proper that the courts of the general government should have cognizance of all matters affecting ambassadors, foreign ministers, and consuls; yet I question much the propriety of giving the supreme court original jurisdiction in all cases of this kind.

Ambassadors, and other public ministers, claim, and are entitled by the law of nations, to certain privileges, and exemptions, both for their persons and their servants.

The meanest servant of an ambassador is exempted by the law of nations from being sued for debt. Should a suit be brought against such an one by a citizen, through inadvertency or want of information, he will be subject to an action in the supreme court. All the officers concerned in issuing or executing the process will be liable to like actions. Thus may a citizen of a state be compelled, at great expence and inconveniency, to defend himself against a suit, brought against him in the supreme court, for inadvertently commencing an action against the most menial servant of an ambassador for a just debt.

The appellate jurisdiction granted to the supreme court, in this paragraph, has justly been considered as one of the most objectionable parts of the constitution: under this power, appeals may be had from the inferior courts to the supreme, in

every case to which the judicial power extends, except in the
few instances in which the supreme court will have original
jurisdiction.

By this article, appeals will lie to the supreme court, in all
criminal as well as civil causes. This I know, has been disputed
by some; but I presume the point will appear clear to any
one, who will attend to the connection of this paragraph with
the one that precedes it. In the former, all the cases, to which
the power of the judicial shall extend, whether civil or criminal, are enumerated. There is no criminal matter, to which the
judicial power of the United States will extend; but such as
are included under some one of the cases specified in this section. For this section is extended to define all the cases, of
every description, to which the power of the judicial shall
reach. But in all these cases it is declared, the supreme court
shall have appellate jurisdiction, except in those which affect
ambassadors, other public ministers and consuls, and those in
which a state shall be a party. If then this section extends the
power of the judicial, to criminal cases, it allows appeals in
such cases. If the power of the judicial is not extended to
criminal matters by this section, I ask, by what part of this
system does it appear, that they have any cognizance of them?

I believe it is a new and unusual thing to allow appeals in
criminal matters. It is contrary to the sense of our laws, and
dangerous to the lives and liberties of the citizen. As our law
now stands, a person charged with a crime has a right to a fair
and impartial trial by a jury of his country, and their verdict is
final. If he is acquitted no other court can call upon him to
answer for the same crime. But by this system, a man may
have had ever so fair a trial, have been acquitted by ever so
respectable a jury of his country; and still the officer of the
government who prosecutes, may appeal to the supreme
court. The whole matter may have a second hearing. By this
means, persons who may have disobliged those who execute
the general government, may be subjected to intolerable oppression. They may be kept in long and ruinous confinement,
and exposed to heavy and insupportable charges, to procure
the attendence of witnesses, and provide the means of their
defence, at a great distance from their places of residence.

I can scarcely believe there can be a considerate citizen of

the United States, that will approve of this appellate jurisdiction, as extending to criminal cases, if they will give themselves time for reflection.

Whether the appellate jurisdiction as it respects civil matters, will not prove injurious to the rights of the citizens, and
destructive of those privileges which have ever been held
sacred by Americans, and whether it will not render the administration of justice intolerably burthensome, intricate, and
dilatory, will best appear, when we have considered the
nature and operation of this power.

It has been the fate of this clause, as it has of most of those,
against which unanswerable objections have been offered, to
be explained different ways, by the advocates and opponents
to the constitution. I confess I do not know what the advocates of the system, would make it mean, for I have not been
fortunate enough to see in any publication this clause taken
up and considered. It is certain however, they do not admit
the explanation which those who oppose the constitution give
it, or otherwise they would not so frequently charge them
with want of candor, for alledging that it takes away the trial
by jury, appeals from an inferior to a superior court, as practised in the civil law courts, are well understood. In these
courts, the judges determine both on the law and the fact;
and appeals are allowed from the inferior to the superior
courts, on the whole merits: the superior tribunal will re-
examine all the facts as well as the law, and frequently new
facts will be introduced, so as many times to render the cause
in the court of appeals very different from what it was in the
court below.

If the appellate jurisdiction of the supreme court, be understood in the above sense, the term is perfectly intelligible. The
meaning then is, that in all the civil causes enumerated, the
supreme court shall have authority to re-examine the whole
merits of the case, both with respect to the facts and the law
which may arise under it, without the intervention of a jury;
that this is the sense of this part of the system appears to me
clear, from the express words of it, "in all the other cases before mentioned, the supreme court shall have appellate jurisdiction, both as to law and fact, &c." Who are the supreme
court? Does it not consist of the judges? and they are to have

the same jurisdiction of the fact as they are to have of the law. They will therefore have the same authority to determine the fact as they will have to determine the law, and no room is left for a jury on appeals to the supreme court.

If we understand the appellate jurisdiction in any other way, we shall be left utterly at a loss to give it a meaning; the common law is a stranger to any such jurisdiction: no appeals can lie from any of our common law courts, upon the merits of the case; the only way in which they can go up from an inferior to a superior tribunal is by habeas corpus before a hearing, or by certiorari, or writ of error, after they are determined in the subordinate courts; but in no case, when they are carried up, are the facts re-examined, but they are always taken as established in the inferior court.

(To be continued.)

(Continued.)

It may still be insisted that this clause does not take away the trial by jury on appeals, but that this may be provided for by the legislature, under that paragraph which authorises them to form regulations and restrictions for the court in the exercise of this power.

The natural meaning of this paragraph seems to be no more than this, that Congress may declare, that certain cases shall not be subject to the appellate jurisdiction, and they may point out the mode in which the court shall proceed in bringing up the causes before them, the manner of their taking evidence to establish the facts, and the method of the courts proceeding. But I presume they cannot take from the court the right of deciding on the fact, any more than they can deprive them of the right of determining on the law, when a cause is once before them; for they have the same jurisdiction as to fact, as they have as to the law. But supposing the Congress may under this clause establish the trial by jury on appeals. It does not seem to me that it will render this article much less exceptionable. An appeal from one court and jury, to another court and jury, is a thing altogether unknown in the laws of our state, and in most of the states in the union. A practice of this kind prevails in the eastern states; actions are there commenced in the inferior courts, and an appeal lies from them on the whole merits to the superior courts: the consequence is well known, very few actions are determined in the lower courts; it is rare that a case of any importance is not carried by appeal to the supreme court, and the jurisdiction of the inferior courts is merely nominal; this has proved so burthensome to the people in Massachusetts, that it was one of the principal causes which excited the insurrection in that state, in the year past; very few sensible and moderate men in that state but what will admit, that the inferior courts are almost entirely useless, and answer very little purpose, save only to accumulate costs against the poor debtors who are already unable to pay their just debts.

But the operation of the appellate power in the supreme judicial of the United States, would work infinitely more mischief than any such power can do in a single state.

The trouble and expence to the parties would be endless and intolerable. No man can say where the supreme court are to hold their sessions, the presumption is, however, that it must be at the seat of the general government: in this case parties must travel many hundred miles, with their witnesses and lawyers, to prosecute or defend a suit; no man of midling fortune, can sustain the expence of such a law suit, and therefore the poorer and midling class of citizens will be under the necessity of submitting to the demands of the rich and the lordly, in cases that will come under the cognizance of this court. If it be said, that to prevent this oppression, the supreme court will set in different parts of the union, it may be replied, that this would only make the oppression somewhat more tolerable, but by no means so much as to give a chance of justice to the poor and midling class. It is utterly impossible that the supreme court can move into so many different parts of the Union, as to make it convenient or even tolerable to attend before them with witnesses to try causes from every part of the United states; if to avoid the expence and inconvenience of calling witnesses from a great distance, to give evidence before the supreme court, the expedient of taking the deposition of witnesses in writing should be adopted, it would not help the matter. It is of great importance in the distribution of justice that witnesses should be examined face to face, that the parties should have the fairest opportunity of cross examining them in order to bring out the whole truth; there is something in the manner in which a witness delivers his testimony which cannot be committed to paper, and which yet very frequently gives a complexion to his evidence, very different from what it would bear if committed to writing, besides the expence of taking written testimony would be enormous; those who are acquainted with the costs that arise in the courts, where all the evidence is taken in writing, well known that they exceed beyond all comparison those of the common law courts, where witnesses are examined viva voce.

The costs accruing in courts generally advance with the grade of the court; thus the charges attending a suit in our common pleas, is much less than those in the supreme court, and these are much lower than those in the court of chancery; indeed the costs in the last mentioned court, are in many cases so exorbitant and the proceedings so dilatory that the suitor had almost as well give up his demand as to prosecute his suit. We have just reason to suppose, that the costs in the supreme general court will exceed either of our courts; the officers of the general court will be more dignified than those of the states, the lawyers of the most ability will practice in them, and the trouble and expence of attending them will be greater. From all these considerations, it appears, that the expence attending suits in the supreme court will be so great, as to put it out of the power of the poor and midling class of citizens to contest a suit in it.

From these remarks it appears, that the administration of justice under the powers of the judicial will be dilatory; that it will be attended with such an heavy expence as to amount to little short of a denial of justice to the poor and middling class of people who in every government stand most in need of the protection of the law; and that the trial by jury, which has so justly been the boast of our fore fathers as well as ourselves is taken away under them.

These extraordinary powers in this court are the more objectionable, because there does not appear the least necessity for them, in order to secure a due and impartial distribution of justice.

The want of ability or integrity, or a disposition to render justice to every suitor, has not been objected against the courts of the respective states: so far as I have been informed, the courts of justice in all the states, have ever been found ready, to administer justice with promptitude and impartiality according to the laws of the land; It is true in some of the states, paper money has been made, and the debtor authorised to discharge his debts with it, at a depreciated value, in others, tender laws have been passed, obliging the creditor to receive on execution other property than money in discharge of his demand, and in several of the states laws have been made unfavorable to the creditor and tending to render property insecure.

But these evils have not happened from any defect in the judicial departments of the states; the courts indeed are bound to take notice of these laws, and so will the courts of the general government be under obligation to observe the laws made by the general legislature; not repugnant to the constitution; but so far have the judicial been from giving undue latitude of construction to laws of this kind, that they have invariably strongly inclined to the other side. All the acts of our legislature, which have been charged with being of this complexion, have uniformly received the strictest construction by the judges, and have been extended to no cases but to such as came within the strict letter of the law. In this way, have our courts, I will not say evaded the law, but so limited it in its operation as to work the least possible injustice: the same thing has taken place in Rhode-Island, which has justly rendered herself infamous, by her tenaciously adhering to her paper money system. The judges there gave a decision, in opposition to the words of the Statute, on this principle, that a construction according to the words of it, would contradict the fundamental maxims of their laws and constitution.

No pretext therefore, can be formed, from the conduct of the judicial courts which will justify giving such powers to the supreme general court, for their decisions have been such as to give just ground of confidence in them, that they will firmly adhere to the principles of rectitude, and there is no necessity of lodging these powers in the courts, in order to guard against the evils justly complained of, on the subject of security of property under this constitution. For it has provided, "that no state shall emit bills of credit, or make any thing but gold and silver coin a tender in payment of debts." It has also declared, that "no state shall pass any law impairing the obligation of contracts."—These prohibitions give the most perfect security against those attacks upon property which I am sorry to say some of the states have but too wantonly made, by passing laws sanctioning fraud in the debtor against his creditor. For "this constitution will be the supreme law of the land, and the judges in every state will be bound thereby; any thing in the constitution and laws of any state to the contrary notwithstanding."

The courts of the respective states might therefore have been securely trusted, with deciding all cases between man and man, whether citizens of the same state or of different states, or between foreigners and citizens, and indeed for ought I see every case that can arise under the constitution or laws of the United States, ought in the first instance to be tried in the court of the state, except those which might arise between states, such as respect ambassadors, or other public ministers, and perhaps such as call in question the claim of lands under grants from different states. The state courts would be under sufficient controul, if writs of error were allowed from the state courts to the supreme court of the union, according to the practice of the courts in England and of this state, on all cases in which the laws of the union are concerned, and perhaps to all cases in which a foreigner is a party.

This method would preserve the good old way of administering justice, would bring justice to every man's door, and preserve the inestimable right of trial by jury. It would be following, as near as our circumstances will admit, the practice of the courts in England, which is almost the only thing I would wish to copy in their government.

But as this system now stands, there is to be as many inferior courts as Congress may see fit to appoint, who are to be authorised to originate and in the first instance to try all the cases falling under the description of this article; there is no security that a trial by jury shall be had in these courts, but the trial here will soon become, as it is in Massachusetts' inferior courts, mere matter of form; for an appeal may be had to the supreme court on the whole merits. This court is to have power to determine in law and in equity, on the law and the fact, and this court is exalted above all other power in the government, subject to no controul, and so fixed as not to be removeable, but upon impeachment, which I shall hereafter shew, is much the same thing as not to be removeable at all.

To obviate the objections made to the judicial power it has been said, that the Congress, in forming the regulations and exceptions which they are authorised to make respecting the appellate jurisdiction, will make provision against all the evils which are apprehended from this article. On this I would re-mark, that this way of answering the objection made to the power, implies an admission that the power is in itself im-proper without restraint, and if so, why not restrict it in the first instance.

The just way of investigating any power given to a govern-ment, is to examine its operation supposing it to be put in exercise. If upon enquiry, it appears that the power, if exer-cised, would be prejudicial, it ought not to be given. For to answer objections made to a power given to a government, by saying it will never be exercised, is really admitting that the power ought not to be exercised, and therefore ought not to be granted.

Joseph Spencer to James Madison, Enclosing John Leland's Objections

Orange County, Virginia, February 28, 1788

The Federal Constitution, has it Enimyes in Orange as well as in other parts, Col. Thos. Barber offers as a Candedit for our March Election, he is as grate an Enimy to it as he posably can be, & if not as grate as any it has, as grate as his abiliteys will alow him to be, which if our County men admired his Politickes no more than I do, the Constitution would have but Little to fear from that Quarter, but his unwared Labours riding his Carquits & the Instruments he makes use of to Obtain his Election, misrepresents things in such Horred carrecters that the weker clas of the people are much predegessed agains it. by which meens he has many which as yet, appears grately in favour of him, amoungs his Friends appears, in a General way the Baptus's, the Prechers of that Society are much alarm'd fearing relegious liberty is not Sufficiently secur'd thay pretend to other objections but that I think is the principle objection, could that be removed by sum one Caperable of the Task. I think thay would become friends to it, that body of people has become very formible in pint of Elections, as I can think of no Gentln. of my Acquaintance so Suitible to the Task as your Self. I have taken the liberty to Request it of you, several of your Conections in Orange Joines me in oppinion, thinking it would answer a Valuable purpus for I am Cartain that pople relye much on your integerity & Candure, Mr. Leeland & Mr. Bledsoe and Sanders are the most publick men of that Society in Orange, therefore as Mr. Leeland Lyes in your Way home from Fredricksburg to Orange would advise you'l call on him & spend a few Howers in his Company, in Clos'd youl receive his objections, which was Sent by me to, Barber, a Coppy I tooke, this copy was first Design'd for Capt Walker, but as I hoped youl be in this state in a few days thought proper to Send it to you, by which means youl be made Acquainted with their objections & have time to Consider them should you think it an Object worth yr Attention, my fears are that Except you & yr friends do Exerte yr Selves Very much youl not obtain yr Election in Orange Such are the predegeses of the people for in short there is nothing so Vile, but what the Constitution is Charged with, hope to See you in Orange in a few days

———

According, to your request, I have send you my objections to the *Fœderal Constitution*, which are as follows,

1st. There is no Bill Rights, whenever Number of men enter into a State of Socity, a Number of individual Rights must be given up to Socity, but there should always be a memorial of those not surrendred, otherwise every natural & domestic Right becomes alianable, which raises Tyranny at once, & this is as necessary in one Form of Goverment as in another—

2nd. There is a Contradiction in the Constitution, we are first inform'd that all Legislative Powers therein granted shall be Vested in a Congress, composed of *two houses*, & yet afterwards all the power that lies between a Majority two thirds, which is one Sixth part, is taken from these *two Houses*, and given to one man, who is not only chosen two removes from the people, but also the head of the executive Department—

3rd. The House of Representatives is the only free, direct Representation of the body of the people, & yet in Treaties which are to be some of the Supreme Laws of the Land, this House has no Voice—

4th. The time place & Manner of chusing the Members of the Lower house is intirely at the Mercy of Congress, if they Appoint Pepin or Japan, or their ten Miles Square for the place, no man can help it.—how can Congress guarantee to each state a republican form of Government, when every principle of Republicanism is Sapped—

5th. The Senators are chosen for Six years, & when they are once Chosen, they are impeachable to nun but themselves, No Counterpoize is left in the hands of the People, or even in

Legislative Bodys to check them, Vote as they will, there they sit, paying themselves at Pleasure—

6th I utterly oppose any Division in Legislative Body, the more Houses, the more parties,—the more they are Divided; the more the Wisdom is Scattered, sometimes one house may prevent the Error of another & the same stands true of twenty Houses But the Question is, whether they do more good then harm the Business is cartainly thereby retarded & the Expence inhansed

7th. We are not informed whether Votes in all cases in the lower house are to be by Members or by States,—I Question wheather a man could find out the Riddle by plowing with Sampsons Heifer, if each Member is not to have a Vote why are they to be chosen according to the Numbers of Inhabitants, & why should Virginia be at ten-times the Expence of Deleware for the same power, if the Votes are always to be by States, why is it not Expressed as in the choise of a President, in cartain Cases, If each member is to have a Vote, Why is it Expressed concarning Senators, & not Concarning Representatives, this Blank appears to me, to be designed, to encourage the Small States with hops of Equality, & the Large States with Hopes of Superiority—

8ly. We have no assurance that the liberty of the press will be allowed under this Constitution—

9ly. We have been always taught that it was dangerous Mixing the Legislative & Executive powers together in the same body of People but in this Constitution, we are taught better, or worse—

10ly. What is dearest of all—*Religious Liberty*, is not Sufficiently Secured, No religious test is required as a Qualification to fill any office under the United States, but if a Majority of Congress with the presedent favour one Systom more then another, they may oblige all others to pay to the Support of their System as Much as they please, & if Oppression dose not ensue, it will be owing to the Mildness of Administration & not to any Constitutional defense, & if the Manners of People are so far Corrupted, that they cannot live by republican principles, it is Very Dangerous leaving religious Liberty at their Marcy—

Rhode Island's Assembly Refuses to Call a Convention and Submits the Constitution Directly to the People

Providence, February 29 and March 1, 1788

FRIDAY, *February* 29, 1788.   A. M.

The House proceeded in hearing private Petitions, until they adjourned for Dinner.

P. M.

A Motion was made by Mr. *Sayles* [*Smithfield*] and seconded by Mr. *Childs* [*Warren*] that the House do now proceed to the Consideration of the Dispatches from Congress, on the Subject of the proposed Federal Constitution.—Upon which Mr. Joslyn [*West-Greenwich*] made a Motion to the following Purport:—"That the Constitution for the United States, proposed by the late Federal Convention, be submitted to the Freemen of the several Towns in this State, in Town-Meetings assembled, for their Decision; and that the Yeas and Nays be registered in the several Towns, in the same Manner as it is now done for the Choice of General Officers."—This Motion was seconded by Mr. *Hazard* [*Charlestown*.]

After a pretty lengthy Discussion of the Propriety of submitting it in this Way, the Vote was finally put—Whether it should be submitted to a Convention, chosen as in the other States—or to the People at large, and was carried against a Convention, by a Majority of 28—15 voting for a Convention, and 43 for submitting it to the People at large.

In Course of discussing this Question, it was observed—That by the proposed Constitution the People were called upon to surrender a Part of their Liberties; that they were the best Judges what Part they ought to give up:—That the Legislature had no legal Right to appoint a Convention to alter the Constitution:—That they were not deputed for that Purpose:—That the Citizens of some other States, had by the

270

Means of appointing Conventions, been decoyed into an Adoption of the Constitution, when, it was asserted, at least Two-Thirds of the Inhabitants of some of the States that had agreed to it, were against the Constitution:—That submitting it to every Individual Freeholder of the State was the only Mode by which the *true* Sentiments of the People could be collected.—It was replied—That this Mode was without Precedent on the Face of the Earth:—That all the United States, except this, had appointed Conventions; and that we ought to pay some Deference to the Opinions, at least of those in the different States who oppose the new Constitution, if not of those who wish it adopted—in not one of which such a Motion as this had been made:—That by Meeting in Convention the Sentiments of the best Men in the State would be collected;—the different *Interests* would there be represented—the *Mechanics* might there shew how far it would be advantageous or disadvantageous for *their* particular Interest to have it adopted or rejected: The *Farmers*—the *Merchants*—might in the same Manner be satisfied: All this would be lost by Meeting in the different Towns, in each of which but *one Interest* or at most but *two*, could be considered.

The principal Speakers were, for a Convention—Mr. *Bradford*, Mr. *Marchant*, Mr. *Champlin*, Mr. *Arnold*, and Mr. *Bourne*:—For referring it to the several Town-Meetings—Mr. *Hazard*, Mr. *Joslyn*, and Mr. *Comstock*.—After the Question was decided, Mr. *Hazard*, Mr. *Joslyn*, and Mr. *Sheldon* were appointed a Committee to draft a Bill, agreeable to the Vote, and lay the same before the House.—Adjourned to Saturday Morning.

SATURDAY, *March* 1, 1788.   A. M.

The House proceeded to hear private Petitions.—Just before they adjourned for Dinner, the Committee appointed last Evening reported a Bill, which was read, and ordered to lie on the Table.

P. M.

The Bill for submitting the Federal Constitution to the People at large, reported by the Committee, was taken up for Debate—when Mr. *Whipple* [*Cranston*] motioned, as an Amendment, that the People at large, when the Constitution

is before them in Town-Meeting, have Liberty to propose a
Convention, which Motion was seconded by Mr. *Bourne*
[*Providence*] but the Speaker said, this was contrary to the
Rules of the House—as their Sense on that Subject had been
fully taken the preceding Evening by the Vote, Whether it
should be submitted to the Towns or a Convention.

Upon this, Mr. *Marchant* [*Newport*] stated a Motion in
Writing, to this Purport:—"That when the Federal Constitution is before the People in Town-Meeting, that any Freeman or Freeholder of the State may, instead of giving his
Yea or Nay on the Question, give his Voice for calling a Convention of the State, by Delegates, to take up and discuss the
Subject."

This Motion met the same Opposition from the Speaker,
and some of the Members, as that made by Commodore
Whipple, and on the same Ground.—It was said, that the
Sense of the House had been already taken on the Subject:—
That the People could, if they saw fit, give Instructions to
their Representatives in General Assembly to have a Convention called, and if there should be a Majority of them, no
Doubt the House would agree to call one; but the Bill was
drawn agreeable to the Sense of the House—and, at present,
there was no Need of calling on the People to vote for a Convention—it would be distracting the State, already much convulsed by Parties, and answer no good Purpose whatever.

It was replied—That no Doubt many Persons in each
Town in the State would think a Convention chosen pur-
posely to discuss the Subject, would be more eligible than
voting singly, either to adopt or reject the Constitution—and
would the House undertake to deprive such of the Privilege
of having a Convention called;—it had been said it was submitted to the People at large, in Deference to the Privileges of
the Citizens—but if this Mode was adopted, many would be
deprived of their Privileges.

After a lengthy and warm Debate, in which Mr. *Bradford*,
Mr. *Marchant*, Mr. *Arnold*, Mr. *Champlin*, and Mr. *Bourne*, in
Favour of the Amendment, and Mr. *Hazard*, Mr. *Joslyn*, Mr.
Comstock, and Mr. *Sheldon*, against it, exerted themselves
pretty strenuously, the Question was put—not, whether the
proposed Amendment should be adopted—but, whether the

Bill should pass—and was carried by a Majority of 30—42 voting for the Bill, and 12 against it.—Those who voted against the Bill generally declaring that with the Amendment they would not oppose it.

After the Bill was passed, a Motion was made and seconded, That it be amended—but it was lost by a Majority of 20—16 voting for the Motion, and 36 against it.

In the Evening a Vote was passed, directing the Hon. *Peleg Arnold*, and *Jonathan J. Hazard*, Esq'rs. Two of the Delegates from this State, to proceed immediately to New-York, and take their Seats in Congress; and a Grant on the Treasury for a Sum of Money was made each of them. A Vote was also past, directing the General-Treasurer to pay a third Quarter Part on the public Securities, to all Persons applying for the same.——Some private Business closed the Session.

WHEN the aforementioned Bill, for referring the proposed National Constitution to the several Town-Meetings, came before the Upper House, it did not meet with the concurrence of all the Members. —The following is a very brief statement of the arguments on the question of concurrence. —It was objected, that the whole body of the people, individually and collectively, have a right to be consulted, and to give their voices in forming a Constitution, by which they are to be governed —That as the body of the people collectively considered, and who form the State, consists of a number of individuals, all personally interested in the proposed government, they ought to have an opportunity of meeting and consulting together, on the propriety and expediency of adopting it —of rejecting it —of proposing amendments, or any other measures they may think will promote the public good —That as it is inconvenient, and perhaps even impossible, in a State no larger than this for all the individuals to assemble together, it was therefore necessary from the nature of things to introduce the idea of representation, in which case the mode of calling upon the people to join in appointing agents, or representatives, for themselves in a Convention of the whole, appears the only proper method. —That in this way every man who chooses it may personally aid and give his voice in the formation and establishment of a body, which coming from every part of the State could conveniently meet, consult and act together, and repre-

senting all parts of the community, with all the different interests, trades and professions, and having the collected sense and wisdom of a free people, could reason, confer with and convince each other, that finally they might judge and determine what was best for the whole —That the proposed Bill, though it gave every person an opportunity to enter his assent or dissent, precluded all the before-mentioned advantages arising from a general Convention, and excluded the light and information which one part of the State could afford to the other by means thereof—That it gave opportunity for misrepresentations to be made, to influence a decision, either one way or the other, and had a tendency to throw the State into parties opposed to each other, to raise jealousies and animosities, without any apparent benefit therefrom, especially if some towns, as would probably be the case, should be generally in favour of the proposed Constitution, while others were as generally opposed to it, without knowing the particular motives of each other's conduct, or having the means, by argumentation and neighbourly conference, of persuading each other into an harmonious concurrence in such measures as would probably promote the real interest and happiness of the whole. —It was also argued, that taking the sense of the people in the manner proposed by the Bill, was not complying with the recommendation of the Convention, or of Congress, and that it tended to deprive the people at large in this State, of that weight and influence in forming or directing the national government of the United States, which they would have by means of a Convention —That this measure was unprecedented in history—and that after the question was taken in this way, it could not be considered as decisive, because not taken from the people in their assembled collective capacity, the only mode in which a major vote is considered to be binding on the minority—a sentiment advanced and established by the writings of Puffendorf, Grotius, and the greatest civilians, on the nature and origin of government.

On the other hand, in favour of the Bill, besides what is contained in the preamble, it was argued, that as this State had not sent delegates to the Convention at Philadelphia, and had not, as a State, joined in forming the proposed Constitution, the business was reduced simply to this question—Will this State agree to this Constitution or not?—*That had this State joined in the appointment of the Convention at Philadelphia, the matter would have rested on a different footing, as such an appointment would have implied the assent of the people to alterations or amendments of the Confederation; in which case a Convention might be proper to ratify or reject it—That the people individually have a right to determine for themselves, whether they will consent to any alterations in the constitutional form of their government; and as they had not been consulted upon the matter, it was therefore proper to refer the proposed national Constitution to them, as individuals, that they might declare, whether it was agreeable to them or not, which would appear on the question being taken in the manner proposed by the Bill—That in either case a Convention could then be called, to ratify and establish the proposed Constitution, if a majority of the people were in favour of it.—But if it appeared that they were not in favour of it as it stands, to propose such alterations or amendments, or other measures, as a majority of the Convention empowered for that purpose might agree to—That submitting the Constitution to the consideration of the freemen in the manner pointed out by this Bill, was the only proper mode of clearing the way, and opening a door for a State Convention, if the people in general should think one necessary:—It was also argued, That as no provision is made by the Convention, at Philadelphia, for alterations or amendments, it was uncertain whether it would answer any purpose to propose them; so that a Convention might be attended only with a fruitless expence, and that the sense of the people could be more fully and better taken in their respective towns, than by a Convention, who possibly might act contrary to the sentiments and wishes of their constituents.*

The question, of concurrence in favour of the Bill becoming a law, was finally carried by a great majority.

The Freemen of Providence Submit Eight Reasons for Calling a Convention

March 26, 1788

Proceedings of the Town of Providence on the FEDERAL CONSTITUTION.

At a TOWN-MEETING *of the* FREEMEN *of the Town of* PROVI-DENCE, *legally assembled on the* 24th *Day of March, A. D.* 1788.

The Hon. JABEZ BOWEN, Esq; Moderator.

RESOLVED, That David Howell, John I. Clark, Thomas Arnold, Theodore Foster, and Benjamin Bourne, Esquires, be, and they are hereby appointed, a Committee to draught a Petition to the Honorable the General Assembly, that a Convention of Delegates may be recommended by the Legislature of this State, to be convened, agreeably to the concurrent Resolutions of the Convention of the United States and of Congress, for considering and deciding on the new Constitution.

A true copy:
Witness,   DANIEL COOKE, T. Clerk.

At a TOWN-MEETING *of the* FREEMEN *of the Town of* PROVI-DENCE, *legally assembled* (*by Adjournment*) *at the State-House, on the* 26th *Day of March, A. D.* 1788.

WHEREAS the Committee appointed on the 24th instant, to draught a Petition to the Honorable the General Assembly, that a Convention of Delegates may be recommended by the Legislature, to be called for considering the Constitution for the United States, transmitted by Congress to this State, have this day made their report; which, having had two several readings, Resolved, That the same be received: And it is further resolved unanimously, That a copy thereof be made out and signed by the Clerk, in behalf of this meeting, and delivered to the Deputies of this town to be preferred to the Honorable the General Assembly, to be holden (by adjournment) at East-Greenwich, in the County of Kent, on the last Monday in March instant.

A true copy:

Witness,   DANIEL COOKE, T. Clerk.

The Petition above referred to, is in the words following, to wit: ──

To the Honorable the GENERAL ASSEMBLY of the State of RHODE-ISLAND, &c.,

The PETITION *of the* FREEMEN *of the Town of* PROVIDENCE, *in Town-Meeting legally assembled (by Adjournment) on the 26th Day of March, A. D.* 1788,

HUMBLY SHEWETH,

THAT your Petitioners being assembled in pursuance of an act passed by the Legislature of this State, at their session in February last, *submitting to the consideration of the freemen of this State the report of the Convention of Delegates for a Constitution for the United States, as agreed on in Philadelphia the 17th of September, A. D.* 1787—and feeling themselves deeply impressed with the weight and magnitude of the subject, under reference to them, beg leave, with most respectful deference, to lay before the Honorable Legislature the unanimous result of their most calm and deliberate considerations and discussions on this subject.

The formation of a Constitution, or fundamental laws for a State, your Petitioners consider as the most arduous, as well as most important work to which the people can be called: It therefore seems to require not only the exercise of the wisdom and experience of all the people, but that this wisdom and experience should have full scope to display itself to advantage; and that all the Members should severally be put into a situation to profit and be edified by each other.—The most natural and simple idea of the mode of proceeding in this business, among a people resolved into a state of nature, would seem to be, that all the people should be assembled on some spacious plain, to consult on the subject, discuss and adopt a Constitution for themselves. In antient times, and in small republics, this measure has been taken with success; but in the present case, where is the spot commodious for assembling all the freemen of this State?—And where is the man who could be heard to advantage by such a numerous assembly?—In this method therefore in vain do we seek for the benefit of the wisdom of our friends in other parts of the State, to assist our reason and guide our judgment in this momentous affair.

These observations will yet become more striking when applied to the Federal Union, and the doctrine of *Representation* will force itself on our minds in an instant. Such is the weakness of the human mind in its most improved state, and such the shortness of human life, that it has been found necessary to divide and parcel out the business thereof, into various hands, to the end, that each may avail himself of the skill and experience of all others, in their various occupations, and a mutual dependence on each other become the interest and safety of all.

Your Petitioners apprehend that Representation is a fundamental principle in the existing Constitution of this State.— The laws which operate throughout the State are made by Representatives of the people, and could not be regularly made by an assembly of all the freemen, or acting at home in their several Town-Meetings: In neither of which cases, could the parties to be affected more immediately by such laws have an opportunity to be heard with convenience, and to have their reasons examined and discussed with candour and deliberation.—When therefore a subject of universal concernment offers itself for the consideration and discussion of the freemen of the State, and which cannot regularly be passed upon by the ordinary Representatives, assembled in their legislative capacity, in orderly pursuance of the existing principle of Representation, other Representatives for the special purpose of deciding thereon, as it would seem to your Petitioners, should be appointed.

It doth not appear to your Petitioners, that either the Federal Convention or Congress have attempted to deprive the freemen of this State of the benefits to be expected from an examination, discussion and decision on the subject now under reference to them, by a State Convention for that special purpose.

The great Federal Convention, held at Philadelphia, resolved that their work should *"be laid before the United States in Congress assembled;"* and the President's letter adds, that it is *"submitted to the consideration of the United States in Congress assembled;"* by which expressions it was clearly open to amendments by Congress at their pleasure; and we are informed that such amendments were in fact proposed in Congress, but not adopted.

The same great Convention further give their opinion, that after their work shall have passed through the hands of Congress, it should be *"submitted to a Convention of Delegates, chosen in each State by the people thereof, under the recommendation of its Legislature."*—This submission being in general terms cannot be understood as confining such Convention to adopt or reject it in gross, and as precluding the consideration or proposal of amendments, nor has in fact been so understood by the States of Virginia and Massachusetts; before the Convention of the former it is to be laid by order of their Legislature, for free and full discussion—and the Convention of the latter have actually proposed several amendments.

The whole agency of Congress in this affair seems to have been to lay it before the States as they received it from the Convention. If therefore the freemen of any State are precluded from the benefit of proposing amendments it must be done by their own Legislature, and by no other body of men who have taken measures relative to this work.

From the prevailing opinion throughout this Union, from the acts of Congress, as well as of most of the Legislatures of these States, and particularly from the acts of this State, granting to Congress the power to levy and collect an impost, and to regulate trade, as well as from the actual embarrassments of public affairs, and private distress and ruin of many individuals, your Petitioners presume themselves authorized to believe, that the old Confederation of the United States is not adequate to all the purposes of the Federal Union.—And whether the proposed new Constitution is the greatest improvement thereon, remains a question to be resolved by this State in common with her sister States in the Union. The most eligible mode of proceeding in this business therefore is the simple point of enquiry.

It occurs to your Petitioners that the mode pointed out by the act under present consideration is inexpedient and improper, because,

1st. In this mode the sea-port towns cannot hear and examine the arguments of their brethren in the country on this subject, nor can they in return be possessed of our views thereof; so that each separate interest will act under an impression of private and local motives only, uninformed of those reasons and arguments which might lead to measures of common utility and public good.

2dly. Not only will much information be denied in this mode, but a full hearing of the cause will be impossible: For other States are interested, and their interests in many cases opposite to ours.—How far it may be proper to sacrifice a State interest to obtain federal protection requires great and deep thought; and how much power ought to be vested in Congress to enable them to vindicate the national honor is not easily determined by those who are best acquainted with the actual circumstances of both the friends and enemies of the United States; yet every individual freeman ought to investigate these great questions in some good degree before he can decide on this Constitution: The time therefore to be spent in this business would prove a great tax on the freemen to be assembled in Town-Meetings, which must be kept open not only three days but three months or more, in proportion as the people at large have more or less information.

3dly. All the letters and papers containing the information aforesaid could not be conveniently copied and dispersed into all the towns in this State, to be read to all the freemen; and in case they should decide without an entire knowledge of the public affairs of the Union there could be no security for a just decision.

4thly. The mode pointed out may exclude many of the freemen from voting at all. Votes are only to be taken by yea and nay. All persons therefore who are not ripe for judging by themselves, and wish to devolve it on a Convention are excluded from a voice; as likewise all others who may be decidedly in favour of certain amendments, and not willing to vote individually by yea or nay. The votes and influence of both these descriptions of citizens will be necessarily ex-

cluded: And as those only who vote can bind themselves individually, how are those to be bound who do not vote? They
are not represented, nor can they be bound under that idea by
the doings of their neighbours; so that after three-quarters of
the State may have individually voted for the new Constitution, a principle is yet to be fought for to bind the other
quarter.

5thly. This mode of voting is in other respects indecisive:
For the United States in Congress assembled will not receive
and count the votes of individuals, nor will they take a certif-
icate thereof from the General Assembly as a warrant to them
to bind the State: They can only attend to the voice of a
Convention duly authorized to act on the subject, and to bind
all the individuals in the State, in virtue of having been appointed their Representatives for this purpose, agreeably to
the line pointed out by the Federal Convention. To what purpose then are all the towns to be put to this great expence of
time and trouble, to investigate and vote on this important
national concernment, when all their doings will be void, and
a Convention must be finally had, before Congress can receive
any information from the State, whether the new Constitution has been adopted or rejected.

6thly. This method of voting deprives this State of the
privilege of proposing amendments, which can be done and
agreed to in a Convention only. After having been excluded
from a hearing, by the policy of the State, in the formation of
the proposed Constitution, would it not be a repetition of
injury to the freemen of this State to deny them the privilege
of proposing such amendments as they might judge necessary,
and of discussing the Constitution in the same mode as
adopted by all the other States?—Have they not a right, as
composing one member of the Union, to have their voice
heard on this subject, before a Constitution shall be adopted
by all their sister States, to which they must finally submit?—
This argument, in the view of your Petitioners, will gain
strength from the suggestion thrown out by some in justification of the present mode, that the people are more enlightened here than elsewhere, and have a greater sense of
freedom: If this suggestion is well founded, their voice was
more wanted in the Federal Convention, and their remarks

and improvements in a State Convention, to be brought forward and ingrafted with the Constitution are more necessary.—Have not the freemen of our sister States a right to claim this service at our hands, and have not the freemen of this State a right to *demand* it?

7thly. The present Congress, a body known and acknowledged by this State, having recommended the calling a Convention for this purpose, and twelve States having complied therewith, your Petitioners cannot avoid expressing their regret, that a mode of deciding on this question so novel, ineffectual, and injurious to the people of this State should have been substituted in the stead of one recommended by a legal body, and sanctioned by such great authorities; and which in every point of view promises to be the best and only mode of putting an end to this business.

8thly. Your Petitioners will only add, that in all events a Convention will become necessary. This State however sovereign and independent cannot exist without a connexion with her sister States: and if Convention be not held at a period when the proceedings of this State might have an influence on the Federal Councils, and the doings of other States, one must of necessity be held sooner or later to join in the general American Confederacy, after having lost all opportunity of influencing, or having any direction in the formation of that Confederacy.

Whether on the whole it be adviseable to adopt, reject, or amend, the proposed Constitution your Petitioners beg leave to decline deciding in their individual capacities, for the foregoing reasons, which they have thought necessary to lay before your honorable body in explanation of their conduct on this occasion. And they beg leave to offer the strongest assurance of their sincere love to their country and attachment to the liberties thereof, as well as of their ardent wish for the establishment of an efficient Federal Government, on such principles as may secure to the States their necessary jurisdictions and power, and to individual citizens their just rights and privileges. And to accomplish these great objects in the most regular, safe and satisfactory manner, your Petitioners HUMBLY PRAY, this Honorable General Assembly to recommend the calling a Convention in this State, at such time and place as they in their wisdom may judge most for the public welfare.

And as in duty bound will ever pray, &c.

> *Signed by the unanimous order, and in behalf*
> *of the Freemen of the Town of Providence,*
> *legally warned and assembled in Town-*
> *Meeting as aforesaid,*
>
> Per   DANIEL COOKE, T. Clerk.

"A Columbian Patriot" [Mercy Otis Warren], Observations on the Constitution

Boston, February 1788

Mankind may amuse themselves with theoretick systems of liberty, and trace its social and moral effects on sciences, virtue, industry, and every improvement of which the human mind is capable; but we can only discern its true value by the practical and wretched effects of slavery; and thus dreadfully will they be realized, when the inhabitants of the Eastern States are dragging out a miserable existence, *only* on the gleanings of their fields; and the Southern, blessed with a softer and more fertile climate, are languishing in hopeless poverty; and when asked, what is become of the flower of their crop, and the rich produce of their farms—they may answer in the hapless stile of the Man of *La Mancha*,—"The steward of my Lord has seized and sent it to *Madrid*."—Or, in the more literal language of truth, The *exigencies* of government require that the collectors of the revenue should transmit it to the *Federal City*.

Animated with the firmest zeal for the interest of this country, the peace and union of the American States, and the freedom and happiness of a people who have made the most costly sacrifices in the cause of liberty,—who have braved the power of Britain, weathered the convulsions of war, and waded thro' the blood of friends and foes to establish their independence and to support the freedom of the human mind; I cannot silently witness this degradation without calling on them, before they are compelled to blush at their own servitude, and to turn back their languid eyes on their lost liberties—to consider, that the character of nations generally changes at the moment of revolution.—And when patriotism is discountenanced and publick virtue becomes the ridicule of the sycophant—when every man of liberality, firmness, and

penetration, who cannot lick the hand stretched out to oppress, is deemed an enemy to the State—then is the gulph of
despotism set open, and the grades to slavery, though rapid,
are scarce perceptible—then genius drags heavily its iron
chain—science is neglected, and real merit flies to the shades
for security from reproach—the mind becomes enervated,
and the national character sinks to a kind of apathy with only
energy sufficient to curse the breast that gave it milk, and as
an elegant writer observes, "To bewail every new birth as an
encrease of misery, under a government where the mind is
necessarily debased, and talents are seduced to become the
panegyrists of usurpation and tyranny." He adds, "that even
sedition is not the most indubitable enemy to the publick welfare; but that its most dreadful foe is despotism, which always
changes the character of nations for the worse, and is productive of nothing but vice, that the tyrant no longer excites to
the pursuits of glory or virtue; it is not talents, it is baseness
and servility that he cherishes, and the weight of arbitrary
power destroys the spring of emulation."* If such is the influence of government on the character and manners, and undoubtedly the observation is just, must we not subscribe to
the opinion of the celebrated *Abbé Mablé*? "That there are
disagreeable seasons in the unhappy situation of human affairs, when policy requires both the intention and the power
of doing mischief to be punished; and that when the senate
proscribed the memory of *Cæsar* they ought to have put *Anthony* to death, and extinguished the hopes of *Octavius*." Self
defence is a primary law of nature, which no subsequent law
of society can abolish; this primæval principle, the immediate
gift of the Creator, obliges every one to remonstrate against
the strides of ambition, and a wanton lust of domination, and
to resist the first approaches of tyranny, which at this day
threaten to sweep away the rights for which the brave sons of
America have fought with an heroism scarcely paralleled even
in ancient republicks. It may be repeated, they have purchased
it with their blood, and have gloried in their independence
with a dignity of spirit, which has made them the admiration
of philosophy, the pride of America, and the wonder of

*Helvitius.

Europe. It has been observed, with great propriety, that "the virtues and vices of a people when a revolution happens in their government, are the measure of the liberty or slavery they ought to expect—An heroic love for the publick good, a profound reverence for the laws, a contempt of riches, and a noble haughtiness of soul, are the only foundations of a free government."* Do not their dignified principles still exist among us? Or are they extinguished in the breasts of Americans, whose fields have been so recently crimsoned to repel the potent arm of a foreign Monarch, who had planted his engines of slavery in every city, with design to erase the vestiges of freedom in this his last asylum. It is yet to be hoped, for the honour of human nature, that no combinations either foreign or domestick have thus darkned this Western hemisphere.—On these shores freedom has planted her standard, diped in the purple tide that flowed from the veins of her martyred heroes; and here every uncorrupted American yet hopes to see it supported by the vigour, the justice, the wisdom and unanimity of the people, in spite of the deep-laid plots, the secret intrigues, or the bold effrontery of those interested and avaricious adventurers for place, who intoxicated with the ideas of distinction and preferment, have prostrated every worthy principle beneath the shrine of ambition. Yet these are the men who tell us republicanism is dwindled into theory—that we are incapable of enjoying our liberties—and that we must have a master.—Let us retrospect the days of our adversity, and recollect who were then our friends; do we find them among the sticklers for aristocratick authority? No, they were generally the same men who now wish to save us from the distractions of anarchy on the one hand, and the jaws of tyranny on the other; where then were the class who now come forth importunately urging that our political salvation depends on the adoption of a system at which freedom spurns?—Were not some of them hidden in the corners of obscurity, and others wrapping themselves in the bosom of our enemies for safety? Some of them were in the arms of infancy; and others speculating for fortune, by sporting with public money; while a few, a very few of them were mag-

*Abbe Mable.

nanimously defending their country, and raising a character, which I pray heaven may never be sullied by aiding measures derogatory to their former exertions. But the revolutions in principle which time produces among mankind, frequently exhibits the most mortifying instances of human weakness; and this alone can account for the extraordinary appearance of a few names, once distinguished in the honourable walks of patriotism, but now found on the list of the Massachusetts assent to the ratification of a Constitution, which, by the undefined meaning of some parts, and the ambiguities of expression in others, is dangerously adapted to the purposes of an immediate *aristocratic tyranny*; that from the difficulty, if not impracticability of its operation, must soon terminate in the most *uncontrouled despotism*.

All writers on government agree, and the feelings of the human mind witness the truth of these political axioms, that man is born free and possessed of certain unalienable rights— that government is instituted for the protection, safety, and happiness of the people, and not for the profit, honour, or private interest of any man, family, or class of men—That the origin of all power is in the people, and that they have an incontestible right to check the creatures of their own creation, vested with certain powers to guard the life, liberty and property of the community: And if certain selected bodies of men, deputed on these principles, determine contrary to the wishes and expectations of their constituents, the people have an undoubted right to reject their decisions, to call for a revision of their conduct, to depute others in their room, or if they think proper, to demand further time for deliberation on matters of the greatest moment: it therefore is an unwarrantable stretch of authority or influence, if any methods are taken to preclude this reasonable, and peaceful mode of enquiry and decision. And it is with inexpressible anxiety, that many of the best friends to the Union of the States—to the peaceable and equal participation of the rights of nature, and to the glory and dignity of this country, behold the insiduous arts, and the strenuous efforts of the partisans of arbitrary power, by their vague definitions of the best established truths, endeavoring to envelope the mind in darkness the concomitant of slavery, and to lock the strong chains of domestic despotism on a

country, which by the most glorious and successful struggles
is but newly emancipated from the sceptre of foreign dominion.—But there are certain seasons in the course of human
affairs, when Genius, Virtue, and Patriotism, seems to nod
over the vices of the times, and perhaps never more remarkably, than at the present period; or we should not see such a
passive disposition prevail in some, who we must candidly
suppose, have liberal and enlarged sentiments; while a supple
multitude are paying a blind and idolatrous homage to the
opinions of those who by the most precipitate steps are tread-
ing down their dear bought privileges; and who are endeavouring by all the arts of insinuation, and influence, to betray
the people of the United States, into an acceptance of a most
complicated system of government; marked on the one side
with the *dark, secret* and *profound intrigues*, of the statesman,
long practised in the purlieus of despotism; and on the other,
with the ideal projects of *young ambition*, with its wings just
expanded to soar to a summit, which imagination has painted
in such gawdy colours as to intoxicate the *inexperienced votary*,
and send *him* rambling from State to State, to collect materials to construct the ladder of preferment.

i. But as a variety of objections to the *heterogeneous phantom*, have been repeatedly laid before the public, by men of
the best abilities and intentions; I will not expatiate long on a
Republican *form* of government, founded on the principles
of monarchy—a democratick branch with the *features* of aristocracy—and the extravagance of nobility pervading the
minds of many of the candidates for office, with the poverty
of peasantry hanging heavily on them, and insurmountable,
from their taste for expence, unless a generous provision
should be made in the arrangement of the civil list, which
may enable them with the champions of their cause to *"sail
down the new pactolean channel."* Some gentlemen with laboured zeal, have spent much time in urging the necessity of
government, from the embarrassments of trade—the want of
respectability abroad and confidence in the public engagements at home:—These are obvious truths which no one denies; and there are few who do not unite in the general wish
for the restoration of public faith, the revival of commerce,
arts, agriculture, and industry, under a lenient, peaceable and

energetick government: But the most sagacious advocates for the party have not by fair discusion, and rational argumentation, evinced the necessity of adopting this many-headed monster; of such motley mixture, that its enemies cannot trace a feature of Democratick or Republican extract; nor have its friends the courage to denominate it a Monarchy, an Aristocracy, or an Oligarchy, and the favoured bantling must have passed through the short period of its existence without a name, had not Mr. *Wilson*, in the fertility of his genius, suggested the happy epithet of a *Federal Republic.*—But I leave the field of general censure on the secrecy of its birth, the rapidity of its growth, and the fatal consequences of suffering it to live to the age of maturity, and will particularize some of the most weighty objections to its passing through this continent in a gigantic size.—It will be allowed by every one that the fundamental principle of a free government, is the equal representation of a free people—And I will *first* observe with a justly celebrated writer, "That the principal aim of society is to protect individuals in the absolute rights which were vested in them by the immediate laws of nature, but which could not be preserved in peace, without the mutual intercourse which is gained by the institution of friendly and social communities." And when society has thus deputed a certain number of their equals to take care of their personal rights, and the interest of the whole community, it must be considered that responsibility is the great security of integrity and honour; and that annual election is the basis of responsibility.—Man is not immediately corrupted, but power without limitation, or amenability, may endanger the brightest virtue—whereas a frequent return to the bar of their Constituents is the strongest check against the corruptions to which men are liable, either from the intrigues of others of more subtle genius, or the propensities of their own hearts,—and the gentlemen who have so warmly advocated in the late Convention of the Massachusetts, the change from annual to biennial elections, may have been in the same predicament, and perhaps with the same views that Mr. *Hutchinson* once acknowledged himself, when in a letter to *Lord Hillsborough*, he observed, "that the grand difficulty of making a change in government against the general bent of the people had caused him to turn his thoughts to a variety of plans, in order to find one that might be executed in spite of opposition," and the first he proposed was that, "instead of annual, the elections should be only once in three years:" but the Minister had not the hardiness to attempt such an innovation, even in the revision of colonial charters: nor has any one ever defended Biennial, Triennial, or Septennial, Elections, either in the British House of Commons, or in the debates of Provincial assemblies, on general and free principles: but it is unnecessary to dwell long on this article, as the best political writers have supported the principles of annual elections with a precision, that cannot be confuted, though they may be darkned, by the sophistical arguments that have been thrown out with design, to undermine all the barriers of freedom.

2. There is no security in the profered system, either for the rights of conscience, or the liberty of the Press: Despotism usually while it is gaining ground, will suffer men to think, say, or write what they please; but when once established, if it is thought necessary to subserve the purposes of arbitrary power, the most unjust restrictions may take place in the first instance, and an *imprimator* on the Press in the next, may silence the complaints, and forbid the most decent remonstrances of an injured and oppressed people.

3. There are no well defined limits of the Judiciary Powers, they seem to be left as a boundless ocean, that has broken over the chart of the Supreme Lawgiver *"thus far shalt thou go and no further,"* and as they cannot be comprehended by the clearest capacity, or the most sagacious mind, it would be an Herculean labour to attempt to describe the dangers with which they are replete.

4. The Executive and the Legislative are so dangerously blended as to give just cause of alarm, and every thing relative thereto, is couched in such ambiguous terms—in such vague and indifinite expression, as is a sufficient ground without any other objection, for the reprobation of a system, that the authors dare not hazard to a clear investigation.

5. The abolition of trial by jury in civil causes.—This mode of trial the learned Judge Blackstone observes, "has been coeval with the first rudiments of civil government, that property, liberty and life, depend on maintaining in its legal force

the constitutional trial by jury." He bids his readers pauze, and with Sir Matthew Hale observes, how admirably this mode is adapted to the investigation of truth beyond any other the world can produce. Even the party who have been disposed to swallow, without examination, the proposals of the *secret conclave*, have started on a discovery that this essential right was curtailed; and shall a privilege, the origin of which may be traced to our Saxon ancestors—that has been a part of the law of nations, even in the fewdatory systems of France, Germany and Italy—and from the earliest records has been held so sacred, both in ancient and modern Britain, that it could never be shaken by the introduction of Norman customs, or any other conquests or change of government— shall this inestimable privilege be relinquished in America— either thro' the fear of inquisition for unaccounted thousands of public monies in the hands of some who have been officious in the fabrication of the *consolidated system*, or from the apprehension that some future delinquent possessed of more power than integrity, may be called to a trial by his peers in the hour of investigation?

6. Though it has been said by Mr. *Wilson* and many others, that a Standing-Army is necessary for the dignity and safety of America, yet freedom revolts at the idea, when the Divan, or the Despot, may draw out his dragoons to suppress the murmurs of a few, who may yet cherish those sublime principles which call forth the exertions, and lead to the best improvement of the human mind. It is hoped this country may yet be governed by milder methods than are usually displayed beneath the bannerets of military law.—Standing armies have been the nursery of vice and the bane of liberty from the Roman legions, to the establishment of the artful Ximenes, and from the ruin of the Cortes of Spain, to the planting the British cohorts in the capitals of America:—By the edicts of authority vested in the sovereign power by the proposed constitution, the militia of the country, the bulwark of defence, and the security of national liberty is no longer under the controul of civil authority; but at the rescript of the Monarch, or the aristocracy, they may either be employed to extort the enormous sums that will be necessary to support the civil list—to maintain the regalia of power—and the splendour of

the most useless part of the community, or they may be sent into foreign countries for the fulfilment of treaties, stipulated by the President and two thirds of the Senate.

7. Notwithstanding the delusory promise to guarantee a Republican form of government to every State in the Union—If the most discerning eye could discover any meaning at all in the engagement, there are no resources left for the support of internal government, or the liquidation of the debts of the State. Every source of revenue is in the monopoly of Congress, and if the several legislatures in their enfebled state, should against their own feelings be necessitated to attempt a dry tax for the payment of their debts, and the support of internal police, even this may be required for the purposes of the general government.

8. As the new Congress are empowered to determine their own salaries, the requisitions for this purpose may not be very moderate, and the drain for public moneys will probably rise past all calculation: and it is to be feared when America has consolidated its despotism, the world will witness the truth of the assertion—"that the pomp of an eastern monarch may impose on the vulgar who may estimate the force of a nation by the magnificence of its palaces; but the wise man, judges differently, it is by that very magnificence he estimates its weakness. He sees nothing more in the midst of this imposing pomp, where the tyrant sets enthroned, than a sumptuous and mournful decoration of the dead; the apparatus of a fastuous funeral, in the centre of which is a cold and lifeless lump of unanimated earth, a phantom of power ready to disappear before the enemy, by whom it is despised!"

9. There is no provision for a rotation, nor any thing to prevent the perpetuity of office in the same hands for life; which by a little well timed bribery, will probably be done, to the exclusion of men of the best abilities from their share in the offices of government.—By this neglect we lose the advantages of that check to the overbearing insolence of office, which by rendering him ineligible at certain periods, keeps the mind of man in equilibrio, and teaches him the feelings of the governed, and better qualifies him to govern in his turn.

10. The inhabitants of the United States, are liable to be draged from the vicinity of their own county, or state, to an-

swer to the litigious or unjust suit of an adversary, on the most distant borders of the Continent: in short the appelate jurisdiction of the Supreme Federal Court, includes an unwarrantable stretch of power over the liberty, life, and property of the subject, through the wide Continent of America.

11. One Representative to thirty thousand inhabitants is a very inadequate representation; and every man who is not lost to all sense of freedom to his country, must reprobate the idea of Congress altering by law, or on any pretence whatever, interfering with any regulations for the time, places, and manner of choosing our own Representatives.

12. If the sovereignty of America is designed to be elective, the circumscribing the votes to only ten electors in this State, and the same proportion in all the others, is nearly tantamount to the exclusion of the voice of the people in the choice of their first magistrate. It is vesting the choice solely in an aristocratic junto, who may easily combine in each State to place at the head of the Union the most convenient instrument for despotic sway.

13. A Senate chosen for six years will, in most instances, be an appointment for life, as the influence of such a body over the minds of the people will be coequal to the extensive powers with which they are vested, and they will not only forget, but be forgotten by their constituents—a branch of the Supreme Legislature thus set beyond all responsibility is totally repugnant to every principle of a free government.

14. There is no provision by a bill of rights to guard against the dangerous encroachments of power in too many instances to be named: but I cannot pass over in silence the insecurity in which we are left with regard to warrants unsupported by evidence—the daring experiment of granting *writs of assistance* in a former arbitrary administration is not yet forgotten in the Massachusetts; nor can we be so ungrateful to the memory of the patriots who counteracted their operation, as so soon after their manly exertions to save us from such a detestable instrument of arbitrary power, to subject ourselves to the insolence of any petty revenue officer to enter our houses, search, insult, and seize at pleasure. We are told by a gentleman of too much virtue and real probity to suspect he has a design to deceive—"that the whole constitution is a

declaration of rights"—but mankind must think for them-selves, and to many very judicious and discerning characters, the whole constitution with very few exceptions appears a perversion of the rights of particular states, and of private cit-izens.—But the gentleman goes on to tell us, "that the pri-mary object is the general government, and that the rights of individuals are only incidentally mentioned, and that there was a clear impropriety in being very particular about them." But, asking pardon for dissenting from such respectable au-thority, who has been led into several mistakes, more from his prediliction in favour of certain modes of government, than from a want of understanding or veracity. The rights of indi-viduals ought to be the primary object of all government, and cannot be too securely guarded by the most explicit declara-tions in their favor. This has been the opinion of the Hamp-dens, the Pyms, and many other illustrious names, that have stood forth in defence of English liberties; and even the Ital-ian master in politicks, the subtle and renouned Machiavel acknowledges, that no republic ever yet stood on a stable foundation without satisfying the common people.

15. The difficulty, if not impracticability, of exercising the equal and equitable powers of government by a single legisla-ture over an extent of territory that reaches from the Mis-sisippi to the Western lakes, and from them to the Atlantic ocean, is an insuperable objection to the adoption of the new system.—Mr. *Hutchinson*, the great champion for arbitrary power, in the multitude of his machinations to subvert the liberties of this country, was obliged to acknowledge in one of his letters, that, "from the extent of country from north to south, the scheme of one government was impracticable." But if the authors of the present visionary project, can by the arts of deception, precipitation and address, obtain a majority of suffrages in the conventions of the states to try the hazardous experiment, they may then make the same inglorious boast with this insidious politician, who may perhaps be their model, that "the union of the colonies was pretty well broken, and that he hoped never to see it renewed."

16. It is an indisputed fact, that not one legislature in the United States had the most distant idea when they first ap-pointed members for a convention, entirely commercial, or

when they afterwards authorized them to consider on some amendments of the Federal union, that they would without any warrant from their constituents, presume on so bold and daring a stride, as ultimately to destroy the state governments, and offer a *consolidated system*, irreversible but on conditions that the smallest degree of penetration must discover to be impracticable.

17. The first appearance of the article which declares the ratification of nine states sufficient for the establishment of the new system, wears the face of dissention, is a subversion of the union of the Confederated States, and tends to the introduction of anarchy and civil convulsions, and may be a means of involving the whole country in blood.

18. The mode in which this constitution is recommended to the people to judge without either the advice of Congress, or the legislatures of the several states, is very reprehensible—it is an attempt to force it upon them before it could be thoroughly understood, and may leave us in that situation, that in the first moments of slavery the minds of the people agitated by the remembrance of their lost liberties, will be like the sea in a tempest, that sweeps down every mound of security.

But it is needless to enumerate other instances, in which the proposed constitution appears contradictory to the first principles which ought to govern mankind; and it is equally so to enquire into the motives that induced to so bold a step as the annihilation of the independence and sovereignty of the thirteen distinct states.—They are but too obvious through the whole progress of the business, from the first shutting up the doors of the federal convention and resolving that no member should correspond with gentlemen in the different states on the subject under discussion; till the trivial proposition of *recommending* a few amendments was artfully ushered into the convention of the Massachusetts. The questions that were then before that honorable assembly were profound and important, they were of such magnitude and extent, that the consequences may run parallel with the existence of the country; and to see them waved and hastily terminated by a measure too absurd to require a serious refutation, raises the honest indignation of every true lover of his country. Nor are they less grieved that the ill policy and arbitrary disposition of some of the sons of America has thus precipitated to the contemplation and discussion of questions that no one could rationally suppose would have been agitated among us, till time had blotted out the principles on which the late revolution was grounded; or till the last traits of the many political tracts, which defended the seperation from Britain, and the rights of men were consigned to everlasting oblivion. After the severe conflicts this country has suffered, it is presumed that they are disposed to make every reasonable sacrifice before the altar of peace. — But when we contemplate the nature of men and consider them originally on an equal footing, subject to the same feelings, stimulated by the same passions, and recollecting the struggles they have recently made, for the security of their civil rights; it cannot be expected that the inhabitants of the Massachusetts, can be easily lulled into a fatal security, by the declamatory effusions of gentlemen, who, contrary to the experience of all ages would perswade them there is no danger to be apprehended, from vesting discretionary powers in the hands of man, which he may, or may not abuse. The very suggestion, that we ought to trust to the precarious hope of amendments and redress, after we have voluntarily fixed the shackles on our own necks should have awakened to a double degree of caution. — This people have not forgotten the artful insinuations of a former Governor, when pleading the unlimited authority of parliament before the legislature of the Massachusetts; nor that his arguments were very similar to some lately urged by gentlemen who boast of opposing his measure, *"with halters about their necks."*

We were then told by him, in all the soft language of insinuation, that no form of government of human construction can be perfect—that we had nothing to fear—that we had no reason to complain—that we had only to acquiesce in their illegal claims, and to submit to the requisitions of parliament, and doubtless the lenient hand of government would redress all grievances, and remove the oppressions of the people: — Yet we soon saw armies of mercenaries encamped on our plains—our commerce ruined—our harbours blockaded— and our cities burnt. It may be replied, that this was in consequence of an obstinate defence of our privileges; this may be true; and when the *"ultima ratio"* is called to aid, the weakest must fall. But let the best informed historian produce an instance when bodies of men were intrusted with power, and the proper checks relinquished, if they were ever found destitute of ingenuity sufficient to furnish pretences to abuse it. And the people at large are already sensible, that the liberties which America has claimed, which reason has justified, and which have been so gloriously defended by the sword of the brave; are not about to fall before the tyranny of foreign conquest: it is native usurpation that is shaking the foundations of peace, and spreading the sable curtain of despotism over the United States. The banners of freedom were erected in the wilds of America by our ancestors, while the wolf prowled for his prey on the one hand, and more savage man on the other; they have been since rescued from the invading hand of foreign power, by the valor and blood of their posterity; and there was reason to hope they would continue for ages to illumine a quarter of the globe, by nature kindly seperated from the proud monarchies of Europe, and the infernal darkness of Asiatic slavery.—And it is to be feared we shall soon see this country rushing into the extremes of confusion and violence, in consequence of the proceedings of a set of gentlemen, who disregarding the purposes of their appointment, have assumed powers unauthorised by any commission, have unnecessarily rejected the confederation of the United States, and annihilated the sovereignty and independence of the individual governments.—The causes which have inspired a few men assembled for very different purposes with such a degree of temerity as to break with a single stroke the union of America, and disseminate the seeds of discord through the land may be easily investigated, when we survey the partizans of monarchy in the state conventions, urging the adoption of a mode of government that militates with the former professions and exertions of this country, and with all ideas of republicanism, and the equal rights of men.

Passion, prejudice, and error, are characteristics of human nature; and as it cannot be accounted for on any principles of philosophy, religion, or good policy; to these shades in the human character must be attributed the mad zeal of some, to precipitate to a blind adoption of the measures of the late federal convention, without giving opportunity for better information to those who are misled by influence or ignorance into erroneous opinions.—Litterary talents may be prostituted, and the powers of genius debased to subserve the purposes of ambition, or avarice; but the feelings of the heart will dictate the language of truth, and the simplicity of her accents will proclaim the infamy of those, who betray the rights of the people, under the specious, and popular pretence of *justice*, *consolidation*, and *dignity*.

It is presumed the great body of the people unite in sentiment with the writer of these observations, who most devoutly prays that public credit may rear her declining head, and remunerative justice pervade the land; nor is there a doubt if a free government is continued, that time and industry will enable both the public and private debtor to liquidate their arrearages in the most equitable manner. They wish to see the Confederated States bound together by the most indissoluble union, but without renouncing their seperate sovereignties and independence, and becoming tributaries to a consolidated fabrick of aristocratick tyranny.—They wish to see government established, and peaceably holding the reins with honour, energy, and dignity; but they wish for no *federal city* whose *"cloud cap't towers"* may screen the state culprit from the hand of justice; while its exclusive jurisdiction may protect the riot of armies encamped within its limits.—They deprecate discord and civil convulsions, but they are not yet generally prepared with the ungrateful Israelites to ask a King, nor are their spirits sufficiently broken to yield the best of their olive grounds to his servants, and to see their sons appointed to run before his chariots—It has been observed by a zealous advocate for the new system, that most governments are the result of fraud or violence, and this with design to recommend its acceptance—but has not almost every step towards its fabrication been fraudulent in the extreme? Did not the prohibition strictly enjoined by the general Convention, that no member should make any communication to his Constituents, or to gentlemen of consideration and abilities in the other States, bear evident marks of fraudulent designs?—This circumstance is regretted in strong terms by Mr. Martin, a member from Maryland, who acknowledges "He had no idea that all the wisdom, integrity, and virtue of the States was contained in that Convention, and that he wished to have corresponded with gentlemen of eminent political characters abroad, and to give their sentiments due weight"—he adds, "so extremely solicitous were they, that their proceedings should not transpire, that the members were prohibited from taking copies of their resolutions, or extracts from the Journals, without express permission, by vote."—And the hurry with which it has been urged to the acceptance of the people, without giving time, by adjournments, for better information, and more unanimity has a deceptive appearance; and if finally driven to resistance, as the only alternative between that and servitude, till in the confusion of discord, the reins should be seized by the violence of some enterprizing genius, that may sweep down the last barrier of liberty, it must be added to the score of criminality with which the fraudulent usurpation at Philadelphia, may be chargeable.—Heaven avert such a tremendous scene! and let us still hope a more happy termination of the present ferment:—may the people be calm, and wait a legal redress; may the mad transport of some of our infatuated capitals subside; and every influential character through the States, make the most prudent exertions for a new general Convention, who may vest adequate powers in Congress, for all national purposes, without annihilating the individual governments, and drawing blood from every pore by taxes, impositions and illegal restrictions.—This step might again re-establish the Union, restore tranquility to the ruffled mind of the inhabitants, and save America from distresses, dreadful even in contemplation.—"The great art of governing is to lay aside all prejudices and attachments to particular opinions, classes or individual characters; to consult the spirit of the people; to give way to it; and in so doing, to give it a turn capable of inspiring those sentiments, which may induce them to relish a change, which an alteration of circumstances may hereafter make necessary."—The education of the advocates for monarchy should have taught them, and their memory should have suggested that "monarchy is a species of government fit only for a people too much corrupted by luxury, avarice, and a passion for pleasure, to have any love for their country, and whose vices the fear of punish-

ment alone is able to restrain; but by no means calculated for
a nation that is poor, and at the same time tenacious of their
liberty—animated with a disgust to tyranny—and inspired
with the generous feelings of patriotism and liberty, and at
the same time, like the ancient Spartans have been hardened
by temperance and manly exertions, and equally despising the
fatigues of the field, and the fear of enemies,"—and while
they change their ground they should recollect, that Aristocracy is still a more formidable foe to public virtue, and the
prosperity of a nation—that under such a government her
patriots become mercenaries—her soldiers, cowards, and the
people slaves.—Though several State Conventions have assented to, and ratified, yet the voice of the people appears at
present strong against the adoption of the Constitution.—By
the chicanery, intrigue, and false colouring of those who
plume themselves, more on their education and abilities, than
their political, patriotic, or private virtues—by the imbecility
of some, and the duplicity of others, a majority of the Convention of Massachusetts have been flattered with the ideas of
amendments, when it will be too late to complain—While
several very worthy characters, too timid for their situation,
magnified the hopeless alternative, between the dissolution of
the bands of all government, and receiving the proffered system *in toto*, after long endeavouring to reconcile it to their
consciences, swallowed the indigestible penacea, and in a kind
of sudden desperation lent their signature to the dereliction of
the honorable station they held in the Union, and have broken over the solemn compact, by which they were bound to
support their own excellent constitution till the period of revision.—Yet Virginia, equally large and respectable, and who
have done honour to themselves, by their vigorous exertions
from the first dawn of independence, have not yet acted upon
the question; they have wisely taken time to consider before
they introduce innovations of a most dangerous nature:—her
inhabitants are brave, her burgesses are free, and they have a
Governor who dares to think for himself, and to speak his
opinion (without first pouring libations on the altar of popularity) though it should militate with some of the most accomplished and illustrious characters.

Maryland, who has no local interest to lead her to adopt,

will doubtless reject the system—I hope the same characters still live, and that the same spirit which dictated to them a wise and cautious care, against sudden revolutions in government, and made them the last State that acceded to the independence of America, will lead them to support what they so deliberately claimed.—Georgia apprehensive of a war with the Savages, has acceded in order to insure protection.—Pennsylvania has struggled through much in the same manner, as the Massachusetts, against the manly feelings, and the masterly reasonings of a very respectable part of the Convention: They have adopted the system, and seen some of its authors burnt in effigy—their towns thrown into riot and confusion, and the minds of the people agitated by apprehension and discord.

New-Jersey and Delaware have united in the measure, from the locality of their situation, and the selfish motives which too generally govern mankind; the Federal City, and the seat of government, will naturally attract the intercourse of strangers—the youth of enterprize, and the wealth of the nation to the central States.

Connecticut has pushed it through with the precipitation of her neighbour, with few dissentient voices;—but more from irritation and resentment to a sister State, perhaps partiality to herself in her commercial regulations, than from a comprehensive view of the system, as a regard to the welfare of all.—But New-York has motives, that will undoubtedly lead her to a rejection, without being afraid to appeal to the understanding of mankind, to justify the grounds of their refusal to adopt a Constitution, that even the framers dare not risque to the hazard of revision, amendment, or reconsideration, least the whole superstructure should be demolished by more skilful and discreet architects.—I know not what part the Carolinas will take; but I hope their determinations will comport with the dignity and freedom of this country—their decisions will have great weight in the scale.—But equally important are the small States of New-Hampshire and Rhode-Island:—New-York, the Carolinas, Virginia, Maryland, and these two lesser States may yet support the liberties of the Continent; if they refuse a ratification, or postpone their proceedings till the spirits of the community have time to cool, there is little doubt but the wise measure of another federal convention will be adopted, when the members would have the advantage of viewing, at large, through the medium of truth, the objections that have been made from various quarters; such a measure might be attended with the most salutary effects, and prevent the dread consequences of civil feuds.—But even if some of those large states should hastily accede, yet we have frequently seen in the story of revolution, relief spring from a quarter least expected.

Though the virtues of a Cato could not save Rome, nor the abilities of a Padilla defend the citizens of Castile from falling under the yoke of Charles; yet a *Tell* once suddenly rose from a little obscure city, and boldly rescued the liberties of his country.—Every age has its Bruti and its Decii, as well as its Cæsars and Sejani:—The happiness of mankind depends much on the modes of government, and the virtues of the governors; and America may yet produce characters who have genius and capacity sufficient to form the manners and correct the morals of the people, and virtue enough to lead their country to freedom. Since her dismemberment from the British empire, America has, in many instances, resembled the conduct of a restless, vigorous, luxurious youth, prematurely emancipated from the authority of a parent, but without the experience necessary to direct him to act with dignity or discretion. Thus we have seen her break the shackles of foreign dominion, and all the blessings of peace restored on the most honourable terms: She acquired the liberty of framing her own laws, choosing her own magistrates, and adopting manners and modes of government the most favourable to the freedom and happiness of society. But how little have we availed ourselves of these superior advantages: The glorious fabric of liberty successfully reared with so much labour and assiduity totters to the foundation, and may be blown away as the bubble of fancy by the rude breath of military combinations, and politicians of yesterday.

It is true this country lately armed in opposition to regal despotism—impoverished by the expences of a long war, and unable immediately to fulfil their public or private engagements, have appeared in some instances, with a boldness of spirit that seemed to set at defiance all authority, government, or order, on the one hand; while on the other, there has been, not only a secret wish, but an open avowal of the necessity of drawing the reins of government much too taught, not only for republicanism, but for a wise and limited monarchy.— But the character of this people is not averse to a degree of subordination: the truth of this appears from the easy restoration of tranquility, after a dangerous insurrection in one of the states; this also evinces the little necessity of a complete revolution of government throughout the union. But it is a republican principle that the majority should rule; and if a spirit of moderation could be cultivated on both sides, till the voice of the people at large could be fairly heard it should be held sacred.— And if, on such a scrutiny, the proposed constitution should appear repugnant to their character and wishes; if they, in the language of a late elegant pen, should acknowledge that "no confusion in my mind, is more terrible to them than the stern disciplined regularity and vaunted police of arbitary governments, where every heart is depraved by fear, where mankind dare not assume their natural characters, where the free spirit must crouch to the slave in office, where genius must repress her effusions, or like the Egyptian worshippers, offer them in sacrifice to the calves in power, and where the human mind, always in shackles, shrinks from every generous effort." Who would then have the effrontery to say, it ought not to be thrown out with indignation, however some respectable names have appeared to support it.— But if after all, on a dispassionate and fair discussion, the people generally give their voice for a voluntary dereliction of their privileges, let every individual who chooses the active scenes of life, strive to support the peace and unanimity of his country, though every other blessing may expire—And while the statesman is plodding for power, and the courtier practising the arts of dissimulation without check—while the rapacious are growing rich by oppression, and fortune throwing her gifts into the lap of fools, let the sublimer characters, the philosophic lovers of freedom who have wept over her exit, retire to the calm shades of contemplation, there they may look down with pity on the inconsistency of human nature, the revolutions of states, the rise of kingdoms, and the fall of empires.

"Giles Hickory" [*Noah Webster*] *III*

American Magazine (New York), February 1788

The constitution of Virginia, like that of Connecticut, stands on the true principles of a Republican Representative Government. It is not shackled with a Bill of Rights, and every part of it, is at any time, alterable by an ordinary legislature. When I say *every part* of the constitution is alterable, I would except the right of elections, for the representatives have not power to prolong the period of their own delegation. This is not numbered among the rights of legislation, and deserves a separate consideration. This right is not vested in the legislature—it is in the people at large—it cannot be alienated without changing the form of government. Nay the right of election is not only the *basis*, but the *whole frame* or essence of a republican constitution—it is not merely *one*, but it is the *only* legislative or constitutional act, which the people at large can with propriety exercise.

The simple principle for which I contend is this—That in a representative democracy, the delegates chosen for legislators ought, at all times, to be competent to every possible act of legislation *under that form of government*; but not to *change that form*. Besides it is contrary to all our ideas of *deputation* or *agency for others*, that the person acting should have the power of extending the period of agency beyond the time specified in his commission. The representative of a people is, as to his powers, in the situation of an Attorney, whose letters commission him to do every thing which his constituent could do, were he on the spot; but for a limited time only. At the expiration of that time his powers cease; and a representative has no more right to extend that period, than a plenipotentiary has to renew his commission. The British Parliament, by prolonging the period of their existence from one to three, and from three to seven years, committed an unjust act—an act however which has been confirmed by the acquiescence of the nation, and thus received the highest constitutional sanction. I am sensible that the Americans are much concerned for the liberties of the British nation; and the act for making Parliaments septennial is often mentioned as an arbitrary oppressive act, destructive of English liberty.* The English are doubtless obliged to us for our tender concern for their happiness—yet for myself I entertain no such ideas—The English have generally understood and advocated their rights as well as any nation, and I am confident that the nation enjoys as much happiness and freedom, and much more tranquility, under septennial Parliaments, than they would with annual elections. Corruption to obtain offices will ever attend wealth; it is generated with it—grows up with it—and will, always fill a country with violent factions and illegal practices. Such are the habits of the people, that money will have a principal influence in carrying elections; and such vast sums are necessary for the purpose, that if elections were annual, none but a few of the wealthiest men could defray the expense—the landholders of moderate estates would not offer themselves as candidates—and thus in fact annual elections, with the present habits of the people, would actually diminish the influence of the commons, by throwing the advantage into the hands of a corrupt ministry, and a few overgrown nabobs. Before annual elections would be a blessing to the English, their habits must be changed—but this cannot be effected by human force. I wish my countrymen would believe that other nations understand and can guard their privileges, without any lamentable outcries from this side of the Atlantic. Government will always take its complexion from the habits of the people—habits are continually changing from age to age—a body of legislators taken from the people, will generally represent these habits at the time when they are chosen—hence these two important conclusions, 1st That a legislative body should be frequently renewed and always taken from the people—2d That a government which is perpetual, or incapable

*The septennial act was judged the only guard against a popish reign, and therefore highly popular.

of being accommodated to every change of national habits, must in time become a *bad* government.

With this view of the subject, I cannot suppress my surprise at the reasoning of Mr. Jefferson on this very point.* He considers it as a defect in the constitution of Virginia, that *it can be altered by an ordinary legislature.* He observes that the Convention which framed the present Constitution of the State, "received no powers in their creation which were not given to every legislature before and since. So far and no farther authorised, they organized the government by the ordinance entitled a Constitution or form of government. It pretends to no higher authority than the other ordinances of the same session; it does not say, that it shall be perpetual; that it shall be unalterable by other legislatures; that it shall be transcendant above the powers of those, who they knew would have equal powers with themselves."

But suppose the framers of this ordinance had said, that it should be *perpetual* and *unalterable*; such a declaration would have been void. Nay altho the people themselves had individually and unanimously declared the ordinance perpetual, the declaration would have been invalid. One Assembly cannot pass an act, binding upon a subsequent Assembly of equal authority;† and the people in 1776 had no authority, and consequently could delegate none, to pass a single act which the people in 1777 could not repeal and annul. And Mr. Jefferson himself, in the very next sentence, assigns a reason, which is an unanswerable argument in favor of my position, and a complete refutation of his own. These are his words. "Not only the silence of the instrument is a proof they thought it would be alterable, but their own practice also: for this very convention, meeting as a House of Delegates in General Assembly with the new Senate in the autumn of that year, passed acts of Assembly in contradiction to their ordinance of government; and *every Assembly from that time to this has done the same.*"

Did Mr. Jefferson reflect upon the inference that would be justly drawn from these facts? Did he not consider that he was furnishing his opponents with the most effectual weapons

*Notes on Virginia, page 197. Lond. Edit. Query 13.
†Contracts, where a Legislature is a party, are excepted.

against himself? The acts passed by *every subsequent Assembly in contradiction to the first ordinance*, prove that all the Assemblies were *fallible* men; and consequently not competent to make *perpetual Constitutions* for future generations. To give Mr. Jefferson, and the other advocates for *unchangeable Constitutions*, the fullest latitude in their argument, I will suppose every freeman in Virginia could have been assembled to deliberate upon a form of government, and that the present form, or even one more perfect, had been the result of their Councils—and that they had declared it unalterable. What would have been the consequence? Experience would probably have discovered, what is the fact—and what forever will be the case—that *Conventions* are not possessed of *infinite wisdom*—that the wisest men cannot devise a perfect system of government. Suppose then that after all this solemn national transaction, and a formal declaration that their proceedings should be unalterable, a single article of the constitution should be found to interfere with some national benefit—some material advantage; where would be the power to change or reform that article? In the same general Assembly of all the people, and in no other body. But must a State be put to this inconvenience, to find a remedy for every defect of constitution?

Suppose, however, the *Convention* had been empowered to declare the form of government *unalterable*: What would have been the consequence? Mr. Jefferson himself has related the consequence. Every succeeding Assembly has found errors or defects in that frame of government, and has happily applied a remedy. But had not every Legislature had power to make these alterations, Virginia must have gone thro the farce and the trouble of calling an *extraordinary* Legislature, to do that which an *ordinary* Legislature could do just as well, in their annual session; or those errors must have remained in the constitution, to the injury of the State.

The whole argument for bills of rights and unalterable constitutions rest on two suppositions, viz. that the Convention which frames the government, is *infallible*; and that future Legislatures will be *less honest—less wise—* and *less attentive to the interest of the State*, than a present Convention: The first supposition is *always false*, and the last is *generally* so. A declaration of perpetuity, annexed to a form of government, implies a supposition of *perfect wisdom and probity* in the framers; which is both arrogant and impudent—and it implies a supposed power in them, to abridge the power of a succeeding Convention and of the future state or body of people. The last supposition is, in every possible instance of legislation, *false*; and an attempt to exercise such a power, a high handed act of tyranny. But setting aside the argument, grounded on a want of power in one Assembly to abridge the power of another, what occasion have we to be so jealous of future Legislatures? Why should we be so anxious to guard the future rights of a nation? Why should we not distrust the people and the Representatives of the present age, as well as those of future ages, in whose acts we have not the smallest interest? For my part, I believe that the people and their Representatives, two or three centuries hence, will be as honest, as wise, as faithful to themselves, and will understand their rights as well, and be as able to defend them, as the people are at this period. The contrary supposition is absurd.

I know it is said that other nations have lost their liberties by the ambitious designs of their rulers, and we may do the same. The experience of other nations furnishes the ground of all the arguments used in favor of an unalterable constitution. The advocates seem determined that posterity shall not lose their liberty, even if they should be willing and desirous to surrender it. If a few declarations on parchment will secure a single blessing to posterity, which they would otherwise lose, I resign the argument and will receive a thousand declarations. Yet so thoroughly convinced am I of the opposite tendency and effect of such unalterable declarations, that, were it possible to render them valid, I should deem every article an infringment of civil and political liberty. I should consider every article as a restriction which might impose some duty which in time might cease to be useful and necessary, while the obligation of performing it might remain; or which in its operation might prove pernicious, by producing effects which were not expected, and could not be foreseen. There is no one single right, no privilege which is commonly deemed fundamental, which may not, by an unalterable establishment, preclude some amendment, some improvement in the future administration of government. And unless the advocates for unalterable constitutions of government, can prevent all changes in the wants, the inclinations, the habits and the circumstances of people, they will find it difficult, even with all their declarations of unalterable rights, to prevent changes in government. A paper-declaration is a very feeble barrier against the force of national habits, and inclinations.

The loss of liberty, as it is called, in the kingdoms of Europe, has, in several instances, been a mere change of government, effected by a change of habits, and in some instances this change has been favorable to liberty. The government of Denmark was changed from a mixed form, like that of England, to an absolute monarchy, by a solemn deliberate act of the people, or States. Was this a loss of liberty? So far from it, that the change removed the oppressions of faction, restored liberty to the subject and tranquility to the kingdom. The change was a blessing to the people. It indeed lodged a power in the Prince to dispose of life and property; but at the same time it lodged in him a *power to defend both*—a power which before was lodged *no where*—and it is infinitely better that such a power should be vested in a *single hand*, than that it should *not exist at all*. The monarchy of France has grown out of a number of petty States and lordships; yet it is a fact, proved by history and experience, that the subjects of that kingdom have acquired liberty, peace and happiness in proportion to the diminution of the powers of the petty sovereignties, and the extension of the prerogatives of the Monarch. It is said that Spain lost her liberties under the reign of Charles Vth; but I question the truth of the assertion; it is probable that the subject has gained as much by an abridgement of the powers of the nobility, as he lost by an annihilation of the Cortez. The United Netherlands fought with more bravery and perseverance to preserve their rights, than any other people, since the days of Leonidas; and yet no sooner established a government, so jealously guarded as to defeat its own designs, and prevent the good effects of government, that they neglected its principles—the freemen resigned the privilege of election, and committed their liberties to a rich aristocracy.

There was no compulsion—no external force in producing

this revolution; but the form of government, which had been established on paper, and solemnly ratified, was not suited to the genius of the subjects. The burghers had a right of electing their rulers; but they voluntarily neglected it; and a *bill of rights*, a *perpetual constitution* on parchment guaranteeing that right, was a useless form of words, because opposed to the temper of the people. The government assumed a complexion, more correspondent to their habits, and tho in theory no constitution is more cautiously guarded against an infringement of popular privileges, yet in practice it is a real aristocracy.

The progress of government in England has been the reverse—The people have been gaining freedom by intrenching upon the powers of the nobles and the royal prerogatives. These changes in government do not proceed from *bills of rights, unalterable forms* and *perpetual establishments*—liberty is never secured by such paper declarations; nor lost for want of them.—The truth in Government originates in necessity, and takes its form and structure from the genius and habits of the people; and if on paper a form is not accommodated to those habits, it will assume a new form, in spite of all the formal sanctions of the supreme authority of a State. Were the monarchy of France to be dissolved, and the wisest system of republican government ever invented, solemnly declared, by the King and his council, to be the constitution of the kingdom; the people, with their present habits, would refuse to receive it; and resign their privileges to their beloved sovereign. But so opposite are the habits of the Americans, that an attempt to erect a monarchy or an aristocracy over the United States, would expose the authors to the loss of their heads.* The truth is, the people of Europe, since they became civilized, have, in no kingdom, possessed the true principles of liberty. They could not therefore lose what they never possessed. There has been, from time immemorial, some rights of government—some prerogatives vested in some man or body of men, independent of the suffrages of the body of the subjects.

---

*Some jealous people ignorantly call the proposed Constitution of Federal Government an *aristocracy*. If such men are honest their ignorance deserves pity—There is not a feature of true aristocracy in the Constitution; the whole frame of Government is a pure Representative Republic.

This circumstance distinguishes the governments of Europe and of all the world, from those of America. There has been in the free nations of Europe an incessant struggle between freedom or national rights, and hereditary prerogatives. The contest has ended variously in different kingdoms; but generally in depressing the power of the nobility; ascertaining and limiting the prerogatives of the crown, and extending the privileges of the people. The Americans have seen the records of their struggles, and without considering that the objects of the contest *do not exist in this country*; they are laboring to guard rights which there is no party to attack. They are as jealous of their rights, as if there existed here a King's prerogatives or the powers of nobles, independent of their own will and choice, and ever eager to swallow up their liberties. But there is *no man* in America, who claims any rights but what are common to *every man*—there is no man who has an interest in invading popular privileges, because his attempt to curtail another's rights, would expose his own to the same abridgement. The jealousy of people in this country has no proper object against which it can rationally arm them—it is therefore directed *against themselves*, or against an invasion which they *imagine* may happen in future ages. The contest for *perpetual bills of rights* against a future tyranny, resembles Don Quixotes fighting windmills; and I never can reflect on the declamation about an *unalterable constitution* to guard certain rights, without wishing to add another article as necessary as those that are generally mentioned; viz, "that no future Convention or Legislature shall cut their own throats, or those of their constituents." While the habits of the Americans remain as they are, the people will choose their Legislature from their own body—that Legislature will have an interest inseperable from that of the people—and therefore an act to restrain their power in any article of legislation, is as unnecessary as an act to prevent them from committing suicide.

Mr. Jefferson, in answer to those who maintain that the form of government in Virginia is unalterable, because it is called a *constitution*, which, ex vi termini, means an act above the power of the ordinary Legislature, asserts that *constitution, statute, law* and *ordinance* are synonymous terms and con-

vertible, as they are used by writers on government; Constitu-
tio dicitur jus quod a principe conditur, Constitutum, quod
ab imperatoribus rescriptum statutumve est. Statutum, idem
quod lex.* Here the words *constitution, statute* and *law* are
defined by each other—They were used as convertible terms
by all former writers whether Roman or British; and before
the terms of the civil law were introduced, our Saxon ancestors used the correspondent English words, *bid* and *set.*†
From hence he concludes that no inference can be drawn
from the meaning of the word, that a *constitution* has a higher
authority than a law or statute. This conclusion of Mr. Jefferson is just.

He quotes Lord Coke also to prove that any Parliament can
abridge, suspend or qualify the acts of a preceding Parliament.
It is a maxim in their laws, that "Leges posteriores priores
contrarias abrogant." After having fully proved that *constitution, statute, law* and *ordinance* are words of similar import,
and that the constitution of Virginia is at any time alterable
by the ordinary Legislature, he proceeds to prove the danger
to which the rights of the people are exposed for want of an
unalterable form of government. The first proof of this danger
he mentions, is, the power which the Assembly exercises of
determining its own quorum. The British Parliament fixes its
own quorum.—The former Assemblies of Virginia did the
same. During the war the Legislature determined that *forty*
members should be a quorum to proceed to business, altho
not a fourth part of the whole house. The danger of delay, it
was judged, would warrant the measure. This precedent, our
writer supposes, is subversive of the principles of the government, and dangerous to liberty.

It is a dictate of natural law that a *majority should govern*;
and the principle is universally received and established in all
societies, where no other mode has been arbitrarily fixed. This
natural right cannot be alienated *in perpetuum*; for altho a
Legislature, or even the body of the people may resign the
powers of government to forty or to four men, when they
please, yet they may likewise resume them at pleasure.

*Calvini Lexicon Juridicum.
†See Laws of the Saxon Kings.

The people may, if they please, create a dictator on an emergency in war, but his creation would not *destroy*, but merely *suspend* the natural right of the *Lex majoris partis*. Thus forty members, a Minority of the Legislature of Virginia, were empowered during a dangerous invasion, to legislate for the State; but any subsequent Assembly might have divested them of that power. During the operation of the law, vesting them with this power, their acts were binding upon the State; because their power was derived from the general sense of the State—it was actually derived from a legal majority. But that majority could, at any moment, resume the power and practice of their natural right.

It is a standing law of Connecticut that forty men should be a quorum of the House of Representatives, which consists of about 170 members. The date of this law, I cannot find; but presume it must have existed for half a century; and I am confident that it never excited a murmur, or a suspicion that the liberties of the people were in danger. Yet this law creates an oligarchy; it is an infringement of natural right; it subjects the State to the possibility, and even the probability of being governed at times by a minority. The acquiescence of the State, in the existence of the law, gives validity, and even the sanction of a majority, to the acts of that minority; but the majority may at any time resume their natural right, and make the assent of more than half of the members, necessary to give validity to their determinations.

The danger therefore arising from a power in the Assembly to determine their own quorum, is merely ideal; for no law can be perpetual—the authority of a majority of the people or of their Representatives, is always competent to repeal any act that it found unjust or inconvenient. The acquiescence however of the people of the States mentioned, and that in one of them for a long course of years, under an oligarchy; or their submission to the power of a minority, is an incontestible proof of what I have before observed, that *theories* and *forms of government* are *empty things*—that the spirit of a government springs immediately from the temper of the people—and the exercise of it will generally take its tone from their feelings. It proves likewise that a *union of interests* between the rulers and the people, which union will always coexist with free elections, is not only the *best*, but the *only* security for their liberties which they can wish for and demand. The government of Connecticut is a solid proof of these truths. The Assembly of that State have always had power to abolish trial by jury, to restrain the liberty of the press, to suspend the habeas corpus act, to maintain a standing army, in short to command every engine of despotism; yet by some means or other it happens that the rights of the people are not invaded, and the subjects have generally been better satisfied with the laws, than the people of any other State. The reason is, the Legislature is a part of the people, and has the *same interest*. If a law should prove bad, the Legislature can repeal it; but in the *unalterable* bills of rights in some of the States, if an article should prove wrong and oppressive, an ordinary Legislature cannot repeal or amend it; and the State will hardly think of calling a special convention for so trifling a purpose. In a future paper, I shall take notice of some articles, in several of the State constitutions, which are glaring infractions of the first rights of freemen; yet they affect not a majority of the community, and centuries may elapse before the evil can be redressed, and a respectable class of men restored to the enjoyment of their rights.

To prove the want of an *unalterable constitution* in Virginia, Mr. Jefferson informs us that in 1776, during the distressed circumstances of the State, a proposition was made in the House of Delegates to create a Dictator, invested with every power, legislative, executive and judicial, civil and military. In June, 1781, under a great calamity, the proposition was repeated, and was near being passed. By the warmth he discovers in reprobating this proposal, one must suppose that the creation of a Dictator even for a few months, would have buried every remain of freedom. Yet he seems to allow that the step would have been justified, had there existed an *irresistable necessity*.

Altho it is possible that a case may happen in which the creation of a Dictator might be the only resort to save life, liberty, property, and the State, as it happened in Rome more than once; yet I should dread his power as much as any man, were I not convinced that the same men that appointed him, could, in a moment, strip him of his tremendous authority. A

Dictator, with an army superior to the strength of the State, would be a despot; but Mr. Jefferson's fears seem grounded on the authority derived from the Legislature. A concession of power from the Legislature, or the people, is a voluntary suspension of a natural *unalienable* right; and is resumeable at the expiration of the period specified, or the moment it is abused. A State can never alienate a *natural right*—for it cannot legislate for those who are not in existence. It may consent to suspend that right for great and temporary purposes; but were every freeman in Virginia to assent to the creation of a *perpetual Dictator*, the act in itself would be void. The expedient of creating a Dictator is dangerous, and no free people would willingly resort to it—but there may be times when this expedient is necessary to save a State from ruin, and when every man in a State would cheerfully give his suffrage for adopting it. At the same time, a temporary investiture of unlimited powers in one man, may be abused—it may be an influential precedent—and the continuance of it may furnish the dictator with the means of perpetuating his office. The distress of a people must be extreme, before a serious thought of a Dictator can be justifiable. But the people who create, can annihilate a Dictator; their right to govern themselves cannot be resigned by any act whatever, altho extreme cases may vindicate them in suspending the exercise of it. Even prescription cannot exist against this right; and every nation in Europe has a natural right to depose its King and take the government into its own hands.

"Publius," The Federalist LXIII
[James Madison]

Independent Journal (New York), March 1, 1788

To the People of the State of New-York.

A *fifth* desideratum illustrating the utility of a senate, is the want of a due sense of national character. Without a select and stable member of the government, the esteem of foreign powers will not only be forfeited by an unenlightened and variable policy, proceeding from the causes already mentioned; but the national councils will not possess that sensibility to the opinion of the world, which is perhaps not less necessary in order to merit, than it is to obtain, its respect and confidence.

An attention to the judgment of other nations is important to every government for two reasons: The one is, that independently of the merits of any particular plan or measure, it is desireable on various accounts, that it should appear to other nations as the offspring of a wise and honorable policy: The second is, that in doubtful cases, particularly where the national councils may be warped by some strong passion, or momentary interest, the presumed or known opinion of the impartial world, may be the best guide that can be followed. What has not America lost by her want of character with foreign nations? And how many errors and follies would she not have avoided, if the justice and propriety of her measures had in every instance been previously tried by the light in which they would probably appear to the unbiassed part of mankind.

Yet however requisite a sense of national character may be, it is evident that it can never be sufficiently possessed by a numerous and changeable body. It can only be found in a number so small, that a sensible degree of the praise and blame of public measures may be the portion of each individual; or in an assembly so durably invested with public trust, that the pride and consequence of its members may be sensibly incorporated with the reputation and prosperity of the community. The half-yearly representatives of Rhode-Island, would probably have been little affected in their deliberations on the iniquitous measures of that state, by arguments drawn from the light in which such measures would be viewed by foreign nations, or even by the sister states; whilst it can scarcely be doubted, that if the concurrence of a select and stable body had been necessary, a regard to national character alone, would have prevented the calamities under which that misguided people is now labouring.

I add as a *sixth* defect, the want in some important cases of a due responsibility in the government to the people, arising from that frequency of elections, which in other cases produces this responsibility. This remark will perhaps appear not only new but paradoxical. It must nevertheless be acknowledged, when explained, to be as undeniable as it is important.

Responsibility in order to be reasonable must be limited to objects within the power of the responsible party; and in order to be effectual, must relate to operations of that power, of which a ready and proper judgment can be formed by the constituents. The objects of government may be divided into two general classes; the one depending on measures which have singly an immediate and sensible operation; the other depending on a succession of well chosen and well connected measures, which have a gradual and perhaps unobserved operation. The importance of the latter description to the collective and permanent welfare of every country needs no explanation. And yet it is evident, that an assembly elected for so short a term as to be unable to provide more than one or two links in a chain of measures, on which the general welfare may essentially depend, ought not to be answerable for the final result, any more than a steward or tenant, engaged for one year, could be justly made to answer for places or improvements, which could not be accomplished in less than half a dozen years. Nor is it possible for the people to estimate the *share* of influence which their annual assemblies may respectively have on events resulting from the mixed transactions of several years. It is sufficiently difficult to preserve a personal responsibility in the members of a *numerous* body, for such acts of the body as have an immediate, detached and palpable operation on its constituents.

The proper remedy for this defect must be an additional body in the legislative department, which, having sufficient permanency to provide for such objects as require a continued attention, and a train of measures, may be justly and effectually answerable for the attainment of those objects.

Thus far I have considered the circumstances which point out the necessity of a well constructed senate, only as they relate to the representatives of the people. To a people as little blinded by prejudice, or corrupted by flattery, as those whom I address, I shall not scruple to add, that such an institution may be sometimes necessary, as a defence to the people against their own temporary errors and delusions. As the cool and deliberate sense of the community ought in all governments, and actually will in all free governments, ultimately prevail over the views of its rulers; so there are particular moments in public affairs, when the people stimulated by some irregular passion, or some illicit advantage, or misled by the artful misrepresentations of interested men, may call for measures which they themselves will afterwards be the most ready to lament and condemn. In these critical moments, how salutary will be the interference of some temperate and respectable body of citizens, in order to check the misguided career, and to suspend the blow meditated by the people against themselves, until reason, justice and truth, can regain their authority over the public mind? What bitter anguish would not the people of Athens have often escaped, if their government had contained so provident a safeguard against the tyranny of their own passions? Popular liberty might then have escaped the indelible reproach of decreeing to the same citizens, the hemlock on one day, and statues on the next.

It may be suggested that a people spread over an extensive region, cannot like the crouded inhabitants of a small district, be subject to the infection of violent passions; or to the danger of combining in pursuit of unjust measures. I am far from denying that this is a distinction of peculiar importance. I have on the contrary endeavoured in a former paper, to shew that it is one of the principal recommendations of a confederated republic. At the same time this advantage ought not to be considered as superseding the use of auxiliary precautions. It may even be remarked that the same extended situation which will exempt the people of America from some of the dangers incident to lesser republics, will expose them to the inconveniency of remaining for a longer time, under the influence of those misrepresentations which the combined industry of interested men may succeed in distributing among them.

It adds no small weight to all these considerations, to recollect, that history informs us of no long lived republic which had not a senate. Sparta, Rome and Carthage are in fact the only states to whom that character can be applied. In each of the two first there was a senate for life. The constitution of the senate in the last, is less known. Circumstantial evidence makes it probable that it was not different in this particular from the two others. It is at least certain that it had some quality or other which rendered it an anchor against popular fluctuations; and that a smaller council drawn out of the senate was appointed not only for life; but filled up vacancies itself. These examples, though as unfit for the imitation, as they are repugnant to the genius of America, are notwithstanding, when compared with the fugitive and turbulent existence of other antient republics, very instructive proofs of the necessity of some institution that will blend stability with liberty. I am not unaware of the circumstances which distinguish the American from other popular governments, as well antient as modern; and which render extreme circumspection necessary in reasoning from the one case to the other. But after allowing due weight to this consideration, it may still be maintained that there are many points of similitude which render these examples not unworthy of our attention. Many of the defects as we have seen, which can only be supplied by a senatorial institution, are common to a numerous assembly frequently elected by the people, and to the people themselves. There are others peculiar to the former, which require the controul of such an institution. The people can never wilfully betray their own interests: But they may possibly be betrayed by the representatives of the people; and the danger will be evidently greater where the whole legislative trust is lodged in the hands of one body of men, than where the concurrence of separate and dissimilar bodies is required in every public act.

The difference most relied on between the American and other republics, consists in the principle of representation, which is the pivot on which the former move, and which is supposed to have been unknown to the latter, or at least to the antient part of them. The use which has been made of this difference, in reasonings contained in former papers, will have shewn that I am disposed neither to deny its existence nor to undervalue its importance. I feel the less restraint therefore in observing that the position concerning the ignorance of the antient government on the subject of representation is by no means precisely true in the latitude commonly given to it. Without entering into a disquisition which here would be misplaced, I will refer to a few known facts in support of what I advance.

In the most pure democracies of Greece, many of the executive functions were performed not by the people themselves, but by officers elected by the people, and *representing* the people in their *executive* capacity.

Prior to the reform of Solon, Athens was governed by nine Archons, annually *elected by the people at large*. The degree of power delegated to them seems to be left in great obscurity. Subsequent to that period, we find an assembly first of four and afterwards of six hundred members, annually *elected by the people*; and *partially* representing them in their *legislative* capacity; since they were not only associated with the people in the function of making laws; but had the exclusive right of originating legislative propositions to the people. The senate of Carthage also, whatever might be its power or the duration of its appointment, appears to have been *elective* by the suffrages of the people. Similar instances might be traced in most if not all the popular governments of antiquity.

Lastly in Sparta, we meet with the Ephori, and in Rome with the Tribunes; two bodies, small indeed in number, but annually *elected by the whole body of the people*, and considered as the *representatives* of the people, almost in their *plenipotentiary* capacity. The Cosme of Crete were also annually *elected by the people*; and have been considered by some authors as an institution analogous to those of Sparta and Rome; with this difference only that in the election of that representative body, the right of suffrage was communicated to a part only of the people.

From these facts, to which many others might be added, it is clear that the principle of representation was neither unknown to the antients, nor wholly overlooked in their political constitutions. The true distinction between these and the American Governments lies *in the total exclusion of the people in their collective capacity* from any share in the *latter*, and not in the *total exclusion of representatives of the people*, from the administration of the *former*. The distinction however thus qualified must be admitted to leave a most advantageous superiority in favor of the United States. But to ensure to this advantage its full effect, we must be careful not to separate it from the other advantage, of an extensive territory. For it cannot be believed that any form of representative government, could have succeeded within the narrow limits occupied by the democracies of Greece.

In answer to all these arguments, suggested by reason, illustrated by other examples, and enforced by our own experience, the jealous adversary of the constitution will probably content himself with repeating, that a senate appointed not immediately by the people, and for the term of six years, must gradually acquire a dangerous preeminence in the government, and finally transform it into a tyrannical aristocracy.

To this general answer the general reply ought to be sufficient; that liberty may be endangered by the abuses of liberty, as well as by the abuses of power; that there are numerous instances of the former as well as of the latter; and that the former rather than the latter is apparently most to be apprehended by the United States. But a more particular reply may be given.

Before such a revolution can be effected, the senate, it is to be observed, must in the first place corrupt itself; must next corrupt the state legislatures, must then corrupt the house of representatives, and must finally corrupt the people at large. It is evident that the senate must be first corrupted, before it can attempt an establishment of tyranny. Without corrupting the state legislatures, it cannot prosecute the attempt, because the periodical change of members would otherwise regenerate the whole body. Without exerting the means of corruption with equal succession the house of representatives, the opposition of that co-equal branch of the government would inevitably defeat the attempt; and without corrupting the people themselves, a succession of new representatives would speedily restore all things to their pristine order. Is there any man who can seriously persuade himself, that the proposed senate can, by any possible means within the compass of human address, arrive at the object of a lawless ambition, through all these obstructions?

If reason condemns the suspicion, the same sentence is pronounced by experience. The constitution of Maryland furnishes the most apposite example. The senate of that state is elected, as the federal senate will be, indirectly by the people; and for a term less by one year only, than the federal senate. It is distinguished also by the remarkable prerogative of filling up its own vacancies within the term of its appointment: and at the same time, is not under the controul of any such rotation, as is provided for the federal senate. There are some other lesser distinctions, which would expose the former to colorable objections that do not lie against the latter. If the federal senate therefore really contained the danger which has been so loudly proclaimed, some symptoms at least of a like danger ought by this time to have been betrayed by the senate of Maryland; but no such symptoms have appeared. On the contrary the jealousies at first entertained by men of the same description with those who view with terror the correspondent part of the federal constitution, have been gradually extinguished by the progress of the experiment; and the Maryland constitution is daily deriving from the salutary operations of this part of it, a reputation in which it will probably not be rivalled by that of any state in the union.

But if any thing could silence the jealousies on this subject, it ought to be the British example. The senate there, instead of being elected for a term of six years, and of being unconfined to particular families or fortunes, is an hereditary assembly of opulent nobles. The house of representatives, instead of being elected for two years and by the whole body of the people, is elected for seven years; and in very great proportion, by a very small proportion of the people. Here unquestionably ought to be seen in full display, the aristocratic usurpations and tyranny, which are at some future period to be exemplified in the United States. Unfortunately however for the antifederal argument in the British history informs us, that this hereditary assembly has not even been able to defend itself against the continual encroachments of the house of representatives; and that it no sooner lost the support of the monarch, than it was actually crushed by the weight of the popular branch.

As far as antiquity can instruct us on this subject, its examples support the reasoning which we have employed. In Sparta the Ephori, the annual representatives of the people, were found an overmatch for the senate for life, continually gained on its authority, and finally drew all power into their own hands. The tribunes of Rome, who were the representatives of the people, prevailed, it is well known, in almost every contest with the senate for life, and in the end gained the most complete triumph over it. This fact is the more remarkable, as unanimity was required in every act of the tribunes, even after their number was augmented to ten. It proves the irresistable force possessed by that branch of a free government, which has the people on its side. To these examples might be added that of Carthage, whose senate, according to the testimony of Polybius, instead of drawing all power into its vortex, had at the commencement of the second punic war, lost almost the whole of its original portion.

Besides the conclusive evidence resulting from this assemblage of facts, that the federal senate will never be able to transform itself, by gradual usurpations, into an independent and aristocratic body; we are warranted in believing that if such a revolution should ever happen from causes which the foresight of man cannot guard against, the house of representatives with the people on their side will at all times be able to bring back the constitution to its primitive form and principles. Against the force of the immediate representatives of the people, nothing will be able to maintain even the constitutional authority of the senate, but such a display of enlightened policy, and attachment to the public good, as will divide with that branch of the legislature, the affections and support of the entire body of the people themselves.

"Publius," The Federalist LXV
[Alexander Hamilton]

New-York Packet, March 7, 1788

To the People of the State of New-York.

The remaining powers, which the plan of the Convention allots to the Senate, in a distinct capacity, are comprised in their participation with the Executive in the appointment to offices, and in their judicial character as a court for the trial of impeachments. As in the business of appointments the Executive will be the principal agent, the provisions relating to it will most properly be discussed in the examination of that department. We will therefore conclude this head with a view of the judicial character of the Senate.

A well constituted court for the trial of impeachments, is an object not more to be desired than difficult to be obtained in a government wholly elective. The subjects of its jurisdiction are those offences which proceed from the misconduct of public men, or in other words from the abuse or violation of some public trust. They are of a nature which may with peculiar propriety be denominated POLITICAL, as they relate chiefly to injuries done immediately to the society itself. The prosecution of them, for this reason, will seldom fail to agitate the passions of the whole community, and to divide it into parties, more or less friendly, or inimical, to the accused. In many cases, it will connect itself with the pre-existing factions, and will inlist all their animosities, partialities, influence and interest on one side, or on the other; and in such cases there will always be the greatest danger, that the decision will be regulated more by the comparitive strength of parties than by the real demonstrations of innocence or guilt.

The delicacy and magnitude of a trust, which so deeply concerns the political reputation and existence of every man engaged in the administration of public affairs, speak for themselves. The difficulty of placing it rightly in a government resting entirely on the basis of periodical elections will as readily be perceived, when it is considered that the most conspicuous characters in it will, from that circumstance, be too often the leaders, or the tools of the most cunning or the most numerous faction; and on this account can hardly be expected to possess the requisite neutrality towards those, whose conduct may be the subject of scrutiny.

The Convention, it appears, thought the Senate the most fit depositary of this important trust. Those who can best discern the intrinsic difficulty of the thing will be least hasty in condemning that opinion; and will be most inclined to allow due weight to the arguments which may be supposed to have produced it.

What it may be asked is the true spirit of the institution itself? Is it not designed as a method of NATIONAL INQUEST into the conduct of public men? If this be the design of it, who can so properly be the inquisitors for the nation, as the representatives of the nation themselves? It is not disputed that the power of originating the inquiry, or in other words of preferring the impeachment ought to be lodged in the hands of one branch of the legislative body; will not the reasons which indicate the propriety of this arrangement, strongly plead for an admission of the other branch of that body to a share in the inquiry? The model, from which the idea of this institution has been borrowed, pointed out that course to the Convention: In Great Britain, it is the province of the house of commons to prefer the impeachment; and of the house of lords to decide upon it. Several of the State constitutions have followed the example. As well the latter as the former seem to have regarded the practice of impeachments, as a bridle in the hands of the legislative body upon the executive servants of the government. Is not this the true light in which it ought to be regarded?

Where else, than in the Senate could have been found a tribunal sufficiently dignified, or sufficiently independent? What other body would be likely to feel *confidence enough in its own situation*, to preserve unawed and uninfluenced the necessary impartiality between an *individual* accused, and the *representatives of the people, his accusers*?

Could the Supreme Court have been relied upon as answering this description? It is much to be doubted whether the members of that tribunal would, at all times, be endowed with so eminent a portion of fortitude, as would be called for in the execution of so difficult a task; & it is still more to be doubted, whether they would possess the degree of credit and authority, which might, on certain occasions, be indispensable, towards reconciling the people to a decision, that should happen to clash with an accusation brought by their immediate representatives. A deficiency in the first would be fatal to the accused; in the last, dangerous to the public tranquility. The hazard in both these respects could only be avoided, if at all, by rendering that tribunal more numerous than would consist with a reasonable attention to œconomy. The necessity of a numerous court for the trial of impeachments is equally dictated by the nature of the proceeding. This can never be tied down by such strict rules, either in the delineation of the offence by the prosecutors, or in the construction of it by the Judges, as in common cases serve to limit the discretion of courts in favor of personal security. There will be no jury to stand between the Judges, who are to pronounce the sentence of the law and the party who is to receive or suffer it. The awful discretion, which a court of impeachments must necessarily have, to doom to honor or to infamy the most confidential and the most distinguished characters of the community, forbids the commitment of the trust to a small number of persons.

These considerations seem alone sufficient to authorise a conclusion, that the Supreme Court would have been an improper substitute for the Senate, as a court of impeachments. There remains a further consideration which will not a little strengthen this conclusion. It is this—The punishment, which may be the consequence of conviction upon impeachment, is not to terminate the chastisement of the offender. After having been sentenced to a perpetual ostracism from the esteem and confidence, the honors and emoluments of his country; he will still be liable to prosecution and punishment in the ordinary course of law. Would it be proper that the persons, who had disposed of his fame and his most valuable rights as a citizen in one trial, should in another trial, for the same offence, be also the disposers of his life and his fortune? Would there not be the greatest reason to apprehend, that error in the first sentence would be the parent of error in the second sentence? That the strong bias of one decision would be apt to overrule the influence of any new lights, which might be brought to vary the complexion of another decision? Those, who know any thing of human nature, will not hesitate to answer these questions in the affirmative; and will be at no loss to perceive, that by making the same persons Judges in both cases, those who might happen to be the objects of prosecution would in a great measure be deprived of the double security, intended them by a double trial. The loss of life and estate would often be virtually included in a sentence, which, in its terms, imported nothing more than dismission from a present, and disqualification for a future office. It may be said, that the intervention of a jury, in the second instance, would obviate the danger. But juries are frequently influenced by the opinions of Judges. They are sometimes induced to find special verdicts which refer the main question to the decision of the court. Who would be willing to stake his life and his estate upon the verdict of a jury, acting under the auspices of Judges, who had predetermined his guilt?

Would it have been an improvement of the plan, to have united the Supreme Court with the Senate, in the formation of the court of impeachments? This Union would certainly have been attended with several advantages; but would they not have been overballanced by the signal disadvantage, already stated, arising from the agency of the same Judges in the double prosecution to which the offender would be liable? To a certain extent, the benefits of that Union will be obtained from making the Chief Justice of the Supreme Court the President of the court of impeachments, as is proposed to be done in the plan of the Convention; while the inconveniences of an intire incorporation of the former into the latter will be substantially avoided. This was perhaps the prudent mean. I forbear to remark upon the additional pretext for clamour, against the Judiciary, which so considerable an augmentation of its authority would have afforded.

Would it have been desirable to have composed the court for the trial of impeachments of persons wholly distinct from the other departments of the government? There are weighty arguments, as well against, as in favor of such a plan. To some minds, it will not appear a trivial objection, that it could tend to increase the complexity of the political machine; and to add a new spring to the government, the utility of which would at best be questionable. But an objection, which will not be thought by any unworthy of attention, is this—A court formed upon such a plan would either be attended with a heavy expence, or might in practice be subject to a variety of casualties and inconveniencies. It must either consist of permanent officers stationary at the seat of government, and of course entitled to fixed and regular stipends, or of certain officers of the State governments, to be called upon whenever an impeachment was actually depending. It will not be easy to imagine any third mode materially different, which could rationally be proposed. As the court, for reasons already given, ought to be numerous; the first scheme will be reprobated by every man, who can compare the extent of the public wants, with the means of supplying them; the second will be espoused with caution by those, who will seriously consider the difficulty of collecting men dispersed over the whole union; the injury to the innocent, from the procrastinated determination of the charges which might be brought against them; the advantage to the guilty, from the opportunities which delay would afford to intrigue and corruption; and in some cases the detriment to the State, from the prolonged inaction of men, whose firm and faithful execution of their duty might have exposed them to the persecution of an intemperate or designing majority in the House of Representatives. Though this latter supposition may seem harsh, and might not be likely often to be verified; yet it ought not to be forgotten, that the dæmon of faction will at certain seasons extend his sceptre over all numerous bodies of men.

But though one or the other of the substitutes which have been examined, or some other that might be devised, should be thought preferable to the plan, in this respect, reported by the Convention, it will not follow, that the Constitution ought for this reason to be rejected. If mankind were to resolve to agree in no institution of government, until every part of it had been adjusted to the most exact standard of perfection, society would soon become a general scene of anarchy, and the world a desart. Where is the standard of perfection to be found? Who will undertake to unite the discordant opinions of a whole community, in the same judgment of it; and to prevail upon one conceited projector to renounce his *infallible* criterion, for the *fallible* criterion of his more *conceited neighbor*? To answer the purpose of the adversaries of the Constitution, they ought to prove, not merely, that particular provisions in it are not the best, which might have been imagined; but that the plan upon the whole is bad and pernicious.

John Page to Thomas Jefferson

Rosewell, Virginia, March 7, 1788

. . . I have long wished for a leisure Hour to write to you, but really could not command one till now; when by means of an uncommon spell of severe Weather, & a deep Snow, I am caught at Home alone, having left my Family at York, to attend on the Election of Delegates to serve in Convention in June next—I came over, offered my Services to the Freeholders in a long Address which took me an Hour & an half to deliver it, in which I explained the Principles of the Plan of the fœderal Constitution & shewed the Defects of the Confederation declaring myself a Friend to the former; & that I wished it might be adopted without losing Time in fruitless Attempts to make Amendments which might be made with more probability of Success in the Manner pointed out by the Constitution itself—I candidly confessed that I had been at first an Enemy to the Constitution proposed, & had endeavoured to fix on some Plan of Amendments; but finding that Govr. Randolph, Col. Mason, & Col. Lee differed in their Ideas of Amendments, & not one of them agreed with me in Objections, I began to suspect that our Objections were founded on wrong Principles; or that we should have agreed; & therefore I set to work; & examined over again the Plan of the Constitution; & soon found, that the Principles we had applied were such as might apply to the Government of a single State, but not to the complicated Government, of 13, perhaps 30 States which were to be *united*, so as to be *one* in Interest Strength & Glory; & yet to be severally sovereign & independent, as to their municipal Laws, & local Circumstances (except in a few Instances which might clash with the general Good); that such a general Government was necessary as could command the Means of mutual Support, more effectually than mere Confederacies Leagues & Alliances, that is, a Government which for fœderal Purposes should have all the

Activity Secresy & Energy which the best regulated Governments in the World have; & yet that this, should be brought
about, without establishg a Monarchy or an Aristocracy; &
without violating the [   ] Principles of democratical Governments. I say I confessed, that, when I considered, that this
was to be the Nature of the Government which was necessary
to be adopted in the United States I found that the Objections which might be made [   ] a single State thus governed, would not apply to this great delicate & complicated
Machinery of Government, & that the Plan proposed by the
Convention was perhaps the best which could be devised—I
have run myself out of Breath in a long winded Sentence, &
lost a deal of Time in telling you what I might as well have
said in three Words,—vizt, that after all my Trouble the Freeholders left me far behind, Warner Lewis & Thos. Smith on
the Lists of Candidates. I had however this Consolation, that
I was not rejected on Account of my Attachment to the Constitution—for those two Gentlemen openly avowed the same
Sentiments which I had declared in my Address to the People.
Many of my Friends were very much mortified at the Disappointment we met with, & thought they comforted me by
telling me of the extreme badness of the Weather which they
said prevented many Freeholders from attending on the Election, but I comforted myself with the Reflection that I had
adhered to my Resolution of treating the Freeholders like free
Men; having never insulted them upon such Occasions by Solicitations & Caresses; & that they would now see clearly the
Impropriety of engaging their Votes; & I comfort myself
now, with the Reflection, that I shall have a little more Leisure to attend to my Affairs & to my Friends. . . .

"Publius," The Federalist LXVIII [Alexander Hamilton]

Independent Journal (New York), March 12, 1788

To the People of the State of New-York.

The mode of appointment of the chief magistrate of the United States is almost the only part of the system, of any consequence, which has escaped without severe censure, or which has received the slightest mark of approbation from its opponents. The most plausible of these, who has appeared in print, has even deigned to admit, that the election of the president is pretty well guarded.* I venture somewhat further; and hesitate not to affirm, that if the manner of it be not perfect, it is at least excellent. It unites in an eminent degree all the advantages; the union of which was to be desired.

It was desireable, that the sense of the people should operate in the choice of the person to whom so important a trust was to be confided. This end will be answered by committing the right of making it, not to any pre-established body, but to men, chosen by the people for the special purpose, and at the particular conjuncture.

It was equally desirable, that the immediate election should be made by men most capable of analizing the qualities adapted to the station, and acting under circumstances favourable to deliberation and to a judicious combination of all the reasons and inducements, which were proper to govern their choice. A small number of persons, selected by their fellow citizens from the general mass, will be most likely to possess the information and discernment requisite to such complicated investigations.

It was also peculiarly desirable, to afford as little opportu-

*Vide Federal Farmer.

nity as possible to tumult and disorder. This evil was not least to be dreaded in the election of a magistrate, who was to have so important an agency in the administration of the government, as the president of the United States. But the precautions which have been so happily concerted in the system under consideration, promise an effectual security against this mischief. The choice of *several* to form an intermediate body of electors, will be much less apt to convulse the community, with any extraordinary or violent movements, than the choice of *one* who was himself to be the final object of the public wishes. And as the electors, chosen in each state, are to assemble and vote in the state, in which they are chosen, this detached and divided situation will expose them much less to heats and ferments, which might be communicated from them to the people, than if they were all to be convened at one time, in one place.

Nothing was more to be desired, than that every practicable obstacle should be opposed to cabal, intrigue and corruption. These most deadly adversaries of republican government might naturally have been expected to make their approaches from more than one quarter, but chiefly from the desire in foreign powers to gain an improper ascendant in our councils. How could they better gratify this, than by raising a creature of their own to the chief magistracy of the union? But the convention have guarded against all danger of this sort with the most provident and judicious attention. They have not made the appointment of the president to depend on any pre-existing bodies of men who might be tampered with before hand to prostitute their votes; but they have referred it in the first instance to an immediate act of the people of America, to be exerted in the choice of persons for the temporary and sole purpose of making the appointment. And they have excluded from eligibility to this trust, all those who from situation might be suspected of too great devotion to the president in office. No senator, representative, or other person holding a place of trust or profit under the United States, can be of the number of the electors. Thus, without corrupting the body of the people, the immediate agents in the election will at least enter upon the task, free from any sinister byass. Their transient existence, and their detached situation, already

taken notice of, afford a satisfactory prospect of their continuing so, to the conclusion of it. The business of corruption,
when it is to embrace so considerable a number of men, requires time, as well as means. Nor would it be found easy
suddenly to embark them, dispersed as they would be over
thirteen states, in any combinations, founded upon motives,
which though they could not properly be denominated corrupt, might yet be of a nature to mislead them from their
duty.

Another and no less important desideratum was, that the
executive should be independent for his continuance in office
on all, but the people themselves. He might otherwise be
tempted to sacrifice his duty to his complaisance for those
whose favor was necessary to the duration of his official consequence. This advantage will also be secured, by making his
re-election to depend on a special body of representatives, deputed by the society for the single purpose of making the
important choice.

All these advantages will be happily combined in the plan
devised by the convention; which is, that the people of each
state shall choose a number of persons as electors, equal to the
number of senators and representatives of such state in the
national government, who shall assemble within the state and
vote for some fit person as president. Their votes, thus given,
are to be transmitted to the seat of the national government;
and the person who may happen to have a majority of the
whole number of votes will be the president. But as a majority of the votes might not always happen to centre on one
man and as it might be unsafe to permit less than a majority
to be conclusive, it is provided, that in such a contingency,
the house of representatives shall select out of the candidates,
who shall have the five highest numbers of votes, the man
who in their opinion may be best qualified for the office.

This process of election affords a moral certainty, that the
office of president, will never fall to the lot of any man, who is
not in an eminent degree endowed with the requisite qualifications. Talents for low intrigue and the little arts of popularity may alone suffice to elevate a man to the first honors in a
single state; but it will require other talents and a different
kind of merit to establish him in the esteem and confidence of

the whole union, or of so considerable a portion of it as would be necessary to make him a successful candidate for the distinguished office of president of the United States. It will not be too strong to say, that there will be a constant probability of seeing the station filled by characters pre-eminent for ability and virtue. And this will be thought no inconsiderable recommendation of the constitution, by those, who are able to estimate the share, which the executive in every government must necessarily have in its good or ill administration. Though we cannot acquiesce in the political heresy of the poet who says—

> "For forms of government let facts contest—
> That which is best administered is best."

—yet we may safely pronounce, that the true test of a good government is its aptitude and tendency to produce a good administration.

The vice-president is to be chosen in the same manner with the president; with this difference, that the senate is to do, in respect to the former, what is to be done by the house of representatives, in respect to the latter.

The appointment of an extraordinary person, as vice president, has been objected to as superfluous, if not mischievous. It has been alledged, that it would have been preferable to have authorised the senate to elect out of their own body an officer, answering that description. But two considerations seem to justify the ideas of the convention in this respect. One is, that to secure at all times the possibility of a definitive resolution of the body, it is necessary that the president should have only a casting vote. And to take the senator of any state from his seat as senator, to place him in that of president of the senate, would be to exchange, in regard to the state from which he came, a constant for a contingent vote. The other consideration is, that as the vice-president may occasionally become a substitute for the president, in the supreme executive magistracy, all the reasons, which recommend the mode of election prescribed for the one, apply with great, if not with equal, force to the manner of appointing the other. It is remarkable, that in this as in most other instances, the objection, which is made, would be against the constitution of this state. We have a Lieutenant Governor chosen by the people at large, who presides in the senate, and is the constitutional substitute for the Governor in casualties similar to those, which would authorise the vice-president to exercise the authorities and discharge the duties of the president.

"Publius," The Federalist LXIX
[Alexander Hamilton]

New-York Packet, March 14, 1788

To the People of the State of New-York.

I proceed now to trace the real characters of the proposed executive as they are marked out in the plan of the Convention. This will serve to place in a strong light the unfairness of the representations which have been made in regard to it.

The first thing which strikes our attention is that the executive authority, with few exceptions, is to be vested in a single magistrate. This will scarcely however be considered as a point upon which any comparison can be grounded; for if in this particular there be a resemblance to the King of Great-Britain, there is not less a resemblance to the Grand Signior, to the Khan of Tartary, to the man of the seven mountains, or to the Governor of New-York.

That magistrate is to be elected for *four* years; and is to be re-eligible as often as the People of the United States shall think him worthy of their confidence. In these circumstances, there is a total dissimilitude between *him* and a King of Great-Britain; who is an *hereditary* monarch, possessing the crown as a patrimony descendible to his heirs forever; but there is a close analogy between *him* and a Governor of New-York, who is elected for *three* years, and is re-eligible without limitation or intermission. If we consider how much less time would be requisite for establishing a dangerous influence in a single State, than for establishing a like influence throughout the United States, we must conclude that a duration of *four* years for the Chief Magistrate of the Union, is a degree of permanency far less to be dreaded in that office, than a duration of *three* years for a correspondent office in a single State.

The President of the United States would be liable to be impeached, tried, and upon conviction of treason, bribery, or other high crimes or misdemeanors, removed from office; and would afterwards be liable to prosecution and punishment in the ordinary course of law. The person of the King of Great-Britain is sacred and inviolable: There is no constitutional tribunal to which he is amenable; no punishment to which he can be subjected without involving the crisis of a national revolution. In this delicate and important circumstance of personal responsibility, the President of confederated America would stand upon no better ground than a Governor of New-York, and upon worse ground than the Governors of Maryland and Delaware.

The President of the United States is to have power to return a bill, which shall have passed the two branches of the Legislature, for re-consideration; but the bill so returned is to become a law, if upon that re-consideration it be approved by two thirds of both houses. The King of Great Britain, on his part, has an absolute negative upon the acts of the two houses of Parliament. The disuse of that power for a considerable time past, does not affect the reality of its existence; and is to be ascribed wholly to the crown's having found the means of substituting influence to authority, or the art of gaining a majority in one or the other of the two houses, to the necessity of exerting a prerogative which could seldom be exerted without hazarding some degree of national agitation. The qualified negative of the President differs widely from this absolute negative of the British sovereign; and tallies exactly with the revisionary authority of the Council of revision of this State, of which the Governor is a constituent part. In this respect, the power of the President would exceed that of the Governor of New-York; because the former would possess singly what the latter shares with the Chancellor and Judges. But it would be precisely the same with that of the Governor of Massachusetts, whose constitution, as to this article, seems to have been the original from which the Convention have copied.

The President is to be the "Commander in Chief of the army and navy of the United States, and of the militia of the several States, when called into the actual service of the United States. He is to have power to grant reprieves and pardons for offences against the United States, *except in cases of impeachment*; to recommend to the consideration of Congress such measures as he shall judge necessary and expedient; to convene on extraordinary occasions both houses of the Legislature, or either of them, and in case of disagreement between them *with respect to the time of adjournment*, to adjourn them to such time as he shall think proper; to take care that the laws be faithfully executed; and to commission all officers of the United States." In most of these particulars the power of the President will resemble equally that of the King of Great-Britain and the Governor of New-York. The most material points of difference are these—First; the President will have only the occasional command of such part of the militia of the nation, as by legislative provision may be called into the actual service of the Union—The King of Great-Britain and the Governor of New-York have at all times the entire command of all the militia within their several jurisdictions. In this article therefore the power of the President would be inferior to that of either the Monarch or the Governor.—Secondly; the President is to be Commander in Chief of the army and navy of the United States. In this respect his authority would be nominally the same with that of the King of Great-Britain, but in substance much inferior to it. It would amount to nothing more than the supreme command and direction of the military and naval forces, as first General and Admiral of the confederacy; while that of the British King extends to the *declaring* of war and to the *raising* and *regulating* of fleets and armies; all which by the Constitution under consideration would appertain to the Legislature.* The Governor of New-York on the other hand, is by the Constitution of the State vested only with the command of its militia and navy. But the

*A writer in a Pennsylvania paper, under the signature of *Tamony* has asserted that the King of Great-Britain owes his prerogatives as Commander in Chief to an annual mutiny bill.—The truth is on the contrary that his prerogative in this respect is immemorial, and was only disputed "contrary to all reason and precedent," as Blackstone, vol. I, p. 262, expresses it, by the long parliament of Charles the first, but by the statute the 13, of Charles second, ch. 6, it was declared to be in the King alone, for that the sole supreme government and command of the militia within his Majesty's realms and dominions, and of all forces by sea and land, and of all forts and places of strength, *ever was and is* the undoubted right of his Majesty and his royal predecessors Kings and Queens of England, and that both or either House of Parliament cannot nor ought to pretend to the same.

Constitutions of several of the States, expressly declare their Governors to be the Commanders in Chief as well of the army as navy; and it may well be a question whether those of New-Hampshire and Massachusetts, in particular, do not in this instance confer larger powers upon their respective Governors, than could be claimed by a President of the United States. — Thirdly; the power of the President in respect to pardons would extend to all cases, *except those of impeachment*. The Governor of New-York may pardon in all cases, even in those of impeachment, except for treason and murder. Is not the power of the Governor in this article, on a calculation of political consequences, greater than that of the President? All conspiracies and plots against the government, which have not been matured into actual treason, may be screened from punishment of every kind, by the interposition of the prerogative of pardoning. If a Governor of New-York therefore should be at the head of any such conspiracy, until the design had been ripened into actual hostility, he could ensure his accomplices and adherents an entire impunity. A President of the Union on the other hand, though he may even pardon treason, when prosecuted in the ordinary course of law, could shelter no offender in any degree from the effects of impeachment & conviction. Would not the prospect of a total indemnity for all the preliminary steps be a greater temptation to undertake and persevere in an enterprise against the public liberty than the mere prospect of an exemption from death and confiscation, if the final execution of the design, upon an actual appeal to arms, should miscarry? Would this last expectation have any influence at all, when the probability was computed that the person who was to afford that exemption might himself be involved in the consequences of the measure; and might be incapacitated by his agency in it, from affording the desired impunity. The better to judge of this matter, it will be necessary to recollect that by the proposed Constitution the offence of treason is limitted "to levying war upon the United States, and adhering to their enemies, giving them aid and comfort," and that by the laws of New-York it is confined within similar bounds. — Fourthly; the President can only adjourn the national Legislature in the single case of disagreement about the time of adjournment. The British monarch may prorogue or even dissolve the Parliament. The Governor of New-York may also prorogue the Legislature of this State for a limited time; a power which in certain situations may be employed to very important purposes.

The President is to have power with the advice and consent of the Senate to make treaties; provided two thirds of the Senators present concur. The King of Great-Britain is the sole and absolute representative of the nation in all foreign transactions. He can of his own accord make treaties of peace, commerce, alliance, and of every other description. It has been insinuated, that his authority in this respect is not conclusive, and that his conventions with foreign powers are subject to revision, and stand in need of the ratification of Parliament. But I believe this doctrine was never heard of 'till it was broached upon the present occasion. Every jurist* of that kingdom, and every other man acquainted with its constitution knows, as an established fact, that the prerogative of making treaties exists in the crown in its utmost plenitude; and that the compacts entered into by the royal authority have the most complete legal validity and perfection, independent of any other sanction. The Parliament, it is true, is sometimes seen employing itself in altering the existing laws to conform them to the speculations in a new treaty; and this may have possibly given birth to the imagination that its co-operation was necessary to the obligatory efficacy of the treaty. But this parliamentary interposition proceeds from a different cause; from the necessity of adjusting a most artificial and intricate system of revenue and commercial laws to the changes made in them by the operation of the treaty; and of adapting new provisions and precautions to the new state of things, to keep the machine from running into disorder. In this respect therefore, there is no comparison between the intended power of the President, and the actual power of the British sovereign. The one can perform alone, what the other can only do with the concurrence of a branch of the Legislature. It must be admitted that in this instance the power of the fœderal executive would exceed that of any State execu-

*Vide Blackstone's Commentaries, page 257.

tive. But this arises naturally from the exclusive possession by the Union of that part of the sovereign power, which relates to treaties. If the confederacy were to be dissolved, it would become a question, whether the executives of the several States were not solely invested with that delicate and important prerogative.

The President is also to be authorised to receive Ambassadors and other public Ministers. This, though it has been a rich theme of declamation, is more a matter of dignity than of authority. It is a circumstance, which will be without consequence in the administration of the government, and it was far more convenient that it should be arranged in this manner, than that there should be a necessity of convening the Legislature, or one of its branches, upon every arrival of a foreign minister; though it were merely to take the place of a departed predecessor.

The President is to nominate and *with the advice and consent of the Senate* to appoint Ambassadors and other public Ministers, Judges of the Supreme Court, and in general all officers of the United States established by law and whose appointments are not otherwise provided for by the Constitution. The King of Great-Britain is emphatically and truly stiled the fountain of honor. He not only appoints to all offices, but can create offices. He can confer titles of nobility at pleasure; and has the disposal of an immense number of church preferments. There is evidently a great inferiority, in the power of the President in this particular, to that of the British King; nor is it equal to that of the Governor of New-York, if we are to interpret the meaning of the constitution of the State by the practice which has obtained under it. The power of appointment is with us lodged in a Council composed of the Governor and four members of the Senate chosen by the Assembly. The Governor *claims* and has frequently *exercised* the right of nomination, and is *entitled* to a casting vote in the appointment. If he really has the right of nominating, his authority is in this respect equal to that of the President, and exceeds it in the article of the casting vote. In the national government, if the Senate should be divided, no appointment could be made: In the government of New-York, if the

Council should be divided the Governor can turn the scale and confirm his own nomination.* If we compare the publicity which must necessarily attend the mode of appointment by the President and an entire branch of the national Legislature, with the privacy in the mode of appointment by the Governor of New-York, closeted in a secret apartment with at most four, and frequently with only two persons, and if we at the same time consider how much more easy it must be to influence the small number of which a Council of Appointment consist than the considerable number of which the national Senate would consist, we cannot hesitate to pronounce, that the power of the Chief Magistrate of this State in the disposition of offices must in practice be greatly superior to that of the Chief Magistrate of the Union.

Hence it appears, that except as to the concurrent authority of the President in the article of treaties, it would be difficult to determine whether that Magistrate would in the aggregate, possess more or less power than the Governor of New-York. And it appears yet more unequivocally that there is no pretence for the parallel which has been attempted between him and the King of Great-Britain. But to render the contrast, in this respect, still more striking, it may be of use to throw the principal circumstances of dissimilitude into a closer groupe.

The President of the United States would be an officer elected by the people for *four* years. The King of Great-Britain is a perpetual and *hereditary* prince. The one would be amenable to personal punishment and disgrace: The person of the other is sacred and inviolable. The one would have a *qualified* negative upon the acts of the legislative body: The other has an *absolute* negative. The one would have a right to command the military and naval forces of the nation: The other in addition to this right, possesses that of *declaring* war, and of *raising* and *regulating* fleets and armies by his own authority. The one would have a concurrent power with a

---

*Candor however demands an acknowledgment, that I do not think the claim of the Governor to a right of nomination well founded. Yet it is always justifiable to reason from the practice of a government till its propriety has been constitutionally questioned. And independent of this claim, when we take into view the other considerations and pursue them through all their consequences, we shall be inclined to draw much the same conclusion.

branch of the Legislature in the formation of treaties: The other is the *sole possessor* of the power of making treaties. The one would have a like concurrent authority in appointing to offices: The other is the sole author of all appointments. The one can infer no privileges whatever: The other can make denizens of aliens, noblemen of commoners, can erect corporations with all the rights incident to corporate bodies. The one can prescribe no rules concerning the commerce or currency of the nation: The other is in several respects the arbiter of commerce, and in this capacity can establish markets and fairs, can regulate weights and measures, can lay embargoes for a limited time, can coin money, can authorise or prohibit the circulation of foreign coin. The one has no particle of spiritual jurisdiction: The other is the supreme head and Governor of the national church!—What answer shall we give to those who would persuade us that things so unlike resemble each other?—The same that ought to be given to those who tell us, that a government, the whole power of which would be in the hands of the elective and periodical servants of the people, is an aristocracy, a monarchy, and a despotism.

"Publius," The Federalist LXX [Alexander Hamilton]

Independent Journal (New York), March 15, 1788

To the People of the State of New-York.

There is an idea, which is not without its advocates, that a vigorous executive is inconsistent with the genius of republican government. The enlightened well wishers to this species of government must at least hope that the supposition is destitute of foundation; since they can never admit its truth, without at the same time admitting the condemnation of their own principles. Energy in the executive is a leading character in the definition of good government. It is essential to the protection of the community against foreign attacks: It is not less essential to the steady administration of the laws, to the protection of property against those irregular and high handed combinations, which sometimes interrupt the ordinary course of justice to the security of liberty against the enterprises and assaults of ambition, of faction and of anarchy. Every man the least conversant in Roman history knows how often that republic was obliged to take refuge in the absolute power of a single man, under the formidable title of dictator, as well against the intrigues of ambitious individuals, who aspired to the tyranny, and the seditions of whole classes of the community, whose conduct threatened the existence of all government, as against the invasions of external enemies, who menaced the conquest and destruction of Rome.

There can be no need however to multiply arguments or examples on this head. A feeble executive implies a feeble execution of the government. A feeble executive is but another phrase for a bad execution: And a government ill executed, whatever it may be in theory, must be in practice a bad government.

Taking it for granted, therefore, that all men of sense will agree in the necessity of an energetic executive; it will only remain to inquire, what are the ingredients which constitute this energy—how far can they be combined with those other ingredients which constitute safety in the republican sense? And how far does this combination characterise the plan, which has been reported by the convention?

The ingredients, which constitute energy in the executive, are first unity, secondly duration, thirdly an adequate provision for its support, fourthly competent powers.

The circumstances which constitute safety in the republican sense are, 1st. a due dependence on the people, secondly a due responsibility.

Those politicians and statesmen, who have been the most celebrated for the soundness of their principles, and for the justness of their views, have declared in favor of a single executive and a numerous legislative. They have with great propriety considered energy as the most necessary qualification of the former, and have regarded this as most applicable to power in a single hand; while they have with equal propriety considered the latter as best adapted to deliberation and wisdom, and best calculated to conciliate the confidence of the people and to secure their privileges and interests.

That unity is conducive to energy will not be disputed. Decision, activity, secrecy, dispatch will generally characterise the proceeding of one man, in a much more eminent degree, than the proceedings of any greater number; and in proportion as the number is increased, these qualities will be diminished.

This unity may be destroyed in two ways; either by vesting the power in two or more magistrates of equal dignity and authority; or by vesting it ostensibly in one man, subject in whole or in part to the controul and co-operation of others, in the capacity of counsellors to him. Of the first the two consuls of Rome may serve as an example; of the last we shall find examples in the constitutions of several of the states. New-York and New-Jersey, if I recollect right, are the only states, which have entrusted the executive authority wholly to single men.* Both these methods of destroying the unity of

*New-York has no council except for the single purpose of appointing to offices; New-Jersey has a council, whom the governor may consult. But I think from the terms of the constitution their resolutions do not bind him.

the executive have their partisans; but the votaries of an executive council are the most numerous. They are both liable, if not to equal, to similar objections; and may in most lights be examined in conjunction.

The experience of other nations will afford little instruction on this head. As far however as it teaches any thing, it teaches us not to be inamoured of plurality in the executive. We have seen that the Achæns on an experiment of two Prætors, were induced to abolish one. The Roman history records many instances of mischiefs to the republic from the dissentions between the consuls, and between the military tribunes, who were at times substituted to the consuls. But it gives us no specimens of any peculiar advantages derived to the state, from the circumstance of the plurality of those magistrates. That the dissentions between them were not more frequent, or more fatal, is matter of astonishment; until we advert to the singular position in which the republic was almost continually placed and to the prudent policy pointed out by the circumstances of the state, and pursued by the consuls, of making a division of the government between them. The Patricians engaged in a perpetual struggle with the Plebians for the preservation of their antient authorities and dignities; the consuls, who were generally chosen out of the former body, were commonly united by the personal interest they had in the defence of the privileges of their order. In addition to this motive of union, after the arms of the republic had considerably expanded the bounds of its empire, it became an established custom with the consuls to divide the administration between themselves by lot; one of them remaining at Rome to govern the city and its environs; the other taking the command in the more distant provinces. This expedient must no doubt have had great influence in preventing those collisions and rivalships, which might otherwise have embroiled the peace of the republic.

But quitting the dim light of historical research, and attaching ourselves purely to the dictates of reason and good sense, we shall discover much greater cause to reject than to approve the idea of plurality in the executive, under any modification whatever.

Wherever two or more persons are engaged in any common enterprize or pursuit, there is always danger of difference of opinion. If it be a public trust or office in which they are cloathed with equal dignity and authority, there is peculiar danger of personal emulation and even animosity. From either and especially from all these causes, the most bitter dissentions are apt to spring. Whenever these happen, they lessen the respectability, weaken the authority, and distract the plans and operations of those whom they divide. If they should unfortunately assail the supreme executive magistracy of a country, consisting of a plurality of persons, they might impede or frustrate the most important measures of the government, in the most critical emergencies of the state. And what is still worse, they might split the community into the most violent and irreconcilable factions, adhering differently to the different individuals who composed the magistracy.

Men often oppose a thing merely because they have had no agency in planning it, or because it may have been planned by those whom they dislike. But if they have been consulted and have happened to disapprove, opposition then becomes in their estimation an indispensable duty of self love. They seem to think themselves bound in honor, and by all the motives of personal infallibility to defeat the success of what has been resolved upon, contrary to their sentiments. Men of upright, benevolent tempers have too many opportunities of remarking with horror, to what desperate lengths this disposition is sometimes carried, and how often the great interests of society are sacrificed to the vanity, to the conceit and to the obstinacy of individuals, who have credit enough to make their passions and their caprices interesting to mankind. Perhaps the question now before the public may in its consequences afford melancholy proofs of the effects of this despicable frailty, or rather detestable vice in the human character.

Upon the principles of a free government, inconveniencies from the source just mentioned must necessarily be submitted to in the formation of the legislature; but it is unnecessary and therefore unwise to introduce them into the constitution of the executive. It is here too that they may be most pernicious—In the legislature, promptitude of decision is oftener an evil than a benefit. The differences of opinion, and the jarrings of parties in that department of the government, though they may sometimes obstruct salutary plans, yet often promote deliberation and circumspection; and serve to check excesses in the majority. When a resolution too is once taken, the opposition must be at an end. That resolution is a law, and resistance to it punishable. But no favourable circumstances palliate or atone for the disadvantages of dissention in the executive department. Here they are pure and unmixed. There is no point at which they cease to operate. They serve to embarrass and weaken the execution of the plan or measure, to which they relate, from the first step to the final conclusion of it. They constantly counteract those qualities in the executive, which are the most necessary ingredients in its composition, vigour and expedition, and this without any counterballancing good. In the conduct of war, in which the energy of the executive is the bulwark of the national security, every thing would be to be apprehended from its plurality.

It must be confessed that these observations apply with principal weight to the first case supposed, that is to a plurality of magistrates of equal dignity and authority; a scheme the advocates for which are not likely to form a numerous sect: But they apply, though not with equal, yet with considerable weight, to the project of a council, whose concurrence is made constitutionally necessary to the operations of the ostensible executive. An artful cabal in that council would be able to distract and to enervate the whole system of administration. If no such cabal should exist, the mere diversity of views and opinions would alone be sufficient to tincture the exercise of the executive authority with a spirit of habitual feebleness and delatoriness.

But one of the weightiest objections to a plurality in the executive, and which lies as much against the last as the first plan, is that it tends to conceal faults, and destroy responsibility. Responsibility is of two kinds, to censure and to punishment. The first is the most important of the two; especially in an elective office. Man, in public trust, will much oftener act in such a manner as to render him unworthy of being any longer trusted, than in such a manner as to make him obnoxious to legal punishment. But the multiplication of the executive adds to the difficulty of detection in either case. It often becomes impossible, amidst mutual accusations, to determine on whom the blame or the punishment of a pernicious measure, or series of pernicious measures ought really to fall. It is shifted from one to another with so much dexterity, and under such plausible appearances, that the public opinion is left in suspense about the real author. The circumstances which may have led to any national miscarriage or misfortune are sometimes so complicated, that where there are a number of actors who may have had different degrees and kinds of agency, though we may clearly see upon the whole that there has been mismanagement, yet it may be impracticable to pronounce to whose account the evil which may have been incurred is truly chargeable.

"I was overruled by my council.—The council were so divided in their opinions, that it was impossible to obtain any better resolution on the point." These and similar pretexts are constantly at hand, whether true or false. And who is there that will either take the trouble or incur the odium of a strict scrutiny into the secret springs of the transaction? Should there be found a citizen zealous enough to undertake the unpromising task, if there happen to be a collusion between the parties concerned, how easy is it to cloath the circumstances with so much ambiguity, as to render it uncertain what was the precise conduct of any of those parties?

In the single instance in which the governor of this state is coupled with a council, that is in the appointment to offices, we have seen the mischiefs of it in the view now under consideration. Scandalous appointments to important offices have been made. Some cases indeed have been so flagrant, that ALL PARTIES have agreed in the impropriety of the thing. When enquiry has been made, the blame has been laid by the governor on the members of the council; who on their part have charged it upon his nomination: While the people remain altogether at a loss to determine by whose influence their interests have been commited to hands so unqualified, and so manifestly improper. In tenderness to individuals, I forbear to descend to particulars.

It is evident from these considerations, that the plurality of the executive tends to deprive the people of the two greatest securities they can have for the faithful exercise of any delegated power; first, the restraints of public opinion, which lose their efficacy as well on account of the division of the censure attendant on bad measures among a number, as on account of the uncertainty on whom it ought to fall; and secondly, the opportunity of discovering with facility and clearness the misconduct of the persons they trust, in order either to their removal from office, or to their actual punishment, in cases which admit of it.

In England the king is a perpetual magistrate; and it is a maxim, which has obtained for the sake of the public peace, that he is unaccountable for his administration, and his person sacred. Nothing therefore can be wiser in that kingdom than to annex to the king a constitutional council, who may be responsible to the nation for the advice they give. Without this there would be no responsibility whatever in the executive department; an idea inadmissible in a free government. But even there the king is not bound by the resolutions of his council, though they are answerable for the advice they give. He is the absolute master of his own conduct, in the exercise of his office; and may observe or disregard the council given to him at his sole discretion.

But in a republic, where every magistrate ought to be personally responsible for his behaviour in office, the reason which in the British constitution dictates the propriety of a council not only ceases to apply, but turns against the institution. In the monarchy of Great-Britain, it furnishes a substitute for the prohibited responsibility of the chief magistrate; which serves in some degree as a hostage to the national justice for his good behaviour. In the American republic it would serve to destroy, or would greatly diminish the intended and necessary responsibility of the chief magistrate himself.

The idea of a council to the executive, which has so generally obtained in the state constitutions, has been derived from that maxim of republican jealousy, which considers power as safer in the hands of a number of men than of a single man. If the maxim should be admitted to be applicable to the case, I should contend that the advantage on that side would not counterballance the numerous disadvantages on the opposite side. But I do not think the rule at all applicable to the executive power. I clearly concur in opinion in this particular with a writer whom the celebrated Junius pronounces to be "deep, solid and ingenious," that, "the executive power is more easily confined when it is one:"* That it is far more safe there should be a single object for the jealousy and watchfulness of the people; and in a word that all multiplication of the executive is rather dangerous than friendly to liberty.

A little consideration will satisfy us, that the species of security sought for in the multiplication of the executive is unattainable. Numbers must be so great as to render combination difficult; or they are rather a source of danger than of security. The united credit and influence of several individuals must be more formidable to liberty than the credit and influence of either of them separately. When power therefore is placed in the hands of so small a number of men, as to admit of their interests and views being easily combined in a common enterprise, by an artful leader, it becomes more liable to abuse and more dangerous when abused, than if it be lodged in the hands of one man; who from the very circumstance of his being alone will be more narrowly watched and more readily suspected, and who cannot unite so great a mass of influence as when he is associated with others. The Decemvres of Rome, whose name denotes their number,† were more to be dreaded in their usurpation than any ONE of them would have been. No person would think of proposing an executive much more numerous than that body, from six to a dozen have been suggested for the number of the council. The extreme of these numbers is not too great for an easy combination; and from such a combination America would have more to fear, than from the ambition of any single individual. A council to a magistrate, who is himself responsible for what he does, are generally nothing better than a clog upon his good intentions; are often the instruments and accomplices of his bad, and are almost always a cloak to his faults.

I forbear to dwell upon the subject of expence; though it be evident that if the council should be numerous enough to answer the principal end, aimed at by the institution, the

*De Loslme.
†Ten.

salaries of the members, who must be drawn from their home to reside at the seat of government, would form an item in the catalogue of public expenditures, too serious to be incurred for an object of equivocal utility.

I will only add, that prior to the appearance of the constitution, I rarely met with an intelligent man from any of the states, who did not admit as the result of experience, that the UNITY of the Executive of this state was one of the best of the distinguishing features of our constitution.

Comte de Moustier to Comte de Montmorin

New York, March 16, 1788

The general expectation has been singularly disappointed by the resolution made by the Convention of the State of Newhampshire to adjourn to the third tuesday of June, which will be the 17th. The majority of votes against the new Constitution there was 70. to 40. It seems certain that most of the members of the Convention, who have voted against the Constitution were bound by the instructions of their constituents, which forced them to vote contrary to the belief, with which the federalists inspired them afterwards, in the necessity and usefulness of the new plan. It is only in this way that one can explain the adherence of a great number to the proposition of the minority to adjourn to reconsider the proposed Constitution after having allowed the people the time to give new instructions to their representatives. This motion passed with a plurality of 53. to 51.

The State of Rhodeisland, which for a long time has separated itself from the others by the singularity of its conduct and where the common people entirely dominate, made a rather peculiar resolution. Instead of taking the advice of the people through the channel of its representatives in a general Convention, the Legislature has submitted the examination of the new federal Constitution to the conventicles formed in each district. The majority of the districts must decide on its adoption. The Demagogues, who govern the people by flattering them, undoubtedly hope in this way to cause the rejection of the Constitution, whose design is to curb their excesses. However they could be deluded in their expectation, if the Quakers who are quite numerous in that State align themselves with the Federalists for fear of the abuse of paper money, the terrible weapon, with which the demagogues attack and destroy the propertied class in general.

The fear of little security for their property disturbs all who possess any; the eagerness to acquire property or to be absolved of their debts arouses a great number of opponents to the new Constitution. Those of this opinion find in paper money a means to free themselves or to become rich by forcing the acceptance of this imaginary money, which they create and abolish at will, when they are able to dominate the State Legislatures. Thus one can count among the Federalists the majority of landowners and among the Antifederalists the Bankrupts, the men of bad faith, the needy and the men who could not exercise any power whatsoever in their States, except if it did not exist in the general Government. The generality of the people divide themselves among their Leaders. Until now there seemed to be more moderation among the Federalists than among their adversaries. But every day it becomes more difficult to judge what the outcome of this power struggle will be. Just as a Government can be built that is solid, united, durable, it is equally possible for one to see it dissipate into the shadow of a body which until now seemed invested with the power of the Confederation. The dissolution of Congress is an event as likely to happen as its regeneration. Interested observers consequently cannot stop themselves from speculating according to these two hypotheses.

It would be principally in a political report that the difference between the consolidation or the division of the American Confederation would be touched. . . .

"Publius," The Federalist LXXI
[Alexander Hamilton]

New-York Packet, March 18, 1788

To the People of the State of New-York.

Duration in office has been mentioned as the second requisite to the energy of the executive authority. This has relation to two objects: To the personal firmness of the Executive Magistrate in the employment of his constitutional powers; and to the stability of the system of administration which may have been adopted under his auspices.—With regard to the first, it must be evident, that the longer the duration in office, the greater will be the probability of obtaining so important an advantage. It is a general principle of human nature, that a man will be interested in whatever he possesses, in proportion to the firmness or precariousness of the tenure, by which he holds it; will be less attached to what he holds by a momentary or uncertain title, than to what he enjoys by a durable or certain title; and of course will be willing to risk more for the sake of the one, than for the sake of the other. This remark is not less applicable to a political privilege, or honor, or trust, than to any article of ordinary property. The inference from it is, that a man acting in the capacity of Chief Magistrate, under a consciousness, that in a very short time he *must* lay down his office, will be apt to feel himself too little interested in it, to hazard any material censure or perplexity, from the independent exertion of his powers, or from encountering the ill-humors, however transient, which may happen to prevail either in a considerable part of the society itself, or even in a predominant faction in the legislative body. If the case should only be, that he *might* lay it down, unless continued by a new choice; and if he should be desirous of being continued, his wishes conspiring with his fears would tend still more powerfully to corrupt his integrity, or debase his fortitude. In either

357

case feebleness and irresolution must be the characteristics of the station.

There are some, who would be inclined to regard the servile pliancy of the executive to a prevailing current, either in the community, or in the Legislature, as its best recommendation. But such men entertain very crude notions, as well of the purposes for which government was instituted, as of the true means by which the public happiness may be promoted. The republican principle demands, that the deliberate sense of the community should govern the conduct of those to whom they entrust the management of their affairs; but it does not require an unqualified complaisance to every sudden breese of passion, or to every transient impulse which the people may receive from the arts of men, who flatter their prejudices to betray their interests. It is a just observation, that the people commonly *intend* the PUBLIC GOOD. This often applies to their very errors. But their good sense would despise the adulator, who should pretend that they always *reason right* about the *means* of promoting it. They know from experience, that they sometimes err; and the wonder is, that they so seldom err as they do; beset as they continually are by the wiles of parasites and sycophants, by the snares of the ambitious, the avaricious, the desperate; by the artifices of men, who possess their confidence more than they deserve it, and of those who seek to possess, rather than to deserve it. When occasions present themselves in which the interests of the people are at variance with their inclinations, it is the duty of the persons whom they have appointed to be the guardians of those interests, to withstand the temporary delusion, in order to give them time and opportunity for more cool and sedate reflection. Instances might be cited, in which a conduct of this kind has saved the people from very fatal consequences of their own mistakes, and has procured lasting monuments of their gratitude to the men, who had courage and magnanimity enough to serve them at the peril of their displeasure.

But however inclined we might be to insist upon an unbounded complaisance in the executive to the inclinations of the people, we can with no propriety contend for a like complaisance to the humors of the Legislature. The latter may sometimes stand in opposition to the former; and at other times the people may be entirely neutral. In either supposition, it is certainly desirable that the executive should be in a situation to dare to act his own opinion with vigor and decision.

The same rule, which teaches the propriety of a partition between the various branches of power, teaches us likewise that this partition ought to be so contrived as to render the one independent of the other. To what purpose separate the executive, or the judiciary, from the legislative, if both the executive and the judiciary are so constituted as to be at the absolute devotion of the legislative? Such a separation must be merely nominal and incapable of producing the ends for which it was established. It is one thing to be subordinate to the laws, and another to be dependent on the legislative body. The first comports with, the last violates, the fundamental principles of good government; and whatever may be the forms of the Constitution, unites all power in the same hands. The tendency of the legislative authority to absorb every other, has been fully displayed and illustrated by examples, in some preceding numbers. In governments purely republican, this tendency is almost irresistable. The representatives of the people, in a popular assembly, seem sometimes to fancy that they are the people themselves; and betray strong symptoms of impatience and disgust at the least sign of opposition from any other quarter; as if the exercise of its rights by either the executive or judiciary, were a breach of their privilege and an outrage to their dignity. They often appear disposed to exert an imperious controul over the other departments; and as they commonly have the people on their side, they always act with such momentum as to make it very difficult for the other members of the government to maintain the balance of the Constitution.

It may perhaps be asked how the shortness of the duration in office can affect the independence of the executive on the legislative, unless the one were possessed of the power of appointing or displacing the other? One answer to this enquiry may be drawn from the principle already remarked, that is from the slender interest a man is apt to take in a short lived advantage, and the little inducement it affords him to expose himself on account of it to any considerable inconvenience or hazard. Another answer, perhaps more obvious, though not more conclusive, will result from the consideration of the influence of the legislative body over the people, which might be employed to prevent the re-election of a man, who by an upright resistance to any sinister project of that body, should have made himself obnoxious to its resentment.

It may be asked also whether a duration of four years would answer the end proposed, and if it would not, whether a less period which would at least be recommended by greater security against ambitious designs, would not for that reason be preferable to a longer period, which was at the same time too short for the purpose of inspiring the desired firmness and independence of the magistrate?

It cannot be affirmed, that a duration of four years or any other limited duration would completely answer the end proposed; but it would contribute towards it in a degree which would have a material influence upon the spirit and character of the government. Between the commencement and termination of such a period there would always be a considerable interval, in which the prospect of annihilation would be sufficiently remote not to have an improper effect upon the conduct of a man endued with a tolerable portion of fortitude; and in which he might reasonably promise himself, that there would be time enough, before it arrived, to make the community sensible of the propriety of the measures he might incline to pursue. Though it be probable, that as he approached the moment when the public were by a new election to signify their sense of his conduct, his confidence and with it, his firmness would decline; yet both the one and the other would derive support from the opportunities, which his previous continuance in the station had afforded him of establishing himself in the esteem and good will of his constituents. He might then hazard with safety, in proportion to the proofs he had given of his wisdom and integrity, and to the title he had acquired to the respect and attachment of his fellow citizens. As on the one hand, a duration of four years will contribute to the firmness of the executive in a sufficient degree to render it a very valuable ingredient in the composition; so on the other, it is not long enough to justify any alarm for the public liberty. If a British House of Commons, from the most feeble beginnings, *from the mere power of assenting or disagreeing to the imposition of a new tax*, have by rapid strides, reduced the prerogatives of the crown and the privileges of the nobility within the limits they conceived to be compatible with the principles of a free government; while they raised themselves to the rank and consequence of a coequal branch of the Legislature; if they have been able in one instance to abolish both the royalty and the aristocracy, and to overturn all the ancient establishments as well in the church as State; if they have been able on a recent occasion to make the monarch tremble at the prospect of an innovation* attempted by them; what would be to be feared from an elective magistrate of four years duration, with the confined authorities of a President of the United States? What but that he might be unequal to the task which the Constitution assigns him?—I shall only add that if his duration be such as to leave a doubt of his firmness, that doubt is inconsistent with a jealousy of his encroachments.

*This was the case with respect to Mr. Fox's India bill which was carried in the House of Commons, and rejected in the House of Lords, to the entire satisfaction, as it is said, of the people.

"Publius," The Federalist LXXII
[Alexander Hamilton]

Independent Journal (New York), March 19, 1788

To the People of the State of New-York.

The ADMINISTRATION of government, in its largest sense, comprehends all the operations of the body politic, whether legislative, executive or judiciary, but in its most usual and perhaps in its most precise signification, it is limited to executive details, and falls peculiarly within the province of the executive department. The actual conduct of foreign negotiations, the preparatory plans of finance, the application and disbursement of the public monies, in conformity to the general appropriations of the legislature, the arrangement of the army and navy, the direction of the operations of war; these and other matters of a like nature constitute what seems to be most properly understood by the administration of government. The persons therefore, to whose immediate management these different matters are committed, ought to be considered as the assistants or deputies of the chief magistrate; and, on this account, they ought to derive their offices from his appointment, at least from his nomination, and ought to be subject to his superintendence. This view of the subject will at once suggest to us the intimate connection between the duration of the executive magistrate in office, and the stability of the system of administration. To reverse and undo what has been done by a predecessor is very often considered by a successor, as the best proof he can give of his own capacity and desert; and, in addition to this propensity, where the alteration has been the result of public choice, the person substituted is warranted in supposing, that the dismission of his predecessor has proceeded from a dislike to his measures, and that the less he resembles him the more he will recommend himself to the favor of his constituents. These considerations, and the influence of personal confidences and attachments, would be likely to induce every new president to promote a change of men to fill the subordinate stations; and these causes together could not fail to occasion a disgraceful and ruinous mutability in the administration of the government.

With a positive duration of considerable extent, I connect the circumstance of re-eligibility. The first is necessary to give to the officer himself the inclination and the resolution to act his part well, and to the community time and leisure to observe the tendency of his measures, and thence to form an experimental estimate of their merits. The last is necessary to enable the people, when they see reason to approve of his conduct, to continue him in the station, in order to prolong the utility of his talents and virtues, and to secure to the government, the advantage of permanency in a wise system of administration.

Nothing appears more plausible at first sight, nor more ill founded upon close inspection, than a scheme, which in relation to the present point has had some respectable advocates—I mean that of continuing the chief magistrate in office for a certain time, and then excluding him from it, either for a limited period, or for ever after. This exclusion whether temporary or perpetual would have nearly the same effects; and these effects would be for the most part rather pernicious than salutary.

One ill effect of the exclusion would be a diminution of the inducements to good behaviour. There are few men who would not feel much less zeal in the discharge of a duty, when they were conscious that the advantages of the station, with which it was connected, must be relinquished at a determinate period, then when they were permitted to entertain a hope of *obtaining* by *meriting* a continuance of them. This position will not be disputed, so long as it is admitted that the desire of reward is one of the strongest incentives of human conduct, or that the best security for the fidelity of mankind is to make their interest coincide with their duty. Even the love of fame, the ruling passion of the noblest minds, which would prompt a man to plan and undertake extensive and arduous enterprises for the public benefit, requiring considerable time to mature and perfect them, if he could flatter himself with the prospect of being allowed to finish what he had begun, would on the contrary deter him from the undertaking, when he foresaw that he must quit the scene, before he could accomplish the work, and must commit that, together with his own reputation, to hands which might be unequal or unfriendly to the task. The most to be expected from the generality of men, in such a situation, is the negative merit of not doing harm instead of the positive merit of doing good.

Another ill effect of the exclusion would be the temptation to sordid views, to peculation, and in some instances, to usurpation. An avaricious man, who might happen to fill the offices, looking forward to a time when he must at all events yield up the emoluments he enjoyed, would feel a propensity, not easy to be resisted by such a man, to make the best use of the opportunity he enjoyed, while it lasted; and might not scruple to have recourse to the most corrupt expedients to make the harvest as abundant as it was transient; though the same man probably, with a different prospect before him, might content himself with the regular perquisites of his situation, and might even be unwilling to risk the consequences of an abuse of his opportunities. His avarice might be a guard upon his avarice. Add to this, that the same man might be vain or ambitious as well as avaricious. And if he could expect to prolong his honors, by his good conduct, he might hesitate to sacrifice his appetite for them to his appetite for gain. But with the prospect before him of approaching and inevitable annihilation, his avarice would be likely to get the victory over his caution, his vanity or his ambition.

An ambitious man too, when he found himself seated on the summit of his country's honors, when he looked forward to the time at which he must descend from the exalted eminence forever; and reflected that no exertion of merit on his part could save him from the unwelcome reverse: Such a man, in such a situation, would be much more violently tempted to embrace a favorable conjuncture for attempting the prolongation of his power, at every personal hazard, than if he had the probability of answering the same end by doing his duty.

Would it promote the peace of the community, or the

stability of the government, to have half a dozen men who had had credit enough to be raised to the seat of the supreme magistracy, wandering among the people like discontented ghosts, and sighing for a place which they were destined never more to possess?

A third ill effect of the exclusion would be the depriving the community of the advantage of the experience gained by the chief magistrate in the exercise of his office. That experience is the parent of wisdom is an adage, the truth of which is recognized by the wisest as well as the simplest of mankind. What more desireable or more essential than this quality in the governors of nations? Where more desirable or more essential than in the first magistrate of a nation? Can it be wise to put this desirable and essential quality under the ban of the constitution; and to declare that the moment it is acquired, its possessor shall be compelled to abandon the station in which it was acquired, and to which it is adapted? This nevertheless is the precise import of all those regulations, which exclude men from serving their country, by the choice of their fellow citizens, after they have, by a course of service filled themselves for doing it with a greater degree of utility.

A fourth ill effect of the exclusion would be the banishing men from stations, in which in certain emergencies of the state their presence might be of the greatest moment to the public interest or safety. There is no nation which has not at one period or another experienced an absolute necessity of the services of particular men, in particular situations, perhaps it would not be too strong to say, to the preservation of its political existence. How unwise therefore must be every such self-denying ordinance, as serves to prohibit a nation from making use of its own citizens, in the manner best suited to its exigences and circumstances! Without supposing the personal essentiality of the man, it is evident that a change of the chief magistrate, at the breaking out of a war, or at any similar crisis, for another even of equal merit, would at all times be detrimental to the community; inasmuch as it would substitute inexperience to experience, and would tend to unhinge and set afloat the already settled train of the administration.

A fifth ill effect of the exclusion would be, that it would operate as a constitutional interdiction of stability in the administration. By *necessitating* a change of men, in the first office in the nation, it would necessitate a mutability of measures. It is not generally to be expected, that men will vary; and measures remain uniform. The contrary is the usual course of things. And we need not be apprehensive there will be too much stability, while there is even the option of changing; nor need we desire to prohibit the people from continuing their confidence, where they think it may be safely placed, and where by constancy on their part, they may obviate the fatal inconveniences of fluctuating councils and a variable policy.

These are some of the disadvantages, which would flow from the principle of exclusion. They apply most forcibly to the scheme of a perpetual exclusion; but when we consider that even a partial exclusion would always render the re-admission of the person a remote and precarious object, the observations which have been made will apply nearly as fully to one case as to the other.

What are the advantages premised to counterballance these disadvantages? They are represented to be 1st. Greater independence in the magistrate: 2dly. Greater security to the people. Unless the exclusion be perpetual there will be no pretence to infer the first advantage. But even in that case, may he have no object beyond his present station to which he may sacrifice his independence? May he have no connections, no friends, for whom he may sacrifice it? May he not be less willing, by a firm conduct, to make personal enemies, when he acts under the impression, that a time is fast approaching, on the arrival of which he not only MAY, but MUST be exposed to their resentments, upon an equal, perhaps upon an inferior footing? It is not an easy point to determine whether his independence would be most promoted or impaired by such an arrangement.

As to the second supposed advantage, there is still greater reason to entertain doubts concerning it. If the exclusion were to be perpetual, a man of irregular ambition, of whom alone there could be reason in any case to entertain apprehensions, would with infinite reluctance yield to the necessity of taking his leave forever of a post, in which his passion for power and pre-eminence had acquired the force of habit. And if he had been fortunate or adroit enough to conciliate the good will of the people he might induce them to consider as a very odious and unjustifiable restraint upon themselves, a provision which was calculated to debar them of the right of giving a fresh proof of their attachment to a favorite. There may be conceived circumstances, in which this disgust of the people, seconding the thwarted ambition of such a favourite, might occasion greater danger to liberty, than could ever reasonably be dreaded from the possibility of a perpetuation in office, by the voluntary suffrages of the community, exercising a constitutional privilege.

There is an excess of refinement in the idea of disabling the people to continue in office men, who had entitled themselves, in their opinion, to approbation and confidence; the advantages of which are at best speculative and equivocal; and are overbalanced by disadvantages far more certain and decisive.

"A Freeman" to the Freeholders and Freemen of Rhode Island

Newport Herald (Rhode Island), March 20, 1788

A question of great magnitude is submitted to your decision on the fourth Monday of this month, *that of deciding in town-meeting upon the proposed Federal Constitution*—six states have already ratified it, and the others, excepting this, have appointed conventions.—This alteration of the mode of decision subjects us to great inconveniences in investigating the truth, for it cannot be expected that our information can be so extensive in separate meetings as in a collective one; besides, we are liable to be imposed on by artful and designing men, whose only prospect is in a state of anarchy, and are excluded from the benefits which frequently result from accommodations.—We are not only deprived by the Legislature *of an unalienable right*, that of determining whether we would decide ourselves on the constitution, or refer it to a convention of our appointment, where it might have a complete discussion—but insidious men have been incited to circulate falsehood after falsehood to destroy this fabric of order, justice and liberty, and flushed with their apparent success, they have presumed so far on our ignorance as to declare, that the Federal Constitution is more despotic than the British.—Let us therefore, my fellow citizens, candidly compare these two constitutions, and then we shall not hesitate to pronounce the superior excellence of the Federal Constitution;—for this purpose I have impartially selected from the celebrated Judge Blackstone, the powers of the British Government, and contrasted those of Congress under the proposed constitution with them.

BRITISH CONSTITUTION.	PROPOSED CONSTITUTION FOR THE UNITED STATES OF AMERICA.
The Parliament.	*The Congress.*
They are the supreme Legislative, their powers are absolute, and extend to an abolition of Magna Charta itself.	Their powers are not supreme, nor absolute, it being defined by the Constitution: and all powers therein not granted, are retained by the State Legislatures.
Its constituent parts are the King's Majesty, the Lords Spiritual and Temporal, and the Commons, each of which parts has a negative in making Laws.	Congress consists of a Senate and House of Representatives; the President may disapprove of Bills; but if upon reconsideration, they are approved by two-thirds of the two Houses, they become Laws, notwithstanding his disapprobation.
The King.	*The President,*
By the positive Constitution of the Kingdom the Crown hath ever been descendible, and so continues by becoming hereditary in the Prince, to whom it is limited.	Is elected by the people for the term of four years only, consequently these States are not exposed to the disadvantages and dangers of hereditary descent.
The Constitution of England not only views the King as absolute in perpetuity, but in perfection. *The King can do no wrong,* is an established maxim.	The Constitution of the United States supposes that a President may do wrong, and have provided that he shall be removed from office on impeachment and conviction of high crimes and misdemeanors.

The King has the sole right of sending and receiving Ambassadors, of making treaties, of proclaiming war or peace, of issuing reprisals, of granting safe conduct.

The President cannot, without the advice and consent of the Senate, appoint Ambassadors, nor make treaties. The powers of declaring war, raising armies, and granting safe conducts, are vested in Congress only.

The King is considered as the General of the Kingdom, may raise fleets and armies, build forts, confine his subjects within the realm, or recall them from foreign parts.

The President is only Commander in Chief of fleets and armies, when called into actual service: he cannot confine our citizens within the States, nor oblige them to return from foreign parts.

The King is the supreme Head of the Church, and receives appeals in all ecclesiastical causes.

The King hath the power to prorogue, nay to dissolve the Parliament.

The Constitution disclaims the exercise of any such powers.

The President hath no power to adjourn Congress, but in cases of disagreement between the Senate and Representatives. The President cannot dissolve them.

The House of Lords.

The Lords who compose this House were originally created by the King and, excepting the sixteen elected by Scotland, retain their seats for life, their powers descending to their heirs. The King may also constitute Lords at pleasure. The House of Lords are not only vested with Legislative powers, but are the High Court of Appeals in civil causes.

The Senate,

Hold not their seats for life, nor are their powers descendible to their heirs; but they are elected by the State Legislatures for six years only: They are liable to be removed for malconduct by impeachment, & are not vested with judicial powers.

The Commons,
Are elected for seven years, and not more than one-twentieth part of the natural free subjects of Great-Britain are privileged to be electors or hold any office of honor or trust under the Crown.

The Representatives,
Are elected for two years only, by the independent freemen of these United States, who compose a great majority of the citizens. No further requisites are necessary to invest citizens with the privileges of freemen, than a small freehold that is prescribed by our particular State Laws; and when admitted free, they are capable of electing and being elected to any office of honor & trust within the United States.

State of Rhode-Island, &c. March 14.

"Brutus" XV

New York Journal, March 20, 1788

(Continued.)

I said in my last number, that the supreme court under this constitution would be exalted above all other power in the government, and subject to no controul. The business of this paper will be to illustrate this, and to shew the danger that will result from it. I question whether the world ever saw, in any period of it, a court of justice invested with such immense powers, and yet placed in a situation so little responsible. Certain it is, that in England, and in the several states, where we have been taught to believe, the courts of law are put upon the most prudent establishment, they are on a very different footing.

The judges in England, it is true, hold their offices during their good behaviour, but then their determinations are subject to correction by the house of lords; and their power is by no means so extensive as that of the proposed supreme court of the union.—I believe they in no instance assume the authority to set aside an act of parliament under the idea that it is inconsistent with their constitution. They consider themselves bound to decide according to the existing laws of the land, and never undertake to controul them by adjudging that they are inconsistent with the constitution—much less are they vested with the power of giving an *equitable* construction to the constitution.

The judges in England are under the controul of the legislature, for they are bound to determine according to the laws passed by them. But the judges under this constitution will controul the legislature, for the supreme court are authorised in the last resort, to determine what is the extent of the powers of the Congress; they are to give the constitution an explanation, and there is no power above them to sit aside their judgment. The framers of this constitution appear to have followed that of the British, in rendering the judges independent, by granting them their offices during good behaviour, without following the constitution of England, in instituting a tribunal in which their errors may be corrected; and without adverting to this, that the judicial under this system have a power which is above the legislative, and which indeed transcends any power before given to a judicial by any free government under heaven.

I do not object to the judges holding their commissions during good behaviour. I suppose it a proper provision provided they were made properly responsible. But I say, this system has followed the English government in this, while it has departed from almost every other principle of their jurisprudence, under the idea, of rendering the judges independent; which, in the British constitution, means no more than that they hold their places during good behaviour, and have fixed salaries, they have made the judges *independent*, in the fullest sense of the word. There is no power above them, to controul any of their decisions. There is no authority that can remove them, and they cannot be controuled by the laws of the legislature. In short, they are independent of the people, of the legislature, and of every power under heaven. Men placed in this situation will generally soon feel themselves independent of heaven itself. Before I proceed to illustrate the truth of these assertions, I beg liberty to make one remark— Though in my opinion the judges ought to hold their offices during good behaviour, yet I think it is clear, that the reasons in favour of this establishment of the judges in England, do by no means apply to this country.

The great reason assigned, why the judges in Britain ought to be commissioned during good behaviour, is this, that they may be placed in a situation, not to be influenced by the crown, to give such decisions, as would tend to increase its powers and prerogatives. While the judges held their places at the will and pleasure of the king, on whom they depended not only for their offices, but also for their salaries, they were subject to every undue influence. If the crown wished to carry a favorite point, to accomplish which the aid of the courts of law was necessary, the pleasure of the king would be signified to the judges. And it required the spirit of a martyr, for the judges to determine contrary to the king's will.—They were absolutely dependent upon him both for their offices and livings. The king, holding his office during life, and transmitting it to his posterity as an inheritance, has much stronger inducements to increase the prerogatives of his office than those who hold their offices for stated periods, or even for life. Hence the English nation gained a great point, in favour of liberty. When they obtained the appointment of the judges, during good behaviour, they got from the crown a concession, which deprived it of one of the most powerful engines with which it might enlarge the boundaries of the royal prerogative and encroach on the liberties of the people. But these reasons do not apply to this country, we have no hereditary monarch; those who appoint the judges do not hold their offices for life, nor do they descend to their children. The same arguments, therefore, which will conclude in favor of the tenor of the judge's offices for good behaviour, lose a considerable part of their weight when applied to the state and condition of America. But much less can it be shewn, that the nature of our government requires that the courts should be placed beyond all account more independent, so much so as to be above controul.

I have said that the judges under this system will be *independent* in the strict sense of the word: To prove this I will shew—That there is no power above them that can controul their decisions, or correct their errors. There is no authority that can remove them from office for any errors or want of capacity, or lower their salaries, and in many cases their power is superior to that of the legislature.

1st. There is no power above them that can correct their errors or controul their decisions—The adjudications of this court are final and irreversible, for there is no court above them to which appeals can lie, either in error or on the merits.—In this respect it differs from the courts in England, for there the house of lords is the highest court, to whom appeals, in error, are carried from the highest of the courts of law.

2d. They cannot be removed from office or suffer a dimuni-tion of their salaries, for any error in judgement or want of capacity.

It is expressly declared by the constitution,—"That they shall at stated times receive a compensation for their services which shall not be diminished during their continuance in office."

The only clause in the constitution which provides for the removal of the judges from offices, is that which declares, that "the president, vice-president, and all civil officers of the United States, shall be removed from office, on impeachment for, and conviction of treason, bribery, or other high crimes and misdemeanors." By this paragraph, civil officers, in which the judges are included, are removable only for crimes. Trea-son and bribery are named, and the rest are included under the general terms of high crimes and misdemeanors.—Errors in judgement, or want of capacity to discharge the duties of the office, can never be supposed to be included in these words, *high crimes and misdemeanors*. A man may mistake a case in giving judgment, or manifest that he is incompetent to the discharge of the duties of a judge, and yet give no evi-dence of corruption or want of integrity. To support the charge, it will be necessary to give in evidence some facts that will shew, that the judges commited the error from wicked and corrupt motives.

3d. The power of this court is in many cases superior to that of the legislature. I have shewed, in a former paper, that this court will be authorised to decide upon the meaning of the constitution, and that, not only according to the natural and obvious meaning of the words, but also according to the spirit and intention of it. In the exercise of this power they will not be subordinate to, but above the legislature. For all the departments of this government will receive their powers, so far as they are expressed in the constitution, from the peo-ple immediately, who are the source of power. The legislature can only exercise such powers as are given them by the con-stitution, they cannot assume any of the rights annexed to the judicial, for this plain reason, that the same authority which vested the legislature with their powers, vested the judicial with theirs—both are derived from the same source, both therefore are equally valid, and the judicial hold their powers independently of the legislature, as the legislature do of the judicial.—The supreme court then have a right, independent of the legislature, to give a construction to the constitution and every part of it, and there is no power provided in this system to correct their construction or do it away. If, therefore, the legislature pass any laws, inconsistent with the sense the judges put upon the constitution, they will declare it void; and therefore in this respect their power is superior to that of the legislature. In England the judges are not only subject to have their decisions set aside by the house of lords, for error, but in cases where they give an explanation to the laws or constitution of the country, contrary to the sense of the parliament, though the parliament will not set aside the judgement of the court, yet, they have authority, by a new law, to explain a former one, and by this means to prevent a reception of such decisions. But no such power is in the legislature. The judges are supreme—and no law, explanatory of the constitution, will be binding on them.

From the preceding remarks, which have been made on the judicial powers proposed in this system, the policy of it may be fully developed.

I have, in the course of my observation on this constitution, affirmed and endeavored to shew, that it was calculated to abolish entirely the state governments, and to melt down the states into one entire government, for every purpose as well internal and local, as external and national. In this opinion the opposers of the system have generally agreed—and this has been uniformly denied by its advocates in public. Some individuals, indeed, among them, will confess, that it has this tendency, and scruple not to say, it is what they wish; and I will venture to predict, without the spirit of prophecy, that if it is adopted without amendments, or some such precautions as will ensure amendments immediately after its adoption, that the same gentlemen who have employed their talents and abilities with such success to influence the public mind to adopt this plan, will employ the same to persuade the people, that it will be for their good to abolish the state governments as useless and burdensome.

Perhaps nothing could have been better conceived to facilitate the abolition of the state governments than the constitution of the judicial. They will be able to extend the limits of the general government gradually, and by insensible degrees, and to accomodate themselves to the temper of the people. Their decisions on the meaning of the constitution will commonly take place in cases which arise between individuals, with which the public will not be generally acquainted; one adjudication will form a precedent to the next, and this to a following one. These cases will immediately affect individuals only; so that a series of determinations will probably take place before even the people will be informed of them. In the mean time all the art and address of those who wish for the change will be employed to make converts to their opinion. The people will be told, that their state officers, and state legislatures are a burden and expence without affording any solid advantage, for that all the laws passed by them, might be equally well made by the general legislature. If to those who will be interested in the change, be added, those who will be under their influence, and such who will submit to almost any change of government, which they can be persuaded to believe will ease them of taxes, it is easy to see, the party who will favor the abolition of the state governments would be far from being inconsiderable.—In this situation, the general legislature, might pass one law after another, extending the general and abridging the state jurisdictions, and to sanction their proceedings would have a course of decisions of the judicial to whom the constitution has committed the power of explaining the constitution.—If the states remonstrated, the constitutional mode of deciding upon the validity of the law, is with the supreme court, and neither people, nor state legislatures, nor the general legislature can remove them or reverse their decrees.

Had the construction of the constitution been left with the legislature, they would have explained it at their peril; if they exceed their powers, or sought to find, in the spirit of the constitution, more than was expressed in the letter, the people from whom they derived their power could remove them, and do themselves right; and indeed I can see no other remedy that the people can have against their rulers for encroachments of this nature. A constitution is a compact of a people with their rulers; if the rulers break the compact, the people have a right and ought to remove them and do themselves justice; but in order to enable them to do this with the greater facility, those whom the people chuse at stated periods, should have the power in the last resort to determine the sense of the compact; if they determine contrary to the understanding of the people, an appeal will lie to the people at the period when the rulers are to be elected, and they will have it in their power to remedy the evil; but when this power is lodged in the hands of men independent of the people, and of their representatives, and who are not, constitutionally, accountable for their opinions, no way is left to controul them but *with a high hand and an outstretched arm.*

"Publius," The Federalist LXXIV
[Alexander Hamilton]

New-York Packet, March 25, 1788

To the People of the State of New-York.

The President of the United States is to be "Commander in Chief of the army and navy of the United States, and of the militia of the several States *when called into the actual service* of the United States." The propriety of this provision is so evident in itself; and it is at the same time so consonant to the precedents of the State constitutions in general, that little need be said to explain or enforce it. Even those of them, which have in other respects coupled the Chief Magistrate with a Council, have for the most part concentred the military authority in him alone. Of all the cares or concerns of government, the direction of war most peculiarly demands those qualities which distinguish the exercise of power by a single hand. The direction of war implies the direction of the common strength; and the power of directing and employing the common strength, forms an usual and essential part in the definition of the executive authority.

"The President may require the opinion in writing of the principal officer in each of the executive departments upon any subject relating to the duties of their respective offices." This I consider as a mere redundancy in the plan; as the right for which it provides would result of itself from the office.

He is also to be authorised "to grant reprieves and pardons for offences against the United States *except in cases of impeachment*." Humanity and good policy conspire to dictate, that the benign prerogative of pardoning should be as little as possible fettered or embarrassed. The criminal code of every country partakes so much of necessary severity, that without

379

an easy access to exceptions in favor of unfortunate guilt, justice would wear a countenance too sanguinary and cruel. As the sense of responsibility is always strongest in proportion as it is undivided, it may be inferred that a single man would be most ready to attend to the force of those motives, which might plead for a mitigation of the rigor of the law, and least apt to yield to considerations, which were calculated to shelter a fit object of its vengeance. The reflection, that the fate of a fellow creature depended on his *sole fiat*, would naturally inspire scrupulousness and caution: The dread of being accused of weakness or connivance would beget equal circumspection, though of a different kind. On the other hand, as men generally derive confidence from their numbers, they might often encourage each other in an act of obduracy, and might be less sensible to the apprehension of suspicion or censure for an injudicious or affected clemency. On these accounts, one man appears to be a more eligible dispenser of the mercy of the government than a body of men.

The expediency of vesting the power of pardoning in the President has, if I mistake not, been only contested in relation to the crime of treason. This, it has been urged, ought to have depended upon the assent of one or both of the branches of the legislative body. I shall not deny that there are strong reasons to be assigned for requiring in this particular the concurrence of that body or of a part of it. As treason is a crime levelled at the immediate being of the society, when the laws have once ascertained the guilt of the offender, there seems a fitness in refering the expediency of an act of mercy towards him to the judgment of the Legislature. And this ought the rather to be the case, as the supposition of the connivance of the Chief Magistrate ought not to be entirely excluded. But there are also strong objections to such a plan. It is not to be doubted that a single man of prudence and good sense, is better fitted, in delicate conjunctures, to balance the motives, which may plead for and against the remission of the punishment, than any numerous body whatever. It deserves particular attention, that treason will often be connected with seditions, which embrace a large proportion of the community; as lately happened in Massachusetts. In every such case, we might expect to see the representation of the people tainted with the same spirit, which had given birth to the offence. And when parties were pretty equally matched, the secret sympathy of the friends and favorers of the condemned person, availing itself of the good nature and weakness of others, might frequently bestow impunity where the terror of an example was necessary. On the other hand, when the sedition had proceeded from causes which had inflamed the resentments of the major party, they might often be found obstinate and inexorable, when policy demanded a conduct of forbearance and clemency. But the principal argument for reposing the power of pardoning in this case in the Chief Magistrate is this—In seasons of insurrection or rebellion, there are often critical moments, when a well timed offer of pardon to the insurgents or rebels may restore the tranquility of the commonwealth; and which, if suffered to pass unimproved, it may never be possible afterwards to recall. The dilatory process of convening the Legislature, or one of its branches, for the purpose of obtaining its sanction to the measure, would frequently be the occasion of letting slip the golden opportunity. The loss of a week, a day, an hour, may sometimes be fatal. If it should be observed that a discretionary power with a view to such contingencies might be occasionally confered upon the President; it may be answered in the first place, that it is questionable whether, in a limited constitution, that power could be delegated by law; and in the second place, that it would generally be impolitic before-hand to take any step which might hold out the prospect of impunity. A proceeding of this kind, out of the usual course, would be likely to be construed into an argument of timidity or of weakness, and would have a tendency to embolden guilt.

James Madison to Eliza House Trist

Orange County, Virginia, March 25, 1788

The badness of the roads & some other delays retarded the completion of my journey till the day before yesterday. I called at Col Syms in Alexanda. but had not the pleasure of seeing either him or his lady. He was not at home though in Town and I was so hurried that I could halt a few minutes only; and she was confined to her chamber by indisposition. — I had the satisfaction to find all my friends well on my arrival; and the chagrin to find the County filled with the most absurd and groundless prejudices against the fœderal Constitution. I was therefore obliged at the election which succeeded the day of my arrival to mount for the first time in my life, the rostrum before a large body of the people, and to launch into a harangue of some length in the open air and on a very windy day. What the effect might be I cannot say, but either from that experiment or the exertion of the fœderalists or perhaps both, the misconceptions of the Government were so far corrected that two federalists one of them myself were elected by a majority of nearly 4 to one. It is very probable that a very different event would have taken place as to myself if the efforts of my friends had not been seconded by my presence. The elections as yet are not sufficiently known to authorize any judgment on the probable complexion of the Convention. As far as I have heard of them they are not discouraging; but I have heard little from the great district of Country which is said to be most tainted with antifederalism. I am so taken up with company that I cannot at present add more than my sincerest wishes for your happiness. Adieu.

"Publius," The Federalist LXXV
[Alexander Hamilton]

Independent Journal (New York), March 26, 1788

To the People of the State of New-York.

The president is to have power "by and with the advice and consent of the senate, to make treaties, provided two-thirds of the senators present concur." Though this provision has been assailed on different grounds, with no small degree of vehemence, I scruple not to declare my firm persuasion, that it is one of the best digested and most unexceptionable parts of the plan. One ground of objection is, the trite topic of the intermixture of powers; some contending that the president ought alone to possess the power of making treaties; and others, that it ought to have been exclusively deposited in the senate. Another source of objection is derived from the small number of persons by whom a treaty may be made: Of those who espouse this objection, a part are of opinion that the house of representatives ought to have been associated in the business, while another part seems to think that nothing more was necessary than to have substituted two-thirds of *all* the members of the senate to two-thirds of the members *present*. As I flatter myself the observations made in a preceding number, upon this part of the plan, must have sufficed to place it to a discerning eye in a very favourable light, I shall here content myself with offering only some supplementary remarks, principally with a view to the objections which have been just stated.

With regard to the intermixture of powers, I shall rely upon the explanations already given, in other places, of the true sense of the rule, upon which that objection is founded; and shall take it for granted, as an inference from them, that the union of the executive with the senate, in the article of treaties, is no infringement of that rule. I venture to add that the particular nature of the power of making treaties indicates a peculiar propriety in that union. Though several writers on the subject of government place that power in the class of executive authorities, yet this is evidently an arbitrary disposition: For if we attend carefully to its operation, it will be found to partake more of the legislative than of the executive character, though it does not seem strictly to fall within the definition of either of them. The essence of the legislative authority is to enact laws, or in other words to prescribe rules for the regulation of the society. While the execution of the laws and the employment of the common strength, either for this purpose or for the common defence, seem to comprise all the functions of the executive magistrate. The power of making treaties is plainly neither the one nor the other. It relates neither to the execution of the subsisting laws, nor to the enaction of new ones, and still less to an exertion of the common strength. Its objects are CONTRACTS with foreign nations, which have the force of law, but derive it from the obligations of good faith. They are not rules prescribed by the sovereign to the subject, but agreements between sovereign and sovereign. The power in question seems therefore to form a distinct department, and to belong properly neither to the legislative nor to the executive. The qualities elsewhere detailed, as indispensable in the management of foreign negotiations, point out the executive as the most fit agent in those transactions; while the vast importance of the trust, and the operation of treaties as laws, plead strongly for the participation of the whole or a part of the legislative body in the effect of making them.

However proper or safe it may be in governments where the executive magistrate is an hereditary monarch, to commit to him the entire power of making treaties, it would be utterly unsafe and improper to entrust that power to an elective magistrate of four years duration. It has been remarked upon another occasion, and the remark is unquestionably just, that an hereditary monarch, though often the oppressor of his people, has personally too much at stake in the government to be in any material danger of being corrupted by foreign powers. But a man raised from the station of a private citizen to the rank of chief magistrate, possessed of but a moderate or slender fortune, and looking forward to a period not very remote, when he may probably be obliged to return to the station from which he was taken, might sometimes be under temptations to sacrifice his duty to his interest, which it would require superlative virtue to withstand. An avaricious man might be tempted to betray the interests of the state to the acquisition of wealth. An ambitious man might make his own aggrandisement, by the aid of a foreign power, the price of his treachery to his constituents. The history of human conduct does not warrant that exalted opinion of human virtue which would make it wise in a nation to commit interests of so delicate and momentous a kind as those which concern its intercourse with the rest of the world to the sole disposal of a magistrate, created and circumstanced, as would be a president of the United States.

To have entrusted the power of making treaties to the senate alone, would have been to relinquish the benefits of the constitutional agency of the president, in the conduct of foreign negotiations. It is true, that the senate would in that case have the option of employing him in this capacity; but they would also have the option of letting it alone; and pique or cabal might induce the latter rather than the former. Besides this, the ministerial servant of the senate could not be expected to enjoy the confidence and respect of foreign powers in the same degree with the constitutional representative of the nation; and of course would not be able to act with an equal degree of weight or efficacy. While the union would from this cause lose a considerable advantage in the management of its external concerns, the people would lose the additional security, which would result from the co-operation of the executive. Though it would be imprudent to confide in him solely so important a trust; yet it cannot be doubted, that his participation in it would materially add to the safety of the society. It must indeed be clear to a demonstration, that the joint possession of the power in question by the president and senate would afford a greater prospect of security, than the separate possession of it by either of them. And whoever has maturely weighed the circumstances, which must concur in the appointment of a president will be satisfied, that the office will always bid fair to be filled by men of such characters as to render their concurrence in the formation of treaties peculiarly desirable, as well on the score of wisdom as on that of integrity.

The remarks made in a former number, which has been alluded to in an other part of this paper, will apply with conclusive force against the admission of the house of representatives to a share in the formation of treaties. The fluctuating and taking its future increase into the account, the multitudinous composition of that body, forbid us to expect in it those qualities which are essential to the proper execution of such a trust. Accurate and comprehensive knowledge of foreign politics; a steady and systematic adherence to the same views; a nice and uniform sensibility to national character, decision, *secrecy* and dispatch; are incompatible with the genius of a body so valuable and so numerous. The very complication of the business by introducing a necessity of the concurrence of so many different bodies, would of itself afford a solid objection. The greater frequency of the calls upon the house of representatives, and the greater length of time which it would often be necessary to keep them together when convened, to obtain their sanction in the progressive stages of a treaty, would be source of so great inconvenience and expence, as alone ought to condemn the project.

The only objection which remains to be canvassed is that which would substitute the proportion of two thirds of all the members composing the senatorial body to that of two thirds of the members *present*. It has been shewn under the second head of our inquiries that all provisions which require more than the majority of any body to its resolutions have a direct tendency to embarrass the operations of the government and an indirect one to subject the sense of the majority to that of the minority. This consideration seems sufficient to determine our opinion, that the convention have gone as far in the endeavour to secure the advantage of numbers in the formation of treaties as could have reconciled either with the activity of the public councils or with a reasonable regard to the major sense of the community. If two thirds of the whole number of members had been required, it would in many cases from the non attendance of a part amount in practice to a necessity of unanimity. And the history of every political establishment in which this principle has prevailed is a history of impotence, perplexity and disorder. Proofs of this position might be adduced from the examples of the Roman tribuneship, the Polish diet and the states general of the Netherlands; did not an example at home render foreign precedents unnecessary.

To require a fixed proportion of the whole body would not in all probability contribute to the advantages of a numerous agency, better than merely to require a proportion of the attending members. The former by making a determinate number at all times requisite to a resolution diminishes the motives to punctual attendance. The latter by making the capacity of the body to depend on a *proportion* which may be varied by the absence or presence of a single member, has the contrary effect. And as, by promoting punctuality, it tends to keep the body complete, there is great likelihood that its resolutions would generally be dictated by as great a number in this case as in the other; while there would be much fewer occasions of delay. It ought not to be forgotten that under the existing confederation two members *may* and usually *do* represent a state; whence it happens that Congress, who now are solely invested with *all the powers* of the union, rarely consists of a greater number of persons than would compose the intended senate. If we add to this, that as the members vote by states, and that where there is only a single member present from a state, his vote is lost, it will justify a supposition that the active voices in the senate, where the members are to vote individually, would rarely fall short in number of the active voices in the existing Congress. When in addition to these considerations we take into view the co-operation of the president, we shall not hesitate to infer that the people of America would have greater security against an improper use of the power of making treaties, under the new constitution, than they now enjoy under the confederation. And when we proceed still one step further, and look forward to the probable augmentation of the senate, by the erection of new states, we shall not only perceive ample ground of confidence in the sufficiency of the members, to whose agency that power will be entrusted; but we shall probably be led to conclude that a body more numerous than the senate would be likely to become, would be very little fit for the proper discharge of the trust.

"Publius," The Federalist LXXVI
[Alexander Hamilton]

New-York Packet, April 1, 1788

To the People of the State of New York.

The President is "to *nominate* and by and with the advice
and consent of the Senate to appoint Ambassadors, other
public Ministers and Consuls, Judges of the Supreme Court,
and all other officers of the United States, whose appointments are not otherwise provided for in the Constitution. But
the Congress may by law vest the appointment of such inferior officers as they think proper in the President alone, or in
the Courts of law, or in the heads of departments. The President shall have power to fill up *all vacancies* which may happen *during the recess of the Senate*, by granting commissions
which shall *expire* at the end of their next session."

It has been observed in a former paper, "that the true test
of a good government is its aptitude and tendency to produce
a good administration." If the justness of this observation be
admitted, the mode of appointing the officers of the United
States contained in the foregoing clauses, must when examined be allowed to be entitled to particular commendation. It
is not easy to conceive a plan better calculated than this, to
produce a judicious choice of men for filling the offices of the
Union; and it will not need proof, that on this point must
essentially depend the character of its administration.

It will be agreed on all hands, that the power of appointment in ordinary cases ought to be modified in one of three
ways. It ought either to be vested in a single man—or in a
select assembly of a moderate number—or in a single man
with the concurrence of such an assembly. The exercise of it
by the people at large, will be readily admitted to be impracticable; as, waving every other consideration it would leave

them little time to do any thing else. When therefore mention is made in the subsequent reasonings of an assembly or body of men, what is said must be understood to relate to a select body or assembly of the description already given. The people collectively from their number and from their dispersed situation cannot be regulated in their movements by that systematic spirit of cabal and intrigue, which will be urged as the chief objections to reposing the power in question in a body of men.

Those who have themselves reflected upon the subject, or who have attended to the observations made in other parts of these papers, in relation to the appointment of the President, will I presume agree to the position that there would always be great probability of having the place supplied by a man of abilities, at least respectable. Premising this, I proceed to lay it down as a rule, that one man of discernment is better fitted to analise and estimate the peculiar qualities adapted to particular offices, than a body of men of equal, or perhaps even of superior discernment.

The sole and undivided responsibility of one man will naturally beget a livelier sense of duty and a more exact regard to reputation. He will on this account feel himself under stronger obligations, and more interested to investigate with care the qualities requisite to the stations to be filled, and to prefer with impartiality the persons who may have the fairest pretentions to them. He will have *fewer* personal attachments to gratify than a body of men, who may each be supposed to have an equal number, and will be so much the less liable to be misled by the sentiments of friendship and of affection. A single well directed man by a single understanding, cannot be distracted and warped by that diversity of views, feelings and interests, which frequently distract and warp the resolutions of a collective body. There is nothing so apt to agitate the passions of mankind as personal considerations, whether they relate to ourselves or to others, who are to be the objects of our choice or preference. Hence, in every exercise of the power of appointing to offices by an assembly of men, we must expect to see a full display of all the private and party likings and dislikes, partialities and antipathies, attachments and animosities, which are felt by those who compose the assembly. The choice which may at any time happen to be made under such circumstances will of course be the result either of a victory gained by one party over the other, or of a compromise between the parties. In either case, the intrinsic merit of the candidate will be too often out of sight. In the first, the qualifications best adapted to uniting the suffrages of the party will be more considered than those which fit the person for the station. In the last the coalition will commonly turn upon some interested equivalent—"Give us the man we wish for this office, and you shall have the one you wish for that." This will be the usual condition of the bargain. And it will rarely happen that the advancement of the public service will be the primary object either of party victories or of party negociations.

The truth of the principles here advanced seems to have been felt by the most intelligent of those who have found fault with the provision made in this respect by the Convention. They contend that the President ought solely to have been authorized to make the appointments under the Fœderal Government. But it is easy to shew that every advantage to be expected from such an arrangement would in substance be derived from the power of *nomination*, which is proposed to be conferred upon him; while several disadvantages which might attend the absolute power of appointment in the hands of that officer, would be avoided. In the act of nomination his judgment alone would be exercised; and as it would be his sole duty to point out the man, who with the approbation of the Senate should fill an office, his responsibility would be as complete as if he were to make the final appointment. There can in this view be no difference between nominating and appointing. The same motives which would influence a proper discharge of his duty in one case would exist in the other. And as no man could be appointed, but upon his previous nomination, every man who might be appointed would be in fact his choice.

But might not his nomination be overruled? I grant it might, yet this could only be to make place for another nomination by himself. The person ultimately appointed must be the object of his preference, though perhaps not in the first degree. It is also not very probable that his nomination would often be overruled. The Senate could not be tempted by the preference they might feel to another to reject the one proposed; because they could not assure themselves that the person they might wish would be brought forward by a second or by any subsequent nomination. They could not even be certain that a future nomination would present a candidate in any degree more acceptable to them: And as their dissent might cast a kind of stigma upon the individual rejected; and might have the appearance of a reflection upon the judgment of the chief magistrate; it is not likely that their sanction would often be refused, where there were not special and strong reasons for the refusal.

To what purpose then require the co-operation of the Senate? I answer that the necessity of their concurrence would have a powerful, though in general a silent operation. It would be an excellent check upon a spirit of favoritism in the President, and would tend greatly to preventing the appointment of unfit characters from State prejudice, from family connection, from personal attachment, or from a view to popularity. And, in addition to this, it would be an efficacious source of stability in the administration.

It will readily be comprehended, that a man, who had himself the sole disposition of offices, would be governed much more by his private inclinations and interests, than when he was bound to submit the propriety of his choice to the discussion and determination of a different and independent body; and that body an entire branch of the Legislature. The possibility of rejection would be a strong motive to care in proposing. The danger to his own reputation, and, in the case of an elective magistrate, to his political existence, from betraying a spirit of favoritism, or an unbecoming pursuit of popularity, to the observation of a body, whose opinion would have great weight in forming that of the public, could not fail to operate as a barrier to the one and to the other. He would be both ashamed and afraid to bring forward for the most distinguished or lucrative stations, candidates who had no other merit, than that of coming from the same State to which he particularly belonged, or of being in some way or other personally allied to him, or of possessing the necessary insignificance and pliancy to render them the obsequious instruments of his pleasure.

To this reasoning, it has been objected, that the President by the influence of the power of nomination may secure the compliance of the Senate to his views. The supposition of universal venality in human nature is little less an error in political reasoning than the supposition of universal rectitude. The institution of delegated power implies that there is a portion of virtue and honor among mankind, which may be a reasonable foundation of confidence. And experience justifies the theory: It has been found to exist in the most corrupt periods of the most corrupt governments. The venality of the British House of Commons has been long a topic of accusation against that body, in the country to which they belong, as well as in this; and it cannot be doubted that the charge is to a considerable extent well founded. But it is as little to be doubted that there is always a large proportion of the body, which consists of independent and public spirited men, who have an influential weight in the councils of the nation. Hence it is (the present reign not excepted) that the sense of that body is often seen to controul the inclinations of the monarch, both with regard to men and to measures. Though it might therefore be allowable to suppose, that the executive might occasionally influence some individuals in the Senate; yet the supposition that he could in general purchase the integrity of the whole body would be forced and improbable. A man disposed to view human nature as it is, without either flattering its virtues or exaggerating its vices, will see sufficient ground of confidence in the probity of the Senate, to rest satisfied not only that it will be impracticable to the Executive to corrupt or seduce a majority of its members; but that the necessity of its co-operation in the business of appointments will be a considerable and salutary restraint upon the conduct of that magistrate. Nor is the integrity of the Senate the only reliance. The constitution has provided some important guards against the danger of executive influence upon the legislative body: It declares that "No Senator, or representative shall, during the time *for which he was elected*, be appointed to any civil office under the United States, which shall have been created, or the emoluments whereof shall have been encreased during such time; and no person holding any office under the United States shall be a member of either house during his continuance in office."

"Publius," The Federalist LXXVII
[Alexander Hamilton]

Independent Journal (New York), April 2, 1788

To the People of the State of New York.

It has been mentioned as one of the advantages to be expected from the co-operation of the senate, in the business of appointments, that it would contribute to the stability of the administration. The consent of that body would be necessary to displace as well as to appoint. A change of the chief magistrate therefore would not occasion so violent or so general a revolution in the officers of the government, as might be expected if he were the sole disposer of offices. Where a man in any station had given satisfactory evidence of his fitness for it, a new president would be restrained from attempting a change, in favour of a person more agreeable to him, by the apprehension that the discountenance of the senate might frustrate the attempt, and bring some degree of discredit upon himself. Those who can best estimate the value of a steady administration will be most disposed to prize a provision, which connects the official existence of public men with the approbation or disapprobation of that body, which from the greater permanency of its own composition, will in all probability be less subject to inconstancy, than any other member of the government.

To this union of the senate with the president, in the article of appointments, it has in some cases been objected, that it would serve to give the president an undue influence over the senate; and in others, that it would have an opposite tendency; a strong proof that neither suggestion is true.

To state the first in its proper form is to refute it. It amounts to this—The president would have an improper *influence over* the senate; because the senate would have the power of *restraining* him. This is an absurdity in terms. It cannot admit of a doubt that the intire power of appointment would enable him much more effectually to establish a dangerous empire over that body, than a mere power of nomination subject to their controul.

Let us take a view of the converse of the proposition—"The senate would influence the executive." As I have had occasion to remark in several other instances, the indistinctness of the objection forbids a precise answer. In what manner is this influence to be exerted? In relation to what objects? The power of influencing a person, in the sense in which it is here used, must imply a power of conferring a benefit upon him. How could the senate confer a benefit upon the president by the manner of employing their right of negative upon his nominations? If it be said they might sometimes gratify him by an acquiescence in a favorite choice, when public motives might dictate a different conduct; I answer that the instances in which the president could be personally interested in the result, would be too few to admit of his being materially affected by the compliances of the senate. The POWER which can *originate* the disposition of honors and emoluments, is more likely to attract than to be attracted by the POWER which can merely obstruct their course. If by influencing the president be meant *restraining* him, this is precisely what must have been intended. And it has been shewn that the restraint would be salutary, at the same time that it would not be such as to destroy a single advantage to be looked for from the uncontrouled agency of that magistrate. The right of nomination would produce all the good of that of appointment and would in a great measure avoid its ills.

Upon a comparison of the plan for the appointment of the officers of the proposed government with that which is established by the constitution of this state a decided preference must be given to the former. In that plan the power of nomination is unequivocally vested in the executive. And as there would be a necessity for submitting each nomination to the judgement of an entire branch of the legislature, the circumstances attending an appointment, from the mode of conducting it, would naturally become matters of notoriety; and the public would be at no loss to determine what part had been performed by the different actors. The blame of a bad nomination would fall upon the president singly and absolutely. The censure of rejecting a good one would lie entirely at the door of the senate; aggravated by the consideration of their having counteracted the good intentions of the executive. If an ill appointment should be made the executive for nominating and the senate for approving would participate though in different degrees in the opprobrium and disgrace.

The reverse of all this characterises the manner of appointment in this state. The council of appointment consists of from three to five persons, of whom the governor is always one. This small body, shut up in a private apartment, impenetrable to the public eye, proceed to the execution of the trust committed to them. It is known that the governor claims the right of nomination, upon the strength of some ambiguous expressions in the constitution; but it is not known to what extent, or in what manner he exercises it; nor upon what occasions he is contradicted or opposed. The censure of a bad appointment, on account of the uncertainty of its author, and for want of a determinate object, has neither poignancy nor duration. And while an unbounded field for cabal and intrigue lies open, all idea of responsibility is lost. The most that the public can know is, that the governor claims the right of nomination: That *two* out of the considerable number of *four* men can too often be managed without much difficulty: That if some of the members of a particular council should happen to be of an uncomplying character, it is frequently not impossible to get rid of their opposition, by regulating the times of meeting in such a manner as to render their attendance inconvenient: And that, from whatever cause it may proceed, a great number of very improper appointments are from time to time made. Whether a governor of this state avails himself of the ascendant he must necessarily have, in this delicate and important part of the administration, to prefer to offices men who are best qualified for them: Or whether he prostitutes that advantage to the advancement of persons, whose chief merit is their implicit devotion to his will, and to the support of a despicable and dangerous system of personal influence, are questions which unfortunately for the community can only be the subjects of speculation and conjecture.

Every mere council of appointment, however constituted, will be a conclave, in which cabal and intrigue will have their full scope. Their number, without an unwarrantable increase of expence, cannot be large enough to preclude a facility of combination. And as each member will have his friends and connections to provide for, the desire of mutual gratification will beget a scandalous bartering of votes and bargaining for places. The private attachments of one man might easily be satisfied; but to satisfy the private attachments of a dozen, or of twenty men, would occasion a monopoly of all the principal employments of the government, in a few families, and would lead more directly to an aristocracy or an oligarchy, than any measure that could be contrived. If to avoid an accumulation of offices, there was to be a frequent change in the persons, who were to compose the council, this would involve the mischiefs of a mutable administration in their full extent. Such a council would also be more liable to executive influence than the senate, because they would be fewer in number, and would act less immediately under the public inspection. Such a council in fine as a substitute for the plan of the convention, would be productive of an increase of expence, a multiplication of the evils which spring from favouritism and intrigue in the distribution of the public honors, a decrease of stability in the administration of the government, and a diminution of the security against an undue influence of the executive. And yet such a council has been warmly contended for as an essential amendment in the proposed constitution.

I could not with propriety conclude my observations on the subject of appointments, without taking notice of a scheme, for which there has appeared some, though but a few advocates; I mean that of uniting the house of representatives in the power of making them. I shall however do little more than mention it, as I cannot imagine that it is likely to gain the countenance of any considerable part of the community. A body so fluctuating, and at the same time so numerous, can never be deemed proper for the exercise of that power. Its unfitness will appear manifest to all, when it is recollected that in half a century it may consist of three or four hundred persons. All the advantages of the stability, both of the executive and of the senate, would be defeated by this union; and infinite delays and embarrassments would be occasioned. The example of most of the states in their local constitutions, encourages us to reprobate the idea.

The only remaining powers of the executive, are comprehended in giving information to congress of the state of the union; in recommending to their consideration such measures as he shall judge expedient; in convening them, or either branch, upon extraordinary occasions; in adjourning them when they cannot themselves agree upon the time of adjournment; in receiving ambassadors and other public ministers; in faithfully executing the laws; and in commissioning all the officers of the United States.

Except some cavils about the power of convening *either* house of the legislature and that of receiving ambassadors, no objection has been made to this class of authorities; nor could they possibly admit of any. It required indeed an insatiable avidity for censure to invent exceptions to the parts which have been excepted to. In regard to the power of convening either house of the legislature, I shall barely remark, that in respect to the senate at least, we can readily discover a good reason for it. As this body has a concurrent power with the executive in the article of treaties, it might often be necessary to call it together with a view to this object, when it would be unnecessary and improper to convene the house of representatives. As to the reception of ambassadors, what I have said in a former paper will furnish a sufficient answer.

We have now compleated a survey of the structure and powers of the executive department, which, I have endeavoured to show, combines, as far as republican principles would admit, all the requisites to energy. The remaining enquiry is: does it also combine the requisites to safety in the republican sense—a due dependence on the people—a due responsibility? The answer to this question has been anticipated in the investigation of its other characteristics, and is satisfactorily deducible from these circumstances, the election of the president once in four years by persons immediately chosen by the people for that purpose; and from his being at all times liable to impeachment, trial, dismission from office, incapacity to serve in any other; and to the forfeiture of life and estate by subsequent prosecution in the common course of law. But these precautions, great as they are, are not the only ones, which the plan of the convention has provided in favor of the public security. In the only instances in which the abuse of the executive authority was materially to be feared, the chief magistrate of the United States would by that plan be subjected to the controul of a branch of the legislative body. What more could be desired by an enlightened and reasonable people?

"K." [Benjamin Franklin] to the Editor

Federal Gazette (Philadelphia), April 8, 1788

A zealous Advocate for the propos'd Federal Constitution, in a certain public Assembly, said, that "the Repugnance of a great part of Mankind to good Government was such, that he believed, that, if an angel from Heaven was to bring down a Constitution form'd there for our Use, it would nevertheless meet with violent Opposition." He was reprov'd for the suppos'd Extravagance of the Sentiment; and he did not justify it. Probably it might not have immediately occur'd to him, that the Experiment had been try'd, and that the Event was recorded in the most faithful of all Histories, the Holy Bible; otherwise he might, as it seems to me, have supported his Opinion by that unexceptionable Authority.

The Supreme Being had been pleased to nourish up a single Family, by continued Acts of his attentive Providence, till it became a great People; and, having rescued them from Bondage by many Miracles, performed by his Servant Moses, he personally deliver'd to that chosen Servant, in the presence of the whole Nation, a Constitution and Code of Laws for their Observance; accompanied and sanction'd with Promises of great Rewards, and Threats of severe Punishments, as the Consequence of their Obedience or Disobedience.

This Constitution, tho' the Deity himself was to be at its Head (and it is therefore call'd by Political Writers a *Theocracy*), could not be carried into Execution but by the Means of his Ministers; Aaron and his Sons were therefore commission'd to be, with Moses, the first establish'd Ministry of the new Government.

One would have thought, that this Appointment of Men, who had distinguish'd themselves in procuring the Liberty of

their Nation, and had hazarded their Lives in openly opposing the Will of a powerful Monarch, who would have retain'd
that Nation in Slavery, might have been an Appointment acceptable to a grateful People; and that a Constitution fram'd
for them by the Deity himself might, on that Account, have
been secure of a universal welcome Reception. Yet there were
in every one of the *thirteen Tribes* some discontented, restless
Spirits, who were continually exciting them to reject the propos'd new Government, and this from various Motives.

Many still retained an Affection for Egypt, the Land of
their Nativity; and these, whenever they felt any Inconvenience or Hardship, tho' the natural and unavoidable Effect
of their Change of Situation, exclaim'd against their Leaders
as the Authors of their Trouble; and were not only for returning into Egypt, but for stoning their deliverers.* Those in-
clin'd to idolatry were displeas'd that their *Golden Calf* was
destroy'd. Many of the Chiefs thought the new Constitution
might be injurious to their particular Interests, that the
profitable Places would be *engrossed by the Families and Friends
of Moses and Aaron,* and others equally well-born excluded.†
In Josephus and the Talmud, we learn some Particulars, not so
fully narrated in the Scripture. We are there told, "That Corah
was ambitious of the Priesthood, and offended that it was
conferred on Aaron; and this, as he said, by the Authority of
Moses only, *without the Consent of the People.* He accus'd
Moses of having, by various Artifices, fraudulently obtain'd
the Government, and depriv'd the People of their Liberties;
and of *conspiring* with Aaron to perpetuate the Tyranny in
their Family. Thus, tho' Corah's real Motive was the Sup-
planting of Aaron, he persuaded the People that he meant
only the *Public Good*; and they, moved by his Insinuations,
began to cry out, 'Let us maintain the Common Liberty of
our *respective Tribes*; we have freed ourselves from the Slavery
impos'd on us by the Egyptians, and shall we now suffer our-

*Numbers, ch. xiv.

†Numbers, ch. xiv, verse 3. "And they gathered themselves together against
Moses and Aaron, and said unto them, 'Ye take too much upon you, seeing
all the congregation are holy, *every one of them*; wherefore, then, lift ye up
yourselves above the congregation?' "

selves to be made Slaves by Moses? If we must have a Master, it were better to return to Pharaoh, who at least fed us with Bread and Onions, than to serve this new Tyrant, who by his Operations has brought us into Danger of Famine.' Then they called in question the *Reality of his Conference* with God; and objected the *Privacy of the Meetings*, and the *preventing any of the People from being present* at the Colloquies, or even approaching the Place, as Grounds of great Suspicion. They accused Moses also of *Peculation*; as embezzling part of the Golden Spoons and the Silver Chargers, that the Princes had offer'd at the Dedication of the Altar,* and the Offerings of Gold by the common People,† as well as most of the Poll-Tax;‡ and Aaron they accus'd of pocketing much of the Gold of which he pretended to have made a molten Calf. Besides *Peculation*, they charg'd Moses with *Ambition*; to gratify which Passion he had, they said, deceiv'd the People, by promising to bring them *to* a land flowing with Milk and Honey; instead of doing which, he had brought them *from* such a Land; and that he thought light of all this mischief, provided he could make himself an *absolute Prince*.§ That, to support the new Dignity with Splendor in his Family, the partial Poll-Tax already levied and given to Aaron‖ was to be follow'd by a general one,¶ which would probably be augmented from time to time, if he were suffered to go on promulgating new Laws, on pretence of new occasional Revelations of the divine Will, till their whole Fortunes were devour'd by that Aristocracy."

Moses deny'd the Charge of Peculation; and his Accusers were destitute of Proofs to support it; tho' *Facts*, if real, are in their Nature capable of Proof. "I have not," said he (with holy Confidence in the Presence of his God), "I have not

*Numbers, ch. vii.

†Exodus, ch. xxxv, verse 22.

‡Numbers, ch. iii, and Exodus, ch. xxx.

§Numbers, ch. xvi, verse 13. "Is it a small thing that thou hast brought us up out of a land that floweth with milk and honey, to kill us in the wilderness, except thou make thyself altogether a prince over us?"

‖Numbers, ch. iii

¶Exodus, ch. xxx.

taken from this People the value of an Ass, nor done them any other Injury." But his Enemies had made the Charge, and with some Success among the Populace; for no kind of Accusation is so readily made, or easily believ'd, by Knaves as the Accusation of Knavery.

In fine, no less than two hundred and fifty of the principal Men, "famous in the Congregation, Men of Renown,"* heading and exciting the Mob, worked them up to such a pitch of Frenzy, that they called out, "Stone 'em, stone 'em, and thereby *secure our Liberties*; and let us chuse other Captains, that may lead us back into Egypt, in case we do not succeed in reducing the Canaanites!"

On the whole, it appears, that the Israelites were a People jealous of their newly-acquired Liberty, which Jealousy was in itself no Fault; but, when they suffer'd it to be work'd upon by artful Men, pretending Public Good, with nothing really in view but private Interest, they were led to oppose the Establishment of the *New Constitution*, whereby they brought upon themselves much Inconvenience and Misfortune. It appears further, from the same inestimable History, that, when after many Ages that Constitution was become old and much abus'd, and an Amendment of it was propos'd, the populace, as they had accus'd Moses of the Ambition of making himself a *Prince*, and cried out, "Stone him, stone him;" so, excited by their High Priests and SCRIBES, they exclaim'd against the Messiah, that he aim'd at becoming King of the Jews, and cry'd out, *"Crucify him, Crucify him."* From all which we may gather, that popular Opposition to a public Measure is no Proof of its Impropriety, even tho' the Opposition be excited and headed by Men of Distinction.

To conclude, I beg I may not be understood to infer, that our General Convention was divinely inspired, when it form'd the new federal Constitution, merely because that Constitution has been unreasonably and vehemently opposed; yet I must own I have so much Faith in the general Government of the world by *Providence*, that I can hardly conceive a Transaction of such momentous Importance to the Welfare of

*Numbers, ch. xvi.

Millions now existing, and to exist in the Posterity of a great Nation, should be suffered to pass without being in some degree influenc'd, guided, and governed by that omnipotent, omnipresent, and beneficent Ruler, in whom all inferior Spirits live, and move, and have their Being.

K.

"To Be or Not To Be? Is the Question"

New Hampshire Gazette (Portsmouth), April 16, 1788

Can you, my fellow countrymen, on a question of existence as a nation hesitate in your decision? whether to be united and powerful, each supporting the dignity of the other; or to be divided into petty States, each seeking and contending for its own local advantages; and like the bundle of twigs which seperated, was easily destroyed by an old and infirm man. *Unite* or *die* has been a successful motto to this country; never was it more applicable than at this moment.

To have *energy*, we must *give power*; to *preserve liberty, that power* must have *sufficient checks*. As I am satisfied, (and no man is more jealous of his rights than myself,) that the Fœderal Constitution is wisely formed to give the one, without sacrificing the other; and that all ambitious and designing men must meet with their just reward for the *very attempt* to encroach on the *rights* we *have preserved*; I shall only shew at present the *certain* advantages that must accrue to the eastern States, if the new government is established.—Navigation, but more particularly ship building, was a great object before and during the war; this is entirely lost.—The question is how are we to restore them? I answer—By adopting the Constitution we not only restore the latter, but increase the former: for by the exclusion of foreigners from the southern States, the navigating of not less than 50,000 tons, or 166 vessels of 300 tons each, will fall to our lot: I say ours, for tho' the exclusive priviledge will not be granted by Congress, yet providence has blessed us with a preeminence which the enterprize of New-Englandmen will not neglect.—The sea port towns will again be filled with vessels *built* in their *own* ports, and *navigated* by their *own* sailors.—The oppressive hand of distress will once more be removed, and success will smile on honest industry.—My heart is warmed with the *happy* prospect, but when I anticipate the benefits the farmer is to participate in, I am filled *with joy*.

Towns and country have so near a connection with, and

depend so much on each other, that they cannot be advantaged singly.—Towns are made populous by manufactories or commerce:—manufactories and exports are the farmers markets. If ships are built it must be with timber and men, the first must be procured *in*, the latter must be fed *from* the *country*.—There are few exports in the New-England States, but the *farmer* has his concern in and *most* of them are the immediate produce of his own labour—Will the channels for these exports encrease?—Undoubtedly.—*Union* at home will give respectability abroad; this, with the inconvenience foreign powers must suffer from a proper regulation of commerce by Congress, will oblige them to enter into treaties, which will open ports on conditions of mutual advantage, and give vend to the produce of our soil; now the conditions are *their own*, or we are *totally excluded*.—Many are the reasons and powerful, why the Fœderal Constitution should meet with the warm support of the *country*. An increased revenue, from a proper and universal regulation of trade, will render needless so large a *dry tax* as we have been subject to. Imposts on *foreign woolens* or *other* manufactories, will be advantageous to this country, either in the consumption of the *raw material*, or to the manufactories as such.—Confidence between individuals will be establish'd, money more easily obtained; and farms of course more generally improved. Lands will increase in value, as we increase in wealth and industry.—Good laws, and a steady government will invite property as well as people to us.—Having full confidence in the good sense of my fellow citizens;—no doubt remains in my mind but they will adopt a system so well calculated to secure our liberties as individuals, and establish our dignity as a nation:—They will aid in finishing the glorious work begun, and not tarnish the reputation they have established for wholesome laws and honest government, by adopting the conduct of a neighbouring State.—From the best information as yet obtained, Maryland, Virginia and South-Carolina are decidedly in favour:—Accounts from New-York are favourable. Let us then be cautious, that we do not stand alone in rejecting what every State in general Convention has already approved, and in State Conventions, as far as it has been considered, adopted.

"Fabius" [John Dickinson], "Observations on the Constitution Proposed by the Federal Convention" III

Pennsylvania Mercury and Universal Advertiser
(Philadelphia), April 17, 1788

The Writer of this Address hopes, that he will now be thought so disengaged from the objections against the part of the principle assumed, concerning *the power of the people*, that he may be excused for recurring to his assertion, that— *the power of the people* pervading the proposed system, together with *the strong confederation of the states*, will form an adequate security against *every* danger that has been apprehended.

It is a mournful, but may be a useful truth, that the liberty of *single republics* has generally been destroyed by *some of the citizens*, and of *confederated republics*, by *some of the associated states*.

It is more pleasing, and may be more profitable to reflect, that, their tranquility and prosperity have commonly been promoted, in proportion to the strength of their government for protecting *the worthy* against *the licentious*.

As in forming a political society, each individual *contributes* some of his rights, in order that he may, from *a common stock* of rights, derive greater benefits, than he could from merely *his own*; so, in forming a confederation, each political society should *contribute* such a share of their rights, as will, from *a common stock* of rights, produce the largest quantity of benefits for them.

But, *what is that share?* and, *how to be managed?* Momentous questions! Here, flattery is treason; and error, destruction.

Are they unanswerable? No. Our most gracious Creator

does not *condemn* us to sigh for unattainable blessedness: But one thing he *demands*—that we should seek for it in *his* way, and not in *our own*.

Humility and *benevolence* must take place of *pride* and *over-weening selfishness*. Reason, then rising above these mists, will discover to us, that we cannot be true to ourselves, without being true to others—that to be solitary, is to be wretched—that to love our neighbours as ourselves, is to love ourselves in the best manner—that to give, is to gain—and, that we never consult our own happiness more effectually, than when we most endeavour to correspond with the Divine designs, by communicating happiness, as much as we can, to our fellow-creatures. INESTIMABLE TRUTH! sufficient, if they do not barely ask what it is, to melt tyrants into men, and to sooth the inflamed minds of a multitude into mildness—sufficient to overflow this earth with unknown felicity—INESTIMABLE TRUTH! which our Maker, in his providence, enables us, not only to talk and write about, but to adopt in practice of vast extent, and of instructive example.

Let us now enquire, if there be not some *principle, simple* as the laws of nature in other instances, from which, as from a source, the many benefits of society are deduced.

We may with reverence say, that our Creator designed men for society, because otherwise they cannot be happy. They cannot be happy without freedom; nor free without security; that is, without the *absence of fear*; nor thus secure, without society. The conclusion is strictly syllogistic—that men cannot be free without society. Of course, they cannot be *equally free* without society, which freedom produces the greatest happiness.

As these premises are invincible, we have advanced a considerable way in our enquiry upon this deeply interesting subject. If we can determine, what share of his rights, every individual must contribute to the common stock of rights in forming a society, for obtaining *equal freedom*, we determine at the same time, what share of their rights each political society must contribute to the common stock of rights in forming a confederation, which is only a larger society, for obtaining *equal freedom*: For, if the deposit be not proportioned to the magnitude of the association in the latter case, it will generate the same mischief among the component parts of it, from their inequality, that would result from a defective contribution to association in the former case, among the component parts of it, from their inequality.

Each individual then must contribute such a share of his rights, as is necessary for attaining that SECURITY that is essential to freedom; and he is bound to make this contribution by the law of his nature; that is, by the command of his creator; therefore, *he must submit his will, in what concerns all, to the will of the whole society*. What does he lose by this submission? The power of doing injuries to others—the dread of suffering injuries from them—and, the incommodities of mental or bodily weakness.—What does he gain by it? The aid of those associated with him—protection against injuries from them or others—a capacity of enjoying his undelegated rights to the best advantage—a repeal of his fears—and tranquility of mind—or, in other words, that *perfect liberty* better described in the Holy Scriptures, than any where else, in these expressions—"When *every* man shall *sit* under his vine, and under his fig-tree, and NONE SHALL MAKE HIM AFRAID."

The like submission, with a correspondent expansion and accommodation, must be made between states, for obtaining the like benefits in a confederation. Men are the materials of both. As the largest number is but a junction of units,—a confederation is but an assembly of *individuals*. The sanction of that *law* of his nature, upon which the happiness of a man depends in society, must attend him in confederation, or he becomes unhappy; for confederation should promote the happiness of *individuals*, or it does not answer the intended purpose. Herein there is a progression, not a contradiction. As man, he becomes a citizen; as a citizen, he becomes a *federalist*. The generation of one, is not the destruction of the other. He carries into society his naked rights: These thereby improved, he carries into confederation. If that sacred law before mentioned, is not here observed, the confederation would not be *real*, but *pretended*. He would confide, and be deceived.

The dilemma is inevitable. There must either be *one* will, or *several* wills. If but *one* will, *all* the people are concerned; if *several* wills, *few* comparatively are concerned. Surprizing! that this doctrine should be contended for by those, who declare, that the constitution is not founded on a *bottom broad enough*; and, though THE WHOLE PEOPLE of the United States are to be TREBLY represented in it in THREE DIFFERENT MODES of representation, and their servants will have the most advantageous situation and opportunities of acquiring all requisite information for the welfare of *the whole union*, yet insist for a privilege of *opposing, obstructing*, and *confounding* all their measures taken with common consent for the general weal, by the delays, negligences, rivalries, or other selfish views of *parts* of the union.

Thus, while one state should be relied upon by the union for giving aid, upon a recommendation of Congress, to another in distress, the latter might be ruined; and the state relied upon, might suppose, it would gain by such an event.

When any persons speak of a confederation, do they, or do they not acknowledge, that the *whole* is *interested* in the safety of *every* part—in the *agreement* of *parts*—in the *relation* of *parts* to *one another*—to *the whole*—or, to *other societies*? If they do—then, the *authority* of the *whole*, must be co-extensive with its *interests*—and if it is, the *will* of *the whole* must and *ought* in *such cases* to govern.

If they do not acknowledge, that *the whole* is *thus interested*, the conversation should cease. Such persons mean not a confederation, but something else.

As to the idea, that this superintending sovereign will must of consequence destroy the subordinate sovereignties of the several states, it is begging a concession of the question, by inferring that a manifest and great *usefulness* must necessarily end in *abuse*; and not only so, but it requires an extinction of *the principle of all society*: for, the subordinate sovereignties, or, in other words, the undelegated rights of the several states, in a confederation, stand upon the very same foundation with the undelegated rights of individuals in a society, the *federal sovereign will* being *composed* of the *subordinate sovereign wills* of the several confederated states. If as some persons seem to think, *a bill of rights* is *the best security* of rights, the sovereignties of the several states have *this* best security by the proposed constitution, & more than *this* best security, for they are not barely *declared* to be rights, but are taken into it as *component parts*, for *their* perpetual preservation by *themselves*. In short, the government of each state is, and is to be, *sovereign* and *supreme* in *all* matters that *relate* to each state *only*. It is to be *subordinate* barely in *those* matters that *relate* to *the whole*; and it will be their own faults, if the several states suffer the *federal sovereignty* to interfere in things of their respective jurisdictions. An instance of such interference with regard to *any single state*, will be a dangerous *precedent* as *to all*, and therefore will be guarded against *by all*, as the trustees or servants of the several states will not dare, if they retain their senses, so to violate the *independent sovereignty* of their respective states, that justly darling object of *American* affections, to which they are responsible, besides being endeared by all the charities of life.

The common sense of mankind agrees to the devolution of individual wills in society; and if it has not been as universally assented to in confederation, the reasons are evident, & worthy of being retained in remembrance by *Americans*. They were, want of opportunities, or the loss of them, through defects of knowledge and virtue. The principle however has been sufficiently vindicated in imperfect combinations, as their prosperity has generally been commensurate to its operation.

How beautifully and forcibly does the inspired Apostle Saint *Paul*, argue upon a sublimer subject, with a train of reasoning strictly applicable to the present? His words are— "If the foot shall say, because I am not the hand, I am not of the body; is it therefore not of the body? and if the ear shall say, because I am not the eye, I am not of the body; is it therefore not of the body?" As plainly inferring, as could be done in that allegorical manner, the strongest censure of such partial discontents and dissentions, especially, as his meaning is enforced by his description of the *benefits* of *union* in these expressions—"But, *now* they are *many members*, yet but *one body*: and the eye CANNOT say to the hand, *I have no need of thee*; nor again, the head to the feet, *I have no need of you*."

When the commons of *Rome* upon a rupture with the senate, seceded in arms at the *Mons sacer*, *Menenius Agrippa* used the like allusion to the human body, in his famous apologue of a quarrel among some of the members. The unpolished but honest-hearted *Romans* of that day, understood him, and were appeased. They returned to the city, and—the world was conquered.

Another comparison has been made by the statesman and the learned, between a natural and a political *body*; and no wonder indeed, when the title of the latter was borrowed from the resemblance. It has therefore been justly observed, that if a mortification takes place in one or some of the limbs, and the rest of the body is sound, remedies may be applied, and not only the contagion prevented from spreading, but the diseased part or parts saved by the connection with the body, & restored to former usefulness. When general putrefaction prevails, death is to be expected. History sacred and prophane tells us, that, CORRUPTION OF MANNERS IS THE VERY BASIS OF SLAVERY.

"Plough Jogger"

Newport Herald (Rhode Island), April 17, 1788

Mr. EDES,
Please to give the following production of a plough jogger a place in your useful paper, and you'll oblige one of your constant readers.

Having lately perused the articles of the old confederation, it appeared to me like a forsaken, neglected, and despised friend.

The federalists forsake it as having done nearly all the good it can.

The antifederalists neglect and despise it, although they say hold to it, as its principal foundation is virtue, and the people have not virtue enough to be governed in a right manner by so mild a constitution—that instead of their morals being re-formed under it, they corrupt more and more, as I conceive: for where is the faith pledged to supply the continental trea-sury to enable Congress to keep their faith, both foreign and domestic.

I have been much in favor of the old confederation, and thought it almost a miracle that so good a system of govern-ment should be formed at the first; and while I had the honor to be a member of our General Assembly, watched every in-novation against it, thinking that there was virtue enough in the people and myself to do well under so mild a constitu-tion; but my experience has taught me another lesson,—I have found my mistake in being against giving Congress more power.

I now begin to see the necessity of a more efficient govern-ment, which may be consistent with the liberties of the peo-ple; but I fear some people have wrong notions of liberty— That can't be pure liberty where the government gives the subject liberty to do wrong, to cheat and defraud his neigh-bor, or a foreigner, and the power to withhold the means of supporting good government. Let us be familiar, it is demonstrable by a family; although the father, or master, may prefer mildness in his family, yet necessity obliges him sometimes to use rigorous measures; and we are told that foolishness is bound up in the heart of a child, but the rod of correction shall drive it from him: and what son is there whom the father chasteneth not? The great Governor of the Universe has given him the power; our depraved natures require it should be so. We are the same creatures in government, and need similar means, tho' in a more extensive manner: we may think when we arrive to manhood we can do without rigorous measures; but if so, what is meant by the sword the magistrate bears, that he don't bear in vain? but is to prove a terror to evil doers, and a praise to them that do well; they are said to be GOD's ministers, and He that has all power no doubt means they should have power, not to do wrong but to administer justice in his fear, consistent with his law: but some may say they are willing they should have power to do us good, but not wrong. If they were perfect as the great Governor you need not be afraid; but whether our fears don't originate as much from our own imperfections I leave you to judge; however, I think every possible check ought to be put upon them that have the supreme power (in our politics) so as not to prevent their doing all the good they can.—But this is a delicate point, it is almost impossible, but that they may abuse their power, if they are bad enough: this shews the necessity of our choosing good men, men that regard the public good more than their own humour, or supporting any party.—Most all agree something is necessary to be done to give energy to our public affairs.—But what that something is we seem unhappily divided about,—and some breathe out threats to those that act their sentiments, and also complain of arbitrary government, while they hold out an arbitrary spirit themselves.—Witness the threats against my privileges and property (though not by men of my own town) the times look dubious (or more the conduct of men) If we unite we may stand; but if we divide we fall: I think it proper either to dissolve the being of a Congress (if so what will be our fate) or give Congress more power; that instead of the states separate having a negative upon Congress, Congress may have a negative upon the respective states: that they as a disinterested body may settle all our concerns upon the large scale. —I think the proposed Constitution needs many checks. Massachusetts have proposed several by way of amendments: but I think there needs more or some others, although I gave my voice in favour of it, choosing rather it should be adopted than rejected: therefore these were my words, of two evils I shall choose the least, therefore put me down yea,—thinking, as I had reason to believe the good of my country was the grand object in the proposed Constitution, and as they appear needful, alterations would be made accordingly.

Exeter, *April* 14. 1788.

Benjamin Rush to David Ramsay

Columbian Herald (Charleston, S.C.), April 19, 1788

Extract of a letter from Dr. RUSH, *of Philadelphia, lately received by gentleman of this city.*

DEAR SIR,

"I presume before this time you have heard, and rejoiced in the auspicious events of the ratification of the federal government by *six* of the United States.

"The objections which have been urged against the federal constitution from its wanting a bill of rights, have been reasoned and ridiculed out of credit in every state that has adopted it. There can be only *two* sureties for liberty in any government, viz. *representation* and *checks*. By the first, the rights of the people, and by the second, the rights of representation are effectually secured. Every part of a free constitution hangs upon these two points, and *these* form the two capital features of the proposed constitution of the United States. Without them, a volume of rights would avail nothing, and with them a declaration of rights is absurd and unnecessary; for the PEOPLE where their liberties are committed to an equal representation, and to a compound legislature (such as we observe in the new government) will always be the sovereigns of their rulers, and hold all their rights in their own hands. To hold them at the mercy of their servants, is disgraceful to the dignity of freemen. Men who call for a bill of rights, have not recovered from the habits they acquired under the monarchical government of Great-Britain.

"I have the same opinion with the antifederalists of the danger of trusting arbitrary power to any single body of men; but no such power will be committed to our new rulers. Neither the house of representatives, the senate, or the president can perform a single legislative act by themselves. An hundred principles in man will lead them to watch, to check and to oppose each other, should an attempt be made by either of them upon the liberties of the people. If we may judge of their conduct, by what we have so often observed in all the state governments, the members of the federal legislature will much oftener injure their constituents by voting agreeably to their inclinations, than *against* them.

"But are we to consider men entrusted with power as the receptacles of *all* the depravity of human nature? By no means. The people do not part with their full proportions of it. Reason and revelation both deceive us, if they are all wise and virtuous. Is not history as full of the vices of the people, as it is of the crimes of the kings? what is the present *moral* character of the citizens of the United States? I need not discover it. It proves too plainly, that the people are as much disposed to vice as their rulers, and that nothing but a vigorous and efficient government can prevent their degenerating into savages, or devouring each other like beasts of prey.

"A simple democracy, has been very aptly compared by Mr. Ames of Massachusetts, to a volcano that contained within its bowels the fiery materials of its own destruction. A citizen of one of the Cantons of Switzerland in the year 1776, refused to drink in my presence "the commonwealth of America" as a toast, and gave as a reason for it, "that a simple democracy was the devil's own government."—The experience of the American states under the present confederation has in too many instances justified these two accounts of a simple popular government.

"It would have been a truth, if Mr. Locke had not said it, that where there is no *law*, there can be no *liberty*, and nothing deserves the name of law but that which is certain, and universal in its operation upon all the members of the community.

"To look up to a government that establishes justice, insures order, cherishes virtue, secures property, and protects from every species of violence, affords a pleasure, that can only be exceeded by looking up in all circumstances to an overuling providence.—Such a pleasure I hope is before us, and our posterity under the influence of the new government.

"The dimensions of the human mind, are apt to be regulated by the extent and objects of the government under which it is formed. Think then my friend, of the expansion and dignity the American mind will acquire, by having its powers transferred from the contracted objects of a state to the unbounded objects of a national government!—A citizen and a legislator of the free and UNITED STATES of America, will be one of the first characters in the world.

"I would not have you suppose, after what I have written, that I believe the new government to be without faults. I can see them, but *not* in *any* of the writings or speeches of any of the persons who are opposed to it. But who ever saw any thing perfect come from the hands of man? It realises notwithstanding in a great degree, every wish I ever entertained in every stage of the revolution for the happiness of my country, for you know that I have acquired no new opinions on principles upon the subject of republics, by the sorrowful events we have lately witnessed in America.—In the year 1776, I lost the confidence of the people of Pennsylvania, by openly exposing the dangers of a simple democracy, and declaring myself an advocate for a government composed of three legislative branches.

"Adieu—from dear sir, yours sincerely."

George Washington to John Armstrong

Mount Vernon, Virginia, April 25, 1788

From some cause or other which I do not know your favor of the 20th of February did not reach me till very lately. This must apologize for its not being sooner acknowledged. — Altho Colo Blain forgot to call upon me for a letter before he left Philadelphia, yet I wrote a few lines to you previous to my departure from that place; whether they ever got to your hands or not you best know. —

I well remember the observation you made in your letter to me of last year, "that my domestic retirement must suffer an interruption". — This took place, notwithstanding it was utterly repugnant to my feelings, my interest and my wishes; I sacrificed every private consideration and personal enjoyment to the earnest and pressing solicitations of those who saw and knew the alarming situation of our public concerns, and had no other end in view but to promote the interest of their Country; and conceiving that under those circumstances, and at so critical a moment, an absolute refusal to act, might, on my part, be construed as a total dereliction of my Country, if imputed to no worse motives. — Altho' you say the same motives induce you to think that another tour of duty of this kind will fall to my lot, I cannot but hope that you will be disappointed, for I am so wedded to a state of retirement; and find the occupations of a rural life so congenial; with my feelings, that to be drawn unto public at the advanced age, would be a sacrifice that could admit of no compensation.

Your remarks on the impressions which will be made on the manners and sentiments of the people by the example of those who are first called to act under the proposed Government are very just; and I have no doubt but (if the proposed Constitution obtains) those persons who are chosen to administer it will have wisdom enough to discern the influence which their examples as rulers and legislators may have on the body of the people, and will have virtue enough to pursue that line of conduct which will most conduce to the happiness of their Country;—and as the first transactions of a nation, like those of an individual upon his enterance into life, make the deepest impression and are to form the leading traits in its character, they will undoubtedly pursue those measures which will best tend to the restoration of public and private faith and of consequence promote our national respectability and individual welfare.—

That the proposed Constitution will admit of amendments is acknowledged by its warmest advocates but to make such amendments as may be proposed by the several States the condition of its adoption would, in my opinion amount to a compleat rejection of it; for upon examination of the objections which are made by the opponents in different States and the amendments which have been proposed, it will be found that what would be a favourite object with one State is the very thing which is strenuously opposed by another;—the truth is, men are too apt to be swayed by local prejudices, and those who are so fond of amendments which have the particular interest of their own State in view cannot extend their ideas to the general welfare of the Union—they do not consider that for every sacrifice which they make they receive an ample compensation by the sacrifices which are made by other States for their benefit—and that those very things which they give up will operate to their advantage through the medium of the general interest.—In addition to these considerations it should be remembered that a constitutional door is open for such amendments as shall be thought necessary by nine States.—When I reflect upon these circumstances I am surprized to find that any person who is acquainted with the critical state of our public affairs, and knows the veriety of views, interests, feelings and prejudices which must be consulted and conciliated in framing a general Government for these States, and how little propositions in themselves so opposite to each other, will tend to promote that desireable an end, can wish to make amendments the ultimatum for adopting the offered system.

I am very glad to find that the opposition in your State, however formidable it has been represented, is, generally speaking, composed of such characters as cannot have an extensive influence; their fort, as well as that of those of the same class in other States seems to lie in misrepresentation, and a desire to inflame the passions and to alarm the fears by noisy declamation rather than to convince the understanding by some arguments or fair and impartial statements—Baffled in their attacks upon the constitution they have attempted to vilify and debase the Characters who formed it, but even here I trust they will not succeed.—Upon the whole I doubt whether the opposition to the Constitution will not ultimately be productive of more good than evil; it has called forth, in its defence, abilities (which would not perhaps have been otherwise exerted) that have thrown new lights upon the science of Government, they have given the rights of man a full and fair discussion, and have explained them in so clear and forcible a manner as cannot fail to make a lasting impression upon those who read the best publications on the subject, and particularly the pieces under the signiture of Publius.—There will be a greater weight of abilities opposed to the system in the convention of this State than there has been in any other, but notwithstanding the unwearied pains which have been taken, and the vigorous efforts which will be made in the Convention to prevent its adoption, I have not the smallest doubt but it will obtain here.—

I am sorry to hear that the College in your neighbourhood is in so declining a state as you represent it, and that it is likely to suffer a farther injury by the loss of Dr. Nisbet whom you are afraid you shall not be able to support in a proper manner on account of the scarcity of Cash which prevents parents from sending their Children hither. This is one of the numerous evils which arise from the want of a general regulating power, for in a Country like this where equal liberty is enjoyed, where every man may reap his own harvest, which by proper attention will afford him much more that what is necessary for his own consumption, and where there is so ample a field for every mercantile and mechanical exertion, if there cannot be money found to answer the common purposes of education, not to mention the necessary commercial circulation, it is evident that there is something amiss in the ruling political power which requires a steady, regulating and energetic hand to connect and control. That money is not to be had, every mans experience tells him, and the great fall in the price of property is an unequivocal, and melancholy proof of it; when, if that property was well secured—faith and justice well preserved—a stable government well administered,—and confidence restored,—the tide of population and wealth would flow to us, from every part of the Globe, and, with a due sense of the blessing, make us the happiest people upon earth—

"Fabius" [*John Dickinson*], *"Observations on the Constitution Proposed by the Federal Convention" VIII*

Pennsylvania Mercury and General Advertiser
(Philadelphia), April 29, 1788

The proposed confederation offers to us a system of diversified representation in the legislative, executive, and judicial departments, as essentially necessary to the good government of an extensive republican empire. Every argument to recommend it, receives new force, by contemplating events, that must take place. The number of states in *America* will encrease. If not united to the present, the consequences are evident. If united, it must be by a plan that will communicate *equal liberty* and assure *just protection* to them. These ends can never be attained, but by *a close combination* of the several states.

It has been asserted, that a very extensive territory cannot be ruled by a government of republican form. What is meant by this proposition? Is it intended to abolish all ideas of connection, and to precipitate us into the miseries of division, either as single states, or partial confederacies? To stupify us into despondence, that destruction may certainly seize us? The fancy of poets never feign'd so dire a *Metamorphosis*, as is now held up to us. The *Ægis* of their *Minerva* was only said to turn men into stones. This spell is to turn "a band of brethren," into a monster, preying upon itself, and prey'd upon by all its enemies.

If hope is not to be abandoned, common sense teaches us to attempt the best means of preservation. This is all that men can do, and this they ought to do. Will it be said, that any kind of disunion, or a connection tending to it, is preferable to a firm union? Or, is there any charm in that despotism, which is said, to be alone competent to the rule of such an empire? There is no evidence of fact, nor any deduction of reason, that justifies the assertion. It is true, that extensive territory has in general been arbitrarily governed; and it is as true, that a number of republics, in such territory, *loosely connected*, must inevitably rot into despotism. Such territory has never been governed by a confederacy of republics. Granted. But, where was there ever a confederacy of republics, in such territory, united, as these states are to be by the proposed constitution? Where was there ever a confederacy, in which, the sovereignty of each state was *equally represented* in one legislative body, the people of each state *equally represented* in another, and the sovereignties & people of all the states *conjointly represented* in a third branch? Or, in which, no law could be made, but by the agreement of three such branches? Or, in which, the appointment to federal offices was vested in a chief magistrate chosen as our president is to be, with the concurrence of a senate elected by the sovereignties of each state? Or, in which, the other acts of the executive department were regulated, as they are to be with us? Or, in which, the fœderal judges were to hold their offices independently and *during good behaviour*? Or, in which, the authority over the militia and troops was so distributed and controuled, as it is to be with us? Or, in which, the people were so drawn together by religion, blood, language, manners and customs, undisturbed by former feuds or prejudices? Or, in which, the affairs relating to the whole union, were to be managed by an assembly of several representative bodies, invested with different powers that became efficient only in concert, without their being embarrassed by attention to other business? Or, in which, a provision was made for the fœderal revenue, without recurring to coertion, the miserable expedient of every other confederacy that has existed, an expedient always attended with odium, & often with a delay productive of irreparable damage? Where was there ever a confederacy, that thus adhered to *the first principle of society*, obliging by its direct authority every individual, to contribute, when the public good necessarily required it, a just proportion of aid to the support of the commonwealth protecting him—without disturbing him in the discharge of the duties owing by him to the state of which he is an inhabitant; and at the same time so amply, so anxiously provided, for bringing the interests, and even the wishes of *every sovereignty* and of *every person* of the union, under all their various modifications and impreshons, into their full operation and efficacy in the national councils? The instance never existed. The conclusion ought not to be made. It is without premises.

It has been said, that the varied representation of sovereignties and people in the legislature, was a mere compromise.

This is a great and dangerous mistake. The equal representation of each state in one branch of the legislature, was an original substantive proposition, as the writer is instructed, made in Convention, very soon after the draft offered by *Virginia*, to which state United *America* is much indebted not only in other respects, but for her merit in the origination and prosecution of this momentous business.

The proposition was expressly made upon this principle, that a territory of such extent as that of United *America*, could not be *safely and advantageously governed*, but by a combination of republics, each retaining all the rights of supreme sovereignty, excepting such as ought to be contributed to the union; that for the securer preservation of these sovereignties, they ought to be represented in a body by themselves, and with equal suffrage; and that they would be annihilated, if both branches of the legislature were to be formed of representatives of the people, in proportion to the number of inhabitants in each state.

The principle appears to be well founded in reason, Why cannot a very extensive territory be ruled by a government of republican form? Because, its power must languish through distance of parts. Granted, if it be not a "body by joints and bands having nourishment ministered and knit together." If it be such a body, the objection is removed. Instead of such a perfect body, framed upon the principle that commands men to associate, and societies to confederate; that which by communicating and extending happiness, corresponds with the gracious intentions of our maker towards us his creatures; what is proposed? Truly, that the natural legs and arms of this body should be cut off, because they are too weak, and their places supplied by stronger limbs of wood and iron.

Arbitrary princes rule extensive territories, by sending vice-roys to govern certain districts.

America is, and will be, divided into several sovereign states, each possessing every power proper for governing within its own limits for its own purposes, and also for acting as a member of the union.

They will be civil and military stations, conveniently planted throughout the empire, with lively and regular communications. A stroke, a touch upon any part, will be immediately felt by the whole. *Rome* famed for imperial arts, had a glimpse of this great truth; and endeavoured, as well as her hardhearted policy would permit, to realize it in her COLO-NIES. They were miniatures of the capital: But wanted the vital principal of sovereignty, and were too small. They were melted down into, or overwhelmed by the nations around them. Were they now existing, they might be called, little stat-ues—something like to our living originals. *These* will bear a remarkable resemblance to the mild features of patriarchal government, in which each son ruled his own household, and in other matters the whole family was directed by the common ancestor.

Will a people thus happily situated, and attached as they will naturally be, with an ardor of affection to their own state, ever desire to exchange their condition, for subjection to an absolute ruler; or can they ever look but with veneration, or act but with deference to that union, that alone can, under providence, preserve them from such subjection?

Can any government be devised, that will be more suited to citizens, who wish for equal freedom and common prosperity? better calculated for preventing corruption of manners? for advancing the improvements that endear or adorn life? or that can be more conformed to the nature and understanding, to the best and the last end of man? What harvests of happiness may grow from the seeds of liberty that are now sowing? The cultivation will indeed demand continual care, unceasing diligence, and frequent conflicts with difficulties. This too is consonant to the laws of our nature. As we pass through night into day, so we do through trouble into joy. Generally, the higher the prize, the deeper the suffering. We die into immortality. To object against the benefits offered to us by our

Creator, by excepting to the terms annexed, is a crime to be equalled only by its folly.

Delightful are the prospects that will open to the view of United *America*—her sons well prepared to defend their own happiness, and ready to relieve the misery of others—her fleets formidable, but only to the unjust—her revenue sufficient, yet unoppressive—her commerce affluent, without debasing—peace and plenty within her borders—and the glory that arises from a proper use of power, encircling them.

Whatever regions may be destined for servitude, let us hope, that some portions of this land may be blessed with liberty; let us be convinced, that nothing short of such an union as has been proposed, can preserve the blessing, and therefore let us be resolved to adopt it.

As to alterations, a little experience will cast more light upon the subject, than a multitude of debates. Whatever qualities are possessed by those who object, they will have the candor to confess, that they will be encountered by opponents, not in any respect inferior, and yet differing from them in judgment, upon every point they have mentioned.

Such untired industry to serve their country, did the delegates to the federal convention exert, that they not only laboured to form the best plan they could, but, provided for making at any time amendments on the authority of the people, without shaking the stability of the government. For this end, the Congress, whenever two thirds of both houses shall deem it necessary, shall propose amendments to the constitution, or, on the application of the legislatures of two thirds of the several states, SHALL call a convention for proposing amendments, which, in either case, shall be valid to all intents and purposes, as part of the constitution, when ratified by the legislatures of three-fourths of the several states, or by conventions in three-fourths thereof, as one or the other mode of ratification may be proposed by Congress.

Thus, by a gradual progress, as has been done in *England*, we may from time to time introduce every improvement in our constitution, that shall be suitable to our situation. For this purpose, it may perhaps be adviseable, for every state, as it sees occasion, to form with the utmost deliberation, drafts of alterations respectively required by them, and to enjoin their representatives, to employ every proper method to obtain a ratification.

In this way of proceeding the undoubted sense of every state, collected in the coolest manner, not the sense of individuals, will be laid before the whole union in Congress, and that body will be enabled with the clearest light that can be afforded by every part of it, and with the least occasion of irritation, to compare and weigh the sentiments of all United *America*; forthwith to adopt such alterations as are recommended by general unanimity; by degrees to devise modes of conciliation upon contradictory propositions; and to give the revered advice of our common country, upon those, if any such there should be, that in her judgment are inadmissible, because they are incompatible with the happiness of these states.

It cannot be with reason apprehended, that Congress will refuse to act upon any articles calculated to promote the *common welfare*, tho' they may be unwilling to act upon such as are designed to advance PARTIAL *interests*: but, whatever their sentiments may be, they MUST call a Convention for proposing amendments, on applications of two-thirds of the legislatures of the several states.

May those good citizens, who have sometimes turned their thoughts towards a second Convention, be pleased to consider, that there are men who speak as they do, yet do not mean as they do. These borrow the sanction of their respected names, to conceal desperate designs. May they also consider, whether persisting in the suggested plan, in preference to the constitutional provision, may not kindle flames of jealousy and discord, which all their abilities and virtues can never extinguish.

A Grand Procession in Honor of Ratification

Maryland Journal (Baltimore), May 6, 1788

As soon as it was known in Town that the Constitution for the United States of America, was ratified, and our Convention dissolved, the Joy of the People was extreme. Every Class and Order of Citizens, wishing to give some Demonstration of their Feelings, it was agreed to form a grand Procession, expressive of their Satisfaction, and the high Importance of the Occasion.—The Mechanics, anticipating, under the new Government, an Increase of their different Manufactures, from the Operation of uniform Duties, on similar Articles imported into the United States, vied with each other in their Preparations.—The Merchants, and those concerned in Shipbuilding, contemplating the Revival, Extension, and Protection of Trade and Navigation, and the Re establishment of Credit, by securing an impartial Administration of Justice between Citizens of different States, were no less anxious to forward the Measure. In short, every Citizen, who wished to live under a Government, capable of protecting his Person and Property, united with the Farmers, Mechanics and Merchants, to form the most interesting Scene ever exhibited in this Part of the World.

At Nine in the Morning of the first Instant, the various Preparations being completed, the Procession, consisting of about Three Thousand People, was formed on Philpot's-Hill, under the Direction of Captains Plunket and Moore. At a Signal of Seven Guns, from Major Smith's and Capt. Furnival's Park of Artillery, which was answered by Three Huzzas, the whole Line moved to Fell's-Point; and from thence, through the principal Streets of the Town, amidst the Acclamations of a prodigious Number of Spectators, to Federal-

Hill, where they were received by a Salute of Seven Guns, and partook of an Entertainment provided for the Purpose.—They were seated at a circular Table of 3600 Feet, with the Devices and Standards of the respective Orders, displayed in the most regular Manner, exhibiting to the Town and Shipping in the Harbour, the Appearance of a most brilliant Encampment.—The Repast was elegantly disposed, and consisted entirely of the Productions of this Country. It was closed with Thirteen Toasts, (drank in the excellent Ale of Messrs. Peters and Company) accompanied by as many Federal Discharges.

TOASTS.

1. The Majesty of the People.
2. The late Convention.
3. Congress.
4. The Seven States which have adopted the Federal Constitution.
5. A speedy Ratification by the remaining Six, without Amendments.
6. George Washington.
7. His Most Christian Majesty, and our other Allies.
8. The virtuous Sixty-three of the Maryland Convention.
9. The Agriculture, Manufactories and Commerce of America.
10. The Memory of those who have fallen in Defence of America.
11. The worthy Minority of Massachusetts.
12. May the American Flag be respected in every Quarter of the Globe.
13. A Continuance of Unanimity among the Inhabitants of Baltimore-Town.

The Business of the Day being thus far completed, the several Classes of Citizens returned, in separate Divisions, to their respective Stations, and continued their Rejoicings in a Variety of rational and elevated Pleasures.

ORDER of PROCESSION.*
FARMERS.†

1st.—Foresters, with Axes, Mattocks, &c.

2d.—Two Sowers, Messrs. Stansbury and Smith.

3d.—A Plough ornamented, drawn by Two white Horses, and guided by Mr. Jonzee Selman—Motto, "Venerate the Plough."

4th.—An Harrow, drawn by Two black Horses.

5th.—A Number of very respectable Farmers from the Country, preceded by Messrs Harry Dorsey Gough, James Gittings, John Egor Howard, and John Cradock, the Four Federal Candidates for the County, followed by Men with Sickles, Sithes, Rakes, Pitchforks, and other Implements of Husbandry.

6th.—A Cart, loaded with fresh-cut Grass.

MILLERS and INSPECTORS of FLOUR—in their proper Habit.

FRENCH BURR MILLSTONE-MAKERS—preceded by Mr. George James, with a decorated Millstone incessantly turning in the Air, on an Axis, by the Power of Four beautiful Continental Flags, which produced the Effect of Sails.

BUTCHERS—in white Frocks, uniformly neat, with the Arms and Implements of their Order—preceded by Messrs. Brown and Tinker, and closed by Messrs. Smith and Tonstill.

BAKERS—preceded by Messrs. Brown and Myers—A Flag, carried by Mr. Clopper, displaying Two Men Hand-in-Hand;—Thirteen Loaves;—Thirteen Stars and Thirteen Stripes;—the rising Sun;—Sheaf of Wheat.—Motto, "May our Country never want Bread."

BREWERS and DISTILLERS—preceded by Messrs. Peters and Johonnot.—A Still, Worm, Tubs, &c.

BLACKSMITHS and NAILERS—preceded by Messrs. M'Clellan, Johnston, and Lawrence.—A Travelling Forge,

---

*The Expence of this Procession amounted to Six Hundred Pounds, independently of what the different Orders expended in their Preparations.

†In forming the Line of Procession, the distinct Orders were arranged promiscuously, Equality being the Basis of the Constitution.

drawn by Horses: Journeymen and Apprentices at work, in the different Branches;—Colours flying—Mottoes,

> "May ev'ry Federal Heart,
> Encourage Vulcan's Art.
> And
> While Industry prevails,
> We need no foreign Nails."

HOUSE-CARPENTERS—preceded by Mr. Harbough.—A grand Tower,—supported by Seven Architects, with Thirteen Fronts, on which were suspended, Tools emblematic of the respective States—Thirteen Stories, Thirteen Pillars, Thirteen Arches, Thirteen Pediments, Thirteen Spires, with Flags displayed on Seven, and Thirteen Flutes.—In the grand Column, a Battery of Thirty-nine Guns, from which were answered the Salutes of the Park.—On the Column—portrayed, Andrew Palladio, and his Excellency General Washington, under the Flags of the Union.

PAINTERS, GLAZIERS and MANUFACTURERS of GLASS—preceded by Messrs. Carlisle and Kuhn.—A Figure of Peter Coeck, with his Pallet, Pencils, &c. painted on Canvas, and a *Michael*, with his Pallet and Pencils, taking Sketches on a Piece of prepared Canvas, Two Boys attending him; all in a Carriage, drawn by a Horse.—On the back Part of the Carriage, a Paint-Stone fixed, with a Painter grinding Colours, followed by Painters, with Heraldry Books, Pallets and Guilding-Cushions, all decorated, proper—The Glaziers with a Sash fixed on a Staff, and glazed with Thirteen Panes—In the Center-Pane, a Portrait of General Washington—Glass Trumpets—and Fame descending.

MASONS—preceded by ——, habited in Aprons;—Trowels, Squares, Plumbs, Hods, &c.—The Grand Royal Temple elevated on Supporters.

STONE-CUTTERS—with their QUARRIERS—preceded by Mr. M'Glathery.—Emblems, &c.

PLASTERERS—preceded by Messrs. Collins and Littlejohn.—A Flag, displaying a Whitewash Brush, Trowel, a Bundle of Laths, &c.

CABINETMAKERS, preceded by Messrs. Bankson and Lawson.—An Ensign, representing a Cabinet.—Motto, "May our Cabinet be enriched by an Union of the States."

COACHMAKERS—preceded by Mr. Finlater.—Emblems, &c.

WHEELWRIGHTS and TURNERS—preceded by Mr. Emmit.—A Spinning-Wheel, supported on Five Columns, and decorated.—Motto, "Industry."

COOPERS—preceded by Mr. Duncan.—Men at work in a Carriage drawn by Horses, under a golden Figure, representing Bacchus on a Cask, &c.

TANNERS and CURRIERS—preceded by Messrs. Brown and Jones.—Implements, &c.

SHOEMAKERS—preceded by Messrs. Wilson and Sloan. —A Flag, displaying King Crispin, in his Robes, with a Boot in his Hand.—A Boot and Crown.—Colours flying, Music, &c.

SADDLERS and HARNESSMAKERS—preceded by Messrs. Gordon and Coulter.—An elegant Horse, richly caparisoned, and led by Two Negroes, in white, with black Velvet Jockey-Caps, Silver Tassels, Half-boots, &c.

HATTERS—preceded by Messrs. Shields and J. Gray.— Skins and Hats displayed upon an Obelisk, at the Base of which appeared a Beaver and a Fox.—Mottoes, "With the Industry of the Beaver, we will support the Federal Constitution."—"With the Eye of the Fox, we will watch and guard our Rights."

TAILORS—preceded by Messrs. Speck, Martin and Borland.—A Flag displaying Adam and Eve in the Garden of Eden;—Thirteen Stars, &c.

STAYMAKERS—preceded by Mr. Bourchet.—A Flag, displaying a spread Pair of Stays;—Thirteen Stars, on a white Field.

COMBMAKERS—preceded by Mr. John Lenvill.—A large Comb elevated on a Standard.—Tools decorated, &c.

BARBERS—preceded by Messrs. Clements and Brydon. —Busts,—A Goddess, surrounded by Sons of Freedom:—a Figure presenting to the Goddess the new Constitution:—the Goddess inclining with a Smile of

Approbation.—Motto, "May our Trade succeed, and the Union enrich us."

SILVERSMITHS and WATCHMAKERS—preceded by Messrs. Levely, Clarke, and Rice.—A Flag, representing the different Articles of their Manufactures—Motto, "No Importation and we shall live":—Under it, a Bee-Hive—Motto,—"If encouraged."

COPPERSMITHS—preceded by Messrs. Clemm and Raburg.—A Still with Head and Worm complete, Scales, &c.—Motto, "May our Industry be rewarded."

BRASS-FOUNDERS, Cutlers, Plumbers, Whitesmiths, and Gunsmiths—preceded by Mr. Wier, &c.—Three large Candlesticks, disposed in a triangular Manner, supported by a Column, with Thirteen Stripes displayed.—Jack, Bell, Andirons, Fender, Grate, Shovel and Tongs, Rifles, Gunlocks, &c.

TALLOW-CHANDLERS—preceded by Messrs. Liston and Ellerton:—A Frame, bearing Seven Candles;—a Wedge of Soap in the Centre.—A Flag;—Thirteen Stripes; Seven Stars;—a Chandler, making Candles.—Motto, "Let your Light so shine."

PRINTERS—Mr. Goddard and Mr. Hayes.—A Figure, Guttemberg—Compositors, &c. with Volumes, American Productions—Mercuries, distributing Copies of the new Constitution, *without Amendments*.

PILOTS—preceded by Captain John Pitt, with Lead and Line, sounding the Channel.

SHIP FEDERALIST.

JOSHUA BARNEY, Esq; Commander,

Mr. COOPER, First Lieutenant.

Completely officered and manned, rigged and sailed; borne on a Carriage drawn by Horses. She displayed the Flag of the United States, and was fully dressed. Being the Seventh Ship in the Line, and having weathered the most dangerous Cape in the Voyage, she lay to, under Seven Sails, during the Repast, on Federal-Hill, throwing out Signals, and expecting the Arrival of the other Six.

SEA-CAPTAINS and MARINERS—preceded by Captains John Winning and Henry Johnson.—Emblems, Quadrant and Compass.

DRAYMEN—preceded by Mr. Jeffers.—A Dray decorated, on which was a Hogshead of Beer, a Flag-Staff in the Bung-Hole, the Flag displaying Thirteen Stripes, &c. drawn by one Horse.

CONSULS.

MERCHANTS and TRADERS—preceded by the Hon. William Smith, Esq;

VINTNERS—preceded by Messrs. Hepburn and Yeiser. A Bunch of Grapes, with a Flag—Motto, "We lead to Joy, Jollity, and real Independence."—"Follow us to real Joy!—We alone dispense the Blessing."

SHIP-CARPENTERS—preceded by Mr. Stodder.—A Shipyard,—One Ship on the Stocks; Thirteen Men at Work.—Draught of a Ship complete, decorated.—Carpenters, with Axes, Adzes, &c.

SHIP-JOINERS—preceded by Messrs. Joseph and James Biays.—Representation,—The Stern of the Ship Federalist;—Binnacle, Compasses, Planes, &c.—Thirteen Stars, and Thirteen Stripes.

CARVERS and GILDERS—preceded by Mr. Brown.—Emblem, Figure of his Excellency Governor Smallwood.

ROPEMAKERS—preceded by Messrs. Dugan and Smith.—A Spinning-Wheel, with Thirteen Whirls, drawn by Thirteen Labourers—Thirteen Workmen, with Hemp round their Waists, occupied.—Queen Catherine portrayed in the Field of a large Flag.

RIGGERS—preceded by Mr. Pine.—Implements of their Order: knotting and splicing.

BLOCKMAKERS—preceded by Mr. John M'Myers.—A Machine.—Cleaver, with Blocks wedged in.—A Person at work.—A Flag; Thirteen different kinds of Blocks, in the Field.

SAILMAKERS, with their Tools—preceded by Mr. William Jacobs.—A portable Sail-Loft; Duck, &c.—Men at work.

MATHEMATICAL INSTRUMENT-MAKERS—preceded by Mr. Dorsey. — Emblems, — Land-Compass, Spy-Glass, &c.

SHIP-CHANDLERS—preceded by Mr. Thomas Johnson, and others.—Half-Hour Glasses, Log-Reel and Line,

Atlas, Compass, Scale and Dividers, Sea Chart, Tinder-Box, Lead-Line, Log-Board, Hand-Trumpet, Epitome, and Spy-Glass.

BOATBUILDERS—preceded by Mr. Davis,—A fore Frame of a Boat, &c.

SURGEONS and PHYSICIANS.

CLERGY.

BENCH and BAR.

MEMBERS OF CONVENTION — Messrs. M'Henry, Coulter, Hanson, Sprigg, Gilpin, Hollingsworth, Heron, Evans, Sulivane, Richardson, and Done.

The Procession was attended by a Band of Music, under the Direction of the celebrated Performer, Mr. Boyer.

The Evening was ushered in by a splendid Bonfire on Federal-Hill.—An allegoric transparent Painting, finely illuminated, was exhibited by Mr. Peale, in the Front of the Court-House.—Mr. Starck's superb Building was handsomely illuminated, where a grand Ball concluded the Festivities of the Day.

We exult in the Happiness of adding, that every Part of this variegated, pleasing and august Scene, was conducted with the most perfect Regularity, Order and Harmony. No unfortunate Accident interrupted the general Joy—no gloomy Thought obstructed the finest Expansions of the human Mind!—Every Eye sparkled, every Heart glowed with Rapture, upon this brilliant Occasion.—The Happiness of each Order, the Happiness of each Individual, the Happiness of every Spectator, was increased by the Consciousness of heightening the Felicity of others.—Those Diffidences which make up Reserve, and check the Progress of social Intercourse, when local Character hath not assumed its proper Tone, retired at the Approach of mutual Confidence, and were absorbed in the Plenitude of Unanimity.—Every Citizen of the United States—every Citizen of the World, who was inspired by the general Sentiment, was embraced with the warmest Feelings of Benevolence, Hospitality and Friendship.—Beauty, Elegance and Taste were exhibited in all their Lustre, by the delicate Fair, whose irresistible Charms attract us to—A FEDERAL UNION.—May the Infant Mind, in its first Impressions, receive the great Ideas of the present Moment,

—may it be nurtured in the clearest Perceptions of their superior Utility;—and, when all human Institutions shall terminate in the Acquisition of their Objects, Virtue and Happiness,—may Heaven itself approve the Wisdom of *our* FEDERAL CONSTITUTION.

J. Hector St. John Crèvecoeur to
Comte de la Luzerne

New York, May 16, 1788

According to the orders that I received by your dispatch of 17 November, I have the honor to transmit to you three copies of the new Constitution. I was getting ready to send you a literal translation when I saw it inserted in the European post No. 4, 5, 6 and 7.

The Convention of Maryland has just adopted this new system of government by a majority of 63 to 11; according to the most authentic letters recently received from South Carolina, it seems very likely that that state will adopt it also. As for Virginia, North Carolina, New Hampshire, and New York, any definite opinion cannot yet be formed, their Conventions not sitting until the months of June and July. The Federalists and the Anties (as they are called here) spare no means to make the choice of the people fall on the persons whose principles are kindred to those of their party. The Election of the City of Alexandria had been kept open for three days, in order to give the partisans of the new Constitution, and General Washington's friends, time to be able to make him agree to be elected as one of the members of the *State Convention* but always restrained by his modesty, he constantly refused to do it. It is said that he fears that he would appear to be too zealous a federalist, he is not accused of working for himself, since he cannot be unaware that if the new Constitution takes place, he is destined to become the first *great President* under it, this conduct is very [   ] to those who maintain that his presence alone in the Convention, would have carried [   ] twenty votes. The greatest opposition on the part of the Antifederalists is expected in this last [   ]: This party counts among its members several very popular people it is true, but the other prides itself, and justly so, on having the most

439

organized leaders, and the best orators. One awaits the outcome of this period of Conventions; that of South Carolina,
was to begin on the 12th of this month; that of this state is set
for 17 June; that of Virginia for the first week, that of New
Hampshire for the last of the same month, and lastly that of
North Carolina for the 4th of July.

But although it is very probable that nine or even ten states
will accept this new form I am far however from conceiving
that it will be able to have much vigor for a long time; it is
very probable that the Delegates who will compose the first
federal Congress, will be specially instructed by their constituents, not to be a party to any act of Legislation before having obtained the ratification of different clauses (amendments)
which, holding to the localities of the confederated states, will
all be contradictory; and then how to subject a people to the
dominion of laws, who for so long have not experienced their
salutary curb, who confuse a license without bounds with the
name of Liberty, who believe that one can be free without
government and rich without effort; how to restrain a people
who inhabit a continent as vast and unlimited, a people
whose habits are so changed, because the upheaval in customs
and opinions occasioned by its separation from Europe has
created a sort of interregnum, a void, which can only be replaced after a long passage of time; perhaps even this century
will not witness the entire restoration of a perfect tranquility
and calm; the next generation will imperceptibly acquire a
greater respect for these new forms; and these happy customs,
finally becoming national, will contribute to spreading their
salutary influences. Judging these people by their present personality, by the geographic situation of all these states, I
believe that their union will never be able to be very close,
unless it finally becomes the result of force and violence; the
inclination for emigration, the facility with which they leave
the dwellings of their fathers in order to go beyond the
Mountains, all these reasons will make the proposed consolidation difficult.

One of the sources of all the misfortunes that I observe
here, resulting from the peace, the Americans had believed
that the revolution was accomplished when it had only begun; because although independent from Europe in its gov-

ernment, this country still nevertheless depends on it for the greater part of its customs, and, unfortunately, for its credit, and whose deadly poison makes itself felt everywhere.

Even if this new Constitution is adopted by a sufficient number of states, it must be expected that it will be fought by the opposition which is forming on all sides; one side, devotedly attached to their sovereignty and to their independence, regards as sacrilege the efforts the federalists are making to decrease them, [   ] party, destined to form the general government; others fear for the impartiality of the new courts of law that it is proposed to establish, call these new principles budding tyranny, and fill the gazettes with a flood of declamations addressed to the passions, much more than to the reason of the readers; another class, composed of those who occupy lucrative places in each of these states, which can be called the Oligarchical party, seeing only in this new order of things the end of their mercenary and ambitious lives, sends forth loud cries and endeavors to spread alarm on all sides; and finally, the others, carried away by the perversity of human nature, fear the return of order, and would wish to plunge the entire engine into anarchy and confusion.

It would thus be flattering oneself needlessly to believe that reason alone operates this great marvel, the contrary is to be feared, that [   ] the ordinary sort of men, they can only receive a uniform and coercive government by means of violence, and in that case the union will be destroyed; the southern states, whose interests are so different from, which are so jealous of, and which dread so much the energy, activity and industry of the inhabitants of the North, will form alliances in Europe; then all will be irrevocably lost. That is what all its democratic forms will possibly lead to, which are so grand on paper, but which will have been deadly and deceitful dreams. It is thus not on their Constitutions, but on the facts and on the present state of their morals that one must judge the nation, which, although new, is nevertheless corrupted with so much rapidity; and how could the individual citizens be honest, when the government was able to support a ruinous war only by transactions which so strongly compromised the public credit, which necessarily aroused fraud and greed. The subsequent conduct of almost all these states since the peace, was not helped by their paper money, which put the crowning glory on all these misfortunes. How intimate are the ties which exist between the morals of a nation and the value of its money. I see only one hope, and it is based on the unexpected help of some even more unfortunate circumstances than those in which they find themselves today, which will finally make them open their eyes to the absurdity of wanting to preserve all the rights of independence and sovereignty for each one of these states, without giving any of them to the general government. This disastrous opinion which has occasioned so many errors since the peace still militates against the [   ] principles of the social contract. If the sky's color blinds them, if they reject this favorable occasion of obtaining a government which promises them dignity and happiness, it is not possible to predict what form sooner or later will come out of the midst of this disorder and anarchy; in less than three months they will cross the Rubicon, and we shall see what course the federalists will adopt.

James Madison to George Nicholas

Orange County, Virginia, May 17, 1788

DEAR SIR

I received your favor of the 9th. inst: several days ago, but have never been able till this moment to comply with the request it makes on the subject of the Mississippi.

Many considerations induce me to believe that there is not at present any dangerous disposition to sacrifice the right of the U. S. to the common use of that navigation. The discussions and enquiries which have taken place on that subject, have had a sensible influence on many opinions which had been formed under very partial and erroneous views of it. I have reason to believe particularly that the project will not again have the patronage of one very influencial quarter. I find also that in States whose delegates had the strongest leaning towards the project, there are more weighty characters who warmly disapprove of it. I may add that some circumstances of a nature not to be particularized, are within my knowledge, which have more effect than any thing I have mentioned, in justifying the opinion I have expressed. These remarks will themselves suggest that they are communicated in confidence.

As far as any disposition may remain to form a treaty with Spain unfriendly to the views of the Western people I think it will be evidently diminished by the establishment of the new Constitution.

The great argument used by the advocates for a temporary cession of the American right was that the Union could not cause the right to be respected by Spain, that it was dishonorable to assert a right and at the same time leave another nation in the full and quiet possession of it, and that to exchange it was to get something for nothing. The force of this reasoning will vanish with the national impotency of our present situation.

The more intimate and permanent the Union be made, the greater will be the sympathy between the whole and each particular part; and consequently the less likely will the whole be to give up the rights or interests of any particular part. Many seem to have been led by the supposed inability of the existing confederation to retain the Western settlements under the general authority, to consider that part of the U. S. as a foreign country, and the other part as at liberty for that reason to pay an exclusive regard to its own particular interests. If the proposed Government will have energy enough to maintain the Union of the Atlantic States, it will be soon perceived, I think, that it will be equally capable at least, to bind together the Western and Atlantic States.

The protection and security which the new Government promises to purchasers of the fœderal lands, will have several consequences extremely favorable to the rights and interests of the Western Country. It will accelerate the population & formation of new States there, and of course increase its weight in the general scale. It will encourage adventurers of character and talents who will not only add much to that weight, but will leave behind them friends and connections who will feel a variety of motives to stand up for whatever concerns the Western Country. It will induce many who will remain at home to speculate in that field with a view of selling out afterwards, or of providing for their children. These with all their friends will form a new class of advocates for their Western brethren. To such causes we are to ascribe the peculiar attachment which Virginia has shewn to the navigation of the Mississippi. The same causes will produce the same effect, wherever they may operate. The disposition of the New England people to emigrate into the Western Country has already shewn itself under every discouragement of the present crisis. A very considerable quantity of public land has been already contracted for by persons of influence in that Country, who are actually carrying out settlers for their purchases. This circumstance has probably contributed to the relaxation of that quarter in the business of a Spanish Treaty. In a very short time if due provision be made for the safety & order of the settlements N. W. of the Ohio the Muskingum will be as well known, and inspire as much solicitude in N. England, as Kentucky does here.

As the establishment of the new Govt. will thus promote the sale of the public lands, it must for the same reason enhance their importance as a fund for paying off the public debts, and render the navigation of the Mississippi still more an object of national concern. Add to this that the new Government, by substantiating the domestic debt, will render the vacant territory a more necessary, as well as more productive fund for discharging it.

On these considerations principally I ground my opinion that the disposition to cede the Mississippi will be much less under the new than it may be under the old system. I am no less persuaded that the form of the new system will present greater obstacles to the measure than exist under the old. The present Congress possess the same powers as to treaties, as will be possessed by the New Government. $\frac{2}{3}$ of the Senate will also be required, as $\frac{2}{3}$ of Congs. now is. The only difference which relates to the Senate is that $\frac{2}{3}$ of a majority of that body will suffice; whereas in Congs. there must be $\frac{2}{3}$ of the whole number of votes. This at first view seems to be a material difference; but in practice it will be found if I mistake not, to be much less so. The representation in the Senate will be generally full for this very reason that a majority will make a quorum, and $\frac{2}{3}$ of that number be competent to a decision. The apprehension of important decisions in a thin House will be a spur to the attendance of the members. It will be an additional spur that decisions when made will have real efficacy. In Congs. the case is different in both respects. So great a proportion of the whole body must concur in every act, particularly in important acts that the absent States find almost as great a security in their absence as in their presence, against measures which they dislike. And they well know that as the measures of Congs. depend for their efficacy on the State legislatures, it is of little consequence in general how questions may be decided. From these causes proceeds the difficulty of keeping up a competent representation.

In calculating the probability of an event depending on the opinion of a body of men, it is necessary to take into view the degree of mutability in the component members of the body. It is obvious that every change of members produces a new chance of the event. If we try the danger to the Mississippi under the old and under the new system by comparing them in relation to this principle, the friends of the Mississippi cannot hesitate to embrace the latter. If the first choice should produce a Senate opposed to the sacrifice of that object, it can not be sacrificed for two years, the danger from a new election of the whole number, can happen but once in six years, and as the same members are re-eligible from time to time, the danger from a change may possibly not happen during the lives of the members. On the other hand the members of Congress may be changed at pleasure, they hold their places at most from year to year, and the entire body necessarily undergoes a revolution once in three years. How many chances does such a body present in a period of six years for the turning up of any particular opinion.

To compleat the comparison between the two bodies another difference is to be noted. In the Senate the States will be represented each by two members who are to vote per capita. In Congress the representation consists of an uncertain number, generally three or five, any two of whom can give the vote of the State. From this peculiarity in the Constitution of Congress, two observations result. 1. If any two out of the three, five or more members happen to concur in any particular opinion and happen to attend together without their colleagues or with not more than one of them, their opinion becomes the vote of the State. It is easy to see how this must multiply the chances of any particular measure in Congress. Where the measure may depend on a few wavering or divided States, this circumstance is of material importance. On the very subject of the Mississippi I have seen the opinion of a State in Congress depending altogether on the casual attendance of these or those members of the same deputation, and sometimes varying more than once in the course of a few days. Even in the Virginia deputation the vote of the State *might* have been given in opposition to the sense of a majority of the delegates in appointment. 2. Although 9 *States* which are ⅔ of the whole must concur in Treaties made by Congress, yet it may happen that of the *members* present less than ⅔, the proportion absolutely necessary in the Senate, may give an affirmative decision. If each delegation contain 5 members present, 27 can carry the point, who amount to ⅗ only of the whole number. If the delegations contain each 3 members only, the point may be carried by not more than ⅖.

But the circumstance most material to be remarked in a comparative examination of the two systems, is the security which the new one affords by making the concurrence of the President necessary to the validity of Treaties. This is an advantage which may be pronounced conclusive. At present the will of a single body can make a Treaty. If the new Government be established no treaty can be made without the joint consent of two distinct and independent wills. The president also being elected in a different mode, and under a different influence from that of the Senate, will be the more apt and the more free to have a will of his own. As a single magistrate too responsible for the events of his administration, his pride will the more naturally revolt against a measure which might bring on him the reproach not only of partiality, but of a dishonorable surrender of a national right. His duration and re-eligibility are other circumstances which diminish the danger to the Mississippi. If the first election should produce either a Senate or a President opposed to the scheme of giving up the river, it must be safe for a considerable time, the danger can only return at considerable intervals, and there will always be at least a double chance of avoiding it.

I consider the House of Reps. as another obstacle afforded by the new Constitution. It is true that this branch is not of necessity to be consulted in the forming of Treaties. But as its approbation and co-operation may often be necessary in carrying treaties into full effect; and as the support of the Government and of the plans of the President & Senate in general must be drawn from the purse which they hold, the sentiments of this body cannot fail to have very great weight, even when the body itself may have no constitutional authority. There are two circumstances in the structure of the House of Reps. which strengthen the argument in this case. The one is that its members will be taken more diffusively from each State than the members of Congs. have generally been. The latter being appointed by the State legislatures, and considered as representatives of the States in their political capacities, have been appointed with little or no regard to local situation, and have of course been taken in most of the States from the commercial and maritime situations which have generally presented the best choice of characters. The House of Reps. on the other hand must consist by a large majority of inland & Western members. This is a difference of some moment in my opinion, on the subject under consideration. The other circumstance is that the people of America being proportionally represented in this branch, that part of America which is supposed to be most attached to the Mississippi, will have a greater share in the representation than they have in Congress, where the number of States only prevails. So that under the new System every Treaty must be made by 1. the authority of the Senate in which the States are to vote equally. 2 that of the President who represents the people & the States in a compounded ratio. and 3. under the influence of the H. of Reps. who represent the people alone.

After all perhaps the comparative merits of the two systems in relation to the point in view depend less on what they may probably omit to do, than on their ability to effect what it is proper they should do. The Western strength is unable at present to command the use of the Mississippi. Within a certain period it will be able. Neither the new nor the old system will be able by any acts or Treaties whatever, very long to protract this period. What ought to be desired therefore by the Western people is not so much that no treaty should be made, as that some treaty should be made which will procure them an immediate and peaceable use of the river. The Present Congs. if ever so well disposed is wholly and notoriously incompetent to this task. Their successors, if the new Government take place, will be able to hold a language which no nation having possessions in America will think it prudent to disregard; and which will be able to have a due effect on Spain in particular.

Besides these considerations which relate to a particular object, there are others which I should suppose ought to recommend the proposed Constitution to the Western Citizens.

They have a common interest in obtaining the advantages

promised by a good general Government, as well as in avoiding the mischeifs of that anarchy which now hovers over us.

If not the number, at least the character of emigrants to that Country, as well from Europe as the elder States, will depend on the degree of security provided there for private rights and public order.

The new Govt. and that alone will be able to take the requisite measures for getting into our hands the Western posts which will not cease to instigate the Savages, as long as they remain in British hands. It is said also that the Southern Indians are encouraged and armed by the Spaniards for like incursions on that side. A respectable Government would have equal effect in putting an end to that evil. These are considerations which must I should think have great weight with men of reflection.

It seems probable that even if the Mississippi were open, it would be used as a channel for exportation only or cheifly, and that the returns will be imported more cheaply & conveniently through the Atlantic States. On this supposition the Western inhabitants, like those of the non-importing States on the Atlantic, will be taxed by other States as long as the present system continues. This must necessarily be the case prior to the opening of the Mississippi. The effect of this oppression on N. Jersey, Connecticut & Delaware are well known.

The idea of an exportation down the Mississippi, and an importation through the channels I have mentioned, has always appeared to me to be warranted by the probable interest and arrangements of the Western people and to furnish a strong inducement to the Atlantic States to contend for the navigation of that river. The imports of every Country must be pretty nearly limited by the amount of its exports. Without the use of the Mississippi the Western Country will export little or nothing. The Atlantic Country will of course have little or no profit from supplying them with imports, at least after the money carried thither by emigrants shall be exhausted. Open the Mississippi, and the amount of imports will yield a profit to the Atlantic merchants which must be contemplated with great avidity.

I have no particular materials or calculations for determining the revenue that may be drawn from the general imports. It does not appear to me to be necessary to go much into details on the subject. As far as it may, the Custom-House returns of Virga. may give proper data. We know in general that the annual amount may be rated at about four millions sterling and upwards. Five perCt. on this which is less than is raised in any other Country except Holland, will be a most precious resource. We know too that there are several particular articles on which enumerated duties may be superadded. From an estimate I saw in N. York, the rum imported there amounted to one million of Gallons. As a part of N. Jersey & of Connecticut are supplied from that port, N. York may perhaps import ⅙ of the whole quantity consumed in the U. States. According to this calculation one shilling per Gallon wd. yield a million of dollars. Other articles might be selected.

I have the pleasure to find that Mr. Brown will befriend the Constitution as far as his influence will extend. Mr. Griffin tells me so. I am sorry that the returns from Kentucky will render an exertion of it necessary. It is much to be feared that the members may come fettered not only with prejudices but with instructions. I beg you to excuse the marks of hurry with which I have written. The hope of finding a conveyance from the Church at which Mr. Waddel preaches, limited me to a space of time which did not admit of correctness. Inclosed are a few papers recd. a few days ago, from Mr. Griffin. With sincere esteem I am Dr Sir Your Obedt. servt.

"An American" [*Tench Coxe*]

Pennsylvania Gazette (Philadelphia), May 21, 1788

To the Honorable the MEMBERS *of the* CONVENTION *of* VIRGINIA.

By the special delegation of the people of your respectable commonwealth, you are shortly to determine on the fate of the proposed constitution of fœderal government. First invited to that important measure by the resolutions of your legislature, from the wisest considerations, America, confiding in the steadiness of your patriotism, and feeling that new weight is daily given to your original inducements, doubts not it is now to receive your sanction. But before the awful determination which is to call *the American union* once more into political existence shall be finally taken, permit one of the most respectful of your countrymen to trespass a few minutes on your time and patience.

The qualities of the proposed government have been so fully explained, and it will receive such further exposition in your honorable body, that it is needless to attempt a regular discussion of the subject. This paper shall therefore be confined to *a few particular considerations* that have been already mentioned by others, or which may now be suggested for the first time.

It has been urged by some sensible and respectable men, that your populous state will not be properly represented in the fœderal senate. Permit me to remind you, that while you have but one vote of thirteen in the present union, you will have twelve in ninety one in the new confederacy. Suffer me to observe too, that as the United States are *free governments*, it might not have been very unreasonable if the people of Virginia could have given only the same number of votes at

451

an election for foederal purposes, as they can give at *a state election*. If the citizens of Virginia find it *wise and prudent*, that *free* persons *only* shall be taken into consideration in electing their *state* legislature, would it appear extraordinary that citizens of the United States should think *the same rule* proper in electing the *foederal* representatives. By the present arrangement, you may enjoy the weight and power of *five* votes and a half for 168,000 slaves, being three fifths of your whole number of blacks. Were these to be deducted from the votes of Virginia in the foederal house of representatives, it would leave little more than one vote in thirteen in that house. In the present Congress, as before observed, and in the proposed senate, a thirteenth vote is allotted to Virginia. Taking the number of free citizens, which is the proper rule of representation in *free governments*, Virginia, in the foederal representation, would have about as many votes as New York, and *fewer* than Massachusetts or Pennsylvania. It will be proper to consider too the effect of the erection of Kentucke into a separate state, and of her becoming another member of the new confederacy. When that *certain event* shall take place, Virginia will fall *considerably short* of the proportion of one in fourteen of the free white inhabitants of the United States. Impartially considering this true state of things, the opinion that Virginia will hold a share of the powers of the new government, less than she is entitled to, will appear to be erroneous. If, on examination, these facts shall be found to be stated with accuracy and candor, and the observations and reasonings upon them shall appear just and fair, we confidently trust your honorable house will not consider the proposed constitution as exceptionable in that particular.

Objections have been made by some very respectable gentlemen of your state to the power of Congress, under the new foederal constitution, to regulate trade *"by a bare majority."* In a *free* government, *the voice of the people*, expressed by the votes of *a majority*, must be *the rule*, or we shall be left without any *certain* rule to determine what is politically right. To depart from it, *is establishing tyranny by law*. It would be *a solemn renunciation* of the forms and substance of liberty; and our affairs, *on this dangerous principle*, must rapidly hasten to *an oligarchy*—the most dreadful of all governments. It would be in vain to say we might be restrained by *one third* in commercial cases, and *free* in all others. The precedent *once established*, it requires no prophetic gift to say *where it would end*. But, independent of the violation of *the great principle of free governments*, the objection, and apprehensions arising from it, are founded on a misconception of the true nature of affairs in all the states. *The landed interest* must ever possess *a commanding majority* in the state and fœderal legislatures. It was supposed the objection ought to have great weight in the five southern states: But we do not find it has been *even mentioned* in the Maryland or Georgia conventions, the only two which have yet determined on the constitution, nor was it noticed in New-Jersey or Delaware, which are *the least commercial* members of the confederacy. Four of the *agricultural* states have considered this objection and these fears as unfounded, for they have adopted the constitution with *only eleven dissentient votes*.

The rejection of the government by the state of Virginia, should eight states have previously adopted it, is a matter (permit me respectfully to observe) the possible consequences of which should be most seriously considered. Should a ninth state ratify the constitution after you have declined to do so, it will become a *binding compact—an operative system*. The American states would *deeply* regret a circumstance, that should place a most respectable member of the present union, and *a natural born elder sister*, in the character of *an alien*; and a late and reluctant adoption, not arising altogether from free choice and *natural affection*, would exceedingly abate that cordial joy, which will flow throughout the land at the early adoption of the proposed constitution by your ancient state, whence *the first call to independence* was boldly given, and whence *first arose this great attempt to cement and invigorate our union*.

The United States, whatever has been the cause of past events, may certainly become *a nation of great respectability and power*. But such is the effect of our *distracted* politics, and of *the feebleness of our general government*, that foreign powers *openly* declare their unwillingness to treat with us, while our affairs remain *on the present footing*. However favorable or friendly they may think our intentions towards them, they know *we have not constitutional powers* to execute *our own* desires, even within *our own jurisdiction*. Senators of no inconsiderable reputation in the British Parliament have told the world, they can make *no fixed arrangements* with us under the *present* confederation. The Ministers of France, which nation has lately evinced the continuance of her friendship by new privileges to our trade, declare they cannot proceed to *the extent* of their desires, since *no power exists to treat upon national ground*. The Court of Spain too, however they might be influenced by *a firm and respectable union*, will never listen to our demands *for the navigation of the Missisippi*, while we remain in *our present unconnected situation*. We are no object *even of respect* to them, much less of *apprehension*; and should the present constitution be rejected, they will laugh at all future attempts to continue or invigorate the union. Our Minister at that Court expects to effect *no arrangements there*, without an efficient government being *first adopted here*.

It has been objected to the proposed fœderal constitution, that it tends to render our country more vulnerable, by admitting the further importation of slaves. To persons not accurately acquainted with the whole of the American constitutions, this objection may appear of weight. But when it is canvassed before so enlightened an assembly as the Convention of Virginia, the mistake will be instantly discovered. It will be remembered that ten of the states, and Virginia among the number, have already prohibited the further importation of slaves, and that the power of the legislature of *each state*, even after the adoption of the constitution, will not only remain *competent to prohibition of the slave trade*, but (if they find the measure wise and safe) to the emancipation of the slaves already among us. It may be added further, that the exercise of this power of the state governments can *in no wise* be controuled or restrained by the fœderal legislature.

Should the present attempt to infuse new vigor into the general government fail of success, partial confederacies must at once follow. The states on the Delaware, central in their situation, and (though not superabundantly rich) perfectly independent in their resources, will find themselves bound together by their position on the globe, by a perfect similarity of manners and interests, by the preservation of their common peace and safety, and by the innumerable ties of blood and marriage subsisting between them. A frank and liberal concession of the impost on the part of Pennsylvania will render the inducements complete. The sentiments of the state of Maryland on the proposed government, their existing connections with Pennsylvania and Delaware, from each of whom they are divided *only by an imaginary line*, will turn their inclinations that way. Rather than connect themselves with a southern country, between which and them a great natural boundary is interposed, and which is rendered vulnerable by 280,000 slaves, they will find it prudent, as well as agreeable, to join their northern neighbours. Should Pennsylvania offer to aggrandize the ports of Maryland, by opening to her the extensive navigation of Susquehanna, whose various branches water many millions of acres of fertile lands, *prudence and interest* will powerfully persuade Maryland to join the middle confederacy. Should the views and propositions of this central and consolidated connexion be *liberal and just*, accessions of very considerable importance may be hoped for from the northern and southern states. What particular benefits then can Virginia reasonably expect from that dissolution of the confederacy, which must follow the rejection of the proposed plan.

The various parts of the North-American continent are formed by nature for the most intimate union. The facilities of our navigation render the communication between the ports of Georgia and New-Hampshire infinitely more expeditious and practicable, than between those of Provence and Picardy, in *France*; Cornwall and Caithness, in *Great-Britain*; or Galicia and Catalonia, in *Spain*. The canals proposed at South-key, Susquehanna and Delaware, will open a communication from the Carolinas to the western countries of Pennsylvania and New-York. The improvements of Potowmack will give a passage from those southern states to the western parts of Virginia, Maryland, Pennsylvania, and even to the lakes. The canals of Delaware and Chessapeak will open the communication from South-Carolina to New-Jersey, Delaware, the most populous parts of Pennsylvania, and the midland counties of New-York. These important works might be effected for two hundred thousand guineas, and America would thereby be converted into *a cluster of large and fertile islands*, easily communicating with each other, without expence, and in many instances without the uncertainty or dangers of the sea. The voice of nature therefore directs us to be *affectionate associates in peace, and firm supporters in war*. As we cannot mistake her injunctions, to disobey them would be criminal.

The distracted state of our affairs has exceedingly retarded population and manufactures, and interrupted the influx of knowledge and riches. At the return of peace, the European world viewed America with the tender and respectful admiration of a lover to his mistress. Their peasantry and manufacturers, their merchants and philosophers, were seized with an irresistable desire to visit our shores, and many of them looked towards this country as another land of promise, to spend the remainder of their days. What has prevented their realising these fond ideas? The insecurity of property, the breach or delay of public and private obligations, paper tenders, insurrections against state governments of our own choice, contentions among the states, and a total disregard of the most reasonable and just demands of the general government. They know us to be a people capable of great exertions. They saw we possessed a country replete with the means of private happiness and national importance, but they saw too that these inestimable properties of the Americans and their dominions were not brought into any use, from *the defects of our political arrangements, and the enormous abuses in our administration*. Their beloved mistress having fallen from the heights of virtue, and become *a wanton*, they turned from her with disgust and bitterness. Ye friends of religion and morality! ye lovers of liberty and mankind! will ye not seize this opportunity proffered you by the bounty of Heaven, and save your country from contempt and wretchedness?

The voice of the people, say the most noble champions of freedom, *is the voice of God*. Before the ratification of the new government by the state of Maryland, the constituents of the conventions which had then adopted it were *a majority of the free people of the United States*. Viewing us as one nation, the constitution had then received *the solemn authoritative sanction of the people*. But as Maryland has *since* added her number, and as it is next to certain that the adoption of South-Carolina will take place before the rising of your honorable house, you will view the constitution *as ratified by nearly two thirds of the union*. After that event you will find too, that of eight conventions, which have determined on it, *all* have given it their approbation, and among them *two*, containing larger numbers of free citizens than *any three* that are yet to decide. Rhode-Island, we know, has rejected the government in an informal way; but we cannot injure you *even for a moment*, by supposing that *their principles and conduct* could ever have insinuated themselves into your minds. We trust you will concur with us in thinking, that as the considerate approbation of *the wise and good* is a fair argument in favor of a public measure, so is its deliberate rejection by *the weak and wicked*.

The capacities of some parts of America are admirably adapted to supply the wants of others. New-England, destitute of iron and deficient in grain, can be plentifully supplied with both by the middle states. Possessed of the fisheries, and strongly inclined to ship building and navigation, they can be furnished with the choicest timber from the Carolinas and Georgia. The southern states, so intersected by great waters as to lie exposed to the depredations of the most contemptible fleets, and crouded with *a dangerous species of population*, when proper arrangements shall be made and occasion shall require, can rely on the most useful and friendly aid from the north. The future wars among the naval powers of Europe will probably be *general*. When the house of Bourbon shall contend with Great-Britain for the dominion of the ocean, Holland, Sweden, Denmark and Portugal, will seldom be unconcerned spectators. The prosperity of agriculture in the southern states, in the event of a general war in Europe, will depend on *the shipping of the middle and eastern states*, for the belligerent powers will navigate under a very high insurance, and their ships will moreover be a precarious dependence, from the innumerable accidents of war. It may be said, the southern states will have shipping of their own, of which there can be no doubt, *so far as the state of commerce may render them profitable in time of peace*, but the sudden and vigorous exertions of the states inhabited by free whites can alone furnish *an immediate supply* for the retiring vessels of belligerent foreigners.

Were we to suppose *for a moment* that Virginia had rejected the proposed constitution, and that Georgia, South-Carolina and Maryland were members of the new confederacy, the agricultural interests of Virginia would be exceedingly injured. The supplies of tobacco, furs, flour, cotton, corn, naval stores and timber, required for the consumption, manufactures, and ships of the new union, would doubtless be taken from the states that belonged to it, while the interfering produce of Virginia probably would not be admitted, or if admitted would be liable to *the foreign impost of five per cent*. Every hundred of her tobacco would pay one fourth of a dollar in Boston, New-York or Philadelphia, every barrel of her flour one fifth of a dollar, every hundred weight of her cotton a dollar and two thirds, every bushel of her corn above a penny sterling; a tax greatly superior in value to the revenue imposed, under her present laws, on the exportation of her own produce. Besides this, the expence of maintaining a *separate* establishment in government *at home and abroad* would come heavily on Virginia and those states that might join a partial confederacy. This expence, we may almost venture to affirm, would be *insupportable*, especially when we consider the present state of money matters *in every part of America*. Should Virginia entertain the idea of a lesser confederacy, would it not be wise to consider who would probably unite in it, and upon what terms? From the debates in the Connecticut and Massachusetts Conventions, as well as the dispositions and habits of those genuine republicans, is it probable that they would consent to give you a share of power *greater* than your number of free white inhabitants—or is it probable that your nearest neighbour, North Carolina, would consent to it, without your paying into *the common treasury* the neat proceeds of all duties on imports and exports, a great part of which is raised on *their consumption* of foreign articles, and the produce of *their farms*? It would now be in vain, should New-York refuse a share of her impost to Connecticut and New-Jersey, or Pennsylvania a share of her's to New-Jersey and

Delaware, or Virginia a share of her's to North Carolina. It is an idea as *just*, as it is generous and liberal, that the imposts of the United States should go into *a common treasury*, belonging to all who pay them, by being the consumers. If North-Carolina has a clear conception of her most evident interests, *she must make this article a sine qua non in any compact that may be proposed to her by your state*.

It will be urged, perhaps, that property should be represented, and that though Virginia has only 252,000 free inhabitants, your representation should still be greater than that of Massachusetts and Pennsylvania, because you are richer. But surely this argument will not be urged by the friends of *equal liberty among the people*. It will not be objected *openly* against the proposed constitution, that it secures *the equal liberties of the poor*. But suppose for a moment a claim for a representation of property were admissable before an assembly of *the free and equal citizens of America*, will not Virginia enjoy the advantage of two votes *more* in the fœderal government than either Massachusetts or Pennsylvania, though each of those states has 108,000 free citizens *more than yours*. If we were represented *by that only rule of republics*, for your *ten* representatives, Massachusetts would have *more than fourteen*, and Pennsylvania the same number, while both of them are limited to *eight*. Here then we see *the balance of property* said to be in favor of Virginia has procured her three fourths as much *extra* power, as *the lives, liberties and property of all the people of Massachusetts or Pennsylvania*. Power has been given to your state *with no sparing hand*. You (suffer me respectfully to say so) of all the members of the union, appear to have the least cause of complaint. Permit me to remind you of the objections made *on this ground* by Mr. Martin, of Maryland. The opposition *there* asserted that the great states had too large a share of power, and you have the most of all. The same sentiments were urged in the Connecticut Convention. Is it probable then that an allotment of power *more favorable to you* would be made by a new Convention? I submit to your candor whether you ought to ask a greater share. A comparison, in point of wealth and resources, between your state and any other, is a matter I wish to touch with delicacy. I mean not to offend, but you would despise a freeman, that would decline *the decent expression of his thoughts* on so momentous an occasion. I would submit to you, whether the energy of 250,000 whites in a southern climate, surrounded by more than as many slaves, can be, *or rather whether it is*, equal to that of the same number in a northern climate? Whether two or three negroes in Virginia will be found equal to one yeoman or manufacturer of Pennsylvania or Massachusetts? Whether the ships, mercantile capitals, houses, and monied corporations of Philadelphia, with her growing manufactures and connexions in foreign commerce, may not be placed in the scale against *the balance* of wealth you may be thought to possess, when Kentucke shall become an independent member of the American union.

But, gentlemen, it will be improper to trespass longer on your valuable time, devoted as it is to the most important concerns of VIRGINIA,—AMERICA,—AND MANKIND. Let me entreat you only to bear in mind *the wide difference* that exists in *the opinions and views* of those who oppose the new constitution. *You will find they differ as much from each other, as they dissent from the friends of the plan.* Were there no other people in America but the opposers of the proposed government, it will appear, on a fair statement of their various views and objections, that any constitution which could be formed, on the principles of those in some states, would meet with as much disapprobation by those in others, as they have deemed it necessary to shew to the propositions of the Fœderal Convention. Consider then, in the event of your rejection, *in what a condition we shall be left—into what a situation we may be thrown! Thirteen jarring* sovereignties—*two or three contending* confederacies—or *a feeble* union—will be *the miserable and hopeless alternatives*. The measure of foreign contempt will be *filled up*. Insult will naturally follow, and then injuries *abroad*—while the certain dangers to liberty, property and peace, *at home*, will sink every American, *however firm*, into despondency, or drive him to despair. But this will be too much.—The Convention of Virginia will never be instrumental in bringing such evils on the United States. No.—We will confidently hope that those among you, who do not altogether approve the proposed government, will yet concur in the measure, to save their country from anarchy and ruin. *They will remember the provision to obtain amendments, and will recollect that the power will continue with the people at large in all time to come.*

May 21st, 1788.

Richard Henry Lee to Edmund Pendleton

Chantilly, Virginia, May 26, 1788

The manner in which we have together struggled for the just rights of human nature, with the friendly correspondence that we have maintained, entitles us, I hope, to the most unreserved confidence in each other upon the subject of human rights and the liberty of our country. It is probable that yourself, no more than I do, propose to be hereafter politically engaged; neither therefore expecting to gain or fearing to loose, the candid part of mankind will admit us to be *impartial* Judges, at least of the arduous business that calls you to Richmond on the 2d. of next month

I do not recollect to have met with a sensible and candid Man who has not admitted that it would be both safer and better if amendments were made to the Constitution proposed for the government of the U. States; but the friends to the idea of amendments divide about the mode of obtaining them—Some thinking that a second Convention might do the business, whilst others fear that the attempt to remedy by another Convention would risk the whole. I have been informed that you wished Amendments, but disliked the plan of another Convention. The just weight that you have Sir in the Councils of your Country may put it in your power to save from Arbitrary Rule a great and free people. I have used the words Arbitrary Rule because great numbers fear that this *will* be the case, when they consider that it *may* be so under the new proposed System, and reflect on the unvarying progress of power in the hands of frail Man. To accomplish the ends of Society by being equal to Contingencies infinite, demands the deposit of power great and extensive indeed in the hands of Rulers. So great, as to render abuse probable, unless prevented by the most careful precautions: among

462

which, the freedom & frequency of elections, the liberty of
the Press, the Trial by Jury, and the Independency of the
Judges, seem to be so capital & essential; that they ought to
be secured by a Bill of Rights to regulate the discretion of
Rulers in a legal way, restraining the progress of Ambition &
Avarice within just bounds. Rulers must act by subordinate
Agents generally, and however the former may be secure from
the pursuits of Justice, the latter are forever kept in Check by
the trial by Jury where that exists "in all its Rights". This most
excellent security against oppression, is an universal, powerful
and equal protector of *all*. But the benefit to be derived from
this System is most effectually to be obtained from a well
informed and enlightened people. Here arrises the necessity
for the freedom of the Press, which is the happiest Organ of
communication ever yet devised, the quickest & surest means
of conveying intelligence to the human Mind.

I am grieved to be forced to think, after the most mature
consideration of the subject, that the proposed Constitution
leaves the three essential Securities before stated, under the
mere pleasure of the new Rulers! And why should it be so
Sir, since the violation of these cannot be necessary to *good*
government, but will be always extremely convenient for bad.
It is a question deserving intense consideration, whether the
State Sovereignties ought not to be supported, perhaps in the
way proposed by Massachusetts in their 1st. 3d. & 4th
Amendments. Force & Opinion seem to be the two ways
alone by which Men can be governed—the latter appears the
most proper for a free people—but remove that and obedience, I apprehend, can only be found to result from *fear* the
Offspring of *force*. If this be so, can Opinion exist among the
great Mass of Mankind without compitent knowledge of
those who govern, and can that knowledge take place in a
Country so extensive as the territory of the U. States which is
stated by Capt. Hutchins at a Million of square miles, whilst
the empire of Germany contains but 192,000, and the kingdom of France but 163,000 square miles. The almost infinite
variety of climates, Soils, productions, manners, customs &
interests renders this still more difficult for the general government of one Legislature; but very practicable to Confederated States united for mutual safety & happiness, each

contributing to the federal head such a portion of its sovereignty as would render the government fully adequate to these purposes and *No more*. The people would govern themselves more easily, the laws of each State being well adapted to its own genius and circumstances; the liberties of the U. States would probably be more secure than under the proposed plan, which, carefully attended to will be found capable of annihilating the State Sovereignties by finishing the operations of their State governments under the general Legislative right of commanding Taxes without restraint. So that the productive Revenues that the States may happily fall upon for their own support can be seized by superior power supported by the Congressional Courts of Justice, and by the sacred obligation of Oath imposed on all the State Judges to regard the laws of Congress as supreme over the laws and Constitutions of the States! Thus circumstanced we shall probably find resistance vain, and the State governments as feeble and contemptible as was the Senatorial power under the Roman Emperors—The *name* existed but the *thing* was gone. I have observed Sir that the sensible and candid friends of the proposed plan agree that amendments would be proper, but fear the consequences of another Convention. I submit the following as an effectual compromise between the Majorities, and the formidable Minorities that generally prevail.

It seems probable that the determinations of four States will be materially influenced by what Virginia shall do—This places a strong obligaton on our country to be unusually cautious and circumspect in our Conventional conduct. The Mode that I would propose is something like that pursued by the Convention Parliament of England in 1688. In our Ratificaton insert plainly and strongly such amendments as can be agreed upon, and say; that the people of Virginia do insist upon and mean to retain them as their undoubted rights and liberties which they intend not to part with; and if these are not obtained and secured by the Mode pointed out in the 5th. article of the Convention plan in two years after the meeting of the new Congress, that Virginia shall be considered as disengaged from this Ratification. In the 5th. article it is stated that two thirds of Congress may propose amendments, which being approved by three fourths of the Legislatures become parts of the Constitution—So that the new Congress may obtain the amendments of Virginia without risking the convulsion of Conventions. Thus the beneficial parts of the new System may be retained, and a just security be given for Civil Liberty; whilst the friends of the System will be gratified in what they say is necessary, to wit, the putting the government in motion, when, as they again say, amendments may and ought to be made. The good consequences resulting from this method will probably be, that the undetermined States may be brought to harmonize, and the formidable minorities in many assenting States be quieted by so friendly and reasonable an accommodation. In this way may be happily prevented the perpetual oppositon that will inevitably follow (the total adoption of the plan) from the State Legislatures; and united exertions take place. In the formation of these amendments Localities ought to be avoided as much as possible. The danger of Monopolized Trade may be avoided by calling for the consent of 3 fourths of the U. States on regulations of Commerce. The trial by Jury to be according to the course of proceeding in the State where the cause criminal or civil is tried, and confining the Supreme federal Court to the jurisdiction of Law excluding Fact. To prevent surprises, and the fixing of injurious laws, it would seem to be prudent to declare against the making [   ] laws until the experience of two years at least shall have [   ] their utility. It being much more easy to get a good Law [   ] than a bad one repealed. The amendments of Massachusetts [   ] to be good so far as they go, except the 2d. and extending the 7th. to foreigners as well as the Citizens of other States in this Union. For their adoption the aid of that powerful State may be secured. The freedom of the Press is by no means sufficiently attended to by Massachusetts, nor have they remedied the want of responsibility by the impolitic combination of President & Senate. No person, I think, can be alarmed at that part of the above proposition which proposes our discharge if the requisite Amendments are not made; because, in all human probability it will be the certain means of securing their adoption for the following reasons—N.C. N.Y. R.I. & N.H. are the 4 States that are to determine after Virginia, and there being abundant reason to suppose that they will be much influenced by our determination; if they, or 3 of them join us, I presume it cannot be fairly imagined that the rest, suppose 9, will hesitate a moment to make Amendments which are of general nature, clearly for the safety of Civil Liberty against the future designs of despotism to destroy it; and which indeed is requir'd by at least half of most of those States who have adopted the new Plan; and which finally obstruct not good but bad government.

It does appear to me, that in the present temper of America, if the Massachusetts amendments, with those herein suggested being added, & were inserted in the form of our ratification as before stated, that Virginia may safely agree, and I believe that the most salutary consequences would ensue. I am sure that America and the World too look with anxious expectations at us, if we change the Liberty that we have so well deserved for elective Despotism we shall suffer the evils of the change while we labor under the contempt of Mankind—I pray Sir that God may bless the Convention with wisdom, maturity of Counsel, and constant care of the public liberty; and that he may have you in his holy keeping. I find that as usual, I have written to *you* a long letter—but you are good and the subject is copious—I like to reason with a reasonable Man, but I disdain to notice those Scribblers in the Newspapers altho they have honored me with their abuse—My attention to them will never exist whilst there is a Cat or a Spaniel in the House!

"Publius," The Federalist LXXVIII
[Alexander Hamilton]

New York, May 28, 1788

We proceed now to an examination of the judiciary department of the proposed government.

In unfolding the defects of the existing confederation, the utility and necessity of a federal judicature have been clearly pointed out. It is the less necessary to recapitulate the considerations there urged; as the propriety of the institution in the abstract is not disputed: The only questions which have been raised being relative to the manner of constituting it, and to its extent. To these points therefore our observations shall be confined.

The manner of constituting it seems to embrace these several objects—1st. The mode of appointing the judges. 2d. The tenure by which they are to hold their places. 3d. The partition of the judiciary authority between different courts, and their relations to each other.

First. As to the mode of appointing the judges: This is the same with that of appointing the officers of the union in general, and has been so fully discussed in the two last numbers, that nothing can be said here which would not be useless repetition.

Second. As to the tenure by which the judges are to hold their places: This chiefly concerns their duration in office; the provisions for their support; and the precautions for their responsibility.

According to the plan of the convention, all the judges who may be appointed by the United States are to hold their offices *during good behaviour*, which is conformable to the most approved of the state constitutions; and among the rest, to that of this state. Its propriety having been drawn into question by the adversaries of that plan, is no light symptom of the rage for objection which disorders their imaginations and judgments. The standard of good behaviour for the continuance in office of the judicial magistracy is certainly one of the most valuable of the modern improvements in the practice of government. In a monarchy it is an excellent barrier to the despotism of the prince: In a republic it is a no less excellent barrier to the encroachments and oppressions of the representative body. And it is the best expedient which can be devised in any government, to secure a steady, upright and impartial administration of the laws.

Whoever attentively considers the different departments of power must perceive, that in a government in which they are separated from each other, the judiciary, from the nature of its functions, will always be the least dangerous to the political rights of the constitution; because it will be least in a capacity to annoy or injure them. The executive not only dispenses the honors, but holds the sword of the community. The legislature not only commands the purse, but prescribes the rules by which the duties and rights of every citizen are to be regulated. The judiciary on the contrary has no influence over either the sword or the purse, no direction either of the strength or of the wealth of the society, and can take no active resolution whatever. It may truly be said to have neither Force nor Will, but merely judgment; and must ultimately depend upon the aid of the executive arm even for the efficacy of its judgments.

This simple view of the matter suggests several important consequences. It proves incontestibly that the judiciary is beyond comparison the weakest of the three departments of power;* that it can never attack with success either of the other two; and that all possible care is requisite to enable it to defend itself against their attacks. It equally proves, that though individual oppression may now and then proceed from the courts of justice, the general liberty of the people can never be endangered from that quarter: I mean, so long as the judiciary remains truly distinct from both the legislative

---

*The celebrated Montesquieu speaking of them says, "of the three powers above mentioned, the JUDICIARY is next to nothing." Spirit of Laws, vol. 1, page 186.

and executive. For I agree that "there is no liberty, if the power of judging be not separated from the legislative and executive powers."* And it proves, in the last place, that as liberty can have nothing to fear from the judiciary alone, but would have every thing to fear from its union with either of the other departments; that as all the effects of such an union must ensue from a dependence of the former on the latter, notwithstanding a nominal and apparent separation; that as from the natural feebleness of the judiciary, it is in continual jeopardy of being overpowered, awed or influenced by its co-ordinate branches; and that as nothing can contribute so much to its firmness and independence, as permanency in office, this quality may therefore be justly regarded as an indispensable ingredient in its constitution; and in a great measure as the citadel of the public justice and the public security.

The complete independence of the courts of justice is peculiarly essential in a limited constitution. By a limited constitution I understand one which contains certain specified exceptions to the legislative authority; such for instance as that it shall pass no bills of attainder, no *ex post facto* laws, and the like. Limitations of this kind can be preserved in practice no other way than through the medium of the courts of justice; whose duty it must be to declare all acts contrary to the manifest tenor of the constitution void. Without this, all the reservations of particular rights or privileges would amount to nothing.

Some perplexity respecting the right of the courts to pronounce legislative acts void, because contrary to the constitution, has arisen from an imagination that the doctrine would imply a superiority of the judiciary to the legislative power. It is urged that the authority which can declare the acts of another void, must necessarily be superior to the one whose acts may be declared void. As this doctrine is of great importance in all the American constitutions, a brief discussion of the grounds on which it rests cannot be unacceptable.

There is no position which depends on clearer principles, than that every act of a delegated authority, contrary to the tenor of the commission under which it is exercised, is void.

*Idem. page 181.

No legislative act therefore contrary to the constitution can be valid. To deny this would be to affirm that the deputy is greater than his principal; that the servant is above his master; that the representatives of the people are superior to the people themselves; that men acting by virtue of powers may do not only what their powers do not authorise, but what they forbid.

If it be said that the legislative body are themselves the constitutional judges of their own powers, and that the construction they put upon them is conclusive upon the other departments, it may be answered, that this cannot be the natural presumption, where it is not to be collected from any particular provisions in the constitution. It is not otherwise to be supposed that the constitution could intend to enable the representatives of the people to substitute their *will* to that of their constituents. It is far more rational to suppose that the courts were designed to be an intermediate body between the people and the legislature, in order, among other things, to keep the latter within the limits assigned to their authority. The interpretation of the laws is the proper and peculiar province of the courts. A constitution is in fact, and must be, regarded by the judges as a fundamental law. It therefore belongs to them to ascertain its meaning as well as the meaning of any particular act proceeding from the legislative body. If there should happen to be an irreconcileable variance between the two, that which has the superior obligation and validity ought of course to be preferred; or in other words, the constitution ought to be preferred to the statute, the intention of the people to the intention of their agents.

Nor does this conclusion by any means suppose a superiority of the judicial to the legislative power. It only supposes that the power of the people is superior to both; and that where the will of the legislature declared in its statutes, stands in opposition to that of the people declared in the constitution, the judges ought to be governed by the latter, rather than the former. They ought to regulate their decisions by the fundamental laws, rather than by those which are not fundamental.

This exercise of judicial discretion in determining between two contradictory laws, is exemplified in a familiar instance. It not uncommonly happens, that there are two statutes existing at one time, clashing in whole or in part with each other, and neither of them containing any repealing clause or expression. In such a case, it is the province of the courts to liquidate and fix their meaning and operation: So far as they can by any fair construction be reconciled to each other; reason and law conspire to dictate that this should be done. Where this is impracticable, it becomes a matter of necessity to give effect to one, in exclusion of the other. The rule which has obtained in the courts for determining their relative validity is that the last in order of time shall be preferred to the first. But this is mere rule of construction, not derived from any positive law, but from the nature and reason of the thing. It is a rule not enjoined upon the courts by legislative provision, but adopted by themselves, as consonant to truth and propriety, for the direction of their conduct as interpreters of the law. They thought it reasonable, that between the interfering acts of an *equal* authority, that which was the last indication of its will, should have the preference.

But in regard to the interfering acts of a superior and subordinate authority, of an original and derivative power, the nature and reason of the thing indicate the converse of that rule as proper to be followed. They teach us that the prior act of a superior ought to be preferred to the subsequent act of an inferior and subordinate authority; and that, accordingly, whenever a particular statute contravenes the constitution, it will be the duty of the judicial tribunals to adhere to the latter, and disregard the former.

It can be of no weight to say, that the courts on the pretence of a repugnancy, may substitute their own pleasure to the constitutional intentions of the legislature. This might as well happen in the case of two contradictory statutes; or it might as well happen in every adjudication upon any single statute. The courts must declare the sense of the law; and if they should be disposed to exercise WILL instead of JUDGMENT, the consequence would equally be the substitution of their pleasure to that of the legislative body. The observation, if it proved any thing, would prove that there ought to be no judges distinct from that body.

If then the courts of justice are to be considered as the

bulwarks of a limited constitution against legislative encroachments, this consideration will afford a strong argument for the permanent tenure of judicial offices, since nothing will contribute so much as this to that independent spirit in the judges, which must be essential to the faithful performance of so arduous a duty.

This independence of the judges is equally requisite to guard the constitution and the rights of individuals from the effects of those ill humours which the arts of designing men, or the influence of particular conjunctures, sometimes disseminate among the people themselves, and which, though they speedily give place to better information and more deliberate reflection, have a tendency in the mean time to occasion dangerous innovations in the government, and serious oppressions of the minor party in the community. Though I trust the friends of the proposed constitution will never concur with its enemies* in questioning that fundamental principle of republican government, which admits the right of the people to alter or abolish the established constitution whenever they find it inconsistent with their happiness; yet it is not to be inferred from this principle, that the representatives of the people, whenever a momentary inclination happens to lay hold of a majority of their constituents incompatible with the provisions in the existing constitution, would on that account be justifiable in a violation of those provisions; or that the courts would be under a greater obligation to connive at infractions in this shape, than when they had proceeded wholly from the cabals of the representative body. Until the people have by some solemn and authoritative act annulled or changed the established form, it is binding upon themselves collectively, as well as individually; and no presumption, or even knowledge of their sentiments, can warrant their representatives in a departure from it, prior to such an act. But it is easy to see that it would require an uncommon portion of fortitude in the judges to do their duty as faithful guardians of the constitution, where legislative invasions of it had been instigated by the major voice of the community.

*Vide Protest of the minority of the convention of Pennsylvania, Martin's speech, &c.

But it is not with a view to infractions of the constitution only that the independence of the judges may be an essential safeguard against the effects of occasional ill humours in the society. These sometimes extend no farther than to the injury of the private rights of particular classes of citizens, by unjust and partial laws. Here also the firmness of the judicial magistracy is of vast importance in mitigating the severity, and confining the operation of such laws. It not only serves to moderate the immediate mischiefs of those which may have been passed, but it operates as a check upon the legislative body in passing them; who, perceiving that obstacles to the success of an iniquitous intention are to be expected from the scruples of the courts, are in a manner compelled by the very motives of the injustice they meditate, to qualify their attempts. This is a circumstance calculated to have more influence upon the character of our governments, than but few may be aware of. The benefits of the integrity and moderation of the judiciary have already been felt in more states than one; and though they may have displeased those whose sinister expectations they may have disappointed, they must have commanded the esteem and applause of all the virtuous and disinterested. Considerate men of every description ought to prize whatever will tend to beget or fortify that temper in the courts; as no man can be sure that he may not be to-morrow the victim of a spirit of injustice, by which he may be a gainer to-day. And every man must now feel that the inevitable tendency of such a spirit is to sap the foundations of public and private confidence, and to introduce in its stead, universal distrust and distress.

That inflexible and uniform adherence to the rights of the constitution and of individuals, which we perceive to be indispensable in the courts of justice, can certainly not be expected from judges who hold their offices by a temporary commission. Periodical appointments, however regulated, or by whomsoever made, would in some way or other be fatal to their necessary independence. If the power of making them was committed either to the executive or legislature, there would be danger of an improper complaisance to the branch which possessed it; if to both, there would be an unwillingness to hazard the displeasure of either; if to the people, or to

persons chosen by them for the special purpose, there would
be too great a disposition to consult popularity, to justify a
reliance that nothing would be consulted but the constitution
and the laws.

There is yet a further and a weighty reason for the permanency of the judicial offices; which is deducible from the nature of the qualifications they require. It has been frequently
remarked with great propriety, that a voluminous code of
laws is one of the inconveniences necessarily connected with
the advantages of a free government. To avoid an arbitrary
discretion in the courts, it is indispensable that they should be
bound down by strict rules and precedents, which serve to
define and point out their duty in every particular case that
comes before them; and it will readily be conceived from the
variety of controversies which grow out of the folly and wickedness of mankind, that the records of those precedents must
unavoidably swell to a very considerable bulk, and must demand long and laborious study to acquire a competent
knowledge of them. Hence it is that there can be but few men
in the society, who will have sufficient skill in the laws to
qualify them for the stations of judges. And making the
proper deductions for the ordinary depravity of human nature, the number must be still smaller of those who unite the
requisite integrity with the requisite knowledge. These considerations apprise us, that the government can have no great
option between fit characters; and that a temporary duration
in office, which would naturally discourage such characters
from quitting a lucrative line of practice to accept a seat on
the bench, would have a tendency to throw the administration of justice into hands less able, and less well qualified to
conduct it with utility and dignity. In the present circumstances of this country, and in those in which it is likely to be
for a long time to come, the disadvantages on this score
would be greater than they may at first sight appear; but it
must be confessed that they are far inferior to those which
present themselves under the other aspects of the subject.

Upon the whole there can be no room to doubt that the
convention acted wisely in copying from the models of those
constitutions which have established *good behaviour* as the tenure of their judicial offices in point of duration; and that so

far from being blameable on this account, their plan would have been inexcuseably defective if it had wanted this important feature of good government. The experience of Great Britain affords an illustrious comment on the excellence of the institution.

"Publius," The Federalist LXXX
[Alexander Hamilton]

New York, May 28, 1788

To judge with accuracy of the proper extent of the federal judicature, it will be necessary to consider in the first place what are its proper objects.

It seems scarcely to admit of controversy that the judiciary authority of the union ought to extend to these several descriptions of causes. 1st. To all those which arise out of the laws of the United States, passed in pursuance of their just and constitutional powers of legislation; 2d. to all those which concern the execution of the provisions expressly contained in the articles of union; 3d. to all those in which the United States are a party; 4th. to all those which involve the PEACE of the CONFEDERACY, whether they relate to the intercourse between the United States and foreign nations, or to that between the States themselves; 5th. to all those which originate on the high seas, and are of admiralty or maritime jurisdiction; and lastly, to all those in which the state tribunals cannot be supposed to be impartial and unbiassed.

The first point depends upon this obvious consideration that there ought always to be a constitutional method of giving efficacy to constitutional provisions. What for instance would avail restrictions on the authority of the state legislatures, without some constitutional mode of enforcing the observance of them? The states, by the plan of the convention are prohibited from doing a variety of things; some of which are incompatible with the interests of the union, and others with the principles of good government. The imposition of duties on imported articles, and the emission of paper money, are specimens of each kind. No man of sense will believe that such prohibitions would be scrupulously regarded, without some effectual power in the government to restrain or correct the infractions of them. This power must either be a direct negative on the state laws, or an authority in the federal courts, to over-rule such as might be in manifest contravention of the articles of union. There is no third course that I can imagine. The latter appears to have been thought by the convention preferable to the former, and I presume will be most agreeable to the states.

As to the second point, it is impossible by any argument or comment to make it clearer than it is in itself. If there are such things as political axioms, the propriety of the judicial power of a government being co-extensive with its legislative, may be ranked among the number. The mere necessity of uniformity in the interpretation of the national laws, decides the question. Thirteen independent courts of final jurisdiction over the same causes, arising upon the same laws, is a hydra in government, from which nothing but contradiction and confusion can proceed.

Still less need be said in regard to the third point. Controversies between the nation and its members or citizens, can only be properly referred to the national tribunals. Any other plan would be contrary to reason, to precedent, and to decorum.

The fourth point rests on this plain proposition, that the peace of the WHOLE ought not to be left at the disposal of a PART. The union will undoubtedly be answerable to foreign powers for the conduct of its members. And the responsibility for an injury ought ever to be accompanied with the faculty of preventing it. As the denial or perversion of justice by the sentences of courts, as well as in any other manner, is with reason classed among the just causes of war, it will follow that the federal judiciary ought to have cognizance of all causes in which the citizens of other countries are concerned. This is not less essential to the preservation of the public faith, than to the security of the public tranquility. A distinction may perhaps be imagined between cases arising upon treaties and the laws of nations, and those which may stand merely on the footing of the municipal law. The former kind may be supposed proper for the federal jurisdiction, the latter for that of the states. But it is at least problematical whether an unjust sentence against a foreigner, where the subject of controversy was wholly relative to the *lex loci*, would not, if unredressed, be an aggression upon his sovereign, as well as one which violated the stipulations in a treaty or the general laws of nations. And a still greater objection to the distinction would result from the immense difficulty, if not impossibility, of a practical discrimination between the cases of one complection and those of the other. So great a proportion of the cases in which foreigners are parties involve national questions, that it is by far most safe and most expedient to refer all those in which they are concerned to the national tribunals.

The power of determining causes between two states, between one state and the citizens of another, and between the citizens of different states, is perhaps not less essential to the peace of the union than that which has been just examined. History gives us a horrid picture of the dissentions and private wars which distracted and desolated Germany prior to the institution of the IMPERIAL CHAMBER by Maximilian, towards the close of the fifteenth century; and informs us at the same time of the vast influence of the institution in appeasing the disorders and establishing the tranquility of the empire. This was a court invested with authority to decide finally all differences between the members of the Germanic body.

A method of terminating territorial disputes between the states, under the authority of the federal head, was not unattended to, even in the imperfect system by which they have been hitherto held together. But there are many other sources, besides interfering claims of boundary, from which bickerings and animosities may spring up among the members of the union. To some of these we have been witnesses in the course of our past experience. It will readily be conjectured that I allude to the fraudulent laws which have been passed in too many of the states. And though the proposed constitution established particular guards against the repetition of those instances which have heretofore made their appearance, yet it is warrantable to apprehend that the spirit which produced them will assume new shapes that could not be foreseen, nor specifically provided against. Whatever practices may have a tendency to disturb the harmony between the states, are proper objects of federal superintendence and control.

It may be esteemed the basis of the union, that "the citizens of each state shall be entitled to all the privileges and immunities of citizens of the several states." And if it be a just principle that every government *ought to possess the means of executing its own provisions by its own authority*, it will follow, that in order to the inviolable maintenance of that equality of privileges and immunities to which the citizens of the union will be entitled, the national judiciary ought to preside in all cases in which one state or its citizens are opposed to another state or its citizens. To secure the full effect of so fundamental a provision against all evasion and subterfuge, it is necessary that its construction should be committed to that tribunal, which, having no local attachments, will be likely to be impartial between the different states and their citizens, and which, owing its official existence to the union, will never be likely to feel any bias inauspicious to the principles on which it is founded.

The fifth point will demand little animadversion. The most bigotted idolizers of state authority have not thus far shewn a disposition to deny the national judiciary the cognizance of maritime causes. These so generally depend on the laws of nations, and so commonly affect the rights of foreigners, that they fall within the considerations which are relative to the public peace. The most important part of them are by the present confederation submitted to federal jurisdiction.

The reasonableness of the agency of the national courts in cases in which the state tribunals cannot be supposed to be impartial, speaks for itself. No man ought certainly to be a judge in his own cause, or in any cause in respect to which he has the least interest or bias. This principle has no inconsiderable weight in designating the federal courts as the proper tribunals for the determination of controversies between different states and their citizens. And it ought to have the same operation in regard to some cases between the citizens of the same state. Claims to land under grants of different states, founded upon adverse pretensions of boundary, are of this description. The courts of neither of the granting states could be expected to be unbiassed. The laws may have even prejudged the question, and tied the courts down to decisions in favour of the grants of the state to which they belonged. And even where this had not been done, it would be natural that the judges, as men, should feel a strong predilection to the claims of their own government.

Having thus laid down and discussed the principles which ought to regulate the constitution of the federal judiciary, we will proceed to test, by these principles, the particular powers of which, according to the plan of the convention, it is to be composed. It is to comprehend, "all cases in law and equity arising under the constitution, the laws of the United States, and treaties made, or which shall be made under their authority; to all cases affecting ambassadors, other public ministers and consuls; to all cases of admiralty and maritime jurisdiction; to controversies to which the United States shall be a party; to controversies between two or more states, between a state and citizens of another state, between citizens of different states, between citizens of the same state claiming lands under grants of different states, and between a state or the citizens thereof, and foreign states, citizens and subjects." This constitutes the entire mass of the judicial authority of the union. Let us now review it in detail. It is then to extend,

First. To all cases in law and equity *arising under the constitution* and *the laws of the United States.* This corresponds to the two first classes of causes which have been enumerated as proper for the jurisdiction of the United States. It has been asked what is meant by "cases arising under the constitution," in contradistinction from those "arising under the laws of the United States." The difference has been already explained. All the restrictions upon the authority of the state legislatures, furnish examples of it. They are not, for instance, to emit paper money; but the interdiction results from the constitution, and will have no connection with any law of the United States. Should paper money, notwithstanding, be emitted, the controversies concerning it would be cases arising upon the constitution, and not upon the laws of the United States, in the ordinary signification of the terms. This may serve as a sample of the whole.

It has also been asked, what need of the word "equity"?

What equitable causes can grow out of the constitution and laws of the United States? There is hardly a subject of litigation between individuals, which may not involve those ingredients of *fraud, accident, trust* or *hardship*, which would render the matter an object of equitable, rather than of legal jurisdiction, as the distinction is known and established in several of the states. It is the peculiar province, for instance, of a court of equity to relieve against what are called hard bargains: These are contracts, in which, though there may have been no direct fraud or deceit, sufficient to invalidate them in a court of law; yet there may have been some undue and unconscionable advantage taken of the necessities or misfortunes of one of the parties, which a court of equity would not tolerate. In such cases, where foreigners were concerned on either side, it would be impossible for the federal judicatories to do justice without an equitable, as well as a legal jurisdiction. Agreements to convey lands claimed under the grants of different states, may afford another example of the necessity of an equitable jurisdiction in the federal courts. This reasoning may not be so palpable in those states where the formal and technical distinction between LAW and EQUITY is not maintained as in this state, where it is exemplified by every day's practice.

The judiciary authority of the union is to extend—

Second. To treaties made, or which shall be made under the authority of the United States, and to all cases affecting ambassadors, other public ministers and consuls. These belong to the fourth class of the enumerated cases, as they have an evident connection with the preservation of the national peace.

Third. To cases of admiralty and maritime jurisdiction. These form altogether the fifth of the enumerated classes of causes proper for the cognizance of the national courts.

Fourth. To controversies to which the United States shall be a party. These constitute the third of those classes.

Fifth. To controversies between two or more states, between a state and citizens of another state, between citizens of different states. These belong to the fourth of those classes, and partake in some measure of the nature of the last.

Sixth. To cases between the citizens of the same state, *claiming lands under grants of different states*. These fall within the last class, and *are the only instance in which the proposed constitution directly contemplates the cognizance of disputes between the citizens of the same state.*

Seventh. To cases between a state and the citizens thereof, and foreign states, citizens, or subjects. These have been already explained to belong to the fourth of the enumerated classes, and have been shewn to be in a peculiar manner the proper subjects of the national judicature.

From this review of the particular powers of the federal judiciary, as marked out in the constitution, it appears, that they are all comfortable to the principles which ought to have governed the structure of that department, and which were necessary to the perfection of the system. If some partial inconveniencies should appear to be connected with the incorporation of any of them into the plan, it ought to be recollected that the national legislature will have ample authority to make such *exceptions* and to prescribe such regulations as will be calculated to obviate or remove these inconveniencies. The possibility of particular mischiefs can never be viewed by a well-informed mind as a solid objection to a general principle, which is calculated to avoid general mischiefs, and to obtain general advantages.

"Publius," The Federalist LXXXI [*Alexander Hamilton*]

New York, May 28, 1788

Let us now return to the partition of the judiciary authority between different courts, and their relations to each other.

"The judicial power of the United States is (by the plan of the convention) to be vested in one supreme court, and in such inferior courts as the congress may from time to time ordain and establish."*

That there ought to be one court of supreme and final jurisdiction is a proposition which has not been, and is not likely to be contested. The reasons for it have been assigned in another place, and are too obvious to need repetition. The only question that seems to have been raised concerning it, is whether it ought to be a distinct body, or a branch of the legislature. The same contradiction is observable in regard to this matter, which has been remarked in several other cases. The very men who object to the senate as a court of impeachments, on the ground of an improper intermixture of powers, advocate, by implication at least, the propriety of vesting the ultimate decision of all causes in the whole, or in a part of the legislative body.

The arguments or rather suggestions, upon which this charge is founded, are to this effect: "The authority of the proposed supreme court of the United States, which is to be a separate and independent body, will be superior to that of the legislature. The power of construing the laws, according to the *spirit* of the constitution, will enable that court to mould them into whatever shape it may think proper; especially as its

*Article 3. Sec. 1.

483

decisions will not be in any manner subject to the revision or correction of the legislative body. This is as unprecedented as it is dangerous. In Britain, the judicial power in the last resort, resides in the house of lords, which is a branch of the legislature; and this part of the British government has been imitated in the state constitutions in general. The parliament of Great-Britain, and the legislatures of the several states, can at any time rectify by law, the exceptionable decisions of their respective courts. But the errors and usurpations of the supreme court of the United States will be uncontrolable and remediless." This, upon examination, will be found to be altogether made up of false reasoning upon misconceived fact.

In the first place, there is not a syllable in the plan under consideration, which *directly* empowers the national courts to construe the laws according to the spirit of the constitution, or which gives them any greater latitude in this respect, than may be claimed by the courts of every state. I admit however, that the constitution ought to be the standard of construction for the laws, and that wherever there is an evident opposition, the laws ought to give place to the constitution. But this doctrine is not deducible from any circumstance peculiar to the plan of the convention; but from the general theory of a limited constitution; and as far as it is true, is equally applicable to most, if not to all the state governments. There can be no objection therefore, on this account, to the federal judicature, which will not lie against the local judicatures in general, and which will not serve to condemn every constitution that attempts to set bounds to the legislative discretion.

But perhaps the force of the objection may be thought to consist in the particular organization of the proposed supreme court; in its being composed of a distinct body of magistrates, instead of being one of the branches of the legislature, as in the government of Great-Britain and in that of this state. To insist upon this point, the authors of the objection must renounce the meaning they have laboured to annex to the celebrated maxim requiring a separation of the departments of power. It shall nevertheless be conceded to them, agreeably to the interpretation given to that maxim in the course of these papers, that it is not violated by vesting the ultimate power of judging in a *part* of the legislative body. But though this be not an absolute violation of that excellent rule; yet it verges so nearly upon it, as on this account alone to be less eligible than the mode preferred by the convention. From a body which had had even a partial agency in passing bad laws, we could rarely expect a disposition to temper and moderate them in the application. The same spirit, which had operated in making them, would be too apt to operate in interpreting them: Still less could it be expected, that men who had infringed the constitution, in the character of legislators, would be disposed to repair the breach, in the character of judges. Nor is this all: Every reason, which recommends the tenure of good behaviour for judicial offices, militates against placing the judiciary power in the last resort in a body composed of men chosen for a limited period. There is an absurdity in referring the determination of causes in the first instance to judges of permanent standing, and in the last to those of a temporary and mutable constitution. And there is a still greater absurdity in subjecting the decisions of men selected for their knowledge of the laws, acquired by long and laborious study, to the revision and control of men, who for want of the same advantage cannot but be deficient in that knowledge. The members of the legislature will rarely be chosen with a view to those qualifications which fit men for the stations of judges; and as on this account there will be great reason to apprehend all the ill consequences of defective information; so on account of the natural propensity of such bodies to party divisions, there will be no less reason to fear, that the pestilential breath of faction may poison the fountains of justice. The habit of being continually marshalled on opposite sides, will be too apt to stifle the voice both of law and of equity.

These considerations teach us to applaud the wisdom of those states, who have committed the judicial power in the last resort, not to a part of the legislature, but to distinct and independent bodies of men. Contrary to the supposition of those, who have represented the plan of the convention in this respect as novel and unprecedented, it is but a copy of the constitutions of New-Hampshire, Massachusetts, Pennsylvania, Delaware, Maryland, Virginia, North-Carolina, South-

Carolina and Georgia; and the preference which has been given to these models is highly to be commended.

It is not true, in the second place, that the parliament of Great Britain, or the legislatures of the particular states, can rectify the exceptionable decisions of their respective courts, in any other sense than might be done by a future legislature of the United States. The theory neither of the British, nor the state constitutions, authorises the revisal of a judicial sentence, by a legislative act. Nor is there any thing in the proposed constitution more than in either of them, by which it is forbidden. In the former as well as in the latter, the impropriety of the thing, on the general principles of law and reason, is the sole obstacle. A legislature without exceeding its province cannot reverse a determination once made, in a particular case; though it may prescribe a new rule for future cases. This is the principle, and it applies in all its consequences, exactly in the same manner and extent, to the state governments, as to the national government, now under consideration. Not the least difference can be pointed out in any view of the subject.

It may in the last place be observed that the supposed danger of judiciary encroachments on the legislative authority, which has been upon many occasions reiterated, is in reality a phantom. Particular misconstructions and contraventions of the will of the legislature may now and then happen; but they can never be so extensive as to amount to an inconvenience, or in any sensible degree to affect the order of the political system. This may be inferred with certainty from the general nature of the judicial power; from the objects to which it relates; from the manner in which it is exercised; from its comparative weakness, and from its total incapacity to support its usurpations by force. And the inference is greatly fortified by the consideration of the important constitutional check, which the power of instituting impeachments, in one part of the legislative body, and of determining upon them in the other, would give to that body upon the members of the judicial department. This is alone a complete security. There never can be danger that the judges, by a series of deliberate usurpations on the authority of the legislature, would hazard the united resentment of the body entrusted with it, while this body was possessed of the means of punishing their presumption by degrading them from their stations. While this ought to remove all apprehensions on the subject, it affords at the same time a cogent argument for constituting the senate a court for the trial of impeachments.

Having now examined, and I trust removed the objections to the distinct and independent organization of the supreme court, I proceed to consider the propriety of the power of constituting inferior courts,* and the relations which will subsist between these and the former.

The power of constituting inferior courts is evidently calculated to obviate the necessity of having recourse to the supreme court, in every case of federal cognizance. It is intended to enable the national government to institute or *authorise* in each state or district of the United States, a tribunal competent to the determination of matters of national jurisdiction within its limits.

But why, it is asked, might not the same purpose have been accomplished by the instrumentality of the state courts? This admits of different answers. Though the fitness and competency of those courts should be allowed in the utmost latitude; yet the substance of the power in question, may still be regarded as a necessary part of the plan, if it were only to empower the national legislature to commit to them the cognizance of causes arising out of the national constitution. To confer the power of determining such causes upon the existing courts of the several states, would perhaps be as much "to constitute tribunals," as to create new courts with the like power. But ought not a more direct and explicit provision to have been made in favour of the state courts? There are, in my opinion, substantial reasons against such a provision: The most discerning cannot foresee how far the prevalency of a local spirit may be found to disqualify the local tribunals for

---

*This power has been absurdly represented as intended to abolish all the county courts in the several states, which are commonly called inferior courts. But the expressions of the constitution are to constitute "tribunals INFERIOR TO THE SUPREME COURT," and the evident design of the provision is to enable the institution of local courts subordinate to the supreme, either in states or larger districts. It is ridiculous to imagine that county courts were in contemplation.

the jurisdiction of national causes; whilst every man may discover that courts constituted like those of some of the states, would be improper channels of the judicial authority of the union. State judges, holding their offices during pleasure, or from year to year, will be too little independent to be relied upon for an inflexible execution of the national laws. And if there was a necessity for confiding the original cognizance of causes arising under those laws to them, there would be a correspondent necessity for leaving the door of appeal as wide as possible. In proportion to the grounds of confidence in, or diffidence of the subordinate tribunals, ought to be the facility or difficulty of appeals. And well satisfied as I am of the propriety of the appellate jurisdiction in the several classes of causes to which it is extended by the plan of the convention, I should consider every thing calculated to give in practice, an *unrestrained course* to appeals as a source of public and private inconvenience.

I am not sure but that it will be found highly expedient and useful to divide the United States into four or five, or half a dozen districts; and to institute a federal court in each district, in lieu of one in every state. The judges of these courts, with the aid of the state judges, may hold circuits for the trial of causes in the several parts of the respective districts. Justice through them may be administered with ease and dispatch; and appeals may be safely circumscribed within a very narrow compass. This plan appears to me at present the most eligible of any that could be adopted, and in order to it, it is necessary that the power of constituting inferior courts should exist in the full extent in which it is to be found in the proposed constitution.

These reasons seem sufficient to satisfy a candid mind, that the want of such a power would have been a great defect in the plan. Let us now examine in what manner the judicial authority is to be distributed between the supreme and the inferior courts of the union.

The supreme court is to be invested with original jurisdiction, only "in cases affecting ambassadors, other public ministers and consuls, and those in which A STATE shall be a party." Public ministers of every class, are the immediate representatives of their sovereigns. All questions in which they are concerned, are so directly connected with the public peace, that as well for the preservation of this, as out of respect to the sovereignties they represent, it is both expedient and proper, that such questions should be submitted in the first instance to the highest judicatory of the nation. Though consuls have not in strictness a diplomatic character, yet as they are the public agents of the nations to which they belong, the same observation is in a great measure applicable to them. In cases in which a state might happen to be a party, it would ill suit its dignity to be turned over to an inferior tribunal.

Though it may rather be a digression from the immediate subject of this paper, I shall take occasion to mention here, a supposition which has excited some alarm upon very mistaken grounds: It has been suggested that an assignment of the public securities of one state to the citizens of another, would enable them to prosecute that state in the federal courts for the amount of those securities. A suggestion which the following considerations prove to be without foundation.

It is inherent in the nature of sovereignty, not to be amenable to the suit of an individual *without its consent*. This is the general sense and the general practice of mankind; and the exemption, as one of the attributes of sovereignty, is now enjoyed by the government of every state in the union. Unless therefore, there is a surrender of this immunity in the plan of the convention, it will remain with the states, and the danger intimated must be merely ideal. The circumstances which are necessary to produce an alienation of state sovereignty, were discussed in considering the article of taxation, and need not be repeated here. A recurrence to the principles there established will satisfy us, that there is no colour to pretend that the state governments, would by the adoption of that plan, be divested of the privilege of paying their own debts in their own way, free from every constraint but that which flows from the obligations of good faith. The contracts between a nation and individuals are only binding on the conscience of the sovereign, and have no pretensions to a compulsive force. They confer no right of action independent of the sovereign will. To what purpose would it be to authorise suits against states, for the debts they owe? How could recoveries be enforced? It is evident that it could not be done without waging war against the contracting state; and to ascribe to the federal courts, by mere implication, and in destruction of a pre-existing right of the state governments, a power which would involve such a consequence, would be altogether forced and unwarrantable.

Let us resume the train of our observations; we have seen that the original jurisdiction of the supreme court would be confined to two classes of causes, and those of a nature rarely to occur. In all other causes of federal cognizance, the original jurisdiction would appertain to the inferior tribunals, and the supreme court would have nothing more than an appellate jurisdiction, "with such *exceptions*, and under such *regulations* as the congress shall make."

The propriety of this appellate jurisdiction has been scarcely called in question in regard to matters of law; but the clamours have been loud against it as applied to matters of fact. Some well intentioned men in this state, deriving their notions from the language and forms which obtain in our courts, have been induced to consider it as an implied super-sedure of the trial by jury, in favour of the civil law mode of trial, which prevails in our courts of admiralty, probates and chancery. A technical sense has been affixed to the term "appellate," which in our law parlance is commonly used in reference to appeals in the course of the civil law. But if I am not misinformed, the same meaning would not be given to it in any part of New-England. There an appeal from one jury to another is familiar both in language and practice, and is even a matter of course, until there have been two verdicts on one side. The word "appellate" therefore will not be understood in the same sense in New-England as in New-York, which shews the impropriety of a technical interpretation derived from the jurisprudence of any particular state. The expression taken in the abstract, denotes nothing more than the power of one tribunal to review the proceedings of another, either as to the law or fact, or both. The mode of doing it may depend on ancient custom or legislative provision, (in a new government it must depend on the latter) and may be with or without the aid of a jury, as may be judged adviseable. If therefore the re-examination of a fact, once determined by a jury, should in any case be admitted under the proposed constitution, it may be so regulated as to be done by a second jury, either by remanding the cause to the court below for a second trial of the fact, or by directing an issue immediately out of the supreme court.

But it does not follow that the re-examination of a fact once ascertained by a jury, will be permitted in the supreme court. Why may it not be said, with the strictest propriety, when a writ of error is brought from an inferior to a superior court of law in this state, that the latter has jurisdiction of the fact, as well as the law? It is true it cannot institute a new enquiry concerning the fact, but it takes cognizance of it as it appears upon the record, and pronounces the law arising upon it.* This is jurisdiction of both fact and law, nor is it even possible to separate them. Though the common law courts of this state ascertain disputed facts by a jury, yet they unquestionably have jurisdiction of both fact and law; and accordingly, when the former is agreed in the pleadings, they have no recourse to a jury, but proceed at once to judgment. I contend therefore on this ground, that the expressions, "appellate jurisdiction, both as to law and fact," do not necessarily imply a re-examination in the supreme court of facts decided by juries in the inferior courts.

The following train of ideas may well be imagined to have influenced the convention in relation to this particular provision. The appellate jurisdiction of the supreme court (may it have been argued) will extend to causes determinable in different modes, some in the course of the COMMON LAW, and others in the course of the CIVIL LAW. In the former, the revision of the law only, will be, generally speaking, the proper province of the supreme court; in the latter, the re-examination of the fact is agreeable to usage, and in some cases, of which prize causes are an example, might be essential to the preservation of the public peace. It is therefore necessary, that the appellate jurisdiction should, in certain cases, extend in the broadest sense to matters of fact. It will not answer to make an express exception of cases, which shall have been originally tried by a jury, because in the courts of

*This word is a compound of JUS and DICTIO, juris, dictio, or a speaking or pronouncing of the law.

some of the states, *all causes* are tried in this mode;* and such
an exception would preclude the revision of matters of fact, as
well where it might be proper, as where it might be improper.
To avoid all inconveniencies, it will be safest to declare generally, that the supreme court shall possess appellate jurisdiction, both as to law and *fact*, and that this jurisdiction shall be
subject to such *exceptions* and regulations as the national legislature may prescribe. This will enable the government to
modify it in such a manner as will best answer the ends of
public justice and security.

This view of the matter, at any rate puts it out of all doubt
that the supposed *abolition* of the trial by jury, by the operation of this provision, is fallacious and untrue. The legislature
of the United States would certainly have full power to provide that in appeals to the supreme court there should be no
re-examination of facts where they had been tried in the original causes by juries. This would certainly be an authorised
exception; but if for the reason already intimated it should be
thought too extensive, it might be qualified with a limitation
to such causes only as are determinable at common law in that
mode of trial.

The amount of the observations hitherto made on the authority of the judicial department is this—that it has been
carefully restricted to those causes which are manifestly
proper for the cognizance of the national judicature, that in
the partition of this authority a very small portion of original
jurisdiction has been reserved to the supreme court, and the
rest consigned to the subordinate tribunals—that the supreme court will possess an appellate jurisdiction both as to
law and fact in all the cases referred to them, but subject to
any *exceptions* and *regulations* which may be thought adviseable; that this appellate jurisdiction does in no case *abolish* the
trial by jury, and that an ordinary degree of prudence and
integrity in the national councils will insure us solid advantages from the establishment of the proposed judiciary, without exposing us to any of the inconveniencies which have
been predicted from that source.

*I hold that the states will have concurrent jurisdiction with the subordi-
nate federal judicatories, in many cases of federal cognizance, as will be explained in my next paper.

"Publius," The Federalist LXXXII *[Alexander Hamilton]*

New York, May 28, 1788

The erection of a new government, whatever care or wisdom may distinguish the work, cannot fail to originate questions of intricacy and nicety; and these may in a particular manner be expected to flow from the establishment of a constitution founded upon the total or partial incorporation of a number of distinct sovereignties. 'Tis time only that can mature and perfect so compound a system, can liquidate the meaning of all the parts, and can adjust them to each other in a harmonious and consistent WHOLE.

Such questions accordingly have arisen upon the plan proposed by the convention, and particularly concerning the judiciary department. The principal of these respect the situation of the state courts in regard to those causes, which are to be submitted to federal jurisdiction. Is this to be exclusive, or are those courts to possess a concurrent jurisdiction? If the latter, in what relation will they stand to the national tribunals? These are inquiries which we meet with in the mouths of men of sense, and which are certainly intitled to attention.

The principles established in a former paper* teach us, that the states will retain all *pre-existing* authorities, which may not be exclusively delegated to the federal head; and that this exclusive delegation can only exist in one of three cases; where an exclusive authority is in express terms granted to the union; or where a particular authority is granted to the union, and the exercise of a like authority is prohibited to the states, or where an authority is granted to the union with which a

*Vol. 1, No. XXXII.

similar authority in the states would be utterly incompatible. Though these principles may not apply with the same force to the judiciary as to the legislative power; yet I am inclined to think that they are in the main just with respect to the former as well as the latter. And under this impression I shall lay it down as a rule that the state courts will *retain* the jurisdiction they now have, unless it appears to be taken away in one of the enumerated modes.

The only thing in the proposed constitution, which wears the appearance of confining the causes of federal cognizance to the federal courts is contained in this passage—"The JUDI-CIAL POWER of the United States *shall be vested* in one supreme court, and in *such* inferior courts as the congress shall from time to time ordain and establish." This might either be construed to signify, that the supreme and subordinate courts of the union should alone have the power of deciding those causes, to which their authority is to extend; or simply to denote that the organs of the national judiciary should be one supreme court and as many subordinate courts as congress should think proper to appoint, or in other words, that the United States should exercise the judicial power with which they are to be invested through one supreme tribunal and a certain number of inferior ones to be instituted by them. The first excludes, the last admits the concurrent jurisdiction of the state tribunals: And as the first would amount to an alienation of state power by implication, the last appears to me the most natural and the most defensible construction.

But this doctrine of concurrent jurisdiction is only clearly applicable to those descriptions of causes of which the state courts have previous cognizance. It is not equally evident in relation to cases which may grow out of, and be *peculiar* to the constitution to be established: For not to allow the state courts a right of jurisdiction in such cases can hardly be considered as the abridgement of a pre-existing authority. I mean not therefore to contend that the United States in the course of legislation upon the objects entrusted to their direction may not commit the decision of causes arising upon a particular regulation to the federal courts solely, if such a measure should be deemed expedient; but I hold that the state courts will be divested of no part of their primitive jurisdiction, further than may relate to an appeal; and I am even of opinion, that in every case in which they were not expressly excluded by the future acts of the national legislature, they will of course take cognizance of the causes to which those acts may give birth. This I infer from the nature of judiciary power, and from the general genius of the system. The judiciary power of every government looks beyond its own local or municipal laws, and in civil cases lays hold of all subjects of litigation between parties within its jurisdiction though the causes of dispute are relative to the laws of the most distant part of the globe. Those of Japan not less than of New-York may furnish the objects of legal discussion to our courts. When in addition to this, we consider the state governments and the national governments as they truly are, in the light of kindred systems and as parts of ONE WHOLE, the inference seems to be conclusive that the state courts would have a concurrent jurisdiction in all cases arising under the laws of the union, where it was not expressly prohibited.

Here another question occurs—what relation would subsist between the national and state courts in these instances of concurrent jurisdiction? I answer that an appeal would certainly lie from the latter to the supreme court of the United States. The constitution in direct terms, gives an appellate jurisdiction to the supreme court in all the enumerated cases of federal cognizance, in which it is not to have an original one; without a single expression to confine its operation to the inferior federal courts. The objects of appeal, not the tribunals from which it is to be made, are alone contemplated. From this circumstance and from the reason of the thing it ought to be construed to extend to the state tribunals. Either this must be the case, or the local courts must be excluded from a concurrent jurisdiction in matters of national concern, else the judiciary authority of the union may be eluded at the pleasure of every plaintiff or prosecutor. Neither of these consequences ought without evident necessity to be involved; the latter would be intirely inadmissible, as it would defeat some of the most important and avowed purposes of the proposed government, and would essentially embarrass its measures. Nor do I perceive any foundation for such a supposition. Agreeably to the remark already made, the national and state systems are to be regarded as ONE WHOLE. The courts of the latter will of course be natural auxiliaries to the execution of the laws of the union, and an appeal from them will as naturally lie to that tribunal, which is destined to unite and assimilate the principles of national justice and the rules of national decisions. The evident aim of the plan of the convention is that all the causes of the specified classes, shall for weighty public reasons receive their original or final determination in the courts of the union. To confine therefore the general expressions giving appellate jurisdiction to the supreme court to appeals from the subordinate federal courts, instead of allowing their extension to the state courts, would be to abridge the latitude of the terms, in subversion of the intent, contrary to every sound rule of interpretation.

But could an appeal be made to lie from the state courts to the subordinate federal judicatories? This is another of the questions which have been raised, and of greater difficulty than the former. The following considerations countenance the affirmative. The plan of the convention in the first place authorises the national legislature "to constitute tribunals inferior to the supreme court."* It declares in the next place that, "the JUDICIAL POWER of the United States *shall be vested* in one supreme court and in such inferior courts as congress shall ordain and establish"; and it then proceeds to enumerate the cases to which this judicial power shall extend. It afterwards divides the jurisdiction of the supreme court into original and appellate, but gives no definition of that of the subordinate courts. The only outlines described for them are that they shall be "inferior to the supreme court" and that they shall not exceed the specified limits of the federal judiciary. Whether their authority shall be original or appellate or both is not declared. All this seems to be left to the discretion of the legislature. And this being the case, I perceive at present no impediment to the establishment of an appeal from the state courts to the subordinate national tribunals; and many advantages attending the power of doing it may be imagined. It would diminish the motives to the multiplication of federal courts, and would admit of arrangements calculated

*Section 8th, Article 1st.

to contract the appellate jurisdiction of the supreme court. The state tribunals may then be left with a more entire charge of federal causes; and appeals in most cases in which they may be deemed proper instead of being carried to the supreme court, may be made to lie from the state courts to district courts of the union.

SOME FINAL THOUGHTS

"Publius," The Federalist LXXXV
[Alexander Hamilton]

New York, May 28, 1788

According to the formal division of the subject of these papers, announced in my first number, there would appear still to remain for discussion, two points, "the analogy of the proposed government to your own state constitution," and "the additional security, which its adoption will afford to republican government, to liberty and to property." But these heads have been so fully anticipated and exhausted in the progress of the work, that it would now scarcely be possible to do any thing more than repeat, in a more dilated form, what has been heretofore said; which the advanced stage of the question, and the time already spent upon it conspire to forbid.

It is remarkable, that the resemblance of the plan of the convention to the act which organizes the government of this state holds, not less with regard to many of the supposed defects, than to the real excellencies of the former. Among the pretended defects, are the re-eligibility of the executive, the want of a council, the omission of a formal bill of rights, the omission of a provision respecting the liberty of the press: These and several others, which have been noted in the course of our inquiries, are as much chargeable on the existing constitution of this state, as on the one proposed for the Union. And a man must have slender pretensions to consistency, who can rail at the latter for imperfections which he finds no difficulty in excusing in the former. Nor indeed can there be a better proof of the insincerity and affectation of some of the zealous adversaries of the plan of the convention among us, who profess to be the devoted admirers of the government under which they live, than the fury with which they have attacked that plan, for matters in regard to which our own constitution is equally, or perhaps more vulnerable.

The additional securities to republican government, to liberty and to property, to be derived from the adoption of the plan under consideration, consist chiefly in the restraints which the preservation of the union will impose on local factions and insurrections, and on the ambition of powerful individuals in single states, who might acquire credit and influence enough, from leaders and favorites, to become the despots of the people; in the diminution of the opportunities to foreign intrigue, which the dissolution of the confederacy would invite and facilitate; in the prevention of extensive military establishments, which could not fail to grow out of wars between the states in a disunited situation; in the express guarantee of a republican form of government to each; in the absolute and universal exclusion of titles of nobility; and in the precautions against the repetition of those practices on the part of the state governments, which have undermined the foundations of property and credit, have planted mutual distrust in the breasts of all classes of citizens, and have occasioned an almost universal prostration of morals.

Thus have I, my fellow citizens, executed the task I had assigned to myself; with what success, your conduct must determine. I trust at least you will admit, that I have not failed in the assurance I gave you respecting the spirit with which my endeavours should be conducted. I have addressed myself purely to your judgments, and have studiously avoided those asperities which are too apt to disgrace political disputants of all parties, and which have been not a little provoked by the language and conduct of the opponents of the constitution. The charge of a conspiracy against the liberties of the people, which has been indiscriminately brought against the advocates of the plan, has something in it too wanton and too malignant not to excite the indignation of every man who feels in his own bosom a refutation of the calumny. The perpetual charges which have been rung upon the wealthy, the well-born and the great, have been such as to inspire the disgust of all sensible men. And the unwarrantable concealments and misrepresentations which have been in various ways practiced to keep the truth from the public eye, have been of a nature to demand the reprobation of all honest men. It is not impossible that these circumstances may have occasionally betrayed me into intemperances of expression which I did not intend: It is certain that I have frequently felt a struggle between sensibility and moderation, and if the former has in some instances prevailed, it must be my excuse that it has been neither often nor much.

Let us now pause and ask ourselves whether, in the course of these papers, the proposed constitution has not been satisfactorily vindicated from the aspersions thrown upon it, and whether it has not been shewn to be worthy of the public approbation, and necessary to the public safety and prosperity. Every man is bound to answer these questions to himself, according to the best of his conscience and understanding, and to act agreeably to the genuine and sober dictates of his judgment. This is a duty, from which nothing can give him a dispensation. 'Tis one that he is called upon, nay, constrained by all the obligations that form the bands of society, to discharge sincerely and honestly. No partial motive, no particular interest, no pride of opinion, no temporary passion or prejudice, will justify to himself, to his country or to his posterity, an improper election of the part he is to act. Let him beware of an obstinate adherence to party. Let him reflect that the object upon which he is to decide is not a particular interest of the community, but the very existence of the nation. And let him remember that a majority of America has already given its sanction to the plan, which he is to approve or reject.

I shall not dissemble, that I feel an intire confidence in the arguments, which recommend the proposed system to your adoption; and that I am unable to discern any real force in those by which it has been opposed. I am persuaded, that it is the best which our political situation, habits and opinions will admit, and superior to any the revolution has produced.

Concessions on the part of the friends of the plan, that it has not a claim to absolute perfection, have afforded matter of no small triumph to its enemies. Why, say they, should we adopt an imperfect thing? Why not amend it, and make it perfect before it is irrevocably established? This may be plausible enough, but it is only plausible. In the first place I remark, that the extent of these concessions has been greatly exaggerated. They have been stated as amounting to an admission, that the plan is radically defective; and that, without material alterations, the rights and the interests of the community cannot be safely confided to it. This, as far as I have understood the meaning of those who make the concessions, is an intire perversion of their sense. No advocate of the measure can be found who will not declare as his sentiment, that the system, though it may not be perfect in every part, is upon the whole a good one, is the best that the present views and circumstances of the country will permit, and is such an one as promises every species of security which a reasonable people can desire.

I answer in the next place, that I should esteem it the extreme of imprudence to prolong the precarious state of our national affairs, and to expose the union to the jeopardy of successive experiments, in the chimerical pursuit of a perfect plan. I never expect to see a perfect work from imperfect man. The result of the deliberations of all collective bodies must necessarily be a compound as well of the errors and prejudices, as of the good sense and wisdom of the individuals of whom they are composed. The compacts which are to embrace thirteen distinct states, in a common bond of amity and union, must as necessarily be a compromise of as many dissimilar interests and inclinations. How can perfection spring from such materials?

The reasons assigned in an excellent little pamphlet lately published in this city* are unanswerable to shew the utter improbability of assembling a new convention, under circumstances in any degree so favourable to a happy issue, as those in which the late convention met, deliberated and concluded. I will not repeat the arguments there used, as I presume the production itself has had an extensive circulation. It is certainly well worthy the perusal of every friend to his country. There is however one point of light in which the subject of amendments still remains to be considered; and in which it has not yet been exhibited to public view. I cannot resolve to conclude, without first taking a survey of it in this aspect.

*Intitled "An Address to the people of the state of New-York."

It appears to me susceptible of absolute demonstration, that it will be far more easy to obtain subsequent than previous amendments to the constitution. The moment an alteration is made in the present plan, it becomes, to the purpose of adoption, a new one, and must undergo a new decision of each state. To its complete establishment throughout the union, it will therefore require the concurrence of thirteen states. If, on the contrary, the constitution proposed should once be ratified by all the states as it stands, alterations in it may at any time be effected by nine states. Here then the chances are as thirteen to nine* in favour of subsequent amendments, rather than of the original adoption of an intire system.

This is not all. Every constitution for the United States must inevitably consist of a great variety of particulars, in which thirteen independent states are to be accommodated in their interests or opinions of interest. We may of course expect to see, in any body of men charged with its original formation, very different combinations of the parts upon different points. Many of those who form the majority on one question may become the minority on a second, and an association dissimilar to either may constitute the majority on a third. Hence the necessity of moulding and arranging all the particulars which are to compose the whole in such a manner as to satisfy all the parties to the compact; and hence also an immense multiplication of difficulties and casualties in obtaining the collective assent to a final act. The degree of that multiplication must evidently be in a ratio to the number of particulars and the number of parties.

But every amendment to the constitution, if once established, would be a single proposition, and might be brought forward singly. There would then be no necessity for management or compromise, in relation to any other point, no giving nor taking. The will of the requisite number would at once bring the matter to a decisive issue. And consequently whenever nine† or rather ten states, were united in the desire of a particular amendment, that amendment must infallibly take

*†It may rather be said TEN, for though two-thirds may set on foot the measure, three-fourths must ratify.

place. There can therefore be no comparison between the facility of effecting an amendment, and that of establishing in the first instance a complete constitution.

In opposition to the probability of subsequent amendments it has been urged, that the persons delegated to the administration of the national government, will always be disinclined to yield up any portion of the authority of which they were once possessed. For my own part I acknowledge a thorough conviction that any amendments which may, upon mature consideration, be thought useful, will be applicable to the organization of the government, not to the mass of its powers; and on this account alone, I think there is no weight in the observation just stated. I also think there is little weight in it on another account. The intrinsic difficulty of governing THIRTEEN STATES at any rate, independent of calculations upon an ordinary degree of public spirit and integrity, will, in my opinion, constantly *impose* on the national rulers the *necessity* of a spirit of accommodation to the reasonable expectations of their constituents. But there is yet a further consideration, which proves beyond the possibility of doubt, that the observation is futile. It is this, that the national rulers, whenever nine states concur, will have no option upon the subject. By the fifth article of the plan the congress will be *obliged*, "on the application of the legislatures of two-thirds of the states, (which at present amounts to nine) to call a convention for proposing amendments, which *shall be valid* to all intents and purposes, as part of the constitution, when ratified by the legislatures of three-fourths of the states, or by conventions in three-fourths thereof." The words of this article are peremptory. The congress "*shall* call a convention." Nothing in this particular is left to the discretion of that body. And of consequence all the declamation about their disinclination to a change, vanishes in air. Nor however difficult it may be supposed to unite two-thirds or three-fourths of the state legislatures, in amendments which may affect local interests, can there be any room to apprehend any such difficulty in a union on points which are merely relative to the general liberty or security of the people. We may safely rely on the disposition of the state legislatures to erect barriers against the encroach-ments of the national authority.

If the foregoing argument is a fallacy, certain it is that I am myself deceived by it; for it is, in my conception, one of those rare instances in which a political truth can be brought to the test of mathematical demonstration. Those who see the mat-ter in the same light with me, however zealous they may be for amendments, must agree in the propriety of a previous adoption, as the most direct road to their own object.

The zeal for attempts to amend, prior to the establishment of the constitution, must abate in every man, who, is ready to accede to the truth of the following observations of a writer, equally solid and ingenious: "To balance a large state or soci-ety (says he) whether monarchial or republican, on general laws, is a work of so great difficulty, that no human genius, however comprehensive, is able by the mere dint of reason and reflection, to effect it. The judgments of many must unite in the work: EXPERIENCE must guide their labour: TIME must bring it to perfection: And the FEELING of inconve-niences must correct the mistakes which they *inevitably* fall into, in their first trials and experiments."* These judicious reflections contain a lesson of moderation to all the sincere lovers of the union, and ought to put them upon their guard against hazarding anarchy, civil war, a perpetual alienation of the states from each other, and perhaps the military despotism of a victorious demagogue, in the pursuit of what they are not likely to obtain, but from TIME and EXPERIENCE. It may be in me a defect of political fortitude, but I acknowledge, that I cannot entertain an equal tranquillity with those who affect to treat the dangers of a longer continuance in our present situation as imaginary. A NATION without a NA-TIONAL GOVERNMENT is, in my view, an awful spectacle. The establishment of a constitution, in time of profound peace, by the voluntary consent of a whole people, is a PRODIGY, to the completion of which I look forward with trembling anxiety. I can reconcile it to no rules of prudence to let go the hold we now have, in so arduous an enterprise, upon seven out of the thirteen states; and after having passed over so considerable a

*Hume's Essays, vol. I, page 128.—The rise of arts and sciences.

part of the ground to recommence the course. I dread the more the consequences of new attempts, because I KNOW that POWERFUL INDIVIDUALS, in this and in other states, are enemies to a general national government, in every possible shape.

David Ramsay's Oration at Charleston, South Carolina

delivered May 27, 1788, printed *Columbian Herald*
(Charleston, S.C.), June 5, 1788

I congratulate you my fellow-citizens on the ratification of the new constitution. This event, replete with advantages, promises to repay us for the toils, dangers and waste of the late revolution. Merely to have established independence was but half the work assigned to this generation. Without an efficient government to protect our rights, in vain have our heroes spilt their blood in emancipating us from Great-Britain; that the blessings of such a government have not yet descended upon us is a melancholly truth too universally known and felt to be disguised. I will not wound your feelings on this festive day, by recapitulating our national distresses since the peace. When we thought our sufferings were ended, we found them only to be varied; nor is it wonderful that constitutions hastily instituted by young politicians and in the tumult of war, should not fully answer their ends in time of peace—Expiring credit, languishing commerce, with a group of concommitant evils, proclaimed aloud something to be fundamentally wrong.—The spirit of the country was once more roused. Unattacked by foreign force—unconvulsed by domestic violence, America called forth her sons to meet and form a constitution for the future good government of her widely extended settlements. To combine in one system, thirteen states differing in climate, soil and manners, and impelled by variant interests, was the arduous work assigned to this band of patriots. Heaven smiled on their deliberations, and inspired their councils with a spirit of conciliation: hence arose a system, which seems well calculated to make us happy at home and respected abroad. The *legislative powers* are re-solveable into this principle, that the sober second thoughts and dispassionate voice of the people, shall be the law of the land. The *executive* department amounts to no more than that the man of the people shall carry into effect the will of the people. The *judicial* declares, that where impartial trials from the nature of the case cannot be expected from state tribunals, there the federal judiciary shall interpose. All this power is derived from the people, and at fixed periods returns to them. No privileges are conferred on the rich or the few, but what they hold in common with the poor and the many. All distinctions of birth, rank and titles are forever excluded. Public offices are open to merit and talents wherever found, and nought forbids the poorest man in the community from attaining to the highest honors.

One of the many advantages we may expect from the adoption of this constitution, is a protecting navy. What is there at present to secure our sea-coast from being laid under contribution by a few frigates? Are either the treasuries of the continent or of the individual states sufficiently replenished to command the means of defence? We have hitherto lain at the mercy of the most inconsiderable maritime powers, and even of a single daring pirate; but we have now well-grounded hopes of an alteration in our favor.

Nothing is more likely to secure a people from foreign attacks than a preparedness for repelling them. On this principle the militia arrangements of the new constitution promise a long exemption from foreign war.—What European power will dare to attack us, when it is known that the yeomanry of the country uniformly armed and disciplined, may on any emergency be called out to our defence by one legislature, and commanded by one person? Tradition informs us, that about forty years ago France meditated an invasion of New-England; but on reading the militia law of Massachusetts, declined the attempt. If this was the case under the wholesome regulations of one state, what room is there to fear invasion when an union of force and uniformity of system extends from New-Hampshire to Georgia? Domestic violence will on the same principles be either prevented or controled—faction will not dare to disturb the peace of a single state, nor will any aspiring leader presume to oppose lawful authority, when it is known that the strength of the whole is subjected to the will of one legislature, and may be called forth under the direction of one man for the safety of each part. How widely different would be our case under a loose federal government, or the more pernicious system of two or more separate confederacies? Let us for a moment suppose these states detached from a common head—what a field for European intrigue? It would be their interest to play off one state or confederacy against another, and to keep us at constant variance. Standing armies would then be multiplied without end, for the defence of the respective parts—good militia arrangements will for the most part be sufficient for our defence when united, but they would be far short of that purpose when our most inveterate enemies might be our next neighbours. After we had weakened ourselves with mutual devastation, we could expect no better fate than that of Poland, to be distributed as apendages to the sovereigns of Europe. To disunite the states of America, would be to entail discord and wars on our unoffending posterity, and turn a band of brethren into a monster, preying upon itself, and preyed upon by all its enemies. How much wiser that policy which embraces our whole extent of territory in one efficient system? This is not only the path to safety but to greatness. While our government was nerveless, nothing could be undertaken which required a persevering unity of design. Much may be done to improve our inland navigation and facilitate our intercourse with each other: but who would expend his capital on any project of this kind, while legislative assemblies claimed and exercised the right of making ex post facto laws? Under the stability and energy which our new constitution promises, methinks I see the rivers of these states wedded to each other. The western country attached to the sea-coast, while turn-pike roads enable travellers with ease and expedition to traverse the whole of our country. These beneficial improvements must have been in a great degree relinquished, unless one legislative power had pervaded the whole of the United States.

Under the same patronage, justice will again lift up her head. While legislative assemblies interfered between debtors and creditors, what security could there be for property? He that sold, did not know that he should ever get the stipulated price: he that parted with his money could not tell when it would be replaced—hence a total want of confidence and of credit. From this day forward, these evils will be done away; creditors knowing that they can recover payment, will be less disposed to distress their debtors than when under a fluctuating system which might induce them to make the most of present opportunities, lest future laws should create new impediments to the course of justice. Debtors, despairing of farther legislative indulgences, and knowing that they can be compelled to pay, will be stimulated to double exertions for acquiring the means of discharging their debts. The gold and silver which have long rusted in the desks of the cautious, will once more see the light and add to the circulating medium of our country. That useful order of men, formerly called money lenders will be revived, and the distresses of the unfortunate relieved without sacrificing their property, or administering to the rapacity of usurers. Time would fail me in dilating at full length on that section of the constitution which declares, that "no state shall emit bills of credit, make any thing but gold and silver a tender in payment of debts, pass any bill of attainder or ex post facto law, impairing the obligation of contracts." This will restore credit; and credit is a mine of real wealth, far surpassing those of Mexico and Peru. It will soon bring back the good old times under which we formerly flourished and were happy.

Our new constitution will also make us respected abroad. What have these states to fear? What may they not hope for when united under one protecting head? The wealth and colonies of the most powerful nations of Europe are near our borders. In case of their future contentions, these states will stand on high ground; that scale into which they throw their weight, must, in the ordinary course of events, infallibly preponderate. The contiguity of our harbours to their territories, and that marine which will grow out of our new constitution, will enable us to hold the balance among European sovereigns. While they contend for their American possessions, those whom the United States favor will be favored, and those whom they chuse to depress will be depressed. Far be it from me to wish this country to be involved in the labyrinth of European politics, but it is both our duty and interest to improve local advantages for procuring us that respect abroad, which will promote our happiness at home. Under such circumstances, and when our citizens can be brought to act in unison, what beneficial treaties may we not expect? At present our commerce is fettered by those very powers which under the new constitution will, for their own sakes, court our friendship. For a long series of years we shall be principally a nation of farmers and planters, and disposed to purchase many manufactures from Europe. To old countries overstocked with inhabitants, and abounding with manufactures, the privilege of supplying our growing numbers with those articles we want to purchase and they to sell, will be an object for which they can afford a valuable consideration; the equivalent which might have been commanded on this account we have hitherto lost, from the want of an efficient government. It is not more melancholy than true, that the inhabitants of this state, in consequence of our deranged police, are now paying nearly as much of the taxes of Great-Britain, as they pay to support their own government. The public benefits which will flow from a constitutional ability to direct the commerce of these states on well regulated permanent principles, will enable us once more to raise our heads and assume our proper rank among the nations. Hitherto, while we were under an unbraced confederation of states, the members of the confederacy could not be brought to draw together, and in consequence thereof our ships have rotted, our commerce has either been abandoned or carried on to our prejudice.

The good consequences which may be expected to result from our new constitution, will also extend to agriculture and manufactures. The stability of government will enhance the value of real property. Our protected commerce will open new channels for our native commodities, and give additional value to the soil, by increasing the demand for its productions. At the same time, judicious arrangements of bounties and duties, will give encouragement to such manufactures as suit our country.

That coasting trade, which under state regulations, would probably have been a source of contention, will, when directed by one legislature, become a nursery for seamen and a cement of our union. Bound together by one general government, we may defy the arts and intrigues of Europe. Commanding our own resources and acting in concert, we can form a little world within ourselves, and smile at those who are jealous of our rising greatness; their efforts against us would resemble waves dashing themselves into foam against a rock. It would be easy to enumerate a variety of other particulars, and from each of them point out advantages that will result from adopting the new constitution. We thereby become a nation, and may hope for a national character. Hitherto our manners, customs and dress have been regulated by those of Europe: But, united under one head, our people will have something original of their own, from which they may copy, and save that money which is now absurdly expended in following the fashions of foreign countries; these may well accord with their policy, but are apparent from ours.

On the whole, to separate from Britain was the least considerable object of the late revolution, and amounted to nothing more than to acquire a capacity for taking care of ourselves. To pull down one form of government without substituting something in its place that would answer the great ends for which men enter into society, would have been to trifle with posterity. The event which we are this day celebrating, acquits us of that heavy charge. The fathers of our country have proposed, and we have adopted a constitution which promises to embrace in one comprehensive system of liberty, safety and happiness the inhabitants of that vast extent of territory which reaches from the Atlantic to the Missisippi, and from the lakes of Canada to the river St. Mary. Judging of the future by the past, a child born on this day, has a prospect of living to see the time when fifty millions of freemen will enjoy the blessings of government under the administration of the president of the United States. Our new constitution is of that expansive nature as to admit of a communication of its privileges to that group of new states, which, ere long will be planted in our Western territory; provision is made for receiving them into the union as fast as they are formed. This is founded on such generous principles, as will divert them from foreign connexions or separate confederacies. What a God-like work, to embrace our grow-ing numbers and extending settlements in one efficient system of government. This our new constitution promises; and from the humanity of the age and the liberal principles of its policy, it is likely to perform. Within one century, the citizens of the United States will probably be five times as numerous as the inhabitants of Great-Britain. Had not the present con-stitution, or something equivalent been adopted, no one can compute the confusion and disorder which would probably have taken place from the jarring interests of such an ungov-erned multitude. The articles of confederation were of too feeble a texture to bind us together, or to ward off threatened evils. Had it not been wisely resolved to introduce a more energetic system, the states must soon have crumbled to pieces; in that case what was to protect the weak from the strong? What was to restrain some adventurous Cromwell from grasping our liberties and establishing himself on a throne of despotism? One Cromwell, did I say—more prob-ably there would have been a score, and each contending for the sovereignty through our desolated country, bleeding in a thousand veins. Thanks to Heaven, far different are our pros-pects; united under one head, the force of the union will soon bring an aspiring individual or overbearing state to reason and moderation. We shall be protected from foreign invasion and restrained from warring on one another. At the same time agriculture, commerce and the useful arts of life will be cherished and protected by federal arrangements pervading all the states, and raising them to an eminence unattainable in any circumstances of separation.

We have now in our view the fairest prospects of political happiness; the wisdom, energy and well poised ballances of our new system, promise to confute the assertions of those who maintain "that there are incurable evils inherent in every form of republican government." From the federal house of representatives we may expect a sympathy with the wants and wishes of the people—from the senate, wisdom, unity of de-sign and a permanent system of national happiness.—from the executive, secrecy, vigor and dispatch. In short, our new constitution is a happy combination of the simple forms of government and as free from the inconveniences of each, as could be expected from the inseparable imperfection of all human institutions. It unites liberty with safety, and promises the enjoyment of all the rights of civil society, while it leads us up the steep ascent to national greatness.

Before I conclude, I beg leave to inculcate a sentiment which cannot be too often presented to the view of the public. No form of government can make a vicious and ignorant people happy.—When the majority of our citizens becomes corrupt, even our well ballanced constitution cannot save us from slavery and ruin. Let it therefore be the unceasing study of all who love their country, to promote virtue and dispense knowledge through the whole extent of our settlements. Without them our growing numbers will soon degenerate into barbarism; but with them the citizens of the United States bid fair for possessing, under the new constitution, as great a share of happiness, as any nation has hitherto enjoyed.

Simeon Baldwin's Oration at New Haven, July 4, 1788

New Haven, Connecticut, 1788

The love of liberty, and a thirst for power, have ever been distinguished passions in the history of mankind. More blood and treasure have been expended in the struggles of freedom against the grasp of oppression, than in all the wars which have originated from other sources. But the instances are rare, of those who have enjoyed the blessings for which they contended. The soldier has frequently triumphed over the vanquished armies of the tyrant; but the citizen has, hitherto, been ignorant of those principles of government, which guard the rights of the people, and preserve an equilibrium between the extremes of despotism and anarchy.

Liberty was the darling object of the first settlers of this country. Animated with the hope of enjoying those civil and religious rights, which Heaven designed for the virtuous, they bade adieu to the joys of a more social life, and, surrounded with the horrors of death in a thousand different shapes, they took possession of the fair territory we now inhabit. In the anticipation of liberty, plenty and peace, they braved all dangers and all hardships.

By the great distance of this country from Europe, Heaven seems to have designed it for the seat of an independent people; and the exertions of the first inhabitants who were but little assisted by the parent state intitled them to the privilege. This privilege however they never claimed, nor would their posterity have ever assumed it, had not their rising greatness been oppressed, by those whom they had ever viewed as the guardians of their national infancy, and into whose stores their filial affection induced them to pour the riches of this western world.

It was a circumstance peculiarly fortunate for us, that during many years after the settlement of this country, policy suspended the lash of tyranny, 'till the posterity of the first settlers had become habituated to the enjoyment of liberty, and by a population too rapid for the calculations of Britain, had scattered themselves over the fertile soil of this extensive country.

Without vanity we may glory in those virtues which we inherited from our ancestors. Though simple in manners, they were men of independent sentiment and strict virtue. They loved their freedom and they loved their posterity, and with their own knowledge and sentiments, took pleasure in improving our minds and meliorating our hearts.

In this stage of our society, we viewed the happiness of Britain, as intimately connected with ours. We considered her as the parent state, and chearfully afforded her all the profits of our commerce, and every assistance to increase her national glory. With fervor we united in our prayers to heaven for her prosperity, until the late cloud of ministerial oppression began to obscure our liberties. The British nation had long been oppressed by an overgrown nobility, and loaded with the weight of an enormous debt. Their court had become habituated to the luxuries of a declining nation, and was perplexed with the numerous applications of hungry placemen. They envied our ease, grew jealous of our increasing strength, and determined that these colonies should bear the burthen of their extravagance. The plan of oppression was artfully devised, and carried on, at first, by slow and almost imperceptible degrees. Under the most plausible pretexts, our charters were wrested from us, and our free republics changed into royal governments. Creatures of the crown supplied the places of those whom freemen once elected—the administration of justice was obstructed—salutary laws were rejected, and others imposed upon us better adapted to a system of despotism. A standing army was quartered in these colonies to awe us into compliance; and then they assumed the high prerogative of imposing duties and taxes on us at pleasure. Policy, 'tis true, fixed the sums upon a very moderate scale; but it is alarming to freemen to hear of taxes and of laws from a court in which we have no representation. These measures were the dictates of a tyrannic spirit, and the sons of freedom with manly firmness, withstood these unwarrantable claims of power. They knew it would be a more difficult task to enslave a free people than to straiten the chains that have once been riveted. Though firm and unshaken they did not disdain the mild language of humble intreaty. Whole districts and provinces repeatedly bent the knee to the inexorable monarch of Britain. His answer was the *thunder of war*—and the reply of patriots was LIBERTY OR DEATH—LIBERTY OR DEATH was in a moment echoed from every rank of citizens in the united colonies. History cannot boast a similar instance of a people inhabiting an extensive territory—divided by so many clashing interests and deep-rooted prejudices, uniting in a moment in a measure the noblest that men in society ever undertake.

The horrors of that slavery which the freeborn sons of America could not brook, and the animation which the hope of freedom inspired, left no time to reflect on our destitute situation. Destitute of the implements of war and of military stores—without money the strength of war—without men who ever experienced a regular campaign—totally unacquainted with the manufactures necessary for the existence of an army, and without a single ally, we contended with a nation whose stores were replete with the instruments of slaughter—whose credit commanded the banks of nations—whose soldiers had been trained to the art of war, and whose armies had made the powers of Europe tremble. Reflection would have thrown us into despair; and indeed, "if the Lord himself had not been on our side when men rose up against us, they had swallowed us up quick."

In this critical moment the Representatives of the United States in Congress assembled, boldly cut the gordian knot. In the name of the people, they "assumed that separate and equal station among the powers of the earth, to which the laws of nature and nature's God, entitled them." While we celebrate that distinguished day, the clear manifestation of providential beneficence in this event, calls for gratitude and joy. The world confess'd it nobly done, and Heaven has ratified the deed.

The European nations beheld the contest with anxiety, and viewed the political balance of power, which preserves the peace of empires, as depending on the event. The noblest principles influenced their measures. They considered the war not the effect of a licentious rebellion against the proper exercise of government, but the effort of virtue struggling in her own defence. The charms of liberty shone with new beauty even in the courts of despotic governments. They revered the cause in which the unalienable rights of mankind, and the dignity of man was defended. They generously supplied our wants—They divided the power of Britain, and the blood of foreign heroes was mingled with the blood of our patriots in defence of freedom.

The numerous incidents of the war, from the *battle of Lexington* to the *capture of Cornwallis*, are too well known and have been too sensibly realized to admit of any comment. Most of us have been anxious spectators—many in this assembly peculiar sufferers and some distinguished actors in those interesting scenes. It was ever a peculiar circumstance following the most gloomy fortune of the war, that success and glory crowned the redoubled efforts of our arms. Three times have the victorious armies of our enemy, with rapid career spread the desolation of war, almost to the centre of our country, and twice has it been emphatically proved by the capture of two powerful British armies, that captivity may be led captive.

In a review of those memorable events, we mourn the untimely deaths of departed heroes, and lament that our charters of freedom were sealed with their blood. Their wounds, their sufferings and their deaths have enhanced the price of freedom.

Peculiar has been the loss of this city in the deaths of many useful and respectable inhabitants. Among the tombs of her slain who have been devoted victims to the rage of tyrannic slaughter, we shall find those of the venerable father, the amiable consort, and the worthy citizen. There we shall find the manes of WOOSTER, that bold and generous patriot. To the shining virtues of the citizen, in him were united the distinguished talents of the soldier. In early life he made the profession of arms his choice. The flower of his days and the prime of his life were employed in the service of Britain. Her glory was then the glory of his country. But the moment she formed the plan of despotism, his generous soul swell'd with indignation, and a rational conviction that the rights of the colonies were invaded, influenced him to take an early and decided part in favour of liberty. Despising the emoluments of a pension when in competition with the freedom of his fellow-citizens, with the ardor of a patriot he re-assumed the armour of his youth, and boldly facing the enemies of his country's freedom the renowned warrior died.

While we pay the tribute of a tear to the memory of the dead, it would be a pleasing task, and civilized nations have ever considered it a useful employment, to celebrate the virtues of distinguished benefactors, who have survived the slaughter of war and triumphed in the freedom of their country. But it would be impossible to do justice to the merits of those patriots who performed conspicuous parts on the theatre of those actions we this day commemorate. My friends, words cannot do it. It is among the dark shades of our national character, that their fellow-citizens have been so reluctant to bestow the honours and rewards of their meritorious services. The *real friends* of their country still experience the feelings of gratitude and the influence of justice. And there is a reward of which malice cannot deprive the soldier. The reflection that they have done their duty, is a source of happiness more refined than that which arises "from the blaze of glory—the arm of power—or the golden lure of wealth"— Some faithful Ramsay, some American Livy or Tacitus, will transmit their names, their virtues, and their noble deeds to posterity; by whom they will be revered as the most distinguished benefactors of mankind, and eminent examples for future patriots.

A part of the debt which the citizen owes to the soldier and to his country, is, to complete the revolution and to secure its blessings, by a liberal, free, and efficacious government. In vain have we struggled against the grasp of despotism, if we degenerate into licentiousness and anarchy.

The declaration of independence, dissolved the political bands—it cut the nerves of former compacts. The ardor of patriotism in pursuit of the darling object of our wishes, was the only link which held us together. But liberty cannot long exist without government. To bring order out of confusion, and to secure the blessings of society, by the establishment of legal authority, was the laborious attempt of our wise politicians in the midst of invasion and the carnage of war. Most of the States adopted energetic forms of government, and yet favourable in the highest degree to the rights of mankind. A federal system was a more difficult task. The necessity of a national government we had never experienced—against its abuse we were then contending. Prejudices and fears therefore must be combated in the accumulation of federal authority. Accustomed to comply with the recommendations and to grant the requisitions of Congress, the people thought they should never need their commands. They could not see the necessity of coercive power, nor of a revenue under the controul of our national council. Thus circumstanced, the wisdom of Congress was necessarily confined to a system, adapted to those sentiments of the people.

It is necessary in a good government, that the *legislature* should be so formed as not to enact laws without due deliberation—that the *judicial* be competent to the administration of justice, and that the *executive* have energy to carry their decisions into execution. The nerves of the whole body politic should concenter in the supreme executive; and the great council of the nation, under due restrictions, ought to command the purse and the sword; or in vain will they weild the sceptre of government. To what purpose should a legislative enact laws if nobody is obliged to obey them? To what purpose make contracts which they can never fulfil? To what purpose remonstrate against the encroachments, the insults—the abuses of other nations, when they have not the appearance of power to oppose them? O my country! thy glory hath been tarnished by the consequences of a confederation totally deficient in these particulars. The resolves of that illustrious body of men, who form the nerveless council of our union, are disregarded at home and despised abroad. Our commerce languishes. Public credit is no more; and the glory of the United-States—where is it? It expired with that patriot warmth which once united our councils, opened our purses, and strengthened our arms without the force of law.

Happy for us there is an ultimate point of national depression, beyond which human nature cannot sink. The degrees of depression will ever be in proportion to the knowledge and refinement of the people. The great bulk of mankind, when they have the means of knowledge, and time to deliberate, in general adopt right political sentiments—Our union, in opposition to the claims of Britain, is a proof of this observation, and a more recent instance is afforded us, from the appointment of that illustrious council of sages who convened, to frame anew the constitution of the United States. The people were sensible that our former confederacy was inadequate to the great objects of a federal union—they were convinced that a more efficacious government was necessary—and they have nobly attempted the change.

To the honour of these states, among the great national events which history preserves for posterity, it will be recorded, that they effected this change in government, in the most calm, deliberate and constitutional method. They despised those mad, tumultuous actions which disgraced many of the great revolutions of antiquity. They acted as became a free and independent people.

Men who were truly the representatives of the people, and the fathers of our empire—whose salutary counsels we had experienced in our most perilous circumstances—whose virtue supported them with fortitude, in "those times which tried men's souls"—who had given proof of their patriotism in the declaratory act of independence—who had approved themselves equal to the greatest negociations in the courts of Europe—who had conducted our armies, rescued millions from the hand of oppression, and triumphantly returned to the joys of private life. Men whose interest was the interest of their country, were deputed by the suffrages of freemen, to give an expiring nation life—to rescue our liberties from the grave of anarchy, and to frame a constitution which might spread and secure the benign influence of freedom and peace to the millions of our posterity. Never—never before did men deliberate upon so interesting an object!

Revolutions in government have in general been the tumultuous exchange of one tyrant for another, or the elevation of a few aspiring nobles upon the ruins of a better system. Never before has the collected wisdom of any nation been permitted quietly to deliberate, and determine upon the form of government best adapted to the genius, views and circumstances of the citizens. Never before have the people of any nation been permitted, candidly to examine, and then deliberately adopt or reject the constitution proposed.

For a moment turn your attention to that venerable body—examine the characters of those illustrious sages, eminent for political wisdom and unsullied virtue—see them unfolding the volumes of antiquity, and carefully examining the various systems of government, which different nations have experienced, and judiciously extracting the excellence of each—listen to the irresistible reasons which they urge—mark the peculiar amity which distinguishes their debates—hear the mutual concessions of private interest to the general good, while they keep steadily in view the great object of their counsels, the firm CONSOLIDATION of our union—and then glory, Americans, in the singular unanimity of that illustrious assembly of patriots, in the most finished form of government that ever blessed a nation.

By the Constitution of the United States, all the essential rights of freemen, and the dignity of individual States are secured. The people have the mediate or immediate election of their rulers—to the people they are amenable for their conduct, and can constitutionally be removed by the frequency of election. While the voice of the people is heard in the House of Representatives, the independent sovereignty of the several States will be guarded by the wisdom of the Senate, and the disinterested penetration of the President will balance the influence and prevent the encroachments of each. In this beautiful gradation we find all those checks which are necessary for the stability of republican government, and the due deliberation of the most perfect legislature. Instead of the mad collections of the populace, we shall have a representation accurately calculated upon the numbers and property of the constituents. There will be as little connection between the executive and legislative as the good of government requires, and a total separation of the judicial from both. In each of these particulars, our constitution far exceeds those of the celebrated republics of Greece or Rome. These principles were admired by the wise politicians of antiquity, but had never been reduced to practice: of consequence their republics were of short duration, and while they lasted were perpetually torn by tumultuous seditions, with their train of numerous and tragical incidents.

The checks and balances of different orders, have the same effect in the regularity of government, as the political balance of power in the peace and happiness of nations. Europe has experienced the advantages of this, ever since the union of nations opposed the aspiring Charles V. If the principle had been earlier understood, the world would never have experienced the mad career of an Alexander, nor would the proud Romans so often have triumphed over the armies of the vanquished—nor would the weaker nations, victims to the lust of dominion in the powerful, so often have experienced the rage of war and the tyranny of conquest.

In these States the balance of property is wholly in favour of the people—Merit is the criterion of eminence, and the aristocratic influence is founded in superior wisdom and virtue.

I should weary the patience of my audience, were I to attempt those encomiums which are due to this monument of wisdom. Perhaps it is not the best possible. But we boldly assert that in theory it appears to be the best form of government that has ever been offered to the world. It has been admired by millions, ratified and adopted by the enlightened freemen of *ten* states, and rejected by none who have constitutionally deliberated upon it—Language cannot praise it more.

I am peculiarly happy, my friends, that in addition to the general joy, which usually dilates the heart of every friend of his country on the celebration of this day, I may congratulate this federal assembly, on this most interesting event, the establishment of this constitution—an event, if possible, more interesting than independence itself. That gave us birth as a nation—This will give duration and happiness to our existence. The rubicon is now passed. Better prospects are before us. Experience has taught us the necessary lessons—to lop off the libertinism of juvenile independence, to strengthen the basis of our system of government—to correct the disordered parts, and to give greater stability and energy to all its operations.

From the adoption of this constitution, we have every thing to hope—nothing to fear. The powers of Congress are solely directed to national objects.—They are accurately defined and can extend to nothing which is not expressly delegated to them. In other nations, and in the several States in particular, the legislatures have power in every thing not expressly excepted: These exceptions in a good form of government comprehend the essentials of liberty.

The laws of every nation will wear the complexion of the constitution, and in a good government, will uniformly promote the great objects of political society: the protection of the estates, families, persons, fame, and lives of the subjects.

From such a system of government and laws, we may flatter ourselves with the most pleasing prospects. No nation ever yet united in itself all those superior advantages for social dignity. All the influential causes of greatness conspire and indicate the future glory of America. The soil of these States is extremely fertile—the territory is sufficiently extensive, and we are bless'd with an internal navigation which is unparalleled, and open to the world. An uncommon spirit of enterprize is populating our country with astonishing rapidity and enlarging the dominion of these States without the horrors of conquest. Our commerce is free to all nations. Manufactures are daily increasing, and that spirit of industry, which is the strength of government and the friend of virtue, is every where visible. A general intercourse has, in a great measure, removed local attachments and prejudices, and has given a refinement to the manners of the people, not accompanied, we hope, with those vices, which usually attend the same degree of refinement in other nations. The United States are peculiarly happy in a general diffusion of knowledge and in the prospect of greater improvement. Science cannot flourish in a land that is blasted with a tyrant's breath.—She is the companion of freedom, the child of independence. Dependency of government insensibly carries with it, a fatal dependency of mind—Men are too apt to think, that superior power is necessarily connected with superior wisdom, and for modes of acting and modes of thinking, with reverence look up to those on whom they are dependent. Even in these States, we have found it a more difficult task to root out those unnatural prepossessions, which tend to idolize the persons and productions of foreigners, to the prejudice of humble merit among ourselves, than to break the chain of political oppression—A single blow of the decisive sword destroys the one—the slow progress of reason and mental improvement the other. Divested of these prejudices we should be surprized were we to enumerate all the efforts of genius which have signalized Americans, since independence animated them to noble exertions. Witness the numerous mechanical inventions—witness those laborious productions, which will convey to posterity the close reasoning of the theologian, the experiments and inductions of the philosopher, the accuracy of the grammarian, the unsullied veracity of the historian, the bold imagery of the painter, the sublime flights of the poet, and those researches of the profound politician, which have taught the senators of Europe political wisdom, and the citizens of the world the road to freedom and peace.

If such effusions of genius distinguish the infancy of this nation, what may we expect when she shall ripen into manhood!

Our language is a channel of more information than any other language on earth. The press is uncontrouled, and a free toleration of sentiments distinguishes the happy government of these States.

In this country is completed that happy alliance of national blessings, which a lively imagination must have painted for the foundation of a glorious empire. It would not require the warmth of enthusiasm to embellish the piece. I leave it to the lively fancy of my audience to enjoy the animating prospect which we have pursued through the rough paths of war and the revolutions of government.

The best system of government cannot insure freedom, riches, and national respect, without the vigilance, the industry and the virtuous exertions of the people. The labours of the patriot and the friend of humanity are not yet completed. It is their task to remove those blemishes which have hitherto sullied the glory of these States. We may feed our vanity with the pompous recital of noble atchievements—we may pride ourselves in the excellency of our government—we may boast of the anticipated glories of the western continent:—But virtue will mourn that injustice and ingratitude have, in too many instances, had the countenance of law—Humanity will mourn that an odious slavery, cruel in itself, degrading to the dignity of man, and shocking to human nature, is tolerated, and in many instances practised with barbarian cruelty.—Yes, even in this land of boasted freedom, this asylum for the oppressed, that inhuman practice has lost its horrors by the sanction of custom.

To remedy this evil will be a work of time.—God be thanked it is already begun. Most of the southern & middle states have made salutary provision by law for the future emancipation of this unfortunate race of men, and it does honnour to the candour and philanthropy of the southern states, that they consented to that liberal clause in our new constitution evidently calculated to abolish a slavery upon which they calculated their riches. It is the duty of every friend to his country to lead his fellow citizens to rational reflections upon these interesting subjects to abolish as much as possible the vices peculiar to us as a nation and as individuals, and to disseminate still farther those principles of wisdom and virtue which form the pillars of republican government.

Let not the enjoyment of peace and the pride of independence lead us to security and dissipation. But in view of those blessings which have heretofore animated us, let us be ambitious to perform well the duty of good citizens of a free government. Let us attentively guard our political constitutions as the most sacred bulwark of national independence and freedom. Let us ever be watchful of our liberties by attending to the choice of our rulers. Let us make merit the passport to honour, and the confidence of the people the reward of meritorious services. Let us be industrious in our employments, benevolent in our intentions, and diffusive in our exertions. Let us endeavour to perform our parts nobly, and to discharge our duty to our God, our country and ourselves, like true patriots and benevolent christians. We shall then in the smiles of heaven, reap the fruit of all our toil. We shall enjoy respectability abroad, peace, liberty and prosperity at home, and shall give occasion for posterity to celebrate the day, that gave birth to this nation, and INDEPENDENCE to the UNITED STATES of AMERICA.

"Phocion"

United States Chronicle (Providence, R.I.), July 17, 1788

To the PEOPLE *of the State of* RHODE-ISLAND.
Fathers, Brothers, Friends, and Fellow-Citizens,

The period has now arrived when ten of the States, of the late Confederacy, have withdrawn from you, or you from them; and there is the utmost probability that we shall hear, in a short time, that the eleventh and twelfth States have also joined the other ten.—We shall then be left in a contending world, to shift for ourselves, surrounded by great, powerful and confederated neighbours. This critical situation claims your immediate and most serious attention. I anxiously wish that some able person would undertake particularly to point out, on the one hand, the peculiar advantages which will result to us, as a people, from the adoption of the new national Constitution, and on the other, the certain destruction which will probably come upon us, if we should not join in the grand American Confederacy. A multiplicity of avocations will permit me to make only a few cursory and hasty remarks, dictated however by the purest and most sincere regard for your real welfare and happiness.

Groundless reports, designed misrepresentations, and absolute falsehoods have been used to raise *innumerable visionary spectres without substance* to affright the people, and to prevent them from cooly and dispassionately considering the merits of this excellent Constitution.—Such a jealousy hath thereby been excited that it is extremely difficult for a man of the purest and best intentions to obtain attention, and more difficult to obtain confidence, if he suggests any thing contrary to the reigning opinion, and he must have some considerable degree of courage to attempt it. But as I well know the good sense of the people in general, in this State, who during the late war were as forward and zealous in the common cause of our "dear country," as any in United America,—whose unremitted exertions were such as repeatedly gained them the applause and the thanks of the illustrious Commander in Chief, and will merit and obtain commemoration in the pages of history—I cannot but hope their candour and moderation will procure a cool and dispassionate consideration of the following remarks.

Let us reflect a moment on the peculiarly happy situation which this State will enjoy, compared with the other States, in point of commerce and intercourse with the world at large, *in case she should join in the General Confederacy.* This State is embowelled by a great and excellent bay of water, leading a great distance towards the heart of the country, and furnishing at Newport one of the finest harbours for shipping on the Atlantic ocean.—And in case this State should adopt the new Constitution, it will soon become the great entreport and mart of New-England.—It consists almost wholly of one great extended line of sea-port towns, lying around the noble bay of Narragansett. Let us in contemplation travel round the extensive shore. Beginning at Connecticut and going round the bay to the northward and eastward, we shall find the towns lying in the following order:—*Westerly, Charlestown, South-Kingstown, North-Kingstown, East-Greenwich, Warwick, Cranston* and *Providence,* on the main land upon the west side of the bay:—*Barrington, Warren, Bristol, Tiverton* and *Little-Compton,* on the main land upon the east side of the bay:— the islands on *Newport, Middletown, Portsmouth, Jamestown* and *New-Shoreham:*—In the whole EIGHTEEN towns, every one of which are washed by the waters of the great Atlantic ocean.— These make almost two-thirds of the towns in the State—for there are but TWELVE other towns in the State, viz.—in the county of Washington, *Exeter, Richmond* and *Hopkinton;*—in the county of Kent, *West-Greenwich* and *Coventry;*—and in the county of Providence, *Scituate, Foster, Gloucester, Smithfield, Cumberland, North-Providence* and *Johnston.* These twelve may be called the inland towns of the State—from the remotest of which a person may ride, in less than four hours, to some one of the principal market-towns on the bay; so that the above-mentioned inland country towns in this State may rather be considered as the environs, suburbs, or parts of the great towns which must unavoidably arise round this noble bay, *should this State become a part of the General Confederacy.*—And in proportion as the large sea-port towns increase in numbers and wealth, in the same proportion will all the country towns increase also in their value and population. No people were ever more blinded to their own interest than the people of this State have been with respect to the new Constitution.—The system of government now proposed is beyond all comparison better for the State of Rhode-Island than the Five Per Cent. Impost System of 1781; yet we find that many who advocated that system are zealous opposers of this. By the regulations to be established, pursuant to the new Constitution, all State impediments or barriers are taken away, and a free, unfettered trade to all the inland country will be opened to the sea-port towns of this State, in the same manner as to Boston, New-York or any other sea-ports on the continent; and of course there will be nothing to prevent the sea-port towns of this State from enjoying all the advantages naturally arising to them in point of situation for commerce. Under the old Confederation, the trade of Rhode-Island government might be confined within her own limits by the restrictions, duties and embargoes of the neighbouring States.—But by the proposed Constitution, the whole extended country is opened to her industrious and enterprizing spirit, and she will experience all the advantages of her sea-ports and harbours which she could if the whole country was within her jurisdiction. The people in the eastern parts of Connecticut, of the western parts of Massachusetts and of the southern parts of Vermont, will find the ports of Rhode-Island State most convenient to resort to for trade, which will therefore naturally center here. Rhode-Island has lost all her trade to Connecticut in consequence of the duties and restrictions imposed by Connecticut on our trade thither—and the citizens of this State have been obliged to pay silver and gold, altogether the last season, for the beef, pork and produce of Connecticut, which were heretofore paid for in goods, imported by our own people.—This is palpably striking to every man's observation, and will account for the vanishing of a great part of the business which used to be transacted in this State, but is now transferred from it.—But if we should join the new Confederacy, our former inland commerce must necessarily be restored, and business of all kinds must revive and flourish through the State.

Under the new Constitution there will be nothing to prevent the town of Providence from becoming a large city.—She will have all the privileges which a town at the head of a great river always has of carrying on manufactures to advantage, and of being the principal mart of the adjacent country on every side.—She is planted near 50 miles inland, towards the heart of the country, from the general line of the ocean. Twice every 24 hours the friendly tide heaves a due proportion of the waters of the Atlantic into the bay, on which the town is built, by the flowing and re-flowing whereof the air is rendered salubrious, and a passage is opened for her navigation and commerce to every quarter of the world. The spirit and enterprize of her merchants have been such as to do honour to themselves, the town, and the State, and have shewn them capable of any commercial undertaking. This town being in the direct way between the cities of New-York and Boston; and the passage from New-York to Providence being cheap, safe, and commodious by water, and the navigation around Nantucket and Cape-Cod dangerous and tedious, will always necessarily cause Providence to be a great thoroughfare for people, goods, and business between the capital towns of Boston and New-York. From all these considerations, is it not probable that, under the new Constitution, the town of Providence will become (what Antwerp was heretofore to the adjacent country on the river Scheldt) *one of the principal marts of New-England*?

But there is another consideration of vast importance to the people of this State, which will probably be a consequence of the new Constitution, in case of its adoption here. The time will come when this country shall have grown populous, rich and powerful, that she will act in some degree as all other commercial countries.—She will in process of time promote the establishment of a NAVY. And there is not an harbour from one end of the continent to the other so likely to be the place of its common rendezvous as THE HARBOUR OF NEW-PORT. The navigation to and from Newport will always be easy and open to the middle and southern States, and to the West Indies. New-England will probably furnish a considerable part of the men and ships.—As they will belong to the continent at large, they will be placed where they can be most safe, most at hand, and best answer the purposes of a navy: —AND NEWPORT MUST THEREFORE BE TO THE UNITED STATES, WHAT BREST IS TO FRANCE, OR SPITHEAD, OR PORTSMOUTH IS TO ENGLAND; and will therefore also probably become a great market town.——From the view we have taken of this State we find it but little more than one great sea-port, eighteen of her thirty towns adjoining upon it; and he must be but a short-sighted politician indeed who cannot see that it will proportionably benefit the people of every town in the State, if they can find a ready market for the articles their industry may enable them to have for sale.

There is another argument in favour of this State's adopting the new Constitution, which I do not recollect to have seen in print, or to have heard orally mentioned.—The smaller States have been much more unanimous on the question of ratifying the new Constitution than the larger ones— *New-Jersey, Delaware* and *Georgia* having adopted it without a dissenting voice, and *Connecticut* and *Maryland* with remarkable unanimity.—There is a natural and powerful reason for this. Those wise and judicious States clearly saw that if the Constitution was rejected, in the hurly-burly of confusion and anarchy which would arise, they should be swallowed up by their more powerful neighbours. They were informed, and they were informed truly, *that it was the wish of the larger States not to allow them an equal voice in the administration of the Continental Government. —That this was the principal source of contention in the great Convention at Philadelphia. —That it was carried to such serious lengths, that the Delegates were more than once on the eve of breaking up, and returning to their several States, with the melancholy tale that they could not agree. —That owing to the unwearied and most indefatigable exertions, day after day, of that patriot and true friend of his country, the Hon. Doctor* SAMUEL W. JOHNSON, *of Connecticut, with a few others, it was finally agreed that the small States should retain their equal voice in the Senate, and should be represented in the House of Deputies in proportion to their numbers. —That it was with very great reluctance the large States agreed to this, which nothing induced them to consent to, but the firm and fixed determination of the smaller States to risque the horrible and tremendous consequences of having no central government, rather than yield that favourite point, so highly important to them.* —This we have found to be one of the principal objections of the antifederalists of Pennsylvania, Massachusetts and Virginia. — It was therefore wise and prudent in the smaller States to agree to this Form of Government, when they were sure that they never could obtain a better, and that attempting it by another Convention would end in worse than Babel confusion. What is more than all, they saw that this Confederacy being once established, *their equal voice in the Senate would be forever secured.* — For notwithstanding this most free and liberal Constitution provides in the 5th article for amendments and alterations *at any time,* on the application of two-thirds of the Legislatures of the several States; yet this is expressly provided, whatever other alterations shall be made, "THAT NO STATE WITHOUT ITS CONSENT SHALL BE DEPRIVED OF ITS EQUAL SUFFRAGE IN THE SENATE." — It would therefore have been extremely injudicious for the smaller States to oppose a Constitution which gives them so respectable an ascendancy, and which when once established they can in no event be deprived of without their consent, though any other alterations may be made. This argument will apply with its full force to the State of Rhode-Island, which has been generally estimated at only a fiftieth part of the Union, and if we include the territory westward of the Ohio, is not a two-hundredth part; yet in the new Confederacy will in the Senate be equal with Massachusetts, Pennsylvania, Virginia, or South-Carolina, and will have a thirteenth part of the controul of the general Government of the Confederacy. — A privilege which one would think she would not hesitate at accepting, *and which it will not be prudent for her too long to delay.* A word to the wise is sufficient. May gracious Heaven grant that party-spirit, feuds and animosities may speedily be banished from among us, and that *we may know the things which belong to our peace, before they are hid from our eyes.*

July 12th, 1788.

"Solon, Junior" [*David Howell*]

Providence Gazette (Rhode Island), August 9, 1788

"In MODERATION *placing all my Glory,*
While Tories call me Whig, and Whigs a Tory."

POPE.

Under all governments where the people have any considerable influence, but especially under democracies, there is a
pervading influential principle superior to all constitutions
and laws on paper—I mean, *the spirit of the times.*

The constitution of England has been nearly the same for
ages, yet how different the condition of the people under it in
different reigns? Even some of their laws lie dormant at times,
maugre all their armies. There is a majesty in the people, and
a sovereignty in their voice, that prostrate all other authority.
Hardy indeed is that Magistrate, who dare execute a law
against the decided opinion of all his neighbours.

I shall not undertake to assert, that this *popular impetus* is
always right—I well know, that bad Kings and bad Ministers
in England have executed the most villainous measures amidst
the acclamations of the people. But these delusions are short-
lived, as being commonly founded in misinformation—or at
least a false notion of their interest; and as soon as the veil is
removed from the minds of the people, their resentment falls
on the authors of the cheat.

The grievances, frauds and irregularities, of the present day,
are the natural result of the depravity of manners and idleness
let in upon us by the late war.—It is no less folly to charge
the whole of them on the deficiency of our present governments or constitutions, than it is to expect a radical cure from
any constitution whatever.—They are evils that grow out of
the manners and habits of the mass of the people—they flow
from causes too operative, it is to be feared, to be suddenly
checked by *any* form of government.

Will not the administration of the new government receive its tincture from this spirit of the times? Will not the people appoint men to administer it in conformity to their views? I am not yet convinced that any government can save us without reformation of manners.

A careful education of youth, and strict family government, will operate like leaven—and lay a foundation to hope for better fruit from the rising generation, than ought to have been expected from the generality of those at present on the stage, had we considered the dissipation of the times when their manners were forming. Children that are taught obedience to their parents, and subordination to their superiors, and in early life initiated in habits of virtue and industry, will not fail to make good citizens.—Civil government may lop off the excrescences of vice; but good education establishes principles in the mind, and prevents the vicious shoots. Let every man, therefore, who glories in being a federalist, consider that true federalism, like charity, ought to begin *at home*.

An abundance of proof lies within our own observation, of the prevalance of the spirit of the times over the dead letter of laws and constitutions.—During the war, and while that was the rage of the day, was not an act passed for putting every freeman in the State under martial law, to be inflicted by a General over whom even the Legislature had no controul?— yet the people bore it—and those who complained of its being *unconstitutional* were answered, that *the safety of the people is the highest law*.

A more recent instance is also in point.—When the rage of the times turned on forcing paper money into circulation— the principles of the *penal laws* became *constitutional*—a trial by jury must be laid aside.—Hardy indeed was that Court, and obstinate to a great degree, which opposed the tide of power—and gave up themselves a sacrifice to a cause by which they could gain nothing! Such were and such are the times—while to fill up the measure of absurdity, the same men who framed that *penal law*, and demolished that Court for not executing it, cry down the New Federal Constitution, because it does not secure *a trial by jury in all cases*!

Had that privilege been ever so safe on paper, and had a phrenzy seized the administration familiar to that under which this State at a certain time laboured, could not a penal law have passed Congress, and been enforced by a Federal Court—or a Federal Army—unless, indeed, they should have found the unconquerable spirit of an ADAMS in that Court, to humble the pride of trumped power?

Whatever the New Federal Constitution is in itself, *its administration* is all that can ever affect the people.—That may be made *safe and easy*—or *cruel and oppressive*, by the administrators for the time being—and much will depend on the *spirit of the times.*

As this Constitution provides the means of altering itself—supposing it right now, the principles and manners of the times would be our chief security for its remaining so—and admitting it to be defective now, is there not reason to hope, that it will soon be made such as the good sense and virtue of the people choose to have it?

> *"For* forms of government *let fools contest:*
> *That form that's* best administer'd *is best."*

While others sharpen the point of the satyric pen, and by stirring up the angry passions of men add fuel to the flame of party—to sooth and sweeten the tempers of fellow-citizens—to warm their bosoms with brotherly love, and to unite them in pursuing the real good of their distracted country, shall be the pleasing task of

SOLON, *junior.*

The Ratifications and Resolutions of Seven State Conventions

adopted February 6–August 2, 1788,
printed early September 1788

RATIFICATION *of the* CONSTITUTION *by the* CONVENTION *of the* STATE *of* NEW-YORK.

We the delegates of the people of the state of New-York, duly elected and met in Convention, having maturely considered the Constitution for the United States of America, agreed to on the seventeenth day of September, in the year one thousand seven hundred and eighty-seven, by the Convention then assembled at Philadelphia, in the Commonwealth of Pennsylvania (a copy whereof precedes these presents) and having also seriously and deliberately considered the present situation of the United States, DO declare and make known,

That all power is originally vested in and consequently derived from the people, and that government is instituted by them for their common interest, protection and security.

That the enjoyment of life, liberty, and the pursuit of happiness are essential rights which every government ought to respect and preserve.

That the powers of government may be reassumed by the people, whensoever it shall become necessary to their happiness; that every power, jurisdiction and right, which is not by the said Constitution clearly delegated to the Congress of the United States, or the departments of the government thereof, remains to the people of the several states, or to their respective state governments, to whom they may have granted the same; and that those clauses in the said constitution, which declare that Congress shall not have or exercise certain powers, do not imply that Congress is entitled to any powers not given by the said Constitution; but such clauses are to be construed either as exceptions to certain specified powers, or as inserted merely for greater caution.

That the people have an equal, natural and unalienable right, freely and peaceably to exercise their religion according to the dictates of conscience; and that no religious sect or society ought to be favored or established by law in preference of others.

That the people have a right to keep and bear arms; that a well regulated militia, including the body of the people *capable of bearing arms*, is the proper, natural, and safe defence of a free state.

That the militia should not be subject to martial law except in time of war, rebellion or insurrection.

That standing armies in time of peace are dangerous to liberty, and ought not to be kept up, except in cases of necessity, and that at all times the military should be under strict subordination to the civil power.

That in the time of peace no soldier ought to be quartered in any house without the consent of the owner; and in time of war only by the civil magistrate, in such manner as the laws may direct.

That no person ought to be taken, imprisoned or disseized of his freehold, or exiled or deprived of his privileges, franchises, life, liberty or property, but by due process of law.

That no person ought to be put twice in jeopardy of life or limb for one and the same offence, nor, unless in case of impeachment, be punished more than once for the same offence.

That every person restrained of his liberty is entitled to an enquiry into the lawfulness of such restraint, and to a removal thereof if unlawful, and that such enquiry and removal ought not to be denied or delayed, except when, on account of public danger, the Congress shall suspend the privilege of the writ of habeas corpus.

That excessive bail ought not to be required, nor excessive fines imposed; nor cruel or unusual punishments inflicted.

That (except in the government of the land and naval forces, and of the militia when in actual service, and in cases of impeachment) a presentment or indictment by a grand jury ought to be observed as a necessary preliminary to the trial of all crimes cognizable by the judiciary of the United States; and such trial should be speedy, public, and by an impartial jury of the county where the crime was committed; and that no person can be found guilty without the unanimous consent of such jury. But in cases of crimes not committed within any county of any of the United States, and in cases of crimes committed within any county in which a general insurrection may prevail, or which may be in the possession of a foreign enemy, the enquiry and trial may be in such county as the Congress shall by law direct; which county in the two cases last mentioned, should be as near as conveniently may be to that county in which the crime may have been committed. And that in all criminal prosecutions, the accused ought to be informed of the cause and nature of his accusation, to be confronted with his accusers and the witnesses against him, to have the means of producing his witnesses, and the assistance of council for his defence, and should not be compelled to give evidence against himself.

That the trial by jury in the extent that it obtains by the common law of England is one of the greatest securities to the rights of a free people, and ought to remain inviolate.

That every freeman has a right to be secure from all unreasonable searches and seizures of his person, his papers or his property: and therefore, that all warrants to search suspected places, or seize any freeman, his papers or property, without information upon oath or affirmation of sufficient cause, are grievous and oppressive; and that all general warrants (or such in which the place or person suspected are not particularly designated) are dangerous and ought not to be granted.

That the people have a right peaceably to assemble together to consult for their common good, or to instruct their representatives, and that every person has a right to petition or apply to the legislature for redress of grievances.

That the freedom of the press ought not to be violated or restrained.

That there should be once in four years, an election of the President and Vice-President, so that no officer who may be appointed by the Congress to act as President, in case of the removal, death, resignation or inability of the President and

Vice-President, can in any case continue to act beyond the termination of the period for which the last President and Vice-President were elected.

That nothing contained in the said Constitution, is to be construed to prevent the legislature of any state from passing laws at its discretion, from time to time, to divide such state into convenient districts, and to apportion its representatives to, and among such districts.

That the prohibition contained in the said Constitution, against *ex post facto* laws, extends only to laws concerning crimes.

That all appeals in causes, determinable according to the course of the common law, ought to be by writ of error, and not otherwise.

That the judicial power of the United States, in cases in which a State may be a party, does not extend to criminal prosecutions, or to authorise any suit, by any person against a State.

That the judicial power of the United States, as to controversies between citizens of the same State, claiming lands under grants of different States, is not to be construed to extend to any other controversies between them, except those which relate to such lands, so claimed, under grants of different States.

That the jurisdiction of the Supreme Court of the United States, or of any other Court to be instituted by the Congress, is not in any case to be encreased, enlarged, or extended, by any fiction, collusion, or mere suggestion; and that no treaty is to be construed, so to operate, as to alter the Constitution of any State.

UNDER these impressions, and declaring that the rights aforesaid cannot be abridged or violated, and that the explanations aforesaid are consistent with the said Constitution, and in confidence that the amendments which shall have been proposed to the said Constitution will receive an early and mature consideration: WE, the said delegates, in the name and in behalf of the People of the State of New-York, DO, by these presents, assent to and RATIFY the said Constitution. In full confidence, nevertheless, that until a Convention shall be called and convened for proposing amendments to the said

Constitution, the militia of this State will not be continued in service out of this State for a longer term than six weeks, without the consent of the legislature thereof; that the Congress will not make or alter any regulation in this State, respecting the times, places, and manner of holding elections for senators or representatives, unless the legislature of this State shall neglect or refuse to make laws or regulations for the purpose, or from any circumstance be incapable of making the same; and that in those cases such power will only be exercised until the legislature of this State shall make provision in the premises; that no excise will be imposed on any article of the growth, production or manufacture of the United States, or any of them, within this State, ardent spirits excepted; and that the Congress will not lay direct taxes within this state, but when the monies arising from the impost and excise shall be insufficient for the public exigencies, nor until Congress shall first have made a requisition upon this State to assess, levy and pay the amount of such requisition made agreeably to the census fixed in the said Constitution, in such way and manner as the legislature of this State shall judge best; but that in such case, if the State shall neglect or refuse to pay its proportion, pursuant to such requisition, then the Congress may assess and levy this State's proportion, together with interest at the rate of six per centum per annum, from the time at which the same was required to be paid.

DONE in Convention at Poughkeepsie, in the county of Dutchess, in the State of New-York, the 26th day of July, in the year of our Lord one thousand seven hundred and eighty-eight.

By order of the Convention,

GEO. CLINTON, President.

Attested, JOHN M'KESSON, } Secretaries.
          ABM. B. BANCKER,

AND the Convention do, in the name and behalf of the people of the State of New-York, enjoin it upon their representatives in the Congress, to exert all their influence and use all reasonable means to obtain a ratification of the following amendments to the said Constitution in the manner prescribed therein; and in all laws to be passed by the Congress in the mean time, to conform to the spirit of the said amendments as far as the Constitution will admit.

That there shall be one representative for every thirty thousand inhabitants, according to the enumeration or census mentioned in the Constitution, until the whole number of representatives amounts to two hundred, after which that number shall be continued or encreased, but not diminished, as Congress shall direct, and according to such ratio as the Congress shall fix, in conformity to the rule prescribed for the apportionment of representatives and direct taxes.

That the Congress do not impose any excise on any article (except ardent spirits) of the growth, production or manufacture of the United States, or any of them.

That Congress do not lay direct taxes, but when the monies arising from the impost and excise, shall be insufficient for the public exigencies, nor then, until Congress shall first have made a requisition upon the States, to assess, levy and pay their respective proportion of such requisition, agreeably to the census fixed in the said Constitution, in such way and manner, as the Legislature of the respective States shall judge best; and in such case, if any State shall neglect or refuse to pay its proportion, pursuant to such requisition, then Congress may assess and levy such State's proportion, together with interest, at the rate of six per centum, per annum, from the time of payment, prescribed in such requisition.

That the Congress shall not make or alter any regulation, in any state, respecting the times, places and manner of holding elections for senators or representatives, unless the legislature of such state shall neglect or refuse to make laws or regulations for the purpose, or from any circumstance, be incapable of making the same, and then only, until the legislature of such state shall make provision in the premises; provided that Congress may prescribe the time for the election of representatives.

That no persons, except natural born citizens, or such as were citizens on or before the fourth day of July, 1776, or such as held commissions under the United States during the war, and have at any time, since the 4th of July, 1776, become citizens of one or other of the United States, and who shall be freeholders, shall be eligible to the places of President, Vice-President, or members of either house of the Congress of the United States.

That the Congress do not grant monopolies, or erect any company with exclusive advantages of commerce.

That no standing army or regular troops shall be raised, or kept up in time of peace, without the consent of two thirds of the senators and representatives present in each house.

That no money be borrowed on the credit of the United States without the assent of two thirds of the senators and representatives present in each house.

That the Congress shall not declare war without the concurrence of two thirds of the senators and representatives present in each house.

That the privilege of the *Habeas Corpus* shall not by any law be suspended for a longer term than six months, or until twenty days after the meeting of the Congress next following the passing the act for such suspension.

That the right of the Congress to exercise exclusive legislation over such district, not exceeding ten miles square, as may by cession of a particular state, and the acceptance of Congress, become the seat of the government of the United States, shall not be so exercised as to exempt the inhabitants of such district from paying the like taxes, imposts, duties and excises, as shall be imposed on the other inhabitants of the state in which such district may be; and that no person shall be privileged within the said district from arrest for crimes committed, or debts contracted out of the said district.

That the right of exclusive legislation with respect to such places as may be purchased for the erection of forts, magazines, arsenals, dock yards, and other needful buildings, shall not authorise the Congress to make any law to prevent the laws of the states respectively in which they may be, from extending to such places in all civil and criminal matters, except as to such persons as shall be in the service of the United States; nor to them with respect to crimes committed without such places.

That the compensation for the senators and representatives be ascertained by standing laws; and that no alteration of the existing rate of compensation shall operate for the benefit of the representatives, until after a subsequent election shall have been had.

That the journals of the Congress shall be published at least once a year, with the exception of such parts relating to treaties or military operations, as in the judgment of either house shall require secrecy: and that both houses of Congress shall always keep their doors open during their session, unless the business may in their opinion require secrecy. That the yeas and nays shall be entered on the journals whenever two members in either house may require it.

That no capitation tax shall ever be laid by the Congress.

That no person be eligible as a senator for more than six years in any term of twelve years; and that the legislatures of the respective states may recall their senators or either of them, and elect others in their stead, to serve the remainder of the time for which the senators so recalled were appointed.

That no senator or representative shall, during the time for which he was elected, be appointed to any office under the authority of the United States.

That the authority given to the executives of the states to fill the vacancies of senators be abolished, and that such vacancies be filled by the respective legislatures.

That the power of Congress to pass uniform laws concerning bankruptcy, shall only extend to merchants and other traders; and that the states respectively may pass laws for the relief of other insolvent debtors.

That no person shall be eligible to the office of president of the United States, a third time.

That the executive shall not grant pardons for treason, unless with the consent of the Congress; but may, at his discretion, grant reprieves to persons convicted of treason, until their causes can be laid before the Congress.

That the president or person exercising his powers for the time being, shall not command an army in the field in person, without the previous desire of the Congress.

That all letters patent, commissions, pardons, writs and process of the United States, shall run in the name of *the People of the United States*, and be tested in the name of the President of the United States, or the person exercising his powers for the time being, or the first judge of the court out of which the same shall issue, as the case may be.

That the Congress shall not constitute, ordain, or establish any tribunals or inferior courts, with any other than appellate jurisdiction, except such as may be necessary for the trial of causes of admiralty, and maritime jurisdiction, and for the trial of piracies and felonies committed on the high seas; and in all other cases to which the judicial power of the United States extends, and in which the supreme court of the United States has not original jurisdiction, the causes shall be heard, tried, and determined, in some one of the state courts, with the right of appeal to the supreme court of the United States, or other proper tribunal to be established for that purpose, by the Congress, with such exceptions, and under such regulations as the Congress shall make.

That the court for the trial of impeachments shall consist of the senate, the judges of the supreme court of the United States, and the first or senior judge, for the time being, of the highest court of general and ordinary common law jurisdiction, in each state; that the Congress shall, by standing laws, designate the courts in the respective states answering this description, and in the states having no courts exactly answering this description, shall designate some other court, preferring such, if any there be, whose judge or judges may hold their places during good behaviour: provided that no more than one judge, other than judges of the supreme court of the United States, shall come from one state. That the Congress be authorised to pass laws for compensating the said judges for such services, and for compelling their attendance; and that a majority at least of the said judges shall be requisite to constitute the said court. That no person impeached shall sit as a member thereof—that each member shall, previous to the entering upon any trial, take an oath or affirmation, honestly and impartially to hear and determine the cause; and that a majority of the members present shall be necessary to a conviction.

That persons aggrieved by any judgment, sentence or decree of the supreme court of the United States, in any cause in which that court has original jurisdiction, with such exceptions and under such regulations as the Congress shall make concerning the same, shall upon application have a commission, to be issued by the President of the United States, to such men learned in the law as he shall nominate, and by and with the advice and consent of the senate appoint not less than seven, authorising such commissioners, or any seven or more of them, to correct the errors in such judgment, or to review such sentence, and decree as the case may be, and to do justice to the parties in the premises.

That no judge of the supreme court of the United States shall hold any other office under the United States, or any of them.

That the judicial power of the United States shall extend to no controversies respecting land, unless it relate to claims of territory or jurisdiction between states, or to claims of land between individuals, or between states and individuals under the grants of different states.

That the militia of any state shall not be compelled to serve without the limits of the state for a longer term than six weeks, without the consent of the legislature thereof.

That the words *without the consent of the Congress,* in the seventh clause of the ninth section of the first article of the constitution be expunged.

That the senators and representatives, and all executive and judicial officers of the United States, shall be bound by oath or affirmation not to infringe or violate the constitutions or rights of the respective states.

That the legislatures of the respective states may make provision by law, that the electors of the election districts, to be by them appointed, shall choose a citizen of the United States, who shall have been an inhabitant of such district for the term of one year immediately preceding the time of his election, for one of the representatives of such state.

DONE in Convention, at Poughkeepsie, in the county of Dutchess, in the State of New-York, the 26th day of July, in the year of our Lord one thousand seven hundred and eighty-eight.

By order of the Convention

GEO. CLINTON, President.

Attested, JOHN M'KESSON, } Secretaries.
ABM. B. BANCKER,

In Convention at Poughkeepsie, state of New-York,
July 26, 1788.
(C I R C U L A R)

SIR:

We the members of the Convention of this state, have deliberately and maturely considered the Constitution proposed for the United States. Several articles in it appears so exceptionable to a majority of us, that nothing but the fullest confidence of obtaining a revision of them by a General Convention, and an invincible reluctance to separating from our sister states, could have prevailed upon a sufficient number to ratify it, without stipulating for previous amendments. We all unite in opinion that such a revision will be necessary to recommend it to the approbation and support of a numerous body of our constituents. We observe that amendments have been proposed, and are anxiously desired by several of the states as well as by this, and we think it of great importance that effectual measures be immediately taken for calling a Convention to meet at a period not far remote: for we are convinced, that the apprehensions and discontents which those articles occasion cannot be removed or allayed unless an act to provide for it, be among the first that shall be passed by the new Congress. As it is essential that an application for the purpose should be made to them by two thirds of the states, we earnestly exhort and request the legislature of your state to take the earliest opportunity of making it. We are persuaded that a similar one will be made by our legislature at their next session, and we ardently wish and desire, that the other states may concur in adopting and promoting the measure. It cannot be necessary to observe that no government however constructed can operate well unless it possesses the confidence and good will of the great body of the people; and as we desire nothing more than that the amendments proposed by this or other states be submitted to the consideration and decision of a General Convention, we flatter ourselves that motives of mutual affection and conciliation will conspire with the obvious dictates of sound policy to induce even such of the states as may be content with every article in the Constitution, to gratify the reasonable desires of that numerous class of American citizens, who are anxious to obtain amendments of some of them.

Our amendments will manifest that none of them originated in local views as they are such as, if acceded to, must equally affect every state in the Union. Our attachment to our sister states and the confidence we repose in them cannot be more forcibly demonstrated, than by acceding to a government, which many of us think very imperfect, and devolving the power of determining whether that government shall be rendered perpetual in its present form, or altered agreeable to our wishes, on a minority of the states with whom we unite.

We request the favor of your Excellency to lay this letter before the legislature of your state, and we are persuaded that your regard for our national harmony and good government will induce you to promote a measure which we are unanimous in thinking very conducive to those interesting objects.

We have the honor to be, With the highest respect, Your Excellency's most obedient servants,

By the unanimous order of the Convention,

GEO. CLINTON, President.

His Excellency the GOVERNOR of VIRGINIA.

———————

Ratification of the Fœderal Constitution of the Commonwealth of Massachusetts,

In CONVENTION of the Delegates of the People of the Commonwealth of MASSACHUSETTS, Feb. 6, 1788.

The Convention having impartially discussed and fully considered the Constitution for the United States of America, reported to Congress by the Convention of Delegates from the United States of America, and submitted to us by a resolution of the General Court of the said Commonwealth, passed the 25th day of October last past; and acknowledging with grateful hearts the goodness of the supreme ruler of the universe, in affording the people of the United States, in the course of his providence, an opportunity, deliberately and peaceably, without fraud or surprise, of entering into an explicit and solemn compact with each other, by assenting to and ratifying a new Constitution, in order to form a more perfect union, establish justice, insure domestic tranquility, provide for the common defence, promote the general welfare, and secure the blessings of liberty to themselves and their posterity; do, in the name and in behalf of the people of the commonwealth of Massachusetts, *assent to* and *ratify* the said *Constitution for the United States of America*.

And as it is the opinion of this Convention, that certain amendments and alterations in the said Constitution would remove the fears and quiet the apprehensions of many of the good people of this commonwealth, and more effectually guard against an undue administration of the Fœderal Government; the Convention do therefore recommend that the following alterations and provisions be introduced into the said Constitution:

First, That it be explicitly declared, that all powers not expressly delegated by the aforesaid Constitution, are reserved to the several states, to be by them exercised.

Secondly, That there shall be one representative to every thirty thousand persons, according to the census mentioned in the Constitution, until the whole number of the representatives amount to 200.

Thirdly, That Congress do not exercise the powers vested in them by the 4th sect. of 1st art. but in cases when a state neglect or refuse to make regulations therein mentioned, or shall make regulations subversive of the rights of the people, to a free and equal representation in Congress, agreeable to the Constitution.

Fourthly, That Congress do not lay direct taxes but when the monies arising from the impost and excise are insufficient for the public exigencies; nor then, until Congress shall have first made a requisition upon the States, to assess, levy, and pay their respective proportions of such requisition, agreeably to the census fixed in the said Constitution, in such way and manner as the legislature of the state shall think best—and in such case, if any state shall neglect or refuse to pay its proportion, pursuant to such requisition, then Congress may assess and levy such state's proportion, together with interest thereon, at the rate of six per cent. per annum, from the time of payment prescribed in such requisition.

Fifthly, That Congress erect no company of merchants, with exclusive advantages of commerce.

Sixthly, That no person shall be tried for any crime by which he may incur an infamous punishment, or loss of life, until he be first indicted by a grand jury, except in such cases as may arise in the government and regulation of the land and naval forces.

Seventhly, The Supreme Judicial Fœderal Court shall have no jurisdiction of causes between citizens of different states, unless the matter in dispute, whether it concerns the reality or personality, be of the value of 3000 dollars at the least; nor shall the fœderal judicial powers extend to any actions between citizens of different states, where the matter in dispute, whether it concerns the reality or personality, is not of the value of 1500 dollars at the least.

Eighthly, In civil actions, between citizens of different states, every issue of fact arising in actions at common law shall be tried by a jury, if the parties, or either of them, request it.

Ninthly, Congress shall, at no time, consent, that any person, holding an office of trust or profit, under the United States, shall accept of a title of nobility, or any other title or office, from any king, prince, or foreign state.

AND the Convention do, in the name and in behalf of the people of this commonwealth, enjoin it upon their representatives in Congress, at all times, until the alterations and provisions aforesaid have been considered, agreeably to the fifth article of the said Constitution, to exert all their influence, and use all reasonable and legal methods to obtain a ratification of the said alterations and provisions, in such manner as is provided in said article.

And that the United States in Congress assembled, may have due notice of the assent and ratification of said Constitution by this Convention;

It is RESOLVED, That the assent and ratification aforesaid be engrossed on parchment, together with the recommendation and injunction aforesaid, and with this resolution, and that his Excellency JOHN HANCOCK, Esq; President, and the Honorable WILLIAM CUSHING, Esq; Vice-President of this Convention, transmit the same, countersigned by the Secretary of the Convention, under their hands and seals, to the United States in Congress assembled.

(Signed)   JOHN HANCOCK, President.
                            W. CUSHING, Vice-President.
(Countersigned)
GEO. RICHD. MINOT, Secretary.

———————

IN CONVENTION of the DELEGATES of the People of the State of NEW-HAMPSHIRE, June the Twenty-first, 1788.

The Convention having impartially discussed and fully considered the Constitution for the United States of America, reported to the Congress by the Convention of Delegates from the United States of America, and submitted to us by a resolution of the General Court of said State, passed the fourteenth day of December last past, and acknowledging with grateful hearts the goodness of the Supreme Ruler of the Universe, in affording the people of the United States in the course of his Providence, an opportunity, deliberately and peaceably, without fraud or surprise, of entering into an explicit and solemn compact with each other, by assenting to and ratifying a new Constitution, in order to form a more perfect Union, establish justice, ensure domestic tranquility, provide for the common defence, promote the general welfare, and secure the blessings of liberty to themselves and their posterity—DO, in the name and behalf of the people of the State of New-Hampshire, assent to and ratify the said Constitution for the United States of America. And as it is the opinion of this Convention that certain amendments and alterations in the said Constitution would remove the fears and quiet the apprehensions of many of the good people of this state, and more effectually guard against an undue administration of the Fœderal Government, the Convention do therefore recommend that the following alterations and provisions be introduced into the said Constitution:

1st. That it be explicitly declared, that all powers not expressly and particularly delegated by the aforesaid constitution, are reserved to the several states, to be by them exercised.

2d. That there shall be one representative to every 30,000 persons, according to the census mentioned in the constitution, until the whole number of the representatives amounts to 200.

3d. That Congress do not exercise the powers vested in them by the 4th section of the 1st article but in cases when a state shall neglect or refuse to make regulations therein mentioned, or shall make regulations contrary to a free and equal representation.

4th. That Congress do not lay direct taxes, but when the money arising from the impost, excise, and their other resources are insufficient for the public exigencies; nor then, until Congress shall have first made a requisition upon the states to assess, levy and pay their respective proportions of such requisition, agreeably to the census fixed in the said constitution, in such way and manner as the legislature of the state shall think best; and in such case if any state shall neglect or refuse to pay its proportion, pursuant to such requisition, then Congress may assess and levy such state's proportion—together with interest thereon at the rate of 6 per cent. per annum, from the time of payment prescribed in such requisition.

5th. That Congress erect no company of merchants with exclusive advantages of commerce.

6th. That no person shall be tried for any crime by which he may incur an infamous punishment, or loss of life, until he be first indicted by a grand jury; except in such cases as may arise in the government and regulation of the land and naval forces.

7th. All common law causes between citizens of different states shall be commenced in the common law courts of the respective states—and no appeal shall be allowed to the fœderal court in such cases, unless the sum or value of the thing in controversy amount to 3000 dollars.

8th. In civil actions between citizens of different states, every issue of fact arising in actions at common law, shall be tried by a jury, if the parties or either of them request it.

9th. Congress shall at no time consent that any person holding an office of trust or profit under the United States, shall accept of a title of nobility, or any other title or office from any king, prince, or foreign state.

10th. That no standing army shall be kept up in time of peace, unless with the consent of three-quarters of the members of each branch of Congress—nor shall soldiers in time of peace be quartered upon private houses, without the consent of the owners.

11th. Congress shall make no laws touching religion, or to infringe the rights of conscience.

12th. Congress shall never disarm any citizen, unless such as are or have been in actual rebellion.

AND THE CONVENTION DO, in the name and behalf of the people of this State, enjoin it upon the Representatives in Congress, at all times until the alterations and provisions aforesaid have been considered agreeably to the fifth article of the said constitution, to exert all their influence, and use all reasonable and legal methods to obtain a ratification of the said alterations and provisions, in such manner as is provided in the said article. And, that the United States in Congress assembled may have due notice of the assent and ratification of the said Constitution by this Convention—It is resolved that the assent and ratification aforesaid, be engrossed on parchment, together with the recommendation and injunction aforesaid, and with this resolution: and that John Sullivan, Esquire, President of Convention, and John Langdon, Esquire, President of the State, transmit the same, countersigned by the Secretary of Convention and the Secretary of the State, under their hands and seals, to the United States in Congress assembled.

JOHN SULLIVAN, President of the Convention.
JOHN LANGDON, President of the State
By Order,   JOHN CALFE, Secretary of Convention.
JOSEPH PEARSON, Secretary of State.

In CONVENTION of the DELEGATES of the PEOPLE of the STATE of MARYLAND, April 28, 1788.

We, the Delegates of the People of the state of Maryland, having fully considered the Constitution of the United States of America, reported by Congress, by the Convention of deputies from the United States of America, held in Philadelphia, on the 17th September, 1787, and submitted to us by a resolution of the General Assembly of Maryland, in November session, 1787, do, for ourselves, and in the name and on the behalf of the people of this State, assent to and ratify the said Constitution. In witness whereof we have hereunto subscribed our names,

TUESDAY, *April* 29, 1788.

RESOLVED, that the proceedings of this Convention to the vote for assenting to and ratifying the proposed plan of fœderal government for the United States, and the yeas and nays be fairly engrossed, signed by the President, and attested by the clerk and assistant clerk: And that the President request the Governor and Council, to transmit the same proceedings, together with the ratification of the same fœderal government, subscribed by the members of this Convention, to the United States in Congress assembled.

The Committee were now called upon to report, when the house was informed that, although the Committee had acceded to several of the propositions referred to them, nevertheless they could come to no agreement to make any report.

Upon this a vote of thanks was moved to the President and carried.

It was then moved "that this Convention adjourn without day." The yeas and nays appear as follow:— YEAS 47— NAYS 27.

Proposed Amendments.

THAT it be declared that all persons entrusted with the legislative or executive powers of government, are the trustees and servants of the public, and as such accountable for their conduct:

WHEREFORE, whenever the ends of government are preverted, and public liberty manifestly endangered, and all other means of redress are ineffectual, the people may, and of right ought, to object to, reform the old, or establish a new government—That the doctrine of non-resistance against arbitrary power and oppression is absurd, slavish, and destructive of the good and happiness of mankind—That it be declared, that every man hath a right to petition the legislature, for the redress of grievances, in a peaceable and orderly manner— That in all criminal prosecutions every man hath a right to be informed of the accusation against him, to have a copy of the indictment or charge in due time (if required) to prepare for his defence, to be allowed council, to be confronted with the witnesses against him, to have process for his witnesses, to examine the witnesses for and against him, on oath, and to a speedy trial, by an impartial jury.

That no freeman ought to be taken, or imprisoned, or deprived of his freehold, liberties or privileges, or outlawed or exiled, or in any manner destroyed, or deprived of his life, liberty or property, but by the lawful judgment of his Peers, or by the law of the land.

That no power of suspending laws, or the execution of laws, unless derived from the legislature, ought to be exercised or allowed.

That all warrants, without oath, or affirmation of a person conscientiously scrupulous of taking an oath, to search suspected places, or to seize any person, or his property, are grievous and oppressive; and all general warrants, to search suspected places, or to apprehend any person suspected, without naming or describing the place or person in special, are dangerous and ought not to be granted.

That there be no appeal to the Supreme Court of Congress in a criminal case.

Congress shall have no power to alter or change the regulations respecting the times, places, or manner of holding elections for senators or representatives.

All imposts and duties laid by Congress, shall be placed to the credit of the state in which the same be collected, and shall be deducted out of such state's quota of the common or general expences of government.

No member of Congress shall be eligible to any office of trust, or profit, under Congress, during the time for which he shall be chosen.

That there be no national religion established by law; but that all persons be equally entitled to protection in their religious liberty.

That Congress shall not lay direct taxes on land, or other property, without a previous requisition of the respective quotas of the states, and a failing, within a limited time, to comply therewith.

In all cases of trespasses, torts, abuses of power, personal wrongs, and injuries done on land, or within the body of a county, the party injured shall be entitled to trial by jury, in the state where the offence shall be committed; and the state courts, in such cases, shall have concurrent jurisdiction with the Fœderal Courts; and there shall be no appeal, excepting on matters of law.

That the Supreme Fœderal Court shall not admit of fictions, to extend its jurisdiction; nor shall citizens of the same state, having controversies with each other, be suffered to make collusive assignments of their rights, to citizens of another state, for the purpose of defeating the jurisdiction of the state courts; nor shall any matter, or question, already determined in the state courts, be revived or agitated in the Fœderal Courts; that there be no appeal from law, or fact, to the Supreme Court, where the claim, or demand, does not exceed three hundred pounds sterling.

That no standing army shall be kept up in time of peace, unless with the consent of three-fourths of the members of each branch of Congress: Nor shall soldiers, in time of peace, be quartered upon private houses, without the consent of the owners.

No law of Congress, or treaties, shall be effectual to repeal or abrogate the constitutions, or bill of rights, of the states, or any of them, or any part of the said constitutions, or bills of rights.

Militia not to be subject to the rules of Congress, nor marched out of the state, without consent of the legislature of such state.

That Congress have no power to lay a poll tax.

That the people have a right to freedom of speech, of writing and publishing their sentiments, and therefore that the freedom of the press ought not to be restrained, and the printing presses ought to be free to examine the proceedings of government, and the conduct of its officers.

That Congress shall exercise no power but what is expressly delegated by the Constitution.

That the President shall not command the army, in person, without the consent of Congress.

> True extract from the minutes of the Convention, of the State of Maryland.
>
> WILLIAM HARWOOD, Clk. Con.

Done in Convention, April 26, 1788.

RATIFICATION of the CONSTITUTION, by
the STATE of SOUTH-CAROLINA, May 23, 1788.

Yesterday the Convention determined that a Committee should be appointed to consider if any and what amendments ought to be made in the new Constitution, previous to putting the grand question.

The members of the Committee were Mr. E. Rutledge, Mr. Bee, Mr. Pringle, Judge Pendleton, Rev. Mr. Cummings, Mr. Hunter, Col. Huger, Col. Hill, and Mr. William Wilson.

The Committee reported in nearly the following words:

As the obtaining the following amendments *would tend to remove the apprehensions of some of the good people of this state*, and confirm the blessings intended by the said Constitution, We do declare, that as the right to regulate elections to the Fœderal Legislature, and to direct the manner, times, and places of holding the same is, and ought to remain to all posterity, a fundamental right,

Resolved, That in the opinion of this Convention, the general government of the United States ought not to interfere therein, but in cases where the legislatures shall refuse or neglect to execute that branch of their duty to the Constitution.

Resolved, That in the opinion of this Convention, the 3d section of article 6th, should be amended, by inserting the word "other" between the words *no* and *religious*.

Resolved, That the general government of the United States ought never to impose direct taxes but where the monies arising from the duties, imposts and excise are insufficient for the public exigencies; nor then, until Congress shall have made a requisition upon the states to assess, levy, and pay their respective proportions of such requisitions, and in case such state shall neglect or refuse to pay its proportion, pursuant to such requisition, then Congress may assess and levy such state's proportion, together with interest thereon, after the rate of six per cent. per annum, from the time of payment prescribed by such requisitions.

Resolved, That the states respectively, do retain every power not expressly delegated by this Constitution to the general government of the Union.

Resolved, That it be a standing instruction to such delegates as many hereafter be elected, to represent this state in the general government, to use every possible and necessary exertion to obtain an alteration of the Constitution, conformable to the aforegoing resolutions.

May 24. Yesterday the Convention went through the new Constitution, and also the proposed amendments published yesterday; after which it was moved, That this Convention do assent to and ratify the Constitution agreed to on the 17th of September last, by the Convention of the United States of America held at Philadelphia.

The yeas and nays being called for, there appeared to be, for the ratification, 149. Against it, 73.

Form of Ratification, which was read and agreed to by the Convention of Virginia.

We the Delegates of the people of Virginia, duly elected in pursuance of a recommendation from the General Assembly, and now met in Convention, having fully and freely investigated and discussed the proceedings of the Fœderal Convention, and being prepared as well as the most mature deliberation hath enabled us, to decide thereon, DO, in the name and in behalf of the people of Virginia, declare and make known that the powers granted under the Constitution, being derived from the people of the United States may be resumed by them whensoever the same shall be perverted to their injury or oppression, and that every power not granted thereby remains with them and at their will: that therefore no right of any denomination, can be cancelled, abridged, restrained or modified, by the Congress, by the senate or house of representatives acting in any capacity, by the President or any department or officer of the United States, except in those instances in which power is given by the Constitution for those purposes: and that among other essential rights, the liberty of conscience and of the press cannot be cancelled, abridged, restrained or modified by any authority of the United States.

With these impressions, with a solemn appeal to the searcher of hearts for the purity of our intentions, and under the conviction, that, whatsoever imperfections may exist in the Constitution, ought rather to be examined in the mode prescribed therein, than to bring the Union into danger by a delay, with a hope of obtaining amendments, previous to the ratification:

We the said Delegates, in the name and in behalf of the People of Virginia, do by these presents assent to, and ratify the Constitution recommended on the seventeenth day of September, one thousand seven hundred and eighty-seven, by the Fœderal Convention for the Government of the United States; hereby announcing to all those whom it may concern, that the said Constitution is binding upon the said People, according to an authentic copy hereto annexed, in the words following:

[*Here followed the Constitution.*]

Mr. Wythe reported, from the Committee appointed, such amendments to the proposed Constitution of Government for the United States, as were by them deemed necessary to be recommended to the consideration of the Congress which shall first assemble under the said Constitution, to be acted upon according to the mode prescribed in the fifth article thereof; and he read the same in his place, and afterwards delivered them in at the clerk's table, where the same were again read, and are as followeth;

That there be a Declaration or Bill of Rights asserting and securing from encroachment the essential and unalienable rights of the people in some such manner as the following:

1st. That there are certain natural rights of which men, when they form a social compact, cannot deprive or divest their posterity, among which are the enjoyment of life, and liberty, with the means of acquiring, possessing and protecting property, and pursuing and obtaining happiness and safety.

2d. That all power is naturally vested in, and consequently derived from, the people; that magistrates therefore are their trustees, and agents, and at all times amenable to them.

3d. That government ought to be instituted for the common benefit, protection and security of the people; and that the doctrine of non-resistance against arbitrary power and oppression, is absurd, slavish, and destructive to the good and happiness of mankind.

4th. That no man or set of men are entitled to exclusive or separate public emoluments or privileges from the community, but in consideration of public services; which not being descendible, neither ought the offices of magistrate, legislator or judge, or any other public office to be hereditary.

5th. That the legislative, executive, and judiciary powers of government should be separate and distinct, and that the members of the two first may be restrained from oppression by feeling and participating the public burthens, they should at fixed periods be reduced to a private station, return into the mass of the people; and the vacancies be supplied by certain and regular elections; in which all or any part of the former members to be eligible or ineligible, as the rules of the Constitution of Government, and the laws shall direct.

6th. That elections of representatives in the legislature ought to be free and frequent, and all men having sufficient evidence of permanent common interest with, and attachment to the community, ought to have the right of suffrage: and no aid, charge, tax or fee can be set, rated, or levied upon the people without their own consent, or that of their representatives, so elected, nor can they be bound by any law, to which they have not in like manner assented for the public good.

7th. That all power of suspending laws, or the execution of laws by any authority without the consent of the representatives, of the people in the legislature, is injurious to their rights, and ought not to be exercised.

8th. That in all criminal and capital prosecutions, a man hath a right to demand the cause and nature of his accusation, to be confronted with the accusers and witnesses, to call for evidence and be allowed counsel in his favor, and to a fair and speedy trial by an impartial jury of his vicinage, without whose unanimous consent he cannot be found guilty (except in the government of the land and naval forces) nor can he be compelled to give evidence against himself.

9th. That no freeman ought to be taken, imprisoned, or disseized of his freehold, liberties, privileges or franchises, or outlawed, or exiled, or in any manner destroyed or deprived of his life, liberty, or property, but by the law of the land.

10th. That every freeman restrained of his liberty is entitled to a remedy to enquire into the lawfulness thereof, and to remove the same, if unlawful, and that such remedy ought not to be denied nor delayed.

11th. That in controversies respecting property, and in suits between man and man, the ancient trial by jury, is one of the greatest securities to the rights of the people, and ought to remain sacred and inviolable.

12th. That every freeman ought to find a certain remedy by recourse to the laws for all injuries and wrongs he may receive in his person, property, or character. He ought to obtain right and justice freely without sale, completely and without denial, promptly and without delay, and that all establishments, or regulations contravening these rights, are oppressive and unjust.

13th. That excessive bail ought not to be required, nor excessive fines imposed, nor cruel and unusual punishments inflicted.

14th. That every freeman has a right to be secure from all unreasonable searches, and seizures of his person, his papers, and property; all warrants therefore to search suspected places, or seize any freeman, his papers or property, without information upon oath (or affirmation of a person religiously scrupulous of taking an oath) of legal and sufficient cause, are grievous and oppressive, and all general warrants to search suspected places, or to apprehend any suspected person without specially naming or describing the place or person, are dangerous and ought not to be granted.

15th. That the people have a right peaceably to assemble together to consult for the common good, or to instruct their representatives; and that every freeman has a right to petition or apply to the Legislature for redress of grievances.

16th. That the people have a right to freedom of speech, and of writing and publishing their sentiments; that the freedom of the press is one of the greatest bulwarks of liberty, and ought not to be violated.

17th. That the people have a right to keep and bear arms: that a well regulated militia composed of the body of the people trained to arms, is the proper, natural and safe defence of a free state. That standing armies in time of peace are dangerous to liberty, and therefore ought to be avoided, as far as the circumstances and protection of the community will admit; and that in all cases, the military should be under strict subordination to and governed by the civil power.

18th. That no soldier in time of peace ought to be quartered in any house without the consent of the owner, and in time of war in such manner only as the laws direct.

19th. That any person religiously scrupulous of bearing arms ought to be exempted upon payment of an equivalent to employ another to bear arms in his stead.

20th. That religion, or the duty which we owe to our Creator, and the manner of discharging it, can be directed only by reason and conviction, not by force or violence, and therefore all men have an equal, natural and unalienable right to the free exercise of religion according to the dictates of conscience, and that no particular religious sect or society ought to be favored or established by law in preferrence to others.

AMENDMENTS to the CONSTITUTION.

1st. That each state in the Union shall respectively retain every power, jurisdiction and right, which is not by this Constitution delegated to the Congress of the United States, or to the departments of the Fœderal Government.

2d. That there shall be one representative for every thirty thousand, according to the enumeration or census mentioned in the Constitution, until the whole number of representatives amounts to two hundred; after which that number shall be encreased as Congress shall direct, upon the principles fixed in the Constitution, by apportioning the representatives of each state to some greater number of people from time to time as population encreases.

3d. When the Congress shall lay direct taxes or excises, they shall immediately inform the Executive power of each State, of the quota of such state according to the census herein directed, which is proposed to be thereby raised; and if the Legislature of any State shall pass a law which shall be effectual for raising such quota at the time required by Congress, the taxes and excises laid by Congress, shall not be collected in such State.

4th. That the members of the Senate and House of Representatives shall be ineligible to, and incapable of holding any civil office under the authority of the United States, during the time for which they shall respectively be elected.

5th. That the journals of the proceedings of the Senate and House of Representatives shall be published at least once in every year, except such parts thereof relating to treaties, alliances, or military operations, as in their judgment require secrecy.

6th. That a regular statement and account of the receipts and expenditures of all public money, shall be published at least once in every year.

7th. That no commercial treaty shall be ratified without the concurrence of two-thirds of the whole number of the members of the Senate; and no treaty, ceding, contracting, restraining or suspending the territorial rights or claims of the United States, or any of them, or their, or any of their rights or claims to fishing in the American seas, or navigating the American rivers, shall be made, but in cases of the most urgent and extreme necessity, nor shall any such treaty be ratified without the concurrence of three-fourths of the whole number of the members of both houses respectively.

8th. That no navigation law or law regulating commerce shall be passed without the consent of two-thirds of the members present, in both houses.

9th. That no standing army or regular troops shall be raised, or kept up in time of peace, without the consent of two-thirds of the members present, in both houses.

10th. That no soldier shall be inlisted for any longer term than four years, except in time of war, and then for no longer term than the continuance of the war.

11th. That each state respectively shall have the power to

provide for organizing, arming, and disciplining its own militia, whensoever Congress shall omit or neglect to provide for the same. That the militia shall not be subject to martial law, except when in actual service in time of war, invasion or rebellion, and when not in the actual service of the United States, shall be subject only to such fines, penalties and punishments as shall be directed or inflicted by the laws of its own state.

12th. That the exclusive power of legislation given to Congress over the Fœderal Town and its adjacent district, and other places, purchased or to be purchased by Congress of any of the states, shall extend only to such regulations as respect the police and good government thereof.

13th. That no person shall be capable of being President of the United States for more than eight years in any term of sixteen years.

14th. That the judicial power of the United States shall be vested in one Supreme Court, and in such Courts of Admiralty as Congress may from time to time ordain and establish in any of the different states: The judicial power shall extend to all cases in law and equity arising under treaties made, or which shall be made under the authority of the United States; to all cases affecting ambassadors, other foreign ministers and consuls; to all cases of admiralty and maritime jurisdiction; to controversies to which the United States shall be a party; to controversies between two or more states, and between parties claiming lands under the grants of different states. In all cases affecting ambassadors, other foreign ministers and consuls, and those in which a state shall be a party, the Supreme Court shall have original jurisdiction; in all other cases before mentioned, the Supreme Court shall have appellate jurisdiction, as to matters of law only: except in cases of equity, and of admiralty and maritime jurisdiction, in which the Supreme Court shall have appellate jurisdiction both as to law and fact, with such exceptions and under such regulations as the Congress shall make: But the judicial power of the United States shall extend to no case where the cause of action shall have originated before the ratification of this Constitution; except in disputes between states about their territory; disputes between persons claiming lands under the grants of different states, and suits for debts due to the United States.

15th. That in criminal prosecutions, no man shall be restrained in the exercise of the usual and accustomed right of challenging or excepting to the jury.

16th. That Congress shall not alter, modify, or interfere in the times, places, or manner of holding elections for Senators and Representatives, or either of them, except when the Legislature of any state shall neglect, refuse, or be disabled by invasion or rebellion to prescribe the same.

17th. That those clauses which declare that Congress shall not exercise certain powers, be not interpreted in any manner whatsoever, to extend the powers of Congress; but that they may be construed either as making exceptions to the specified powers where this shall be the case, or otherwise, as inserted merely for greater caution.

18th. That the laws ascertaining the compensation of senators and representatives for their services, be postponed in their operation, until after the election of representatives immediately succeeding the passing thereof; that excepted, which shall first be passed on the subject.

19th. That some tribunal other than the senate be provided for trying impeachments of senators.

20th. That the salary of a judge shall not be encreased or diminished during his continuance in office otherwise than by general regulations of salary, which may take place on a revision of the subject at stated periods of not less than seven years, to commence from the time such salaries shall be first ascertained by Congress.

AND the Convention do, in the name and behalf of the people of this commonwealth, enjoin it upon their representatives in Congress to exert all their influence and use all reasonable and legal methods to obtain a RATIFICATION of the foregoing alterations and provisions in the manner provided by the fifth article of the said Constitution; and in all congressional laws to be passed in the meantime, to conform to the spirit of these amendments as far as the said Constitution will admit.

And so much of the said amendments as is contained in the

first twenty articles, constituting the Bill of Rights, being again read;

Resolved, That this Convention doth concur therein.

The other amendments to the said proposed Constitution contained in twenty-one articles, being then again read, a motion was made, and the question being put, to amend the same by striking out the third article, containing these words;

"When the Congress shall lay direct taxes or excises, they shall immediately inform the Executive power of each state, of the quota of such state according to the census herein directed, which is proposed to be thereby raised; and if the Legislature of any state shall pass a law which shall be effectual for raising such quota at the time required by Congress, the taxes and excises laid by Congress shall not be collected in such state."

It passed in the negative,

A Y E S . . . . 65.
N O E S . . . . 85.

STATE of NORTH-CAROLINA
In CONVENTION, *August* 2, 1788.

RESOLVED, That a Declaration of Rights, asserting and securing from encroachment the great Principles of civil and religious Liberty, and the unalienable Rights of the People, together with amendments to the most ambiguous and exceptionable parts of the said Constitution of Government, ought to be laid before Congress, or the Convention of the States that shall or may be called for the purpose of amending the said Constitution, for their consideration, previous to the Ratification of the Constitution aforesaid, on the part of the State of North-Carolina.

Declaration of Rights.

1st. THAT there are certain natural rights of which men, when they form a social compact, cannot deprive or divest their posterity, among which are the enjoyment of life, and liberty, with the means of acquiring, possessing and protecting property, and pursuing and obtaining happiness and safety.

2d. That all power is naturally vested in, and consequently derived from the people; that magistrates therefore are their trustees, and agents, and at all times amenable to them.

3d. That Government ought to be instituted for the common benefit, protection and security of the people; and that the doctrine of non resistance against arbitrary power and oppression is absurd, slavish, and destructive to the good and happiness of mankind.

4th. That no man or set of men are entitled to exclusive or separate public emoluments or privileges from the community, but in consideration of public services; which not being descendible, neither ought the offices of Magistrate, Legislator or Judge, or any other public office, to be hereditary.

5th. That the Legislative, Executive and Judiciary powers of government should be separate and distinct, and that the members of the two first may be restrained from oppression by feeling and participating the public burthens, they should at fixed periods be reduced to a private station, return into the mass of the people; and the vacancies be supplied by certain and regular elections; in which all or any part of the former members to be eligible or ineligible, as the rules of the Constitution of Government, and the laws shall direct.

6th. That elections of representatives in the legislature ought to be free and frequent, and all men having sufficient evidence of permanent common interest with, and attachment to the community, ought to have the right of suffrage: and no aid, charge, tax or fee can be set, rated, or levied upon the people without their own consent, or that of their representatives, so elected, nor can they be bound by any law, to which they have not in like manner assented for the public good.

7th. That all power of suspending laws, or the execution of laws by any authority without the consent of the representatives, of the people in the legislature, is injurious to their rights, and ought not to be exercised.

8th. That in all capital and criminal prosecutions, a man hath a right to demand the cause and nature of his accusation, to be confronted with the accusers and witnesses, to call for evidence and be allowed counsel in his favor, and to a fair and speedy trial by an impartial jury of his vicinage, without whose unanimous consent he cannot be found guilty (except in the government of the land and naval forces) nor can he be compelled to give evidence against himself.

9th. That no freeman ought to be taken, imprisoned, or disseized of his freehold, liberties, privileges or franchises, or outlawed, or exiled, or in any manner destroyed or deprived of his life, liberty, or property, but by the law of the land.

10th. That every freeman restrained of his liberty is entitled to a remedy to enquire into the lawfulness thereof, and to remove the same, if unlawful, and that such remedy ought not to be denied nor delayed.

11th. That in controversies respecting property, and in suits between man and man, the ancient trial by jury is one of the greatest securities to the rights of the people, and ought to remain sacred and inviolable.

12th. That every freeman ought to find a certain remedy by recourse to the laws for all injuries and wrongs he may receive in his person, property, or character. He ought to obtain right and justice freely without sale, completely and without denial, promptly and without delay, and that all establishments, or regulations contravening these are oppressive and unjust.

13th. That excessive bail ought not to be required, nor excessive fines imposed, nor cruel and unusual punishments inflicted.

14th. That every freeman has a right to be secure from all unreasonable searches, and seizures of his person, his papers, and his property; all warrants therefore to search suspected places, or seize any freeman, his papers or property, without information upon oath (or affirmation of a person religiously scrupulous of taking an oath) of legal and sufficient cause, are grievous and oppressive, and all general warrants to search suspected places, or to apprehend any suspected person without specially naming or describing the place or person, are dangerous and ought not to be granted.

15th. That the people have a right peaceably to assemble together to consult for the common good, or to instruct their representatives; and that every freeman has a right to petition or apply to the Legislature for redress of grievances.

16th. That the people have a right to freedom of speech, and of writing and publishing their sentiments; that the freedom of the press is one of the greatest bulwarks of liberty, and ought not to be violated.

17th. That the people have a right to keep and bear arms: that a well regulated militia composed of the body of the people trained to arms, is the proper, natural and safe defence of a free state. That standing armies in time of peace are dangerous to liberty, and therefore ought to be avoided, as far as the circumstances and protection of the community will admit; and that in all cases, the military should be under strict subordination to and governed by the civil power.

18th. That no soldier in time of peace ought to be quartered in any house without the consent of the owner, and in time of war in such manner only as the laws direct.

19th. That any person religiously scrupulous of bearing arms ought to be exempted upon payment of an equivalent to employ another to bear arms in his stead.

20th. That religion, or the duty which we owe to our Creator, and the manner of discharging it, can be directed only by reason and conviction, not by force or violence, and therefore all men have an equal, natural and unalienable right to the free exercise of religion according to the dictates of conscience, and that no particular religious sect or society ought to be favored or established by law in preference to others.

AMENDMENTS to the CONSTITUTION

1st. That each state in the Union shall respectively retain every power, jurisdiction and right, which is not by this Constitution delegated to the Congress of the United States, or to the departments of the Fœderal Government.

2d. That there shall be one representative for every thirty thousand, according to the enumeration or census mentioned in the Constitution, until the whole number of representatives amounts to two hundred; after which that number shall be continued or encreased as Congress shall direct, upon the principles fixed in the Constitution, by apportioning the representatives of each state to some greater number of people from time to time as population encreases.

3d. When Congress shall lay direct taxes or excises, they shall immediately inform the Executive power of each State, of the quota of such state according to the census herein directed, which is proposed to be thereby raised; and if the Legislature of any State shall pass a law which shall be effectual for raising such quota at the time required by Congress, the taxes and excises laid by Congress, shall not be collected in such State.

4th. That the members of the Senate and House of Representatives shall be ineligible to, and incapable of holding any civil office under the authority of the United States, during the time for which they shall respectively be elected.

5th. That the journals of the proceedings of the Senate and House of Representatives shall be published at least once in every year, except such parts thereof relating to treaties, alliances, or military operations, as in their judgment require secrecy.

6th. That a regular statement and account of the receipts and expenditures of all public money, shall be published at least once in every year.

7th. That no commercial treaty shall be ratified without the concurrence of two-thirds of the whole number of the members of the Senate; and no treaty ceding, contracting, or restraining or suspending the territorial rights or claims of the United States, or any of them, or their, or any of their rights or claims to fishing in the American seas, or navigating the American rivers, shall be made, but in cases of the most urgent and extreme necessity, nor shall any such treaty be ratified without the concurrence of three-fourths of the whole number of the members of both houses respectively.

8th. That no navigation law or law regulating commerce shall be passed without the consent of two-thirds of the members present, in both houses.

9th. That no standing army or regular troops shall be raised, or kept up in time of peace, without the consent of two-thirds of the members present, in both houses.

10th. That no soldier shall be inlisted for any longer term than four years, except in time of war, and then for no longer term than the continuance of the war.

11th. That each state respectively shall have the power to provide for organizing, arming, and disciplining its own militia, whensoever Congress shall omit or neglect to provide for the same. That the militia shall not be subject to martial law, except when in actual service in time of war, invasion, or rebellion, and when not in the actual service of the United States, shall be subject only to such fines, penalties and punishments as shall be directed or inflicted by the laws of its own state.

12th. That Congress shall not declare any State to be in rebellion without the consent of at least two-thirds of all the members present of both houses.

13th. That the exclusive power of legislation given to Congress over the Fœderal Town and its adjacent district, and other places, purchased or to be purchased by Congress of any of the states, shall extend only to such regulations as respect the police and good government thereof.

14th. That no person shall be capable of being President of the United States for more than eight years in any term of sixteen years.

15th. That the judicial power of the United States shall be vested in one Supreme Court, and in such Courts of Admiralty as Congress may from time to time ordain and establish in any of the different states: The judicial power shall extend to all cases in law and equity arising under treaties made, or which shall be made under the authority of the United States; to all cases affecting ambassadors, other foreign ministers and consuls; to all cases of admiralty and maritime jurisdiction; to controversies to which the United States shall be a party; to controversies between two or more states, and between parties claiming lands under the grants of different states. In all cases affecting ambassadors, other foreign ministers and consuls, and those in which a state shall be a party, the Supreme Court shall have original jurisdiction; in all other cases before mentioned, the Supreme Court shall have appellate jurisdiction, as to matters of law only: except in cases of equity, and of admiralty and maritime jurisdiction, in which the Supreme

Court shall have appellate jurisdiction both as to law and fact, with such exceptions and under such regulations as the Congress shall make: But the judicial power of the United States shall extend to no case where the cause of action shall have originated before the ratification of this Constitution; except in disputes between states about their territory; disputes between persons claiming lands under the grants of different states, and suits for debts due to the United States.

16th. That in criminal prosecutions, no man shall be restrained in the exercise of the usual and accustomed right of challenging or excepting to the jury.

17th. That Congress shall not alter, modify, or interfere in the times, places, or manner of holding elections for Senators and Representatives, or either of them, except when the Legislature of any state shall neglect, refuse, or be disabled by invasion or rebellion to prescribe the same.

18th. That those clauses which declare that Congress shall not exercise certain powers, be not interpreted in any manner whatsoever, to extend the powers of Congress; but that they may be construed either as making exceptions to the specified powers where this shall be the case, or otherwise, as inserted merely for greater caution.

19th. That the laws ascertaining the compensation of senators and representatives for their services, be postponed in their operation, until after the election of representatives immediately succeeding the passing thereof; that excepted, which shall first be passed on the subject.

20th. That some tribunal other than the senate be provided for trying impeachments of senators.

21st. That the salary of a judge shall not be encreased or diminished during his continuance in office otherwise than by general regulations of salary, which may take place on a revision of the subject at stated periods of not less than seven years, to commence from the time such salaries shall be first ascertained by Congress.

22d. That Congress erect no company of merchants with exclusive advantages of commerce.

23d. That no treaties which shall be directly opposed to the existing laws of the United States in Congress assembled, shall be valid until such laws shall be repealed, or made conformable to such treaty; nor shall any treaty be valid which is contradictory to the Constitution of the United States.

24th. That the latter part of the 5th paragraph of the 9th section of the first article be altered to read thus—'Nor shall vessels bound to a particular State be obliged to enter or pay duties in any other; nor when bound from any one of the States be obliged to clear in another.'

25th. That Congress shall not directly or indirectly, either by themselves or through the judiciary, interfere with any one of the states in the redemption of paper money already emited and now in circulation, or in liquidating and discharging the public securities of any one of the States: But each and every State shall have the exclusive right of making such laws and regulations for the above purposes, as they shall think proper.

26th. That Congress shall not introduce foreign troops into the United States without the consent of two-thirds of the members present of both Houses.

Mr. Iredell seconded by Mr. John Skinner moved, that this report be amended, by striking out all the words of the said report, except the two first, viz. "Resolved that," And that the following words be inserted in their room, viz.

This Convention having fully deliberated on the Constitution, proposed for the future government of the United States of America, by the Fœderal Convention lately held at Philadelphia, on the seventeenth day of September last, and having taken into their serious and solemn consideration the present critical situation of America, which induces them to be of opinion, that though certain amendments to the said Constitution may be wished for, yet that those amendments should be proposed subsequent to the ratification on the part of this state, and not previous to it: They do therefore, on behalf of the state of North-Carolina, and the good people thereof, and by virtue of the authority to them delegated, ratify the said Constitution on the part of this state. And they do at the same time recommend, that as early as possible, the following amendments to the said Constitution may be proposed for the consideration and adoption of the several States in the Union, in one of the modes prescribed by the fifth article thereof.

AMENDMENTS.

1st. Each State in the Union shall, respectively, retain every power, jurisdiction and right, which is not by this Constitution delegated to the Congress of the United States, or to the departments of the General Government; nor shall the said Congress, nor any department of the said government exercise any act of authority over any individual in any of the said States, but such as can be justified under some power, particularly given in this Constitution; but the said Constitution shall be considered at all times a solemn instrument, defining the extent of their authority, and the limits of which they cannot rightfully in any instance exceed.

2d. There shall be one representative for every thirty thousand, according to the enumeration, or census mentioned in the Constitution, until the whole number of representatives amounts to two hundred; after which that number shall be continued or increased as Congress shall direct, upon the principles fixed in the Constitution, by apportioning the representatives of each state to some greater number of people, from time to time, as population increases.

3d. Each state, respectively, shall have the power to provide for organizing, arming, and disciplining its own militia, whensoever Congress shall omit or neglect to provide for the same. The militia shall not be subject to martial law, except when in actual service in time of war, invasion or rebellion; and when they are not in the actual service of the United States, they shall be subject only to such fines, penalties, and punishments as shall be directed or inflicted by the laws of its own state.

4th. The Congress shall not alter, modify, or interfere in the times, places, or manner of holding elections for senators and representatives, or either of them, except when the legislature of any state shall neglect, refuse or be disabled by invasion, or rebellion, to prescribe the same.

5th. The laws ascertaining the compensation of senators and representatives for their services, shall be postponed in their operation, until after the election of representatives immediately succeeding the passing thereof; that excepted which shall first be passed on the subject.

6th. Instead of the following words in the 9th section of the first article, viz. "Nor shall vessels bound to or from one state, be obliged to enter, clear or pay duties in another," (The meaning of which is, by many deemed not sufficiently explicit) It is proposed, that the following shall be substituted: "No vessel bound to one state shall be obliged to enter or pay duties to which such vessel may be liable at any port of entry, in any other state than that to which such vessel is bound: Nor shall any vessel bound from one state be obliged to clear or pay duties to which such vessel shall be liable at any port of clearance, in any other state than that from which such vessel is bound."

This motion made by Mr. Iredell being objected to, the question was put, "Will the Convention adopt that amendment or not?" and it was negatived: Whereupon the yeas and nays were required by Mr. Iredell, seconded by Mr. Steele, and were, yeas 84.—nays 183.—The yeas on this question are nays upon the concurrence, and the nays, yeas, except Mr. A. Neale, who voted on this question in favor of the amendment, but did not vote on the concurrence, owing to indisposition.

DEBATES IN THE STATE
RATIFYING CONVENTIONS

South Carolina, May 12–24, 1788
Virginia, June 2–27, 1788
New York, June 17–July 26, 1788
North Carolina, July 21–August 4, 1788

Charles Cotesworth Pinckney Explains America's Unique Structure of Freedom

May 14, 1788

The following Speech of the Honorable Mr. Charles Pinckney's, as delivered in the late Convention of this state, and published in the City Gazette, on the 3d inst, we have taken the liberty to re publish.

Mr. PRESIDENT,

After so much has been said with respect to the powers possessed by the late convention, to form and propose a new system—after so many observations have been made on its leading principles, as well in the house of representatives as in the conventions of other states, whose proceedings have been published, it will be as unnecessary for me again minutely to examine a subject which has been so thoroughly investigated, as it would be difficult to carry you into a field that has not been sufficiently explored.

Having, however, had the honor of being associated in the delegation from this state, and presuming on the indulgence of the house, I shall proceed to make some observations which appear to me as necessary to a full and candid discussion of the system before us. It seems to be generally confessed, that of all sciences, that of government or of politics is most difficult. In the old world, as far as the lights of history extend, from the earliest ages to the present, we find them in the constant exercise of all the forms with which the world is still furnished. We have seen among the ancients as well as the moderns—monarchies limited, and absolute aristocracies—republics of a single state, and federal unions; but notwithstanding all their experience, how imperfect at this moment is their knowledge of government? How little is the true doc-

577

trine of representation understood? How few states enjoy what we term freedom? How few governments answer these great ends of public happiness, which we seem to expect from our own?

In reviewing such of the European states as we are best acquainted with, we may with truth affirm, that there is but one among the most important, which confirms to its citizens their civil liberties or provides for the security of private rights; but as if it had been fated that we should be the first perfectly free people the world had ever seen—even the government I have alluded to, withholds from a part of its subjects the equal enjoyment of their religious liberties. How many thousands of the subjects of Great-Britain at this moment labour under civil disabilities, merely on account of their religious persuasions? To the liberal and enlightened mind the rest of Europe afford a melancholly picture of the depravity of human nature, and of the total subversion of those rights without which we should suppose no people could be happy or content.

We have been taught here to believe that all power of right belongs to THE PEOPLE—that it flows immediately from them, and is delegated to their officers for the public good—that our rulers are the servants of the people, amenable to their will, and created for their use. How different are the governments of Europe? There the people are the servants and subjects of their rulers. There merit and talents have little or no influence, but all the honors and offices of government are swallowed up by birth, by fortune, or by rank.

From the European world no precedents are to be drawn for a people who think they are capable of governing themselves. Instead of receiving instruction from them, we may with pride assert, that new as this country is in point of settlement; inexperienced as she must be upon questions of government, she still has held forth more useful lessons to the old world—she has made them more accquainted with their own rights, than they had been otherwise for centuries.—It is with pride I repeat, that old and experienced as they are, they are indebted to us for light and refinement upon points of all others the most interesting.

Had the American revolution not happened, would Ireland

at this time enjoy her present rights of commerce and legislation? Would the subjects of the emperor in the Netherlands have persumed to contend for and ultimately secure the privileges they demanded? Would the parliament of Paris have resisted the edicts of their monarch, and justified this step in a language that would do honor to the freest people? Nay, I may add, would a becoming sense of liberty, and of the rights of mankind, have so generally pervaded that kingdom, had not their knowledge of America led them to the investigation? Undoubtedly not. Let it be therefore our boast, that we have already taught some of the oldest and wisest nations to explore their rights as men; and let it be our prayer, that the effects of our revolution may never cease to operate, until they have unshackled all the nations that have firmness enough to resist the fetters of despotism. Without a precedent, and with the experience of but a few years, were the convention called upon to form a system for a people, differing from all others we are acquainted with. The first knowledge necessary for us to acquire, was a knowledge of the people for whom this system was to be formed. For unless we were acquainted with their situation, their habits, opinions and resources, it would be impossible to form a government upon adequate or practicable principles. If we examine the reasons which have given rise to the distinctions of rank that at present prevail in Europe, we shall find that none of them do, or in all probability ever will, exist in the union. The only distinction that may take place is that of wealth. Riches, no doubt, will ever have their influence, and where they are suffered to increase to large amounts in a few hands, there they may become dangerous to the public; particularly when from the cheapness of labor, and from the scarcity of money, a great proportion of the people are poor. These however are dangers that I think we have very little to apprehend; for these reasons—One is from the destruction of the right of primogeniture, by which means the estates of intestates are equally to be divided among all their children—a provision no less consonant to the principles of a republican government, than it is to those of general equity and parental affection; to endeavour to raise a name by accumulating property in one branch of a family at the expence of others, *equally related and deserving*, is a vanity no *less unjust and cruel*, than dangerous to the interest of liberty; it is a practice no wise state will ever encourage or tolerate.

In the northern and eastern states such distinctions among children are seldom heard of. Laws have been long since passed in all of them destroying the right of primogeniture; and as laws never fail to have a powerful influence upon the manners of a people, we may suppose that in future an equal division of property among children will in general take place in all the states, and one means of amassing inordinate wealth in the hands of individuals be, as it ought, for ever removed.

Another reason is, that in the eastern and northern states, the landed property is nearly equally divided. Very few have large bodies, and there are few of them that have not small tracts; the greater part of the people are employed in cultivating their own lands; the rest in handicrafts and commerce. They are frugal in their manner of living, plain tables, cloathing, and furniture prevail in their houses, and expensive appearances avoided. Among the landed interest it may be truly said there are few of them rich, or few of them very poor; nor while the states are capable of supporting so many more inhabitants than they contain at present—while so vast a territory on our frontier remains uncultivated and unexplored—while the means of subsistence are so much within every man's power, are those dangerous distinctions of fortune to be expected which at present prevail in other countries.

The people of the union may be classed as follows:

Commercial men—who will be of consequence or not in the political scale, as commerce may be made an object of the attention of government. As far as I am able to judge, and presuming that proper sentiments will ultimately prevail me upon this subject, it does not appear to me that the commercial line will ever have much influence in the politics of the union. Foreign trade is one of the enemies against which we must be extremely guarded, more so than against any other, as none will ever have a more unfavorable operation.—I consider it as the root of our present public distress—as the plentiful source from which our future national calamities will flow, unless great care is taken to prevent it. Divided as we are from the old world, we should have nothing to do with

their politics, and as little as possible with their commerce—
they can never improve, but must inevitably corrupt us.

Another class is that of professional men, who from their
education and pursuits must ever have a considerable influence, while your government retains the republican principle,
and its affairs are agitated in assemblies of the people.

The third—with whom I will connect the mechanical as
generally attached to them, are the landed interest, the owners
and cultivators of the soil—the men attached to the truest
interests of their country, from those motives which always
bind and secure the affections of nations. In these consist the
great body of the people; and here rests, and I hope will ever
continue, all the authority of our government.

I remember once to have seen in the writings of a very
celebrated author on national wealth, the following remark.
"Finally, says he, there are but three ways for a nation to
acquire wealth—the first is *by war*, as the Romans did in
plundering their conquered neighbours—this *is robbery*; the
second is in *commerce*, which is *generally cheating*; the third is
agriculture, the only honest way; wherein a man receives a
real increase of the seed thrown into the ground, in a kind of
continual miracle, wrought by the hand of God in his favor,
as a reward for his innocent life and virtuous industry."

I do not agree with him so far as to suppose that commerce
is generally cheating. I think there are some kinds of commerce not only fair and valuable, but such as ought to be
encouraged by government. I agree with him in this general
principle, *that all the great objects of government should be sub-
servient to the increase of agriculture, and the support of the
landed interest; and that commerce should only be so far attended
to, as it may serve to improve and strengthen it—that the object of
a republic is to render its citizens virtuous and happy; and that an
unlimited foreign commerce can seldom fail to have a contrary
tendency.*

These classes compose the people of the union, and fortunately for their harmony they may be said in a great measure
to be connected with and dependent upon each other.

The merchant is dependent upon the planter as the pur-
chaser of his imports, and as furnishing him with the means
of his remittances—the professional men depend upon both

for employment in their respective pursuits, and are in their turn useful to both. The landholder, though the most independent of the three, is still in some measure obliged to the merchant for furnishing him *at home* with a ready sale for his productions.

From this mutual dependence, and the statement I have made respecting the situation of the people of the union, I am led to conclude, that *mediocrity of fortune* is a leading feature in our national character—that most of the causes which lead to distinctions of fortune among other nations being removed and causes of equality existing with us, which are not to be found among them, we may with safety assert, that the great body of national wealth is nearly equal in the hands of the people, among whom there are few dangerously rich, or few miserably poor—that we may congratulate ourselves with living under the blessings of a mild and equal government, which knows no distinctions but those of merit or of talents —under a government whose honors and offices are *equally open* to the exertions of *all her citizens, and which adopts virtue and worth for her own wheresoever she can find them.*

Another distinguishing feature in our union is its division into individual states, differing in extent of territory, manners, population and products.

Those who are acquainted with the eastern states; their reasons of their original migration, and the present habits and principles, well know that they are essentially different from those of the middle and southern states; that they retain all those opinions respecting religion and government which first induced their ancestors to cross the Atlantic, and that they are perhaps more purely republican in habit and sentiment than any other part of the union. The inhabitants of New York, and the eastern part of New Jersey, originally Dutch settlements, seem to have altered less than might have been expected in the course of a century. Indeed the greatest part of New-York may still be considered as a Dutch settlement, the people in the interior country generally using that language in their families, and having very little varied their ancient customs. Pennsylvania and Delaware are nearly one half inhabited by Quakers, whose passive principles upon questions of government, and rigid opinions in private life, render them extremely different from either the eastern or southern states. Maryland was originally a Roman Catholic colony, and a great number of their inhabitants, some of them the most wealthy and cultivated, are still of this persuasion. It is unnecessary for me to state the striking difference in sentiment and habit, which must always exist between the independence of the east, the Calvinists and Quakers of the middle states, and the Roman Catholics of Maryland; but striking as this is, it is not to be compared with the difference that there is between the inhabitants of the *northern and southern states*; when I say southern states, I mean Maryland and the states to the southward of her; here we may truly observe nature has drawn a strong mark of distinction in the habits and manners of the people as she has in their climates and productions—The southern citizen beholds with a kind of surprize the simple manners of the east, and is too often induced to entertain undeserved opinions of the apparent purity of the Quaker—while they in their turn seem concerned at what they term the extravagance and dissipation of their southern friends, and reprobate as an unpardonable, moral and political evil the dominion they hold over a part of the human race.

The inconveniencies which too frequently attend these differences in habits and opinions among the citizens that compose the union, are not a little encreased by the variety of their state governments; for as I have already observed, the constitutions or laws under which a people live, never fail to have a powerful effect upon their manners. We know that all the states have adhered in their forms to the republican principles, though they have differed widely in their opinions of the mode best calculated to preserve it.—In Pennsylvania and Georgia the whole powers of government are lodged in a legislative body of a single branch, over which there is no controul; nor are their executives or judicials, from their connection and necessary dependence on the legislature capable of strictly executing their respective offices. In all the other states, except Maryland, Massachusetts and New-York, they are only so far improved as to have a legislature with two branches, which compleatly involve and swallow up all the powers of their government. In neither of these are the judicial or executive placed in that firm or independent situation which can alone secure the safety of the people, or the just administration of the laws. In Maryland one branch of their legislature is a senate, chosen for *five years*, by electors chosen by the people; the knowledge and firmness which this body have upon all occasions displayed, not only in the exercise of their legislative duties, but in withstanding and defeating such of the projects of the other house as appeared to them founded in local and personal motives, have long since convinced me that the senate of Maryland is the best model of a senate that has yet been offered to the union—that it is capable of correcting many of the vices of the other parts of their constitution, and in a great measure atoning for those defects which in common with the states I have mentioned, are but too evident in their execution—*the want of stability and independence in the judicial and executive departments.*

In Massachusetts we find the principle of legislation more improved by the revisionary power which is given to their government, and the independence of their judges.

In New York the same improvement in legislation has taken place as in Massachusetts, but here from the executive being elected by the great body of the people,—holding his office for three years, and being re-eligible—from the appointment to offices being taken from the legislature, and placed in a select council—I think their constitution upon the whole, is the best in the union. Its faults are the want of permanent salaries to their judges, and giving to their executive the nomination to offices, which is in fact giving him the appointment. It does not, however, appear to me that this can be strictly called a vice of their system, as I have always been of opinion, that the insisting upon the right to nominate, *was an usurpation* of their executives, not warranted by the letter or meaning of the constitution.

These are the outlines of their various forms, in few of which are their executive or judicial departments wisely constructed, or that solid distinction adopted between the branches of their legislature, which can alone provide for the influence of different principles in their operation.

Much difficulty was expected from the extent of country to be governed.—All the republics we read of, either in the ancient or modern world, have been extremely limited in territory—we know of none a tenth part so large as the United States. Indeed we are hardly able to determine, from the lights we are furnished with, whether the governments we have heard of under the names of republics really deserved them, or whether the ancients ever had any just or proper ideas upon the subject. Of the doctrine of representation, the fundamental of a republic, they certainly were ignorant. If they were in possession of any other safe or practicable principles, they have long since been lost and forgotten to the world. Among the other honors therefore that have been reserved for the American union, not the least inconsiderable of them, is that of defining a mixed system by which a people may govern themselves, possessing all the virtue and benefits, and avoiding all the dangers and inconveniences of the three simple forms. I have said, that the ancient confederacies, as far as we are acquainted with them, covered but an inconsiderable territory. Among the moderns, in our sense of the words, there is no such system as a confederate republic; there are indeed some small states whose interior governments are democratic, but these are too inconsiderable to afford information. The Swiss Cantons are only connected by alliances; the Germanic body is merely an association of potentates, most of them absolute in their own dominions; and as to the United Netherlands, it is such a confusion of states and assemblies, that I have always been at a loss what speces of government to term it; according to my idea of the word, it is not a republic, for I consider it as indispensible in a republic, that all authority should flow from the people. In the United Netherlands the people have no interference, either in the election of their magistrates, or the affairs of government.

From the experiment therefore never having been fairly made, opinions have been entertained, and sanctioned by high authorities, that republics are only suited to small societies. This opinion has its advocates among all those who not having a sufficient share of industry or talents to investigate for themselves, easily adopt the opinions of such authors as are supposed to have written with ability upon the subject, but I am led to believe other opinions begin to prevail.— Opinions more to be depended upon, because they result from juster principles.

We begin now to suppose that the evils of a republic—dissention, tumult and faction, are more dangerous in small societies than in large confederate states. In the first, the people are easily assembled and inflamed—are always opposed to those convulsive tumults of infatuation and enthusiasm, which often overturn all public order. In the latter, the multitude will be less imperious, and consequently less inconstant, because the extensive territory of each republic, and the number of its citizens will not permit them all to be assembled at one time, and in one place—the sphere of government being enlarged, it will not easily be in the power of factious and designing men to infect the whole people—it will give an opportunity to the more temperate and prudent part of the society to correct the licentiousness and injustice of the rest. We have strong proofs of the truth of this opinion in the examples of Rhode-Island and Massachusetts. Instances which have perhaps been critically afforded by an all merciful providence, to evince the truth of a position extremely important to our present enquiries. In the former the most contracted society in the union, we have seen their licentiousness so far prevail as to seize the reins of government, and oppress the people by laws the most infamous that have ever disgraced a civilized nation. In the latter, where the sphere was enlarged, similar attempts have been rendered abortive by the zeal and activity of those who were opposed to them.

As the constitution before you is intended to represent states as well as citizens, I have thought it necessary to make these remarks, because there are no doubt a great number of the members of this body, who from their particular pursuits have not had an opportunity of minutely investigating them; and because it will be impossible for the house fairly to determine whether the government is a proper one, or not, unless they are in some degree acquainted with the people and states for whose use it is instituted.

For a people thus situated is a government to be formed—a people who have the justest opinions of their civil and religious rights, and who have risqued every thing in defending and asserting them.

In every government there necessarily exists a power from

which there is no appeal, and which for that reason may be termed absolute and uncontroulable.

The person or assembly in whom this power resides, is called the sovereign or supreme power of the state. With us the *Sovereignty of the union is in the People*.

One of the best political and moral writers* I have met with, enumerates three principal forms of government, which he says are to be regarded rather as the simple forms, by some combination and intermixture of which all actual governments are composed, than as any where existing in a pure and elementary state.

These forms are—

1st. Despotism or absolute Monarchy, where the legislature is in a single person.

2d. An Aristocracy, where the legislature is in a select assembly, the members of which either fill up by election the vacancies in their own body, or succeed to it by inheritance, property, tenure of lands, or in respect of some personal right or qualification.

3d. A Republic, where the people at large either collectively or by representation form the legislature.

The separate advantages of *Monarchy* are, unity of council, decision, secrecy, and dispatch—the military strength and energy resulting from these qualities of government: The exclusion of popular and Aristocratical contentions—the preventing by a known rule of succession all competition for the supreme power, thereby repressing the dangerous hope and intrigues of aspiring citizens.

The dangers of a *Monarchy* are, tyranny, expence, exaction, military domination, unnecessary wars,—ignorance in the governors of the interest and accomodation of the people, and a consequent deficiency of salutary regulations—want of constancy and uniformity in the rules of government, and proceeding from thence in security of person and property.

The separate advantage of an *Aristocracy* is the wisdom which may be expected from experience and education—a permanent council naturally possesses experience, and the

*Paley, a deacon of Carlisle, 2 vols. 174 & 175.

members will always be educated with a view to the stations they are destined by their birth to occupy.

The mischiefs of an *Aristocracy* are dissentions in the ruling orders of the state—an oppression of the lower orders by the privileges of the higher, and by laws partial to the separate interests of the law makers.

The advantages of a *Republic* are liberty, exemption from needless restrictions—equal laws—public spirit—averseness to war—frugality—above all, the opportunities which they afford to men of every description of producing their abilities and councils to public observation, and the exciting to the service of the commonwealth the faculties of its best citizens.

The evils of a *Republic* are dissentions—tumults—faction—the attempts of ambitious citizens to possess power—the confusion and clamour which are the inevitable consequences of propounding questions of state to the discussion of large popular assemblies—the delay and disclosure of the public councils, and too often the imbecility of the laws.

A *mixed government* is composed by the combination of two or more of the simple forms above described; and in whatever proportion each form enters into the constitution of a government, in the same proportion may both the advantages and evils which have been attributed to that form, be expected.

The citizens of the United States would reprobate, with indignation, the idea of a monarchy; but the essential qualities of a monarch—unity of councils—vigor—secrecy and dispatch, are qualities essential in every government.

While therefore, we have reserved to the people *the fountain* of all power, the periodical election of their first magistrate; while we have defined his authorities, and bound them to such limits as will effectually prevent his usurping others dangerous to the general welfare; we have at the same time endeavoured to infuse into this department, that degree of vigor which will enable the president to execute the laws *with energy and dispatch*.

By constructing the senate upon rotative principles, we have removed, as will be shewn on another occasion, all danger of an *aristocratic influence*, while, by electing the members for six years, we hope that we have given to this part of the system all the advantages of an *aristocracy — wisdom — experience — and a consistency of measures.*

The house of representatives, in which the people of the union are proportionably represented, are to be biennially elected by them; those appointments are sufficiently short to render the member as dependent as he ought to be upon his constituent.

They are the moving spring of the system, — with them all grants of money are to originate — on them depend the wars we shall be engaged in — the fleets and armies we shall raise and support — the salaries we shall pay — in short, on them depend the appropriations of money, and consequently all the arrangements of government. With the powerful influence of the purse, they will be always able to restrain the usurpations of the other departments, while their own licentiousness will, in its turn, be checked and corrected by them. I trust, that when we proceed to review the system by sections, it will be found to contain all those necessary provisions and restraints, which while they enable the general government to guard and protect our common rights as a nation — to restore to us those blessings of commerce and mutual confidence which have been so long removed and impaired — will secure to us those rights, which, as the citizens of a state, will make us content and happy at home — as the citizens of the union respectable abroad.

How differently Mr. President, is this government constructed from any we have yet known among us.

In their individual capacities as citizens, the people are proportionably represented *in the house of representatives.* Here they who are to support the expences of government have purse strings in their hands. Here the people hold and feel that they possess an influence sufficiently powerful to prevent any undue attempt of the other branches; to maintain that weight in the political scale which as the source of all authority they should ever possess. Here too the states, whose existence as such we have often heard predicted as precarious, will find in the senate *the guards of their rights as political associations,* a sure protection.

On them, I mean the *state systems,* rests the general fabric; on their foundation is this magnificent structure of freedom erected—each depending upon, supporting and protecting the other, nor, so intimate is the connexion, can the one be removed without prostrating the other in ruin—like the head and the body, separate them and they die.

Far be it from me to suppose, that such an attempt should ever be made—the good sense and virtue of our country forbid the idea. To the union we will look up as to the temple of our freedom—a temple founded in the affections, and supported by the virtue of the people—here we will point out our gratitude to the author of all good, for suffering us to participate in the rights of a people who *govern themselves*. Is there at this moment a nation upon earth that enjoys this right—where the true principles of representation are understood and practised, and where all authority flows from and returns at stated periods to the people? I answer there is not. Can a government be said to be free where these rights do not exist? It cannot. On what depends the enjoyment of these rare, these inestimable privileges? On the firmness—on the power of the union to protect them.

How grateful then should we be, that at this important period—a period important, not to us alone, but to the general rights of mankind, so much harmony and concession should prevail throughout the states—that the public opinion should be so much actuated by candor and an attention to their general interests—that disdaining to be governed by the narrow motives of state policy, they have liberally determined to dedicate a part of their advantages to the support of that government from which they received them.

To the philosophic mind how new and awful an instance do the United States at present exhibit in the political world?— They exhibit, sir, the first instance of a people, who being dissatisfied with their government—unattacked by foreign force, and undisturbed by domestic uneasiness—coolly and deliberately resort to the virtue and good sense of their country for a correction of their public errors.

It must be obvious, that without a superintending government, it is impossible the liberties of this country can long be secured.

Single and unconnected, how weak and contemptible are the largest of our states—how unable to protect themselves from external or domestic insult—how incompetent to national purposes would our partial unions be?—how liable to intestine wars and confusion?—how little able to secure the blessings of peace?

Let us therefore be careful in strengthening the union—let us remember that we are bounded by vigilant and attentive neighbours, who view with a jealous eye our rise to empire.

Let us remember that we are bound in gratitude to our northern brethren to aid them in the recovery of those rights which they have lost in obtaining for us an extension of our commerce and the security of our liberties—Let us not be unmindful, that those who are weak and may expect support, must, in their turn, be ready to afford it.

We are called upon to execute an important trust—to examine the principles of the constitution before you, and, in the name of the people, to receive or reject it. I have no doubt we shall do this with attention and harmony, and flatter myself that, at the conclusion of our discussions, we shall find that it is not only expedient, but safe and honorable to adopt it.

Patrick Dollard Fears a Corrupt, Despotic Aristocracy

May 22, 1788

It being mentioned in convention, that it would be proper to know, from gentlemen, what were the sentiments of their constituents, with regard to the new constitution. Mr. Dollard, a member from Prince Frederick's parish, made the following speech, to which his colleague Mr. Tweed added.

Mr. President,

I rise with the greatest diffidence to speak on this occasion, not only knowing myself unequal to the task, but believing this to be the most important question that ever the good people of this state were called together to deliberate upon. This constitution has been ably supported, and ingeniously glossed over by many able and respectable gentlemen in this house, whose reasoning, aided by the most accurate eloquence, might strike conviction even in the pre-determined breast, had they a good cause to support. Conscious that they have not, and also conscious of my inabilities to point out the consequences of its defects, which have in some measure been defined by able gentlemen in this house, I shall therefore confine myself within narrow bounds, that is, concisely to make known the sense and language of my constituents. The people of Prince Frederick's parish, whom I have the honor to represent, are a brave, honest and industrious people. In the late bloody contest they bore a conspicuous part, when they fought, bled and conquered, in defence of their civil rights and privileges, which they expected to transmit untainted to their posterity. They are nearly to a man opposed to this new constitution, because, they say, they have omitted to insert a bill of rights therein, ascertaining and fundamentally establishing the unalienable rights of men, without a full, free and secure enjoyment of which there can be no liberty, and over which it is not necessary that a good government should have the controul. They say, that they are by no means against vesting congress with ample and sufficient powers, but to make over to them or any set of men, their birthright comprized in Magna Charta, which this new constitution absolutely does, they can never agree to. Notwithstanding this they have the highest opinion of the virtue and abilities of the honorable gentlemen from this state, who represented us in the general convention; and also a few other distinguished characters, whose names will be transmitted with honor to future ages; but I believe at the same time, they are but mortal, and therefore liable to err; and as the virtue and abilities of those gentlemen will consequently recommend their being first employed in jointly conducting the reins of this government, they are led to believe it will commence in a moderate aristocracy, but that it will in its future operations produce a monarchy, or a corrupt and oppressive aristocracy they have no manner of doubt. Lust of dominion is natural in every soil, and the love of power and superiority is as prevailing in the United States at present as in any part of the earth; yet in this country, depraved as it is, there still remains a strong regard for liberty: an American bosom is apt to glow at the sound of it, and the splendid merit of preserving that best gift of God, which is mostly expelled every country in Europe, might stimulate indolence, and animate even luxury herself to consecrate at the altar of freedom. My constituents are highly alarmed at the large and rapid strides which this new government has taken towards despotism. They say it is big with political mischiefs, and pregnant with a greater variety of impending woes to the good people of the southern states, especially South-Carolina, than all the plagues supposed to issue from the poisonous box of Pandora. They say it is particularly calculated for the meridian of despotic aristocracy—that it evidently tends to promote the ambitious views of a few able and designing men, and enslave the rest; that it carries with it the appearance of an old phrase formerly made use of in despotic reigns, and especially by archbishop Laud in the reign of Charles the 1st, that is *"non resistance."* They say they will resist against it—that they will not accept of it unless compelled by force of arms, which this new constitution plainly threatens; and then, they say, your standing army, like Turkish Janizaries enforcing despotic laws, must ram it down their throats with the points of Bayonets. They warn the gentlemen of this convention, as the guardians of their liberty, to beware how they will be accessary to the disposal of, or rather sacrificing their dear bought rights and privileges. This is the sense and language, Mr. President, of the people; and it is an old saying, and I believe, a very true one, that the general voice of the people is the voice of God. The general voice of the people to whom I am responsible is against it; I shall never betray the trust reposed in me by them, therefore shall give it my hearty dissent.

Patrick Henry's Opening Speech: A Wrong Step Now and the Republic Will Be Lost Forever

June 4, 1788

Mr. *Henry*—Mr. Chairman.—The public mind, as well as my own, is extremely uneasy at the proposed change of Government. Give me leave to form one of the number of those who wish to be thoroughly acquainted with the reasons of this perilous and uneasy situation—and why we are brought hither to decide on this great national question. I consider myself as the servant of the people of this Commonwealth, as a centinel over their rights, liberty, and happiness. I represent their feelings when I say, that they are exceedingly uneasy, being brought from that state of full security, which they enjoyed, to the present delusive appearance of things. A year ago the minds of our citizens were at perfect repose. Before the meeting of the late Federal Convention at Philadelphia, a general peace, and an universal tranquillity prevailed in this country;—but since that period they are exceedingly uneasy and disquieted. When I wished for an appointment to this Convention, my mind was extremely agitated for the situation of public affairs. I conceive the republic to be in extreme danger. If our situation be thus uneasy, whence has arisen this fearful jeopardy? It arises from this fatal system—it arises from a proposal to change our government:—A proposal that goes to the utter annihilation of the most solemn engagements of the States. A proposal of establishing 9 States into a confederacy, to the eventual exclusion of 4 States. It goes to the annihilation of those solemn treaties we have formed with foreign nations. The present circumstances of France—the good offices rendered us by that kingdom, require our most faithful and most punctual adherence to our treaty with her.

We are in alliance with the Spaniards, the Dutch, the Prussians: Those treaties bound us as thirteen States, confederated together—Yet, here is a proposal to sever that confederacy. Is it possible that we shall abandon all our treaties and national engagements?—And for what? I expected to have heard the reasons of an event so unexpected to my mind, and many others. Was our civil polity, or public justice, endangered or sapped? Was the real existence of the country threatened—or was this preceded by a mournful progression of events? This proposal of altering our Federal Government is of a most alarming nature: Make the best of this new Government— say it is composed by any thing but inspiration—you ought to be extremely cautious, watchful, jealous of your liberty; for instead of securing your rights you may lose them forever. If a wrong step be now made, the republic may be lost forever. If this new Government will not come up to the expectation of the people, and they should be disappointed—their liberty will be lost, and tyranny must and will arise. I repeat it again, and I beg Gentlemen to consider, that a wrong step made now will plunge us into misery, and our Republic will be lost. It will be necessary for this Convention to have a faithful historical detail of the facts, that preceded the session of the Federal Convention, and the reasons that actuated its members in proposing an entire alteration of Government—and to demonstrate the dangers that awaited us: If they were of such awful magnitude, as to warrant a proposal so extremely perilous as this, I must assert, that this Convention has an absolute right to a thorough discovery of every circumstance relative to this great event. And here I would make this enquiry of those worthy characters who composed a part of the late Federal Convention. I am sure they were fully impressed with the necessity of forming a great consolidated Government, instead of a confederation. That this is a consolidated Government is demonstrably clear, and the danger of such a Government, is, to my mind, very striking. I have the highest veneration for those Gentlemen,—but, Sir, give me leave to demand, what right had they to say, *We, the People*. My political curiosity, exclusive of my anxious solicitude for the public welfare, leads me to ask, who authorised them to speak the language of, *We, the People*, instead of *We, the States*? States are the characteristics, and the soul of a confederation. If the States be not the agents of this compact, it must be one great consolidated National Government of the people of all the States. I have the highest respect for those Gentlemen who formed the Convention, and were some of them not here, I would express some testimonial of my esteem for them. America had on a former occasion put the utmost confidence in them: A confidence which was well placed: And I am sure, Sir, I would give up any thing to them; I would chearfully confide in them as my Representatives. But, Sir, on this great occasion, I would demand the cause of their conduct.—Even from that illustrious man, who saved us by his valor, I would have a reason for his conduct—that liberty which he has given us by his valor, tells me to ask this reason,—and sure I am, were he here, he would give us that reason: But there are other Gentlemen here, who can give us this information. The people gave them no power to use their name. That they exceeded their power is perfectly clear. It is not mere curiosity that actuates me—I wish to hear the real actual existing danger, which should lead us to take those steps so dangerous in my conception. Disorders have arisen in other parts of America, but here, Sir, no dangers, no insurrection or tumult, has happened—every thing has been calm and tranquil. But notwithstanding this, we are wandering on the great ocean of human affairs. I see no landmark to guide us. We are running we know not whither. Difference in opinion has gone to a degree of inflammatory resentment in different parts of the country—which has been occasioned by this perilous innovation. The Federal Convention ought to have amended the old system—for this purpose they were solely delegated: The object of their mission extended to no other consideration. You must therefore forgive the solicitation of one unworthy member, to know what danger could have arisen under the present confederation, and what are the causes of this proposal to change our Government.

Governor Edmund Randolph Explains Why He Now Supports the Constitution with Amendments

June 4, 1788

Governor *Randolph*—Mr. Chairman.—Had the most enlightened Statesman whom America has yet seen, foretold but a year ago, the crisis which has now called us together, he would have been confronted by the universal testimony of history: for never was it yet known, that in so short a space, by the peaceable working of events, without a war, or even the menace of the smallest force, a nation has been brought to agitate a question, an error in the issue of which, may blast their happiness. It is therefore to be feared, left to this trying exigency, the best wisdom should be unequal, and here, (if it were allowable to lament any ordinance of nature) might it be deplored, that in proportion to the magnitude of a subject, is the mind intemperate. Religion, the dearest of all interests, has too often sought proselytes by fire, rather than by reason; and politics, the next in rank, are too often nourished by passion, at the expence of the understanding.—Pardon me, however, for expecting one exception to this tendency of mankind—From the dignity of this Convention, a mutual toleration, and a persuasion that no man has a right to impose his opinion on others. Pardon me too, Sir, if I am particularly sanguine in my expectations from the chair—It well knows what is order, how to command obedience, and that political opinions may be as honest on one side as on the other. Before I press into the body of the argument, I must take the liberty of mentioning the part I have already borne in this great question: But let me not here be misunderstood. I come not to apologize to any individual within these walls, to the Convention as a body, or even to my fellow citizens at large—Having obeyed the impulse of duty, having satisfied my conscience, and I trust, my God, I shall appeal to no other tribunal; nor do I come a candidate for popularity: My manner of life, has never yet betrayed such a desire. The highest honors and emoluments of this Commonwealth, are a poor compensation for the surrender of personal independence. The history of England, from the revolution, and that of Virginia, for more than twenty years past, shew the vanity of a hope, that general favor should ever follow the man, who without partiality or prejudice, praises or disapproves the opinions of friends or of foes: Nay, I might enlarge the field, and declare from the great volume of human nature itself, that to be moderate in politics, forbids an ascent to the summit of political fame. But I come hither regardless of allurements; to continue as I have begun, to repeat my earnest endeavours for a firm energetic government, to enforce my objections to the Constitution, and to concur in any practical scheme of amendments; but I never will assent to any scheme that will operate a dissolution of the Union, or any measure which may lead to it. This conduct may possibly be upbraided as injurious to my own views; if it be so, it is at least, the natural offspring of my judgment. I refused to sign, and if the same were to return, again would I refuse. Wholly to adopt or wholly to reject, as proposed by the Convention, seemed too hard an alternative to the citizens of America, whose servants we were, and whose pretensions amply to discuss the means of their happiness, were undeniable. Even if adopted under the terror of impending anarchy, the government must have been without that safest bulwark, the hearts of the people— and if rejected because the chance for amendments was cut off, the Union would have been irredeemably lost. This seems to have been verified by the event in Massachusetts; but our Assembly have removed these inconveniences, by propounding the Constitution to our full and free enquiry. When I withheld my subscription, I had not even a glimpse of the genius of America, relative to the principles of the new Constitution. Who, arguing from the preceding history of Virginia, could have divined that she was prepared for the important change? In former times indeed, she transcended every Colony in professions and practices of loyalty; but she opened a perilous war, under a democracy almost as pure as representation would admit: She supported it under a Constitution which subjects all rule, authority and power, to the Legislature: Every attempt to alter it had been baffled: The increase of Congressional power, had always excited an alarm. I therefore would not bind myself to uphold the new Constitution, before I had tried it by the true touchstone; especially too, when I foresaw, that even the members of the General Convention, might be instructed by the comments of those who were without doors. But I had moreover objections to the Constitution, the most material of which, too lengthy in the detail, I have as yet but barely stated to the public, but shall explain when we arrive at the proper points. Amendments were consequently my wish; these were the grounds of my repugnance to subscribe, and were perfectly reconcileable with my unalterable resolution, to be regulated by the spirit of America, if after our best efforts for amendments they could not be removed. I freely indulge those who may think this declaration too candid, in believing, that I hereby depart from the concealment belonging to the character of a Statesman. Their censure would be more reasonable, were it not for an unquestionable fact, that the spirit of America depends upon a combination of circumstances, which no individual can controul, and arises not from the prospect of advantages which may be gained by the arts of negociation, but from deeper and more honest causes.

As with me the only question has ever been, between previous, and subsequent amendments, so will I express my apprehensions, that the postponement of this Convention, to so late a day, has extinguished the probability of the former without inevitable ruin to the Union, and the Union is the anchor of our political salvation; and I will assent to the lopping of this limb (meaning his arm) before I assent to the dissolution of the Union.—I shall now follow the Honorable Gentleman (Mr. *Henry*) in his enquiry. Before the meeting of the Federal Convention, says the Honorable Gentleman, we rested in peace; a miracle it was, that we were so: Miraculous must it appear to those who consider the distresses of the war, and the no less afflicting calamities, which we suffered in the succeeding peace;—be so good as to recollect how we fared under the confederation. I am ready to pour forth sentiments of the fullest gratitude to those Gentlemen who framed that system. I believe they had the most enlightened heads in this western hemisphere:—Notwithstanding their intelligence, and earnest solicitude, for the good of their country, this system has proved totally inadequate to the purpose, for which it was devised: But, Sir, this was no disgrace to them; the subject of confederations was then new, and the necessity of speedily forming some government for the States, to defend them against the pressing dangers, prevented, perhaps, those able Statesmen from making that system as perfect as more leisure and deliberation might have enabled them to do: I cannot otherwise conceive how they could have formed a system, that provided no means of enforcing the powers which were nominally given it. Was it not a political farce, to pretend to vest powers, without accompanying them with the means of putting them in execution? This want of energy was not a greater solecism than the blending together, and vesting in one body, all the branches of Government. The utter inefficacy of this system was discovered the moment the danger was over, by the introduction of peace: The accumulated public misfortunes that resulted from its inefficacy, rendered an alteration necessary; this necessity was obvious to all America: Attempts have accordingly been made for this purpose. I have been a witness to this business from its earliest beginning. I was honored with a seat in the small Convention held at Annapolis. The members of that Convention thought unanimously, that the controul of commerce should be given to Congress, and recommended to their States to extend the improvement to the whole system. The members of the General Convention were particularly deputed to meliorate the confederation. On a thorough contemplation of the subject, they found it impossible to amend that system: What was to be done? The dangers of America, which will be shewn at another time by a particular enumeration, suggested the expedient of forming a new plan: The confederation has done a great deal for us, we all allow, but it was the danger of a powerful enemy, and the spirit of America, Sir, and not any energy in that system that carried us through that perilous war: For what were its best arms? The greatest exertions were made, when the danger was most imminent. This system was not signed till March, 1781, Maryland having not acceded to it before; yet the military atchievements and other exertions of America, previous to that period, were as brilliant, effectual, and successful, as they could have been under the most energetic Government. This clearly shews, that our perilous situation was the cement of our Union—How different the scene when this peril vanished, and peace was restored! The demands of Congress were treated with neglect. One State complained that another had not paid its quotas as well as itself. Public credit gone—for I believe were it not for the private credit of individuals we should have been ruined long before that time. Commerce languishing—produce falling in value, and justice trampled under foot. We became contemptible in the eyes of foreign nations; they discarded us as little wanton bees who had played for liberty, but who had not sufficient solidity or wisdom to secure it on a permanent basis, and were therefore unworthy of their regard. It was found that Congress could not even enforce the observance of treaties. That treaty under which we enjoy our present tranquillity was disregarded. Making no difference between the justice of paying debts due to people here, and that of paying those due to people on the other side of the Atlantic. I wished to see the treaty complied with, by the payment of the British debts, but have not been able to know why it has been neglected. What was the reply to the demands and requisitions of Congress? You are too contemptible, we will despise and disregard you. I shall endeavor to satisfy the Gentleman's political curiosity. Did not our compliance with any demand of Congress depend on our own free will?—If we refused, I know of no coercive force to compel a compliance:—After meeting in Convention, the deputies from the States communicated their information to one another: On a review of our critical situation, and of the impossibility of introducing any degree of improvement into the old system; what ought they to have done? Would it not have been treason to return without proposing some scheme to relieve their distressed country? The Honorable Gentleman asks, why we should adopt a system, that shall annihilate and destroy our treaties with France, and other nations? I think, the misfortune is, that these treaties are violated already, under the Honorable Gentleman's favorite system. I conceive that our engagements with foreign nations are not at all affected by this system, for the sixth article expressly provides, that "all debts contracted, and engagements entered into, before the adoption of this Constitution, shall be as valid against the United States under this Constitution, as under the Confederation." Does this system then, cancel debts due to or from the continent? Is it not a well known maxim that no change of situation can alter an obligation once rightly entered into? He also objects because nine States are sufficient to put the Government in motion: What number of States ought we to have said? Ought we to have required, the concurrence of all the thirteen? Rhode-Island, in rebellion against integrity; Rhode-Island plundering all the world by her paper money, and notorious for her uniform opposition to every federal duty, would then have it in her power to defeat the Union; and may we not judge with absolute certainty from her past conduct, that she would do so? Therefore, to have required the ratification of all the thirteen States would have been tantamount to returning without having done any thing. What other number would have been proper? Twelve? The same spirit that has actuated me in the whole progress of the business, would have prevented me from leaving it in the power of any one State to dissolve the Union: For would it not be lamentable, that nothing could be done for the defection of one State? A majority of the whole would have been too few. Nine States therefore seem to be a most proper number. The Gentleman then proceeds, and inquires, why we assumed the language of "We, the People." I ask why not? The Government is for the people; and the misfortune was, that the people had no agency in the Government before. The Congress had power to make peace and war, under the old Confederation. Granting passports, by the law of nations, is annexed to this power; yet Congress was reduced to the humiliating condition of being obliged to send deputies to Virginia to solicit a passport. Notwithstanding the exclusive power of war, given to Congress, the second article of the Confederation was interpreted to forbid that body to grant a passport for tobacco; which during the war, and in pursuance of engagements made at little York, was to have been sent into New-York. What harm is there in consulting the people, on the construction of a Government by which they are to be bound? Is it unfair? Is it unjust? If the Government is to be binding on the people, are not the people the proper persons to examine its merits or defects? I take this to be one of the least and most trivial objections that will be made to the Constitution—it carries the answer with itself. In the whole of this business, I have acted in the strictest obedience to the dictates of my conscience, in discharging what I conceive to be my duty to my country. I refused my signature, and if the same reasons operated on my mind, I would still refuse; but as I think that those eight States which have adopted the Constitution will not recede, I am a friend to the Union.

George Mason Fears for
the Rights of the People

June 4, 1788

Mr. *George Mason.* — Mr. Chairman — Whether the Constitution be good or bad, the present clause clearly discovers, that it is a National Government, and no longer a confederation. I mean that clause which gives the first hint of the General Government laying direct taxes. The assumption of this power of laying direct taxes, does of itself, entirely change the confederation of the States into one consolidated Government. This power being at discretion, unconfined, and without any kind of controul, must carry every thing before it. The very idea of converting what was formerly a confederation, to a consolidated Government, is totally subversive of every principle which has hitherto governed us. This power is calculated to annihilate totally the State Governments. Will the people of this great community submit to be individually taxed by two different and distinct powers? Will they suffer themselves to be doubly harrassed? These two concurrent powers cannot exist long together; the one will destroy the other: The General Government being paramount to, and in every respect more powerful than, the State governments, the latter must give way to the former. Is it to be supposed that one National Government will suit so extensive a country, embracing so many climates, and containing inhabitants so very different in manners, habits, and customs? It is ascertained by history, that there never was a Government, over a very extensive country, without destroying the liberties of the people: History also, supported by the opinions of the best writers, shew us, that monarchy may suit a large territory, and despotic Governments ever so extensive a country; but that popular Governments can only exist in small territories. Is there a single example, on the face of the earth, to support a contrary opinion? Where is there one exception to this general rule? Was there ever an instance of a general National Government extending over so extensive a country, abounding in such a variety of climates, &c. where the people retained their liberty? I solemnly declare, that no man is a greater friend to a firm Union of the American States than I am: But, Sir, if this great end can be obtained without hazarding the rights of the people, why should we recur to such dangerous principles? Requisitions have been often refused, sometimes from an impossibility of complying with them; often from that great variety of circumstances which retard the collection of monies, and, perhaps, sometimes from a wilful design of procrastinating. But why shall we give up to the National Government this power, so dangerous in its nature, and for which its members will not have sufficient information?—Is it not well known, that what would be a proper tax in one State would be grievous in another? The Gentleman who hath favored us with an eulogium in favor of this system, must, after all the encomiums he has been pleased to bestow upon it, acknowledge, that our Federal Representatives must be unacquainted with the situation of their constituents: Sixty-five members cannot possibly know the situation and circumstances of all the inhabitants of this immense continent: When a certain sum comes to be taxed, and the mode of levying to be fixed, they will lay the tax on that article which will be most productive, and easiest in the collection, without consulting the real circumstances or convenience of a country, with which, in fact, they cannot be sufficiently acquainted. The mode of levying taxes is of the utmost consequence, and yet here it is to be determined by those who have neither knowledge of our situation, nor a common interest with us, nor a fellow feeling for us:—The subjects of taxation differ in three-fourths; nay, I might say with truth, in four-fifths of the States:—If we trust the National Government with an effectual way of raising the necessary sums, 'tis sufficient; every thing we do further is trusting the happiness and rights of the people: Why then should we give up this dangerous power of individual taxation? Why leave the manner of laying taxes to those, who in the nature of things, cannot be acquainted with the situation of those on whom they are to impose them, when it can be done by those who are well acquainted with it? If instead of giving this oppressive power, we give them such an effectual alternative as will answer the purpose, without encountering the evil and danger that might arise from it, then I would chearfully acquiesce: And would it not be far more eligible? I candidly acknowledge the inefficacy of the confederation; but requisitions have been made, which were impossible to be complied with: Requisitions for more gold and silver than were in the United States: If we give the General Government the power of demanding their quotas of the States, with an alternative of laying direct taxes, in case of non compliance, then the mischief would be avoided; and the certainty of this conditional power would, in all human probability, prevent the application, and the sums necessary for the Union would be then laid by the States; by those who know how it can best be raised; by those who have a fellow-feeling for us. Give me leave to say, that the same sum raised one way with convenience and ease, would be very oppressive another way: Why then not leave this power to be exercised by those who know the mode most convenient for the inhabitants, and not by those who must necessarily apportion it in such manner as shall be oppressive? With respect to the representation so much applauded, I cannot think it such a full and free one as it is represented; but I must candidly acknowledge, that this defect results from the very nature of the Government. It would be impossible to have a full and adequate representation in the General Government; it would be too expensive and too unweildy: We are then under the necessity of having this a very inadequate representation: Is this general representation to be compared with the real, actual, substantial representation of the State Legislatures? It cannot bear a comparison. To make representation real and actual, the number of Representatives ought to be adequate; they ought to mix with the people, think as they think, feel as they feel, ought to be perfectly amenable to them, and thoroughly acquainted with their interest and condition: Now these great ingredients are, either not at all, or in so small a degree, to be found in our Federal Representatives, that we have no real, actual, substantial representation; but I acknowledge it results from the nature of the Government: The necessity of this inconvenience may appear a sufficient reason not to argue against it: But, Sir, it clearly shews, that we ought to give power with a sparing hand to a Government thus imperfectly constructed. To a Government, which, in the nature of things, cannot but be defective, no powers ought to be given, but such as are absolutely necessary: There is one thing in it which I conceive to be extremely dangerous. Gentlemen may talk of public virtue and confidence; we shall be told that the House of Representatives will consist of the most virtuous men on the Continent, and that in their hands we may trust our dearest rights. This, like all other assemblies, will be composed of some bad and some good men; and considering the natural lust of power so inherent in man, I fear the thirst of power will prevail to oppress the people:—What I conceive to be so dangerous, is the provision with respect to the number of Representatives: It does not expressly provide, that we shall have one for every 30,000, but that the number shall not exceed that proportion: The utmost that we can expect (and perhaps that is too much) is, that the present number shall be continued to us:—"The number of Representatives shall not exceed one for every 30,000." Now will not this be complied with, although the present number should never be increased; nay, although it should be decreased? Suppose Congress should say, that we should have one for every 200,000, will not the Constitution be complied with? For one for every 200,000 does not exceed one for every 30,000. There is a want of proportion that ought to be strictly guarded against: The worthy Gentleman tells us, we have no reason to fear; but I always fear for the rights of the people: I do not pretend to inspiration, but I think, it is apparent as the day, that the members will attend to local partial interests to prevent an augmentation of their number: I know not how they will be chosen, but whatever be the mode of choosing, our present number is but ten: And suppose our State is laid off in ten districts; those Gentlemen who shall be sent from those districts will lessen their own power and influence, in their respective districts, if they increase their number; for the greater the number of men among whom any given quantum of power is divided, the less the power of each individual. Thus they will have a local interest to prevent the increase of, and perhaps they will lessen their own number: This is evident on the face of the Constitution—so loose an expression ought to be guarded against; for Congress will be clearly within the requisition of the Constitution, although the number of Representatives should always continue what it is now, and the population of the country should increase to an immense number. Nay, they may reduce the number from 65, to one from each State, without violating the Constitution; and thus the number which is now too small, would then be infinitely too much so: But my principal objection is, that the confederation is converted to one general consolidated Government, which, from my best judgment of it (and which perhaps will be shewn in the course of this discussion, to be really well founded) is one of the worst curses that can possibly befal a nation. Does any man suppose, that one general National Government can exist in so extensive a country as this? I hope that a Government may be framed which may suit us, by drawing the line between the general and State Governments, and prevent that dangerous clashing of interest and power, which must, as it now stands, terminate in the destruction of one or the other. When we come to the Judiciary, we shall be more convinced, that this Government will terminate in the annihilation of the State Governments: The question then will be, whether a consolidated Government can preserve the freedom, and secure the great rights of the people.

If such amendments be introduced as shall exclude danger, I shall most gladly put my hand to it. When such amendments, as shall, from the best information, secure the great essential rights of the people, shall be agreed to by Gentlemen, I shall most heartily make the greatest concessions, and concur in any reasonable measure to obtain the desirable end of conciliation and unanimity. An indispensible amendment in this case, is, that Congress shall not exercise the power of raising direct taxes till the States shall have refused to comply with the requisitions of Congress. On this condition it may be granted, but I see no reason to grant it unconditionally; as the States can raise the taxes with more ease, and lay them on the inhabitants with more propriety, than it is possible for the General Government to do. If Congress hath this power without controul, the taxes will be laid by those who have no fellow-feeling or acquaintance with the people. This is my objection to the article now under consideration. It is a very great and important one. I therefore beg Gentlemen seriously to consider it. Should this power be restrained, I shall with-draw my objections to this part of the Constitution: But as it stands, it is an objection so strong in my mind, that its amendment is with me, a *sine qua non*, of its adoption. I wish for such amendments, and such only, as are necessary to se-cure the dearest rights of the people.

James Madison Replies to Patrick Henry, Defending the Taxing Power and Explaining Federalism

June 6, 1788

Mr. *Madison* then arose (but he spoke so low that his exordium could not be heard distinctly.)—I shall not attempt to make impressions by any ardent professions of zeal for the public welfare: We know the principles of every man will, and ought to be judged, not by his professions and declarations, but by his conduct; by that criterion I mean in common with every other member to be judged; and should it prove unfavorable to my reputation, yet it is a criterion, from which I will by no means depart. Comparisons have been made between the friends of this Constitution, and those who oppose it: Although I disapprove of such comparisons, I trust, that in points of truth, honor, candour, and rectitude of motives, the friends of this system, here, and in the other States, are not inferior to its opponents.—But professions of attachment to the public good, and comparisons of parties, ought not to govern or influence us now. We ought, Sir, to examine the Constitution on its own merits solely: We are to enquire whether it will promote the public happiness;—its aptitude to produce this desireable object, ought to be the exclusive subject of our present researches. In this pursuit, we ought not to address our arguments to the feelings and passions, but to those understandings and judgments which were selected by the people of this country, to decide this great question, by a calm and rational investigation. I hope that Gentlemen, in displaying their abilities, on this occasion, instead of giving opinions, and making assertions, will condescend to prove and demonstrate, by a fair and regular discussion.—It gives me pain to hear Gentlemen continually distorting the natural construction of language; for, it is sufficient if any human production can stand a fair discussion. Before I proceed to make some additions to the reasons which have been adduced by my honorable friend over the way, I must take the liberty to make some observations on what was said by another Gentleman, (Mr. *Henry.*) He told us, that this Constitution ought to be rejected, because it endangered the public liberty, in his opinion, in many instances. Give me leave to make one answer to that observation—Let the dangers which this system is supposed to be replete with, be clearly pointed out. If any dangerous and unnecessary powers be given to the general Legislature, let them be plainly demonstrated, and let us not rest satisfied with general assertions of dangers, without examination. If powers be necessary, apparent danger is not a sufficient reason against conceding them. He has suggested, that licentiousness has seldom produced the loss of liberty; but that the tyranny of rulers has almost always effected it. Since the general civilization of mankind, I believe there are more instances of the abridgment of the freedom of the people, by gradual and silent encroachments of those in power, than by violent and sudden usurpations:—But on a candid examination of history, we shall find that turbulence, violence, and abuse of power, by the majority trampling on the rights of the minority, have produced factions and commotions, which, in republics, have more frequently than any other cause, produced despotism. If we go over the whole history of ancient and modern republics, we shall find their destruction to have generally resulted from those causes. If we consider the peculiar situation of the United States, and what are the sources of that diversity of sentiments which pervades its inhabitants, we shall find great danger, that the same causes may terminate here, in the same fatal effects, which they produced in those republics. This danger ought to be wisely guarded against: Perhaps in the progress of this discussion it will appear, that the only possible remedy for those evils, and means of preserving and protecting the principles of republicanism, will be found in that very system which is now exclaimed against as the parent of oppression. I must confess, I have not been able to find his usual consistency, in the Gentleman's arguments on this occasion:—He informs us that the people of this country are at perfect repose;—that every man enjoys the fruits of his labor, peaceably and securely, and that every thing is in perfect tranquillity and safety. I wish sincerely, Sir, this were true. If this be their happy situation, why has every State acknowledged the contrary? Why were deputies from all the States sent to the General Convention? Why have complaints of national and individual distresses been echoed and re-echoed throughout the Continent? Why has our General Government been so shamefully disgraced, and our Constitution violated? Wherefore have laws been made to authorise a change, and wherefore are we now assembled here? A Federal Government is formed for the protection of its individual members. Ours was attacked itself with impunity. Its authority has been disobeyed and despised. I think I perceive a glaring inconsistency in another of his arguments. He complains of this Constitution, because it requires the consent of at least three-fourths of the States to introduce amendments which shall be necessary for the happiness of the people. The assent of so many, he urges as too great an obstacle, to the admission of salutary amendments; which he strongly insists, ought to be at the will of a bare majority—We hear this argument, at the very moment we are called upon to assign reasons for proposing a Constitution, which puts it in the power of nine States to abolish the present inadequate, unsafe, and pernicious Confederation! In the first case he asserts, that a majority ought to have the power of altering the Government when found to be inadequate to the security of public happiness. In the last case, he affirms, that even three-fourths of the community have not a right to alter a Government, which experience has proved to be subversive of national felicity! Nay, that the most necessary and urgent alterations cannot be made without the absolute unanimity of all the States. Does not the thirteenth article of the Confederation expressly require, that no alteration shall be made without the unanimous consent of all the States? Could any thing in theory, be more perniciously improvident and injudicious, than this submission of the will of the majority to the most trifling minority? Have not experience and practice actually manifested this theoretical inconvenience to be extremely impolitic? Let me mention one fact, which I conceive must carry conviction to the mind of any one—The smallest State in the Union has obstructed every attempt to reform the Government—That little member has repeatedly disobeyed and counteracted the general authority; nay, has even supplied the enemies of its country with provisions. Twelve States had agreed to certain improvements which were proposed, being thought absolutely necessary to preserve the existence of the General Government; but as these improvements, though really indispensible, could not by the Confederation be introduced into it without the consent of every State; the refractory dissent of that little State prevented their adoption. The inconveniences resulting from this requisition, of unanimous concurrence in alterations in the Confederation, must be known to every member in this Convention; 'tis therefore needless to remind them of them. Is it not self-evident, that a trifling minority ought not to bind the majority? Would not foreign influence be exerted with facility over a small minority? Would the Honorable Gentleman agree to continue the most radical defects in the old system, because the petty State of Rhode-Island would not agree to remove them? He next objects to the exclusive legislation over the district where the seat of the Government may be fixed. Would he submit that the Representatives of this State should carry on their deliberations under the controul of any one member of the Union? If any State had the power of legislation over the place where Congress should fix the General Government; this would impair the dignity, and hazard the safety of Congress. If the safety of the Union were under the controul of any particular State, would not foreign corruption probably prevail in such a State, to induce it to exert its controuling influence over the members of the General Government? Gentlemen cannot have forgotten the disgraceful insult which Congress received some years ago. When we also reflect, that the previous cession of particular States is necessary, before Congress can legislate exclusively any where, we must, instead of being alarmed at this part, heartily approve of it. But the honorable member sees great danger in the provision concerning the militia: This I conceive to be an additional security to our liberty, without diminishing the power of the States, in any considerable degree—It appears to me so highly expedient, that I should imagine it would have found advocates even in the warmest friends of the present system: The authority of training the militia, and appointing the officers, is reserved to the States. Congress ought to have the power of establishing an uniform discipline through the States; and to provide for the execution of the laws, suppress insurrections, and repel invasions: These are the only cases wherein they can interfere with the militia; and the obvious necessity of their having power over them in these cases, must convince any reflecting mind. Without uniformity of discipline military bodies would be incapable of action:—Without a general controuling power to call forth the strength of the Union, to repel invasions, the country might be over-run and conquered by foreign enemies—Without such a power, to suppress insurrections, our liberties might be destroyed by domestic faction, and domestic tyranny be established.—The honorable member then told us, that there was no instance of power once transferred, being voluntarily renounced. Not to produce European examples, which may probably be done before the rising of this Convention; have we not seen already in seven States (and probably in an eighth State) Legislatures surrendering some of the most important powers they possessed? But, Sir, by this Government, powers are not given to any particular set of men— They are in the hands of the people—delegated to their Representatives chosen for short terms. To Representatives responsible to the people, and whose situation is perfectly similar to their own:—As long as this is the case we have no danger to apprehend. When the Gentleman called our recollection to the usual effects of the concession of powers, and imputed the loss of liberty generally to open tyranny, I wish he had gone on further. Upon a review of history he would have found, that the loss of liberty very often resulted from factions and divisions;—from local considerations, which eternally lead to quarrels—He would have found internal dissentions to have more frequently demolished civil liberty, than a tenacious disposition in rulers, to retain any stipulated powers. (Here Mr. *Madison* enumerated the various means whereby nations had lost their liberty.)—The power of raising and supporting armies is exclaimed against, as dangerous and unnecessary. I wish there was no necessity of vesting this power in the General Government. But suppose a foreign nation to declare war against the United States, must not the general Legislature have the power of defending the United States? Ought it to be known to foreign nations, that the General Government of the United States of America has no power to raise or support an army, even in the utmost danger, when attacked by external enemies? Would not their knowledge of such a circumstance stimulate them to fall upon us? If, Sir, Congress be not invested with this power, any powerful nation, prompted by ambition or avarice, will be invited, by our weakness, to attack us; and such an attack, by disciplined veterans, would certainly be attended with success, when only opposed by irregular, undisciplined militia.— Whoever considers the peculiar situation of this country; the multiplicity of its excellent inlets and harbours, and the uncommon facility of attacking it, however much he may regret the necessity of such a power, cannot hesitate a moment in granting it. One fact may elucidate this argument. In the course of the late war, when the weak parts of the Union were exposed, and many States were in the most deplorable situation, by the enemy's ravages: The assistance of foreign nations was thought so urgently necessary for our protection, that the relinquishment of territorial advantages was not deemed too great a sacrifice for the acquisition of one ally. This expedient was admitted with great reluctance even by those States who expected most advantages from it. The crises however at length arrived, when it was judged necessary for the salvation of this country, to make certain cessions to Spain; whether wisely, or otherwise, is not for me to say; but the fact was, that instructions were sent to our Representative at the Court of Spain, to empower him to enter into negotiations for that purpose: How it terminated is well known. This fact shews the extremities to which nations will recur in cases of imminent danger, and demonstrates the necessity of making ourselves more respectable. The necessity of making dangerous cessions, and of applying to foreign aid, ought to be excluded. The honorable member then told us, there are heart-burnings in the adopting States, and that Virginia may, if she does not come into the measure, continue in amicable confederacy with the adopting States. I wish as seldom as possible to contradict the assertions of Gentlemen, but I can venture to affirm, without danger of being in an error, that there is the most satisfactory evidence, that the satisfaction of those States is increasing every day, and that in that State where it was adopted only by a majority of nineteen, there is not one-fifth of the people dissatisfied. There are some reasons which induce us to conclude, that the grounds of proselytism extend every where—its principles begin to be better understood—and the inflammatory violence, wherewith it was opposed by designing, illiberal, and unthinking minds, begins to subside. I will not enumerate the causes from which, in my conception, the heart-burnings of a majority of its opposers have originated. Suffice it to say, that in all they were founded on a misconception of its nature and tendency. Had it been candidly examined, and fairly discussed, I believe, Sir, that but a very inconsiderable minority of the people of the United States would have opposed it. With respect to the Swiss, which the Honorable Gentleman has proposed for our example, as far as historical authority may be relied upon, we shall find their Government quite unworthy of our imitation. I am sure if the honorable member had adverted to their history and Government, he never would have quoted their example here: He would have found, that instead of respecting the rights of mankind, their Government (at least of several of their cantons) is one of the vilest aristocracies that ever was instituted: The peasants of some of their cantons are more oppressed and degraded, than the subjects of any Monarch in Europe: Nay, almost as much so, as those of any Eastern despot. It is a novelty in politics, that from the worst of systems, the happiest consequences should ensue: Their aristocratical rigor, and the peculiarity of their situation, have so long supported their Union: Without the closest alliance and amity, dismemberment might follow: Their powerful and ambitious neighbours would immediately avail themselves of their least jarrings. As we are not circumstanced like them, no conclusive precedent can be drawn from their situation. I trust, the Gentleman does not carry his idea so far as to recommend a separation from the adopting States. This Government may secure our happiness; this is at least as probable, as that it shall be oppressive. If eight States have, from a persuasion of its policy and utility adopted it, shall Virginia shrink from it without a full conviction of its danger and inutility? I hope she will never shrink from any duty: I trust she will not determine without the most serious reflection and deliberation. I confess to you, Sir, were uniformity of religion to be introduced by this system, it would, in my opinion, be ineligible; but I have no reason to conclude, that uniformity of Government will produce that of religion. This subject is, for the honor of America, perfectly free and unshackled: The Government has no jurisdiction over it—The least reflection will convince us, there is no danger to be feared on this ground. But we are flattered with the probability of obtaining previous amendments. This calls for the most serious attention of this House. If amendments are to be proposed by one State, other States have the same right, and will also propose alterations. These cannot but be dissimilar, and opposite in their nature. I beg leave to remark, that the Governments of the different States are in many respects dissimilar in their structure—Their Legislative bodies are not similar—Their Executives are more different. In several of the States the first Magistrate is elected by the people at large—In others, by joint ballot of the members of both branches of the Legislature—And in others, in other different manners. This dissimilarity has occasioned a diversity of opinion on the theory of Government, which will, without many reciprocal concessions, render a concurrence impossible. Although the appointment of an Executive Magistrate, has not been thought destructive to the principles of democracy in any of the States, yet, in the course of the debate, we find objections made to the Federal Executive: It is urged that the President will degenerate into a tyrant. I intended, in compliance with the call of the honorable member, to explain the reasons of proposing this Constitution, and develop its principles; but I shall postpone my remarks, till we hear the supplement which he has informed us, he intends to add to what he has already said. Give me leave to say something of the nature of the Government, and to shew that it is safe and just to vest it with the power of direct taxation. There are a number of opinions; but the principal question is, whether it be a federal or consolidated Government: In order to judge properly of the question before us, we must consider it minutely in its principal parts. I conceive myself, that it is of a mixed nature:—It is in a manner unprecedented: We cannot find one express example in the experience of the world:—It stands by itself. In some respects, it is a Government of a federal nature; in others it is of a consolidated nature. Even if we attend to the manner in which the Constitution is investigated, ratified, and made the act of the people of America, I can say, notwithstanding what the Honorable Gentleman has alledged, that this Government is not completely consolidated,—nor is it entirely federal. Who are parties to it? The people—but not the people as composing one great body—but the people as composing thirteen sovereignties: Were it as the Gentleman asserts, a consolidated Government, the assent of a majority of the people would be sufficient for its establishment, and as a majority have adopted it already, the remaining States would be bound by the act of the majority, even if they unanimously reprobated it: Were it such a Government as it is suggested, it would be now binding on the people of this State, without having had the privilege of deliberating upon it: But, Sir, no State is bound by it, as it is, without its own consent. Should all the States adopt it, it will be then a Government established by the thirteen States of America, not through the intervention of the Legislatures, but by the people at large. In this particular respect the distinction between the existing and proposed Governments is very material. The existing system has been derived from the dependent derivative authority of the Legislatures of the States; whereas this is derived from the superior power of the people. If we look at the manner in which alterations are to be made in it, the same idea is in some degree attended to. By the new system a majority of the States cannot introduce amendments; nor are all the States required for that purpose; three-fourths of them must concur in alterations; in this there is a departure from the federal idea. The members to the national House of Representatives are to be chosen by the people at large, in proportion to the numbers in the respective districts. When we come to the Senate, its members are elected by the States in their equal and political capacity; but had the Government been completely consolidated, the Senate would have been chosen by the people in their individual capacity, in the same manner as the members of the other House. Thus it is of a complicated

nature, and this complication, I trust, will be found to exclude
the evils of absolute consolidation, as well as of a mere confederacy. If Virginia were separated from all the States, her
power and authority would extend to all cases: In like manner
were all powers vested in the General Government, it would
be a consolidated Government: But the powers of the Federal
Government are enumerated; it can only operate in certain
cases: It has Legislative powers on defined and limited objects, beyond which it cannot extend its jurisdiction. But the
honorable member has satirized with peculiar acrimony, the
powers given to the General Government by this Constitution. I conceive that the first question on this subject is,
whether those powers be necessary; if they be, we are reduced
to the dilemma of either submitting to the inconvenience, or,
losing the Union. Let us consider the most important of these
reprobated powers; that of direct taxation is most generally
objected to: With respect to the exigencies of Government,
there is no question but the most easy mode of providing for
them will be adopted. When therefore direct taxes are not
necessary, they will not be recurred to. It can be of little advantage to those in power to raise money in a manner oppressive to the people. To consult the conveniences of the people,
will cost them nothing, and in many respects will be advantageous to them. Direct taxes will only be recurred to for great
purposes. What has brought on other nations those immense
debts, under the pressure of which many of them labour? Not
the expences of their governments, but war. If this country
should be engaged in war (and I conceive we ought to provide for the possibility of such a case) how would it be carried
on? By the usual means provided from year to year? As our
imports will be necessary for the expences of Government,
and other common exigencies, how are we to carry on the
means of defence? How is it possible a war could be supported without money, or credit? And would it be possible
for a Government to have credit, without having the power
of raising money? No, it would be impossible for any Government in such a case to defend itself. Then, I say, Sir, that it
is necessary to establish funds for extraordinary exigencies,
and give this power to the General Government—for the
utter inutility of previous requisitions on the States is too well

known. Would it be possible for those countries whose finances and revenues are carried to the highest perfection, to carry on the operations of Government on great emergencies, such as the maintenance of a war, without an uncontrouled power of raising money? Has it not been necessary for Great-Britain, notwithstanding the facility of the collection of her taxes, to have recourse very often to this and other extraordinary methods of procuring money? Would not her public credit have been ruined, if it was known that her power to raise money was limited? Has not France been obliged on great occasions to use unusual means to raise funds? It has been the case in many countries, and no Government can exist, unless its powers extend to make provisions for every contingency. If we were actually attacked by a powerful nation, and our General Government had not the power of raising money, but depended solely on requisitions, our condition would be truly deplorable: — If the revenue of this Commonwealth were to depend on twenty distinct authorities, it would be impossible for it to carry on its operations. This must be obvious to every member here: I think therefore, that it is necessary for the preservation of the Union, that this power should be given to the General Government: — But it is urged, that its consolidated nature, joined to the power of direct taxation, will give it a tendency to destroy all subordinate authority; that its increasing influence will speedily enable it to absorb the State Governments. I cannot think this will be the case. If the General Government were wholly independent of the Governments of the particular States, then indeed usurpation might be expected to the fullest extent: But, Sir, on whom does this General Government depend? It derives its authority from those Governments, and from the same sources from which their authority is derived. The members of the Federal Government are taken from the same men from whom those of the State Legislatures are taken. If we consider the mode in which the Federal Representatives will be chosen, we shall be convinced, that the general will never destroy the individual Governments; and this conviction must be strengthened by an attention to the construction of the Senate. — The Representatives will be chosen, probably under the influence of the members of the State Legislatures; but there is not the least probability that the election of the latter will be influenced by the former. One hundred and sixty members represent this Commonwealth in one branch of the Legislature, are drawn from the people at large, and must ever possess more influence than the few men who will be elected to the General Legislature. The reasons offered on this subject, by a Gentleman on the same side (Mr. *Nicholas*) are unanswerable, and have been so full, that I shall add but little more on the subject. Those who wish to become Federal Representatives, must depend on their credit with that class of men who will be the most popular in their counties, who generally represent the people in the State Governments: They can, therefore, never succeed in any measure contrary to the wishes of those on whom they depend. It is almost certain, therefore, that the deliberations of the members of the Federal House of Representatives, will be directed to the interests of the people of America. As to the other branch, the Senators will be appointed by the Legislatures, and though elected for six years, I do not conceive they will so soon forget the source from which they derive their political existence. This election of one branch of the Federal, by the State Legislatures, secures an absolute dependence of the former on the latter. The biennial exclusion of one-third, will lessen the facility of a combination, and may put a stop to intrigues. I appeal to our past experience, whether they will attend to the interests of their constituent States. Have not those Gentlemen who have been honored with seats in Congress, *often signalized themselves by their attachment* to their States? I wish this government may answer the expectation of its friends, and foil the apprehensions of its enemies. I hope the patriotism of the people will continue, and be a sufficient guard to their liberties. I believe its tendency will be, that the State Governments will counteract the general interest, and ultimately prevail. The number of the Representatives is yet sufficient for our safety, and will gradually increase—and if we consider their different sources of information, the number will not appear too small.

Patrick Henry Replies to Governor Randolph

June 7, 1788

Mr. *Henry.* —I have thought, and still think, that a full investigation of the actual situation of America, ought to precede any decision on this great and important question. That Government is no more than a choice among evils, is acknowledged by the most intelligent among mankind, and has been a standing maxim for ages. If it be demonstrated that the adoption of the new plan is a little or a trifling evil, then, Sir, I acknowledge that adoption ought to follow: But, Sir, if this be a truth that its adoption may entail misery on the free people of this country, I then insist, that rejection ought to follow. Gentlemen strongly urge its adoption will be a mighty benefit to us: But, Sir, I am made of such incredulous materials that assertions and declarations, do not satisfy me. I must be convinced, Sir. I shall retain my infidelity on that subject, till I see our liberties secured in a manner perfectly satisfactory to my understanding.

There are certain maxims by which every wise and enlightened people will regulate their conduct. There are certain political maxims, which no free people ought ever to abandon. Maxims of which the observance is essential to the security of happiness. It is impiously irritating the avenging hand of Heaven, when a people who are in the full enjoyment of freedom, launch out into the wide ocean of human affairs, and desert those maxims which alone can preserve liberty. Such maxims, humble as they are, are those only which can render a nation safe or formidable. Poor little humble republican maxims have attracted the admiration and engaged the attention of the virtuous and wise in all nations, and have stood the shock of ages. We do not now admit the validity of maxims, which we once delighted in. We have since adopted maxims of a different but more *refined nature*: New maxims which tend to the prostration of republicanism.

We have one, Sir, *That all men are by nature free and independent, and have certain inherent rights, of which, when they enter into society, they cannot by any compact deprive or divest their posterity.* We have a set of maxims of the same spirit, which must be beloved by every friend to liberty, to virtue, to mankind. Our Bill of Rights contains those admirable maxims.

Now, Sir, I say, let us consider, whether the picture given of American affairs ought to drive us from those beloved maxims.

The Honorable Gentleman (Governor *Randolph*) has said, that it is too late in the day for us to reject this new plan: That system which was once execrated by the Honorable member, must now be adopted, let its defects be ever so glaring. That Honorable member will not accuse me of want of candour, when I cast in my mind what he has given the public,* and compare it to what has happened since. It seems to me very strange and unaccountable, that that which was the object of his execration, should now receive his encomiums. Something extraordinary must have operated so great a change in his opinion. *It is too late in the day?* Gentlemen must excuse me, if they should declare again and again, that it was too late, and I should think differently. I never can believe, Sir, that it is too late to save all that is precious. If it be proper, and independently of every external consideration, wisely constructed, let us receive it: But, Sir, shall its adoption by eight States induce us to receive it, if it be replete with the most dangerous defects? They urge that subsequent amendments are safer than previous amendments, and that they will answer the same ends. At present we have our liberties and privileges in our own hands. Let us not relinquish them. Let us not adopt this system till we see them secured. There is some small possibility, that should we follow the conduct of Massachusetts, amendments might be obtained. There is a small possibility of amending any Government; but, Sir, shall we abandon our most inestimable rights, and rest their security on a mere possibility? The Gentleman fears the loss of the Union. If eight States have ratified it unamended, and we should rashly imitate their precipitate example, do we not

---

*Alluding to his Excellency's letter on that subject to the Speaker of the House of Delegates.

thereby disunite from several other States? Shall those who have risked their lives for the sake of union, be at once thrown out of it? If it be amended, every State will accede to it; but by an imprudent adoption in its defective and dangerous state, a schism must inevitably be the consequence: I can never, therefore, consent to hazard our most unalienable rights on an absolute uncertainty. You are told there is no peace, although you fondly flatter yourselves that all is peace —No peace—a general cry and alarm in the country— Commerce, riches, and wealth vanished—Citizens going to seek comforts in other parts of the world—Laws insulted— Many instances of tyrannical legislation. These things, Sir, are new to me. He has made the discovery—As to the administration of justice, I believe that failures in commerce, &c. cannot be attributed to it. My age enables me to recollect its progress under the old Government. I can justify it by saying, that it continues in the same manner in this State, as it did under former Government. As to other parts of the Continent, I refer that to other Gentlemen. As to the ability of those who administer it, I believe they would not suffer by a comparison with those who administered it under the royal authority. Where is the cause of complaint if the wealthy go away? Is this added to the other circumstances, of such enormity, and does it bring such danger over this Commonwealth as to warrant so important, and so awful a change in so precipitate a manner? As to insults offered to the laws, I know of none. In this respect I believe this Commonwealth would not suffer by a comparison with the former Government. The laws are as well executed, and as patiently acquiesced in, as they were under the royal administration. Compare the situation of the country—Compare that of our citizens to what they were then, and decide whether persons and property are not as safe and secure as they were at that time. Is there a man in this Commonwealth, whose person can be insulted with impunity? Cannot redress be had here for personal insults or injuries, as well as in any part of the world—as well as in those countries where Aristocrats and Monarchs triumph and reign? Is not the protection of property in full operation here? The contrary cannot with truth be charged on this Commonwealth. Those severe charges which are exhibited against it, appear to me totally groundless. On a fair investigation, we shall be found to be surrounded by no real dangers. We have the animating fortitude and persevering alacrity of republican men, to carry us through misfortunes and calamities. 'Tis the fortune of a republic to be able to withstand the stormy ocean of human vicissitudes. I know of no danger awaiting us. Public and private security are to be found here in the highest degree. Sir, it is the fortune of a free people, not to be intimidated by imaginary dangers. Fear is the passion of slaves. Our political and natural hemispheres are now equally tranquil. Let us recollect the awful magnitude of the subject of our deliberation. Let us consider the latent consequences of an erroneous decision—and let not our minds be led away by unfair misrepresentations and uncandid suggestions. There have been many instances of uncommon lenity and temperance used in the exercise of power in this Commonwealth. I could call your recollection to many that happened during the war and since—But every Gentleman here must be apprized of them.

The Honorable member has given you an elaborate account of what he judges tyrannical legislation, and an *ex post facto law* (in the case of Josiah Philips.) He has misrepresented the facts. That man was not executed by a tyrannical stroke of power. Nor was he a Socrates. He was a fugitive murderer and an out-law—a man who commanded an infamous banditti, at a time when the war was at the most perilous stage. He committed the most cruel and shocking barbarities. He was an enemy to the human name.—Those who declare war against the human race, may be struck out of existence as soon as they are apprehended. He was not executed according to those beautiful legal ceremonies which are pointed out by the laws, in criminal cases. The enormity of his crimes did not entitle him to it. I am truly a friend to legal forms and methods; but, Sir, the occasion warranted the measure. A pirate, an out-law, or a common enemy to all mankind, may be put to death at any time. It is justified by the laws of nature and nations. The Honorable member tells us then, that there are burnings and discontents in the hearts of our citizens in general, and that they are dissatisfied with their Government. I have no doubt the Honorable member believes this to be the case, because he says so. But I have the comfortable assurance, that it is a certain fact, *that it is not so.* The middle and lower ranks of people have not those illumined ideas, which the well-born are so happily possessed of—They cannot so readily perceive latent objects. The microscopic eyes of modern States-men can see abundance of defects in old systems; and their illumined imaginations discover the necessity of a change. They are captivated by the parade of the number ten—The charms of the ten miles square.—Sir, I fear this change will ultimately lead to our ruin. My fears are not the force of imagination—They are but too well founded. I tremble for my country: But, Sir, I trust, I rely, and I am confident, that this political speculation has not taken so strong a hold of men's minds, as some would make us believe.

The dangers which may arise from our geographical situation, will be more properly considered awhile hence. At present, what may be surmised on the subject, with respect to the adjacent States, is merely visionary. Strength, Sir, is a relative term. When I reflect on the natural force of those nations that might be induced to attack us, and consider the difficulty of the attempt and uncertainty of the success, and compare thereto the relative strength of our country, I say that we are strong. We have no cause to fear from that quarter—We have nothing to dread from our neighboring States. The superiority of our cause would give us an advantage over them, were they so unfriendly or rash as to attack us. As to that part of the community, which the Honorable Gentlemen spoke of as being in danger of being separated from us: What incitement or inducement could its inhabitants have to wish such an event? It is a matter of doubt whether they would derive any advantage to themselves, or be any loss to us by such a separation. Time has been, and may yet come, when they will find it their advantage and true interest to be united with us. There is no danger of a dismemberment of our country, unless a Constitution be adopted which will enable the Government to plant enemies on our backs. By the Confederation, the rights of territory are secured. No treaty can be made without the consent of nine States. While the consent of nine States is necessary to the cession of territory you are safe. If it be put in the power of a less number, you will most infallibly lose the Mississippi. As long as we can preserve our unalienable rights, we are in safety. This new Constitution will involve in its operation the loss of the navigation of that valuable river. The Honorable Gentleman cannot be ignorant of the *Spanish transactions.*—A treaty had been nearly entered into with Spain, to relinquish that navigation. That relinquishment would absolutely have taken place, had the consent of seven States been sufficient. The Honorable Gentleman told us then, that eight States having adopted this system, we cannot suppose they will recede on our account. I know not what they may do; but this I know, that a people of infinitely less importance, than those of Virginia, stood the terror of war.—Vermont, Sir, withstood the terror of thirteen States. Maryland did not accede to the Confederation till the year, 1781. These two States, feeble as they are comparatively to us, were not afraid of the whole Union. Did either of these States perish? No, Sir, they were admitted freely into the Union. Will not Virginia then be admitted? I flatter myself that those States who have ratified the new plan of Government will open their arms and chearfully receive us, although we should propose certain amendments as the conditions on which we should ratify it. During the late war, all the States were in pursuit of the same object. To obtain that object they made the most strenuous exertions. They did not suffer trivial considerations to impede its acquisition. Give me leave to say, that if the smallest States in the Union were admitted into it, after having unreasonably procrastinated their accession; the greatest and most mighty State in the Union, will be easily admitted, when her reluctance to an immediate accession to this system, is founded on the most reasonable grounds. When I call this the most mighty State in the Union, do I not speak the truth? Does not Virginia surpass every State in the Union, in number of inhabitants, extent of territory, felicity of position, and affluence and wealth? Some infatuation hangs over men's minds, that they will inconsiderately precipitate into measures the most important, and give not a moment's deliberation to others, nor pay any respect to their opinions. Is this federalism? Are these the beloved effects of the federal spirit, that its votaries will never accede to the just propositions of others? Sir, were there nothing objectionable in it but that, I would vote against it. I desire to have nothing to do with such men as will obstinately refuse to change their opinion. Are our opinions not to be regarded? I hope that you will recollect, that you are going to join with men who will pay no respect even to this State.

Switzerland consists of thirteen cantons expressly confederated for national defence. They have stood the shock of 400 years: That country has enjoyed internal tranquillity most of that long period. Their dissentions have been comparatively, to those of other countries, very few. What has passed in the neighbouring countries? Wars, dissentions, and intrigues. Germany involved in the most deplorable civil war, thirty years successively—Continually convulsed with intestine divisions, and harrassed by foreign wars. France with her mighty monarchy perpetually at war. Compare the peasants of Switzerland with those of any other mighty nation: You will find them far more happy—for one civil war among them, there have been five or six among other nations—Their attachment to their country, and to freedom—their resolute intrepidity in their defence; the consequent security and happiness which they have enjoyed, and the respect and awe which these things produced in their bordering nations, have signalized these republicans. Their valor, Sir, has been active; every thing that sets in motion the springs of the human heart, engaged them to the protection of their inestimable privileges. They have not only secured their own liberty, but have been the arbiters of the fate of other people. Here, Sir, contemplate the triumph of republican Governments over the pride of monarchy. I acknowledge, Sir, that the necessity of national defence has prevailed in invigorating their councils and arms, and has been in a considerable degree the means of keeping these honest people together. But, Sir, they have had wisdom enough to keep together and render themselves formidable. Their heroism is proverbial. They would heroically fight for their Government, and their laws. One of the illumined sons of these times would not fight for those objects. Those virtuous and simple people have not a mighty and splendid President—nor enormously expensive navies and armies to support. No, Sir, those brave republicans have acquired their reputation no less by their undaunted intrepidity, than by the wisdom of their frugal and œconomical policy. Let us follow their example, and be equally happy. The Honorable member advises us to adopt a measure which will destroy our Bill of Rights. For, after hearing his picture of nations, and his reasons for abandoning all the powers retained to the States by the confederation, I am more firmly persuaded of the impropriety of adopting this new plan in its present shape.

I had doubts of the power of those who went to the Convention; but now we are possessed of it, let us examine it— When we trusted the great object of revising the Confederation to the greatest, the best, and most enlightened of our citizens, we thought their deliberations would have been solely confined to that revision. Instead of this, a new system, totally different in its nature and vesting the most extensive powers in Congress, is presented. Will the ten men you are to send to Congress, be more worthy than those seven were? If power grew so rapidly in their hands, what may it not do in the hands of others? If those who go from this State will find power accompanied with temptation, our situation must be truly critical. When about forming a Government, if we mistake the principles, or commit any other error, the very circumstance promises that power will be abused. The greatest caution and circumspection are therefore necessary—Nor does this proposed system in its investigation here, deserve the least charity.

The Honorable member says, that the National Government is without energy. I perfectly agree with him;—and when he cried out, *Union*, I agreed with him: But I tell him not to mistake the end for the means. The end is Union. The most capital means, I suppose, are an army, and navy: On a supposition I will acknowledge this; still the bare act of agreeing to that paper, though it may have an amazing influence, will not pay our millions. There must be things to pay debts. What these things are, or how they are to be produced, must be determined by our political wisdom and œconomy.

The Honorable Gentleman alledges, that previous amendments will prevent the junction of our riches from producing great profits and emoluments which would enable us to pay our public debts, by excluding us from the Union. I believe, Sir, that a previous ratification of a system notoriously and confessedly defective, will endanger our riches—our liberty—our all.—Its defects are acknowledged—They cannot be denied. The reason offered by the Honorable Gentleman for adopting this defective system, is the adoption by eight States. I say, Sir, that if we present nothing but what is reasonable in the shape of amendments they will receive us. Union is as necessary for them as for us. Will they then be so unreasonable as not to join us? If such be their disposition, I am happy to know it in time.

The Honorable member then observed, that nations will expend millions for commercial advantages—That is, that they will deprive you of every advantage if they can. Apply this another way.—Their cheaper way—instead of laying out millions in making war upon you, will be to corrupt your Senators. I know that if they be not above all price, they may make a sacrifice of our commercial interests. They may advise your President to make a treaty that will not only sacrifice all your commercial interests, but throw prostrate your Bill of Rights. Does he fear that their ships will out number ours on the ocean, or that nations whose interest comes in contrast with ours, in the progress of their guilt, will perpetrate the vilest expedients to exclude us from a participation in commercial advantages? Does he advise us, in order to avoid this evil, to adopt a Constitution, which will enable such nations to obtain their ends by the more easy mode of contaminating the principles of our Senators? Sir, if our Senators will not be corrupted it will be because they will be good men; and not because the Constitution provides against corruption, for there is no real check secured in it, and the most abandoned and profligate acts may with impunity be committed by them.

With respect to Maryland—What danger from thence? I know none. I have not heard of any hostility premeditated or committed. Nine-tenths of the people have not heard of it. Those who are so happy as to be illumined, have not informed their fellow-citizens of it. I am so valiant as to say, that no danger can come from that source, sufficient to make me abandon my republican principles.—The Honorable Gentleman ought to have recollected, that there were no tyrants in America, as there are in Europe.—The citizens of republican borders are only terrible to tyrants—Instead of being dangerous to one another, they mutually support one another's liberties. We might be confederated with the adopting States, without ratifying this system. No form of Government renders a people more formidable.—A confederacy of States joined together becomes strong as the United Netherlands.—The Government of Holland (execrated as it is) proves that the present Confederation is adequate to every purpose of human association. There are seven Provinces confederated together for a long time, containing numerous opulent cities and many of the finest ports in the world.—The recollection of the situation of that country, would make me execrate monarchy. The singular felicity and success of that people are unparalleled—Freedom has done miracles there in reclaiming land from the ocean. It is the richest spot on the face of the globe. Have they no men or money? Have they no fleets or armies? Have they no arts or sciences among them? How did they repel the attacks of the greatest nations in the world? How have they acquired their amazing affluence and power? Did they consolidate Government, to effect these purposes as we do? No, Sir, they have triumphed over every obstacle and difficulty; and have arrived at the summit of political felicity, and of uncommon opulence, by means of a confederacy; that very Government which Gentlemen affect to despise. They have, Sir, avoided a consolidation as the greatest of evils. They have lately, it is true, made one advance to that fatal progression. This misfortune burst on them by iniquity and artifice. *That Stadtholder, that Executive Magistrate*, contrived it in conjunction with other European nations. It was not the choice of the people. Was it owing to *his energy* that this happened? If two provinces have paid nothing, what have not the rest done? And have not these two provinces made other exertions? Ought they, to avoid this inconvenience, to have consolidated their different States, and have a ten miles square? Compare that little spot, nurtered by liberty, with the fairest country in the world. Does not Holland possess a powerful navy and army, and a full treasury? They did not acquire these by debasing the principles and trampling on the rights of their citizens. Sir, they acquired these by their industry, œconomy, and by the freedom of their Government. Their commerce is the most extensive in Europe: Their credit is un-

equalled: Their felicity will be an eternal monument of the
blessings of liberty: Every nation in Europe is taught by them
what they are, and what they ought to be. The contrast between those nations and this happy people, is the most splendid spectacle for republicans. The greatest cause of exultation
and triumph to the sons of freedom. While other nations,
precipitated by the rage of ambition or folly, have, in the pursuit of the most magnificent projects, rivetted the fetters of
bondage on themselves and descendants, these republicans secured their political happiness and freedom. Where is there a
nation to be compared to them? Where is there now, or
where was there ever a nation, of so small a territory, and so
few in number, so powerful—so wealthy—so happy? What
is the cause of this superiority? Liberty, Sir, the freedom of
their Government. Though they are now unhappily in some
degree consolidated, yet they have my acclamations, when put
in contrast with those millions of their fellow-men who lived
and died slaves. The dangers of a consolidation ought to be
guarded against in this country. I shall exert my poor talents
to ward them off. Dangers are to be apprehended in whatever
manner we proceed; but those of a consolidation are the most
destructive. Let us leave no expedient untried to secure happiness; but whatever be our decision, I am consoled, if American liberty will remain entire only for half a century—and I
trust that mankind in general, and our posterity in particular,
will be compensated for every anxiety we now feel.

Another Gentleman tells us, that no inconvenience will result from the exercise of the power of taxation by the General
Government; that two shillings out of ten may be saved by
the impost; and that four shillings may be paid to the federal
collector, and four to the State collector. A change of Government will not pay money. If from the probable amount of the
impost, you take the enormous and extravagant expences,
which will certainly attend the support of this great Consolidated Government, I believe you will find no reduction of the
public burthens by this new system. The splendid maintenance of the President and of the members of both Houses;
and the salaries and fees of the swarm of officers and dependants on the Government will cost this Continent immense
sums. Double sets of collectors will double the expence. To

these are to be added oppressive excise-men and custom-house officers. Sir, the people have an hereditary hatred to custom-house officers. The experience of the mother country leads me to detest them. They have introduced their baneful influence into the administration and destroyed one of the most beautiful systems that ever the world saw. Our fore-fathers enjoyed liberty there while that system was in its purity—but it is now contaminated by influence of every kind.

The stile of the Government (we the people) was intro-duced perhaps to recommend it to the people at large, to those citizens who are to be levelled and degraded to the lowest degree; who are likened to a *herd**; and who by the operation of this *blessed* system are to be transformed from respectable independent citizens, to abject, dependent subjects or slaves. The Honorable Gentleman has anticipated what we are to be reduced to, by degradingly assimilating our citizens to a herd.—(Here Governor *Randolph* arose, and declared that he did not use that word to excite any odium, but merely to convey an idea of a multitude.)—Mr. *Henry* replied, that it made a deep impression on his mind, and that he verily be-lieved, that system would operate as he had said.—He then continued. I will exchange that *abominable* word for requisi-tions—requisitions which Gentlemen affect to despise, have nothing degrading in them. On this depends our political prosperity. I never will give up that *darling* word requisi-tions—My country may give it up—A majority may wrest it from me, but I will never give it up till my grave. Requisi-tions are attended with one singular advantage. They are at-tended by deliberation.—They secure to the States the benefit of correcting oppressive errors. If our Assembly thought req-uisitions erroneous—If they thought the demand was too great, they might at least supplicate Congress to reconsider,—that it was a little too much. The power of direct taxation was called by the Honorable Gentleman the soul of the Govern-ment: Another Gentleman, called it the lungs of the Govern-ment. We all agree, that it is the most important part of the

---

*Governor Randolph had cursorily mentioned the word *herd* in his second speech.

body politic. If the power of raising money be necessary for the General Government, it is no less so for the States. If money be the vitals of Congress, is it not precious for those individuals from whom it is to be taken? Must I give my soul—my lungs, to Congress? Congress must have our souls. The State must have our souls. This is dishonorable and disgraceful. These two co-ordinate, interferring unlimited powers of harrassing the community, are unexampled: It is unprecedented in history: They are the visionary projects of modern politicians: Tell me not of imaginary means, but of reality: This political solecism will never tend to the bene-fit of the community. It will be as oppressive in practice as it is absurd in theory. If you part with this which the Honorable Gentleman tells you is the soul of Congress, you will be in-evitably ruined. I tell you, they shall not have the soul of Vir-ginia. They tell us, that one collector may collect the Federal and State taxes. The General Government being paramount to the State Legislatures; if the Sheriff is to collect for both; his right hand for the Congress, his left for the State; his right hand being paramount over the left, his collections will go to Congress. We will have the rest. Defficiencies in collections will always operate against the States. Congress being the par-amount supreme power, must not be disappointed. Thus Congress will have an unlimited, unbounded command over the soul of this Commonwealth. After satisfying their un-controuled demands, what can be left for the States? Not a sufficiency even to defray the expence of their internal admin-istration. They must therefore glide imperceptibly and gradu-ally out of existence. This, Sir, must naturally terminate in a consolidation. If this will do for other people, it never will do for me.

If we are to have one Representative for every 30,000 souls it must be by implication. The Constitution does not posi-tively secure it. Even say it is a natural implication, why not give us a right to that proportion in express terms, in lan-guage that could not admit of evasions or subterfuges? If they can use implication *for* us, they can also use implication *against* us. We are *giving* power, they are *getting* power, judge then, on which side the implication will be used. When we once put it in their option to assume constructive power, danger will follow. Trial by jury and liberty of the press, are also on this foundation of implication. If they encroach on these rights, and you give your implication for a plea, you are cast; for they will be justified by the last part of it, which gives them full power, "To make all laws which shall be necessary and proper to carry their powers into execution." Implication is dangerous, because it is unbounded: If it be admitted at all, and no limits be prescribed, it admits of the utmost extension. They say that every thing that is not given is retained. The reverse of the proposition is true by implication. They do not carry their implication so far when they speak of the general welfare. No implication when the sweeping clause comes. Implication is only necessary when the existence of privileges is in dispute. The existence of powers is sufficiently established. If we trust our dearest rights to implication, we shall be in a very unhappy situation.

Implication in England has been a source of dissention. There has been a war of implication between the King and people. For 100 years did the mother country struggle under the uncertainty of implication. The people insisted that their rights were implied: The Monarch denied the doctrine. Their Bill of Rights in some degree terminated the dispute. By a bold implication, they said they had a right to bind us in all cases whatsoever. This constructive power we opposed, and successfully. Thirteen or fourteen years ago, the most important thing that could be thought of, was to exclude the possibility of construction and implication. These, Sir, were then deemed perilous. The first thing that was thought of, was a Bill of Rights. We were not satisfied with your constructive argumentative rights.

Mr. *Henry* then declared, a Bill of Rights indispensably necessary; that a general positive provision should be inserted in the new system, securing to the States and the people, every right which was not conceded to the General Government; and that every implication should be done away. It being now late, he concluded by observing, that he would resume the subject another time.

Henry Lee's Sharp Reply to Patrick Henry's Attacks on the Constitution

June 9, 1788

Mr. *Lee*, of *Westmoreland.*—Mr. Chairman.—When I spoke before, and called on the Honorable Gentleman (Mr. *Henry*) to come forward and give his reasons for his opposition, in a systematic manner; I did it from a love of order, and respect for the character of the Honorable Gentleman; having no other motives, but the good of my country. As he seemed so solicitous that the truth should be brought before the Committee on this occasion, I thought I could not do more properly, than to call on him for his reasons for standing forth the champion of opposition. I took the liberty to add, that the subject belonged to the judgments of the Gentlemen of the Committee, and not to their passions. I am obliged to him for his politeness in this Committee; but as the Honorable Gentleman seems to have discarded in a great measure, solid argument and strong reasoning, and has established a new system of throwing those bolts, which he has so peculiar a dexterity at discharging; I trust I shall not incur the displeasure of the Committee, by answering the Honorable Gentleman in the desultory manner in which he has treated the subject. I shall touch a few of those *luminous* points which he has entertained us with. He told us the other day, that the enemies of the Constitution were firm supporters of liberty; and implied that its friends were not republicans. This may have been calculated to make impressions disadvantageous to those Gentlemen who favor this new plan of Government; and impressions of that kind are not easily eradicated. I conceive that I may say with truth, that the friends of that paper are true republicans, and by no means less attached to liberty, than those who oppose it. The verity of this does not depend on my assertion, but on the lives, and well known characters of different Gentlemen in different parts of the Continent.— I trust the friends of that Government, will oppose the efforts of despotism as well as its opposers.

Much is said by Gentlemen out of doors. They ought to urge all their objections here. I hope they will offer them here. I shall confine myself to what is said here. In all his rage for democracy, and zeal for the rights of the people, how often does he express his admiration of that King and Parliament over the Atlantic? But we republicans are contemned and despised. Here, Sir, I conceive that *implication* might operate against himself.

He tells us that he is a staunch republican, and that he adores liberty. I believe him, and when I do so, I wonder that he should say, that a Kingly Government is superior to that system which we admire.—He tells you that it cherishes a standing army, and that militia alone ought to be depended upon for the defence of every free country.—There is not a Gentleman in this House—There is no man without these walls (not even the Gentleman himself) who admires the militia more than I do. Without vanity I may say, I have had different experience of their service, from that of the Honorable Gentleman. It was my fortune to be a soldier of my country. In the discharge of my duty, I knew the worth of militia. I have seen them perform feats that would do honor to the first veterans, and submitting to what would daunt German soldiers. I saw what the Honorable Gentleman did not see—Our men fighting with the troops of that King which he so much admires. I have seen proofs of the wisdom of that paper on your table. I have seen incontrovertible evidence that militia cannot always be relied upon. I could enumerate many instances, but one will suffice. Let the Gentleman recollect the action of Guildford. The American regular troops behaved there with the most gallant intrepidity. What did the militia do? The greatest numbers of them fled. Their abandonment of the regulars occasioned the loss of the field. Had the line been supported that day, Cornwallis, instead of surrendering at York, would have laid down his arms at Guildford.

This plan provides for the public defence as it ought to do. Regulars are to be employed when necessary; and the service of the militia will always be made use of. This, Sir, will promote agricultural industry and skill, and military discipline and science.

I cannot understand the implication of the Honorable Gentleman, that because Congress may arm the militia, the States cannot do it: Nor do I understand the reverse of the proposition. The States are by no part of the plan before you, precluded from arming and disciplining the militia, should Congress neglect it. In the course of Saturday, and some previous harangues, from the terms in which some of the Northern States were spoken of, one would have thought that the love of an American was in some degree criminal; as being incompatible with a proper degree of affection for a Virginian. The people of America, Sir, are one people. I love the people of the North, not because they have adopted the Constitution; but, because I fought with them as my countrymen, and because I consider them as such.—Does it follow from hence, that I have forgotten my attachment to my native State? In all local matters I shall be a Virginian: In those of a general nature, I shall not forget that I am an American.

He has called on the House to expose the catalogue of evils which would justify this change of the Government. I appeal to Gentlemen's candour, has not a most mournful detail been unfolded here?

In the course of the debates, I have heard from those Gentlemen who have advocated the new system, an enumeration, which drew groans from my very soul; but which did not draw one sigh from the Honorable Gentleman over the way. Permit me to ask, if there be an evil which can visit mankind, so injurious and oppressive in its consequence and operation, as a tender law? If Pandora's box were on one side of me, and a tender law on the other, I would rather submit to the box than to the tender law. The principle, evil as it is, is not so base and pernicious as the application. It breaks down the moral character of your people—robs the widow of her maintenance, and defrauds the offspring of his food. The widow and orphans are reduced to misery, by receiving in a depreciated value, money which the husband and father had lent out of friendship. This reverses the natural course of things. It robs the industrious of the fruits of their labor, and often enables the idle and rapacious to live in ease and comfort at the expence of the better part of the community. Was there not another evil but the possibility of continuing such palpable injustice, I would object to the present system. But, Sir, I will out of many more, mention another. How are your domestic creditors situated? I will not go to the general creditors. I mean the military creditor—The man who, by the vices of your system, is urged to part with his money for a trivial consideration—The poor man who has the paper in his pocket, for which he can receive little or nothing. There is a greater number of these meritorious men than the Honorable Gentleman believes. These unfortunate men are compelled to receive paper instead of gold—Paper, which nominally represents something, but which in reality represents almost nothing. A proper Government could do them justice, but the present one cannot do it. They are therefore forced to part with that paper which they fought for, and get less than a dollar for 20 shillings. I would for my part, and I hope every other Gentleman here would, submit to the inconvenience; but when I consider that the widows of gallant heroes, with their numerous offspring, are labouring under the most distressing indigence, and that these poor unhappy people will be relieved by the adoption of this Constitution, I am still more impressed with the necessity of this change.

But says the Honorable Gentleman, we are in peace. Does he forget the insurrection in Massachusetts? Perhaps he did not extend his philanthropy to that quarter. I was then in Congress, and had a proper opportunity to know the circumstances of this event. Had *Shays* been possessed of abilities, he might have established that favorite system of the Gentleman—*King, Lords and Commons.* Nothing was wanting to bring about a revolution, but a great man to head the insurgents; but fortunately he was a worthless Captain. There were 30,000 stand of arms nearly in his power, which were defended by a pensioner of this country. It would have been sufficient had he taken this deposit. He failed in it; but even after that failure, it was in the power of a great man to have taken it. But he wanted design and knowledge. Will you trust to the want of design and knowledge? Suppose another insurrection headed by a different man; what will follow? Under a man of capacity, the favourite Government of that Gentleman might have been established in Massachusetts and extended to Virginia.

But, Sir, this is a Consolidated Government, he tells us, and most feelingly does he dwell on the imaginary dangers of this pretended consolidation. I did suppose that an Honorable Gentleman whom I do not now see (Mr. *Madison*) had placed this in such a clear light, that every man would have been satisfied with it.

If this were a Consolidated Government, ought it not to be ratified by a majority of the people as individuals, and not as States? Suppose Virginia, Connecticut, Massachusetts, and Pennsylvania had ratified it; these four States being a majority of the people of America, would, by their adoption, have made it binding on all the States, had this been a Consolidated Government. But it is only the Government of those seven States who have adopted it. If the Honorable Gentleman will attend to this, we shall hear no more of consolidation.

Direct taxation is another objection, on which the Honorable Gentleman expatiates. This has been answered by several able Gentlemen; but as the Honorable Gentleman reverts to the subject, I hope I will be excused in saying a little on it. If Union be necessary, direct taxes are also necessary for its support. If it be an inconvenience, it results from the Union; and we must take its disadvantages with it: Besides, it will render it unnecessary to recur to the sanguinary method which some Gentlemen are said to admire. Had the Amphyctionic Council had the power contained in that paper, would they have sent armies to levy money? Will the Honorable Gentleman say, that it is more eligible and humane, to collect money by carrying fire and sword through the country, than by the peaceable mode of raising money of the people through the medium of an officer of peace, when it is necessary?

But says he, "The President will enslave you—Congress will trample on your liberties—A few regiments will appear —Mr. Chief Justice must give way—Our mace bearer is no match for a regiment." It was inhuman to place an individual against a whole regiment. A *few* regiments will not avail—I trust the supporters of the Government would get the better of *many* regiments. Were so mad an attempt made, the people would assemble in thousands, and drive 30 times the number of their few regiments. We would then do, as we have already done, with the regiments of that King which he so often tells us of.

The public liberty, says he, is designed to be destroyed.— What does he mean? Does he mean that we who are friends to that Government, are not friends to liberty? No man dares to say so. Does he mean that he is a greater admirer of liberty than we are? Perhaps so. But I undertake to say, that when it will be necessary to struggle in the cause of freedom; he will find himself equalled by thousands of those who support this Constitution. The purse of the people of Virginia is not given up by that paper: They can take no more of our money than is necessary to pay our share of the public debts, and provide for the general welfare. Were it otherwise, no man would be louder against it than myself.

He has represented our situation, as contradistinguished from the other States. What does he mean? I ask if it be fair to attempt to influence Gentlemen by particular applications to local interests? I say it is not fair. Am I to be told, when I come to deliberate on the interest of Virginia, that it obstructs the interest of the county of Westmoreland? Is this obstruction a sufficient reason to neglect the collective interests of Virginia? Were it of a local nature, it would be right to prefer it; but being of a general nature, the local interests must give way. I trust then that Gentlemen will consider, that the object of their deliberations is of a general nature. I disregard the argument, which insinuated the propriety of attending to localities; and I hope that the Gentlemen to whom it was addressed, regard too much the happiness of the community to be influenced by it.

But he tells you, that the Mississippi is insecure unless you reject this system, and that the transactions relating to it, were carried on under a veil of secrecy. His arguments on this subject are equally as defective, as those I have just had under consideration. But I feel myself called on by the Honorable Gentleman to come forward and tell the truth about the transactions respecting the Mississippi. In every action of my life, in which I have been concerned, whether as the soldier or politician, the good of my country was my first wish. I have attended not only to the good of the United States, but also to that of particular districts. There are men of integrity and truth here, who were also then in Congress. I call on them to put me right with respect to those transactions. As far as I could gather from what was then passing, I believe there was not a Gentleman in that Congress, who had an idea of surrendering the navigation of that river. They thought of the best mode of securing it: Some thought one way, and some another way. I was one of those men who thought the mode which has been alluded to, the best to secure it. I shall never deny that it was my opinion. I was one peculiarly interested. I had a fortune in that country, purchased, not by *paper money*, but by gold, to the amount of 8,000 pounds. But private interest could not have influenced me. The public welfare was my criterion in my opinions. I united private interest to the public interest, not of the whole people of Virginia, but of the United States. I thought I was promoting the real interest of the people. But says he, it was under the veil of secrecy. There was no peculiar or uncommon desire manifested of concealing those transactions. They were carried on in the same manner with others of the same nature, and consonant to the principles of the Confederation. I saw no anxiety on the occasion. I wish he would send to the President to know their secrets. He would be gratified fully.

The Honorable member this day, among other things, gave us a statement, of those States that have passed the new system, of those who have not, and of those who would probably not pass it. He called his assertions *facts*; but I expected he would shew us something to prove their existence.

He tells us, that New-Hampshire and Rhode-Island have refused it. Is that a *fact*? It is not a *fact*. New-Hampshire has not refused it. That State postponed her ultimate decision till she could know what Massachusetts would do: And whatever the Gentleman may say of borderers, the people of that State were very right in conducting themselves as they did. With respect to Rhode-Island, I hardly know any thing. That small State has so rebelled against justice, and so knocked down the bulwarks of probity, rectitude and truth, that nothing rational or just can be expected from her. She has not however, I believe, called a Convention to deliberate on it, much less formally refused it. From her situation it is evident, that she must adopt it, unless she departs from the primary maxims of human nature, which are those of self-preservation. New-York and North-Carolina are so high in opposition, he tells us, that they will certainly reject it. Here is another of his *facts*; and he says, he has the highest authority. As he dislikes the *veil of secrecy*, I beg he would tell us that high authority from which he gets this fact. Has he official communications? Have the Executives of those States informed him? Has our Executive been apprised of it? I believe not. I hold his unsupported authority in contempt.

Pennsylvania, Delaware and New-Jersey have adopted, but says he, they were governed by local considerations.—What are these local considerations? The Honorable Gentleman draws advantages from every source, but his arguments operate very often against himself. I admire the State of Pennsylvania—She deserves the attachment of every lover of his country. Poor Pennsylvania, says he, has been tricked into it. What an insult! The Honorable Gentleman would not say so of an individual—I know his politeness too well. Will he insult the majority of a free country? Pennsylvania is a respectable State. Though not so extensive as Virginia, she did as much as any State, in proportion, during the war; and has done as much since the peace. She has done as much in every situation, and her citizens have been as remarkable for their virtue and science, as those of any State. The Honorable Gentleman has told you, that Pennsylvania has been tricked into it; and, in so saying, has insulted the majority of a free country, in a manner in which I would not dare to insult any private Gentleman. The other adopting States have not been tricked into it, it seems.—Why? The Honorable Gentleman cannot tell us why these *have not* been tricked into it, no more than he can tell why Pennsylvania *has* been tricked into it. Is it because of their superior power and respectability; or, is it the consequence of their local situation?—But the State of New-York has too much virtue to be governed by local considerations. He insinuates this by his assertion that she will not regard the example of the other States. How can he, without being inconsistent, and without perverting facts, pretend to say, that New-York is not governed by local considerations in

her opposition? Is she not influenced by the local consideration of retaining that impost of which he says, Connecticut
and New-Jersey wish to get a participation?—What does he
say of North-Carolina? How will local considerations affect
her? If the principle be uniform, she will be led by the local
consideration of wishing to get a participation of the impost
of the importing States. Is it to be supposed, that she will be
so blind to her own interest as to depart from this principle?

When he attempted to prove, that you ought not to adopt
that paper which I admire, he told you that it was untrodden
ground. This objection goes to the adoption of any Government. The British Government ought to be proposed
perhaps. It is trodden ground. I know not of any reason to
operate against a system, because it is untrodden ground. The
Honorable Gentleman objects to the publication from time to
time, as being ambiguous and uncertain. Does not *from time
to time*, signify convenient time? If it admits of an extension of
time, does it not equally admit of publishing the accounts at
very short periods? For argument sake, say they may postpone the publications of the public accounts to the expiration
of every ten years: Will their constituents be satisfied with this
conduct? Will they not discard them, and elect other men
who will publish the accounts as often as they ought? It is
also in their power to publish every ten days. Is it not more
probable, that they will do their duty, than that they will neglect it, especially as their interest is inseparably connected
with their duty? He says they may conceal them for a century.
Did you ever hear so trivial and so captious an argument? I
felt when the great genius of the Gentleman nodded on that
occasion. Another objection of the Honorable Gentleman,
(whom I cannot follow through all his windings and turn-
ings) is, that those parts of the Constitution which are in favour of privileges, are not so clearly expressed as those parts
which concede powers. I beg your attention, because this is a
leading distinction. As long as the privilege of representation
is well secured, our liberties cannot be easily endangered. I
conceive this is secured in this country more fully than in any
other. How are we the people of America, as land-holders,
compared to the people of all the world besides? Vassalage is
not known here. A small quantity of land entitles a man to a

freehold—Land is pretty equally divided. And the law of descents in this country, will carry this division farther and farther; perhaps even to an extreme. This of itself secures that great privilege. Is it so in any other country? Is it so in England? We differ in this, from all other countries. I admire this paper in this respect. It does not impair our right of suffrage. Whoever will have a right to vote for a Representative to our Legislature, will also have a right to vote for a Federal Representative. This will render that branch of Congress very democratic. We have a right to send a certain proportion. If we do not exert that right, it will be our folly.

It was necessary to provide against licentiousness, which is so natural to our climate. I dread more from the licentiousness of the people, than from the bad government of rulers. Our privileges are not however in danger: They are better secured than any bill of rights could have secured them.

I say that this new system shews in stronger terms than words could declare, that the liberties of the people are secure. It goes on the principle that all power is in the people, and that rulers have no powers but what are enumerated in that paper. When a question arises with respect to the legality of any power, exercised or assumed by Congress, it is plain on the side of the governed. *Is it enumerated in the Constitution?* If it be, it is legal and just. It is otherwise arbitrary and unconstitutional. Candour must confess, that it is infinitely more attentive to the liberties of the people than any State Government.

(Mr. *Lee* then said, that under the State Governments the people reserved to themselves certain enumerated rights, and that the rest were vested in their rulers. That consequently the powers reserved to the people, were but an inconsiderable exception from what was given to their rulers. But that in the Federal Government the rulers of the people were vested with certain defined powers, and that what was not delegated to those rulers were retained by the people. The consequence of this, he said, was, that the limited powers were only an exception to those which still rested in the people, that the people therefore knew what they had given up, and could be in no danger. He exemplified the proposition in a familiar manner. He observed, that if a man delegated certain powers to an agent, it would be an insult upon common sense, to suppose, that the agent could legally transact any business for his principal, which was not contained in the commission whereby the powers were delegated. But that if a man empowered his representative or agent to transact all his business, except certain enumerated parts, the clear result was, that the agent could lawfully transact every possible part of his principal's business except the enumerated parts; and added, that these plain propositions were sufficient to demonstrate the inutility and *folly*, were he permited to use the expression, of Bills of Rights.) He then continued,—I am convinced that that paper secures the liberty of Virginia, and of the United States.—I ask myself, if there be a single power in it, which is not necessary for the support of the Union; and as far as my reasoning goes, I say, that if you deprive it of one single power contained in it, it will be *"Vox et præterea nihil."* Those who are to go to Congress will be the servants of the people. They are created and deputed by us, and removeable by us. Is there a greater security than this in our State Government? To fortify this security, is there not a constitutional remedy in the Government, to reform any errors which shall be found inconvenient? Although the Honorable Gentleman has dwelt so long upon it, he has not made it appear otherwise.—The Confederation can neither render us happy at home, nor respectable abroad; I conceive this system will do both. The two Gentlemen who have been in the Grand Convention have proved incontestibly, that the fears arising from the powers of Congress, are groundless. Having now gone through some of the principal parts of the Gentleman's harangue, I shall take up but a few moments in replying to its conclusion.

I contend for myself, and the friends of the Constitution, that we are as great friends to liberty as he or any other person; and that we will not be behind in exertions in its defence, when it is invaded. For my part, I trust, that young as I am, I will be trusted in the support of freedom, as far as the Honorable Gentleman. I feel that indignation and contempt with respect to his previous amendments, which he expresses against posterior amendments. I can see no danger from a previous ratification. I see infinite dangers from previous amendments. I shall give my suffrage for the former, because I think the *happiness* of my country depends upon it. To maintain and secure that happiness, the first object of my wishes, I shall brave all storms and political dangers.

James Madison on Direct Taxation by the Federal Government

June 11, 1788

Mr. *Madison.*—Mr. Chairman,—It was my purpose to resume before now, what I had left unfinished, concerning the necessity of a radical change of our system. The intermission which has taken place, has discontinued the progress of the argument, and has given opportunity to others to advance arguments on different parts of the plan. I hope we shall steer our course in a different manner from what we have hitherto done. I presume that vague discourses and mere sports of fancy, not relative to the subject at all, are very improper on this interesting occasion. I hope these will be no longer attempted, but that we shall come to the point. I trust we shall not go out of order, but confine ourselves to the clause under consideration. I beg Gentlemen would observe this rule. I shall endeavour not to depart from it myself.

The subject of direct taxation is perhaps one of the most important that can possibly engage our attention, or that can be involved in the discussion of this question. If it be to be judged by the comments made upon it, by the opposers and favourers of the proposed system, it requires a most clear and critical investigation. The objections against the exercise of this power by the General Government, as far as I am able to comprehend them, are founded upon the supposition of its being unnecessary, impracticable, unsafe and accumulative of expence. I shall therefore consider, 1st, how far it may be necessary; 2dly, how far it may be practicable; 3dly, how far it may be safe, as well with respect to the public liberty at large, as to the State Legislatures; and 4thly, with respect to œconomy. First then, is it necessary? I must acknowledge that I concur in opinion with those Gentlemen who told you, that this branch of revenue was essential to the salvation of the Union. It appears to me necessary, in order to secure that punctuality which is necessary in revenue matters. Without punctuality individuals will give it no confidence; without

which it cannot get resources. I beg Gentlemen to consider
the situation of this country, if unhappily the Government
were to be deprived of this power. Let us suppose for a moment, that one of those powers which may be unfriendly to
us, should take advantage of our weakness, which they will be
more ready to do when they know the want of this resource
in our Government. Suppose it should attack us, what forces
could we oppose to it? Could we find safety in such forces as
we could call out? Could we call forth a sufficient number,
either by draughts, or any other way, to repel a powerful enemy? The inability of the Government to raise and support
regular troops, would compel us to depend on militia. It
would be then necessary to give this power to the Government, or run the risk of a national annihilation. It is my firm
belief, that if a hostile attack were made this moment on the
United States, it would flash conviction on the minds of the
citizens of the United States, of the necessity of vesting the
Government with this power, which alone can enable it to
protect the community. I do not wish to frighten the members of this Convention into a concession of this power, but
to bring to their minds those considerations which demonstrate its necessity. If we were secured from the possibility, or
the probability of danger, it might be unnecessary. I shall not
review that concourse of dangers which may probably arise at
remote periods of futurity, nor all those which we have immediately to apprehend, for this would lead me beyond the
bounds which I prescribed myself. But I will mention one
single consideration drawn from fact itself. I hope to have
your attention. By the treaty between the United States and
his Most Christian Majesty, among other things it is stipulated, that the great principle on which the armed neutrality
in Europe was founded, should prevail in case of future wars.
The principle is this, that free ships shall make free goods, and
that vessels and goods shall be both free from condemnation.
Great-Britain did not recognize it. While all Europe was
against her, she held out without acceding to it. It has been
considered for some time past, that the flames of war, already
kindled, would spread, and that France and England were
likely to draw those swords which were so recently put up.
This is judged probable. We should not be surprised in a

short time, to consider ourselves as a neutral nation—France on one side, and Great-Britain on the other—What is the situation of America? She is remote from Europe, and ought not to engage in her politics or wars. The American vessels, if they can do it with advantage, may carry on the commerce of the contending nations. It is a source of wealth which we ought not to deny to our citizens. But, Sir, is there not infinite danger, that in despite of all our caution we shall be drawn into the war? If American vessels have French property on board, Great-Britain will seize them. By this means we shall be obliged to relinquish the advantage of a neutral nation, or be engaged in a war. A neutral nation ought to be respectable, or else it will be insulted and attacked. America in her present impotent situation would run the risk of being drawn in as a party in the war, and loose the advantage of being neutral. Should it happen that the British fleet should be superior, have we not reason to conclude, from the spirit displayed by that nation to us and to all the world, that we should be insulted in our own ports, and our vessels seized? But if we be in a respectable situation—If it be known that our Government can command the whole resources of the Union, we shall be suffered to enjoy the great advantages of carrying on the commerce of the nations at war; for none of them would be willing to add us to the number of their enemies. I shall say no more on this point, there being others which merit your consideration.

The expedient proposed by the Gentlemen opposed to this clause, is, that requisitions shall be made, and if not complied with in a certain time, that then taxation shall be recurred to. I am clearly convinced, that whenever requisitions shall be made, they will disappoint those who put their trust in them. One reason to prevent the concurrent exertions of all the States, will arise from the suspicion, in some States, of delinquency in others. States will be governed by the motives that actuate individuals.

When a tax law is in operation in a particular State, every citizen, if he knows of the energy of the laws to enforce payment, and that every other citizen is performing his duty, will chearfully discharge his duty; but were it known that the citizens of one district were not performing their duty, and that it was left to the policy of the Government to make them come up with it, the citizens of the other districts would be very supine and careless in making provisions for payment. Our own experience makes the illustration more natural. If requisitions be made on thirteen different States, when one deliberates on the subject, she will know that all the rest will deliberate upon it also. This, Sir, has been a principal cause of the inefficacy of requisitions heretofore, and will hereafter produce the same evil. If the Legislatures are to deliberate on this subject, (and the Honorable Gentleman opposed to this clause, thinks their deliberation necessary) is it not presume-able, that they will consider peculiar local circumstances? In the General Council, on the contrary, the sense of all America will be drawn to a single point. The collective interest of the Union at large, will be known and pursued. No local views will be permitted to operate against the general welfare. But when propositions would come before a particular State, there is every reason to believe, that qualifications of the requisitions would be proposed—compliance might be promised, and some instant remittances might be made. This will cause delays, which in the first instance will produce disappointment. This also will make failures every where else. This I hope will be considered with the attention it deserves. The public creditors will be disappointed, and more pressing. Requisitions will be made for purposes equally pervading all America; but the exertions to make compliances will probably be not uniform in the States. If requisitions be made for future occasions; for putting the States in a state of military defence, or to repel an invasion, will the exertions be uniform and equal in all the States? Some parts of the United States are more exposed than others. Will the least exposed States exert themselves equally? We know that the most exposed will be more immediately interested, and will make less sacrifices in making exertions. I beg Gentlemen to consider that this argument will apply with most effect to the States which are most defenceless and exposed. The Southern States are most exposed, whether we consider their situation, or the smallness of their population. And there are other circumstances which render them still more vulnerable, which do not apply to the Northern States. They are therefore more interested in giving the Government a power to command the whole strength of the Union in cases of emergency. Do not Gentlemen conceive that this mode of obtaining supplies from the States, will keep alive animosities between the General Government and particular States? Where the chances of failures are so numerous as thirteen, by the thirteen States, disappointment in the first place, and consequent animosity, must inevitably take place.

Let us consider the alternative proposed by Gentlemen instead of the power of laying direct taxes. After the States shall have refused to comply, weigh the consequences of the exercise of this power by Congress. When it comes in the form of a punishment, great clamours will be raised among the people against the Government; hatred will be excited against it. It will be considered as an ignominious stigma on the State. It will be considered at least in this light by the State where the failure is made, and these sentiments will no doubt be diffused through the other States. Now let us consider the effect, if collectors are sent where the State Governments refuse to comply with requisitions. It is too much the disposition of mankind not to stop at one violation of duty. I conceive that every requisition that will be made on any part of America, will kindle a contention between the delinquent member, and the General Government. Is there no reason to suppose divisions in the Government (for seldom does any thing pass with unanimity) on the subject of requisitions? The parts least exposed will oppose those measures which may be adopted for the defence of the weakest parts. Is there no reason to presume, that the Representatives from the delinquent State will be more likely to foster disobedience to the requisitions of the Government, than study to recommend them to the public?

There is, in my opinion, another point of view in which this alternative will produce great evil. I will suppose, what is very probable, that partial compliances will be made. A difficulty here arises which fully demonstrates its impolicy. If a part be paid, and the rest withheld, how is the General Government to proceed? They are to impose a tax, but how shall it be done in this case? Are they to impose it by way of punishment, on those who have paid, as well as those who have not? All these considerations taken in view (for they are not visionary or fanciful speculations) will, perhaps, produce this consequence. The General Government to avoid those disappointments which I first described, and to avoid the contentions and embarrassments which I last described, will, in all probability, throw the public burdens on those branches of revenue which will be more in their power. They will be continually necessitated to augment the imposts. If we throw a disproportion of the burdens on that side, shall we not discourage commerce, and suffer many political evils? Shall we not increase that disproportion on the Southern States, which for some time will operate against us? The Southern States, from having fewer manufactures, will import and consume more. They will therefore pay more of the imposts. The more commerce is burdened, the more the disproportion will operate against them. If direct taxation be mixed with other taxes, it will be in the power of the General Government to lessen that inequality. But this inequality will be increased to the utmost extent, if the General Government have not this power. There is another point of view in which this subject affords us instruction. The imports will decrease in time of war. The Honorable Gentleman who spoke yesterday, said, that the imposts would be so productive, that there would be no occasion of laying taxes. I will submit two observations to him and the Committee. First: In time of war the imposts will be less; and as I hope we are considering a Government for a perpetual duration, we ought to provide for every future contingency. At present our importations bear a full proportion to the full amount of our sales, and to the number of our inhabitants; but when we have inhabitants enough, our imports will decrease; and as the national demands will increase with our population, our resources will increase as our wants increase. The other consideration which I will submit on this part of the subject is this:—I believe that it will be found in practice, that those who fix the public burdens, will feel a greater degree of responsibility when they are to impose them on the citizens immediately, than if they were only to say what sum should be paid by the States. If they exceed the limits of propriety, universal discontentment and clamour will arise. Let us suppose they were to collect the taxes from the citizens of America—would they not consider their circumstances? Would they not attentively consider what could be done by the citizens at large? Were they to exceed in their demands, what were reasonable burdens, the people would impute it to the right source, and look on the imposers as odious. When I consider the nature of the various objections brought against this clause, I should be led to think, that the difficulties were such that Gentlemen would not be able to get over them, and that the power, as defined in the plan of the Convention, was impracticable. I shall trouble them with a few observations on that point.

It has been said, that ten men deputed from this State, and others in proportion from other States, will not be able to adjust direct taxes so as to accommodate the various citizens in thirteen States.

I confess I do not see the force of this observation. Could not ten intelligent men, chosen from ten districts from this State, lay direct taxes on a few objects in the most judicious manner? It is to be conceived, that they would be acquainted with the situation of the different citizens of this country. Can any one divide this State into any ten districts so as not to contain men of sufficient information? Could not one man of knowledge be found in a district? When thus selected, will they not be able to carry their knowledge into the General Council? I may say with great propriety, that the experience of our own Legislature demonstrates the competency of Congress to lay taxes wisely. Our Assembly consists of considerably more than a hundred, yet from the nature of the business, it devolves on a much smaller number. It is through their sanction, approved of by all the others. It will be found that there are seldom more than ten men who rise to high information on this subject. Our Federal Representatives, as has been said by the Gentleman, (Mr. *Marshall*) who entered into the subject with a great deal of ability, will get information from the State Governments. They will be perfectly well informed of the circumstances of the people of the different States, and the mode of taxation that would be most convenient for them, from the laws of the States. In laying taxes, they may even refer to the State systems of taxation. Let it not be forgotten, that there is a probability, that that ignorance which is complained of in some parts of America, will be continually diminishing. Let us compare the degree of knowledge which the people had in time past, to their present information. Does not our own experience teach us, that the people are better informed than they were a few years ago? The citizen of Georgia knows more now of the affairs of New-Hampshire, than he did before the revolution, of those of South-Carolina. When the Representatives from the different States are collected together, to consider this subject, they will interchange their knowledge with one another, and will have the laws of each State on the table. Besides this, the intercourse of the States will be continually increasing. It is now much greater than before the revolution. My honorable friend over the way, (Mr. *Monro*) yesterday, seemed to conceive, as an insuperable objection, that if land were made the particular object of taxation, it would be unjust, as it would exonerate the commercial part of the community—That if it were laid on trade, it would be unjust in discharging the landholders; and that any exclusive selection would be unequal and unfair. If the General Government were tied down to one object, I confess the objection would have some force in it. But if this be not the case, it can have no weight. If it should have a general power of taxation, they could select the most proper objects, and distribute the taxes in such a manner, as that they should fall in a due degree on every member of the community. They will be limited to fix the proportion of each State, and they must raise it in the most convenient and satisfactory manner to the public.

The honorable member considered it as another insuperable objection, that uniform laws could not be made for thirteen States, and that dissonance would produce inconvenience and oppression. Perhaps it may not be found, on due enquiry, to be so impracticable as he supposes. But were it so, where is the evil of different laws operating in different States, to raise money for the General Government? Where is the evil of such laws? There are instances in other countries, of different laws operating in different parts of the country, without producing any kind of oppression. The revenue-laws are different in England and Scotland in several respects. Their laws relating to custom, excises, and trade, are similar; but those respecting direct taxation are dissimilar. There is a land-tax in England, and a land-tax in Scotland, but the laws concerning them are not the same. It is much heavier in proportion, in the former than in the latter. The mode of collection is different—yet this is not productive of any national inconvenience. Were we to conclude from the objections against the proposed plan, this dissimilarity, in that point alone, would have involved those kingdoms in difficulties. In England itself, there is a variety of different laws operating differently in different places.

I will make another observation on the objection of my honorable friend. He seemed to conclude, that concurrent collections under different authorities, were not reducible to practice. I agree that were they independent of the people, the argument would be good. But they must serve one common master. They must act in concert, or the defaulting party must bring on itself the resentment of the people. If the General Government be so constructed, that it will not dare to impose such burdens, as will distress the people, where is the evil of its having a power of taxation concurrent with the States? The people would not support it were it to impose oppressive burdens. Let me make one more comparison of the State Governments to this plan. Do not the States impose taxes for local purposes? Does the concurrent collection of taxes, imposed by the Legislatures for general purposes, and of levies laid by the counties for parochial and county purposes, produce any inconvenience or oppression? The collection of these taxes is perfectly practicable, and consistent with the views of both parties. The people at large are the common superior of the State Governments, and the General Government. It is reasonable to conclude, that they will avoid interferences for two causes—To avoid public oppression, and to render the collections more productive. I conceive they will be more likely to produce disputes, in rendering it convenient for the people, than run into interfering regulations.

In the third place I shall consider, whether the power of taxation to be given the General Government be safe: And first, whether it be safe as to the public liberty in general. It would be sufficient to remark, that they are, because, I conceive, the point has been clearly established by more than one

Gentleman who has spoken on the same side of the question. In the decision of this question, it is of importance to examine, whether elections of Representatives by great districts of freeholders be favourable to fidelity in Representatives. The greatest degree of treachery in Representatives, is to be apprehended where they are chosen by the least number of electors; because there is a greater facility of using undue influence, and because the electors must be less independent. This position is verified in the most unanswerable manner, in that country to which appeals are so often made, and sometimes instructively. Who are the most corrupt members in Parliament? Are they not the inhabitants of small towns and districts? The supporters of liberty are from the great counties. Have we not seen that the Representatives of the city of London, who are chosen by such thousands of voters, have continually studied and supported the liberties of the people, and opposed the corruption of the Crown? We have seen continually that most of the members in the ministerial majority are drawn from small circumscribed districts. We may therefore conclude, that our Representatives being chosen by such extensive districts, will be upright and independent. In proportion as we have security against corruption in Representatives, we have security against corruption from every other quarter whatsoever. I shall take a view of certain subjects which will lead to some reflections, to quiet the minds of those Gentlemen who think that the individual Governments will be swallowed up by the General Government. In order to effect this, it is proper to compare the State Governments to the General Government with respect to reciprocal dependence, and with respect to the means they have of supporting themselves, or of encroaching on one another. At the first comparison we must be struck with these remarkable facts. The General Government has not the appointment of a single branch of the individual Governments, or of any officers within the States, to execute their laws. Are not the States integral parts of the General Government? Is not the President chosen under the influence of the State Legislatures? May we not suppose that he will be complaisant to those from whom he has his appointment, and from whom he must have his re-appointment? The Senators are appointed altogether by the Legislatures.

My honorable friend apprehended a coalition between the President, Senate, and House of Representatives against the States. This could be supposed only from a similarity of the component parts.

A coalition is not likely to take place, because its component parts are heterogeneous in their nature. The House of Representatives is not chosen by the State Governments, but under the influence of those who compose the State Legislature. Let us suppose ten men appointed to carry the Government into effect, there is every degree of certainty, that they would be indebted for their re-election, to the members of the Legislatures. If they derive their appointment from them, will they not execute their duty to them? Besides this, will not the people (whose predominant interest will ultimately prevail) feel great attachment to the State Legislatures? They have the care of all local interests—Those familiar domestic objects, for which men have the strongest predilection. The General Government on the contrary, has the preservation of the aggregate interests of the Union—objects, which being less familiar, and more remote from men's notice, have a less powerful influence on their minds. Do we not see great and natural attachments arising from local considerations? This will be the case in a much stronger degree in the State Governments, than in the General Government. The people will be attached to their State Legislatures from a thousand causes; and into whatever scale the people at large will throw themselves, that scale will preponderate. Did we not perceive in the early stages of the war, when Congress was the idol of America, and when in pursuit of the object most dear to America, that they were attached to their States? Afterwards the whole current of their affection was to the States, and would be still the case were it not for the alarming situation of America.

At one period of the Congressional history, they had power to trample on the States. When they had that fund of paper money in their hands, and could carry on all their measures without any dependence on the States, was there any disposition to debase the State Governments? All that municipal authority which was necessary to carry on the administration of the Government, they still retained unimpaired. There was no attempt to diminish it.

I am led by what fell from my honorable friend yesterday to take this supposed combination in another view. Is it supposed, that the influence of the General Government will facilitate a combination between the members? Is it supposed, that it will preponderate against that of the State Governments? The means of influence consists in having the disposal of gifts and emoluments, and in the number of persons employed by, and dependent upon a Government. Will any Gentleman compare the number of persons, which will be employed in the General Government, with the number of those which will be in the State Governments? The number of dependents upon the State Governments will be infinitely greater than those on the General Government. I may say with truth, that there never was a more œconomical Government in any age or country; nor which will require fewer hands, or give less influence.

Let us compare the members composing the Legislative, Executive, and Judicial powers in the General Government, with those in the States, and let us take into view the vast number of persons employed in the States; from the chief officers to the lowest, we will find the scale preponderating so much in favor of the States, that while so many persons are attached to them, it will be impossible to turn the balance against them. There will be an irresistible bias towards the State Governments. Consider the number of militia officers, the number of Justices of the Peace, the number of the members of the Legislatures, and all the various officers for districts, towns, and corporations, all intermixing with, and residing among the people at large. While this part of the community retains their affection to the State Governments, I conceive that the fact will be, that the State Governments, and not the General Government, will preponderate. It cannot be contradicted that they have more extensive means of influence. I have my fears as well as the Honorable Gentleman— But my fears are on the other side. Experience, I think, will prove (though there be no infallible proof of it here) that the powerful and prevailing influence of the States, will produce such attention to local considerations as will be inconsistent with the advancement of the interests of the Union. But I choose rather to indulge my hopes than fears, because I flatter myself, if inconveniences should result from it, that the clause which provides amendments will remedy them. The combination of powers vested in those persons, would seem conclusive in favor of the States.

The powers of the General Government relate to external objects, and are but few. But the powers in the States relate to those great objects which immediately concern the prosperity of the people. Let us observe also, that the powers in the General Government are those which will be exercised mostly in time of war, while those of the State Governments will be exercised in time of peace. But I hope the time of war will be little compared to that of peace. I should not complete the view which ought to be taken of this subject, without making this additional remark, that the powers vested in the proposed Government, are not so much an augmentation of powers in the General Government, as a change rendered necessary, for the purpose of giving efficacy to those which were vested in it before. It cannot escape any Gentleman, that this power in theory, exists in the Confederation, as fully as in this Constitution. The only difference is this, that now they tax States, and by this plan they will tax individuals. There is no theoretic difference between the two. But in practice there will be an infinite difference between them. The one is an ineffectual power: The other is adequate to the purpose for which it is given. This change was necessary for the public safety.

Let us suppose for a moment, that the acts of Congress requiring money from the States, had been as effectual as the paper on the table—Suppose all the laws of Congress had had complete compliance, will any Gentleman say, as far as we can judge from past experience, that the State Governments would have been debased, and all consolidated and incorporated in one system? My imagination cannot reach it. I conceive, that had those acts that effect which all laws ought to have, the States would have retained their sovereignty.

It seems to be supposed, that it will introduce new expences and burdens on the people. I believe it is not necessary here to make a comparison between the expences of the present and of the proposed Government. All agree that the General Government ought to have power for the regulation of commerce. I will venture to say, that very great improvements and very œconomical regulations will be made. It will be a principal object to guard against smuggling, and such other attacks on the revenue as other nations are subject to. We are now obliged to defend against those lawless attempts, but from the interfering regulations of different States, with little success. There are regulations in different States which are unfavourable to the inhabitants of other States, and which militate against the revenue. New-York levies money from New-Jersey by her imposts. In New-Jersey, instead of co-operating with New-York, the Legislature favors violations on her regulations. This will not be the case when uniform regulations will be made.

Requisitions though ineffectual are unfriendly to œconomy.—When requisitions are submitted to the States, there are near 2500 or 2000 persons deliberating on the mode of payment. All these, during their deliberation, receive public pay. A great proportion of every session, in every State, is employed to consider whether they will pay at all, and in what mode. Let us suppose 1500 persons are deliberating on this subject. Let any one make a calculation—It will be found that a very few days of their deliberation will consume more of the public money, than one year of that of the General Legislature. This is not all, Mr. Chairman. When general powers will be vested in the General Government, there will be less of that mutability which is seen in the Legislation of the States. The consequence will be a great saving of expence and time. There is another great advantage which I will but barely mention. The greatest calamity to which the United States can be subject, is a vicissitude of laws, and continual shifting and changing from one object to another, which must expose the people to various inconveniences. This has a certain effect, of which sagacious men always have, and always will make an advantage. From whom is this advantage made? From the industrious farmers and tradesmen, who are ignorant of the means of making such advantages. The people will not be exposed to these inconveniences under an uniform and steady course of Legislation. But they have been so heretofore. The history of taxation of this country is so fully and well known to every member of this Committee, that I shall say no more of it.

We have hitherto discussed the subject very irregularly. I dare not dictate to any Gentleman, but I hope we shall pursue that mode of going through the business, which the House resolved. With respect to a great variety of arguments made use of, I mean to take notice of them when we come to those parts of the Constitution to which they apply. If we exchange this mode, for the regular way of proceeding, we can finish it better in one week than in one month.

James Madison on Concurrent Taxation and the Future of the American West

June 12, 1788

Mr. *Madison.*—Mr. Chairman,—Finding, Sir, that the clause more immediately under consideration still meets with the disapprobation of the Honorable Gentleman over the way (Mr. *Grayson*) and finding that the reasons of the opposition as farther developed are not satisfactory to myself and others who are in favor of the clause; I wish that it may meet with the most thorough and complete investigation. I beg the attention of the Committee, in order to obviate what fell from the Honorable Gentleman. He set forth that by giving up the power of taxation, we should give up every thing, and still insists on requisitions being made on the States, and that then, if they be not complied with, Congress shall lay direct taxes by way of penalty. Let us consider the dilemma which arises from this doctrine. Either requisitions will be efficacious or they will not. If they will be efficacious, then I say, Sir, we gave up every thing as much as by direct taxation. The same amount will be paid by the people as by direct taxes.—If they be not efficatious where is the advantage of this plan? In what respect will it relieve us from the inconveniences which we have experienced from requisitions? The power of laying direct taxes by the General Government is supposed by the Honorable Gentleman to be chimerical and impracticable. What is the consequence of the alternative he proposes? We are to rely upon this power to be ultimately used as a penalty to compel the States to comply. If it be chimerical and impracticable in the first instance, it will be equally so when it will be exercised as a penalty. A reference was made to concurrent executions as an instance of the possibility of interference between the two Governments. (Here Mr. *Madison* spoke so low that he could not be distinctly heard.) This has been experienced under the State Governments without involving any inconvenience. But it may be answered, that under the State Governments, concurrent executions cannot produce the inconvenience here dreaded, because they are executed by the same officer. Is it not in the power of the General Government to employ the State officers? Is nothing to be left to future legislation, or must every thing be immutably fixed in the Constitution? Where exclusive power is given to the Union, there can be no interference. Where the General and State Legislatures have concurrent power, such regulations will be made as shall be found necessary to exclude interferences and other inconveniences. It will be their interest to make such regulations.

It has been said, that there is no similarity between petty corporations and independent States. I admit that in many points of view there is a great disimilarity, but in others, there is a striking similarity between them, which illustrates what is before us. Have we not seen in our own country (as has been already suggested in the course of the debates) concurrent collections of taxes going on at once, without producing any inconvenience? We have seen three distinct collections of taxes, for three distinct purposes. Has it not been possible for collections of taxes, for parochial, county and State purposes, to go on at the same time? Every Gentleman must know that this is now the case, and though there be a subordination in these cases which will not be in the General Government, yet in practice it has been found, that these different collections have been concurrently carried on, with convenience to the people, without clashing with one another, and without deriving their harmony from the circumstance of being subordinate to one Legislative body. The taxes will be laid for different purposes. The members of the one Government as well as of the other, are the agents of, and subordinate to the people. I conceive that the collections of the taxes of the one will not impede those of the other, and that there can be no interference. This concurrent collection appears to me neither chimerical nor impracticable. He compares resistance of the people to collectors, to refusal of requisitions. This goes against all Government. It is as much as to urge, that there should be no Legislature. The Gentlemen who favored us with their observations on this subject, seemed to have reasoned on a supposition, that the General Government was confined by the paper on your table to lay general uniform taxes. Is it necessary that there should be a tax on any given article throughout the United States? It is represented to be oppressive, that the States who have slaves and make tobacco, should pay taxes on these for Federal wants, when other States who have them not would escape. But does the Constitution on the table admit of this? On the contrary, there is a proportion to be laid on each State according to its population. The most proper articles will be selected in each State. If one article in any State should be deficient, it will be laid on another article. Our State is secured on this foundation. — Its proportion will be commensurate to its population. This is a constitutional scale, which is an insuperable bar against disproportion, and ought to satisfy all reasonable minds. — If the taxes be not uniform, and the Representatives of some States contribute to lay a tax of which they bear no proportion, is not this principle reciprocal? Does not the same principle hold in our State Government in some degree? It has been found inconvenient to fix on uniform objects of taxation in this State, as the back parts are not circumstanced like the lower parts of the country. In both cases the reciprocity of the principle will prevent a disposition in one part to oppress the other. My honorable friend seems to suppose that Congress, by the possession of this ultimate power as a penalty, will have as much credit and will be as able to procure any sums, on any emergency, as if they were possessed of it in the first instance; and that the votes of Congress will be as competent to procure loans, as the votes of the British Commons. Would the votes of the British House of Commons have that credit which they now have, if they were liable to be retarded in their operation, and perhaps rendered ultimately nugatory as those of Congress must be by the proposed alternative? When their vote passes, it usually receives the concurrence of the other branch, and it is known that there is sufficient energy in the Government, to carry it into effect. But here the votes of Congress are in the first place dependent on the compliance of 13 different bodies, and after non compliance, are liable to be opposed and defeated, by the jealousy of the States against the exercise of this power, and by the opposition of the people which may be expected, if this power be exercised by Congress after partial compliances. These circumstances being known, Congress could not command one shilling.—My honorable friend seems to think that we ought to spare the present generation, and throw our burthens upon posterity. I will not contest the equity of this reasoning, but I must say that good policy as well as views of œconomy, strongly urge us even to distress ourselves to comply with our most solemn engagements. We must make effectual provision for the payment of the interest of our public debts. In order to do justice to our creditors, and support our credit and reputation; we must lodge power some where or other for this purpose. As yet the United States have not been able by any energy contained in the old system, to accomplish this end. Our creditors have a right to demand the principal, but would be satisfied with a punctual payment of the interest. If we have been unable to pay the interest, much less shall we be able to discharge the principal. It appears to me that the whole reasoning used on this occasion shews, that we ought to adopt this system to enable us to throw our burdens on posterity. The honorable member spoke of the Decemviri at Rome as having some similitude to the ten Representatives who are to be appointed by this State. I can see no point of similitude here, to enable us to draw any conclusion. For what purpose were the Decemviri appointed? They were invested with a plenipotentiary commission to make a code of laws. By whom were they appointed? By the people at large?—My memory is not infallible, but it tells me they were appointed by the Senate. I believe in the name of the people. If they were appointed by the Senate and composed of the most influential characters among the Nobles, can any thing be inferred from that against our Federal Representatives? Who made a discrimination between the Nobles and the people?—The Senate. Those men totally perverted the powers which were given them for the purpose above specified, to the subversion of the public liberty. Can we suppose that a similar usurpation might be made, by men appointed in a totally different manner? As their circumstances were totally dissimilar I conceive that no arguments drawn from that source, can apply to this Government. I do not thoroughly comprehend the reasoning of my honorable friend, when he tells us, that the Federal Government will predominate, and that the State interest will be lost; when at the same time he tells us, that it will be a faction of seven States.—If seven States will prevail *as States*, I conceive that state influence will prevail. If state influence under the present feeble Government has prevailed, I think that a remedy ought to be introduced by giving the General Government power to suppress it.

He supposed that my argument with respect to a future war between Great-Britain and France was fallacious. The other nations of Europe have acceded to that neutrality while Great-Britain opposed it. We need not expect in case of such a war, that we should be suffered to participate of the profitable emoluments of the carrying trade, unless we were in a respectable situation. Recollect the last war.—Was there ever a war in which the British nation stood opposed to so many nations? All the belligerent nations in Europe, with near one half of the British empire, were united against it. Yet that nation, though defeated, and humbled beyond any previous example, stood out against this. From her firmness and spirit in such desperate circumstances, we may divine what her future conduct may be. I did not contend that it was necessary for the United States to establish a navy for that sole purpose, but instanced it as one reason out of several, for rendering ourselves respectable. I am no friend to naval or land armaments in time of peace, but if they be necessary, the calamity must be submitted to. Weakness will invite insults. A respectable Government will not only intitle us to a participation of the advantages which are enjoyed by other nations, but will be a security against attacks and insults. It is to avoid the calamity of being obliged to have large armaments that we should establish this Government. The best way to avoid danger, is to be in a capacity to withstand it.

The impost, we are told, will not diminish, because the emigrations to the Westward will prevent the increase of population.—He has reasoned on this subject justly to a certain degree. I admit that the imposts will increase till population becomes so great as to compel us to recur to manufactures. The period cannot be very far distant, when the unsettled parts of America will be inhabited. At the expiration of twenty-five years hence, I conceive that in every part of the United States, there will be as great a population as there is

now in the settled parts. We see already, that in the most populous parts of the Union, and where there is but a medium,
manufactures are beginning to be established. Where this is
the case the amounts of importations will begin to diminish.
Although the impost may even increase during the term of
twenty-five years, yet when we are preparing a Government
for perpetuity, we ought to found it on permanent principles
and not on those of a temporary nature.

Holland is a favorite quotation with honorable members on
the other side of the question. Had not their sentiments been
discovered by other circumstances, I should have concluded
from their reasonings on this occasion, that they were friends
to the Constitution. I should suppose that they had forgotten
which side of the question they were on. Holland has been
called a Republic, and a Government friendly to liberty.
Though it may be greatly superior to some other Governments in Europe, still it is not a Republic, or a Democracy.
Their Legislature consist in some degree of men who legislate
for life. Their Councils consists of men who hold their offices
for life, who fill up offices and appoint their salaries themselves. The people have no agency mediate or immediate in
the Government. If we look at their history we shall find, that
every mischief which has befallen them, has resulted from the
existing Confederacy. If the Stadtholder has been productive
of mischief—if we ought to guard against such a Magistrate
more than any evil, let me beseech the Honorable Gentleman
to take notice of what produced that, and those troubles
which have interrupted their tranquillity from time to time—
The weakness of their Confederacy produced both. When the
French arms were ready to overpower their Republic, and
were feeble in the means of defence, which was principally
owing to the violence of parties, they then appointed a
Stadtholder, who sustained them. If we look at more recent
events, we shall have a more pointed demonstration that their
political infelicity arises from the imbicility of their Government. In the late disorders the States were almost equally divided, three Provinces on one side, three on the other, and
the other divided—one party inclined to the Prussians, and
the other to the French. The situation of France did not admit of their interposing immediately in their disputes by an

army—That of the Prussians did. A powerful and large army marched into Holland and compelled the other party to surrender. We know the distressing consequences to the people. What produced those disputes and the necessity of foreign interference, but the debility of their Confederacy? We may be warned by their example, and shun their fate, by removing the causes which produced their misfortunes.

My honorable friend has referred to the transactions of the Federal Council with respect to the navigation of the Mississippi. I wish it was consistent with delicacy and prudence to lay a complete view of the whole matter before this Committee. The history of it is singular and curious, and perhaps its origin ought to be taken into consideration. I will touch on some circumstances, and introduce nearly the substance of most of the facts relative to it, that I may not seem to shrink from explanation. It was soon perceived, Sir, after the commencement of the war with Britain, that among the various objects that would affect the happiness of the people of America, the navigation of the Mississippi was one. Throughout the whole history of foreign negotiation, great stress was laid on its preservation. In the time of our greatest distresses, and particularly when the Southern States were the scene of war, the Southern States cast their eyes around to be relieved from their misfortunes. It was supposed that assistance might be obtained for the relinquishment of that navigation. It was thought that for so substantial a consideration, Spain might be induced to afford decisive succour. It was opposed by the Northern and Eastern States. They were sensible that it might be dangerous to surrender this important right, particularly to the inhabitants of the Western country. But so it was, that the Southern States were for it, and the Eastern States opposed it. Since obtaining that happy peace, which secures to us all our claims, this subject has been taken again into consideration, and deliberated upon in the Federal Government. A temporary relinquishment has been agitated. Several members from the different States, but particularly from the Northern, were for a temporary surrender, because it would terminate disputes, and at the end of the short period for which it was to be given, the right would revert of course to those who had given it up. And for this temporary surrender some commercial advantages were offered. For my part, I considered that this measure, though founded on considerations plausible and honorable, was yet not justifiable but on grounds of inevitable necessity. I must declare in justice to many characters who were in Congress, that they declared that they never would enter into the measure unless the situation of the United States was such as could not prevent it.

I suppose that the adoption of this Government will be favorable to the preservation of the right to that navigation. Emigrations will be made from those parts of the United States which are settled, to those parts which are unsettled. If we afford protection to the Western country, we will see it rapidly peopled. Emigrations from some of the Northern States have been lately increased. We may conclude, as has been said by a Gentleman on the same side (Mr. *Nicholas*) that those who emigrate to that country, will leave behind them all their friends and connections as advocates for this right.

What was the cause of those States being the champions of this right when the Southern States were disposed to surrender it? The preservation of this right will be for the general interest of the Union. The Western country will be settled from the North as well as from the South, and its prosperity will add to the strength and security of the Union. I am not able to recollect all those circumstances which would be necessary to give Gentlemen a full view of the subject. I can only add, that I conceive that the establishment of the new Government will be the best possible means of securing our rights as well in the Western parts as elsewhere. I will not sit down till I make one more observation on what fell from my honorable friend. He says, that the true difference between the States lies in this circumstance—that some are carrying States and others productive, and that the operation of the new Government will be, that there will be a plurality of the former to combine against the interest of the latter, and that consequently it will be dangerous to put it in their power to do so. I would join with him in sentiments, if this were the case.—Were this within the bounds of probability, I should be equally alarmed, but I think that those States which are contradistinguished as carrying States, from the non-importing States will be but few. I suppose the Southern States will be considered by all, as under the latter description. Some other States have been mentioned by an honorable member on the same side, which are not considered as carrying States. New-Jersey and Connecticut can by no means be enumerated among the carrying States. They receive their supplies through New-York. Here then is a plurality of non-importing States. I could add another if necessary. Delaware, though situated upon the water, is upon the list of non-carrying States. I might say that a great part of New-Hampshire is so. I believe a majority of the people of that State receive their supplies from Massachusetts, Rhode-Island, and Connecticut. Might I not add all those States which will be admitted here-after into the Union? These will be non-carrying States, and will support Virginia in case the carrying States will attempt to combine against the rest. This objection must therefore fall to the ground. My honorable friend has made several other remarks, but I will defer saying any more till we come to those parts to which his objections refer.

Patrick Henry Elaborates His Main Objections, and James Madison Responds

June 12, 1788

Mr. *Henry.*—Mr. Chairman,—Once more I find it necessary to trespass on your patience. An Honorable Gentleman several days ago observed, that the great object of this Government, was justice. We were told before, that the greater consideration was Union. However, the consideration of justice seems to have been what influenced his mind when he made strictures on the proceedings of the Virginia Assembly. I thought the reasons of that transaction had been sufficiently explained. It is exceedingly painful to me to be objecting, but I must make a few observations. I shall not again review the catalogue of dangers which the Honorable Gentleman entertained us with. They appear to me absolutely imaginary. They have in my conception proved to be such. But sure I am, that the dangers of this system are real, when those who have no similar interests with the people of this country, are to legislate for us—when our dearest interests are left in the power of those whose advantage it may be to infringe them. How will the quotas of troops be furnished? *Hated* as requisitions are, your Federal officers cannot collect troops like dollars, and carry them in their pockets. You must make those *abominable* requisitions for them, and the scale will be in proportion to the number of your blacks, as well as your whites, unless they violate the constitutional rule of apportionment. This is not calculated to rouse the fears of the people. It is founded in truth. How oppressive and dangerous must this be to the Southern States who alone have slaves? This will render their proportion infinitely greater than that of the Northern States. It has been openly avowed that this shall be the rule. I will appeal to the judgments of the Committee, whether there be danger.—The Honorable Gentleman said, that there was no precedent for *this* American revolution. We have precedents in abundance. They have been drawn from Great-Britain. Tyranny has arisen there in the same manner in which it was introduced among the Dutch. The tyranny of Philadelphia may be like the tyranny of George the IIId. I believe this similitude will be incontestibly proved before we conclude.

The Honorable Gentleman has endeavored to explain the opinion of Mr. Jefferson our common friend, into an advice to adopt this new Government. What are his sentiments? He wishes nine States to adopt, and that four States may be found somewhere to reject it? Now, Sir, I say, if we pursue his advice, what are we to do?—To prefer form to substance? For, give me leave to ask what is the substantial part of his counsel? It is, Sir, that four States should *reject*. They tell us, that from the most authentic accounts, New-Hampshire will adopt it. When I denied this, Gentlemen said they were absolutely certain of it. Where then will four States be found to reject, if we adopt it? If we do, the counsel of this enlightened and worthy countryman of ours, will be thrown away,—and for what? He wishes to secure amendments and a Bill of Rights, if I am not mistaken. I speak from the best information, and if wrong, I beg to be put right. His amendments go to that despised thing *a Bill of Rights*, and all the rights which are dear to human nature—Trial by jury, the liberty of religion, and the press, &c.—Do not Gentlemen see, that if we adopt under the idea of following Mr. Jefferson's opinion, we amuse ourselves with the shadow, while the substance is given away? If Virginia be for adoption, what States will be left, of sufficient respectability and importance, to secure amendments by their rejection? As to North Carolina it is *a poor despised place*. Its dissent will not have influence to introduce any amendments.—Where is the American spirit of liberty? Where will you find attachment to the rights of mankind, when Massachusetts the great Northern State, Pennsylvania the great middle State, and Virginia the great Southern State, shall have adopted this Government? Where will you find magnanimity enough to reject it? Should the remaining States have this magnanimity, they will not have sufficient weight to have the Government altered. This State has weight and importance. Her example will have powerful influence—Her rejection will procure amendments—Shall we by our adoption hazard the loss of amendments?—Shall we forsake that importance and respectability which our station in America commands, in hopes that relief will come from an obscure part of the Union? I hope my countrymen will spurn at the idea. The necessity of amendments is universally admitted. It is a word which is re-echoed from every part of the Continent. A majority of those who hear me, think amendments are necessary. Policy tells us they are necessary. Reason, self-preservation, and every idea of propriety, powerfully urge us to secure the dearest rights of human nature—Shall we in direct violation of these principles, rest this security upon the uncertainty of its being obtained by a few States more weak, and less respectable than ourselves—and whose virtue and magnanimity may be overborne by the example of so many adopting States?—*Poor* Rhode-Island and North-Carolina, and even New-York, surrounded with Federal walls on every side, may not be magnanimous enough to reject, and if they do reject it, they will have but little influence to obtain amendments. I ask, if amendments be necessary, from whence can they be so properly proposed as from this State? The example of Virginia is a powerful thing, particularly with respect to North-Carolina, whose supplies must come *through* Virginia. Every possible opportunity of procuring amendments is gone—Our power and political salvation is gone, if we ratify unconditionally. The important right of making treaties is upon the most dangerous foundation. The President with a few Senators possess it in the most unlimited manner, without any real responsibility, if from sinister views they should think proper to abuse it. For they may keep all their measures in the most profound secrecy as long as they please. Were we not told that war was the case wherein secrecy was most necessary? But by the paper on your table, their secrecy is not limited to this case only. It is as unlimited and unbounded as their powers. Under the abominable veil of political secrecy and contrivance, your most valuable rights may be sacrificed by a most corrupt faction, without having the satisfaction of knowing who injured you. They are bound by honor and conscience to act with integrity, but they are under no constitutional restraint. The navigation of the Mississippi, which is of so much importance to the happiness of the people of this country, may be lost by the operation of that paper. There are seven States now decidedly opposed to this navigation. If it be of the highest consequence to know who they are who shall have voted its relinquishment, the Federal veil of secrecy will prevent that discovery. We may labor under the magnitude of our miseries without knowing or being able to punish those who produced them. I did not wish that transactions relative to treaties should when unfinished, be exposed; but that it should be known after they were concluded, who had advised them to be made, in order to secure some degree of certainty that the public interest shall be consulted in their formation.

We are told that all powers not given are reserved. I am sorry to bring forth hackneyed observations. But, Sir, important truths lose nothing of their validity or weight, by frequency of repetition. The English history is frequently recurred to by Gentlemen. Let us advert to the conduct of the people of that country. The people of England lived without a declaration of rights, till the war in the time of Charles Ist. That King made usurpations upon the rights of the people. Those rights were in a great measure before that time undefined. Power and privilege then depended on implication and logical discussion. Though the declaration of rights was obtained from that King, his usurpations cost him his life. The limits between the liberty of the people, and the prerogative of the King, were still not clearly defined. The rights of the people continued to be violated till the Steward family was banished in the year 1688. The people of England magnanimously defended their rights, banished the tyrant, and prescribed to William Prince of Orange, *by the Bill of Rights*, on what terms he should reign. And this Bill of Rights put an end to all construction and implication. Before this, Sir, the situation of the public liberty of England was dreadful. For upwards of a century the nation was involved in every kind of calamity, till the Bill of Rights put an end to all, by defining the rights of the people, and limiting the King's prerogative. Give me leave to add (if I can add any thing to so splendid an example) the conduct of the American people. They Sir, thought a *Bill of Rights* necessary. It is alledged that several States, in the formation of their governments, omitted a Bill of Rights. To this I answer, that they had the substance of a

Bill of Rights contained in their Constitutions, which is the same thing. I believe that Connecticut has preserved by her Constitution her royal charter, which clearly defines and secures the great rights of mankind—Secure to us the great important rights of humanity, and I care not in what form it is done. Of what advantage is it to the American Congress to take away this great and general security? I ask of what advantage is it to the public or to Congress to drag an unhappy debtor, not for the sake of justice, but to gratify the malice of the plaintiff, with his witnesses to the Federal Court, from a great distance? What was the principle that actuated the Convention in proposing to put such dangerous powers in the hands of any one? Why is the trial by jury taken away? All the learned arguments that have been used on this occasion do not prove that it is secured. Even the advocates for the plan do not all concur in the certainty of its security. Wherefore is religious liberty not secured? One Honorable Gentleman who favors adoption, said that he had had his fears on the subject. If I can well recollect, he informed us that he was perfectly satisfied by the powers of reasoning (with which he is so happily endowed) that those fears were not well grounded. There is many a religious man who knows nothing of argumentative reasoning;—there are many of our most worthy citizens, who cannot go through all the labyrinths of syllogistic argumentative deductions, when they think that the rights of conscience are invaded. This sacred right ought not to depend on constructive logical reasoning. When we see men of such talents and learning, compelled to use their utmost abilities to convince themselves that there is no danger, is it not sufficient to make us tremble? Is it not sufficient to fill the minds of the ignorant part of men with fear? If Gentlemen believe that the apprehensions of men will be quieted, they are mistaken; since our best informed men are in doubt with respect to the security of our rights. Those who are not so well informed will spurn at the Government. When our common citizens, who are not possessed with such extensive knowledge and abilities, are called upon to change their Bill of Rights, (which in plain unequivocal terms, secures their most valuable rights and privileges) for construction and implication, will they implicitly acquiesce? Our Declaration of Rights tells us,

"That all men are by nature free and independent, &c." (Here Mr. *Henry* read the Declaration of Rights.) Will they exchange these Rights for logical reasons? If you had a thousand acres of land, dependent on this, would you be satisfied with logical construction? Would you depend upon a title of so disputable a nature? The present opinions of individuals will be buried in entire oblivion when those rights will be thought of. That sacred and lovely thing Religion, ought not to rest on the ingenuity of logical deduction. Holy Religion, Sir, will be prostituted to the lowest purposes of human policy. What has been more productive of mischief among mankind than Religious disputes. Then here, Sir, is a foundation for such disputes, when it requires learning and logical deduction to perceive that religious liberty is secure. The Honorable member told us that he had doubts with respect to the judiciary department. I hope those doubts will be explained.—He told us that his object was Union. I admit that the reality of Union and not the name, is the object which most merits the attention of every friend to his country. He told you that you should hear many great *sounding words* on our side of the question. We have heard the *word Union* from him. I have heard no word so often pronounced in this House as he did this. I admit that the American Union is dear to every man—I admit that every man who has three grains of information, must know and think that Union is the best of all things. But as I said before, we must not mistake the end for the means. If he can shew that the rights of the Union are secure, we will consent. It has been sufficiently demonstrated that they are not secured. It sounds mighty prettily to Gentlemen to curse paper money and honestly pay debts. But apply to the situation of America, and you will find there are thousands and thousands of contracts, whereof equity forbids an exact literal performance. Pass that government, and you will be bound hand and foot. There was an immense quantity of depreciated continental paper money in circulation at the conclusion of the war. This money is in the hands of individuals to this day. The holders of this money may call for the nominal value, if this government be adopted. This State may be compelled to pay her proportion of that currency pound for pound. Pass this government and you will be carried to the

Federal Court (if I understand that paper right) and you will be compelled to pay shilling for shilling. I doubt on the subject, at least as a public man, I ought to have doubts. A State may be sued in the Federal Court by the paper on your table. It appears to me then, that the holder of the paper money may require shilling for shilling. If there be any latent remedy to prevent this, I hope it will be discovered.

The precedent, with respect to the Union between England and Scotland, does not hold. The Union of Scotland speaks in plain and direct terms. Their privileges were particularly secured. It was expressly provided, that they should retain their own particular laws. Their nobles have a right to choose Representatives to the number of sixteen.—I might thus go on and specify particulars, but it will suffice to observe generally, that their rights and privileges were expressly and unequivocally reserved.—The power of direct taxation was not given up by the Scotch people. There is no trait in that Union which will maintain their arguments. In order to do this, they ought to have proved that Scotland united without securing their rights, and afterwards got that security by subsequent amendments. Did the people of Scotland do this? No, Sir, like a sensible people, they trusted nothing to hazard. If they have but 45 members, and those be often corrupted, these defects will be greater here. The number will be smaller, and they will be consequently the more easily corrupted. Another Honorable Gentleman advises us to give this power, in order to exclude the necessity of going to war. He wishes to establish national credit I presume—and imagines that if a nation has public faith and shews a disposition to comply with her engagements, she is safe among ten thousand dangers. If the Honorable Gentleman can prove that this paper is calculated to give us public faith, I will be satisfied. But if you be in constant preparation for war, on such airy and imaginary grounds, as the mere possibility of danger, your government must be military, which will be inconsistent with the enjoyment of liberty. But, Sir, we must become formidable, and have a strong government to protect us from the British nation. Will the paper on the table prevent the attacks of the British navy, or enable us to raise a fleet equal to the British fleet? The British have the strongest fleet in Europe, and can strike any where. It is the utmost folly to conceive, that that paper can have such an operation. It will be no less so to attempt to raise a powerful fleet. With respect to requisitions, I beseech Gentlemen to consider the importance of the subject. We who are for amendments propose, (as has been frequently mentioned) that a requisition shall be made for £. 200,000 for instance, instead of direct taxation, and that if it be not complied with, then it shall be raised by direct taxes. We do not wish to have strength to refuse to pay them, but to possess the power of raising the taxes in the most easy mode for the people. But says he, you may delay us by this mode.— Let us see if there be not sufficient to counterbalance this evil. The oppression arising from taxation, is not from the amount but, from the mode—a thorough acquaintance with the condition of the people, is necessary to a just distribution of taxes. The whole wisdom of the science of Government, with respect to taxation, consists in selecting that mode of collection which will best accommodate the convenience of the people. When you come to tax a great country, you will find that ten men are too few to settle the manner of collection. One capital advantage which will result from the proposed alternative is this, that there will be necessary communications between your ten members in Congress, and your 170 Representatives here. If it goes through the hands of the latter, they will know how much the citizens *can* pay, and by looking at the paper on your table, they will know how much they *ought* to pay. No man is possessed of sufficient information to know how much we can or ought to pay.

We might also remonstrate, if by mistake or design, they should call for a greater sum than our proportion. After a remonstrance, and a free investigation between our Representatives here, and those in Congress, the error would be removed.

Another valuable thing which it will produce is, that the people will pay the taxes chearfully. It is supposed, that this would occasion a waste of time, and be an injury to public credit. This would only happen if requisitions should not be complied with. In this case the delay would be compensated by the payment of interest, which with the addition of the credit of the State to that of the General Government, would in a great measure obviate this objection. But if it had all the force which it is supposed to have, it would not be adequate to the evil of direct taxation. But there is every probability that requisitions would be then complied with. Would it not then be our interest, as well as duty, to comply? After non-compliance, there would be a general acquiescence in the exercise of this power. We are fond of giving power, at least power which is constitutional. Here is an option to pay according to your own mode, or otherwise. If you give probability fair play, you must conclude, that they would be complied with. Would the Assembly of Virginia by refusal, destroy the country and plunge the people into miseries and distress? If you give your reasoning faculty fair play, you cannot but know, that payment must be made when the consequence of a refusal would be an accumulation of inconveniences to the people. Then they say, that if requisitions be not complied with, in case of a war, the destruction of the country may be the consequence; that therefore, we ought to give the power of taxation to the Government to enable it to protect us. Would not this be another reason for complying with requisitions, to prevent the country from being destroyed? You tell us, that unless requisitions be complied with, your commerce is gone. The prevention of this also, will be an additional reason to comply.

He tells us, that responsibility is secured by direct taxation. Responsibility instead of being increased, will be lost for ever by it. In our State Government, our Representatives may be severally instructed by their constituents. There are no persons to counteract their operations. They can have no excuse for deviating from our instructions. In the General Government other men have power over the business. When oppressions may take place, our Representatives may tell us, *We contended for your interest, but we could not carry our point, because the Representatives from Massachusetts, New Hampshire, Connecticut, &c. were against us.* Thus, Sir, you may see, that there is no real responsibility. He further said, that there was such a contrariety of interests, as to hinder a consolidation. I will only make one remark—There is a variety of interests— Some of the States owe a great deal on account of paper money—Others very little—Some of the Northern States

have collected and barrelled up paper money. Virginia has
sent thither her cash long ago. There is little or none of the
Continental paper money retained in this State. Is it not their
business to appreciate this money? Yes,—and it will be your
business to prevent it. But there will be a majority against
you, and you will be obliged to pay your share of this money
in its nominal value. It has been said by several Gentlemen,
that the freeness of elections would be promoted by throwing
the country into large districts. I contend, Sir, that it will have
a contrary effect. It will destroy that connection that ought to
subsist between the electors and the elected. If your elections
be by districts instead of counties, the people will not be acquainted with the candidates. They must therefore be directed
in the elections by those who know them. So that instead of a
confidential connection between the electors and the elected,
they will be absolutely unacquainted with each other. A common man must ask a man of influence how he is to proceed,
and for whom he must vote. The elected, therefore, will be
careless of the interest of the electors. It will be a common job
to extort the suffrages of the common people for the most
influential characters. The same men may be repeatedly
elected by these means. This, Sir, instead of promoting the
freedom of elections, leads us to an Aristocracy. Consider the
mode of elections in England. Behold the progress of an election in an English shire. A man of an enormous fortune will
spend 30,000 l. or 40,000 l. to get himself elected. This is
frequently the case. Will the Honorable Gentleman say, that a
poor man, as enlightened as any man in the island, has an
equal chance with a rich man, to be elected? He will stand no
chance though he may have the finest understanding of any
man in the shire. It will be so here. Where is the chance that a
poor man can come forward with the rich? The Honorable
Gentleman will find that instead of supporting Democratical
principles, it goes absolutely to destroy them. The State Governments, says he, will possess greater advantages than the
General Government, and will consequently prevail. His
opinion and mine are diametrically opposite. Bring forth the
Federal allurements, and compare them with the poor contemptible things that the State Legislatures can bring forth.
On the part of the State Legislatures, there are Justices of

Peace and militia officers—And even these Justices and officers, are bound by oath in favour of the Constitution. A constable is the only man who is not obliged to swear paramount allegiance to this beloved Congress. On the other hand, there are rich, fat Federal emoluments—your rich, snug, fine, fat Federal offices—The number of collectors of taxes and excises will outnumber any thing from the States. Who can cope with the excisemen and taxmen? There are none in this country, that can cope with this class of men alone. But, Sir, is this the only danger? Would to Heaven that it were. If we are to ask which will last the longest—the State or the General Government, you must take an army and a navy into the account. Lay these things together, and add to the enumeration the superior abilities of those who manage the General Government. Can then the State Governments look it in the face? You dare not look it in the face now, when it is but in *embryo*. The influence of this Government will be such, that you never can get amendments; for if you propose alterations, you will affront them. Let the Honorable Gentleman consider all these things and say, whether the State Governments will last as long as the Federal Government. With respect to excises, I can never endure them. They have been productive of the most intolerable oppressions every where. Make a probable calculation of the expence attending the Legislative, Executive, and Judiciary. You will find that there must be an immense increase of taxes. We are the same mass of people we were before.—In the same circumstances—The same pockets are to pay—The expences are to be increased—What will enable us to bear this augmentation of taxes? The mere form of the Government will not do it. A plain understanding cannot conceive how the taxes can be diminished, when our expences are augmented, and the means of paying them not increased.

With respect to our tax-laws, we have purchased a little knowledge by sad experience upon the subject. Reiterated experiments have taught us what can alleviate the distresses and suit the convenience of the people. But we are now to throw away that system, by which we have acquired this knowledge, and send ten men to legislate for us.

The Honorable Gentleman was pleased to say, that the representation of the people was the vital principle of this Government. I will readily agree that it ought to be so.—But I contend that this principle is only nominally, and not substantially to be found there. We contended with the British about representation; they offered us such a representation as Congress now does. They called it a virtual representation. If you look at that paper you will find it so there. Is there but a virtual representation in the upper House? The States are represented *as States*, by two Senators each. This is virtual, not actual. They encounter you with Rhode-Island and Delaware. This is not an actual representation. What does the term representation signify? It means that a certain district—a certain association of men should be represented in the Government for *certain ends*. These ends ought not to be impeded or obstructed in any manner. Here, Sir, this populous State has not an adequate share of legislative influence. The two petty States of Rhode-Island and Delaware, which together are infinitely inferior to this State, in extent and population, have double her weight, and can counteract her interest. I say, that the representation in the Senate, as applicable to States, is not actual. Representation is not therefore the vital principle of this Government—So far it is wrong.

Rulers are the servants and agents of the people—The people are their masters—Does the new Constitution acknowledge this principle? Trial by jury is the best appendage of freedom—Does it secure this? Does it secure the other great rights of mankind? Our own Constitution preserves these principles. The Honorable Gentleman contributed to form that Constitution: The applauses so justly due to it, should, in my opinion, go to the condemnation of that paper.

With respect to the failures and errors of our Government, they might have happened in any Government.—I do not justify what merits censure, but I shall not degrade my country. As to deviations from justice, I hope they will be attributed to the errors of the head, and not to those of the heart.

The Honorable Gentleman did our Judiciary honour in saying, that they had firmness to counteract the Legislature in some cases. Yes, Sir, our Judges opposed the acts of the Legislature. We have this land mark to guide us.—They had fortitude to declare that they were the Judiciary and would oppose unconstitutional acts. Are you sure that your Federal Judiciary will act thus? Is that Judiciary so well constructed and so independent of the other branches, as our State Judiciary? Where are your land-marks in this Government? I will be bold to say you cannot find any in it. I take it as the highest encomium on this country, that the acts of the Legislature, if unconstitutional, are liable to be opposed by the Judiciary.

Then the Honorable Gentleman said, that the two Judiciaries and Legislatures, would go in a parallel line and never interfere—That as long as each was confined to its proper objects, that there would be no danger of interference—That like two parallel lines as long as they continued in their parallel direction they never would meet. With submission to the Honorable Gentleman's opinion, I assert, that there is danger of interference, because no line is drawn between the powers of the two Governments in many instances; and, where there is a line, there is no check to prevent the one from encroaching upon the powers of the other. I therefore contend that they must interfere, and that this interference must subvert the State Government, as being less powerful. Unless your Government have checks, it must inevitably terminate in the destruction of your privileges. I will be bold to say, that the British Government has real checks. I was attacked by Gentlemen, as if I had said that I loved the British Government better than our own. I never said so. I said that if I were obliged to relinquish a Republican Government, I would chuse the British Monarchy. I never gave the preference to the British or any other Government, when compared to *that* which the Honorable Gentleman assisted to form. I was constrained to say what I said. When two disagreeable objects present themselves to the mind, we choose that which has the least deformity.

As to the Western Country, notwithstanding our representation in Congress, and notwithstanding any regulation that may be made by Congress, it may be lost. The seven Northern States are determined to give up the Mississippi. We are told that in order to secure the navigation of that river, it was necessary to give it up twenty-five years to the Spaniards, and that thereafter we should enjoy it forever without any interruption from them. This argument resembles that which recommends adopting first and then amending. I think the reverse of what the Honorable Gentleman said on this subject. Those seven States are decidedly against it. He tells us, that it is the policy of the whole Union to retain it. If men were wise, virtuous, and honest, we might depend on an adherence to this policy.—Did we not know of the fallibility of human nature, we might rely on the present structure of this Government.—We might depend that the rules of propriety, and the general interest of the Union would be observed. But the depraved nature of man is well known. He has a natural biass towards his own interest, which will prevail over every consideration, unless it be checked. It is the interest and inclination of the seven Northern States to relinquish this river. If you enable them to do so, will the mere propriety of consulting the interest of the other six States, refrain them from it? Is it imagined, that Spain will, after a peaceable possession of it for thirty years, give it up to you again? Can credulity itself hope, that the Spaniards who wish to have it for that period, wish to clear the river for you? What is it they wish?—To clear the river?—For whom? America saw the time when she had the reputation of common sense at least. Do you suppose they will restore it to you after thirty years? If you do, you depart from that rule. Common observation tells you, that it must be the policy of Spain to get it first, and then retain it forever. If you give it up, in my poor estimation, they will never voluntarily restore it. Where is the man who will believe that after clearing the river, strengthening themselves, and increasing the means of retaining it, the Spaniards will tamely surrender it?

With respect to the concurrent collections of parochial, county, and State taxes, which the Honorable Gentleman has instanced as a proof of the practicability of the concurrent collection of taxes by the General and State Governments, the comparison will not stand examination. As my honorable friend has said, these concurrent collections come from one power. They irradiate from the same center. They are not co-equal or co-extensive. There is no clashing of powers between them. Each is limited to its own particular objects, and all subordinate to one supreme controuling power—The Legislature.—The County Courts have power over the county and parish collections, and can constantly redress any injuries or oppressions committed by the collectors. Will this be the case in the Federal Courts? I hope they will not have Federal Courts in every county. If they will, the State Courts will be debased and stripped of their cognizance, and utterly abolished. Yet, if there be no power in the county to call them to account, they will more flagrantly trample on your rights. Does the Honorable Gentleman mean that the Thirteen States will have thirteen different tax-laws? Is this the expedient which is to be substituted to the unequal and unjust one of uniform taxes? If so, many horrors present themselves to my mind. They may be imaginary, but it appears to my mind to be the most abominable system that could be imagined. It will destroy every principle of responsibility: It will be destructive of that fellow-feeling, and consequent confidence, which ought to subsist between the Representatives and the represented. We shall then be taxed by those who bear no part of the taxes themselves, and who consequently will be regardless of our interest in imposing them upon us. The efforts of our ten men will avail very little when opposed by the Northern majority. If our ten men be disposed to sacrifice our interests, we cannot detect them. Under the colour of being outnumbered by the Northern Representatives, they can always screen themselves. When they go to the General Government, they may make a bargain with the Northern Delegates. They may agree to tax our citizens in any manner which may be proposed by the Northern members; in consideration of which the latter may make them some favorite concessions. The Northern States will never assent to regulations promotive of the Southern aggrandisement. Notwithstanding what Gentlemen say of the probable virtue of our Representatives, I dread the depravity of human nature. I wish to guard against it by proper checks, and trust nothing to accident or chance. I will never depend on so slender a protection as the possibility of being represented by virtuous men.

Will not thirteen different objects of taxation in the thirteen different States, involve us in an infinite number of inconveniences and absolute confusion? There is a striking difference, and great contrariety of interests between the States. They are naturally divided into carrying and productive States. This is an actual existing distinction which cannot be altered. The former are more numerous, and must prevail. What then will be the consequence of their contending interests, if the taxation of America is to go on in thirteen different shapes? This Government subjects every thing to the Northern majority. Is there not then a settled purpose to check the Southern interest? We thus put unbounded power over our property in hands not having a common interest with us. How can the Southern members prevent the adoption of the most oppressive mode of taxation in the Southern States, as there is a majority in favor of the Northern States? Sir, this is a picture so horrid, so wretched, so dreadful, that I need no longer dwell upon it.—Mr. *Henry* then concluded by remarking, that he dreaded the most iniquitous speculation and stock-jobbing, from the operation of such a system.

Mr. *Madison*,—Mr. Chairman.—Pardon me for making a few remarks on what fell from the Honorable Gentleman last up:—I am sorry to follow the example of Gentlemen in deviating from the rule of the House:—But as they have taken the utmost latitude in their objections, it is necessary that those who favor the Government should answer them.—But I wish as soon as possible to take up the subject regularly. I will therefore take the liberty to answer some observations which have been irregularly made, though they might be more properly answered when we came to discuss those parts of the Constitution to which they respectively refer.—I will, however, postpone answering some others till then.—If there be that terror in direct taxation, that the States would comply with requisitions to guard against the Federal Legislature; and if, as Gentlemen say, this State will always have it in her power to make her collections speedily and fully, the people will be compelled to pay the same amount as quickly and punctually as if raised by the General Government. It has been amply proved, that the General Government can lay taxes as conveniently to the people as the State Governments, by imitating the State systems of taxation.—If the General Government have not the power of collecting its own revenues, in the first instance, it will be still dependent on the State Governments in some measure; and the exercise of this power after refusal, will be inevitably productive of injustice and confusion, if partial compliances be made before it is driven to assume it.—Thus, Sir, without relieving the people in the smallest degree, the alternative proposed will impair the efficacy of the Government, and will perpetually endanger the tranquillity of the Union.

The honorable member's objection with respect to requisitions of troops will be fully obviated at another time.—Let it suffice now to say, that it is altogether unwarrantable, and founded upon a misconception of the paper before you. But the honorable member, in order to influence our decision, has mentioned the opinion of a citizen who is an ornament to this State. When the name of this distinguished character was introduced, I was much surprised.—Is it come to this then, that we are not to follow our own reason?—Is it proper to introduce the opinions of respectable men not within these walls?—If the opinion of an important character were to weigh on this occasion, could we not adduce a character equally great on our side?—Are we who (in the Honorable Gentleman's opinion) are not to be governed by an *erring world*, now to submit to the opinion of a citizen beyond the Atlantic? I believe that were that Gentleman now on this floor, he would be *for* the adoption of this Constitution. I wish his name had never been mentioned.—I wish every thing spoken here relative to his opinion may be suppressed if our debates should be published. I know that the delicacy of his feelings will be wounded when he will see in print what has, and may be said, concerning him on this occasion. I am in some measure acquainted with his sentiments on this subject. It is not right for me to unfold what he has informed me. But I will venture to assert, that the clause now discussed, is not objected to by Mr. Jefferson:—He approves of it, because it enables the Government to carry on its operations. He admires several parts of it, which have been reprobated with vehemence in this House. He is captivated with the equality of suffrage in the Senate, which the Honorable Gentleman (Mr. *Henry*) calls the rotten part of this Constitution. But whatever be the opinion of that illustrious citizen, considerations of personal delicacy should dissuade us from introducing it here.

The honorable member has introduced the subject of religion.—Religion is not guarded—There is no Bill of Rights declaring that religion should be secure.—Is a Bill of Rights a security for religion? Would the Bill of Rights in this State exempt the people from paying for the support of one particular sect, if such sect were exclusively established by law? If there were a majority of one sect, a Bill of Rights would be a poor protection for liberty. Happily for the States, they enjoy the utmost freedom of religion. This freedom arises from that multiplicity of sects, which pervades America, and which is the best and only security for religious liberty in any society. For where there is such a variety of sects, there cannot be a majority of any one sect to oppress and persecute the rest. Fortunately for this Commonwealth, a majority of the people are decidedly against any exclusive establishment—I believe it to be so in the other States. There is not a shadow of right in the General Government to intermeddle with religion.—Its least interference with it would be a most flagrant usurpation.—I can appeal to my uniform conduct on this subject, that I have warmly supported religious freedom.—It is better that this security should be depended upon from the General Legislature, than from one particular State. A particular State might concur in one religious project.—But the United States abound in such a vast variety of sects, that it is a strong security against religious persecution, and is sufficient to authorise a conclusion, that no one sect will ever be able to out number or depress the rest.

I will not travel over that extensive tract, which the honorable member has traversed.—I shall not now take notice of all his desultory objections.—As occasions arise I shall answer them.

It is worthy of observation on this occasion, that the Honorable Gentleman himself, seldom fails to contradict the arguments of Gentlemen on that side of the question.—For example, he strongly complains that the Federal Government from the number of its members will make an addition to the public expence, too formidable to be borne; and yet he and other Gentlemen on the same side, object that the number of Representatives is too small, though ten men are more than we are entitled to under the existing system! How can these contradictions be reconciled? If we are to adopt any efficient

Government at all, how can we discover or establish such a system, if it be thus attacked?—Will it be possible to form a rational conclusion upon contradictory principles? If arguments of a contradictory nature were to be brought against the wisest and most admirable system, to the formation of which human intelligence is competent, it never could stand them.

He has accrimoniously inveighed against the Government, because such transactions as Congress think require secrecy, may be concealed—and particularly those which relate to treaties. He admits that when a treaty is forming, secrecy is proper; but urges that when actually made, the public ought to be made acquainted with every circumstance relative to it. The policy of not divulging the most important transactions, and negotiations of nations, such as those which relate to warlike arrangements and treaties, is universally admitted. The Congressional proceedings are to be occasionally published, including *all receipts and expenditures* of public money, of which no part can be used, but in consequence of appropriations made by law. This is a security which we do not enjoy under the existing system.—That part which authorises the Government to with-hold from the public knowledge what in their judgment may require secrecy, is imitated from the Confederation—that very system which the Gentleman advocates.

No treaty has been formed, and I will undertake to say, that none *will* be formed under the old system, which will secure to us the actual enjoyment of the navigation of the Mississippi. Our weakness precludes us from it. We *are* entitled to it. But it is not under an inefficient Government that we shall be able to avail ourselves fully of that right.—I most conscientiously believe, that it will be far better secured under the new Government, than the old, as we will be more able to enforce our right. The people of Kentucky will have an additional safe-guard from the change of system. The strength and respectability of the Union will secure them in the enjoyment of that right, till that country becomes sufficiently populous. When this happens they will be able to retain it in spite of every opposition.

I never can admit that seven States are disposed to sur-

render that navigation.—Indeed it never was the case.—
Some of their most distinguished characters are decidedly opposed to its relinquishment. When its cession was proposed
by the Southern States, the Northern States opposed it. They
still oppose it. New-Jersey directed her Delegates to oppose it,
and is strenuously against it. The same sentiments pervade
Pennsylvania:—At least I am warranted to say so, from the
best information which I have. Those States, added to the
Southern States, would be a majority against it.

The Honorable Gentleman, to obviate the force of my observations with respect to concurrent collections of taxes
under different authorities, said, that there was no interference
between the concurrent collections of parochial, county, and
State taxes, because they all irradiated from the same centre;
but that this was not the case with the General Government.
—To make use of the Gentleman's own term, the concurrent
collections under the authorities of the General Government
and State Governments, all irradiate from the people at large.
The people is their common superior. The sense of the people
at large is to be the predominant spring of their actions. This
is a sufficient security against interference.

Our attention was called to our commercial interest, and at
the same time the landed interest was said to be in danger. If
those ten men who are to be chosen, be elected by landed
men, and have land themselves, can the electors have anything
to apprehend?—If the commercial interest be in danger, why
are we alarmed about the carrying trade?—Why is it said,
that the carrying States will preponderate, if commerce be in
danger?—With respect to speculation, I will remark that
stock-jobbing has more or less prevailed in all countries, and
ever will in some degree, notwithstanding any exertions to
prevent it. If you judge from what has happened under
the existing system, any change would render a melioration
probable.

James Monroe Questions James Madison on Congressional Control of Elections to the House and Senate

June 14, 1788

Mr. *Monroe* wished that the Honorable Gentleman, who had been in the Federal Convention, would give information respecting the clause concerning elections. He wished to know why Congress had an ultimate controul over the time, place, and manner of elections of Representatives, and the time and manner of that of Senators; and also why there was an exception as to the *place* of electing Senators.

Mr. *Madison*,—Mr. Chairman.—The reason of the exception was, that if Congress could fix the *place* of choosing the Senators, it might compel the State Legislatures to elect them in a different place from that of their usual sessions, which would produce some inconvenience, and was not necessary for the object of regulating the elections. But it was necessary to give the General Government a controul over the time and manner of choosing the Senators, to prevent its own dissolution.

With respect to the other point, it was thought that the regulation of time, place, and manner of electing the Representatives, should be uniform throughout the Continent. Some States might regulate the elections on the principles of equality, and others might regulate them otherwise. This diversity would be obviously unjust. Elections are regulated now unequally in some States; particularly South-Carolina, with respect to *Charleston*, which is represented by 30 Members. Should the people of any State, by any means be deprived of the right of suffrage, it was judged proper that it should be remedied by the General Government. It was found impossible to fix the time, place, and manner, of the election of Representatives in the Constitution. It was found necessary to leave the regulation of these, in the first place, to the State Governments, as being best acquainted with the situation of the people, subject to the controul of the General Government, in order to enable it to produce uniformity, and prevent its own dissolution. And considering the State Governments and General Government as distinct bodies, acting in different and independent capacities for the people, it was thought the particular regulations should be submitted to the former, and the general regulations to the latter. Were they exclusively under the controul of the State Governments, the General Government might easily be dissolved. But if they be regulated properly by the State Legislatures, the Congressional controul will very probably never be exercised. The power appears to me satisfactory, and as unlikely to be abused as any part of the Constitution.

Patrick Henry's Objections to a National Army and James Madison's Reply

June 16, 1788

Mr. *Henry* thought it necessary and proper that they should take a collective view of this whole section, and revert again to the first clause. He adverted to the clause which gives Congress the power of raising armies, and proceeded as follows. To me this appears a very alarming power, when unlimitted. They are not only to raise, but to support armies; and this support is to go to the utmost abilities of the United States. If Congress shall say, that the general welfare requires it, they may keep armies continually on foot. There is no controul on Congress in raising or stationing them. They may billet them on the people at pleasure. This unlimited authority is a most dangerous power: Its principles are despotic. If it be unbounded, it must lead to despotism. For the power of the people in a free Government, is supposed to be paramount to the existing power.

We shall be told, that in England, the King, Lords, and Commons, have this power—That armies can be raised by the Prince alone, without the consent of the people. How does this apply here? Is this Government to place us in the situation of the English? Should we suppose this Government to resemble King, Lords, and Commons, we of this State, should be like an English county. An English county cannot controul the Government. Virginia cannot controul the Government of Congress no more than the county of Kent can controul that of England. Advert to the power thoroughly. One of our first complaints under the former Government, was the quarterring of troops upon us. This was one of the principal reasons for dissolving the connection with Great-Britain. Here we may have troops in time of peace. They may be billeted in any manner—to tyrannize, oppress, and crush us.

We are told, we are afraid to trust ourselves.—That our own Representatives—Congress, will not exercise their powers oppressively.—That we will not enslave ourselves.— That the militia cannot enslave themselves, &c. Who has en- slaved France, Spain, Germany, Turkey, and other countries which groan under tyranny? They have been enslaved by the hands of their own people. If it will be so in America, it will be only as it has been every where else. I am still persuaded that the power of calling forth the militia to execute the laws of the Union, &c. is dangerous.—We requested the Gentle- man to shew the cases where the militia would be wanting to execute the laws. Have we received a satisfactory answer? When we consider this part, and compare it to other parts, which declare that Congress may declare war; and that the Presi- dent shall command the regular troops, militia, and navy, we will find great danger. Under the order of Congress, they shall suppress insurrections. Under the order of Congress, they shall be called to execute the laws. It will result of course, that this is to be a Government of force. Look at the part which speaks of excises and you will recollect, that those who are to collect excises and duties, are to be aided by military force. They have power to call them out, and to provide for arming, organizing, and disciplining them.—Consequently they are to make militia laws for this State.—The Honorable Gentleman has said, that the militia should be called forth to quell riots. Have we not seen this business go on very well to this day, without military force? It is a long established principle of the common law of England, that civil force is sufficient to quell riots. To what length may it not be carried? A law may be made, that if twelve men assemble, if they do not disperse, they may be fired upon. I think it is so in England. Does not this part of the paper bear a strong aspect? The Honorable Gentleman, from his knowledge, was called upon to shew the instances, and he told us the militia may be called out to quell riots.—They may make the militia travel, and act under a Colonel, or perhaps under a Constable. Who are to determine whether it be a riot or not? Those who are to execute the laws of the union? If they have power to execute their laws in this manner, in what situation are we placed?—Your men who go to Congress are not restrained by a Bill of Rights. They are not restrained from inflicting unusual and severe punish- ments: Though the Bill of Rights of Virginia forbids it—

What will be the consequence? They may inflict the most cruel and ignominious punishments on the militia, and they will tell you it is necessary for their discipline.

Give me leave to ask another thing. Suppose an exciseman will demand leave to enter your cellar or house, by virtue of his office; perhaps he may call on the militia to enable him to go. If Congress be informed of it, will they give you redress? They will tell you, that he is executing the laws under the authority of the continent at large, which must be obeyed; for that the Government cannot be carried on without exercising severity. If, without any reservation of rights, or controul, you are contented to give up your rights, I am not. There is no principle to guide the Legislature to restrain them from inflicting the utmost severity of punishment. Will Gentlemen voluntarily give up their liberty? With respect to calling the militia to execute every execution indiscriminately, it is un-precedented. Have we ever seen it done in any free country? Was it ever so in the mother country? It never was so in any well regulated country. It is a Government of force, and the genius of despotism expressly. It is not proved that this power is necessary; and if it be unnecessary, shall we give it up?

Mr. *Madison*,—Mr. Chairman.—I will endeavor to follow the rule of the House; but must pay due attention to the observations which fell from the Gentleman. I should con-clude, from abstracted reasoning, that they were ill founded. I should think, that if there were any object, which the General Government ought to command, it would be the direction of the national forces. And as the force which lies in militia is most safe, the direction of that part ought to be submitted to, in order to render another force unnecessary. The power objected to is necessary, because it is to be employed for national purposes. It is necessary to be given to every Government. This is not opinion, but fact. The highest au-thority may be given;—That the want of such authority in the Government protracted the late war, and prolonged its calamities.

He says, that one ground of complaint at the beginning of the revolution, was, that a standing army was quartered upon us. This was not the whole complaint. We complained be-cause it was done without the local authority of this country,

—without the consent of the people of America. As to the exclusion of standing armies in the Bills of Rights of the States, we shall find, that though in one or two of them, there is something like a prohibition, yet in most of them it is only provided, that no armies shall be kept up without the Legislative authority; that is, without the consent of the community itself. Where is the impropriety of saying we shall have an army if necessary? Does not the notoriety of this constitute security? If inimical nations were to fall upon us when defenceless, what would be the consequence? Would it be wise to say, that we should have no defence? Give me leave to say, that the only possible way to provide against standing armies, is, to make them unnecessary. The way to do this, is to organize and discipline our militia, so as to render them capable of defending the country against external invasions, and internal insurrections. But it is urged, that abuses may happen.— How is it possible to answer objections against possibility of abuses? It must strike every logical reasoner, that these cannot be entirely provided against. I really thought that the objection to the militia was at an end. Was there ever a Constitution, in which, if authority was vested, it must not have been executed by force, if resisted? Was it not in the contemplation of this State, when contemptuous proceedings were expected, to recur to something of this kind? How is it possible to have a more proper resource than this? That the laws of every country ought to be executed, cannot be denied. That force must be used if necessary, cannot be denied. Can any Government be established, that will answer any purpose whatever, unless force be provided for executing its laws? The Constitution does not say that a standing army shall be called out to execute the laws. Is not this a more proper way? The militia ought to be called forth to suppress smugglers. Will this be denied? The case actually happened at Alexandria. There were a number of smugglers, who were too formidable for the civil power to overcome. The militia quelled the sailors, who, otherwise, would have perpetrated their intentions. Should a number of smugglers have a number of ships, the militia ought to be called forth to quell them. We do not know but what there may be combinations of smugglers in Virginia hereafter. We all know the use made of the Isle of Man. It was a general depositary of contraband goods. The Parliament found the evil so great, as to render it necessary to wrest it out of the hands of its possessor.

The Honorable Gentleman says, it is a Government of force. If he means *military* force, the clause under consideration proves the contrary. There never was a Government without force. What is the meaning of Government? An institution to make people do their duty. A Government leaving it to a man to do his duty, or not, as he pleases, would be a new species of Government, or rather no Government at all. The ingenuity of the Gentleman is remarkable, in introducing the riot-act of Great-Britain.—That act has no connection, or analogy, to any regulation of the militia: Nor is there any thing in the Constitution to warrant the General Government to make such an act. It never was a complaint in Great-Britain, that the militia could be called forth. If riots should happen, the militia are proper to quell it, to prevent a resort to another mode.—As to the infliction of ignominious punishments, we have no ground of alarm, if we consider the circumstances of the people at large. There will be no punishments so ignominious as have been inflicted already. The militia law of every State to the north of Maryland, is less rigorous than the particular law of this State. If a change be necessary to be made by the General Government, it will be in our favor. I think that the people of those States would not agree to be subjected to a more harsh punishment than their own militia laws inflict. An observation fell from a Gentleman, on the same side with myself, which deserves to be attended to. If we be dissatisfied with the national Government—If we should choose to renounce it, this is an additional safe-guard to our defence. I conceive that we are peculiarly interested in giving the General Government as extensive means as possible to protect us. If there be a particular discrimination between places in America, the Southern States are, from their situation and circumstances, most interested in giving the national Government the power of protecting its members.—(Here Mr. *Madison* made some other observations; but spoke so very low, that his meaning could not be comprehended.)—An act passed a few years ago, in this State, to enable the Government to call forth the militia to enforce the laws, when a powerful combination should take place to oppose them. This is the same power which the Constitution is to have. There is a great deal of difference between calling forth the militia, when a combination is formed to prevent the execution of the laws, and the Sheriff or Constable carrying with him a body of militia to execute them in the first instance; which is a construction not warranted by the clause. There is an act also in this State, empowering the officers of the customs to summon *any* persons to assist them when they meet with obstruction in executing their duty. This shews the necessity of giving the Government power to call forth the militia when the laws are resisted. It is a power vested in every Legislature in the Union, and which is necessary to every Government.—He then moved, that the Clerk should read those acts,—which were accordingly read.

Patrick Henry and James Madison Debate Constructive Rights and the Uses of the Militia

---

June 16, 1788

Mr. *Henry* still retained his opinion, that the States had no right to call forth the militia to suppress insurrections, &c.—But the right interpretation (and such as the nations of the earth had put upon the concession of power) was, that when power was given, it was given exclusively. He appealed to the Committee, if power was not confined in the hands of a *few* in almost all countries of the world. He referred to their candour, if the construction of conceded power, was not an exclusive concession in nineteen-twentieth parts of the world. The nations which retained their liberty, were comparatively few. America would add to the number of the oppressed nations, if she depended on constructive rights, and argumentative implication: That the powers given to Congress were exclusively given, was very obvious to him. The rights which the States had must be founded on the restrictions on Congress.—He asked, if the doctrine which had been so often circulated, that rights not given were retained, was true, why there were negative clauses to restrain Congress? He told Gentlemen, that these clauses were sufficient to shake all their implications. For, says he, if Congress had no power but what was given them, why restrict them by negative words? Is not the clear implication this—that if these restrictions were not inserted, they could have performed what they prohibit? The worthy Member had said, that Congress ought to have power to protect all, and had given this system the highest encomium. But still insisted that the power over the militia was concurrent.—To obviate the futility of this doctrine, Mr. *Henry* alledged that it was not reducible to practice. Examine it, says he—Reduce it to practice. Suppose an insurrection in Virginia, and suppose there be danger apprehended of an insurrection in another State, from the exercise of the Government; or suppose a national war, and there be discontents among the people of this State that produces or threatens an insurrection; suppose Congress in either case, demands a number of militia; will they not be obliged to go? Where are your reserved rights, when your militia go to a neighbouring State? Which call is to be obeyed, the Congressional call, or the call of the State Legislature? The call of Congress must be obeyed. I need not remind this Committee that the sweeping clause will cause their demands to be submitted to.—This clause enables them "to make all laws which shall be necessary and proper to carry into execution all the powers vested by this Constitution in the Government of the United States, or in any department or officer thereof."—Mr. Chairman, I will turn to another clause, which relates to the same subject, and tends to shew the fallacy of their argument. The tenth section, of the first article, to which reference was made by the worthy Member, militates against himself. It says, that "no State shall engage in war, unless actually invaded." If you give this clause a fair construction, what is the true meaning of it? What does this relate to? Not domestic insurrections, but war. If the country be invaded, a State may go to war; but cannot suppress insurrections. If there should happen an insurrection of slaves, the country cannot be said to be invaded.—They cannot therefore suppress it, without the interposition of Congress. The fourth section, of the fourth article, expressly directs, that in case of domestic violence, Congress shall protect the States on application of the Legislature or Executive; and the eighth section, of the first article, gives Congress power, to call forth the militia to quell insurrections: There cannot therefore be a concurrent power. The State Legislatures ought to have power to call forth the efforts of militia when necessary. Occasions for calling them out may be urgent, pressing, and instantaneous. The States cannot now call them, let an insurrection be ever so perilous, without an application to Congress. So long a delay may be fatal.

There are three clauses which prove beyond a possibility of doubt, that Congress, and *Congress only*, can call forth the militia. The clause giving Congress power to call them out to suppress insurrections, &c.—that which restrains a State from engaging in war, except when actually invaded,—and that which requires Congress to protect the States against domestic violence, render it impossible, that a State can have power to intermeddle with them. Will not Congress find refuge for their actions in these clauses? With respect to the concurrent jurisdiction, it is a political monster of absurdity. We have passed that clause which gives Congress an unlimitted authority over the national wealth; and here is an unbounded controul over the national strength. Notwithstanding this clear and unequivocal relinquishment of the power of controuling the militia, you say the States retain it for the very purposes given to Congress. Is it fair to say, that you gave the power of arming the militia, and at the same time say you reserve it? This great national Government ought not to be left in this condition. If it be, it will terminate in the destruction of our liberties.

Mr. *Madison*,—Mr. Chairman.—Let me ask this Committee, and the Honorable Member last up, what we are to understand from this reasoning? The power must be vested in Congress, or in the State Governments; or there must be a division or concurrence.—He is against division—It is a political monster. He will not give it to Congress for fear of oppression. Is it to be vested in the State Governments? If so, where is the provision for general defence? If ever America should be attacked, the States would fall successively. It will prevent them from giving aid to their sister States.—For, as each State will expect to be attacked, and wish to guard against it, each will retain its own militia for its own defence. Where is this power to be deposited then, unless in the General Government, if it be dangerous to the public safety to give it exclusively to the States? If it must be divided, let him shew a better manner of doing it than that which is in the Constitution. I cannot agree with the other Honorable Gentleman, that there is no check. There is a powerful check in that paper. The State Governments are to govern the militia, when not called forth for general national purposes; and Congress is to govern such part only as may be in the actual service of the Union. Nothing can be more certain and positive than this. It expressly empowers Congress to govern them when in the service of the United States. It is then clear, that the States govern them when they are not. With respect to suppressing insurrections, I say that those clauses which were mentioned by the Honorable Gentleman, are compatible with a concurrence of the power. By the first, Congress is to call them forth to suppress insurrections and repel invasions of foreign powers. A concurrence in the former case is necessary, because a whole State may be in insurrection against the Union. What has passed will perhaps justify this apprehension. The safety of the Union, and particular States, requires that the General Government should have power to repel foreign invasions. The fourth section, of the fourth article, is perfectly consistent with the exercise of the power by the States. The words are, "The United States shall guarantee to every State in this Union, a Republican form of Government, and shall protect each of them against invasion; and on application of the Legislature, or of the Executive, (when the Legislature cannot be convened) against domestic violence."— The word *invasion* here, after power had been given in the former clause to repel *invasions*, may be thought tautologous, but it has a different meaning from the other. This clause speaks of a particular State. It means that it shall be protected from invasion by other States. A Republican Government is to be guaranteed to each State, and they are to be protected from invasion from other States, as well as from foreign powers: And on application by the Legislature or Executive, as the case may be, the militia of other States are to be called to suppress domestic insurrections. Does this bar the States from calling forth their own militia? No.—But it gives them a supplementary security to suppress insurrections and domestic violence. The other clause runs in these words, "No State shall, without the consent of Congress, lay any duty on tonnage, keep troops or ships of war in time of peace, enter into any agreement or compact with another State, or with a foreign power, or engage in war, unless actually invaded, or in such imminent danger as will not admit of delay." They are restrained from making war, unless invaded, *or in imminent danger*.—When in such danger, they are not restrained. I can perceive no competition in these clauses. They cannot be said to be repugnant to a concurrence of the power. If we object to the Constitution in this manner, and consume our time in verbal criticism, we shall never put an end to the business.

George Mason and James Madison Debate the Slave-Trade Clause

Mr. *George Mason*,—Mr. Chairman.—This is a fatal section, which has created more dangers than any other.—The first clause, allows the importation of slaves for twenty years. Under the royal Government, this evil was looked upon as a great oppression, and many attempts were made to prevent it; but the interest of the African merchants prevented its prohibition. No sooner did the revolution take place, than it was thought of. It was one of the great causes of our separation from Great-Britain. Its exclusion has been a principal object of this State, and most of the States in the Union. The augmentation of slaves weakens the States; and such a trade is diabolical in itself, and disgraceful to mankind. Yet by this Constitution it is continued for twenty years. As much as I value an union of all the States, I would not admit the Southern States into the Union, unless they agreed to the discontinuance of this disgraceful trade, because it would bring weakness and not strength to the Union. And though this infamous traffic be continued, we have no security for the property of that kind which we have already. There is no clause in this Constitution to secure it; for they may lay such a tax as will amount to manumission. And should the Government be amended, still this detestable kind of commerce cannot be discontinued till after the expiration of twenty years.—For the fifth article, which provides for amendments, expressly excepts this clause. I have ever looked upon this as a most disgraceful thing to America. I cannot express my detestation of it. Yet they have not secured us the property of the slaves we have already. So that "They have done what they ought not to have done, and have left undone what they ought to have done."

Mr. *Madison*,—Mr. Chairman.—I should conceive this clause to be impolitic, if it were one of those things which could be excluded without encountering greater evils.—The Southern States would not have entered into the Union of America, without the temporary permission of that trade. And if they were excluded from the Union, the consequences might be dreadful to them and to us. We are not in a worse situation than before. That traffic is prohibited by our laws, and we may continue the prohibition. The Union in general is not in a worse situation. Under the articles of Confederation, it might be continued forever: But by this clause an end may be put to it after twenty years. There is therefore an amelioration of our circumstances. A tax may be laid in the mean time; but it is limited, otherwise Congress might lay such a tax as would amount to a prohibition. From the mode of representation and taxation, Congress cannot lay such a tax on slaves as will amount to manumission. Another clause secures us that property which we now possess. At present, if any slave elopes to any of those States where slaves are free, he becomes emancipated by their laws. For the laws of the States are uncharitable to one another in this respect. But in this Constitution, "No person held to service, or labor, in one State, under the laws thereof, escaping into another, shall in consequence of any law or regulation therein, be discharged from such service or labor; but shall be delivered up on claim of the party to whom such service or labour may be due."— This clause was expressly inserted to enable owners of slaves to reclaim them. This is a better security than any that now exists. No power is given to the General Government to interpose with respect to the property in slaves now held by the States. The taxation of this State being equal only to its representation, such a tax cannot be laid as he supposes. They cannot prevent the importation of slaves for twenty years; but after that period they can. The Gentlemen from South-Carolina and Georgia argued in this manner:—"We have now liberty to import this species of property, and much of the property now possessed, has been purchased, or otherwise acquired, in contemplation of improving it by the assistance of imported slaves. What would be the consequence of hindering us from it? The slaves of Virginia would rise in value, and we would be obliged to go to your markets." I need not

expatiate on this subject. Great as the evil is, a dismemberment of the Union would be worse. If those States should
disunite from the other States, for not indulging them in the
temporary continuance of this traffic, they might solicit and
obtain aid from foreign powers.

Governor Edmund Randolph on the "Necessary and Proper" Clause, Implied Powers, and Bills of Rights

June 17, 1788

Governor *Randolph*,—Mr. Chairman.—The general review which the Gentleman has taken of the ninth section, is so inconsistent, that in order to answer him, I must with your permission, who are the custos of order here, depart from the rule of the House in some degree. I declared some days ago that I would give my suffrage for this Constitution, not because I considered it without blemish, but because the critical situation of our country demanded it. I invite those who think with me to vote for the Constitution.—But where things occur in it which I disapprove of, I shall be candid in exposing my objections.

Permit me to return to that clause, which is called by Gentlemen the sweeping clause. I observed yesterday, that I conceived the construction which had been put on this clause by the advocates of the Constitution was too narrow; and that the construction put upon it by the other party, was extravagant. The intermediate explanation appears to me most rational. The former contend, that it gives no supplementary power; but only enables them to make laws to execute the delegated powers, or in other words, that it only involves the powers incidental to those expressly delegated.—By incidental powers they mean those which are necessary for the principal thing.—That the incident is inseparable from the principal, is a maxim in the construction of laws.—A Constitution differs from a law.—For a law only embraces one thing—But a Constitution embraces a number of things, and is to have a more liberal construction. I need not recur to the Constitutions of Europe for a precedent to direct my explication of this clause, because in Europe there is no Constitution wholly in writing. The European Constitutions sometimes consist in detached statutes or ordinances:—Sometimes they are on record, and sometimes they depend on immemorial tradition. The American Constitutions are singular, and their construction ought to be liberal. On this principle what should be said of the clause under consideration (*the sweeping clause*.) If incidental powers be those only which are necessary for the principal thing, the clause would be superfluous.

Let us take an example of a single department: For instance that of the President, who has certain things annexed to his office. Does it not reasonably follow, that he must have some incidental powers? The principle of incidental powers extends to all parts of the system. If you then say, that the President has incidental powers, you reduce it to tautology. I cannot conceive that the fair interpretation of these words is as the Honorable Member says.

Let me say, that, in my opinion, the adversaries of the Constitution wander equally from the true meaning. If it would not fatigue the House too far, I would go back to the question of reserved rights. The Gentleman supposes, that compleat and unlimited legislation is vested in the Congress of the United States. This supposition is founded on false reasoning. What is the present situation of this State? She has possession of all rights of sovereignty, except those given to the Confederation. She *must* delegate powers to the Confederate Government. It is necessary for her public happiness. Her weakness compels her to confederate with the twelve other Governments. She trusts certain powers to the General Government in order to support, protect, and defend the Union. Now is there not a demonstrable difference between the principle of the State Government, and the General Government? There is not a word said in the State Government of the powers given to it, because they are general. But in the general Constitution, its powers are enumerated. Is it not then fairly deducible, that it has no power but what is expressly given it? For if its powers were to be general, an enumeration would be needless.

But the insertion of the negative restrictions has given cause of triumph it seems, to Gentlemen. They suppose, that it demonstrates that Congress are to have powers by implication. I will meet them on that ground. I persuade myself, that every exception here mentioned, is an exception not from general powers, but from the particular powers therein vested. To what power in the General Government is the exception made, respecting the importation of negroes? Not from a general power, but from a particular power expressly enumerated. This is an exception from the power given them of regulating commerce. He asks, where is the power to which the prohibition of suspending the *habeas corpus* is an exception. I contend that by virtue of the power given to Congress to regulate courts, they could suspend the writ of *habeas corpus.*—This is therefore an exception to that power.

The third restriction is, that "No bill of attainder, or *ex post facto* law shall be passed."—This is a manifest exception to another power. We know well that attainders, and *ex post facto* laws, have always been the engines of criminal jurisprudence. This is therefore an exception to the criminal jurisdiction vested in that body.

The fourth restriction is, that no capitation, or other direct tax shall be laid, unless in proportion to the census before directed to be taken. Our debates shew from what power this is an exception.

The restrictions in the fifth clause, are an exception to the power of regulating commerce.

The restriction of the sixth clause, that no money shall be drawn from the treasury, but in consequence of appropriations made by law, is an exception to the power of paying the debts of the United States; for the power of drawing money from the treasury is consequential of that of paying the public debts.

The next restriction is, that no titles of nobility shall be granted by the United States. If we cast our eyes to the manner in which titles of nobility first originated, we shall find this restriction founded on the same principles. These sprung from military and civil offices: Both are put in the hands of the United States, and therefore I presume it to be an exception to that power.

The last restriction restrains any persons in office from accepting of any present or emolument, title or office, from any foreign Prince or State. It must have been observed before, that though the Confederation had restricted Congress from exercising any powers not given them, yet they inserted it, not from any apprehension of usurpation, but for greater security. This restriction is provided to prevent corruption. All men have a natural inherent right of receiving emoluments from any one, unless they be restrained by the regulations of the community. An accident which actually happened, operated in producing the restriction. A box was presented to our Ambassador by the King of our allies. It was thought proper, in order to exclude corruption and foreign influence, to prohibit any one in office from receiving or holding any emoluments from foreign States. I believe, that if at that moment, when we were in harmony with the King of France, we had supposed that he was corrupting our Ambassador, it might have disturbed that confidence, and diminished that mutual friendship, which contributed to carry us through the war.

The Honorable Gentleman observed, that Congress might define punishments, from petty larceny to high treason. This is an unfortunate quotation for the Gentleman; because treason is expressly defined in the third section, of the third article, and they can add no feature to it. They have not cognizance over any other crime, except piracies, felonies committed on the high seas, and offences against the law of nations.

But the rhetoric of the Gentleman has highly coloured the dangers of giving the General Government an indefinite power of providing for the general welfare. I contend that no such power is given. They have power "To lay and collect taxes, duties, imposts, and excises, to pay the debts and provide for the common defence and general welfare of the United States." Is this an independent, separate, substantive power, to provide for the general welfare of the United States?—No, Sir.—They can lay and collect taxes, &c.—For what?—To pay the debts and provide for the general welfare. Were not this the case the following part of the clause would be absurd. It would have been treason against common language. Take it altogether, and let me ask if the plain interpretation be not this—a power to lay and collect taxes, &c. in order to provide for the general welfare, and pay debts.

On the subject of a Bill of Rights, the want of which has been complained of, I will observe that it has been sanctified by such reverend authority, that I feel some difficulty in going against it. I shall not, however, be deterred from giving my opinion on this occasion, let the consequence be what it may. At the beginning of the war we had no certain Bill of Rights: For our charter cannot be considered as a Bill of Rights. It is nothing more than an investiture in the hands of the Virginian citizens, of those rights which belonged to the British subjects. When the British thought proper to infringe our rights, was it not necessary to mention in our Constitution, those rights which ought to be paramount to the power of the Legislature? Why are the Bill of Rights distinct from the Constitution? I consider Bills of Rights in this view, that the Government should use them when there is a departure from its fundamental principles, in order to restore them. This is the true sense of a Bill of Rights. If it be consistent with the Constitution, or contains additional rights, why not put it in the Constitution? If it be repugnant to the Constitution, there will be a perpetual scene of warfare between them. The Honorable Gentleman has praised the Bill of Rights of Virginia, and called it his guardian angel, and vilified this Constitution for not having it. Give me leave to make a distinction between the Representatives of the people of a particular country, who are appointed as the ordinary Legislature, having no limitation to their powers, and another body arising from a compact and certain delineated powers. Were a Bill of Rights necessary in the former, it would not in the latter; for the best security that can be in the latter is the express enumeration of its powers. But let me ask the Gentleman where his favourite rights are violated? They are not violated by the tenth section, which contains restrictions on the States. Are they violated by the enumerated powers? (Here his Excellency read from the eighth to the twelfth article of the Declaration of Rights.)—Is there not provision made in this Constitution for the trial by jury in criminal cases? Does not the third article provide, that the trial of all crimes shall be by jury, and held in the State where the said crimes shall have been committed? Does it not follow, that the cause and nature of the accusation must be produced, because otherwise they cannot proceed on the cause? Every one knows, that the witnesses must be brought before the jury, or else the prisoner will be discharged. Calling for evidence in his favor is co-incident to his trial. There is no suspicion, that less than twelve jurors will be thought sufficient. The only defect is, that there is no speedy trial.—Consider how this could have been amended. We have heard complaints against it, because it is supposed the jury is to come from the State at large. It will be in their power to have juries from the vicinage. And would not the complaints have been louder, if they had appointed a Federal Court to be had in every county in the State?—Criminals are brought in this State from every part of the country to the General Court, and jurors from the vicinage are summoned to the trials. There can be no reason to prevent the General Government from adopting a similar regulation.

As to the exclusion of excessive bail and fines, and cruel and unusual punishments, this would follow of itself without a Bill of Rights. Observations have been made about watchfulness over those in power, which deserve our attention. There must be a combination—We must presume corruption in the House of Representatives, Senate, and President, before we can suppose that excessive fines can be imposed, or cruel punishments inflicted. Their number is the highest security.— Numbers are the highest security in our own Constitution, which has attracted so many eulogiums from the Gentleman. Here we have launched into a sea of suspicions. How shall we check power?—By their numbers. Before these cruel punishments can be inflicted, laws must be passed, and Judges must judge contrary to justice. This would excite universal discontent, and detestation of the Members of the Government. They might involve their friends in the calamities resulting from it, and could be removed from office. I never desire a greater security than this, which I believe to be absolutely sufficient.

That general warrants are grievous and oppressive, and ought not to be granted, I fully admit. I heartily concur in expressing my detestation of them. But we have sufficient security here also. We do not rely on the integrity of any one particular person or body; but on the number and different orders of the Members of the Government: Some of them having necessarily the same feelings with ourselves. Can it be believed, that the Federal Judiciary would not be independent enough to prevent such oppressive practices? If they will not do justice to persons injured, may they not go to our own State Judiciaries and obtain it?

Gentlemen have been misled to a certain degree, by a general declaration, that the trial by jury was gone. We see that in the most valuable cases, it is reserved. Is it abolished in civil cases? Let him put his finger on the part where it is abolished. The Constitution is silent on it.—What expression would you wish the Constitution to use, to establish it? Remember we were not making a Constitution for Virginia alone, or we might have taken Virginia for our directory. But we were forming a Constitution for thirteen States. The trial by jury is different in different States. In some States it is excluded in cases in which it is admitted in others. In Admiralty causes it is not used. Would you have a jury to determine the case of a capture? The Virginian Legislature thought proper to make an exception of that case. These depend on the law of nations, and no twelve men that could be picked up would be equal to the decision of such a matter.

Then, Sir, the freedom of the press is said to be insecure. God forbid that I should give my voice against the freedom of the press. But I ask, (and with confidence that it cannot be answered) where is the page where it is restrained? If there had been any regulation about it, leaving it insecure, then there might have been reason for clamours. But this is not the case. If it be, I again ask for the particular clause which gives liberty to destroy the freedom of the press.

He has added religion to the objects endangered in his conception. Is there any power given over it? Let it be pointed out. Will he not be contented with the answer which has been frequently given to that objection? That variety of sects which abounds in the United States is the best security for the freedom of religion. No part of the Constitution, even if strictly construed, will justify a conclusion, that the General Government can take away, or impair the freedom of religion.

The Gentleman asks with triumph, shall we be deprived of these valuable rights? Had there been an exception, or express infringement of those rights, he might object.—But I conceive every fair reasoner will agree, that there is no just cause to suspect that they will be violated.

But he objects, that the common law is not established by

the Constitution. The wisdom of the Convention is displayed by its omission; because the common law ought not to be immutably fixed. Is it established in our own Constitution, or the Bill of Rights which has been resounded through the House? It is established only by an act of the Legislature, and can therefore be changed as circumstances may require it. Let the Honorable Gentleman consider what would be the destructive consequences of its establishment in the Constitution. Even in England, where the firmest opposition has been made to encroachments upon it, it has been frequently changed. What would have been our dilemma if it had been established?—Virginia has declared, that children shall have equal portions of the real estates of their intestate parents, and it is consistent to the principles of a Republican Government.—The immutable establishment of the common law, would have been repugnant to that regulation. It would in many respects be destructive to republican principles, and productive of great inconveniencies. I might indulge myself, by shewing many parts of the common law which would have this effect. I hope I shall not be thought to speak ludicrously, when I say, that the *writ* of *burning heretics*, would have been revived by it. It would tend to throw real property in few hands, and prevent the introduction of many salutary regulations. Thus, were the common law adopted in that system, it would destroy the principles of Republican Government. But it is not excluded. It may be established by an act of the Legislature. Its defective parts may be altered, and it may be changed and modified as the convenience of the public may require it.

I said when I opened my observations, that I thought the friends of the Constitution were mistaken, when they supposed the powers granted by the last clause of the eighth section, to be merely incidental; and that its enemies were equally mistaken when they put such an extravagant construction upon it.

My objection is, that the clause is ambiguous, and that that ambiguity may injure the States. My fear is, that it will by gradual accessions gather to a dangerous length. This is my apprehension, and I disdain to disown it. I will praise it where it deserves it, and censure it where it appears defective.

But, Sir, are we to reject it, because it is ambiguous in some particular instances? I cast my eyes to the actual situation of America; I see the dreadful tempest, to which the present calm is a prelude, if disunion takes place. I see the anarchy which must happen if no energetic Government be established. In this situation, I would take the Constitution were it more objectionable than it is. — For if anarchy and confusion follow disunion, an enterprising man may enter into the American throne. I conceive there is no danger. The Representatives are chosen by and from among the people. They will have a fellow-feeling for the farmers and planters. The twenty-six Senators, Representatives of the States, will not be those desperadoes and horrid adventurers which they are represented to be. The State Legislatures, I trust, will not forget the duty they owe to their country so far, as to choose such men to manage their federal interests. I trust, that the Members of Congress themselves, will explain the ambiguous parts: And if not, the States can combine in order to insist on amending the ambiguities. I would depend on the present actual feelings of the people of America, to introduce any amendment which may be necessary. I repeat it again, though I do not reverence the Constitution, that its adoption is necessary to avoid the storm which is hanging over America, and that no greater curse can befal her, than the dissolution of the political connection between the States. Whether we shall propose previous or subsequent amendments, is now the only dispute. It is supererogation to repeat again the arguments in support of each. — But I ask Gentlemen, whether, as eight States have adopted it, it be not safer to adopt it, and rely on the probability of obtaining amendments, than by a rejection to hazard a breach of the Union? I hope to be excused for the breach of order which I have committed.

George Mason on the President:
He Will Serve for Life and Be Corrupted by Foreign Powers

June 17, 1788

Mr. *George Mason*,—Mr. Chairman.—There is not a more important article in the Constitution than this. The great fundamental principle of responsibility in republicanism is here sapped. The President is elected without rotation.—It may be said that a new election may remove him, and place another in his stead. If we judge from the experience of all other countries, and even our own, we may conclude, that as the President of the United States may be re-elected, so he will. How is it in every Government where rotation is not required? Is there a single instance of a great man not being re-elected? Our Governor is obliged to return after a given period, to a private station. It is so in most of the States. This President will be elected time after time—He will be continued in office for life.—If we wish to change him, the great powers in Europe will not allow us.

The Honorable Gentleman my colleague in the late Federal Convention, mentions with applause those parts of which he had expressed his approbation; but when he comes to those parts of which he had expressed his disapprobation, he says not a word. If I am mistaken, let me be put right. I shall not make use of his name, but in the course of this investigation, I shall use the arguments of that Gentleman against it.

Will not the great powers of Europe, as France and Great-Britain, be interested in having a friend in the President of the United States; and will they not be more interested in his election, than in that of the King of Poland? The people of Poland have a right to displace their King. But do they ever do it? No. Prussia and Russia, and other European powers, would not suffer it. This clause will open a door to the dangers and misfortunes which the people of Poland undergo. The powers of Europe will interpose, and we shall have a civil

718

war in the bowels of our country, and be subject to all the horrors and calamities of an elective Monarchy. This very executive officer, may, by consent of Congress, receive a stated pension from European Potentates. This is an idea not altogether new in America. It is not many years ago, since the revolution, that a foreign power offered emoluments to persons holding offices under our Government. It will moreover be difficult to know, whether he receives emoluments from foreign powers or not. The Electors who are to meet in each State to vote for him, may be easily influenced. To prevent the certain evils of attempting to elect a new President, it will be necessary to continue the old one. The only way to alter this, would be to render him ineligible after a certain number of years, and then no foreign nation would interfere to keep *in* a man who was utterly ineligible. Nothing is so essential to the preservation of a Republican Government, as a periodical rotation. Nothing so strongly impels a man to regard the interest of his constituents, as the certainty of returning to the general mass of the people, from whence he was taken; where he must participate in their burdens. It is a great defect in the Senate, that they are not ineligible at the end of six years. The biennial exclusion of one third of them, will have no effect, as they can be re-elected. Some stated time ought to be fixed, when the President ought to be reduced to a private station. I should be contented that he might be elected for eight years: But I would wish him to be capable of holding the office only eight years, out of twelve or sixteen years. But as it now stands, he may continue in office for life; or in other words, it will be an elective Monarchy.

George Mason Fears the Power of the Federal Courts: What Will Be Left to the States?

June 19, 1788

Mr. *George Mason*,—Mr. Chairman.—I had some hopes that the candour and reason of the warmest friends of this Constitution would have led them to point out objections so important. They must occur, more or less, to the mind of every one. It is with great reluctance I speak of this department, as it lies out of my line. I should not tell my sentiments upon it, did I not conceive it to be so constructed as to destroy the dearest rights of the community. After having read the first section, Mr. *Mason* asked, what is there left to the State Courts? Will Gentlemen be pleased, candidly, fairly, and without sophistry, to shew us what remains? There is no limitation. It goes to every thing. The inferior Courts are to be as numerous as Congress may think proper. They are to be of whatever nature they please. Read the second section, and contemplate attentively the extent of the jurisdiction of these Courts; and consider if there be any limits to it. I am greatly mistaken if there be any limitation whatsoever, with respect to the nature or jurisdiction of these Courts. If there be any limits, they must be contained in one of the clauses of this section; and I believe, on a dispassionate discussion, it will be found that there is none of any check. All the laws of the United States are paramount to the laws and Constitution of any single State. "The Judicial power shall extend to all cases in law and equity, arising under this Constitution." What objects will not this expression extend to? Such laws may be formed, as will go to every object of private property.—When we consider the nature of these Courts, we must conclude, that their effect and operation will be utterly to destroy the State Governments. For they will be the judges how far their laws will operate. They are to modify their own Courts, and you can make no State law to counteract them. The discrimination between their Judicial power and that of the States, exists therefore but in name.—To what disgraceful and dangerous length does the principle of this go? For if your State Judiciaries are not to be trusted with the administration of common justice, and decision of disputes respecting property between man and man, much less ought the State Governments to be trusted with the power of legislation. The principle itself goes to the destruction of the legislation of the States, whether or not it was intended. As to my own opinion, I most religiously and conscientiously believe, that it was intended, though I am not absolutely certain. But I think it will destroy the State Governments, whatever may have been the intention. There are many Gentlemen in the United States who think it right, that we should have one great national consolidated Government, and that it was better to bring it about slowly and imperceptibly, rather than all at once. This is no reflection on any man, for I mean none. To those who think that one national consolidated Government would be best for America, this extensive Judicial authority will be agreeable; but I hope there are many in this Convention of a different opinion, and who see their political happiness resting on their State Governments. I know, from my own knowledge, many worthy Gentlemen of the former opinion.—(Here Mr. *Madison* interrupted Mr. *Mason*, and demanded an unequivocal explanation. As those insinuations might create a belief, that every Member of the late Federal Convention was of that opinion, he wished him to tell who the Gentlemen were, to whom he alluded.)—Mr. *Mason* then replied—I shall never refuse to explain myself. It is notorious that this is a prevailing principle.—It was at least the opinion of many Gentlemen in Convention, and many in the United States. I do not know what explanation the Honorable Gentleman asks. I can say with great truth, that the Honorable Gentleman, in private conversation with me, expressed himself against it: Neither did I ever hear any of the Delegates from this State advocate it.

Mr. *Madison* declared himself satisfied with this, unless the Committee thought themselves entitled to ask a further explanation.

After some desultory remarks, Mr. *Mason* continued.—I have heard that opinion advocated by Gentlemen, for whose abilities, judgment, and knowledge, I have the highest reverence and respect. I say that the general description of the Judiciary involves the most extensive jurisdiction. Its cognizance in all cases arising under the system, and the laws of Congress, may be said to be unlimited. In the next place it extends to treaties made, or which shall be made, under their authority. This is one of the powers which ought to be given them. I also admit that they ought to have Judicial cognizance in all cases affecting Ambassadors, foreign Ministers and Consuls, as well as in cases of maritime jurisdiction. There is an additional reason now to give them this last power: Because Congress besides the general powers, are about to get that of regulating commerce with foreign nations. This is a power which existed before, and is a proper subject of federal jurisdiction. The next power of the Judiciary is also necessary under some restrictions.—Though the decision of controversies to which the United States shall be a party, may at first view seem proper, it may without restraint, be extended to a dangerously oppressive length. The next, with respect to disputes between two or more States, is right. I cannot see the propriety of the next power, in disputes between a State and the citizens of another State. As to controversies between citizens of different States, their power is improper and inadmissible. In disputes between citizens of the same State, claiming lands under the grants of different States, the power is proper.—It is the only case in which the Federal Judiciary ought to have appellate cognizance of disputes between private citizens. Unless this was the case, the suit must be brought and decided in one, or the other State, under whose grants the lands are claimed, which would be injurious, as the decision must be consistent with the grant.

The last clause is still more improper. To give them cognizance in disputes between a State and the citizens thereof, is utterly inconsistent with reason or good policy.

Here Mr. *Nicholas* arose, and informed Mr. *Mason*, that his interpretation of this part was not warranted by the words.

Mr. *Mason* replied, that if he recollected rightly, the propriety of the power as explained by him, had been contended for; but that as his memory had never been good, and was now much impaired from his age, he would not insist on that interpretation. He then proceeded.—Give me leave to advert to the operation of this Judicial power. Its jurisdiction in the first case will extend to all cases affecting revenue, excise and custom-house officers. If I am mistaken I will retract.—"All cases in law and equity arising under this Constitution, and the laws of the United States," take in all the officers of Government. They comprehend all those who act as collectors of taxes, excisemen, &c. It will take in of course what others do to them, and what is done by them to others. In what predicament will our citizens then be? We know the difficulty we are put in by our own Courts, and how hard it is to bring officers to justice even in them. If any of the Federal officers should be guilty of the greatest oppressions, or behave with the most insolent and wanton brutality to a man's wife or daughter, where is this man to get relief? If you suppose in the inferior Courts, they are not appointed by the States. They are not men in whom the community can place confidence. It will be decided by Federal Judges. Even suppose the poor man should be able to obtain judgment in the inferior Court, for the greatest injury, what justice can he get on appeal? Can he go 400 or 500 miles? Can he stand the expence attending it? On this occasion they are to judge of fact as well as law. He must bring his witnesses where he is not known, where a new evidence may be brought against him, of which he never heard before, and which he cannot contradict.

The Honorable Gentleman who presides here, has told us, that the Supreme Court of Appeals must embrace every object of maritime, Chancery, and common law controversy. In the two first, the indiscriminate appellate jurisdiction as to fact, must be generally granted; because otherwise it could exclude appeals in those cases. But why not discriminate as to matters of fact in common law controversies?—The Honorable Gentleman has allowed that it was dangerous, but hopes regulations will be made to suit the convenience of the people.—But mere hope is not a sufficient security. I have said that it appears to me (though I am no lawyer) to be very dangerous. Give me leave to lay before the committee an amendment, which I think convenient, easy, and proper.— (Here Mr. *Mason* proposed an alteration nearly the same as the first part of the fourteenth amendment recommended by the Convention, which see at the conclusion.)—Thus, Sir, after limiting the cases in which the Federal Judiciary could interpose, I would confine the appellate jurisdiction to matters of law only, in common law controversies.

It appears to me, that this will remove oppressions, and answer every purpose of an appellate power.

A discrimination arises between common law trials and trials by Courts of Equity and Admiralty.—In these two last, depositions are committed to record, and therefore on an appeal the whole fact goes up; the equity of the whole case, comprehending fact and law, is considered, and no new evidence requisite. Is it so in Courts of common law? There evidence is only given *viva voce*. I know not a single case, where there is an appeal of fact as to common law. But I may be mistaken. Where there is an appeal from an inferior to a Superior Court, with respect to matters of fact, a new witness may be introduced, who is perhaps suborned by the other party, a thousand miles from the place where the first trial was had. These are some of the inconveniencies, and insurmountable objections against this general power being given to the Federal Courts. Gentlemen will perhaps say, there will be no occasion to carry up the evidence by *viva voce* testimony, because Congress may order it to be admitted to writing, and transmitted in that manner with the rest of the record. 'Tis true they may, but it is as true that they may not. But suppose they do. Little conversant as I am in this subject, I know there is a great difference between *viva voce* evidence given at the bar, and testimony given in writing. I leave it to Gentlemen more conversant in these matters, to discuss it. They are also to have cognizance in controversies to which the United States shall be a party. This power is superadded, that there might be no doubt, and that all cases arising under the Government might be brought before the Federal Court. Gentlemen will not, I presume, deny that all revenue and excise controversies, and all proceedings relative to the duties of the officers of Government, from the highest to the lowest, may, and must be brought by these means to the Federal Courts; in the first instance, to the inferior Federal Court, and afterwards to the Superior Court.—Every fact proved with respect to these, in the Court below, may be revived in the Superior Court.—But this appellate jurisdiction is to be under the regulations of Congress.—What these regulations may be, God only knows.

Their jurisdiction further extends to controversies between citizens of different States.—Can we not trust our State Courts with the decision of these?—If I have a controversy with a man in Maryland—if a man in Maryland has my bond for 100 l. are not the State Courts competent to try it?—Is it suspected that they would enforce the payment if unjust, or refuse to enforce it if just?—The very idea is ridiculous. What carry me a thousand miles from home—from my family, and business, where perhaps, it will be impossible for me to prove that I paid it?—Perhaps I have a respectable witness who saw me pay the money:—But I must carry him 1000 miles to prove it, or be compelled to pay it again. Is there any necessity for this power?—It ought to have no unnecessary or dangerous power. Why should the Federal Courts have this cognizance?—Is it because one lives on one side of the Potowmack, and the other on the other?—Suppose I have your bond for 1000 l.—If I have any wish to harrass you, or if I be of a litigious disposition, I have only to assign it to a Gentleman in Maryland. This assignment will involve you in trouble and expence. What effect will this power have between British creditors and the citizens of this State?—This is a ground on which I shall speak with confidence. Every one who heard me speak on the subject, knows, that I always spoke for the payment of the British debts. I wish every honest debt to be paid. Though I would wish to pay the British creditor, yet I would not put it in his power to gratify private malice to our injury. Let me be put right if I be mistaken. But there is not, in my opinion, a single British creditor, but who can bring his debtors to the Federal Court. There are a thousand instances where debts have been paid, and yet must by this appellate cognizance be paid again. Are these imaginary cases?—Are they only possible cases, or are they certain and inevitable?—"To controversies between a State, and the citizens of another State."—How will their jurisdiction in this case do? Let Gentlemen look at the Westward. Claims respecting those lands, every liquidated account, or other claim against this State, will be tried before the Federal Court. Is not this disgraceful?—Is this State to be brought to the bar of justice like a delinquent individual?—Is the sovereignty of the State to be arraigned like a culprit, or private offender?—Will the States undergo this mortification? I think this power perfectly unnecessary. But let us pursue this subject further. What is to be done if a judgment be obtained against a State?—Will you issue a *fieri facias*? It would be ludicrous to say, that you could put the State's body in jail. How is the judgment then to be inforced? A power which cannot be executed, ought not to be granted. Let us consider the operation of the last subject of its cognizance.—Controversies between a State, or the citizens thereof, and foreign States, citizens or subjects.—There is a confusion in this case. This much, however, may be raised out of it—that a suit will be brought against Virginia.—She may be sued by a foreign State.—What reciprocity is there in it?—In a suit between Virginia and a foreign State, is the foreign State to be bound by the decision?—Is there a similar privilege given to us in foreign States?—Where will you find a parallel regulation? How will the decision be enforced?—Only by the *ultima ratio regum*. A dispute between a foreign citizen or subject, and a Virginian cannot be tried in our own Courts, but must be decided in the Federal Court. Is this the case in any other country?—Are not men obliged to stand by the laws of the country where the disputes are?—This is an innovation which is utterly unprecedented and unheard of.—Cannot we trust the State Courts with disputes between a Frenchman, or an Englishman, and a citizen; or with disputes between two Frenchmen? This is disgraceful: It will annihilate your State Judiciary: It will prostrate your Legislature.

Thus, Sir, it appears to me that the greater part of these powers are unnecessary, and dangerous, as tending to impair and ultimately destroy the State Judiciaries, and by the same principle, the legislation of the State Governments. To render it safe there must be an amendment, such as I have pointed out. After mentioning the original jurisdiction of the Supreme Court, which extends to but three cases, it gives it appellate jurisdiction in all the other cases mentioned, both as to law and fact, indiscriminately, and without limitation. Why not remove the cause of fear and danger? But it is said, that the regulations of Congress will remove these. I say, that, in my opinion, they will have a contrary effect, and will utterly annihilate your State Courts.—Who are the Court?—The Judges. It is a familiar distinction. We frequently speak of a Court in contradistinction to a jury. I think the Court are to be the Judges of this.—The Judges on the bench, are to be Judges of fact and law, with such exceptions, &c. as Congress shall make. Now give me leave to ask—is not a jury excluded absolutely?—By way of illustration, were Congress to say that a jury, instead of the Court, should judge the fact, will not the Court be still judges of the fact consistently with this Constitution? Congress may make such a regulation, or may not. But suppose they do, what sort of a jury would they have in the ten miles square? I would rather a thousand times be tried by a Court than by such a jury. This great palladium of national safety, which is secured to us by our own Government, will be taken from us in those Courts; or if it be reserved, it will be but in name, and not in substance. In the Government of Virginia, we have secured an impartial jury of the vicinage. We can except to jurors, and peremptorily challenge them in criminal trials. If I be tried in the Federal Court for a crime which may affect my life, have I a right of challenging or excepting to the jury? Have not the best men suffered by weak and partial juries? This sacred right ought therefore to be secured. I dread the ruin that will be brought on 30,000 of our people with respect to disputed lands. I am personally endangered as an inhabitant of the *Northern Neck*. The people of that part will be obliged, by the operation of this power, to pay the quitrents of their lands. Whatever other Gentlemen may think, I consider this as a most serious alarm. It will little avail a man to make a profession of his candour. It is to his character and reputation they will appeal. Let Gentlemen consider my public and private character.—To these I wish Gentlemen to appeal for an interpretation of my motives and views. Lord Fairfax's title was clear and undisputed.—After the revolution, we taxed his lands as private property. After his death an act of Assembly was made, in 1782, to sequester the quitrents due at his death, in the hands of his debtors: Next year an act was made restoring them to the executor of the proprietor. Subsequent to this the treaty of peace was made, by which it was agreed, that there should be no further confiscations. But after this an act of Assembly passed, confiscating this whole property. As Lord Fairfax's title was indisputably good, and as treaties are to be the supreme law of the land, will not his representatives be able to recover all in the Federal Court? How will Gentlemen like to pay additional tax on the lands in the Northern Neck? This the operation of this system will compel them to do. They now are subject to the same taxes that other citizens are, and if the quitrents be recovered in the Federal Court, they are doubly taxed. This may be called an assertion, but, were I going to my grave, I would appeal to Heaven that I think it true. How will a poor man, who is injured or dispossessed unjustly, get a remedy? Is he to go to the Federal Court, 7 or 800 miles? He might as well give his claim up. He may grumble, but finding no relief, he will be contented.

Again, all that great tract of country between the Blue Ridge and the Allegany mountains, will be claimed, and probably recovered in the Federal Court, from the present possessors, by those companies who have a title to them.—These lands have been sold to a great number of people.—Many settled on them, on terms which were advertised. How will this be with respect to *ex post facto* laws? We have not only confirmed the title of those who made the contracts, but those who did not, by a law in 1779, on their paying the original price. Much was paid in a depreciated value, and much was not paid at all.—Again, the great Indiana purchase which was made to the Westward, will, by this judicial power, be rendered a cause of dispute. The possessors may be ejected from those lands. That company paid a consideration of 10,000 l. to the Crown, before the lands were taken up. I have heard Gentlemen of the law say, (and I believe it is right) that after the consideration was paid to the Crown, the purchase was legally made, and ought to be valid. That company may come in, and shew that they have paid the money, and have a full right to the land. Of the Indiana company I need not say much. It is well known that their claims will be brought before these Courts. Three or four counties are settled on the lands to which that company claims a title, and have long enjoyed it peaceably. All these claims before those Courts, if they succeed, will introduce a scene of distress and confusion never heard of before. Our peasants will be like those mentioned by *Virgil*, reduced to ruin and misery, driven from their farms, and obliged to leave their country.—

—*Nos patriam fugimus—et dulcia linquimus arva.*—

Having mentioned these things, give me leave to submit an amendment which I think would be proper and safe, and would render our citizens secure in their possessions justly held. I mean, Sir, "That the Judicial power shall extend to no case where the cause of action shall have originated before the ratification of this Constitution, except in suits for debts due to the United States, disputes between States about their territory, and disputes between persons claiming lands under the grants of different States." In these cases there is an obvious necessity for giving it a retrospective power. I have laid before you my idea on the subject, and expressed my fears, which I most conscientiously believe to be well founded.

John Marshall on the Fairness and Jurisdiction of the Federal Courts

June 20, 1788

Mr. *John Marshall*,—Mr. Chairman.—This part of the plan before us, is a great improvement on that system from which we are now departing. Here are tribunals appointed for the decision of controversies, which were before, either not at all, or improperly provided for.—That many benefits will result from this to the members of the collective society, every one confesses. Unless its organization be defective, and so constructed as to injure, instead of accommodating the convenience of the people, it merits our approbation. After such a candid and fair discussion by those Gentlemen who support it—after the very able manner in which they have investigated and examined it, I conceived it would be no longer considered as so very defective, and that those who opposed it, would be convinced of the impropriety of some of their objections.—But I perceive they still continue the same opposition. Gentlemen have gone on an idea, that the Federal Courts will not determine the causes which may come before them, with the same fairness and impartiality, with which other Courts decide. What are the reasons of this supposition?—Do they draw them from the manner in which the Judges are chosen, or the tenure of their office?—What is it that makes us trust our Judges?—Their independence in office, and manner of appointment. Are not the Judges of the Federal Court chosen with as much wisdom, as the Judges of the State Governments?—Are they not equally, if not more independent?—If so, shall we not conclude, that they will decide with equal impartiality and candour?—If there be as much wisdom and knowledge in the United States, as in a particular State, shall we conclude that that wisdom and knowledge will not be equally exercised in the selection of the Judges?

The principle on which they object to the Federal jurisdiction, seems to me to be founded on a belief, that there will not be a fair trial had in those Courts. If this Committee will consider it fully, they will find it has no foundation, and that we are as secure there as any where else. What mischief results from some causes being tried there?—Is there not the utmost reason to conclude, that Judges wisely appointed, and independent in their office, will never countenance any unfair trial?—What are the subjects of its jurisdiction? Let us examine them with an expectation that causes will be as candidly tried there, as elsewhere, and then determine. The objection, which was made by the Honorable member who was first up yesterday (Mr. *Mason*) has been so fully refuted, that it is not worth while to notice it. He objected to Congress having power to create a number of Inferior Courts according to the necessity of public circumstances. I had an apprehension that those Gentlemen who placed no confidence in Congress, would object that there might be no Inferior Courts. I own that I thought, that those Gentlemen would think there would be no Inferior Courts, as it depended on the will of Congress, but that we should be dragged to the centre of the Union. But I did not conceive, that the power of increasing the number of Courts could be objected to by any Gentleman, as it would remove the inconvenience of being dragged to the centre of the United States. I own that the power of creating a number of Courts, is, in my estimation, so far from being a defect, that it seems necessary to the perfection of this system. After having objected to the number and mode, he objected to the subject matter of their cognizance.—(Here Mr. *Marshall* read the 2d section.)—These, Sir, are the points of Federal jurisdiction to which he objects, with a few exceptions. Let us examine each of them with a supposition, that the same impartiality will be observed there, as in other Courts, and then see if any mischief will result from them.— With respect to its cognizance in all cases arising under the Constitution and the laws of the United States, he says, that the laws of the United States being paramount to the laws of particular States, there is no case but what this will extend to. Has the Government of the United States power to make laws on every subject?—Does he understand it so?—Can they make laws affecting the mode of transferring property, or contracts, or claims between citizens of the same State? Can they go beyond the delegated powers? If they were to make a law not warranted by any of the powers enumerated, it would be considered by the Judges as an infringement of the Constitution which they are to guard:—They would not consider such a law as coming under their jurisdiction.—They would declare it void. It will annihilate the State Courts, says the Honorable Gentleman. Does not every Gentleman here know, that the causes in our Courts are more numerous than they can decide, according to their present construction? Look at the dockets.—You will find them crouded with suits, which the life of man will not see determined. If some of these suits be carried to other Courts, will it be wrong? They will still have business enough. Then there is no danger, that particular subjects, small in proportion, being taken out of the jurisdiction of the State Judiciaries, will render them useless and of no effect. Does the Gentleman think that the State Courts will have no cognizance of cases not mentioned here? Are there any words in this Constitution which excludes the Courts of the States from those cases which they now possess? Does the Gentleman imagine this to be the case? Will any Gentleman believe it? Are not controversies respecting lands claimed under the grants of different States, the only controversies between citizens of the same State, which the Federal Judiciary can take cognizance of? The case is so clear, that to prove it would be an useless waste of time. The State Courts will not lose the jurisdiction of the causes they now decide. They have a concurrence of jurisdiction with the Federal Courts in those cases, in which the latter have cognizance.

How disgraceful is it that the State Courts cannot be trusted, says the Honorable Gentleman! What is the language of the Constitution? Does it take away their jurisdiction? Is it not necessary that the Federal Courts should have cognizance of cases arising under the Constitution, and the laws of the United States? What is the service or purpose of a Judiciary, but to execute the laws in a peaceable orderly manner, without shedding blood, or creating a contest, or availing yourselves of force? If this be the case, where can its jurisdiction be more necessary than here? To what quarter will you look for protection from an infringement on the Constitution, if you will not give the power to the Judiciary? There is no other body that can afford such a protection. But the Honorable Member objects to it, because, he says, that the officers of the Government will be screened from merited punishment by the Federal Judiciary. The Federal Sheriff, says he, will go into a poor man's house, and beat him, or abuse his family, and the Federal Court will protect him. Does any Gentleman believe this? Is it necessary that the officers will commit a trespass on the property or persons of those with whom they are to transact business? Will such great insults on the people of this country be allowable? Were a law made to authorise them, it would be void. The injured man would trust to a tribunal in his neighbourhood. To such a tribunal he would apply for redress, and get it. There is no reason to fear that he would not meet that justice there, which his country will be ever willing to maintain. But on appeal, says the Honorable Gentleman, what chance is there to obtain justice? This is founded on an idea, that they will not be impartial. There is no clause in the Constitution which bars the individual member injured, from applying to the State Courts to give him redress. He says that there is no instance of appeals as to fact in common law cases. The contrary is well known to you, Mr. Chairman, to be the case in this Commonwealth. With respect to mills, roads, and other cases, appeals lye from the Inferior to the Superior Court, as to fact as well as law. It is a clear case, that there can be no case in common law, in which an appeal as to fact might be proper and necessary? Can you not conceive a case where it would be productive of advantages to the people at large, to submit to that tribunal the final determination, involving facts as well as law? Suppose it should be deemed for the convenience of the citizens, that those things which concerned foreign Ministers, should be tried in the Inferior Courts—If justice would be done, the decision would satisfy all. But if an appeal in matters of fact could not be carried to the Superior Court, then it would result, that such cases could not be tried before the Inferior Courts, for fear of injurious and partial decisions.

But, Sir, where is the necessity of discriminating between the three cases of chancery, admiralty, and common law? Why not leave it to Congress? Will it enlarge their powers? Is it necessary for them wantonly to infringe your rights? Have you any thing to apprehend, when they can in no case abuse their power without rendering themselves hateful to the people at large? When this is the case, something may be left to the Legislature freely chosen by ourselves, from among ourselves, who are to share the burdens imposed upon the community, and who can be changed at our pleasure. Where power may be trusted, and there is no motive to abuse it, it seems to me to be as well to leave it undetermined, as to fix it in the Constitution.

With respect to disputes between a State, and the citizens of another State, its jurisdiction has been decried with unusual vehemence. I hope no Gentleman will think that a State will be called at the bar of the Federal Court. Is there no such case at present? Are there not many cases in which the Legislature of Virginia is a party, and yet the State is not sued? It is not rational to suppose, that the sovereign power shall be dragged before a Court. The intent is, to enable States to recover claims of individuals residing in other States. I contend this construction is warranted by the words. But, say they, there will be partiality in it if a State cannot be defendant—if an individual cannot proceed to obtain judgment against a State, though he may be sued by a State. It is necessary to be so, and cannot be avoided. I see a difficulty in making a State defendant, which does not prevent its being plaintiff. If this be only what cannot be avoided, why object to the system on that account? If an individual has a just claim against any particular State, is it to be presumed, that on application to its Legislature, he will not obtain satisfaction? But how could a State recover any claim from a citizen of another State, without the establishment of these tribunals?

The Honorable Member objects to suits being instituted in the Federal Courts by the citizens of one State, against the citizens of another State. Were I to contend, that this was necessary in all cases, and that the Government without it would be defective, I should not use my own judgment. But are not the objections to it carried too far? Though it may not in general be absolutely necessary, a case may happen, as has been observed, in which a citizen of one State ought to be able to recur to this tribunal, to recover a claim from the citizen of another State. What is the evil which this can produce?—Will he get more than justice there?—The independence of the Judges forbids it. What has he to get?— Justice. Shall we object to this, because a citizen of another State can obtain justice without applying to our State Courts? It may be necessary with respect to the laws and regulations of commerce, which Congress may make. It may be necessary in cases of debt, and some other controversies. In claims for land it is not necessary, but it is not dangerous. In the Court of which State will it be instituted, said the Honorable Gentleman? It will be instituted in the Court of the State where the defendant resides,—where the law can come at him, and no where else. By the laws of which State will it be determined, said he? By the laws of the State where the contract was made. According to those laws, and those only, can it be decided. Is this a novelty?—No—it is a principle in the jurisprudence of this Commonwealth. If a man contracted a debt in the East-Indies, and it was sued for here, the decision must be consonant to the laws of that country.—Suppose a contract made in Maryland, where the annual interest is at six per centum; and a suit instituted for it in Virginia—What interest would be given now, without any Federal aid?—The interest of Maryland most certainly; and if the contract had been made in Virginia, and suit brought in Maryland, the interest of Virginia must be given without doubt.—It is now to be governed by the laws of that State where the contract was made. The laws which governed the contract at its formation, govern it in its decision. To preserve the peace of the Union only, its jurisdiction in this case ought to be recurred to.—Let us consider that when citizens of one State carry on trade in another State, much must be due to the one from the other, as is the case between North-Carolina and Virginia. Would not the refusal of justice to our citizens, from the Courts of North-Carolina, produce disputes between the States? Would the Federal Judiciary swerve from their duty in order to give partial and unjust decisions?

The objection respecting the assignment of a bond to a citizen of another State, has been fully answered. But suppose it were to be tried as he says, what could be given more than was actually due in the case he mentioned? It is *possible*, in our

Courts as they now stand, to obtain a judgment for more than justice. But the Court of Chancery grants relief. Would it not be so in the Federal Court? Would not depositions be taken, to prove the payments, and if proved, would not the decision of the Court be accordingly?

He objects in the next place to its jurisdiction in controversies between a State, and a foreign State. Suppose, says he, in such a suit, a foreign State is cast, will she be bound by the decision? If a foreign State brought a suit against the Commonwealth of Virginia, would she not be barred from the claim if the Federal Judiciary thought it unjust? The previous consent of the parties is necessary. And, as the Federal Judiciary will decide, each party will acquiesce. It will be the means of preventing disputes with foreign nations. On an attentive consideration of these Courts, I trust every part will appear satisfactory to the Committee.

The exclusion of trial by jury in this case, he urged to prostrate our rights. Does the word Court only mean the Judges? Does not the determination of a jury, necessarily lead to the judgment of the Court? Is there any thing here which gives the Judges exclusive jurisdiction of matters of fact? What is the object of a jury trial? To inform the Court of the facts. When a Court has cognizance of facts, does it not follow, that they can make enquiry by a jury? It is impossible to be otherwise. I hope that in this country, where impartiality is so much admired, the laws will direct facts to be ascertained by a jury. But, says the Honorable Gentleman, the juries in the ten miles square will be mere tools of parties, with which he would not trust his person or property; which, he says, he would rather leave to the Court. Because the Government may have a district ten miles square, will no man stay there but the tools and officers of the Government?—Will no body else be found there?—Is it so in any other part of the world, where a Government has Legislative power?—Are there none but officers and tools of the Government of Virginia in Richmond?—Will there not be independent merchants, and respectable Gentlemen of fortune, within the ten miles square?—Will there not be worthy farmers and mechanics? Will not a good jury be found there as well as any where else?—Will the officers of the Government become improper to be on a jury?—What is it to the Government, whether this man or that man succeeds?—It is all one thing. Does the Constitution say, that juries shall consist of officers, or that the Supreme Court shall be held in the ten miles square? It was acknowledged by the Honorable Member, that it was secure in England. What makes it secure there?—Is it their Constitution?—What part of their Constitution is there, that the Parliament cannot change?—As the preservation of this right is in the hands of Parliament, and it has ever been held sacred by them, will the Government of America be less honest than that of Great-Britain? Here a restriction is to be found. The jury is not to be brought out of the State. There is no such restriction in that Government; for the laws of Parliament decide every thing respecting it. Yet Gentlemen tell us, that there is safety there, and nothing here but danger. It seems to me, that the laws of the United States will generally secure trials by a jury of the vicinage, or in such manner as will be most safe and convenient for the people.

But it seems that the right of challenging the jurors, is not secured in this Constitution. Is this done by our own Constitution, or by any provision of the English Government? Is it done by their Magna Charta, or Bill of Rights? This privilege is founded on their laws. If so, why should it be objected to the American Constitution, that it is not inserted in it? If we are secure in Virginia, without mentioning it in our Constitution, why should not this security be found in the Federal Court?

The Honorable Gentleman said much about the quitrents in the Northern Neck. I will refer it to the Honorable Gentleman himself. Has he not acknowledged, that there was no complete title? Was he not satisfied, that the right of the legal representative of the proprietor did not exist at the time he mentioned? If so, it cannot exist now. I will leave it to those Gentlemen who come from that quarter. I trust they will not be intimidated on this account, in voting on this question. A law passed in 1782, which secures this. He says that many poor men may be harrassed and injured by the representative of Lord Fairfax. If he has no right, this cannot be done. If he has this right and comes to Virginia, what laws will his claims be determined by? By those of this State. By what tribunals will they be determined? By our State Courts. Would not the poor man, who was oppressed by an unjust prosecution, be abundantly protected and satisfied by the temper of his neighbours, and would he not find ample justice? What reason has the Honorable Member to apprehend partiality or injustice? He supposes, that if the Judges be Judges of both the Federal and State Courts, they will incline in favour of one Government. If such contests should arise, who could more properly decide them, than those who are to swear to do justice? If we can expect a fair decision any where, may we not expect justice to be done by the Judges of both the Federal and State Governments? But, says the Honorable Member, laws may be executed tyrannically. Where is the independency of your Judges? If a law be executed tyrannically in Virginia, to what can you trust? To your Judiciary. What security have you for justice? Their independence. Will it not be so in the Federal Court?

Gentlemen ask what is meant by law cases, and if they be not distinct from facts. Is there no law arising on cases in equity and admiralty? Look at the acts of Assembly.—Have you not many cases, where law and fact are blended? Does not the jurisdiction in point of law as well as fact, find itself completely satisfied in law and fact? The Honorable Gentleman says, that no law of Congress can make any exception to the Federal appellate jurisdiction of fact as well as law. He has frequently spoken of technical terms, and the meaning of them. What is the meaning of the term *exception*? Does it not mean an alteration and diminution? Congress is empowered to make exceptions to the appellate jurisdiction, as to law and fact, of the Supreme Court.—These exceptions certainly go as far as the Legislature may think proper, for the interest and liberty of the people.—Who can understand this word, *exception*, to extend to one case as well as the other? I am persuaded, that a reconsideration of this case will convince the Gentleman, that he was mistaken. This may go to the cure of the mischief apprehended. Gentlemen must be satisfied, that this power will not be so much abused as they have said.

The Honorable Member says, that he derives no consolation from the wisdom and integrity of the Legislature, because we call them to rectify defects which it is our duty to remove. We ought well to weigh the good and evil before we determine—We ought to be well convinced, that the evil will be really produced before we decide against it. If we be convinced that the good greatly preponderates, though there be small defects in it, shall we give up that which is really good, when we can remove the little mischief it may contain, in the plain easy method pointed out in the system itself?

I was astonished when I heard the Honorable Gentleman say, that he wished the trial by jury to be struck out entirely. Is there no justice to be expected by a jury of our fellow citizens? Will any man prefer to be tried by a Court, when the jury is to be of his countrymen, and probably of his vicinage? We have reason to believe the regulations with respect to juries will be such as shall be satisfactory. Because it does not contain all, does it contain nothing? But I conceive that this Committee will see there is safety in the case, and that there is no mischief to be apprehended.

He states a case, that a man may be carried from a federal to an antifederal corner, (and *vice versa*) where men are ready to destroy him. Is this probable? Is it presumeable that they will make a law to punish men who are of different opinions in politics from themselves? Is it presumeable, that they will do it in one single case, unless it be such a case as must satisfy the people at large? The good opinion of the people at large must be consulted by their Representatives; otherwise mischiefs would be produced, which would shake the Government to its foundation. As it is late, I shall not mention all the Gentleman's argument: But some parts of it are so glaring, that I cannot pass them over in silence. He says that the establishment of these tribunals, and more particularly in their jurisdiction of controversies between citizens of these States, and foreign citizens and subjects, is like a retrospective law. Is there no difference between a tribunal which shall give justice and effect to an existing right, and creating a right that did not exist before? The debt or claim is created by the individual. He has bound himself to comply with it. Does the creation of a new Court amount to a retrospective law?

We are satisfied with the provision made in this country on the subject of trial by jury. Does our Constitution direct trials to be by jury? It is required in our Bill of Rights, which is not a part of the Constitution. Does any security arise from hence? Have you a jury when a judgment is obtained on a replevin bond, or by default? Have you a jury when a motion is made for the Commonwealth, against an individual; or when a motion is made by one joint obligor against another, to recover sums paid as security? Our Courts decide in all these cases, without the intervention of a jury; yet they are all civil cases. The Bill of Rights is merely recommendatory. Were it otherwise, the consequence would be, that many laws which are found convenient, would be unconstitutional. What does the Government before you say? Does it exclude the Legislature from giving a trial by jury in civil cases? If it does not forbid its exclusion, it is on the same footing on which your State Government stands now. The Legislature of Virginia does not give a trial by jury where it is not necessary. But gives it wherever it is thought expedient. The Federal Legislature will do so too, as it is formed on the same principles.

The Honorable Gentleman says, that unjust claims will be made, and the defendant had better pay them than go to the Supreme Court. Can you suppose such a disposition in one of your citizens, as that to oppress another man, he will incur great expences? What will he gain by an unjust demand? Does a claim establish a right? He must bring his witnesses to prove his claim. If he does not bring his witnesses, the expences must fall upon him. Will he go on a calculation that the defendant will not defend it; or cannot produce a witness? Will he incur a great deal of expence, from a dependance on such a chance? Those who know human nature, black as it is, must know, that mankind are too well attached to their interest to run such a risk. I conceive, that this power is absolutely necessary, and not dangerous; that should it be attended by little inconveniences, they will be altered, and that they can have no interest in not altering them. Is there any real danger?— When I compare it to the exercise of the same power in the Government of Virginia, I am persuaded there is not. The Federal Government has no other motive, and has every reason of doing right, which the Members of our State Legislature have. Will a man on the Eastern Shore, be sent to be tried in Kentuckey; or a man from Kentuckey be brought to the Eastern Shore to have his trial? A Government by doing this, would destroy itself. I am convinced, the trial by jury will be regulated in the manner most advantageous to the community.

John Dawson's Fears for the Future

Mr. *Dawson.* — Mr. Chairman, — When a nation is about to make a change in its political character, it behoves it to summon the experience of ages which have passed, to collect the wisdom of the present day, to ascertain clearly those great principles of equal liberty, which secure the rights, the liberties, and properties of the people. Such is the situation of the United States at this moment. We are about to make such a change.

The Constitution proposed for the government of the United States, has been a subject of general discussion; and while many able and honorable gentlemen within these walls, have, in the development of the various parts, delivered their sentiments with that freedom which will ever mark the citizens of an independent State, and with that ability which will prove to the world their eminent talents; I, Sir, although urged by my feelings, have forbore to say any thing on my part, from a satisfactory impression of the inferiority of my talents, and from a wish to acquire every information which might assist my judgment in forming a decision on a question of such magnitude. But, Sir, as it involves in its fate the interest of so extensive a country, every sentiment which can be offered deserves its proportion of public attention. I shall therefore avoid any apology for now rising although uncommon propriety might justify it, and rather trust to the candour of those who hear me: Indeed I am induced to come forward, not from any apprehension that my opinions will have weight, but in order to discharge that duty which I owe to myself, and to those I have the honor to represent.

The defects of the articles by which we are at present confederated, have been echoed and re-echoed, not only from every quarter of this House, but from every part of the continent. At the framing of those articles, a common interest excited us to unite for the common good: But no sooner did this principle cease to operate, than the defects of the system were sensibly felt. Since then the seeds of civil dissension have been gradually opening, and political confusion has pervaded the States. During the short time of my political life, having been fully impressed with the truth of these observations, when a proposition was made by Virginia to invite the sister States to a General Convention, at Philadelphia, *to amend these defects*, I readily gave my assent; and when I considered the very respectable characters who formed that body—when I reflected that they were, most of them, those sages and patriots, under whose banners and by whose councils, it had been rescued from impending danger, and placed among the nations of the earth—when I also turned my attention to that illustrious character, *to immortalize whose memory, Fame shall blow her trump* to the latest ages—I say, when I weighed all these considerations, I was almost persuaded to declare in favour of the proposed plan, and to exert my slender abilities in its favour. But, when I came to investigate it impartially, on the immutable principles of government, and to exercise that reason, with which the God of Nature hath endowed me, and which I will ever freely use, I was convinced of this important, though melancholy truth, "that the greatest men may err," and that their errors are sometimes of the greatest magnitude. I was persuaded that, although the proposed plan contains many things excellent, yet by the adoption of it, as it now stands, the liberties of America, in general; the property of Virginia in particular; would be endangered.

These being my sentiments; sentiments which I offer with the diffidence of a young politician, but with the firmness of a republican; which I am ready to change when I am convinced they are founded in error; but which I will support until that conviction—I should be a traitor to my country and unworthy that freedom, for which I trust I shall ever remain an advocate, was I to declare my entire approbation to the plan, as it now stands, or assent to its ratification without previous amendments.

During the deliberations of this Convention, several gentlemen of eminent talents, have exerted themselves to prove the necessity of the Union, by presenting to our view the relative situation of Virginia to the other States: The melancholy representation made to day, and frequently before, by an Honorable Gentleman (Governor *Randolph*) of our State, reduced, in his estimation, to the lowest degree of degradation, must now haunt the recollection of any gentlemen in this Committee, how far he has drawn the picture to the life, or where it is too highly coloured, rests with them to determine. To Gentlemen, however, Sir, of their abilities, the task was easy, and perhaps I may add unnecessary. It is a truth admitted on all sides, and I presume there is not a Gentleman, who hears me, who is not a friend to a Union of the Thirteen States.

But, Sir, an opinion is gone abroad (from whence it originated, or by whom it is supported, I will not venture to say) that the opponents to the paper on your table, are enemies to the Union; it may not therefore be improper for me to declare, that *I am* a warm friend to a firm, federal, energetic Government; that I consider a confederation of the States, on republican principles, as a security to their mutual interest, and a disunion as injurious to the whole: But I shall lament exceedingly, when a confederation of independent States shall be converted into a consolidated Government; for when that event shall happen, I shall consider the history of American liberty as short as it has been brilliant, and we shall afford one more proof to the favorite maxim of tyrants, "that mankind cannot govern themselves."

An Honorable Gentleman (Col. *H. Lee*) came forward some days since, with all the powers of eloquence, and all the warmth of enthusiasm—after discanting on some military operations to the South, of which he was a spectator, and pronouncing sentence of condemnation on a Mr. *Shays*, to the North—as a military character, he boldly throws the gauntlet and defies the warmest friend to the opposition to come forth, and say that the friends to the system on your table, are not also friends to republican liberty. Arguments, Sir, in this House, should ever be addressed to the reason, and should be applied to the system itself, and not to those who either support or oppose it. *I*, however, dare come forth, and tell that Honorable Gentleman, not with the military warmth of a young soldier, but with the firmness of a republican, that in my humble opinion, had the paper now on your table, and which is so ably supported, been presented to our view ten years ago (when the *American spirit* shone forth in the meridian of glory, and rendered us the wonder of an admiring world) it would have been considered as containing principles incompatible with republican liberty, and therefore doomed to infamy.

Having, Sir, made these loose observations, and having proved, I flatter myself, to this Honorable Convention, the motives from which my opposition to the proposed system originated; may I now be permitted to turn my attention, for a very few moments, to the system itself, and to point out some of the leading parts, most exceptionable in my estimation, and to which my original objections have not been removed, by the debate, but rather confirmed.

If we grant to Congress the power of direct taxation; if we yield to them the sword, and if we also invest them with the Judicial authority; two questions of the utmost importance, immediately present themselves to our inquiries—whether these powers will not be oppressive in their operations, and aided by other parts of the system, convert the Thirteen Confederate States into one consolidated government—and, whether any country, as extensive as North-America, and where climates, dispositions, and interests, are so essentially different, can be governed under one consolidated plan, except by the introduction of despotic principles—The warmest friends, Sir, to the Government, some of those who formed, signed, and have recommended it; some of those who have enthusiastically supported it in every quarter of this Continent; have answered my first query in the affirmative: They have admitted that it possesses few federal features and will ultimately end in a consolidated Government—a truth which in my opinion they would have denied in vain, for every article, every section, every clause, and almost every line, prove that it will have this tendency: And if this position has, during the course of the long and learned debates on this head, been established to the satisfaction of the Convention; I apprehend that the authority of all eminent writers on the subject, and the experience of all ages, cannot be controverted, and that it will be admitted that no government, formed on the principles of freedom, can pervade all North America.

This, Sir, is my great objection; an objection general in its nature, because it operates on the whole system; an objection which I early formed, which I flattered myself would have been removed, but which hath obliged me to say, has been confirmed by the observations which have been made by many learned Gentlemen, and which it would be tedious for me now to recapitulate.

That the Legislative, Executive, and Judicial powers, should be separate and distinct, in all free governments, is a political fact, so well established, that I presume I shall not be thought arrogant, when I affirm, that no country ever did, or ever can, long remain free, where they are blended. All the States have been in this sentiment, when they formed their State Constitutions, and therefore have guarded against the danger; and every school-boy in politics must be convinced of the propriety of the observation—and yet by the proposed plan, the Legislative and Executive powers are closely united; the Senate, who compose one part of the Legislature, are also as council to the President, the Supreme Head, and are concerned in passing laws, which they themselves are to execute.

The wisdom, Sir, of many nations, has induced them to enlarge the powers of their rulers, but there are very few instances of the relinquishment of power or the abridgement of authority, on the part of the governors. The very first clause of the eighth section of the first article, which gives to Congress the power "to lay and collect taxes, duties, imposts, excises, &c. &c." appears to me to be big with unnecessary danger, and to reduce human nature, to which I would willingly pay a compliment did not the experience of all ages rise up against me, to too great a test. The arguments, Sir, which have been urged by some Gentlemen, that the impost will defray all expences, in my estimation, cannot be supported; and common sense will never assent to the assertions which have been made, that the government will not be an additional expence to this country. Will not the support of an army and navy—will not the establishment of a multiplicity of offices in the Legislative, Executive, and particularly the Judiciary departments, most of which will be of a national character, and must be supported with a superior degree of dignity and credit, be prodigious additions to the national expence? And, Sir, if the States are to retain, even the shadow of sovereignty, the expence thence arising must also be defrayed, and will be very considerable.

I come now, Sir, to speak of a clause, to which our attention has been frequently called, and on which many Gentlemen have already delivered their sentiments; a clause, in the estimation of some, of little consequence, and which rather serves as a pretext for scuffling for votes, but which, in my opinion, is one of the most important contained in the system, and to which there are many and weighty objections. I refer to the clause, empowering the President, by and with the consent of two thirds of the Senators present, to make treaties.—If, Sir, the dismemberment of empire—if the privation of the most essential national rights, and the very existence of a people, depend on this clause, surely, Sir, it merits the most thorough investigation; and if, on that investigation, it appears that those great rights are endangered, it highly behoves us to amend it in such manner as will prevent the evils which may arise from it as it now stands. My objections to it do not arise from a view of the particular situation of the western part of this State, although certainly we are bound, by every principle, to attend to the interest of our fellow-citizens in that quarter, but from an apprehension that the principle pervades all America, and that in its operation, it will be found highly injurious to the Southern States. It will, I presume, be readily admitted, that the dismemberment of empire is the highest act of sovereign authority, the exercise of which can be authorized only by absolute authority: Exclusive then, Sir, of any consideration which arises from the particular system of American politics, the guard established against the exercise of this power is by far too slender. The President with the concurrence of two-thirds of the Senate present, may make a treaty, by which any territory may be ceded or the navigation of any river surrendered; thereby granted to five States the exercise of a right acknowledged to be the highest act of sovereignty—to fifteen men, not the representatives of the country to be ceded, but, as has already happened, men whose interest and policy it may be to make such surrender. Admitting for a moment, that this point is as well guarded by the proposed plan, as by the old Articles of Confederation, to which however common sense can never assent, have we not already had cause to tremble, and ought we not to guard against the accomplishment of a scheme, to which nothing but an inattention to the general interest of America, and a selfish regard to the interest of particular States, could have given rise: Surely, Sir, we ought; and since we have already seen a diabolical attempt made to surrender the navigation of a river, the source of which is as yet unknown, and on which depends the importance of the southern part of America—since we have every reason to believe that the same principle which at first dictated this measure still exists and will forever operate—it is our duty; a duty we owe to ourselves; which we owe to the southern part of America, and which we owe to the natural rights of mankind, to guard against it in such manner as will forever prevent its accomplishment. This, Sir, is not done by the clause, nor will it rest on that sure footing which I wish and which the importance of the subject demands, until the concurrence of three-fourths *of all the Senators*, shall be requisite to ratify a treaty respecting the cession of territory; the surrender of the navigation of rivers, or the use of the American seas.

That sacred palladium of liberty, the freedom of the press, the influence of which is so great that it is the opinion of the ablest writers, that no country can remain long in slavery where it is restrained, has not been expressed, nor are the liberties of the people ascertained and protected by any declaration of rights—that inestimable privilege, the most important which freemen can enjoy, the trial by jury in all civil cases has not been guarded by the system—and while they have been inattentive to these all important considerations, they have made provision for the introduction of standing armies in time of peace—These, Sir, ever have been used as the grand machines to suppress the liberties of the people, and will ever awaken the jealousy of republicans, so long as liberty is dear and tyranny odious to mankind.

Congress, Sir, have the power "to declare war," and also to raise and support armies, and if we suppose them to be a representation of the States, the *nexus imperii* of the British Constitution is here lost—there the King has the power of declaring war, and the Parliament that of raising money to support it. Governments ought not to depend on an army for their support, but ought to be so formed as to have the confidence, respect and affection of the citizens—Some degree of virtue, Sir, must exist, or freedom cannot live—A standing army will introduce idleness and extravagance, which will be followed by their sure concomitant vices—In a country extensive, like ours, the power of the sword is more sensibly felt, than in a small community—the advantages, Sir, of military science and discipline cannot be exerted unless a proper number of soldiers are united in one body, and actuated by one soul. The tyrant of a single town, or a small district, would soon discover that an hundred armed soldiers were a weak defence against ten thousand peasants or citizens: but ten thousand well disciplined soldiers will command, with despotic sway, millions of subjects, and will strike terror into the most numerous populace. It was this, Sir, which enabled the Prætorean bands of Rome, whose number scarcely amounted to ten thousand, after having violated the sanctity of the throne, by the attrocious murder of a most excellent Emperor, to dishonor the majesty of it, by proclaiming that the Roman Empire—the mistress of the world—was to be disposed of to the highest bidder, at public auction;—and to their licentious frenzy may be attributed the *first* cause of the decline and fall of that mighty Empire—We ought therefore strictly to guard against the establishment of an army, whose only occupation would be idleness, whose only effort the introduction of vice and dissipation, and who would, at some future day deprive us of our liberties, as a reward for past favors, by the introduction of some military despot.

I had it in contemplation, to have made some observations on the disposition of the judicial powers, but as my knowledge in that line is confined, and as the subject has been so ably handled by other Gentlemen, and the defects clearly developed, and as their arguments remain unanswered, I shall say nothing on that head;—the want of responsibility to the people from their Representatives, would furnish matter of ample discussion, but I pass it over in silence, only observing that it is a grand, and indeed a *daring* fault, and one which sanctions with security the most tyrannic edicts, of a despotic ruler. The ambiguous terms in which all rights are secured to the people, and the clear and comprehensive language used, when power is granted to Congress, also affords matter for suspicions and objections, but the able manner in which, my very worthy, my very eloquent, and truly patriotic friend and co-adjutor, whose name shall ever be hallowed in the temple of liberty, has handled this subject, would render any observations from me, tedious and unnecessary.

Permit me then to conclude by reminding Gentlemen who appeal to history to prove the excellence of the proposed plan, that their mode of comparison is unjust—"Wealth and extent of territory, says the great Montesquieu, have a relation to Government, and the manners and customs of the people are closely connected with it." The same system of policy which might have been excellent in the Governments of antiquity, would not probably suit *us* at the present day—The question therefore which should be agitated, is not whether the proposed Constitution is better or worse than those which have from time to time existed, but whether it is calculated to secure our liberties and happiness at the present stage of the world.

For my own part, after an impartial investigation of it, and after a close attention, and candid consideration of the arguments which have been used, I am impressed with an opinion, that it is not—I am persuaded, that by adopting it, and then proposing amendments, that unfortunate traveller liberty is more endangered than the Union of the States will be by first proposing these amendments. I am so far an enthusiast in favor of liberty, that I never will trust the sacred deposit to other hands, nor will I exchange it for any earthly consideration—and I have such a fixed aversion to the bitter cup of slavery, that in my estimation a draught is not sweetened, whether administered by the hand of a Turk, a Briton, or an American.

Impressed then, Sir, with these sentiments, and governed by these principles, I shall decidedly give my vote in favor of previous amendments;—but, Sir, should the question be decided contrary to my wishes, the first wish of my heart is, that that decision may promote the happiness and prosperity of the country so dear to us all.

Zachariah Johnston, "of the Middle Rank," Favors Ratification Without Previous Amendments

June 25, 1788

Mr. *Zachariah Johnson*,—Mr. Chairman.—I am now called upon to decide the greatest of all questions,—a question which may involve the felicity or misery of myself and posterity. I have hitherto listened attentively to the arguments adduced by both sides, and attended to hear the discussion of the most complicated parts of the system by Gentlemen of great abilities. Having now come to the ultimate stage of the investigation, I think it my duty to declare my sentiments on the subject. When I view the necessity of Government among mankind, and its happy operation when judiciously constructed, and when I view the principles of this Constitution, and the satisfactory and liberal manner in which they have been developed by the Gentleman in the Chair, and several other Gentlemen; and when I view on the other hand, the strained construction which has been put, by the Gentlemen on the other side, on every word and syllable, in endeavouring to prove oppressions which can never possibly happen, my judgment is convinced of the safety and propriety of this system. This conviction has not arisen from a blind acquiescence or dependence on the assertions and opinions of others, but from a full persuasion of its rectitude, after an attentive and mature consideration of the subject; the arguments of other Gentlemen having only confirmed the opinion which I had previously formed, and which I was determined to abandon, should I find it to be ill founded.

As to the principle of representation, I find it attended to in this Government in the fullest manner.—It is founded on absolute equality. When I see the power of electing the Representatives—the principal branch—in the people at large—in those very persons who are the constituents of the State Legislatures; when I find that the other branch is chosen by the

State Legislatures; that the Executive is eligible in a secondary degree by the people likewise, and that the terms of elections are short, and proportionate to the difficulty, and magnitude of the objects which they are to act upon; and when in addition to this, I find that no person holding *any office* under the United States shall be a Member of either branch—I say, when I review all these things, that I plainly see a security of the liberties of this country, to which we may safely trust. Were this Government defective in this fundamental principle of representation, it would be so radical, that it would admit of no remedy.

I shall consider several other parts which are much objected to. As to the regulation of the militia, I feel myself doubly interested. Having a numerous offspring, I am careful to prevent the establishment of any regulation, that might entail oppression on them. When Gentlemen of high abilities in this House, and whom I respect, tell us that the militia may be subjected to martial law in time of peace, and whensoever Congress may please, I am much astonished. My judgment is astray and exceedingly undiscerning, if it can bear such a construction. Congress has only the power of arming, and disciplining them. The States have the appointment of the officers, and the authority of training the militia according to the discipline prescribed by Congress. When called into the actual service of the United States, they shall be subject to the marching orders of the United States.—Then, and then only it ought to be so.—When we advert to the plain and obvious meaning of the words, without twisting and torturing their natural signification, we must be satisfied that this objection is groundless. Had we adverted to the true meaning, and not gone further, we should not be here to-day, but would have come to a decision long ago. We are also told, that religion is not secured—that religious tests are not required.—You will find that the exclusion of tests, will strongly tend to establish religious freedom. If tests were required—and if the church of England or any other were established, I might be excluded from any office under the Government, because my conscience might not permit me to take the test required. The diversity of opinions and variety of sects in the United States, have justly been reckoned a great security with respect to religious liberty. The difficulty of establishing an uniformity of religion in this country is immense.—The extent of the country is very great. The multiplicity of sects is very great likewise.—The people are not to be disarmed of their weapons—They are left in full possession of them. The Government is administered by the Representatives of the people voluntarily and freely chosen. Under these circumstances, should any one attempt to establish their own system, in prejudice of the rest, they would be universally detested and opposed, and easily frustrated. This is a principle which secures religious liberty most firmly.—The Government will depend on the assistance of the people in the day of distress. This is the case in all Governments. It never was otherwise. They object to this Government, because it is strong and energetic; and with respect to the rich and poor, that it will be favorable to the one and oppressive to the other. It is right it should be energetic. This does not shew that the poor shall be more oppressed than the rich. Let us examine it. If it admits that private and public justice should be done, it admits what is just. As to the indolent and fraudulent, nothing will reclaim these, but the hand of force and compulsion. Is there any thing in this Government which will shew that it will bear hardly and unequally on the honest and industrious part of the community? I think not. As to the mode of taxation, the proportion of each State being known, cannot be exceeded. And such proportion will be raised in the most equitable manner of the people, according to their ability. There is nothing to warrant a supposition that the poor will be equally taxed with the wealthy and opulent.

I shall make a comparison, to illustrate my observations, between the State and the General Governments. In our State Government so much admired by the worthy Gentleman over the way, though there are 1700 militia in some counties, and but 150 in others, yet every county sends two Members to assist in Legislating for the whole community.—There is this disproportion between the respectable county of *Augusta*, which I have the honor to represent, and the circumscribed narrow county of *Warwick*; yet *Augusta* has no more Legislative influence than *Warwick*! Will any Gentleman tell us, that this is a more equal representation than is fixed in the Constitution, whereby 30,000 are to send one Representative in whatever place they may reside?—By the same State system the poor in many instances pay as much as the rich. Many laws occur to my mind, where I could shew you, that the representation and taxation bears hard on those who live in large remote back counties. The mode of taxation is more oppressive to us than to the rest of the community. Last fall when the principle of taxation was debated, it was determined that tobacco should be received in discharge of taxes; but this did not relieve us, for it would not fetch what it cost us, as the distance is so great, and the carriage so difficult.—Other specific articles were not received in payment of taxes, so that we had no other alternative than to pay specie, which was a peculiar hardship.—I could point out many other disadvantages which we labour under, but I shall not now fatigue the House.

It is my lot to be among the poor people. The most that I can claim, or flatter myself with, is to be of the middle rank—I wish no more, for I am contented. But I shall give my opinion unbiassed, and uninfluenced—without erudition or eloquence, but with firmness and candour. And in so doing, I will satisfy my conscience.—If this Constitution be bad, it will bear equally as hard on me, as on any Member of the society—It will bear hard on my children, who are as dear to me, as any man's children can be to him. Having their felicity and happiness at heart, the vote I shall give in its favor, can only be imputed to a conviction of its utility and propriety.

When I look for responsibility, I fully find it in that paper. When the Members of the Government depend on ourselves for their appointment, and will bear an equal share of the burthens imposed on the people—when their duty is inseparably connected with their interest, I conceive there can be no danger. Will they forfeit the friendship and confidence of their countrymen, and counteract their own interests? As they will probably have families, they cannot forget them—When one of them sees that providence has given him a numerous family, he will be averse to lay taxes on his own posterity. They cannot escape them. They will be as liable to be taxed as any other persons in the community.—Neither is he sure, that he shall enjoy the place again, if he breaks his faith. When I take these things into consideration, I think there is sufficient responsibility.

As to the amendments now on your table, besides the impropriety of proposing them to be obtained previous to ratification, they appear to me, to be evidently and clearly objectionable.—Look at the bill of rights; it is totally mutilated and destroyed, in that paper.—The 15th article of the bill of rights of Virginia is omitted entirely in his proposed bill of rights. That article says, "That no free Government, or the blessing of liberty, can be preserved to any people, but by a firm adherence to justice, moderation, temperance, frugality and virtue, and by frequent recurrence to fundamental principles."—This article is the best of the whole—Take away this, and all is gone. Look at the first article of our bill of rights. It says that all men are by nature equally free and independent. Does that paper acknowledge this? No,—It denies it.

They tell us that they see a progressive danger of bringing about emancipation. The principle has begun since the revolution. Let us do what we will, it will come round. Slavery has been the foundation of that impiety and dissipation which have been so much disseminated among our countrymen. If it were totally abolished, it would do much good.

Gentlemen say that we destroy our own principles by subsequent amendments. They say that it is acting inconsistent with our reasons—Let us examine this position. Here is a principle of united wisdom founded on mutual benefits; and as experience may shew defects, we stipulate, that when they will happen, they shall be amended—That when a majority finds defects, we will search a remedy and apply it. There are two ways of amending it, pointed out in the system itself—When introduced either way, they are to be binding.

I am happy to see that happy day approaching, when we lose sight of dissentions and discord, which are one of the greatest sources of political misfortunes. Division is a dreadful thing. This Constitution may have defects. There can be no human institution without defects. We must go out of this world to find it otherwise. The annals of mankind do not shew us one example of a perfect Constitution.

When I see such a diversity of opinions among Gentlemen

on this occasion, it brings to my recollection, a portion of history which strongly warns us to be moderate and cautious. The historical facts to which I allude, happened in a situation similar to our own. When the Parliament of England beheaded King *Charles* the first, conquered their enemies, obtained liberty and established a kind of a republic, one would think that they would have had sufficient wisdom and policy to preserve that freedom and independence, which they had with such difficulty acquired. What was the consequence?— That they would not bend to the sanction of laws, or legal authority.—For the want of an efficient and judicious system of republican Government, confusion and anarchy took place. Men became so lawless, so destitute of principles, and so utterly ungovernable, that to avoid greater calamities, they were driven to the expedient of sending for the son of that Monarch whom they had beheaded, that he might become their master. This is like our situation in some degree. It will completely resemble it, should we lose our liberty as they did. It warns and cautions us to shun their fate, by avoiding the causes which produced it: Shall we lose our blood and treasure which we lost in the revolution and permit anarchy and misery to complete the ruin of this country? Under these impressions, and for these reasons, I am for adopting the Constitution without previous amendments. I will go any length afterwards to reconcile it to Gentlemen by proposing subsequent amendments. The great and wise State of Massachusetts has taken this step. The great and wise State of Virginia might safely do the same. I am contented to rest my happiness on that footing.

Melancton Smith and Alexander Hamilton Debate Representation, Aristocracy, and Interests

June 21, 1788

Mr. *M. Smith.* I had the honor yesterday of submitting an amendment to the clause under consideration, with some observations in support of it. I hope I shall be indulged in making some additional remarks in reply to what has been offered by the honorable gentleman from New-York.

He has taken up much time in endeavouring to prove that the great defect in the old confederation was, that it operated upon states instead of individuals. It is needless to dispute concerning points on which we do not disagree: It is admitted that the powers of the general government ought to operate upon individuals to a certain degree. How far the powers should extend, and in what cases to individuals is the question. As the different parts of the system will come into view in the course of our investigation, an opportunity will be afforded to consider this question; I wish at present to confine myself to the subject immediately under the consideration of the committee. I shall make no reply to the arguments offered by the hon. gentleman to justify the rule of apportionment fixed by this clause: For though I am confident they might be easily refuted, yet I am persuaded we must yield this point, in accommodation to the southern states. The amendment therefore proposes no alteration to the clause in this respect.

The honorable gentleman says, that the clause by obvious construction fixes the representation. I wish not to torture words or sentences. I perceive no such obvious construction. I see clearly, that on the one hand the representatives cannot exceed one for thirty thousand inhabitants; and on the other, that whatever larger number of inhabitants may be taken for

757

the rule of apportionment, each state shall be entitled to send one representative. Every thing else appears to me in the discretion of the legislature. If there be any other limitation, it is certainly implied. Matters of such moment should not be left to doubtful construction. It is urged that the number of representatives will be fixed at one for 30,000, because it will be the interest of the larger states to do it. I cannot discern the force of this argument.—To me it appears clear, that the relative weight of influence of the different states will be the same, with the number of representatives at 65 as at 600, and that of the individual members greater. For each member's share of power will decrease as the number of the house of representatives increases.—If therefore this maxim be true, that men are unwilling to relinquish powers which they once possess, we are not to expect that the house of representatives will be inclined to enlarge the numbers. The same motive will operate to influence the president and senate to oppose the increase of the number of representatives; for in proportion as the weight of the house of representatives is augmented, they will feel their own diminished: It is therefore of the highest importance that a suitable number of representatives should be established by the constitution.

It has been observed by an honorable member, that the eastern states insisted upon a small representation on the principles of œconomy.—This argument must have no weight in the mind of a considerate person. The difference of expence, between supporting a house of representatives sufficiently numerous, and the present proposed one would be about 20 or 30,000 dollars per annum. The man who would seriously object to this expence, to secure his liberties, does not deserve to enjoy them. Besides, by increasing the number of representatives, we open a door for the admission of the substantial yeomanry of your country; who, being possessed of the habits of œconomy, will be cautious of imprudent expenditures, by which means a much greater saving will be made of public money than is sufficient to support them. A reduction of the number of the state legislatures might also be made, by which means there might be a saving of expence much more than sufficient for the purpose of supporting the general legislature.—For, as under this system all the powers of legislation relating to our general concerns, are vested in the general government, the powers of the state legislatures will be so curtailed, as to render it less necessary to have them so numerous as they now are.

But an honorable gentleman has observed that it is a problem that cannot be solved, what the proper number is which ought to compose the house of representatives, and calls upon me to fix the number. I admit this is a question that will not admit of a solution with mathematical certainty—few political questions will—yet we may determine with certainty that certain numbers are too small or too large. We may be sure that ten is too small and a thousand too large a number—every one will allow that the first number is too small to possess the sentiments, be influenced by the interests of the people, or secure against corruption: A thousand would be too numerous to be capable of deliberating.

To determine whether the number of representatives proposed by this Constitution is sufficient, it is proper to examine the qualifications which this house ought to possess, in order to exercise their powers discreetly for the happiness of the people. The idea that naturally suggests itself to our minds, when we speak of representatives is, that they resemble those they represent; they should be a true picture of the people; possess the knowledge of their circumstances and their wants; sympathize in all their distresses, and be disposed to seek their true interests. The knowledge necessary for the representatives of a free people, not only comprehends extensive political and commercial information, such as is acquired by men of refined education, who have leisure to attain to high degrees of improvement, but it should also comprehend that kind of acquaintance with the common concerns and occupations of the people, which men of the middling class of life are in general much better competent to, than those of a superior class. To understand the true commercial interests of a country, not only requires just ideas of the general commerce of the world, but also, and principally, a knowledge of the productions of your own country and their value, what your soil is capable of producing, the nature of your manufactures, and the capacity of the country to increase both. To exercise the power of laying taxes, duties and excises with discretion requires something more than an acquaintance with the abstruse parts of the system of finance. It calls for a knowledge of the circumstances and ability of the people in general, a discernment how the burdens imposed will bear upon the different classes.

From these observations results this conclusion that the number of representatives should be so large, as that while it embraces men of the first class, it should admit those of the middling class of life. I am convinced that this Government is so constituted, that the representatives will generally be composed of the first class in the community, which I shall distinguish by the name of the natural aristocracy of the country. I do not mean to give offence by using this term. I am sensible this idea is treated by many gentlemen as chimerical. I shall be asked what is meant by the natural aristocracy—and told that no such distinction of classes of men exists among us. It is true it is our singular felicity that we have no legal or hereditary distinctions of this kind; but still there are real differences: Every society naturally divides itself into classes. The author of nature has bestowed on some greater capacities than on others—birth, education, talents and wealth, create distinctions among men as visible and of as much influence as titles, stars and garters. In every society, men of this class will command a superior degree of respect—and if the government is so constituted as to admit but few to exercise the powers of it, it will, according to the natural course of things, be in their hands. Men in the middling class, who are qualified as representatives, will not be so anxious to be chosen as those of the first. When the number is so small the office will be highly elevated and distinguished—the stile in which the members live will probably be high—circumstances of this kind, will render the place of a representative not a desirable one to sensible, substantial men, who have been used to walk in the plain and frugal paths of life.

Besides, the influence of the great will generally enable them to succeed in elections—it will be difficult to combine a district of country containing 30 or 40,000 inhabitants, frame your election laws as you please, in any one character; unless it be in one of conspicuous, military, popular, civil or legal talents. The great easily form associations; the poor and middling class form them with difficulty. If the elections be by plurality, as probably will be the case in this state, it is almost certain, none but the great will be chosen—for they easily unite their interest—The common people will divide, and their divisions will be promoted by the others. There will be scarcely a chance of their uniting, in any other but some great man, unless in some popular demagogue, who will probably be destitute of principle. A substantial yeoman of sense and discernment, will hardly ever be chosen. From these remarks it appears that the government will fall into the hands of the few and the great. This will be a government of oppression. I do not mean to declaim against the great, and charge them indiscriminately with want of principle and honesty.—The same passions and prejudices govern all men. The circumstances in which men are placed in a great measure give a cast to the human character. Those in middling circumstances, have less temptation—they are inclined by habit and the company with whom they associate, to set bounds to their passions and appetites—if this is not sufficient, the want of means to gratify them will be a restraint—they are obliged to employ their time in their respective callings—hence the substantial yeomanry of the country are more temperate, of better morals and less ambition than the great. The latter do not feel for the poor and middling class; the reasons are obvious—they are not obliged to use the pains and labour to procure property as the other.—They feel not the inconveniences arising from the payment of small sums. The great consider themselves above the common people—entitled to more respect—do not associate with them—they fancy themselves to have a right of pre-eminence in every thing. In short, they possess the same feelings, and are under the influence of the same motives, as an hereditary nobility. I know the idea that such a distinction exists in this country is ridiculed by some—But I am not the less apprehensive of danger from their influence on this account—Such distinctions exist all the world over—have been taken notice of by all writers on free government—and are founded in the nature of things. It has been the principal care of free governments to guard against the encroachments of the great. Common observation and experience prove the existence of such distinctions. Will any one say, that there does not exist in this country the pride of family, of wealth, of talents; and that they do not command influence and respect among the common people? Congress, in their address to the inhabitants of the province of Quebec, in 1775, state this distinction in the following forcible words quoted from the Marquis Beccaria. "In every human society, there is an essay continually tending to confer on one part the height of power and happiness, and to reduce the other to the extreme of weakness and misery. The intent of good laws is to oppose this effort, and to diffuse their influence universally and equally." We ought to guard against the government being placed in the hands of this class—They cannot have that sympathy with their constituents which is necessary to connect them closely to their interest: Being in the habit of profuse living, they will be profuse in the public expences. They find no difficulty in paying their taxes, and therefore do not feel public burthens: Besides if they govern, they will enjoy the emoluments of the government. The middling class, from their frugal habits, and feeling themselves the public burdens, will be careful how they increase them.

But I may be asked, would you exclude the first class in the community, from any share in legislation? I answer by no means—they would be more dangerous out of power than in it—they would be factious—discontented and constantly disturbing the government—it would also be unjust—they have their liberties to protect as well as others—and the largest share of property. But my idea is, that the Constitution should be so framed as to admit this class, together with a sufficient number of the middling class to control them. You will then combine the abilities and honesty of the community—a proper degree of information, and a disposition to pursue the the public good. A representative body, composed principally of respectable yeomanry is the best possible security to liberty.—When the interest of this part of the community is pursued, the public good is pursued, because the body of every nation consists of this class. And because the interest of both the rich and the poor are involved in that of the middling class. No burden can be laid on the poor, but what will sensibly affect the middling class. Any law rendering property insecure, would be injurious to them.—When therefore this class of society pursue their own interest, they promote that of the public, for it is involved in it.

In so small a number of representatives, there is great danger from corruption and combination. A great politician has said that every man has his price. I hope this is not true in all its extent—But I ask the gentlemen to inform, what government there is, in which it has not been practised? Notwithstanding all that has been said of the defects in the Constitution of the antient Confederacies of the Grecian Republics, their destruction is to be imputed more to this cause than to any imperfection in their forms of government. This was the deadly poison that effected their dissolution. This is an extensive country, increasing in population and growing in consequence. Very many lucrative offices will be in the grant of the government, which will be the object of avarice and ambition. How easy will it be to gain over a sufficient number, in the bestowment of these offices, to promote the views and purposes of those who grant them! Foreign corruption is also to be guarded against. A system of corruption is known to be the system of government in Europe. It is practised without blushing. And we may lay it to our account it will be attempted amongst us. The most effectual as well as natural security against this, is a strong democratic branch in the legislature frequently chosen, including in it a number of the substantial, sensible yeomanry of the country. Does the house of representatives answer this description? I confess, to me they hardly wear the complexion of a democratic branch— they appear the mere shadow of representation. The whole number in both houses amounts to 91—Of these 46 make a quorum; and 24 of those being secured, may carry any point. Can the liberties of three millions of people be securely trusted in the hands of 24 men? Is it prudent to commit to so small a number the decision of the great questions which will come before them? Reason revolts at the idea.

The honorable gentleman from New York has said that 65 members in the house of representatives are sufficient for the present situation of the country, and taking it for granted that they will increase as one for 30,000, in 25 years they will amount to 200. It is admitted by this observation that the number fixed in the Constitution, is not sufficient without it is augmented. It is not declared that an increase shall be made, but is left to the discretion of the legislature, by the gentleman's own concession; therefore the Constitution is imperfect. We certainly ought to fix in the Constitution those things which are essential to liberty. If any thing falls under this description, it is the number of the legislature. To say, as this gentleman does, that our security is to depend upon the spirit of the people, who will be watchful of their liberties, and not suffer them to be infringed, is absurd. It would equally prove that we might adopt any form of government. I believe were we to create a despot, he would not immediately dare to act the tyrant; but it would not be long before he would destroy the spirit of the people, or the people would destroy him. If our people have a high sense of liberty, the government should be congenial to this spirit—calculated to cherish the love of liberty, while yet it had sufficient force to restrain licentiousness. Government operates upon the spirit of the people, as well as the spirit of the people operates upon it—and if they are not comfortable to each other, the one or the other will prevail. In a less time than 25 years, the government will receive its tone. What the spirit of the country may be at the end of that period, it is impossible to foretel: Our duty is to frame a government friendly to liberty and the rights of mankind, which will tend to cherish and cultivate a love of liberty among our citizens. If this government becomes oppressive it will be by degrees: It will aim at its end by disseminating sentiments of government opposite to republicanism; and proceed from step to step in depriving the people of a share in the government. A recollection of the change that has taken place in the minds of many in this country in the course of a few years, ought to put us upon our guard. Many who are ardent advocates for the new system, reprobate republican principles as chimerical and such as ought to be expelled from society. Who would have thought ten years ago, that the very men who risqued their lives and fortunes in support of republican principles, would now treat them as the fictions of fancy?—A few years ago we fought for liberty—We framed a general government on free principles—We placed the state legislatures, in whom the people have a full and fair representation, between Congress and the people. We were then, it is true, too cautious; and too much restricted the powers of the general government. But now it is proposed to go into the contrary, and a more dangerous extreme; to remove all barriers; to give the New Government free access to our pockets, and ample command of our persons; and that without providing for a genuine and fair representation of the people. No one can say what the progress of the change of sentiment may be in 25 years. The same men who now cry up the necessity of an energetic government, to induce a compliance with this system, may in much less time reprobate this in as severe terms as they now do the confederation, and may as strongly urge the necessity of going as far beyond this, as this is beyond the Confederation.—Men of this class are increasing—they have influence, talents and industry—It is time to form a barrier against them. And while we are willing to establish a government adequate to the purposes of the union, let us be careful to establish it on the broad basis of equal liberty.

Mr. *Hamilton* then reassumed his argument. When, said he, I had the honor to address the committee yesterday, I gave a history of the circumstances which attended the Convention, when forming the Plan before you. I endeavored to point out to you the principles of accommodation, on which this arrangement was made; and to shew that the contending interests of the States led them to establish the representation as it now stands. In the second place I attempted to prove, that, in point of number, the representation would be perfectly secure.

Sir, no man agrees more perfectly than myself to the main principle for which the gentlemen contend. I agree that there should be a broad democratic branch in the national legislature. But this matter, Sir, depends on circumstances; It is impossible, in the first instance to be precise and exact with regard to the number; and it is equally impossible to determine to what point it may be proper in future to increase it. On this ground I am disposed to acquiesce. In my reasonings on the subject of government, I rely more on the interests and the opinions of men, than on any speculative parchment provisions whatever. I have found, that Constitutions are more

or less excellent as they are more or less agreeable to the natural operation of things: — I am therefore disposed not to
dwell long on curious speculations, or pay much attention to
modes and forms; but to adopt a system, whose principles
have been sanctioned by experience; adapt it to the real state
of our country; and depend on probable reasonings for its
operation and result. I contend that sixty-five and twenty-six
in two bodies afford perfect security, in the present state of
things; and that the regular progressive enlargement, which
was in the contemplation of the General Convention, will
leave not an apprehension of danger in the most timid and
suspicious mind. It will be the interest of the large states to
increase the representation: This will be the standing instruction to their delegates. — But, say the gentlemen, the
Members of Congress will be interested not to increase the
number, as it will diminish their relative influence. In all their
reasoning upon the subject, there seems to be this fallacy: —
They suppose that the representative will have no motive of
action, on the one side, but a sense of duty; or on the other,
but corruption: — They do not reflect, that he is to return to
the community; that he is dependent on the will of the people, and that it cannot be his interest to oppose their wishes.
Sir, the general sense of the people will regulate the conduct
of their representatives. I admit that there are exceptions to
this rule: There are certain conjunctures, when it may be necessary and proper to disregard the opinions which the majority of the people have formed: But in the general course of
things, the popular views and even prejudices will direct the
actions of the rulers.

All governments, even the most despotic, depend, in a
great degree, on opinion. In free republics, it is most peculiarly the case: In these, the will of the people makes the
essential principle of the government; and the laws which
control the community, receive their tone and spirit from the
public wishes. It is the fortunate situation of our country, that
the minds of the people are exceedingly enlightened and refined: Here then we may expect the laws to be proportionably
agreeable to the standard of perfect policy; and the wisdom of
public measures to consist with the most intimate conformity
between the views of the representative and his constituent. If

the general view of the people be for an increase, it undoubtedly must take place: They have it in their power to instruct their representatives; and the State Legislatures, which appoint the Senators, may enjoin it also upon them. Sir, if I believed that the number would remain at sixty-five, I confess I should give my vote for an amendment; though in a different form from the one proposed.

The amendment proposes a ratio of one for twenty thousand: I would ask, by what rule or reasoning it is determined, that one man is a better representative for twenty than thirty thousand? At present we have three millions of people; in twenty-five years, we shall have six millions; and in forty years, nine millions: And this is a short period, as it relates to the existence of States. Here then, according to the ratio of one for thirty thousand, we shall have, in forty years, three hundred representatives. If this be true, and if this be a safe representation, why be dissatisfied? why embarrass the Constitution with amendments, that are merely speculative and useless. I agree with the gentleman, that a very small number might give some colour for suspicion: I acknowledge, that ten would be unsafe; on the other hand, a thousand would be too numerous. But I ask him, why will not ninety-one be an adequate and safe representation? This at present appears to be the proper medium. Besides, the President of the United States will be himself the representative of the people. From the competition that ever subsists between the branches of government, the President will be induced to protect their rights, whenever they are invaded by either branch. On whatever side we view this subject, we discover various and powerful checks to the encroachments of Congress. The true and permanent interests of the members are opposed to corruption: Their number is vastly too large for easy combination: The rivalship between the houses will forever prove an insuperable obstacle: The people have an obvious and powerful protection in their own State governments: Should any thing dangerous be attempted, these bodies of perpetual observation, will be capable of forming and conducting plans of regular opposition. Can we suppose the people's love of liberty will not, under the incitement of their legislative leaders, be roused into resistance, and the madness of tyranny be extinguished at a blow? Sir, the danger is too distant; it is beyond all rational calculations.

It has been observed by an honorable gentleman, that a pure democracy, if it were practicable, would be the most perfect government. Experience has proved, that no position in politics is more false than this. The ancient democracies, in which the people themselves deliberated, never possessed one feature of good government.—Their very character was tyranny; their figure deformity:—When they assembled, the field of debate presented an ungovernable mob, not only incapable of deliberation, but prepared for every enormity. In these assemblies, the enemies of the people brought forward their plans of ambition systematically. They were opposed by their enemies of another party; and it became a matter of contingency, whether the people subjected themselves to be led blindly by one tyrant or by another.

It was remarked yesterday, that a numerous representation was necessary to obtain the confidence of the people. This is not generally true. The confidence of the people will easily be gained by a good administration. This is the true touchstone. I could illustrate the position, by a variety of historical examples, both ancient and modern. In Sparta, the Ephori were a body of magistrates, instituted as a check upon the senate, and representing the people. They consisted of only five men: But they were able to protect their rights, and therefore enjoyed their confidence and attachment. In Rome, the people were represented by three Tribunes, who were afterwards increased to ten. Every one acquainted with the history of that republic, will recollect how powerful a check to the senatorial encroachments, this small body proved; how unlimited a confidence was placed in them by the people whose guardians they were; and to what a conspicuous station in the government, their influence at length elevated the Plebians. Massachusetts has three hundred representatives; New-York has sixty-five. Have the people in this state less confidence in their representation, than the people of that? Delaware has twenty-one. Do the inhabitants of New York feel a higher confidence than those of Delaware? I have stated these examples, to prove that the gentleman's principle is not just. The popular confidence depends on circumstances very distinct from considerations of number. Probably the public attachment is more strongly secured by a train of prosperous events, which are the result of wise deliberation and vigorous execution, and to which large bodies are much less competent than small ones. If the representative conducts with propriety, he will necessarily enjoy the good will of the constituent. It appears then, if my reasoning be just, that the clause is perfectly proper, upon the principles of the gentleman who contends for the amendment: as there is in it the greatest degree of present security, and a moral certainty of an increase equal to our utmost wishes.

It has been farther, by the gentlemen in opposition, observed, that a large representation is necessary to understand the interests of the people—This principle is by no means true in the extent to which the gentleman seems to carry it. I would ask, why may not a man understand the interests of thirty as well as of twenty? The position appears to be made upon the unfounded presumption, that all the interests of all parts of the community must be represented. No idea is more erroneous than this. Only such interests are proper to be represented, as are involved in the powers of the General Government. These interests come compleatly under the observation of one, or a few men; and the requisite information is by no means augmented in proportion to the increase of number. What are the objects of the Government? Commerce, taxation, &c. In order to comprehend the interests of commerce, is it necessary to know how wheat is raised, and in what proportion it is produced in one district and in another? By no means. Neither is this species of knowledge necessary in general calculations upon the subject of taxation. The information necessary for these purposes, is that which is open to every intelligent enquirer; and of which, five men may be as perfectly possessed as fifty. In royal governments, there are usually particular men to whom the business of taxation is committed. These men have the forming of systems of finance; and the regulation of the revenue. I do not mean to recommend this practice. It proves however, this point; that a few individuals may be competent to these objects; and that large numbers are not necessary to perfection in the science of taxation. But, granting for a moment, that this minute and local knowledge the gentlemen contend for, is necessary, let us see, if under the New Constitution, it will not probably be found in the representation. The natural and proper mode of holding elections, will be to divide the state into districts, in proportion to the number to be elected. This state will consequently be divided at first into six. One man from each district will probably possess all the knowledge the gentlemen can desire. Are the senators of this state more ignorant of the interests of the people, than the assembly? Have they not ever enjoyed their confidence as much? Yet, instead of six districts, they are elected in four; and the chance of their being collected from the smaller divisions of the state consequently diminished. Their number is but twenty-four; and their powers are co-extensive with those of the assembly, and reach objects, which are most dear to the people—life, liberty and property.

Sir, we hear constantly a great deal, which is rather calculated to awake our passions, and create prejudices, than to conduct us to truth, and teach us our real interests.—I do not suppose this to be the design of the gentlemen.—Why then are we told so often of an aristocracy? For my part, I hardly know the meaning of this word as it is applied. If all we hear be true, this government is really a very bad one. But who are the aristocracy among us? Where do we find men elevated to a perpetual rank above their fellow citizens; and possessing powers entirely independent of them? The arguments of the gentlemen only go to prove that there are men who are rich, men who are poor, some who are wise, and others who are not—That indeed every distinguished man is an aristocrat.—This reminds me of a description of the aristocrats, I have seen in a late publication, styled the Federal Farmer.—The author reckons in the aristocracy, all governors of states, members of Congress, chief magistrates, and all officers of the militia.—This description, I presume to say, is ridiculous.—The image is a phantom. Does the new government render a rich man more eligible than a poor one? No. It requires no such qualification. It is bottomed on the broad and equal principle of your state constitution.

Sir, if the people have it in their option, to elect their most meritorious men; is this to be considered as an objection? Shall the constitution oppose their wishes, and abridge their most invaluable privilege? While property continues to be pretty equally divided, and a considerable share of information pervades the community; the tendency of the people's suffrages, will be to elevate merit even from obscurity—As riches increase and accumulate in few hands;—as luxury prevails in society; virtue will be in a greater degree considered as only a graceful appendage of wealth, and the tendency of things will be to depart from the republican standard. This is the real disposition of human nature: It is what, neither the honorable member nor myself can correct—It is a common misfortune, that awaits our state constitution, as well as all others.

There is an advantage incident to large districts of election, which perhaps the gentlemen, amidst all their apprehensions of influence and bribery, have not adverted to. In large districts, the corruption of the electors is much more difficult:— Combinations for the purposes of intrigue are less easily formed: Factions and cabals are little known. In a small district, wealth will have a more complete influence; because the people in the vicinity of a great man, are more immediately his dependants, and because this influence has fewer objects to act upon. It has been remarked, that it would be disagreeable to the middle class of men to go to the seat of the new government. If this be so, the difficulty will be enhanced by the gentleman's proposal. If his arguments be true, it proves that the larger the representation is, the less will be your choice of having it filled. But, it appears to me frivolous to bring forward such arguments as these. It has answered no other purpose, than to induce me, by way of reply, to enter into discussions, which I consider as useless, and not applicable to our subject.

It is a harsh doctrine, that men grow wicked in proportion as they improve and enlighten their minds. Experience has by no means justified us in the supposition, that there is more virtue in one class of men than in another. Look through the rich and the poor of the community; the learned and the ignorant.—Where does virtue predominate? The difference indeed consists, not in the quantity but kind of vices, which are incident to the various classes; and here the advantage of character belongs to the wealthy. Their vices are probably more favorable to the prosperity of the state, than those of the indigent; and partake less of moral depravity.

After all, Sir, we must submit to this idea, that the true principle of a republic is, that the people should choose whom they please to govern them. Representation is imperfect, in proportion as the current of popular favour is checked.—This great source of free government, popular election, should be perfectly pure, and the most unbounded liberty allowed. Where this principle is adhered to; where, in the organization of the government, the legislative, executive and judicial branches are rendered distinct; where again the legislative is divided into separate houses, and the operations of each are controuled by various checks and balances, and above all, by the vigilance and weight of the state governments; to talk of tyranny, and the subversion of our liberties, is to speak the language of enthusiasm. This balance between the national and the state governments ought to be dwelt on with peculiar attention, as it is of the utmost importance.—It forms a double security to the people. If one encroaches on their rights, they will find a powerful protection in the other.—Indeed they will both be prevented from overpassing their constitutional limits, by a certain rivalship, which will ever subsist between them.—I am persuaded, that a firm union is as necessary to perpetuate our liberties, as it is to make us respectable; and experience will probably prove, that the national government will be as natural a guardian of our freedom, as the state legislatures themselves.

Suggestions, Sir, of an extraordinary nature, have been frequently thrown out in the course of the present political controversy. It gives me pain to dwell on topics of this kind; and I wish they might be dismissed. We have been told, that the old Confederation has proved inefficacious, only because intriguing and powerful men, aiming at a revolution, have been forever instigating the people, and rendering them disaffected with it. This, Sir, is a false insinuation—The thing is impossible. I will venture to assert, that no combination of designing men under Heaven, will be capable of making a government unpopular, which is in its principles a wise and good one; and vigorous in its operations.

The Confederation was framed amidst the agitation and tumult of society.—It was composed of unsound materials put together in haste. Men of intelligence discovered the feebleness of the structure, in the first stages of its existence; but the great body of the people, too much engrossed with their distresses, to contemplate any but the immediate causes of them, were ignorant of the defects of their Constitution.—But, when the dangers of war were removed, they saw clearly what they had suffered, and what they had yet to suffer from a feeble form of government. There was no need of discerning men to convince the people of their unhappy situation—the complaint was co-extensive with the evil, and both were common to all classes of the community. We have been told, that the spirit of patriotism and love of liberty are almost extinguished among the people; and that it has become a prevailing doctrine, that republican principles ought to be hooted out of the world. Sir, I am confident that such remarks as these are rather occasioned by the heat of argument, than by a cool conviction of their truth and justice. As far as my experience has extended, I have heard no such doctrine, nor have I discovered any diminution of regard for those rights and liberties, in defence of which, the people have fought and suffered. There have been, undoubtedly, some men who have had speculative doubts on the subject of government; but the principles of republicanism are founded on too firm a basis to be shaken by a few speculative and sceptical reasoners. Our error has been of a very different kind. We have erred through excess of caution, and a zeal false and impracticable. Our counsels have been destitute of consistency and stability. I am flattered with a hope, Sir, that we have now found a cure for the evils under which we have so long labored. I trust, that the proposed Constitution affords a genuine specimen of representative and republican government—and that it will answer, in an eminent degree, all the beneficial purposes of society.

The honorable *Melancton Smith* rose and observed, that the gentleman might have spared many of his remarks in answer to the ideas he had advanced. The only way to remedy and correct the faults in the proposed Constitution was, he imagined, to increase the representation and limit the powers. He admitted that no precise number could be fixed on. His object only was to augment the number in such a degree as to render the government more favorable to liberty. The gentleman had charged his argument, that it would be the interest of the Congress to diminish the number of representatives, as being puerile. It was only made in answer to another of the gentleman's, which he thought equally weak; that it would be their interest to increase it. It appeared to him, he said, evident that the relative interests of the states would not be in the least degree increased by augmenting the numbers. The honorable member had assured the committee that the states would be checks upon the general government, and had pledged himself to point out and demonstrate the operation of these checks. For his own part, he could see no possibility of checking a government of independent powers, which extended to all objects and resources without limitation. What he lamented was that no constitutional checks were provided; such checks as would not leave the exercise of government to the operation of causes, which in their nature are variable and uncertain.

The honorable member had observed that the confidence of the people was not necessarily connected with the number of their rulers, and had cited the Ephori of Sparta, and the Tribunes in Rome, as examples. But it ought to be considered, that in both these places, the people were to contend with a body of hereditary nobles: They would, therefore, naturally have confidence in a few men who were their leaders in the constant struggle for liberty. The comparison between the representations of several states did not better apply. New-York had but sixty-five representatives in assembly—But because sixty-five was a proper representation of two hundred and forty thousand, did it follow that it was also sufficient for three millions? The state legislatures had not the powers of the general government, and were not competent to those important regulations which might endanger liberty.

The gentleman, continued Mr. *Smith*, had ridiculed his idea of an aristocracy, and had entered into a definition of the word: He himself agreed to this definition; but the dispute was not of words but things. He was convinced, that in every society there were certain men exalted above the rest. These men he did not consider as destitute of morality or virtue. —He only insisted that they could not feel sympathetically the wants of the people.

Robert R. Livingston, Melancton Smith, and John Jay Debate Aristocracy, Representation, and Corruption

June 23, 1788

Mr. Chancellor *Livingston*. The gentleman from Dutchess appears to have misapprehended some of the ideas which dropped from me: My argument was, that a republic might very properly be formed by a league of states; but that the laws of the general legislature must act, and be enforced upon individuals. I am contending for this species of government. The gentlemen who have spoken in opposition to me, have either misunderstood or perverted my meaning: But, Sir, I flatter myself, it has not been misunderstood by the convention at large.

If we examine the history of federal republics, whose legislative powers were exercised only on states, in their collective capacity; we shall find in their fundamental principles, the seeds of domestic violence and consequent annihilation. This was the principal reason why I thought the old confederation would be forever impracticable.

Much has been said, Sir, about the number which ought to compose the house of representatives, and the question has been debated with great address by the gentlemen on both sides of the house. It is agreed, that the representative body should be so small, as to prevent the disorder inseparable from the deliberations of a mob; and yet sufficiently numerous, to represent the interests of the people; and to be a safe depository of power. There is, unfortunately, no standard, by which we can determine this matter. Gentlemen who think that a hundred may be the medium, in which the advantages of regular deliberation, and the safety of the people are united, will probably be disposed to support the plan as it stands; others, who imagine that no number less than three or four hundred can ensure the preservation of liberty, will contend for an alteration. Indeed, these effects depend so much upon contingency, and upon circumstances totally unconnected with the idea of number; that we ought not to be surprized at the want of a standing criterion. On so vague a subject, it is very possible that the opinions of no two gentlemen in this assembly, if they were governed by their own original reflections, would entirely coincide. I acknowledge myself one of those who suppose the number expressed in the constitution to be about the proper medium; and yet future experience may induce me to think it too small or too large. When I consider the objects and powers of the general government, I am of an opinion that one hundred men may at all times be collected, of sufficient information and integrity, to manage well the affairs of the union. Some gentlemen suppose, that to understand and provide for the general interests of commerce and manufactures, our legislatures ought to know how all commodities are produced, from the first principle of vegetation to the last polish of mechanical labour; that they ought to be minutely acquainted with all the process of all the arts: if this were true, it would be necessary, that a great part of the British house of commons should be woolen drapers: Yet, we seldom find such characters in that celebrated assembly.

As to the idea of representing the feelings of the people, I do not entirely understand it, unless by their feelings is meant their interests. They appear to me to be the same thing. But if they have feelings which do not rise out of their interests, I think they ought not to be represented. What! Shall the unjust, the selfish, the unsocial feelings be represented? Shall the vices, the infirmities, the passions of the people be represented? Government, Sir, would be a monster: Laws made to encourage virtue and maintain peace, would have a preposterous tendency to subvert the authority and outrage the principles, on which they were founded: Besides, the feelings of the people are so variable and inconstant, that our rulers should be chosen every day: People have one sort of feelings to day, another to-morrow; and the voice of the representative must be incessantly changing in correspondence with these feelings: This would be making him a political weathercock.

The honorable gentleman from Dutchess [Mr. *Smith*] who has so copiously declaimed against all declamation, has pointed his artillery against the rich and the great. I am not interested in defending rich men: But what does he mean by telling us that the rich are vicious and intemperate. Will he presume to point out to us the class of men in which intemperance is not to be found? Is there less intemperence in feeding on beef than on turtle; or in drinking rum than wine? I think the gentleman does not reason from facts: If he will look round among the rich men of his acquaintance, I fancy he will find them as honest and virtuous as any class in the community—He says the rich are unfeeling—I believe they are less so than the poor: For it seems to me probable that those who are most occupied by their own cares and distresses, have the least sympathy with the distresses of others. The sympathy of the poor is generally selfish; that of the rich a more disinterested emotion.

The gentleman further observes, that ambition is peculiarly the vice of the wealthy. But, have not all classes of men their objects of ambition? Will not a poor man contend for a constable's staff with as much assiduity and eagerness as a man of rank will aspire to the chief magistracy? The great offices in a state are beyond the view of the poor and ignorant man: He will therefore contemplate a humbler office as the highest alluring object of ambition: He will look, with equal envy, on a successful competitor; and will equally sacrifice to the attainment of his wishes, the duty he owes to his friends or to the public. But, says the gentleman, the rich will be always brought forward: They will exclusively enjoy the suffrages of the people.—For my own part, I believe that if two men of equal abilities set out together in life, one rich, the other of small fortune, the latter will generally take the lead in your government. The rich are ever objects of envy; and this, more or less, operates as a bar to their advancement. What is the fact? Let us look around us: I might mention gentlemen in office who have not been advanced for their wealth; I might instance in particular the honorable gentleman who presides over this state, who was not promoted to the chief magistracy for his riches, but his virtue.

The gentleman, sensible of the weakness of this reasoning, is obliged to fortify it by having recourse to the phantom aristocracy. I have heard much of this. I always considered it as the bugbear of the party. We are told, that in every country there is a natural aristocracy, and that this aristocracy consists of the rich and the great: Nay, the gentleman goes further, and ranks in this class of men, the wise, the learned, and those eminent for their talents or great virtues. Does a man possess the confidence of his fellow-citizens for having done them important services? He is an aristocrat—Has he great integrity? Such a man will be greatly trusted; he is an aristocrat. Indeed, to determine that one is an aristocrat, we need only be assured that he is a man of merit. But, I hope we have many such—I hope, Sir, we are all aristocrats. So sensible am I of that gentleman's talents, integrity and virtue, that we might at once hail him the first of the nobles, the very prince of the Senate.—But who, in the name of common sense, will he have to represent us? Not the rich; for they are sheer aristocrats. Not the learned, the wise, the virtuous, for they are all aristocrats. Who then? Why, those who are not virtuous; those who are not wise; those who are not learned: These are the men, to whom alone we can trust our liberties. He says further we ought not to choose these aristocrats, because the people will not have confidence in them; that is, the people will not have confidence in those who best deserve and most possess their confidence. He would have his government composed of other classes of men: Where will he find them? Why, he must go out into the highways, and pick up the rogue and the robber: He must go to the hedges and ditches and bring in the poor, the blind and the lame. As the gentleman has thus settled the definition of aristocracy, I trust that no man will think it a term of reproach: For who among us would not be wise? Who would not be virtuous? Who would not be above want? How, again, would he have us guard against aristocracy? Clearly by doubling the representation, and sending twelve aristocrats, instead of six. The truth is, in these republican governments we know no such ideal distinctions.—We are all equally aristocrats. Offices, emoluments, honors are open to all.

Much has been said by the gentleman about corruption: He calculates that twenty-four may give the voice of Congress.—That is, they will compose a bare majority of a bare quorum of both houses. He supposes here the most singular, and I might add, the most improbable combination of events: First, there is to be a power in the government who has the means, and whose interest it is to corrupt—Next, twenty-four men are to compose the legislature; and these twenty-four, selected by their fellow citizens as the most virtuous, are all, in violation of their oath and their real interests, to be corrupted. Then he supposes the virtuous minority inattentive, regardless of their own honor, and the good of their country; making no alarm, no struggle: A whole people, suffering the injury of a ruinous law, yet ignorant, inactive, and taking no measures to redress the grievance.

Let us take a view of the present Congress. The gentleman is satisfied with our present federal government, on the score of corruption. Here he has confidence: Though each state may delegate seven, they generally send no more than three; consequently, thirty-nine men may transact any business under the old government; while, the new legislature, which will be in all probability constantly full, will consist of ninety-one. But, say the gentlemen, our present Congress have not the same powers.—I answer they have the very same. Congress have the power of making war and peace, of levying money and raising men; they involve us in a war at their pleasure; they may negociate loans to any extent, and make unlimited demands upon the states. Here, the gentleman comes forward, and says, that the states are to carry these powers into execution; and they have the power of non-compliance. But is not every state bound to comply? What power have they to controul Congress in the exercise of those rights, which they have pledged themselves to support? It is true, they have broken, in numerous instances, the compact by which they were obligated; and they may do it again: But, will the gentleman draw an argument of security from the facility of violating their faith? Suppose there should be a majority of creditor states, under the present government; might they not combine and compel us to observe the covenant, by which we had bound ourselves?

We are told, that this constitution gives Congress the power over the purse and the sword. Sir, have not all good governments this power? Nay, does any one doubt, that under the old confederation, Congress holds the purse and the sword? How many loans did they procure, which we are bound to pay? How many men did they raise, which we were bound to maintain? How will gentlemen say, that that body, which indeed is extremely small, can be more safely trusted than a much larger body, possessed of the same authority?— What is the ground of such entire confidence in the one— what the cause of so much jealousy of the other?

An honorable member from New-York, has viewed the subject of representation in a point of light which had escaped me; and which I think clear and conclusive. He says, that the state of Delaware must have one; and as that state will not probably increase for a long time, it will be the interest of the larger states to determine the ratio, by the number which Delaware contains. The gentlemen in opposition say, suppose Delaware contains fifty thousand, why not fix the ratio at sixty thousand? Clearly, because by this, the other states will give up a sixth part of their interests. The members of Congress, also, from a more private motive, will be induced to augment the representation. The chance of their own re-election will increase with the number of their colleagues.

It has been further observed, that the sense of the people is for a larger representation; and that this ought to govern us:—That the people generally are of opinion, that even our House of Assembly is too small.—I very much doubt this fact. As far as my observation has extended, I have found a very different sentiment prevail. It seems to be the predominant opinion, that sixty-five is fully equal, if not superior to the exigencies of our state government: And I presume, that the people have as much confidence in their Senate of twenty-four, as in their Assembly of sixty five. All these considerations have united to give my mind the most perfect conviction, that the number specified in the constitution, is fully adequate to the present wants and circumstances of our country; and that this number will be increased to the satisfaction of the most timid and jealous.

Honorable Mr. *Smith*. I did not intend to make any more observations on this article. Indeed, I have heard nothing to day, which has not been suggested before, except the polite reprimand I have received for my declamation. I should not have risen again, but to examine who proved himself the greatest declaimer. The gentleman wishes me to describe what I meant, by representing the feelings of the people. If I recollect right, I said the representative ought to understand, and govern his conduct by the true interest of the people.—I believe I stated this idea precisely. When he attempts to explain my ideas, he explains them away to nothing; and instead of answering, he distorts, and then sports with them. But he may rest assured, that in the present spirit of the Convention, to irritate is not the way to conciliate. The gentleman, by the false gloss he has given to my argument, makes me an enemy to the rich: This is not true. All I said, was, that mankind were influenced, in a great degree, by interests and prejudices:—That men, in different ranks of life, were exposed to different temptations—and that ambition was more peculiarly the passion of the rich and great. The gentleman supposes the poor have less sympathy with the sufferings of their fellow creatures; for that those who feel most distress themselves, have the least regard to the misfortunes of others:—Whether this be reasoning or declamation, let all who hear us determine. I observed that the rich were more exposed to those temptations, which rank and power hold out to view; that they were more luxurious and intemperate, because they had more fully the means of enjoyment; that they were more ambitious, because more in the hope of success. The gentleman says my principle is not true; for that a poor man will be as ambitious to be a constable, as a rich man to be a governor:—But he will not injure his country so much by the party he creates to support his ambition.

The next object of the gentleman's ridicule is my idea of an aristocracy; and he indeed has done me the honor, to rank me in the order. If then I am an aristocrat, and yet publicly caution my countrymen against the encroachments of the aristocrats, they will surely consider me as one of their most disinterested friends. My idea of aristocracy is not new:—It is embraced by many writers on government:—I would refer the gentleman for a definition of it to the honorable *John Adams*, one of our natural aristocrats. This writer will give him a description the most ample and satisfactory. But I by no means intended to carry my idea of it to such a ridiculous length as the gentleman would have me; nor will any of my expressions warrant the construction he imposes on them. My argument was, that in order to have a true and genuine representation, you must receive the middling class of people into your government—such as compose the body of this assembly. I observed, that a representation from the United States could not be so constituted, as to represent completely the feelings and interests of the people; but that we ought to come as near this object as possible. The gentlemen say, that the exactly proper number of representatives is so indeterminate and vague, that it is impossible for them to ascertain it with any precision. But surely, they are able to see the distinction between twenty and thirty. I acknowledged that a complete representation would make the legislature too numerous; and therefore, it is our duty to limit the powers, and form checks on the government, in proportion to the smallness of the number.

The honorable gentleman next animadverts on my apprehensions of corruption, and instances the present Congress, to prove an absurdity in my argument. But is this fair reasoning? There are many material checks to the operations of that body, which the future Congress will not have. In the first place, they are chosen annually:—What more powerful check! They are subject to recal: Nine states must agree to any important resolution, which will not be carried into execution, till it meets the approbation of the people in the state legislatures. Admitting what he says, that they have pledged their faith to support the acts of Congress: yet, if these be contrary to the essential interests of the people, they ought not to be acceded to for they are not bound to obey any law, which tends to destroy them.

It appears to me, that had economy been a motive for making the representation small; it might have operated more properly in leaving out some of the offices which this constitution requires. I am sensible that a great many of the common people, who do not reflect, imagine that a numerous representation involves a great expence:—But they are not aware of the real security it gives to an œconomical management in all the departments of government.

The gentleman further declared, that as far his acquaintance extended, the people thought sixty-five a number fully large enough for our State Assembly; and hence inferred, that sixty-five is to two hundred and forty thousand, as sixty-five is to three millions.—This is curious reasoning.

I feel that I have troubled the committee too long. I should not indeed have risen again upon this subject, had not my ideas been grossly misrepresented.

The honorable Mr. *Jay*. I will make a few observations on this article, Mr. Chairman, though I am sensible it may not appear very useful to travel over the field, which has been already so fully explored.

Sir, it seems to be on all sides agreed, that a strong, energetic, federal government, is necessary for the United States. It has given me pleasure to hear such declarations come from all parts of the house. If gentlemen are of this opinion, they give us to understand that such a government is the favorite object of their desire; and also that it can be instituted; That, indeed, it is both necessary and practicable; or why do they advocate it.

The gentleman last on the floor, has informed us, that according to his idea of a complete representation, the extent of our country is too great for it.—[Here he called on Mr. *Smith*, to know if he had mistaken him; who replied—My idea is not that a proper representation for a strong federal government is unattainable; but that such a representation, under the proposed constitution, is impracticable.] Sir, continued Mr. *Jay*, I now understand the gentleman in a different sense—However, what I shall say will reach equally his explanation. I take it, that no federal government is worth having, unless it can provide for the general interests of the United States. If this constitution be so formed as to answer these purposes, our object is obtained. The providing for the general interests of the Union requires certain powers in government, which the gentleman seems to be willing it should possess; that is, the important powers of war and peace. These powers are peculiarly interesting—Their operation reaches objects the most dear to the people; and every man is concerned in them. Yet; for the exercise of these powers the gentleman does not think a very large representation necessary: But, Sir, if the proposed constitution provides for a representation adequate to the purposes I have described, why not adequate to all other purposes of a federal government? The adversaries of the plan seem to consider the general government, as possessing all the minute and local powers of the state governments. The direct inference from this, according to their principle, would be that the federal representation should be proportionably large: In this state, as the gentleman says, we have sixty-five: If the national representation is to be extended in proportion, what an unwieldy body shall we have! If the United States contain three millions of inhabitants, in this ratio, the Congress must consist of more than eight hundred. But, Sir, let us examine whether such a number is necessary or reasonable—What are the objects of our state legislatures? Innumerable things of small moment occupy their attention—matters of a private nature, which require much minute and local information. The objects of the general government are not of this nature—They comprehend the interests of the States in relation to each other, and in relation to foreign powers. Surely there are many men in this state, fully informed of the general interests of its trade, its agriculture, its manufactures: Is any thing more than this necessary? Is it requisite that our representatives in Congress should possess any particular knowledge of the local interests of the county of Suffolk, distinguished from those of Orange and Ulster? The Senate is to be composed of men, appointed by the state legislatures: They will certainly choose those who are most distinguished for their general knowledge: I presume they will also instruct them; that there will be a constant correspondence supported between the senators and the state executives, who will be able, from time to time, to afford them all that particular information, which particular circumstances may require. I am in favour of large representations: Yet, as the minds of the people are so various on this subject, I think it best to let things stand as they are. The people in Massachusetts are satisfied with two hundred: The gentlemen require three hundred: Many others suppose either number unnecessarily large.—There is no point on which men's opinions vary more materially. If the matter be doubtful, and much may be rationally said on both sides, gentlemen ought not to be very strenuous on such points. The convention, who decided this question, took all these different opinions into consideration, and were directed by a kind of necessity of mutual accommodation, and by reasons of expediency: It would therefore be unfair to censure them. Were I asked if the number corresponds exactly with my own private judgment, I should answer, no.—But I think it is best, under our present circumstances, to acquiesce. Yet, Sir, if I could be convinced that danger would probably result from so small a number, I should certainly withhold my acquiescence—But whence will this danger arise? Sir, I am not fearful of my countrymen: We have yet known very little of corruption:—We have already experienced great distresses and difficulties: We have seen perilous times; when it was the interest of Great-Britain to hold out the most seducing temptations to every man worth gaining. I mention this as a circumstance to shew, that in case of a war with any foreign power, there can be little fear of corruption; and I mention it to the honor of the American character.—At the time I allude to, how many men had you in Congress? Generally fewer than sixty-five.

Sir, all the arguments offered on the other side serve to shew, that it will be easier to corrupt under the old, than under the new government: Such arguments, therefore, do not seem to answer the gentleman's purpose. In the federal government, as it now stands, there are but thirteen votes, though there may be sixty or seventy voices.—Now, what is the object of corruption? To gain votes. In the new government there are to be ninety-one votes. Is it easier to buy many than a few? In the present Congress, you cannot declare war, make peace, or do any other important act, without the concurrence of nine states. There are rarely more than nine present. A full Congress is an extraordinary thing. Is it necessary to declare war, or pass a requisition for money to support it? A foreign Prince says, this will be against my interest—I must prevent it—How? By having recourse to corruption. If there are eleven states on the floor, it will be necessary to corrupt three: What measure shall I take? Why, it is common for each state to have no more than two members in Congress. I will take off one, and the vote of that state is lost: I will take off three, and their most important plan is defeated. Thus in the old government, it is only necessary to bribe the few: In the new government, it is only necessary to corrupt the many. Where lies the greater security? The gentleman says, the election is annual, and you may recall your delegates when you please. But how are you to form your opinion of his conduct? He may excuse himself from acting, without giving any reason. Nay, on a particular emergency, he has only to go home, for which he may have a thousand plausible reasons to offer, and you have no mode of compelling his attendance.—To detect corruption is at all times difficult; but, under these circumstances, it appears almost impossible. I give out these hints to shew, that on the score of corruption, we have much the best chance under the new constitution: and that if we do not reach perfection, we certainly change for the better. But, Sir, suppose corruption should infect one branch of the government, for instance, the house of representatives; what a powerful check you have in the senate! You have a double security—You have two chances in your favor to one against you. The two houses will naturally be in a state of rivalship: This will make them always vigilant, quick to discern a bad measure, and ready to oppose it. Thus the chance of corruption is not only lessened by an increase of the number, but vastly diminished by the necessity of concurrence. This is the peculiar excellence of a division of the legislature.

Sir, I argue from plain facts—Here is no sophistry; no construction; no false glosses, but simple inferences from the obvious operation of things. We did not come here to carry points. If the gentleman will convince me I am wrong, I will submit. I mean to give them my ideas frankly upon the subject. If my reasoning is not good, let them shew me the folly of it. It is from this reciprocal interchange of ideas, that the truth must come out. My earnest wish is, that we may go home attended with the pleasing consciousness that we have industriously and candidly sought the truth, and have done our duty. I cannot conclude, without repeating, that though I prefer a large representation, yet considering our present situation, I see abundant reason to acquiesce in the wisdom of the general convention, and to rest satisfied, that the representation will increase in a sufficient degree, to answer the wishes of the most zealous advocates for liberty.

The hon. Mr. *Smith* rose and said. It appeared to him probable, that it would be the interest of the state having the least number of inhabitants, to make its whole number the measure of the representation: That it would be the interest of Delaware, supposing she has forty thousand, and consequently only one vote, to make this whole number the ratio: So, if she had fifty thousand, or any number under sixty thousand. The interest also of some other of the small states would correspond with hers; and thus, the representation would be reduced in proportion to the increase of Delaware. He still insisted, that the number of representatives might be diminished.

He would make one observation more, upon the gentleman's idea of corruption. His reasoning, he said, went only to prove that the present Congress might be restrained from doing good, by the wilful absence of two or three members. It was rare, he said, that the people were oppressed by a government's not doing; and little danger to liberty could flow from that source.

Gilbert Livingston Warns Against Giving the Senate Power Too Profusely

June 24, 1788

Convention assembled; and being resolved into a committee, the first paragraph of the third section of the first article was read, when Mr. *G. Livingston* rose, and addressed the chair.

He in the first place considered the importance of the senate, as a branch of the legislature, in three points of view.

First, they would possess legislative powers, co-extensive with those of the house of representatives, except with respect to originating revenue laws; which, however, they would have power to reject or amend, as in the case of other bills. Secondly, they would have an importance, even exceeding that of the representative house, as they would be composed of a smaller number, and possess more firmness and system. Thirdly, their consequence: and dignity would still farther transcend those of the other branch, from their longer continuance in office. These powers, Mr. *Livingston* contended, rendered the senate a dangerous body.

He went on, in the second place, to enumerate and animadvert on the powers, with which they were cloathed in their judicial capacity; and in their capacity of council to the president, and in the forming of treaties. In the last place, as if too much power could not be given to this body, they were made, he said, a council of appointment; by whom, ambassadors and other officers of state were to be appointed. These are the powers, continued he, which are vested in this small body of twenty-six men: In some cases, to be exercised by a bare quorum, which is fourteen; a majority of which number again, is eight. What are the checks provided to balance this great mass of powers? Our present Congress cannot serve longer than three years in six: They are at any time subject to recall. These and other checks were considered as necessary, at a period which I choose to honor with the name of virtuous. Sir, I venerate the spirit with which every thing was done, at the trying time in which the confederation was formed. America then, had a sufficiency of this virtue to resolve to resist, perhaps, the first nation in the universe, even unto bloodshed. What was her aim? equal liberty and safety. What ideas had she of this equal liberty? Read them in her articles of confederation. True it is, Sir, there are some powers wanted to make the glorious compact complete: But, Sir, let us be cautious, that we do not err more on the other hand, by giving power too profusely when perhaps it will be too late to recall it. Consider, Sir, the great influence which this body armed at all points will have. What will be the effect of this? Probably, a security of their re-election, as long as they please. Indeed, in my view, it will amount nearly to an appointment for life. What will be their situation in a federal town? Hallowed ground! Nothing so unclean as state laws to enter there; surrounded, as they will be, by an impenetrable wall of adamant and gold; the wealth of the whole country flowing into it—[Here a member who did not fully understand, called out to know what WALL the gentleman meant: On which he turned and replied, "A wall of Gold—of adamant, which will flow in from all parts of the continent." At which flowing metaphor, a great laugh in the house.] The gentleman continued. Their attention to their various business, will probably require their constant attendance.—In this Eden, will they reside, with their families, distant from the observation of the people. In such a situation, men are apt to forget their dependence—lose their sympathy, and contract selfish habits. Factions will be apt to be formed, if the body becomes permanent. The senators will associate only with men of their own class; and thus become strangers to the condition of the common people. They should not only return, and be obliged to live with the people, but return to their former rank of citizenship, both to revive their sense of dependence, and to gain a knowledge of the state of their country. This will afford opportunity to bring forward the genius and information of the states; and will be a stimulus to acquire political abilities. It will be a means of diffusing a more general knowledge of the measures and spirit of administration. These things will confirm the people's confidence in government. When they see those who have been high in office, residing among them, as private citizens, they will feel more forcibly, that the government is of their own choice. The members of this branch, having the idea impressed on their minds, that they are soon to return to the level, whence the suffrages of the people raised them; this good effect will follow: They will consider their interests as the same with those of their constituents; and that they legislate for themselves as well as others. They will not conceive themselves made to receive, enjoy and rule; nor the people solely to earn, pay and submit.

Mr. Chairman, I have endeavored, with as much perspicuity and candor as I am master of, shortly to state my objections to this clause—I would wish the committee to believe that they are not raised for the sake of opposition; but that I am very sincere in my sentiments in this important investigation. The senate, as they are now constituted, have little or no check on them. Indeed, Sir, too much is put into their hands. When we come to that part of the system which points out their powers, it will be the proper time to consider this subject more particularly.

I think, Sir, we must relinquish the idea of safety under this government, if the time for service is not further limited, and the power of recall given to the state legislatures. I am strengthened in my opinion, on this point, by an observation made yesterday by an honorable member from New-York, to this effect:—"That there should be no fear of corruption of the members in the house of representatives; especially, as they are, in two years, to return to the body of the people." I therefore move, that the committee adopt the following resolution as an amendment to this clause.

"*Resolved,* That no person shall be eligible as a senator for more than six years in any term of twelve years, and that it shall be in the power of the legislature of the several states, to recall their senators, or either of them, and to elect others in their stead, to serve for the remainder of the time for which such senator or senators so recalled were appointed."

Robert R. Livingston Replies to Gilbert Livingston's "Dreamings of a Distempered Fancy"

June 24, 1788

Mr. *Chancellor Livingston*. The amendment appears to have in view two objects: That a rotation shall be established in the senate; and that its members shall be subject to recall by the state legislatures. It is not contended, that six years is too long a time for the senators to remain in office: Indeed this cannot be objected to, when the purposes for which this body is instituted, are considered. They are to form treaties with foreign nations: This requires a comprehensive knowledge of foreign politics, and an extensive acquaintance with characters, whom, in this capacity, they have to negociate with; together with such an intimate conception of our best interests, relative to foreign powers, as can only be derived from much experience in this business. What singular policy, to cut off the hand which has just qualified itself for action! But, says the gentleman, as they are the representatives of the states, those states should have a controul. Will this principle hold good? The members of the lower house are the representatives of the people. Have the people any power to recall them? What would be the tendency of the power contended for? Clearly this.—The state legislatures being frequently subject to factious and irregular passions, may be unjustly disaffected, and discontented with their delegates; and a senator may be appointed one day and recalled the next. This would be a source of endless confusion. The senate are indeed designed to represent the state governments; but they are also the representatives of the United States, and are not to consult the interest of any one state alone, but that of the Union.— This could never be done, if there was a power of recall: For sometimes it happens, that small sacrifices are absolutely indispensable for the general good and safety of the confederacy: but if a senator should presume to consent to these sacrifices, he could be immediately recalled. This reasoning turns on the idea, that a state not being able to comprehend the interests of the whole, would, in all instances, adhere to her own, even to the hazard of the Union.

I should disapprove of this amendment, because it would open so wide a door for faction and intrigue, and afford such scope for the arts of an evil ambition. A man might go to the senate with an incorruptible integrity, and the strongest attachment to the interest of his state: But if he deviated, in the least degree, from the line which a prevailing party in a popular assembly had marked for him, he would be immediately recalled. Under these circumstances, how easy would it be for an ambitious, factious demagogue to misrepresent him; to distort the features of his character, and give a false colour to his conduct! How easy for such a man to impose upon the public, and influence them to recall and disgrace their faithful delegate!—The general government may find it necessary to do many things, which some states might never be willing to consent to. Suppose Congress should enter into a war to protect the fisheries, or any of the northern interests; the southern states, loaded with their share of the burthen, which it would be necessary to impose, would condemn their representatives in the senate for acquiescing in such a measure. There are a thousand things which an honest man might be obliged to do, from a conviction that it would be for the general good, which would give great dissatisfaction to his constituents.

Sir, all the argument drawn from an imaginary prospect of corruption, have little weight with me. From what source is this corruption to be derived? One gentleman tells you, that this dreadful senate is to be surrounded by a wall of adamant—of gold; and that this wall is to be a liquid one, and to flow in from all quarters. Such arguments as these seem rather to be the dreamings of a distempered fancy, than the cool rational deductions of a deliberate mind. Whence is this corruption to be derived? Are the people to corrupt the senators with their own gold? Is bribery to enter the federal city, with the amazing influx of adamant, the gentleman so pathetically contemplates? Are not Congress to publish from time to time, an account of their receipts and expenditures? Can there be

any appropriations of money by the senate, without the concurrence of the assembly? And can we suppose that a majority
of both houses can be corrupted? At this rate we must suppose a miracle indeed.

But to return—The people are the best judges who ought
to represent them. To dictate and controul them; to tell them
who they shall not elect, is to abridge their natural rights.
This rotation is an absurd species of ostracism—a mode of
proscribing eminent merit, and banishing from stations of
trust those who have filled them with the greatest faithfulness.
Besides, it takes away the strongest stimulus to public virtue—the hope of honors and rewards. The acquisition of
abilities is hardly worth the trouble, unless one is to enjoy the
satisfaction of employing them for the good of one's country.
We all know that experience is indispensibly necessary to good
government.—Shall we then drive experience into obscurity?
I repeat, that this is an absolute abridgement of the people's
rights.

As to the senate's rendering themselves perpetual, or establishing such a power, as to prevent their being removed, it
appears to me chimerical.—Can they make interest with their
legislatures, who are themselves varying every year, sufficient
for such a purpose? Can we suppose two senators will be able
to corrupt the whole legislature of this state? The idea, I say,
is chimerical—The thing is impossible.

Alexander Hamilton Defends the Senate: A Small, Independent, Discerning Body to Check the Passions of the People

June 24, 1788

Honorable Mr. *Hamilton.* I am persuaded, Mr. Chairman, that I in my turn, shall be indulged, in addressing the committee—We all, with equal sincerity, profess to be anxious for the establishment of a republican government, on a safe and solid basis—It is the object of the wishes of every honest man in the United States, and I presume I shall not be disbelieved, when I declare, that it is an object of all others the nearest and most dear to my own heart. The means of accomplishing this great purpose become the most important study, which can interest mankind. It is our duty to examine all those means with peculiar attention, and to chuse the best and most effectual. It is our duty to draw from nature, from reason, from examples, the justest principles of policy, and to pursue and apply them in the formation of our government. We should contemplate and compare the systems, which, in this examination, come under our view, distinguish, with a careful eye, the defects and excellencies of each, and discarding the former, incorporate the latter, as far as circumstances will admit, into our constitution. If we pursue a different course and neglect this duty, we shall probably disappoint the expectations of our country and of the world.

In the commencement of a revolution, which received its birth from the usurpations of tyranny, nothing was more natural, than that the public mind should be influenced by an extreme spirit of jealousy. To resist these encroachments, and to nourish this spirit, was the great object of all our public and private institutions. The zeal for liberty became predominant and excessive. In forming our confederation, this passion alone seemed to actuate us, and we appear to have had no other view than to secure ourselves from despotism. The object certainly was a valuable one, and deserved our utmost attention: But, Sir, there is another object, equally important, and which our enthusiasm rendered us little capable of regarding—I mean a principle of strength and stability in the organization of our government, and vigor in its operations. This purpose could never be accomplished but by the establishment of some select body, formed peculiarly upon this principle. There are few positions more demonstrable than that there should be in every republic, some permanent body to correct the prejudices, check the intemperate passions, and regulate the fluctuations of a popular assembly. It is evident that a body instituted for these purposes must be so formed as to exclude as much as possible from its own character, those infirmities, and that mutability which it is designed to remedy. It is therefore necessary that it should be small, that it should hold its authority during a considerable period, and that it should have such an independence in the exercise of its powers, as will divest it as much as possible of local prejudices. It should be so formed as to be the center of political knowledge, to pursue always a steady line of conduct, and to reduce every irregular propensity to system. Without this establishment, we may make experiments without end, but shall never have an efficient government.

It is an unquestionable truth, that the body of the people in every country desire sincerely its prosperity: But it is equally unquestionable, that they do not possess the discernment and stability necessary for systematic government. To deny that they are frequently led into the grossest errors by misinformation and passion, would be a flattery which their own good sense must despise. That branch of administration especially, which involves our political relation with foreign states, a community will ever be incompetent to. These truths are not often held up in public assemblies—but they cannot be unknown to any who hear me. From these principles it follows that there ought to be two distinct bodies in our government—one which shall be immediately constituted by and peculiarly represent the people, and possess all the popular features; another formed upon the principles, and for the purposes before explained. Such considerations as these induced the convention who formed your state constitution, to institute a senate upon the present plan. The history of ancient and modern republics had taught them, that many of the evils which these republics suffered arose from the want of a certain balance and mutual controul indispensible to a wise administration—They were convinced that popular assemblies are frequently misguided by ignorance, by sudden impulses and the intrigues of ambitious men; and that some firm barrier against these operations was necessary: They, therefore, instituted your senate, and the benefits we have experienced, have fully justified their conceptions.

Now, Sir, what is the tendency of the proposed amendment? To take away the stability of government by depriving the senate of its permanency: To make this body subject to the same weakness and prejudices, which are incident to popular assemblies, and which it was instituted to correct; and by thus assimilating the complexion of the two branches, destroy the balance between them. The amendment will render the senator a slave to all their capricious humors among the people. It will probably be here suggested, that the legislatures—not the people—are to have the power of recall. Without attempting to prove that the legislatures must be in a great degree the image of the multitude, in respect to federal affairs, and that the same prejudices and factions will prevail; I insist, that in whatever body the power of recall is vested, the senator will perpetually feel himself in such a state of vassalage and dependence, that he never can possess that firmness which is necessary to the discharge of his great duty to the union.

Gentlemen, in their reasoning, have placed the interests of the several states, and those of the United States in contrast—This is not a fair view of the subject—They must necessarily be involved in each other. What we apprehend is, that some sinister prejudice, or some prevailing passion, may assume the form of a genuine interest. The influence of these is as powerful as the most permanent conviction of the public good; and against this influence we ought to provide. The local interests of a state ought in every case to give way to the interests of the Union: For when a sacrifice of one or the other is necessary, the former becomes only an apparent, partial interest, and should yield, on the principle that the small good ought never to oppose the great one. When you assemble from your several counties in the legislature, were every member to be guided only by the apparent interest of his county, government would be impracticable. There must be a perpetual accommodation and sacrifice of local advantage to general expediency—But the spirit of a mere popular assembly would rarely be actuated by this important principle. It is therefore absolutely necessary that the senate should be so formed, as to be unbiassed by false conceptions of the real interests, or undue attachment to the apparent good of their several states.

Gentlemen indulge too many unreasonable apprehensions of danger to the state governments—They seem to suppose, that the moment you put men into the national council, they become corrupt and tyrannical, and lose all their affection for their fellow-citizens. But can we imagine that the senators will ever be so insensible of their own advantage, as to sacrifice the genuine interest of their constituents? The state governments are essentially necessary to the form and spirit of the general system. As long, therefore, as Congress have a full conviction of this necessity, they must, even upon principles purely national, have as firm an attachment to the one as to the other. This conviction can never leave them, unless they become madmen. While the constitution continues to be read, and its principles known, the states must, by every rational man, be considered as essential component parts of the union; and therefore the idea of sacrificing the former to the latter is totally inadmissible.

The objectors do not advert to the natural strength and resources of the state governments, which will ever give them an important superiority over the general government. If we compare the nature of their different powers, or the means of popular influence which each possesses, we shall find the advantage entirely on the side of the states. This consideration, important as it is, seems to have been little attended to. The aggregate number of representatives throughout the states may be two thousand. Their personal influence will therefore be proportionably more extensive than that of one or two hundred men in Congress. The state establishments of civil and military officers of every description, infinitely surpassing in number any possible correspondent establishments in the general government, will create such an extent and complication of attachments, as will ever secure the predilection and support of the people. Whenever, therefore, Congress shall meditate any infringement of the state constitutions, the great body of the people will naturally take part with their domestic representatives. Can the general government withstand such a united opposition? Will the people suffer themselves to be stripped of their privileges? Will they suffer their legislatures to be reduced to a shadow and a name? The idea is shocking to common sense.

From the circumstances already explained, and many others which might be mentioned, results a complicated, irresistable check, which must ever support the existence and importance of the state governments. The danger, if any exists, flows from an opposite source.—The probable evil is, that the general government will be too dependent on the state legislatures, too much governed by their prejudices, and too obsequious to their humours; that the states, with every power in their hands, will make encroachments on the national authority, till the union is weakened and dissolved.

Every member must have been struck with an observation of a gentleman from Albany. Do what you will, says he, local prejudices and opinions will go into the government. What! shall we then form a constitution to cherish and strengthen these prejudices? Shall we confirm the distemper instead of remedying it? It is undeniable that there must be a controul somewhere. Either the general interest is to controul the particular interests, or the contrary. If the former, then certainly the government ought to be so framed, as to render the power of controul efficient to all intents and purposes; if the latter, a striking absurdity follows: The controuling powers must be as numerous as the varying interests, and the operations of government must therefore cease: For the moment you accommodate these differing interests, which is the only way to set the government in motion, you establish a general controuling power. Thus, whatever constitutional provisions are made to the contrary, every government will be at last driven to the necessity of subjecting the partial to the universal interest. The gentlemen ought always, in their reasoning, to distinguish between the real, genuine good of a state, and the opinions and prejudices which may prevail respecting it:

The latter may be opposed to the general good, and consequently ought to be sacrificed; the former is so involved in it, that it never can be sacrificed. Sir, the main design of the convention, in forming the senate, was to prevent fluctuations and cabals: With this view, they made that body small, and to exist for a considerable period. Have they executed this design too far? The Senators are to serve six years. This is only two years longer than the senators of this state hold their places. One third of the members are to go out every two years; and in six, the whole body may be changed. Prior to the revolution, the representatives in the several colonies were elected for different periods; for three years, for seven years, &c. Were those bodies ever considered as incapable of representing the people, or as too independent of them? There is one circumstance which will have a tendency to increase the dependence of the senators on the states, in proportion to the duration of their appointments. As the state legislatures are in continual fluctuation, the senator will have more attachments to form, and consequently a greater difficulty of maintaining his place, than one of shorter duration. He will therefore be more cautious and industrious to suit his conduct to the wishes of his constituents.

Sir, when you take a view of all the circumstances which have been recited, you will certainly see, that the senators will constantly look up to the state governments, with an eye of dependence and affection. If they are ambitious to continue in office, they will make every prudent arrangement for this purpose, and, whatever may be their private sentiments of politics, they will be convinced, that the surest means of obtaining a re-election will be a uniform attachment to the interests of their several states.

The gentlemen to support their amendment have observed that the power of recall, under the old government, has never been exercised. There is no reasoning from this. The experience of a few years, under peculiar circumstances, can afford no probable security that it never will be carried into execution, with unhappy effects. A seat in congress has been less an object of ambition; and the arts of intrigue, consequently, have been less practised. Indeed, it has been difficult to find men, who were willing to suffer the mortifications, to which so feeble a government and so dependent a station exposed them.

Sir, if you consider but a moment the purposes, for which the senate was instituted, and the nature of the business which they are to transact, you will see the necessity of giving them duration. They, together with the President, are to manage all our concerns with foreign nations: They must understand all their interests, and their political systems. This knowledge is not soon acquired—But a very small part is gained in the closet. Is it desirable then that new and unqualified members should be continually thrown into that body? When public bodies are engaged in the exercise of general powers, you cannot judge of the propriety of their conduct, but from the result of their systems. They may be forming plans, which require time and diligence to bring to maturity. It is necessary, therefore, that they should have a considerable and fixed duration, that they may make their calculations accordingly. If they are to be perpetually fluctuating, they can never have that responsibility which is so important in republican governments. In bodies subject to frequent changes, great political plans must be conducted by members in succession: A single assembly can have but a partial agency in them, and consequently cannot properly be answerable for the final event. Considering the senate therefore with a view to responsibility, duration is a very interesting and essential quality. There is another view, in which duration in the senate appears necessary. A government, changeable in its policy, must soon lose its sense of national character, and forfeit the respect of foreigners—Senators will not be solicitous for the reputation of public measures, in which they have had but a temporary concern, and will feel lightly the burthen of public disapprobation, in proportion to the number of those who partake of the censure. Our political rivals will ever consider our mutable counsels as evidence of deficient wisdom, and will be little apprehensive of our arriving at any exalted station in the scale of power. Such are the internal and external disadvantages which would result from the principle contended for. Were it admitted, I am firmly persuaded, Sir, that prejudices would govern the public deliberations, and passions rage in the counsels of the union. If it were necessary, I could illustrate my subject by historical facts: I could travel through an extensive field of detail, and demonstrate that wherever the fatal principle of—the head suffering the controul of the members, has operated, it has proved a fruitful source of commotions and disorder.

This, Sir, is the first fair opportunity that has been offered, of deliberately correcting the errors in government. Instability has been a prominent and very defective feature in most republican systems.—It is the first to be seen, and the last to be lamented by a philosophical enquirer. It has operated most banefully in our infant republics. It is necessary that we apply an immediate remedy, and eradicate the poisonous principle from our government. If this be not done, Sir, we shall feel, and posterity will be convulsed by a painful malady.

Melancton Smith and Alexander Hamilton
Debate Rotation in the Senate

Mr. *Smith* resumed his argument as follows. The amendment embraces two objects: First, that the senators shall be eligible for only six years in any term of twelve years; Second, that they shall be subject to the recall of the legislatures of their several states. It is proper that we take up these points separately. I concur with the honorable gentleman, that there is a necessity for giving this branch a greater stability than the house of representatives. I think his reasons are conclusive on this point. But, Sir, it does not follow from this position that the senators ought to hold their places during life. Declaring them ineligible during a certain term after six years, is far from rendering them less stable than is necessary. We think the amendment will place the senate in a proper medium between a fluctuating and a perpetual body. As the clause now stands, there is no doubt that the senators will hold their office perpetually; and in this situation, they must of necessity lose their dependence and attachment to the people. It is certainly inconsistent with the established principles of republicanism, that the senate should be a fixed and unchangeable body of men. There should be then some constitutional provision against this evil. A rotation I consider as the best possible mode of affecting a remedy. The amendment will not only have a tendency to defeat any plots, which may be formed against the liberty and authority of the state governments, but will be the best means to extinguish the factions which often prevail, and which are sometimes so fatal in legislative bodies. This appears to me an important consideration. We have generally found, that perpetual bodies have either combined in some scheme of usurpation, or have been torn and distracted with cabals—Both have been the source of misfortunes to the state. Most people acquainted with history will acknowledge these facts. Our Congress would have been a fine field for party spirit to act in—That body would undoubtedly have suffered all the evils of faction, had it not been secured by the rotation established by the articles of the confederation. I think a rotation in the government is a very important and truly republican institution. All good republicans, I presume to say will treat it with respect.

It is a circumstance strongly in favor of rotation, that it will have a tendency to diffuse a more general spirit of emulation, and to bring forward into office the genius and abilities of the continent—The ambition of gaining the qualifications necessary to govern, will be in some proportion to the chance of success. If the office is to be perpetually confined to a few, other men of equal talents and virtue, but not possessed of so extensive an influence, may be discouraged from aspiring to it. The more perfectly we are versed in the political science, the more firmly will the happy principles of republicanism be supported. The true policy of constitutions will be to increase the information of the country, and disseminate the knowledge of government as universally as possible. If this be done, we shall have, in any dangerous emergency, a numerous body of enlightened citizens, ready for the call of their country. As the constitution now is, you only give an opportunity to two men to be acquainted with the public affairs. It is a maxim with me, that every man employed in a high office by the people, should from time to time return to them, that he may be in a situation to satisfy them with respect to his conduct and the measures of administration. If I recollect right, it was observed by an honorable member from New York, that this amendment would be an infringement of the natural rights of the people. I humbly conceive, if the gentleman reflects maturely on the nature of his argument, he will acknowledge its weakness. What is government itself, but a restraint upon the natural rights of the people? What constitution was ever devised, that did not operate as a restraint on their original liberties? What is the whole system of qualifications, which take place in all free governments, but a restraint? Why is a certain age made necessary? Why a certain term of citizenship? This constitution itself, Sir, has restraints innumerable.—The amendment, it is true, may exclude two of the best men: but it can rarely happen, that the state will sustain any material loss by this. I hope and believe that we shall always have more than two men, who are capable of discharging the duty of a senator. But if it should so happen that the state possessed only two capable men, it will be necessary that they should return home, from time to time, to inspect and regulate our domestic affairs. I do not conceive that the state can suffer any inconvenience. The argument indeed might have some weight were the representation very large: But as the power is to be exercised upon only two men, the apprehensions of the gentlemen are entirely without foundation.

With respect to the second part of the amendment, I would observe that as the senators are the representatives of the state legislatures, it is reasonable and proper that they should be under their controul. When a state sends an agent commissioned to transact any business, or perform any service, it certainly ought to have a power to recall him. These are plain principles, and so far as they apply to the case under examination, they ought to be adopted by us. Form this government as you please, you must at all events lodge in it very important powers: These powers must be in the hands of a few men, so situated as to produce a small degree of responsibility. These circumstances ought to put us upon our guard; and the inconvenience of this necessary delegation of power should be corrected, by providing some suitable checks.

Against this part of the amendment a great deal of argument has been used, and with considerable plausibility. It is said if the amendment takes place, the senators will hold their office only during the pleasure of the state legislatures, and consequently will not possess the necessary firmness and stability. I conceive, Sir, there is a fallacy in this argument, founded upon the suspicion that the legislature of a state will possess the qualities of a mob, and be incapable of any regular conduct. I know that the impulses of the multitude are inconsistent with systematic government. The people are frequently incompetent to deliberate discussion, and subject to errors and imprudencies. Is this the complexion of the state legislatures? I presume it is not. I presume that they are never actuated by blind impulses—that they rarely do things hastily and without consideration. My apprehension is that the power of recall would not be exercised as often as it ought. It is highly improbable that a man, in whom the state has confided, and

who has an established influence, will be recalled, unless his
conduct has been notoriously wicked.—The arguments of the
gentleman therefore, do not apply in this case. It is further
observed, that it would be improper to give the legislatures
this power, because the local interests and prejudices of the
states ought not to be admitted into the general government;
and that if the senator is rendered too independent on his
constituents, he will sacrifice the interests of the Union to the
policy of his state. Sir, the senate has been generally held up
by all parties as a safe guard to the rights of the several states.
In this view, the clossest connection between them has been
considered as necessary. But now it seems we speak a different
language—We now look upon the least attachment to their
states as dangerous—We are now for separating them, and
rendering them entirely independent, that we may root out
the last vestige of state sovereignty.

An honorable gentleman from New-York observed yesterday, that the states would always maintain their importance
and authority, on account of their superior influence over the
people. To prove this influence, he mentioned the aggregate
number of the state representatives throughout the continent.
But I ask him, how long the people will retain their confidence for two thousand representatives, who shall meet once
in a year to make laws for regulating the heighth of your
fences and the repairing of your roads? Will they not by and
by be saying,—Here, we are paying a great number of men
for doing nothing: We had better give up all the civil business
of our state with its powers to congress, who are sitting all
the year round: We had better get rid of the useless burthen.
That matters will come to this at last, I have no more doubt
than I have of my existence. The state governments, without
object or authority, will soon dwindle into insignificance, and
be despised by the people themselves. I am, sir, at a loss to
know how the state legislatures will spend their time. Will
they make laws to regulate agriculture? I imagine this will be
best regulated by the sagacity and industry of those who prac-
tise it. Another reason offered by the gentleman is, that the
states will have a greater number of officers than the general
government. I doubt this. Let us make a comparison. In the
first place, the federal government must have a compleat set of

judicial officers of different ranks throughout the continent: Then, a numerous train of executive officers, in all the branches of the revenue, both internal and external, and all the civil and military departments. Add to this, their salaries will probably be larger and better secured than those of any state officers. If these numerous offices are not at once established, they are in the power of congress, and will all in time be created. Very few offices will be objects of ambition in the states. They will have no establishments at all to correspond with some of those I have mentioned—In other branches, they will have the same as congress. But I ask, what will be their comparative influence and importance? I will leave it, sir, to any man of candour, to determine whether there will not probably be more lucrative and honorable places in the gift of congress than in the disposal of the states all together. But the whole reasoning of the gentlemen rests upon the principle that the states will be able to check the general government, by exciting the people to opposition: It only goes to prove, that the state officers will have such an influence over the people, as to impell them to hostility and rebellion. This kind of check, I contend, would be a pernicious one; and certainly ought to be prevented. Checks in government ought to act silently, and without public commotion. I think that the harmony of the two powers should by all means be maintained: If it be not, the operation of government will be baneful— One or the other of the parties must finally be destroyed in the conflict. The constitutional line between the authority of each should be so obvious, as to leave no room for jealous apprehensions or violent contests.

It is further said, that the operation of local interests should be counteracted; for which purpose, the senate should be rendered permanent. I conceive that the true interest of every state is the interest of the whole; and that if we should have a well regulated government, this idea will prevail. We shall indeed have few local interests to pursue, under the new constitution: because it limits the claims of the states by so close a line, that on their part there can be little dispute, and little worth disputing about. But, sir, I conceive that partial interests will grow continually weaker, because there are not those fundamental differences between the real interests of the several states, which will long prevent their coming together and becoming uniform.

Another argument advanced by the gentlemen is, that our amendment would be the means of producing factions among the electors: That aspiring men would misrepresent the conduct of a faithful senator; and by intrigue, procure a recall, upon false grounds, in order to make room for themselves. But, sir, men who are ambitious for places will rarely be disposed to render those places unstable. A truly ambitious man will never do this, unless he is mad. It is not to be supported that a state will recall a man once in twenty years, to make way for another. Dangers of this kind are very remote: I think they ought not to be brought seriously into view.

More than one of the gentlemen have ridiculed my apprehensions of corruption. How, say they, are the people to be corrupted? By their own money? Sir, in many countries, the people pay money to corrupt themselves: why should it not happen in this? Certainly, the congress will be as liable to corruption as other bodies of men. Have they not the same frailties, and the same temptations? With respect to the corruption arising from the disposal of offices, the gentlemen have treated the argument as insignificant. But let any one make a calculation, and see whether there will not be good offices enough, to dispose of to every man who goes there, who will then freely resign his seat: for, can any one suppose, that a member of congress would not go out and relinquish his four dollars a day, for two, or three thousand pounds a year? It is here objected than no man can hold an office created during the time he is in Congress—But it will be easy for a man of influence, who has in his eye a favorite office previously created and already filled, to say to his friend, who holds it—Here—I will procure you another place of more emolument, provided you will relinquish yours in favor of me. The constitution appears to be a restraint, when in fact it is none at all. I presume, sir, there is not a government in the world in which there is a greater scope for influence and corruption in the disposal of offices. Sir, I will not declaim, and say all men are dishonest; but I think that, in forming a constitution, if we presume this, we shall be on the safest side. This extreme is certainly less dangerous than the other. It is wise to multiply checks to a greater degree than the present state of things requires. It is said that corruption has never taken place under the old government—I believe, gentlemen hazard this assertion without proofs. That it has taken place in some degree is very probable. Many millions of money have been put into the hands of government, which have never yet been accounted for: The accounts are not yet settled, and Heaven only knows when they will be.

I have frequently observed a restraint upon the state governments, which Congress never can be under, construct that body as you please. It is a truth, capable of demonstration, that the nearer the representative is to his constituent, the more attached and dependent he will be—In the states, the elections are frequent, and the representatives numerous: They transact business in the midst of their constituents, and every man may be called upon to account for his conduct. In this state the council of appointment are elected for one year.—The proposed constitution establishes a council of appointment who will be perpetual—Is there any comparison between the two governments in point of security? It is said that the governor of this state is always eligible: But this is not in point. The governor of this state is limited in his powers—Indeed his authority is small and insignificant, compared to that of the senate of the United States.

The Hon. Mr. *Hamilton*. Mr. Chairman, in debates of this kind it is extremely easy, on either side, to say a great number of plausible things. It is to be acknowledged, that there is even a certain degree of truth in the reasonings on both sides. In this situation, it is the province of judgment and good sense to determine their force and application, and how far the arguments advanced on one side, are balanced by those on the other. The ingenious dress, in which both may appear, renders it a difficult task to make this decision, and the mind is frequently unable to come to a safe and solid conclusion. On the present question, some of the principles on each side are admitted, and the conclusions drawn from them denied, while other principles, with their inferences, are rejected altogether. It is the business of the committee to seek the truth in this labyrinth of argument.

There are two objects in forming systems of government—
Safety for the people, and energy in the administration. When
these objects are united, the certain tendency of the system
will be to the public welfare. If the latter object be neglected,
the people's security will be as certainly sacrificed, as by disregarding the former. Good constitutions are formed upon a
comparison of the liberty of the individual with the strength
of government: If the tone of either be too high, the other
will be weakened too much. It is the happiest possible mode
of conciliating these objects, to institute one branch peculiarly
endowed with sensibility, another with knowledge and firmness. Through the opposition and mutual controul of these
bodies, the government will reach, in its regular operations,
the perfect balance between liberty and power. The arguments of the gentlemen chiefly apply to the former branch—
the house of representatives. If they will calmly consider the
different nature of the two branches, they will see that the
reasoning which justly applies to the representative house,
will go to destroy the essential qualities of the senate. If the
former is calculated perfectly upon the principles of caution,
why should you impose the same principles upon the latter,
which is designed for a different operation? Gentlemen, while
they discover a laudable anxiety for the safety of the people,
do not attend to the important distinction I have drawn. We
have it constantly held up to us, that as it is our chief duty to
guard against tyranny, it is our policy to form all the branches
of government for this purpose. Sir, it is a truth sufficiently
illustrated by experience, that when the people act by their
representatives, they are commonly irresistable. The gentleman admits the position, that stability is essential to the government, and yet enforces principles, which if true, ought to
banish stability from the system. The gentleman observes that
there is a fallacy in my reasoning, and informs us that the
legislatures of the states—not the people, are to appoint the
senators. Does he reflect, that they are the immediate agents
of the people; that they are so constituted, as to feel all their
prejudices and passions, and to be governed, in a great degree, by their misapprehensions? Experience must have taught
him the truth of this. Look through their history. What factions have arisen from the most trifling causes? What in-

trigues have been practised for the most illiberal purposes? Is not the state of Rhode-Island, at this moment, struggling under difficulties and distresses, for having been led blindly by the spirit of the multitude? What is her legislature but the picture of a mob? In this state we have a senate, possessed of the proper qualities of a permanent body: Virginia, Maryland, and a few other states, are in the same situation: The rest are either governed by a single democratic assembly, or have a senate constituted entirely upon democratic principles— These have been more or less embroiled in factions, and have generally been the image and echo of the multitude. It is difficult to reason on this point, without touching on certain delicate cords. I could refer you to periods and conjunctures, when the people have been governed by improper passions, and led by factious and designing men. I could shew that the same passions have infected their representatives. Let us beware that we do not make the state legislatures a vehicle, in which the evil humors may be conveyed into the national system. To prevent this, it is necessary that the senate should be so formed, as in some measure to check the state government, and preclude the communication of the false impressions which they receive from the people. It has been often repeated, that the legislatures of the states can have only a partial and confined view of national affairs; that they can form no proper estimate of great objects which are not in the sphere of their interests. The observation of the gentleman therefore cannot take off the force of my argument.

Sir, the senators will constantly be attended with a reflection, that their future existence is absolutely in the power of the states. Will not this form a powerful check? It is a reflection which applies closely to their feelings and interests; and no candid man, who thinks deliberately, will deny that it would be alone a sufficient check. The legislatures are to provide the mode of electing the President, and must have a great influence over the electors. Indeed they convey their influence, through a thousand channels, into the general government. Gentlemen have endeavoured to shew that there will be no clashing of local and general interests—They do not seem to have sufficiently considered the subject. We have in this state a duty of six pence per pound on salt, and it operates lightly and with advantage: But such a duty would be very burthensome to some of the states. If Congress should, at any time, find it convenient to impose a salt tax, would it not be opposed by the eastern states? Being themselves incapable of feeling the necessity of the measure, they could only feel its apparent injustice. Would it be wise to give the New-England States a power to defeat this measure by recalling their senators who may be engaged for it? I beg the gentlemen once more to attend to the distinction between the real and apparent interests of the states. I admit that the aggregate of individuals constitutes the government—yet every state is not the government: Every petty district is not the government.— Sir, in our state legislatures, a compromise is frequently necessary between the interests of counties: The same must happen in the general government between states. In this, the few must yield to the many; or, in other words, the particular must be sacrificed to the general interest. If the members of Congress are too dependent on the state legislatures, they will be eternally forming secret combinations from local views. This is reasoning from the plainest principles.—Their interest is interwoven with their dependence, and they will necessarily yield to the impression of their situation. Those who have been in Congress have seen these operations. The first question has been—How will such a measure affect my constituents, and consequently, how will the part I take affect my re-election? This consideration may be in some degree proper; but to be dependent from day to day, and to have the idea perpetually present would be the source of innumerable evils. Six years, sir, is a period short enough for a proper degree of dependence. Let us consider the peculiar state of this body, and see under what impressions they will act. One third of them are to go out at the end of two years; two thirds at four years, and the whole at six years. When one year is elapsed, there is a number who are to hold their places for one year, others for three, and others for five years. Thus, there will not only be a constant and frequent change of members; but there will be some whose office is near the point of expiration, and who from this circumstance, will have a lively sense of their dependence. The biennial change of members is an excellent invention for increasing the difficulty of combination. Any scheme of usurpation will lose, every two years, a number of its oldest advocates, and their places will be supplied by an equal number of new, unaccommodating and virtuous men. When two principles are equally important, we ought if possible to reconcile them, and sacrifice neither. We think that safety and permanency in this government are completely reconcileable. The state governments will have, from the causes I have described, a sufficient influence over the senate, without the check for which the gentlemen contend.

It has been remarked that there is an inconsistency in our admitting that the equal vote in the senate was given to secure the rights of the states, and at the same time holding up the idea, that their interests should be sacrificed to those of the union. But the committee certainly perceive the distinction between the rights of a state and its interests. The rights of a state are defined by the constitution, and cannot be invaded without a violation of it; but the interests of a state have no connection with the constitution, and may be in a thousand instances constitutionally sacrificed. A uniform tax is perfectly constitutional; and yet it may operate oppressively upon certain members of the union. The gentlemen are afraid that the state governments will be abolished. But, Sir, their existence does not depend upon the laws of the United States. Congress can no more abolish the state governments, than they can dissolve the union. The whole constitution is repugnant to it, and yet the gentlemen would introduce an additional useless provision against it. It is proper that the influence of the states should prevail to a certain extent. But shall the individual states be the judges how far? Shall an unlimited power be left them to determine in their own favor? The gentlemen go into the extreme: Instead of a wise government, they would form a fantastical Utopia: But, Sir, while they give it a plausible, popular shape, they would render it impracticable. Much has been said about factions. As far as my observation has extended, factions in Congress have arisen from attachment to state prejudices. We are attempting by this constitution to abolish factions, and to unite all parties for the general welfare.—That a man should have the power, in private life, of recalling his agent, is proper; because in the business in which he is engaged, he has no other object but to gain the approbation of his principal. Is this the case with the senator? Is he simply the agent of the state? No: He is an agent for the union, and he is bound to perform services necessary to the good of the whole, though his state should condemn them.

Sir, in contending for a rotation, the gentlemen carry their zeal beyond all reasonable bounds. I am convinced that no government, founded on this feeble principle, can operate well. I believe also that we shall be singular in this proposal. We have not felt the embarassments resulting from rotation, that other states have; and we hardly know the strength of their objections to it. There is no probability that we shall ever persuade a majority of the states to agree to this amendment. The gentlemen deceive themselves—The amendment would defeat their own design. When a man knows he must quit his station, let his merit be what it may; he will turn his attention chiefly to his own emolument: Nay, he will feel temptations, which few other situations furnish; to perpetuate his power by unconstitutional usurpations. Men will pursue their interests—It is as easy to change human nature, as to oppose the strong current of the selfish passions. A wise legislator will gently divert the channel, and direct it, if possible, to the public good.

It has been observed, that it is not possible there should be in a state only two men qualified for senators. But, sir, the question is not, whether there may be no more than two men; but whether, in certain emergencies, you could find two equal to those whom the amendment would discard. Important negociations, or other business to which they shall be most competent, may employ them, at the moment of their removal. These things often happen. The difficulty of obtaining men, capable of conducting the affairs of a nation in dangerous times, is much more serious than the gentlemen imagine.

As to corruption, sir, admitting in the president a disposition to corrupt; what are the instruments of bribery? It is said, he will have in his disposal a great number of offices: But how many offices are there, for which a man would relinquish the senatorial dignity? There may be some in the judicial, and some in the other principal departments: But there are very few, whose respectability can in any measure balance that of the office of senator. Men who have been in the senate once, and who have a reasonable hope of a re-election, will not be easily bought by offices. This reasoning shews that a rotation would be productive of many disadvantages—Under particular circumstances, it might be extremely inconvenient, if not fatal to the prosperity of our country.

Melancton Smith Fears the Federal Taxing Power and the Capacity of Any Free Government to Rule So Vast a Nation

June 27, 1788

The hon. Mr. *Smith* rose.—We are now come to a part of the system, which requires our utmost attention, and most careful investigation. It is necessary that the powers vested in government should be precisely defined, that the people may be able to know whether it moves in the circle of the constitution. It is the more necessary in governments like the one under examination; because Congress here is to be considered as only part of a complex system. The state governments are necessary for certain local purposes; The general government for national purposes: The latter ought to rest on the former, not only in its form, but in its operations. It is therefore of the highest importance, that the line of jurisdiction should be accurately drawn: It is necessary, sir, in order to maintain harmony between the governments, and to prevent the constant interference which must either be the cause of perpetual differences, or oblige one to yield, perhaps unjustly, to the other. I conceive the system cannot operate well, unless it is so contrived, as to preserve harmony. If this be not done, in every contest, the weak must submit to the strong. The clause before us is of the greatest importance: It respects the very vital principle of government: The power is the most efficient and comprehensive that can be delegated; and seems in some measure to answer for all others. I believe it will appear evident, that money must be raised for the support of both governments: If therefore you give to one or the other, a power which may in its operation become exclusive; it is obvious, that one can exist only at the will of the other; and must ultimately be sacrificed. The powers of the general government extend to the raising of money, in all possible ways, except by duties on exports; to the laying taxes on imports, lands, buildings, and even on persons. The individual states in

816

time will be allowed to raise no money at all: The United States will have a right to raise money from every quarter. The general government has moreover this advantage. All disputes relative to jurisdiction must be decided in a federal court.

It is a general maxim, that all governments find a use for as much money as they can raise. Indeed they have commonly demands for more: Hence it is, that all, as far as we are acquainted, are in debt. I take this to be a settled truth, that they will all spend as much as their revenue; that is, will live at least up to their income. Congress will ever exercise their powers, to levy as much money as the people can pay. They will not be restrained from direct taxes, by the consideration that necessity does not require them. If they forbear, it will be because the people cannot answer their demands. There will be no possibility of preventing the clashing of jurisdictions, unless some system of accomodation is formed. Suppose taxes are laid by both governments on the same article: It seems to me impossible, that they can operate with harmony. I have no more conception that in taxation two powers can act together; than that two bodies can occupy the same place. They will therefore not only interfere; but they will be hostile to each other. Here are to be two lists of all kinds of officers—supervisors, assessors, constables, &c. imployed in this business. It is unnecessary that I should enter into a minute detail, to prove that these complex powers cannot operate peaceably together, and without one being overpowered by the other. One day, the continental collector calls for the tax; He seizes a horse: The next day, the state collector comes, procures a replevin and retakes the horse, to satisfy the state tax. I just mention this, to shew that people will not submit to such a government, and that finally it must defeat itself.

It must appear evident, that there will be a constant jarring of claims and interests. Now will the states in this contest stand any chance of success? If they will, there is less necessity for our amendment. But, consider the superior advantages of the general government: Consider their extensive, exclusive revenues; the vast sums of money they can command, and the means they thereby possess of supporting a powerful standing force. The states, on the contrary, will not have the command of a shilling, or a soldier. The two governments will be like two men contending for a certain property: The one has no interest but that which is the subject of the controversy; while the other has money enough to carry on the law-suit for twenty years. By this clause unlimited powers in taxation are given: Another clause declares, that Congress shall have power to make all laws necessary to carry the constitution into effect. Nothing therefore is left to construction; but the powers are most express. How far the state legislature will be able to command a revenue, every man, on viewing the subject, can determine. If he contemplates the ordinary operation of causes, he will be convinced that the powers of the confederacy will swallow up those of the members. I do not suppose that this effect will be brought about suddenly—As long as the people feel universally and strongly attached to the state governments, Congress will not be able to accomplish it: If they act prudently, their powers will operate and be increased by degrees. The tendency of taxation, tho' it be moderate, is to lessen the attachment of the citizens—If it becomes oppressive, it will certainly destroy their confidence. While the general taxes are sufficiently heavy, every attempt of the states to enhance them, will be considered as a tyrannical act, and the people will lose their respect and affection for a government, which cannot support itself, without the most grievous impositions upon them. If the constitution is accepted as it stands, I am convinced, that in seven years as much will be laid against the state governments, as is now said in favour of the proposed system.

Sir, I contemplate the abolition of the state constitutions as an event fatal to the liberties of America. These liberties will not be violently wrested from the people; they will be undermined and gradually consumed. On subjects of this kind we cannot be too critical. The investigation is difficult, because we have no examples to serve as guides. The world has never seen such a government over such a country. If we consult authorities in this matter, they will declare the impracticability of governing a free people, on such an extensive plan. In a country, where a portion of the people live more than twelve hundred miles from the center, I think that one body cannot possibly legislate for the whole. Can the legislature frame a system of taxation that will operate with uniform advantages? Can they carry any system into execution? Will it not give occasion for an innumerable swarm of officers, to infest our country and consume our substance? People will be subject to impositions, which they cannot support, and of which their complaints can never reach the government.

Another idea is in my mind, which I think conclusive against a simple government for the United States. It is not possible to collect a set of representatives, who are acquainted with all parts of the continent. Can you find men in Georgia who are acquainted with the situation of New-Hampshire? Who know what taxes will best suit the inhabitants; and how much they are able to bear? Can the best men make laws for a people of whom they are entirely ignorant? Sir, we have no reason to hold our state governments in contempt, or to suppose them incapable of acting wisely. I believe they have operated more beneficially than most people expected, who considered that those governments were erected in a time of war and confusion, when they were very liable to errors in their structure. It will be a matter of astonishment to all unprejudiced men hereafter, who shall reflect upon our situation, to observe to what a great degree good government has prevailed. It is true some bad laws have been passed in most of the states; but they arose more from the difficulty of the times, than from any want of honesty or wisdom. Perhaps there never was a government, which in the course of ten years did not do something to be repented of. As for Rhode-Island, I do not mean to justify her—She deserves to be condemned—If there were in the world but one example of political depravity, it would be her's: And no nation ever merited or suffered a more genuine infamy, than a wicked administration has attached to her character. Massachusetts also has been guilty of errors: and has lately been distracted by an internal convulsion. Great-Britain, notwithstanding her boasted constitution, has been a perpetual scene of revolutions and civil war—Her parliaments have been abolished; her kings have been banished and murdered. I assert that the majority of the governments in the union have operated better than any body had reason to expect: and that nothing but experience and habit is wanting, to give the state laws all the stability and wisdom necessary to make them respectable. If these things be true, I think we ought not to exchange our condition, with a hazard of losing our state constitutions. We all agree that a general government is necessary: But it ought not to go so far, as to destroy the authority of the members. We shall be unwise, to make a new experiment in so important a matter, without some known and sure grounds to go upon. The state constitutions should be the guardians of our domestic rights and interests; and should be both the support and the check of the federal government. The want of the means of raising a general revenue has been the principal cause of our difficulties. I believe no man will doubt that if our present Congress had money enough, there would be few complaints of their weakness. Requisitions have perhaps been too much condemned. What has been their actual operation? Let us attend to experience, and see if they are such poor, unproductive things, as is commonly supposed. If I calculate right, the requisitions for the ten years past, have amounted to thirty-six millions of dollars; of which twenty-four millions, or two thirds, have been actually paid. Does not this fact warrant a conclusion that some reliance is to be placed on this mode? Besides, will any gentleman say that the states have generally been able to collect more than two thirds of their taxes from the people? The delinquency of some states has arisen from the fluctuations of paper money, &c. Indeed it is my decided opinion, that no government in the difficult circumstances, which we have passed thro', will be able to realize more than two thirds of the taxes it imposes. I might suggest two other considerations which have weight with me—There has probably been more money called for, than was actually wanted, on the expectation of delinquencies; and it is equally probable, that in a short course of time the increasing ability of the country will render requisitions a much more efficient mode of raising a revenue. The war left the people under very great burthens, and oppressed with both public and private debts. They are now fast emerging from their difficulties. Many individuals without doubt still feel great inconveniences; but they will find a gradual remedy. Sir, has any country which has suffered distresses like ours, exhibited within a few years, more striking marks of improvement and prosperity? How its population has grown; How its agriculture, commerce and manufactures have been extended and improved! How many forests have been cut down; How many wastes have been cleared and cultivated; How many additions have been made to the extent and beauty of our towns and cities! I think our advancement has been rapid. In a few years, it is to be hoped, that we shall be relieved from our embarrassments; and unless new, calamities come upon us, shall be flourishing and happy. Some difficulties will ever occur in the collection of taxes by any mode whatever. Some states will pay more; some less. If New-York lays a tax, will not one county or district furnish more, another less than its proportion? The same will happen to the United States, as happens in New-York, and in every other country.—Let them impose a duty equal and uniform—those districts, where there is plenty of money, will pay punctually: Those, in which money is scarce, will be in some measure delinquent. The idea that Congress ought to have unlimited powers, is entirely novel; I never heard of it, till the meeting of this convention. The general government once called on the states, to invest them with the command of funds adequate to the exigencies of the union: but they did not ask to command all the resources of the states—They did not wish to have a controul over all the property of the people. If we now give them this controul, we may as well give up the state governments with it. I have no notion of setting the two powers at variance; nor would I give a farthing for a government, which could not command a farthing. On the whole, it appears to me probable, that unless some certain, specific source of revenue is reserved to the states, their governments, with their independence will be totally annihilated.

Melancton Smith Writes to Nathan Dane, Reconsidering His Position on Ratification and Amendments

Poughkeepsie, N.Y., June 28, 1788

Dear Sir

I am favoured with yours of the 24th Inst—The accession of New Hampshire will have no other effect upon our convention, than softning them to consider what is proper to be done, in the present situation of things, if it has that—Indeed I can scarcely perceive any effect it has had—And the most I fear is that there will not be a sufficient degree of moderation in some of our most influential men, calmly to consider the circumstances in which we are, and to accommodate our decisions to those circumstances—You have had too much experience in public life not to know, that pride, passion, and interested motive, have great influence in all public bodies— They no doubt have their influence in this—From my own situation, perhaps, more than from any better principle, I feel none of these, except, it is probable, a wish to support the party with whom I am connected as far as is consistent with propriety—But, I know, my great object is, to procure such amendments in this government, as to prevent its attaining the ends, for which it appears to me, and to you calculated—I am therefore very anxious to procure good amendments—I had rather recommend substantial amendments, than adopt it conditionally with unimportant ones, leaving our critical situation out of the question—I do not find these endeavors sufficiently seconded—The principal labor of managing the Controversy lies upon me—hitherto the amendments proposed are substantial, they will continue so—but as no question is taken on any, it is questionable whether, the most important will not be yielded, under the Idea of making previous conditional amendments—When I am persuaded, if we can agree, to make the condition, a subsequent one, that is, to take place in one or two years after adoption or the

822

ratification to become void, we can accommodate with the advocates of the constitution far more substantial amendmt—

I inclose you the amendments as far as they have been offered—The last has been the subject of two days debate —and will take some days more—Mr. Hamilton and the Chancellor have spoken largely in favour of the Article—Mr Lansing and myself have advocated the amendment—The speech published for the Chancellor is the substance of what he delivered—He and I have come in contact several times— but he has ceased hostilities—He is a wretched reasoner, very frequently—

Hamilton is the champion, he speaks frequently, very long and very vehemently—has, like publius, much to say not very applicable to the subject—I wish you to communicate any observations you may think useful.

Alexander Hamilton Discusses Federal Taxation and Denies That His Views Are Influenced by Personal Ambition

June 28, 1788

Mr. *Hamilton*. The honorable gentleman from Ulster has given a turn to the introduction of those papers, which was never in our contemplation. He seems to insinuate that they were brought forward, with a view of shewing an inconsistency in the conduct of some gentlemen—perhaps of himself. Sir, the exhibition of them had a very different object. It was to prove that this state once experienced hardships and distresses to an astonishing degree, for want of the assistance of the other states. It was to shew the evils we suffered since, as well as before the establishment of the confederation, from being compelled to support the burthen of the war; That requisitions have been unable to call forth the resources of the country; That requisitions have been the cause of a principal part of our calamities; that the system is defective and rotten, and ought forever to be banished from our government. It was necessary, with deference to the honorable gentleman, to bring forward these important proofs of our argument, without consulting the feelings of any man.

That the human passion should flow from one extreme to another, I allow is natural.—Hence the mad project of creating a dictator.—But it is equally true, that this project was never ripened into a deliberate and extensive design. When I heard of it, it met my instant disapprobation. The honorable gentleman's opposition too is known and applauded. But why bring these things into remembrance? Why affect to compare this temporary effusion with the serious sentiments our fellow citizens entertained of the national weaknesses? The gentleman has made a declaration of his wishes for a strong federal government. I hope this is the wish of all. But why has he not given us his ideas of the nature of this government, which is the object of his wishes? Why does he not describe it? We

824

have proposed a system, which we supposed would answer the purposes of strength and safety—The gentleman objects to it, without pointing out the grounds, on which his objections are founded, or shewing us a better form. These general surmises never lead to the discovery of truth. It is to be desired, that the gentleman would explain particularly the errors in this system, and furnish us with their proper remedies. The committee remember that a grant of an impost to the United States, for twenty-five years, was requested by Congress. Though this was a very small addition of power to the federal government, it was opposed in this state, without any reason being offered. The dissent of New-York and Rhode-Island frustrated a most important measure. The gentleman says, he was for granting the impost; yet he acknowledges, he could not agree to the mode recommended. But it was well known, that Congress had declared, that they could not receive the accession of the states, upon any other plan than that proposed. In such case, propositions for altering the plan amounted to a positive rejection. At this time, Sir, we were told it was dangerous to grant powers to Congress—Did this general argument indicate a disposition to grant the impost in any shape? I should myself have been averse to the granting of very extensive powers: But the impost was justly considered as the only means of supporting the union.—We did not then contemplate a fundamental change in government. From my sense of the gentlemen's integrity, I am bound to believe, that they are attached to a strong united government; and yet I find it difficult to draw this conclusion from their conduct or their reasonings.

Sir, with respect to the subject of revenue, which was debated yesterday, it was asserted that in all matters of taxation, except in the article of imposts, the united and individual states had a concurrent jurisdiction; that the state governments had an independent authority, to draw revenue from every source but one. The truth of these positions will appear on a slight investigation. I maintain, that the word *supreme* imports no more than this; that the constitution, and laws made in pursuance thereof, cannot be controuled or defeated by any other law. The acts of the United States therefore will be absolutely obligatory, as to all the proper objects and powers of the general government. The states as well as individuals are bound by these laws—but the laws of Congress are restricted to a certain sphere, and when they depart from this sphere, they are no longer supreme or binding. In the same manner the states have certain independent powers, in which their laws are supreme: For example, in making and executing laws concerning the punishment of certain crimes, such as murder, theft, &c. the states cannot be controuled. With respect to certain other objects, the powers of the two governments are concurrent, and yet supreme. I instanced, yesterday, a tax on any specific article. Both might lay the tax; both might collect it without clashing or interference. If the individual should be unable to pay both, the first seizure would hold the property. Here the laws are not in the way of each other; they are independent and supreme.—The case is like that of two creditors: Each has a distinct demand; the debtor is held equally for the payment of both. Their suits are independent; and if the debtor cannot pay both, he who takes the first step, secures his debt. The individual is precisely in the same situation, whether he pays such a sum to one, or to two. No more will be required of him to supply the public wants, than he has ability to afford. That the states have an undoubted right to lay taxes in all cases in which they are not prohibited, is a position founded on the obvious and important principle in confederated governments, that whatever is not expressly given to the federal head, is reserved to the members. The truth of this principle must strike every intelligent mind. In the first formation of government by the association of individuals, every power of the community is delegated, because the government is to extend to every possible object; Nothing is reserved, but the unalienable rights of mankind: But when a number of these societies unite for certain purposes, the rule is different, and from the plainest reason: They have already delegated their sovereignty, and their powers to their several governments; and these cannot be recalled, and given to another, without an express act. I submit to the committee whether this reasoning is not conclusive. Unless therefore we find that the powers of taxation are exclusively granted, we must conclude, that there remains a concurrent authority. Let us then enquire if the constitution gives such exclusive powers to the general government. Sir, there is not a syllable in it, that favours this idea;—Not a word importing an exclusive grant, except in the article of imposts. I am supported in my general position, by this very exception. If the states are prohibited from laying duties on imports, the implication is clear. Now, what proportion will the duties on imports bear to the other ordinary resources of the country? We may now say, one third; but this will not be the case long. As our manufactures increase, foreign importations must lessen. Here are two thirds at least of the resources of our country open to the state governments. Can it be imagined then, that the states will lose their existence or their importance for want of revenues? The propriety of Congress possessing an exclusive power over the impost appears from the necessity of their having a considerable portion of our resources, to pledge as a fund for the reduction of the debts of the United States. When you have given a power of taxation to the general government, none of the states individually will be holden for the discharge of the federal obligations: The burthen will be on the union.

The gentleman says, that the operation of the taxes will exclude the states, on this ground, that the demands of the community are always equal to its resources; that Congress will find a use for all the money the people can pay. This observation, if designed as a general rule, is in every view unjust.—Does he suppose the general government will want all the money the people can furnish; and also that the state governments will want all the money the people can furnish? What contradiction is this? But if this maxim be true, how does the wealth of a country ever increase? How are the people enabled to accumulate fortunes? Do the burthens regularly augment, as its inhabitants grow prosperous and happy.—But if indeed all the resources are required for the protection of the people, it follows that the protecting power should have access to them. The only difficulty lies in the want of resources: If they are adequate, the operation will be easy:—If they are not, taxation must be restrained: Will this be the fate of the state tax alone? Certainly not—The people will say no—What will be the conduct of the national rulers? The consideration will not be, that our imposing the tax will destroy the states, for this cannot be effected; but that it will distress the people, whom we represent, and whose protectors we are.—It is unjust to suppose that they will be altogether destitute of virtue and prudence; It is unfair to presume that the representatives of the people will be disposed to tyrannize, in one government more than in another. If we are convinced that the national legislature will pursue a system of measures unfavorable to the interests of the people, we ought to have no general government at all. But if we unite, it will be for the accomplishment of great purposes: These demand great resources, and great powers. There are certain extensive and uniform objects of revenue, which the United States will improve, and to which, if possible they will confine themselves. Those objects which are more limited, and in respect to which, the circumstances of the states differ, will be reserved for their use: A great variety of articles will be in this last class of objects, to which only the state laws will properly apply. To ascertain this division of objects is the proper business of legislation: It would be absurd to fix it in the constitution, both because it would be too extensive and intricate, and because alteration of circumstances must render a change of the division indispensible. Constitutions should consist only of general provisions: The reason is, that they must necessarily be permanent, and that they cannot calculate for the possible changes of things. I know that the states must have their resources; but I contend that it would be improper to point them out particularly in the constitution.

Sir, it has been said that a poll-tax is a tyrannical tax: But the legislature of this state can lay it, whenever they please. Does then our constitution authorize tyranny? I am as much opposed to a capitation, as any man: Yet who can deny, that there may exist certain circumstances, which will render this tax necessary. In the course of a war, it may be necessary to lay hold of every resource: and, for a certain period, the people may submit to it. But on removal of the danger, or the return of peace, the general sense of the community would abolish it. The United Netherlands were obliged, on an emergency, to give up one half of their property to the government. It has been said, that it will be impossible to exercise this power of taxation: If it cannot be exercised, why be alarmed at it? But the gentlemen say that the difficulty of executing it with moderation will necessarily drive the government into despotic measures. Here again they are in the old track of jealousy and conjecture. Whenever the people feel the hand of despotism, they will not regard forms and parchments. But the gentlemen's premises are as false as their conclusion. No one reason can be offered, why the exercise of the power should be impracticable: No one difficulty can be pointed out, which will not apply to our state governments. Congress will have every means of knowledge, that any legislature can have. From general observation, and from the revenue systems of the several states, they will derive information as to the most eligible modes of taxation. If a land tax is the object, cannot Congress procure as perfect a valuation as any other assembly? Can they not have all the necessary officers for assessment and collection? Where is the difficulty? Where is the evil? They never can oppress a particular state, by an unequal imposition; because the constitution has provided a fixed ratio, a uniform rule, by which this must be regulated. The system will be founded upon the most easy and equal principles—to draw as much as possible from direct taxation; to lay the principal burthens on the wealthy, &c. Even ambitious and unprincipled men will form their system so, as to draw forth the resources of the country in the most favorable and gentle methods; because such will be ever the most productive. They never can hope for success, by adopting those arbitrary modes, which have been used in some of the states.

A gentleman yesterday passed many encomiums on the character and operations of the state governments. The question has not been, whether their laws have produced happy or unhappy effects: The character of our confederation is the subject of our controversy. But the gentleman concludes too hastily. In many of the states, government has not had a salutary operation. Not only Rhode-Island, but several others have been guilty of indiscretions and misconduct—of acts, which have produced misfortune and dishonor. I grant that the government of New-York has operated well; and I ascribe it to the influence of those excellent principles, in which the proposed constitution and our own are so congenial. We are sensible that private credit is much lower in some states, than it is in ours. What is the cause of this? Why is it at the present period, so low even in this state? Why is the value of our land depreciated? It is said there is a scarcity of money in the community: I do not believe this scarcity to be so great, as is represented. It may not appear; It may be retained by its holders; but nothing more than stability and confidence in the government is requisite to draw it into circulation. It is acknowledged that the general government has not answered its purposes. Why? We attribute it to the defects of the revenue system. But the gentlemen say, the requisitions have not been obeyed, because the states were impoverished. This is a kind of reasoning that astonished me. The records of this state—the records of Congress prove that, during the war, New-York had the best reason to complain of the non-compliance of the other states. I appeal to the gentlemen—Have the states, who have suffered least, contributed most? No sir—the fact is directly the reverse. This consideration is sufficient entirely to refute the gentlemen's reasoning. Requisitions will ever be attended with the same effects. This depends on principles of human nature, that are as infallible as any mathematical calculations. States will contribute or not, according to their circumstances and interests: They will all be inclined to throw off the burthens of government upon their neighbours. These positions have been so fully illustrated and proved in former stages of this debate, that nothing need be added. Unanswerable experience—stubborn facts have supported and fixed them. Sir, to what situation is our Congress now reduced! It is notorious, that with the utmost difficulty they maintain their ordinary officers, and support the mere form of a federal government. How do we stand with respect to foreign nations? It is a fact, that should strike us with surprize and with shame, that we are obliged to borrow money, in order to pay the interest of our debts.—It is a fact, that these debts are every day accumulating by compound interest. This, sir, will one day endanger the peace of our country, and expose us to vicisitudes the most alarming. Such is the character of requisitions; Such the melancholy, dangerous condition, to which they have reduced us. Now, sir, after this full and fair experiment, with what countenance do gentlemen come forward, to recommend the ruinous principle, and make it the basis of a new government? Why do they affect to cherish this political demon, and present it once more to our embraces? The gentleman observes, that we cannot, even in a single state, collect the whole of a tax; Some countries will necessarily be deficient: In the same way, says he, some states will be delinquent. If this reasoning were just, I should expect to see the states pay, like the counties, in proportion to their ability; which is not the fact.

I shall proceed now more particularly to the proposition before the committee. This clearly admits, that the unlimited power of taxation, which I have been contending for, is proper. It declares that after the states have refused to comply with the requisitions, the general government may enforce its demands. While the gentlemen's proposal admits my principle, in its fullest latitude, the whole course of their argument is against it. The mode they point out would involve all the inconveniences, against which they would wish to guard. Suppose the gentlemen's scheme should be adopted; Would not all the resources of the country be equally in the power of Congress? The states cannot have but one opportunity of refusal. After having passed through the empty ceremony of a requisition, the general government can enforce all its demands, without limitation or resistance. The states will either comply, or they will not. If they comply, they are bound to collect the whole of the tax from the citizens. The people must pay it. What then will be the disadvantage of its being levied and collected by Congress, in the first instance? It has been proved, as far as probabilities can go, that the federal government will, in general, take the laws of the several states as its rule, and pursue those measures, to which the people are most accustomed. But if the states do not comply, what is the consequence? If the power of compulsion be a misfortune to the states, they must now suffer it, without opposition or complaint. I shall shew too, that they must feel it in an aggravated degree. It may frequently happen, that, though the states formally comply with the requisitions, the avails will not be fully realized by Congress: The states may be dilatory in the collection and payment, and may form excuses for not paying the whole: There may be also partial compliances, which will subject the Union to inconveniences. Congress therefore in laying the tax will calculate for these losses and inconveniences: They will make allowances for the delays and delinquencies of the states, and apportion their burthens accordingly: They will be induced to demand more than their actual wants. In these circumstances the requisitions will be made upon calculations in some measure arbitrary. Upon the constitutional plan, the only enquiry will be—how much is actually wanted; and how much can the object bear, or the people pay? On the gentlemen's scheme, it will be—what will be the probable deficiencies of the states? for we must increase our demands in proportion, whatever the public wants may be, or whatever may be the abilities of the people. Now suppose the requisition is totally rejected, it must be levied upon the citizens, without reserve. This will be like inflicting a penalty upon the states: It will place them in the light of criminals. Will they suffer this? Will Congress presume so far?—If the states solemnly declare they will not comply, does not this imply a determination not to permit the exercise of the coercive power? The gentlemen cannot escape the dilemma, into which their own reasoning leads them. If the states comply, the people must be taxed; If they do not comply, the people must equally be taxed: The burthen, in either case, will be the same; the difficulty of collecting the same. Sir, if these operations are merely harmless and indifferent, why play the ridiculous farce? If they are inconvenient, why subject us to their evils? It is infinitely more eligible, to lay a tax originally, which will have uniform effects throughout the Union; which will operate equally and silently. The United States will then be able to ascertain their resources, and to act with vigor and decision: All hostility between the governments will be prevented: The people will contribute regularly and gradually, for the support of government; and all odious, retrospective enquiries will be precluded.

But, the ill effects of the gentlemen's plan do not terminate here. Our own state will suffer peculiar disadvantages from the measure. One provision in the amendment is, that no direct taxes shall be laid till after the impost and excise shall be found insufficient for the public exigencies; and that no excise shall be laid on articles of the growth or manufacture of the United States. Sir, the favorable maritime situation of this state, and our large and valuable tracts of unsettled land, will ever lead us to commerce and agriculture as our proper objects. Unconfined, and tempted by the prospect of easy subsistance and independence, our citizens, as the country populates, will retreat back, and cultivate the western parts of our state. Our population, though extensive, will never be crowded, and consequently we shall remain an importing and agricultural state. Now, what will be the operation of the proposed plan?—The general government, restrained by the constitution from a free application to other resources, will push imposts to an extreme. Will excessive impositions on our commerce be favorable to the policy of this state? Will they not directly oppose our interests. Similar will be the operation of the other clause of the amendment, relative to excise. Our neighbours not possessed of our advantages for commerce and agriculture, will become manufacturers: Their property will, in a great measure, be vested in the commodities of their own production: But a small proportion will be in trade, or in lands. Thus, on the gentlemen's scheme, they will be almost free from burthens, while we shall be loaded with them. Does not the partiality of this strike every one? Can gentlemen, who are laboring for the interest of their state, seriously bring forward such propositions? It is the interest of New-York, that those articles should be taxed, in the production of which, the other states exceed us. If we are not a manufacturing people, excises on manufactures will ever be for our advantage. This position is indisputable. Sir, I agree, that it is not good policy to lay excises to any considerable amount, while our manufactures are in their infancy—but are they always to be so? In some of the states, they already begin to make considerable progress. In Connecticut such encouragement is given, as will soon distinguish that state. Even at the present period, there is one article, from which, a revenue may very properly be drawn: I speak of ardent spirits. New-England manufactures more than a hundred gallons to our one—consequently, an excise on spirits at the still-head would make those states contribute in a vastly greater proportion than ourselves. In every view, excises on domestic manufactures would benefit New-York. But the gentlemen would defeat the advantages of our situation, by drawing upon us all the burthens of government. The nature of our union requires, that we should give up our state impost: The amendment would forfeit every other advantage. This part of the constitution should not be touched. The excises were designed as a recompence to the importing states, for relinquishing their imposts. Why then should we reject the benefits conferred upon us? Why should we run blindly against our own interest?

Sir, I shall no further enlarge on this argument—My exertions have already exhausted me. I have persevered, from an anxious desire to give the committee the most complete conception of this subject. I fear however, that I have not been so successful, as to bestow upon it that full and clear light, of which it is susceptible. I shall conclude with a few remarks, by way of apology. I am apprehensive, Sir, that in the warmth of my feelings, I may have uttered expressions, which were too vehement. If such has been my language, it was from the habit of using strong phrases to express my ideas; and, above all, from the interesting nature of the subject. I have ever condemned those cold, unfeeling hearts, which no object can animate. I condemn those indifferent mortals, who either never form opinions, or never make them known. I confess, Sir, that on no subject, has my breast been filled with stronger emotions, or more anxious concern. If any thing has escaped me, which may be construed into a personal reflection, I beg the gentlemen, once for all, to be assured, that I have no design to wound the feelings of any one who is opposed to me. While I am making these observations, I cannot but take notice of some expressions, which have fallen, in the course of the debate. It has been said, that ingenious men may say ingenious things, and that those, who are interested in raising the few upon the ruins of the many may give to every cause an appearance of justice. I know not whether these insinuations allude to the characters of any, who are present, or to any of the reasonings in this house. I presume that the gentlemen would not ungenerously impute such motives to those, who differ from themselves. I declare, I know not any set of men who are to derive peculiar advantages from this constitution. Were any permanent honors or emoluments to be secured to the families of those who have been active in this cause, there might be some ground for suspicion. But what reasonable man, for the precarious enjoyment of rank and power, would establish a system, which would reduce his nearest friends and his posterity to slavery and ruin? If the gentlemen reckon me among the obnoxious few; If they imagine, that I contemplate, with an ambitious eye, the immediate honors of the government; yet, let them consider, that I have my friends—my family—my children, to whom the ties of nature and of habit have attached me. If, to day, I am among the favoured few; my children, to-morrow, may be among the oppressed many: These dearest pledges of my patriotism may, at a future day, be suffering the severe distresses, to which my ambition has reduced them. The changes in the human conditions are uncertain and frequent. Many, on whom fortune has bestowed her favours, may trace their family to a more unprosperous station; and many who are now in obscurity, may look back upon the affluence and exalted rank of their ancestors. But I will no longer trespass on your indulgence. I have troubled the committee with these observations, to shew that it cannot be the wish of any reasonable man, to establish a government unfriendly to the liberties of the people. Gentlemen ought not then to presume, that the advocates of this constitution are influenced by ambitious views—The suspicion, Sir, is unjust; the charge is uncharitable.

Robert R. Livingston Compares the Antifederalists to "Children Making Bubbles with a Pipe"

July 1, 1788

The hon. *Chancellor Livingston.*—When this subject came into discussion, on Friday, Mr. Chairman, I did myself the honor to express my sentiments to the committee. I considered the amendment, as it would affect the general government, and was favored with the support of my honorable colleague, who went more largely and ably into the argument, and added weight to the ideas I had suggested. I shall now confine myself to a few cursory and general observations on the reasoning of our opponents. I do not think it my duty to attempt to reconcile the gentlemen with each other. They advance opposite principles, and they argue differently. As they do not appear to have any fixed maxims, in their politics, it is not to be wondered at, that they talk at random and run into inconsistencies. The gentleman from Dutchess went into a defence of the state governments: He painted their good qualities in very warm colours; described their stability, their wisdom, their justice, their affection for the people. This was undoubtedly proper; for it was necessary to his argument. On the contrary, another gentleman took up the matter in a different point of view: He said the government of New-York, which had been acknowledged one of the best, was quite imperfect: But this was all right, for it answered his purpose. A gentleman from New-York had remarked a great resemblance between the government of this state, and the new constitution. To condemn the former therefore, was giving a dead blow at the proposed system. But, sir, tho' we may pardon the gentlemen for differing from each other, yet it is difficult to excuse their differing from themselves. As these inconsistencies are too delicate to dwell on, I shall mention but a few. Their amendment declares that Congress shall lay direct taxes, and the whole drift of their argument is against it. In their reasoning direct taxes are odious and useless things: In their amendment they are necessary and proper. Thus their arguments and their motion are at variance. But this is not the only contradiction. The gentlemen say that Congress will be avaricious, and will want every farthing of the people's property. One from Washington tells you that taxation will shut out the light of Heaven, and will pick your pockets. With these melancholy ideas, no wonder he mourns for the fair damsel of American liberty, harrassed with oppressive laws, shut up in a dismal dungeon, robbed of the light of Heaven, and by a beautiful anticlimax, robbed of the money in her pocket. Yet, says the gentleman, tho' Congress will do all this, they cannot do it. You are told that the collection of the tax is impracticable. Is then this great mischief to arise from an impracticable thing? It is the reasoning among all reasoners, that from nothing nothing comes; and yet this nothing is to destroy the state governments, and swallow up the state revenues: The tax, which cannot realize a farthing, is to rob the citizens of all their property. This is fine reasoning. To what shall I compare it? Shall I liken it to children in the market-place, or shall I liken it to children making bubbles with a pipe? Shall I not rather compare it to two boys upon a balanced board—One goes up, the other down; and so they go up and down, down and up, till the sport is over, and the board is left exactly on the balance, in which they found it. But, let us see if we cannot, from all this rubbish, pick out something which may look like reasoning. I confess I am embarrassed by their mode of arguing. They tell us that the state governments will be destroyed, because they will have no powers left them. This is new—Is the power over property nothing? Is the power of life and death no power? Let me ask, what powers this constitution would take from the states? Have the state governments the power of war and peace, of raising troops, and making treaties? The power of regulating commerce we possess: But the gentlemen admit that we improperly possess it. What then is taken away? Have not the states the right of raising money, and regulating the militia? and yet these objects could never have employed your legislatures, four or five months in the year. What then have they been about? making laws to regulate the height of fences, and the repairing of roads? If this be true, take the power out of their hands—They have been unworthy servants—They have not deserved your confidence. Admit that the power of raising money should be taken from them; does it follow, that the people will lose all confidence in their representatives? There are but two objects, for which money must be raised: the support of the general governments, and that of the states, and they have an equal right to levy and collect their taxes. But if, as the amendment proposes, they should be obliged to grant all that Congress should call for; if they are to be compelled to comply with the requisitions without limitation; they would be, on the gentlemen's principles, in a pitiable situation indeed. The mode alone would be in their discretion. Is this the mighty matter about which we differ? Contend about modes! I am sorry to say, sir, that a rigid adherence to modes in this state, has been the cause of great injustice to individuals, and has hurt the confidence of the people: It has led this state, on one occasion, to raise the expectations of public creditors, and to sink them again, by an unwarrantable breach of faith. Sir, if the power of regulating the militia, of raising money, of making and executing all the civil and criminal laws—laws which affect the life, liberty and property of individuals, can ensure or deserve the confidence and respect of the people, I think the gentleman's argument falls to the ground.

Much has been said, Sir, about the sword and the purse. These words convey very confused ideas, on the gentleman's application of them. The honorable member from New-York has fully explained their meaning, as applied to the British government. His reasoning was so conclusive, that it seems to have carried conviction to every mind:—The gentleman from Dutchess, to elude it has made use of a singular shift. Says he, the general government and state governments form one government. Let us see how this matter stands. The states of Pennsylvania and New-York form two distinct governments; But New-York, Pennsylvania and the general government together form one government; The United States and New-York make another government; The United States and Connecticut another, and so on.—To the gentleman's optics, these things may be clear; but to me they are utter darkness.

We have thirteen distinct governments, and yet they are not thirteen governments, but one government. It requires the ingenuity of St. Athanasius to understand this political mystery. Were the gentleman a minister of the gospel, I might have faith; but, I confess, my reason is much too weak for it. Sir, we are attempting to build one government out of thirteen; preserving however the states, as parts of the system, for local purposes, and to give it support and beauty. The truth is, the states, and the United States have distinct objects. They are both supreme. As to national objects, the latter is supreme; as to internal and domestic objects, the former. I can easily conceive of two joint tenures, and of joint jurisdictions without controul. If I wanted an example, I might instance the mine, Mr. Chairman in which you and others have a joint property and concurrent jurisdiction. But why should the states hold the purse? How are they to use it? They have not to pay the civil list, to maintain the army or navy—what will they do with it? What is the sword which the gentlemen talk of? How is Congress to defend us without a sword? You will also keep that—How shall it be handled? Shall we all take hold of it? I never knew, till now, the design of a curious image I have seen at the head of one of our newspapers. I am now convinced, that the idea was prophetic in the printer. It was a figure of thirteen hands, in an awkward position, grasping a perpendicular sword.—As the arms, which supported it, were on every side, I could see no way of moving it, but by drawing it through, with the hazard of dangerously cutting the fingers.—For my own part, I should be for crying hands off.—But this sword of the gentleman's is a visionary sword—a mere empty pageant; and yet they would never trust it out of the state scabbard, lest it should wound somebody. They wish for checks against what can do no harm— They contend for a phantom. Gentlemen should consider their arguments, before they come here. Sir, our reasoning on this ground is conclusive. If it be necessary, to trust our defence to the union, it is necessary that we should trust it with the sword to defend us, and the purse to give the sword effect. I have heard not a shadow of an argument, to shake the truth of this. But gentlemen will talk—It is expected.—It is necessary that they should support, in this house, the

opinions they have propagated out of doors; but which perhaps they had themselves too hastily formed.

Sir, one word with respect to excise. When I addressed the
committee on Friday last, I observed that the amendment
would operate with great inconvenience; that at a future period, this would be a manufacturing country; and then there
would be many proper objects of excise: But the gentleman,
in answer to this, says we ought not to look forward to a
future period. What! must this then be the government of a
day? It is the third time, we have been making governments,
and God grant it may be the last.

Melancton Smith Mocks
Robert R. Livingston's "Comic Talents" and Replies to His "Misrepresentation"

July 2, 1788

The hon. Mr. *Smith*. Mr. Chairman, the honorable gentleman, who spoke yesterday, animadverted, in a very ludicrous manner, upon my arguments; and endeavored to place them in a ridiculous point of view. Perhaps it was necessary that the convention should be diverted with something fanciful, and that they should be relieved from the tediousness of a dull debate, by a few flashes of merriment. I suppose it was for this purpose, that the gentleman was induced to make so handsome a display of his comic talents, to the no small entertainment of the ladies and gentlemen without the bar. It is well known, that in theatrical exhibitions, the farce succeeds the tragedy. Now, as another honorable gentleman [Mr. Duane] had, but the day before, called to our minds, in a most dismal picture, the tragic scenes of war, devastation and bloodshed; it was entirely proper that our feelings should be relieved from the shocking impression, by a light and musical play. I think the gentleman has acquitted himself admirably. However, his attack seems to have thrown him off his guard, and to have exposed him to his own weapons. The gentleman might well have turned his strictures upon his own contradictions; for at one time, he argues that a federal republic is impracticable; at another, he argues that the proposed government is a federal republic: At one time, he says the old confederation has no powers at all; at another, he says it has nearly as many as the one proposed. He seems to be an enemy to creeds; and yet, with respect to concurrent jurisdiction, he presents us with his creed, which we are bound to believe. Let us hear it. "I believe that the general government is supreme, and that the state governments are supreme, and yet they are not two supremes, but one supreme; and this cannot be doubted." He says, there is a concurrent jurisdiction in your mine, Mr. Chairman, and yet you do not concur; for the gentleman himself claims the soil, and there seems to be a difference between you. But as the honorable gentleman considers his harrangue as containing some reasoning, I shall take notice of a few of his remarks.

The gentleman has said, that the committee seemed to be convinced by the arguments of an honorable member from New-York. I suppose it was only a fancy of the moment that struck him, of which he probably can give no better account than the rest of us. I can only say for myself, that the more I hear and reflect, the more convinced I am of the necessity of amendments. Whether the committee have received conviction, can easily be settled by a vote.

The gentleman from Washington had said that even the state of New-York was not a perfect form—In the course of my argument, I observed that the state legislatures were competent to good government, and that it was not proper to exchange governments, at so great a risk. Where is the mighty contradiction? I said that the state governments were proper depositaries of power, and were the proper guardians of the people. I did not say that any government was perfect, nor did I ascribe any extraordinary qualities to the states. The gentleman endeavors to fix another contradiction upon me. He charges me with saying, that direct taxes are dangerous, and yet impracticable. This is an egregious misrepresentation. My declaration was, that general direct taxes would be extremely difficult, in the apportionment and collection, and that this difficulty would push the general government into despotic measures. The gentleman also ridicules our idea of the states losing their powers. He says this constitution adds little or no power to the union; and consequently takes little or nothing from the states. If this be true, what are the advocates of the system contending about? It is the reasoning among all reasoners, that nothing to something adds nothing. If the new plan does not contain any new powers, why advocate it? If it does, whence are they taken? The honorable member cannot understand our argument about the sword and the purse, and asks, why should the states hold them? I say the state governments ought to hold the purse, to keep people's hands out of it. With respect to the sword, I say you must handle it, through your general government: But the states must have some agency, or the people will not be willing to put their hands to it. It is observed that we must talk a great deal; and that is necessary to support here what we have said out of doors. Sir, I conceive that we ought to talk of this subject every where.—Several gentlemen have observed, that it is necessary these powers should be vested in Congress, that they may have funds to pledge for the payment of debts. This argument has not the least weight in my mind. The government ought not to have it in their power, to borrow with too great facility. The funds, which we agree to lodge with Congress, will be sufficient for as much as they ought to borrow.

I submit to the candor of the committee, whether any evidence of the strength of a cause is afforded, when gentlemen, instead of reasoning fairly, assert roundly; and use all the powers of ridicule and rhetoric, to abuse their adversaries. Any argument may be placed in a ridiculous light, by taking only detached parts. I wish, Mr. Chairman, that ridicule may be avoided. It can only irritate the passions, and has no tendency to convince the judgment.

Nathan Dane Writes to Melancton Smith, Recommending That New York Unconditionally Ratify

New York City, July 3, 1788

Dear Sir,

In my last letter I briefly gave my opinion on the questions you stated to me; now being more at leisure sensible that the peculiar situation of our Government at this time is a matter of common concern and highly interesting to us all; and that we have the same object in view, the peaceable establishment of a general Government on genuine federal and republican principles, I shall in this be more particular, and submit to your consideration several observations with that candor and frankness with which we have always communicated our sentiments to each other relative to the important subject in question—

The Constitution of the United States is now established by the people of ten States, and a day of course must soon be fixed, when all proceedings under the Confederation shall cease—The line of conduct which shall now be pursued by the three States which have not as yet ratified is become particularly and deeply interesting to them, and to the whole Confederacy—As things are now circumstanced will it not be clearly for their interest and happiness, as well as for the interest and happiness of all the union to adopt the Constitution proposing such amendments as they may think essential—the situation of the States is now critical—as the Constitution is already established there can be no previous amendments; and a State which has not ratified, and wishes to be in the union, appears to have but this alternative before her;—either to accede with recommending certain alterations, or to make them a condition of her accession, and the probable consequence of either Step must be considered—I take it for granted that New York and the other two States wish to form a part of an American Confederacy—the readiness with which they

844

Joined in the revolution, and acceded to the articles of Confederation; their open and general professions, and their past exertions to the support of the union Justify the opinion—In all our late political discussions, a separation of the States, or Separate Confederacies, have Scarcely, to my knowledge, been Seriously mentioned—Admitting that Rhode Island, New York, and North Carolina all withhold their assent to the Constitution, and propose similar amendments, their situation is such, far removed from each other, and surrounded by ratifying States, that they never can think of confederating among themselves—Each one of them must be considered as Standing alone—but we have no reason to suppose that any one of those States has a wish to Stand alone, in Case she can Confederate on principles agreeable to her—If I understand the politics of these three States, they are Strongly attached to governments founded in freedom and compact, and possess a Just aversion to those which are the result of force and violence—they will, therefore, be the last States which will adopt measures tending to foment parties, and give passion an ascendancy over reason, or to hazard Steps that may, in the end, lead to a civil war, and consequently to the Government of the prevailing party established by the longest Sword—It is not to be pretended that the ratifying States will have any Just cause to make war upon any non ratifying State, merely because she does not accede to a national compact, where she has a right to act according to her discretion—nor ought we to presume that hostilities will be commenced by any party without some plausible or Just provocation—But the ratifying and non ratifying States will immediately have opposite Interests, which, in the nature of things, they will pursue— the longer they shall remain Separate the more their assertions and friendship for each other will decrease—and counteracting laws and a disposition for coercive measures will take place—the affairs of the Country will have a propensity to extremities and a thousand accidents may give rise to hostilities—The question in the ratifying States being settled, it is probable the parties in them will gradually unite—In the States where the question shall remain unsettled, and the contest continue between the parties in them, as it undoubtedly will, in what manner they shall Join the union, they will grow more hostile to each other; and from what appears to be their present temper and situation, and if we reason from experience and from the character of men we must conclude, it is at least highly probable that they will have recourse to arms, or to contentions extremely injurious to their common Interest, at no very distant period And what must be the issue of force, or of such contentions between the parties in any State is not difficult to foresee—If the other States should not interfere, those parties must decide their contest by themselves—If the party called federal shall prevail, they bring the State into the union unconditionally, or establish a State Government of their own, probably, on their own principles—If the other party shall prevail they will keep the State out of the union, unless the federal Constitution, which can hardly be presumed, shall in the mean time be made agreeable to them, and they will of necessity add a degree of severity to their laws and measures very incompatible with those principles of freedom they now contend for—this presents a disagreeable Scene in either event—But should the other States interfere, or a civil war by any accident become general between the advocates and opposers of the Constitution, throughout the United States, which is the probable consequence of any hostile beginnings, what must be the issue? our people tho enlightened are high Spirited—one party, when both are nearly ruined, may prevail, not in accommodating and fixing a government in freedom and compact, but in force and violence,—and may we not expect a more severe high toned partial system established to secure the victorious party, at least a system more despotic than the old one we lay aside, or the one we are adopting—Were there any great number of men heartly attached to the Confederation, their success might establish it—but this in its present form seems to have but few or no advocates—Were there any great number of men attached to it with certain defined alterations in it, their success might establish it when so altered—but we have not agreed in those alterations—and if we may Judge from experience, and what appears to be the public opinion, it is more difficult to mould the Confederation to the wishes of the people than the Constitution—the Community in fact consists of two parties, the advocates, who are for establishing the Constitution in its present form, and the opposers, who generally if I understand them consider it as a tolerable basis, but as an imperfect and unguarded system unless amended—Were the advocates well attached to the system their success might establish it but this is not the Case—we know that many of them and those too, who would have the most influence, from their abilities, address, and activity, in producing a Government, never will agree to a system so favourable to liberty and republicanism even as the one proposed, if by any means they can get one more favourable to themselves, and unfavourable to the body of the people. If the other party those who wish to have the system but amended, succeed, and they were agreed in the amendments their success might establish the plan so amended—but no set of amendments have been agreed upon, and different ones have been proposed by different Conventions—You will, therefore, I am confident, agree with me that the friends of liberty and of Governments founded in compact cannot reasonably expect any good consequences from force and violence—the very means are hostile to the end proposed—Our object is to improve the plan proposed: to Strengthen and secure its democratic features; to add checks and guards to it; to secure equal liberty by proper Stipulations to prevent any undue exercise of power, and to establish beyond the power of faction to alter, a genuine federal republic to effect this great and desirable object the peace of the Country must be preserved, candor cherished, information extended and the doors of accommodation constantly kept open—the votes of the people will I think avail them much more in establishing a government favourable to them—than any violent or forceable proceedings—It is to be considered that five States have adopted the Constitution without proposing any amendments—we have seen the amendments proposed in the Conventions of four States—and certain it is there appears to be too little in reality proposed to be gained by the amendments to Justify parties in those States carrying matters to extremities—nor will any one, two, or three States ever expect the others to meet them in amendments, but on the principles of accommodation —whatever amendments any State may propose, I am persuaded you are too well acquainted with men, not to be sensible that passion, opinion, and self will must have a constant influence in their conduct relative to them, that when terms are rigidly insisted on by one party, they are generally opposed by terms rigidly insisted on by the other   It cannot be proper for any State positively to say to the others, that unless they precisely agree to the alterations she proposes she will not accede to the Union—this would be rather dictating—a State may take a question upon the Constitution simply as it stands and express its sense of it in its present form—she may then annex recommended amendments and adopt it with them, or make them the Condition of her accession to the Union. I flatter myself, after a State has expressed her Sense upon the simple proposition you will prefer the mode of adopting with recommendatory amendments annexed—the new system must soon go into operation and some of the most important laws be made in the first Congress, and essential amendments be recommended by it—the State that adopts this mode comes into the Union armed with the declared Sentiments of her people, and will immediately have a voice in the federal Councils—she there will avail herself of all her influence, and of the advantages of accommodating principles in bringing the other States to accord with her sentiments—whereas if she adopts conditionally she will not have a voice in those Councils during the most interesting period—party Spirit will, probably, reign in her bosom, and ill will constantly gain ground between her and the other States—and it is in my mind almost an absolute certainty that she must forever remain out of the union, or relinquish some of her conditions—It cannot be presumed that any two of the three States will precisely agree in the same Alterations, and should they do it, it is not probable that all the States will agree exactly to them—there are many and able advocates for valuable amendments, and a good system of laws in every State and may they not prevail should all the States meet in the first Congress but should some of them Stand out, and those in which those amendments and laws have the most friends—the federal republicans or men who wish to cement the union of the States on republican principles will be divided, and have but a part of their Strength in Congress, where they ought to have the whole—When measures of any sort become necessary in a Community, it is generally wise to take a part in them, and to bring them as near to our opinions as we can in the first instance, and I have ever thought since a federal Convention was agreed on that Rhode Island and certain individuals who were appointed to that Convention, missed it exceedingly in not attending it—they might clearly, had they attended, have engrafted many of the principles and checks they now contend for, into the System—and have given it those features and securities which as it now appears, would meet the approbation of the people in General—they saw a Constitution of some kind was to be made, and before it had taken a fixed direction was the time for exertions—You as well as others know it to be a fact that some parts of the Constitution most complained of, were obtained with much address and after repeated trials, and which never could have been carried had the States and members, I refer to, attended the federal Convention—for any State now to Stand out and oppose appears to me to be but a repetition of the same error—I might add many more observations but I think I need not dwell longer on these points—Even when a few States had adopted without any alterations, the ground was materially changed; and now it is totally shifted—tho I retain my opinion respecting the feeble features, the extensive powers, and defective parts of the System, yet circumstanced as we are, I confess, I feel no impropriety in urging the three States to accede—men in all the States who wish to establish a free, equal, and efficient government, to the exclusion of anarchy, corruption, faction, and oppression ought in my opinion to unite in their exertions in making the best of the Constitution now established; to preserve inviolate the liberties of America, and to promote the happiness of the people by Just and equal laws and an equitable administration; to add constitutional security to those liberties on every proper occasion are still the objects of all good men—this now appears to be the way to disappoint those men who discover a disposition to make a bad use of a Constitution in many parts not well guarded, and to use its powers to corrupt and selfish purposes—a good Constitution is capable of affording much security to the rights of the people, and ought to be aimed at with unremitted attention—But ought we to expect any Constitution under which the people may, with Safety, relax in any considerable degree in their attention to public measures?—can they be secure under any Constitution unless attentive themselves, and unless some of their able leaders are their real friends and their faithful guardians

Tho I think our people have examined the system in question with candor and freedom and discovered a strong attachment to liberty—Yet I would by no means so far rely upon their exertions and vigilance as to lose sight of those Constitutional securities which may be obtained by time and experience—while we veiw the conduct of rulers with candor, we ought to watch their movements with an Eagle's eye, and guard and secure the temple of freedom with unceasing attention—

To conclude ought we not now to give additional weight to the plea in favor of the Constitution drawn from the peculiarity of our situation, and which when less urgent and pressing appears again and again to have saved the system? and tho the system may be abused by bad men, ought we not to recollect that the road to lasting fame in this Country has generally been Justice, and Integrity, prudence and moderation, political information and industry & that there is more than an equal chance that this will continue to be the case? Attempts to palm upon our people vice for virtue, the mere shew of talents for real abilities, and the arts and puffs of party for a well earned reputation have generally failed—and what is wanting but to excite the attention of this intelligent people to render such attempts always unsuccessful? all these and many other considerations ought to have their Just weight in deciding the great question before us—

Melancton Smith Replies to Nathan Dane, Agreeing with His Arguments

Poughkeepsie, N.Y., c. July 15, 1788

My dear Sir,

I have received yours, and thank you for them—We have gone through the proposal of amendments, and are now deliberating what to do with them—In this we do not accord in sentiments, but I am not without hopes, we shall become of one mind—

I entirely accord with you in opinion, and shall if necessary avow them—Time and patience is necessary to bring our party to accord, which I ardently wish—

I have no time to copy the amendments proposed nor to answer Mr. Osgoods friendly Letter, for which I beg you to thank him—I beg you to use your influence to defer the organization of the New Governmt until we decide—You may be assured, that time & great industry is requisite, to bring us to act properly—My task is arduous and disagreable—You shall hear more by the next oportunity

Melancton Smith Speaks in Support of Ratification Without Condition

---

July 23, 1788

On Wednesday the Convention finished the consideration of the amendments, and took up the proposition of adopting the Constitution with three conditions annexed. Mr. Jones moved to insert the words *in full confidence*, instead of the words *upon condition*. Mr. M. Smith rose and declared his determination to vote against a condition. He urged that however it might otherwise be presumed he was consistent in his principles and conduct. He was as thoroughly convinced then as he ever had been, that the Constitution was radically defective—amendments to it had always been the object of his pursuit, and until Virginia came in, he had reason to believe they might have been obtained previous to the operation of the Government. He was now satisfied they could not, and it was equally the dictate of reason and duty to quit his first ground, and advance so far as that they might be received into the Union. He should hereafter pursue his important and favorite object of amendments, with equal zeal as before, but in a practicable way; which was only in the mode prescribed by the Constitution. On the first suggestion of the plan then under consideration, he thought it might have answered the purpose; but from the reasonings of gentlemen in opposition to it, and whose opinions alone would deservedly have vast weight in the national councils, as well as from the sentiments of persons abroad, he was now persuaded the proposition would not be received, however doubtful it might appear, considered merely as an abstract and speculative question. The thing must now be abandoned as fallacious, for if persisted in, it would certainly prove in the event, only a dreadful deception to those who were serious for joining the Union. He then placed in a striking and affecting light, the situation of this State in case we should not be received by Congress. Convulsions in the Southern part, factions and discord in the rest. The strength of his own party, who were seriously anxious for amending the Government, would be dissipated; their union lost—their object probably defeated—and they would, to use the simple figurative language of scripture, be dispersed like sheep on a mountain. He therefore concluded that it was no more than a proper discharge of his public duty, as well as the most advisable way of obtaining the great end of his opposition, to vote against any proposition which would not be received as a ratification of the Constitution.

Five Speakers Debate Congressional Control of Congressional Elections

<hr>

July 25, 1788

<hr>

Mr. *Spencer*—Mr. Chairman, It is with great reluctance that I rise upon this important occasion. I have considered with some attention the subject before us. I have paid attention to the Constitution itself, and to the writings on both sides. I considered it on one side as well as on the other, in order to know whether it would be best to adopt it or not. I would not wish to insinuate any reflections on those gentlemen who formed it. I look upon it as a great performance. It has a great deal of merit in it, and it is perhaps as much as any set of men could have done. Even if it be true what gentlemen have observed, that the gentlemen who were Delegates to the federal Convention, were not instructed to form a new Constitution, but to amend the Confederation. This will be immaterial, if it be proper to be adopted. It will be of equal benefit to us, if proper to be adopted in the whole, or in such parts as will be necessary, whether they were expressly delegated for that purpose or not. This appears to me to be a reprehensible clause; because it seems to strike at the state Legislatures, and seems to take away that power of elections, which reason dictates they ought to have among themselves. It apparently looks forward to a consolidation of the government of the United States, when the state Legislatures may entirely decay away. This is one of the grounds which have induced me to make objections to the new form of government. It appears to me that the state governments are not sufficiently secured, and that they may be swallowed up by the great mass of powers given to Congress. If that be the case, such power should not be given; for from all the notions which we have concerning our happiness and well-being, the state governments are the basis of our happiness, security and prosperity. A large extent of country ought to be divided into such a number of states, as that the people may conveniently carry on their own government. This will render the government perfectly agreeable to the genius and wishes of the people. If the United States were to consist of ten times as many states, they might all have a degree of harmony. Nothing would be wanting but some cement for their connection. On the contrary, if all the United States were to be swallowed up by the great mass of powers given to Congress, the parts that are more distant in this great empire would be governed with less and less energy. It would not suit the genius of the people to assist in the government. Nothing would support government in such a case as that but military coercion. Armies would be necessary in different parts of the United States. The expence which they would cost, and the burdens which they would make necessary to be laid upon the people, would be ruinous. I know of no way that is likely to produce the happiness of the people, but to preserve, as far as possible, the existence of the several states, so that they shall not be swallowed up. It has been said, that the existence of the state governments is essential to that of the general government, because they choose the Senators. By this clause it is evident, that it is in the power of Congress to make any alterations, except as to the place of choosing Senators. They may alter the time from six to twenty years, or to any time; for they have an unlimited controul over the time of elections. They have also an absolute controul over the election of the Representatives. It deprives the people of the very mode of choosing them. It seems nearly to throw the whole power of election into the hands of Congress. It strikes at the mode, time and place of choosing Representatives. It puts all but the place of electing Senators, into the hands of Congress. This supercedes the necessity of continuing the state Legislatures. This is such an article as I can give no sanction to, because it strikes at the foundation of the government on which depends the happiness of the states, and the general government. It is with reluctance I make the objection. I have the highest veneration for the characters of the framers of this Constitution. I mean to make objections only which are necessary to be made. I would not take up time unnecessarily. As to this matter, it strikes at the foundation of every thing. I may say more when we come to that part which points out the mode of doing without the agency of the state Legislatures.

Mr. *Iredell*—Mr. Chairman, I am glad to see so much candour and moderation. The liberal sentiments expressed by the honourable gentleman who spoke last, command my respect. No time can be better employed than in endeavouring to remove, by fair and just reasoning, every objection which can be made to this Constitution. I apprehend, that the honourable gentleman is mistaken as to the extent of the operation of this clause. He supposes, that the controul of the general government over elections looks forward to a consolidation of the states; and that the general word, *time*, may extend to twenty, or any number of years. In my humble opinion, this clause does by no means warrant such a construction. We ought to compare other parts with it. Does not the Constitution say, that Representatives shall be chosen every second year? The right of choosing them, therefore, reverts to the people every second year. No instrument of writing ought to be construed absurdly, when a rational construction can be put upon it. If Congress can prolong the election to any time they please, why is it said, that Representatives shall be chosen every second year? *They must be chosen every second year;* but whether in the month of March or January, or any other month, may be ascertained at a future time, by regulations of Congress. The word *time*, refers only to the particular month and day within the two years. I heartily agree with the gentleman, that if any thing in this Constitution tended to the annihilation of the state governments, instead of exciting the admiration of any man, it ought to excite his resentment and execration. No such wicked intention ought to be suffered. But the gentlemen who formed the Constitution had no such object; nor do I think there is the least ground for that jealousy. The very existence of the general government depends on that of the state governments. The state Legislatures are to choose the Senators. Without a Senate there can be no Congress. The state Legislatures are also to direct the manner of choosing the President. Unless, therefore, there are state Legislatures to direct that manner, no President can be chosen.

The same observation may be made as to the House of Representatives, since, as they are to be chosen by the electors of the most numerous branch of each state Legislature. If there are no state Legislatures, there are no persons to choose the House of Representatives. Thus it is evident, that the very existence of the general government depends on that of the state Legislatures, and of course, that their continuance cannot be endangered by it.

An occasion may arise when the exercise of this ultimate power in Congress may be necessary: As for instance, if a state should be involved in war, and its Legislature could not assemble, as was the case of South-Carolina, and occasionally of some other states, during the late war. It might also be useful for this reason—lest a few powerful states should combine, and make regulations concerning elections, which might deprive many of the electors of a fair exercise of their rights, and thus injure the community, and occasion great dissatisfaction: And it seems natural and proper that every government should have in itself the means of its own preservation. A few of the great states might combine to prevent any election of Representatives at all, and thus a majority might be wanting to do business; but it would not be so easy to destroy the government by the non-election of Senators, because one-third only are to go out at a time, and all the states will be equally represented in the Senate. It is not probable this power would be abused; for if it should be, the state Legislatures would immediately resent it; and their authority over the people will always be extremely great. These reasons induce me to think, that the power is both necessary and useful. But I am sensible great jealousy has been entertained concerning it: And as, perhaps, the danger of a combination, in the manner I have mentioned, to destroy or distress the general government, is not very probable, it may be better to incur this risk, than occasion any discontent, by suffering the clause to continue as it now stands. I should, therefore, not object to the recommendation of an amendment similar to that of other states, that this power in Congress should only be exercised when a state Legislature neglected, or was disabled from making the regulations required.

Mr. *Spencer*—Mr. Chairman, I did not mean to insinuate,

that designs were made by the honourable gentlemen who composed the federal Constitution, against our liberties. I only meant to say, that the words in this place were exceeding vague. It may admit of the gentleman's construction; but it may admit of a contrary construction. In a matter of so great moment, words ought not to be so vague and indeterminate. I have said, that the states are the basis on which the government of the United States ought to rest, and which must render us secure. No man wishes more for a federal government than I do. I think it necessary for our happiness: But at the same time, when we form a government which must entail happiness or misery on posterity, nothing is of more consequence than settling it so as to exclude animosity and a contest between the general and individual governments. With respect to the mode here mentioned, they are words of very great extent. This clause provides, that a Congress may at any time alter such regulations, except as to the places of choosing Senators. These words are so vague and uncertain, that it must ultimately destroy the whole liberty of the United States. It strikes at the very existence of the states, and supercedes the necessity of having them at all. I would therefore wish to have it amended in such a manner, as that the Congress should not interfere but when the states refused or neglected to regulate elections.

Mr. *Bloodworth*—Mr. Chairman, I trust that such learned arguments as are offered to reconcile to our minds such dangerous powers will not have the intended weight. The House of Representatives is the only democratical branch. This clause may destroy representation entirely. What does it say? The times, places and manner of holding elections for Senators and Representatives, shall be prescribed in each state by the Legislature thereof; but the Congress may at any time, by law, make or alter such regulations, except as to the places of choosing Senators. Now, Sir, does not this clause give an unlimited and unbounded power to Congress over the times, places and manner of choosing Representatives? They may make the time of election so long, the place so inconvenient, and the manner so oppressive, that it will entirely destroy representation. I hope gentlemen will exercise their own understanding on this occasion, and not let their judgment be led away by these shining characters, for whom, however, I have the highest respect. This Constitution, if adopted in its present mode, must end in the subversion of our liberties. Suppose it takes place in North-Carolina, can farmers elect then? No, Sir. The elections may be in such a manner that men may be appointed who are not Representatives of the people. This may exist, and it ought to be guarded against. As to the place, suppose Congress should order the elections to be held in the most inconvenient place, in the most inconvenient district; could every person entitled to vote attend at such a place? Suppose they should order it to be laid off into so many districts, and order the election to be held within each district; yet may not their power over the manner of election enable them to exclude from voting every description of men they please? The democratic branch is so much endangered, that no arguments can be made use of to satisfy my mind to it. The honourable gentleman has amused us with learned discussions, and told us he will condescend to propose amendments. I hope the Representatives of North-Carolina will never swallow the Constitution till it is amended.

Mr. *Goudy*—Mr. Chairman, The invasion of the states is urged as a reason for this clause. But why did they not mention that it should be only in cases of invasion? But that was not the reason in my humble opinion. I fear it was a combination against our liberties. I ask, when we give them the purse in one hand, and the sword in another, what power have we left? It will lead to an aristocratical government, and establish tyranny over us. We are freemen, and we ought to have the privileges of such.

Governor *Johnston*—Mr. Chairman, I do not impute any impure intentions to the gentlemen who formed this Constitution. I think it unwarrantable in any one to do it. I believe, that were there twenty Conventions appointed, and as many Constitutions formed, we never could get men more able and disinterested than those who formed this, nor a Constitution less exceptionable than that which is now before you. I am not apprehensive that this article will be attended with all the fatal consequences, which the gentleman conceives. I conceive that Congress can have no other power than the states had.

The states, with regard to elections, must be governed by the articles of the Constitution; so must Congress. But, I believe, the power, as it now stands, is unnecessary. I should be perfectly satisfied with it in the mode recommended by the worthy Member on my right hand: Although I should be extremely cautious to adopt any Constitution that would endanger the rights and privileges of the people. I have no fear in adopting this Constitution, and then proposing amendments. I feel as much attachment to the rights and privileges of my country as any man in it; and if I thought any thing in this Constitution tended to abridge these rights, I would not agree to it. I cannot conceive that this is the case. I have not the least doubt but it will be adopted by a very great majority of the states: For states who have been as jealous of their liberties as any in the world, have adopted it; and they are some of the most powerful states. We shall have the assent of all the states in getting amendments. Some gentlemen have apprehensions, that Congress will immediately conspire to destroy the liberties of their country. The men, of whom Congress will consist, are to be chosen from among ourselves. They will be in the same situation with us. They are to be bone of our bone, and flesh of our flesh. They cannot injure us without injuring themselves. I have no doubt but we shall choose the best men in the community. Should different men be appointed, they are sufficiently responsible. I therefore think, that no danger is to be apprehended.

The Debate on Congressional Elections
Continued: Britain and America Contrasted

Mr. *Caldwell*—Mr. Chairman, Those things which can be, may be. We know that in the British government, the Members of Parliament were eligible only for three years. They determined they might be chosen for seven years. If Congress can alter the time, manner and place, I think it will enable them to do what the British Parliament once did. They have declared, that the elections of Senators are for six years, and of Representatives for two years. But they have said there was an exception to this general declaration, *viz.* that Congress can alter them. If the Convention only meant that they should alter them in such a manner as to prevent a discontinuation of the government, why have they not said so? It must appear to every gentleman in this Convention, that they can alter the elections to what time they please: And if the British Parliament did once give themselves the power of sitting four years longer than they had a right to do, Congress, having a standing army, and the command of the militia, may, with the same propriety, make an act to continue the Members for twenty years, or even for their natural lives. This construction appears perfectly rational to me. I shall therefore think that this Convention will never swallow such a government, without securing us against danger.

Mr. *Maclaine*—Mr. Chairman, The reverend gentleman from Guilford, has made an objection which astonishes me more than any thing I have heard. He seems to be acquainted with the history of England, but he ought to consider whether his historical references apply to this country. He tells us of triennial elections being changed to septennial elections. This is a historical fact we well know, and the occasion on which it happened, is equally well known. They talk as loudly of constitutional rights and privileges in England, as we do here, but they have no written constitution. They have a common law, which has been altered from year to year, for a very long period—Magna Charta, and Bill of Rights. These they look upon as their constitution. Yet this is such a constitution as it is universally considered Parliament can change. Blackstone, in his admirable Commentaries, tells us, that the power of the Parliament is transcendent and absolute, and can do and undo every thing that is not naturally impossible. The act, therefore, to which the reverend gentleman alludes, was not unconstitutional. Has any man said that the Legislature can deviate from this Constitution? The Legislature is to be guided by the Constitution. They cannot travel beyond its bounds. The reverend gentleman says, that though the Representatives are to be elected for two years, they may pass an act prolonging their appointment for twenty years, or for natural life, without any violation of the Constitution. Is it possible for any common understanding or sense, to put this construction upon it? Such an act, Sir, would be a palpable violation of the Constitution. Were they to attempt it, Sir, the country would rise against them. After such an unwarrantable suggestion as this, any objection may be made to this Constitution. It is necessary to give power to the government. I would ask that gentleman who is so afraid it will destroy our liberties, why he is not as much afraid of our state Legislature? For they have much more power than we are now proposing to give this general government. They have an unlimited controul over the purse and sword—yet no complaints are made. Why is he not afraid that our Legislature will call out the militia to destroy our liberties? Will the militia be called out by the general government to enslave the people—to enslave their friends, their families, themselves? The idea of the militia being made use of as an instrument to destroy our liberties, is almost too absurd to merit a refutation. It cannot be supposed that the Representatives of our general government will be worse men than the Members of our state government. Will we be such fools as to send our greatest rascals to the general government? We must be both fools as well as villains to do so.

Governor *Johnston*—Mr. Chairman, I shall offer some observations on what the gentleman said. A parallel has been drawn between the British Parliament and Congress. The powers of Congress are all circumscribed, defined, and clearly laid down. So far they may go, but no farther. But, Sir, what are the powers of the British Parliament? They have no written Constitution in Britain. They have certain fundamental principles and legislative acts, securing the liberty of the people: But these may be altered by their Representatives, without violating their Constitution, in such manner as they may think proper. Their Legislature existed long before the science of government was well understood. From very early periods you find their Parliament in full force. What is their Magna Charta? It is only an act of Parliament. Their Parliament can at any time, alter the whole, or any part of it. In short, it is no more binding on the people than any other act which has passed. The power of the Parliament is, therefore, unbounded. But, Sir, can Congress alter the Constitution? They have no such power. They are bound to act by the Constitution. They dare not recede from it. At the moment that the time for which they are elected expires, they may be removed. If they make bad laws, they *will* be removed, for they will be no longer worthy of confidence. The British Parliament can do every thing they please. Their Bill of Rights is only an act of Parliament, which may be at any time altered or modified, without a violation of the Constitution. The people of Great-Britain have no Constitution to controul their Legislature.— The King, Lords and Commons can do what they please.

Mr. *Caldwell* observed, that whatever nominal powers the British Parliament might possess, yet they had infringed the liberty of the people in the most flagrant manner, by giving themselves power to continue four years in Parliament longer than they had been elected for—That though they were only chosen for three years by their constituents, yet they passed an act, that Representatives should, for the future, be chosen for seven years—That this Constitution would have a dangerous tendency—That this clause would enable them to prolong their continuance in office as long as they pleased—And that if a Constitution was not agreeable to the people, its operation could not be happy.

James Iredell on the Necessity for a Peacetime Army

July 26, 1788

Mr. *Iredell*—Mr. Chairman, This clause is of so much importance, that we ought to consider it with the most serious attention. It is a power vested in Congress, which, in my opinion, is absolutely indispensable; yet there have been, perhaps, more objections made to it, than any other power vested in Congress. For my part, I will observe generally, that so far from being displeased with that jealousy and extreme caution with which gentlemen consider every power proposed to be given to this government, they give me the utmost satisfaction. I believe the passion for liberty is stronger in America than in any other country in the world: Here every man is strongly impressed with its importance, and every breast glows for the preservation of it. Every jealousy, not incompatible with the indispensable principles of government, is undoubtedly to be commended: But these principles must, at all events, be observed. The powers of government ought to be competent to the public safety. This, indeed, is the primary object of all governments. It is the duty of gentlemen who form a Constitution, to take care that no power should be wanting which the safety of the community requires. The exigencies of the country must be provided for, not only in respect to common and usual cases, but for occasions which do not frequently occur. If such a provision is not made, critical occasions may arise, when there must be either an usurpation of power, or the public safety eminently endangered; for besides the evils attending the frequent change of a Constitution, the case may not admit of so slow a remedy. In considering the powers that ought to be vested in any government, possible abuses ought not to be pointed out, without at the same time considering their use. No power of any kind or degree can be given, but what may be abused: We have therefore only to consider, whether any particular power is absolutely necessary. If it be, the power must be given and we must run the risk of the abuse, considering our risk of this evil, as one of the conditions of the imperfect state of human nature, where there is no good without the mixture of some evil. At the same time it is undoubtedly our duty to guard against abuses as much as possible. In America, we enjoy peculiar blessings: The people are distinguished by the possession of freedom in a very high degree, unmixed with those oppressions the freest countries in Europe suffer. But we ought to consider that in this country as well as others, it is equally necessary to restrain and suppress internal commotions, and to guard against foreign hostility. There is I believe, no government in the world without a power to raise armies. In some countries in Europe, a great force is necessary to be kept up to guard against those numerous armies maintained by many sovereigns there; where an army belonging to one government alone, sometimes amounts to two hundred thousand or four hundred thousand men. Happily we are situated at a great distance from them, and the inconsiderable power to the north of us is not likely soon to be very formidable. But though our situation places us at a remote danger, it cannot be pretended we are in no danger at all. I believe there is no man who has written on this subject, but has admitted that this power of raising armies is necessary in time of war; but they do not choose to admit of it in a time of peace. It is to be hoped that in time of peace, there will not be occasion at any time, but for a very small number of forces; possibly a few garrisons may be necessary to guard the frontiers, and an insurrection like that lately in Massachusetts, might require some troops. But a time of war is the time when the power would probably be exerted to any extent. Let us, however, consider the consequences of a limitation of this power to a time of war only. One moment's consideration will shew the impolicy of it in the most glaring manner. We certainly ought to guard against the machinations of other countries. We know not what designs may be entertained against us; but surely when known, we ought to endeavour to counteract their effects; such designs may be entertained in a time of profound peace as well as after a declaration of war. Now suppose, for instance, our government had received certain intelligence that the British government had formed a scheme to attack New-York next April, with ten thousand men; would it not be proper immediately to prepare against it? and by so doing the scheme might be defeated. But if Congress had no such power, because it was a time of peace, the place must fall the instant it was attacked, and it might take years to recover what might at first have been seasonably defended. This restriction, therefore, cannot take place with safety to the community, and the power must of course be left to the direction of the general government. I hope there will be little necessity for the exercise of this power; and I trust that the universal resentment and resistance of the people will meet every attempt to abuse this or any other power. That high spirit for which they are distinguished, I hope will ever exist, and it probably will as long as we have a republican form of government. Every man feels a consciousness of personal equality and independence: Let him look at any part of the continent, he can see no superiors. This personal independence is the surest safe-guard of the public freedom. But is it probable that our own Representatives, chosen for a limited time, can be capable of destroying themselves, their families, and fortunes, even if they have no regard to their public duty? When such considerations are involved, surely it is very unlikely that they will attempt to raise an army against the liberties of their country. Were we to establish an hereditary nobility, or a set of men who were to have exclusive privileges, then indeed our jealousy might be well grounded. But fortunately we have no such. The restriction contended for, of no standing army in time of peace, forms a part of our own state Constitution. What has been the consequence? In December, 1786, the Assembly flagrantly violated it, by raising two hundred and one men for two years, for the defence of Davidson county. I do not deny that the intention might have been good, and that the Assembly really thought the situation of that part of the country required such a defence. But this makes the argument still stronger against the impolicy of such a restriction, since our own experience points out the danger resulting from it: For I take it for granted, that we could not at that time be said to be in a state of war. Dreadful might the condition of this country be, without this power. We must trust our friends or trust our enemies. There is one restriction on this power, which I believe is the only one that ought to be put upon it. Though Congress are to have the power of raising and supporting armies, yet they cannot appropriate money for that purpose for a longer time than two years. Now we will suppose that the majority of the two Houses should be capable of making a bad use of this power, and should appropriate more money to raise an army than is necessary. The appropriation we have seen cannot be constitutional for more than two years: Within that time it might command obedience. But at the end of the second year from the first choice, the whole House of Representatives must be re-chosen, and also one-third of the Senate. The people being inflamed with the abuse of power of the old Members, would turn them out with indignation. Upon their return home they would meet the universal execrations of their fellow-citizens—Instead of the grateful plaudits of their country, so dear to every feeling mind, they would be treated with the utmost resentment and contempt:—Their names would be held in everlasting infamy; and their measures would be instantly reprobated and changed by the new Members. In two years, a system of tyranny certainly could not succeed in the face of the whole people; and the appropriation could not be with any safety for less than that period. If it depended on an annual vote, the consequence might be, that at a critical period, when military operations were necessary, the troops would not know whether they were entitled to pay or not, and could not safely act till they knew that the annual vote had passed. To refuse this power to the government, would be to invite insults and attacks from other nations. Let us not, for God's sake, be guilty of such indiscretion as to trust to our enemies mercy, but give, as is our duty, a sufficient power to government to protect their country, guarding at the same time against abuses as well as we can. We well know what this country suffered by the ravages of the British army during the war. How could we have been saved but by an army? Without that resource we should soon have felt the miserable consequences; and this day, instead of having the honour, the greatest any people ever enjoyed, to choose a government which our reason recommends, we should have been groaning under the most intolerable tyranny that was ever felt. We ought not to think these dangers are entirely over. The British government is not friendly to us: They dread the rising glory of America: They tremble for the West-Indies, and their colonies to the north of us: They have counteracted us on every occasion since the peace. Instead of a liberal and reciprocal commerce, they have attempted to confine us to a most narrow and ignominious one. Their pride is still irritated with the disappointment of their endeavours to enslave us. They know that on the record of history their conduct towards us must appear in the most disgraceful light. Let it also appear on the record of history, that America was equally wise and fortunate in peace as well as in war. Let it be said, that with a temper and unanimity unexampled, they corrected the vices of an imperfect government, and framed a new one on the basis of justice and liberty: That though all did not concur in approving the particular structure of this government, yet that the minority peaceably and respectfully submitted to the decision of the greater number. This is a spectacle so great, that if it should succeed, this must be considered the greatest country under Heaven; for there is no instance of any such deliberate change of government in any other nation that ever existed. But how would it gratify the pride of our enemy to say: "We could not conquer you, but you have ruined yourselves. You have foolishly quarrelled about trifles. You are unfit for any government whatever. You have separated from us, when you were unable to govern yourselves, and you now deservedly feel all the horrors of anarchy." I beg pardon for saying so much. I did not intend it when I began. But the consideration of one of the most important parts of the plan excited all my feelings on the subject. I speak without any affectation in expressing my apprehension of foreign dangers—the belief of them is strongly impressed on my mind. I hope therefore the gentlemen of the committee will excuse the warmth with which I have spoken. I shall now take leave of the subject. I flatter myself that gentlemen will see that this power is absolutely necessary, and must be vested somewhere; that it can be vested no where so well as in the general government, and that it is guarded by the only restriction which the nature of the thing will admit of.

Mr. *Hardiman* desired to know, if the people were attacked

or harrassed in any part of the state, if on the frontiers for instance, whether they must not apply to the state Legislature for assistance?

Mr. *Iredell* replied, that he admitted that application might be immediately made to the state Legislature, but that by the plan under consideration, the strength of the union was to be exerted to repel invasions of foreign enemies and suppress domestic insurrections; and that the possibility of an instantaneous and unexpected attack in time of profound peace, illustrated the danger of restricting the power of raising and supporting armies.

James Iredell on the Presidency, Spies, the Pardoning Power, and Impeachment

July 28, 1788

The second section of the second article read.

Mr. *Iredell*—Mr. Chairman, This part of the Constitution has been much objected to. The office of superintending the execution of the laws of the union, is an office of the utmost importance. It is of the greatest consequence to the happiness of the people of America, that the person to whom this great trust is delegated should be worthy of it. It would require a man of abilities and experience: It would also require a man who possessed in a high degree the confidence of his country. This being the case, it would be a great defect in forming a Constitution for the United States, if it was so constructed that by any accident an improper person could have a chance to obtain that office. The Committee will recollect, that the President is to be elected by Electors appointed by each state, according to the number of Senators and Representatives to which the state may be entitled in the Congress: That they are to meet on the same day throughout all the states, and vote by ballot for two persons, one of whom shall not be an inhabitant of the same state with themselves. These votes are afterwards to be transmitted under seal to the seat of the general government. The person who has the greatest number of votes, if it be a majority of the whole, will be the President. If more than one have a majority, and equal votes, the House of Representatives are to choose one of them. If none have a majority of votes, then the House of Representatives are to choose which of the persons they think proper, out of the five highest on the list. The person having the next greatest number of votes is to be the Vice President, unless two or more should have equal votes, in which case the Senate is to choose one of them for Vice-President. If I recollect right, these are the principal characteristics. Thus, Sir, two men will be in office at the same time. The President, who possesses in the highest degree the confidence of his country; and the Vice-

President, who is thought to be the next person in the union most fit to perform this trust. Here, Sir, every contingency is provided for. No faction or combination can bring about the election. It is probable, that the choice will always fall upon a man of experienced abilities and fidelity. In all human probability, no better mode of election could have been devised.

The rest of the first section read without any observations. Second section read.

Mr. *Iredell*—Mr. Chairman, I was in hopes that some other gentleman would have spoken to this clause. It conveys very important powers, and ought not to be passed by. I beg leave in as few words as possible to speak my sentiments upon it. I believe most of the Governors of the different states, have powers similar to those of the President. In almost every country the Executive has the command of the military forces. From the nature of the thing, the command of armies ought to be delegated to one person only. The secrecy, dispatch and decision which are necessary in military operations, can only be expected from one person. The President therefore is to command the military forces of the United States, and this power I think a proper one; at the same time it will be found to be sufficiently guarded. A very material difference may be observed between this power, and the authority of the King of Great-Britain under similar circumstances. The King of Great-Britain is not only the Commander in Chief of the land and naval forces, but has power in time of war to raise fleets and armies. He has also authority to declare war. The President has not the power of declaring war by his own authority, nor that of raising fleets and armies: These powers are vested in other hands. The power of declaring war is expressly given to Congress, that is, to the two branches of the Legislature, the Senate composed of Representatives of the state Legislatures, the House of Representatives deputed by the people at large. They have also expressly delegated to them, the powers of raising and supporting armies, and of providing and maintaining a navy.

With regard to the militia, it must be observed, that though he has the command of them when called into the actual service of the United States, yet he has not the power of calling them out. The power of calling them out, is vested in Congress, for the purpose of executing the laws of the union. When the militia are called out for any purpose, some person must command them; and who so proper as that person who has the best evidence of his possessing the general confidence of the people? I trust therefore, that the power of commanding the militia when called forth into the actual service of the United States, will not be objected to.

The next part which says, "That he may require the opinion in writing of the principal officers," is in some degree substituted for a Council. He is only to consult them if he thinks proper. Their opinion is to be given him in writing. By this means he will be aided by their intelligence, and the necessity of their opinions being in writing, will render them more cautious in giving them, and make them responsible should they give advice manifestly improper. This does not diminish the responsibility of the President himself. They might otherwise have colluded, and opinions have been given too much under his influence.

It has been the opinion of many gentlemen, that the President should have a Council. This opinion probably has been derived from the example in England. It would be very proper for every gentleman to consider attentively, whether that example ought to be imitated by us. Altho' it be a respectable example, yet in my opinion very satisfactory reasons can be assigned for a departure from it in this Constitution.

It was very difficult, immediately on our separation from Great-Britain, to disengage ourselves entirely from ideas of government we had been used to. We had been accustomed to a Council under the old government, and took it for granted we ought to have one under the new. But examples ought not to be implicitly followed; and the reasons which prevail in Great-Britain for a Council, do not apply equally to us. In that country the executive authority is vested in a magistrate who holds it by birth-right. He has great powers and prerogatives; and it is a constitutional maxim, *that he can do no wrong*. We have experienced that he can do wrong, yet no man can say so in his own country. There are no courts to try him for any crimes; nor is there any constitutional method of depriving him of his throne. If he loses it, it must be by a general resistance of his people contrary to *forms* of law, as at the revolution which took place about a hundred years ago. It is therefore of the utmost moment in that country, that whoever is the instrument of any act of government should be personally responsible for it, since the King is not; and for the same reason, that no act of government should be exercised but by the instrumentality of some person, who can be accountable for it. Every thing therefore that the King does must be by some *advice*, and the adviser of course answerable. Under our Constitution we are much happier. No man has an authority to injure another with impunity. No man is better than his fellow-citizens, nor can pretend to any superiority over the meanest man in the country. If the President does a single act, by which the people are prejudiced, he is punishable himself, and no other man merely to screen him. If he commits any misdemeanor in office, he is impeachable, removable from office, and incapacitated to hold any office of honour, trust or profit. If he commits any crime, he is punishable by the laws of his country, and in capital cases may be deprived of his life. This being the case, there is not the same reason here for having a Council, which exists in England. It is, however, much to be desired, that a man who has such extensive and important business to perform, should have the means of some assistance to enable him to discharge his arduous employment. The advice of the principal executive officers, which he can at all times command, will in my opinion answer this valuable purpose. He can at no time want advice, if he desires it, as the principal officers will always be on the spot. Those officers from their abilities and experience, will probably be able to give as good, if not better advice, than any Counsellors would do; and the solemnity of the advice in writing, which must be preserved, would be a great check upon them.

Besides these considerations, it was difficult for the Convention to prepare a Council that would be unexceptionable. That jealousy which naturally exists between the different states, enhanced this difficulty. If a few Counsellors were to be chosen from the northern, southern or middle states, or from a few states only, undue preference might be given to those particular states from which they should come. If to avoid this difficulty, one Counsellor should be sent from each state, this would require great expence, which is a consideration at this time of much moment, especially as it is probable, that by the method proposed, the President may be equally well advised without any expence at all.

We ought also to consider, that had he a Council, by whose advice he was bound to act, his responsibility in all such cases must be destroyed. You surely would not oblige him to follow their advice, and punish him for obeying it. If called upon on any occasion of dislike, it would be natural for him to say, "You know my Council are men of integrity and ability: I could not act against their opinions, though I confess my own was contrary to theirs." This, Sir, would be pernicious. In such a situation, he might easily combine with his Council, and it might be impossible to fix a fact upon him. It would be difficult often to know, whether the President or Counsellors were most to blame. A thousand plausible excuses might be made, which would escape detection. But the method proposed in the Constitution creates no such embarrassment. It is plain and open. And the President will personally have the credit of good, or the censure of bad measures; since, though he may ask advice, he is to use his own judgment in following or rejecting it. For all these reasons I am clearly of opinion, that the clause is better as it stands than if the President were to have a Council. I think every good that can be derived from the institution of a Council, may be expected from the advice of these officers, without its being liable to the disadvantages to which it appears to me the institution of a Council would be.

Another power that he has is to grant pardons, except in cases of impeachment. I believe it is the sense of a great part of America, that this power should be exercised by their Governors. It is in several states on the same footing that it is here. It is the genius of a republican government, that the laws should be rigidly executed without the influence of favour or ill-will: That when a man commits a crime, however powerful he or his friends may be, yet he should be punished for it; and on the other hand, though he should be universally hated by his country, his real guilt alone as to the particular charge is to operate against him. This strict and scrupulous observance of justice is proper in all governments, but it is particularly indispensable in a republican one; because in such a government, the law is superior to every man, and no man is superior to another. But though this general principle be unquestionable, surely there is no gentleman in the committee, who is not aware that there ought to be exceptions to it; because there may be many instances, where though a man offends against the *letter* of the law, yet peculiar circumstances in his case may entitle him to mercy. It is impossible for any general law to foresee and provide for all possible cases that may arise, and therefore an inflexible adherence to it in every instance, might frequently be the cause of very great injustice. For this reason, such a power ought to exist somewhere; and where could it be more properly vested, than in a man who had received such strong proofs of his possessing the highest confidence of the people? This power however only refers to offences against the United States, and not against particular states. Another reason for the President possessing this authority, is this: It is often necessary to convict a man by means of his accomplices: We have sufficient experience of that in this country. A criminal would often go unpunished, were not this method to be pursued against him. In my opinion, till an accomplice's own danger is removed, his evidence ought to be regarded with great diffidence. If in civil causes of property, a witness must be entirely disinterested, how much more proper is it he should be so in cases of life and death! This power is naturally vested in the President, because it is his duty to watch over the public safety, and as that may frequently require the evidence of accomplices to bring great offenders to justice, he ought to be entrusted with the most effectual means of procuring it.

I beg leave farther to observe, that for another reason I think there is a propriety in leaving this power to the general discretion of the executive magistrate, rather than to fetter it in any manner which has been proposed. It may happen, that many men, upon plausible pretences, may be seduced into very dangerous measures against their country. They may aim by an insurrection to redress imaginary grievances, at the same time believing, upon false suggestions, that their exertions are necessary to save their country from destruction. Upon cool reflection however, they possibly are convinced of their error, and clearly see thro' the treachery and villainy of their leaders. In this situation, if the President possessed the power of pardoning, they probably would immediately throw themselves on the equity of the government, and the whole body be peaceably broke up. Thus, at a critical moment, the President might prevent perhaps a civil war. But if there was no authority to pardon, in that delicate exigency, what would be the consequence? The principle of self-preservation would prevent their parting. Would it not be natural for them to say, "We shall be punished if we disband. Were we sure of mercy we would peaceably part. But we know not that there is any chance of this. We may as well meet one kind of death as another. We may as well die in the field as at the gallows." I therefore submit to the committee, if this power be not highly necessary for such a purpose. We have seen a happy instance of the good effect of such an exercise of mercy in the state of Massachusetts, where very lately there was so formidable an insurrection. I believe a great majority of the insurgents were drawn into it by false artifices. They at length saw their error, and were willing to disband. Government, by a wise exercise of lenity, after having shewn its power, generally granted a pardon; and the whole party were dispersed. There is now as much peace in that country as in any state in the union.

A particular instance which occurs to me, shews the utility of this power very strongly. Suppose we were involved in war. It would be then necessary to know the designs of the enemy. This kind of knowledge cannot always be procured but by means of *spies*, a set of wretches whom all nations despise, but whom all employ; and as they would assuredly be used against us, a principle of self defence would urge and justify the use of them on our part. Suppose therefore the President could prevail upon a man of some importance to go over to the enemy, in order to give him secret information of his measures. He goes off privately to the enemy. He feigns resentment against his country for some ill usage, either real or pretended, and is received possibly into favour and confidence. The people would not know the purpose for which he was employed. In the mean time he secretly informs the President of the enemy's designs, and by this means, perhaps those designs are counteracted, and the country saved from destruction. After his business is executed, he returns into his own country, where the people, not knowing he had rendered them any service, are naturally exasperated against him for his supposed treason. I would ask any gentleman whether the President ought not to have the power of pardoning this man. Suppose the concurrence of the Senate, or any other body was necessary, would this obnoxious person be properly safe? We know in every country there is a strong prejudice against the executive authority. If a prejudice of this kind, on such an occasion, prevailed against the President, the President might be suspected of being influenced by corrupt motives, and the application in favour of this man be rejected. Such a thing might very possibly happen when the prejudices of party were strong, and therefore no man so clearly entitled as in the case I have supposed, ought to have his life exposed to so hazardous a contingency.

The power of impeachment is given by this Constitution, to bring great offenders to punishment. It is calculated to bring them to punishment for crimes which it is not easy to describe, but which every one must be convinced is a high crime and misdemeanor against the government. This power is lodged in those who represent the great body of the people, because the occasion for its exercise will arise from acts of great injury to the community, and the objects of it may be such as cannot be easily reached by an ordinary tribunal. The trial belongs to the Senate, lest an inferior tribunal should be too much awed by so powerful an accuser. After a trial thus solemnly conducted, it is not probable that it would happen once in a thousand times, that a man actually convicted, would be entitled to mercy; and if the President had the power of pardoning in such a case, this great check upon high officers of state would lose much of its influence. It seems therefore proper, that the general power of pardoning should be abridged in this particular instance. The punishment annexed to conviction on impeachment, can only be removal from office, and disqualification to hold any place of honour, trust or profit. But the person convicted is further liable to a trial at common law, and may receive such common law punishment as belongs to a description of such offences, if it be one punishable by that law. I hope, for the reasons I have stated, that the whole of this clause will be approved by the committee. The regulations altogether, in my opinion, are as wisely contrived as they could be. It is impossible for imperfect beings to form a perfect system. If the present one may be productive of possible inconveniences, we are not to reject it for that reason, but inquire whether any other system could be devised which would be attended with fewer inconveniences, in proportion to the advantages resulting. But we ought to be exceedingly attentive in examining, and still more cautious in deciding, lest we should condemn what may be worthy of applause, or approve of what may be exceptionable. I hope, that in the explanation of this clause, I have not improperly taken up the time of the committee.

Samuel Spencer Objects to the Powers of the Senate and Fears It Will Control the President

July 28, 1788

Mr. *Spencer*—Mr. Chairman, I rise to declare my disapprobation of this likewise. It is an essential article in our Constitution, that the legislative, the executive and the supreme judicial powers of government, ought to be forever separate and distinct from each other. The Senate in the proposed government of the United States, are possessed of the legislative authority in conjunction with the House of Representatives. They are likewise possessed of the sole power of trying all impeachments, which not being restrained to the officers of the United States, may be intended to include all the officers of the several states in the union. And by this clause they possess the chief of the executive power—they are in effect to form treaties, which are to be the law of the land, and they have obviously in effect the appointment of all the officers of the United States; the President may nominate, but they have a negative upon his nomination, till he has exhausted the number of those he wishes to be appointed: He will be obliged finally to acquiesce in the appointment of those which the Senate shall nominate, or else no appointment will take place. Hence it is easy to perceive, that the President, in order to do any business, or to answer any purpose in his department of his office, and to keep himself out of perpetual hot water, will be under a necessity to form a connection with that powerful body, and be contented to put himself at the head of the leading members who compose it. I do not expect at this day, that the outline and organization of this proposed government will be materially altered. But I cannot but be of opinion, that the government would have been infinitely better and more secure, if the President had been provided with a standing Council, composed of one Member from each of the states, the duration of whose office might have been the same as that of the President's office, or for any other period that might have been thought more proper. For it can hardly be supposed, that if two Senators can be sent from each state, who are fit to give counsel to the President, that one such cannot be found in each state, qualified for that purpose. Upon this plan, one half the expence of the Senate, as a standing Council to the President in the recess of Congress, would evidently be saved; each state would have equal weight in this Council, as it has now in the Senate: And what renders this plan the more eligible is, that two very important consequences would result from it, which cannot result from the present plan. The first is, that the whole executive department, being separate and distinct from that of the legislative and judicial, would be amenable to the justice of the land—the President and his Council, or either or any of them, might be impeached, tried and condemned for any misdemeanor in office. Whereas on the present plan proposed, the Senate who are to advise the President, and who in effect are possessed of the chief executive power, let their conduct be what it will, are not amenable to the public justice of their country; if they may be impeached, there is no tribunal invested with jurisdiction to try them. It is true that the proposed Constitution provides, that when the President is tried the Chief-Justice shall preside. But I take this to be very little more than a farce. What can the Senate try him for? For doing that which they have advised him to do, and which without their advice he would not have done. Except what he may do in a military capacity, when I presume he will be entitled to be tried by a court-martial of General officers, he can do nothing in the executive department without the advice of the Senate, unless it be to grant pardons, and adjourn the two Houses of Congress to some day to which they cannot agree to adjourn themselves, probably to some term that may be convenient to the leading Members of the Senate. I cannot conceive therefore, that the President can ever be tried by the Senate with any effect, or to any purpose, for any misdemeanor in his office, unless it should extend to high treason, or unless they should wish to fix the odium of any measure on him, in order to exculpate themselves; the latter of which I cannot suppose will ever happen.

Another important consequence of the plan I wish had taken place, is, that the office of the President being thereby unconnected with that of the legislative, as well as the judicial, he would enjoy that independence which is necessary to form the intended check upon the acts passed by the Legislature before they obtain the sanction of laws. But on the present plan, from the necessary connection of the President's office with that of the Senate, I have little ground to hope, that his firmness will long prevail against the overbearing power and influence of the Senate, so far as to answer the purpose of any considerable check upon the acts they may think proper to pass in conjunction with the House of Representatives. For he will soon find, that unless he inclines to compound with them, they can easily hinder and controul him in the principal articles of his office. But if nothing else could be said in favour of the plan of a standing Council to the President, independent of the Senate, the dividing the power of the latter would be sufficient to recommend it; it being of the utmost importance toward the security of the government, and the liberties of the citizens under it. For I think it must be obvious to every unprejudiced mind, that the combining in the Senate, the power of legislation with a controuling share in the appointment of all the officers of the United States, except those chosen by the people, and the power of trying all impeachments that may be found against such officers, invests the Senate at once with such an enormity of power, and with such an overbearing and uncontroulable influence, as is incompatible with every idea of safety to the liberties of a free country, and is calculated to swallow up all other powers, and to render that body a despotic aristocracy.

James Iredell on Impeachment:
"It Must Be for an Error of the Heart, and Not of the Head"

July 28, 1788

Mr. *Iredell*—Mr. Chairman, The objections to this clause deserve great consideration. I believe it will be easy to obviate the objections against it, and that it will be found to have been necessary, for the reasons stated by the gentleman from Halifax, to vest this power in some body composed of Representatives of states, where their voices should be equal: For in this case the sovereignty of the states is particularly concerned; and the great caution of giving the states an equality of suffrage in making treaties, was for the express purpose of taking care of that sovereignty, and attending to their interests, as political bodies, in foreign negociations. It is objected to as improper, because if the President or Senate should abuse their trust, there is not sufficient responsibility, since he can only be tried by the Senate, by whose advice he acted; and the Senate cannot be tried at all. I beg leave to observe, that when any man is impeached, it must be for an error of the heart, and not of the head. God forbid, that a man in any country in the world, should be liable to be punished for want of judgment. This is not the case here. As to errors of the heart there is sufficient responsibility. Should these be committed, there is a ready way to bring him to punishment. This is a responsibility which answers every purpose that could be desired by a people jealous of their liberty. I presume that if the President, with the advice of the Senate, should make a treaty with a foreign power, and that treaty should be deemed unwise, or against the interest of the country, yet if nothing could be objected against it but the difference of opinion between them and their constituents, they could not justly be obnoxious to punishment. If they were punishable for exercising their own judgment, and not that of their constituents, no man who regarded his reputation would accept the office either of a Senator or President. Whatever mistake a man may make, he ought not to be punished for it, nor his posterity rendered infamous. But if a man be a villain, and wilfully abuses his trust, he is to be held up as a public offender, and ignominiously punished.

A public officer ought not to act from a principle of fear. Were he punishable for want of judgment, he would be continually in dread. But when he knows that nothing but real guilt can disgrace him, he may do his duty firmly if he be an honest man, and if he be not, a just fear of disgrace, may perhaps, as to the public, have nearly the effect of an intrinsic principle of virtue. According to these principles, I suppose the only instances in which the President would be liable to impeachment, would be where he had received a bribe, or had acted from some corrupt motive or other. If the President had received a bribe without the privity or knowledge of the Senate, from a foreign power, and had, under the influence of that bribe, had address enough with the Senate, by artifices and misrepresentations, to seduce their consent to a pernicious treaty—if it appeared afterwards that this was the case, would not that Senate be as competent to try him as any other persons whatsoever? Would they not exclaim against his villainy? Would they not feel a particular resentment against him for their being made the instrument of his treacherous purposes? In this situation, if any objection could be made against the Senate as a proper tribunal, it might more properly be made by the President himself, lest their resentment should operate too strongly, rather than by the public, on the ground of a supposed partiality. The President must certainly be punishable for giving false information to the Senate. He is to regulate all intercourse with foreign powers, and it is his duty to impart to the Senate every material intelligence he receives. If it should appear that he has not given them full information, but has concealed important intelligence which he ought to have communicated, and by that means induced them to enter into measures injurious to their country, and which they would not have consented to had the true state of things been disclosed to them—In this case, I ask whether, upon an impeachment for a misdemeanor upon such an account, the Senate would probably favour him? With respect to the impeachability of the Senate, that is a matter of doubt. There have been no instances of impeachment for legislative misdemeanors: And we shall find, upon examination, that the inconveniences resulting from such impeachments, would more than preponderate the advantages. There is no greater honour in the world, than being the representative of a free people—There is no trust on which the happiness of the people has a greater dependence. Yet, whoever heard of impeaching a Member of the Legislature for any legislative misconduct? It would be a great check on the public business, if a Member of the Assembly was liable to punishment for his conduct as such. Unfortunately it is the case, not only in other countries but even in this, that divisions and differences in opinion will continually arise. On many questions, there will be two or more parties. These often judge with little charity of each other, and attribute every opposition to their own system to an ill motive. We know this very well from experience; but, in my opinion, this constant suspicion is frequently unjust. I believe in general, both parties really think themselves right, and that the majority of each commonly act with equal innocence of intention. But, with the usual want of charity in these cases, how dangerous would it be to make a Member of the Legislature liable to impeachment! A mere difference of opinion might be interpreted by the malignity of party, into a deliberate, wicked action. It, therefore, appears to me at least very doubtful, whether it would be proper to render the Senate impeachable at all; especially as in the branches of executive government, where their concurrence is required, the President is the primary agent, and plainly responsible; and they in fact are but a Council to validate proper, or restrain improper, conduct in him.—But if a Senator is impeachable, it could only be for corruption, or some other wicked motive; in which case, surely those Senators who had acted from upright motives, would be competent to try him. Suppose there had been such a Council as was proposed, consisting of thirteen, one from each state, to assist the President in making treaties, &c. more general alarm would have been excited, and stronger opposition made to this Constitution, than even at present—The power of the President would have appeared more formidable, and the states would have lost one half of their security; since, instead of two Representatives, which each has now for those purposes, they would have had but one. A gentleman from New-Hanover has asked, whether it is not the practice in Great-Britain to submit treaties to Parliament, before they are esteemed valid. The King has the sole authority, by the laws of that country, to make treaties. After treaties are made, they are frequently discussed in the two Houses of Parliament; where, of late years, the most important measures of government have been narrowly examined. It is usual to move for an address of approbation; and such has been the complaisance of Parliament for a long time, that this seldom hath been with-held. Sometimes they pass an act in conformity to the treaty made: But this I believe is not for the mere purpose of confirmation, but to make alterations in a particular system, which the change of circumstances requires. The constitutional power of making treaties is vested in the crown; and the power with whom a treaty is made, considers it as binding without any act of Parliament, unless an alteration by such is provided for in the treaty itself, which I believe is sometimes the case. When the treaty of peace was made in 1763, it contained stipulations for the surrender of some islands to the French. The islands were given up, I believe, without any act of Parliament. The power of making treaties is very important, and must be vested somewhere, in order to counteract the dangerous designs of other countries, and to be able to terminate a war when it is begun. Were it known that our government was weak, two or more European powers might combine against us. Would it not be politic to have some power in this country, to obviate this danger by a treaty? If this power was injudiciously limited, the nations where the power was possessed without restriction, would have greatly the advantage of us in negociation; and every one must know, according to modern policy, of what moment an advantage in negociation is. The honourable Member from Anson said, that the accumulation of all the different branches of power in the Senate, would be dangerous. The experience of other countries shews that this fear is without foundation. What is the Senate of Great-Britain opposed to the House of Commons, although it be composed of an hereditary nobility, of vast fortunes, and entirely independent of the people? Their weight is far inferior to that of the Commons. Here is a strong instance of the accumulation of powers of the different branches of government without producing any inconvenience. That Senate, Sir, is a separate branch of the Legislature, is the great constitutional Council of the Crown, and decides on lives and fortunes in impeachments, besides being the ultimate tribunal for trying controversies respecting private rights. Would it not appear that all these things should render them more formidable than the other House? Yet the Commons have generally been able to carry every thing before them. The circumstance of their representing the great body of the people, alone gives them great weight. This weight has great authority added to it, by their possessing the right (a right given to the people's Representatives in Congress) of exclusively originating money bills. The authority over money will do every thing. A government cannot be supported without money. Our Representatives may at any time compel the Senate to agree to a reasonable measure, by with-holding supplies till the measure is consented to. There was a great debate in the Convention, whether the Senate should have an equal power of originating money bills. It was strongly insisted by some that they should; but at length a majority thought it unadviseable, and the clause was passed as it now stands. I have reason to believe our own Representatives had a great share in establishing this excellent regulation, and in my opinion they deserve the public thanks for it. It has been objected, that this power must necessarily injure the people, inasmuch as a bare majority of the Senate might alone be assembled, and eight would be sufficient for a decision. This is on a supposition that many of the Senators would neglect attending. It is to be hoped that the gentlemen who will be honored with seats in Congress, will faithfully execute their trust, as well in attending as in every other part of their duty. An objection of this sort, will go against all government whatever. Possible abuse and neglect of attendance, are objections which may be urged against any government which the wisdom of man is able to construct. When it is known of how much importance attendance is, no Senator would dare to incur the universal resentment of his fellow-citizens, by grossly absenting himself from his duty. Do gentlemen mean that it ought to have been provided by the Constitution, that the whole body should attend before particular business was done? Then it would be in the power of a few men, by neglecting to attend, to obstruct the public business, and possibly bring on the destruction of their country. If this power be improperly vested, it is incumbent on gentlemen to tell us in what body it could be more safely and properly lodged. I believe, on a serious consideration, it will be found that it was necessary, for the reasons mentioned by the gentleman from Halifax, to vest the power in the Senate or in some other body representing equally the sovereignty of the states, and that the power, as given in the Constitution, is not likely to be attended with the evils which some gentlemen apprehend. The only real security of liberty in any country, is the jealousy and circumspection of the people themselves. Let them be watchful over their rulers. Should they find a combination against their liberties, and all other methods appear insufficient to preserve them, they have, thank God, an ultimate remedy. That power which created the government, can destroy it. Should the government, on trial, be found to want amendments, those amendments can be made in a regular method, in a mode prescribed by the Constitution itself. Massachusetts, South-Carolina, New-Hampshire, and Virginia, have all proposed amendments; but they all concurred in the necessity of an immediate adoption. A constitutional mode of altering the Constitution itself, is perhaps, what has never been known among mankind before. We have this security, in addition to the natural watchfulness of the people, which I hope will never be found wanting. The objections I have answered, deserved all possible attention, and for my part I shall always respect that jealousy which arises from the love of public liberty.

Samuel Spencer and William R. Davie Debate the Need for a Bill of Rights and the Jurisdiction of the Federal Courts

---

July 29, 1788

Mr. *Spencer*—Mr. Chairman, I hope to be excused for making some observations on what was said yesterday, by gentlemen in favour of these two clauses. The motion which was made that the committee should rise, precluded me from speaking then. The gentlemen have shewed much moderation and candour in conducting this business: But I still think that my observations are well founded, and that some amendments are necessary. The gentlemen said all matters not given up by this form of government, were retained by the respective states. I know that it ought to be so; it is the general doctrine, but it is necessary that it should be expressly declared in the Constitution, and not left to mere construction and opinion. I am authorised to say it was heretofore thought necessary. The Confederation says expressly, that all that was not given up by the United States, was retained by the respective states. If such a clause had been inserted in this Constitution, it would have superceded the necessity of a bill of rights. But that not being the case, it was necessary that a bill of rights, or something of that kind, should be a part of the Constitution. It was observed, that as the Constitution is to be a delegation of power from the several states to the United States, a bill of rights was unnecessary. But it will be noticed that this is a different case. The states do not act in their political capacities, but the government is proposed for individuals. The very caption of the Constitution shews that this is the case. The expression, "We the people of the United States," shews that this government is intended for individuals; there ought therefore to be a bill of rights. I am ready to acknowledge that the Congress ought to have the power of executing its laws. Heretofore, because all the laws of the Confederation were binding on the states in their political

888

capacities, courts had nothing to do with them; but now the thing is entirely different. The laws of Congress will be binding on individuals, and those things which concern individuals will be brought properly before the courts. In the next place, all the officers are to take an oath to carry into execution this general government, and are bound to support every act of the government, of whatever nature it may be. This is a fourth reason for securing the rights of individuals. It was also observed, that the Federal Judiciary and the courts of the states under the federal authority, would have concurrent jurisdiction with respect to any subject that might arise under the Constitution. I am ready to say that I most heartily wish that whenever this government takes place, the two jurisdictions and the two governments, that is, the general and the several state governments, may go hand in hand, and that there may be no interference, but that every thing may be rightly conducted. But I will never concede that it is proper to divide the business between the two different courts. I have no doubt but there is wisdom enough in this state to decide the business in a proper manner, without the necessity of federal assistance to do our business. The worthy gentleman from Edenton, dwelt a considerable time on the observations on a bill of rights, contending that they were proper only in monarchies, which were founded on different principles from those of our government; and therefore, though they might be necessary for others, yet they were not necessary for us. I still think that a bill of rights is necessary. This necessity arises from the nature of human societies. When individuals enter into society, they give up some rights to secure the rest. There are certain human rights that ought not to be given up, and which ought in some manner to be secured. With respect to these great essential rights, no latitude ought to be left. They are the most inestimable gifts of the great Creator, and therefore ought not be destroyed, but ought to be secured. They ought to be secured to individuals in consideration of the other rights which they give up to support society.

The trial by jury has been also spoken of. Every person who is acquainted with the nature of liberty, need not be informed of the importance of this trial. Juries are called the bulwarks of our rights and liberty; and no country can ever be enslaved as long as those cases which affect their lives and property, are to be decided in a great measure, by the consent of twelve honest, disinterested men, taken from the respectable body of yeomanry. It is highly improper that any clause which regards the security of the trial by jury should be any way doubtful. In the clause that has been read, it is ascertained that criminal cases are to be tried by jury, in the states wherein they are committed. It has been objected to that clause, that it is not sufficiently explicit. I think that it is not. It was observed, that one may be taken at a great distance. One reason of the resistance to the British government was, because they required that we should be carried to the country of Great-Britain, to be tried by juries of that country. But we insisted on being tried by juries of the vicinage in our own country. I think it therefore proper, that something explicit should be said with respect to the vicinage.

With regard to that part that the Supreme Court shall have appellate jurisdiction both as to law and fact, it has been observed, that though the Federal Court might decide without a jury, yet the court below, which tried it, might have a jury. I ask the gentleman what benefit would be received in the suit by having a jury trial in the court below, when the verdict is set aside in the Supreme Court. It was intended by this clause that the trial by jury should be suppressed in the superior and inferior courts. It has been said in defence of the omission concerning the trial by jury in civil cases, that one general regulation could not be made—that in several cases the Constitution of several states did not require a trial by jury; for instance, in cases of equity and admiralty, whereas in others it did; and that therefore it was proper to leave this subject at large. I am sure that for the security of liberty they ought to have been at the pains of drawing some line. I think that the respectable body who formed the Constitution, should have gone so far as to put matters on such a footing as that there should be no danger. They might have provided that all those cases which are now triable by a jury, should be tried in each state by a jury, according to the mode usually practised in such state. This would have been easily done if they had been at the trouble of writing five or six lines. Had it been done, we should have been entitled to say that our rights and liberties were not endangered. If we adopt this clause as it is, I think, notwithstanding what gentlemen have said, that there will be danger. There ought to be some amendments to it, to put this matter on a sure footing. There does not appear to me to be any kind of necessity that the Federal Court should have jurisdiction in the body of the country. I am ready to give up that in the cases expressly enumerated, an appellate jurisdiction, except in one or two instances, might be given. I wish them also to have jurisdiction in maritime affairs, and to try offences committed on the high seas. But in the body of a state, the jurisdiction of the courts in that state might extend to carry into execution the laws of Congress. It must be unnecessary for the Federal Courts to do it, and would create trouble and expence which might be avoided. In all cases where appeals are proper, I will agree that it is necessary there should be one Supreme Court. Were those things properly regulated, so that the Supreme Court might not be oppressive, I should have no objection to it.

Mr. *Davy*—Mr. Chairman, Yesterday and to day I have given particular attention to the observations of the gentleman last up. I believe, however, that before we take into consideration these important clauses, it will be necessary to consider in what manner laws can be executed. For my own part, I know but two ways in which the laws can be executed by any government. If there be any other, it is unknown to me. The first mode is coercion by military force, and the second is coercion through the judiciary. With respect to coercion by force, I shall suppose that it is so extremely repugnant to the principles of justice and the feelings of a free people, that no man will support it. It must in the end terminate in the destruction of the liberty of the people. I take it, therefore, that there is no rational way of enforcing the laws but by the instrumentality of the Judiciary. From these premises we are left only to consider how far the jurisdiction of the Judiciary ought to exend. It appears to me that the Judiciary ought to be competent to the decision of any question arising out of the Constitution itself. On a review of the principles of all free governments, it seems to me also necessary that the judicial power should be co-extensive with the legislative. It is necessary in all governments, but particularly in a federal government, that its judiciary should be competent to the decision of all questions arising out of the Constitution. If I understand the gentleman right, his objection was not to the defined jurisdiction, but to the general jurisdiction, which is expressed thus, "The judicial power shall extend to all cases in law and equity arising under this Constitution, the laws of the United States, and treaties made or which shall be made under their authority," and also to the appellate jurisdiction in some instances. Every Member who has read the Constitution with attention, must observe that there are certain fundamental principles in it, both of a positive and negative nature, which, being intended for the general advantage of the community, ought not to be violated by any future legislation of the particular states. Every Member will agree that the positive regulations ought to be carried into execution, and that the negative restrictions ought not to be disregarded or violated. Without a Judiciary, the injunctions of the Constitution may be disobeyed, and the positive regulations neglected or contravened. There are certain prohibitory provisions in this Constitution, the wisdom and propriety of which must strike every reflecting mind, and certainly meet with the warmest approbation of every citizen of this state. It provides, "That no state shall, without the consent of Congress, lay any imposts or duties on imports or exports, except what may be absolutely necessary for executing its inspection laws—that no preference shall be given by any regulation of commerce or revenue, to the ports of one state over those of another—and that no state shall emit bills of credit—make any thing but gold and silver coin a tender in payments of debts—pass any bill of attainder, ex post facto law, or law impairing the obligation of contracts." These restrictions ought to supercede the laws of particular states. With respect to the prohibitory provisions, that no duty or impost shall be laid by any particular state, which is so highly in favour of us and the other non-importing states, the importing states might make laws laying duties notwithstanding, and the Constitution might be violated with impunity, if there were no power in the general government to correct and counteract such laws.

This great object can only be safely and completely obtained by the instrumentality of the Federal Judiciary. Would not Virginia, who has raised many thousand pounds out of our citizens by her imposts, still avail herself of the same advantage if there were no constitutional power to counteract her regulations? If cases arising under the Constitution were left to her own courts, might she not still continue the same practices? But we are now to look for justice to the controuling power of the Judiciary of the United States. If the Virginians were to continue to oppress us by laying duties, we can be relieved by a recurrence to the general Judiciary. This restriction in the Constitution, is a fundamental principle which is not to be violated, but which would have been a dead letter were there no Judiciary constituted to enforce obedience to it. Paper money and private contracts were in the same condition. Without a general controuling Judiciary, laws might be made in particular states to enable its citizens to defraud the citizens of other states. Is it probable that if a citizen of South-Carolina owed a sum of money to a citizen of this state, that the latter would be certain of recovering the full value in their courts? That state might in future, as they have already done, make pine-barren acts to discharge their debts. They might say that our citizens should be paid in sterile in-arable lands, at an extravagant price. They might pass the most iniquitous instalment laws, procrastinating the payment of debts due from their citizens, for years—nay, for ages. Is it probable that we should get justice from their own judiciary, who might consider themselves obliged to obey the laws of their own state? Where then are we to look for justice? To the Judiciary of the United States. Gentlemen must have observed the contracted and narrow minded regulations of the individual states, and their predominant disposition to advance the interests of their own citizens to the prejudice of others. Will not these evils be continued if there be no restraint? The people of the United States have one common interest—they are all members of the same community, and ought to have justice administered to them equally in every part of the continent, in the same manner, with the same dispatch, and on the same principles. It is therefore absolutely necessary that the Judiciary of the union, should have jurisdiction in all cases arising in law and equity under the Constitution. Surely there should be somewhere a constitutional authority for carrying into execution constitutional provisions, otherwise, as I have already said, they would be a dead letter.

With respect to their having jurisdiction of all cases arising under the laws of the United States, although I have a very high respect for the gentleman, I heard his objection to it with surprise. I thought, if there were any political axiom under the sun, it must be that the judicial power ought to be co-extensive with the legislative. The federal government ought to possess the means of carrying the laws into execution. This position will not be disputed. A government would be a *felo de se* to put the execution of its laws under the controul of any other body. If laws are not to be carried into execution by the interposition of the Judiciary, how is it to be done? I have already observed, that the mind of every honest man who has any feeling for the happiness of his country, must have the highest repugnance to the idea of military co-ercion. The only means then, of enforcing obedience to the legislative authority, must be through the medium of the officers of peace. Did the gentleman carry his objection to the extension of the judicial power to treaties? It is another principle which I imagine will not be controverted, that the general Judiciary ought to be competent to the decision of all questions which involve the general welfare or the peace of the union. It was necessary that treaties should operate as laws upon individuals. They ought to be binding upon us the moment they are made. They involve in their nature, not only our own rights but those of foreigners. If the rights of foreigners were left to be decided ultimately by thirteen distinct judiciaries, there would necessarily be unjust and contradictory decisions. If our courts of justice did not decide in favour of foreign citizens and subjects when they ought, it might involve the whole union in a war. There ought, therefore, to be a paramount tribunal, which should have ample power to carry them into effect. To the decision of all causes which might involve the peace of the union, may be referred also, that of controversies between the citizens or subjects of foreign states and the citizens of the United States. It has been laid down by all writers, that the denial of justice is one of the just causes of war. If these controversies were left to the decision of particular states, it would be in their power at any time, to involve the whole continent in a war, usually the greatest of all national calamities. It is certainly clear, that where the peace of the union is affected, the general Judiciary ought to decide. It has generally been given up, that all cases of admiralty and maritime jurisdiction should also be determined by them. It has been equally ceded by the strongest opposers to this government, that the Federal Courts should have cognizance of controversies between two or more states; between a state and the citizens of another state, and between the citizens of the same state claiming lands under the grant of different states. Its jurisdiction in these cases is necessary, to secure impartiality in decisions, and preserve tranquility among the states. It is impossible that there should be impartiality when a party affected is to be Judge.

The security of impartiality is the principal reason for giving up the ultimate decision of controversies between citizens of different states. It is essential to the interest of agriculture and commerce, that the hands of the states should be bound from making paper money, instalment laws, or *pine-barren acts*. By such iniquitous laws the merchant or farmer may be defrauded of a considerable part of his just claims. But in the federal court real money will be recovered with that speed which is necessary to accommodate the circumstances of individuals. The tedious delays of judicial proceedings at present in some states, are ruinous to creditors. In Virginia many suits are twenty or thirty years spun out by legal ingenuity, and the defective construction of their judiciary. A citizen of Massachusetts or this country might be ruined before he could recover a debt in that state. It is necessary therefore in order to obtain justice, that we recur to the Judiciary of the United States, where justice must be equally administered, and where a debt may be recovered from the citizen of one state as soon as from the citizen of another.

As to a bill of rights, which has been brought forward in a manner I cannot account for, it is unnecessary to say any thing. The learned gentleman has said, that by a concurrent jurisdiction the laws of the United States must necessarily clash with the laws of the individual states, in consequence of which the laws of the states will be obstructed, and the state governments absorbed. This cannot be the case. There is not one instance of a power given to the United States, whereby the internal policy or administration of the states is affected. There is no instance that can be pointed out, wherein the internal policy of the state can be affected by the Judiciary of the United States. He mentioned impost laws. It has been given up on all hands, that if there was a necessity of a Federal Court, it was on this account. Money is difficult to be got into the treasury. The power of the Judiciary to enforce the federal laws is necessary to facilitate the collection of the public revenues. It is well known in this state with what reluctance and backwardness Collectors pay up the public monies. We have been making laws after laws to remedy this evil and still find them ineffectual. Is it not therefore necessary to enable the general government to compel the delinquent receivers to be punctual? The honourable gentleman admits that the general government ought to legislate upon individuals instead of states. Its laws will otherwise be ineffectual, but particularly with respect to treaties. We have seen with what little ceremony the states violated the peace with Great-Britain. Congress had no power to enforce its observance. The same cause will produce the same effect. We need not flatter ourselves that similar violations will always meet with equal impunity. I think he must be of opinion upon more reflection, that the jurisdiction of the federal Judiciary could not have been constructed otherwise with safety or propriety. It is necessary that the Constitution should be carried into effect, that the laws should be executed, justice equally done to all the community, and treaties observed. These ends can only be accomplished by a general paramount Judiciary. These are my sentiments, and if the honourable gentleman will prove them erroneous, I shall readily adopt his opinions.

Andrew Bass Thinks the Constitution Is "Uncommonly Difficult, or Absolutely Unintelligible"; Maclaine and Iredell Respond

July 29, 1788

Mr. *Bass* took a general view of the original and appellate jurisdiction of the Federal Court. He considered the Constitution neither necessary nor proper. He declared that the last part of the first paragraph of the second section, appeared to him totally inexplicable. He feared that dreadful oppression would be committed by carrying people too great a distance to decide trivial causes. He observed that gentlemen of the law and men of learning did not concur in the explanation or meaning of this Constitution. For his part, he said, he could not understand it, although he took great pains to find out its meaning, and although he flattered himself with the possession of common sense and reason. He always thought that there ought to be a compact between the governors and governed: Some called this a compact, others said it was not. From the contrariety of opinions, he thought the thing was either uncommonly difficult, or absolutely unintelligible. He wished to reflect on no gentleman, and apologized for his ignorance, by observing that he never went to school, and had been born blind; but he wished for information, and supposed that every gentleman would consider his desire as laudable.

Mr. *Maclaine* first, and then Mr. *Iredell*, endeavoured to satisfy the gentleman by a particular explanation of the whole paragraph. It was observed, that if there should be a controversy between this state and the Kings of France or Spain, it must be decided in the Federal Court. Or if there should arise a controversy between the French King or any other foreign power, or one of their subjects or citizens, and one of our citizens, it must be decided there also. The distinction between the words *citizen* and *subject* was explained—that the former related to individuals of popular governments; the latter to those of monarchies. As for instance, a dispute between this state or a citizen of it, and a person in Holland. The word foreign citizen would properly refer to such person. If the dispute was between this state and a person in France or Spain, the word foreign subject would apply to this—and all such controversies might be decided in the Federal Court—That the words *citizens* or *subjects* in that part of the clause, could only apply to *foreign citizens* or *foreign subjects*, and another part of the Constitution made this plain, by confining disputes in general between citizens of the same state, to the single case of their claiming lands under grants of different states.

James Iredell and Timothy Bloodworth Debate the Supremacy of the Constitution and of Federal Law

---

July 29, 1788

Article sixth. First clause read without any observation. Second clause read.

Mr. *Iredell*—This clause is supposed to give too much power, when in fact it only provides for the execution of those powers which are already given in the foregoing articles. What does it say? That "this Constitution, and the laws of the United States which shall be made in pursuance thereof, and all treaties made or which shall be made under the authority of the United States, shall be the supreme law of the land; and the Judges in every state shall be bound thereby, any thing in the constitution of laws of any state to the contrary notwithstanding." What is the meaning of this, but that as we have given power we will support the execution of it? We should act like children to give power and deny the legality of executing it. It is saying no more than that when we adopt the government we will maintain and obey it; in the same manner as if the Constitution of this state had said, that when a law is passed in conformity to it we must obey that law. Would this be objected to? Then when the Congress passes a law consistent with the Constitution, it is to be binding on the people. If Congress under pretence of executing one power, should in fact usurp another, they will violate the Constitution. I presume therefore that this explanation, which appears to me the plainest in the world, will be entirely satisfactory to the committee.

Mr. *Bloodworth*—Mr. Chairman, I confess his explanation is not satisfactory to me—I wish the gentleman had gone further. I readily agree, that it is giving them no more power than to execute their laws. But how far does this go? It appears to me to sweep off all the Constitutions of the states. It is a total repeal of every act and Constitution of the states. The Judges are sworn to uphold it. It will produce an abolition of the state governments. Its sovereignty absolutely annihilates them.

Mr. *Iredell*—Mr. Chairman, Every power delegated to Congress, is to be executed by laws made for that purpose. It is necessary to particularise the powers intended to be given in the Constitution, as having no existence before. But after having enumerated what we give up, it follows of course, that whatever is done by virtue of that authority, is legal without any new authority or power. The question then under this clause, will always be—whether Congress has exceeded its authority? If it has not exceeded it we must obey, otherwise not. This Constitution when adopted will become a part of our state Constitution, and the latter must yield to the former only in those cases where power is given by it. It is not to yield to it in any other case whatever. For instance, there is nothing in the Constitution of this state establishing the authority of a Federal Court. Yet the Federal Court when established, will be as constitutional as the Superior Court is now under our Constitution.—It appears to me merely a general clause, the amount of which is, that when they pass an act, if it be in the execution of a power given by the Constitution, it shall be binding on the people, otherwise not. As to the sufficiency or extent of the power, that is another consideration, and has been discussed before.

Mr. *Bloodworth*, This clause will be the destruction of every law which will come in competition with the laws of the United States. Those laws and regulations which have been or shall be made in this state, must be destroyed by it if they come in competition with the powers of Congress. Is it not necessary to define the extent of its operation? Is not the force of our tender laws destroyed by it? The worthy gentleman from Wilmington has endeavoured to obviate the objection as to the Constitution's destroying the credit of our paper money and paying debts in coin, but unsatisfactorily to me. A man assigns by legal fiction a bond to a man in another state—Could that bond be paid by money? I know it is very easy to be wrong. I am conscious of being frequently so. I endeavour to be open to conviction. This clause seems to me too general, and I think its extent ought to be limited and defined. I should suppose every reasonable man would think some amendment to it was necessary.

Henry Abbot and James Iredell Debate the Ban on Religious Tests: Could Not the Pope Be President?

July 30, 1788

Mr. *Henry Abbot*, after a short exordium which was not distinctly heard, proceeded thus—Some are afraid, Mr. Chairman, that should the Constitution be received, they would be deprived of the privilege of worshipping God according to their consciences, which would be taking from them a benefit they enjoy under the present Constitution. They wish to know if their religious and civil liberties be secured under this system, or whether the general government may not make laws infringing their religious liberties. The worthy member from Edenton mentioned sundry political reasons why treaties should be the supreme law of the land. It is feared by some people, that by the power of making treaties, they might make a treaty engaging with foreign powers to adopt the Roman catholic religion in the United States, which would prevent the people from worshipping God according to their own consciences. The worthy member from Halifax has in some measure satisfied my mind on this subject. But others may be dissatisfied. Many wish to know what religion shall be established. I believe a majority of the community are Presbyterians. I am for my part against any exclusive establishment, but if there were any, I would prefer the Episcopal. The exclusion of religious tests is by many thought dangerous and impolitic. They suppose that if there be no religious test required, Pagans, Deists and Mahometans might obtain offices among us, and that the Senate and Representatives might all be Pagans. Every person employed by the general and state governments is to take an oath to support the former. Some are desirous to know how, and by whom they are to swear, since no religious tests are required—whether they are to swear by Jupiter, Juno, Minerva, Proserpine or Pluto. We ought to be suspicious of our liberties. We have felt the effects of oppressive measures, and know the happy consequences of being jealous of our rights. I would be glad some gentleman would endeavour to obviate these objections, in order to satisfy the religious part of the society. Could I be convinced that the objections were well founded, I would then declare my opinion against the Constitution. [Mr. *Abbot* added several other observations, but spoke too low to be heard.]

Mr. *Iredell*—Mr. Chairman, Nothing is more desireable than to remove the scruples of any gentleman on this interesting subject: Those concerning religion are entitled to particular respect. I did not expect any objection to this particular regulation, which in my opinion, is calculated to prevent evils of the most pernicious consequences to society. Every person in the least conversant in the history of mankind, knows what dreadful mischiefs have been committed by religious persecutions. Under the colour of religious tests the utmost cruelties have been exercised. Those in power have generally considered all wisdom centered in themselves, that they alone had a right to dictate to the rest of mankind, and that all opposition to their tenets was profane and impious. The consequence of this intolerant spirit has been, that each church has in turn set itself up against every other, and persecutions and wars of the most implacable and bloody nature have taken place in every part of the world. America has set an example to mankind to think more modestly and reasonably; that a man may be of different religious sentiments from our own, without being a bad member of society. The principles of toleration, to the honour of this age, are doing away those errors and prejudices which have so long prevailed even in the most intolerant countries. In the Roman catholic countries, principles of moderation are adopted, which would have been spurned at a century or two ago. I should be sorry to find, when examples of toleration are set even by arbitrary governments, that this country, so impressed with the highest sense of liberty, should adopt principles on this subject, that were narrow and illiberal. I consider the clause under consideration as one of the strongest proofs that could be adduced, that it was the intention of those who formed this system, to establish a general religious liberty in America. Were we to judge from the examples of religious tests in other countries, we should be persuaded that they do not answer the purpose for which they are intended. What is the consequence of such in England? In that country no man can be a Member in the House of Commons, or hold any office under the Crown, without taking the sacrament according to the rites of the church. This in the first instance must degrade and profane a rite, which never ought to be taken but from a sincere principle of devotion. To a man of base principles, it is made a mere instrument of civil policy. The intention was to exclude all persons from offices, but the members of the church of England. Yet it is notorious, that Dissenters qualify themselves for offices in this manner, though they never conform to the church on any other occasion; and men of no religion at all, have no scruple to make use of this qualification. It never was known that a man who had no principles of religion, hesitated to perform any rite when it was convenient for his private interest. No test can bind such a one. I am therefore clearly of opinion, that such a discrimination would neither be effectual for its own purposes, nor if it could, ought it by any means to be made. Upon the principles I have stated, I confess the restriction on the power of Congress in this particular has my hearty approbation. They certainly have no authority to interfere in the establishment of any religion whatsoever, and I am astonished that any gentleman should conceive they have. Is there any power given to Congress in matters of religion? Can they pass a single act to impair our religious liberties? If they could, it would be a just cause of alarm. If they could, Sir, no man would have more horror against it than myself. Happily no sect here is superior to another. As long as this is the case, we shall be free from those persecutions and distractions with which other countries have been torn. If any future Congress should pass an act concerning the religion of the country, it would be an act which they are not authorised to pass by the Constitution, and which the people would not obey. Every one would ask, "Who authorised the government to pass such an act? It is not warranted by the Constitution, and is a barefaced usurpation." The power to make treaties can never be supposed to include a right to establish a foreign religion among ourselves, though it might authorise a toleration of others.

But it is objected, that the people of America may perhaps chuse Representatives who have no religion at all, and that Pagans and Mahometans may be admitted into offices. But how is it possible to exclude any set of men, without taking away that principle of religious freedom which we ourselves so warmly contend for? This is the foundation on which persecution has been raised in every part of the world. The people in power were always in the right, and every body else wrong. If you admit the least difference, the door to persecution is opened. Nor would it answer the purpose, for the worst part of the excluded sects would comply with the test, and the best men only be kept out of our counsels. But it is never to be supposed that the people of America will trust their dearest rights to persons who have no religion at all, or a religion materially different from their own. It would be happy for mankind if religion was permitted to take its own course, and maintain itself by the excellence of its own doctrines. The divine author of our religion never wished for its support by worldly authority. Has he not said, *that the gates of hell shall not prevail against it*? It made much greater progress for itself, than when supported by the greatest authority upon earth.

It has been asked by that respectable gentleman [Mr. Abbot] what is the meaning of that part, where it is said, that the United States shall *guarantee* to every state in the union a republican form of government, and why a *guarantee* of *religious freedom* was not included. The meaning of the guarantee provided was this—There being thirteen governments confederated, upon a republican principle, it was essential to the existence and harmony of the confederacy that each should be a republican government, and that no state should have a right to establish an aristocracy or monarchy. That clause was therefore inserted to prevent any state from establishing any government but a republican one. Every one must be convinced of the mischief that would ensue, if any state had a right to change its government to a monarchy. If a monarchy was established in any one state, it would endeavour to subvert the freedom of the others, and would probably by degrees succeed in it. This must strike the mind of every person here who recollects the history of Greece when she had confederated governments. The King of Macedon by his arts and intrigues got himself admitted a member of the Amphyctionic council, which was the superintending government of the Grecian republics, and in a short time he became master of them all. It is then necessary that the members of a confederacy should have similar governments. But consistently with this restriction the states may make what change in their own governments they think proper. Had Congress undertaken to guarantee *religious freedom*, or any particular species of it, they would then have had a pretence to interfere in a subject they have nothing to do with. Each state, so far as the clause in question does not interfere, must be left to the operation of its own principles.

There is a degree of jealousy which it is impossible to satisfy. Jealousy in a free government ought to be respected: But it may be carried to too great an extent. It is impracticable to guard against all *possible* danger of people's chusing their officers indiscreetly. If they have a right to chuse, they may make a bad choice. I met by accident with a pamphlet this morning, in which the author states as a very serious danger, that the Pope of Rome might be elected President. I confess this never struck me before, and if the author had read all the qualifications of a President, perhaps his fears might have been quieted. No man but a native, and who has resided fourteen years in America, can be chosen President. I know not all the qualifications for a Pope, but I believe he must be taken from the college of Cardinals, and probably there are many previous steps necessary before he arrives at this dignity. A native of America must have very singular good fortune, who after residing fourteen years in his own country, should go to Europe, enter into Romish orders, obtain the promotion of Cardinal, afterwards that of Pope, and at length be so much in the confidence of his own country, as to be elected President. It would be still more extraordinary if he should give up his Popedom for our Presidency. Sir, it is impossible to treat such idle fears with any degree of gravity. Why is it not objected, that there is no provision in the Constitution against electing one of the Kings of Europe President? It would be a clause equally rational and judicious.

I hope that I have in some degree satisfied the doubts of the gentleman. This article is calculated to secure universal religious liberty, by putting all sects on a level, the only way to prevent persecution. I thought nobody would have objected to this clause, which deserves in my opinion the highest approbation. This country has already had the honour of setting an example of civil freedom, and I trust it will likewise have the honour of teaching the rest of the world the way to religious freedom also. God grant both may be perpetuated to the end of time.

Rev. David Caldwell and Samuel Spencer Continue the Debate on Religious Toleration

July 30, 1788

Mr. *Caldwell* thought that some danger might arise. He imagined it might be objected to in a political as well as in a religious view. In the first place, he said there was an invitation for Jews, and Pagans of every kind, to come among us. At some future period, said he, this might endanger the character of the United States. Moreover, even those who do not regard religion, acknowledge that the Christian religion is best calculated of all religions to make good members of society, on account of its morality. I think then, added he, that in a political view, those gentlemen who formed this Constitution, should not have given this invitation to Jews and Heathens. All those who have any religion are against the emigration of those people from the eastern hemisphere.

Mr. *Spencer* was an advocate for securing every unalienable right, and that of worshipping God according to the dictates of conscience in particular. He therefore thought that no one particular religion should be established. Religious tests, said he, have been the foundation of persecutions in all countries. Persons who are conscientious will not take the oath required by religious tests, and will therefore be excluded from offices, though equally capable of discharging them as any member of the society. It is feared, continued he, that persons of bad principles, Deists, Atheists, &c. may come into this country, and there is nothing to restrain them from being eligible to offices. He asked if it was reasonable to suppose that the people would chuse men without regarding their characters. Mr. *Spencer* then continued thus—Gentlemen urge that the want of a test admits the most vicious characters to offices. I desire to know what test could bind them. If they were of such principles, it would not keep them from enjoying those offices. On the other hand, it would exclude from offices conscientious and truly religious people, though equally capable as others. Conscientious persons would not take such an oath, and would be therefore excluded. This would be a great cause of objection to a religious test. But in this case as there is not a religious test required, it leaves religion on the solid foundation of its own inherent validity, without any connexion with temporal authority, and no kind of oppression can take place. I confess it strikes me so. I am sorry to differ from the worthy gentleman. I cannot object to this part of the Constitution. I wish every other part was as good and proper.

James Iredell Urges Ratification, and a Vote Is Taken

July 30, 1788

Mr. *Willie Jones* was against ratifying in the manner proposed. He had attended, he said, with great patience to the debates of the speakers on both sides of the question. One party said the Constitution was all perfection. The other party said it wanted a great deal of perfection. For his part, he thought so. He treated the dangers which were held forth in case of non adoption, as merely ideal and fanciful. After adding other remarks, he moved that the previous question might be put, with an intention, as he said, if that was carried, to introduce a resolution which he had in his hand, and which he was then willing to read if gentlemen thought proper, stipulating for certain amendments to be made previous to the adoption by this state.

Governor *Johnston* begged gentlemen to recollect, that the proposed amendments could not be laid before the other states unless we adopted and became part of the union.

Mr. *Taylor* wished that the previous question might be put as it would save much time. He feared the motion first made was a manœuvre or contrivance to impose a Constitution on the people, which a majority disapproved of.

Mr. *Iredell* wished the previous question should be withdrawn, and that they might debate the first question. The great importance of the subject, and the respectability of the gentleman who made the motion, claimed more deference and attention than to decide it in the very moment it was introduced by getting rid of it by the previous question. A decision was now presented in a new form by a gentleman of great influence in the House, and gentlemen ought to have time to consider before they voted precipitately upon it.

A desultory conversation now arose. Mr. *J. Galloway* wished the question to be postponed till to-morrow morning.

Mr. *J. McDowall* was for immediately putting the question.

—Several gentlemen expatiated on the evident necessity of amendments.

Governor *Johnston* declared, that he disdained all manœuvres and contrivance; that an intention of imposing an improper system on the people, contrary to their wishes, was unworthy of any man. He wished the motion to be fairly and fully argued and investigated. He observed, that the very motion before them proposed amendments to be made. That they were proposed as they had been in other states. He wished therefore that the motion for the previous question should be withdrawn.

Mr. *Willie Jones* could not withdraw his motion. Gentlemens arguments, he said, had been listened to attentively, but he believed no person had changed his opinion. It was unnecessary then to argue it again. His motion was not conclusive. He only wished to know what ground they stood on, whether they should ratify it unconditionally or not.

Mr. *Spencer* wished to hear the arguments and reasons for and against the motion. Although he was convinced the House wanted amendments, and that all had nearly determined the question in their own minds, he was for hearing the question argued, and had no objection to the postponement of it till to-morrow.

Mr. *Iredell* urged the great importance of consideration. That the consequence of the previous question, if carried, would be an exclusion of this state out of the union. He contended that the House had no right to make a conditional ratification, and if excluded from the union, they could not be assured of an easy admission at a future day, though the impossibility of existing out of the union must be obvious to every thinking man. The gentleman from Halifax had said, that his motion would not be conclusive. For his part, he was certain it would be tantamount to an immediate decision. He trusted gentlemen would consider the propriety of debating the first motion at large.

Mr. *Person* observed, that the previous question would produce no inconvenience. The other party, he said, had all the debating to themselves, and would probably have it again, if they insisted on further argument. He saw no propriety in putting it off till to-morrow, as it was not customary for a committee to adjourn with two questions before them.

Mr. *Shepherd* declared, that though he had made up his mind, and believed other gentlemen had done so, yet he had no objection to giving gentlemen an opportunity of displaying their abilities, and convincing the rest of their error if they could. He was for putting it off till to-morrow.

Mr. *Davie* took notice that the gentleman from Granville had frequently used ungenerous insinuations, and had taken much pains out of doors to irritate the minds of his countrymen against the Constitution. He called upon gentlemen to act openly and above board, adding that a contrary conduct on this occasion, was extremely despicable. He came thither, he said, for the common cause of his country, and knew no party, but wished the business to be conducted with candour and moderation. The previous question he thought irregular, and that it ought not to be put till the other question was called for. That it was evidently intended to preclude all further debate, and to precipitate the committee upon the resolution which it had been suggested was immediately to follow, which they were not then ready to enter upon. That he had not fully considered the consequences of a conditional ratification, but at present they appeared to him alarmingly dangerous, and perhaps equal to those of an absolute rejection.

Mr. *Willie Jones* observed, that he had not intended to take the House by surprise: That though he had his motion ready, and had heard of the motion which was intended for ratification, he waited till that motion should be made, and had afterwards waited for some time, in expectation that the gentleman from Halifax, and the gentleman from Edenton, would both speak to it. He had no objection to adjourning, but his motion would be still before the House.

Here there was a great cry for the question.

Mr. *Iredell*, [The cry for the question still continuing.] Mr. Chairman, I desire to be heard, notwithstanding the cry of "the question, the question." Gentlemen have no right to prevent any Member from speaking to it if he thinks fit. [The House subsided into order.] Unimportant as I may be myself, my constituents are as respectable as those of any Member in the House. It has indeed, Sir, been my misfortune to be under the necessity of troubling the House much oftener than I wished, owing to a circumstance which I have greatly regretted, that so few gentlemen take a share in our debates, though many are capable of doing so with propriety. I should have spoken to the question at large before, if I had not fully depended on some other gentleman doing it, and therefore I did not prepare myself by taking notes of what was said. However, I beg leave now to make a few observations. I think this Constitution safe. I have not heard a single objection which in my opinion shewed that it was dangerous. Some particular parts have been objected to, and amendments pointed out. Though I think it perfectly safe, yet with respect to any amendments which do not destroy the substance of the Constitution, but will tend to give greater satisfaction, I should approve of them, because I should prefer that system which would most tend to conciliate all parties. On these principles I am of opinion, that some amendments should be proposed.

The general ground of the objections seems to be, that the powers proposed to the general government, may be abused. If we give no power but such as may not be abused, we shall give none; for all delegated powers may be abused. There are two extremes equally dangerous to liberty. These are *tyranny* and *anarchy*. The medium between these two is the true government to protect the people. In my opinion, this Constitution is well calculated to guard against both these extremes. The possibility of general abuses ought not to be urged, but particular ones pointed out. A gentleman who spoke some time ago [Mr. Lenoir] observed that the government might make it treason to write against the most arbitrary proceedings. He corrected himself afterwards, by saying he meant *misprision* of *treason*. But in the correction he committed as great a mistake as he did at first. Where is the power given to them to do this? They have power to define and punish piracies and felonies committed on the high seas, and offences against the law of nations. They have no power to define any other crime whatever. This will shew how apt gentlemen are to commit mistakes. I am convinced on the part of the worthy Member, it was not designed, but arose merely from inattention.

Mr. *Lenoir* arose and declared, that he meant that those

punishments might be inflicted by them within the ten miles square, where they would have exclusive powers of legislation.

Mr. *Iredell* continued—They are to have exclusive power of legislation; but how? Wherever they may have this district, they must possess it from the authority of the state within which it lies: And that state may stipulate the conditions of the cession. Will not such state take care of the liberties of its own people. What would be the consequence if the seat of the government of the United States, with all the archives of America, was in the power of any one particular state? Would not this be most unsafe and humiliating? Do we not all remember that in the year 1783, a band of soldiers went and insulted Congress? The sovereignty of the United States was treated with indignity. They applied for protection to the state they resided in, but could obtain none. It is to be hoped such a disgraceful scene will never happen again, but that for the future the national government will be able to protect itself. The powers of the government are particularly enumerated and defined: they can claim no others but such as are so enumerated. In my opinion they are excluded as much from the exercise of any other authority as they could be by the strongest negative clause that could be framed. A gentleman has asked, what would be the consequence if they had the power of the purse and sword? I ask, in what government under Heaven are these not given up to some authority or other? There is a necessity of giving both the purse and the sword to every government, or else it cannot protect the people. But have we not sufficient security that those powers shall not be abused? The immediate power of the purse is in the immediate Representatives of the people, chosen every two years, who can lay no tax on their constituents but what they are subject to at the same time themselves. The power of taxation must be vested somewhere. Do the committee wish it to be as it has been? Then they must suffer the evils which they have done. Requisitions will be of no avail. No money will be collected but by means of military force. Under the new government taxes will probably be much lighter than they can be under our present one. The impost will afford vast advantages, and greatly relieve the people from direct taxation. In time of peace it is supposed by many the imposts may be alone sufficient: But in time of war, it cannot be expected they will. Our expences would be much greater, and our ports might be blocked up by the enemy's fleet. Think then of the advantage of a national government possessed of energy and credit. Could government borrow money to any advantage without the power of taxation? If they could secure funds, and wanted immediately for instance 100,000 l. they might borrow this sum, and immediately raise only money to pay the interest of it. If they could not, the 100,000 l. must be instantly raised however distressing to the people, or our country perhaps over-run by the enemy. Do not gentlemen see an immense difference between the two cases? It is said that there ought to be jealousy in mankind. I admit it as far as is consistent with prudence. But unlimited jealousy is very pernicious. We must be contented if powers be as well guarded as the nature of them will permit. In regard to amending before or after adoption, the difference is very great. I beg leave to state my idea of that difference. I mentioned one day before, the adoption by ten states. When I did so, it was not to influence any person with respect to the merits of the Constitution, but as a reason for coolness and deliberation. In my opinion, when so great a majority of the American people have adopted it, it is a strong evidence in its favour: For it is not probable that ten states would have agreed to a bad Constitution. If we do not adopt, we are no longer in the union with the other states. We ought to consider seriously before we determine our connection with them. The safety and happiness of this state depend upon it. Without that union what would have been our condition now? A striking instance will point out this very clearly: At the beginning of the late war with Great-Britain, the Parliament thought proper to stop all commercial intercourse with the American provinces. They passed a general prohibitory act, from which New-York and North-Carolina were at first excepted. Why were they excepted? They had been as active in opposition as the other states; but this was an expedient to divide the northern from the middle states, and to break the heart of the southern. Had New-York and North-Carolina been weak enough to fall into this snare, we probably should not now have been an independent people. [Mr. *Person* called to order, and intimated that the gentleman meant to reflect on the opposers of the Constitution, as if they were friendly to the British interest. Mr. *Iredell* warmly resented the interruption, declaring he was perfectly in order, that it was disorderly to interrupt him, and in respect to Mr. *Person*'s insinuation as to his intention, he declared in the most solemn manner he had no such, being well assured the opposers of the Constitution were equally friendly to the independence of America, as its supporters. He then proceeded.] I say they endeavoured to divide us. North-Carolina and New-York had too much sense to be taken in by their artifices. Union enabled us then to defeat all their endeavours: Union will enable us to defeat all the machinations of our enemies hereafter. The friends of their country must lament our present unhappy divisions. Most free countries have lost their liberties by means of dissentions among themselves. They united in war and danger: When peace and apparent security came, they split into factions and parties, and thereby became a prey to foreign invaders. This shews the necessity of union. In urging the danger of disunion so strongly, I beg leave again to say, that I mean not to reflect on any gentleman whatsoever, as if his wishes were directed to so wicked a purpose. I am sure such an insinuation as the gentleman from Granville supposed I intended, would be utterly unjust, as I know some of the warmest opposers of Great-Britain, are now among the warmest opponents of the proposed Constitution. Such a suggestion never entered into my head, and I can say with truth, that warmly as I am attached to this Constitution, and though I am convinced that the salvation of our country depends upon the adoption of it, I would not procure it success by one unworthy action or one ungenerous word. A gentleman has said that we ought to determine in the same manner as if no state had adopted the Constitution. The general principle is right, but we ought to consider our peculiar situation. We cannot exist by ourselves. If we imitate the examples of some respectable states that have proposed amendments subsequent to their ratification, we shall add our weight to have these amendments carried, as our Representatives will be in Congress to enforce them. Gentlemen entertain a jealousy of the eastern states. To withdraw ourselves from the southern

states, will be encreasing the northern influence. The loss of
one state may be attended with particular prejudice. It will be
a good while before amendments of any kind can take place,
and in the mean time if we do not adopt we shall have no
share or agency in their transactions, though we may be ultimately bound by them. The first session of Congress will
probably be the most important of any for many years. A
general code of laws will then be established in execution of
every power contained in the Constitution. If we ratify and
propose amendments, our Representatives will be there to act
in this important business. If we do not our interest may suffer, nor will the system be afterwards altered merely to accommodate our wishes. Besides that, one House may prevent a
measure from taking place, but both must concur in repealing
it. I therefore think an adoption proposing subsequent
amendments, far safer and more desireable than the other
mode. Nor do I doubt that every amendment, not of a local
nature, nor injuring essentially the material powers of the
Constitution, but principally calculated to guard against misconstruction, the real liberties of the people, will be readily
obtained.

The previous question, after some desultory conversation,
was now put. For it 183. Against it 84.—Majority in favour of
the motion 99.

The Declaration of Independence

In CONGRESS, July 4, 1776.
The unanimous Declaration
of the thirteen united States of America,

When in the Course of human events, it becomes necessary for one people to dissolve the political bands which have connected them with another, and to assume among the powers of the earth, the separate and equal station to which the Laws of Nature and of Nature's God entitle them, a decent respect to the opinions of mankind requires that they should declare the causes which impel them to the separation.—We hold these truths to be self-evident, that all men are created equal, that they are endowed by their Creator with certain unalienable Rights, that among these are Life, Liberty and the pursuit of Happiness.—That to secure these rights, Governments are instituted among Men, deriving their just powers from the consent of the governed,—That whenever any Form of Government becomes destructive of these ends, it is the Right of the People to alter or to abolish it, and to institute new Government, laying its foundation on such principles and organizing its powers in such form, as to them shall seem most likely to effect their Safety and Happiness. Prudence, indeed, will dictate that Governments long established should not be changed for light and transient causes; and accordingly all experience hath shewn, that mankind are more disposed to suffer, while evils are sufferable, than to right themselves by abolishing the forms to which they are accustomed. But when a long train of abuses and usurpations, pursuing invariably the same Object evinces a design to reduce them under absolute Despotism, it is their right, it is their duty, to throw off such Government, and to provide new Guards for their future security.— Such has been the patient sufferance of these Colonies; and such is now the necessity which constrains them to alter their former Systems of Government. The history of the present King of Great Britain is a history of repeated injuries and usurpations, all having in direct object the establishment of an absolute Tyranny over these States. To prove this, let Facts be submitted to a candid world.— He has refused his

Assent to Laws, the most wholesome and necessary for the public good.—He has forbidden his Governors to pass Laws of immediate and pressing importance, unless suspended in their operation till his Assent should be obtained; and when so suspended, he has utterly neglected to attend to them. —He has refused to pass other Laws for the accommodation of large districts of people, unless those people would relinquish the right of Representation in the Legislature, a right inestimable to them and formidable to tyrants only.—He has called together legislative bodies at places unusual, uncomfortable, and distant from the depository of their public Records, for the sole purpose of fatiguing them into compliance with his measures.—He has dissolved Representative Houses repeatedly, for opposing with manly firmness his invasions on the rights of the people.—He has refused for a long time, after such dissolutions, to cause others to be elected; whereby the Legislative powers, incapable of Annihilation, have returned to the People at large for their exercise; the State remaining in the mean time exposed to all the dangers of invasion from without, and convulsions within.—He has endeavoured to prevent the population of these States; for that purpose obstructing the Laws for Naturalization of Foreigners; refusing to pass others to encourage their migrations hither, and raising the conditions of new Appropriations of Lands.—He has obstructed the Administration of Justice, by refusing his Assent to Laws for establishing Judiciary powers —He has made Judges dependent on his Will alone, for the tenure of their offices, and the amount and payment of their salaries.—He has erected a multitude of New Offices, and sent hither swarms of Officers to harrass our people, and eat out their substance.—He has kept among us, in times of peace, Standing Armies without the Consent of our legislatures.—He has affected to render the Military independent of and superior to the Civil power.—He has combined with others to subject us to a jurisdiction foreign to our constitution, and unacknowledged by our laws; giving his Assent to their Acts of pretended Legislation:—For Quartering large bodies of armed troops among us:—For protecting them, by a mock Trial, from punishment for any Murders which they should commit on the Inhabitants of these States:—For calling off our Trade with all parts of the world:—For imposing Taxes on us without our Consent:—For depriving us in many cases, of the benefits of Trial by Jury:—For transporting us beyond Seas to be tried for pretended offences—For abolishing the free System of English Laws in a neighbouring Province, establishing therein an Arbitrary government, and enlarging its Boundaries so as to render it at once an example and fit instrument for introducing the same absolute rule into these Colonies:—For taking away our Charters, abolishing our most valuable Laws and altering fundamentally the Forms of our Governments:—For suspending our own Legislatures, and declaring themselves invested with power to legislate for us in all cases whatsoever.—He has abdicated Government here, by declaring us out of his Protection and waging War against us.—He has plundered our seas, ravaged our Coasts, burnt our towns, and destroyed the Lives of our people.—He is at this time transporting large Armies of foreign Mercenaries to compleat the works of death, desolation and tyranny, already begun with circumstances of Cruelty & perfidy scarcely paralleled in the most barbarous ages, and totally unworthy the Head of a civilized nation.—He has constrained our fellow Citizens taken Captive on the high Seas to bear Arms against their Country, to become the executioners of their friends and Brethren, or to fall themselves by their Hands.—He has excited domestic insurrections amongst us, and has endeavoured to bring on the inhabitants of our frontiers, the merciless Indian Savages, whose known rule of warfare, is an undistinguished destruction of all ages, sexes and conditions. In every stage of these Oppressions We have Petitioned for Redress in the most humble terms: Our repeated Petitions have been answered only by repeated injury. A Prince, whose character is thus marked by every act which may define a Tyrant, is unfit to be the ruler of a free people. Nor have We been wanting in attentions to our Brittish brethren. We have warned them from time to time of attempts by their legislature to extend an unwarrantable jurisdiction over us. We have reminded them of the circumstances of our emigration and settlement here. We have appealed to their native justice and magnanimity, and we have conjured them by the ties of our common kindred to disavow these usurpations,

which, would inevitably interrupt our connections and correspondence   They too have been deaf to the voice of justice and
of consanguinity. We must, therefore, acquiesce in the necessity, which denounces our Separation, and hold them, as we
hold the rest of mankind, Enemies in War, in Peace Friends.—

We, therefore, the Representatives of the united States of
America, in General Congress, Assembled, appealing to the
Supreme Judge of the world for the rectitude of our intentions, do, in the Name, and by Authority of the good People
of these Colonies, solemnly publish and declare, That these
United Colonies are, and of Right ought to be Free and Independent States; that they are Absolved from all Allegiance to
the British Crown, and that all political connection between
them and the State of Great Britain, is and ought to be totally
dissolved; and that as Free and Independent States, they have
full Power to levy War, conclude Peace, contract Alliances, establish Commerce, and to do all other Acts and Things which
Independent States may of right do.— And for the support of
this Declaration, with a firm reliance on the protection of divine Providence, we mutually pledge to each other our Lives,
our Fortunes and our sacred Honor.

John Hancock

Josiah Bartlett
Wm Whipple
Saml Adams
John Adams
Robt Treat Paine
Elbridge Gerry
Step. Hopkins
William Ellery
Roger Sherman
Saml Huntington
Wm Williams
Oliver Wolcott
Matthew Thornton
Wm Floyd
Phil. Livingston
Fran^s. Lewis
Lewis Morris
Richd Stockton
Jno Witherspoon
Fra^s. Hopkinson
John Hart
Abra Clark
Robt Morris
Benjamin Rush
Benj. Franklin
John Morton
Geo Clymer
Ja^s. Smith
Geo. Taylor
James Wilson
Geo. Ross

Cæsar Rodney
Geo Read
Tho M:Kean
Samuel Chase
W^m. Paca
Thos. Stone
Charles Carroll of Carrollton
George Wythe
Richard Henry Lee
Th Jefferson
Benj Harrison
Th^s Nelson Jr.
Francis Lightfoot Lee
Carter Braxton
Wm Hooper
Joseph Hewes
John Penn
Edward Rutledge
Thos Heyward Junr
Thomas Lynch Junr.
Arthur Middleton
Button Gwinnett
Lyman Hall
Geo Walton

The Articles of Confederation

To all to whom these Presents shall come, we the under signed Delegates of the States affixed to our Names send greeting. Whereas the Delegates of the United States of America in Congress assembled did on the fifteenth day of November in the Year of our Lord One Thousand Seven Hundred and Seventy seven, and in the Second Year of the Independence of America agree to certain articles of Confederation and perpetual Union between the States of New-hampshire, Massachusetts-bay, Rhodeisland and Providence Plantations, Connecticut, New York, New Jersey, Pennsylvania, Delaware, Maryland, Virginia, North-Carolina, South-Carolina and Georgia in the Words following, viz, "Articles of Confederation and perpetual Union between the States of Newhampshire, Massachusetts-bay, Rhodeisland and Providence Plantations, Connecticut, New-York, New-Jersey, Pennsylvania, Delaware, Maryland, Virginia, North-Carolina, South-Carolina and Georgia.

Article I.   The Stile of this confederacy shall be "The United States of America."

Article II.   Each state retains its sovereignty, freedom and independence, and every Power, Jurisdiction and right, which is not by this confederation expressly delegated to the United States, in Congress assembled.

Article III.   The said states hereby severally enter into a firm league of friendship with each other, for their common defence, the security of their Liberties, and their mutual and general welfare, binding themselves to assist each other, against all force offered to, or attacks made upon them, or any of them, on account of religion, sovereignty, trade, or any other pretence whatever.

Article IV.   The better to secure and perpetuate mutual friendship and intercourse among the people of the different states in this union, the free inhabitants of each of these states, paupers, vagabonds and fugitives from Justice excepted, shall be entitled to all privileges and immunities of free citizens in the several states; and the people of each state shall have free ingress and regress to and from any other state, and shall enjoy therein all the privileges of trade and commerce, subject to the same duties, impositions and restrictions as the inhabitants thereof respectively, provided that such restriction shall not extend so far as to prevent the removal of property imported into any state, to any other state of which the Owner is an inhabitant; provided also that no imposition, duties or restriction shall be laid by any state, on the property of the united states, or either of them.

If any Person guilty of, or charged with treason, felony, or other high misdemeanor in any state, shall flee from Justice, and be found in any of the united states, he shall upon demand of the Governor or executive power, of the state from which he fled, be delivered up and removed to the state having jurisdiction of his offence.

Full faith and credit shall be given in each of these states to the records, acts and judicial proceedings of the courts and magistrates of every other state.

Article V. For the more convenient management of the general interests of the united states, delegates shall be annually appointed in such manner as the legislature of each state shall direct, to meet in Congress on the first Monday in November, in every year, with a power reserved to each state, to recal its delegates, or any of them, at any time within the year, and to send others in their stead, for the remainder of the Year.

No state shall be represented in Congress by less than two, nor by more than seven Members; and no person shall be capable of being a delegate for more than three years in any term of six years; nor shall any person, being a delegate, be capable of holding any office under the united states, for which he, or another for his benefit receives any salary, fees or emolument of any kind.

Each state shall maintain its own delegates in a meeting of the states, and while they act as members of the committee of the states.

In determining questions in the united states, in Congress assembled, each state shall have one vote.

Freedom of speech and debate in Congress shall not be impeached or questioned in any Court, or place out of Congress, and the members of congress shall be protected in their persons from arrests and imprisonments, during the time of their going to and from, and attendance on congress, except for treason, felony, or breach of the peace.

Article VI. No state without the Consent of the united states in congress assembled, shall send any embassy to, or receive any embassy from, or enter into any conferrence, agreement, alliance or treaty with any King prince or state; nor shall any person holding any office of profit or trust under the united states, or any of them, accept of any present, emolument, office or title of any kind whatever from any king, prince or foreign state; nor shall the united states in congress assembled, or any of them, grant any title of nobility.

No two or more states shall enter into any treaty, confederation or alliance whatever between them, without the consent of the united states in congress assembled, specifying accurately the purposes for which the same is to be entered into, and how long it shall continue.

No state shall lay any imposts or duties, which may interfere with any stipulations in treaties, entered into by the united states in congress assembled, with any king, prince or state, in pursuance of any treaties already proposed by congress, to the courts of France and Spain.

No vessels of war shall be kept up in time of peace by any state, except such number only, as shall be deemed necessary by the united states in congress assembled, for the defence of such state, or its trade; nor shall any body of forces be kept up by any state, in time of peace, except such number only, as in the judgment of the united states, in congress assembled, shall be deemed requisite to garrison the forts necessary for the defence of such state; but every state shall always keep up a well regulated and disciplined militia, sufficiently armed and accoutred, and shall provide and constantly have ready for use, in public stores, a due number of field pieces and tents, and a proper quantity of arms, ammunition and camp equipage.

No state shall engage in any war without the consent of the united states in congress assembled, unless such state be actually invaded by enemies, or shall have received certain advice of a resolution being formed by some nation of Indians to invade such state, and the danger is so imminent as not to admit of a delay, till the united states in congress assembled can be consulted: nor shall any state grant commissions to any ships or vessels of war, nor letters of marque or reprisal, except it be after a declaration of war by the united states in congress assembled, and then only against the kingdom or state and the subjects thereof, against which war has been so declared, and under such regulations as shall be established by the united states in congress assembled, unless such state be infested by pirates, in which case vessels of war may be fitted out for that occasion, and kept so long as the danger shall continue, or until the united states in congress assembled shall determine otherwise.

Article VII.   When land-forces are raised by any state for the common defence, all officers of or under the rank of colonel, shall be appointed by the legislature of each state respectively by whom such forces shall be raised, or in such manner as such state shall direct, and all vacancies shall be filled up by the state which first made the appointment.

Article VIII.   All charges of war, and all other expences that shall be incurred for the common defence or general welfare, and allowed by the united states in congress assembled, shall be defrayed out of a common treasury, which shall be supplied by the several states, in proportion to the value of all land within each state, granted to or surveyed for any Person, as such land and the buildings and improvements thereon shall be estimated according to such mode as the united states in congress assembled, shall from time to time direct and appoint. The taxes for paying that proportion shall be laid and levied by the authority and direction of the legislatures of the several states within the time agreed upon by the united states in congress assembled.

Article IX.   The united states in congress assembled, shall have the sole and exclusive right and power of determining on peace and war, except in the cases mentioned in the sixth article—of sending and receiving ambassadors—entering into treaties and alliances, provided that no treaty of commerce shall be made whereby the legislative power of the respective states shall be restrained from imposing such imposts and duties on foreigners, as their own people are subjected to, or from prohibiting the exportation or importation of any species of goods or commodities whatsoever—of establishing rules for deciding in all cases, what captures on land or water shall be legal, and in what manner prizes taken by land or naval forces in the service of the united states shall be divided or appropriated—of granting letters of marque and reprisal in times of peace—appointing courts for the trial of piracies and felonies committed on the high seas and establishing courts for receiving and determining finally appeals in all cases of captures, provided that no member of congress shall be appointed a judge of any of the said courts.

The united states in congress assembled shall also be the last resort on appeal in all disputes and differences now subsisting or that hereafter may arise between two or more states concerning boundary, jurisdiction or any other cause whatever; which authority shall always be exercised in the manner following. Whenever the legislative or executive authority or lawful agent of any state in controversy with another shall present a petition to congress stating the matter in question and praying for a hearing, notice thereof shall be given by order of congress to the legislative or executive authority of the other state in controversy, and a day assigned for the appearance of the parties by their lawful agents, who shall then be directed to appoint by joint consent, commissioners or judges to constitute a court for hearing and determining the matter in question: but if they cannot agree, congress shall name three persons out of each of the united states, and from the list of such persons each party shall alternately strike out one, the petitioners beginning, until the number shall be reduced to thirteen; and from that number not less than seven, nor more than nine names as congress shall direct, shall in the presence of congress be drawn out by lot, and the persons whose names shall be so drawn or any five of them, shall be commissioners or judges, to hear and finally determine the controversy, so always as a major part of the judges who shall hear the cause shall agree in the determination: and if either party shall neglect to attend at the day appointed, without shewing reasons, which congress shall judge sufficient, or being present shall refuse to strike, the congress shall proceed to nominate three persons out of each state, and the secretary of congress shall strike in behalf of such party absent or refusing; and the judgment and sentence of the court to be appointed, in the manner before prescribed, shall be final and conclusive; and if any of the parties shall refuse to submit to the authority of such court, or to appear or defend their claim or cause, the court shall nevertheless proceed to pronounce sentence, or judgment, which shall in like manner be final and decisive, the judgment or sentence and other proceedings being in either case transmitted to congress, and lodged among the acts of congress for the security of the parties concerned: provided that every commissioner, before he sits in judgment, shall take an oath to be administered by one of the judges of the supreme or superior court of the state, where the cause shall be tried, "well and truly to hear and determine the matter in question, according to the best of his judgment, without favour, affection or hope of reward:" provided also that no state shall be deprived of territory for the benefit of the united states.

All controversies concerning the private right of soil claimed under different grants of two or more states, whose jurisdictions as they may respect such lands, and the states which passed such grants are adjusted, the said grants or either of them being at the same time claimed to have originated antecedent to such settlement of jurisdiction, shall on the petition of either party to the congress of the united states, be finally determined as near as maybe in the same manner as is before prescribed for deciding disputes respecting territorial jurisdiction between different states.

The united states in congress assembled shall also have the sole and exclusive right and power of regulating the alloy and value of coin struck by their own authority, or by that of the respective states—fixing the standard of weights and measures throughout the united states—regulating the trade and managing all affairs with the Indians, not members of any of the states, provided that the legislative right of any state within its own limits be not infringed or violated—establishing and regulating post-offices from one state to another, throughout all the united states, and exacting such postage on the papers passing thro' the same as may be requisite to defray the expences of the said office—appointing all officers of the land forces, in the service of the united states, excepting regimental officers—appointing all the officers of the naval forces, and commissioning all officers whatever in the service of the united states—making rules for the government and regulation of the said land and naval forces, and directing their operations.

The united states in congress assembled shall have authority to appoint a committee, to sit in the recess of congress, to be denominated "A Committee of the States," and to consist of one delegate from each state; and to appoint such other committees and civil officers as may be necessary for managing the general affairs of the united states under their direction—to appoint one of their number to preside, provided that no person be allowed to serve in the office of president more than one year in any term of three years; to ascertain the necessary sums of Money to be raised for the service of the united states, and to appropriate and apply the same for defraying the public expences—to borrow money, or emit bills on the credit of the united states, transmitting every half year to the respective states an account of the sums of money so borrowed or emitted,—to build and equip a navy—to agree upon the number of land forces, and to make requisitions from each state for its quota, in proportion to the number of white inhabitants in such state; which requisition shall be binding, and thereupon the legislature of each state shall appoint the regimental officers, raise the men and cloath, arm and equip them in a soldier like manner, at the expence of the united states, and the officers and men so cloathed, armed and equipped shall march to the place appointed, and within the time agreed on by the united states in congress assembled: But if the united states in congress assembled shall, on consideration of circumstances judge proper that any state should not raise men, or should raise a smaller number than its quota, and that any other state should raise a greater number of men than the quota thereof, such extra number shall be raised, officered, cloathed, armed and equipped in the same manner as the quota of such state, unless the legislature of such state shall judge that such extra number cannot be safely spared out of the same, in which case they shall raise officer, cloath, arm and equip as many of such extra number as they judge can be safely spared. And the officers and men so cloathed, armed and equipped, shall march to the place appointed, and within the time agreed on by the united states in congress assembled.

The united states in congress assembled shall never engage in a war, nor grant letters of marque and reprisal in time of peace, nor enter into any treaties or alliances, nor coin money, nor regulate the value thereof, nor ascertain the sums and expences necessary for the defence and welfare of the united states, or any of them, nor emit bills, nor borrow money on the credit of the united states, nor appropriate money, nor agree upon the number of vessels of war, to be built or purchased, or the number of land or sea forces to be raised, nor appoint a commander in chief of the army or navy, unless nine states assent to the same: nor shall a question on any other point, except for adjourning from day to day be determined, unless by the votes of a majority of the united states in congress assembled.

The congress of the united states shall have power to adjourn to any time within the year, and to any place within the united states, so that no period of adjournment be for a longer duration than the space of six Months, and shall publish the Journal of their proceedings monthly, except such parts thereof relating to treaties, alliances or military operations, as in their judgment require secresy; and the yeas and nays of the delegates of each state on any question shall be entered on the Journal, when it is desired by any delegate; and the delegates of a state, or any of them, at his or their request shall be furnished with a transcript of the said Journal, except such parts as are above excepted, to lay before the legislatures of the several states.

Article X.   The committee of the states, or any nine of them, shall be authorized to execute, in the recess of congress, such of the powers of congress as the united states in congress assembled, by the consent of nine states, shall from time to time think expedient to vest them with; provided that no power be delegated to the said committee, for the exercise of which, by the articles of confederation, the voice of nine states in the congress of the united states assembled is requisite.

Article XI.   Canada acceding to this confederation, and joining in the measures of the united states, shall be admitted into, and entitled to all the advantages of this union: but no other colony shall be admitted into the same, unless such admission be agreed to by nine states.

Article XII.   All bills of credit emitted, monies borrowed and debts contracted by, or under the authority of congress, before the assembling of the united states, in pursuance of the present confederation, shall be deemed and considered as a charge against the united states, for payment and satisfaction whereof the said united states, and the public faith are hereby solemnly pledged.

Article XIII.   Every state shall abide by the determinations of the united states in congress assembled, on all questions which by this confederation are submitted to them. And the Articles of this confederation shall be inviolably observed by every state, and the union shall be perpetual; nor shall any alteration at any time hereafter be made in any of them; unless such alteration be agreed to in a congress of the united states, and be afterwards confirmed by the legislatures of every state.

And Whereas it hath pleased the Great Governor of the World to incline the hearts of the legislatures we respectively represent in congress, to approve of, and to authorize us to ratify the said articles of confederation and perpetual union. Know Ye that we the undersigned delegates, by virtue of the power and authority to us given for that purpose, do by these presents, in the name and in behalf of our respective constituents, fully and entirely ratify and confirm each and every of the said articles of confederation and perpetual union, and all and singular the matters and things therein contained: And we do further solemnly plight and engage the faith of our respective constituents, that they shall abide by the determinations of the united states in congress assembled, on all questions, which by the said confederation are submitted to them. And that the articles thereof shall be inviolably observed by the states we respectively represent, and that the union shall be perpetual. In Witness whereof we have hereunto set our hands in Congress. Done at Philadelphia in the state of Pennsylvania the ninth Day of July in the Year of our Lord one Thousand seven Hundred and Seventy-eight, and in the third year of the independence of America.

Josiah Bartlett
John Wentworth Junr
    August 8th 1778

On the Part & behalf
of the State of
New Hampshire

John Hancock
Samuel Adams
Elbridge Gerry
Francis Dana
James Lovell
Samuel Holten

On the part and behalf
of the State of
Massachusetts Bay

William Ellery
Henry Marchant
John Collins

On the part and behalf of
the State of Rhode-Island
and Providence Plantations

Roger Sherman
Samuel Huntington
Oliver Wolcott
Titus Hosmer
Andrew Adams

on the Part and behalf
of the State of
Connecticut

Jas. Duane
Fras. Lewis
Wm: Duer.
Gouvr. Morris

On the Part and Behalf
of the State of New York

Jno Witherspoon
Nathl. Scudder
} On the Part and in Behalf of the State of New Jersey Novr. 26. 1778.—

Robt Morris.
Daniel Roberdeau
Jona: Bayard Smith.
William Clingan
Joseph Reed   July 1778
} On the part and behalf of the State of Pennsylvania

Thos M:Kean   Feby 22, 1779
John Dickinson   May 5th– 1779
Nicholas Van Dyke,
} On the part & behalf of the State of Delaware

John Hanson   March 1st, 1781
Daniel Carroll   do
} on the part and behalf of the State of Maryland

Richard Henry Lee
John Banister
Thomas Adams
Jno Harvie
Francis Lightfoot Lee
} On the Part and Behalf of the State of Virginia

John Penn, July 21st 1778
Corns. Harnett
Jno. Williams
} on the part and Behalf of the State of No. Carolina

Henry Laurens.
William Henry Drayton
Jno. Mathews
Richd. Hutson
Thos: Heyward Junr:
} On the part & behalf of the State of South-Carolina

Jno Walton   24th. July 1778
Edwd. Telfair.
Edwd Langworthy.
} On the part & behalf of the State of Georgia

Letter from the Constitutional Convention to the President of Congress

In Convention, September 17, 1787.

SIR, WE have now the honor to submit to the consideration of the United States in Congress assembled, that Constitution which has appeared to us the most adviseable.

The friends of our country have long seen and desired, that the power of making war, peace and treaties, that of levying money and regulating commerce, and the correspondent executive and judicial authorities should be fully and effectually vested in the general government of the Union: but the impropriety of delegating such extensive trust to one body of men is evident—Hence results the necessity of a different organization.

It is obviously impracticable in the foederal government of these States; to secure all rights of independent sovereignty to each, and yet provide for the interest and safety of all—Individuals entering into society, must give up a share of liberty to preserve the rest. The magnitude of the sacrifice must depend as well on situation and circumstance, as on the object to be obtained. It is at all times difficult to draw with precision the line between those rights which must be surrendered, and those which may be reserved; and on the present occasion this difficulty was encreased by a difference among the several States as to their situation, extent, habits, and particular interests.

In all our deliberations on this subject we kept steadily in our view, that which appears to us the greatest interest of every true American, the consolidation of our Union, in which is involved our prosperity, felicity, safety, perhaps our national existence, This important consideration, seriously and deeply impressed on our minds, led each State in the Convention to be less rigid on points of inferior magnitude, than might have been otherwise expected; and thus the Constitution, which we now present, is the result of a spirit of amity, and of that mutual deference and concession which the peculiarity of our political situation rendered indispensible.

That it will meet the full and entire approbation of every State is not perhaps to be expected; but each will doubtless consider, that had her interests been alone consulted, the consequences might have been particularly disagreeable or injurious to others; that it is liable to as few exceptions as could reasonably have been expected, we hope and believe; that it may promote the lasting welfare of that country so dear to us all, and secure her freedom and happiness, is our most ardent wish.

With great respect, WE have the honor to be SIR, Your Excellency's most Obedient and humble servants.

> George Washington, President.
> By unanimous Order of the
> Convention

Resolutions of the Convention Concerning the Ratification and Implementation of the Constitution

In Convention Monday September 17th. 1787.

Present The States of New Hampshire, Massachusetts, Connecticut, Mr. Hamilton from New York, New Jersey, Pennsylvania, Delaware, Maryland, Virginia, North Carolina, South Carolina and Georgia.

RESOLVED, That the preceeding Constitution be laid before the United States in Congress assembled, and that it is the Opinion of this Convention, that it should afterwards be submitted to a Convention of Delegates, chosen in each State by the People thereof, under the Recommendation of its Legislature, for their Assent and Ratification; and that each Convention assenting to, and ratifying the Same, should give Notice thereof to the United States in Congress assembled.

Resolved, That it is the Opinion of this Convention, that as soon as the Conventions of nine States shall have ratified this Constitution, the United States in Congress assembled should fix a Day on which Electors should be appointed by the States which shall have ratified the same, and a Day on which the Electors should assemble to vote for the President, and the Time and Place for commencing Proceedings under this Constitution. That after such Publication the Electors should be appointed, and the Senators and Representatives elected: That the Electors should meet on the Day fixed for the Election of the President, and should transmit their Votes certified, signed, sealed and directed, as the Constitution requires, to the Secretary of the United States in Congress assembled, that the Senators and Representatives should convene at the Time and Place assigned; that the Senators should appoint a President of the Senate, for the sole Purpose of receiving, opening and counting the Votes for President; and, that after he shall be chosen, the Congress, together with the President, should, without Delay, proceed to execute this Constitution.

By the Unanimous Order of the Convention

W. Jackson Secretary.   Go: Washington Presidt.

The Constitution

[*The footnotes in this appendix, keyed to the line number on the page, indicate portions of the Constitution that have been altered by subsequent amendment.*]

We the People of the United States, in Order to form a more perfect Union, establish Justice, insure domestic Tranquility, provide for the common defence, promote the general Welfare, and secure the Blessings of Liberty to ourselves and our Posterity, do ordain and establish this Constitution for the United States of America.

Article. I.

Section. 1. All legislative Powers herein granted shall be vested in a Congress of the United States, which shall consist of a Senate and House of Representatives.

Section. 2. The House of Representatives shall be composed of Members chosen every second Year by the People of the several States, and the Electors in each State shall have the Qualifications requisite for Electors of the most numerous Branch of the State Legislature.

No Person shall be a Representative who shall not have attained to the Age of twenty five Years, and been seven Years a Citizen of the United States, and who shall not, when elected, be an Inhabitant of that State in which he shall be chosen.

Representatives and direct Taxes shall be apportioned among the several States which may be included within this Union, according to their respective Numbers, which shall be determined by adding to the whole Number of free Persons, including those bound to Service for a Term of Years, and excluding Indians not taxed, three fifths of all other Persons. The actual Enumeration shall be made within three Years after the first Meeting of the Congress of the United States, and within every subsequent Term of ten Years, in such Manner as

940.25–30 Representatives . . . other Persons.] Changed regarding representation by the Fourteenth Amendment; changed regarding taxation by the Sixteenth Amendment.

they shall by Law direct. The Number of Representatives shall not exceed one for every thirty Thousand, but each State shall have at Least one Representative; and until such enumeration shall be made, the State of New Hampshire shall be entitled to chuse three, Massachusetts eight, Rhode-Island and Providence Plantations one, Connecticut five, New-York six, New Jersey four, Pennsylvania eight, Delaware one, Maryland six, Virginia ten, North Carolina five, South Carolina five, and Georgia three.

When vacancies happen in the Representation from any State, the Executive Authority thereof shall issue Writs of Election to fill such Vacancies.

The House of Representatives shall chuse their Speaker and other Officers; and shall have the sole Power of Impeachment.

Section. 3.   The Senate of the United States shall be composed of two Senators from each State, chosen by the Legislature thereof, for six Years; and each Senator shall have one Vote.

Immediately after they shall be assembled in Consequence of the first Election, they shall be divided as equally as may be into three Classes. The Seats of the Senators of the first Class shall be vacated at the Expiration of the second Year, of the second Class at the Expiration of the fourth Year, and of the third Class at the Expiration of the sixth Year, so that one third may be chosen every second Year; and if Vacancies happen by Resignation, or otherwise, during the Recess of the Legislature of any State, the Executive thereof may make temporary Appointments until the next Meeting of the Legislature, which shall then fill such Vacancies.

No Person shall be a Senator who shall not have attained to the Age of thirty Years, and been nine Years a Citizen of the United States, and who shall not, when elected, be an Inhabitant of that State for which he shall be chosen.

The Vice President of the United States shall be President of the Senate, but shall have no Vote, unless they be equally divided.

941.16–17   chosen by the Legislature thereof,] Changed by the Seventeenth Amendment.

941.25–29   and if Vacancies . . . Vacanies.] Changed by the Seventeenth Amendment.

The Senate shall chuse their other Officers, and also a President pro tempore, in the Absence of the Vice President, or when he shall exercise the Office of President of the United States.

The Senate shall have the sole Power to try all Impeachments. When sitting for that Purpose, they shall be on Oath or Affirmation. When the President of the United States is tried, the Chief Justice shall preside: And no Person shall be convicted without the Concurrence of two thirds of the Members present.

Judgment in Cases of Impeachment shall not extend further than to removal from Office, and disqualification to hold and enjoy any Office of honor, Trust or Profit under the United States: but the Party convicted shall nevertheless be liable and subject to Indictment, Trial, Judgment and Punishment, according to Law.

Section. 4.   The Times, Places and Manner of holding Elections for Senators and Representatives, shall be prescribed in each State by the Legislature thereof; but the Congress may at any time by Law make or alter such Regulations, except as to the Places of chusing Senators.

The Congress shall assemble at least once in every Year, and such Meeting shall be on the first Monday in December, unless they shall by Law appoint a different Day.

Section. 5.   Each House shall be the Judge of the Elections, Returns and Qualifications of its own Members, and a Majority of each shall constitute a Quorum to do Business; but a smaller Number may adjourn from day to day, and may be authorized to compel the Attendance of absent Members, in such Manner, and under such Penalties as each House may provide.

Each House may determine the Rules of its Proceedings, punish its members for disorderly Behaviour, and, with the Concurrence of two thirds, expel a Member.

Each House shall keep a Journal of its Proceedings, and from time to time publish the same, excepting such Parts as may in their Judgment require Secrecy; and the Yeas and

942.23   be on . . . December,] Changed by the Twentieth Amendment.

Nays of the Members of either House on any question shall, at the Desire of one fifth of those Present, be entered on the Journal.

Neither House, during the Session of Congress, shall, without the Consent of the other, adjourn for more than three days, nor to any other Place than that in which the two Houses shall be sitting.

Section. 6. The Senators and Representatives shall receive a Compensation for their Services, to be ascertained by Law, and paid out of the Treasury of the United States. They shall in all Cases, except Treason, Felony and Breach of the Peace, be privileged from Arrest during their Attendance at the Session of their respective Houses, and in going to and returning from the same; and for any Speech or Debate in either House, they shall not be questioned in any other Place.

No Senator or Representative shall, during the Time for which he was elected, be appointed to any civil Office under the Authority of the United States which shall have been created, or the Emoluments whereof shall have been increased during such time; and no Person holding any Office under the United States, shall be a Member of either House during his Continuance in Office.

Section. 7. All Bills for raising Revenue shall originate in the House of Representatives; but the Senate may propose or concur with Amendments as on other Bills.

Every Bill which shall have passed the House of Representatives and the Senate shall, before it become a Law, be presented to the President of the United States; If he approve he shall sign it, but if not he shall return it, with his Objections to that House in which it shall have originated, who shall enter the Objections at large on their Journal, and proceed to reconsider it. If after such Reconsideration two thirds of that House shall agree to pass the Bill, it shall be sent, together with the Objections, to the other House, by which it shall likewise be reconsidered, and if approved by two thirds of that House, it shall become a Law. But in all such Cases the Votes of both Houses shall be determined by yeas and Nays, and the Names of the Persons voting for and against the Bill shall be entered on the Journal of each

House respectively. If any Bill shall not be returned by the President within ten Days (Sundays excepted) after it shall have been presented to him, the Same shall be a Law, in like Manner as if he had signed it, unless the Congress by their Adjournment prevent its Return, in which Case it shall not be a Law.

Every Order, Resolution, or Vote to which the Concurrence of the Senate and House of Representatives may be necessary (except on a question of Adjournment) shall be presented to the President of the United States; and before the Same shall take Effect, shall be approved by him, or being disapproved by him, shall be repassed by two thirds of the Senate and House of Representatives, according to the Rules and Limitations prescribed in the Case of a Bill.

Section. 8.   The Congress shall have Power To lay and collect Taxes, Duties, Imposts and Excises, to pay the Debts and provide for the common Defence and general Welfare of the United States; but all Duties, Imposts and Excises shall be uniform throughout the United States;

To borrow Money on the credit of the United States;

To regulate Commerce with foreign Nations, and among the several States, and with the Indian Tribes;

To establish an uniform Rule of Naturalization, and uniform Laws on the subject of Bankruptcies throughout the United States;

To coin Money, regulate the Value thereof, and of foreign Coin, and fix the Standard of Weights and Measures;

To provide for the Punishment of counterfeiting the Securities and current Coin of the United States;

To establish Post Offices and post Roads;

To promote the Progress of Science and useful Arts, by securing for limited Times to Authors and Inventors the exclusive Right to their respective Writings and Discoveries;

To constitute Tribunals inferior to the supreme Court;

To define and punish Piracies and Felonies committed on the high Seas, and Offences against the Law of Nations;

To declare War, grant Letters of Marque and Reprisal, and make Rules concerning Captures on Land and Water;

To raise and support Armies, but no Appropriation of Money to that Use shall be for a longer Term than two Years;

To provide and maintain a Navy;

To make Rules for the Government and Regulation of the land and naval Forces;

To provide for calling forth the Militia to execute the Laws of the Union, suppress Insurrections and repel Invasions;

To provide for organizing, arming, and disciplining, the Militia, and for governing such Part of them as may be employed in the Service of the United States, reserving to the States respectively, the Appointment of the Officers, and the Authority of training the Militia according to the discipline prescribed by Congress;

To exercise exclusive Legislation in all Cases whatsoever, over such District (not exceeding ten Miles square) as may, by Cession of particular States, and the Acceptance of Congress, become the Seat of the Government of the United States, and to exercise like Authority over all Places purchased by the Consent of the Legislature of the State in which the same shall be, for the Erection of Forts, Magazines, Arsenals, dock-Yards, and other needful Buildings; —And

To make all Laws which shall be necessary and proper for carrying into Execution the foregoing Powers, and all other Powers vested by this Constitution in the Government of the United States, or in any Department or Officer thereof.

Section. 9. The Migration or Importation of such Persons as any of the States now existing shall think proper to admit, shall not be prohibited by the Congress prior to the Year one thousand eight hundred and eight, but a Tax or duty may be imposed on such Importation, not exceeding ten dollars for each Person.

The Privilege of the Writ of Habeas Corpus shall not be suspended, unless when in Cases of Rebellion or Invasion the public Safety may require it.

No Bill of Attainder or ex post facto Law shall be passed.

No Capitation, or other direct, Tax shall be laid, unless in

Proportion to the Census or Enumeration herein before directed to be taken.

No Tax or Duty shall be laid on Articles exported from any State.

No Preference shall be given by any Regulation of Commerce or Revenue to the Ports of one State over those of another: nor shall Vessels bound to, or from, one State, be obliged to enter, clear, or pay Duties in another.

No Money shall be drawn from the Treasury, but in Consequence of Appropriations made by Law; and a regular Statement and Account of the Receipts and Expenditures of all public Money shall be published from time to time.

No Title of Nobility shall be granted by the United States: And no Person holding any Office of Profit or Trust under them, shall, without the Consent of the Congress, accept of any present, Emolument, Office, or Title, of any kind whatever, from any King, Prince, or foreign State.

Section. 10.   No State shall enter into any Treaty, Alliance, or Confederation; grant Letters of Marque and Reprisal; coin Money; emit Bills of Credit; make any Thing but gold and silver Coin a Tender in Payment of Debts; pass any Bill of Attainder, ex post facto Law, or Law impairing the Obligation of Contracts, or grant any Title of Nobility.

No State shall, without the Consent of the Congress, lay any Imposts or Duties on Imports or Exports, except what may be absolutely necessary for executing it's inspection Laws: and the net Produce of all Duties and Imposts, laid by any State on Imports or Exports, shall be for the Use of the Treasury of the United States; and all such Laws shall be subject to the Revision and Controul of the Congress.

No State shall, without the Consent of Congress, lay any Duty of Tonnage, keep Troops, or Ships of War in time of Peace, enter into any Agreement or Compact with another State, or with a foreign Power, or engage in War, unless actually invaded, or in such imminent Danger as will not admit of delay.

945.38–946.2 No Capitation . . . taken.] Changed by the Sixteenth Amendment.

Article. II.

Section. I. The executive Power shall be vested in a President of the United States of America. He shall hold his Office during the Term of four Years, and, together with the Vice President, chosen for the same Term, be elected, as follows

Each State shall appoint, in such Manner as the Legislature thereof may direct, a Number of Electors, equal to the whole Number of Senators and Representatives to which the State may be entitled in the Congress: but no Senator or Representative, or Person holding an Office of Trust or Profit under the United States, shall be appointed an Elector.

The Electors shall meet in their respective States and vote by Ballot for two Persons, of whom one at least shall not be an Inhabitant of the same State with themselves. And they shall make a List of all the Persons voted for, and of the Number of Votes for each; which List they shall sign and certify, and transmit sealed to the Seat of the Government of the United States, directed to the President of the Senate. The President of the Senate shall, in the Presence of the Senate and House of Representatives, open all the Certificates, and the Votes shall then be counted. The Person having the greatest Number of Votes shall be the President, if such Number be a Majority of the whole Number of Electors appointed; and if there be more than one who have such Majority, and have an equal Number of Votes, then the House of Representatives shall immediately chuse by Ballot one of them for President; and if no Person have a Majority, then from the five highest on the List the said House shall in like Manner chuse the President. But in chusing the President, the Votes shall be taken by States, the Representation from each State having one Vote; A quorum for this Purpose shall consist of a Member or Members from two thirds of the States, and a Majority of all the States shall be necessary to a Choice. In every Case, after the Choice of the President, the Person having the greatest Number of Votes of the Electors shall be the Vice President. But if there should remain two or more who have equal

Votes, the Senate shall chuse from them by Ballot the Vice President.

The Congress may determine the Time of chusing the Electors, and the Day on which they shall give their Votes; which Day shall be the same throughout the United States.

No Persons except a natural born Citizen, or a Citizen of the United States, at the time of the Adoption of this Constitution, shall be eligible to the Office of President; neither shall any Person be eligible to that Office who shall not have attained to the Age of thirty five Years, and been fourteen Years a Resident within the United States.

In Case of the Removal of the President from Office, or of his Death, Resignation, or Inability to discharge the Powers and Duties of the said Office, the Same shall devolve on the Vice President, and the Congress may by Law provide for the Case of Removal, Death, Resignation or Inability, both of the President and Vice President, declaring what Officer shall then act as President, and such Officer shall act accordingly, until the Disability be removed, or a President shall be elected.

The President shall, at stated Times, receive for his Services, a Compensation, which shall neither be encreased nor diminished during the Period for which he shall have been elected, and he shall not receive within that Period any other Emolument from the United States, or any of them.

Before he enter on the Execution of his Office, he shall take the following Oath or Affirmation:—"I do solemnly swear (or affirm) that I will faithfully execute the Office of President of the United States, and will to the best of my Ability, preserve, protect and defend the Constitution of the United States."

Section. 2.   The President shall be Commander in Chief of the Army and Navy of the United States, and of the Militia of the several States, when called into the actual Service of the United States; he may require the Opinion, in writing, of the principal Officer in each of the executive Departments, upon any Subject relating to the Duties of their respective Offices,

947.14–948.2 The Electors . . . Vice President.] Changed by the Twelfth Amendment.
948.12–19 In Case . . . elected.] Changed by the Twenty-fifth Amendment.

and he shall have Power to grant Reprieves and Pardons for Offences against the United States, except in Cases of Impeachment.

He shall have Power, by and with the Advice and Consent of the Senate, to make Treaties, provided two thirds of the Senators present concur; and he shall nominate, and by and with the Advice and Consent of the Senate, shall appoint Ambassadors, other public Ministers and Consuls, Judges of the supreme Court, and all other Officers of the United States, whose Appointments are not herein otherwise provided for, and which shall be established by Law: but the Congress may by Law vest the Appointment of such inferior Officers, as they think proper, in the President alone, in the Courts of Law, or in the Heads of Departments.

The President shall have Power to fill up all Vacancies that may happen during the Recess of the Senate, by granting Commissions which shall expire at the End of their next Session.

Section. 3. He shall from time to time give to the Congress Information of the State of the Union, and recommend to their Consideration such Measures as he shall judge necessary and expedient; he may, on extraordinary Occasions, convene both Houses, or either of them, and in Case of Disagreement between them, with Respect to the Time of Adjournment, he may adjourn them to such Time as he shall think proper; he shall receive Ambassadors and other public Ministers; he shall take Care that the Laws be faithfully executed, and shall Commission all the Officers of the United States.

Section. 4. The President, Vice President and all civil Officers of the United States, shall be removed from Office on Impeachment for, and Conviction of Treason, Bribery, or other high Crimes and Misdemeanors.

Article. III.

Section. 1. The judicial Power of the United States, shall be vested in one supreme Court, and in such inferior Courts as the Congress may from time to time ordain and establish. The Judges, both of the supreme and inferior Courts, shall hold their Offices during good Behaviour, and shall, at stated Times, receive for their Services, a Compensation, which shall not be diminished during their Continuance in Office.

Section. 2.   The judicial Power shall extend to all Cases, in Law and Equity, arising under this Constitution, the Laws of the United States, and Treaties made, or which shall be made, under their Authority;—to all Cases affecting Ambassadors, other public Ministers and Consuls;—to all Cases of admiralty and maritime Jurisdiction;—to Controversies to which the United States shall be a Party;—to Controversies between two or more States—between a State and Citizens of another State;—between Citizens of different States,—between Citizens of the same State claiming Lands under Grants of different States, and between a State, or the Citizens thereof, and of foreign States, Citizens or Subjects.

In all Cases affecting Ambassadors, other public Ministers and Consuls, and those in which a State shall be Party, the supreme Court shall have original Jurisdiction. In all the other Cases before mentioned, the supreme Court shall have appellate Jurisdiction, both as to Law and Fact, with such Exceptions, and under such Regulations as the Congress shall make.

The Trial of all Crimes, except in Cases of Impeachment, shall be by Jury; and such Trial shall be held in the State where the said Crimes shall have been committed; but when not committed within any State, the Trial shall be at such Place or Places as the Congress may by Law have directed.

Section. 3.   Treason against the United States, shall consist only in levying War against them, or in adhering to their Enemies, giving them Aid and Comfort. No Person shall be convicted of Treason unless on the Testimony of two Witnesses to the same overt Act, or on Confession in open Court.

The Congress shall have Power to declare the Punishment of Treason, but no Attainder of Treason shall work Cor-

950.12–16   between a State . . . Subjects] Jurisdiction over suits brought against states by citizens of another state, or by foreigners, was addressed by the Eleventh Amendment.

ruption of Blood, or Forfeiture except during the Life of the Person attainted.

Article. IV.

Section. 1. Full Faith and Credit shall be given in each State to the public Acts, Records, and judicial Proceedings of every other State. And the Congress may by general Laws prescribe the Manner in which such Acts, Records and Proceedings shall be proved, and the Effect thereof.

Section. 2. The Citizens of each State shall be entitled to all privileges and Immunities of Citizens in the several States.

A Person charged in any State with Treason, Felony, or other Crime, who shall flee from Justice, and be found in another State, shall on Demand of the executive Authority of the State from which he fled, be delivered up, to be removed to the State having Jurisdiction of the Crime.

No Person held to Service or Labour in one State, under the Laws thereof, escaping into another, shall, in Consequence of any Law or Regulation therein, be discharged from such Service or Labour, but shall be delivered up on Claim of the Party to whom such Service or Labour may be due.

Section. 3. New States may be admitted by the Congress into this Union; but no new State shall be formed or erected within the Jurisdiction of any other State; nor any State be formed by the Junction of two or more States, or Parts of States, without the Consent of the Legislatures of the States concerned as well as of the Congress.

The Congress shall have Power to dispose of and make all needful Rules and Regulations respecting the Territory or other Property belonging to the United States; and nothing in this Constitution shall be so construed as to Prejudice any Claims of the United States, or of any particular State.

951.17–22 No Person . . . due.] Changed by the Thirteenth Amendment.

Section. 4. The United States shall guarantee to every State in this Union a Republican Form of Government, and shall protect each of them against Invasion; and on Application of the Legislature, or of the Executive (when the Legislature cannot be convened) against domestic Violence.

Article. V.

The Congress, whenever two thirds of both Houses shall deem it necessary, shall propose Amendments to this Constitution, or, on the Application of the Legislatures of two thirds of the several States, shall call a Convention for proposing Amendments, which, in either Case, shall be valid to all Intents and Purposes, as Part of this Constitution, when ratified by the Legislatures of three fourths of the several States, or by Conventions in three fourths thereof, as the one or the other Mode of Ratification may be proposed by the Congress; Provided that no Amendment which may be made prior to the Year One thousand eight hundred and eight shall in any Manner affect the first and fourth Clauses in the Ninth Section of the first Article; and that no State, without its Consent, shall be deprived of it's equal Suffrage in the Senate.

Article. VI.

All Debts contracted and Engagements entered into, before the Adoption of this Constitution, shall be as valid against the United States under this Constitution, as under the Confederation.

This Constitution, and the Laws of the United States which shall be made in Pursuance thereof; and all Treaties made, or which shall be made, under the Authority of the United States, shall be the supreme Law of the Land; and the Judges in every State shall be bound thereby, any Thing in the Constitution or Laws of any State to the Contrary notwithstanding.

The Senators and Representatives before mentioned, and the Members of the several State Legislatures, and all executive and judicial Officers; both of the United States and of the several States, shall be bound by Oath or Affirmation, to support this Constitution; but no religious Test shall ever be required as a Qualification to any Office or public Trust under the United States.

Article. VII.

The Ratification of the Conventions of nine States, shall be sufficient for the Establishment of this Constitution between the States so ratifying the Same.

DONE in Convention by the Unanimous Consent of the States present the Seventeenth Day of September in the Year of our Lord one thousand seven hundred and Eighty seven and of the Independance of the United States of America the Twelfth In Witness whereof We have hereunto subscribed our Names,

Attest William Jackson Secretary

Go: Washington—Presidt.
and deputy from Virginia

Delaware
{ Geo: Read
Gunning Bedford junr
John Dickinson
Richard Bassett
Jaco: Broom

New Hampshire
{ John Langdon
Nicholas Gilman

Massachusetts
{ Nathaniel Gorham
Rufus King

Maryland
{ James McHenry
Dan of St Thos. Jenifer
Danl Carroll

Connecticut
{ Wm: Saml. Johnson
Roger Sherman

New York . . . Alexander Hamilton

Virginia
{ John Blair—
James Madison Jr.

North Carolina
{ Wm. Blount
Richd. Dobbs Spaight.
Hu Williamson

New Jersey
{ Wil: Livingston
David Brearley
Wm. Paterson.
Jona: Dayton

South Carolina
{ J. Rutledge
Charles Cotesworth
Pinckney
Charles Pinckney
Pierce Butler

Georgia
{ William Few
Abr Baldwin

Pensylvania
{ B Franklin
Thomas Mifflin
Robt Morris
Geo. Clymer
Thos. FitzSimons
Jared Ingersoll
James Wilson
Gouv. Morris

ARTICLES in Addition to, and Amendment of, the Constitution of the United States of America, proposed by Congress, and ratified by the Legislatures of the several States, pursuant to the fifth Article of the original Constitution.

Article I.

Congress shall make no law respecting an establishment of religion, or prohibiting the free exercise thereof; or abridging the freedom of speech, or of the press; or the right of the people peaceably to assemble, and to petition the Government for a redress of grievances.

Article II.

A well regulated Militia, being necessary to the security of a free State, the right of the people to keep and bear Arms, shall not be infringed.

Article III.

No Soldier shall, in time of peace be quartered in any house, without the consent of the Owner, nor in time of war, but in a manner to be prescribed by law.

Article IV.

The right of the people to be secure in their persons, houses, papers, and effects, against unreasonable searches and seizures, shall not be violated, and no Warrants shall issue, but upon probable cause, supported by Oath or affirmation, and particularly describing the place to be searched, and the persons or things to be seized.

Article V.

No person shall be held to answer for a capital, or otherwise infamous crime, unless on a presentment or indictment of a Grand Jury, except in cases arising in the land or naval forces, or in the Militia, when in actual service in time of War or public danger; nor shall any person be subject for the same offence to be twice put in jeopardy of life or limb; nor shall be compelled in any criminal case to be a witness against himself, nor be deprived of life, liberty, or property, without due process of law; nor shall private property be taken for public use, without just compensation.

Article VI.

In all criminal prosecutions, the accused shall enjoy the right to a speedy and public trial, by an impartial jury of the State and district wherein the crime shall have been committed, which district shall have been previously ascertained by law, and to be informed of the nature and cause of the accusation; to be confronted with the witnesses against him; to have compulsory process for obtaining witnesses in his favor, and to have the Assistance of Counsel for his defence.

Article VII.

In Suits at common law, where the value in controversy shall exceed twenty dollars, the right of trial by jury shall be preserved, and no fact tried by a jury, shall be otherwise re-examined in any Court of the United States, than according to the rules of the common law.

Article VIII.

Excessive bail shall not be required, nor excessive fines imposed, nor cruel and unusual punishments inflicted.

Article IX.

The enumeration in the Constitution, of certain rights, shall not be construed to deny or disparage others retained by the people.

Article X.

The powers not delegated to the United States by the Constitution, nor prohibited by it to the States, are reserved to the States respectively, or to the people.

Articles I.–X. proposed to the states by Congress, September 25, 1789
Ratification completed, December 15, 1791
Ratification declared, March 1, 1792

Article XI.

The Judicial power of the United States shall not be construed to extend to any suit in law or equity, commenced or prosecuted against one of the United States by Citizens of another State, or by Citizens or Subjects of any Foreign State.

Proposed to the states by Congress, March 4, 1794
Ratification completed, February 7, 1795
Ratification declared, January 8, 1798

Article XII.

The Electors shall meet in their respective states, and vote by ballot for President and Vice-President, one of whom, at least, shall not be an inhabitant of the same state with themselves; they shall name in their ballots the person voted for as President, and in distinct ballots the person voted for as Vice-President, and they shall make distinct lists of all persons voted for as President, and of all persons voted for as Vice-President, and of the number of votes for each, which lists they shall sign and certify, and transmit sealed to the seat of the government of the United States, directed to the President of the Senate;—The President of the Senate shall, in the presence of the Senate and House of Representatives, open all the certificates and the votes shall then be counted;—The person having the greatest number of votes for President, shall be the President, if such number be a majority of the whole number of Electors appointed; and if no person have such majority, then from the persons having the highest numbers not exceeding three on the list of those voted for as President, the House of Representatives shall choose immediately, by ballot, the President. But in choosing the President, the votes shall be taken by states, the representation from each state having one vote; a quorum for this purpose shall consist of a member or members from two-thirds of the states, and a majority of all the states shall be necessary to a choice. And if the House of Representatives shall not choose a President whenever the right of choice shall devolve upon them, before the fourth day of March next following, then the Vice-President shall act as President, as in the case of the death or other constitutional disability of the President.—The person having the greatest number of votes as Vice-President, shall be the Vice-President, if such number be a majority of the whole number of Electors appointed, and if no person have a majority, then from the two highest numbers on the list, the Senate shall choose the Vice-President; a quorum for the purpose shall consist of two-thirds of the whole number of Senators, and a majority of the whole number shall be necessary to a choice. But no person constitutionally ineligible to the office of President shall be eligible to that of Vice-President of the United States.

Proposed to the states by Congress, December 9, 1803
Ratification completed, June 15, 1804
Ratification declared, September 25, 1804

Article XIII.

SECTION 1.   Neither slavery nor involuntary servitude, except as a punishment for crime whereof the party shall have been duly convicted, shall exist within the United States, or any place subject to their jurisdiction.

SECTION 2.   Congress shall have power to enforce this article by appropriate legislation.

Proposed to the states by Congress, January 31, 1865
Ratification completed, December 6, 1865
Ratification declared, December 18, 1865

Article XIV.

SECTION 1.   All persons born or naturalized in the United States, and subject to the jurisdiction thereof, are citizens of the United States and of the State wherein they reside. No

957.2–7   And if . . . President.—] Changed by the Twentieth Amendment.

State shall make or enforce any law which shall abridge the privileges or immunities of citizens of the United States; nor shall any State deprive any person of life, liberty, or property, without due process of law; nor deny to any person within its jurisdiction the equal protection of the laws.

SECTION 2. Representatives shall be apportioned among the several States according to their respective numbers, counting the whole number of persons in each State, excluding Indians not taxed. But when the right to vote at any election for the choice of electors for President and Vice President of the United States, Representatives in Congress, the Executive and Judicial officers of a State, or the members of the Legislature thereof, is denied to any of the male inhabitants of such State, being twenty-one years of age, and citizens of the United States, or in any way abridged, except for participation in rebellion, or other crime, the basis of representation therein shall be reduced in the proportion which the number of such male citizens shall bear to the whole number of male citizens twenty-one years of age in such State.

SECTION 3. No person shall be a Senator or Representative in Congress, or elector of President and Vice President, or hold any office, civil or military, under the United States, or under any State, who, having previously taken an oath, as a member of Congress, or as an officer of the United States, or as a member of any State legislature, or as an executive or judicial officer of any State, to support the Constitution of the United States, shall have engaged in insurrection or rebellion against the same, or given aid or comfort to the enemies thereof. But Congress may by a vote of two-thirds of each House, remove such disability.

SECTION 4. The validity of the public debt of the United States, authorized by law, including debts incurred for payment of pensions and bounties for services in suppressing insurrection or rebellion, shall not be questioned. But neither the United States nor any State shall assume or pay any debt or obligation incurred in aid of insurrection or rebellion

958.13–14   male inhabitants . . . twenty-one years of age] Regarding voting rights and sex, see the Nineteenth Amendment; regarding voting rights and age, see the Twenty-sixth Amendment.

against the United States, or any claim for the loss or emancipation of any slave; but all such debts, obligations and claims shall be held illegal and void.

SECTION 5. The Congress shall have power to enforce, by appropriate legislation, the provisions of this article.

Proposed to the states by Congress, June 13, 1866
Ratification completed, July 9, 1868
Ratification declared, July 28, 1868

Article XV.

SECTION 1. The right of citizens of the United States to vote shall not be denied or abridged by the United States or by any State on account of race, color, or previous condition of servitude.

SECTION 2. The Congress shall have power to enforce this article by appropriate legislation.

Proposed to the states by Congress, February 26, 1869
Ratification completed, February 3, 1870
Ratification declared, March 30, 1870

Article XVI.

The Congress shall have power to lay and collect taxes on incomes, from whatever source derived, without apportionment among the several States, and without regard to any census or enumeration.

Proposed to the states by Congress, July 12, 1909
Ratification completed, February 3, 1913
Ratification declared, February 25, 1913

Article XVII.

The Senate of the United States shall be composed of two Senators from each State, elected by the people thereof, for six years; and each Senator shall have one vote. The electors in each State shall have the qualifications requisite for electors of the most numerous branch of the State legislatures.

When vacancies happen in the representation of any State in the Senate, the executive authority of such State shall issue writs of election to fill such vacancies: *Provided,* That the legislature of any State may empower the executive thereof to make temporary appointments until the people fill the vacancies by election as the legislature may direct.

This amendment shall not be so construed as to affect the election or term of any Senator chosen before it becomes valid as part of the Constitution.

Proposed to the states by Congress, May 13, 1912
Ratification completed, April 8, 1913
Ratification declared, May 31, 1913

Article XVIII.

SECTION 1.   After one year from the ratification of this article the manufacture, sale, or transportation of intoxicating liquors within, the importation thereof into, or the exportation thereof from the United States and all territory subject to the jurisdiction thereof for beverage purposes is hereby prohibited.

SEC. 2.   The Congress and the several States shall have concurrent power to enforce this article by appropriate legislation.

SEC. 3.   This article shall be inoperative unless it shall have been ratified as an amendment to the Constitution by the legislatures of the several States, as provided in the Constitution, within seven years from the date of the submission hereof to the States by the Congress.

Proposed to the states by Congress, December 18, 1917
Ratification completed, January 16, 1919
Ratification declared, January 29, 1919

Article XIX.

The right of citizens of the United States to vote shall not be denied or abridged by the United States or by any State on account of sex.

Congress shall have power to enforce this article by appropriate legislation.

Proposed to the states by Congress, June 4, 1919
Ratification completed, August 18, 1920
Ratification declared, August 26, 1920

960.10–23   Article XVIII. . . . Congress] Repealed by the Twenty-first Amendment.

Article XX.

SECTION 1.   The terms of the President and Vice President shall end at noon on the 20th day of January, and the terms of Senators and Representatives at noon on the 3d day of January, of the years in which such terms would have ended if this article had not been ratified; and the terms of their successors shall then begin.

SEC. 2.   The Congress shall assemble at least once in every year, and such meeting shall begin at noon on the 3d day of January, unless they shall by law appoint a different day.

SEC. 3.   If, at the time fixed for the beginning of the term of the President, the President elect shall have died, the Vice President elect shall become President. If a President shall not have been chosen before the time fixed for the beginning of his term, or if the President elect shall have failed to qualify, then the Vice President elect shall act as President until a President shall have qualified; and the Congress may by law provide for the case wherein neither a President elect nor a Vice President elect shall have qualified, declaring who shall then act as President, or the manner in which one who is to act shall be selected, and such person shall act accordingly until a President or Vice President shall have qualified.

SEC. 4.   The Congress may by law provide for the case of the death of any of the persons from whom the House of Representatives may choose a President whenever the right of choice shall have devolved upon them, and for the case of the death of any of the persons from whom the Senate may choose a Vice President whenever the right of choice shall have devolved upon them.

SEC. 5.   Sections 1 and 2 shall take effect on the 15th day of October following the ratification of this article.

SEC. 6.   This article shall be inoperative unless it shall have been ratified as an amendment to the Constitution by the legislatures of three-fourths of the several States within seven years from the date of its submission.

Proposed to the states by Congress, March 2, 1932
Ratification completed, January 23, 1933
Ratification declared, February 6, 1933

Article XXI.

SECTION 1.   The eighteenth article of amendment to the Constitution of the United States is hereby repealed.

SECTION 2.   The transportation or importation into any State, Territory, or possession of the United States for delivery or use therein of intoxicating liquors, in violation of the laws thereof, is hereby prohibited.

SECTION 3.   This article shall be inoperative unless it shall have been ratified as an amendment to the Constitution by conventions in the several States, as provided in the Constitution, within seven years from the date of the submission hereof to the States by the Congress.

Proposed to the states by Congress, February 20, 1933
Ratification completed, December 5, 1933
Ratification declared, December 5, 1933

Article XXII.

SECTION 1.   No person shall be elected to the office of the President more than twice, and no person who has held the office of President, or acted as President, for more than two years of a term to which some other person was elected President shall be elected to the office of the President more than once. But this Article shall not apply to any person holding the office of President when this Article was proposed by the Congress, and shall not prevent any person who may be holding the office of President, or acting as President, during the term within which this Article becomes operative from holding the office of President or acting as President during the remainder of such term.

SEC. 2.   This article shall be inoperative unless it shall have been ratified as an amendment to the Constitution by the legislatures of three-fourths of the several States within seven years from the date of its submission to the States by the Congress.

Proposed to the states by Congress, March 21, 1947
Ratification completed, February 27, 1951
Ratification declared, March 1, 1951

Article XXIII.

SECTION I.   The District constituting the seat of Government of the United States shall appoint in such manner as the Congress may direct:

A number of electors of President and Vice President equal to the whole number of Senators and Representatives in Congress to which the District would be entitled if it were a State, but in no event more than the least populous State; they shall be in addition to those appointed by the States, but they shall be considered, for the purposes of the election of President and Vice President, to be electors appointed by a State; and they shall meet in the District and perform such duties as provided by the twelfth article of amendment.

SEC. 2.   The Congress shall have power to enforce this article by appropriate legislation.

Proposed to the states by Congress, June 17, 1960
Ratification completed, March 29, 1961
Ratification declared, April 3, 1961

Article XXIV.

SECTION I.   The right of citizens of the United States to vote in any primary or other election for President or Vice President, for electors for President or Vice President, or for Senator or Representative in Congress, shall not be denied or abridged by the United States or any State by reason of failure to pay any poll tax or other tax.

SEC. 2.   The Congress shall have power to enforce this article by appropriate legislation.

Proposed to the states by Congress, August 27, 1962
Ratification completed, January 23, 1964
Ratification declared, February 4, 1964

Article XXV.

SECTION I.   In case of the removal of the President from office or of his death or resignation, the Vice President shall become President.

SEC. 2.   Whenever there is a vacancy in the office of the Vice President, the President shall nominate a Vice President who shall take office upon confirmation by a majority vote of both Houses of Congress.

SEC. 3.   Whenever the President transmits to the President pro tempore of the Senate and the Speaker of the House of Representatives his written declaration that he is unable to discharge the powers and duties of his office, and until he transmits to them a written declaration to the contrary, such powers and duties shall be discharged by the Vice President as Acting President.

SEC. 4.   Whenever the Vice President and a majority of either the principal officers of the executive departments or of such other body as Congress may by law provide, transmit to the President pro tempore of the Senate and the Speaker of the House of Representatives their written declaration that the President is unable to discharge the powers and duties of his office, the Vice President shall immediately assume the powers and duties of the office as Acting President.

Thereafter, when the President transmits to the President pro tempore of the Senate and the Speaker of the House of Representatives his written declaration that no inability exists, he shall resume the powers and duties of his office unless the Vice President and a majority of either the principal officers of the executive department or of such other body as Congress may by law provide, transmit within four days to the President pro tempore of the Senate and the Speaker of the House of Representatives their written declaration that the President is unable to discharge the powers and duties of his office. Thereupon Congress shall decide the issue, assembling within forty-eight hours for that purpose if not in session. If the Congress, within twenty-one days after receipt of the latter written declaration, or, if Congress is not in session, within twenty-one days after Congress is required to assemble, determines by two-thirds vote of both Houses that the President is unable to discharge the powers and duties of his office, the Vice President shall continue to discharge the same as Acting President; otherwise, the President shall resume the powers and duties of his office.

Proposed to the states by Congress, July 6, 1965
Ratification completed, February 10, 1967
Ratification declared, February 23, 1967

Article XXVI.

SECTION 1.   The right of citizens of the United States, who are eighteen years of age or older, to vote shall not be denied or abridged by the United States or by any State on account of age.

SEC. 2.   The Congress shall have power to enforce this article by appropriate legislation.

Proposed to the states by Congress, March 23, 1971
Ratification completed, July 1, 1971
Ratification declared, July 5, 1971

Article XXVII.

No law, varying the compensation for the services of the Senators and Representatives, shall take effect, until an election of Representatives shall have intervened.

Proposed to the states by Congress, September 25, 1789
Ratification completed, May 7, 1992
Ratification declared, May 18, 1992

Biographical Notes

Speakers, Writers, and Letter Recipients

HENRY ABBOT (c. 1740–1791)   Born in London, son of the Reverend John Abbot (a canon of St. Paul's Cathedral). Ran away to America in the mid-1750s and settled in Pasquotank (later Camden) County, North Carolina. Became a Baptist in 1758 and was an itinerant evangelist in northeastern North Carolina until 1761, when he became pastor of the Tar River Baptist Church in Granville County. By 1765, he had been ordained pastor of Shiloh Baptist Church in Pasquotank County. In 1769, he participated in the formation of the Kehukee Baptist Association of reformed, or Particular, Baptists. Sometime between 1766 and 1772, he married Mariam Caroon Lurry Wilson, who had two sons by a previous marriage. In 1776, he represented Pasquotank County in the provincial congress that endorsed American independence. Served on legislative committees for defense and for drafting a new state constitution and declaration of rights. Introduced bill permitting non-established clergy to perform marriages. Was recruiting officer for his county. Generally recognized as the author of 19th article of state declaration of rights, affirming that "all men have natural and inalienable rights to worship almighty God according to the dictates of their own conscience." Attended ratifying conventions at Hillsborough in 1788 and Fayetteville in 1789 and supported ratification with amendments. In 1790, owned six slaves and 300 acres of land. Died in May 1791 after a brief illness.

JOHN ARMSTRONG (1717–1795)   Born October 13, 1717, in Brookborough Parish, County Fermanagh, Ireland, son of James Armstrong. Married Rebecca Lyon of Enniskillen in the same county (their son, General John Armstrong, an aide to Mercer and Horatio Gates and the author of the Newburgh Addresses of 1783, married a sister of Robert R. Livingston; later served as diplomat under Jefferson and secretary of war under Madison). They moved to the Cumberland district in Pennsylvania. Armstrong, as surveyor, laid out the town of Carlisle. Served successfully in French and Indian War as captain and lieutenant colonel. Commissioned brigadier general in the Continental Army in May 1776, and then major general and commander of the Pennsylvania militia. Served in the Continental Congress 1779–80. Supported ratification of the Constitution. When Washington wrote him (letter of April 25, 1788), Armstrong was retired and living in Carlisle, Pennsylvania, where he died on March 9, 1795.

SIMEON BALDWIN (1761–1851)   Born in Norwich, Connecticut, December 14, 1761, son of Bethiah Barker and Ebenezer Baldwin (farmer and blacksmith). Graduated from Yale College in 1781. Continued studies for one year and taught school in New Haven. Became tutor at Yale for three years and studied law. Admitted to the bar of New Haven in 1786. In July 1787, he married Rebecca Sherman, daughter of Roger Sherman, with whom he had four children. After her death, he married her sister, Elizabeth Sherman Burr, with whom he had five more children. Baldwin practiced law in New Haven. He was city clerk of New Haven from 1789 to 1800, and was clerk of the U.S. District and Circuit Courts for Connecticut from 1790 to 1803. Secretary of Connecticut Academy of Arts and Sciences in 1800. Elected to U.S. House of Representatives in 1803 as a Federalist; served one term, declining to run for reelection. Resumed federal clerkship in 1805, but was removed in 1806. Served as associate judge of state superior court 1806–18. President of commission that located Farmington Canal, 1822–30. Elected mayor of New Haven in 1826. He died in New Haven on May 26, 1851. His son, Roger Sherman Baldwin (1793–1863), was governor and senator from Connecticut.

NATHANIEL BARRELL (1732–1831)   Born in Boston, son of Ruth Greene and John Barrell (wealthy Boston merchant and shipowner). Nathaniel Barrell engaged in business in Portsmouth, New Hampshire, in the 1750s. In 1758, he married Sally Sayward, only child of Jonathan Sayward, with whom he had eleven children. In 1759, he was a lieutenant in General Wolfe's expedition against Quebec. From 1760 to 1763, he was in London, where he was presented to George III. He returned to Portsmouth and served in the provincial council of New Hampshire from 1763 to 1765. In 1764, he adopted the doctrines of Robert Sandeman and John Glass, which stressed obedience to civil authority and forbade taking up arms. During the Stamp Act crisis in 1765, the Sandemanians came under suspicion of being Tories, and their church in Portsmouth was destroyed by rioters. Barrell suffered losses, closed his business in Portsmouth, and moved to York, district of Maine, to the estate of his father-in-law, who was also suspected of Tory sympathies. He took no part in political or military affairs during the Revolution. At the town meeting in 1787 to elect delegates to the Massachusetts ratifying convention, Barrell spoke vehemently against ratification, saying "he would sooner lose his Arm than put his Assent to the new proposed Constitution," and was elected one of two delegates from York. His reading of Pelatiah Webster's *The Weakness of Brutus Exposed*, and the efforts of his brother Joseph Barrell, George Thatcher, and others, induced him to change his mind, and he spoke and voted in favor of ratification. He afterwards served one term as representative from York in the General Court in 1794. He died April 3, 1831, at the age of 99.

ANDREW BASS (1734–1791)   Born in Craven County, North Carolina, in 1734, son of Anne and Andrew Bass (owner of large estates in Craven and Dobbs counties). Settled in southern Dobbs County on land inherited from his father and established a successful medical practice. Married Alice Anne Rhodes, with whom he had two daughters. Represented Dobbs County in third provincial congress at Hillsborough in 1775 and fifth provincial congress at Halifax in 1776, which drafted the new state constitution. Elected to state house of representatives from Dobbs County in 1777. In 1779, Wayne County was formed from western half of Dobbs, and Bass was elected from Wayne County to state senate in 1780, 1781, and 1782. He also served as justice of the peace. In 1787, he sold land to the county to be used for new town of Waynesborough, county seat until 1847. Delegate from Wayne County to ratifying convention of 1788, where he opposed ratification. In 1788–89, Bass tried to collect money for cattle he had sold to the state during the Revolution that had been captured by Cornwallis before Bass was paid. In 1790, he owned 432 acres of land and 27 slaves. He died in 1791 and was buried in old Waynesborough cemetery.

JEREMY BELKNAP (1744–1798)   Born June 4, 1744, in Boston, Massachusetts, son of Sarah Byles and Joseph Belknap (a leather-dresser and furrier). Graduated from Harvard College in 1762. Taught school at Milton, Massachusetts, and Portsmouth and Greenland, New Hampshire. Studied for the ministry. Became pastor of the Congregational church in Dover, New Hampshire, in 1766. Married Ruth Eliot of Cornhill, Boston, in 1767. Favored independence after passage of Boston Port Act in 1774. Resigned pastorate in Dover in 1786. Accepted post at the Federal Street Church in Boston early in 1787 and remained there until his death. Served as minister of the Long Lane Meeting House, where the Massachusetts ratifying convention met in 1788. Wrote *History of New Hampshire* (published in three volumes, 1784–92) and other works, including *American Biography* (2 volumes, 1794, 1798). Helped to found Massachusetts Historical Society in 1791 (incorporated 1794). Vigorously opposed slavery and the slave trade. He died June 20, 1798.

TIMOTHY BLOODWORTH (1736–1814)   Born in 1736 in New Hanover County, North Carolina. Worked as a wheelwright, cobbler, farmer, doctor, preacher, and teacher and became a political and agricultural leader in the lower Cape Fear region. Member of the committee of safety for New Hanover County in 1775. Made muskets and bayonets for Continental Army in 1776. Justice of county court in 1777. Elected to state house of commons in 1778 and 1779, and supported harsh measures against Loyalists. Treasurer of Wilmington District in 1781 and 1782. Appointed commissioner of confiscated property in 1783. Served as delegate to Continental Congress from 1786 to August 13, 1787, when he resigned; returned to North Carolina to oppose adoption of the Constitution. Delegate from New Hanover County to North Carolina ratifying conventions of 1788 and 1789, where he opposed ratification. Continued active opposition as a state senator 1788–89, and agreed to work with New York's John Lamb to secure amendments to the Constitution. In 1790, he owned nine slaves and 4,266 acres of land. Elected to U.S. House of Representatives in First Congress, served 1790–91. Member of state house of representatives in 1793 and 1794. Elected to U.S. Senate, served 1795–1801, and was an active Republican. Appointed collector of customs at Wilmington in 1807, and served until his death in Washington, North Carolina, on August 24, 1814.

JOHN BROWN (1757–1837)   Born on September 12, 1757, in Staunton, Virginia, son of Margaret (daughter of John Preston) and John Brown (a Presbyterian minister). Attended College of New Jersey (later Princeton), but left to join Washington's forces during retreat through New Jersey in 1776. Later served with Rockbridge, Virginia, soldiers under Lafayette. Left the army and attended William and Mary College. Studied law under supervision of Thomas Jefferson and was admitted to bar in 1782. Moved to district of Kentucky in 1782, first to Danville, but later to Frankfort, where he settled and established law practice. Elected to state senate from Kentucky in 1784 and served until 1788. Member of the Continental Congress in 1787 and 1788. Advocated statehood for Kentucky and attended Kentucky statehood convention of 1788. Delegate from Kentucky to Virginia ratifying convention in 1788, where he opposed ratification. Elected to First and Second Congresses, served from 1789 to 1792. When Kentucky became a state in 1792, Brown was elected to U.S. Senate, where he served until 1805 and was president pro tempore from October 1803 to March 1805. In 1799, married Margaretta, daughter of John Mason of New York, who was Lafayette's chaplain during the Revolution. In 1805, he returned to Kentucky and resumed practice of law. His home, Liberty Hall in Frankfort, was built from plans drawn by Jefferson. He died in Frankfort on August 28, 1837.

SAMUEL BRYAN (1759–1821)   Born September 30, 1759, in Philadelphia, eldest son of Elizabeth Smith and George Bryan, provincial politician and judge of supreme court. Assisted father in business and public affairs and lived in his house in Philadelphia. Appointed secretary of state council of censors in 1784. Served as clerk of state assembly from 1784 to 1786. In October 1787, during Pennsylvania ratifying convention, began secret authorship of "Centinel" columns, published in Philadelphia newspapers *Independent Gazetteer* and *Freeman's Journal*, opposing ratification. Series continued through November 1789; after federal Constitution was adopted, unsuccessfully defended the Pennsylvania constitution of 1776 against the new state constitution, which was ultimately adopted. In December 1790, was unsuccessful candidate for post of clerk of state senate and for appointment as secretary of commonwealth. In July 1795, Governor Thomas Mifflin appointed him state register general. Moved in 1799 to Lancaster, the new state capital. Governor Thomas McKean appointed him state comptroller general in 1801, and removed him from office in 1805. Unsuccessful candidate for collector of port of Philadelphia and state treasurer in 1807. In 1809, moved back to Philadelphia and became register of wills, serving until his death, in Chester County, on October 6, 1821.

DAVID CALDWELL (1725–1824)   Born March 22, 1725, in Lancaster County, Pennsylvania, son of Ann Stewart and Andrew Caldwell (a Scots farmer who immigrated to America from Ireland in 1718). Caldwell worked as a carpenter between 1742 and 1750, experienced a religious conversion, and began to study for the ministry. Attended College of New Jersey (now

Princeton) and graduated in 1761. Ordained Presbyterian minister in Trenton in 1765. In 1766, moved to North Carolina and married Rachel Craighead, with whom he had at least eleven children. A good friend of Benjamin Rush, whom he had met at college, Caldwell also was a practicing physician. In 1768, he became pastor of two churches in Buffalo and Alamance, North Carolina, where he farmed, taught a school in classics, and was active in politics. Represented Guilford County in the provincial congress of 1776. Served on the committee to draft a new state constitution and is credited with authorship of the articles that declared clergymen ineligible to serve in the state legislature and barred non-Protestants from holding public office. Delegate from Guilford County to North Carolina ratifying convention of 1788, where he opposed ratification. In 1790, he owned eight slaves and 791 acres of land. Supported the War of 1812, and continued to teach and preach until 1820. He died on August 25, 1824.

GEORGE CLINTON (1739–1812)   Born July 26, 1739, in Little Britain, Ulster County, New York, son of Charles Clinton (born in Longford, Ireland). In 1758, served on the privateer *Defiance* and as subaltern in father's regiment in expedition that captured and destroyed Fort Frontenac on Lake Ontario. Studied law with William Smith in New York, and practiced in Ulster County. Elected to the provincial assembly in 1768. Married Cornelia Tappen, of a prominent Ulster County family closely aligned with Gilbert Livingston and Melancton Smith, in February 1770. Elected delegate to the Second Continental Congress in 1775. Appointed brigadier general of militia in December 1775. Supported separation from Great Britain, but was absent on military duty when Declaration of Independence was signed. Served in militia until 1777, when he resigned and was commissioned brigadier general in Continental Army. Elected governor of New York in 1777, defeating Philip Schuyler, and was reelected for six successive terms through 1795, defeating John Jay in 1786 and 1792 and Robert Yates (whom he later appointed chief justice of New York) in 1789. Presided over the New York ratifying convention in June 1788, where he opposed ratification. Helped convince John Jay to write a circular to other states seeking a second convention to amend the Constitution. Appointed Aaron Burr state attorney general in 1789 and helped secure his election to Senate in 1791. His daughter Cornelia Tappen married Edmond Charles Genêt, the former French minister to the U.S., in 1794. Declined to seek reelection in 1795, but ran for governor again in 1800, was elected, and served until 1804. In 1804, he was elected vice-president of the United States under Jefferson, and was reelected under Madison in 1808. He died on April 20, 1812.

TENCH COXE (1755–1824)   Born May 22, 1755, in Philadelphia, son of Mary Francis and William Coxe (merchant). Attended College of Philadelphia (now University of Pennsylvania) and studied law. Entered father's business and in 1776 became a partner in firm of Coxe, Furman & Coxe. Resigned from the Pennsylvania militia in 1776, joined the British Army under Howe, and returned with them to Philadelphia in 1777. After the departure of the British, Coxe was arrested by the patriots, paroled, and joined the patriot cause. He was married twice, first to Catherine McCall of Philadelphia, who died without children, and then to Rebecca, daughter of Charles Coxe of New Jersey, with whom he had children. He was a delegate to the Annapolis Convention in 1786 and to the Continental Congress in 1787 and 1788. Wrote pamphlets in support of the proposed Constitution. Appointed assistant secretary of the treasury in 1789. Appointed commissioner of revenue in 1792 and served until his removal by John Adams in 1797. Became a staunch Republican. Appointed purveyor of public supplies by Jefferson in 1803, and held office until it was abolished in 1812. Remained friends with Jefferson and Madison for the rest of his life. Coxe believed in economic development through manufacturing, tariffs, and the free flow of interstate commerce. He encouraged cotton production and manufacturing, and purchased extensive tracts in western Pennsylvania coal fields. He died in Philadelphia on July 16, 1824.

MICHEL-GUILLAUME-JEAN DE (J. HECTOR ST. JOHN) CRÈVECOEUR (1735–1813)   Born January 31, 1735, near Caen, in Normandy, son of Marie-Anne-Thérèse Blouet and Guillaume Jean de Crèvecoeur. Received some education in England. Immigrated to Canada in 1754, explored the area of the Great Lakes and Ohio River, and served with the French Army under Montcalm in the Seven Years War. Migrated to New York in 1759, and became a British subject in 1765. Married Mehetable Tippet of Yonkers in 1769 and lived on a farm at Pine Hills in Orange County, New York. In 1780 he returned to Europe, staying in Ireland and England before going to France. Essays, *Letters from an American Farmer* (published in England in 1782), extolled the virtues and freedom of rural American life and probed the character of "the American, this new man." Sympathized with the Loyalists during the Revolution, although he corresponded with Washington and knew Franklin and Jefferson (who would attend the marriage of his daughter America-Françes to Louis-Guillaume Otto, comte de Mosloy, in April 1790). Returned to America in 1783 to find his house burned, his wife dead, and his children gone (they were eventually found). Served as French consul for New York, New Jersey, and Connecticut 1783–90. Returned to France for the remainder of his life. Died at Sarcelles on November 12, 1813.

NATHAN DANE (1752–1835)   Born December 29, 1752, in Ipswich, Massachusetts, son of Abigail Burnham and Daniel Dane (farmer). Attended common schools and graduated from Harvard College in 1778. Read law with Judge William Wetmore at Salem and taught school at Beverly, Massachusetts. Married Mrs. Mary Brown in November 1779. Admitted to the bar in 1782. Practiced law in Beverly and was elected to state house of representatives 1782–85. Delegate to the Continental Congress from 1785 to 1788. Helped draft the Northwest Ordinance and prepared the article prohibiting slavery north of the Ohio River. Opposed the Constitution when it was first reported and was unsuccessful candidate for delegate to Massachusetts ratifying convention. By July 1788, when ratification was assured, he supported the Constitution with subsequent amendments, and his letters to Melancton Smith helped secure ratification in New York. In 1790, 1791, and 1794–97, he was elected to the state senate. In 1812, with Joseph Story and Judge William Prescott, revised and published the Massachusetts Colonial and Provincial Laws. Presidential elector for DeWitt Clinton in 1812. Delegate to the Hartford Convention in 1814. Elected delegate to state constitutional convention of 1820, but his deafness prevented his attendance. In 1823, published his *General Abridgment and Digest of American Law, with Occasional Notes and Comments* (8 volumes). Died in Beverly, February 15, 1835.

WILLIAM RICHARDSON DAVIE (1756–1820)   Born at Egremont, Cumberlandshire, England, June 20, 1756, son of Archibald Davie. Taken by his father in 1763 to Waxhaw settlement, South Carolina, and was adopted by his maternal uncle, William Richardson, a Presbyterian clergyman. Attended Queen's Museum College in Charlotte, North Carolina, and entered College of New Jersey (now Princeton), where he graduated in 1776. Began study of law at Salisbury, North Carolina. Served in Revolution under General Allen Jones in Camden region, 1777–78. Helped raise regiment of cavalry and rose to rank of major. Joined Pulaski's division and was wounded in 1779. Began practice of law in 1780 while recovering. Resumed military service in 1780 as colonel under Gates, and was appointed commissary general by Greene. Settled in Halifax, North Carolina, and married Sarah Jones, daughter of his former commander and niece of Willie Jones. Sarah owned a large farm, and eventually the couple had six children. Traveled court circuit and became one of the most important lawyers in the state. Active in North Carolina legislature from 1786 until 1798. Delegate to the Constitutional Convention in Philadelphia in 1787. A staunch Federalist, he was elected a delegate from Halifax to the North Carolina ratifying convention of 1788. Delegate to second ratifying convention in 1789, where he introduced the ratification bill that led to North Carolina's joining the union. He was a leading figure in the establishment of the University of North Carolina in 1789. In 1790, owned 36 slaves. Elected governor of North Carolina in 1798. Denounced the Virginia and Kentucky Resolutions. Appointed brigadier general by President Adams and peace commissioner to France in 1799 with Oliver Ellsworth and William Vans Murray. Ran for U.S. Congress in 1803, but lost to Jeffersonian candidate. Retired to his plantation, Tivoli, on the Catawba River, South Carolina, in 1805. Opposed the War of 1812, and publicly defended New England Federalists. He died at Camden on November 29, 1820.

JOHN DAWSON (1762–1814)   Born in 1762 in Virginia, son of Mary Waugh and Musgrave Dawson (minister at Raleigh parish, Amelia County, and St. Mary's parish, Caroline County, educated at Oxford; two uncles, William and Thomas Dawson, were presidents of the College of William and Mary). Graduated from Harvard College in 1782. Studied law and was admitted to bar. Known as "Beau" Dawson for his dress and manners. Settled in Fredericksburg and represented Spotsylvania County in the Virginia House of Delegates from 1786 to 1789. Delegate to Virginia ratifying convention in 1788, where he opposed ratification. Elected to Virginia state council in 1789. Presidential elector for Washington in 1792. Elected to U.S. House of Representatives in 1797, and reelected eight times through 1814. A Jeffersonian in politics, he opposed the Alien and Sedition Acts. He never married, and owned no slaves. Served as aide to generals Jacob Brown and Andrew Jackson in War of 1812. Died in Washington, D.C., on March 31, 1814.

JOHN DICKINSON (1732–1808)   Born November 8, 1732, on father's estate Crosiadoré near Trappe, Talbot County, Maryland, son of Mary Cadwalader of Philadelphia and Samuel Dickinson of Talbot County, Maryland. Family moved to estate near Dover, Delaware, in 1740. Dickinson studied law in Philadelphia under John Moland in 1750. Went to the Middle Temple in London to continue his studies from 1753 to 1757. Admitted to the bar in Pennsylvania in 1757. Served in the Delaware state assembly 1760–61 and became speaker. Elected from Philadelphia to Pennsylvania State Assembly in 1762 and 1764. Supported the Proprietary party in Pennsylvania and opposed Franklin's Royalist party; feared a royal charter granted by the British ministry would be worse than proprietary control. Defeated for reelection in 1764. Delegate to the Stamp Act Congress in New York in 1765, where he drafted the Declaration of Rights. Took James Wilson as law student in 1766. Wrote and published the influential series *Letters from a Farmer in Pennsylvania*, 1767–68, in support of the colonial cause. Supported Non-Importation Agreements. Elected to Pennsylvania State Assembly in 1770 and served until 1776. In July 1770, he married Mary, daughter of Isaac Norris (wealthy merchant and leader of the Quaker party of Philadelphia). Was chairman of the Philadelphia committee of correspondence in 1774. Member of the First Continental Congress; served only one week in October 1774, during which time he wrote a petition to the king and the address to the people of Canada. Member of Second Continental Congress in 1775. Wrote second petition to the king, still hoping for reconciliation; also wrote a large part of the "Declaration of the Causes of taking up Arms." Voted against separation from Great Britain and did not sign Declaration of Independence. As chairman of committee wrote draft of the Articles of Confederation in June. Joined his militia regiment at Elizabethtown, but resigned when he was not reelected to the next Continental Congress. Resigned from Pennsylvania State Assembly in 1776. Elected to Continental Congress from Delaware in November 1776, but declined to serve. When the British Army advanced on Philadelphia, he left for his estate in Delaware. Took part in battle of Brandywine in September 1777. Elected to Continental Congress from Delaware in 1779 and took his seat but resigned that same year. President of state of Delaware 1782–83. President of the Pennsylvania executive council 1783–85. With Benjamin Rush, in 1783 helped found and endow Dickinson College in Carlisle, Pennsylvania, donating extensive library he had inherited from his father-in-law.

Delegate from Delaware to the Annapolis Convention in 1786 and Constitutional Convention in Philadelphia in 1787. Wrote "Fabius" letters supporting ratification. Presided at the Delaware constitutional convention in 1792. Received LL.D. from the College of New Jersey (now Princeton) in 1796. Wrote further "Fabius" letters in 1797, supporting American alliance with France. Remained friendly to Jefferson. Published *The Political Writings of John Dickinson* in 1801. Died in Wilmington, Delaware, February 14, 1808.

PATRICK DOLLARD (1746–1800) Born in Ireland in 1746. Immigrated to South Carolina in 1770. Kept an inn and helped supply South Carolina militia in the early 1780s. Ultimately owned a plantation. Opposed the Constitution in the South Carolina ratifying convention in 1788. Served in the state assembly 1789–90, and was a justice for the Georgetown District in 1790.

BENJAMIN FRANKLIN (1706–1790) Born January 17, 1706, in Boston, son of Abiah Folger and Josiah Franklin (a candle and soap maker who had emigrated from England in 1683). Attended Boston Grammar School 1714–15 and George Brownell's English school 1715–16. Worked in his father's shop, and was apprenticed to his brother James Franklin's printing business in 1718, where he worked on newspapers *The Boston Gazette* and *New-England Courant*, which published his anonymous "Silence Dogood" letters. In 1723, he ran away to New York, but failed to find work and moved on to Philadelphia. Encouraged by Governor William Keith to open a printing shop, he sailed for London in 1724 to purchase materials. In London, he worked as a typesetter and published *A Dissertation on Liberty and Necessity, Pleasure and Pain* in 1725. Returned to Philadelphia in 1726 and worked as clerk, bookkeeper, and printer. Bought newspaper *The Pennsylvania Gazette* in 1729, which became most widely read paper in colonies. Published *A Modest Enquiry into the Nature and Necessity of a Paper Currency* in 1729. Son William Franklin born out of wedlock to unidentified mother around 1730. Formed common-law union with Deborah Read Rogers, who had been deserted by her husband and with whom he had a son (died 1736) and daughter. Became Freemason, organized Library Company of Philadelphia, published German-language newspaper *Philadelphische Zeitung*, and *Poor Richard's Almanack*. Proposed first fire protection society and system of night watchmen for Philadelphia. Printed George Whitfield's journals and sermons, paper currency of Pennsylvania and New Jersey, and *General Magazine* (first in colonies). Designed Franklin stove in winter of 1740–41. Published *A Proposal for Promoting Useful Knowledge* in 1743, leading to founding of American Philosophical Society. Experimented with electricity beginning in 1745, and proved that lightning was form of electricity in 1750. Elected to Common Council of Philadelphia in 1748, alderman in 1751, and member of Pennsylvania Assembly in 1751. Appointed deputy postmaster general of North America in 1753. Negotiated treaty at Carlisle with Ohio Indians. Drew first known American political cartoon, a snake cut in sections with legend "Join or Die," in 1754. Attended Albany Congress on frontier defense and proposed a plan for colonial union.

Arranged supplies and transport for General Braddock's expedition against Fort Duquesne, drafted militia bill passed by assembly in 1755, and organized frontier defenses. Elected member of Royal Society of London in 1756. Appointed Pennsylvania agent to England in 1757, and sailed to London, where his acquaintances eventually included David Hume, Samuel Johnson, Captain James Cook, Lord Granville, Joseph Priestley, James Boswell, and Adam Smith. Returned to Philadelphia in 1762. Denounced massacre of Christian Indians in Lancaster County by "Paxton Boys," who subsequently marched on Philadelphia, were met by Franklin, and dispersed. Elected speaker of assembly in 1764. Helped organize opposition to Stamp Act. Defeated for reelection to assembly in 1764, and was appointed colonial agent in London. Philadelphia house threatened by mob protesting Stamp Act. Examined by House of Commons regarding colonial resistance in 1766, and his answers helped lead to repeal of Stamp Act. Became colonial agent for Georgia, New Jersey, and Massachusetts. In 1772, he clandestinely acquired letters of Massachusetts governor Thomas Hutchinson and lieutenant governor Peter Oliver recommending repressive measures and relayed them to Thomas Cushing, who laid them before provincial assembly, exacerbating crisis in Boston. Involved in several unsuccessful attempts to reconcile colonies with Britain. Returned to Philadelphia in 1775 and was chosen delegate to Second Continental Congress, where he was active on many committees, including the one that drafted Declaration of Independence. Advocated proportional representation in debates over Articles of Confederation. Named commissioner to France (with Silas Deane and Arthur Lee) and assumed post in December 1776. Negotiated French aid to colonies and treaty of alliance. Became sole minister to France in September 1778. Responding to Vergennes' complaints that John Adams's letters to him were insulting, sent copies of their correspondence to Congress in 1780, contributing to Adams's hostility to Franklin and to France. Appointed (with Jefferson, John Adams, John Jay, and Henry Laurens) to negotiate peace with Great Britain in 1781; treaty was eventually signed September 3, 1783. Negotiated treaties with European powers, including Prussia (signed July 9, 1785). Returned to Philadelphia in September 1785 and was elected president of Pennsylvania Supreme Executive Council. Named president of Pennsylvania Abolition Society in 1787. Served as Pennsylvania delegate to Constitutional Convention in Philadelphia, where he was both an active participant and a conciliating presence. Retired as president of state executive council in 1788, ending public career. Continued efforts for abolition of slavery, including petitions presented to Congress in 1789 and 1790. Died in Philadelphia on April 17, 1790.

WILLIAM GOUDY (c. 1745–1798)   Goudy (also spelled Gowdy) was an early settler of Guilford County, North Carolina. He became justice of the peace, and was elected to five terms in the state house of commons (1780–82, 1787, and 1788) and two terms in the state senate (1786 and 1789). His second wife was Jean Paisley White, and he had at least six children. Delegate from Guilford County to North Carolina ratifying convention of 1788, where he opposed ratification. In 1790, he owned no slaves and 1,220 acres of land. In 1791, he was elected to the council of state, and died in office in 1791.

ALEXANDER HAMILTON (1755–1804)   Born January 11, 1755 (Hamilton later said he was born in 1757), in Nevis, in the West Indies, son of Rachel Fawcett Lavien (daughter of a French Huguenot physician and wife of John Lavien, a German merchant from whom she was divorced in 1758) and James Hamilton (younger son of the Laird of Cambuskeith, The Grange, Ayrshire, Scotland). Moved to St. Croix in 1765; father deserted mother, and she opened small store to support the family (she died in 1769). Hamilton clerked in counting house of Cruger and Beekman, 1766–72, and so impressed his employers and the Reverend Hugh Knox (who published letter by Hamilton about hurricane in 1772) that they sent him to America in October 1772 to obtain an education. Stayed with the William Livingston family while studying at Dr. Barber's preparatory school in Elizabethtown, New Jersey. President Witherspoon of the College of New Jersey (now Princeton) refused his request to take an accelerated course, and he entered King's College (now Columbia) in 1773. Defended Boston Tea Party in speech and in newspaper and became pamphleteer for the patriot cause. Appointed captain of artillery by the provincial congress of New York in March 1776. Campaigned in Long Island, Manhattan, and New Jersey. He quickly won the confidence of Washington and became the general's aide in 1777 with a promotion to lieutenant colonel. Took part in battles at Brandywine, Germantown, and Monmouth. With John Laurens, was witness against General Charles Lee at his court martial. Wintered with army at Valley Forge and Morristown. Acted as interpreter between Washington and French officers. Married Elizabeth, daughter of General Philip Schuyler, in December 1780. Given a command under Lafayette in 1781 and led successful attack on British redoubt at Yorktown. An early advocate of a strong national government, wrote pamphlets and sent letters to the Continental Congress suggesting plans for a national bank and a continental convention to strengthen government. Studied law in Albany under several lawyers, including Robert Troup, who became a lifelong friend, and passed the bar in early summer 1782. Appointed receiver for continental taxes for New York in 1782. Elected to the Continental Congress 1782–83, where he worked closely with Madison and superintendent of finance Robert Morris. Helped start and became a director of the Bank of New York in 1784 (it began operations immediately, but was not chartered until 1792). Elected to the New York Assembly in 1786. Attended Annapolis Convention on interstate commerce, where he drafted the call for a Constitutional Convention to meet in Philadelphia in May 1787. Elected delegate, with John Lansing and Robert Yates (both of whom opposed strong national government), to the Constitutional Convention in Philadelphia in 1787, where he argued for strong national government modeled on the English system, with a president and senate elected for life. Signed Constitution. As "Publius," with James Madison and John Jay, published a series of articles called *The Federalist*, defending the Constitution. Elected to Continental Congress in early 1788, and to the New York ratifying convention in Poughkeepsie, where he continued his advocacy. Appointed secretary of the treasury by Washington in 1789 with support of Madison and Robert Morris. Began vigorous and controversial program for assumption of state debts, creation of national bank, and support for manufactures. Dismayed by Madison's opposition to the assumption bill, finally made a deal with Jefferson and Madison to have the capital located on the Potomac in exchange for their help. Became a major figure in Washington's administration. Awarded honorary degrees from Dartmouth, Harvard, and Columbia, and a new college was named after him. Began bitter rivalry with Thomas Jefferson in cabinet. Accompanied Washington to western Pennsylvania in 1794 and took leading role in suppression of Whiskey Rebellion. Retired as secretary of the treasury in January 1795 for financial reasons. Defended Jay's Treaty with England in 1795, though not happy with all its provisions, and was attacked by hostile crowds. Continued active in politics, advising Washington and helping draft his "Farewell Address." In 1796 tried to influence election to make Thomas Pinckney president rather than John Adams. In autumn 1797, published confession of adulterous affair to establish that he had not indulged in financial wrongdoings while secretary of the treasury. Was consulted on all policies by members of Adams's cabinet, Thomas Pickering, James McHenry, and Oliver Wolcott. When war tensions increased with France, was appointed major general, second in command to Washington, despite Adams's protest. Angry attack, *Letter from Alexander Hamilton concerning the Public Conduct and Character of John Adams, Esq., President of the United States*, published in newspapers in 1800 to Federalists' dismay. Returned to law practice when war threat was over. Son Philip killed in a duel in November 1801 fought with a Jeffersonian lawyer. Used influence to prevent Aaron Burr from becoming governor of New York and was challenged to duel by him. Accepted challenge and was shot by Burr in Weehawken, New Jersey, on July 11, 1804. Died in New York City on July 12, 1804.

THOMAS HARDIMAN (1750–1833)   Hardiman (also spelled Hardeman) was born in Albemarle County, Virginia, on January 8, 1750. Settled in North Carolina west of the Allegheny Mountains before the Revolution. In 1770, he married Mary Perkins (1754–98), with whom he had most or all of his thirteen children. Joined militia company of Captain William Bean and served as a private at the battle of King's Mountain in October 1780. Settled in Davidson County (now Tennessee), and was elected to North Carolina House of Commons in 1788. Delegate to state ratifying convention of 1788, where he opposed ratification. In 1790, he owned nearly 4,000 acres of land. Member of Tennessee state constitutional convention in 1796. Elected to Tennessee General Assembly in 1797, and served until 1799. In 1799, he married the widow Susan Perkins Marr. He died in Davidson County, Tennessee, on June 14, 1833.

PATRICK HENRY (1736–1799)   Born May 29, 1736, in Hanover County, Virginia, son of Sarah Winston and John Henry, from Aberdeen, Scotland (vestryman of the Anglican church, justice of the peace, colonel in the militia, and owner of a plantation). Studied Latin with his father and enjoyed reading Latin classics. Became storekeeper in Hanover County. Married Sarah Shelton in 1754, and the couple worked a 300-acre plantation. When their house and furniture burned, Henry again tried storekeeping unsuccessfully in 1757. He began study of law and was admitted to the bar after little training, in 1760. Continued study on his own and became one of Virginia's foremost lawyers. Became a freeholder in Louisa County, and was elected from that district to the Virginia House of Burgesses in 1765. During Stamp Act crisis, took active role in overcoming objections of representatives from Tidewater region. From 1765 to 1770, continued to gain influence and exercise power in the assembly. Delegate from Virginia to the First Continental Congress in 1774. Helped organize and took part in the Revolutionary conventions in Virginia 1774–76, delivering his famous speech with the words "give me liberty or give me death" to the state convention in March 1775. In April 1775, when he learned that Lord Dunmore, the governor, had seized the ammunition of the colony at Williamsburg, he delayed his attendence at the Second Continental Congress, marched on Williamsburg with militia from Hanover, and returned the munitions to colonial control. In 1776, took part in drafting of new Virginia constitution and passage of resolution authorizing Continental Congress to declare independence. Elected governor of Virginia for three terms 1776–79 and two terms 1784–86. Though they had earlier been friends, Henry turned against Thomas Jefferson after Jefferson's two terms as governor (1779–81). After death of his first wife (in 1775), married Dorothy Dandridge. Following the war, Henry favored forgiving and restoring the Loyalists in Virginia and opposed Madison's effort to separate church and state. Declined appointment to the Constitutional Convention in Philadelphia in 1787. Delegate to Virginia ratifying convention in 1788, where he strongly opposed ratification. His influence in the state legislature gave him control over the election of senators from Virginia in 1788, and he prevented James Madison's election to the Senate and made his election to the House of Representatives difficult. Argued in the courts against payment of British debts. In 1791, the father of many children and grandchildren and not in good health, he retired from politics and law to his new plantation, Red Hill, on the Staunton River. Declined to serve in the U.S. Senate, as Washington's secretary of state, and as chief justice of the Supreme Court. Became increasingly conservative and hostile to Jefferson, Madison, and many of his old supporters. Elected as a Federalist to the Virginia House of Delegates in 1799, but died before serving, on June 6, 1799.

JEREMIAH HILL (1747–1820)   Born April 30, 1747, in Biddeford, district of Maine, son of Sarah Smith and Jeremiah Hill (sawmill owner). Entered Harvard College in 1766; was expelled in 1768 for breaking a tutor's windows. Returned to Biddeford and in 1772 married Mary Emery, with whom he had at least twelve children. In May 1775, he was captain in Colonel Scammon's Maine regiment, and according to tradition he commanded a company at

Bunker Hill. Appointed captain in the 18th Continental Infantry in 1776 and served with it two years, including at the battle of Saratoga. In 1779, he was appointed adjutant general under Solomon Lovell of the expedition of Massachusetts militia against the British outpost at Castine, Maine, on the Penobscot River. After storming outlying British batteries, the expedition was defeated by a British fleet with reinforcements. Remained in the army until the end of 1783 and became a member of the Society of the Cincinnati. Held various town offices in Biddeford and was justice of the peace for York County. Elected representative to the Massachusetts General Court in 1787 and 1788. Hill afterwards became collector of impost and excise for York, collector of the port of Biddeford and Saco, inspector of the port, collector of revenue, and collector of customs. He was also appointed judge of quorum and court of common pleas. Elected representative from Biddeford in the Massachusetts General Court in 1809 and 1812–14. Died at Biddeford on June 11, 1820.

FRANCIS HOPKINSON (1737–1791)   Born October 2, 1737, in Philadelphia, son of English parents Mary Johnson and Thomas Hopkinson (successful lawyer, political and civic leader). First graduate of College of Philadelphia (now University of Pennsylvania) in 1757. Learned to play harpsichord in 1754 and performed in public by 1757. Composed music and wrote poems. Studied law under provincial attorney general Benjamin Chew and was admitted to the bar of the supreme court of Pennsylvania in 1761. Appointed collector of customs at Salem, New Jersey, in 1763. Visited England in 1766 to seek political advancement through influence of friends and relatives, but was unsuccessful. Became friends there with Benjamin Franklin and Benjamin West and returned in 1767. In 1768, married Ann Borden of Bordentown, New Jersey. Opened shop for English imported dry goods, and became collector of customs at New Castle, Delaware. Moved to Bordentown, New Jersey, and resumed successful practice of law. Member of provincial council 1774–76. Delegate from New Jersey to the Continental Congress in 1776. Signed Declaration of Independence. Designed state seal of New Jersey, other seals, and the American flag in 1777. During the Revolution he wrote pamphlets and political satires and served on various war boards. Judge of the admiralty court of Pennsylvania 1779–89. Member of the New Jersey ratifying convention of 1787, where he strongly supported ratification. Organized parade and ratification celebration in Philadelphia on July 4, 1788. Appointed judge of United States District Court for Eastern Pennsylvania in 1789. Died suddenly on May 9, 1791.

DAVID HOWELL (1747–1824)   Born January 1, 1747, in Morristown, New Jersey, son of Sarah and Aaron Howell. Prepared for college with the Reverend Isaac Eaton in Hopewell at first Baptist academy in the colonies, where he met fellow student James Manning. Attended College of New Jersey (now Princeton) and graduated in 1766. Accepted post of tutor at Rhode Island College (now Brown University), recently founded by his friend Manning in Warren, Rhode Island (moved to Providence in 1770). Studied law and was admitted to the bar in 1768. In 1770, married Mary Brown, daughter of Baptist pastor Jeremiah Brown, with whom he had five children. Taught mathematics, natural philosophy, Latin, Greek, and law until 1779, when he resigned because of wartime disruptions. Continued affiliation with college until his death. Elected deputy from Providence to the Rhode Island legislature in 1779. In 1780 and 1781, he was justice of the court of common pleas for Providence County, and in 1781 was appointed to the state superior court. Wrote articles opposing proposed amendment to Articles of Confederation allowing Congress to levy impost. Delegate from Rhode Island to Continental Congress, served from 1782 to 1785. With Jefferson, drafted Northwest Ordinance in 1784 and became a warm admirer of him. Again appointed to the state superior court 1786–87. Not reappointed after disagreement with legislature over constitutionality of paper money act in case of *Trevett* v. *Weeden*. In 1789, was a founder and first president of the Providence Abolition Society. Supported ratification of the Constitution, and was relieved when Rhode Island finally adopted it in 1790. Appointed by Washington to commission on Canadian boundary in 1796. In 1812, Madison appointed him judge of the U.S. District Court for Rhode Island, where he served until his death in Providence on July 29, 1824.

HARRY INNES (1752–1816)   Born January 4, 1752 (old style), in Caroline County, Virginia, son of Catherine Richards and Robert Innes (clergyman who had emigrated from Scotland). Educated at Donald Robertson's school, with his brother James, James Madison, and Edmund Pendleton. Studied law and was admitted to the bar. Moved to Bedford County and established successful law practice. Administered powder mills and lead mines for Virginia committee of safety, 1776–77. Became tax collector in his county, and was so successful that Benjamin Harrison appointed him supervisor of six counties through the end of the war. Married Elizabeth Calloway of Bedford County, who died in 1791. Appointed attorney general for the district of Kentucky in 1784 and moved there in 1785. Supported Patrick Henry's opposition to Constitution. Promoted cotton manufacturing in the district and set up factory in Danville in 1790. Member of Kentucky constitutional convention of 1792, where he supported resolution abolishing slavery that narrowly failed to pass. Appointed judge of U.S. District Court for Kentucky in 1789; served until his death. Married Mrs. Ann Shields, with whom he had a daughter, Maria, who married John J. Crittenden. His friendship with James Wilkinson and Benjamin Sebastian seemed to implicate him in their treasonable negotiations with Spain. He was attacked in the Federalist press and responded with a series of libel actions. Refused to issue warrant for Aaron Burr in 1806. Died in Frankfort, Kentucky, on September 20, 1816.

JAMES IREDELL (1751–1799)   Born October 5, 1751, in Lewes, England, son of Margaret McCulloh and Francis Iredell (Bristol merchant). Iredell went to Edenton, North Carolina, as British comptroller of customs in 1768. Studied law with Samuel Johnston and married Johnston's sister, Hannah, in

July 1773. Admitted to the bar in 1771. Collector of the port of Edenton 1774–76. Wrote articles in support of the American cause, but hoped that differences could be resolved and there would be no need to separate from England. Drafted law establishing state court system in 1776. Appointed judge of superior court in 1777. Elected state attorney general 1779–81. Elected to the council of state in 1787, which appointed him to compile and revise the state's laws, a work he completed in 1791. A fervent Federalist, Iredell wrote "Marcus" letters supporting adoption of the Constitution. Delegate from Edenton to North Carolina ratifying convention of 1788, where he led unsuccessful effort for ratification. In 1790, he owned over 4,500 acres of land and eight slaves. Appointed in 1790 by Washington to the U.S. Supreme Court, with responsibility to ride the southern circuit. Took James Wilson into his home when Wilson was trying to salvage his financial status and was hiding from creditors. Iredell's health was weakened by the strenuous work and hard circuit traveling; he died at his home in Edenton on October 20, 1799.

JOHN JAY (1745–1829)   Born December 12, 1745, in New York City, son of Mary Van Cortlandt of Dutch ancestry and Peter Jay (wealthy merchant of French Huguenot descent). Soon after his birth, the family moved to farm at Rye, Westchester County. Four older brothers and sisters suffered mental or physical problems. Tutored at home and attended New Rochelle grammar school taught by French-speaking pastor of the Huguenot church, Peter Stouppe. Graduated from King's College (now Columbia University) in 1764, and became close friend of classmate Robert R. Livingston. Studied law in offices of Benjamin Kissam and was admitted to the bar in 1768. Entered into partnership with Livingston until 1771. Clerk of boundary commission to settle dispute between New Jersey and New York 1769–70. In April 1774, he married Sarah Van Brugh, daughter of William Livingston, an early supporter of colonial cause. In May 1774, as member of committee to draft response to closing of Boston port, called for meeting of delegates from all colonies to consult on course of action. Elected delegate from New York to First Continental Congress, traveled to Philadelphia in September 1774 with William Livingston, delegate from New Jersey. Signed the Association Agreement on non-importation and wrote *Address to the People of Great Britain*. In New York, he worked on committees to enforce the Association Agreements, organized a convention to elect delegates to the Second Continental Congress when the provincial assembly refused. Elected to both Revolutionary provincial congress and appointed to committee of safety. Attended Second Continental Congress in 1775 still hoping for reconciliation. Took active part in Congress, supporting measures for defense and apprehension of Tories. Served on secret committee of foreign correspondence and discouraged states from sending further petitions to the king. Commissioned colonel of regiment of state militia. Left Continental Congress in late April 1776 to return to New York because of the ill health of his wife and parents. Elected to New York provincial congress and authorized state delegation to sign Declaration of Independence. During British invasion of New York, served with Gilbert Livingston, Robert R. Livingston, and Robert Yates on secret committee to defend Hudson River from British naval incursions. Chairman of secret committee for detecting conspiracies, served with various members, including Melancton Smith. Moved family from Rye to Fishkill, New York, as British and Loyalists approached. Helped draft New York state constitution in 1777. Elected member of state council of safety. Appointed state chief justice in 1777 (resigned in August 1779). Elected president of Continental Congress in December 1778. Appointed by Congress minister plenipotentiary to Spain in September 1779, took his family with him and served from January 1780 to May 1782, though frustrated by lack of progress. Sent in June 1782 to join Franklin in Paris to negotiate terms of peace with England (other American commissioners, John Adams and Henry Laurens, arrived much later; Adams became a strong Jay supporter and helped with final details). The delegation did not follow Congress's orders to negotiate treaty under aegis of France and carried on the negotiations with England alone; resulting treaty was much more favorable than expected, but Robert R. Livingston, secretary of foreign affairs in Congress, was unhappy that France had not been more involved in negotiations, and friendship with him cooled. Visited England before returning home in 1784 to find that Continental Congress had appointed him secretary of foreign affairs, a position he held 1785–89. He reorganized and strengthened the office; he angered southern states when he recommended signing a treaty with Spain that would give up free navigation of the Mississippi for a period of 25 years. In 1785, he was a founder and became first president of the New York Society for Promoting the Manumission of Slaves, with Alexander Hamilton as one of its counselors. Jay had owned slaves, which he purchased and set free after a certain period. Convinced by diplomatic problems under the Confederation that a stronger central government was necessary. Wrote five of the *Federalist* papers. Supported ratification in the New York ratifying convention, and helped win over some Antifederalists by agreeing to write a circular letter to other states in support of a convention to propose amendments. Appointed by Washington as the first Chief Justice of the U.S. Supreme Court in 1789. Continued to act as secretary of foreign affairs in the new government until Jefferson's return from France in 1790. Received honorary LL.D. degree from Harvard College in 1790. Unsuccessful Federalist candidate for governor of New York in 1792, when accusations of fraud were made against Clinton. In April 1794, when war with England seemed likely, he was appointed minister plenipotentiary to England. Returned to United States in 1795 after signing treaty that was strongly attacked by many Americans. Resigned as Chief Justice in June 1795. Elected governor of New York and served two terms 1795–1801. In April 1799, signed bill for emancipation of slaves. Retired to his farm at Bedford, Westchester County, 40 miles from New York City; he was often consulted on matters of policy by many old friends and occasionally took part in meetings with them. He died on May 17, 1829, the last survivor of those who had attended the First Continental Congress.

THOMAS JEFFERSON (1743–1826)   Born April 13, 1743, at Shadwell,
Goochland (now Albemarle) County, Virginia, son of Jane Randolph and
Peter Jefferson (surveyor, landowner, mapmaker, and magistrate). After death
of mother's cousin, William Randolph, his father managed Randolph plantation at Tuckahoe on James River. Attended plantation school at Tuckahoe
and Latin school conducted by the Reverend William Douglas at Shadwell
from 1752 to 1758. After father died in 1757, attended school of the Reverend
James Maury in Fredericksville 1758–60. Attended College of William and
Mary from 1760 to 1762 and studied with mathematics professor William
Small. In 1762, began study of law under George Wythe. Inherited 2,750 acres
from father's estate in 1764. Admitted to Virginia bar in 1767 and began practice of law. In 1769, began building Monticello, country seat near Charlottesville, Virginia. Elected to house of burgesses from Albemarle County in 1769,
and served until its dissolution in 1776. In 1772, he married Martha Wayles
Skelton, with whom he had six children, four of whom died in childhood. In
1773, inherited large tracts of land and large debts from estate of father-in-law,
John Wayles. Active in organizing resistance to British authority and committees of correspondence, and in 1774 published *A Summary View of the Rights
of British America*. In 1775 and 1776, served as Virginia delegate to Continental
Congress in Philadelphia, where he drafted the Declaration of Independence,
adopted July 4, 1776. He also drafted a new state constitution for Virginia,
which was not adopted. Elected to Virginia House of Delegates from Albemarle County in 1776, served until 1779. Elected governor of Virginia in 1779;
reelected in 1780. During Benedict Arnold's invasion of Virginia in 1781, he
organized colonial defenses and narrowly escaped capture by British troops
under General Tarleton (his conduct was later investigated and exonerated by
house of delegates). His wife died in 1782. Appointed by Congress commissioner to negotiate peace with Great Britain in 1782, but because of extreme
cold and ice, was unable to leave Philadelphia to take up post. Served in
Continental Congress 1783–84. Appointed in 1784 to join John Adams and
Benjamin Franklin as minister to negotiate treaties with European powers. In
1785, succeeded Franklin as minister to France (post held until 1789) and published *Notes on the State of Virginia* in Paris. He received a copy of proposed
Constitution in November 1787, and supported its ratification, but urged
Madison and others to add a bill of rights. Published *Observations on the
Whale-Fishery* in 1788. Attended sessions of Estates General at Versailles and
witnessed riots and massacres in Paris July–September 1789. Returned to
America in 1790, and was appointed first secretary of state in Washington's
administration. Opposed formation of national bank as unconstitutional in
1791, but Washington was convinced by secretary of treasury Alexander
Hamilton to sign bill chartering it. In 1792, private note referring to "political
heresies" of Vice-President John Adams was published without authorization
as preface to Thomas Paine's *Rights of Man*. Disputes with Hamilton continued over removal of British troops from western posts, continuation of treaty
obligations with French republic, and retaliation against discriminatory British trade policies. Resigned as secretary of state at the end of 1793 and re-

turned to farming at Monticello. Denounced Jay's Treaty in 1795 and was seen as the leader of opposition to Federalist policies. Elected vice-president of the United States in 1796, finishing second to John Adams in electoral balloting. In 1797, he assumed leadership of Republican party. In 1798, he worked to prevent war with France following revelations of XYZ Affair and drafted Kentucky Resolutions (passed by Kentucky legislature) declaring Alien and Sedition Acts unconstitutional. In 1800, he ran the first national campaign for president between organized political parties and defeated John Adams. When Republican vice-presidential candidate Aaron Burr received the same number of electoral votes as Jefferson, election was thrown into the House of Representatives, which elected Jefferson president on 36th ballot. Published *A Manual of Parliamentary Practice* in 1801. Inaugurated as president in March 1801. Dispatched naval squadron to Mediterranean to protect American vessels against Barbary pirates. Encouraged Republicans to repeal Judiciary Act of 1801, enacted by lame-duck Federalists to expand federal court system. Sent James Monroe as minister plenipotentiary on special mission to join American minister Robert R. Livingston in France to negotiate purchase of New Orleans and free navigation of the Mississippi, resulting in Louisiana Purchase; treaty concluded in 1803. Commissioned Meriwether Lewis and William Clark to explore Louisiana Purchase; their expedition returned in 1806. Reelected president in landslide in 1804. Called for impeachment and removal of Supreme Court Justice Samuel Chase, who was acquitted by Senate in 1805. Concluded peace treaty with Tripoli in 1805 and maintained American neutrality in European war. Succeeded in passage of Non-Importation Act of 1806 to apply commercial pressure on Great Britain. In November 1806, he issued proclamation warning against the Burr conspiracy to separate western territories and attack Mexico. Burr, defended by Edmund Randolph and Luther Martin, was acquitted of charges of treason in 1807 trial, with John Marshall presiding. In 1807, he refused to submit Monroe-Pinckney Treaty with Britain to Senate because of lack of guarantee against impressment and more open trade agreement. After incident in which HMS *Leopard* fired on, disabled, and boarded USS *Chesapeake*, he had the Embargo Act passed in December 1807, suspending all foreign commerce. Declined requests to seek third term as president. Signed Non-Intercourse Act in March 1809, repealing embargo and restoring trade with all nations except England and France. Retired to Monticello in 1809, kept up a large correspondence, and continued his efforts to establish system of general education. In 1811, he published a translation of Destutt de Tracy's *A Commentary and Review of Montesquieu's Spirit of the Laws*. Resumed correspondence with John Adams, leading to a reconciliation in 1812. In 1814, he sold his library to the United States; it became foundation of Library of Congress. In 1817–19, he was instrumental in founding University of Virginia at Charlottesville. In 1820, he denounced the Missouri Compromise, predicting it would exacerbate sectional rivalries. In 1823, he warmly approved the message that outlined the Monroe Doctrine, declaring western hemisphere closed to European expansion. Among his unpublished works were an *Autobiography, The Life and*

Morals of Jesus of Nazareth, and *Anas* (a collection of memoranda from his government service). Died at Monticello, July 4, 1826.

SAMUEL JOHNSTON (1733–1816)   Born December 15, 1733, in Dundee, Scotland, son of Helen Scrymoure and Samuel Johnston. In 1736, the family immigrated to North Carolina, where their kinsman Gabriel Johnston was governor. Attended school in New Haven, Connecticut. Went to Edenton, North Carolina, to study law in 1754 and settled there. Married Frances Cathcart of Edenton. Elected to state assembly in 1759, and served continuously for the next sixteen years. His sister Hannah married James Iredell in 1773. Opposed the Stamp Act and sided with the patriot cause during the Revolution. Moderator of state revolutionary convention in 1775. Helped draft North Carolina constitution in 1776. Elected to state senate in 1779. Delegate from North Carolina to Continental Congress 1780–82, elected its president but declined to serve. Elected governor of North Carolina in 1787 and reelected in 1788 and 1789. Presided at North Carolina ratifying convention in 1788 at Hillsborough, which rejected the Constitution, and at convention in 1789 at Fayetteville, which ratified it. Resigned as governor to become U.S. senator in 1789. Served in Senate until 1793 as a Federalist, but favored Madison's plan for paying off the national debt over Hamilton's. In 1790, he owned over 8,000 acres of land and 96 slaves. Judge of state superior court from 1800 to 1803. Died near Edenton on August 17, 1816.

ZACHARIAH JOHNSTON (1742–1800)   Born in 1742 near Staunton, Virginia, son of William Johnston (an Ulster Scot Presbyterian who had immigrated to Pennsylvania and settled in Virginia). He married Ann Robertson, with whom he had at least eleven children, and became a prosperous farmer before the Revolution. Commissioned captain in the Virginia militia in 1776, was active in defense of the frontier and in the campaign against Cornwallis in 1781. Elected representative from Augusta County to the Virginia House of Delegates in 1778, and reelected annually through 1791. Opposed the issue of paper money and, as chairman of the committee on religion that included James Madison, led successful effort to adopt the Virginia statute on religious freedom in 1786. Delegate to the Virginia ratifying convention of 1788, where he actively supported ratification. Presidential elector in 1789. Declined to run for U.S. Congress. Moved to Rockbridge County in 1792, and elected to house of delegates 1792, 1797, 1798. Spent the last decade of his life promoting plans to connect the rivers of western Virginia with the Potomac. Died in Rockbridge County, Virginia, in January 1800.

WILLIE JONES (1741–1801)   Born in 1741 in Northampton County, North Carolina, son of Sarah Cobb of Virginia and Robin Jones (Lord Granville's agent for his vast properties in North Carolina). Educated in England, studied at Eton, and traveled on the Continent. Returned to North Carolina in the early 1760s and built a large house in the town of Halifax. Became very wealthy planter, businessman, and sportsman. Took part in Alamance campaign against Regulators. In June 1776, he married Mary Montfort. Member of provincial congresses 1774–76, president of state committee of safety in 1776. Member of state constitutional convention in 1776, state house of commons 1776–80, council of state in 1781 and 1787, and state senate in 1782, 1784, and 1788. By early 1780s, he was the state's most powerful political leader. Delegate from North Carolina to Continental Congress 1780–81. Declined to serve as delegate to Constitutional Convention in Philadelphia in 1787. Led opposition in the North Carolina ratifying convention of 1788, and declined election to convention of 1789 that ratified the Constitution. In 1790, he owned nearly 10,000 acres of land and 120 slaves. He was a close friend of Jefferson and became an active Republican. Leading figure in founding of the University of North Carolina. Served on commission to build a state house and lay out the city of Raleigh. Retired from politics to home in Raleigh, where he died June 18, 1801.

HENRY KNOX (1750–1806)   Born July 25, 1750, in Boston, Massachusetts, son of Scots-Irish emigrants from Northern Ireland, Mary Campbell and William Knox (shipmaster). Left school to work in a bookstore in 1762, after his father's death. Opened his own successful shop, The London Bookstore, in 1771. Interested in military affairs, enlisted in a local company and studied strategy. Married Lucy Flucker, daughter of Thomas Flucker, royal secretary of the province, against the families' wishes in June 1774; though they had many children, only three survived him. Enlisted as a volunteer under General Artemas Ward in June 1775, and rose quickly through the ranks to become major general and chief of artillery in the Continental Army. Became close friend of Washington. Organized Society of the Cincinnati. Served as secretary at war under the Articles of Confederation from 1785 until the Constitution took effect. Appointed secretary of war in the Washington administration. Retired to private life at the end of 1794. In 1795, he settled at Montpelier, estate near Thomaston, district of Maine, part of which was inherited by his wife from her grandfather Samuel Waldo and a larger part of which was added by Knox after the Revolution. Engaged in brick, cattle, ship-building, and lumber industries, and speculated heavily in Maine land. Died at Montpelier on October 25, 1806.

MARQUIS DE LAFAYETTE (1757–1834)   Born September 6, 1757, in Chavaniac, Auvergne, France, son of Marie Louise Julie de la Rivière and Gilbert Marquis de Lafayette (colonel in the French grenadiers who died in battle in 1759). Taken to Paris for education in 1768. Mother and grandfather died in 1770, and he inherited a large income and decided to pursue a military career. Arranged marriage to Marie Adrienne Françoise de Noailles took place in April 1774. Learned of American uprising in 1775 and was moved to help their cause. With the German professional soldier John Kalb, he contracted with American agents Silas Deane and Arthur Lee to be received into the Continental Army in 1776. Arrived on the coast of South Carolina in his own ship in June 1777 and proceeded to Philadelphia to meet with the Continental

Congress. At first rebuffed, he offered to serve at his own expense as a volunteer. Appointed major general but not given a command (Kalb was finally
made a brigadier general and died fighting under Gates against Cornwallis in
1780). Appointed to Washington's staff, and they began lifelong friendship. In
his first battle at Brandywine he was slightly wounded in the leg but rejoined
Washington after a month. Appointed to command of division of Virginia
light troops by Congress in December 1777. Fought in various battles and
enjoyed great popularity among the Americans. When the French joined the
war, he helped maintain good relations between the two countries. Returned
to France early in 1779 on leave of absence and was greeted with great ac-
claim. Urged France to send troops and naval forces. Returned to America in
1780 and resumed command of Virginia division. Worked closely with Washington, acted as intermediary between French and American armies, and took
part in the defeat of Cornwallis. Embarked for France in late December 1781.
Received with great enthusiasm and continued to support the American
cause. Prepared to return to America, but when he learned of signing of
preliminary articles of peace, he returned to his home in Auvergne. Named
his son George Washington Lafayette. Made a member of the Society of the
Cincinnati. Became spokesman for republican ideas in France. Revisited
America in 1784 and found a warm welcome wherever he went. In France, he
continued to advocate American causes and worked for the abolition of slavery and the restoration of rights to French Protestants. Often consulted with
Jefferson. Took leading part in early years of the French Revolution. By 1792,
he was forced to flee the country and was captured by the Austrians and
imprisoned at Olmutz, where he remained in prison until 1797. Remained in
exile with his family until 1799, then returned to France and settled at La
Grange, forty miles from Paris. The French Revolution had destroyed his
fortune, but he remained a believer in representative government. Made tri-
umphal tour of America at the invitation of President Monroe in 1824. Took
part in the July 1830 revolution in France. Continued his support of America.
Died May 20, 1834.

CHEVALIER ANNE-CÉSAR DE LA LUZERNE (1741–1791)   Born September, 17, 1741, in Paris, youngest son of César-Antoine de la Luzerne, Comte de
Beuzeville. Educated in military school and appointed Chevalier of the Order
of Malta, which provided an income but bound him to celibacy and military
service. Served in Seven Years War 1756–63, mustered out with rank of colonel in 1775. Began diplomatic career in 1776 as minister plenipotentiary to
Bavaria. In 1779, appointed minister to the United States and sailed with John
and John Quincy Adams to Boston aboard French frigate *Sensible*. Became
ally of George Washington in seeking greater congressional and state support
for Continental Army. Settled in Philadelphia and exerted influence on Continental Congress. Supported ratification of Articles of Confederation, creation of separate department of foreign affairs, and appointment of Robert
R. Livingston as secretary. Influenced selection of Benjamin Lincoln as secretary of war. Claimed to have kept Samuel Cooper, minister of Brattle Street

Church in Boston, and John Sullivan, delegate from New Hampshire, on secret payroll to provide information and influence legislation. Secured appointment of Benjamin Franklin and John Jay as co-commissioners with John Adams to negotiate peace treaty with Great Britain. Elected to American Philosophical Society and American Academy of Arts and Sciences; awarded honorary degrees by Harvard and Dartmouth colleges. Concluded American mission June 21, 1784, and sailed to France, where he secretly married Mademoiselle Angran d'Alleray. Appointed ambassador to Sardinia. Publicly avowed marriage and renounced title of Chevalier in Order of Malta. Made marquis by Louis XVI. Appointed ambassador to England in 1788, and moved to London, where his wife died. In 1790, Washington ordered commemorative medal struck in recognition of services. Died in Southampton, England, September 14, 1791. His body was returned to France for burial but was thrown into the Orne by revolutionaries.

JOHN LAMB (1735–1800)   Born January 1, 1735, in New York City, son of a Dutch mother and Anthony Lamb (transported English convict who became a maker of optical and mathematical instruments). Joined his father in the manufacture of mathematical instruments. Learned Dutch from mother, spoke German and French. Married Catherine Jandine, of Huguenot descent, in November 1755, with whom he had at least three children. Became a prosperous wine merchant, beginning in 1760. After passage of Stamp Act, he became a leader of the Sons of Liberty in New York in 1765 and organized popular resistance that prevented distribution of stamped paper. Member of committee of correspondence and supporter of non-importation agreements. Spoke at meeting to protest assembly's cooperation in provisioning British troops in November 1769. On April 23, 1775, after learning of events at Lexington and Concord, he and Isaac Sears led insurgents who captured New York customs house, prevented ships from leaving the harbor, and seized military stores at Turtle Bay. Commissioned captain of artillery in July 1775, and served under General Robert Montgomery in the invasion of Canada. Wounded and captured at Quebec in December 1775. Paroled in 1776, and officially exchanged in January 1777. Appointed colonel of artillery in Continental Army. Wounded at Campo Hill in April 1777, commanded artillery at West Point 1779–80, and at the siege of Yorktown in 1781. Brevetted brigadier general at end of war. Became a member of the Society of the Cincinnati. Suffered from gout. Elected to New York state legislature. Appointed collector of customs for New York by legislature in 1784. With his son-in-law, Charles Tillinghast, he organized and was president of the Federal Republicans, an Antifederalist association. Corresponded with Patrick Henry, Richard Henry Lee, William Grayson, and others to oppose ratification and subsequently to secure amendments to the Constitution. In 1789, Washington appointed him collector of customs for New York. Resided at 34 Wall Street. Resigned from office in 1797, after discovery of large shortages, probably stolen by a former deputy. Lamb's property was sold to repay the missing funds, and he died in poverty on May 31, 1800.

JOHN LANSING (1754–1829)   Born January 30, 1754, in Albany, son of
Jannetje Waters and Gerrit Jacob Lansing, both of Dutch ancestry. Studied
law with Robert Yates in Albany and James Duane in New York City. Admitted to bar and began practice in Albany in 1775. In 1776–77, was military
secretary to General Philip Schuyler. In April 1781, married Cornelia Ray of
New York City, with whom he had ten children, only five of whom survived
childhood. Prepared law students, including Alexander Hamilton and Aaron
Burr, for admission to bar in 1782. Served in state assembly 1780–86 and 1788.
Delegate from New York to Continental Congress 1784–85. Mayor of Albany
1786–90. Appointed to commissions to settle New York border disputes with
Massachusetts and Vermont. Delegate from New York, with Robert Yates and
Alexander Hamilton, to the Constitutional Convention in Philadelphia in
1787. With Yates, he left the convention on July 10, 1787; the convention, he
said, had exceeded its instructions by proposing a new system of government
rather than amending the Articles of Confederation. Member of the New
York ratifying convention in 1788, where he opposed ratification. Appointed
associate justice of state supreme court in 1790, and chief justice in 1798. Became state chancellor in 1801, and served until he reached the age limit in 1814.
Resumed law practice in Albany. Became regent of the University of the State
of New York in 1817, and took an interest in Columbia College. On December 12, 1829, while in New York City on business for Columbia College, he
left his hotel to mail some letters and disappeared; his body was never found.
Thurlow Weed later claimed to have evidence proving that Lansing was murdered and establishing the motive.

HUGH LEDLIE (c. 1720–1798)   Captain in Connecticut militia 1761–62.
Invested in western lands and was a director of the Company of Military
Adventurers formed in 1763 to solicit land grants. Storekeeper in Windham,
Connecticut. Organizer of Windham Sons of Liberty in opposition to Stamp
Act in 1765, and important member of state committee of correspondence.
Attended state convention at Hartford in 1766. Kept store in Hartford during
the Revolution, and apparently maintained contacts with people he had corresponded with in Sons of Liberty. Attended conventions in Middletown in
1783 and 1784, which protested pensions for Revolutionary War officers, calling the act a congressional encroachment on state authority, and denounced
the Society of the Cincinnati. Apparently kept a lodging-house in Hartford
where various political figures stayed when visiting the area.

HENRY ("LIGHT-HORSE HARRY") LEE (1756–1818)   Born July 29, 1756,
at Leesylvania, near Dumfries, Prince William County, Virginia, son of Lucy
Grymes and Henry Lee. (Was first cousin once removed of Arthur, Francis
Lightfoot, Richard Henry, and William Lee.) Graduated from the College of
New Jersey (now Princeton) in 1773, where he became friends with fellow
student James Madison. Abandoned plans to study law in London at Middle
Temple. Appointed captain in Theodorick Bland's regiment of Virginia cav-
alry in 1776. In 1777, with his company, he joined the Continental Army.

Established lasting friendship with Washington. Promoted to major in January 1778 and commanded force of cavalry and infantry, known as "Lee's Legion." Fought successfully in many engagements, including raid of Paulus Hook, and was promoted to lieutenant colonel in 1780. Joined Greene's command in the South, where he led legion in Pyle's Massacre and the battles of Guilford Courthouse and Eutaw Springs, and the siege of Yorktown, where he witnessed the surrender of Cornwallis on October 19, 1781. Took leave from the army in February 1782. Married second cousin, Matilda Lee, heiress of Stratford, in 1782, with whom he had two children who survived him. Helped found the Society of the Cincinnati in 1783. Elected to Virginia House of Delegates in 1785. Delegate from Virginia to the Continental Congress 1785–89. Member of the Virginia ratifying convention of 1788, where he supported ratification. Elected governor of Virginia in 1791 and served 1792–94. Appointed brigadier general and commander of Virginia troops to suppress the Whiskey Rebellion in western Pennsylvania in 1794. Wife Matilda died in 1790 and he married Anne Hill Carter, daughter of Charles Carter of Shirley, in 1793 (their fifth child was Robert E. Lee). Activated as major general in the United States Army in 1798. Elected as a Federalist to the U.S. House of Representatives for one term 1799–1801. Wrote the resolutions read by Marshall on the death of Washington in 1799, describing him as "first in war, first in peace, and first in the hearts of his countrymen." Retired to Stratford and engaged in land speculations. Imprisoned for debt 1809–10, and wrote *Memoirs of the War in the Southern Department of the United States* (published in 1812). Moved with family to Alexandria in 1810, surviving on wife's trust fund. Seriously injured in Baltimore riot in 1812 while attempting to help friend who published the *Federal Republican*, an anti-administration paper. Went to the West Indies in 1813 to recover failing health. Returned to the United States when he realized he was close to death. Died before reaching home on March 25, 1818, on Cumberland Island, Georgia.

RICHARD HENRY LEE (1732–1794)   Born January 20, 1732, at Machodoc in Westmoreland County, Virginia, son of Hannah Ludwell and Thomas Lee. (Was brother of Francis Lightfoot, William, and Arthur Lee, and first cousin once removed to Henry Lee.) Family moved to new home of Stratford around 1740. Tutored at home. Sent to England for education in 1744 and completed course at academy at Wakefield. Returned to Virginia in 1753. Became justice of the peace in Westmoreland County and member of the Virginia House of Burgesses in 1758. Married Anne Aylett of Westmoreland County in December 1757. Established residence at Chantilly, neighboring estate to Stratford. Took active role in colonial affairs and made strong antislavery speech in 1759 (later he was briefly involved in slave trade). Initially sought position of tax collector, but subsequently led protests against the Stamp Act in 1765 and corresponded with John Lamb, Samuel Adams, and others. Continued in the forefront of protests against taxation by Parliament. He was strong in appearance, but suffered from epilepsy and a left hand maimed in a hunting accident. Wife Ann died in 1768 and in 1769 he married

Anne Gaskins Pinckard, widow of Thomas Pinckard (he had nine children with his two wives). Worked closely with Patrick Henry and Thomas Jefferson in the house of burgesses. Organized committees of correspondence in 1773. Delegate from Virginia to First and Second Continental Congresses in 1774 and 1775. Became lifelong friend of Samuel and John Adams. Delegate to Continental Congress in 1776, where he made the motion for independence from England (seconded by John Adams). Signed the Declaration of Independence. Signed the Articles of Confederation and convinced Virginia to surrender its claims on western lands, which made possible their ratification by all 13 states. Resigned from Continental Congress in failing health in 1779. Elected to the Virginia House of Delegates in 1780. Delegate from Virginia to Continental Congress in 1784–87; elected president of Congress in 1784. Took the lead in passage of the Northwest Ordinance, establishing basis on which new states were to be admitted and prohibiting slavery north of the Ohio River. Declined to be a delegate to the Constitutional Convention in Philadelphia in 1787. Member of Virginia ratifying convention of 1788, where he took leading role in opposing ratification. Elected to U.S. Senate in 1789, where he actively supported adoption of the Bill of Rights. Resigned from Senate in October 1792 in poor health. Died at Chantilly on June 19, 1794.

JOHN LELAND (1754–1841)   Born May 14, 1754, in Grafton, Massachusetts, son of Lucy Warren and James Leland. Attended common schools and in 1772 felt called to preach. Baptized by Noah Alden; received Baptist preacher's license in 1774. In September 1776, married Sarah Divine, with whom he had nine children. Moved to Orange, Virginia, and became pastor of two churches in Orange and Culpepper counties. Leader in struggle to disestablish the Episcopal church in Virginia. Became popular preacher during revival of 1787. Nominated to oppose James Madison for seat in Virginia ratifying convention in 1788, but withdrew after he was convinced by Madison that the Constitution did not threaten religious liberty (Leland later supported Madison in election for U.S. Congress). At meeting of Baptist General Committee in Richmond in 1789, proposed resolution calling for abolition of slavery. Moved to Cheshire, Massachusetts, in 1791. Led fight to disestablish Congregational church and worked to amend constitutions of Connecticut and Massachusetts to ensure religious freedom and separation of church and state. In 1792, became co-pastor of the Third Baptist Church in Cheshire. Refused to administer Lord's Supper starting in 1798. Supported Jefferson for president in 1800 and 1804. Elected as Republican to the Massachusetts legislature in 1811. Continued service as preacher, defended Christian revelation against Deism, and composed popular hymns. Died in Cheshire on January 14, 1841.

WILLIAM LENOIR (1751–1839)   Born May 8, 1751, in Brunswick County, Virginia, son of Mourning Crawley and Thomas Lenoir. Father sold Virginia plantation and resettled on farm in Edgecombe County, North Carolina, in 1759. After father's death in 1765, Lenoir, though deprived of formal education, taught himself mathematics and opened elementary school in Brunswick County, Virginia, in 1769. Opened another school in Halifax County, North Carolina, in 1770. In 1771, married Ann Ballard of Halifax County, with whom he had nine children. Unable to support family by teaching school, taught himself surveying. In 1775, moved family to Surry County (district incorporated as Wilkes County in 1778) in western North Carolina, where he established new farm. Appointed to county committee of safety. Enlisted in militia, appointed lieutenant, and commanded ranger company that patrolled Blue Ridge Mountains and defended settlements against Indians. Participated in General Griffith Rutherford's campaign against the Cherokee towns in September 1776. Actively engaged in capture and suppression of Tories, and displayed talent for mustering troops and assembling supplies and arms. Appointed justice of the peace in 1776 (a position he held until his death) and county clerk of court in 1778. Fought in the battle of King's Mountain in October 1780, where he was wounded. Took part in Pyle's Massacre (American victory over Loyalists) in February 1781. Elected to North Carolina House of Commons 1781–84. Elected to state senate 1784–85 and 1787–95, serving as speaker the last five years. Continued in the militia after the Revolution, and in 1795 was commissioned major general of Fifth Division. Delegate from Wilkes County to North Carolina ratifying conventions of 1788 and 1789, where he opposed ratification because of the lack of a bill of rights. Lenoir was an original trustee of the University of North Carolina in 1789 and first president of its board of trustees. In 1790, he owned twelve slaves and 4,439 acres of land. Supplemented income from his farm, Fort Defiance, by operating blacksmith shop, breeding horses, lending money, and land speculation. He died at home in Fort Defiance on May 6, 1839.

BENJAMIN LINCOLN (1733–1810)   Born January 24, 1733, in Hingham, Massachusetts, son of Elizabeth Thaxter (widow of John Norton) and Benjamin Lincoln (maltster and farmer and a member of the General Court). Attended common schools. In January 1756, married Mary Cushing of Pembroke, Massachusetts, with whom he had six sons and five daughters. Became a moderately prosperous farmer. Joined militia in 1755. Elected town clerk in 1757. Became justice of the peace in 1762. Commissioned major in militia in 1763 and lieutenant colonel in 1772. Elected to state legislature in 1772 and 1773 and to provincial congress in 1774 and 1775. Commissioned brigadier general of militia in February 1776. Appointed major general and given command of Massachusetts troops near Boston in August 1776. Assigned to New York, where he won Washington's approval. Appointed major general in the Continental Army in February 1777. In October 1777, played significant role in victory over Burgoyne at Saratoga, where he was wounded in the leg. Forced to remain inactive in Hingham for ten months until he recovered. Appointed by Congress in September 1778 to command of Southern Department. Cooperated with French Army in unsuccessful siege of Savannah, Georgia, in September 1779. Retreated with army to Charleston, South Carolina, where he was trapped by British expedition under Clinton and forced to surrender on

May 12, 1780. Exchanged in time to join Washington's march from New York to Yorktown in September 1781. Commanded division in siege of Yorktown, and stepped forward to accept British surrender (offered by Cornwallis's subordinate) on October 19, 1781. Served as secretary at war under Continental Congress from 1781 to the peace in 1783. Returned to his farm in Hingham, speculated in Maine lands, and was appointed to Massachusetts commission to treat with Penobscot Indians for land purchases in 1784 and 1786. Became president of the Society of the Cincinnati in Massachusetts. Appointed in 1787 to command militia in suppression of Shays' Rebellion in western Massachusetts. Raised money for the campaign through loans from Boston citizens. Delegate from Hingham to Massachusetts ratifying convention in 1788, where he supported ratification. Chosen lieutenant governor by the legislature in 1788, but lost popular election for same post to Samuel Adams in 1789. Appointed collector of the port of Boston by Washington in 1789, served until he resigned in protest over Force Act in 1809. Appointed federal commissioner to treat with Creek Indians regarding borders of the southern states in 1789 and to treat with Indians north of the Ohio River in 1793. John Adams considered Lincoln one of his closest friends. Died at Hingham on May 9, 1810.

GILBERT LIVINGSTON (1742–1806)   Born in 1742 near Poughkeepsie, Dutchess County, New York, son of Susanna Conklin and Henry Livingston (grandson of the first Robert Livingston, Dutchess County clerk and agent for its largest landowner, Henry Beekman, Jr., and through his influence, a member of the provincial assembly 1761–68). Brother of John Henry Livingston, Dutch Reformed minister and first president of Queen's College (now Rutgers University). Studied law and was admitted to the bar. Elected Poughkeepsie supervisor in 1769 and again in 1784. Acted as land agent for his uncle, Robert Gilbert Livingston, a Tory and heir to one-third of the large Beekman estate. Married Catharine, daughter of lawyer Bartholomew Crannell. Member of provincial congress 1775–77, elected by the widest suffrage to date. Elected to state assembly 1777–78 and 1788–89. Served on secret committee to defend the Hudson River from British naval incursions with his second cousin Robert R. Livingston, John Jay, and Robert Yates in 1776. Appointed county surrogate 1778–85 and 1787–1804. Served as chairman of price-fixing committee to counter wartime inflation in 1779–80. Engaged with Peter Tappen in building boats for the army in 1780. After the Revolution, owned a mercantile establishment in partnership with Israel Smith, brother of Melancton, and Peter Tappen. Formed law partnership with Federalist James Kent 1785–93. Member of New York ratifying convention in 1788, where he opposed the Constitution, though he finally supported its ratification with subsequent amendments. He was a presidential elector as a Jeffersonian Republican in 1800. Became Dutchess County Clerk in 1804 and held office until his death in 1806.

ROBERT R. LIVINGSTON (1746–1813)   Born November 27, 1746, in New York City, oldest son of Margaret Beekman and Robert R. Livingston (owner of Clermont estate, judge, and one of the largest landholders in New York). Graduated from King's College (now Columbia University) in 1765 and studied law with cousin William Livingston and William Smith, Jr. Admitted to the bar in 1768. Opened law practice with friend and college classmate John Jay; partnership continued until 1771. In September 1770, married Mary Stevens, daughter of John Stevens of New York (owner of large tracts of land in New Jersey), with whom he had two daughters. Lived in New York City and at Clermont. Appointed recorder of the City of New York in 1773. Took active part in the New York provincial congress 1775–76 and in legislature 1779–80 and 1784–85. Helped draft the New York constitution at the convention in 1777. Elected chancellor of New York (a position he kept until 1801) and member of the council of safety. Served on secret committee to defend the Hudson River from British naval incursions with his second cousin Gilbert Livingston, John Jay, and Robert Yates in 1776. House at Clermont on the Hudson was burned by the British in October 1777. Delegate from New York to the Continental Congress 1775–76. Served on the committee of five (with Jefferson, Adams, Franklin, and Roger Sherman) that drafted the Declaration of Independence, but was absent during its signing. Believed that independence was inevitable, but would have preferred its delay. Served again in Continental Congress 1779–81 and 1784–85, and was active on many committees. Became secretary for foreign affairs 1781–83. Disapproved of the American peace commission (Franklin, John Jay, John Adams, and Henry Laurens) negotiating directly with Britain in disobedience of congressional instructions to work with the advice and approval of France, and his relations with Jay cooled. Delegate from the city and county of New York to the New York ratifying convention in Poughkeepsie in 1788, where he strongly supported ratification. Administered presidential oath to George Washington in 1789. Disappointed with Washington administration's failure to offer him a position and opposed to some of Hamilton's policies, he began moving closer to the Antifederalists in New York. Turned down Washington's offer to appoint him minister to France and opposed Jay's Treaty with Britain. Supported Jefferson for president in 1800, and accepted appointment as minister to France in 1801. Had advanced negotiations for purchase of Louisiana before being joined by special emissary James Monroe to complete the final agreement; returned to America in 1804. With his wife's brother, John Stevens, Jr., engaged in development of the steamboat. Entered into partnership with Robert Fulton and Nicholas J. Roosevelt, and was granted a monopoly for steamboats in New York and on the Mississippi River. Spent remaining years experimenting with agricultural improvements and protecting his steamboat interests. Died at Clermont on February 25, 1813.

RAWLINS LOWNDES (1721–1800)   Born January 1721 in St. Kitts, British West Indies, son of Ruth Rawlins and Charles Lowndes. Family moved to Charleston, South Carolina, because of financial difficulty in 1730. Father died a few years later, and his mother returned to the West Indies, leaving Lowndes in the care of the colony's provost marshal, Robert Hall, with whom he studied law. After Hall's death in 1740, was appointed temporary provost marshal and retained position until 1754. Married Amarinthia Elliott of Rantoules, Stone River, on August 15, 1748. She died in January 1750, and in December 1751 he married Mary Cartwright of Charleston, with whom he had seven children. Elected to South Carolina assembly in 1749, and served almost continuously until the Revolution, including terms as speaker 1763–65 and 1772–75. Resigned as provost marshal in 1754 to begin his own law practice. Appointed associate judge of the court of common pleas in 1766. Wife Mary died in 1770, and in 1773 he married Sarah Jones of Georgia, with whom he had one son. Refused to enforce the use of stamped paper and denied the right of royal council to act as an upper house of the assembly in 1773; was removed from the bench soon after. Opposed independence from Britain and confiscation of Loyalist property. Opposed the drafting of a state constitution, but served on eleven-man committee that wrote the South Carolina constitution of 1776. Opposed changes made by new state constitution in 1778, but served as state president under it when John Rutledge resigned after unsuccessfully vetoing it. Declined to seek reelection in 1779. Opposed the federal Constitution in the state assembly, and declined to serve when elected to the South Carolina ratifying convention. He died August 24, 1800.

JOSEPH McDOWELL (1756–1801)   Born February 15, 1756, in Winchester, Virginia, son of Margaret O'Neal and Joseph McDowell, Scots-Irish immigrants. Moved with his parents in 1758 to Quaker Meadows (near Morganton), Burke County, North Carolina. Educated in common schools and at Augusta Academy (later Washington College, now Washington and Lee University) in Virginia. Like his brothers, became a farmer, trader, and political leader. In 1776, joined older brother Charles McDowell's regiment of militia and participated in campaign against Cherokees under General Griffith Rutherford. Took part in numerous battles against Loyalists and commanded the McDowell regiment in the battle of King's Mountain in October 1780. Continued to fight until 1782, earning the rank of colonel. Elected from Burke County to the North Carolina House of Commons 1785–88. Delegate from Burke County to North Carolina ratifying conventions of 1788 and 1789, where he opposed ratification. In 1790, he owned ten slaves and 2,918 acres of land. Elected to state senate 1791–95. Became a leader of the Republicans in North Carolina. Elected to U.S. House of Representatives 1797–99; opposed the Alien and Sedition Acts. Declined to seek reelection. He was one of the first trustees of the University of North Carolina. Moved to Kentucky in 1800, but returned in 1801 to North Carolina, where he died at Quaker Meadows on February 5, 1801.

ARCHIBALD MACLAINE (1728–1791)   Born December 9, 1728, in Banbridge, Ireland, son of the Reverend Archibald Maclaine (a Presbyterian minister who had emigrated from Lochbuie, Scotland). Served mercantile apprenticeship, and left Ireland for America, arriving in Philadelphia in June 1750. In 1752, he left Philadelphia and settled in Wilmington, North Carolina, where he married Elizabeth Rowan, stepdaughter of Matthew Rowan, president of the council and acting governor, with whom he had six children, two of whom survived childhood. Maclaine attempted to become a merchant, but his business failed and he took up the practice of law, which proved more profitable. In 1759, he was appointed clerk of the supreme court, and he served as town commissioner from 1772 to 1778. An early supporter of the patriot cause, served on the committee of safety for Wilmington from 1774 to 1776, on the committee that called for a provincial congress in 1774, in the provincial congress in 1775 and 1776, and as senator from Brunswick County in 1777 and 1780. He was a member of the committee that drafted the new North Carolina constitution and declaration of rights, and in 1777 drafted the law for establishing the state court system. He declined an appointment as judge of the superior court in 1779, and twice declined nomination for election to the Continental Congress. Maclaine's son-in-law, George Hooper, was a Tory, and Maclaine, who advocated mild measures against Loyalists, was sometimes attacked for his suspected Tory sympathies; in a riot in 1782 in the Bladen County Court, Captain Robert Raiford of the Continental Army assaulted Maclaine with a sword. Maclaine returned to the state legislature from 1783 to 1787, and took part in the attempt to remove state judges from the bench in 1787. He was a delegate from Wilmington to the North Carolina ratifying convention in Hillsborough in 1788, where he spoke and voted in favor of ratification, and wrote articles as "Publicola" in support of the Constitution. He was a member of the Episcopal church, possessed a large library, and was one of the original trustees of the University of North Carolina. He died December 20, 1790, at his home in Wilmington.

JAMES MADISON (1751–1836) Born March 16, 1751, across the Rappahannock River from Port Royal, oldest son of Nelly Conway and James Madison. Family moved when he was an infant to the site of Montpelier in Orange County, Virginia. After education at home, attended boarding school of Donald Robertson (Scots graduate of Aberdeen and Edinburgh universities) 1762–67. Continued study at home with Thomas Martin (a minister boarding at his house) in 1768 before entering the College of New Jersey (now Princeton) in 1769. Studied under college president John Witherspoon and graduated in 1771. Fellow students included Philip Freneau and Hugh Henry Brackenridge. Continued at college another year before returning to Virginia in 1773. In late 1774 became a member of committee of safety for Orange County, chaired by his father and including neighbors Lawrence Taliaferro and Joseph Spencer. Active in raising men and materials to defend against British invasion. Appointed colonel of militia of Orange County under command of father, but never took part in fighting. Member of Virginia convention of 1776 that framed new state government and instructed delegates to the Continental Congress to vote for independence. Strengthened George Mason's wording of freedom of religion clause in state declaration of rights. Elected to Virginia House of Delegates in October 1776 and met Jefferson for the first time. Worked with Jefferson to disestablish church in Virginia. Lost election to legislature in 1777 when he refused to supply the traditional barrel of liquor for voters. Appointed to council of state and held that position January 1778–80. Lived with cousin, the Reverend James Madison. Elected delegate from Virginia to Continental Congress in December 1779 and began attendence in Philadelphia in March 1780. Took active part in questions of cession of western lands. Served on many foreign committees and supported Robert R. Livingston over Arthur Lee for foreign secretary in 1781. Supported Robert Morris's efforts to stabilize Continental finances. With James Wilson, attempted to establish a Library of Congress and drafted list of books needed. Met Hamilton in Congress and worked closely with him to strengthen central government. Wrote address to the states on means of ridding country of debt (published as pamphlet). Left Congress in October 1783, discouraged by its inability to achieve national power: one state was able to block any important national measure, and there seemed no way to finance the repayment of internal and external debts. Elected from Orange County to state house of delegates 1784–87. Traveled with Lafayette to Fort Stanwix to witness Indian treaty in summer of 1784. Elected member of the American Philosophical Society in January 1785. Wrote "Memorial and Remonstrance," petition used to defeat Patrick Henry's tax assessment bill for state support of Christian churches. Secured passage of Jefferson's bill for religious liberty. Attended Annapolis Convention in 1786 and, with Hamilton and others, issued call for a convention of states to be held in Philadelphia in May 1787 to form a new plan of government for the United States. Elected delegate to Continental Congress, where he upheld right of free navigation on the Mississippi River, which was threatened by Jay's negotiations with the Spanish envoy Gardoqui. Delegate to the Constitutional Convention in Philadelphia in 1787, where he drafted the Virginia plan presented to the convention by Randolph. Played major role in guiding the work of the convention and returned to the Continental Congress in New York to aid transmittal of Constitution to the states. Wrote *Federalist* papers (with Hamilton and Jay) to assist the ratification struggle in New York. Awarded LL.D. degree from College of New Jersey (now Princeton). Returned to Orange County and won election to the Virginia ratifying convention of June 1788, where he led the fight for ratification against opposition led by Patrick Henry. Influence of Henry prevented his election to U.S. Senate. Elected to U.S. House of Representatives in 1789, defeating James Monroe. Advised Washington and wrote his inaugural address, then drafted the response from Congress and Washington's reply to it. Played important role in establishing the new government, including defining the duties and title of the president and the creation of departments of foreign affairs, treasury, and war. Introduced Bill of Rights amendments in June 1789 and guided their passage through Congress. In 1790, with Jefferson, made agreement with Hamilton to locate permanent capital on the Potomac River and to credit Virginia for payments on the general war debt. In return, he arranged support in Congress for Hamilton's assumption bill, which he thought unfair to Virginia. Fought unsuccessfully against creation of national bank, which he regarded as unconstitutional.

When the federal government moved to Philadelphia, helped Jefferson convince Freneau to start the *National Gazette* there to counter Hamilton's journal. Wrote articles using term "Republican Party" to describe his and Jefferson's supporters (Hamiltonians were using the term "Federalists"). In 1793, learned that he had been made a "Citizen of France" (with Hamilton and Washington) by the National Assembly. Entered pamphlet war against Hamilton over president's right to declare neutrality and other issues. Married widow Dolley Payne Todd, of Quaker descent (she had one son by previous marriage), in September 1794. Attacked Jay's Treaty in 1795. Submitted Jefferson's name for election as president in 1796 to Republican caucus in Congress. Retired from Congress in 1797 and declined to seek Virginia governorship. Returned to Montpelier to farm and experiment with scientific agriculture. Drafted the Virginia Resolutions opposing the Alien and Sedition Acts in 1798. Appointed secretary of state by Jefferson in 1801 and served until 1809. Issued instructions to Robert R. Livingston for negotiations with France concerning cession of New Orleans and navigation rights on Mississippi River. Wrote the instructions to Monroe, who was sent as minister plenipotentiary to join Livingston's negotiations and sign treaty. Elected first president of the American Board of Agriculture in 1803. In 1806, wrote pamphlet *An Examination of the British Doctrine, which subjects to capture a Neutral Trade Not Open in Time of Peace*, protesting interference with American shipping. Supported Non-Importation Act to apply commercial pressure against Great Britain. With Jefferson, disapproved of treaty with England negotiated by Monroe and William Pinkney and decided not to submit it to the Senate in 1807. Elected president in 1808, defeating George Clinton, Charles Cotesworth Pinckney, and James Monroe. Efforts to raise money for defense were defeated in Congress in 1810. Annexed part of West Florida to the United States. Attempted to negotiate peaceful resolutions to attacks on American shipping by both England and France during Napoleonic Wars. When French appeared to concede some shipping rights, he appointed Joel Barlow minister to France in 1811. Continued efforts to avert crisis with England. Reinstated non-intercourse when England refused to rescind the Orders of Council aimed at American shipping. Dismissed Robert Smith as secretary of state when he learned Smith was conspiring against the administration (Madison had written all diplomatic correspondence himself because of Smith's incompetence). Appointed James Monroe secretary of state. Continued efforts to get Congress to strengthen national defenses. British repeal of Orders in Council arrived too late to prevent Congress from declaring war on England in June 1812. Viciously attacked by Federalist newspapers, but maintained freedom of press and speech throughout the war. Reelected president in 1812 despite setbacks in war. Reluctantly appointed John Armstrong secretary of war on advice of secretary of treasury Albert Gallatin. Appointed William Jones secretary of the navy. Throughout the war, naval victories cheered national prospects. Appointed new generals and reorganized army. Dismayed by disaffection of New England. Appointed John Quincy Adams, Albert Gallatin, and James

A. Bayard as peace commissioners when Russia offered to mediate a settlement with England; this mediation was superseded by direct negotiation, and Madison added Henry Clay and Jonathan Russell to the commission. Became dissatisfied with Armstrong after examining his correspondence and ensured promotion of Andrew Jackson and Jacob Brown to higher ranks than Armstrong had recommended. Washington, D.C., captured and burned by British on August 24, 1814, despite Madison's previous warnings. Dismissed Armstrong as secretary of war and replaced him with Monroe (who continued as acting secretary of state as well). News of peace treaty and Andrew Jackson's victory at New Orleans was received in February 1815. Delivered message to Congress asking for adequate regular army and gradual build-up of navy. Sought and received declaration of war against the Dey of Algiers on February 25, 1815. Appointed Alexander J. Dallas secretary of the treasury and was pleased with his service. Suggested amendment to the Constitution to allow the building of roads and canals. Signed bill creating the second Bank of the United States in April 1816. Refused to run for third term as president in 1816. Left Washington for the last time in April 1817 and traveled part of the way home by steamboat. Tended his farm and was appointed to the board of visitors of Jefferson's Central College (University of Virginia), where he helped choose professors. Worked on codification of English common law into statutes for the American states at request of Jeremy Bentham. Became active member of the American Colonization Society, organized in 1816. Continued active interest in political affairs, carried on large correspondence, responded to frequent requests for advice, and entertained many visitors. Prepared his notes on the debates in the Philadelphia convention of 1787 for publication after his death. After Jefferson's death, became rector of the college. Attended Virginia constitutional convention in Richmond 1829–30. During debates over nullification and state rights that began in 1830, wrote numerous letters and articles supporting union and clarifying intent of Constitution and his own work. Became last survivor of the Philadelphia convention in 1833. Died at Montpelier on June 27, 1836.

JOHN MARSHALL (1755–1835)   Born September 24, 1755, in a log cabin near Germantown in western Prince William County (Fauquier County after 1759) in the Virginia backcountry, son of Mary Randolph Keith and Thomas Marshall (land surveyor, employee and friend of George Washington, member of the house of burgesses in 1759, and sheriff of Fauquier County in 1765). Family moved before Marshall was ten years old to a frame house 30 miles west in a valley of the Blue Ridge Mountains, and they moved again to a larger house in 1773. Educated by his parents, by James Thompson, a Scots deacon, and by Archibald Campbell (who also taught James Monroe). In May 1775, Marshall was appointed lieutenant of the Culpeper Minute Men and fought the Loyalists at Great Bridge. In 1776, he enlisted in the Continental Army and served as a lieutenant in the Third Virginia Regiment under his father, its major. In late 1776, he was promoted and transferred to the Fifteenth Virginia Line. Took part in the battle of Brandy-wine, September 11, 1777, and spent the winter of 1777–78 at Valley Forge. Fought in battle of Monmouth under General Charles Lee, June 28, 1778, and was part of Henry Lee's light infantry that raided Paulus Hook, August 19, 1779. Appointed deputy judge advocate and captain. In 1780, while still in the army, he attended George Wythe's lectures on law at William and Mary College for six weeks (his only formal legal training), received his license to practice (signed by Governor Jefferson), and was admitted to the bar in Fauquier County in August 1780. Awaited orders to return to active duty, but none came and he resigned his commission in 1781. Elected to the state assembly from Fauquier County, where he had established his law practice, and served in 1782 and 1784–85. Served as member of the council of state, but retired from that position when he realized it hurt his law practice. In January 1783, he married Mary Willis Ambler of Yorktown, daughter of Rebecca Burwell and state treasurer Jacquelin Ambler, with whom he had six children who reached maturity. Became a member of the Society of the Cincinnati. One of his close friends was assemblyman James Monroe, who had shared many of his war experiences. Did not seek election to the assembly 1785, but returned as a delegate from Henrico County 1787–88. Led the successful effort in 1787 to send the Constitution to a state convention without binding instructions. Delegate to the Virginia ratifying convention in 1788, where he strongly advocated ratification and made a speech defending federal judicial power. Reelected to house of delegates 1789–90, but did not run again until 1795. Maintained close friendship with George Mason and other Antifederalists despite political disagreements. Supported the Jay Treaty and the policies of Hamilton and Washington, but declined appointment as attorney general in 1795. Accepted John Adams's appointment as minister plenipotentiary (with Charles Cotesworth Pinckney and Elbridge Gerry) on the ill-fated XYZ peace mission to France 1797–98. Though the mission was not successful, it brought him national recognition when the ministers' dispatches were published. Elected to U.S. House of Representatives 1799–1800, where he acted as a moderate Federalist, voting in support of John Adams to send the second peace mission to France and for partial repeal of the Sedition Act. John Adams appointed him to replace the dismissed Thomas Pickering as secretary of state in 1800, and appointed him Chief Justice of the U.S. Supreme Court early in 1801 (he continued to act as secretary of state until Adams's term was over). He served as Chief Justice until 1835 and spoke for the court in cases such as *Marbury* v. *Madison*, *McCulloch* v. *Maryland*, *Cohens* v. *Virginia*, and *Gibbons* v. *Ogden*. Marshall repeatedly affirmed the supremecy of the Constitution over states, broadly interpreted its contract, commerce, and "necessary and proper" clauses, and established the power of the supreme court to judge the constitutionality of state laws and state court decisions. Wrote *The Life of George Washington* (5 volumes, 1804–07). Presided at trial of Aaron Burr (defended by Edmund Randolph and Luther Martin) for treason in circuit court in Richmond in 1807. He opposed the War of 1812. Died in Philadelphia on July 6, 1835.

GEORGE MASON (1725–1792)   Born in 1725 in the Northern Neck of Virginia, son of Ann Thomson and George Mason. Father died when Mason was ten years old, and he was brought up under the guardianship of John Mercer of Marlborough, Stafford County (lawyer and the owner of a large library). Educated by private tutors and by his own reading. In April 1750, married Anne Eilbeck of Mattawoman, Charles County, Maryland, with whom he had nine children. They moved to new home, Gunston Hall, at Dogue's Neck on the Potomac River below Alexandria near Washington's home at Mount Vernon. Mason acted as his own steward and attended the needs of his plantation. He was active in Fairfax County politics, served as trustee of the new town of Alexandria from 1754 until its incorporation in 1779 and as justice on the county court 1747–89. Took part in Truro Parish church activities 1748–85. Though he never became a professional lawyer, he was often asked for advice on public law. From 1752 to 1773, he was a member and treasurer of the Ohio Company for promoting western settlement. Elected to Virginia House of Burgesses in 1758, served until 1761. In 1766, he wrote an open letter to London merchants seeking repeal of the Stamp Act. Wife Anne died in 1773. Washington, also a member of the house of burgesses, would often consult with Mason before going to Williamsburg and ask him to write opinions on various issues. In 1774, Mason drafted the Fairfax Resolves that were eventually adopted by the Continental Congress. Member of the state Revolutionary conventions of 1775 and 1776 and a member of the state committee of safety in 1775. In 1776, he drafted much of the new Virginia state constitution, including its Declaration of Rights. Served in Virginia House of Delegates 1776–81, 1786–87 (absent), and 1787–88. Elected delegate from Virginia to the Continental Congress in 1777, but did not attend. Helped arrange the cession of the Northwest Territory by Virginia to the Confederation and the disestablishment of religion in Virginia. Though a slaveholder himself, consistently opposed the slave trade and denounced slavery. Married Sarah Brent in April 1780. Attended meeting at Mount Vernon in 1785 to coordinate support of Potomac navigation project by Virginia and Maryland. This meeting indirectly led to calling of the Annapolis Convention in 1786, which he did not attend. Chosen delegate from Virginia to the Constitutional Convention in Philadelphia in 1787, where he supported a more effective federal government, but ultimately refused to sign the Constitution. Delegate to Virginia ratifying convention of 1788, where he strongly opposed ratification without prior amendments. In 1790, the Virginia legislature elected him to the U.S. Senate, but he declined to serve. Died at Gunston Hall on October 7, 1792.

JAMES MONROE (1758–1831)   Born April 28, 1758, in Westmoreland County, Virginia, son of Elizabeth Jones and Spence Monroe. Attended school of parson Archibald Campbell (who also taught Marshall) and entered College of William and Mary in 1774, but left in 1776 because of the Revolution. Served as a cadet and was appointed lieutenant, with John Marshall, in the Third Virginia regiment in the Continental Army. In 1776, he participated in the battles of Harlem Heights, White Plains, and Trenton, where he was wounded. Promoted to rank of major and became aide to General Stirling. Served in the battles of Brandywine and Germantown in 1777, wintered at Valley Forge, and fought in the battle of Monmouth in 1778. Appointed military commissioner of Virginia in 1780 with rank of lieutenant colonel. Studied law under Governor Jefferson 1780–81. Licensed to practice law in Virginia in June 1782. Elected to the Virginia legislature from King George County in 1782, and resigned to become member of the council of state. Elected delegate from Virginia to Continental Congress 1783–86, where he led opposition to Jay's recommendation of a treaty with Spain that would forgo claims to free navigation on Mississippi River for 25 years. In February 1786, he married Elizabeth, daughter of Lawrence Kortright, a New York merchant. Delegate from Virginia to the Annapolis Convention in 1786. Practiced law in Fredericksburg in 1787, and returned to the Virginia House of Delegates. Delegate to the Virginia ratifying convention of 1788, where he opposed ratification. Defeated by James Madison in election for U.S. House of Representatives. Elected to U.S. Senate in 1790, where he opposed measures proposed by the Washington administration, including the establishment of a national bank, Gouverneur Morris's appointment as minister to France, and Jay's appointment as special envoy to England. Appointed in 1794 minister plenipotentiary to France, where he obtained the release of Thomas Paine from prison, then nursed him back to health. Somewhat successful in reducing French seizures of American shipping. Angered the administration by refusing to defend Jay's Treaty, and by being too friendly with the French government; was recalled by Secretary of State Pickering in 1796. Elected governor of Virginia 1799–1802. Appointed by Jefferson in 1803 minister plenipotentiary to France, Spain, and England to join Robert R. Livingston in negotiating a treaty to secure free navigation of the Mississippi; discovered on arrival that the vast territory of Louisiana was being offered for sale and participated in negotiations for purchase. Traveled between Spain, France, and England in 1804 on unsuccessful mission to obtain eastern Florida for the United States. Went to England in 1805–06, where he was later joined by William Pinkney, to negotiate commercial treaty; Jefferson and Madison found treaty unsatisfactory because it did not deal with impressment or include broader navigation rights for American commerce, and did not submit it to the Senate. Unsuccessful candidate for president against Madison in 1808, despite support of John Randolph and others. Elected to the Virginia legislature in the fall of 1810, and became governor of Virginia in January 1811. Resigned governorship in November 1811 to become secretary of state under Madison; served until 1817. Also served as secretary of war from August 1814 to March 1815. Elected president of the United States in 1817. Reelected in 1821, receiving all but one electoral vote. During his administration he signed the Missouri Compromise, acquired Florida, and, with advice from Secretary of State John Quincy Adams, recognized the independence of former Spanish colonies in Latin America and wrote the message in December 1823 that has become known as the Monroe Doctrine. Retired to his farm in Loudoun

County, Virginia, in 1825. With Jefferson and Madison, helped found the University of Virginia. He presided at Virginia's constitutional convention in 1829. After the death of his wife in 1830, he moved to New York City to live with his daughter and her husband. He died in New York on July 4, 1831.

ARMAND-MARC, COMTE DE MONTMORIN-SAINT-HÉREM   (1745–1792) Born October 13, 1745, in Paris, France, into an aristocratic family. In 1768 he became gentleman-in-waiting to the dauphin. In 1774, on the accession of Louis XVI, he was appointed minister to the archbishop of Treves. In 1777, he was appointed ambassador to the court of Charles III of Spain, where he successfully negotiated Spanish war assistance against England and befriended John Jay. Returned to France in 1783 and was appointed *commandant* of Brittany. Served there until 1787, when he succeeded Vergennes as foreign minister of France and was named to the Assembly of Notables. As foreign minister in 1787, he unsuccessfully advocated financial and military support for French partisans in the Netherlands. In 1788, he became involved with finance minister Necker in domestic affairs. In June 1789, he and Necker advised the king to pursue moderate constitutional reforms, but Louis XVI rejected their plan, overruled the decrees of the Third Estate, and, on July 11, dismissed Montmorin and the entire Necker ministry. On July 14, 1789, a popular uprising in Paris attacked and seized the Bastille, forcing Louis to recall Montmorin and Necker. After Necker's forced retirement in September 1790, Montmorin became the leading minister and allied himself with the comte de Mirabeau to preserve the monarchy, but his efforts to pursue a moderate course were attacked by both radicals and royalists. After the death of Mirabeau in April 1791, the king and queen made secret plans to escape France and raise an army of invasion. Montmorin unwittingly signed the false passports they used in their abortive flight in June, and although he was cleared of complicity in their flight, his reputation and credibility suffered. He continued in office until November 1791, when he resigned; he continued to advise the king and queen without success. In July 1792, he was publicly accused by Brissot and others of conspiring against the revolution. After the attack on the Tuileries in August 1792, he went into hiding, but was betrayed, arrested, and sent to the Abbaye prison, where he was impaled and hacked to death on September 2, 1792, during the September Massacres.

ELÉONORE FRANÇOIS ELIE, MARQUIS DE MOUSTIER   (1751–1817)   Born May 15, 1751, at Paris, France, of an ancient and noble family. Attended Jesuit college at Heidelberg, completed military apprenticeship at Besançon, and, in 1768, was commissioned underlieutenant in the Royal-Navarre regiment. His brother-in-law, the marquis de Clermont d'Amboise, ambassador to Portugal, took him to Lisbon in 1769, where he became secretary. Accompanied his uncle to Naples in 1775. In 1778, he was made minister to the Elector of Treves. In 1783, he was sent as minister to London to resolve difficulties resulting from the Spanish intervention in the recent war. In 1787, he replaced La Luzerne as minister to the United States, where he served until 1789, when he returned to Paris. He became minister to Prussia in 1790, and in September 1791 was recalled and offered the post of foreign minister by Louis XVI. He declined, fearing his monarchical principles would further compromise the king's position, and accepted briefly the post of ambassador at Constantinople. Almost immediately, he joined the brothers of Louis XVI in exile, and was commissioned by them to negotiate with Prussia and England for intervention on behalf of the Bourbons. His secret correspondence fell into the hands of the revolutionaries and was used as evidence in the condemnation of himself and Louis XVI. After the failure of the Prussian invasion in 1792, he lived in England until 1796, and in Prussia until 1806, working for the restoration of the Bourbon monarchy. He returned to England in 1806 to escape the French occupation of Prussia, and remained there until the restoration of 1814, when he returned to France. He retired to Bailli, near Versailles, where he resided until his death, of apoplexy, on February 1, 1817.

GEORGE NICHOLAS (c. 1754–1799)   Born in Williamsburg, Virginia, about 1754, eldest son of Anne Cary and Robert Carter Nicholas (prominent lawyer, member of houses of burgesses and delegates, judge of chancery and court of appeals, and treasurer of the colony). Attended College of William and Mary in 1772. Commissioned major of Second Virginia Regiment in Continental Army in 1776, achieved rank of lieutenant colonel, and retired in 1778. Married Mary Smith of Baltimore and was admitted to the bar in Virginia in 1778. Elected to Virginia House of Delegates from Williamsburg in 1778 and 1779. Served as aide-de-camp to Governor Thomas Nelson in 1781. Elected to house of delegates from Hanover County in 1781 and 1782. Moved to Albemarle County, Virginia, with his family, mother, and brothers in 1781. Appointed acting attorney general of Virginia in 1781 and 1782. In legislature, he instigated, probably at Patrick Henry's urging, investigation of Governor Jefferson's conduct during British invasion (he later became a close supporter of Jefferson). Member of house of delegates from Albemarle County 1783–84 and 1786–88, supported James Madison's effort to enact statute for religious freedom, and opposed issuing paper money. Delegate from Albemarle County to Virginia ratifying convention of 1788, where he strongly supported ratification. In 1790 moved to district of Kentucky and became involved in land speculations, New Orleans trade, and possibly the Spanish Conspiracy with college classmate Harry Innes and James Wilkinson. Attorney general of District of Kentucky from 1790 to 1792. In 1792, helped draft first state constitution, in which he inserted a clause that land titles should be decided by state supreme court, and became first attorney general of Kentucky. Appointed first professor of law at Transylvania University in Lexington. In 1798, helped secure passage by Kentucky legislature of Kentucky Resolutions (drafted secretly by Thomas Jefferson) protesting passage of Alien and Sedition Acts. He died in June 1799.

JOHN PAGE (1743–1808)   Born April 28, 1743, at Rosewell, Gloucester
County, Virginia, son of Alice Grymes and Mann Page. Educated at private
school and by tutors. Entered grammar school of William and Mary College
when he was thirteen, and remained until 1763, completing the regular
courses in philosophy. Became close friend of classmate Thomas Jefferson.
Served under Washington in expedition against the French and Indians. Married Frances, daughter of Robert Carter Burwell of Isle of Wight County,
around 1765. They had twelve children, five of whom married sons or daughters of Thomas Nelson. Member of Virginia House of Burgesses 1771–73.
Member of state council and committee of public safety. Delegate to convention that drafted state constitution in 1776. Lieutenant governor and member
of the council of state under Patrick Henry 1776–79. Raised regiment of militia from Gloucester County and was made colonel. Lost election for governor by narrow margin to Jefferson in 1779, and became lieutenant governor;
resigned in May 1780. Served in Yorktown campaign in 1781. Elected to state
house of delegates 1781–84, 1785–87, and 1788–89. Lost election as delegate
to the Virginia ratifying convention; at first would have preferred amendments made prior to adoption, but soon felt that prior amendment was not
practicable and supported the Constitution, which itself allowed for future
amendments. In 1786, he owned 160 slaves. His first wife died, and in 1789 he
married Margaret, daughter of William Lowther of Scotland, in New York
City, and had eight more children with her. Elected to U.S. House of Representatives in the first Congress in 1789 and was reelected three times, serving until 1797. Presidential elector for Jefferson in 1800. Elected governor of
Virginia three terms 1802–05. Appointed by Jefferson U.S. commissioner of
loans for Virginia, and served until his death in Richmond on October 11,
1808.

EDMUND PENDLETON (1721–1803)   Born September 9, 1721, in Caroline
County, Virginia, son of Mary Taylor and Henry Pendleton. His father died
the year he was born and his mother remarried. Apprenticed at age 14 to
Benjamin Robinson, clerk of the court of Caroline. Became clerk to the ves-
try of St. Mary's Parish in 1737. Appointed clerk of the Caroline court martial
in 1740. Admitted to the local bar in 1741. In 1742, he married Elizabeth Roy,
who died within the year in childbirth. In June 1743, he married Sarah Pol-
lard, with whom he had no children. Admitted to practice before the general
court in 1745. Appointed justice of the peace for Caroline County in 1751.
Elected to the Virginia House of Burgesses in 1752 and served until 1774.
Opposed Patrick Henry's resolutions during the Stamp Act crisis (as he had
opposed him on other issues), but opened his court without the use of
stamps and stated that parliament had no constitutional authority to pass the
act. In 1773, he was a member of Virginia's committee of correspondence.
Delegate from Virginia to the First Continental Congress in 1774. Member of
all of Virginia's Revolutionary conventions and president of two of them in
1775. President of state committee of safety 1775–76. Hoped that a compromise with Britain was still possible, but drafted the resolves instructing

Virginia's delegates in the Continental Congress to propose independence. With Jefferson and George Wythe, he was placed on a committee to revise the laws of Virginia; he opposed Jefferson's programs for disestablishment of the church and abolition of primogeniture and entail. Elected first speaker of the new Virginia House of Delegates and appointed presiding judge of the court of chancery. When the supreme court of appeals was organized in 1779, became its first president and held that position until his death. Presided at the Virginia ratifying convention of 1788, where he warmly supported ratification. Though an old friend of Washington, he disapproved of the administration's financial and foreign policies and allied himself with the Jeffersonian Republicans. He died in Richmond, on October 26, 1803.

HENRY PENDLETON (1750–1789)   Born in 1750 in Culpeper County, Virginia, son of Nathaniel Greene Pendleton and nephew of Edmund Pendleton. With his brother Nathaniel, joined the Culpeper Minute Men when the Revolution began. Moved to South Carolina and was appointed judge of court of common pleas in 1776. Taken prisoner, he apparently violated parole and left Charleston in 1780 because of threats by Loyalists and refugees there. Fought under Nathaniel Greene at battle of Eutaw Springs in September 1781. Returned to Charleston and was taken prisoner again March 26, 1782. Originated the County Court Act of South Carolina and was one of three judges appointed to revise the laws of the state in 1785. Delegate to South Carolina ratifying convention in 1788, where he supported ratification. Declined to stand for election to U.S. House of Representatives in 1788. Died in the Greenville District of South Carolina on January 10, 1789.

THOMAS PERSON (1733–1800)   Born January 19, 1733, probably in Brunswick County, Virginia, son of Ann and William Person. Around 1740, the family moved to Granville County, North Carolina. Became surveyor for Lord Granville and acquired a landed estate of 82,000 acres in western North Carolina, in what would later become Tennessee. He married Johanna Thomas of Granville County in 1760; they had no children. Became justice of the peace in 1756 and sheriff in 1762. Elected to the provincial assembly in 1764. Arrested for his involvment in the backcountry Regulator movement in 1768, but was released before trial. Represented Granville County in all the provincial congresses, and served on committees that drafted the Halifax Resolution in April 1776 instructing North Carolina delegates to the Continental Congress to vote for independence, that drew up a declaration of rights, and that drafted the state constitution of 1776. He was a member of the state council, and served on the council of safety in 1776. Appointed general of militia, but apparently saw no active duty during the war. Elected to state house of commons 1777–86, 1788–91, 1793–95, and 1797. Elected to state senate 1787 and 1791. By 1785, he owned 89,660 acres of land and 62 slaves. Delegate from Granville County to North Carolina ratifying conventions of 1788 and 1789, where he opposed ratification. Became a founding trustee and benefactor of the University of North Carolina. He died in Franklin County on November 16, 1800.

CHARLES COTESWORTH PINCKNEY (1746–1825)   Born February 25, 1746, in Charleston, South Carolina, son of Elizabeth Lucas (who helped bring indigo cultivation to South Carolina) and Charles Pinckney (chief justice of the province). Brother of Thomas Pinckney (1750–1828) and second cousin of Charles Pinckney (1757–1824). Family moved to England in 1753, when his father was appointed agent of the colony to London. Remained in England after his parents returned to America in 1758 (where his father soon died). Educated at Westminster and Christ Church College, Oxford, attended lectures of William Blackstone, and was admitted to the Middle Temple in 1764. Admitted to the English bar in 1769; practiced briefly before continuing his studies in France. Returned to America in late 1769 and was immediately elected to the colonial assembly. Admitted to the South Carolina bar in early 1770. Married Sarah Middleton, daughter of the second president of the Continental Congress and sister of Arthur Middleton, signer of the Declaration of Independence. Became acting attorney general for Camden, Georgetown, and the Cheraws in 1773. Served in the provincial congress 1775–76, where he advocated disestablishment of the church and served on various committees and the council of safety. Joined the militia and was appointed ranking major when the South Carolina 1st Regiment was organized. Promoted to colonel by September 1776. Appointed aide to Washington and took part in the battles of Brandywine and Germantown in 1777. In 1778 he took part in the campaign in Florida and the unsuccessful siege of Savannah. Taken prisoner after surrender of Charleston in 1780, was exchanged in 1782 and rejoined army; was discharged as brigadier general in 1783. Joined the Society of the Cincinnati (became its third president general in 1805). Elected to the lower house in 1778 and 1782. President of the state senate in 1779. Wife Sarah died in 1784, and he married Mary, daughter of Benjamin Stead. Delegate from South Carolina to the Constitutional Convention of 1787, where he opposed religious tests and proposed that Senate have power to ratify treaties. Delegate to South Carolina ratifying convention, where he supported ratification. Declined Washington's offers to appoint him U.S. Supreme Court justice, secretary of war, and secretary of state. In 1796, he succeeded Monroe as minister to France, but when he arrived he was not formally received and was forced to leave. He was one of the American peace commissioners (with Elbridge Gerry and John Marshall) appointed by Adams in 1797 for mission to France in what became known as the XYZ Affair, and he shared Marshall's view of the proceedings. In 1798, when war with France threatened, he was commissioned major general under Washington and Hamilton (discharged in June 1800). Unsuccessful Federalist candidate for vice-president in 1800 and unsuccessful Federalist candidate for president in 1804 and 1808. Helped found South Carolina College in 1801 and Charleston Bible Society in 1810. He lived at his plantation, Belmont, and in Charleston. Died in Charleston on August 16, 1825.

DAVID RAMSAY (1749–1815)   Born April 2, 1749, in Drumore Township, Lancaster County, Pennsylvania, son of Jane Montgomery and James Ramsay, emigrants from Ireland. Ramsay graduated from the College of New Jersey (now Princeton) in 1765 and worked as a tutor in Maryland and then in Virginia for two years. Entered the Medical College of Philadelphia (now University of Pennsylvania), where he studied with Benjamin Rush, and received his degree in 1773. Practiced medicine for a year in Cecil County, Maryland, before moving to Charleston, South Carolina, in 1774. In February 1775, he married Sabina Ellis of Charleston, who died the next year. Elected to state house of representatives in 1776, and served until 1790. Delivered the first known oration commemorating the Fourth of July in 1778. Served as a surgeon for the Continental Army and was taken prisoner when the British captured Charleston in 1780. Detained in St. Augustine, Florida, for eleven months. Delegate from South Carolina to the Continental Congress 1782–86. In 1783 he married Frances, daughter of John Witherspoon (president of the College of New Jersey and a signer of the Declaration of Independence), who gave birth to a son and died in 1784. In January 1787 he married Martha, daughter of Henry Laurens (former president of the Continental Congress and one of the commissioners who signed the preliminary peace treaty with Great Britain in 1782), and they had eleven children. Delegate to South Carolina ratifying convention, where he supported ratification. Served as president of the state senate 1792, 1794, and 1796. Retired from politics and wrote histories of the American Revolution, South Carolina, and the United States, and a biography of George Washington. He was involved in land speculations and other investments and in 1798 was declared bankrupt, but arranged with creditors to repay them through medical services. Published the memoirs of his wife after her death in 1811. Shot by a mentally deranged man, against whom he had given testimony, and died two days later in Charleston on May 8, 1815.

EDMUND RANDOLPH (1753–1813)   Born August 10, 1753, at Tazewell Hall, near Williamsburg, Virginia, only son of Ariana Jenings and John Randolph (former king's attorney for Virginia). Graduated from the College of William and Mary, studied law with his father, and was admitted to the Virginia bar in 1774. His father left Virginia with Lord Dunmore and other Loyalists in 1775, and Randolph was taken into the home of his uncle, Peyton Randolph, who was the first president of the Continental Congress. In August 1775, he joined the army in Cambridge, Massachusetts, and was appointed aide-de-camp by Washington. Hearing of his uncle's death, he returned to Virginia. In August 1776, he married Elizabeth, daughter of Robert Carter and sister of George Nicolas, and had four children with her. Youngest member of the Virginia convention that adopted the first state constitution. Served as mayor of Williamsburg, clerk of the house of delegates, and attorney general of Virginia. Delegate from Virginia to the Continental Congress 1779–82. Governor of Virginia 1786–88. Delegate to the Annapolis Convention in 1786. Delegate to the Constitutional Convention in Philadelphia in 1787, where he proposed Virginia plan (drafted by Madison) but refused to sign the Constitution as written. Explained his reasons for refusing in a widely publicized letter. As delegate to Virginia ratifying convention in 1788, he surprised many by supporting ratification. Appointed the first attorney general of the United States by Washington in 1789 and served until 1794, during which time Washington relied on him to mediate differences between Jefferson and Hamilton. Appointed secretary of state in 1794 after Jefferson's retirement. Forced to resign in August 1795 after a letter written by retiring French minister Fauchet appeared to implicate Randolph in disloyal behavior (it was intercepted by the English and brought to Washington's attention by other members of the cabinet). Randolph published a pamphlet defending himself in 1795. Moved to Richmond and resumed practice of law. He was senior counsel (with Luther Martin) for Aaron Burr during his trial for treason in federal circuit court before John Marshall in 1807. He died on September 12, 1813.

BENJAMIN RUSH (1746–1813)   Born January 4, 1746, in Byberry Township, outside of Philadelphia, son of Susanna Hall Harvey and her second husband, John Rush (gunsmith and farmer who died in 1751). Attended academy run by Samuel Finley, his mother's sister's husband, in West Nottingham in 1753. Entered College of New Jersey (now Princeton) in spring of 1759 and graduated in 1760. Studied medicine with John Redman, the leading physician in Philadelphia, from February 1761 to July 1766. Attended medical lectures at the College of Philadelphia (now University of Pennsylvania). Attended Edinburgh University and received M.D. degree in 1768. Helped convince Witherspoon to become president of the College of New Jersey in 1768. Spent five months in London in further study of medicine and became a friend of Franklin. Returned to Philadelphia and opened medical practice in 1769. Became the first professor of chemistry at the College of Philadelphia. Elected to the American Philosophical Association. In 1774 (and 1803) helped found the Pennsylvania Society for Promoting the Abolition of Slavery. Met delegates to the First and Second Continental Congresses and became friend of John Adams and Thomas Jefferson. Married Julia, daughter of Richard Stockton, trustee of College of New Jersey and a signer of the Declaration of Independence. He had many children, and six sons and three daughters survived him. Elected to the provincial congress. Delegate from Pennsylvania to the Continental Congress in 1776, where he signed the Declaration of Independence. Not reelected to Continental Congress because of his expressed dislike for the new Pennsylvania constitution. Served as surgeon general in the Continental Army in 1777, but resigned after his complaints to Washington about conditions and medical treatment were not heeded. Joined staff of the Pennsylvania Hospital in 1783. With John Dickinson, helped found Dickinson College in Carlisle, Pennsylvania. Supported various reform movements, including temperance, women's education, and improved treatment for the indigent sick. In 1787, he helped found the Philadelphia College of Physicians. Delegate to Pennsylvania ratifying convention of 1787, where he strongly supported ratification. With James Wilson, campaigned successfully for a new state constitution in 1789. Continued to teach and occupy various chairs after the College of Philadelphia merged with the University of the State of Pennsylvania to become the University of Pennsylvania in 1791. Member of Pennsylvania Democratic Society 1794. Resigned from Philadelphia College of Physicians after dispute over treatment of yellow fever in 1794. Pioneered studies of insanity and wrote *Medical Inquiries and Observations upon the Diseases of the Mind* (1812). Supported Jefferson for president in 1796. Appointed treasurer of the U.S. mint by John Adams in November 1797 and retained that position until his death. Helped bring about reconciliation between Jefferson and Adams in 1812. Died in Philadelphia on April 19, 1813.

EDWARD RUTLEDGE (1749–1800)   Born November 23, 1749, in Christ Church Parish, South Carolina, youngest child of Sarah and Dr. John Rutledge (who had emigrated from Northern Ireland in 1735). Brother of John Rutledge (later justice of the U.S. Supreme Court). Received classical education and read law with his brother. Admitted to the Middle Temple in London in 1767 and called to the English bar in 1772. Returned to South Carolina in 1773 and began to practice law. Married Henrietta, daughter of Henry Middleton (second president of the Continental Congress and signer of the Declaration of Independence), in March 1774, and they had three children. Delegate from South Carolina to the Continental Congress 1774–76. Elected to the first and second provincial congresses 1775–76. Appointed to the board of war of the Continental Congress in June 1776. Favored delaying the vote for independence in June 1776, but on July 2 influenced the South Carolina delegation to vote for the independence resolution and was one of the signers of the Declaration of Independence. With Benjamin Franklin and John Adams, met with Admiral Howe at Staten Island in September 1776 to discuss British terms of reconciliation. Returned to South Carolina and became captain of artillery in the Charleston militia. Elected to state house of representatives in 1778. Elected delegate to Continental Congress in 1779, but instead took part in defense of Port Royal Island at Beaufort in February 1779. Taken prisoner after surrender of Charleston in May 1780 and confined in St. Augustine September 1780–July 1781. Elected to state house of representatives 1782–96. Formed partnership investing in plantations with his wife's brother-in-law, Charles Cotesworth Pinckney, and continued his successful law practice. Delegate to South Carolina ratifying convention of 1788, where he supported ratification. Presidential elector in 1789 and 1792. Member of the state constitutional convention in 1790. Declined appointment as associate justice on Supreme Court offered by Washington in 1791. Wife Henrietta died in April 1792, and he married Mary Shubrick Eveleigh in October 1792. Presidential elector in 1796, voting for Thomas Pinckney and Thomas Jefferson in 1796. Elected to state senate in 1796. Elected governor in 1798. He died in Charleston, January 23, 1800.

WILLIAM SHEPPARD (1746–1822)   An early settler of Surry County, North Carolina. Married Elizabeth Haywood, with whom he had eight children. Commanded troop of cavalry in General Griffith Rutherford's campaign against the Cherokees in September 1776. Colonel of militia during Revolution, active against Tories. State senator from Surry County from 1778 to 1782. Moved to Orange County, North Carolina. Delegate from Orange County to North Carolina ratifying convention of 1788, where he opposed ratification. In 1790, he owned twelve slaves and over 500 acres of land. State senator from Orange County in 1793, 1801, and 1803. Died on February 8, 1822.

MELANCTON SMITH (1744–1798)   Born May 7, 1744, in Jamaica, Long Island, New York, son of Elizabeth Bayles and Samuel Smith. Educated at home. Became storekeeper in Poughkeepsie, Dutchess County, New York, where he began to buy land. Helped organize the Washington Hollow Presbyterian Church in 1769. After the death of his wife, Sarah Smith, in 1770, he married Margaret, daughter of Richbill Mott, in 1771; they had three children. One of ten delegates from Dutchess County to the first provincial congress in 1775. In June 1775, organized and was captain of the first company of minutemen in Dutchess County, with duty to detect Loyalist conspiracies. Appointed on December 20, 1776, major in command of all New York ranger companies. Appointed high sheriff of the county in 1777 and 1779. Bought confiscated Loyalist lands, became a substantial landowner, and speculated in government securities and bonds. With Governor George Clinton's support, became commissary agent for the army. Appointed by Washington in 1782 to commission to settle disputes between army and contractors at West Point and elsewhere. Moved to New York City in 1784 and became both a merchant and a lawyer. Delegate from New York to the Continental Congress 1785–88. Because New York City, a Federalist stronghold, would not send him to the New York ratifying convention in 1788, Smith sought and won election from Dutchess County. He consistently opposed the Constitution without amendments, but, in a move of great importance to the ratification process, finally agreed to give his support after Federalists promised to incorporate a bill of rights and news of ratification by Virginia and New Hampshire reached New York. Part of the compromise consisted of a circular letter, written by John Jay, sent to other states asking for a second Constitutional Convention. Elected to the legislature in 1791. Worked for Clinton's reelection as governor in 1792 and was appointed circuit judge. Died during yellow fever outbreak in New York City, on July 29, 1798.

JOSEPH SPENCER (1745–1829)   A neighbor of James Madison in Orange County, Virginia, and an active Baptist. Married Sarah, daughter of Francis Moore. Organized a company of militia in 1775 and joined the Culpeper Minute Men in the Great Bridge–Norfolk campaign 1775–76. Member of the committee of safety of Orange County 1774–76, with James Madison and Lawrence Taliaferro. Commissioned captain of the 7th Virginia Regiment in the Continental Army on July 4, 1776. Resigned from army in November 1777 with rank of lieutenant colonel, and later received land for his service. Elected to the state assembly 1780–81. Died August 27, 1829.

SAMUEL SPENCER (1734–1793)   Born January 21, 1734, in East Haddam, Connecticut, son of Jerusha Brainerd and Samuel Spencer, both of prominent New Light Presbyterian families. Attended College of New Jersey (now Princeton) from 1755 to 1759. Moved to North Carolina, settled in Anson County, and began practice of law. In 1765 appointed deputy clerk of court of pleas for Anson County. In 1766 married Phillipa Pegues, with whom he had two surviving children. Elected to state assembly in 1766. Colonel of Anson County militia 1768–76; participated in campaigns against Regulators, including battle at Alamance in May 1771. From 1774 to 1776 was county representative in provincial congress and sat on committee that drafted new state constitution and declaration of rights. Became district judge in 1777 and was later appointed to state superior court. In 1787, when court declared act of the assembly unconstitutional in case of *Bayard* v. *Singleton*, legislators attempted unsuccessfully to unseat him. Attended North Carolina ratifying conventions at Hillsborough in 1788 and Fayetteville in 1789, and opposed ratification at both. In 1789, became trustee of the University of North Carolina. In 1790, owned eleven slaves and 2,080 acres of land. Died at home in Anson County on April 20, 1793, of an infected hand wound sustained from attack by a turkey.

JOHN STEVENS, JR. (1749–1838)   Born in New York City in 1749, son of Elizabeth (daughter of James Alexander) and John Stevens (ship owner and merchant with extensive land holdings and political interests in New Jersey). Grew up at Perth Amboy, New Jersey. Received tutoring at home and at Kenersley's College near Woodbridge. Joined family in New York in 1762. Entered King's College (now Columbia) in 1766 and graduated in 1768. Admitted to the New York bar in 1771, but never practiced law. Joined his father in New Jersey political work and acted occasionally as special aide to Governor William Franklin. At the outbreak of the Revolution, commissioned captain in the New Jersey militia and appointed a loan office collector. New Jersey state treasurer 1777–83 and state surveyor general 1782–83. Married Rachel (daughter of John Cox of Bloomsbury, New Jersey) in October 1782, and they had seven children who survived him, including several who became successful inventors. In 1784, he bought a large tract of land (including most of present-day Hoboken) at auction. Lived in New York in winter and at his Hoboken estate, Castle Point, in summer. In 1787 and 1788 wrote "Americanus" essays supporting ratification of the Constitution. Attended demonstration of steamboat by John Fitch and James Rumsey on the Delaware River in 1788 and began serious study of its prospects. Urged friends in Congress to pass the first patent law in April 1790. With his brother-in-law Robert R. Livingston, Nicholas J. Roosevelt, and others, built experimental steamboats 1797–1800. Became consulting engineer for the Manhattan Company, organized by Livingston, Burr, and others to supply city with fresh water and act as a bank. Installed steam pump for company and continued to develop steam-powered engines and build boats. Robert Fulton, Roosevelt, and Livingston were granted a monopoly on steamboat traffic on the Hudson River in 1807. Stevens developed the first ocean-going steamboat and operated steamboats on the Delaware and the Connecticut Rivers and ferries to Hoboken and elsewhere. Began to consider use of steam engine for railroad in 1810 and lobbied states to open ways. Received charter from New Jersey legislature to build railroad from Trenton to New Brunswick in 1815. Organized unsuccessful Pennsylvania Railroad with charter from state legislature in 1823. In 1825, to prove the viability of the steam locomotive, he built a model for demonstrations on his Hoboken estate. It was the first steam locomotive in the United States. Formed Camden & Amboy Railroad Company in 1830. He died in Hoboken on March 6, 1838.

JOHN SULLIVAN (1740–1795)   Born February 17, 1740, in Somersworth, New Hampshire, son of Margery Browne of Cork, Ireland, and John Sullivan of Limerick, both of whom had immigrated to Maine as redemptioners in 1723. Brother of James Sullivan. When he was a child, the family moved to Berwick in the district of Maine, where his father taught school. Sullivan studied law under Samuel Livermore in Portsmouth and practiced in Durham. He married Lydia Worcester in 1760, with whom he had a daughter and three sons who survived him. Appointed major of the New Hampshire militia in 1772. Elected delegate from New Hampshire to the First Continental Congress in 1774. With John Langdon, led militia in capture of British forts at Portsmouth Harbor in late 1774. Delegate to the Second Continental Congress in 1775, where he was commissioned brigadier general in the Continental Army in June. Joined Washington's army at siege of Boston. Promoted to major general in August 1776, was captured at the battle of Long Island that same month. Sent as emissary from British Admiral Howe to the Congress in Philadelphia to offer peace negotiations. Exchanged for British general Richard Prescott in fall of 1776. Fought in battles at Trenton and Princeton and on Staten Island in 1776–77, and spent winter of 1777–78 at Valley Forge. Commanded unsuccessful expedition against Newport, Rhode Island, in 1778. Led successful expedition against Iroquois Six Nations in western New York and Pennsylvania in 1779. Resigned from army November 30, 1779, because of poor health. Awarded honorary degree from Harvard in 1780. Delegate to the Continental Congress 1780–81. Member of the New Hampshire state constitutional convention in 1782. State attorney general 1782–86. Member of the state assembly in 1785. Elected to three terms as president of New Hampshire 1787–89, during which time he took strong measures against Shays' Rebellion. Presided over the New Hampshire ratifying convention in 1788, where he supported ratification. Presidential elector in 1789. Appointed to the U.S. District Court for New Hampshire in 1789; served until his death in Durham on January 23, 1795.

JOSEPH TAYLOR (1742–1815)   Born February 19, 1742, in Virginia, son of Catherine Pendleton and John Taylor, both of prominent Virginia families. Moved to Granville County, North Carolina, before the Revolution. Married Frances Anderson, with whom he had one son, Joseph. Became a lawyer and large-scale planter. Appointed colonel of Granville County Minute Men on September 9, 1775, and colonel of Granville County militia on April 22, 1776. State senator from Granville County in 1781. Delegate to North Carolina ratifying convention of 1788, where he opposed ratification. In 1790, he owned over 2,800 acres of land. Unsuccessful Republican candidate for governor in 1800. Served as presidential elector for Jefferson in 1800 and 1804 and for Madison in 1808. Elected state senator from Granville County in 1803. He died in June 1815.

GEORGE THATCHER (1754–1824)   Born April 12, 1754, in Yarmouth, Massachusetts, son of Anner Lewis and Lieutenant Peter Thatcher. Prepared for college under minister Timothy Hilliard of Barnstable. Graduated from Harvard College in 1776 (in class with Christopher Gore). Served one cruise on privateer. Studied law under Shearjashub Bourne of Cape Cod. Admitted to bar in 1778. Moved to York, district of Maine, and commenced practice. Settled at Biddeford in 1782 and took over practice from James Sullivan. Elected to Massachusetts General Court. In July 1784, married Sarah Savage of Weston, Massachusetts, with whom he had ten children. Delegate from Massachusetts to Continental Congress in 1787. Supported ratification of the Constitution and corresponded with delegates to Massachusetts ratifying convention, journalists, and office-holders, including Christopher Gore, Nathaniel Barrell, Rufus King, Samuel Nasson, William Widgery, Samuel Thompson, Nathan Dane, Samuel Otis, Jeremiah Hill, and Thomas Wait. Elected to U.S. House of Representatives in 1789 and reelected five more terms through 1801. Judge in Maine district 1792–1800. Associate judge of Massachusetts Supreme Court 1800–20. Delegate to Maine constitutional convention in 1819. Judge of Maine Supreme Court 1820–24. About 1815, he began to spell his name "Thacher." Died in Biddeford, Maine, April 6, 1824.

ELIZA HOUSE TRIST (1751–1828)   Born in Philadelphia in 1751 of Quaker parents. In 1774, married Nicholas Trist of County Devon, England, a lieutenant and medical officer in the British Army. Traveled to New York to be with her husband; her son, Hore Browse Trist, was born there in February 1775. Husband resigned his commission in Boston after battle of Bunker Hill in 1775 and bought land in what is today Louisiana. Eliza remained in Philadelphia and helped her widowed mother, Mary House, run boarding house patronized by Robert R. Livingston, James Madison, John F. Mercer, Thomas Jefferson, and other members of Continental Congress. Became lifelong friend of Jefferson and Madison. In December 1783, began horseback journey via Pittsburgh to Natchez in the Louisiana area to join her husband. Wrote diary of her impressions of the frontier for Jefferson. Arrived in July 1784 and found that her husband had died in February. Settled husband's accounts, but had difficulty getting passage home because Spain controlled the area and the route up Mississippi River was closed. Sailed to Jamaica in spring 1785 and from there returned to her mother and son in Philadelphia. Her mother died in 1793, and Jefferson helped secure a small inheritance for her son from English relatives. In 1798, with Jefferson's advice, her son bought Birdwood Plantation, next to Monticello, where she lived with him and his wife. In 1804 Jefferson appointed her son port collector for the lower Mississippi, and she joined him in New Orleans. After her son's death and his wife's remarriage in 1807, she returned to Virginia, where she lived with various friends. In 1823 she moved to Monticello; her eldest grandson married Jefferson's granddaughter in 1824. After Jefferson's death, she continued to live at Monticello until she died, on December 9, 1828.

MERCY OTIS WARREN (1728–1814)   Born September 25, 1728, in Barnstable, Massachusetts, daughter of Mary Allyne and James Otis. Sister of James Otis (orator and lawyer who led the fight against writs of assistance and Stamp Act). In November 1754, she married James Warren, Massachusetts patriot and political leader and later speaker of the state house of representatives. They eventually had five sons. Lived in Plymouth until 1781, when they purchased the house of Loyalist governor Thomas Hutchinson in Milton, where they lived for ten years. Mercy Warren was a fervent patriot and wrote poetry, satirical anti-British plays, and the *History of the Rise, Progress, and Termination of the American Revolution* (3 volumes, 1805). She opposed the Constitution and all her life was suspicious of monarchical and aristocratic tendencies. She espoused Jeffersonian politics and supported the Embargo Act. Maintained lively correspondence with many people active in public affairs, including Samuel Adams, John and Abigail Adams, John Dickinson, Thomas Jefferson, Elbridge Gerry, Henry Knox, and Catharine Macaulay. Her friendship with John Adams was severed for almost five years after he read her description of him in her history, but Gerry helped bring about a reconciliation. Her husband died in November 1808, and she died October 19, 1814, in Plymouth.

GEORGE WASHINGTON (1732–1799)   Born February 22, 1732, at Wakefield, Westmoreland County, Virginia, eldest son of Mary Ball and Augustine Washington (who had two sons from a previous marriage). Family moved in 1735 to Little Hunting Creek, Stafford County, on the Potomac River and later to Ferry Farm, King George County, on the Rappahannock River. Father died in 1743, and Washington lived six years with relatives, including his half-brothers Augustine, in Westmoreland County, and Lawrence, at Mount Vernon. Attended school and studied mathematics and surveying. In 1748, accompanied James Genn to survey lands for Lord Fairfax in Shenandoah Valley. Appointed surveyor for Culpeper County in 1749. Accompanied half-brother Lawrence to Barbados and contracted smallpox before return to Virginia. Lawrence died in 1752, leaving Mount Vernon to him after his wife's death (she moved out and left it to him). Appointed adjutant general of Virginia militia, with rank of major. Commissioned in November 1753 to carry ultimatum demanding evacuation of French posts in Ohio territory and to meet with chiefs of the Six Nations. Traveled overland to forks of Ohio, held council with Six Nations at Logstown, and then proceeded to Fort Le Boeuf on Lake Erie, where he delivered message to French commander. Returned to Virginia in January 1754 and wrote report published in London as *The Journal of Major George Washington* in 1754. Commissioned lieutenant colonel of militia and sent to occupy forks of Ohio in April 1754. Finding French already in possession, built Fort Necessity near Great Meadows, Pennsylvania. Skirmished with French and signed armistice in July 1754. Resigned from militia in late 1754. Appointed aide-de-camp to General Braddock on British expedition against Fort Duquesne at forks of Ohio in 1755. Taken ill, but rejoined army the day before it was surprised by French and Indians at the Monongahela on July 9, 1755. Two horses were shot from under him and four bullets passed through his coat during battle. British force retreated to Great Meadows. Death of Braddock ended his appointment as aide-de-camp. Appointed colonel and commander-in-chief of Virginia forces in fall 1755, with responsibility for defense of the frontier. Defeated for election to Virginia House of Burgesses in 1755 and 1757. Traveled to Boston in February 1756 to resolve status of colonial military commissions. In 1758, cooperated with British general John Forbes in expedition against Fort Duquesne, which French forces abandoned on their approach in November 1758. Resigned from militia. Elected burgess from Frederick County in 1758, and reelected annually through 1774. Married Martha Dandridge Custis, wealthy widow of Daniel Parke Custis, in January 1759, and became farmer and planter at Mount Vernon. An early supporter of patriot causes, often enlisted his neighbor George Mason to write resolutions. Elected delegate from Virginia to First Continental Congress in 1774. Chosen commander of militia of five Virginia counties. Elected delegate to Second Continental Congress in 1775, where on June 15 he was unanimously elected commander-in-chief of all Continental forces. Traveled to Cambridge and assumed command of forces surrounding Boston in early July. Secured authorization from Continental Congress to bombard Boston, and by March 5, 1776, had brought captured cannon from Ticonderoga and entrenched them on Dorchester Heights. British evacuated Boston on March 17, 1776. At request of Congress, moved army to New York to defend against expected British invasion under Howe. Outflanked and defeated by British and Hessians at battle of Long Island on August 27, 1776. Evacuated Brooklyn on August 30 and New York City on September 12, 1776. Withdrew army to Harlem Heights, where it defeated British assault on September 16. Retreated to White Plains, and repulsed British attack on October 28. Forced to abandon Fort Lee, New Jersey, on November 20. Retreated with army to Newark, then New Brunswick, and finally to west bank of Delaware River in early December. British occupied Amboy, New Brunswick, Princeton, and Trenton, and went into winter quarters. On December 25, 1776, Washington led 2,400 troops across Delaware River and surprised and defeated Hessian forces at Trenton. Recrossed Delaware, but returned to Trenton on December 30. British counterattack on January 2, 1777, trapped Washington and army against Delaware River. Americans withdrew under cover of darkness, eluded opposing British forces, and advanced to Princeton, where they defeated smaller British force on January 3. Took army into winter quarters in Watchung Mountains near Morristown. British retreated to New Brunswick and Amboy. Trained and reorganized army into five divisions under major generals Greene, Sullivan, Stephen, Lincoln, and Stirling. Appointed marquis de Lafayette and Alexander Hamilton to his staff in 1777. Skirmished with British army in June 1777 but declined to be drawn into major battle. British evacuated New Jersey and began expedition against Philadelphia by way of Chesapeake Bay. Moved army south of Philadelphia to block British advance. Fought battle of Brandywine on September 11, 1777. British occupied Philadelphia on September 23. Washington attacked British force at Germantown, Pennsylvania, on October 4, but was driven back by reinforcements. British withdrew to Philadelphia. Informed of efforts involving Major General Thomas Conway to replace him as commander-in-chief with Horatio Gates, recent victor at Saratoga. Took army into winter quarters at Valley Forge, where Baron von Steuben was employed in drilling and training. Repeatedly appealed to Continental Congress and the states for provisions and supplies for ill-equipped and malnourished army. Supported proposal to grant Continental officers half pay for life. New British commander Clinton began overland evacuation from Philadelphia in June 1778. Washington followed, intercepted British, and fought inconclusive battle of Monmouth on June 28, 1778. British continued retreat to New York. Washington followed to White Plains and commenced land blockade. In 1779, British advanced up Hudson River and captured uncompleted American fort at Stony Point on June 1. Appointed Anthony Wayne to command attack that recaptured fort on July 16, halting British advance. Focus of British actions shifted to South, and Washington continued to occupy positions around New York City and plan attack in cooperation with French forces under Rochambeau. In August 1781, French and Continental armies were combined near New York City when Washington learned that French admiral De Grasse had sailed for Chesapeake Bay to drive off British fleet and trap Cornwallis and British army at Yorktown, Virginia. Leaving half of Continental Army to hold British in New York, Washington proceeded with other half and French Army to join forces under Lafayette at Yorktown. Washington detoured to Mount Vernon for first visit home in six years. Armies assembled outside Yorktown by September 15, 1781, and commenced successful siege. British army surrendered October 19, 1781, ending major military operations of Revolution. Cornwallis declined to attend surrender, and Washington delegated Benjamin Lincoln to accept sword from British subordinate. Led troops back to Newburgh, New York. Adopted two of wife's orphaned grandchildren. Sent memorial to Congress regarding treatment of army veterans in December 1782 and addressed meeting of potentially rebellious officers at Newburgh in March 1783, stressing patience and duty. Sent circular letter to states seeking justice for officers and men and recommending union of states under federal head. After preliminary peace treaty was signed, Washington fixed the date for cessation of hostilities on April 19, 1783 (anniversary of battle of Lexington). Occupied New York as British evacuated on November 25. Traveled to Annapolis to meet with Con-

tinental Congress and resigned as commander-in-chief December 23, 1783. Retired to private life at Mount Vernon. Visited lands on Kanawha and Ohio
rivers in 1784 and became president of Potomac Company to develop navigation routes to western rivers. Secured passage of bills in Maryland and
Virginia legislatures to perform survey, create joint-stock company, and
undertake construction. Meeting at Mount Vernon indirectly led to convention of states to discuss interstate commerce at Annapolis in 1786, which
called for Constitutional Convention to be held in 1787. Attempted to restore
financial condition of estate, but declined to sell slaves "because I am princi-
pled against this kind of traffic." Named to Virginia delegation to Constitutional Convention in Philadelphia in 1787 and was unanimously elected
president of the convention. Signed and transmitted proposed Constitution
to Continental Congress in September 1787. Supported ratification through
private letters and advised James Madison and others. Unanimously elected
first president of United States by electors from ten states on February 4,
1789. Inaugurated in New York on April 30, 1789. Appointed Thomas Jefferson secretary of state, Alexander Hamilton secretary of treasury, and Henry
Knox secretary of war. Appointments to Supreme Court included successive
chief justices John Jay, John Rutledge, and Oliver Ellsworth, and associate
justices William Cushing, James Wilson, James Iredell, and Samuel Chase.
Wished to retire after first term but was convinced to serve again. Unanimously reelected president by electors from fifteen states in 1792. Issued proclamation of neutrality in European wars on April 22, 1793. Disturbed by
growing dissension between Jefferson and Hamilton, relied on Randolph as
intermediary, and after Jefferson's retirement, appointed Randolph in his
place. Called out militia to suppress Whiskey Rebellion in western Pennsylvania in fall of 1794 and led troops in person. Met with emissaries William
Findley and David Redick at Carlisle before army under Hamilton, Henry
Lee, and Daniel Morgan occupied western Pennsylvania. Pardoned all insurgents who took oath of allegiance. Denounced Democratic Societies for their
alleged role in the rebellion. Pinckney Treaty with Spain in 1795 secured navigation rights on Mississippi River. Appointed John Jay to negotiate differences with Great Britain and though disappointed with elements of it,
succeeded in having Jay's Treaty ratified despite opposition. Refused to supply papers relating to treaty to House of Representatives on grounds it had
no constitutional role in ratification. Despite wish to avoid party factionalism,
found his administration increasingly supported by Federalists and attacked
by Republicans. After Hamilton's retirement, continued to rely on him for
advice; asked him to help write "Farewell Address," published in September
1796; was succeeded as president by John Adams in 1797. Retired to Mount
Vernon. On July 3, 1798, appointed lieutenant general and commander-in-
chief of army being raised in expectation of war with France. Insisted on
Hamilton as second in command over Adams's objections. Died at Mount
Vernon after brief illness (cynache trachealis) on December 14, 1799. Congress
immediately adopted resolutions, delivered by John Marshall and written by
Henry Lee, declaring him "first in war, first in peace, and first in the hearts

of his countrymen," and making February 22 a national holiday. French armies and British fleets flew flags at half-mast. His will granted freedom to Mount Vernon slaves after his wife's death and provided endowment for a national university.

NOAH WEBSTER (1758–1843)   Born October 16, 1758, in West Hartford, Connecticut, son of Mercy Steele and Noah Webster (farmer, justice of the peace, and deacon of the Congregational church). Enjoyed reading at an early age and attended local schools. Attended Yale College and graduated in 1778, though his father had to mortgage his farm to make this possible. Worked as a teacher and clerk and read law under several lawyers. Admitted to the bar in Hartford in 1781. Taught school in Goshen, New York, and prepared a spelling book, the first in a series of publications that included a grammar and a reader, together forming his *Grammatical Institute of the English Language* (changed to *American Language* in later editions). The difficulty of securing copyrights from thirteen separate state governments helped convince him of the need for an effective national government, and he became an active pamphleteer in the Federalist cause. Traveled to various states to obtain copyrights and earned a living by teaching, holding singing schools, and lecturing. Met Benjamin Franklin in Philadelphia in 1786 and discussed a favorite project of simplified spelling. Coined the terms "fœderal" and "antifœderal" for opposing political factions in 1786. Moved to New York to edit the new *American Magazine* in 1787, but the venture did not succeed. Published articles under various pseudonyms ("America," "Giles Hickory," "A Citizen of America") supporting ratification of the Constitution. Moved back to Hartford in 1788 to practice law. Married Rebecca Greenleaf (daughter of William Greenleaf, a Boston merchant) in Boston in October 1789 and eventually had seven children who survived him. Practiced law in Hartford until 1793, when prominent Federalists persuaded him to move to New York and edit a daily newspaper *The Minerva* (later *Commercial Advertiser*) and semi-weekly *The Herald* (later *Spectator*). He remained a Federalist all his life; strongly defended Adams against Hamilton in 1800. In New York, he continued to write on various subjects, including political economy and medicine. In 1803 he moved to New Haven and began work on his dictionary. Published first edition of his *Dictionary of the English Language* in 1806 and the larger *American Dictionary of the English Language* in 1828. Moved to Amherst, Massachusetts, in 1812 and helped found Amherst College in 1821. Served in Massachusetts legislature in 1815 and 1819. Returned to New Haven in 1822. Traveled in France and England to do research in lexicography 1824–25. Died in New Haven on May 28, 1843.

JOHN WILLIAMS (1752–1806)   Born in Barnstable, England, in September 1752. Received classic education and studied medicine and surgery in St. Thomas Hospital, London. Served one year as surgeon's mate on English man-of-war. Immigrated to America in 1773 and settled in New Perth, New York, where he had extensive medical practice and acquired large holdings of land. Married Susanna Turner. Member of provincial congress from 1775 until its dissolution in 1777. Appointed surgeon of state militia in 1775 and colonel of Charlotte County militia regiment in 1776. State senator in 1777, 1778, and 1782–85. State assemblyman in 1781 and 1782. Appointed to first board of regents for New York University in 1784. Appointed brigadier general of militia in 1786. Delegate from counties of Washington and Clinton to state ratifying convention in 1788, where he opposed ratification. Elected to two terms in U.S. House of Representatives 1795–99. Afterwards judge of county court. Helped organize private company to construct Erie Canal, later taken over and completed by state. Died in Salem, New York, July 22, 1806.

WILLIAM WILLIAMS (1731–1811)   Born April 8, 1731, son of Mary Porter of Hadley, Massachusetts, and Solomon Williams (pastor of the First Congregational Church in Lebanon, Connecticut). Graduated from Harvard in 1751 and studied theology for a year under his father. Town clerk of Lebanon 1752–96 and selectman 1760–85. Took part in campaign at Lake George in 1755 on the staff of his father's first cousin Ephraim Williams, who was killed in an ambush. Entered mercantile business. Married Mary (daughter of Jonathan Trumbull the elder and sister of Jonathan Trumbull the younger, both governors of Connecticut), with whom he had three children. Member of the state house of representatives 1757–61, 1763–76, and 1780–84, serving as speaker 1774–75 and 1781–84. Member of the governor's council 1784–1803. During the Revolution he was a member of the state council of safety and helped finance the expedition of Connecticut troops against Ticonderoga in 1775 and again in 1779. Judge of county court 1775–1805, judge of district probate court 1775–1809, and justice of the peace. Delegate from Connecticut to the Continental Congress 1776–77 and 1783–84. Signed the Declaration of Independence. Refused to hear cases for the collection of debts in the winter of 1786–87, maintaining that debtors deserved more time to make good their loans. Delegate to the Connecticut ratifying convention in 1788, where he voted for ratification. He died in Lebanon, on August 2, 1811.

HUGH WILLIAMSON (1735–1819)   Born December 5, 1735, in West Nottingham, Pennsylvania, eldest son of Mary Davison (of Derry, Ireland) and John W. Williamson (a wealthy clothier of Scots descent who emigrated from Dublin, Ireland, in 1730). Intended for the ministry, he was educated for college at New London Cross Roads and Newark, Delaware. Graduated with the first class from the College of Philadelphia (now the University of Pennsylvania) in 1757. Studied theology in Connecticut and preached there for some time. Returned to Philadelphia in 1760 to study medicine and teach mathematics. In 1764 he went to Edinburgh, London, and Utrecht to continue his medical education and received M.D. degree from the University of Utrecht in 1768. Returned to Philadelphia to practice, but found his health too fragile and decided to become a businessman. Elected to the American Philosophical Society in 1768; studied the transits of Venus and Mercury for it. Went to the West Indies to raise subscriptions to start an academy in

Newark, Delaware. Sailed to Boston on his way to Europe and witnessed the Boston Tea Party. Arrived in England with the first official communications of the event, which he delivered to Franklin. He was examined by Lord Dartmouth and the Privy Council. Became friend of Franklin and conducted electrical experiments with him. Read paper at the Royal Society on the electric eel (published 1775). Traveled in Holland and returned to America in December 1776. Settled in Edenton, North Carolina, built up a mercantile business trading with the West Indies, and resumed medical practice. Surgeon general for the North Carolina troops 1779–82; emphasized the need for inoculation against smallpox. While in camp in the Dismal Swamp, he experimented with the effects on health of dress, diet, shelter, and drainage. He was elected to the North Carolina House of Commons in 1782 and 1785. Delegate from North Carolina to the Continental Congress 1782–85, 1787, and 1788. Appointed to settle accounts between the state and federal government. He supported a stronger form of government, opposed paper money, and advocated an excise rather than a land or poll tax. Delegate to the Constitutional Convention of 1787, where he took an active part. Wrote essays in support of ratification. Delegate to the second North Carolina ratifying convention at Fayetteville in 1789; he supported ratification. Elected to the U.S. House of Representatives 1789–93. Married Maria, daughter of Charles Ward Apthorpe, a wealthy New York merchant, in January 1789. Remained in New York and wrote a history of North Carolina and books on literary and scientific subjects, most notably on the climate of the United States. He died in New York City on May 22, 1819, having survived his wife and two sons.

JAMES WINTHROP (1752–1821)   Born March 28, 1752, in Cambridge, Massachusetts, son of Rebecca Townsend and John Winthrop (Harvard mathematician). Graduated from Harvard in 1769 and became librarian in 1770. Fought at battle of Bunker Hill in June 1775, where he was slightly wounded. Appointed register of probate for Middlesex. Passed over for his late father's professorship in 1779 (and again in 1788) because of his eccentricities. In 1780 encouraged students to rebel against the college president. Became an early member of the American Academy of Arts and Sciences, but embarrassed the Academy by publishing fallacious solutions to mathematical problems in their journal. In 1786–87 he was a volunteer in the forces sent to suppress Shays' Rebellion. Resigned as college librarian in 1787 when forced by the college to choose between that post and his job as register of probate. Received an honorary M.A. degree from Dartmouth in 1787. Author of Antifederalist essays published under pseudonym "Agrippa." Appointed judge of common pleas for Middlesex in 1791. Surveyed the area for a proposed Cape Cod canal and was a promoter of the West Boston Bridge and the Middlesex Canal. Presidential elector for Jefferson in 1804. Helped found the Massachusetts Historical Society. Spent remaining years writing on theological and astronomical subjects. He never married. Became overseer of Allegheny College, founded by his friend Timothy Alden, and left the college his large library. Awarded LL.D. degree from Allegheny College in 1817. Died in Cambridge on September 26, 1821.

ROBERT YATES (1738–1801)   Born January 27, 1738, in Schenectady, New York, son of Maria Dunbar and Joseph Yates. Received classical education in New York City and read law with William Livingston (later governor of New Jersey and father-in-law of John Jay). Admitted to the bar in May 1760 at Albany, where he lived and practiced for the rest of his life. Married Jannetje Van Ness in March 1765, with whom he had four children who survived him. Served on the board of alderman 1771–75. Member of the Albany committee of safety. Served in the four provincial congresses and the convention 1775–77, and on the provincial committee of safety. Member (with John Jay, Gilbert Livingston, and Robert R. Livingston) of the secret committee to obstruct British passage of the Hudson River. Served on committee on arrangements for the Continental regiments and chaired the committee to cooperate with General Schuyler. One of the members, with John Jay, who drafted the New York state constitution in 1777. Appointed to the state supreme court 1777–98, chief justice 1790–98. Noted for his fairness to both Whigs and Loyalists. Member of several commissions to settle boundary disputes. Supported George Clinton and led the fight in New York against the federal impost during the 1780s. Delegate from New York to Constitutional Convention in Philadelphia in 1787, which, with John Lansing (who had studied law with him and was related by marriage), he left on July 10, 1787. Attacked the proposed Constitution in pamphlets. Delegate to the New York ratifying convention of 1788, where he opposed ratification. In 1789, with support of Federalists including Alexander Hamilton, ran for governor against his old ally George Clinton, and lost. Lost 1795 election for governor to John Jay. Died September 9, 1801. Twenty years after his death, his widow published his notes from the 1787 Philadelphia convention.

Chronology of Events, 1774–1804

1774   In response to the Boston Tea Party of December 16, 1773, the British Parliament passes four laws that become known in the American colonies as the Coercive Acts. The Boston Port Act, which receives royal assent on March 31, closes Boston harbor, effective June 1, until "peace and obedience to the laws" is restored in the town and its people pay for the destroyed tea. Massachusetts Government Act, signed May 20, abrogates Massachusetts' 1691 royal charter by removing power of appointing the governor's council from the elected assembly and giving it to the king. Act also gives the royal governor power to appoint (or nominate, for the king's assent) all provincial judges and sheriffs, makes the sheriffs responsible for choosing jury panels, and severely restricts town meetings. Administration of Justice Act, signed May 20, allows trials of those accused of committing capital crimes while enforcing the law or collecting revenue to be removed to Britain or Nova Scotia. Quartering Act, signed June 2, allows quartering of troops in occupied dwellings throughout the colonies. (Quebec Act, signed June 22, establishes civil government for Quebec without an elected legislature, grants Roman Catholic Church the right to collect tithes, and potentially extends the province's borders to the Mississippi and Ohio rivers; it is viewed as a hostile measure by many colonists.) General Thomas Gage, commander-in-chief of British forces in North America, is commissioned as royal governor of Massachusetts and arrives in Boston on May 13; British troops begin landing in the city in mid-June.

May–Sept.   Calls for an intercolonial congress to propose common measures of resistance are made in Providence, Philadelphia, New York, and Williamsburg, Virginia, May 17–27. Delegates to the congress are chosen in 12 colonies, June 15–August 25, either by the elected assembly, a committee of correspondence chosen by the assembly, special meetings of town or county representatives, or by a convention called by members of the elected assembly after its dissolution by the royal governor. Meeting of parish delegates in Georgia on August 10 votes against sending delegates to the congress, although it does adopt a declaration of rights and chooses a committee of correspondence. Unable to enforce the law outside of Boston, Gage begins fortifying the city on September 3.

Sept.   Congress (later known as First Continental Congress) opens in Philadelphia on September 5 and is eventually at-

tended by 56 delegates. Peyton Randolph (a delegate from
Virginia) is unanimously elected president (presiding
officer) of the Congress and Charles Thomson (who is not a
delegate) is chosen as its secretary. (Thomson will serve
until the end of the Second Continental Congress in 1789.)
John Adams (Massachusetts) asks if each colony is to have
an equal vote, or whether voting should be made proportional to the population or property of each colony. Patrick
Henry (Virginia) proposes that voting be made proportional
to free population, while John Jay (New York) and others
support giving each colony one vote. Congress adopts rule
giving each colony a single vote and makes its proceedings
secret.

On September 17 Congress endorses Suffolk County
Resolves, recently adopted by a convention in Massachusetts, which declare that no obedience is due the Coercive
Acts and advocate measures of resistance, including the formation of a provincial congress, nonpayment of taxes, the
boycott of British goods, and weekly militia training. Joseph
Galloway (Pennsylvania) submits plan on September 28 for a
union between Great Britain and the colonies that would
create "an inferior and distinct branch of the British legislature" for the government of the "general affairs" of America.
Each colonial assembly would send delegates to serve on a
grand council for three-year terms, while a president-general,
chosen by the king, would have an absolute veto over the
council's acts. Measures pertaining to the colonies could
originate in either the American council or the British Parliament, but the assent of both bodies would be required to
make them law. The plan is defeated by a 6–5 vote (proposal is expunged from official journal on October 22).

Oct.   On October 14 Congress adopts series of declarations and
resolves that denounce the Coercive Acts and Quebec Act as
"impolitic, unjust, and cruel, as well as unconstitutional," call
for the repeal of several other laws passed since 1763, protest
the dissolution of elected assemblies and the royal appointment of colonial councils, and condemn the keeping of a
standing army in the colonies in peacetime, without the consent of colonial legislatures, as "against law." The resolves
enumerate rights that the colonists are entitled to under "the
immutable laws of nature," the English constitution, and
their colonial charters, including life, liberty, and property,
the right to the common law of England, the right to trial by
a local jury, and the right to assemble and petition the king.
They assert that none of these rights can be taken from the
colonists without the consent of their own legislatures, and

claim for the colonial legislatures an "exclusive power of legislation . . . in all cases of taxation and internal polity,"
subject only to royal veto, while "cheerfully" consenting to
acts of Parliament that regulate external commerce for the
benefit of the whole empire.

Oct.   Congress votes on October 18 to create Continental Association, modeled on Virginia Association formed in early August. Its articles pledge the colonies to discontinue the slave
trade and cease importing goods from Great Britain, Ireland,
and the East and West Indies after December 1, 1774, to cease
consuming British goods after March 1, 1775, and, if necessary, to cease all exports (excluding rice) to Britain, Ireland,
and the West Indies after September 10, 1775. The Association
is to be enforced by elected town, city, and county committees, which will punish violators by publicity and boycott.
After preparing addresses to the British people and to the
king, Congress calls on the people of the colonies to elect
deputies to provincial congresses, which in turn will elect delegates to a second Congress, called for May 10, 1775. Congress
adjourns October 26.

Nov.–Dec.   By the end of the year, provincial congresses or conventions have been formed in eight colonies. (Provincial congresses will meet in New York in April 1775 and Georgia in
July 1775. In Pennsylvania the assembly continues under its
1701 proprietary charter until June 1776. Connecticut and
Rhode Island continue to govern themselves under their
royal charters, which grant them a high degree of auton-
omy, including the right to elect their own governors.)

1775   On February 9 Parliament declares Massachusetts to be in rebellion. The House of Commons endorses on February 27 a
conciliatory proposal by ministry of Lord North, under
which Parliament would refrain from laying revenue taxes
upon the colonies if the colonial assemblies agree to levy their
own taxes to support imperial defense. General Gage receives
orders from ministry on April 14 (written January 27 but not
dispatched until March 13) directing him to use force against
the Massachusetts rebels. Revolutionary War begins when
British attempt to destroy military supplies at Concord leads
to fighting with militia at Lexington, Concord, and along the
road back to Boston on April 19. Massachusetts forces begin
siege of city.

May–June   Second Continental Congress meets in Philadelphia on
May 10, with every state except Georgia present. Peyton Randolph is reelected president; after he returns to Virginia for
meeting of its assembly, John Hancock (Massachusetts) is

elected on May 24 (14 men serve as president of the Congress between 1774 and 1789). Massachusetts provincial congress asks Congress for advice on establishing a government during the conflict with Great Britain. Congress responds on June 9 by recommending that the colony elect a new assembly and council to govern itself until the crown agrees to abide by the 1691 charter (new Massachusetts legislature meets in late July, with the council serving as the executive). Congress votes on June 14 to form a Continental army. John Adams nominates George Washington (a Virginia delegate) as its commander, and he is unanimously approved on June 15 (Washington assumes command in Cambridge, Massachusetts, on July 3). To finance army, Congress votes on June 22 to issue of $2 million in paper money not backed by specie and pledges that the "12 Confederated Colonies" will redeem the issue (decides on July 29 that each colony will assume a share of the debt in proportion to its population).

July–Aug. Provincial congress meets in Georgia on July 4 and elects delegates to the Second Congress. On July 5 Congress approves the Olive Branch Petition, a conciliatory message to George III drafted by John Dickinson (Pennsylvania), and on July 6 adopts the Declaration of the Causes and Necessities of Taking Up Arms, drafted by Thomas Jefferson (Virginia) and rewritten by Dickinson. Declaration disavows intention to establish American independence, but asserts that colonists are "resolved to die freemen rather than to live slaves" and states that "foreign assistance is undoubtedly attainable" for the colonial cause. Congress appoints commissioners to negotiate with Indians, July 19, establishes a post office department headed by Benjamin Franklin (Pennsylvania), July 26, and rejects Lord North's proposal for conciliation, July 31, before adjourning on August 2. George III rejects Olive Branch Petition and on August 23 proclaims American colonies to be in rebellion (news reaches Congress on November 9).

Sept.–Dec. Delegates from Georgia join Congress when it reconvenes September 12. Congress begins organizing a navy in October, appoints on November 29 five-member Committee of Correspondence to establish contact with foreign supporters (becomes Committee for Foreign Affairs on April 17, 1777), and on December 6 disavows allegiance to Parliament. British rule continues to collapse throughout the 13 colonies; in Virginia, militia defeats force under Lord Dunmore, the royal governor, at Great Bridge on December 9 (Dunmore will destroy much of Norfolk and retreat to ships in Chesapeake Bay). George III signs Prohibitory Act on December 23, closing off commerce with America and making American ships and crews subject to seizure by the Royal Navy.

1776   On advice of Congress, New Hampshire provincial congress adopts form of government for the colony on January 5.

Jan.   *Common Sense*, pamphlet by Thomas Paine denouncing monarchical rule and advocating an independent American republic, is published in Philadelphia on January 10 (an expanded edition appears February 14); it sells tens of thousands of copies and is widely discussed throughout the colonies.

Mar.–Apr.   Congress votes on March 3 to send Silas Deane to Europe to buy military supplies. British garrison evacuates Boston on March 17 and sails to Nova Scotia. South Carolina provincial congress adopts a plan of government on March 26. Congress opens American ports to all nations except Britain on April 6. North Carolina provincial congress authorizes its delegates on April 12 to vote in Congress for independence, while reserving for North Carolina the "sole and exclusive right" of forming its own constitution and laws.

May   At the urging of his foreign minister the comte de Vergennes, Louis XVI of France authorizes clandestine support of the American insurgents on May 2. (After his arrival in Paris on July 7, Silas Deane will work with Vergennes and Pierre de Beaumarchais in arranging covert shipments of arms, supplies, and money; effort is soon joined by Spain.)

May–June   Rhode Island legislature disavows allegiance to George III on May 4. Under leadership of John Adams and Richard Henry Lee (Virginia), Congress recommends on May 10 that each of the "United Colonies" form a government and on May 15 calls for royal authority in the colonies to be "totally suppressed." On May 15 Virginia convention (successor to the convention called by the assembly after its dissolution by Lord Dunmore in 1774) instructs its delegates in Congress to propose a declaration of independence and the formation of a confederation; it also appoints a committee to prepare a declaration of rights and constitution for Virginia. Following these instructions, Richard Henry Lee submits resolution in Congress on June 7, declaring that "these United Colonies are, and of right ought to be, free and independent States," urging the formation of foreign alliances, and recommending the preparation and transmission of "a plan of confederation" to the colonies for their approval. John Dickinson, James Wilson (Pennsylvania), Robert R. Livingston (New York), and others argue that an immediate declaration of independence would be premature. Congress postpones decision and refers resolution on independence to a committee of five (Franklin, John Adams, Livingston, Jefferson, and Roger Sherman, a Connecticut delegate) on June 11; Jefferson begins drafting a declaration. On June 12 resolution to form an American confederation is submitted to a committee of 13, consisting of one representative from each colony; its chairman, John Dickinson, begins drafting confederation plan.

June

Virginia convention adopts a declaration of rights, drafted by George Mason, on June 12, and a state constitution, drafted largely by George Mason and containing preamble written by Jefferson, on June 29.

July

On July 1 Congress resumes debate on Lee's independence resolution and approves it on July 2, severing all political ties with Great Britain. After revising Jefferson's draft (changes include deletion of passage condemning slave trade), Congress adopts the Declaration of Independence on July 4.

Dickinson committee submits draft of twenty "Articles of Confederation and Perpetual Union" on July 12, under which the states would "enter into a firm League of Friendship" for their "common Defence, the Security of their Liberties, and their mutual and general Welfare." Each state is to retain such of its current laws as it thinks fit, and to have exclusive power over its "internal police, in all matters that shall not interfere with the Articles of Confederation." Inhabitants of each state are to enjoy reciprocal rights, liberties, privileges, and immunities in the other states, including those pertaining to trade. Each state has one vote in Congress, which is to have sole power over foreign affairs, war and peace, admiralty and prize courts, coining money, settling disputes among the states, setting the boundaries of states, including those whose colonial charters claim lands extending to the South Sea (Pacific Ocean), establishing new territories, and maintaining a postal service, while the states retain all taxing power and are allowed to lay import and export duties, subject to treaties made by Congress with foreign states. Common expenses are to be paid out of a central treasury, supported by requisitions on the states, apportioned according to population and levied by the state legislatures. A Council of State, consisting of one delegate from each state, is to manage the general affairs of the Confederation. Troops are to be requisitioned from the states in proportion to their white inhabitants. Major issues are to require approval of nine states, lesser issues seven, and amendments to the Articles must be approved by every state legislature. Delegates to Congress are to be annually appointed by the state legislatures, and may be recalled at any time.

July–Aug.   Congress begins debating draft Articles on July 22. Frank-
                lin, John Adams, James Wilson, and Benjamin Rush (Penn-
                sylvania) argue that representation of the states in Congress
                should be made proportional to their population. Samuel
                Chase (Maryland) moves amendment to count only whites
                when apportioning treasury requisitions, contending that
                slaves should be treated as property, not persons, and that it
                is unfair to tax southern property while exempting northern
                property. His amendment is defeated in a 7–5 vote along
                sectional lines on August 1, with Delaware supporting the
                proposal and Georgia divided. Delegates from states with
                western land claims oppose giving Congress power to set
                state boundaries (Massachusetts, Connecticut, Virginia,
                North and South Carolina, and Georgia have charter claims,
                while New York has a claim based on a treaty with the Iro-
                quois Confederacy). Congress has revised draft of Articles
                printed on August 20, but then postpones further debate.

Aug.–Sept.   British troops land on Long Island, August 22, and win
                battle there on August 27, beginning series of American de-
                feats in the New York region. On September 26 Congress
                appoints Franklin, Jefferson, and Silas Deane as commission-
                ers to negotiate treaties with European powers. (Franklin ar-
                rives in Paris on December 21; Jefferson declines position and
                is replaced by Arthur Lee, who is already in Europe.)

Nov.–Dec.   Fort Washington in upper Manhattan surrenders to the
                British on November 16, and Fort Lee, New Jersey, is evacu-
                ated November 20, beginning Washington's retreat across
                New Jersey. Congress adjourns session in Philadelphia De-
                cember 12 and meets in Baltimore on December 20 (will re-
                convene in Philadelphia on March 12, 1777). Washington's
                army crosses the Delaware on the night of December 25 and
                defeats Hessians at Trenton on the morning of December 26.

July–Dec.   States continue to frame and adopt their own constitu-
                tions, including New Jersey, July 2, Delaware, September 20,
                Pennsylvania, September 28, Maryland, November 9, and
                North Carolina, December 18. (After its adoption the Penn-
                sylvania constitution becomes the focus of a continuing polit-
                ical struggle within the state between its "Constitutionalist"
                supporters and "Republican" opponents. Connecticut and
                Rhode Island revise their colonial charters to eliminate refer-
                ences to royal authority; Connecticut adopts its first state
                constitution in 1818, Rhode Island in 1842.)

1777   Georgia convention adopts state constitution on February 5
                (convention had been elected in October 1776 to draw up a
                plan of government).

April   When Congress resumes discussion of the draft Articles on April 18, Thomas Burke (North Carolina) moves the adoption of a new article declaring that each state "retains its sovereignty, freedom and independence, and every Power, Jurisdiction and right, which is not by this confederation expressly delegated to the United States, in Congress assembled." The amendment is carried in late April over the opposition of James Wilson and Richard Henry Lee.

New York convention (successor to its provincial congress) adopts state constitution on April 20 (none of the state constitutions adopted in 1776–77 are submitted to the people for ratification).

May–July   On May 5 the Massachusetts legislature asks the towns to grant it the power at the next election to frame a constitution; the towns agree, and on June 17 the new legislature resolves itself into a constitutional convention and appoints a drafting committee. Vermont adopts constitution on July 8 that forbids slavery and declares the state independent from both Great Britain and New York (Vermont will not join the United States until 1791).

Sept.–Oct.   Congress ends session in Philadelphia on September 18 (British occupy the city on September 25) and reconvenes in York, Pennsylvania, on September 30 (will remain there until June 27, 1778). In series of votes on the draft Articles of Confederation, Congress defeats on October 7 amendments to make state representation in Congress proportional to population or to contributions to the central treasury; approves on October 14 amendment that changes the basis for apportioning financial requisitions from a state's population to the value of its land and improvements; and votes on October 15 to remove from Congress the power to determine western state boundaries.

Oct.   After series of defeats, British army under General John Burgoyne surrenders to Americans under General Horatio Gates at Saratoga, New York, on October 17 (news of victory strengthens position of the comte de Vergennes, who advocates an open French alliance with the United States).

Oct.–Nov.   Congress further amends draft Articles, limiting the power of congressional commerce treaties to restrict state imposts and replacing the proposed Council of State with a Committee of the States, to sit only when Congress is in recess. A procedure is established for submitting boundary disputes between the states to commissioners selected by Congress, but the commissioners will have no power to enforce their rulings, and no state may be deprived of its territory for the benefit of the United States. On November 15 Congress approves revised Articles of Confederation and submits them to the state legislatures for ratification. The Maryland legislature instructs its congressional delegates on December 22 to secure an amendment to the Articles restoring congressional power to fix western state boundaries. (Advocates of congressional control over state boundaries argue that the land west of the Appalachians will be won from the British and Indians only by the common sacrifice of all the states, and assert that the "landless" states need western land to give as bounties to their soldiers. Opponents of congressional control charge that land speculators, who include many prominent Maryland and Pennsylvania political leaders, are seeking to protect their purchases from being invalidated by the Virginia legislature, which has the strongest claim to authority over the territory northwest of the Ohio River.)

Dec.   Washington begins winter encampment at Valley Forge, Pennsylvania, and appeals to Congress for supplies (will repeatedly ask Congress and the states for money and supplies throughout the war, often with meager results). Issues of Continental paper currency reach $38 million.

1778   American commissioners in Paris sign two treaties with France on February 6. Under their terms, France recognizes the independence of the United States and receives commercial privileges in American markets. In the event that French recognition of the United States leads to war between France and Great Britain, France and the United States pledge to fight and negotiate as allies, with the aim of securing complete American independence. France also renounces all claims to Canada and to land east of the Mississippi in return for an American commitment to help defend French possessions in the West Indies.

Feb.   New Hampshire legislature calls on February 26 for the election of a special convention to draw up a state constitution, which will then be submitted to town meetings and take effect if approved by three-fourths of the state's voters (convention meets on June 10). Massachusetts legislature submits proposed constitution, which lacks a bill of rights, to the town meetings on February 28 for ratification by two-thirds of the freemen; it is eventually rejected by vote of 9,972 to 2,083.

Mar.   South Carolina general assembly approves on March 19 a new constitution to replace the temporary form of government adopted in 1776.

Apr.–Dec.   French fleet sails from Toulon for America on April 11 (it arrives off Delaware Bay on July 8). By April 25 ten states have ratified the Articles; Maryland, New Jersey, and Delaware continue to oppose ratification because of the western land dispute. War breaks out between Britain and France after their naval forces clash in the English Channel on June 17. From June 22 to June 25, Congress considers and rejects 37 motions for changes or amendments to the Articles of Confederation proposed by seven state legislatures. Eight of the ratifying states sign the Articles on July 9 (the other two ratifying states sign by July 24). New Jersey legislature ratifies the Articles of Confederation on November 20. British capture Savannah, Georgia, on December 29, as the major theater of war shifts to the south.

1779   With more than $100 million in circulation, Continental currency trades for specie at 8–1. Delaware legislature ratifies the Articles of Confederation on February 1.

Feb.–June   Massachusetts legislature asks the towns on February 20 if special elections should be held for a new constitutional convention, independent of the legislature (towns agree, and convention meets on September 1). New Hampshire convention elected in 1778 submits proposed constitution to town meetings on June 5; it is rejected by a majority of the voters.

June–Sept.   After entering into alliance with France, Spain declares war on Great Britain on June 21 (Spain does not recognize American independence). After months of debate, Congress approves on August 14 minimum terms to be sought when peace negotiations begin; they include independence, evacuation of British forces, borders extending to the Mississippi in the west and the 31st parallel in the south, and free navigation of the Mississippi (navigation right is especially sought by southerners), but not the protection of fishing rights off Newfoundland (which is of special importance to New England delegates). On September 1 Congress resolves to limit emissions of Continental paper money at $200 million (total issues have reached $160 million). John Jay, president of the Congress, sends circular letter to the states on September 13 urging them to collect taxes in order to pay their requisitions into the common treasury. Congress appoints John Adams as peace negotiator and Jay envoy to Spain on September 27. (During his stay in Madrid from January 1780 to May 1782, Jay will be unable to secure Spanish recognition of American independence, negotiate treaties of alliance or commerce, or secure a significant loan.)

Oct.–Dec.   Autumn session of Virginia legislature ends state taxation of Anglicans in support of their own church and considers two proposed bills concerning religion. One would establish

Christianity in Virginia and levy a general assessment in its support, with taxpayers choosing which denomination their taxes would go to; the other, drafted by Jefferson in 1777, protects the free exercise of "religious opinions or belief" while forbidding taxation to support any religion. Neither law is passed.

1780 Continental currency trades for specie at 40–1. New York legislature offers on February 1 to cede its western lands, claimed through treaty with the Iroquois, to Congress (cession is accepted by Congress in October 1782). An act for the gradual abolition of slavery is passed by the Pennsylvania legislature on March 1 (gradual emancipation laws will be passed in Connecticut and Rhode Island in 1784).

Mar. Massachusetts convention submits new constitution, drafted mainly by John Adams, to the towns on March 2 for ratification. (The constitution is approved by the towns, declared ratified on June 16, and takes effect on October 25, 1780.)

Mar.–Oct. Congress approves plan on March 18 for retiring existing Continental currency, valued by the plan at 40–1 against specie, and replacing it with $10 million in new paper money (plan fails, and by spring 1781 Continental paper money has ceased to circulate). British take 5,000 prisoners when American garrison at Charleston, South Carolina, surrenders on May 12 (the largest American capitulation of the war). American force under Horatio Gates is routed by British and Loyalists at Camden, South Carolina, on August 16; Americans retreat to Hillsborough, North Carolina. Treachery of Benedict Arnold is revealed on September 25. Connecticut cedes most of its western lands on October 10 (cession is accepted in 1786). Congress grants Continental officers half-pay pensions for life on October 21.

1781 Pennsylvania Continental regiments mutiny on January 1 over pay and enlistments (negotiations with Pennsylvania state government end mutiny on January 8, the largest of several Continental mutinies in 1780–81). Virginia legislature offers on January 2 to cede to Congress its lands northwest of the Ohio River, on the condition that new states be eventually formed out of the territory and that purchases made from the Indians by land companies be voided (cession is supported by Jefferson, Madison, and Richard Henry Lee).

Jan.–Mar. Congress begins establishment of executive departments with the creation of the Department of Foreign Affairs on January 10 (executive duties had previously been carried out by various committees of Congress). The Chevalier de la Luzerne, French minister to the United States, responds to pleas from Maryland for French naval protection against British raids in the Chesapeake Bay by urging Maryland to ratify the Articles; the Maryland legislature approves them on February 2. Congress votes February 3 to ask states for power to levy a 5 percent impost on imports in order to pay for the war; measure requires approval of all 13 state legislatures. Departments of War and Finance are established by Congress, February 6, and Robert Morris, a wealthy Pennsylvania merchant, is named superintendent of finance on February 20. Maryland delegates sign the Articles of Confederation on March 1, completing their ratification.

Mar.–May   On March 16 James Madison (Virginia), James Duane (New York), and James Varnum (Rhode Island) propose amending the Articles to give Congress the power to coerce states that defy Congress or fail to fulfill their requisitions (proposal is referred to committee and is never approved). Robert Morris takes office on May 14 after successfully demanding the power to control his subordinates. On May 26 he wins congressional approval for the chartering of a national bank (Bank of North America, first commercial bank in the United States, is chartered December 31) and begins to ease financial crisis with the help of French loans and subsidies and a large Dutch loan guaranteed by France.

May   After American victory at Cowpens, South Carolina (January 17) and drawn battle at Guilford Courthouse, North Carolina (March 15), Lord Cornwallis decides to strengthen British position in the Carolinas by attacking Virginia, a major source of supplies for American forces in the South. On May 20 Cornwallis reaches Petersburg, Virginia, and begins his Virginia campaign.

June   Second convention meets in New Hampshire in June and submits to the voters a new proposed constitution, which calls for indirect election of the state house of representatives; it is rejected.

June–Aug.   Congress names Franklin, Jay, Henry Laurens, and Jefferson as additional peace negotiators (Jefferson declines) and on June 15 revises its instructions, making independence and the preservation of the French alliance the only essential peace terms and requiring the negotiators to take no action without the "knowledge and concurrence" of French ministers and to "govern" themselves by "their advice and opinion." On August 10 Congress chooses Robert R. Livingston over Arthur Lee to be secretary for foreign affairs (French envoy La Luzerne actively supports revision of instructions and Livingston's election).

Sept.–Oct.   French naval victory in Chesapeake Bay on September 5 prevents evacuation of army under Cornwallis from its base at Yorktown, Virginia. American and French armies under Washington and Rochambeau begin siege of Yorktown on September 28. Cornwallis surrenders on October 19, ending major fighting in the Revolutionary War. General Benjamin Lincoln becomes secretary at war on October 30. Morris moves to restore national finances to a specie basis, while states begin confronting problem of their war debts and the depreciation of their own wartime paper money issues.

1782   After the House of Commons votes against continuing the war in America, Lord North resigns as prime minister on March 20. The new ministry of Lord Rockingham opens peace negotiations with Benjamin Franklin in Paris on April 12 (Franklin conducts negotiations independently of the French, despite his congressional instructions).

Feb.–Apr.   In response to uncertainty regarding congressional power to charter a bank, Robert Morris and his allies obtain a state charter for the Bank of North America from the Pennsylvania legislature. With states failing to meet their requisitions, Morris ceases paying interest on Continental loan office certificates (the major form of outstanding federal debt) and tells public creditors that payments cannot be resumed unless the impost is adopted. (Loan officers later begin issuing certificates for interest due, and in April 1784 Congress votes to allow states to pay part of their requisitions with these certificates.)

June–Dec.   New Hampshire convention reconvenes in June and revises the constitution rejected by the towns in 1781 (it is resubmitted in August but again fails to win approval). New York legislature approves in July a resolution, probably drafted by Alexander Hamilton, calling for a national convention to give Congress the power to raise money. Rhode Island refuses on November 1 to ratify the amendment levying the 5 percent impost, which 11 other states have agreed to (Georgia had not yet considered the measure); when Virginia repeals its ratification of the impost on December 7, the measure lapses. Maryland legislature adopts law allowing Maryland holders of Continental loan office certificates to exchange them for state securities.

Nov.   Franklin, John Adams, John Jay, and Henry Laurens sign preliminary peace treaty with Great Britain in Paris on

November 30 (agreement is to be implemented after Anglo-French treaty is negotiated). Its terms provide for: a cessation of hostilities; the evacuation of British forces from American territory; British recognition of an independent United States with borders extending north to the Great Lakes, west to the Mississippi, and south to the 31st parallel; the honoring of debts owed to creditors in the other country; the recognition of American fishing rights off Canada; and a pledge that Congress would "earnestly recommend" to the state legislatures the restoration of the rights and properties of Loyalists.

Dec.

On December 30 a special commission, formed by Congress at Pennsylvania's request to rule on the long-standing dispute between Pennsylvania and Connecticut over the Wyoming Valley in northeastern Pennsylvania, awards jurisdiction to Pennsylvania while recommending that land claims of Connecticut settlers in the region be recognized.

1783

On January 6 Congress receives memorial from Continental Army officers protesting the failure of Congress to pay them and asking that they receive several years' full pay in lieu of the lifetime pensions at half pay granted in 1780. Britain, France, and Spain sign preliminary peace agreement on January 20 (Britain proclaims an end to hostilities on February 4). Robert Morris tells Congress on January 24 that he will resign as superintendent of finance on May 31; Congress begins debating new financial measures and Morris continues in office. Anonymous address is circulated among Continental officers camped at Newburgh, New York, on March 10, denouncing congressional inaction on pay and inciting the army to defy Congress if its demands are not met. Washington condemns the address at an assembly held on March 15 and calls upon his officers to express their loyalty to Congress; they adopt a resolution doing so. Congress commutes officers' pensions to five years full pay on March 22, ratifies the preliminary peace treaty on April 15, and approves on April 18 a new plan for restoring public credit. It calls for levying specific excise duties and a general 5 percent impost for 25 years in order to pay the interest and principal on the national war debt. Collectors of the revenue are to be appointed by the states but would be removable by Congress, and the income collected is to be credited to each state's requisition quota. The plan also calls on the states to pay an additional $1.5 million annually for 25 years toward the discharge of the debt. A proposed amendment to the Articles, submitted to the states on April 18, changes the basis for apportioning requisitions from property to population, with "other persons" (slaves) counted as three-fifths of whites. Financial measure is opposed by Alexander Hamilton (New York), who favors stronger revenue measures, and by the Rhode Island delegates, who oppose any national impost.

May–June   On May 26 Congress furloughs Continental troops who enlisted for the duration of the war. Robert R. Livingston resigns as secretary for foreign affairs on June 5. Washington sends circular letter to state governors and legislatures on June 8, urging adoption of the congressional finance measures and the strengthening of the federal union. Pennsylvania soldiers from the Continental Army surround the State House in Philadelphia, where Congress and the Pennsylvania executive council are meeting, on June 21 and demand back pay. When the Pennsylvania council declines to use the militia to restore order, Congress leaves the city and reconvenes in Princeton, New Jersey, on June 26.

June   New Hampshire convention submits fourth proposed constitution to the voters in June (it is declared ratified on October 31 and goes into effect in June 1784).

July–Sept.   British government issues order on July 2 closing West Indian ports to American shipping and forbidding importation of American produce (Britain will also restrict ability of American ships to enter British ports). Final peace treaty between Great Britain and the United States of America is signed in Paris on September 3 (terms are similar to those of preliminary agreement of November 30, 1782).

Oct.–Nov.   Unable to agree on a single site for a permanent seat of government, Congress votes on October 7 to establish a "federal town" on the Delaware, near Trenton, New Jersey, then approves on October 20 the creation of a second capital on the Potomac, near Georgetown, Maryland, intending to alternate sessions between the two sites. Session in Princeton adjourns November 4 and Congress reconvenes in Annapolis, Maryland, on November 26, planning to move between Annapolis and Trenton until permanent capitals are ready.

Nov.–Dec.   Benjamin Lincoln resigns as secretary at war on November 12. British evacuate New York City on November 25 and Washington leads his troops into the city later in the day. Washington has farewell meeting with his officers on December 4 and then goes to Annapolis, where he addresses Congress on December 23 before resigning his commission.

1784   Congress ratifies final peace treaty on January 14 and calls on states to rescind confiscations of Loyalist property and repeal laws blocking the collection of debts owed British creditors. On March 1 Congress accepts Virginia's cession of its western land north of the Ohio and begins considering a proposal, written by Jefferson, for governing the territory. The plan would create ten new states, each not less than 100 or more than 150 miles square. Their free male inhabitants would temporarily adopt the constitution and laws of one of the original states, and then hold a constitutional convention when the state's free population reached 20,000. When a new state's free population equaled that of the smallest original state, it would join the Confederation on an equal basis, with a single vote in Congress. Each new state would be required to have a republican form of government and to assume a share of the federal debt, and slavery and involuntary servitude would be forbidden in all of the new states after 1800. After deleting the antislavery provision and making minor changes, Congress adopts the plan on April 23 (proposal is forwarded to the states in 1785 along with ordinance on western land sales). On April 30 Congress asks the states to grant it the power to regulate foreign commerce for 15 years so that it can respond to British trade restrictions. John Jay is appointed secretary for foreign affairs on May 7 (will not assume office, vacant since the resignation of Robert R. Livingston in June 1783, until December 21). After the Pennsylvania assembly tries to evict Connecticut settlers from the Wyoming Valley, fighting breaks out in May between settlers and Pennsylvania troops. On June 26 Spain orders the lower Mississippi closed to American navigation until the boundaries of Louisiana and West Florida are settled (the Spanish do not recognize the American frontiers established by the 1783 Anglo-American peace treaty).

June

In *Rutgers* v. *Waddington* Alexander Hamilton argues before the New York Mayor's Court on June 29 that the terms of the 1783 peace treaty are binding on the states and that a New York state law allowing suits against Loyalists should be voided by the court for violating the treaty. Chief Judge James Duane declares that while states cannot "alter or abridge" a treaty ratified by Congress, it would be "subversive of all government" for the court to reject a legislative enactment. The court then issues a ruling favorable to the defendant, asserting that the legislature could not have intended to violate the treaty and that judges should interpret the law accordingly (decision is criticized by the legislature and is widely debated in the press).

Sept.–Dec.   Second session of the Pennsylvania Council of Censors condemns the assembly's actions in the Wyoming Valley, and on September 15 the assembly votes to restore lands to settlers dispossessed in May. Autumn session of Virginia legislature considers new bill for levying a general assessment in support of the Christian religion. It is supported by Patrick Henry, Richard Henry Lee, and Edmund Pendleton, but opposed by James Madison, who succeeds on December 24 in postponing its final consideration until the fall of 1785.

Nov.–Dec.   Robert Morris leaves office as superintendent of finance on November 1 and is eventually replaced by a three-man Board of Treasury (board does not begin work until spring 1785). Congress convenes in Trenton on November 1 and adjourns on December 24 after deciding to meet in New York City until capital on banks of the Delaware is built (holds first session in New York on January 11, 1785, and will continue to meet there for the remainder of the Confederation).

1785   United States defaults on its French loans (will continue with difficulty to make interest payments on Dutch loans negotiated by John Adams in 1782 and 1784). On February 4 the Society for Promoting the Manumission of Slaves is formed in New York, with John Jay as its president and Alexander Hamilton as one of its counselors. (When Hamilton proposes that members begin by freeing their own slaves, the members decline, and the society will concentrate on protecting freed slaves and educating black children.) Congress appoints John Adams as the first American minister to Great Britain on February 24 and names Thomas Jefferson minister to France on March 10, replacing Franklin, who is planning to return to America (Adams and Jefferson are already in Europe, where they have been attempting to negotiate commercial treaties with continental governments). General Henry Knox is appointed secretary at war on March 8, filling position vacant since November 1783.

Mar.   Pennsylvania assembly votes on March 16 to assume payment of the interest on the national debt owed to Pennsylvanians, who own approximately one-third of the domestic national debt. The assumption measure, which is to be funded by selling public lands, levying £200,000 in annual taxes, and issuing £150,000 in paper money, is opposed by advocates of a stronger national government, including Robert Morris and John Dickinson, but is supported by many public creditors. (By the end of 1786 six other states issue paper money. In South Carolina and Pennsylvania, it cannot be used to pay private debts; in New York it can be used to pay creditors who sue; and in North Carolina, Georgia, New Jersey, and Rhode Island, it circulates as full legal tender. Issues are proposed in the other states, and in Maryland the senate defeats paper money bills that pass the house of delegates in December 1785 and December 1786.)

Mar.

Commissioners appointed by the Virginia and Maryland legislatures meet at Mount Vernon, March 25–28, to discuss disputes over navigation of the Potomac River and Chesapeake Bay. After reaching agreement on several commercial and financial measures, the commissioners write to the Pennsylvania executive council, proposing that Pennsylvania join in plans to link the Potomac and Ohio valleys by canals.

Mar.–May

On March 28 Congress begins considering proposed amendment to the Articles giving Congress permanent power to regulate commerce (measure is never approved for submission to the states). Congress passes ordinance for the disposal of western lands on May 20. It calls for surveying townships, six miles square, which will be divided for sale into 640-acre lots at minimum price of $1 an acre. One lot per township is to be reserved for supporting public education (proposal to reserve another lot for supporting the religion of the majority of the township inhabitants is narrowly defeated).

June

In late June Madison writes a "Memorial and Remonstrance" attacking the proposed Virginia bill for a general assessment in support of religion. Memorial is anonymously circulated with the help of George Mason and is signed by over 1,500 people (nearly 11,000 people sign petitions opposing the bill before the October 1785 legislative session opens, and the measure fails to win passage).

July–Dec.

John Adams writes Jay that a commercial treaty with Britain is impossible unless the states adopt uniform retaliatory measures against discriminatory British trading practices. Jay begins talks with Spanish envoy Diego de Gardoqui in July and is instructed by Congress on August 25 to negotiate a treaty recognizing American navigation rights on the Mississippi and the southwestern frontiers established in the 1783 peace treaty. In September the Constitutionalist majority in the Pennsylvania assembly repeals the charter of the Bank of North America and establishes a state loan office to issue paper money to farmers. On November 30 John Adams formally demands the evacuation of British garrisons from the Northwest in compliance with the 1783 treaty. Maryland legislature approves on December 5 agreement reached at Mount Vernon conference and proposes that Delaware join Maryland, Virginia, and Pennsylvania in an interstate navigation compact (Mount Vernon agreement is also ratified by Virginia legislature).

1786   In Virginia Madison wins passage on January 16 of revised version of the statute on religious freedom drafted by Jefferson in 1777 and first debated in 1779. (Madison writes to Jefferson that he hopes "this Country" has "extinguished for ever the ambitious hope of making laws for the human mind.") On January 21 the Virginia legislature calls for a general meeting of the states to consider adopting a uniform system of commercial regulations and appoints five commissioners to attend.

Feb.–May   A committee investigating finances reports to Congress on February 3 that only $2.4 million of the $15.6 million requisitioned from the states since October 1, 1781, has been received. British government informs John Adams on February 28 that they will not evacuate northwestern garrisons until Americans fulfill their treaty obligations to pay British creditors and compensate Loyalists. Pennsylvania and New York legislatures vote to assume principal on national debt owed their citizens, allowing them to exchange federal certificates for state securities. On May 4 the New York legislature approves the 1783 impost while refusing Congress the power to remove state-appointed collectors and insisting that New York paper money be accepted in payment of impost duties; Congress rejects these conditions on August 23. (By summer 1786 the other 12 states have approved the impost, although Pennsylvania vote is conditioned on supplementary funds being provided by all 13 states, a condition Pennsylvania legislature will refuse to drop despite congressional plea in September 1786. Every state except New Hampshire and Rhode Island has ratified the amendment to the Articles changing the basis for apportioning requisitions from property to population. All 13 states have granted Congress the power to regulate commerce for 15 years, but in varying forms that must be reconciled before the power can be exercised.)

May   Rhode Island legislature issues £100,000 in paper money in May and makes it legal tender for all debts. When creditors refuse to accept the money, the legislature establishes penalties for not accepting the money and denies trial by jury to those sued under the act.

July   Farmers in Massachusetts, burdened by debt and requirement to pay rising taxes in specie, petition the legislature for paper money and laws to suspend home and farm foreclosures. The legislature fails to pass significant relief measures before adjourning on July 8, but does grant supplemental funds requested by Congress in 1783 (tax burden is already high due to effort by the state government to quickly pay off its war debt).

Aug.   Jay reports to Congress on August 3 on the terms of a tentative Spanish-American commercial treaty he has negotiated with Gardoqui and recommends that the United States forgo its claim to free navigation of the Mississippi for 25 or 30 years in return for Spanish agreement to the treaty. On August 7, a 12-man committee of the Congress reports seven amendments to the Articles, drafted by Charles Pinckney (South Carolina), Nathan Dane (Massachusetts), and William Samuel Johnson (Connecticut), which would give Congress the power to regulate foreign and interstate commerce and directly levy taxes in states that failed to meet their requisitions, establish a seven-member federal judicial court, and reduce to 11 the number of states needed to approve future federal revenue measures. Amendments are not considered by the full Congress, which begins debating the proposed Jay-Gardoqui treaty. With all of the southern states opposed, on August 29 Congress votes 7–5 (Delaware is absent) to repeal its 1785 instructions requiring Jay to obtain free navigation of the Mississippi (because nine states are needed to ratify a treaty, the negotiations do not progress).

Aug.–Sept.   In Hatfield, Massachusetts, 50 Hampshire County towns meet, August 22–25, and adopt resolutions calling for the abolition of the state senate, reapportionment of the state house of representatives, issuing paper money, a reduction in court fees, changes in the court and tax systems, and moving the state capital from Boston (other county conventions make similar demands). The convention appeals against mob action, but on August 29 armed men prevent a court from sitting at Northampton. Court sessions are also broken up at Worcester, September 5, and Concord and Great Barrington, September 12, in an attempt to block further foreclosures.

Sept.   Convention called by Virginia legislature in January 1786 to consider new commercial regulations meets in Annapolis, September 11–14, and is attended by 12 commissioners from New York, New Jersey, Delaware, Pennsylvania, and Virginia (representatives from New Hampshire, Massachusetts, Rhode Island, and North Carolina do not arrive in time, and Georgia, South Carolina, Connecticut, and Maryland do not appoint delegates). With only five states represented, the meeting does not consider specific proposals regarding commerce, but does unanimously adopt a report, drafted by Hamilton, for transmission to Congress and all 13 states. It proposes that every state appoint representatives to meet in Philadelphia on May 14, 1787, to "devise such further provisions as shall appear to them necessary to render the constitution of the Fœderal Government adequate to the exigencies of the Union; and to report an Act for that purpose" to Congress for its approval, and then to the legislatures of every state for their unanimous confirmation. (Congress receives the report on September 20, refers it to a committee on October 11, and takes no further action before its session ends on November 3.)

In *Trevett* v. *Weeden* the Rhode Island superior court of judicature is asked to void the state's paper money enforcement act because it unconstitutionally abridges the fundamental right to trial by jury guaranteed by the Rhode Island colonial charter (which serves as the state constitution). Court rules on September 25 that it lacks jurisdiction over the case, effectively making the statute unenforceable. (When newspapers report that several of the judges delivered opinions holding the law unconstitutional, the court is summoned before a special session of the legislature and accused of subverting the legislative power; however, a motion to remove the judges fails, and the enforcement act is repealed.)

Sept.–Oct.   Massachusetts governor James Bowdoin orders 600 militiamen under General William Shepard to protect the sitting of the supreme judicial court at Springfield, where they are confronted on September 26 by 500 insurgents, led by former Revolutionary War captain Daniel Shays, who are trying to prevent indictments from being issued for previous court disruptions. (Although Shays never becomes the sole leader of the Massachusetts insurgents, the rebellion becomes associated with him throughout the country.) The court adjourns without taking action. When Congress sends Secretary at War Knox to Massachusetts to investigate the rebellion, Knox reports to Congress, Washington, and others that the insurgents number 12,000–15,000 and seek the common distribution of all property. Although it lacks power under the Articles to intervene in domestic disturbances, Congress authorizes Knox on October 20 to raise 1,340 troops and protect the federal arsenal at Springfield from the rebels, publicly claiming that the troops are to fight Indians along the Ohio River (federal troops are never used and their real purpose soon becomes known). Massachusetts rebels continue to block court sittings in the fall (crowds also resist debt collection in rural areas of New Hampshire, Pennsylvania, Maryland, Virginia, and South Carolina in 1786–87).

Nov.–Dec.   Legislatures appoint delegates to the Philadelphia conven-
                   tion in New Jersey, November 23, Virginia, December 4, and
                   Pennsylvania, December 30 (in Virginia Patrick Henry and
                   Richard Henry Lee will decline appointment).

1787   Delegates to the Philadelphia convention are appointed by
                   legislatures in North Carolina, January 6, and New Hamp-
                   shire, January 17. In New York the legislature adopts on Janu-
                   ary 26 a comprehensive law, drafted by John Lansing, that
                   lists the rights and privileges of citizens.

Jan.–Apr.   Massachusetts governor James Bowdoin calls for 4,400
                   militia to assemble under General Benjamin Lincoln and
                   suppress Shays' rebels. When Shays attempts to seize the
                   Springfield arsenal on January 25, militia under Shepard open
                   fire and kill four rebels. Lincoln pursues the insurgents to
                   Petersham and scatters them on February 4. Shays and other
                   leaders flee to Vermont, and the organized insurrection ends
                   (five men are killed in skirmish near Sheffield on February 27,
                   and unrest continues in western Massachusetts until June).
                   Massachusetts legislature passes disqualification act on Feb-
                   ruary 16, barring most rebels from holding office, voting, or
                   serving as jurors for three years. In April elections in Massa-
                   chusetts Governor Bowdoin is overwhelmingly defeated by
                   John Hancock. Bowdoin and Hancock eventually pardon 14
                   men condemned to death for treason and murder during the
                   rebellion (two rebels are hanged for burglary). The new leg-
                   islature does not levy a direct tax in 1787 and adopts measures
                   that give some relief to debtors.

Feb.–Mar.   Delaware legislature appoints delegates to the Philadelphia
                   convention on February 3 and instructs them not to agree
                   to any change in the equality of state representation in
                   Congress. New session of Congress, designated to meet on
                   November 6, 1786, achieves first regular quorum on Febru-
                   ary 12 and resumes consideration of the Annapolis report.
                   On February 21 it calls for a convention to meet in Philadel-
                   phia on May 14 for "the sole and express purpose of revising
                   the Articles of Confederation" and directs that proposed
                   changes be submitted to Congress for its approval. Dele-
                   gates are appointed in Massachusetts, March 3, New York,
                   March 6, and South Carolina, March 8; in Massachusetts
                   and New York they are instructed by the legislature to limit
                   the convention to revising the Articles. On March 14 Rhode
                   Island legislature refuses to elect delegates (will again decline
                   on May 5 and June 16, despite efforts of legislators from
                   trading towns of Newport and Providence to have state
                   represented).

Mar.–Apr.   While attending Congress in the spring, Madison writes a
                memorandum, "Vices of the Political System of the United
                States," and outlines principles for a new plan of government
                in letters to Jefferson, Edmund Randolph, and Washington.

May   In *Bayard* v. *Singleton* the North Carolina supreme court
                voids a state law requiring the dismissal of recovery suits
                brought against owners of confiscated Loyalist property, rul-
                ing that it violates the right to trial by jury protected by the
                state constitution.

                Connecticut legislature elects convention delegates on May
                17 and instructs them only to revise the existing Articles.
                Maryland legislature elects delegates on May 26. (Of the 74
                delegates chosen by 12 states, 55 will attend the convention at
                one time or another.)

                On May 14 the convention meets in Philadelphia but fails
                to achieve a quorum. Virginia delegates caucus while wait-
                ing for the convention to begin. Quorum is achieved on
                May 25, when seven state delegations are present (delega-
                tions from Connecticut and Massachusetts achieve voting
                quorum on May 28, Georgia on May 31, Maryland on June
                2, and New Hampshire delegates, possibly delayed by lack
                of funds, arrive on July 23; not all delegations will maintain
                a voting quorum throughout the convention). George
                Washington is unanimously elected president of the conven-
                tion and a committee (Hamilton, Charles Pinckney, George
                Wythe) is appointed to prepare rules. Convention adopts
                rules, May 28–29, that make their deliberations secret, give
                each state delegation a single vote, let questions be decided
                by a majority of states present, and allow for the reconsider-
                ation of matters already voted on.

                On May 29 Virginia governor Edmund Randolph opens
                the main deliberations by giving a speech on the defects of
                the Confederation and presenting 15 resolutions, drafted by
                the Virginia caucus, which incorporate many of Madison's
                ideas (resolutions become known as the Virginia plan). The
                resolutions propose establishing a national legislature with
                two branches, in which states would be represented and
                vote in proportion either to their "quotas of contribution"
                or to their free population. The first branch is to be elected
                by the people of the states and would be subject to rotation
                in office and recall, while the second branch is to be elected
                by the first branch, choosing from nominees submitted by
                the respective state legislatures. Each branch would have the
                right to originate legislation. The national legislature would
                have all of the powers of the existing Congress, as well as
                the power to "legislate in all cases to which the separate

States are incompetent," to veto all state laws which it thinks unconstitutional, and "to call forth the force of the Union" against any state failing to fulfill its national obligations. A national executive would be chosen by the national legislature and exercise the executive rights vested in Congress under the Articles of Confederation. The executive would be ineligible for reelection (its term, as well as those of both branches of the legislature, are left unspecified in the resolutions). A national judiciary, with both supreme and inferior tribunals, is to be chosen by the legislature and serve for good behavior (for life, unless removed for misconduct); its jurisdiction would include impeachment of national officers and "questions which may involve the national peace and harmony." The executive and members of the judiciary would form a council of revision with power to examine and veto all acts of the national legislature (including vetoes of state laws); the council's veto could be overridden by an unspecified vote in each legislative branch. New states could be admitted by a less than unanimous vote in the legislature and a "Republican Government" would be guaranteed by the United States to each state. The resolutions also call for continuing the present Congress until the new government takes power, establishing an amendment procedure for the new "Articles of Union" not involving the national legislature, and submitting the new plan of government to special assemblies chosen by the people after it has been approved by Congress. After Randolph speaks, Charles Pinckney (South Carolina) submits his own plan for a new government, and the convention adjourns.

On May 30 the convention resolves itself into a committee of the whole with Nathaniel Gorham (Massachusetts) presiding and begins debating the Virginia resolutions (the Pinckney plan is never discussed by the convention). The first resolution, calling for the Articles of Confederation to be "corrected & enlarged," is challenged by Gouverneur Morris (Pennsylvania), who says that the remaining Virginia resolutions are incompatible with the Articles. Charles Cotesworth Pinckney (South Carolina, a second cousin of Charles Pinckney) and Elbridge Gerry (Massachusetts) question whether the convention has the authority to discuss a system not founded on the principles of the Confederation. After further debate, a resolution calling for establishing "a *national* Government" consisting of "a *supreme* Legislative, Executive & Judiciary" is approved, 6–1. Debate then turns to how representation in the national legislature should be apportioned, but the matter is postponed when George

Read (Delaware) reminds the convention that his delegation has been instructed not to change the equality of state representation provided for by the Articles.

On May 31 the delegates agree to establish a bicameral legislature and begin debating whether the first branch should be elected by the people. Roger Sherman (Connecticut) and Gerry speak against popular election, which is supported by George Mason (Virginia), James Wilson (Pennsylvania), and Madison, and then approved by a 6–2 vote. A debate over the method of electing the second branch, which Wilson suggests should also be chosen by the people, reaches no conclusion.

June

On June 1 the committee of the whole debates the national executive. Wilson moves that it be a single person and is opposed by Randolph, who favors a plural executive; the question is postponed. Wilson also favors having the executive elected by the people, saying that he wishes to make both legislative branches and the executive as independent of the state legislatures as possible. The committee votes 5–4 to create a seven-year term for the executive. On June 2 Wilson proposes that the people vote for electors who will then choose the executive. His motion is defeated, 8–2, and the committee then approves, 8–2, election of the executive by the national legislature. John Dickinson (Delaware) seeks to make the executive removable on request of a majority of the state legislatures, arguing that it is necessary to preserve a role for the states under the new plan. He is opposed by Madison and Wilson and the motion is rejected, 9–1. A single executive is approved, 7–3, on June 4, and Gerry then moves that the executive be given veto power, subject to legislative override. Wilson and Hamilton argue in favor of an absolute veto, but are opposed by Benjamin Franklin, Sherman, Madison, Mason, and others. An executive veto, subject to override by a two-thirds majority in each legislative chamber, is approved 8–2 (override majority is increased to three-fourths on August 15, then changed back to two-thirds on September 12).

On June 6 Charles Pinckney moves for reconsideration of the popular election of the first branch and proposes that it be chosen instead by the state legislatures. During the ensuing debate Madison supports popular election and says that it will help limit the power of the state governments. He argues that in republics there is always a danger of a united majority oppressing a minority, and that the only remedy is to enlarge the republic, increasing the number of contending interests and factions and thus reducing the chances and opportunity for a single oppressive majority to emerge. Pinckney's motion is defeated, 8–3. Dickinson moves on June 7 that the second branch (now referred to as the Senate) be elected by the state legislatures. Wilson again advocates popular election, but the motion is carried 10–0.

When discussion of representation in the national legislature resumes on June 9, New Jersey delegates David Brearly and William Paterson warn that proportional representation will allow Massachusetts, Pennsylvania, and Virginia to dominate the new government. Paterson says that the people of the smaller states will never accept a scheme that abolishes the state equality they possess under the Confederation. On June 11 Roger Sherman proposes that representation in the first branch be in proportion to free population while in the Senate each state would have one vote. His motion for equality in the Senate is defeated, 6–5, with Massachusetts, Pennsylvania, Virginia, North Carolina, South Carolina, and Georgia opposed and Connecticut, New York, New Jersey, Delaware, and Maryland supporting.

On June 13 the committee of the whole ends its deliberations and an amended version of the Virginia plan is prepared in the form of 19 resolutions. It provides for the first branch of the legislature to be elected by the people for three-year terms and the second branch to be chosen by the state legislatures for seven-year terms. Representation of both branches is to be in proportion to the free population and three-fifths of "other persons" (slaves). The national legislature will elect a single executive to serve for a single seven-year term, and the supreme tribunal of the national judiciary will be appointed by the Senate.

William Paterson asks for an adjournment on June 14 so that an alternate plan can be prepared (plan is drafted by New Jersey delegation, along with delegates from Connecticut, New York, Delaware, and Maryland). On June 15 Paterson presents nine resolutions that call for giving the existing Congress power to directly levy imposts and stamp taxes, regulate foreign and interstate trade, and appoint an executive. Congress would also be able to collect requisitions from noncomplying states. A federal judiciary would rule on cases involving foreigners, treaties, and federal trade regulation and revenue collection. All acts of Congress and treaties would be "the supreme law of the respective States" to which "the Judiciary of the several States shall be bound thereby in their decisions, any thing in the respective laws of the Individual States to the contrary notwithstanding." The executive would have the power to compel a state to obey federal law.

On June 16 the convention again resolves into a committee

of the whole. John Lansing (New York) supports the New Jersey plan, saying that it sustains the sovereignty of the states while the Virginia plan destroys state sovereignty. He insists that the convention has no power to supersede the Articles and therefore the states will never adopt the Virginia plan. Wilson replies with a detailed defense of the Virginia plan and says that the convention has the authority to "*conclude nothing*, but to be at liberty to *propose any thing*."

On June 18 Alexander Hamilton speaks for several hours, praising the British constitution as the best in the world, and presenting his own plan for creating an elected assembly, serving for three years, and a Senate, elected for life by electors chosen by the people. A single executive would also serve for life after being indirectly elected by the people and would have an absolute veto. The Senate would have the sole power to declare war, and the national legislature would establish the courts in each state. All state governors would be appointed by the national government and have an absolute veto over legislation in their states.

On June 19 Madison argues that the New Jersey plan will not "remedy the evils" of the Confederation, which include: violations of treaties; encroachments on federal authority; states trespassing against one another; the threat of insurrection by armed minorities, or by minorities of voters allied with "those whose poverty disqualifies them from the suffrage"; the injustice, impotence, and instability of many of the state laws; and the influence of foreign powers within the Union. Madison warns that if the Articles are merely amended to give the Confederation coercive power against recalcitrant members, national power will be used against the weaker states but not against the stronger, and that if the union dissolves for the lack of a new plan, the 13 states either will remain independent and sovereign or will form two or more smaller confederacies. In the first case, Madison predicts that the smaller states will be unable to defend themselves against their larger neighbors; in the second, the larger members of the new confederacies will offer the smaller states no better concessions than does the Virginia plan. After Madison finishes, the committee of the whole votes, 7–3, to adhere to the Virginia plan rather than the New Jersey plan, with New York, New Jersey, and Delaware opposed and Maryland divided.

Debate returns to the place of the states in the new system. Rufus King (Massachusetts) says that the states under the Confederation are not fully sovereign because they cannot make war, peace, or foreign alliances. On June 20 Oliver Ells-

worth (Connecticut) proposes that the phrase "national government" in the first amended resolution be changed to
"Government of the United States," and the convention
unanimously agrees. John Lansing moves to preserve the
Congress as it exists under the Confederation. George Mason
says that the people will not give additional power to a Congress they do not directly elect. The Virginia plan does not
ask the people to surrender power, but to transfer it from
their state representatives to national representatives that they
will directly choose. Luther Martin (Maryland) insists that
the federal government was instituted to support the state
governments, arguing that when the people of America separated from Britain, they chose to form 13 separate sovereignties instead of incorporating themselves into one. The
Lansing motion is defeated, 6–4. On June 21 Wilson argues
that the state and national governments have a shared interest, while Madison again warns that the encroachment of the
states on federal authority is more likely and more dangerous
than the reverse. The convention then changes the terms of
the first legislative branch from three to two years.

On June 25 Charles Pinckney delivers a long speech on the
nature of American society, agreeing with Hamilton's praise
of the British constitution, but arguing that a similar constitution could not be introduced for many centuries in America, where there is greater equality than in any other country.
Pinckney doubts an aristocracy will ever develop in America,
since the landowners, merchants, and professional men,
though divided in their pursuits, have common political interests, and are mutually dependent. On June 26 Madison
again discusses the diversity of interests in America and argues that a Senate serving for long terms will help protect
minorities against majority oppression. Gerry opposes long
senatorial terms, predicting that the people will reject any system that approaches monarchy. The convention approves,
7–4, a six-year term, with one-third of the Senate chosen
every two years.

Luther Martin speaks for several hours on the nature of
government, June 27–28, again contending that the general
government is meant to preserve state governments, not to
govern individuals, and says that he would rather see partial
confederacies than a government instituted according to the
Virginia plan. Madison replies, citing ancient history and the
fates of modern confederacies, and argues that the dissimilar
interests of Massachusetts, Pennsylvania, and Virginia make it
unlikely that they will combine to oppress the smaller states.
Franklin reviews the "small progress" made in five weeks, and

sees in it "a melancholy proof of the imperfection of the Human Understanding." He asks how it is that the delegates, "groping . . . in the dark to find political truth, and scarce able to distinguish it when presented to us" had not thought to call on "the Father of lights to illuminate our understandings." Franklin moves that sessions open with prayer, led by Philadelphia clergy. Hamilton worries that calling in clergy would alert the public to the dissensions within the convention. Hugh Williamson (North Carolina) says the convention has no funds. Randolph proposes that a sermon be preached on July 4, and prayers given each morning subsequently. No action is taken on the proposal.

June–July   On June 29 William Samuel Johnson (Connecticut) says the convention is divided between those who see the states as political societies and those who see them as districts of individual citizens. He urges that the two ideas be combined, with the people represented in one branch of the legislature and the states in the other. His position is not supported. The convention votes 6–4 in favor of proportional representation in the first branch, with Connecticut, New York, New Jersey, and Delaware opposed and Maryland divided. Hamilton, thinking the convention will never produce a strong enough constitution, returns to New York (will resume regular attendance on September 6). Debate on representation continues on June 30, when Gunning Bedford (Delaware) warns that if the large states dissolve the Confederation, the smaller states will find foreign allies. On July 2 Oliver Ellsworth moves that each state have a single vote in the Senate. The convention splits 5–5, with Connecticut, New York, New Jersey, Delaware, and Maryland voting yes and Georgia divided. Charles Cotesworth Pinckney proposes that a committee consisting of one member from each state be appointed to work out a compromise. The proposal is supported by Sherman, Gouverneur Morris, Randolph, and Gerry, opposed by Madison and Wilson, and approved, 10–1, with only Pennsylvania voting no. A committee is elected and the convention adjourns (committee members include Franklin, Gerry, Ellsworth, Paterson, Mason, and Luther Martin).

July   On July 5 the committee reports a compromise proposal. In the first branch of the legislature, each state would have one representative for every 40,000 people (with slaves counted as three-fifths of free citizens); in the second branch, each state would have an equal vote. All money bills would originate in the first branch, and they could not be altered or amended in the second. A new committee is appointed to

propose an exact apportionment of the first branch. Its report
distributes 56 members among the 13 states. Paterson objects
to counting slaves as people, saying that they are treated as
property and that including them in apportionment indirectly
encourages the slave trade. A second committee is appointed
and proposes a new apportionment calling for 65 members.
Rufus King says it favors the South and describes the greatest
difference of interests as being between the southern and
New England states, not the large and small ones. Charles
Cotesworth Pinckney says the proposed apportionment favors the North, which will be able to regulate trade to its
own advantage. New York delegates Robert Yates and John
Lansing, who believe the convention has authority only to
amend the Articles, leave after the July 10 session, and their
state is no longer represented.

In New York the Continental Congress adopts on July 13
the Northwest Ordinance for governing the territory beyond the Ohio River. Largely drafted by Nathan Dane
(Massachusetts) and based in part on Jefferson's plan of
1784, the new law gives Congress the power to appoint a
governor, secretary, and three judges for the territory. When
the territorial population includes 5,000 adult free males, a
territorial legislature will be formed, consisting of an elected
house of representatives and a council appointed by Congress from nominees submitted by the elected territorial representatives. Between three and five states will eventually be
formed from the territory, each to be admitted on full equality with the existing states when its population reaches
60,000. Slavery is prohibited in the territory, and its inhabitants are entitled to freedom of "peaceable" worship, the
writ of habeas corpus, trial by jury, judicial proceedings
according to the common law, and protection from immoderate fines and cruel and unusual punishments. The ordinance also provides for the return of fugitive slaves and
forbids the making of laws interfering with valid existing
private contracts.

As the debate over representation continues in the Philadelphia convention on July 14, Madison and Wilson restate
their opposition to state equality in the Senate. On July 16
an amended compromise resolution is proposed, calling for
a regular census to help reapportion the first branch according to population (with slaves counted as three-fifths of
whites), requiring money bills to originate in the first
branch and not be changed in the second, and giving each
state an equal vote in the Senate. It is approved, 5–4,
with Pennsylvania, Virginia, South Carolina, and Georgia

opposed, and Massachusetts divided. Delegates from the larger states caucus but are unable to agree on a plan for reversing the vote, and when Gouverneur Morris moves on July 17 for reconsideration of the compromise, his motion is not seconded.

The convention begins considering other resolutions reported by the committee of the whole on June 13. Gouverneur Morris and Sherman argue that giving the national legislature power to veto state laws is unnecessary and offensive to the states. Madison defends it as essential to the "efficacy & security" of the new government, but the proposed legislative veto is rejected, 7–3.

Debate turns to whether the national legislature should elect the executive. Gouverneur Morris warns that the executive would become "the mere creature" of the legislature under such a system, and favors election by the people at large. He is supported by Wilson, but opposed by Sherman, Charles Pinckney, and Mason, who says that it would be as "unnatural" to refer the choice of the executive to the people as it would be to "refer a trial of colours to a blind man." Mason argues that the extent of the country would make it impossible for the people to judge the qualifications of candidates. A motion in favor of election by the people is defeated, 9–1. Gouverneur Morris advocates making the executive eligible for reelection as an incentive for good behavior; reeligibility is approved, 6–4.

On July 18 the convention votes 6–2 against having the national judiciary appointed by the executive, then divides, 4–4, on a proposal for the executive to appoint judges with the advice and consent of the Senate. Debate on the executive resumes on July 19, when Madison argues that the executive must be independent of the legislature and favors his indirect election by special electors. Ellsworth moves that the executive be chosen by electors and the convention approves, 6–3; it then votes, 8–2, in favor of the electors being chosen by the state legislatures. The convention also approves a six-year executive term.

On July 21 Wilson and Madison propose that the national judiciary share veto power with the executive. Wilson advocates giving the judiciary power to block laws that are unwise but not unconstitutional, while Madison argues that a shared veto will strengthen the check on legislative power. Gerry opposes the measure, saying it will create an alliance between the executive and judiciary. The motion is defeated, 4–3, and the convention votes, 6–3, in favor of having the Senate appoint judges.

On July 23 the convention debates resolution calling for ratification of the new Constitution by special conventions elected by the people. Ellsworth and Paterson propose submitting the Constitution to the state legislatures. Randolph argues that state legislatures are too often influenced by local demagogues who will be threatened by the new Constitution; Mason and Madison also strongly support ratification by conventions. The Ellsworth motion is defeated, 8–3. Convention then approves, 10–1, giving each state two senators, with each senator having an individual vote.

On July 24 the convention reconsiders the election of the executive and approves election by the national legislature, 7–4, reversing its vote of July 19. Reconsideration of reeligibility leads to suggestions that the executive serve for terms of 11, 15, or 20 years. Further discussion of the executive is postponed, and a committee of detail (John Rutledge of South Carolina, Randolph, Gorham, Ellsworth, and Wilson) is elected and instructed to draft a Constitution. After debating the executive without resolution on July 25, the convention votes, 7–3, in favor of a single seven-year term on July 26. It then submits 23 resolutions derived from the Virginia plan to the committee of detail, which also receives texts of the Pinckney and New Jersey plans, and adjourns until August 6.

July–Aug.   Randolph prepares a draft Constitution, which is examined by the committee, rewritten by Wilson, and again reviewed by the committee. The draft reported by the committee draws on the materials submitted by the convention, as well as state constitutions, the Articles of Confederation, and resolutions in the Continental Congress. It is divided into a preamble and 23 articles, with the preamble beginning "We the People of the States of . . . " and then listing all 13 states. In place of the general definition of legislative power given in the amended Virginia resolutions, the draft Constitution enumerates 17 powers to be vested in the new Congress and also gives the legislature power "to make all laws that shall be necessary and proper" for executing both its enumerated powers and all other powers given to the government of the United States by the Constitution. (The draft also lists several prohibitions on the powers of the states, and includes an article defining the judicial power of the United States.) Copies are printed and distributed to the delegates when the convention reconvenes on August 6.

Aug.   The convention begins a detailed examination and revision of the draft on August 7. Gouverneur Morris proposes uniformly restricting suffrage in elections for the House of

Representatives to freeholders; his amendment is defeated, 7–1, as several delegates argue that it would be impossible to establish an acceptable uniform property qualification. On August 10 the convention votes 7–3 to remove a draft clause giving Congress power to establish uniform property requirements for its own members.

Debate on enumerated legislative powers begins on August 16. Clause giving Congress power to regulate foreign and interstate commerce is unanimously approved. When the convention considers the power to "make war," Charles Pinckney suggests restricting it to the Senate, saying that it will be better qualified than the House of Representatives to judge foreign affairs. Pierce Butler (South Carolina) recommends giving the power to the president, who "will not make war but when the Nation will support it." Madison and Gerry move to replace "make" with "declare," leaving to the president "the power to repel sudden attacks." Their motion is approved, 8–1. Madison and Charles Pinckney each propose an additional list of legislative powers on August 18, and on August 20 Pinckney submits another list, which includes several enumerated restrictions on legislative power; their recommendations are referred to the committee of detail (some of the Madison and Pinckney recommendations are incorporated in the final Constitution). The "necessary and proper" clause is unanimously adopted on August 20.

Luther Martin moves on August 21 to give Congress the power to tax or to prohibit the importation of slaves and calls the slave trade "dishonorable to the American character." Rutledge replies that the question is one of interest, not religion and humanity. Ellsworth says that the "morality or wisdom" of slavery should be left to the states. On August 22 Sherman supports the draft clause forbidding interference with the slave trade. Mason condemns slavery and warns that "providence punishes national sins, by national calamities." He calls for giving the government power to prevent the increase of slavery. Ellsworth replies that morality would suggest freeing slaves already in the country and predicts that an increasing number of poor white laborers will eventually cause slavery to disappear. Rutledge says that North Carolina, South Carolina, and Georgia will never agree to a constitution prohibiting the slave trade. Gouverneur Morris recommends referring the question to a committee, along with draft clauses prohibiting Congress from taxing exports and requiring a two-thirds majority to pass navigation acts (laws regulating maritime commerce). He suggests, "These things may form a bargain among the Northern & Southern States." A committee consisting of a delegate from each state is chosen.

The convention resumes its review of the draft Constitution and adopts a clause forbidding Congress from passing bills of attainder or ex post facto laws (prohibition is extended to the states on August 28). An amended version of the "supreme law" clause, first introduced in the New Jersey plan, is unanimously adopted on August 23.

The convention debates on August 25 the committee report on the slave trade and navigation acts, which recommends that Congress should have the power to end the slave trade after 1800 and to tax the importation of slaves until then. It also recommends striking the draft clause requiring a two-thirds majority to pass navigation laws. Charles Cotesworth Pinckney moves that the slave trade be protected until 1808. Madison objects that 20 years of importation would be "dishonorable," but the motion is approved, 7–4, with New Jersey, Pennsylvania, Delaware, and Virginia opposed. Sherman and Madison object to taxing imported slaves, since it acknowledges that people can be property. King, John Langdon (New Hampshire), and Charles Cotesworth Pinckney say this is the price of securing eventual prohibition of the slave trade. On August 29 the convention debates making navigation laws subject to a simple majority. Mason says that this will make the southern states, who will be a minority in both the House and Senate, subject to the commercial interest of the majority. Madison argues that agricultural interests in the interior of the commercial states, as well as the admission of new agricultural western states, will prevent abuse of the power to make commercial laws. The convention votes 7–4 against a two-thirds majority, with Maryland, Virginia, North Carolina, and Georgia opposed, and then unanimously approves adding a fugitive-slave clause to the Constitution.

After unanimously voting to prohibit religious tests for holding office under the new Constitution, the convention debates how many state ratifications should be sufficient to begin the new government. Wilson recommends seven, Randolph nine, Sherman ten, and Daniel Carroll (Maryland) says that all 13 states must agree to dissolve the Articles of Confederation before the Constitution can go into effect. On August 31 the convention votes to make the ratification of nine states sufficient. Gouverneur Morris says that the Constitution must be ratified quickly, before state officials can intrigue against it; Luther Martin says the people will not ratify it unless they are hurried into it by surprise.

Mason tells the convention that he would sooner chop off his right hand than sign the Constitution as it stands. Sherman proposes the election of a committee consisting of one delegate from each state to report on postponed matters. The committee is chosen, with David Brearly (New Jersey) as its chairman; members include King, Sherman, Gouverneur Morris, Dickinson, and Madison.

Sept.   On September 4 the committee reports an amended article regarding the president, who will now serve for four years and be eligible for reelection. Presidential electors will be chosen in each state in a manner determined by the state legislature, and each state will have electors equal in number to its senators and representatives. Each elector will vote for two candidates, one of whom must not be a resident of their state. If no candidate receives a majority of electoral votes, or if there is a tie, the Senate is to choose a president from among the top five recipients of electoral votes. The candidate receiving the second-highest number of votes will become vice-president.

On September 5 Charles Pinckney says electors will not have sufficient knowledge of the "fittest men" and will vote for an eminent man from their own state. The resulting dispersion of electoral votes will lead to appointment by the Senate, who will repeatedly elect the same man. Mason fears that the proposed system will lead to the president and Senate forming a coalition to subvert the Constitution. Gouverneur Morris believes electors will choose "characters eminent & generally known" when voting for men from out of state, and that this will contribute to electoral majorities. A proposal by Wilson to have both houses of Congress choose the president when there is no electoral majority is defeated, 7–3. Madison and Williamson move that one-third of the electoral vote be sufficient to elect a president; they are defeated, 9–2. Randolph and Wilson warn that giving a role in presidential elections to the Senate will lead to its becoming an aristocracy. On September 6 the convention votes 9–2 in favor of having electors choose the president. Williamson suggests having both houses elect the president when there is no electoral majority, voting by state and not as individuals. Sherman then suggests giving the power to the House of Representatives, with the members from each state having one vote; his motion is seconded by Mason and approved, 10–1.

On September 7 the convention considers other proposals by the committee on postponed matters. It defeats, 10–1, a motion by Wilson to let the House of Representatives share

treaty-making power with the Senate and then approves presidential power to make appointments with the advice and
consent of the Senate. Mason proposes establishing a six-
member council of state to advise the president; his motion,
seconded by Franklin, is defeated 8–3. On September 8 the
convention approves making a two-thirds majority in the
Senate necessary to ratify treaties and gives the Senate power
to amend money bills, which must still originate in the
House. A committee of style (William Samuel Johnson, Gouverneur Morris, Madison, Hamilton, and King) is appointed
to prepare a finished text of the Constitution. Convention
debates draft clause on amendments, which provides for calling a convention if two-thirds of the state legislatures seek an
amendment. Hamilton advocates giving Congress the power
to initiate amendments. Madison moves that amendments be
proposed by Congress when two-thirds of both houses deem
them necessary or when two-thirds of the state legislatures
apply for them, and then be ratified by either three-fourths of
the state legislatures, or by conventions in three-fourths of
the states. His motion is approved, 9–1. Hamilton proposes
submitting the Constitution to the Continental Congress for
approval before it is transmitted to the states. Wilson dis-
agrees, warning that the Congress may refuse its assent, and
the proposal is defeated.

On September 12 the committee of style submits its draft
Constitution, consisting of a preamble and seven articles
(much of the final wording is attributed to Gouverneur Morris). The preamble, rewritten by Morris, now begins "We, the
People of the United States," and introduces language describing the purpose of the Constitution ("to form a more
perfect union . . . "). The committee of style draft also includes a clause prohibiting states from impairing the obligation of contracts, which will be adopted without debate.

Mason and Gerry recommend that a bill of rights be prepared. Sherman says that the Constitution does not repeal
state declarations of rights, which will still be in force and
sufficient to secure the rights of the people. Mason answers
that the laws of the United States are to be paramount to
state bills of rights. The convention votes unanimously
against preparing a bill of rights. On September 13 the committee of style reports two resolutions concerning the ratification and implementation of the Constitution (they are sent to
Congress on September 17, along with a letter drafted by the
committee and signed by Washington). The convention rejects on September 14 a motion by Madison to give Congress
limited power to grant charters of incorporation benefiting

the interest of the United States. On September 15 Mason
objects to the power given to Congress regarding amendments. The convention unanimously votes to give two-thirds
of the state legislatures power to call a convention to propose
amendments.

Randolph, Mason, and Gerry then express their reservations (other delegates opposed to the Constitution have
already left the convention). Randolph proposes that state
ratifying conventions be able to submit amendments for consideration by a second general convention. If this procedure
is not adopted, Randolph will not sign the Constitution and
may oppose it in Virginia. Mason and Gerry also support a
second convention. Mason believes the government being
created will turn into either a monarchy or a tyrannical aristocracy and supports a second convention. Gerry specifically
objects to the reeligibility of the Senate, control by Congress
over places of elections and its own compensation, the possibility that monopolies could be established, the representation of three-fifths of the slaves as if they were freemen, and
the vice-president being made head of the Senate, mixing executive and legislative powers. He adds that the rights of citizens are threatened by the power of the legislature "to make
what laws they may please to call necessary and proper," to
raise armies and money without limit, and to establish courts
capable of trying civil cases without juries. The motion by
Randolph proposing a second convention is unanimously
defeated, and the convention then unanimously adopts the
amended Constitution and orders it engrossed.

On September 17, with the engrossed Constitution ready
to be signed, Benjamin Franklin rises with a written speech,
which James Wilson reads. Franklin confesses that he does
not entirely approve of the Constitution at present, but
doubts that he will never change his mind. He urges unanimous support of the Constitution and hopes that future
thoughts be turned to its good administration. Franklin presents a form of signing, drafted by Gouverneur Morris in the
hope of gaining the signatures of the three dissenters, that
asks delegates to sign as witnesses to the adoption of the
Constitution "by the unanimous consent of the States
present." Gorham, King, and Carroll move one final amendment, proposing that the number of representatives not exceed one for every 30,000 people, instead of the 40,000
presently called for. Washington rises from the chair and for
the first time gives his sentiments on a question before the
convention, supporting the amendment, despite its lateness,
in the hope that it will remove a possible objection to the

Constitution. The amendment is adopted without opposition. Randolph apologizes to Franklin, but says he cannot sign the Constitution. He believes it will be rejected, and by withholding his name he will be able to take steps "consistent with the public good" in the ensuing confusion. Gouverneur Morris and Hamilton reply that they will support the Constitution despite their reservations and see anarchy as the only alternative to its adoption. Franklin asks Randolph, whom he commends for bringing the basic plan forward in May, to reconsider and sign. Randolph says he cannot sign, and warns that attempting to obtain unconditional ratification will produce anarchy and convulsion. Gerry sees a civil war ensuing, especially in Massachusetts, where two parties, one devoted to democracy and the other to the opposite extreme, already confront each other and will collide in the struggle over the Constitution. The convention adopts the form of signing proposed by Franklin and orders the convention journals deposited in the custody of Washington. (The journals are first published in 1819; Madison's notes of the debates, the fullest account by a participant, are posthumously published in 1840.) All of the 41 delegates present, except Gerry, Randolph, and Mason, then sign (Dickinson signs by proxy). Toward the close of the signing Franklin observes that during sessions he had often been unable to tell whether the sun painted on the back of the chair Washington presided from had been "rising or setting: But now at length I have the happiness to know that it is a rising and not a setting Sun." When the signing is completed, the convention dissolves itself.

The Constitution is read in Congress on September 20, and on September 26 debate begins on the ratification procedure proposed by the Constitutional Convention. Richard Henry Lee proposes amendments, but Congress unanimously resolves on September 28 to send the Constitution, along with the resolutions and letter accompanying it, to the state legislatures for submission to conventions elected by the people.

Press debate on the Constitution begins in Philadelphia, where a favorable commentary appears on September 19 and a critical article is published on September 26. (Supporters of the Constitution become known as Federalists and opponents as Antifederalists; most newspapers in the United States support the Federalists.) The first of seven Antifederalist letters by "Cato" appears in New York on September 27 (series runs until January 3, 1788).

Sept.–Oct.   In Pennsylvania the Constitution is supported by Republicans (opponents of the 1776 state constitution) and opposed by Constitutionalists (supporters of the 1776 state constitution). In Philadelphia the Federalist majority in the state assembly calls on September 28 for a state ratifying convention and proposes electing the convention in October. Antifederalist assemblymen object to the early date and prevent a quorum by boycotting the afternoon session (assembly is scheduled to adjourn on September 29; elections for a new assembly are to be held on October 9). On September 29 Federalists order the sergeant at arms to look for absentees, and with the help of a mob two Antifederalists are forcibly brought to the State House. With the necessary two-thirds quorum achieved, the assembly calls for the convention to be elected on November 6 and to meet on November 20. An address from 16 of the "seceding" Antifederalists is published on October 2, attacking the Federalists for their tactics and criticizing the Philadelphia convention for abandoning the Articles of Confederation.

Oct.   Samuel Bryan of Philadelphia publishes the first of his 18 Antifederalist "Centinel" essays in Philadelphia on October 5 (series runs until April 9, 1788). James Wilson defends the Constitution in a speech delivered in the State House Yard in Philadelphia on October 6 (printed version is widely circulated and is the subject of several Antifederalist replies as the press debate intensifies).

In New York the first of 16 Antifederalist essays by "Brutus" appears on October 18 (series runs until April 10, 1788). The first number of *The Federalist* appears in New York on October 27 under the name "Publius" (of the 85 essays published through May 28, 1788, Hamilton writes 51, Madison 29, and John Jay 5; the series appears in several New York newspapers and is collected in two volumes published on March 22 and May 28, 1788). While in New York, Madison corresponds with leading Federalists in Pennsylvania, Massachusetts, and Virginia, as well as with Edmund Randolph, whom he hopes to persuade to support ratification in Virginia.

Oct.–Nov.   On October 17 the Connecticut legislature calls for a ratifying convention to meet on January 3, 1788 (election is held November 12). Massachusetts legislature calls on October 25 for convention to meet on January 9, 1788 (elections are held November 19, 1787–January 7, 1788). Georgia legislature calls on October 26 for convention to meet on December 25 (elections are held December 4–5). Virginia legislature calls on October 31 for a convention to meet on June 2, 1788 (elections are held March 3–27, 1788). New Jersey legislature calls on November 1 for a convention to meet on December 11 (elections are held November 27–December 1).

Nov.   On November 3 a letter from Elbridge Gerry to the Massachusetts legislature explaining why he did not sign the Constitution is published in Boston. Five "Letters from the
Federal Farmer to the Republican" are published as a pamphlet on November 8; it becomes one of the most widely
circulated Antifederalist publications. Delaware legislature
calls on November 10 for a convention to meet on December
3 (election is held on November 26).

Pennsylvania ratifying convention achieves quorum on November 21 and begins debate on November 24, with James
Wilson serving as the main Federalist advocate and Robert
Whitehill, William Findley, and John Smilie leading the opposition. On November 26 convention rejects, 44–24, an
Antifederalist motion to allow voting on individual articles
of the Constitution.

Nov.–Dec.   George Mason's objections to the Constitution, which
have been circulating privately since early October, are published November 21. Luther Martin attacks the Constitution
in a speech before the Maryland legislature on November 29
and gives an account of the proceedings of the Constitutional Convention (expanded version of speech is published
in 12 installments, December 28, 1787–February 8, 1788, and
in pamphlet form as "The Genuine Information" in April
1788). Maryland legislature calls on December 1 for a convention to meet April 21, 1788 (elections are held April 7,
1788). North Carolina legislature calls on December 6 for a
convention to meet on July 21, 1788 (elections are held
March 28–29).

Dec.   On December 7 Delaware convention votes 30–0 to ratify
the Constitution. Robert Whitehill submits 15 amendments to
the Pennsylvania convention on December 12 and proposes
that the convention adjourn so that the people may have time
to consider them. His motion is defeated, 46–23, and the
Constitution is then ratified, 46–23. An "Address and Reasons of Dissent," signed by 21 members of the minority, is
published on December 18 and widely circulated. (Antifederalists continue to oppose ratification in Pennsylvania, and in
March 1788 petitions signed by over 6,000 people in rural
counties are submitted to the assembly, asking it to reject ratification; the assembly takes no action.)

Virginia legislature passes law on December 12 authorizing the Virginia ratifying convention to communicate with
other states regarding amendments to the Constitution. At
the request of the legislature, Governor Randolph transmits
copies of the bill to each state on December 27. (Letter does
not reach Antifederalist New York governor George Clinton

until March 7, 1788; during the ratification contest, some Antifederalists accuse Federalists of tampering with the mails.)

New Hampshire legislature calls on December 14 for a convention to meet on February 13, 1788 (elections are held December 31, 1787–February 12, 1788).

New Jersey convention votes to ratify, 38–0, on December 18.

Jefferson writes to Madison from Paris on December 20, expressing his unhappiness with the lack of a bill of rights in the Constitution and the reeligibility of the president.

On December 27 Virginia governor Edmund Randolph publishes his reasons for not signing the Constitution.

Georgia convention votes to ratify the Constitution, 26–0, on December 31.

1788   Connecticut convention votes to ratify, 128–40, on January 9. Massachusetts convention meets in Boston on January 9, with delegates from the coastal towns generally favoring ratification and delegates from rural counties generally opposed; convention includes delegates from the Maine district. Convention elects Governor John Hancock, who has remained publicly neutral on ratification, as its president, though William Cushing serves as presiding officer while Hancock remains confined with an attack of gout; his absence is seen by some delegates as a political maneuver. On January 14 the convention votes to consider the Constitution clause by clause and begins debate.

South Carolina house of representatives debates Constitution, January 16–19, and unanimously votes to call convention to meet on May 12 (elections are held April 11–12). House votes, 76–75, to hold convention in Charleston (Federalists are strongest in coastal lowlands, while Antifederalists are concentrated in the western uplands).

On January 24 Antifederalists in the Massachusetts convention propose ending the clause-by-clause debate and bringing the entire Constitution to a vote. Samuel Adams says that while he is troubled by some parts of the Constitution, he believes it should be fully considered; the motion for an immediate vote is defeated. Convinced that ratification without amendments of some kind is impossible, Federalist leaders reach agreement with Hancock on a compromise proposal. On January 31 Hancock gives a speech to the convention supporting ratification and recommending nine amendments for adoption by Congress and the states after the Constitution goes into effect. Samuel Adams supports Hancock's proposal and suggests that it will set an example for other states that have yet to ratify.

Feb.

New York legislature calls on February 1 for a convention to meet on June 17 (elections are held April 29–May 3, with the suffrage extended to all male freemen over 21).

A committee of the Massachusetts convention reports on February 4 a revised form of the amendments proposed by Hancock. On February 6 Hancock calls for conciliation in his final speech to the convention, which then votes, 187–168, to ratify the Constitution and recommend nine subsequent amendments.

New Hampshire convention meets on February 13. Federalists hope it will follow example of Massachusetts, but when they discover that many delegates have been instructed by their towns to vote against ratification, they move for an adjournment until June 18. Motion is carried, 56–51, and convention adjourns on February 22.

Mar.

Rhode Island legislature votes on March 1 to hold a popular referendum on the Constitution instead of a ratifying convention. Most Federalists boycott the vote, held in the towns on March 24, and the Constitution is rejected by 2,711 to 239.

In Virginia the result of convention elections, held March 3–27, is uncertain, with a small number of uncommitted delegates seen as likely to determine the outcome.

Apr.

Maryland convention votes on April 26 to ratify the Constitution, 63–11, before tabling amendments proposed by Antifederalists.

May

New York governor George Clinton writes to Randolph on May 8, proposing that the Virginia and New York conventions communicate regarding amendments (when Randolph receives the letter, he and the Virginia council of state decide that it should first be sent to the legislature, and it does not become public until June 26, after the Virginia convention has voted). New York Antifederalist John Lamb writes to Virginia Antifederalists George Mason, Patrick Henry, William Grayson, and Richard Henry Lee on May 18, proposing that Antifederalists in New York, Virginia, and New Hampshire work together to secure amendments before ratification. (Mason, Henry, and Grayson reply favorably on June 9, enclosing a list of proposed amendments, but the response of the New York Antifederalists does not reach Virginia until after its convention votes on ratification.)

South Carolina convention votes on May 23 to ratify the Constitution, 149–73, and recommends four subsequent amendments. With eight states having ratified, only one more ratification is necessary to bring the Constitution into effect, although both Federalists and Antifederalists anticipate that a union without Virginia and New York will be impracticable. Counting of ballots in New York in late May confirms election of 46 Antifederalists and 19 Federalists to the state ratifying convention; all of the Federalists are from New York City or neighboring counties, leading to speculation that the southern counties will secede from the state if the convention rejects the Constitution.

June

Virginia convention meets in Richmond on June 2 (convention includes 14 delegates from the Kentucky district). The convention unanimously elects Edmund Pendleton, a supporter of the Constitution, as president, and then votes on June 3 to consider the Constitution clause by clause in a committee of the whole chaired by Federalist George Wythe (clause-by-clause discussion is moved by Mason and supported by Madison; committee procedure allows Pendleton to join debate). On June 4 Patrick Henry and George Mason attack the Constitution while Edmund Randolph announces that he now supports ratification with recommended subsequent amendments. Madison gives his first extended speech on June 6 and becomes the leading Federalist advocate; other Federalist speakers include Pendleton, George Nicholas, Henry Lee, and John Marshall, while Grayson, John Tyler, Benjamin Harrison, and James Monroe join Mason and Henry in opposing unconditional ratification. Madison also continues correspondence with Hamilton in New York (Hamilton believes prior ratification by Virginia is essential to winning ratification in New York).

New York ratifying convention meets in Poughkeepsie on June 17 and elects Governor George Clinton as its president. On June 19 it approves proposal by Federalist Robert R. Livingston to consider the Constitution clause by clause and begins debate, with Hamilton leading the Federalists and Melancton Smith the Antifederalists.

New Hampshire convention begins second session on June 18 and on June 21 votes, 57–47, to ratify the Constitution and recommend 12 subsequent amendments. Federalists send news of ratification by express rider to New York convention.

Virginia convention ends clause-by-clause consideration on June 23. George Wythe proposes on June 24 that the convention ratify the Constitution and recommend the subsequent adoption of amendments. Henry introduces an alternate resolution, calling for the submission of amendments to other states for their consideration before the Constitution is ratified, and warns of the dangers of unconditional ratification in a speech which concludes during a violent thunderstorm. On

June 25 the Henry resolution is defeated, 88–80, and the Wythe resolution is approved, 89–79. The convention adopts a form of ratification on June 27 that recommends the adoption of 40 amendments and then adjourns.

July   Continental Congress receives New Hampshire act of ratification on July 2. With the necessary nine states having ratified the Constitution, the Congress appoints committee to draft an ordinance for putting it into effect by holding elections for the new government.

Express messenger brings news of Virginia ratification to New York convention on July 2. Convention ends its clause-by-clause debate on July 7. After Antifederalists caucus, John Lansing proposes a form of ratification on July 10 that includes explanatory, conditional, and recommended amendments. John Jay responds on July 11 by proposing unconditional ratification with explanatory and recommended amendments. The convention debates whether a conditional ratification would be accepted by Congress, with Antifederalist leader Melancton Smith expressing doubts on July 17 that conditional ratification is possible. Lansing proposes resolution on July 23 calling for ratification "upon condition" that specified measures be taken. Antifederalist Samuel Jones moves that "upon condition" be replaced by "in full confidence." Smith supports Jones, and the Jones motion is approved, 31–29. On July 24 Lansing proposes that New York reserve the right to secede from the new union if certain amendments are not adopted. After reading a letter from Madison expressing opinion that conditional ratification will leave New York out of the union, Hamilton proposes that the convention send a circular letter to the other states calling for a second general convention to consider amendments. On July 25 Jay reads a circular letter he has written with Lansing and Smith (draft is mainly the work of Jay, who plays a leading role in negotiating a compromise ratification with the Antifederalists). The letter is unanimously approved and the Lansing motion on secession is defeated, 31–28, with Smith, Jones, Gilbert Livingston, and other Antifederalists again voting with the Federalists. The final form of ratification, including explanatory and recommended amendments, is approved, 30–27, on July 26.

July–Aug.   North Carolina convention meets in Hillsborough on July 21, with Antifederalists holding a clear majority (convention includes five delegates from Tennessee, then part of North Carolina). Although the convention votes to consider the Constitution clause by clause, the Antifederalists generally refrain from engaging the Federalists in debate. On July 30

Antifederalist leader Willie Jones proposes that the convention withhold ratification of the Constitution and submit amendments to a second general convention. His resolution is approved, 183–83, on August 2, and the convention adjourns on August 4.

Sept.   Pennsylvania Antifederalists meet at Harrisburg, September 3–6, to propose amendments to the Constitution.

Sept.–Oct.   After prolonged debate over where the new government should meet, Continental Congress passes election ordinance on September 13 that sets dates for choosing presidential electors (January 7, 1789), electing the president (February 4, 1789), and beginning the new government (March 4, 1789), and retains New York City as the capital. (Senators and representatives are elected in the 11 ratifying states, September 30, 1788–July 16, 1789, with Federalists winning majorities in both houses.) Continental Congress achieves its last quorum on October 10.

Oct.   John Lamb, Melancton Smith, and eight other Antifederalists form Federal Republican Society in New York on October 30; society circulates letters within the state urging the election of representatives to the new Congress committed to amending the Constitution and corresponds with Antifederalists in other states in effort to procure a second general convention and to have George Clinton elected vice-president.

Nov.   The Virginia legislature elects Antifederalists Richard Henry Lee and William Grayson to the new Senate on November 8 after Patrick Henry opposes Madison's election, and on November 20 it requests that the new Congress call a second constitutional convention

North Carolina legislature calls on November 30 for a second state ratifying convention to meet on November 16, 1789.

1789   On January 7 presidential electors are chosen in every ratifying state except New York, where dispute between Federalist and Antifederalist chambers of legislature prevents their election (electors are chosen by the voters in four states, nominated by the voters and chosen by the legislature in two states, elected by the legislature in three states, and chosen by the governor and council in one state). Madison runs against James Monroe for seat in House of Representatives from Virginia, promising to work in Congress for amendments protecting essential rights and debating the Constitution with Monroe at joint appearances throughout the district, which includes several Antifederalist counties. On February 2 Madison wins the election, 1,308–972. Electors meet in their states on February 4 and vote for two candidates in balloting for president. George Washington receives votes from all 69 electors and is elected president, and John Adams, with 34 votes, is elected vice-president (John Jay receives nine votes, and 26 votes are scattered among nine other candidates).

Feb.   On February 5 New York state legislature passes resolution calling for a second convention to consider amendments.

Mar.–Apr.   Continental Congress holds last session on March 2, attended by secretary Charles Thomson and a single delegate from New York. First Federal Congress convenes on March 4. Quorum is achieved in both houses on April 6 and electoral votes are counted. George Washington takes the oath of office as the first president of the United States on April 30.

May   After studying the amendments proposed by the state ratifying conventions, Madison tells the House of Representatives on May 4 that he will introduce amendments during the current session. Calls by the Virginia and New York legislatures for a second general convention are laid before the House, May 5–6.

                On May 19 Madison proposes the creation of a Department of Foreign Affairs (later renamed the Department of State), Department of the Treasury, and Department of War. House debates whether executive officers subject to Senate confirmation can be dismissed by the president without the consent of the Senate. Madison argues that full presidential power to remove officials is implied in Article II of the Constitution, and the House adopts his position in 34–20 vote. (Legislation organizing the three executive departments is enacted July 27– September 2. Alexander Hamilton is confirmed as secretary of the treasury on September 11, Henry Knox as secretary of war on September 12, and Thomas Jefferson as secretary of state on September 26; Jefferson takes office on March 22, 1790, following his return from France.)

June   On June 8 Madison moves that the House begin considering amendments. Roger Sherman and other Federalists argue that adopting revenue measures and organizing the government is more important than changing the Constitution, which should be tested by experience before being altered. Madison refers to the widespread demands for a bill of rights made during ratification and argues that it is better for Congress to propose specific amendments than to have the entire Constitution reconsidered. He then recommends incorporating into the text of the Constitution a series of changes, most of which are intended to protect individual rights (proposals include adding new declarations of general principles to the preamble). After Madison presents his amendments, Federalists again argue that their consideration is premature, while

Elbridge Gerry says that the House should consider the full range of amendments proposed by the state conventions; the House postpones action on amendments. (Madison's proposals will be criticized by some Antifederalists, including George Mason, as a diversionary measure designed to forestall attempts to change the structure and powers of the new government.)

July–Aug.   On July 21 Madison again raises question of amendments. The House votes to refer his proposals of June 8, along with all of the amendments proposed by the state ratifying conventions, to an 11–member select committee whose members include Sherman and Madison. On July 28 the committee reports the June 8 Madison proposals in slightly altered form, and the House begins considering them on August 13. Gerry moves on August 18 that they also consider amendments recommended by the state conventions, but his motion is defeated, 34–18. South Carolina Antifederalist Thomas Tudor Tucker moves that amendment reserving "powers not delegated" to the states be changed to read "powers not expressly delegated." Madison objects, arguing that "it was impossible to confine a Government to the exercise of express powers; there must necessarily be admitted powers by implication, unless the constitution descended to recount every minutia." The motion is defeated. Tucker then proposes consideration of 17 amendments altering the powers and structure of the government; this motion is also defeated. Roger Sherman proposes on August 19 that the amendments be added as separate articles at the end of the Constitution, leaving the original text unaltered. His motion is approved, and on August 22 Sherman and two others are appointed to arrange the amendments. They report 17 articles on August 24 that are substantially similar to Madison's original proposals (revisions to preamble are omitted), and the House sends them to the Senate.

Aug.   On August 22 and August 24 President Washington visits the Senate chamber to ask for its advice concerning instructions for commissioners negotiating a treaty with southern Indians. When senators request that he put his questions in writing, Washington complies, but never again returns to ask the Senate for its advice.

Sept.   Senate begins its consideration of the amendments on September 2 and sends its version to the House on September 9. In the Senate version the 17 articles are reduced to 12 by combining some provisions and eliminating an article on the separation of powers and an article forbidding states from infringing the right to jury trial in criminal cases, "the rights of conscience," or the freedom of speech and the press (described by Madison as "the most valuable amendment of the lot"). The Senate also weakens the clause forbidding the establishment of religion. A conference committee, whose six members include Madison, Sherman, and senators Oliver Ellsworth and William Paterson, reports a compromise between the House and Senate versions on September 23 that closely follows the Senate version but restores the prohibition against congressional establishment of religion. It is approved by the House, 37–14, on September 24 and by the Senate on September 25; the 12 amendments are then submitted to the states for ratification.

Judiciary Act, largely drafted by Senator Oliver Ellsworth, becomes law on September 24. It implements Article III of the Constitution by creating a three-tiered federal judiciary, consisting of 13 district courts (one for each of the 11 states that have ratified, with additional courts for the Kentucky district of Virginia and the Maine district of Massachusetts), three circuit courts (in which cases will be heard in each district by two supreme court justices and the district court judge), and a supreme court, consisting of a chief justice and five associate justices (Chief Justice John Jay and five associate justices are confirmed on September 26). The act defines the original and appellate jurisdiction of the federal courts and specifies that cases in the state courts concerning the Constitution, treaties, or laws of the United States must first be decided by a state's highest court before being appealed to the United States Supreme Court. Appeals of state cases are restricted to instances where the state courts rule against the validity of a treaty or federal law; where they rule in favor of a state law that has been challenged as being contrary to the Constitution, treaties, or federal laws; or where they deny the validity of a right or privilege claimed under the Constitution, treaties, or federal law. The act also establishes the office of Attorney General of the United States; Edmund Randolph becomes attorney general on September 26 (Department of Justice is not established until 1870).

Nov.– Dec.   On November 20 New Jersey ratifies all but the second of the proposed amendments (requiring that no law varying congressional compensation can take effect without an election of Representatives having intervened). Second North Carolina convention ratifies the Constitution, 194–77, on November 21 and proposes amendments. Virginia house of delegates approves all 12 amendments on November 30, but Antifederalists in the state senate, who hope to obtain an amendment barring direct taxation by the federal government, oppose ratification. Georgia legislature rejects proposed amendments, but all 12 amendments are ratified by Maryland, December 19, and North Carolina, December 22.

1790   Secretary of the Treasury Hamilton submits a report on public credit to the House on January 14. It calls for funding the $54 million national debt and for federal assumption of $25 million of debt incurred by the states during the Revolutionary War (Hamilton believes assumption will strengthen the allegiance of state creditors to the new union). Holders of depreciated Continental securities will be able to exchange them for new interest-paying bonds at face value, and import and excise taxes will be levied to pay interest on the debt.

Jan.–Feb.   On January 17 the Rhode Island legislature narrowly approves bill calling a ratifying state convention. South Carolina ratifies all 12 proposed amendments on January 18, New Hampshire ratifies all but the second on January 25, and Delaware ratifies all but the first (regulating the numbers of representatives as the population increases, so that there eventually would be not more than one representative for every 50,000 persons, and no fewer than 200 representatives) on January 28. Massachusetts senate approves all but the first two amendments on January 29, and the state house of representatives approves all but the first, second, and twelfth on February 2; however, the two chambers fail to vote on a bill giving joint approval to any amendments, and Massachusetts does not report its partial ratification to the federal government. (Connecticut also fails to ratify the amendments.)

Feb.   Madison opposes Hamilton's funding measure for the national debt, arguing that it rewards speculators and unfairly denies compensation to those original holders of Continental securities, including many impoverished war veterans, who were forced to sell at depreciated prices. He favors discrimination between original and subsequent creditors, which Hamilton opposes as impractical and likely to undermine confidence in federal securities. The House rejects discrimination, 36–13, on February 22 and turns to consideration of assumption of state debts.

Feb.–Mar.   On February 24 New York ratifies all but the second proposed amendment. Pennsylvania ratifies all but the first two proposed amendments March 10.

Mar.–Apr.   Madison leads opposition in the House of Representatives to plan for assuming state debts, arguing that it unfairly discriminates against states, such as Virginia, that have already paid much of their war debt, or believe that they will be creditors of the federal government when Revolutionary War finances are finally settled. Assumption measure is defeated, 31–29, on April 12.

May–June   On May 13 the Senate passes a bill embargoing all trade between the 12 ratifying states and Rhode Island. Rhode Island convention votes to ratify the Constitution, 34–32, on May 29, and proposes a bill of rights and amendments; on June 7 the Rhode Island legislature ratifies all but the second of the 12 amendments proposed by Congress.

June–July   On June 2 House sends bill for funding the national debt to the Senate without assumption measure. In late June, Jefferson, Hamilton, and Madison agree that in exchange for southern support of the assumption measure, northern members of Congress will support moving the capital to Philadelphia for ten years and then permanently establishing it along the Potomac in 1800. The Senate sends bills for moving the capital and for assuming the state debts to the House in July, where they are passed by narrow margins. Virginia house of delegates adopts resolutions in early November condemning assumption of state debts as an exercise of powers not given to the federal government by the Constitution.

Dec.   Congress meets in Philadelphia on December 6. Hamilton submits report to the House on December 14 calling for the chartering of a national bank; the bank would be funded by the government and private investors, receive government deposits, assist the treasury and loan it money, and issue bank notes backed by specie.

1791   Bill chartering Bank of the United States passes Senate on January 20. It is opposed in the House by Madison, who argues that the Constitution does not specifically grant Congress the power to incorporate a bank, and that because the federal government can execute constitutionally specified powers such as collecting taxes and borrowing money without a bank, its incorporation cannot be considered "necessary" under the "necessary and proper" clause. The House passes the bill, 39–20 (all but one of the dissenting votes are from the five southern states). Unsure of the constitutionality of the bank bill, Washington asks Randolph and Jefferson for advisory opinions, then gives them to Hamilton for rebuttal while asking Madison to draft a veto message. In his opinion, Jefferson also finds no specific or general power in the Constitution to incorporate a bank, and argues that while a bank would be "convenient" for executing specified powers, it is not indispensable and therefore not "necessary." Hamilton submits his opinion to Washington on February 23, arguing that "necessary" means useful, not indispensable, and that the "necessary and proper" clause gives Congress implied power to adopt any measure clearly useful in executing a specified power, as long as the measure is not specifically prohibited by the Constitution. Washington signs the bank bill on February 25. Excise tax on distilled spirits, proposed by Hamilton as part of 1790 funding plan, becomes law on March 3.

Mar.–Apr.   Vermont is admitted to the Union on March 4. Before leaving on an extended tour of the South, Washington suggests on April 4 that Jefferson, Hamilton, Knox, and Adams meet in his absence.

Nov.   On November 3 Vermont ratifies all 12 proposed amendments. Antifederalists in Virginia state senate end their opposition, and on December 15 Virginia ratifies all 12 amendments, completing ratification of the third through the twelfth proposed amendments, which become the first ten amendments to the Constitution. (First proposed amendment, concerning apportionment of the House, remains unratified. Second proposed amendment, restricting congressional pay increases, is ratified by six states in 1789–91, by one state in 1873 and one state in 1978, and by 31 states in 1983–92; on May 7, 1992, it becomes the Twenty-seventh Amendment to the Constitution.)

Dec.   On December 5 Hamilton submits a report on manufactures to the House. It advocates encouraging domestic industry by government subsidies and protective tariffs, and finds constitutional authority for spending public funds on manufacturing subsidies in a broad interpretation of the general welfare clause. (Congress implements little of the proposed program, and Madison challenges Hamilton's broad construction as leading to the creation of a federal government of unlimited powers.)

Dec.   Washington begins meeting with Jefferson, Hamilton, Knox, and Randolph to discuss policy (term "cabinet" comes into use by 1793).

1792   On April 5 Washington uses the veto power for the first time, disapproving a bill apportioning representatives on the grounds that it unconstitutionally gives some states more than one representative for every 30,000 persons. The House sustains the veto, and on April 14 a new bill, apportioning representatives on a different basis, becomes law (measure increases the size of the House from 67 to 101).

Mar.–June   After Congress passes law on March 23 giving federal circuit courts responsibility for hearing Revolutionary War pension claims, Chief Justice Jay and justices Cushing, Wilson, Blair, and Iredell express opinion in letters to Washington that the law infringes upon the constitutional independence of the judicial branch, since it requires federal courts to perform nonjudicial duties and subjects their decisions to the nonjudicial review of the secretary of war and the Congress. (In 1793 Congress passes a new pension law that relieves the courts from hearing claims.)

May   On May 2 a militia act becomes law, authorizing the president to call forth state militias in case of insurrection against federal authority, or when a state calls for aid.

June   Kentucky is admitted to the Union on June 1.

June–July   In *Champion and Dickason* v. *Casey*, the U.S. Circuit Court for the district of Rhode Island rules in June that a state law giving debtors a three-year extension in paying their creditors violates the constitutional prohibition against state laws impairing the obligation of contracts (Article I, section 10). On July 11 the state of Georgia is summoned to respond in *Chisholm* v. *Georgia*, a suit brought before the U.S. Supreme Court by a South Carolina executor seeking payment for military supplies bought by Georgia commissioners in 1777. Georgia refuses to contest the suit, claiming that as a sovereign state it cannot be sued without its consent.

Aug.–Dec.   Continuing conflict over foreign and domestic policy between Jefferson and Hamilton becomes increasingly public as each writes or encourages newspaper attacks on the other. Washington tries unsuccessfully to mediate the feud, but does agree to serve a second term at the urging of Hamilton, Jefferson, Madison, and others. In the electoral balloting on December 5 Washington is reelected with the votes of all 132 electors, and Adams is reelected vice-president with 77 votes (George Clinton receives 50 electoral votes, Jefferson four, and Aaron Burr one).

1793   In a 4–1 decision, the Supreme Court rules on February 18 for the plaintiff in *Chisholm* v. *Georgia*, affirming that Article III, section 2 of the Constitution gives federal courts jurisdiction over suits brought against a state by a citizen of another state. An amendment intended to overturn the decision is introduced in both houses of Congress by February 20.

Apr.   Washington calls cabinet meeting on April 19 after learning that the revolutionary French republic has declared war on Great Britain. After Hamilton and Jefferson advocate opposing views, Washington decides to maintain the 1778 treaty of alliance with France (which does not obligate the United States to join France in an offensive war) while issuing a proclamation of neutrality (published April 22). When proclamation is challenged on constitutional grounds by supporters of France, Hamilton defends it in "Pacificus" newspaper articles, arguing that Article II of the Constitution gives the president broad general powers, including the power to negotiate and interpret treaties and to determine new courses in foreign affairs. At the urging of Jefferson, Madison replies in "Helvidius" articles, arguing that the power to interpret treaties and proclaim neutrality is constitutionally vested in Congress. (Controversy over neutrality and relations with France contribute to emergence of two political parties, with supporters of Madison and Jefferson calling themselves Republicans and supporters of Hamilton continuing to call themselves Federalists.)

July   Washington writes to Jay on July 18, asking for the advice of the Supreme Court on 29 legal issues relating to the 1778 treaty of alliance with France. In its reply the court declines to give an advisory opinion, stating that its proper role is restricted to ruling on actual disputes brought before it by litigation.

Dec.   Jefferson resigns as secretary of state, effective December 31 (although Jefferson is succeeded by Randolph, Hamilton becomes Washington's leading adviser on foreign policy).

1794   On March 4 Congress proposes the Eleventh Amendment to the states for ratification. Framed in reaction to *Chisholm* v. *Georgia*, the amendment removes from federal jurisdiction any suit "commenced or prosecuted" against a state by the citizen of another state, or by a foreigner.

Apr.–May   Tensions arising from British seizures of American ships trading with the French West Indies and from British trade with Indians along the northwest frontier result in growing anticipation of an Anglo-American war. In effort to avoid hostilities, Washington nominates Jay on April 16 to serve as a special envoy to Britain. After receiving instructions drafted mainly by Hamilton, Jay sails May 12 (arrives in England on June 8).

Aug.–Sept.   Resistance to excise tax on distilled spirits leads to widespread violence against federal officials in western Pennsylvania during summer. Washington issues proclamation on August 7, calling for the insurgents to disperse and summoning 15,000 militiamen into service, and a second proclamation on September 24, calling for suppression of the insurrection. When the federal force marches into western Pennsylvania, the "Whiskey Rebellion" collapses without further bloodshed. (Two men are later convicted of treason, but are pardoned by Washington.)

Nov.   On November 19 Jay signs treaty in London. Its terms include evacuation of British garrisons from frontier posts in the northwestern United States (a provision of the 1783 peace treaty never carried out by Britain), and establishment of commissions to resolve British claims against American debtors and American claims against British seizures of American commerce.

1795   Hamilton resigns as secretary of the treasury on January 31 (will continue to advise Washington on major issues). Ratification of the Eleventh Amendment is completed on February 7 (amendment is not declared to be in effect until January 8, 1798).

June–Aug.   Washington calls special session of the Senate for June 8. After secret debate, Senate votes, 20–10, on June 24 to ratify Jay's Treaty on condition that article concerning trade with British West Indies is renegotiated. Text of treaty is given to Republican newspaper and published July 1. Treaty is widely attacked for failing to secure American neutral rights, to protect American seamen from impressment, or to obtain compensation for slaves evacuated by the British at the end of the Revolutionary War, and for pledging to keep American ports open to British commerce. Despite misgivings, Washington signs treaty on August 18. Randolph resigns as secretary of state on August 19 after being accused by Washington of soliciting a bribe from the French; with the departure of Randolph, the cabinet becomes entirely Federalist.

1796   Supreme Court rules on March 7 in *Ware* v. *Hylton* that under the supremacy clause of Article VI of the Constitution, a wartime Virginia law allowing the discharge of British debts with paper currency is invalid because it contravenes provision of the 1783 peace treaty calling for payment of British debts at full sterling value. On March 8 the Supreme Court rules for the first time on the constitutionality of a congressional act, deciding in *Hylton* v. *United States* that a federal tax on carriages is an excise tax, not a direct tax, and thus does not have to be apportioned according to population as provided for in Article I, section 9.

Mar.–Apr.   Republicans in the House move to have documents relating to the negotiation of Jay's Treaty submitted by the president, arguing that because the treaty regulates commerce and requires appropriations for its implementation, the House has a constitutional right to examine the merits of the treaty. On March 24 the House calls for the papers in 62–37 vote. Washington replies on March 30, withholding the papers on

the grounds that the House has no constitutional role in ratifying treaties and asserting an executive right to maintain the
confidentiality of diplomatic correspondence. After an intense
debate, House votes 51–48 on April 30 to appropriate money
for implementation of the treaty.

June   Tennessee is admitted to the Union on June 1.

Sept.– Dec.   Washington makes public his decision not to seek a third
term when his farewell address is published on September 19.
In the presidential election, Federalist candidate John Adams
receives 71 electoral votes and is elected president, while Jefferson, the Republican candidate, receives 68 electoral votes
and becomes vice-president. (Federalist Thomas Pinckney receives 59 votes, Republican Aaron Burr 30, and nine other
candidates receive 48 electoral votes.)

1797   Relations with France worsen as French navy increases its
seizures of American ships trading with Britain. On May 31
Adams appoints Charles Cotesworth Pinckney, John Marshall, and Elbridge Gerry as commissioners to negotiate
treaty with France. When the commission arrives in Paris in
October, it is approached by three French diplomatic agents
(referred to in later dispatches as X,Y, and Z), who solicit
$240,000 bribe as precondition for negotiations, but the
American commissioners refuse to pay.

1798   Adams submits dispatches from American commissioners in
France to Congress on April 3, and the Federalist Senate
orders their publication. Revelation of "XYZ Affair" causes
popular furor against France. Administration and Congress
take measures to strengthen the navy (Department of the
Navy is established May 3) and army (Washington is named
its commander and chooses Hamilton as his second in command; Adams reluctantly accepts Hamilton's appointment)
while levying a direct property tax to finance war preparations. Unsure of winning majority support, Adams does not
ask Congress for a declaration of war against France, but
Congress does adopt measure on July 9 authorizing the navy
and privateers to capture armed French ships (limited naval
war with France begins in 1798).

July   Congress also adopts series of alien acts and a sedition act.
The three alien acts, passed June 18– July 6, extend the period
required for naturalization from five to 14 years and give the
president power to expel or, in time of declared war, to im-
prison dangerous aliens (no one is expelled under these laws,
and in 1802 the five-year naturalization period is restored).
Sedition act, which becomes law on July 14 after passing the

House by 44–41 vote, establishes criminal penalties for un-
lawfully opposing the execution of federal laws and makes
publication of "false, scandalous, and malicious writing" attacking the federal government, the president, or the Congress a crime punishable by up to two years in prison and a
fine not exceeding $2,000. (The act departs from the English
common law of seditious libel by allowing defendants to offer the truth of their statements as a defense and by permitting juries to determine if statements are libelous under the
law. During the Adams administration ten Republican editors and printers are convicted under the act in trials conducted by sometimes openly partisan Federalist judges.)

Oct.–Dec.   Jefferson secretly drafts resolutions attacking the Alien and
Sedition Acts and shows them to Madison, who secretly
drafts a second set of more moderate resolutions. Kentucky
legislature adopts the Jefferson resolutions in modified form
on November 10, and the Virginia legislature adopts the
Madison resolutions as originally written on December 24.
Both sets of resolutions condemn the Alien and Sedition Acts
as unconstitutional and assert the right of states to determine
the constitutionality of congressional acts.

Nov.   Kentucky resolutions describe the Constitution as a "compact" made by the states that gives the federal government
only the powers definitely delegated to it, and deny that the
federal government is the "exclusive or final judge" of its own
powers. They assert that constitutionally each state "has an
equal right to judge for itself" when the federal government
has exceeded its delegated powers and to determine "the
mode and measure of redress." Declaring the Alien and Sedition Acts to be "void, and of no force" for asserting un-
enumerated powers reserved to the states by the Tenth
Amendment, the resolutions also denounce the alien acts for
violating the independence of the judiciary and constitutional
guarantees of due process and trial by jury and assert that the
sedition act violates the First Amendment by giving the federal government power to punish press libels, a power constitutionally reserved to the states. The Kentucky resolutions
conclude by asking the other states to unite in seeking repeal
of the Alien and Sedition Acts.

Dec.   Virginia resolutions also describe the Constitution as a
"compact" created by the states under which the federal government can exercise only enumerated powers. When the federal government dangerously exercises powers not granted to
it by the Constitution, the resolutions assert that the states
"have the right, and are in duty bound, to interpose for ar-
resting the progress of the evil" and maintaining the liberties

of the people. The resolutions denounce the alien acts for violating the separation of powers and describe the sedition act as a violation of the First Amendment. They conclude by asking the other states to join in declaring the acts unconstitutional and in working to preserve the liberties of the people.

1799   Adams nominates William Vans Murray as special envoy to France on February 18 in attempt to negotiate end to Franco-American hostilities (Oliver Ellsworth and William Davie are later named as additional negotiators). Peace overture splits Federalist party into Adams and Hamilton factions.

Nov.   In response to Kentucky and Virginia resolutions of 1798, legislatures of Delaware, Rhode Island, Massachusetts, New York, Connecticut, New Hampshire, and Vermont adopt resolutions declaring that only the federal courts have the power to determine the constitutionality of federal laws; some of the resolutions also defend the sedition act. On November 14 the Kentucky legislature adopts a second set of resolutions, declaring its attachment to the union and reaffirming its opposition to the Alien and Sedition Acts. The new resolutions assert that the states which formed the Constitution are "sovereign and independent," with the power to judge violations of it, and that "a nullification, by those sovereignties, of all unauthorized acts done" under the Constitution "is the rightful remedy" for such violations. (Jefferson's original 1798 draft for the Kentucky resolutions, first published in 1832 during the South Carolina nullification crisis, declared that states have a "natural right" to "nullify of their own authority" all unconstitutional "assumptions of power by others" within their own state limits.)

1800   Virginia house of delegates adopts on January 7 a report drafted by Madison on the response to the 1798 Virginia resolutions. In the report Madison writes that the people of the states, "in their highest sovereign capacity," ratified the Constitution and are thus parties to the compact creating the federal government, and that there "can be no tribunal above" the states "to decide in the last resort" whether the compact has been violated. Rejecting claims that under the First Amendment Congress is prohibited only from imposing prior restraints upon the press and therefore can pass laws punishing seditious libels, Madison asserts that the federal government is "destitute" of authority to punish the press, and argues that English doctrines of seditious libel are inappropriate in America, where the executive and legislature are responsible to the people and may justifiably incur their "ha-tred" and "contempt" by failing to discharge the public trust. (Opposition to the Alien and Sedition Acts becomes major Republican issue in the 1800 election campaign.)

May   Adams forces the resignation of Secretary of War James McHenry on May 6 and dismisses Secretary of State Timothy Pickering on May 12 for allying themselves with Hamilton and opposing his reelection (Adams appoints John Marshall to replace Pickering). Hamiltonian Federalists are further an-gered by Adams when he pardons John Fries, a Pennsylvania auctioneer condemned to death for treason, on May 21 against the unanimous opinion of his cabinet (Fries had been convicted of leading an armed band to free prisoners jailed for resisting the 1798 federal property tax).

Sept.   American negotiators in France sign treaty on Septem-ber 30 ending undeclared naval war with France and sus-pending 1778 treaty of alliance. (When the Senate ratifies the treaty on condition that the 1778 treaty be completely abro-gated, France refuses to pay compensation for seizures of American ships; amended treaty goes into effect on Decem-ber 21, 1801.)

Nov.   Congress meets for the first time in new capital city of Washington on November 17.

Dec.   In the presidential election Jefferson and Republican vice-presidential candidate Aaron Burr each receive 73 electoral votes, Adams 65, Federalist vice-presidential candidate Charles Cotesworth Pinckney 64, and John Jay one electoral vote (tie is the result of Republican electors evenly dividing their two votes between Jefferson and Burr in order to pre-serve alliance between Virginia and New York Republican parties and to prevent election of a Federalist vice-president). The tie forces the presidential election into the Federalist-controlled House of Representatives. Although many Feder-alists prefer Burr over Jefferson, Hamilton considers Burr to be more dangerous and urges Federalists to elect Jefferson.

1801   Adams nominates Secretary of State John Marshall to be Chief Justice of the Supreme Court on January 20 (confirmed by the Senate on January 27, Marshall serves in both positions for remainder of the Adams administration).

Feb.   Official counting of electoral vote at joint session of Con-gress on February 11 confirms expected tie. House of Repre-sentatives immediately begins voting for president, with each state delegation having one vote as provided for by Article II, section 1. First ballot gives eight states for Jefferson, six for Burr, and two divided, leaving Jefferson one state short of the nine needed for a majority. Deadlock continues through 35 ballots; on the 36th ballot, held February 17, Jefferson receives the votes of ten states, Burr four, and two states cast blank ballots (Burr becomes vice-president).

Feb.–Mar.   New judiciary act is signed by Adams on February 13, reducing the size of the Supreme Court (after the next vacancy occurs) from six justices to five, relieving Supreme Court justices from circuit duty, creating six judicial circuits and 16 circuit court judges, and establishing five new judicial districts; the act also significantly expands federal jurisdiction. Adams and the Federalist Senate begin rapidly filling new judgeships with Federalists, with some appointees receiving their commissions on March 3; expansion of judicial power and appointments angers Jefferson and the Republicans.

Mar.–Dec.   Jefferson gives conciliatory inaugural address on March 4 and quickly pardons all persons convicted under the sedition act, which had expired on March 3. (During the Jefferson administration several Federalist editors will be prosecuted under state laws for seditious libel.) Jefferson also withholds the commissions of 17 of the 42 justices of the peace for the District of Columbia who were appointed and confirmed to five-year terms after Adams learned of his defeat in the 1800 election, but whose signed and sealed commissions remained undelivered when Jefferson took office (Jefferson believes that the number of appointments was excessive). In December William Marbury, one of the 17 justices of the peace who did not receive his commission, asks the U.S. Supreme Court to issue a writ of mandamus commanding Madison, now secretary of state, to deliver the commission (the Supreme Court is authorized to issue writs of mandamus as part of its original jurisdiction by section 13 of the 1789 judiciary act). The Court orders Madison to show cause why the writ should not be issued.

1802   Encouraged by Jefferson, Republicans in Congress move on January 6 to repeal the judiciary act of 1801 and abolish the newly created circuit judgeships. Federalists denounce the repeal bill as an unconstitutional threat to the independence of the judiciary, since it would remove from office judges appointed for good behavior. Republicans argue that since Article III, section 1 gives Congress the power to establish inferior federal courts, Congress also has the power to abolish them. Some Federalists predict that the Supreme Court will hold the repeal law unconstitutional, while some Republicans deny that the court has the power to determine the unconstitutionality of congressional acts, and criticize the show-cause order issued by the court in the pending case of *Marbury* v. *Madison* as an unconstitutional intrusion by the judiciary into the actions of the executive branch. Repeal measure becomes law on March 8. Congress then passes new judiciary act on April 23 that abolishes the June term of the Supreme Court (postponing until February 1803 any decision in *Marbury* v. *Madison* and on the constitutionality of the repeal act) and returns the Supreme Court justices to circuit duty.

1803   On February 24 the Supreme Court delivers its decision in *Marbury* v. *Madison*, holding an act of Congress unconstitutional for the first time. Chief Justice Marshall, speaking for a unanimous court, rules that Marbury is legally entitled to both his commission and a writ of mandamus commanding its delivery, and that the secretary of state is bound by the law to obey such a writ, but that the Supreme Court cannot issue the writ because section 13 of the 1789 judiciary act, giving the Supreme Court power to issue writs of mandamus as part of its original jurisdiction, unconstitutionally expanded the original jurisdiction of the court beyond the limits specified in Article III, section 2. In his opinion, Marshall defends the power of the judiciary to declare acts of Congress unconstitutional, writing that if the Constitution is to be a "superior paramount law, unchangeable by ordinary means," then legislative acts repugnant to the Constitution must be held void by the courts. In *Stuart* v. *Laird*, decided March 2 with Marshall not participating, the Supreme Court upholds the repeal of the 1801 judiciary act against a challenge that does not raise the question of whether Congress can remove judges appointed for good behavior.

Mar.   Ohio is admitted to the union on March 1.

May–Oct. American negotiators in Paris sign treaty on May 2 purchasing Louisiana from France. Because the Constitution does not provide for the acquisition of foreign territory, Jefferson drafts an amendment authorizing the purchase, but then reluctantly agrees to having the acquisition approved under the existing treaty-making power when advisers warn him that questioning the constitutionality of the treaty could jeopardize its ratification (Senate ratifies treaty October 20).

Dec.   Twelfth Amendment, providing for separate balloting by the electors for president and vice-president, is proposed to the states on December 9.

1804   Ratification of the Twelfth Amendment by the states is completed on June 15 and the amendment is proclaimed in effect by Secretary of State Madison on September 17. (No further amendments to the Constitution will be made until the Thirteenth Amendment, abolishing slavery, is proposed and ratified in 1865 at the close of the Civil War.)

Notes on State Constitutions, 1776–90

VIRGINIA The Virginia convention (successor to the convention called in 1774 after the royal governor dissolved the assembly) adopted a declaration of rights, drafted by George Mason, on June 12, 1776, and a constitution, drafted largely by Mason, on June 29, 1776. The declaration of rights asserted that men have certain inherent rights and that all power is derived from the people. It called for the separation of powers in the state government and enumerated essential rights, including trial by a local jury, the ability to confront witnesses, freedom from the compulsion to give evidence, and the prohibition of excessive bails and fines, cruel and unusual punishments, and general search warrants. Declaration of rights also stated that no man should be deprived of his liberty "except by the law of the land, or the judgment of his peers," that freedom of the press should not be restrained and that all men are equally entitled to the free exercise of religion (draft of clause on religion was revised in convention by James Madison). The constitution established a bicameral general assembly, consisting of a house of delegates, elected annually and possessing the sole power to initiate legislation, and a senate, whose members served four-year terms. (Constitution retained existing property qualification for voting, which required adult males to own 25 acres of settled land or its town equivalent.) The senate had to approve all bills passed by the house and could propose amendments to pending laws, with the exception of money bills, which it was required to accept or reject without alteration. Both chambers annually elected the governor, who served as the executive with the advice of an eight-man council of state, also chosen by the legislature. The governor could serve for only three consecutive terms and had no veto over legislation. State judges were appointed by the general assembly and held their offices during "good behavior" (for life, unless removed for misconduct). State officials were prohibited from being elected to the legislature (prohibition against officials sitting in the legislature was adopted by other states in their constitutions). No provision was made for amending the constitution or distinguishing it from ordinary legislation.

NEW JERSEY Provincial congress, which had been elected to serve as an ordinary legislature, adopted constitution on July 2, 1776. It did not contain a separate declarations of rights, but did protect the right to trial by jury, grant religious toleration, and forbid the establishment of any particular religious sect, although officeholders were required to be Protestants. The constitution established a general assembly and a legislative council, both elected annually. Council members were required to own £1,000 property and members of the assembly £500, while ownership of £50 property was needed to vote. The council could accept or reject, but not alter, money bills passed by the general assembly. A governor was elected annually by a joint ballot of the legislature and had no veto power. All significant appointments were made by the legislature, with judges serving for fixed terms. Some articles of the constitution were declared unannulable, leaving the remainder capable of being changed by ordinary legislation.

DELAWARE   A convention elected for the purpose of framing a new government adopted a declaration of rights on September 11 and a constitution on September 20, 1776. The declarations of rights, similar to those adopted in Virginia and already framed in Pennsylvania, was declared to be unalterable. The constitution established a bicameral legislature elected by adult male taxpayers, with the house of assembly serving for one year and the council serving for three years. A president was elected by a joint ballot of the legislature for three years and was advised by a four-member privy council, with each chamber choosing two members. There was no executive veto. Judges were chosen by the legislature and served for good behavior, while other officials were appointed by the president and council. Officeholders were required to be Christians. While some articles of the constitution were declared unannulable, others could be changed by five-sevenths of the assembly and seven-ninths of the council.

PENNSYLVANIA   A convention elected in July 1776 for the purpose of framing a plan of government approved a state constitution on September 28, 1776, that included a declaration of rights, similar to the one adopted in Virginia but adding a statement that the people have a right to freedom of speech. Legislative powers were vested in a unicameral general assembly, elected by all male taxpayers over 21 and by non-taxpaying sons of freeholders over 21 (the widest suffrage adopted by any state). The assembly was elected annually and no member could serve more than four years in seven; delegates to the Continental Congress were also subject to rotation in office. Assembly members were required to believe in one God and the divine inspiration of the Old and New Testaments. Whenever possible, proposed laws were to be held over to the next session to allow for public discussion before their final enactment. A 12-member executive council was to be elected by the freemen, and two of its members were to be chosen as its president and vice-president by a joint ballot of the assembly and council. The council had no veto power. Supreme court judges served for seven-year terms. Every seven years an elected council of censors would review the actions of the state government and determine if the constitution has been violated. A two-thirds vote of the censors could propose amendments and call for a new convention to consider them, but the assembly had no power to change the constitution.

After its adoption the constitution became the focus of a continuing political struggle within the state between its "Constitutionalist" supporters and "Republican" opponents. The first council of censors, elected in October 1783, began meeting in November to review the state government. Amendments to the 1776 constitution advocated by the Republicans included creating a bicameral legislature, establishing a single executive with a limited veto, appointing judges for terms of good behavior, and abolishing rotation in office. Although the Republicans outnumbered Constitutionalists on the council, they did not have the two-thirds majority required to call a new convention.

In September 1789 the Republicans succeeded in having the assembly call a new constitutional convention. It met from November 24 until February 26, 1790, and drafted a constitution which established a bicameral legislature, replaced the executive council with a governor elected by the voters and possessing a limited veto, and tenured judges for good behavior. It also contained a new bill of rights, which included a provision on freedom of the press, drafted by James Wilson, that allowed juries in libel cases to determine both facts and law. The new constitution was adopted on September 2, 1790.

MARYLAND A convention elected for the purpose of framing a new government adopted a declaration of rights and a constitution on November 9, 1776. The declarations of rights contained provisions similar to those of the Virginia and Pennsylvania declarations, as well as a prohibition against bills of attainder. The constitution established a bicameral legislature, with the house of delegates elected annually by voters with 50 acres freehold or £30 property and the senate indirectly elected by an electoral college. Delegates were required to own £500 property and senators £1,000; all officeholders were required to be Christians. Money bills could be accepted or rejected by the senate but not altered by them. The governor and a five-member council were elected by a joint ballot of the legislature. There was no executive veto, but the governor and council did appoint judges, who served for good behavior, as well as other state officials. Changes to the constitution could be made by a majority of the legislature voting in two consecutive sessions.

NORTH CAROLINA Convention elected to frame a new government adopted a declaration of rights, similar to those of other states, and a constitution on December 18, 1776. The constitution established a house of commons and a senate, both elected annually. Taxpayers could vote for the house of commons, while ownership of 50 acres was needed to vote in senate elections. Members of the house of commons were required to own 100 acres and senators had to own 300 acres. The legislature elected a governor and seven-member council annually. There was no executive veto, and the legislature appointed judges, who served for good behavior, as well as other state officials. Officeholding was restricted to Protestants. No provision was made for amending the constitution.

GEORGIA A convention elected in October 1776 to draw up a plan of government adopted a constitution on February 5, 1777. Legislative power was vested in a unicameral assembly, elected annually, whose members were required to be Protestants owning 250 acres of land or £250 of property. The assembly annually elected a governor, who served for only one year out of three and had no veto or pardoning power, an advisory executive council, chosen from among the assembly members, and a state chief justice. Clergymen were forbidden to sit in the legislature, and the Anglican church was disestablished. The constitution protected the free exercise of religion unless "it be repugnant to the peace and safety of the State," freedom of the press, the right to trial by jury, and the principle of habeas corpus, while forbidding excessive fines or bail. Amendments could be made only by a convention petitioned for by a majority of the voters in a majority of the counties.

In November 1788 a convention framed a new state constitution, which was ratified and amended by subsequent conventions in January and May 1789. The new constitution created a house of representatives, elected for one year, and a senate, elected for three years; the governor, elected by the legislature for a two-year term, could veto legislation, but his veto could be overridden by a two-thirds majority in both chambers.

NEW YORK   A convention acting as the state legislature adopted a constitution on April 20, 1777. Legislative power was vested in an assembly, elected annually by males with £20 freehold, and a senate, whose members served four-year terms and were elected by males with £100 freehold; voters qualified for senate elections also chose the governor, who served for three years. Each year the assembly elected four senators to a council of appointment, on which the governor had the deciding vote. The governor, chancellor, and supreme court judges formed a council of revision, which could veto legislation; a two-thirds majority in both legislative chambers could override the veto. The chancellor and judges of the supreme court held office during good behavior until they retired at age 60. Clergymen were forbidden to hold state office. Liberty of conscience and the right to trial by jury and to counsel in criminal cases were protected, but there was no separate declaration of rights. No provision was made for amending the constitution.

SOUTH CAROLINA   The general assembly approved a new constitution on March 19, 1778, to replace the temporary form of government adopted in 1776. It established a senate and house of representatives, both of which served for two years. Appropriation bills had to originate in the house, and could be rejected, but not altered, by the senate; all other legislation could be drafted or amended in either chamber. Senators were required to have £2,000 freehold, while representatives, as well as all voters, had to be free white males over 21, owning 50 acres of land or a town lot of equivalent value. The legislature jointly elected a governor, lieutenant governor, and eight privy councilors, all of whom were required to have a £10,000 freehold, and who served for two years before becoming ineligible for the same office for the next four years. There was no executive veto. Judges were chosen by a joint legislative ballot and served for good behavior. All officeholders were required to be Protestants, and the "Christian Protestant religion" was established in the state. A majority of both legislative chambers could alter the constitution.

MASSACHUSETTS   A specially elected convention submitted a constitution, drafted mainly by John Adams, to the towns for ratification on March 2, 1780; it was approved and went into effect on October 25, 1780. The first article of its declaration of rights proclaimed that "All men are born free and equal" and have "natural" and "unalienable" rights regarding life, liberty, and property (in several cases tried in 1781 and 1783, Massachusetts judges and juries found slavery incompatible with this article; in 1790 the census reported that there were no longer any slaves in Massachusetts). Article II protected religious "profession or beliefs" against persecution, while Article III allowed the legislature to mandate public support for Protestant denominations, effectively continuing the establishment of the Congregational church. Other articles required that reasonable compensation be given for property taken for public use, protected individuals against being compelled to accuse or furnish evidence against themselves, prohibited unreasonable searches and seizures, bills of attainder, cruel and unusual punishments, ex post facto laws, and excessive fines and bail, guaranteed criminal defendants the right to confront witnesses and to trial by jury, and established the right of the people to assemble, instruct their representatives, and petition the legislature. The "Frame of Government" established a senate and a house of representatives, both elected annually by males over 21 who earned £3 a year from freehold property or had £60 in total property. Senators were required to have £300 freehold or £600 total property, representatives £100 freehold or £200 property. The senate was apportioned among districts according to assessed value of taxable property, while the house of representatives was apportioned according to population. All money bills originated in the house, but could be altered in the senate. The governor, elected annually by the voters, was required to have £1000 freehold, and, like the senators and representatives, had to be a declared Christian. Legislation could be vetoed by the governor, but a two-thirds majority in both legislative chambers could override his veto. The governor appointed all judicial officials and sheriffs, with the advice and consent of nine counselors jointly elected by the legislature from among those chosen to be senators. Judges served for good behavior. A new constitutional convention would be called in 1795 if two-thirds of the electors voted in favor of amendment in a referendum.

NEW HAMPSHIRE   An elected convention submitted a constitution to the towns in June; it was declared ratified on October 31 and went into effect in June 1784. It was closely modeled on the 1780 Massachusetts constitution, although the property qualifications for officeholders were lower than in Massachusetts and every male over 21 who paid a poll tax could vote. Executive power was vested in the president of the state, who presided over and voted in the senate, but lacked a veto over legislation.

CONNECTICUT and RHODE ISLAND revised their colonial charters (granted in 1662 and 1663) in 1776 to eliminate references to royal authority. In both states the governor, deputy governor, and council (which served as the upper house of the legislature) were annually elected by the freemen. The lower house of the legislature was elected by the towns twice a year in Connecticut and annually in Rhode Island. There was no executive veto in either state, and in both states judges were annually chosen by the legislature. Connecticut adopted its first state constitution in 1818, Rhode Island in 1842.

Note on the Texts

This volume collects the texts of newspaper articles, essays, pamphlets, private letters, and speeches written or delivered during the debate over ratification of the Constitution from January 14 to August 9, 1788. The first section of the volume includes 90 items written, delivered, or printed as part of the general ratification debate, including a pamphlet collecting resolutions and proposed amendments from seven state ratifying conventions held between January and August 1788. The second section contains speeches from, and letters pertaining to, the ratifying conventions held in South Carolina, Virginia, New York, and North Carolina between May 12 and August 4, 1788.

Most items in this volume are taken from *The Documentary History of the Ratification of the Constitution*, published by the State Historical Society of Wisconsin: Madison, Wisconsin. This set of volumes is the most comprehensive collection ever made of the debates, representing all viewpoints and presenting texts drawn from original documents, including manuscripts of private letters and notes, articles that appeared in newspapers, broadsides, and pamphlets, and the printed and manuscript records of state ratification conventions. The materials are gathered from the holdings of hundreds of libraries, historical societies, and private collections. Under the editorship of John P. Kaminski and Gaspare J. Saladino, the texts are unmodernized literal reproductions, maintaining the eighteenth-century spelling, punctuation, and word usage of the originals. The project consists of an introductory volume, *Constitutional Documents and Records, 1776–1787* (edited by Merrill Jensen, the project's first editor), and two multi-volume series: the *Ratification of the Constitution by the States* (eventually to include 13 volumes), focusing on the public and private debates in the individual states as well as the debates in the state ratifying conventions, and *Commentaries on the Constitution: Public and Private* (eventually to include 5 volumes), which is a chronological arrangement, day by day, of the public and private commentaries from all thirteen states.

In the present volume the texts from the *Documentary History* follow those established by Kaminski and Saladino, except for a few changes in editorial procedure. Words crossed out with a line through them have been deleted here. Bracketed editorial conjectural readings, in cases where the original text was damaged or difficult to read, are accepted without brackets when that reading seems the only possible one; otherwise the missing words are indicated by a bracketed space, i.e., [   ]. The editors of the *Documentary History* also use angle brackets to indicate parts of articles that other newspapers excerpted and printed for their own use; these brackets have been omitted in the present volume. In cases where the texts of the early printings used as sources have been corrected or revised in later printings (for example, *The Federalist*) or by publication of errata, the editors of the *Documentary History* give the later correction in a footnote or insert the correction in brackets next to the original word; this volume deletes the error and prints the corrected word in the text without brackets.

The texts in the present volume that are not in the *Documentary History* (many of them are scheduled for future *Documentary History* volumes) are taken from the best alternative sources, whenever possible from original appearances in newspapers, pamphlets, or early accounts of the state ratifying conventions. For instance, the texts of the debates in the New York ratifying convention are from the shorthand version by Francis Childs, *Debates and Proceedings of the Convention of the State of New-York*, edited and transcribed by Francis Childs (New York, 1788). The texts of the debates in the North Carolina ratifying convention are from *Proceedings and Debates of the Convention of North-Carolina, Convened at Hillsborough, on Monday the 21st Day of July 1788*, transcribed by David Robertson, and published in Edenton, North Carolina, in 1789. The texts of *The Federalist*, beginning with number LXXVI, are from *The Federalist*, edited by Jacob E. Cooke (Middletown, Connecticut: Wesleyan University Press, 1961). The texts in Cooke's edition, like those in the *Documentary History*, are based on the early newspaper versions rather than the subsequent book editions, except for the last essays, LXXVIII–LXXXV, which appeared in print for the first time in the second volume of *The Federalist: A Collection of Essays, Written in Favour of the New Constitution, as Agreed upon by the Federal Convention, September 17, 1787. In Two Volumes Corrected by the Author, with Additions and Alterations*, edited and printed by John and Archibald McLean, published in New York on May 28, 1788. Cooke prints the earliest text of each essay, showing later corrections and revisions in notes, except for corrections of typographical or other obvious errors, which are incorporated into the text. The text of one letter included in the present volume is from *The Papers of James Madison: Volume II, 7 March 1788–1 March 1789*, edited by Robert A. Rutland, Charles F. Hobson, William M. E. Rachal, and Fredrika J. Teute (Charlottesville: The University Press of Virginia, 1977). The texts of four letters are from original holograph manuscripts. The text of the exchange between Rawlins Lowndes and Edward Rutledge in the South Carolina legislature is from the pamphlet, *Debates Which Arose in the House of Representatives of South Carolina on the Constitution Framed for the United States by a Convention of Delegates Assembled at Philadelphia*, edited by R. Haswell and printed at the *City Gazette* office in Charleston, South Carolina, in 1788.

The following is a list of all the writings included in this volume, in the order of their appearance, giving the source of each text. The *Documentary History* is abbreviated as *DHRC*, and the volume and page number follow. When the article is from *Commentaries on the Constitution: Public and Private*, the item number assigned by that edition is also given (for example, CC:447).

LIST OF SOURCES

Robert Yates and John Lansing, Jr., to Governor George Clinton, January 14, 1788. *DHRC*, XV (1984), 368–70 (CC:447), based on New York *Daily Advertiser*, January 14, 1788.

Hugh Ledlie to John Lamb, January 15, 1788. Holograph manuscript, recipient's copy, Lamb Papers, New-York Historical Society. Courtesy of The New-York Historical Society.

Nathaniel Barrell to George Thatcher, January 15, 1788. *DHRC*, XV (1984), 372–73 (CC:449), based on recipient's copy, Thatcher Papers, Boston Public Library.

Rawlins Lowndes and Edward Rutledge Debate in the South Carolina Legislature, January 16, 1788. *Debates Which Arose in the House of Representatives of South Carolina on the Constitution Framed for the United States by a Convention of Delegates Assembled at Philadelphia*, edited by R. Haswell, (Charleston, S.C., 1788), 15–19.

"Publius," The Federalist XXXIX [James Madison], January 16, 1788. *DHRC*, XV (1984), 380–86 (CC:452), based on New York *Independent Journal*, January 16, 1788.

"An Old State Soldier" I, January 16, 1788. *DHRC*, VIII (1988), 303–08. *Virginia Independent Chronicle*, January 16, 1788.

"Brutus" IX, January 17, 1788. *DHRC*, XV (1984), 393–98 (CC:455), based on *New York Journal*, January 17, 1788.

"Publius," The Federalist XLI [James Madison], January 19, 1788. *DHRC*, XV (1984), 418–25 (CC:463), based on New York *Independent Journal*, January 19, 1788.

Henry Knox to John Sullivan, January 19, 1788. *DHRC*, XV (1984), 416–17 (CC:461), based on recipient's copy, Sullivan Papers, New Hampshire Historical Society.

"Americanus" [John Stevens, Jr.] VII, January 21, 1788. New York *Daily Advertiser*, January 21, 1788.

"Publius," The Federalist XLII [James Madison], January 22, 1788. *DHRC*, XV (1984), 427–33 (CC:466), based on *New-York Packet*, January 22, 1788.

"Publius," The Federalist XLIII [James Madison], January 23, 1788. *DHRC*, XV (1984), 439–46 (CC:469), based on New York *Independent Journal*, January 23, 1788.

"Centinel" [Samuel Bryan] XII, January 23, 1788. *DHRC*, XV (1984), 446–50 (CC:470), based on Philadelphia *Independent Gazetteer*, January 23, 1788.

"Brutus" X, January 24, 1788. *DHRC*, XV (1984), 462–67 (CC:474), based on *New York Journal*, January 24, 1788.

"Publius," The Federalist XLIV [James Madison], January 25, 1788. *DHRC*, XV (1984), 469–75 (CC:476), based on *New-York Packet*, January 25, 1788.

"Publius," The Federalist XLV [James Madison], January 26, 1788. *DHRC*, XV (1984), 476–80 (CC:478), based on New York *Independent Journal*, January 26, 1788.

On the New Constitution, January 28, 1788. *DHRC*, XV (1984), 486 (CC:481), based on *State Gazette of South Carolina*, January 28, 1788.

"Publius," The Federalist XLVI [James Madison], January 29, 1788. *DHRC*, XV (1984), 488–93 (CC:483), based on *New-York Packet*, January 29, 1788.

David Ramsay to Benjamin Lincoln, January 29, 1788. *DHRC*, XV (1984), 487–88 (CC:482), based on recipient's copy, Lincoln Papers, Massachusetts Historical Society.

John Williams to His Constituents, written January 29, 1788, published February 25, 1788. *DHRC*, XVI (1986), 200 (CC:559), based on Albany *Federal Herald*, February 25, 1788.

"Publius," The Federalist XLVII [James Madison], January 30, 1788. *DHRC*, XV (1984), 499–504 (CC:486), based on New York *Independent Journal*, January 30, 1788.

"Brutus" XI, January 31, 1788. *DHRC*, XV (1984), 512–17 (CC:489), based on *New York Journal*, January 31, 1788.

"Publius," The Federalist XLVIII [James Madison], February 1, 1788. *DHRC*, XVI (1986), 3–7 (CC:492), based on *New-York Packet*, February 1, 1788.

"Publius," The Federalist XLIX [James Madison], February 2, 1788. *DHRC*, XVI (1986), 16–19 (CC:495), based on New York *Independent Journal*, February 2, 1788.

"Civis" [David Ramsay] to the Citizens of South Carolina, February 4, 1788. *DHRC*, XVI (1986), 21–27 (CC:498), based on *Columbian Herald* (Charleston), February 4, 1788.

"Agrippa" [James Winthrop] XVIII, February 5, 1788. *Massachusetts Gazette*, February 5, 1788.

"Publius," The Federalist LI [James Madison], February 6, 1788. *DHRC*, XVI (1986), 43–47 (CC:503), based on New York *Independent Journal*, February 6, 1788.

"A. B." [Francis Hopkinson], The Raising: A New Song for Federal Mechanics, February 6, 1788. *DHRC*, XVI (1986), 47–48 (CC:504), based on *Pennsylvania Gazette*, February 6, 1788.

"Brutus" XII, February 7 & 14, 1788. *DHRC*, XVI (1986), 72–75 (CC:510) and 120–22 (CC:530), based on *New York Journal*, February 7 and 14, 1788.

George Washington to the Marquis de Lafayette, February 7, 1788. *DHRC*, XVI (1986), 70–72 (CC:509), based on file copy, Washington Papers, Library of Congress.

"Publius," The Federalist LII [James Madison], February 8, 1788. *DHRC*, XVI (1986), 83–87 (CC:514), based on *New-York Packet*, February 8, 1788.

"Publius," The Federalist LIII [James Madison], February 9, 1788. *DHRC*, XVI (1986), 97–101 (CC:519), based on New York *Independent Journal*, February 9, 1788.

William Williams to the Printer, February 11, 1788. *American Mercury*, February 11, 1788.

"Publius," The Federalist LIV [James Madison], February 12, 1788. *DHRC*, XVI (1986), 107–10 (CC:524), based on *New-York Packet*, February 12, 1788.

"Publius," The Federalist LV [James Madison], February 13, 1788. *DHRC*, XVI (1986), 111–15 (CC:525), based on New York *Independent Journal*, February 13, 1788.

"Publius," The Federalist LVI [James Madison], February 16, 1788. *DHRC*, XVI (1986), 129–32 (CC:533), based on New York *Independent Journal*, February 16, 1788.

"Publius," The Federalist LVII [James Madison], February 19, 1788. *DHRC*, XVI (1986), 145–49 (CC:542), based on *New-York Packet*, February 19, 1788.

Harry Innes to John Brown, February 20, 1788. *DHRC*, XVI (1986), 152–53 (CC:545), based on typescript, Innes Papers, Library of Congress.

"Brutus" XIII, February 21, 1788. *DHRC*, XVI (1986), 172–75 (CC:551), based on *New York Journal*, February 21, 1788.

Hugh Williamson's Speech at Edenton, North Carolina, delivered November 8, 1787, printed February 25, 26, 27, 1788. *DHRC*, XVI (1986), 201–08 (CC:560), based on New York *Daily Advertiser*, February 25, 26, 27, 1788.

"Centinel" [Samuel Bryan] XVI, February 26, 1788. *DHRC*, XVI (1986), 218–20 (CC:565), based on Philadelphia *Independent Gazetteer*, February 26, 1788.

Jeremiah Hill to George Thatcher, c. February 26, 1788. *DHRC*, XVI (1986), 209–10 (CC:561), based on recipient's copy, Chamberlain Collection, Thatcher Papers, Boston Public Library.

"A Deep Laid Scheme to Enslave Us . . . Invented in the Society of the Cincinnati," February 27, 1788. *DHRC*, XVI (1986), 528–29 (Appendix I), based on Philadelphia *Independent Gazetteer*, February 27, 1788.

"Publius," The Federalist LXII [James Madison], February 27, 1788. *DHRC*, XVI (1986), 232–37 (CC:569), based on New York *Independent Journal*, February 27, 1788.

"The Impartial Examiner" I, part 2, February 27, 1788. *DHRC*, VIII (1988), 420–24, based on *Virginia Independent Chronicle*, February 27, 1788.

Benjamin Rush to Jeremy Belknap, February 28, 1788. *DHRC*, XVI (1986), 250–51 (CC:573), based on recipient's copy, Belknap Papers, Massachusetts Historical Society.

"Brutus" XIV, February 28 & March 6, 1788. *DHRC*, XVI (1986), 255–58 (CC:576) and 328–31 (CC:598), based on *New York Journal*, February 28 and March 6, 1788.

Joseph Spencer to James Madison, Enclosing John Leland's Objections, February 28, 1788. *DHRC*, XVI (1986), 252–54 (CC:574), based on recipient's copy, Madison Papers, Library of Congress.

Rhode Island's Assembly Refuses to Call a Convention and Submits the Constitution Directly to the People, February 29 & March 1, 1788. *United States Chronicle* (Providence), March 6, 1788.

The Freemen of Providence Submit Eight Reasons for Calling a Convention, March 26, 1788. *United States Chronicle* (Providence), April 10, 1788.

"A Columbian Patriot" [Mercy Otis Warren], Observations on the Constitution, February 1788. *DHRC*, XVI (1986), 274–89 (CC:581), based on *Observations on the New Constitution, and on the Federal and State Conventions* (Boston, 1788).

"Giles Hickory" [Noah Webster] III, February 1788. *American Magazine*, February 1788.

"Publius," The Federalist LXIII [James Madison], March 1, 1788. *DHRC*, XVI (1986), 292–98 (CC:582), based on New York *Independent Journal*, March 1, 1788.

"Publius," The Federalist LXV [Alexander Hamilton], March 7, 1788. *DHRC*, XVI (1986), 335–39 (CC:601), based on *New-York Packet*, March 7, 1788.

John Page to Thomas Jefferson, March 7, 1788. *DHRC*, XVI (1986), 332–33 (CC:599), based on recipient's copy, Jefferson Papers, Library of Congress.

"Publius," The Federalist LXVIII [Alexander Hamilton], March 12, 1788. *DHRC*, XVI (1986), 376–79 (CC:615), based on New York *Independent Journal*, March 12, 1788.

"Publius," The Federalist LXIX [Alexander Hamilton], March 14, 1788. *DHRC*, XVI (1986), 387–93 (CC:617), based on *New-York Packet*, March 14, 1788.

"Publius," The Federalist LXX [Alexander Hamilton], March 15, 1788. *DHRC*, XVI (1986), 396–402 (CC:619), based on New York *Independent Journal*, March 15, 1788.

Comte de Moustier to Comte de Montmorin, March 16, 1788. *DHRC*, XVI (1986), 402–03 (CC:620), based on recipient's copy (translation), Correspondance Politique, États-Unis, Vol. 33, 152–53, Archives du Ministère des Affaires Étrangères, Paris, France.

"Publius," The Federalist LXXI [Alexander Hamilton], March 18, 1788. *DHRC*, XVI (1986), 411–14 (CC:625), based on *New-York Packet*, March 18, 1788.

"Publius," The Federalist LXXII [Alexander Hamilton], March 19, 1788. *DHRC*, XVI (1986), 422–25 (CC:628), based on New York *Independent Journal*, March 19, 1788.

"A Freeman" to the Freeholders and Freemen of Rhode Island, March 20, 1788. *Newport Herald*, March 20, 1788.

"Brutus" XV, March 20, 1788. *DHRC*, XVI (1986), 431–35 (CC:632), based on *New York Journal*, March 20, 1788.

"Publius," The Federalist LXXIV [Alexander Hamilton], March 25, 1788. *DHRC*, XVI (1986), 479–80 (CC:644), based on *New-York Packet*, March 25, 1788.

James Madison to Eliza House Trist, March 25, 1788. *DHRC*, IX (1990), 603, based on recipient's copy (microfilm), University of Virginia.

"Publius," The Federalist LXXV [Alexander Hamilton], March 26, 1788. *DHRC*, XVI (1986), 481–85 (CC:646), based on New York *Independent Journal*, March 26, 1788.

"Publius," The Federalist LXXVI [Alexander Hamilton], April 1, 1788. *The Federalist*, edited by Jacob E. Cooke (Middletown, Connecticut: Wesleyan University Press, 1961 [1982]), 509–15, based on *New-York Packet*, April 1, 1788. Copyright 1961 Wesleyan University; reprinted by permission of the University Press of New England.

"Publius," The Federalist LXXVII [Alexander Hamilton], April 2, 1788. *The Federalist*, ed. Cooke, 515–21, based on New York *Independent Journal*, April 2, 1788. Copyright 1961 Wesleyan University; reprinted by permission of the University Press of New England.

"K." [Benjamin Franklin] to the Editor, April 8, 1788. *The Writings of Benjamin Franklin*, edited by Albert Henry Smyth (New York: The Macmillan Company, 1905–07), IX, 698–703, based on manuscript, Franklin Papers, Library of Congress.

"To Be or Not To Be? Is the Question," April 16, 1788. *New Hampshire Gazette*, April 16, 1788.

"Fabius" [John Dickinson], "Observations on the Constitution Proposed by the Federal Convention" III, April 17, 1788. *Pennsylvania Mercury*, April 17, 1788.

"Plough Jogger," April 17, 1788. *Newport Herald*, April 17, 1788.

Benjamin Rush to David Ramsay, April 19, 1788. *Columbian Herald* (Charleston), April 19, 1788.

George Washington to John Armstrong, April 25, 1788. *DHRC*, IX (1990), 758–61, based on file copy, Washington Papers, Library of Congress.

"Fabius" [John Dickinson], "Observations on the Constitution Proposed by the Federal Convention" VIII, April 29, 1788. *Pennsylvania Mercury*, April 29, 1788.

A Grand Procession in Honor of Ratification, Baltimore, May 6, 1788. *Maryland Journal*, May 6, 1788.

J. Hector St. John Crèvecoeur to Comte de la Luzerne, May 16, 1788. *DHRC*, XVII (forthcoming).

James Madison to George Nicholas, May 17, 1788. *The Papers of James Madison: Volume 11, 7 March 1788 to 1 March 1789*, edited by Robert A. Rutland, Charles F. Hobson, William M. E. Rachal, and Fredrika J. Teute (Charlottesville: The University Press of Virginia, 1977), 44–51. Copyright 1977

The University Press of Virginia; reprinted by permission of The University Press of Virginia.

"An American" [Tench Coxe], May 21, 1788. *DHRC*, IX (1990), 833–41, based on *Pennsylvania Gazette*, May 21, 1788.

Richard Henry Lee to Edmund Pendleton, May 26, 1788. *DHRC*, IX (1990), 878–81, based on recipient's copy, Huntington Library, San Marino, California.

"Publius," The Federalist LXXVIII [Alexander Hamilton], May 28, 1788. *The Federalist*, ed. Cooke, 521–30, based on *The Federalist: A Collection of Essays, Written in Favour of the New Constitution, as Agreed upon by the Federal Convention, September 17, 1787* (New York, 1788). Copyright 1961 Wesleyan University; reprinted by permission of the University Press of New England.

"Publius," The Federalist LXXX [Alexander Hamilton], May 28, 1788. *The Federalist*, ed. Cooke, 534–41, based on *The Federalist* (1788). Copyright 1961 Wesleyan University; reprinted by permission of the University Press of New England.

"Publius," The Federalist LXXXI [Alexander Hamilton], May 28, 1788. *The Federalist*, ed. Cooke, 541–52, based on *The Federalist* (1788). Copyright 1961 Wesleyan University; reprinted by permission of the University Press of New England.

"Publius," The Federalist LXXXII [Alexander Hamilton], May 28, 1788. *The Federalist*, ed. Cooke, 553–57, based on *The Federalist* (1788). Copyright 1961 Wesleyan University; reprinted by permission of the University Press of New England.

"Publius," The Federalist LXXXV [Alexander Hamilton], May 28, 1788. *The Federalist*, ed. Cooke, 587–95, based on *The Federalist* (1788). Copyright 1961 Wesleyan University; reprinted by permission of the University Press of New England.

David Ramsay's Oration at Charleston, South Carolina, delivered May 27, 1788, printed June 5, 1788. *Columbian Herald* (Charleston), June 5, 1788.

Simeon Baldwin's Oration at New Haven, July 4, 1788. *An Oration Pronounced before the Citizens of New-Haven, July 4th, 1788; in Commemoration of the Declaration of Independence and Establishment of the Constitution of the United States of America* (New Haven, 1788).

"Phocion," July 17, 1788. *United States Chronicle* (Providence), July 17, 1788.

"Solon, Junior" [David Howell], August 9, 1788. *Providence Gazette*, August 9, 1788.

The Ratifications and Resolutions of Seven State Conventions, February 6–August 2, 1788. *The Ratifications of the New Fœderal Constitution, together with the Amendments, proposed by the Several States* (Richmond, 1788).

SOUTH CAROLINA RATIFYING CONVENTION

Charles Cotesworth Pinckney, May 14, 1788. *Columbian Herald* (Charleston), June 9, 1788.

Patrick Dollard, May 22, 1788. *City Gazette* (Charleston), May 29, 1788.

VIRGINIA RATIFYING CONVENTION

Patrick Henry's Opening Speech, June 4, 1788. *DHRC*, IX (1990), 929–31, based on *Debates and Other Proceedings of the Convention of Virginia*, transcribed by David Robertson (Petersburg, 1788 & 1789).

Governor Edmund Randolph, June 4, 1788. *DHRC*, IX (1990), 931–36, based on *Debates and Other Proceedings of the Convention of Virginia*.

George Mason, June 4, 1788. *DHRC*, IX (1990), 936–41, based on *Debates and Other Proceedings of the Convention of Virginia*.

James Madison, June 6, 1788. *DHRC*, IX (1990), 989–98, based on *Debates and Other Proceedings of the Convention of Virginia*.

Patrick Henry, June 7, 1788. *DHRC*, IX (1990), 1035–47, based on *Debates and Other Proceedings of the Convention of Virginia*.

Henry Lee, June 9, 1788. *DHRC*, IX (1990), 1072–81, based on *Debates and Other Proceedings of the Convention of Virginia*.

James Madison, June 11, 1788. *DHRC*, IX (1990), 1142–54, based on *Debates and Other Proceedings of the Convention of Virginia*.

James Madison, June 12, 1788. *DHRC*, X (1992), 1202–09, based on *Debates and Other Proceedings of the Convention of Virginia*.

Patrick Henry and James Madison, June 12, 1788. *DHRC*, X (1992), 1209–26, based on *Debates and Other Proceedings of the Convention of Virginia*.

James Monroe Questions James Madison, June 14, 1788. *DHRC*, X (1992), 1259–60, based on *Debates and Other Proceedings of the Convention of Virginia*.

Patrick Henry and James Madison, June 16, 1788. *DHRC*, X (1992), 1299–1303, based on *Debates and Other Proceedings of the Convention of Virginia*.

Patrick Henry and James Madison, June 16, 1788. *DHRC*, X (1992), 1309–12, based on *Debates and Other Proceedings of the Convention of Virginia*.

George Mason and James Madison, June 17, 1788. *DHRC*, X (1992), 1338–39, based on *Debates and Other Proceedings of the Convention of Virginia*.

Governor Edmund Randolph, June 17, 1788. *DHRC*, X (1992), 1347–54, based on *Debates and Other Proceedings of the Convention of Virginia*.

George Mason, June 17, 1788. *DHRC*, X (1992), 1365–66, based on *Debates and Other Proceedings of the Convention of Virginia*.

George Mason, June 19, 1788. *DHRC*, X (1992), 1401–09, based on *Debates and Other Proceedings of the Convention of Virginia*.

John Marshall, June 20, 1788. *DHRC*, X (1992), 1430–39, based on *Debates and Other Proceedings of the Convention of Virginia*.

John Dawson, June 24, 1788. *DHRC*, X (1992), 1488–95, based on *Debates and Other Proceedings of the Convention of Virginia*.

Zachariah Johnston, June 25, 1788. *DHRC*, X (1992), 1530–34, based on *Debates and Other Proceedings of the Convention of Virginia*.

NEW YORK RATIFYING CONVENTION

Melancton Smith and Alexander Hamilton, June 21, 1788. *Debates and Proceedings of the Convention of the State of New-York*, edited and transcribed by Francis Childs (New York, 1788), 30–42.

Robert R. Livingston, Melancton Smith, and John Jay, June 23, 1788. *Debates and Proceedings of the Convention of the State of New-York* (1788), 51–60.

Gilbert Livingston, June 24, 1788. *Debates and Proceedings of the Convention of the State of New-York* (1788), 60–62.

Robert R. Livingston, June 24, 1788. *Debates and Proceedings of the Convention of the State of New-York* (1788), 63–65.

Alexander Hamilton, June 24, 1788. *Debates and Proceedings of the Convention of the State of New-York* (1788), 70–75.

Melancton Smith and Alexander Hamilton, June 25, 1788. *Debates and Proceedings of the Convention of the State of New-York* (1788), 76–86.

Melancton Smith, June 27, 1788. *Debates and Proceedings of the Convention of the State of New-York* (1788), 92–96.

Melancton Smith to Nathan Dane, June 28, 1788. Holograph manuscript, recipient's copy, Dane Papers, Beverly Historical Society. Courtesy of the Beverly Historical Society and Museum.

Alexander Hamilton, June 28, 1788. *Debates and Proceedings of the Convention of the State of New-York* (1788), 112–19.

Robert R. Livingston, July 1, 1788. *Debates and Proceedings of the Convention of the State of New-York* (1788), 127–30.

Melancton Smith, July 2, 1788. *Debates and Proceedings of the Convention of the State of New-York* (1788), 134–35.

Nathan Dane to Melancton Smith, July 3, 1788. Holograph manuscript (mss 95), John Wingate Thorton Papers, New England Historic Genealogical Society. Courtesy of New England Historic Genealogical Society.

Melancton Smith to Nathan Dane, c. July 15, 1788. Holograph manuscript (mss 95), John Wingate Thorton Papers, New England Historic Genealogical Society. Courtesy of New England Historic Genealogical Society.

Melancton Smith, July 23, 1788. New York *Daily Advertiser*, July 28, 1788.

NORTH CAROLINA RATIFYING CONVENTION

Five Speakers Debate Congressional Control of Congressional Elections, July 25, 1788. *Proceedings and Debates of the Convention of North-Carolina, Convened at Hillsborough, on Monday the 21st Day of July 1788*, transcribed by David Robertson (Edenton, North Carolina, 1789), 72–78.

The Debate on Congressional Elections Continued, July 25, 1788. *Proceedings and Debates of the Convention of North- Carolina* (1789), 84–86.

James Iredell, July 26, 1788. *Proceedings and Debates of the Convention of North-Carolina* (1789), 117–22.

James Iredell, July 28, 1788. *Proceedings and Debates of the Convention of North-Carolina* (1789), 129–37.

Samuel Spencer, July 28, 1788. *Proceedings and Debates of the Convention of North-Carolina* (1789), 139–42.

This volume presents the texts of the documents chosen for inclusion here without change, except for the correction of typographical errors or slips of the pen and the modernization of the use of quotation marks (only beginning and ending quotation marks are provided here, instead of placing a quotation mark at the beginning of every line of a quoted passage). The other conventional features of eighteenth-century spelling and punctuation (including the use of italics for proper names and large and small capitals for emphasis) have been preserved. The following is a list of typographical errors corrected, cited by page and line number: 8.16, my; 25.12, importance. The gentleman had com-/templating a subject of such vast importance. The; 155.26, gentlemen; 156.28, if; 156.38, far; 156.40, reveiwers; 160.27, notwistanding; 161.23, ageee; 179.40, amelisration; 193.13, gentlemen; 193.13, uneasiy; 194.24, chatholic; 227.31, tha; 282.12, of of; 290.6–7, Beinnial; 304.11, per-/period; 304.20, "That; 304.30, where; 306.14–15, trancendant; 310.33, The; 331.16, probablility; 334.12–13, detatched; 352.26, responsiblity; 419.9, I; 504.32, GOVERMENT; 517.11, defence freedom; 525.21, goverment; 547.1, anxions; 547.25, ONNENTION; 553.16–17, governmennt; 554.4, to to; 557.21, apreared; 562.2, Execute; 562.37, solder; 563.10, it; 569.27, suspendg; 570.1, solder; 574.12, bound.; 577.8, *the the*; 584.11, man; 584.39, eitheir; 585.12, sys-; 585.25, spices; 586.4, assmbled; 586.9, the mall; 586.13, apportunity; 587.22, seperate; 593.35, arbishop; 618.25, Magistate; 620.9, jursdiction; 748.37, *imperu*; 758.27, representative; 759.33, hetter; 759.38, producing; 761.25, to to; 774.34, fellow; 777.10–11, goverement; 785.3, goveenment; 787.28, folse; 792.6, establshed; 793.23, in senate; 797.18, thas; 797.19, recallt; 797.20, grea.; 797.22, ant; 797.23, id; 797.24, perpetualln; 797.25, nevey; 797.26, hir;

801.34, wisdon; 805.28, firmnes; 808.2, uniform,; 820.15, operation; 825.19, we we; 829.28, enconiums; 835.22, deople; 835.24, change; 836.30, thro'; 838.6, raised?; 838.16, adehrence; 841.34, too; 871.30, power declaring; 881.12, conjuction.

Notes

In the notes below, the reference numbers denote page and line of this volume (the line count includes headings). No note is made for information found in common desk-reference books such as *Webster's Ninth Collegiate* and *Webster's Biographical* dictionaries. Footnotes within the text were part of the original documents. Quotations from Shakespeare are keyed to *The Riverside Shakespeare*, ed. G. Blakemore Evans (Boston: Houghton Mifflin, 1974). Quotations from the Bible are keyed to the King James Version. Quotations from William Blackstone's *Commentaries on the Laws of England* are keyed to the first edition (4 vols., 1765–69; University of Chicago facsimile edition, 1979). For historical and biographical background see Chronology of Events and Biographical Notes in this volume. For further historical information and references to other studies, see the following volumes in *The Documentary History of the Ratification of the Constitution* (Madison: State Historical Society of Wisconsin): *Constitutional Documents and Records, 1776–1787* (vol. I, 1976), ed. Merrill Jensen, *Ratification of the Constitution by the States—Pennsylvania* (II, 1976), ed. Jensen, *Delaware, New Jersey, Georgia, Connecticut* (III, 1978), ed. Jensen, *Virginia* (VIII–X, 1988–92), ed. John P. Kaminski and Gaspare J. Saladino, and *Commentaries on the Constitution, Public and Private* (XIII–XVI, 1981–86), ed. Kaminski and Saladino; *The Papers of James Madison* (vols. 1–10, Chicago: University of Chicago Press, 1962–77; vols. 11–17, Charlottesville: University Press of Virginia, 1977–91), ed. Robert A. Rutland et. al.; *The Records of the Federal Convention* (3 vols.; New Haven: Yale University Press, 1911), ed. Max Farrand; *Supplement to Max Farrand's The Records of the Federal Convention* (New Haven: Yale University Press, 1987), ed. James H. Hutson and Leonard Rapport; *Encyclopedia of the American Constitution* (4 vols.; New York: Macmillan Publishing Company, 1986), ed. Leonard W. Levy, Kenneth L. Karst, Dennis J. Mahoney; *The Federalist* (Middletown: Wesleyan University Press, 1961), ed. Jacob E. Cooke; *The Federal and State Constitutions, Colonial Charters, and Other Organic Laws of the States, Territories, and Colonies* (7 vols.; Washington, D.C.: Government Printing Office, 1909), ed. Francis N. Thorpe; Gaspare J. Saladino, "The Bill of Rights; A Bibliographic Essay" in *The Bill of Rights and the States: The Colonial and Revolutionary Origins of American Liberties* (Madison: Madison House Publishers, Inc., 1992), ed. Patrick T. Conley and John P. Kaminski; and Bernard Bailyn, "The Ideological Fulfillment of the American Revolution" in *Faces of Revolution: Personalities and Themes in the Struggle for American Independence* (New York:

Alfred A. Knopf, Inc., 1990). The scholarship of *The Documentary History of the Ratification of the Constitution* has been an essential aid in the preparation of this volume.

3.7   *Dec. 21, 1787.*] Yates and Lansing withdrew from participation in the Constitutional Convention and left Philadelphia on July 10, 1787. This letter to Governor Clinton was their first public explanation of their conduct. It was transmitted to the state legislature on January 11, 1788, and appeared in print three days later.

3.16   ⌃ powers delegated to us] See Chronology of Events, February 21–March 6, 1787.

7.3   *Hugh Ledlie*] The letter is signed by Ledlie (who suffered from gout) but is in the handwriting of a secretary to whom he dictated it.

7.8–9   Sears, . . . Hazard] Sears, Robinson, Wiley, and Mott, along with John Lamb, composed the intercolonial committee of correspondence for the New York Sons of Liberty in 1765 and were active in mobilizing resistance to the Stamp Act. Isaac Sears (1730–86), born in New England, was a New York City sea captain, merchant, privateer, leader of the Sons of Liberty 1765–76, member of first and second provincial congresses and the state assembly, who died in Canton, China, while on a commercial voyage; Thomas Robinson (1730–1817), naval captain of New York and Connecticut; William Wiley; Gershom Mott (c. 1743–86), of New Jersey and New York, served during the Revolution in sieges of St. Johns and Quebec under McDougall and was later captain and recruiting officer in Lamb's 1st New York Artillery and the Continental Army; Edward Laight (1721–94), New York City merchant and ironmonger, member of the Sons of Liberty 1765–66, and member of the committee of inspection to enforce non-importation agreements, later withdrew from politics and remained in New York during British occupation; John Morin Scott (1730–84), New York lawyer and pamphleteer, was associated with the New York Sons of Liberty but was probably not a member—he was later a judge, a member of the first and second provincial congresses and state constitutional convention, brigadier general in Continental Army at battle of Long Island 1776, state senator 1777–82, delegate to Continental Congress 1779–83, and member of Society of the Cincinnati; Jonathan J. Hazard (1744–1824) of Newport, a leader of the resistance to the Stamp Act in Rhode Island, paymaster in Continental Army, delegate to Continental Congress 1787–89, member of the state house of representatives 1776–78 and 1790–1805, and (in 1787–88) a vigorous Antifederalist. In 1805 he moved to a Friends' settlement in Oneida County, New York.

7.11   Pintard Williams] In February 1766, New York merchant Lewis Pintard (1732–1818) and customs collector Charles Williams were accused of using stamped paper and were taken by the Sons of Liberty to the Common and forced to apologize; a mob threatened their houses.

7.21–22   Genl. James Wadsworth] James Wadsworth (1730–1817), Yale graduate, Durham lawyer, town clerk, member of the house of representatives 1759–85 (speaker 1784–85) and 1788–89, justice of the peace 1761–86 and 1788–91, justice of quorum 1773–78, member council of safety 1777–82, major general of Connecticut militia 1777–79, judge of New Haven county court 1778–89, delegate to Continental Congress 1783–86, member state executive council 1785–89, state comptroller 1786–87, delegate to ratifying convention of 1788, where he opposed ratification. He refused reappointment to county court in 1789 rather than take the oath to uphold the Constitution.

7.34–8.2   impost . . . the foederal farmer] The 40-page pamphlet *Observations Leading to a Fair Examination of the System of Government Proposed by the Late Convention; and to Several Essential and Necessary Alterations in It. In a Number of Letters from the Federal Farmer to the Republican* was published November 8, 1787 (see *Debate on the Constitution, Part One*, pp. 245–88); by early January it was in its fourth printing. Richard Henry Lee was wrongly thought to be its author. An article in the *Connecticut Courant* of December 24, 1787, entitled "New England: to the Honorable Richard Henry Lee, Esquire" had charged that the pamphlet was distributed throughout Connecticut by the impost collector of New York (John Lamb) in an effort to preserve the state's power to tax interstate commerce. Those charges had been extended in "Connecticutensis: To the People of Connecticut," in *American Mercury* of December 31, 1787.

8.5–6   Lamb . . . Yates's] This enumeration of Antifederalists is taken from Oliver Ellsworth's "Landholder" VIII (December 24, 1787). Marinus Willett (1740–1830), New York City merchant, leader of the Sons of Liberty, lieutenant colonel of New York militia and Continental Army, voted sword by Congress for defense of Fort Stanwix in 1777, sheriff of New York City 1784–88 and 1792–96, and mayor of New York 1807–11; for Melancton Smith, George Clinton, and Robert Yates, see Biographical Notes.

8.31   Mr. Mason, Mr. Geary] George Mason and Elbridge Gerry.

9.22–26   piece aluded . . . Genl. Lee] The article "New England: to the Honorable Richard Henry Lee, Esquire" in the *Connecticut Courant* of December 24, 1787. General Charles Lee of the Continental Army, a retired British officer and no relation to the Lees of Virginia, was court martialed for disobedience and misconduct in 1778 and dismissed from the army in 1780. Richard Henry Lee was never an enemy of George Washington.

9.32   Copper, Wimble] "Copper" was Joseph Hopkins (1730–1801), Waterbury silversmith who (with three others) was granted the right to mint copper coins in 1785; he was town treasurer 1760–64, justice of the peace of New Haven 1760–1801, justice of quorum 1777–1801, member of the house of representatives 1764–77 and 1780–96, judge of probate 1779–1801, and a member of the state council of safety 1781–83. "Wimble" was William Williams (1731–1811) of Lebanon, a delegate to the Continental Congress and signer of the Declaration of Independence, who feared speculators' designs on the state's western lands. Both men were Antifederalists, although they voted for ratification in the Connecticut convention.

9.35   Wrongheads]   A common epithet for Antifederalists; it was first applied to James Wadsworth as early as 1786.

10.7–8   trials . . . Writ]   Shakespeare, *Othello*, III.iii.322–24.

10.8–9   the Wise . . . secure]   William Congreve, *The Way of the World*, end of Act III (xviii).

11.24–26   Duane . . . DeWitt]   James Duane (1733–97), New York City lawyer, delegate to Continental Congress 1774–84 (where he helped draft the Articles of Confederation), first mayor of New York 1784–89, state senator 1782–85 and 1789–90, member New York ratifying convention 1788 (where he voted for ratification), U.S. District Judge 1789–94; Robert R. Livingston (see Biographical Notes); John Haring (1739–1809), Rockland County and New York City lawyer, judge of Orange County 1774–75 and 1778–88, delegate to Continental Congress 1774–75 and 1785–88, member and president of provincial congresses 1775–77, state senator 1781–82, member New York ratifying convention 1788 (where he opposed ratification), state assemblyman 1806; Egbert Benson (1746–1833), Dutchess County lawyer, state attorney general 1777–89, state assemblyman 1777–81 and 1788, delegate to Continental Congress 1784–88, judge of state supreme court 1794–1801, delegate to Annapolis convention 1786, member New York ratifying convention 1788 (where he supported ratification), U.S. Representative 1789–93, U.S. Circuit Court Judge 1801–02, U.S. Representative March–August 1813, and a founder of New-York Historical Society; Simeon DeWitt (1756–1834), geographer for Continental Army 1778–81, surveyor general of New York 1784–1834, regent, vice-chancellor, and chancellor of the University of the State of New York 1798–1834.

12.5   half Joe.]   The Portuguese "johannes" was a gold coin that circulated throughout the Atlantic world; a half-joe was worth approximately eight dollars in 1775.

12.26   Hugh Hughes]   Hugh Hughes (1727–1802), originally of New Jersey, was a member of the New York Sons of Liberty 1765–66 and quartermaster general of New York during the Revolution (Charles Tillinghast was his assistant). He later taught school in New York and was a tutor for John Lamb's children. His brother John Hughes was the stamp agent for Pennsylvania in 1765 and a friend of Franklin. Hugh Hughes was a member of New York assembly in 1784. He wrote six Antifederalist essays published under the name "A Countryman" in the *New York Journal*, November 21, 1787–February 14, 1788, and other essays. In 1788, he lived in Dutchess

County but soon moved to Westchester County where he became a tenant of John Lamb.

13.4   those very men] Oliver Ellsworth, William Samuel Johnson, and Roger Sherman were delegates to the Constitutional Convention and the Connecticut ratifying convention (January 3–9, 1788).

13.34   1/3 . . . 6/8.] One shilling, three pence; six shillings, eight pence (there were 20 shillings in a pound).

13.39–40   20/. . . . 2/6.] One pound (20 shillings); two shillings, six pence. In 1790 the first federal Congress debated the fairness of redeeming at face value public securities which had been bought by speculators at depreciated prices; see Chronology of Events, January–July 1790.

14.35–38   Dr. Franklin . . . Johnson] Benjamin Franklin; his son William Franklin, the exiled royalist governor of New Jersey; Governor William Livingston of New Jersey; William Smith, a Loyalist who had become the chief justice of Quebec; Sir Henry Moore (1713–69), colonial governor of New York 1765–69; and William Samuel Johnson.

15.12   Philip Livingston] He had died in 1778.

15.18–20   Govr. Livingston . . . Landaff] William Livingston published the pamphlet *A Letter to the Right Reverend Father in God, John, Lord Bishop of Landaff* in 1768 in opposition to the creation of an Anglican bishopric in America. Shute Barrington (1734–1826) was Bishop of Llandaff (in Wales) 1760–82.

15.35–37   Harison . . . Washington] In 1775 Congress had appointed Benjamin Franklin and two other delegates, Benjamin Harrison of Virginia and Thomas Lynch, Sr., of South Carolina, to confer with Washington at his headquarters in Cambridge.

16.14–15   pamphlet . . . enclose] "A Citizen of Philadelphia" (Pelatiah Webster), *The Weaknesses of Brutus Exposed: or, some Remarks in Vindication of the Constitution Proposed by the Late Federal Convention, against the Objections and Gloomy Fears of that Writer*, published November 8, 1787 (see *Debate on the Constitution, Part One*, pp. 176–88).

19.4   *South Carolina Legislature*] In South Carolina, debate on the proposed Constitution began in the legislature over the question of whether or not to convene a ratifying convention. Charles Pinckney, who had been one of South Carolina's delegates to the Constitutional Convention, opened the discussion in the state house of representatives on January 16, 1788. After three days of intense debate with the Antifederalists, led by Rawlins Lowndes, the house voted 76 to 75 to hold a convention in Charleston, a Federalist stronghold (a previous motion on calling a convention, location unspecified, had carried unanimously). See David Ramsay's January 29 letter to Benjamin

Lincoln (pp. 117–18 in this volume) and his "Civis" letter of February 4 (pp. 147–54 in this volume).

21.21   Major Butler]   Pierce Butler (1744–1822), former major in British Army, state representative 1778–89, delegate to Continental Congress 1787, delegate to Constitutional Convention 1787 (where he drafted the fugitive slave clause), U.S. Senator 1789–96 and 1802–04, and director of the Bank of the United States.

25.23   two-fifths]   An error for three-fifths (Art. I, sec. 2).

26.3   *The Federalist*]   The *Federalist* essays, Madison wrote, "were written most of them in great haste, and without any special allotment of the different parts of the subject to the several writers. . . . It frequently happened that whilst the printer was putting into type the parts of a number, the following parts were under the pen, & to be finished in time for the press." Yet the resulting 85 essays (the longest series by far of all those written in the ratification debate), even at the time of their publication, were praised by many as a masterpiece of political theory—in Jefferson's words "the best commentary on the principles of government which ever was written." But not all contemporaries, not even all the Federalists, agreed. Rufus King thought Oliver Ellsworth's "Landholder" essays more effective than the *Federalist* essays, and the Federalist judge Alexander Contee Hanson, formerly Washington's private secretary and soon to be chancellor of the state of Maryland, while acknowledging that *The Federalist Papers* (collected in 2 vols., March and May, 1788, by John and Archibald M'Lean) displayed deep penetration and were ingenious and elaborate, found them sophistical in some places, painfully obvious in others, and throughout, prolix and tiresome. He could not get through them, he said: they do not "force the attention rouze the passions, or thrill the nerves." He thought his own short pamphlet, *Remarks on the Proposed Plan of a Federal Government, Addressed to the Citizens of the United States, by Aristides* (January 1788), dedicated to Washington, though perhaps inferior to *The Federalist* as an abstract treatise on government, "as an occasional pamphlet" was "superior" and "more serviceable." *The Federalist Papers*, all addressed to "The People of the State of New-York," were first published from October 27 to May 28, 1788. When the essays were collected in the M'Lean edition (see note 467.5), essay XXXV became essay XXIX (Hamilton placing it by topic rather than date), requiring a change in the numbering of the subsequent essays, and number XXXI was divided into two essays (also on Hamilton's advice) numbered XXXII and XXXIII. This volume uses the numbering of the M'Lean edition, which has become standard. Essays II, III, IV, V, and LXIV have been attributed to John Jay; essays X, XIV, XXXVII–LVIII, LXII, and LXIII to Madison; essays XVIII–XX to Madison, assisted by Hamilton; and the remainder to Hamilton.

27.29–30   one . . . legislature]   Maryland, where the senate was indirectly elected by electors chosen by the people.

33.3   "*An Old . . . I*]   The first of a series of five essays that ran through April 2, 1788. The author was probably George Nicholas, of Charlottesville, Virginia.

33.7   *an Officer . . . army.*]   The essay by "An Officer of the Late Continental Army" (Philadelphia *Independent Gazetteer*, November 6, 1787; see *Debate on the Constitution, Part One*, pp. 97–104) included 23 objections to the Constitution; it was reprinted in at least eight newspapers, the *American Museum* magazine (November 1787), and as a pamphlet and broadside.

34.23   *Omnes . . . licentia.*]   "We are all made worse by licence." Terence, *Heautontimorumenos* (The Self-Tormenter).

40.2   "*Brutus*"]   The author of the 16 Antifederalist "Brutus" essays (*New York Journal*, October 18, 1787–April 10, 1788) is not known. A likely candidate is Robert Yates, the New York delegate to the Constitutional Convention who withdrew in opposition halfway through the proceedings.

41.24   my last number]   "Brutus" VIII, January 10, 1788 (see *Debate on the Constitution, Part One*, pp. 732–36).

42.1   A writer . . . system]   Noah Webster, *An Examination into the Leading Principles of the Federal Constitution Proposed by the Late Convention Held at Philadelphia. With Answers to the Principal Objections that Have Been Raised Against the System*, published October 17, 1787 (see *Debate on the Constitution, Part One*, pp. 129–63).

43.39–40   A writer . . . constitution]   "Publius" (Alexander Hamilton), in *The Federalist XXIV* (*New-York Independent Journal*, December 19, 1787; see *Debate on the Constitution, Part One*, pp. 575–80).

51.17   repeat . . . observations]   Presumably in *The Federalist XXVI*, December 22, 1787, written by Hamilton.

53.36   already . . . explained]   By Hamilton, in *The Federalist XXIX*, January 9, 1788.

58.3   "*Americanus*" . . . *VII*]   This is the last in the "Americanus" series; the first was published November 2, 1787.

58.5   Governor Randolph's letter]   After Virginia's Governor Edmund Randolph refused to sign the Constitution, he said he would make his objections public in due time and that he was undecided whether or not he would favor ratification by the state. On October 10, he wrote but did not send a letter to the speaker of the house of delegates explaining his reasons for not signing. In response to a formal request (December 2) from four Antifederalist members to make public those objections, he sent them the letter, which was published on December 27, 1787, in a 16-page pamphlet that was widely reprinted in newspapers (see *Debate on the Constitution, Part One*, pp. 595–611).

67.22   an antecedent paper]   *The Federalist XIX* (by Madison, assisted by Hamilton), December 8, 1787.

71.7   The *fourth* class]   See page 48.11–21 in this volume.

73.22–25   *new States . . . by it.*]   The Northwest Ordinance, passed by the Continental Congress on July 13, 1787, provided for the creation of three to five states from the Northwest Territory and established procedures for creating territorial and state governments. See Chronology of Events, July 1787.

74.23–28   "As the . . . Amphyctions."]   *The Spirit of the Laws*, Bk. IX, ch. 2.

75.28   A recent . . . event]   For Shays' Rebellion in western Massachusetts (1786–87), see Chronology of Events, July–October 1786 and January–April 1787.

77.15–18   "that should . . . sound."]   *The Spirit of the Laws*, Vol. I, Bk. IX, ch. 1.

82.25–26   seal . . . constitution;]   Referring to Benjamin Rush's speech in the Pennsylvania ratifying convention, December 12, 1787.

83.26–84.3   Under the . . . business.]   Rush's speech (see above note) created a storm of controversy because of its conclusion that the Constitution was God-given and that ratification was the will of heaven. It was reported in the *Pennsylvania Herald* (December 15, see *Debate on the Constitution, Part One*, pp. 869–70) by Alexander J. Dallas, who called it a "new species of *divine right*." Dallas's summary was denounced by the convention's shorthand reporter Thomas Lloyd (1756–1827) as "a gross misrepresentation," and Dallas called Lloyd's criticism a "*gross falsehood*." (Lloyd's version of Rush's speech was published in the *Pennsylvania Gazette*, the Philadelphia *Independent Gazetteer*, and the *Pennsylvania Packet* on December 19.) On December 29, the *Independent Gazetteer* ran both versions side by side with remarks by "P.Q.," who wrote: "I cannot for my life and soul, find any difference in the features of either of these bantlings which have been laid at the Doctor's door." Federalist attacks on Dallas and the versions of the debates he published in the *Herald* resulted in the cancellation of about 100 subscriptions. In early January 1788, Dallas was dismissed as editor of the paper, and its last known edition was published on February 14. Dallas (1759–1817) was a lawyer from the West Indies who had come to Pennsylvania to serve as editor of the *Herald* in 1783; he was later secretary of Pennsylvania 1790–1801, U.S. District Attorney for the Eastern District of Pennsylvania 1801–14, and secretary of the treasury under Madison 1814–16.

84.5–6   Mr. Findley] William Findley (1741–1821), born in Ireland of Scots parentage, immigrated to Pennsylvania in 1762, worked as a weaver, taught school, enlisted in the Continental Army as a private and rose to the rank of captain, settled in Westmoreland County, Pa., and became a state representative, state senator, member of the council of censors and the state supreme executive council, and delegate to the state ratifying convention of 1787, where he helped lead the opposition to ratification. At the outbreak of the Whiskey Rebellion in 1794, he met with Washington in an unsuccessful attempt to mediate grievances. He was a U.S. Representative 1791–99 and 1809–17 and supported the policies of Jefferson and Madison.

86.15   a former paper] "Brutus" VIII, *New York Journal*, January 10, 1788 (see *Debate on the Constitution, Part One*, pp. 732–36).

87.15–18   When . . . well known.] The protests of the army officers in Newburgh, New York, in March 1783, demanding that Congress improve conditions in the army and provide several years' full pay, were written by Major John Armstrong, Jr. It was rumored that Armstrong had acted with the support of Robert Morris, Gouverneur Morris, Alexander Hamilton, and other supporters of a stronger national government. See Chronology of Events, March 1783.

88.21–28   The advocates . . . Britain.] Hamilton's *The Federalist XXIV* (December 19, 1787; see *Debate on the Constitution, Part One*, pp. 575–80).

89.11–15   The advocates . . . disuse.] Hamilton's *The Federalist XXV* (December 21, 1787).

90.40–91.6   The same . . . peace.] *The Federalist XXV*.

91.22–25   It is farther . . . abusing it.] Hamilton's *The Federalist XXVI* (December 22, 1787).

92.3–7   It is further . . . interests.] *The Federalist XXVI*.

92.10   former numbers,] In the *New York Journal*: "Brutus" I (October 15, 1787), III (October 18), and IV (November 29).

100.24   in another place] Hamilton would discuss the executive department in *The Federalist LXVII–LXXVII* (March 11–April 2, 1788) and the judiciary in *The Federalist LXXVIII–LXXXIII* (May 28, 1788). For the essays that appear in this volume, see Index.

102.37–40   Achæan league . . . Lycian confederacy,] The First Achaean League (5th–4th cent. B.C.), a confederation of cities on the Gulf of Corinth, was formed as a protection against pirates. The Second Achaean League, originally four cities, was founded around 280 B.C. primarily under the leadership of Aratus, who brought many of the principal Greek cities into the confederation; votes were proportional to the size and importance of the cities, although in his notes on ancient and modern confederacies, Madison quoted Polybius as writing that the members "enjoyed a perfect equality, each of them sending the same number of delegates to the senate," and wrote that, according to Polybius, the union was weakened by dissensions raised "cheifly thro' the arts of the Kings of Macedon," when the cities devoted themselves to their separate interests rather than acting in concert. The League was dissolved in 147 B.C. after losing a war with Rome. In the same notes, Madison quotes Ubbo Emmius's *Vetus Graecia* on the confederated republic of Lycia, formed around 169 B.C. in southwest Asia Minor. According to Emmius, who cites Strabo, it was composed of 23 cities which managed their own domestic affairs and participated in a common council that deliberated on the affairs of Lycia. The cities were grouped in three ranks, and according to rank had either one, two, or three votes in the council, and also made contributions and performed other duties proportionate to their rank. The council chose a Lychiarch, or chief of the republic, and other magistrates, and established courts of justice. The confederacy lasted until Lycia was annexed by Rome in A.D. 43.

107.4−7   Adams . . . disgrac'd.]   While serving as minister to England, John Adams wrote *Defence of the Constitutions of Government of the United States of America against the attack of M. Turgot* (vols. 1−2, 1787; vol. 3, 1788), a collection of constitutional documents and commentaries on various republics and on American state constitutions, emphasizing the value of strong executives and praising the balance of democratic, aristocratic, and monarchic elements in the English "constitution." First printed in England, Volume I began circulating in America in the winter of 1787 and Volume II in January 1788 (the third volume was sold in the United States beginning in the spring of 1788). Some Antifederalists believed that the first volume had influenced the Constitutional Convention. (Neither Adams nor the book are mentioned in records of the Constitutional Convention, and there is no evidence that it influenced the writing or ratification of the Constitution in any important way.) Critics charged that Adams was advocating a monarchical government with a diminished role for the body of the people and attacked the role he assigned in government to an "aristocracy" of "the rich, the well-born, and the able."

109.32−33   former occasion]   Hamilton's *The Federalist XVII* (December 5, 1787); the essay is also referred to at 111.8 ("already proved").

110.32   elsewhere remarked]   In Hamilton's *The Federalist XXVII* (December 25, 1787; see *Debate on the Constitution, Part One*, pp. 591−94).

117.10−11   Mr Lownds . . . it.]   See pages 19−22 in this volume.

117.31−35   Your delegates . . . importation.]   At the Constitutional Convention, Massachusetts joined South Carolina in the majority in the 7−4 vote to guarantee continuance of the slave trade until 1808 (Art. I, sec. 9; see Chronology, August 1787).

119.5   *John Williams, Esq*]   Williams had voted in the New York senate against convening a state ratifying convention.

122.13   British . . . Montesquieu]   Madison's quotations and references
to Montesquieu in this essay are from *The Spirit of the Laws*, Vol. I, Bk. XI,
ch. 6: "Of the Constitution of England."

131.40–132.15   "From . . . law."]   Loosely quoted from William Blackstone, *Commentaries on the Laws of England* (4 vols., 1765–69), "Introduction," Bk. I, sec. 2, pp. 61–62. In that edition, the quotation from Grotius
reads: "when general decrees of the law come to be applied . . ." (rather
than "when the decrees of the law cannot be applied . . ."); "have excepted"
(rather than "have expressed"); and "fixed precepts" (rather than "fixed principles"). The Latin passage from Grotius may be translated: "The law is not
exact on the subject, but leaves it open to a good man's judgment."

135.1–18   The court . . . nation.]   Paraphrasing and quoting from Blackstone, *Commentaries*, Bk. III, ch. 4, sec. vii, pp. 43–45.

138.38–39   "Notes . . . Virginia."]   Drafted in 1781, privately printed in
France in 1785, and published in revised form in London in 1787. The passage
quoted is from Query XIII.

140.35–36   number of members]   The Pennsylvania state constitution of
1776 established a 12-member supreme executive council, elected by the freemen of the 11 counties and the city of Philadelphia (the creation of seven new
counties had increased its membership to 19 by 1788). All of the other state
constitutions vested executive power in either a single individual, or a single
individual and an advisory council. See also the Notes on State Constitutions
in this volume.

155.4   *"Agrippa" . . . XVIII*]   Winthrop's 18-part "Agrippa" series (November 23, 1787–February 5, 1788) probably had less impact politically than
the more widely known Antifederalist writings that emanated from powerful
political groups in Philadelphia and New York.

155.23–25   Even . . . adverse party.]   In the previous "Agrippa" paper,
published on January 25, Winthrop had made reference to Rhode Island's
intention to alter its legislative election procedures. A bill providing equal
representation for all towns, under discussion in Rhode Island since 1786 and
supported by the "country" party to counteract the legislative influence of
the four mercantile shire towns, had lost by a single vote in the lower house
in November 1787.

155.25–31   A gentleman . . . *state.*]   In the Massachusetts ratifying convention, January 19, 1788, Judge Francis Dana alleged that Rhode Island
planned to reallocate assembly seats "in order to deprive the towns of Newport and Providence of their weight, and that thereby the legislature may
have a power to counteract the will of the majority of the people," and argued that Article I, section 4, was aimed at preventing such practices in federal elections. In the published reports of the convention, however, Dana said
nothing about "a bill lying on a table," only that Rhode Island "has lately

formed a plan . . ." Rufus King, speaking in support of Dana, had said that the plan in Rhode Island "is about to be adopted."

156.37–38   captain M'Daniel]   In a letter to the *Massachusetts Gazette* on January 29, M'Daniel challenged the Rhode Island example: "it is my opinion that this originated no where but in your own imagination."

157.15–16   Adams . . . constitutions,]   See note 107.4–7.

169.9   *our Roof*]   These stanzas are a verse development of Hopkinson's essay "The New Roof" (*Pennsylvania Packet*, December 29, 1787; see *Debate on the Constitution, Part One*, pp. 662–68). When the poem was reprinted in the *Massachusetts Gazette* (February 29, 1788) and the *Massachusetts Centinel* (March 1), it was accompanied by a cartoon (often revised and reprinted) showing six standing pillars, representing the states that had ratified the Constitution, with a seventh, representing New Hampshire, being raised.

175.16   a voluminous writer]   *The Federalist XXXIV* (January 4, 1788, see *Debate on the Constitution, Part One*, pp. 698–703) and *The Federalist XLIV* (pp. 93–100 in this volume).

176.38–177.13   Originally . . . dispute."]   *Commentaries*, Bk. III, ch. 4, sec. vi, pp. 42–43.

178.12   Minister Plenipotentiary of France]   The Comte de Moustier (see pp. 57, 355–56, and the Biographical Notes section in this volume).

180.33–34   Parsons, . . . Sherman]   Samuel Holden Parsons (1737–89), Harvard graduate and lawyer in Lyme, Connecticut, state assemblyman 1762–74, colonel of militia in capture of Ticonderoga and siege of Boston 1775, brigadier general and major general in Continental Army 1776–82, Indian commissioner for Northwest Territory 1785, president Connecticut Society of the Cincinnati, director of the Ohio Company, U.S. Judge of Northwest Territory 1787–89, member state ratifying convention of 1788, where he supported ratification—he died in a canoe accident on Big Beaver River in Northwest Territory; James Mitchell Varnum (1748–89) of Dracut, Massachusetts, became a lawyer in Providence, Rhode Island, colonel and brigadier general of Rhode Island militia 1774–76 (served at siege of Boston and battles of Long Island and White Plains), brigadier general in Continental Army 1776–79 (wintered at Valley Forge), delegate to Continental Congress 1780–87, member of the Society of the Cincinnati, member of the Ohio Company, and U.S. Judge for Northwest Territory 1788–89; Rufus Putnam (1738–1824) of Massachusetts, brigadier general in Continental Army, organizer of the Ohio Company, judge of Northwest Territory 1792–96, U.S. surveyor general 1796–1803; Benjamin Tupper (1738–92), colonel of Massachusetts regiment at Long Island, Saratoga, and Monmouth, organizer of Ohio Company, civil court judge in Ohio Territory 1788–92; Ebenezer Sproat or Sprout (1752–1805), originally of Middleborough, Massachusetts, captain, major, and lieutenant colonel in command of Massachusetts 2d Regiment during Revolution, including battles of Trenton, Princeton, and Monmouth, surveyor in Providence, Rhode Island (where he married daughter of Abraham Whipple), member Ohio Company and one of the original settlers of Marietta, Ohio; Isaac Sherman of Connecticut and the Continental Army was not a member of the Ohio Company.

184.15–23   intermissions . . . another statute] . Charles I ruled without a parliament from 1629 until the lack of money forced him to summon a new one in 1640. The new parliament passed a law in 1641 removing the power to dissolve and summon parliaments from the crown and requiring that no more than three years elapse between the last sitting of one parliament and the summoning and election of a new one. Following the English Civil War and the restoration of Charles II, the first Triennial Act (1664) was passed. It repealed the 1641 statute and recognized the royal prerogative to dissolve and summon parliament, but required that parliament meet at least once every three years. Frequent holdings of parliament were called for in the Bill of Rights (1689), enacted after the overthrow of James II and the accession of William and Mary. The second Triennial Act (1694) required that a new parliament be summoned and elected within three years of the first meeting of its predecessor.

184.29–31   seven years . . . succession] The Septennial Act of 1716 allowed parliaments to last for seven years unless dissolved earlier. Its passage was secured by the Whig ministry in reaction to the party strife during the reign of Queen Anne (1702–14), to which the frequent elections called for by the Triennial Act contributed, and to the attempt by supporters of the Stuart pretender James, including some Tories, to prevent the succession of the Hanoverian George I. After the Whig victory in the 1715 general election and the defeat of the 1715 Jacobite uprising, the ministry sought to extend the life of the current parliament and stabilize the new regime. The act increased the value of seats in the House of Commons and the cost of winning parliamentary elections, and was attacked by reformers in the 18th and 19th centuries. In 1911 the length of parliaments was changed to five years.

185.17–18   octenniel parliaments . . . established.] By the Octennial Act of 1768.

193.4   Mr. BABCOCK] Elisha Babcock (c. 1753–1821), publisher of the *American Mercury* (which he had founded with Joel Barlow) from 1784 until 1820.

193.9   anonymous writers] On January 28, 1788, "Landholder" (Oliver Ellsworth) published an open letter to William Williams, responding to his criticism in the Connecticut ratifying convention of the seventh "Landholder" essay (published in both the *Connecticut Courant* and *American Mercury* on December 17, 1787, see *Debate on the Constitution, Part One*, pp. 521–25), which defended the Constitution's prohibition of religious tests for officeholding; see page 194.26–31 in this volume.

193.23–29   religious test . . . terms,]   "Landholder" (Ellsworth) replied to Williams' letter on March 10, 1788, in the *American Mercury*, saying that, if all Williams had wanted was a religious preamble to the Constitution, "Against preambles, we have no animosity." But, he concluded, there were still "a great number of those odd people who really think they were present" when Williams had defended religious oaths and "have such a strong habit of believing their senses, that they will not be convinced even by evidence which is superior to all sense. But it must be so in this imperfect world."

196.23–24   recently . . . sanction]   On April 18, 1783, the Continental Congress adopted an amendment to the Articles of Confederation changing the basis for apportioning treasury requisitions among the states from property values to population. By the time the Constitutional Convention met, all of the states except New Hampshire and Rhode Island had ratified the amendment.

204.4–5   the observations . . . elections.]   In *The Federalist LII*, pp. 182–86 in this volume.

208.33   elsewhere remarked]   In *The Federalist LIII* (pp. 187–92 in this volume); this essay is also referred to at 210.13 ("on another occasion"), 210.34 ("formerly remarked"), and 216.22 ("We have seen").

210.4–9   The observations . . . state.]   In the M'Lean edition, this paragraph was changed to read: "With regard to the regulation of the militia, there are scarcely any circumstances in reference to which local knowledge can be said to be necessary. The general face of the country, whether mountainous or level, most fit for the operations of infantry or cavalry, is almost the only consideration of this nature that can occur. The art of war teaches general principles of organization, movement, and discipline, which apply universally."

211.39   Burgh's polit. disquis.]   James Burgh, *Political Disquisitions* (3 vols., London, 1774–75; Philadelphia, 1775), I, 48, 45. Burgh (1714–75), born in Scotland, was a political and religious reformer in England; his work was an influential textbook of ideas.

219.5–6   Mr. Lacasagne]   Michael Laccasagne (d. 1797), Louisville merchant, attorney, land speculator, postmaster, town trustee, and a native of France, represented Jefferson County in the January 1787 Kentucky statehood convention.

221.1   Mr. Al Parker]   Alexander Parker, partner in the Lexington, Kentucky, mercantile firm of Alexander and James Parker, attorney, town trustee, trustee of Transylvania Seminary, and member of the Kentucky Society for

Promoting Useful Knowledge, was one of eight surveyors appointed by Congress under the Land Ordinance of 1785.

223.16–19   the clause . . . destructive.]   "Brutus" anticipates the issues disputed in the case of *Chisholm* v. *Georgia* (1793), which eventually led to the Eleventh Amendment to the Constitution (1798).

227.11   *instruct their Representatives.*]   The meeting called for the state legislature to convene a ratifying convention as soon as possible.

228.13–15   literary property . . . Congress.]   In May 1783 the Continental Congress approved a proposal, drafted by Williamson, urging the states to provide copyright protection for authors. Williamson also secured passage of a copyright law in North Carolina in 1785 that extended protection to authors from states with similar laws; it did not delegate copyright powers to Congress.

232.18–233.26   Without . . . commotion.]   This passage was reprinted in newspapers in Massachusetts and, along with the paragraphs cited in the note below, in Connecticut, New Hampshire, and New York.

235.19–236.7   The proposed . . . Man.]   This passage was also reprinted in Boston and Rhode Island newspapers.

237.3   *"Centinel"*]   Eighteen "Centinel" essays, published October 5, 1787, through April 5, 1788, circulated throughout the states in newspaper, pamphlet, and broadside form. At the time, Samuel Bryan's father, George Bryan (1731–91), judge of the supreme court of Pennsylvania and a leading Antifederalist, was thought to be the author. (A second group of "Centinel" essays, XIX–XXIV, October 7–November 24, 1788, advocated electing U.S. Congressmen who would support amendments to the Constitution protecting personal rights and property and states rights, and the last group, XXV–XXXVII, August 27–November 11, 1789, opposed revising the Pennsylvania state constitution of 1776 and criticized the amendments to the federal Constitution proposed by the first U.S. Congress.)

237.32   the *Caledonian*]   James Wilson.

238.28   the late Financier]   Robert Morris (1734–1806), a signer of the Declaration of Independence and a delegate to the Constitutional Convention, was a powerful Pennsylvania merchant associated with the creditor and mercantile interests of the middle colonies. He served on the congressional committees charged with purchasing arms and supplies for the war effort 1775–77 and was superintendent of finance under the Continental Congress 1781–84 and founder of the Bank of North America in 1781. He was often accused by his enemies of using public office for private gain. His conduct was defended in Federalist publications after "Centinel" XVI appeared; Morris himself published denials in early April. He remained in debt to the nation long after he left office, and an official accounting of 1790 listed him as the nation's largest individual debtor.

238.32–35   the others . . . designated—] Subsequent Antifederalist publications identified Thomas Mifflin, William Bingham, and Benjamin Franklin as public defaulters. Federalist replies defended the character and records of the accused men and insisted that the constitutional argument made by "Centinel" was inconsistent with Article IV, section 3: "nothing in this Constitution shall be so construed as to prejudice any claims of the United States." Sometime after March 30, 1788, Franklin wrote, but did not publish, a letter deploring such personal attacks ("nothing is more likely to endanger the liberty of the press, than the abuse of that liberty, by employing it in personal accusation, detraction, and calumny") and criticizing the harshness expressed by both sides of the ratification debate in the Philadelphia press.

241.33   Lincolnians and Shaysites]   Benjamin Lincoln had commanded the Massachusetts militia called out to suppress Shays' Rebellion in 1787; see Chronology of Events, July–October 1786 and January–April 1787.

241.34–35   swords . . . no more.]   Cf. Isaiah 2:4 and Micah 4:3.

242.7   brother Lee]   Silas Lee (1760–1814), Biddeford lawyer and former law student of George Thatcher, fiancé (later husband) of Thatcher's niece Temperance Hedge, state representative 1793, 1797, and 1798, U.S. Representative 1799–1801, U.S. District Attorney for Maine 1802–14.

243.14–28   Time . . . hills.]   This passage was excerpted in the *Massachusetts Centinel* (April 9, 1788) with these remarks: "We give the following, as a specimen of the dirty-dirty tricks of the antifederalists in the Southern States, to impose on the freemen of America—It is extracted from a Philadelphia paper."

243.16–17   society of the Cincinnati,]   The controversial Society of the Cincinnati, an association of officers of the Continental Army, was formed at the suggestion of General Henry Knox in June 1783, and Washington was its first president. Named for the Roman hero Cincinnatus, its stated purpose was to raise funds to protect officers and their families from hardship and to promote closer ties among the states. Membership would be inherited through the eldest son, but when there was no direct descendant, other relatives were eligible. The Cincinnati were widely attacked as a hereditary military aristocracy capable of overthrowing constitutional government. At the May 1784 general meeting, Washington urged the abolition of hereditary membership and other changes designed to allay public apprehensions about the society. His proposal was submitted to the state societies for their approval; the societies were still debating these changes during the ratification debate of 1787–88. After the Constitution was adopted, the Cincinnati became less controversial.

245.25–27   "of a . . . indispensable."] From George Washington's letter, as president of the Constitutional Convention, transmitting the Constitution to the Continental Congress; pp. 937–38 in this volume.

251.6   *(Continued . . . last.)*] Five essays by "The Impartial Examiner" were published, the first in three parts: part 1 on February 20 and part 3, which was signed "P.P.," on March 5. The other four essays were published May 28, June 4, June 11, and June 18, 1788.

252.38–253.2   the nature . . . nation."] *Commentaries on the Laws of England*, Bk. I, ch. 8, sec. ii, pp. 308–10.

264.28–33   Rhode-Island . . . constitution.] The Rhode Island legislature issued paper money in 1786, established penalties for refusing to accept it at face value, and directed that suits brought under the enforcement act be tried by judges without juries. In the case of *Trevett* v. *Weeden*, argued before the state superior court of judicature in September 1786, the defense claimed that the enforcement act unconstitutionally violated the fundamental right to trial by jury guaranteed by the Rhode Island colonial charter (the state did not adopt a constitution until 1842). The court ruled that the suit did not come under its jurisdiction, effectively making the disputed law unenforceable. Newspapers subsequently reported that several of the judges delivered opinions holding the law unconstitutional. See also the Chronology of Events, September 1786.

267.7   Col. Thos. Barber] Thomas Barbour (1735–1825), Orange County planter, neighbor and close friend of James Madison, justice of the peace, member house of burgesses 1769–75, member of Revolutionary conventions of 1774 and 1775, sheriff 1776–77, major and colonel of militia 1778–84, and county lieutenant 1784–86 and 1789–91.

267.29–30   Mr. Bledsoe . . . Sanders] Aaron Bledsoe (c. 1730–1809) was preacher at "North Fork of Pamunkey" near Orange, Virginia; Nathaniel Saunders (d. 1808) was one of the first Baptist preachers in Orange County.

268.1   Capt Walker] James Walker, Culpeper County planter, militia officer in French and Indian War, justice of the peace, member of house of burgesses 1761–67, 1769–71, and 1775, sheriff 1771–72, member Revolutionary convention of March 1775, state senator 1777–79, and an unsuccessful candidate for the Virginia ratifying convention.

269.12–13   plowing . . . Sampsons Heifer] In Judges 14, when Samson's Philistine wife revealed the solution of his riddle to her countrymen, he told them, "If ye had not plowed with my heifer, ye had not found out my riddle."

270.1–3 *Rhode Island's . . . People*] In 1788 Rhode Island had a population of approximately 60,000 in an area of 1,000 square miles. Under the terms of Rhode Island's royal charter of 1663, the power of the legislature was severely limited: representatives in both houses were elected by the towns each year, and the towns commonly bound their representatives by strict instructions, initiated legislation, and ratified or negated legislation by frequent use of the referendum. All significant matters were effectively decided not by the two-house legislature but by the entire voting population in their town meetings, and the assembly prudently consulted the towns before attempting serious initiatives. Public opinion of the Constitution was severely negative, as it had been of every effort to enlarge the power of the central government.

The dominant issue in Rhode Island was the question of debtor relief, primarily in the form of paper money. Opposed mainly by merchants and townsmen in the commercial centers of Providence, Newport, and Portsmouth, paper money, issued as loans on real estate collateral, was supported by a farming population caught in a deepening postwar depression. It would create a badly needed circulating medium, offer debtor relief, and provide a means of postponing and diminishing the repayment of the state's debts. In the spring election of 1786 the "country" party was triumphant. The assembly rescinded the existing tax and excise laws and issued £100,000 of paper money declared to be legal tender. A penalty act provided severe punishments for persons convicted of refusing the paper at face value.

The mercantile party, defeated at the polls, looked to Congress for help and favored the new Constitution, which explicitly prohibited the kinds of fiscal policies that the assembly had enacted. The country majority feared both the power of the enlarged federal government to prevent such popular measures in the future and the immediate effect of ratification on the legal-tender paper already in circulation and on the state's policy of repaying its public debt with depreciated bills. Viewing the Constitution as a threat to the entire relief effort that had been enacted since 1786, the majority in the assembly ignored Congress's request to convene a ratifying convention and referred the matter directly to the entire voting population convened in the town meetings. Newspapers in the main port towns carried denunciations of the move (see, for example, "A Freeman," on March 20, 1788, pp. 368–71 in this volume, and "Phocion," July 17, 1788, pp. 526–32 in this volume). The commercial towns, led by Providence, simply refused to vote, which exaggerated the outcome of the March 24 vote: 2,711 against the Constitution to 239 in favor.

When Washington took the oath of office in April 1789, Rhode Island was independent of the United States. Another year went by before the paper issues of 1786 were redeemed and the state's debts were repaid in depreciated currency. By 1790, the "country" majority was willing to reconsider the issue. A ratifying convention was authorized, and, on May 29, 1790, by a majority of only two votes (34–32), Rhode Island finally joined the newly constituted Union.

270.9   Mr. *Sayles*] Colonel John Sayles (1723–1822), Smithfield attorney, was a delegate to the state ratifying convention of 1790, where he opposed ratification.

270.10   Mr. *Childs*] Cromel Child (1716–90), Warren attorney and collector of impost for Bristol County 1787–90; he voted against calling a ratifying convention at the Warren town meeting of March 24, 1788.

270.13   Mr. *Joslyn*] Thomas Joslyn, Jr., who voted against calling a state ratifying convention in the West Greenwich town meeting of March 24, 1788.

270.20   Mr. *Hazard*] See note 7.8–9.

271.23–27   Mr. *Bradford* . . . Mr. *Sheldon*] William Bradford (1729–1808), Bristol doctor and lawyer, former speaker of the house and deputy governor 1775–78, delegate to Continental Congress but did not serve, delegate to state ratifying convention of 1790, where he supported ratification, U.S. Senator 1793–97 (president pro tempore July–October 1797); Henry Marchant (1741–1796), Newport lawyer, Rhode Island attorney general 1770–77, member of the Sons of Liberty, delegate to Continental Congress 1777–80, 1783, and 1784, signer of the Articles of Confederation, delegate to ratifying convention of 1790, where he led supporters of ratification, U.S. District Judge 1790–96; George Champlin (1738–1809), Newport merchant, officer in the Revolution, alderman 1784–87, delegate to Continental Congress 1785–86, and member of the state ratifying convention in 1790, where he supported ratification; Peleg Arnold (1751–1820), Smithfield tavernkeeper, delegate to Continental Congress 1787–88 (reelected in 1789), and chief justice of the supreme court of Rhode Island 1795–1809; Benjamin Bourne (1755–1808), Providence attorney, quartermaster and ensign in Rhode Island militia during the Revolution, member state ratifying convention of 1790, where he led supporters of ratification, U.S. Representative 1790–96, and U.S. district judge 1801–08; Job Comstock, East Greenwich attorney and collector of impost for Kent County 1787–90, was a delegate to the state ratifying convention of 1790, where he opposed ratification; James Sheldon, Richmond attorney and delegate to state ratifying convention of 1790, where he opposed ratification.

271.39   Mr. *Whipple*] Abraham Whipple (1733–1819), Cranston merchant, had been a privateer in the French and Indian War, engaged in West India trade, served as a commodore in American navy during the Revolution, captured near Charleston, South Carolina, in 1780 and held prisoner for remainder of war. He moved to Marietta, Ohio, with the Ohio Company in 1788.

276.9–11   BOWEN . . . Bourne] Jabez Bowen (1739–1815), Providence attorney, member of the Sons of Liberty, fellow, trustee, and chancellor of

Rhode Island College (became Brown University in 1804) 1768–1815, colonel of militia, deputy governor 1778–86, judge of supreme court, state representative 1790, delegate to state ratifying convention of 1790, where he supported ratification, and U.S. Commissioner of Loans 1789–96; David Howell (1747–1824), Providence lawyer, professor at Rhode Island College, judge of common pleas, delegate to the Continental Congress 1782–85, state attorney general 1789, U.S. District Judge 1812–24; John Innes Clark, Providence attorney and delegate to state ratifying convention of 1790, where he supported ratification; Theodore Foster (1752–1828), Providence lawyer and town clerk, admiralty court judge, U.S. Senator 1790–1803, trustee of Rhode Island College 1794–1822, and state representative 1812–16; for Benjamin Bourne, see note 271.23–27.

284.3   *Observations on the Constitution*] Published as a 19-page pamphlet titled *Observations on the New Constitution, and on the Federal and State Conventions*, this essay was reprinted in newspapers in Pennsylvania and New York, and as a 22-page pamphlet in New York, where it was widely distributed by the Antifederalist county committees in early April, a few weeks before the election of delegates to the state ratifying convention.

284.16   Man of *La Mancha*] In Cervantes' *Don Quixote*.

285.22–27   *Abbé Mablé? . . . Octavius."*] Gabriel Bonnot, Abbé de Mably (1709–85); the quotation is from *Observations sur les Romains* (1751).

285.39   *Helvitius] Claude Adrien Helvétius (1715–71), French writer and philosopher.

288. 33   *pactolean channel*] Pactolus River in Lydia, Asia Minor; according to legend, Midas was cured of his golden touch by bathing in its waters, and its sands contained gold since that time.

289.18–23   writer . . . communities."] Blackstone, *Commentaries*, Bk. I, ch. 1, p. 120, which reads "immutable laws of nature."

289.37–290.4   Mr. *Hutchinson* . . . years:"] Governor Thomas Hutchinson left Massachusetts in 1774 and died in exile in England in 1780. Warren lived in Hutchinson's former house in Milton, which she and her husband had bought when it was confiscated by the state. The quotation is from a private letter of October 1770, discovered by the patriots after his departure and published in the *Boston Gazette*, August 14, 1775. Wills Hill, Earl of Hillsborough, secretary of state for America and president of the Board of Trade 1768–72, was Hutchinson's patron and immediate superior.

290.26–27   *"thus far . . . further,"*] Cf. Job 38:11.

290.38–291.4   Blackstone . . . produce.] *Commentaries*, Bk. III, ch. 23 (the quotation is conflated from pages 349 and 351; the Hale reference is on page 355).

291.31   Ximenes] Francisco Jiménez de Cisneros (1437–1517), Spanish
prelate, inquisitor, and regent.

291.32   Cortes of Spain]   Literally, courts of Spain; the parliaments of the
Spanish kingdoms.

293.31–32   *writs of assistance*]   An act of parliament passed in 1662 gave
customs officers power to search any ship or building they suspected contained contraband goods and, if necessary, to break into chests or boxes during searches. The act also authorized the court of exchequer to issue writs of
assistance to customs officers; the writs called upon justices of the peace,
sheriffs, and constables to assist customs officials in conducting searches on
land. In 1696 the power of customs officers to conduct general searches was
extended by act of parliament to the American colonies. William Shirley, the
royal governor of Massachusetts, issued writs of assistance until 1755, when his
power to grant them was challenged. The Boston customs surveyor then obtained a writ from the superior court of Massachusetts, which exercised the
powers of the court of exchequer within the colony. After the death of
George II in 1760 Massachusetts customs officers petitioned the superior
court to have their writs renewed (writs of assistance expired six months after
the death of the sovereign in whose name they were issued). Their petition
was opposed by Boston merchants, who engaged attorney James Otis
(brother of Mercy Otis Warren) to represent them before the superior court
in February 1761. Otis argued that the 1662 act did not authorize general
searches, and that writs of assistance must specify the place to be searched in
order to be legal under the common law. He also asserted that an act of
parliament contrary to the principles of the English constitution and natural
law was "void," and that it was the duty of the courts to pass unconstitutional
acts into "disuse." The court reserved judgment on the case while its chief
justice, Thomas Hutchinson, wrote to England for information regarding
laws and precedents unavailable in Massachusetts, and then ruled in November 1761 that general writs of assistance were lawful. After Otis denounced
general writs in the press, the Massachusetts legislature passed a law early in
1762 restricting writs of assistance to cases where customs officers swore that
they had specific information about places to be searched, and requiring that
the writs be returned after seven days; Governor Francis Bernard vetoed the
bill. Power to issue general writs of assistance was given to the supreme
courts of American colonies as part of Townshend Acts in 1767, but in many
colonies the courts refused to exercise the power and issued writs only on
specific information. In 1817 John Adams, who had attended the court in 1761,
remembered that Otis had been "a flame of fire" as he argued against the
unconstitutionality of unjust parliamentary acts. Adams wrote: "Then and
there the child Independence was born."

293.39–294.1   gentleman . . . rights"]   Governor James Bowdoin, in a
speech in the Massachusetts ratifying convention, January 23, 1788.

296.25   a former Governor]   Thomas Hutchinson.

296.28–29   gentlemen . . . *necks.*"]   In the Massachusetts ratifying convention on January 18, 1788, Judge Francis Dana had asked if the advocates of the Constitution in the convention could not be trusted since they were the same people who, "with halters about their necks, boldly and intrepidly advocated the rights of America, and of humanity, at home and in foreign countries."

298.23   *"cloud cap't towers"*]   Shakespeare, *The Tempest*, IV. i. 152.

298.28–30   King . . . chariots]   Cf. I Samuel, chapter 8.

298.40–299.8   "He had . . . vote."]   Luther Martin, "The Genuine Information" I (*Maryland Gazette*, December 28, 1787; see *Debate on the Constitution, Part One*, pp. 631–37).

300.36–37   Governor . . . opinion]   See note 58.5.

301.12–14   authors . . . discord.]   On December 26, 1787, a riot broke out in Carlisle, Pennsylvania, when an Antifederalist mob attacked Federalists who had gathered in the town square to celebrate the state's recent ratification of the Constitution (an Antifederalist writer later claimed that Federalists had threatened to break the windows of those refusing to celebrate ratification). After dispersing the Federalists, the Antifederalists burned a copy of the Constitution and cheered the 23 dissenting members of the Pennsylvania state convention. Bearing arms, the Federalists returned to the square on December 27 and celebrated ratification before withdrawing. Antifederalists then burned James Wilson and Thomas McKean in effigy. Other instances of mob action in Pennsylvania during the ratification debate included the seizure of two Antifederalist assemblymen in Philadelphia on September 29, 1787 (see Chronology of Events) and the riot in Philadelphia on November 6, 1787, when a Federalist mob attacked the boarding house where Antifederalist leaders John Smilie and William Findley were staying.

302.14   Decii]   According to Livy (Book 8, ch. 9), the Roman consul Publius Decius Mus, during a battle against the Latins around 340 B.C., "devoted" himself and the enemy to the gods and spirits of the dead, ensuring the Roman people's victory by his own death. A son and grandson of the same name were sometimes said to have performed similar sacrifices.

304.3   *Giles Hickory"*]   Noah Webster wrote four "Giles Hickory" papers for his *American Magazine*; the first appeared in the December 1787 issue (see *Debate on the Constitution, Part One*, pp. 669–72).

304.5–7   Virginia . . . Bill of Rights,]   The Virginia declaration of rights, drafted by George Mason and adopted in 1776, though not formally part of the state constitution, was understood to have constitutional status. Both the declaration and the constitution were adopted by a convention acting as a legislature. The constitution contained no provisions for its own amendment or for distinguishing it from ordinary legislation.

304.33–305.1   British Parliament . . . years,]   See note 184.29–31.

311.36   Mr. Jefferson] In *Notes on the State of Virginia* (1787), Query XIII. The text of the 1787 edition is printed in Thomas Jefferson, *Writings* (New York: The Library of America, 1984), pp. 248–49.

311.38   ex vi termini,]   From the meaning of the term itself.

312.15–16   "Leges . . . abrogant."]   "Later laws repeal former ones which are inconsistent."

312.38   *Calvini Lexicon Juridicum]   Johannes Calvinus (Johann Kahl), a German jurist, published his *Lexicon Juridicum* in 1609. Jefferson owned a 1669 edition.

318.40   a former paper]   *The Federalist X*, November 22, 1787 (see *Debate on the Constitution, Part One*, pp. 404–11), developed further in *The Federalist LI*, February 6, 1788 (pp. 163–68 in this volume).

332.15   Warner . . . Smith]   Warner Lewis (1747–91) owned a plantation at Warner Hall in Gloucester County; he was a presidential elector in 1789. Thomas Smith, merchant, planter, graduate of College of William and Mary, justice of the peace, and member of the house of delegates from Gloucester County 1780–91 and Mathews County 1792–96. Both voted in favor of ratification in the Virginia convention of 1788.

333.34   *Vide Federal Farmer]   *Letters from the Federal Farmer*, III, November 8, 1787 (see *Debate on the Constitution, Part One*, pp. 259–74).

336.12–13   "For forms . . . best."]   Alexander Pope, *An Essay on Man* (1733–34), Epistle III, lines 303–04: "For Forms of Government let fools contest; / Whate'er is best administered is best."

339.10–11   Maryland]   Changed to "Virginia" in the M'Lean edition.

339.18–19   disuse . . . past]   In March 1708 Queen Anne became the last English monarch to use the royal veto when she withheld her assent from the Scottish Militia bill.

339.29–31   Governor . . . Judges.]   Under the New York state constitution of 1777, the governor, chancellor, and judges of the supreme court formed a council of revision with the power to veto legislation within ten days of its passage. The legislature could then revise the law in order to meet the objections of the council, or override the veto by two-thirds majorities in both houses.

343.27–29   New-York . . . under it.]   Article XXIII of the New York state constitution of 1777 provided that the governor serve as president of the council of appointment and "with the advice and consent of the said council, shall appoint" state officers. George Clinton, governor of New York from 1777 to 1795, interpreted the article as giving him the sole power to nominate state officers, with their appointment then depending upon the vote of the senators serving on the council. In 1794 the assembly, which was controlled by Federalists opposed to Clinton, elected a new council, which then asserted a concurrent right to nominate officers and appointed Federalist Egbert Benson to the state supreme court despite Clinton's refusal to nominate him. Clinton retired in 1795 and was succeeded by Federalist John Jay, who had drafted Article XXIII in 1777. Jay also interpreted the article as giving the governor an exclusive right to nominate, and in 1801 came into conflict over this issue with a council chosen by the now Republican-controlled assembly. The constitution was then amended to give both the governor and the senators on the council the right to nominate officers. A new state constitution, framed in 1821, abolished the council of appointment.

353.1−3   Junius . . . one:"*]   The quotations are from the preface (written 1771) to the pseudonymous *Letters of Junius* (1772; first published in the *London Public Advertiser*, Jan. 1769–Jan. 1772), attacking Lord Mansfield, George III, and others. The preface to the *Letters* cited the Swiss jurist Jean Louis Delolme's *The Constitution of England* (1771).

355.20−356.2   Rhodeisland . . . general.]   See note 270.1–3.

361.18−19   Mr. Fox's . . . Lords]   Charles James Fox and Lord North formed a coalition ministry in April 1783 in which Fox served as foreign secretary. In November 1783 Fox proposed placing the East India Company under the control of seven directors and nine assistants. The India Bill nominated 16 men to hold the positions; succeeding directors would be chosen by the king, but serve for fixed terms, not at the pleasure of the crown, while future assistants would be elected by major Company stockholders. Although the bill passed the Houses of Commons by a decisive majority (208–102), it was widely attacked in pamphlets and satirical prints. Its opponents charged that it violated the independence of chartered corporations and was an attempt by Fox to secure a permanent majority in the Commons by controlling the patronage of the East India Company (most of the men nominated in the bill were his allies). George III made it known through an intermediary that he would consider all who voted for the bill in the House of Lords to be his "enemies." On December 17 it was defeated in the Lords, 95–76, and on December 18 the king dismissed the Fox-North coalition and asked William Pitt to form a new ministry. In response the House of Commons resolved, 153–80, that it was a breach of privilege to report the personal opinions of the king on legislation, and resisted the formation of a ministry that did not have majority support in the Commons. After several weeks of uncertain political maneuvering, Parliament was dissolved in March 1784. Pitt then won a strong majority in the ensuing general election.

368.6−8   A question . . . *Constitution*—]   See note 270.1–3.

372.7   my last number]   "Brutus" XIV, February 28–March 6, 1788 (page 258 in this volume).

375.27   a former paper]   "Brutus" XI, January 31, 1788 (page 129 in this volume).

378.13   *with . . . arm.*] Cf. Deuteronomy 26:8 and Jeremiah 21:5.

380.39   lately . . . Massachusetts.] Shays' Rebellion.

382.7   Col Syms] Charles Simms (1755–1819), officer of the Continental Army during the Revolution, member house of delegates from Fairfax County 1785, and member state ratifying convention from Fairfax County 1788, where he voted in favor of ratification.

382.18–22   effect . . . to one.] Of Madison's performance that day, a contemporary (James Duncanson) wrote: "Maddison came in the day before the Election in Orange, & when the People assembled converted them in a speech of an hour & three quarters, delivered at the Court house door before the Pol opened, so that he & James Gordon were chosen by a large majority, to the great mortification of Tom Barbour & that set who got but very few votes." The election was held March 24; Madison received 202 votes, James Gordon, Jr., 187, Thomas Barbour, 56, and Charles Porter, 42.

383.24–25   a preceding number] John Jay's *The Federalist LXIV*, March 5, 1788.

384.24–25   elsewhere detailed,] In *The Federalist LXIV*.

384.35–36   on another occasion,] In Hamilton's *The Federalist XXII*, December 14, 1787 (see *Debate on the Constitution, Part One*, pp. 507–16).

389.18   a former paper] Hamilton's *The Federalist LXVIII*, March 12, 1788 (page 336 in this volume).

399.30   a former paper] Hamilton's *The Federalist LXIX*, March 14, 1788 (page 343 in this volume).

402.22   Corah] Or Korah, in Numbers 16:1–49.

404.28–30   popular Opposition . . . Distinction.] Franklin's satire is an attack not only on the Antifederalists in general but specifically on the opposition to the Constitution that erupted in December 1787 in Carlisle, Pennsylvania (see note 301.12–14). Seven of the 21 Antifederalists arrested for their part in the riot refused parole and were jailed. In early March 1788 several hundred militiamen converged on Carlisle to force the prisoners' release. The charges were dropped at the end of the month, but in the weeks preceding the appearance of Franklin's piece, the affair was the subject of speeches in the Pennsylvania legislature and articles in the newspapers.

408.9   The Writer] Dickinson wrote nine "Fabius" essays at the urging of John Vaughan, a Philadelphia merchant recently arrived from England and an active member of the American Philosophical Society. Vaughan arranged their publication in the *Pennsylvania Mercury and Universal Advertiser*, April 12–May 1, 1788, and reprintings in many newspapers throughout the states, especially in New York, Maryland, Virginia, and South Carolina. He distributed copies personally to major figures like Washington and convinced

Mathew Carey to reprint all nine in his *American Museum* later in 1788. Washington spoke of the author's mastery, dignity, and clarity. "I have no doubt," he wrote, "but an extensive republication . . . would be of utility in removing the impressions which have been made upon the Mind of many by an unfair or partial representation of the proposed constitution, and would afford desirable information upon the subject to those who sought for it." "Fabius" VIII (April 29, 1788) appears on pages 424–29 in this volume.

410.19–20   "When *every* . . . AFRAID."]   Cf. Micah 4:4.

412.26–35   "If the . . . *you*."]   I Corinthians 12:15–16 and 20–21.

412.36–37   *Rome . . . Menenius Agrippa*]   The story of Menenius Agrippa and the parable of the belly and the limbs is given in Livy (Book 2, ch. 32), but is probably mythical and of ancient origin. The first strike or secession of the plebeians occurred in 494 B.C.

417.6–7   *Extract . . . city.*]   Rush circulated this letter widely to justify his opposition to a bill of rights. It was quickly reprinted in several states and appeared in London's *Gentlemen's Magazine* in June.

418.20–21   Mr. Ames]   Fisher Ames, in a speech in the Massachusetts ratifying convention, January 15, 1788.

418.22–23   A citizen . . . Switzerland]   John Joachim Zubly (1724–81), Presbyterian pastor in Savannah, Georgia, member provincial congress 1775, and delegate to the Continental Congress 1775–77. He opposed the Declaration of Independence, was denounced as a traitor by Samuel Chase, resigned from Congress, was banished from Georgia and resided in South Carolina from 1777 to 1779, when he returned to Savannah.

420.8   Colo Blain]   Ephraim Blaine (1741–1808), commissary general of Northern Department during the Revolution, owned land in Cumberland County, Pennsylvania, and was a merchant in Carlisle.

422.29   Dr. Nisbet]   The Reverend Charles Nisbet (1736–1804), longtime pastor at Montrose, Scotland, had come to Carlisle, Pennsylvania, in 1785, at the invitation of Benjamin Rush and John Dickinson, to be the first president of Dickinson College, where he served until his death.

426.31–32   "body . . . together."]   Colossians 2:19.

431.21   Christian Majesty]   Louis XVI of France.

431.22   The virtuous Sixty-three]   The vote for ratification in the Maryland Convention on April 26, 1788, was 63–11.

431.27   Minority of Massachusetts]   Many members of the minority in the Massachusetts convention had pledged their support for the Constitution once it had won ratification in their state. Federalists contrasted their stance with that of the Pennsylvania minority, who had published a widely

circulated Antifederalist address after being defeated at the Pennsylvania convention.

433.21   Peter Coeck] Pieter Koeck (c. 1500–53), Flemish painter, engraver, and architect.

433.22   *Michael*] Michelangelo Buonarotti Simoni (1475–1564), Italian sculptor, painter, architect, and poet.

436.25   Queen Catherine] Catherine of Braganza, wife of Charles II of England.

437.16   Mr. Peale] Charles Willson Peale (1741–1827) of Philadelphia (born in Maryland) had served in the Continental Army, where he began painting portraits of American and French officers. He celebrated American victories and American republicanism in large allegorical transparencies, which were hung in windows. He painted more than 1,000 portraits, including George and Martha Washington, Jefferson, Franklin, John Adams, Robert Morris, Steuben, and Rochambeau.

443.4   May 17, 1788] Nicholas used Madison's arguments from this letter in a speech in the Virginia ratifying convention on western interests, June 13, 1788.

450.18   Mr. Griffin] Cyrus Griffin (1748–1810), state representative from Lancaster County 1777–78, delegate to the Continental Congress 1778–81, 1787, and 1788 (president), judge of the Continental Court of Appeals in Cases of Capture 1780–87, and U.S. District Judge in Virginia 1789–1810.

450.24   Mr. Waddel] The Rev. James Waddel (1739–1805) had been educated and was a tutor in Samuel Finley's New Light Presbyterian School and an organizer of Presbyterian congregations in Virginia since 1761. In 1788, he preached regularly at St. Thomas Episcopal Church in Orange County, Virginia.

459.30–31   objections . . . Mr. Martin,] Luther Martin, *The Genuine Information*, V (*Maryland Gazette*, January 11, 1788); see note 472.38–39.

462.13–14   business . . . Richmond] Pendleton had been elected to the Virginia ratifying convention, where he was chosen to serve as the presiding officer.

463.34   Capt. Hutchins] Thomas Hutchins (1730–89), a native of New Jersey, took part in the French and Indian Wars and was commissioned captain of engineers in the 60th (Royal American) Regiment of the British Army, serving until 1780. He published *A Topographical Description of Virginia, Pennsylvania, Maryland, and Carolina, with Maps* (London, 1778). In London in 1779, he refused a commission to serve in America, was suspected of a treasonable correspondence with Franklin in Paris, was imprisoned for six weeks and released. In May 1781 he was appointed geographer of the Continental Army at Charleston and was made geographer of the United States in

July 1781. In 1783 he helped determine the boundary between Virginia and Pennsylvania and in 1785 surveyed the western lands ceded by the states.

465.28   the 2d. . . . 7th.]   See pages 548 and 549 in this volume.

467.5   New York, May 28, 1788]   The final eight *Federalist* essays (nos. LXXVIII–LXXXV), all written by Hamilton, first appeared in the second volume of the collected edition published by John and Archibald M'Lean in New York on May 28, 1788 (the first volume was published in March); all eight were subsequently printed separately in newspapers. Five of the eight appear together here under the initial publication date.

467.9–10   have been . . . out.]   In Hamilton's *The Federalist XXII*, December 14, 1787, (see *Debate on the Constitution, Part One*, pp. 507–16).

472.38–39   Protest . . . speech,]   "The Address and Reasons of Dissent of the Minority of the Convention of the State of Pennsylvania to their Constituents," probably written by Samuel Bryan ("Centinel"), and signed by 21 of the 23 opponents of ratification in the Pennsylvania ratifying convention, was published in the *Pennsylvania Packet*, December 18, 1787 (see *Debate on the Constitution, Part One*, pp. 526–52), and reprinted in newspapers, magazines, broadsides, and pamphlets. Luther Martin's speech to the Maryland Assembly, delivered November 29, 1787, was printed in the *Maryland Gazette* December 28, 1787–February 8, 1788 (see *Debate on the Constitution, Part One*, pp. 631–61), and was collected with additional materials in a pamphlet titled *The Genuine Information, Delivered to the Legislature of the State of Maryland*, in April 1788 (see *Debate on the Constitution, Part One*, pp. 631–61).

478.18   IMPERIAL . . . Maximilian]   The Imperial Chamber (*Reichskammergericht*) was created by Emperor Maximilian I in 1495 to serve as the supreme court of the Holy Roman Empire. Its members were nominated by the emperor, the imperial electors, and the college of princes of the imperial diet. The *Reichskammergericht* continued until the final dissolution of the empire in 1806.

479.10–12   preside . . . citizens.]   See "Brutus" XIII (February 21, 1788; pages 223.16–226.14 in this volume) and *The Federalist LXXXI* (pages 489.11–490.5 in this volume). In 1793 the U.S. Supreme Court ruled in *Chisholm* v. *Georgia* that under Article III, section 2, federal jurisdiction extended to cases where a state was sued without its own consent by the citizen of another state. Opposition to the decision led to the proposal (1794) and ratification (1795, declared 1798) of the Eleventh Amendment, removing from federal jurisdiction suits "commenced or prosecuted" against states by citizens of other states. In *Cohens* v. *Virginia* (1821) the court ruled that the Eleventh Amendment did not prevent the Supreme Court from deciding appeals brought against states by citizens of another state in cases involving questions of constitutional or federal law; the decision was written by Chief Justice John Marshall.

483.15–16   in another place]   See note 384.35–36.

489.27–28   were discussed . . . taxation]   Hamilton's *The Federalist XXXII* (January 2, 1788; see *Debate on the Constitution, Part One*, pp. 678–81).

490.14–16   appellate jurisdiction . . . fact.]   This issue was addressed by the Seventh Amendment to the Constitution, which states that "no fact tried by a jury, shall be otherwise re-examined in any Court of the United States, than according to the rules of the common law." (Under the common law, appeals courts could order new trials in cases where the original verdict had resulted from an error in the determination of fact. At the second trial the facts would again be examined and determined by a jury.)

501.39   "An Address . . . New-York."]   Written by John Jay and signed "A Citizen of New-York," it was published in New York City on April 15, 1788. The pamphlet concludes:
"Suppose this plan to be rejected, what measures would you propose for obtaining a better? Some will answer, let us appoint another Convention, and as everything has been said and written that can well be said and written on the subject, they will be better informed than the former one was, and consequently be better able to make and agree upon a more eligible one.
"This reasoning is fair, and as far as it goes has weight; but it nevertheless takes one thing for granted, which appears very doubtful; for although the new Convention might have more information, and perhaps equal abilities, yet it does not from thence follow that they would be equally disposed to agree. The contrary of this position is the most probable. You must have observed that the same temper and equanimity which prevailed among the people on the former occasion, no longer exists. We have unhappily become divided into parties; and this important subject has been handled with such indiscreet and offensive acrimony, and with so many little unhandsome artifices and misrepresentations, that pernicious heats and animosities have been kindled, and spread their flames far and wide among us. When therefore it becomes a question who shall be deputed to the new Convention; we cannot flatter ourselves that the talents and integrity of the candidates will determine who shall be elected. Federal electors will vote for Federal deputies, and anti-Federal electors for anti-Federal ones. Nor will either party prefer the most moderate of their adherents, for as the most staunch and active partizans will be the most popular, so the men most willing and able to carry points, to oppose, and divide, and embarrass their opponents, will be chosen. A Convention formed at such a season, and of such men, would be but too exact an epitome of the great body that named them. The same party views, the same propensity to opposition, the same distrusts and jealousies, and the same unaccommodating spirit which prevail without, would be concentred and ferment with still greater violence within. Each deputy would recollect who sent him, and why he was sent; and be too apt to consider himself bound in honor, to contend and act vigorously under the standard of his party, and not hazard their displeasure by prefering compromise to victory. As vice does not

sow the seeds of virtue, so neither does passion cultivate the fruits of reason. Suspicions and resentments create no disposition to conciliate, nor do they infuse a desire of making partial and personal objects bend to general union and the common good. The utmost efforts of that excellent disposition were necessary to enable the late Convention to perform their task; and although contrary causes sometimes operate similar effects, yet to expect that discord and animosity should produce the fruits of confidence and agreement, is to expect 'grapes from thorns, figs from thistles.'

"The States of Georgia, Delaware, Jersey, and Connecticut, have adopted the present plan with unexampled unanimity; they are content with it as it is, and consequently their deputies, being apprized of the sentiments of their Constituents, will be little inclined to make alterations, and cannot be otherwise than averse to changes which they have no reason to think would be agreeable to their people—some other States, tho' less unanimous, have nevertheless adopted it by very respectable majorities; and for reasons so evidently cogent, that even the minority in one of them, have nobly pledged themselves for its promotion and support. From these circumstances, the new Convention would derive and experience difficulties unknown to the former. Nor are these the only additional difficulties they would have to encounter. Few are ignorant that there has lately sprung up a sect of politicians who teach and profess to believe that the extent of our nation is too great for the superintendance of one national Government, and on that principle argue that it ought to be divided into two or three. This doctrine, however mischievous in its tendency and consequences, has its advocates; and, should any of them be sent to the Convention, it will naturally be their policy rather to cherish than to prevent divisions; for well knowing that the institution of any national Government, would blast their favourite system, no measures that lead to it can meet with their aid or approbation.

"Nor can we be certain whether or not any and what foreign influence would, on such an occasion, be indirectly exerted, nor for what purposes—delicacy forbids an ample discussion of this question. Thus much may be said, without error or offence, viz. That such foreign nations as desire the prosperity of America, and would rejoice to see her become great and powerful, under the auspices of a Government wisely calculated to extend her commerce, to encourage her navigation and marine, and to direct the whole weight of her power and resources as her interest and honour may require, will doubtless be friendly to the Union of the States, and to the establishment of a Government able to perpetuate, protect and dignify it. Such other foreign nations, if any such there be, who, jealous of our growing importance, and fearful that our commerce and navigation should impair their own—who behold our rapid population with regret, and apprehend that the enterprising spirit of our people, when seconded by power and probability of success, may be directed to objects not consistent with their policy or interests, cannot fail to wish that we may continue a weak and a divided people.

"These considerations merit much attention, and candid men will judge how far they render it probable that a new Convention would be able either to agree in a better plan, or with tolerable unanimity, in any plan at all. Any plan forcibly carried by a slender majority, must expect numerous opponents among the people, who, especially in their present temper, would be more inclined to reject than adopt any system so made and carried. We should in such case again see the press teeming with publications for and against it; for as the minority would take pains to justify their dissent, so would the majority be industrious to display the wisdom of their proceedings. Hence new divisions, new parties, and new distractions would ensue, and no one can foresee or conjecture when or how they would terminate.

"Let those who are sanguine in their expectations of a better plan from a new Convention, also reflect on the delays and risque to which it would expose us. Let them consider whether we ought, by continuing much longer in our present humiliated condition, to give other nations further time to perfect their restrictive systems of commerce, to reconcile their own people to them, and to fence and guard and strengthen them by all those regulations and contrivances in which a jealous policy is ever fruitful. Let them consider whether we ought to give further opportunities to discord to alienate the hearts of our citizens from one another, and thereby encourage new Cromwells to bold exploits. Are we certain that our foreign creditors will continue patient, and ready to proportion their forbearance to our delays? Are we sure that our distresses, dissentions and weakness will neither invite hostility nor insult? If they should, how ill prepared shall we be for defence! without Union, without Government, without money, and without credit!

"It seems necessary to remind you, that some time must yet elapse, before all the States will have decided on the present plan. If they reject it, some time must also pass before the measure of a new Constitution, can be brought about and generally agreed to. A further space of time will then be requisite to elect their deputies, and send them on to Convention. What time they may expend when met, cannot be divined, and it is equally uncertain how much time the several States may take to deliberate and decide on any plan they may recommend—if adopted, still a further space of time will be necessary to organize and set it in motion:—In the mean time our affairs are daily going on from bad to worse, and it is not rash to say that our distresses are accumulating like compound interest.

"But if for the reasons already mentioned, and others that we cannot now perceive, the new Convention, instead of producing a better plan, should give us only a history of their disputes, or should offer us one still less pleasing than the present, where should we be then? The old Confederation has done its best, and cannot help us; and is now so relaxed and feeble, that in all probability it would not survive so violent a shock. Then 'to your tents Oh Israel!' would be the word. Then every band of union would be severed. Then every State would be a little nation, jealous of its neighbors, and anxious to strengthen itself by foreign alliances, against its former friends. Then farewell to fraternal affection, unsuspecting intercourse; and mutual participation in commerce, navigation, and citizenship. Then would arise mutual restrictions and fears, mutual garrisons,—and standing armies, and all those dreadful evils which for so many ages plagued England, Scotland, Wales, and Ireland, while they continued disunited, and were played off against each other.

"Consider my fellow citizens what you are about, before it is too late—consider what in such an event would be your particular case. You know the geography of your State, and the consequences of your local position. Jersey and Connecticut, to whom your impost laws have been unkind—Jersey and Connecticut, who have adopted the present plan, and expect much good from it—will impute its miscarriage and all the consequent evils to you. They now consider your opposition as dictated more by your fondness for your impost, than for those rights to which they have never been behind you in attachment. They cannot, they will not love you—they border upon you, and are your neighbors; but you will soon cease to regard their neighborhood as a blessing. You have but one port and outlet to your commerce, and how you are to keep that outlet free and uninterrupted, merits consideration. What advantage Vermont in combination with others, might take of you, may easily be conjectured; nor will you be at a loss to perceive how much reason the people of Long Island, whom you cannot protect, have to deprecate being constantly exposed to the depredations of every invader.

"These are short hints—they ought not to be more developed—you can easily in your own mind dilate and trace them through all their relative circumstances and connections.—Pause then for a moment, and reflect whether the matters you are disputing about are of sufficient moment to justify your running such extravagant risques. Reflect that the present plan comes recommended to you by men and fellow citizens who have given you the highest proofs that men can give, of their justice, their love for liberty and their country, of their prudence, of their application, and of their talents. They tell you it is the best that they could form; and that in their opinion, it is necessary to redeem you from those calamities which already begin to be heavy upon us all. You find that not only those men, but others of similar characters, and of whom you have also had very ample experience, advise you to adopt it. You find that whole States concur in the sentiment, and among them are your next neighbors; both whom have shed much blood in the cause of liberty, and have manifested as strong and constant a predilection for a free Republican Government as any State in the Union, and perhaps in the world. They perceive not those latent mischiefs in it, with which some double-sighted politicians endeavor to alarm you. You cannot but be sensible that this plan or constitution will always be in the hands and power of the people, and that if on experiment, it should be found defective or incompetent, they may either remedy its defects, or substitute another in its room. The objectionable parts of it are certainly very questionable, for otherwise there would not be such a contrariety of opinions about them. Experience will better determine such questions than theoretical arguments, and so far as the danger of abuses is urged against the institution of a Government, remember that a power to do good, always involves a power to do harm. We must in the business of Government as well as in all other business, have some degree of confidence, as well as a great degree of caution. Who on a sick bed would refuse medicines from a physician, merely because it is as much in his power to administer deadly poisons, as salutary remedies."

516.27–29   "if the . . . quick."]   Cf. Psalm 124:1–3.

526.6   PEOPLE . . . RHODE-ISLAND]   See note 270.1–3.

528.10–12   The system . . . 1781;]   See Chronology, January–March, 1781, June–December, 1782.

531.2–5   JOHNSON . . . numbers.]   William Samuel Johnson spoke in the Constitutional Convention on June 29, 1787, in favor of proportional representation in the House and equal representation in the Senate. Roger Sherman, another Connecticut delegate, had proposed the same compromise on June 11, and it was supported by the third Connecticut delegate, Oliver Ellsworth. The Convention finally adopted this formula on July 16; it later became known as the "Connecticut Compromise."

532.3–4   we may . . . eyes.]   Cf. Luke 19:42.

533.5–6   "In . . . Tory."]   First Satire of the Second Book of Horace, lines 67–68.

535.17–18   "For . . . best."]   See note 336.12–13.

536.3–4   Ratifications . . . Conventions]   This pamphlet was printed in Richmond, Virginia, in the late summer of 1788 by Augustine Davis, publisher of the Virginia Independent Chronicle, as The Ratifications of the New Fœderal Constitution Together with the Amendments Proposed by the Several States. On September 12 Edmund Randolph sent a copy of the pamphlet to James Madison, who in turn sent a copy to Thomas Jefferson in Paris on October 17. The pamphlet contained an introductory note explaining that the ratifications of Connecticut, New Jersey, Delaware, Pennsylvania, and Georgia, had been omitted because they were unconditional and did not propose any amendments.

540.33–34   JOHN M'KESSON . . . ABM. B. BANCKER]   John McKesson (c. 1735–98) had been secretary of the New York provincial convention of 1775, the first provincial congress in 1775, the convention to draft a state constitution in 1777 (where he supervised the printing), and secretary to the supreme court of New York in 1778, when John Jay was chief justice. Abraham B. Bancker of Ulster County was the son of retired merchant Evert Bancker (1721–1803); his cousin Abraham Bancker (1760–1832), delegate from Richmond County, voted in favor of ratification in the convention. Both Abraham B. Bancker and McKesson were Antifederalists.

550.9   GEO. RICHD. MINOT]   George Richards Minot (1758–1802), a Boston lawyer, was clerk of the state house of representatives and secretary of the ratifying convention. He was later a judge of probate, common pleas, and municipal court, and a founder, librarian, and treasurer of the Massachusetts

Historical Society. He wrote *History of the Insurrection in Massachusetts in 1786* (1788) and *Continuation of the History of the Province of Massachusetts Bay from 1748* (1798).

552.33   JOHN CALFE] John Calfe of Hampstead was clerk of the New Hampshire house of representatives.

552.34   JOSEPH PEARSON] Joseph Pearson of Exeter was secretary of state for New Hampshire.

556.16–17   Bee . . . Wilson.] Thomas Bee (1725–1812), Charleston lawyer and planter, former member and speaker of state assemblies 1762–79, lieutenant governor 1779–80, delegate to Continental Congress 1780–82, appointed U.S. District Judge 1790; John Julius Pringle (1753–1843), Charleston lawyer, state representative 1785–88 (speaker 1787–88), U.S. District Attorney 1789–92, and state attorney general 1792–1808; Henry Pendleton (see Biographical Notes); Francis Cummins (1732–1832), clergyman and former teacher in North and South Carolina and Georgia (Andrew Jackson was one of his pupils); John Hunter (1732–1802), Newberry farmer, state representative 1786–92, U.S. Representative 1793–95, and U.S. Senator 1796–98; Daniel Huger (1742–1799), Charleston lawyer, state representative 1778–80, active in defense of Charleston, delegate to Continental Congress 1786–88, U.S. Representative 1789–93; William Hill (1741–1816), emigrant from Ireland, ironmaster, supplier of cannonballs to Continental Army, lieutenant colonel of militia, and state representative; William Wilson (1740–93), planter in Williamsburg District and Marion District, was a state representative and senator.

572.18   Mr. John Skinner] Delegate from Perquimans County, member state house of commons 1783, state senator 1784–88.

574.16   Mr. Steele] John Steele (1764–1815), Salisbury merchant and supporter of ratification, member state house of commons 1787–88, 1794–95, 1806, and 1811–13, U.S. Representative 1789–93, U.S. Comptroller of Treasury 1796–1802.

574.18–19   Mr. A. Neale] Abner Neale, Craven County farmer and member of the state house of commons 1785–86.

577.1   SOUTH CAROLINA RATIFYING CONVENTION] In South Carolina the formal debate on ratification began in the legislature over the question of whether or not to convene a ratifying convention; see pages 19–25 (and notes) in this volume. After voting unanimously to convene a ratifying convention, the state house of representatives approved, 76–75, holding it in Charleston, a Federalist stronghold, in May.

The state had long favored a stronger central government for practical reasons. Though the interests of the eastern and western sections differed, particularly on the need for a temporary halt of the slave trade (a short-term embargo was in fact instituted for economic reasons in 1787), there was general agreement that the central government could help the state solve its economic problems. Twice the state had favored congressional impost, and it voted for congressional regulation of foreign and interstate commerce to force commercial benefits from Britain. British occupation of the state from 1780 to 1782 had revealed its vulnerability to foreign invasion.

Leading figures, especially Charles Pinckney and Charles Cotesworth Pinckney, had long favored a stronger central power even at the expense of state sovereignty. They had succeeded in protecting the state's vital interests in the Constitutional Convention. While conceding that after twenty years the importation of slaves into the country might be banned, they carefully protected the continued existence of the institution in several provisions of the Constitution. Charles Cotesworth Pinckney declared that "S. Carolina & Georgia cannot do without slaves. . . . If slavery be wrong, it is justified by the example of all the world. . . . In all ages one half of mankind have been slaves." They also succeeded in having slaves counted as people for purposes of representation in the House but otherwise regarded as property. Though they gave up their hoped-for restraints on federal regulation of commerce, which they feared might hurt their ships and merchants, they managed to outlaw export taxes, which they believed could have injured them more severely. They were assured that treaties hostile to their sectional interest, such as the agreement negotiated with Spain by John Jay in 1786 relinquishing the navigation of the Mississippi, could be defeated in the Senate. Behind these arrangements lay the threat that the South would refuse to join the Union—that South Carolina would lead in the creation of a separate southern confederacy linked only loosely with the other states. The negotiated compromises of the Constitutional Convention left leading South Carolinians free to express their nationalistic sentiment and to advocate ratification in the debates of 1788. Antifederalist views remained strong among the representatives of the western regions of the state, but the opposition was unable to overcome the Federalist commitments of the leading figures. South Carolina's short and poorly recorded ratification debate developed as a contest of ideas, of political and constitutional theory, in which the Federalists were easily victorious. (For the form of ratification and recommended amendments, see pp. 556–57 in this volume.)

581.14–15   very celebrated author]   Benjamin Franklin, in "Positions to Be Examined," first published in *De Re Rustica; or, the Repository for Select Papers on Agriculture, Arts, and Manufactures*, I (1769).

587.38   *Paley]   English theologian and philosopher William Paley (1743–1805), Archdeacon of Carlisle; his *Principles of Moral and Political Philosophy* (1785), to which Pinckney refers, has been called the textbook of utilitarianism.

592.8   Mr. Tweed]   Alexander Tweed of Prince Frederick's Parish.

595.1   VIRGINIA RATIFYING CONVENTION]   In 1788, Virginia included the present states of West Virginia and Kentucky and was the largest state of the union in both area and population (the 1790 census showed that it constituted 20 percent of the entire nation, including slaves). George Washington chose not to attend the ratifying convention, but James Madison, George Wythe, George Mason, Governor Edmund Randolph, Patrick Henry, Henry ("Light-Horse Harry") Lee, George Nicholas, Wilson Cary Nicholas—all major public figures—led the convention of 170 delegates, which included two young lawyers and politicians of unusual ability: James Monroe (who opposed the Constitution) and John Marshall (who favored it).

The debates stretched over 24 working days and were fully reported. Attorney David Robertson, seated in the gallery, took shorthand notes, and his resulting publication, *Debates and Other Proceedings of the Convention of Virginia* (3 vols., Petersburg, Va., 1788–89), was the fullest stenographic account of a deliberative body published in the Anglo-American world up to that time. Traffic in the gallery made hearing difficult, and Madison, leader of the Federalists, spoke with "a feebleness of voice," so that Robertson repeatedly had to record that he could not make out what Madison was saying. Robertson omitted several exchanges he considered "desultory," and he failed to attend one day's deliberations. Nevertheless the convention is remarkably well recorded, and the stenographic report conveys the exceptional quality of the debates.

The sides were well-balanced and the outcome was in doubt until the very end. It was clear that the union could not succeed without Virginia, and when the convention met, only eight states had ratified. (Virginia would be the tenth since New Hampshire's second convention ratified while the Virginians were still deliberating.)

Mason and Randolph, as delegates to the Constitutional Convention, had refused to sign the Constitution, and now added to their published explanations (November 21 and December 27, 1787) oral accounts of their decision, face-to-face with their friends, colleagues, and neighbors. Randolph had decided to support the Constitution despite his misgivings, a move that required explanation. The chief debaters on the two sides, Madison and Henry, were as different as two Virginia politicians could have been. Henry was an emotional rhetorician, so given to digressions that Governor Randolph warned, after one speech, that if he continued, "instead of three or six weeks, it will take us six months to decide this question." Many of Henry's speeches lasted over two hours; one stretched over two days. Madison, on the other hand, was weak in voice, logical, succinct, disciplined, and cogent. The strategies on both sides turned on these differences.

The chief hope of the Antifederalists lay in delaying the progress toward ratification, attacking the document as a wholesale violation of republicanism and the purposes of the Revolution, and attaching prior amendments that would necessitate a second national convention. The Federalists wished to show the necessity and safety of every provision in the Constitution, and to convince the many silent members (only 21 of the 170 members spoke during the month-long convention) that the Constitution was consistent with the principles of the Revolution and the only alternative to disunion. They succeeded, but only barely. The crucial vote came June 25 on Henry's proposal to make ratification contingent on the acceptance of a set of prepared amendments, to be submitted to the other states for approval. It lost 88–80, and the vote to ratify (89–79) followed immediately. (For the form of ratification and recommended amendments, see pp. 557–65 in this volume.)

600.8–10   objections . . . public,] See note 58.5.

603.32–34   Congress . . . passport.] Under the terms of the surrender agreement signed at Yorktown in 1781, British traders were allowed to sell their property in Virginia and remove the proceeds. In February 1782 the Continental Congress issued passports allowing British merchants who had sold their goods to the United States government to ship their proceeds in the form of tobacco to New York City (then still under British occupation). Virginia governor Benjamin Harrison refused to honor the documents and referred the matter to Randolph, then the state attorney general, and to the state legislature. Randolph argued that Congress had the power under the Articles of Confederation to issue passports, but the house of delegates disagreed and adopted five resolutions on May 20 protesting the congressional action. Although the resolutions were subsequently amended by the state senate, Congress sent John Rutledge and George Clymer to Virginia to "make such explanations" as needed to secure recognition of the passports. After conferring with the two congressional delegates, both houses of the legislature asked Governor Harrison in mid-June to assist Congress in exporting the tobacco.

603.35–36   second . . . Confederation] See page 926 in this volume.

606.14–15   The Gentleman . . . eulogium] George Nicholas's speech on June 4 preceded Patrick Henry's speech.

612.1   honorable friend] Edmund Randolph spoke before James Madison on June 6.

614.29–30   disgraceful insult] In June 1783 Congress was forced to leave Philadelphia to escape Pennsylvania soldiers demanding back pay. See Chronology of Events, May–June 1783.

616.26–27   cessions to Spain] Spain declared war on Great Britain on June 21, 1779. In September 1779 Congress appointed John Jay as envoy to Spain and instructed him to negotiate a treaty of alliance and secure substantial financial aid while maintaining the American claim to free navigation of the Mississippi. Jay arrived in Spain in January 1780 but was unable to achieve an alliance or negotiate a large loan because of Spanish insistence that the United States surrender its navigation claim. British victories in the South in 1780 and fears that Britain, Spain, and possibly France would negotiate an armistice that would leave Georgia and South Carolina under British occupation caused their delegations to Congress to move in late 1780 for Jay's instructions to be revised. Madison, then a Virginia delegate, wrote to the

Virginia legislature for guidance. The legislature approved changing the Jay instructions on January 2, 1781, after learning that Benedict Arnold had landed at Hampton Roads with a large raiding force. On February 15 Congress approved new instructions, drafted by Madison, that allowed Jay to concede American navigation rights on the river below the 31st parallel in return for a treaty of alliance. Jay offered the cession on the condition that if Spain postponed its acceptance to the time when a general peace was being negotiated, the offer would be withdrawn. The Spanish rejected the offer, insisting instead that the United States concede all navigation rights in the Gulf of Mexico as well. After the British surrender at Yorktown in October 1781 the American claim to navigation on the Mississippi was reasserted by both southern delegates in Congress and the American peace negotiators in Europe. See also note 628.5–6.

624.38–39   his Excellency's . . . Delegates]   See note 58.5.

626.22   Josiah Phillips]   In the previous day's debates Edmund Randolph had illustrated the violations of the Virginia state constitution by the state legislature by citing the condemnation of Josiah Phillips, a bandit leader, on a bill of attainder when Patrick Henry himself had been governor (1778). Such bills, prohibited under Article I, sections 9 and 10, of the proposed Constitution, denied individuals trial under the common law and condemned them by legislative act; although not explicitly prohibited by the Virginia constitution, they implicitly violated several of the provisions of article 8 of the state declaration of rights (see note 678.2). The act attainting Phillips (passed May 30, 1778) condemned him to death for treason unless he surrendered himself before June 30, 1778 (the act charged that Phillips had "levied war" against the state by his depradations). It was drafted by Jefferson, who in 1783 proposed that attainders be banned in a revision of the Virginia constitution. Phillips was apprehended on June 4, 1778, and convicted of robbery in a trial held October 16–21, 1778; he was hanged November 23, 1778. Randolph was then the state attorney general, and it was his decision, according to Jefferson, to try Phillips for robbery under the common law rather than to execute him for treason under the bill of attainder. Jefferson recalled the episode and responded to Randolph's version of events in letters to William Wirt and Louis H. Girardin in 1814–15.

628.5–6   treaty . . . Spain]   On June 26, 1784, Spain closed the lower Mississippi to American navigation until the United States and Spain reached an agreement on the boundaries of Louisiana and the Floridas. In July 1785 Jay, then secretary for foreign affairs, began negotiations with Spanish envoy Diego de Gardoqui on the Mississippi and other issues, and on August 25, 1785, received instructions from Congress to secure American navigation of the river. On August 3, 1786, Jay recommended to Congress that the United States forgo its Mississippi navigation claim for 25 or 30 years in return for a Spanish-American commercial treaty and asked that his instructions be changed. The proposed treaty was supported by delegates from the North, where mercantile areas were suffering from British trade restrictions, and opposed by southern delegates, who considered free navigation essential to western settlement. After a heated debate, Congress amended Jay's instructions on August 29 in a 7–5 vote along sectional lines (Delaware was absent); because the votes of nine states were needed to ratify a treaty under the Articles, the negotiations did not progress and the Jay-Gardoqui commercial treaty was never signed. In 1795 Thomas Pinckney negotiated a treaty with Spain that opened the river to American navigation.

631.31 Maryland . . . danger] In his speech of June 6, Randolph had suggested that if Virginia failed to ratify, Maryland might contest Virginia's navigation rights on the Potomac River, and that the Northern Neck of Virginia (between the Rappahannock and Potomac rivers) might annex itself to Maryland.

633.27 Another Gentleman] George Nicholas.

636.17–22 Bill of Rights] In 1689 parliament offered William and Mary the throne on the condition that they acknowledge the rights and liberties later included in the "Act declaring the Rights and Liberties of the Subject and Setleing the Succession of the Crowne," commonly known as the Bill of Rights, which became law on December 16, 1689. The Bill of Rights established a line of royal succession, barred Catholics from the throne, denounced the abuses of James II, and declared that the crown could not legally suspend or dispense with laws, levy money, or keep a standing army in peacetime without the consent of parliament. It also called for free elections to parliament, frequent holdings of parliament, freedom of speech in parliament, proclaimed the right of subjects to petition the king, and declared that excessive bail and fines ought not to be imposed and that cruel and unusual punishments ought not to be inflicted.

636.37 another time.] Henry's speech was continued at the next session of the convention, June 9, at almost twice the length of the first part. One passage—a peroration on "self-love"—is a notable expression of Henry's attitude to politics:

"Tell me not of checks on paper; but tell me of checks founded on self-love. The English Government is founded on self-love. This powerful irrisistible stimulous of self-love has saved that Government. It has interposed that hereditary nobility between the King and Commons. If the House of Lords assists or permits the King to overturn the liberties of the people, the same tyranny will destroy them; they will therefore keep the balance in the democratic branch. Suppose they see the Commons incroach upon the King; self-love, that great energetic check, will call upon them to interpose: For, if the King be destroyed, their destruction must speedily follow. . . . Compare this with your Congressional checks. I beseech Gentlemen to consider, whether they can say, when trusting power, that a mere patriotic profession will be equally operative and efficacious, as the check of self-love. In considering the experience of ages, is it not seen, that fair disinterested patriotism, and professed attachment to rectitude have never been solely trusted to by an enlightened free people?—If you depend on your President's and Senators' patriotism, you are gone. . . . The real rock of political salvation is *self-love* perpetuated from age to age in every human breast, and manifested in every action. If they can stand the temptations of human nature, you are safe. If you have a good President, Senators and Representatives, there is no danger.—But can this be expected from human nature? . . . A good President, or Senator, or Representative, will have a natural weakness—Virtue will slumber. The wicked will be continually watching: Consequently you will be undone. Where are your checks? . . . If you say, that out of this depraved mass, you can collect luminous characters, it will not avail, unless this luminous breed will be propagated from generation to generation; and even then, if the number of vicious characters will preponderate, you are undone. And that this will certainly be the case, is, to my mind, perfectly clear.—In the British Government there are real balances and checks—In this system, there are only ideal balances. Till I am convinced that there are actual efficient checks, I will not give my assent to its establishment. The President and Senators have nothing to lose. They have not that interest in the preservation of the Government, that the King and Lords have in England. They will therefore be regardless of the interests of the people."

638.29   action of Guildford]   At the start of the battle of Guilford Courthouse, North Carolina (March 15, 1781), the North Carolina militia in the front line had withdrawn precipitously after firing one volley at the advancing British and exposed Lt. Col. Lee's troops to Cornwallis's attack. Lee had tried but failed to stop the militia's retreat.

639.28   tender law]   A law making paper money legal tender for the payment of all obligations, public and private.

647.16   *"Vox et præterea nihil."*]   "Voice and nothing more."

649.15–16   confine . . . consideration.]   The convention had voted on June 3 to consider the Constitution clause by clause in a committee of the whole before voting on ratification.

650.29–31   treaty . . . neutrality]   One of the provisions of the Franco-American treaty of amity and commerce signed in Paris on February 6, 1778, was that "free Ships shall also give a freedom to Goods" (i.e., that neutral ships should be able to carry the nonmilitary goods of belligerent nations without having them seized by other belligerent nations). Britain did not recognize this principle and seized American, French, and Spanish goods carried on neutral ships. In 1780 Russia, Denmark, and Sweden formed the League of Armed Neutrality in an attempt to defend neutral shipping rights, including the principle of free ships making free goods. Six other European nations had joined the League by 1783.

654.22   Honorable Gentleman]   James Monroe.

664.7   Mr. *Grayson*]   William Grayson (c. 1736–90), lawyer from Dumfries, colonel and aide-de-camp to Washington 1776–79 (including battles of Long Island, White Plains, Brandywine, and Monmouth), commissioner of the Board of War 1780–81, member house of delegates 1784–88, delegate to Continental Congress 1785–87 (where he was instrumental in passing Northwest Ordinance), and U.S. Senator 1789–90. He voted against ratification in the convention.

667.19   Decemviri at Rome]   In 451 B.C., at the request of the plebeians, ten patricians (the *decemviri*), including Appius Claudius, were appointed by the Roman senate to prepare a written code of laws and were invested with absolute authority. Ten tables of laws were submitted to the people and ratified. A second commission of *decemviri*, including some plebeians, was appointed in 450, and two further tables of laws (including a formal prohibition of intermarriage between patricians and plebeians) were enacted (together these are known as the Twelve Tables). The following year, according to Livy (Book 3, ch. 44), Appius Claudius abused his authority by seizing Verginia, daughter of a plebeian centurion, but her father killed her to preserve her chastity and the act precipitated a revolution that overthrew the *decemviri*.

669.30–33   French . . . Stadtholder]   After the death of William II of Orange in 1650, five of the seven provinces of the Netherlands did not choose a new stadtholder to replace him (a member of the House of Orange had served as stadtholder since the founding of the United Provinces in 1579). When Louis XIV of France invaded the United Provinces in June 1672 and quickly occupied much of the country, popular discontent with the unpreparedness of Johan de Witt, grand pensionary of the province of Holland and the leading political figure in the republic since 1653, led to the proclamation of William III of Orange as stadtholder in July; de Witt was killed by a mob in August. William rejected the humiliating peace terms offered by Louis and rallied the Dutch behind water barriers created by flooding the countryside. The war continued until 1678, when the French withdrew completely from the United Provinces. After the death of the childless William III in 1702, the stadtholdership of the United Provinces again fell vacant. It was revived in 1747 after the French invasion during the War of Austrian Succession, when William IV was elevated to the position. Although William proved an ineffective military leader, the French withdrew as part of the general peace of 1748.

669.36–670.3   late disorders . . . surrender.]   The Patriots' Movement in the United Provinces received the support of France for its opposition to the stadtholder William V, who was blamed by the Patriots for Dutch defeats in the 1780–84 Anglo-Dutch war. In 1785 William left The Hague in Holland for the less hostile province of Gelderland and the Patriots assumed power in Holland and Utrecht. When Wilhelmina, his wife, attempted to return to Holland in 1787 she was detained at the border. This incident provided the pretext for her brother, Frederick William II of Prussia, to intervene, and a

Prussian army restored William V to power in The Hague. Thousands of Patriots fled to France.

670.9–10   navigation . . . Mississippi.]   See note 628.5–6.

670.31   Southern . . . Eastern]   In the vote in Congress on February 15, 1781, New Hampshire, Rhode Island, Pennsylvania, Delaware, Virginia, South Carolina, and Georgia supported changing Jay's instructions to permit a cession of Mississippi navigation rights. Massachusetts, Connecticut, and North Carolina were opposed, with New York divided and New Jersey and Maryland absent.

671.29–30   honorable friend]   William Grayson.

672.2   honorable member]   Patrick Henry.

673.5   An Honorable Gentleman]   Edmund Randolph.

674.5   The Honorable Gentleman]   Edmund Pendleton.

674.6   opinion . . . Jefferson]   On June 9 Henry had referred to a letter Jefferson had written from Paris saying that the French government, far from planning reprisals against the United States for failing to pay its debts, was expecting to enter into favorable commercial arrangements with the new nation. Henry also alleged that Jefferson advised rejecting the Constitution. Randolph responded on June 10, regretting that Jefferson had been introduced into the debate on the basis of a reported letter, and rejecting the idea that Jefferson was against ratification. Although Jefferson had written several letters in February 1788 suggesting that after the first nine state conventions ratified, the remaining four states should reject the Constitution until a bill of rights was added, by late May 1788 he had come to believe that the Massachusetts plan of unconditional ratification with recommended amendments was a better idea.

677.13   trial . . . away?]   Art. III, sec. 2 (page 978.24–28 in this volume) mandated jury trials for criminal cases under federal jurisdiction but not in civil cases (a deliberate omission, reversed by the Seventh Amendment).

678.2   Declaration of Rights]   Virginia's declaration of rights, adopted June 12, 1776:

"*A* DECLARATION *of* RIGHTS *made by the representatives of the good people of* Virginia, *assembled in full and free Convention; which rights do pertain to them, and their posterity, as the basis and foundation of government.*

"1. That all men are by nature equally free and independent, and have certain inherent rights, of which, when they enter into a state of society, they cannot, by any compact, deprive or divest their posterity; namely, the enjoyment of life and liberty, with the means of acquiring and possessing property, and pursuing and obtaining happiness and safety.

"2. That all power is vested in, and consequently derived from, the people; that magistrates are their trustees and servants, and at all times amenable to them.

"3. That government is, or ought to be, instituted for the common benefit, protection, and security, of the people, nation, or community, of all the various modes and forms of government that is best, which is capable of producing the greatest degree of happiness and safety, and is most effectually secured against the danger of mal-administration; and that whenever any government shall be found inadequate or contrary to these purposes, a majority of the community hath an indubitable, unalienable, and indefeasible right, to reform, alter, or abolish it, in such manner as shall be judged most conducive to the public weal.

"4. That no man, or set of men, are entitled to exclusive or separate emoluments or privileges from the community, but in consideration of publick services; which, not being descendible, neither ought the offices of magistrate, legislator, or judge, to be hereditary.

"5. That the legislative and executive powers of the state should be separate and distinct from the judiciary; and that the members of the two first may be restrained from oppression, by feeling and participating the burthens of the people, they should at fixed periods, be reduced to a private station, return into that body from which they were originally taken, and the vacancies be supplied by frequent, certain, and regular elections, in which all, or any part of the former members, to be again eligible, or ineligible, as the laws shall direct.

"6. That elections of members to serve as representatives of the people, in assembly, ought to be free; and that all men, having sufficient evidence of permanent common interest with, and attachment to, the community, have the right of suffrage, and cannot be taxed or deprived of their property for publick uses without their own consent, or that of their representatives so elected, nor bound by any law to which they have not, in like manner, assented, for the publick good.

"7. That all power of suspending laws, or the execution of laws, by any authority without consent of the representatives of the people, is injurious to their rights, and ought not to be exercised.

"8. That in all capital or criminal prosecutions a man hath a right to demand the cause and nature of his accusation, to be confronted with the accusers and witnesses, to call for evidence in his favour, and to a speedy trial by an impartial jury of his vicinage, without whose unanimous consent he cannot be found guilty, nor can he be compelled to give evidence against himself; that no man be deprived of his liberty except by the law of the land, or the judgment of his peers.

"9. That excessive bail ought not to be required, nor excessive fines imposed, nor cruel and unusual punishments inflicted.

"10. That general warrants, whereby any officer or messenger may be commanded to search suspected places without evidence of a fact committed, or to seize any person or persons not named, or whose offence is not particularly described and supported by evidence, are grievous and oppressive, and ought not to be granted.

"11. That in controversies respecting property, and in suits between man and man, the ancient trial by jury is preferable to any other, and ought to be held sacred.

"12. That the freedom of the press is one of the great bulwarks of liberty, and can never be restrained but by despotick governments.

"13. That a well regulated militia, composed of the body of the people, trained to arms, is the proper, natural, and safe defence of a free state; that standing armies, in time of peace, should be avoided, as dangerous to liberty; and that, in all cases, the military should be under strict subordination to, and governed by, the civil power.

"14. That the people have a right to uniform government; and therefore, that no government separate from, or independent of, the government of *Virginia*, ought to be erected or established within the limits thereof.

"15. That no free government, or the blessing of liberty, can be preserved to any people but by a firm adherence to justice, moderation, temperance, frugality, and virtue, and by frequent recurrence to fundamental principles.

"16. That religion, or the duty which we owe to our CREATOR, and the manner of discharging it, can be directed only by reason and conviction, not by force or violence, and therefore all men are equally entitled to the free exercise of religion, according to the dictates of conscience; and that it is the mutual duty of all to practice Christian forbearance, love, and charity, towards each other."

678.14–15   The Honorable member]   Edmund Randolph.

682.31–32   Honorable Gentleman]   Edmund Pendleton.

684.36   Honorable Gentleman]   Edmund Pendleton.

701.28   worthy member]   John Marshall.

703.34–35   other Honorable Gentleman,]   William Grayson.

706.31–33   "They . . . done."]   Cf. the Anglican *Book of Common Prayer*, "General Confession."

707.2–3   Southern . . . trade.]   See Chronology, August 1787.

709.6   the Gentleman]   Patrick Henry.

710.14   Honorable Member]   James Madison.

710.18   The Gentleman]   Patrick Henry.

718.20–26   Honorable Gentleman . . . it.]   Edmund Randolph rose immediately afterward to explain that he now considered adoption of the Constitution necessary "were it even more defective than it is." He admitted having once opposed the reeligibility of the president, but second thoughts and the opinions of others had led him to change his mind. He had come to see the value of the independence that reeligibility would confer and the continuing concern for public rather than private interests that would result. Randolph added that the possibility of impeachment would help prevent corruption by foreign powers.

722.20–21   disputes . . . State.]   See note 479.10–12, and pp. 734–35 in this volume.

723.39–40   fourteenth amendment . . . Convention,]   See pp. 563–64 in this volume.

726.6–7   *fieri facias* . . . jail.]   "Cause to be done"; that is, a writ ordering the sheriff to confiscate the goods of a debtor and to sell them until the amount of the judgment is raised. If the debt cannot be paid off by this measure, a writ of *capias ad satisfaciendum* may be issued, which provides for the imprisonment of "the body of the debtor" until the debt is satisfied (Blackstone, *Commentaries on the Laws of England*, Bk. III, ch. 26, pp. 412–17).

726.19   *ultima ratio regum*]   "The final argument of kings" (i.e., force); the saying was inscribed on French cannon in the reign of Louis XIV (king 1643–1715).

727.25–28   disputed lands . . . quitrents]   In 1781 Thomas, 6th Lord Fairfax, died in Virginia, leaving to his English heirs the Northern Neck proprietary, a tract of over five million acres of land between the Potomac and Rapidan-Rappahannock rivers. The Virginia assembly declared in 1782 that the Fairfax heirs were "alien enemies" and ordered that quitrents due at the time of Fairfax's death be sequestered until the title to the land was settled; future quitrents would be paid into the state treasury. Although the sequestration was repealed in 1783, the assembly transferred the land papers for the Northern Neck to the state land office in 1785 and discharged all Northern Neck landholders from paying further quitrents. In 1786 the state began issuing grants of unappropriated land within the proprietary (the unappropriated land totaled about 2.5 million acres). Denny Martin, Lord Fairfax's nephew, contested these actions, including the abolition of quitrents, but eventually began to concentrate his efforts on securing title to the manor lands personally used by the 6th Lord (approximately 160,000 acres). After considerable litigation, John Marshall, who had contracted to buy part of the Fairfax manor lands and was serving as Martin's attorney, helped negotiate a legislative settlement in 1796. Under its terms, Martin sold the unappropriated lands to the state in return for confirmation by the assembly of his title to the manor lands. (Because the abolition of quitrents in 1785 was no longer being actively challenged by Martin, the issue of their collection lapsed.)

729.4   *Nos . . . arva.*]   "We flee our native land—and leave our beloved fields." Cf. Virgil, *Eclogues*, I, lines 3–4: "Nos patriæ fines et dulcia linquimus arva / nos patriam fugimus."

737.5   Honorable Member]   Patrick Henry.

738.12   Honorable Member]   Patrick Henry.

748.37   *nexus imperii*]   Binding of power.

757.1   NEW YORK RATIFYING CONVENTION]   New York had long been
embroiled in the question of extending the powers of the federal government.
During the war, with New York City and its surroundings occupied by British troops, New York needed the protection of the federal government. In
1780 Hamilton and Governor George Clinton called for a national convention
to increase Congress's powers, and New York concurred with the Continental
Congress's call for approval of a federal impost in 1781. When that proposal
failed, the state legislature, in 1782, resolved that Congress be given general
taxing power and that a national convention be called to strengthen the powers of the federal government. But after the British occupation ended Governor Clinton's forces favored the enhancement of state power. New York's
state tariff fell heavily on consumers in Connecticut and New Jersey and on
New York City merchants, but yielded about half of the state's revenues,
relieving the majority farming population of property taxes. The sale of Loyalist estates and of unsettled land claims in the west and north, though legally
dubious, further enriched the state's treasury. All of these revenues were im-
periled by the enhancement of congressional powers. Clinton's leadership was
strengthened by the legislature's creation in 1786 of a land bank to assist debtors and farmers in the recession that had overtaken the state. The stake in the
paper money issued by the bank, widespread among farmers, broadened out
to the commercial interests when income generated by the bank was committed to funding the widely held securities that had been issued by the state and
much of the federal debt that was held by New Yorkers. In 1786 and again in
1787 the state, reversing its earlier position, refused to concur in Congress's
second appeal for a federal impost unless the state was given control over its
collectors.

     While major interests within the state made it unlikely that New York
would support an enlargement of Congressional powers, there were important elements centered in the powerful merchant community that increasingly
saw a need to strengthen the central government (such as John Jay, who had
experienced at first hand the nation's feebleness in international relations).
Under Hamilton's leadership they convinced the state legislature to send delegates to the Annapolis convention; they led that delegation, and at Annapolis helped formulate the call for the Constitutional Convention. Two of the
three delegates to Philadelphia—Robert Yates and John Lansing, Jr.—were
strongly Antifederalist, voted consistently for state sovereignty, and quit the
convention halfway through the proceedings when it was clear that a strong
central government would be created. Hamilton, the third delegate, whose
extreme nationalism alienated some Federalists, attended sporadically, but
made significant contributions in the last weeks of the convention and alone
of the New York delegates signed the Constitution.

     Nine months intervened between the publication of the Constitution in
New York and the convening of the state's ratifying convention. Politicians,

public commentators, and writers of all persuasions flooded the state with polemical tracts. Some of the most notable commentaries on the Constitution published anywhere in the country appeared in New York. Strings of pseud-onymous polemics were quickly spun out: "Caesar" responded to "Cato"; "The Federal Farmer" was followed by the first of "Publius's" eighty-five *Federalist* essays; John Jay's *Address to the People of . . . New York* was an-swered by "A Plebeian" (Melancton Smith). All of New York's newspapers entered into the debate, and an Antifederalist publication committee was formed to publish and distribute writings against the Constitution. When the convention met on June 17, the delegates, chosen by the entire body of free adult male citizens, reflected the state's basic Antifederalist position: the Fed-eralists were outnumbered 46 to 19. Led by Melancton Smith, delegate from Dutchess County, the Antifederalists had every expectation of winning the final vote. They were defeated not by the Federalists' arguments (the political influence of the *The Federalist* was negligible) but by the latent divisions within the Antifederalist coalition, the timing of events, and the moderation and statesmanship of Melancton Smith. The convention's decision to debate the Constitution paragraph by paragraph before voting proved to be crucial. As the debates proceeded in New York, decisive votes were being taken else-where. Seven days after the convention met, news arrived that New Hamp-shire (the ninth state) had ratified, allowing the Constitution to be put into effect. On July 2, news of Virginia's ratification was also received. The Anti-federalist majority was faced with a dilemma: if they outvoted the Federalists, New York would be isolated outside the Union, incapable of forming a middle-state confederacy and denied the opportunity of forcing amendments. If they conceded, they would forsake their principles and what they saw as the majority's interests. They turned to complicated compromises: one plan called for ratification with amendments that would cripple essential parts of the Constitution. The Federalists, whose confidence grew daily, rejected this proposal and Melancton Smith's subsequent proposal to ratify with the right to withdraw if a new convention were not called. Finally, on July 23, with the convention aware that Congress would not accept any kind of conditional ratification, a motion was made in the committee of the whole to ratify "in full confidence" that the vital amendments would soon be passed. Smith, though he still believed the Constitution to be radically defective, was aware of Madison's and other leading Federalists' insistence that the Constitution be adopted "*in toto*" and concluded that prior amendments were impossible. The question became whether or not New York would join the Union, within which the Antifederalists could pursue "in a practicable way" the amend-ments they felt were necessary. If they did not ratify outright, leaving amend-ments for the future, he predicted there would be chaos within the state and a breakup of the Clinton coalition, with the prospect that the southern part of the state would secede and join the Union separately. Smith's shift of his vote on this vital motion in the committee of the whole had been anticipated in his private correspondence with Nathan Dane of Massachusetts (June 28, July 3, 15; see pp. 822–23, 844–50, and 851 in this volume), and other Federalists agreed with his reasoning and the motion was approved, 31–29. Three days later, the convention approved the Constitution by a vote of 30 to 27, with the Federalists agreeing to circulate a letter to the other states calling for a general convention to draft the amendments. The debate in New York, both in the public press and the five weeks of convention arguments, had been the most widely publicized of all the ratification discussions. Clinton came to terms with the new political world and served for eight years as vice-president of the government he had hoped would never be created. (For the form of ratification and recommended amendments adopted by the convention, see pp. 536–47 in this volume.)

757.11   honorable . . . New-York.]   Alexander Hamilton.

757.24   rule of apportionment]   Art. I, sec. 2, par. 3 (the "three-fifths clause").

762.6–11   "In every . . . equally."]   The opening sentences of the introduction to *Essay on Crimes and Punishments* (Milan or Livorno, 1764; English translation, 1767) by Cesare Bonesana, Marchese di Beccaria, an argument against capital punishment and maltreatment of prisoners that stimulated action for penal reform throughout Western Europe.

768.3   honorable gentleman,]   John Williams.

770.29–30   aristocrats . . . Federal Farmer.]   "The Federal Farmer" Letter VII, published in *An Additional Number of Letters from the Federal Farmer* ([New York], 1788), estimated the class of aristocrats at 4,000–5,000 men (including state senators, superior judges, "the most eminent professional men, &c., and men of large property"). These were contrasted with "the natural democracy . . . the yeomanry, the subordinate officers, civil and military, the fishermen, mechanics and traders, many of the merchants and professional men," making "two classes, the aristocratical, and democratical, with views . . . widely different."

781.8   honorable . . . New-York,]   Richard Harison (1747–1829), graduate of King's College (Columbia), New York lawyer and U.S. Attorney for the District of New York 1789–1801, voted for ratification.

791.24   honorable . . . New York]   John Jay.

799.21   gentleman from Albany.]   John Lansing, Jr.

804.27   honorable . . . New York,]   Robert R. Livingston.

823.4–7   the last . . . amendment—]   The proposed amendment, introduced by George Livingston on June 24, would have limited eligibility for the Senate to six years in any term of twelve years and made senators subject to recall by their legislatures. Lansing and Hamilton had debated the issue at length on June 24, Smith and Hamilton on the 25th. It was adopted as a recommended amendment in the final form of ratification (see page 543.12–17 in this volume).

824.5   honorable . . . Ulster]   George Clinton.

824.6   those papers]   Earlier in the day Hamilton had introduced into the record resolutions adopted by the New York legislature in 1780–82 to prove that the Confederation's financial system of requisitions upon the states had led New York to suffer "extremes of distress." Clinton replied by stating that he had always desired a stronger central government than that of the Articles of Confederation and had consistently favored a congressional impost, so long as it was enforced by state officials, but that it did not follow that the nation should now accept a dangerous central government with an uncontrollable power to tax. Clinton also alluded to "a dangerous attempt to subvert our liberties, by creating a supreme dictator" during the war, and warned that the people "when wearied with their distresses, will, in the moment of frenzy, be guilty of the most imprudent and desperate measures."

828.28   has been said]   By John Williams, who the day before had cited Montesquieu (cf. *The Spirit of the Laws*, Vol. I, Bk. XIII) to the effect that a poll tax upon the person was indicative of despotism but a property tax was congenial with the spirit of a free government.

831.9–10   proposition . . . committee.]   Introduced on June 26 by John Williams, this proposed amendment became two of the recommended amendments in the final form of ratification. See page 541.11–26 in this volume (the Williams proposal did not contain the exception for "ardent spirits").

836.8   the amendment]   See note 831.9–10.

836.9–10   honorable colleague,]   Alexander Hamilton.

836.23   another gentleman]   John Williams.

837.6   one from Washington]   John Williams.

838.31–32   gentleman from Dutchess]   Melancton Smith.

842.14   gentleman from Washington]   John Williams.

851.14   Mr. Osgoods]   Samuel Osgood (1748–1813), Massachusetts delegate to Continental Congress 1781–84, was appointed to the board of treasury and served 1785–89. He took up permanent residence in New York and was a Republican in politics, aligned with the Clinton party.

852.6   Mr. Jones]   Samuel Jones (1734–1819), Queens County lawyer, state assemblyman 1786–90, recorder of New York City 1789–96, state senator 1791–97, and state comptroller 1797–1800. In the convention, he joined Melancton Smith to vote for ratification with subsequent amendments.

854.1   NORTH CAROLINA RATIFYING CONVENTION]   Of the twelve states that held ratifying conventions before the new federal government was organized, only North Carolina refused to accept the Constitution. The Antifederalist delegation to North Carolina's first ratifying convention far outnumbered the Federalists—but that had also been the case in New York. The Federalists were led by James Iredell, Richard Dobbs Spaight, Archibald Maclaine, and Governor Samuel Johnston, who were the equals of many of the very best Federalist leaders elsewhere. The main Antifederalist leaders— Willie Jones, Timothy Bloodworth, and Samuel Spencer—were not abler or more influential in their state than Patrick Henry, George Clinton, and Samuel Bryan were in theirs. Most of the issues debated were the same as those discussed in the other conventions, and the threatened enforcement of the Peace Treaty (particularly its guarantee of pre-war debts and its required restoration of Loyalist property) was no more worrisome to some North Carolinians than it had been to some Virginians and New Yorkers. By the time the final vote was taken it was known that ten states had already ratified and that the Constitution would go into effect whether North Carolina joined or not. Rejection seemed unlikely to affect the nation's development but very likely to harm the state by isolation. Yet the North Carolina convention not only refused to ratify, but refused by a substantial margin—184–83.

North Carolina differed from the other states in certain ways. It was the fourth largest state in size, including the present states of North Carolina and Tennessee and stretching almost 1,000 miles from the Atlantic coast to the Mississippi River. The settlements west of the coastal region were recent, scattered, and ill-organized. By 1790, 36,000 people, almost 10 percent of the state's total population, lived in the trans-Allegheny region. This sudden population growth and westward movement, begun only in the 1740s, had left small settlements scattered over the countryside, isolated from the eastern villages and the state's single effective coastal port. Newspapers and schools were rare, illiteracy was widespread, and the population was divided along ethnic and religious lines. Scots-Irish, Scots Highlanders, and Germans formed enclaves of their own, and every variety of Protestant dissent was represented. Slaves comprised 25 percent of the population, most of them clustered in the east. Though there were people of some wealth and position, their advantages had been very recently acquired, and no settled leadership had been established. Before the Revolution, government was concentrated in the east, and when the state's agents penetrated into the Piedmont and further west, they were viewed as exploitative, insensitive to local needs, arbitrary, and invulnerable, since the allocation of assembly seats heavily favored the east. In 1768–71, the Regulators in the Piedmont, especially in Orange County, staged an armed uprising against the taxes, courts, and legal processes imposed from the east. The insurrection was suppressed by Governor Tryon and the militia, but western resentment of the eastern establishment persisted.

Through much of the state, all government above the local level was viewed as alien and threatening to liberty. Western elements, led by Thomas Burke of Orange County, drafted a state constitution that would have instituted popular sovereignty in the most radical form. Burke tried to delay the state's acceptance of the Articles of Confederation, and, in the Continental Congress, he was responsible for the second Article which guaranteed the sovereignty of the states and reserved to them the powers not expressly delegated to Congress. Burke and other North Carolinians in Congress, particularly Timothy Bloodworth, also asserted the state's sovereignty in managing its Indian population. North Carolina refused to cede its western territories to the nation, repeal laws that contradicted the terms of the peace treaty with Britain, and pay its requisition into the national treasury. The state also opposed the Jay-Gardoqui negotiations, which would have barred Americans from free use of the Mississippi.

The Antifederalists quickly attacked the Constitution, defeated several leading Federalists for seats in the ratifying convention, and elected some of the most fervent Antifederalists. The Baptist preacher Lemuel Burkitt described the Constitution's federal district as a walled fortress from which would sally forth a vast national army to "enslave the people, who will be gradually disarmed." When the ratifying convention convened, the Antifederalists had a 2–1 majority; they represented the entire west and the numerically superior Presbyterian and Baptist communities. The Federalists, from the eastern counties and towns, represented the interests of the lawyers (but not the judges), the merchants, and the large slave owners. The convention met at Hillsborough, in the western part of the state, and its debates were recorded by David Robertson, who had earlier reported the debates of the Virginia ratifying convention. Federalists sought to convince the western delegates that their interests and those of the east were mutually supportive. Outside authorities were brought in: the Federalists published John Hancock's crucial speech in the Massachusetts convention; the Antifederalists quoted Jefferson's letter (long since repudiated by him) urging four states to reject the Constitution in order to force amendments. In the end, the state's endemic localism, the widespread suspicion of government, and the west's resentment of the east prevailed. The debate ended in a confusion of parliamentary maneuvering, but the issue was never in doubt. The Federalists failed to overcome their opposition's fears, and there were no Antifederalist leaders, like Melancton Smith in New York, willing or able to swing their side's votes. (For the resolutions adopted by the convention at Hillsborough on August 2, 1788, see pp. 565–74 in this volume.)

In April 1789, when the new government of the United States went into operation, North Carolina and Rhode Island, which had refused even to convene a convention, were not part of the Union. North Carolina held a second ratifying convention in Fayetteville in November 1789, by which time the national government was underway and the Bill of Rights had been approved by Congress and sent out to the states. The debates in the second convention were not recorded, but ratification came quickly and decisively (194–77).

862.4–6   Blackstone . . . impossible.] Bk. I, ch. 2, sec. iii, p. 156.

864.8–9   gentleman from Halifax,] William R. Davie.

866.30–32   violated . . . Davidson county.] In an effort to protect new settlements in its western territory, North Carolina in 1786 authorized the formation of a 200-man military force in Davidson and Sumner counties and provided taxes to support it.

876.20–21   Government . . . lenity]   In November 1786 Massachusetts passed an Act of Indemnity pardoning all Shaysite rebels who pledged allegiance to the state government before January 1, 1787. A second act, passed in February 1787, offered pardons to rank and file insurgents, although those who took the oath were to be disenfranchised for three years.

885.3   gentleman from New-Hanover]   Timothy Bloodworth.

885.35   Member from Anson]   Samuel Spencer.

887.10   gentleman from Halifax,]   William R. Davie.

888.7   these two clauses.]   Article III, sections 1 and 2.

889.21–22   gentleman from Edenton,]   James Iredell.

894.13   *felo de se*]   A *felo de se* is "he that deliberately puts an end to his own existence or commits an unlawful malicious act, the consequence of which is his own death." (Blackstone, *Commentaries on the Laws of England*, Bk. IV, ch. 14, sec. iii, p. 189.)

897.9   second section]   Of Article III.

900.34–35   gentleman from Wilmington]   Archibald Maclaine.

902.14   member from Edenton]   James Iredell.

902.20–21   member from Halifax]   William R. Davie.

905.20–21   the gates . . . against it]   Matthew 16:18.

910.4–5   the manner proposed]   Earlier in the day, Governor Johnston had moved that the committee of the whole recommend to the convention that they ratify the Constitution without prior amendments and that amendments "take place in one of the modes prescribed by the Constitution."

910.11   the previous question]   In parliamentary procedure, the "previous question" is the question whether a vote shall be taken on the main question or issue. Moving the previous question stopped further debate on Johnston's motion and required that an immediate vote be taken on whether or not to put the main issue (ratification) to a final vote.

910.33   J. Galloway]   James Gallaway (d. 1798) was born in Scotland, moved to North Carolina before the Revolution, went into business with his uncle, Charles Gallaway, and became a large landowner in the Dan River Valley. James Gallaway represented Guilford County in the house of commons 1783–84 and senate 1784–85 and Rockingham County in the senate 1786–89. An Antifederalist, he opposed the cession of the state's western lands and the calling of a ratifying convention. Both he and his uncle served in the ratifying conventions at Hillsborough in 1788 and Fayetteville in 1789, where they opposed ratification.

912.8   gentleman from Granville] Thomas Person.

912.31   Halifax, . . . Edenton,] William R. Davie and James Iredell.

914.12–13   1783 . . . Congress?] See note 614.29–30.

917.22–24   The previous . . . 99.] For the resolutions that were finally adopted by North Carolina convention at Hillsborough, see pages 565–74 in this volume.

Index

Further information on persons marked with an asterisk (*) is given in the Biographical Notes section.

483–84, 675, 747–48, 752, 801, 826, 879, 881; executive branch, 64, 119, 338–45, 369–70, 379–81, 389–94, 507, 747, 871–78; military, 64–65, 87–88, 133, 616, 780–81, 865–68; legislative branch, 119, 148, 160, 225, 292, 369–71, 383–84, 386, 507, 571, 789, 801, 821, 877–78, 879–81, 886; judiciary branch, 129–35, 171–77, 222–26, 290, 372–78, 507, 891–96; taxation, 133, 780–81, 843; reserved to states, 826, 926, 937 (*See also* Checks and balances; Constitution; Government; Necessary and proper clause; People; Separation of powers; States)
Presbyterians, 902
Presidency, 7, 23, 30, 35, 45, 59–60, 61, 100, 103, 107, 119, 132, 150, 158, 159, 172, 206, 269, 292, 333, 338–45, 346–54, 369, 389–94, 395–400, 417–18, 447, 521, 538, 545, 556, 563, 570, 618, 629, 658–59, 675, 696, 710, 747, 758, 767, 801, 811, 814, 856, 870–78, 879–81, 882–84, 902–8, 939, 942, 943, 944, 947–49, 956–57, 958, 961, 962, 963, 964; term of office, 59, 570, 718–19; qualifications, 161, 335, 541–42, 543, 719, 906 (*See also* Executive branch)
Press, freedom of, 8, 36, 55, 83, 153, 227–28, 268, 290, 463, 465, 524, 538, 555, 561, 568, 636, 674, 715, 748, 954
Primogeniture, 579–80
Pringle, John Julius, 556
Proceedings, published, 543, 562, 569, 645, 691, 933, 942
Property, 119–20, 158, 196–201, 264–65, 287, 314, 346, 355–56, 371, 423, 430, 456, 459, 499, 508, 522, 542, 579–80, 721, 770; security of, 538, 567, 706–7 (*See also* Land; Slavery)
Proserpine, 902
Providence, R.I., 276–83, 529
Providence Gazette, article in, 533–35
Prussia, 596, 669–70, 718
Public opinion, 519, 533–35, 679, 766
"Publius," 422, 823 (*See also Federalist, The*; Hamilton, Alexander; Madison, James)
Pufendorf, Samuel von, 274

Punishments, 72, 158, 537, 549, 551, 560, 567, 573, 626, 696, 697, 712, 714, 883–84, 950, 955
Putnam, Rufus, 180
Pym, John, 294

Quakers, 256–57, 355, 582–83
Quartering, 537, 561, 568, 697, 922, 954
Quebec, 762

*Ramsay, David, 518; letter to B. Lincoln, 117–18; "Civis," 147–54; letter from B. Rush, 417–19; oration at Charleston, 506–13
*Randolph, Edmund, 331; reply by "Americanus," 58–62; speeches in Va. convention, 598–604, 709–17; reply by Henry, 623–36
Read, George, 925, 953
Recall, 791, 792–93, 797–800, 805, 813
Reed, Joseph, 936
Regions, 20–21, 53, 117, 198, 219–21, 231, 233, 284, 449, 457, 460, 527–32, 639, 652, 674, 706, 833, 916; rivalry, 25, 441, 687–88, 692; variety, 61, 463, 506, 582, 605–6, 671–72, 819 (*See also* States)
Religion, freedom of, 42, 161, 166, 183, 193–95, 267–69, 290, 345, 514, 537, 552, 554, 561, 568, 578, 582–84, 598, 618, 674, 677, 678, 690, 715, 752–53, 902–7, 908–9
Religious tests, 193–94, 269, 752, 903–4, 908–9, 953
Representation, 5, 25, 37, 92, 98, 149, 151, 183–86, 196–201, 202–7, 208–12, 245–46, 268–69, 273–74, 278, 293, 304–5, 317, 320–21, 323–24, 411, 417, 425, 451, 585, 645, 684, 751–54, 762, 765–72, 858, 922; ratio and numbers, 541, 551, 548, 607–9, 622, 753–54, 757–64, 765–71, 774, 776–77, 781, 783–88
Representatives, House of, 20, 28, 30, 35, 45, 61, 99, 100, 103, 150, 182–86, 196, 202, 204, 208–12, 213, 239, 268, 329, 371, 383, 398, 417–18, 447, 521, 548, 551, 561, 568, 573, 589, 608, 615, 619, 621–22, 635, 655, 658–59, 667, 693, 717, 758–59, 763, 776, 810, 855–59, 861–62, 870, 879, 886, 902,

CATALOGING INFORMATION

The Debate on the Constitution
    Edited by Bernard Bailyn

    (The Library of America ; 63)
    Includes bibliographical references and indexes.
    Contents: Debates in the press and in private correspondence,
January 14–August 9, 1788; Debates in the state ratifying
conventions: South Carolina, Virginia, New York, North Carolina.
    1. Federalist. 2. United States—Constitutional history.
3. United States—Politics and government—1783–1789. I. Title.
II. Series.
JK155.D33   1993   92-25449
342.73′029—dc20
[347.30229]
ISBN 0–940450–64–X (alk. paper)

This book is set in 10 point Linotron Galliard,
a face designed for photocomposition by Matthew Carter
and based on the sixteenth-century face Granjon. The paper
is acid-free Ecusta Nyalite and meets the requirements for per-
manence of the American National Standards Institute. The binding
material is Brillianta, a 100% woven rayon cloth made by
Van Heek-Scholco Textielfabrieken, Holland. The com-
position is by Haddon Craftsmen, Inc., and The
Clarinda Company. Printing and binding
by R. R. Donnelley & Sons Company.
Designed by Bruce Campbell.

THE LIBRARY OF AMERICA SERIES